Contemporary Authors®

NEW REVISION SERIES

ISSN 0275-7176

Contemporary Authors®

**A Bio-Bibliographical Guide to
Current Writers in Fiction, General Nonfiction,
Poetry, Journalism, Drama, Motion Pictures,
Television, and Other Fields**

DEBORAH A. STRAUB
Editor

**JAMES G. LESNIAK
DONNA OLENDORF
BRYAN RYAN**
Associate Editors

THOMAS WILOCH
Senior Writer

NEW REVISION SERIES
volume 23

GALE RESEARCH COMPANY • BOOK TOWER • DETROIT, MICHIGAN 48226

STAFF

Poetry by Robert Creeley from his books *Later* (© 1975, 1976, 1977, 1978, 1979), *Hello* (© 1976, 1977, 1978), and *Mirrors* (© 1981, 1982, 1983) reprinted by permission of New Directions Publishing Corporation; poetry from *The Collected Poems of Robert Creeley, 1945-1975*, reprinted by permission of University of California Press.

Computerized photocomposition by
Typographics, Incorporated
Kansas City, Missouri

Contents

Indexing note: All *Contemporary Authors New Revision Series* entries are indexed in the *Contemporary Authors* cumulative index, which is bound into the back of even-numbered *Contemporary Authors* original volumes (blue and black cover with orange bands) and available separately as an offprint.

Authors and Media People
Featured in This Volume

John Barth (American novelist, author of short stories, and fiction theorist)—Among Barth's most celebrated works, which Curt Suplee of the *Washington Post* describes as "huge and bawdy intellectual fables," are the novels *The Sot-Weed Factor* and *Giles, Goat-Boy,* the novella collection *Chimera,* and the short story collection *Lost in the Funhouse.*

Bruno Bettelheim (Austrian-born psychiatrist)—A specialist in the treatment of emotionally disturbed children, Bettelheim is the author of *Love Is Not Enough* and *The Uses of Enchantment: The Meaning and Importance of Fairy Tales. The Informed Heart* and *Surviving, and Other Essays* examine his and others' experiences in Nazi death camps from a psychological perspective.

Jane E. Brody (American journalist)—Brody is best known for her nationally syndicated column on personal health. Her titles include *Jane Brody's Nutrition Book* and *Jane Brody's Good Food Book.* (Entry contains interview.)

Elias Canetti (Bulgarian-born author of fiction, nonfiction, plays, and essays)—Canetti, who writes in German, won a 1981 Nobel Prize primarily on the strength of two books, both of which have appeared in English translation—*Auto-da-fe,* a novel, and *Crowds and Power,* a psycho-sociological study of crowd behavior.

Richard Condon (American novelist and screenwriter)—Condon is the author of several popular political thrillers, including *The Manchurian Candidate* and *Winter Kills.* He also wrote the novel *Prizzi's Honor* and collaborated on the award-winning film adaptation. (Entry contains interview.)

Fred J. Cook (American journalist)—Among Cook's numerous investigative reports are *The FBI Nobody Knows, The Corrupted Land: The Social Morality of Modern Americans,* and *Julia's Story: The Tragedy of an Unnecessary Death.* (Entry contains interview.)

Robert Cormier (American novelist)—In his often-controversial novels for young adults, including *The Chocolate War, I Am the Cheese,* and *After the First Death,* Cormier explores such themes as the struggle of individuals with institutions and the abuse of power and authority. (Entry contains interview.)

Robert Creeley (American poet)—Once known primarily for his association with the Black Mountain Poets, Creeley has achieved prominence in his own right as a proponent of free verse that is created specifically to be read aloud. Representative work appears in *For Love* and *The Collected Poems of Robert Creeley, 1945-1975.*

Lois Duncan (American novelist)—Duncan is the author of several popular suspense novels for young adults, among them *I Know What You Did Last Summer, Killing Mr. Griffin,* and *Stranger with My Face.*

Betty Ford (American first lady during the administration of President Gerald R. Ford)—The autobiographical works *The Times of My Life* and *Betty: A Glad Awakening* recount Ford's bout with breast cancer and her struggle to overcome alcoholism and drug addiction.

Doris Kearns Goodwin (American biographer)—Goodwin has published two best-selling studies, *Lyndon Johnson and the American Dream,* which takes a psychoanalytical approach to the life of the thirty-sixth president, and *The Fitzgeralds and the Kennedys: An American Saga,* a multigenerational portrait of President John F. Kennedy's family.

Russell Hoban (American illustrator and fiction writer)—Hoban began his career as an illustrator and author of stories for children. The novel *Riddley Walker* subsequently brought him critical and popular acclaim among adult readers.

Etheridge Knight (American poet)—Knight's work, based in large part on the rhythms of black street talk, blues, and ballads, has been collected in several volumes, including *Poems from Prison, Belly Song and Other Poems,* and *Born of a Woman.*

Jill Krementz (American photojournalist)—In such books as *A Very Young Dancer* and *How It Feels When Parents Divorce,* Krementz uncovers the thoughts and feelings of young people coping with demanding physical regimens or emotional crises. (Entry contains interview.)

Jonathan Kwitny (American journalist)—Kwitny is noted for several extensively documented accounts of corruption in business and government, including *Vicious Circles: The Mafia in the Marketplace* and *The Crimes of Patriots: A True Tale of Dope, Dirty Money, and the CIA.*

Barry Holstun Lopez (American author of nonfiction and fiction)—Lopez's popular natural history titles, such as *Of Wolves and Men* and the 1986 National Book Award-winning *Arctic Dreams,* typically interweave factual material with philosophical discussions on man's place in nature. (Entry contains interview.)

Ved Mehta (Indian-born American author of autobiographies, fiction, and essays)—Mehta, who became blind at the age of four, is often credited with explaining his native land to Americans better than any other writer. Among his autobiographical works are *Face to Face, Vedi,* and *The Ledge between the Streams.*

Czeslaw Milosz (Polish-born American poet and author of fiction and nonfiction)—A victim of both Nazi and Soviet totalitarianism, Milosz writes of man's search for ways to survive spiritually in a world beset by political catastrophe. Books that have been translated into English include *Selected Poems, The Captive Mind,* and *The Seizure of Power.*

Cynthia Ozick (American fiction writer, essayist, and critic)—Ozick is best known for her fiction, which often mixes elements of fantasy, mysticism, comedy, satire, and Judaic law and history. She is the author of *The Pagan Rabbi, and Other Stories* and the novel *The Messiah of Stockholm.* (Entry contains interview.)

Walker Percy (American novelist and author of nonfiction) —In *The Moviegoer, The Last Gentleman, The Second Coming,* and other novels, Percy addresses the predicament facing man in an era when science and technology alleviate physical suffering but offer no solutions to spiritual malaise.

Dudley Randall (American poet and publisher)—A poet of the transitional years in black American literature, Randall helped usher in the modern age as the founder of Broadside Press, a major forum for many Afro-American writers of the 1960s and 1970s. The collection *More to Remember* spans some forty years of Randall's own verse.

Colby Rodowsky (American author of books for children) —Rodowsky writes about families in crisis, usually from an adolescent's point of view. Her notable titles include *What about Me?, The Gathering Room, H, My Name Is Henley,* and *Julie's Daughter.* (Entry contains interview.)

Rosemary Rogers (Ceylonese-born American romance novelist)—One of the best-selling romance writers in the world, Rogers helped popularize the genre with such books as *Sweet Savage Love, Lost Love, Last Love,* and *The Wanton,* all of which feature sexually explicit love scenes. (Entry contains interview.)

Leon Rooke (American author of short stories, novels, and plays)—Rooke, a longtime resident of Canada, is an experimentalist who often fuses realism with surrealism in his works, among them the novels *Fat Woman* and *Shakespeare's Dog* and the short story collections *The Love Parlour* and *The Broad Back of the Angel.*

Nathalie Sarraute (Russian-born French author of novels, essays, criticism, and plays)—In innovative works of fiction such as *Tropisms* and *The Golden Fruits,* Sarraute examines the psychological reality beneath the surface of daily events and conversations, a concept she develops more fully in the essay collection *The Age of Suspicion.*

Martin Cruz Smith (American novelist)—Smith is the author of several best-selling suspense novels, including *Nightwing, Gorky Park,* and *Stallion Gate.* (Entry contains interview.)

Irving Stone (American novelist)—Although they have not met with widespread critical acclaim, Stone's fictionalized biographies of Vincent van Gogh *(Lust for Life)*, Michelangelo *(The Agony and the Ecstasy)*, Sigmund Freud *(The Passions of the Mind)*, and Charles Darwin *(The Origin)* have proven immensely popular with readers. (Entry contains interview.)

Robert Stone (American novelist and screenwriter)—Stone is the author of four novels, *A Hall of Mirrors, Dog Soldiers, A Flag for Sunrise,* and *Children of Light,* all of which are marked by a stringent political tone, biting dialogue, and characters at odds with society and the law. (Entry contains interview.)

Anthony Summers (British journalist)—Summers specializes in uncovering new facts about old cases. Among his meticulously documented studies are *The Files on the Tsar,* which re-examines the fate of the Russian royal family, and *Goddess: The Secret Lives of Marilyn Monroe,* which links both John and Robert Kennedy to the famous actress.

Tad Szulc (Polish-born American journalist)—Szulc has produced investigative reports on a variety of political issues, events, and personages in such widely reviewed books as *The Illusion of Peace: Foreign Policy in the Nixon Years* and *Fidel,* a biography of Cuban leader Fidel Castro. (Entry contains interview.)

Hunter S. Thompson (American journalist)—Thompson's savagely humorous and frenzied accounts of contemporary American culture include *Fear and Loathing in Las Vegas, Fear and Loathing on the Campaign Trail '72,* and *The Great Shark Hunt.*

John Toland (American historian)—Toland, a popular historian who concentrates primarily on the Second World War, has written several best-selling works, among them *The Rising Sun: The Decline and Fall of the Japanese Empire, 1936-1945, Adolf Hitler,* and *Infamy: Pearl Harbor and Its Aftermath.*

Kathleen Woodiwiss (American romance novelist)—Credited with inventing the erotic historical romance, Woodiwiss is the author of *The Flame and the Flower* and *Shanna.* (Entry contains interview.)

Marguerite Yourcenar (Belgian-born fiction writer, essayist, and poet who died in 1987)—Two of her thought-provoking historical novels, translated into English as *Memoirs of Hadrian* and *The Abyss,* are considered classics for their vivid recreations of the past. In 1981, she became the first woman elected to the prestigious Academie Francaise.

Preface

The *Contemporary Authors New Revision Series* provides completely updated information on authors listed in earlier volumes of *Contemporary Authors (CA)*. Entries for active individual authors from *any* volume of *CA* may be included in a volume of the *New Revision Series*. The sketches appearing in *New Revision Series* Volume 23, for example, were selected from more than twenty previously published *CA* volumes.

As always, the most recent *Contemporary Authors* cumulative index continues to be the user's guide to the location of an individual author's listing.

Compilation Methods

The editors make every effort to secure information directly from the authors. Copies of all sketches in selected *CA* volumes published several years ago are routinely sent to the listees at their last-known addresses. Authors mark material to be deleted or changed and insert any new personal data, new affiliations, new writings, new work in progress, new sidelights, and new biographical/critical sources. All returns are assessed, more comprehensive research is done, if necessary, and those sketches requiring significant change are completely updated and published in the *New Revision Series*.

If, however, authors fail to reply or are now deceased, biographical dictionaries are checked for new information (a task made easier through the use of Gale's *Biography and Genealogy Master Index* and other Gale biographical indexes), as are bibliographical sources such as *Cumulative Book Index* and *The National Union Catalog*. Using data from such sources, revision editors select and revise nonrespondents' entries that need substantial updating. Sketches not personally reviewed by the biographees are marked with a dagger (†) to indicate that these listings have been revised from secondary sources believed to be reliable, but they have not been personally reviewed for this edition by the authors sketched.

In addition, reviews and articles in major periodicals, lists of prestigious awards, and, particularly, requests from *CA* users are monitored so that writers on whom new information is in demand can be identified and revised listings prepared promptly.

Format

CA entries provide biographical and bibliographical information in an easy-to-use format. For example, individual paragraphs featuring such rubrics as "Addresses," "Career," and "Awards, honors" ensure that a reader seeking specific information can quickly focus on the pertinent portion of an entry. In sketch sections headed "Writings," the title of each book, play, and other published or unpublished work appears on a separate line, clearly distinguishing one title from another. This same convenient bibliographical presentation is also featured in the "Biographical/Critical Sources" sections of sketches where individual book and periodical titles are listed on separate lines. *CA* readers can therefore quickly scan these often-lengthy bibliographies to find the titles they need.

Comprehensive Revision

All listings in this volume have been revised and/or augmented in various ways, though the amount and type of change vary with the author. In many instances, sketches are totally rewritten, and the resulting *New Revision Series* entries are often considerably longer than the authors' previous listings. Revised entries include additions of or changes in such information as degrees, mailing addresses, literary agents, career items, career-related and civic activities, memberships, work in progress, and biographical/critical sources. They may also include the following:

1) Major new awards—As noted in Barry Holstun Lopez's updated sketch, the National Book Award, the Christopher Book Award, and a National Book Critics Circle award nomination are among the many honors the author received in 1986 for *Arctic Dreams,* his contemplative look at the northern landscape and man's relationship with it. The year 1986 also saw Lopez named recipient of an Award in Literature from the American Academy and Institute of Arts and Letters for his entire body of work. New awards added to science fiction writer John Stewart Williamson's revised *CA* entry include the 1976 Grand Master Award for lifetime achievement from the Science Fiction Writers of America and the 1985 Hugo Award for his autobiography, *Wonder's Child: My Life in Science Fiction.*

2) Extensive bibliographical additions—A few of the prolific authors with updated entries in this volume are Russell Hoban, Jill Krementz, and John Wain. Well over thirty titles were added to writer/illustrator Russell Hoban's sketch, including six adult novels and more than twenty-five works for children. Since her last appearance in *CA* in 1979, photojournalist Jill Krementz has published sixteen books, among them the three in her highly acclaimed "How It Feels" series. Some forty additional titles are listed in the revised entry for British man of letters John Wain, including seven works of fiction, eight poetry collections, five plays, four nonfiction books, and twelve edited volumes.

3) Informative new sidelights—Numerous *CA* sketches contain sidelights, which provide personal dimensions to the listings, supply information about the critical reaction to the authors' works, or both. For instance, in sidelights on John Barth, assistant editor and writer Marilyn K. Basel examines the novelist's inventive storytelling techniques, particularly his method of addressing complex philosophical ideas through bawdy fables or elaborate parodies of old literary forms. "The unpredictable [Barth's] encyclopedic fictions have baffled some critics and bored others," observes Basel, "yet nearly all reviewers recognize his genius."

According to assistant editor Jani Prescott, "Lois Duncan, a popular author of young adult books, has learned to tailor her work to a generation of teens more familiar with television than books." In her sidelights, Prescott looks at such works as *Down a Dark Hall, Killing Mr. Griffin,* and *Stranger with My Face* to demonstrate how Duncan uses suspense, unconventional characters, and plots replete with danger and the supernatural to attract readers conditioned to expect "instant entertainment."

For more than fifty years, Irving Stone has been the "undisputed king of the literary genre he terms 'biographical novel,'" declares Edwin McDowell in the *New York Times Book Review.* In her sidelights on the author of *Lust for Life* and *The Agony and the Ecstasy,* to name only two of his bestsellers, assistant editor Sharon Malinowski notes that "while critics have been somewhat reluctant to appreciate the genre itself..., they nonetheless commend [the] perseverance and meticulous research" that go into each of Stone's detailed portraits of such influential figures as Vincent van Gogh, Michelangelo, Sigmund Freud, and Charles Darwin.

These sketches, as well as others with sidelights by *CA*'s editors, provide informative and enjoyable reading.

Writers of Special Interest

CA's editors make every effort to include in each *New Revision Series* volume a substantial number of revised entries on active authors and media people of special interest to *CA*'s readers. Since the *New Revision Series* also includes sketches on noteworthy deceased writers, a significant amount of work on the part of *CA*'s editors goes into the revision of entries on important deceased authors. Some of the prominent writers, both living and deceased, whose sketches are contained in this volume are noted in the list on pages vii-viii headed Authors and Media People Featured in This Volume.

Exclusive Interviews

CA provides exclusive, primary information on certain authors in the form of interviews. Prepared specifically for *CA,* the never-before-published conversations presented in the section of the sketch headed "*CA* Interview" give users the opportunity to learn the authors' thoughts, in depth, about their craft. Subjects chosen for interviews are, the editors feel, authors who hold special interest for *CA*'s readers.

Authors and journalists in this volume whose sketches contain exclusive interviews are Jane E. Brody, Richard Condon, Fred J. Cook, Robert Cormier, Jill Krementz, Barry Holstun Lopez, Cynthia Ozick, Colby Rodowsky, Rosemary Rogers, Martin Cruz Smith, Irving Stone, Robert Stone, Tad Szulc, and Kathleen Woodiwiss.

Contemporary Authors Autobiography Series

Designed to complement the information in *CA* original and revision volumes, the *Contemporary Authors Autobiography Series* provides autobiographical essays written by important current authors. Each volume contains from twenty to thirty specially commissioned autobiographies and is illustrated with numerous personal photographs supplied by the authors. The range of contemporary writers describing their lives and interests in the *Autobiography Series* encompasses authors such as Dannie Abse, Vance Bourjaily, Doris Grumbach, Elizabeth Forsythe Hailey, Marge Piercy, Frederik Pohl, Alan Sillitoe, William Stafford, Diane Wakoski, and Elie Wiesel. Though the information presented in the autobiographies is as varied and unique as the authors, common topics of discussion include their motivations for writing, the people and experiences that shaped their careers, the rewards they derive from their work, and their impressions of the current literary scene.

Autobiographies included in the *Contemporary Authors Autobiography Series* can be located through both the *CA* cumulative index and the *Contemporary Authors Autobiography Series* cumulative index, which lists not only personal names but also titles of works, geographical names, subjects, and schools of writing.

Contemporary Authors Bibliographical Series

The *Contemporary Authors Bibliographical Series* is a comprehensive survey of writings by and about the most important authors since World War II in the United States and abroad. Each volume concentrates on a specific genre and nationality and features approximately ten major writers. Volume 1, for instance, covers the American novelists James Baldwin, John Barth, Saul Bellow, John Cheever, Joseph Heller, Norman Mailer, Bernard Malamud, Carson McCullers, John Updike, and Eudora Welty. *Bibliographical Series* entries consist of three parts: a primary bibliography that lists works written by the author, a secondary bibliography that lists works about the author, and an analytical bibliographical essay that thoroughly discusses the merits and deficiencies of major critical and scholarly works. Complementing the information in other *CA* volumes, the *Bibliographical Series* is a new key to finding and evaluating information on the lives and writings of those authors who have attracted significant critical attention.

Each author's entry in the *Contemporary Authors Bibliographical Series* can be located through both the *CA* cumulative index and, beginning with Volume 2, the *Contemporary Authors Bibliographical Series* cumulative author index. A cumulative critic index, citing critics discussed in the bibliographical essays, also appears in each *Bibliographical Series* volume.

CA Numbering System

Occasionally questions arise about the *CA* numbering system. Despite numbers like "97-100" and "122," the entire *CA* series consists of only 81 physical volumes with the publication of *CA New Revision Series* Volume 23. The following information notes changes in the numbering system, as well as in cover design, to help users better understand the organization of the entire *CA* series.

***CA* First Revisions**	• 1-4R through 41-44R (11 books) *Cover:* Brown with black and gold trim. There will be no further *First Revisions* because revised entries are now being handled exclusively through the more efficient *New Revision Series* mentioned below.
***CA* Original Volumes**	• 45-48 through 97-100 (14 books) *Cover:* Brown with black and gold trim. • 101 through 122 (22 books) *Cover:* Blue and black with orange bands. The same as previous *CA* original volumes but with a new, simplified numbering system and new cover design.
***CA* New Revision Series**	• *CANR*-1 through *CANR*-23 (23 books) *Cover:* Blue and black with green bands. Includes only sketches requiring extensive change; **sketches are taken from any previously published *CA* volume.**
***CA* Permanent Series**	• *CAP*-1 and *CAP*-2 (2 books) *Cover:* Brown with red and gold trim. There will be no further *Permanent Series* volumes because revised entries are now being handled exclusively through the more efficient *New Revision Series* mentioned above.

CA Autobiography Series	• CAAS-1 through CAAS-7 (7 books)
	Cover: Blue and black with pink and purple bands. Presents specially commissioned autobiographies by leading contemporary writers to complement the information in CA original and revision volumes.
CA Bibliographical Series	• CABS-1 and CABS-2 (2 books)
	Cover: Blue and black with blue bands. Provides comprehensive bibliographical information on published works by and about major modern authors.

Retaining CA Volumes

As new volumes in the series are published, users often ask which CA volumes, if any, can be discarded. The Volume Update Chart on page xiii is designed to assist users in keeping their collections as complete as possible. All volumes in the left column of the chart should be retained to have the most complete, up-to-date coverage possible; volumes in the right column can be discarded if the appropriate replacements are held.

Cumulative Index Should Always Be Consulted

The key to locating an individual author's listing is the CA cumulative index bound into the back of alternate original volumes (and available separately as an offprint). Since the CA cumulative index provides access to *all* entries in the CA series, the latest cumulative index should always be consulted to find the specific volume containing a listee's original or most recently revised sketch.

Those authors whose entries appear in the *New Revision Series* are listed in the CA cumulative index with the designation **CANR-** in front of the specific volume number. For the convenience of those who do not have *New Revision Series* volumes, the cumulative index also notes the specific earlier volumes of CA in which the sketch appeared. Below is a sample index citation for an author whose revised entry appears in a *New Revision Series* volume.

Sagan, Carl (Edward) 1934- CANR-11
Earlier sketch in CA 25-28R

For the most recent information on Sagan, users should refer to Volume 11 of the *New Revision Series,* as designated by "CANR-11"; if that volume is unavailable, refer to CA 25-28 First Revision, as indicated by "Earlier sketch in CA 25-28R," for his 1977 listing. (And if CA 25-28 First Revision is unavailable, refer to CA 25-28, published in 1971, for Sagan's original listing.)

Sketches not eligible for inclusion in a *New Revision Series* volume because the biographee or a revision editor has verified that no significant change is required will, of course, be available in previously published CA volumes. Users should always consult the most recent CA cumulative index to determine the location of these authors' entries.

For the convenience of CA users, the CA cumulative index also includes references to all entries in these related Gale literary series: *Authors in the News, Children's Literature Review, Concise Dictionary of American Literary Biography, Contemporary Literary Criticism, Dictionary of Literary Biography, Something About the Author, Something About the Author Autobiography Series,* and *Twentieth-Century Literary Criticism.*

Acknowledgments

The editors wish to thank Judith S. Baughman and Armida Gilbert for their assistance with copyediting.

Suggestions Are Welcome

The editors welcome comments and suggestions from users on any aspect of the CA series. If readers would like to suggest authors whose CA entries should appear in future volumes of the *New Revision Series,* they are cordially invited to write: The Editors, *Contemporary Authors New Revision Series,* Book Tower, Detroit, MI 48226; or, call toll-free at 1-800-521-0707.

Volume Update Chart

IF YOU HAVE:	YOU MAY DISCARD:
1-4 First Revision (1967)	1 (1962) 2 (1963) 3 (1963) 4 (1963)
5-8 First Revision (1969)	5-6 (1963) 7-8 (1963)
Both 9-12 First Revision (1974) AND *Contemporary Authors Permanent Series,* Volume 1 (1975)	9-10 (1964) 11-12 (1965)
Both 13-16 First Revision (1975) AND *Contemporary Authors Permanent Series,* Volumes 1 and 2 (1975, 1978)	13-14 (1965) 15-16 (1966)
Both 17-20 First Revision (1976) AND *Contemporary Authors Permanent Series,* Volumes 1 and 2 (1975, 1978)	17-18 (1967) 19-20 (1968)
Both 21-24 First Revision (1977) AND *Contemporary Authors Permanent Series,* Volumes 1 and 2 (1975, 1978)	21-22 (1969) 23-24 (1970)
Both 25-28 First Revision (1977) AND *Contemporary Authors Permanent Series,* Volume 2 (1978)	25-28 (1971)
Both 29-32 First Revision (1978) AND *Contemporary Authors Permanent Series,* Volume 2 (1978)	29-32 (1972)
Both 33-36 First Revision (1978) AND *Contemporary Authors Permanent Series,* Volume 2 (1978)	33-36 (1973)
37-40 First Revision (1979)	37-40 (1973)
41-44 First Revision (1979)	41-44 (1974)
45-48 (1974) 49-52 (1975) ↓ ↓ 122 (1988)	NONE: These volumes will not be superseded by corresponding revised volumes. Individual entries from these and all other volumes appearing in the left column of this chart will be revised and included in the *New Revision Series.*
Volumes in the *Contemporary Authors New Revision Series*	NONE: The *New Revision Series* does not replace any single volume of *CA.* All volumes appearing in the left column of this chart must be retained to have information on all authors in the series.

Contemporary Authors

NEW REVISION SERIES

† *Indicates that a listing has been revised from secondary sources believed to be reliable, but has not been personally reviewed for this edition by the author sketched.*

ADAMS, Arthur Gray (Jr.) 1935-

PERSONAL: Born September 23, 1935, in Englewood, N.J.; son of Arthur Gray (a manufacturer's representative) and Jo Dorothy (Joyce) Adams; married Daryl Dubar Hart, December 25, 1956; children: Christopher Joseph, Cynthia Dorothy. *Education:* Brown University, A.B., 1957; graduate study at New York University. *Politics:* Independent. *Religion:* Roman Catholic.

ADDRESSES: Home—116 Deerfield Ter., Mahwah, N.J. 07430.

CAREER: Arthur G. Adams Agency (sales and marketing organization), New York, N.Y., founder and owner, 1959—. Former president and member of board of directors of Lehigh, Erie & Wallkill Transportation Co., Hudson River Navigation Co., and New Jersey Steamboat Co.; past founding president, and member of board of directors of Hudson River Maritime Center. Fellow of Carl Carmer Center for Catskill Mountain and Hudson River Studies, State University of New York College at New Paltz, 1978—. Member of program committee of Hudson Basin Project, Mohonk Consultations on the Earth's Ecosystem, 1980—; lecturer.

MEMBER: National Maritime Historical Society, American Teilhard Association, Hamilton Club (Patterson, N.J.), Steamer Alexander Hamilton Society (former vice-president and member of board of directors), New Jersey Association of Railroad Passengers (co-founder, 1980; member of board of directors), Brown University Club of Northeast New Jersey.

AWARDS, HONORS: Award of merit from State University of New York at New Paltz, 1981.

WRITINGS:

(With Leon R. Greenman and Harriet Greenman) *Guide to the Catskills with Trail Guide and Maps,* Walking News Press, 1975, new edition, 1987.
Guide to the Catskills and the Region Around, Sun Books, 1977.
(Editor) *The Hudson River in Literature,* State University of New York Press, 1980.
The Hudson: A Guidebook to the River, State University of New York Press, 1980.

History of the Hudson River Valley, Lind Graphics, 1982, published as *The Hudson through the Years,* Lind Graphics, 1983, 2nd edition, 1985.
Rip Van Winkle Tour Guide, Purple Mountain Press, 1986.
A Motoring Guide to the Catskills, Purple Mountain Press, 1987.
(With Raymond J. Baxter) *Railroad Ferries of the Hudson and Stories of a Deckhand,* Lind Graphics, 1987.

Associate editor of *Hudson River Archive.*

WORK IN PROGRESS: With R. J. Baxter, a profusely illustrated history-picture book of past and present palatial railroad and ferry terminals along the Hudson shoreline in New Jersey and Manhattan entitled *Palace Terminals of the Hudson;* a fully illustrated and updated edition of *The Hudson: A Guidebook to the River,* tentatively entitled *A Conservationists Guide to the Hudson,* the proceeds of which will be donated to the Hudson River Foundation for research.

SIDELIGHTS: Arthur Gray Adams once told *CA:* "I perceive myself primarily as a historian, geographer, and interpreter of the Catskill-Hudson Region, rather than as a writer. A lifetime of study and travel has given me great insight and understanding of the region and has brought familiarity with much rare documentary material and arcane information. Because the region is at a critical crossroads in its social, environmental, and economic development, the professional decision makers and the general public both require a better and deeper understanding of it in order to make enlightened decisions for the future. Much can be learned from the past.

"It has been my purpose in writing a series of six books to present a full-length portrait of the Catskill-Hudson Region from the perspectives of an economic geographer, a historian, and a transportation professional. This is, of necessity, an interdisciplinary approach. Often academic writers are trapped within the confines of their own special interests and disciplines and career publication requirements. They do not see the forest for the trees. On the other hand, journalists, in an understandable attempt to capture popular superficial interest, often gloss over or ignore very important, but sometimes tedious, details, that can be of interest to such readers as professional transportation planners. An example is the interior vertical clearance of the Holland Tunnel, which my editors wished to cut from the Hudson River guidebook. Subsequently, this item proved of tremendous importance to Department of Transportation planners because of the limitation on the size of trailer trucks which can use the tunnel—a matter of considerable economic significance to New York City.

"I attempt to write in the manner of such past writers as Benson Lossing, N. P. Willis, William Cullen Bryant, and Ernest Ingersoll, whose historical and geographical guidebooks straddled the uneasy line between academic and popular journalism. This, coupled with the large size and complexity of my books, has presented a dilemma to both commercial and academic publishers. On the one hand, while I do not stay within traditional academic formats, I present the academic publisher with the potential of a wider market. On the other hand, commercial publishers sometimes fear that the books are too detailed and 'academic' for the popular market. Interestingly, they have all sold well, and are doing an important job of disseminating vital information not previously available to the general public or planners. In this sense I perceive my writings as a public service rather than a personal creative outlet. It is my sincere hope that these books will help people to better know, understand, and love this beautiful and historic region."

Adams more recently added: "I am presently consulting with corporations interested in undertaking construction/restoration of the palatial Hoboken Ferry Terminal and operation of a revived Hoboken to Manhattan passenger ferry service. I also currently have a picture exhibition at WaveHill Center in the Bronx which will later be shown at the Museum of the City of New York, the World Trade Center, and next year on the Hudson River Ferries. I also consult with WaveHill Center on their Hudson River program and I am extremely busy with all these multifarious activities."

AVOCATIONAL INTERESTS: Playing piano (chamber music), opera, international travel by ship and rail, reading (history, poetry, and "classic" literature), regional planning, national transportation policy, environmental concerns, architecture, landscaping, interior decoration and design.

*   *   *

ADLER, David A. 1947-

PERSONAL: Born April 10, 1947, in New York, N.Y.; son of Sidney G. (a teacher) and Betty (a social worker; maiden name, Straus) Adler; married Renee Hamada (a psychologist), April 8, 1973; two children. *Education:* Queens College of the City University of New York, B.A., 1968; New York University, M.B.A., 1971. *Religion:* Jewish.

ADDRESSES: c/o Holiday House, 18 East 53rd St., New York, N.Y. 10022.

CAREER: Math teacher in New York, N.Y., 1968-77; author of books for young readers, 1972—; senior editor of books for young readers, 1979—.

WRITINGS:

Hanukkah Fun Book, Bonim Books, 1976.
Passover Fun Book, Bonim Books, 1978.
Hanukkah Game Book, Bonim Books, 1978.
Bible Fun Book, Bonim Books, 1979.
Fingerspelling Fun Book, F. Watts, 1981.
A Children's Treasury of Chassidic Tales, Mesorah, 1983.
The Car Sick Zebra and Other Animal Riddles, Holiday House, 1983.

The Twisted Witch and Other Spooky Riddles, Holiday House, 1985.
Eaton Stanley and the Mind Control Experiment, Dutton, 1985.
The Purple Turkey and Other Thanksgiving Riddles, Holiday House, 1986.
Benny, Benny, Baseball Nut, Scholastic, Inc., 1987.
Jewish Holiday Fun, Kar-Ben, 1987.
Rabbit Trouble and the Green Magician, Weekly Reader Books, 1987.
Remember Betsy Floss and Other Colonial American Riddles, Holiday House, 1987.

PICTURE BOOKS

A Little at a Time, Random House, 1976.
The House on the Roof, Kar-Ben, 1976.
The Children of Chelm, Bonim Books, 1979.
You Think It's Fun to Be a Clown!, Doubleday, 1980.
A Picture Book of Jewish Holidays, Holiday House, 1981.
A Picture Book of Passover, Holiday House, 1982.
A Picture Book of Hanukkah, Holiday House, 1982.
My Dog and the Key Mystery, F. Watts, 1982.
Bunny Rabbit Rebus, Crowell, 1983.
My Dog and the Knock Knock Mystery, Holiday House, 1985.
My Dog and the Green Sock Mystery, Holiday House, 1986.
My Dog and the Birthday Mystery, Holiday House, 1987.
I Know I'm a Witch, Holt, 1988.

NONFICTION

Base Five, Crowell, 1975.
3D, 2D, 1D, Crowell, 1975.
Roman Numerals, Crowell, 1977.
Redwoods Are the Tallest Trees in the World, Crowell, 1978.
3-2-1 Number Fun, Doubleday, 1981.
Calculator Fun Book, F. Watts, 1982.
Hyperspace! Facts and Fun from All Over the Universe, Viking, 1982.
Our Amazing Ocean, Troll, 1983.
All About the Moon, Troll, 1983.
World of Weather, Troll, 1983.
Wonders of Energy, Troll, 1983.
Amazing Magnets, Troll, 1983.
Our Golda: The Story of Golda Meir, Viking, 1984.
All Kinds of Money, F. Watts, 1984.
Prices Go Up, Prices Go Down: The Laws of Supply and Demand, F. Watts, 1984.
Inflation: When Prices Go Up, Up, Up, F. Watts, 1985.
Banks: Where the Money Is, F. Watts, 1985.
Martin Luther King Jr.: Free at Last, Holiday House, 1986.
Thomas Jefferson: Father of Our Democracy, Holiday House, 1987.
We Remember the Holocaust, Holt, 1987.
The Number on My Grandfather's Arm, Union of American Hebrew Congregations, 1987.
The Jewish Holidays, Mesorah, 1987.
Breathe In, Breathe Out: All About Your Lungs, F. Watts, 1988.

"CAM JANSEN" SERIES

Cam Jansen and the Mystery of the Stolen Diamonds, Viking, 1980.
. . . and the Mystery of the U.F.O., Viking, 1980.
. . . and the Mystery of the Dinosaur Bones, Viking, 1981.
. . . and the Mystery of the Television Dog, Viking, 1981.
. . . and the Mystery of the Gold Coins, Viking, 1982.
. . . and the Mystery of the Babe Ruth Baseball, Viking, 1982.

. . . and the Mystery of the Circus Clown, Viking, 1983.
. . . and the Mystery of the Monster Movie, Viking, 1984.
. . . and the Mystery of the Carnival Prize, Viking, 1984.
. . . and the Mystery at the Monkey House, Viking, 1985.
. . . and the Mystery of the Stolen Corn Popper, Viking, 1986.
. . . and the Mystery of Flight One Forty-Five, Viking, 1988.

"FOURTH FLOOR TWINS" ADVENTURE SERIES

The Fourth Floor Twins and the Fish Snitch Mystery, Viking, 1985.
. . . and the Fortune Cookie Chase, Viking, 1985.
. . . and the Disappearing Parrot Trick, Viking, 1986.
. . . and the Silver Ghost Express, Viking, 1986.
. . . and the Skyscraper Parade, Viking, 1987.

"JEFFREY'S GHOST" ADVENTURE SERIES

Jeffrey's Ghost and the Leftover Baseball Team, Holt, 1984.
. . . and the Fifth Grade Dragon, Holt, 1985.
. . . and the Ziffel Fair Mystery, Holt, 1987.

SIDELIGHTS: David A. Adler wrote *CA:* "Friends always ask me when I'll write an adult novel. I tell them, 'soon, soon. . . .' But sitting here now, writing this sidelight, I wonder why. I love children's books and there are so many more books for children I want to write. Because of the diversity of the books I write, I am able to vary my work even in a single day from research on a nonfiction book to fiction writing to riddle writing. As my interests have changed, so have the subjects of the books I have written.

"I grew up in a large house, the second oldest of six children. My parents were relaxed and encouraged each of us to develop his own interests. I get many ideas for my fiction from my experiences as a child. My own children also inspire me to write. My greatest pleasure as a writer comes when I watch one of my children enjoying something I have written."

*   *   *

ADLER, Irene
   See STORR, Catherine (Cole)

*   *   *

AIKEN, Joan (Delano) 1924-

PERSONAL: Born September 4, 1924, in Rye, Sussex, England; daughter of Conrad Potter (the poet) and Jessie (MacDonald) Aiken; married Ronald George Brown (a journalist), July 7, 1945 (died, 1955); married Julius Goldstein (a painter),1976; children: (first marriage) John Sebastian, Elizabeth Delano. *Politics:* Liberal. *Religion:* Agnostic.

ADDRESSES: Home—The Hermitage, East St., Petworth, West Sussex GU28 0AB, England; New York, New York. *Agent*—Brandt & Brandt, 1501 Broadway, New York, N.Y. 10036.

CAREER: Associated with British Broadcasting Corp., 1942-43, United Nations Information Office, London, England, 1943-49, *Argosy* magazine, 1955-60, and J. Walter Thompson Advertising Agency, 1961; full-time writer, 1961—.

AWARDS, HONORS: Guardian award, and runner-up for Carnegie Award, 1969, for *The Whispering Mountain;* Mystery Writers of America award, 1972, for *Night Fall.*

WRITINGS:

JUVENILE FICTION

All You've Ever Wanted (also see below), J. Cape, 1953.

More Than You Bargained For (also see below), J. Cape, 1955, Abelard, 1957.
The Kingdom and the Cave, Abelard, 1960.
The Wolves of Willoughby Chase, J. Cape, 1962, Doubleday, 1963.
Black Hearts in Battersea, Doubleday, 1964.
Nightbirds on Nantucket, Doubleday, 1966.
The Whispering Mountain, J. Cape, 1968, Doubleday, 1969.
A Necklace of Raindrops, and Other Stories, J. Cape, 1968, Doubleday, 1969.
A Small Pinch of Weather, and Other Stories, J. Cape, 1969.
Night Fall, Macmillan (London), 1969, Holt, 1970.
Armitage, Armitage, Fly away Home, Doubleday, 1970.
Smoke from Cromwell's Time, and Other Stories, Doubleday, 1970.
The Cuckoo Tree, Doubleday, 1971.
The Kingdom under the Sea, J. Cape, 1971.
All and More (short stories; includes *All You've Ever Wanted* and *More Than You Bargained For*), J. Cape, 1971.
Winterthing: A Child's Play (first produced in London, England, by Puffin Drama Group at Young Vic Theatre, 1970), Holt, 1972.
Arabel's Raven, BBC Publications, 1972, hardcover edition published as *Tales of Arabel's Raven*, J. Cape, 1974, published under original title, Doubleday, 1974.
A Harp of Fishbones (stories), J. Cape, 1972.
The Mooncusser's Daughter (play; first produced in London at Unicorn Theatre, 1973), Viking, 1973.
The Escaped Black Mambo, BBC Publications, 1973.
The Bread Bin, BBC Publications, 1974.
Midnight Is a Place, Viking, 1974.
Not What You Expected (stories), Doubleday, 1974.
Tale of a One-Way Street (stories), J. Cape, 1976, Doubleday, 1980.
The Skin Spinners (poems), Viking, 1976.
A Bundle of Nerves (horror stories), Gollancz, 1976.
Mortimer's Tie, BBC Publications, 1976.
Go Saddle the Sea, Doubleday, 1977.
The Faithless Lollybird (stories), J. Cape, 1977, Doubleday, 1978.
Mice and Mendelson, J. Cape, 1978.
Street (play; first produced in 1977), Viking, 1978.
The Spiral Stair, BBC Publications, 1979.
Mortimer and the Sword Excalibur, BBC Publications, 1979.
Arabel and Mortimer, BBC Publications, 1980.
The Shadow Guests, Delacorte, 1980.
The Stolen Lake, Delacorte, 1981.
"Moon Mill" (play), first produced in London at Unicorn Theatre, 1982.
Mortimer's Portrait on Glass (also see below), BBC Publications, 1982.
The Mystery of Mr. Jones's Disappearing Taxi (also see below), BBC Publications, 1982.
Bridle the Wind, Delacorte, 1983.
Mortimer's Cross (also contains *Mortimer's Portrait on Glass* and *The Mystery of Mr. Jones's Disappearing Taxi*), J. Cape, 1983, Harper, 1984.
The Kitchen Warriors (stories), BBC Publications, 1984.
Up the Chimney Down (stories), J. Cape, 1984, Harper, 1985.
Fog Hounds, Wind Cat, Sea Mice (stories), Macmillan, 1984.
Mortimer Says Nothing (stories), J. Cape, 1985, Harper, 1986.
The Last Slice of Rainbow, J. Cape, 1985.
Past Eight O'Clock (stories), J. Cape, 1986.
Dido and Pa, Delacorte, 1986.
A Goose on Your Grave, Gollancz, in press.

ADULT FICTION

The Silence of Herondale, Doubleday, 1964.

The Fortune Hunters, Doubleday, 1965.

Beware of the Bouquet, Doubleday, 1966 (published in England as *Trouble with Product X,* Gollancz, 1966).

Dark Interval, Doubleday, 1967 (published in England as *Hate Begins at Home,* Gollancz, 1967).

The Ribs of Death, Gollancz, 1967, published as *The Crystal Crow,* Doubleday, 1968.

The Windscreen Weepers, and Other Tales of Horror and Suspense, Gollancz, 1969, published as *Green Flash, and Other Tales of Horror, Suspense, and Fantasy,* Holt, 1971.

The Embroidered Sunset, Doubleday, 1970.

The Butterfly Picnic, Gollancz, 1970, published as *A Cluster of Separate Sparks,* Doubleday, 1972.

Nightly Deadshade, Macmillan, 1971.

Died on a Rainy Sunday, Holt, 1972.

Voices in an Empty House, Doubleday, 1975.

Castle Barebane, Viking, 1976.

Last Movement, Doubleday, 1977.

The Five-Minute Marriage, Gollancz, 1977, Doubleday, 1978.

The Smile of the Stranger, Doubleday, 1978.

A Touch of the Chill: Tales for Sleepless Nights (horror stories), Gollancz, 1979, Delacorte, 1980.

The Weeping Ash, Doubleday, 1980.

The Girl from Paris, Doubleday, 1982 (published as *The Young Lady from Paris,* Gollancz, 1982).

A Whisper in the Night (horror stories), Gollancz, 1982, Delacorte, 1983.

Foul Matter, Doubleday, 1983.

Mansfield Revisited, Gollancz, 1984, Doubleday, 1985.

If I Were You, Doubleday, 1987.

Deception, Gollancz, 1987.

SOUND RECORDINGS

"The Wolves of Willoughby Chase," Caedmon, 1978.

"A Necklace of Raindrops," Caedmon, 1978.

OTHER

(Translator from the French) Sophie De Segur, *The Angel Inn,* J. Cape, 1976, Stemmer House, 1978.

The Way to Write for Children, Elm Tree Books, 1982, St. Martin's, 1983.

SIDELIGHTS: Joan Aiken is best known for inventing the "unhistorical romance, . . . a new genre which far outdoes its conventional counterpart in inventiveness and wit," according to *New Statesman* contributor Patricia Craig. These tales combine traditional elements of fairy tale, romance, and myth with fast-paced action and humor. They are set in an imaginary time period during the reign of King James III in England, described by Susan Dooley in the *Washington Post Book World* as "a surreal version of Dickens' 19th century." Aiken began her alternate history in *The Wolves of Willoughby Chase* and continued it in several other novels, including *Black Hearts in Battersea, Nightbirds on Nantucket,* and *The Stolen Lake.*

As the daughter of the American poet Conrad Aiken and the stepdaughter of the English writer Martin Armstrong, Joan Aiken was surrounded by literary models from birth. At the age of five she decided upon a literary career and began writing her first stories and poems. Her first acceptance came while she was still in school; two of her poems were published in a prestigious little magazine, the *Abinger Chronicle,* edited by E. M. Forster, Sylvia Sprigge, and Max Beerbohm. "They printed my poems but never paid me, which gave me the idea

that poetry was not a remunerative occupation," notes Aiken in the *Something about the Author Autobiography Series.*

Aiken continued to develop her writing after her marriage to journalist Ron Brown, selling several radio scripts and some short stories. When Brown's death in 1955 left her with large debts and two children to support, she went to work as an editor for the stort story magazine *Argosy.* To supplement her editor's wages, she also contributed many short stories to this publication and others. "I worked like a beaver, selling stories to *John Bull, Housewife, Vogue,* any magazine that would take fiction other than the woman's sob-type," the author relates in the *SATA Autobiography Series.* These stories, collected in the volumes *More Than You Bargained For* and *All You've Ever Wanted,* became Aiken's first published books. But writing short stories was beginning to seem like "an uneconomic use of time,"she continues in the *SATA Autobiography Series.* "I wanted to write longer pieces of fiction that would sell for large sums." With that goal in mind she unearthed the manuscript of a novel written at the age of seventeen. Carefully revised, that manuscript became her first published novel, *The Kingdom and the Cave.*

Aiken began creating her scrambled history of England in her next novel, *The Wolves of Willoughby Chase.* Here she introduced what would become the standard elements of several of her novels: an English countryside terrorized by wolves, a colorful London underworld, the Stuart king James III, and the Hanoverian rebels determined to assassinate him. Although *The Wolves of Willoughby Chase* was marketed as a children's book, it was read and enjoyed by adults as well. Its success enabled Aiken to devote herself to writing full-time.

In their book *You're a Brick, Angela! A New Look at Girls' Fiction from 1839 to 1975,* Patricia Craig and Mary Cadogan offer an analysis of Aiken's "unhistorical adventure stories." They believe that these stories have "an exuberance, a pantomimic largeness which is . . . effective. There is nothing original about her plots, but she has brought to bear on them a sensibility which *is* original, if only because of its ability to assimilate, re-channel, enliven, send up, make good use of elements and conventions already traditional. She has effected a fusion of Gothic with Baroque, set off by a manneristic flair for detail."

Cadogan and Craig comment on Aiken's invented time setting: "This device has a great economy: events which take place in an imaginary era obviously are not governed by restrictions of plausibility, either social or temperamental. The period's non-existence serves mainly to emphasize that the stories are not meant to be pegged to the ground, their purpose is to take off as stylishly as possible. In a time that never happened, anything *can* happen."

Aiken's horror and suspense stories have been as highly praised as her fantasy adventures. Georgess McHargue writes of *Died on a Rainy Sunday* in the *New York Times Book Review:* "A thriller by Joan Aiken is like an ice cream cone. Both must be consumed at a single sitting and both leave a cold but pleasurable feeling in the pit of the stomach." *Washington Post Book World* contributor Natalie Babbitt explains that Aiken's stories in this genre "do not, any of them, go in much for the blood and gore that passes for horror in the movies these days, nor do any of them deal flat-out with the supernatural, also a common movie gimmick. Rather they run on the gray edge between order and chaos called so aptly the 'twilight zone' by the old television series."

In any genre, it is Aiken's professional craftsmanship that lifts her stories to the level of fine entertainment, writes *Washington Post Book World* contributor Michael Dirda. He concludes: "Joan Aiken can turn her hand to almost anything—mystery, fantasy, suspense, comedy—and nearly always come up with a winner." Reflecting on her earliest aspirations in her *SATA Autobiography Series* essay, Aiken notes, "With over sixty books listed on the British Public Lending Right register I feel I have achieved my ambition to be a professional writer. I know that my books vary. Some I am proud of; some are mere jobs of work, money-earners; a couple now fill me with slight embarrassment. Which do I love best? A pair of books with Spanish settings—*Go Saddle the Sea* and *Bridle the Wind*. Sometimes when you write a book you can feel it take off and lift away from you into unexplored regions—I felt those two did that."

MEDIA ADAPTATIONS: An adaptation of *Midnight Is a Place*, directed by Chris McMaster, was produced by Southern Television, 1977.

BIOGRAPHICAL/CRITICAL SOURCES:

BOOKS

Books for Children, 1960-1965, American Library Association, 1966.
Cadogan, Mary and Patricia Craig, *You're a Brick, Angela! A New Look at Girls' Fiction from 1839 to 1975*, Gollancz, 1976.
The Children's Bookshelf, Child Study Association of America, Bantam, 1966.
Children's Literature Review, Volume I, Gale, 1976.
Contemporary Literary Criticism, Volume XXXV, Gale, 1985.
Eadkin, Mark K., editor, *Good Books for Children*, Phoenix Books, 1966.
Jones, Cornelia and Olivia R. Way, *British Children's Authors: Interviews at Home*, American Library Association, 1976.
Larrick, Nancy, *A Parent's Guide to Children's Reading*, 3rd edition, Doubleday, 1969.
Something about the Author Autobiography Series, Volume I, Gale, 1986.
Townsend, John Rowe, *A Sense of Story: Essays on Contemporary Writers for Children*, Lippincott, 1971.

PERIODICALS

British Book News, August, 1982.
Calendar, March-October, 1979.
Chicago Tribune, November 9, 1980.
Horn Book, October, 1970, October, 1973, April, 1974, December, 1976.
Junior Bookshelf, August, 1974, June, 1976, October, 1982.
National Observer, September 23, 1968.
New Statesman, December 4, 1981.
New York Times Book Review, July 23, 1967, March 24, 1968, July 23, 1972, May 5, 1974, April 27, 1980, February 14, 1982.
Observer, April 18, 1982.
Punch, August 15, 1984.
Saturday Review, April 18, 1970, April 17, 1971, May 20, 1972.
Times (London), March 5, 1980, February 8, 1982, August 25, 1983, December 27, 1984.
Times Educational Supplement, June 5, 1981.
Times Literary Supplement, June 15, 1967, July 2, 1971, March 28, 1980, July 10, 1987, July 31, 1987.

Washington Post, July 17, 1987.
Washington Post Book World, January 8, 1978, May 22, 1980, July 13, 1980, January 13, 1985, June 9, 1985, November 4, 1986.
The Writer, March, 1980, May, 1982.

—*Sketch by Joan Goldsworthy*

*   *   *

ALBERT, Burton, Jr. 1936-
(Brooks Healey)

PERSONAL: Born September 25, 1936, in Pittsfield, Mass.; son of Burton and Isabel (Deming) Albert; married Lois Bent, July 27, 1963; children: Heather Leigh, Kelley Lynn. *Education:* State Teachers College at North Adams (now North Adams State College), B.S. (magna cum laude), 1958; Duke University, M.A., 1962.

ADDRESSES: Home and office—3 Narrow Brook Rd., Weston, Conn. 06883.

CAREER: Elementary school teacher in Greenwich, Conn., 1958-60, 1962-63; high school teacher of English in Greenwich, 1963-64; Harcourt Brace Jovanovich, Inc., New York, N.Y., assistant editor in language arts, 1964-66; *Reader's Digest*, Educational Division, Pleasantville, N.Y., senior editor and product developer, 1966-76, editorial director, 1976-77; Albert Communications, Weston, Conn., corporate consultant to businesses and schools, 1977—.

MEMBER: National Council of Teachers of English.

WRITINGS:

(Contributor) Melissa Costello and Reginold Fickett, editors, *Essays in American and English Literature*, M.S.S. Information, 1976.
Sure Steps to a New Job, Learning Pyramid, Inc., 1981.

JUVENILES

Codes for Kids, Albert Whitman, 1976.
Monster Riddles, Firefly Book Club, 1976.
More Monster Riddles, Firefly Book Club, 1976.
Puzzle Fun, Firefly Book Club, 1976.
Mine, Yours, Ours, illustrations by Lois Axeman, Albert Whitman, 1977.
More Codes for Kids, Albert Whitman, 1979.
Sharks and Whales, Platt, 1979.
Secrets of Hiding, Macmillan, 1983.
Clubs for Kids, Ballantine, 1983.
Code Busters!, Albert Whitman, 1985.
Top Secret! Codes to Crack, Albert Whitman, 1987.

TEXTBOOKS AND CLASSROOM MATERIALS

(Ghostwriter) *Language for Daily Use Workbook*, Harcourt, 1965.
(Ghostwriter) *Language for Daily Use*, Harcourt, 1966.
(Contributor) Ronald Noland, Jone Wright, and Elizabeth Allen, editors, *An Introduction to Elementary Reading: Selected Materials*, M.S.S. Information, 1971.
(With Donald M. Murray) *Write to Communicate: The Language Arts in Process* (multimedia kit), Levels 3-6, Reader's Digest Educational Division, 1973-74.
Reader's Digest Reading Skills Practice Pads, Level 3 and Advanced, Reader's Digest Educational Division, 1976.
Reader's Digest Reading Skill Builders, Reader's Digest Educational Division, 1977.

Holiday Party Panels, three sets, Instructor Curriculum Materials, 1978.
Houghton Mifflin Reading Program, Levels 6-8, Houghton, 1980.
Houghton Mifflin Spelling Series, Levels 2-3, Houghton, 1981.
Our Country's History, Scholastic Book Services, 1981.

UNDER PSEUDONYM BROOKS HEALEY; ALL JUVENILES

The Giggles and Games Puzzle Book, Firefly Book Club, 1977.
It's True, by George!, Firefly Book Club, 1978.
Star Words, Firefly Book Club, 1978.
The Stranger and the Scarecrow, Firefly Book Club, 1978.
Maze Daze, Firefly Book Club, 1979.

OTHER

Monthly columnist for *Early Years,* 1980-81. Contributor of articles and poems to education and literature journals, and to children's magazines, including *Instructor, Early Years, Today's Education, Jack and Jill, Bitterroot International Poetry Quarterly,* and *Language Arts.*

SIDELIGHTS: ''When young people ask what they can do to improve their writing, I preach what I try to practice,'' Albert Burton, Jr., told *CA.* The communications consultant and children's book writer listed the following tips for young writers: ''Write about what interests *you.* Narrow your subject; write a lot about a little. Be specific; feed hungry readers dollops of detail. Tap all your senses: see, hear, taste, touch, and smell. Show, don't tell. Power your writing with active verbs. Play with words, word order, and a variety of writing forms— from biography and story to poem, label, fable, and more. Cut, cut, cut all that blocks the way to what you want to say. Question your copy from a reader's point of view. Tune in: listen to the music and rhythm of your language. Make each word clear; write exactly what you mean. Be honest and true; leave your voice on the page.''

*   *   *

ALBINSKI, Henry Stephen   1931-

PERSONAL: Born December 31, 1931, in Chicago, Ill.; son of Stephen (a chemical engineer) and Josephine (Wieczorek) Albinski; married Barbara Van Why, January 30, 1954; married second wife, Ethel Bisbicos (a psychologist), September 2, 1967; married third wife, Nan Bowman (a literature academic), February 11, 1984; children: (first marriage) Lawrence; (second marriage) Gillian, Allison. *Education:* University of California, Los Angeles, B.A. (summa cum laude), 1953, M.A., 1955; University of Minnesota, Ph.D., 1959.

ADDRESSES: *Home*—803 Cornwall Dr., State College, Pa. 16801. *Office*—Department of Political Science, Pennsylvania State University, University Park, Pa. 16802.

CAREER: University of Minnesota, Minneapolis, instructor in political science, 1959; Pennsylvania State University, University Park, instructor, 1959-61, assistant professor, 1961-65, associate professor, 1965-68, professor of political science, 1968—, director of Office of Australian Studies, 1980-81, director of Australian Studies Center, 1982-87, director of Australia-New Zealand Studies Center, 1987—. Visiting fellow, Australian National University, Research School of Pacific Studies, 1963-64, 1978-79; visiting professor, University of Western Ontario, 1969, University of Queensland, 1970, University of Sydney, and Flinders University of South Australia, both 1974-75, University of Melbourne, 1985-86. Con-

sultant, Research Analysis Corp., 1968-70, Institute for Defense Analyses, 1969, Georgetown University Center for Strategic and International Studies, 1972-73, U.S. Department of State, and Research Council, Pacific Forum. Political risk-assessment consultant, Frost and Sullivan, Inc., 1980—.

MEMBER: International Studies Association, American Political Science Association, Australasian Political Studies Association, New Zealand Political Studies Association, Australian Studies Association (executive overseas board member, 1986—), British Australian Studies Association, Middle Atlantic Conference for Canadian Studies, Canadian Institute for Strategic Studies, Association for Canadian Studies in the United States, Canadian Political Science Association, United States Naval Institute, Inter-University Seminar on Armed Forces and Society.

AWARDS, HONORS: Rockefeller Foundation grant, 1963-64; Institute of Humanistic Studies of Pennsylvania State University fellowship, 1968; senior Fulbright scholar, 1974-75, 1979; Hoover Institution fellow, 1984—.

WRITINGS:

Australia and the China Problem during the Korean War Period, Department of International Relations, Australian National University, 1964.
Australian Policies and Attitudes toward China, Princeton University Press, 1965.
The Australian Labor Party and the Aid to Parochial Schools Controversy, Pennsylvania State University Press, 1966.
(Contributor) *Writings on Canadian-American Studies,* Committee on Canadian-American Studies, Michigan State University, 1967.
(Editor with L. K. Pettit) *European Political Processes: Essays and Readings,* Allyn & Bacon, 1968, 2nd edition, 1974.
(Contributor) Jan Prybyla, editor, *Communism at the Crossroads,* Pennsylvania State University Press, 1968.
(Contributor) Richard Preston, editor, *Contemporary Australia: Studies in History, Politics and Economics,* Duke University Press, 1969.
(Contributor) *American Studies Conference Proceedings,* New South Wales Department of Education, 1970.
Politics and Foreign Policy in Australia, Duke University Press, 1970.
Australia in Southeast Asia: Interest, Capacity, and Acceptability, Research Analysis Corp., 1970.
(Editor and contributor) *Asian Political Processes,* Allyn & Bacon, 1971.
(Contributor) Arthur Stahnke, editor, *China's Trade with the West,* Praeger, 1972.
Canadian and Australian Politics in Comparative Perspective, Oxford University Press, 1973.
(Contributor) Prybyla, editor, *The Pentagon of Power,* Pennsylvania State University Press, 1973.
(Contributor) Roy Forward, editor, *Public Policy in Australia,* F. W. Cheshire, 1974.
Australian External Policy under Labor, University of Queensland Press and University of British Columbia Press, 1977.
(Contributor) Preston, editor, *Perspectives on Revolution and Evolution,* Duke University Press, 1979.
(Contributor) John Henderson and others, editors, *Beyond New Zealand: The Foreign Policy of a Small State,* Methuen, 1980.

(Contributor) R. Hayburn and B. Webb, editors, *Economic Strategies and Foreign Policy*, University of Otago, 1980.

(Contributor) James Roherty, editor, *Defense Policy Formation*, Carolina Academic Press, 1980.

(Contributor) Larry Bowman and Ian Clark, editors, *The Indian Ocean in Global Politics*, Westview Press, 1981.

(Contributor) Haus Indorf and others, editors, *Lines of Communication and Security*, National Defense University Press, 1981.

(Contributor) Ramon Myers, editor, *An American Foreign Policy for Asia*, Hoover Institution Press, 1982.

(Contributor) William Tow and William Feeney, editors, *U.S. Alliance System in the Indo-Pacific Region*, Westview Press, 1982.

The Australian-American Security Relationship, University of Queensland Press and St. Martin's Press, 1982.

(Contributor) J. E. Starron and A. C. Waldek, editors, *Maritime Resources of the Indian and Pacific Oceans*, National Defense University Press, 1983.

(Contributor) William Dowdy and Russell Trood, editors, *The Indian Ocean: Perspectives on a Strategic Arena*, Duke University Press, 1985.

(Contributor) Claude Buss, editor, *National Security Interests in the Pacific Basin*, Hoover Institution Press, 1985.

(Contributor) Stephen Graubard, editor, *Australia: Terra Incognita?*, Angus and Robertson, 1985.

(Contributor) Robert Kiste and Richard Herr, editors, *The Pacific in the Year 2000*, Center for Asian and Pacific Studies, University of Hawaii, 1985.

(Contributor) David Radock, editor, *Assessing Corporate Political Risk*, Rowman and Littlefield, 1986.

(Contributor) Lloyd R. Vasey, editor, *Strategic Imperatives and Western Responses in the South and Southwest Pacific*, Pacific Forum, 1986.

ANZUS, the United States, and Pacific Security, Asia Society/University Press of America, 1987.

(Contributor) F. A. Mediansky and A. C. Palfreeman, editors, *An Introduction to Australian Foreign Policy*, Pergamon Press, in press.

(Contributor) Jay A. Sigler, editor, *International Handbook on Race Relations*, Greenwood Press, in press.

Contributor of articles and reviews to professional journals in the United States, Australia, Canada, and New Zealand. Editorial board, *Australian Journal of Politics and History;* editorial advisory board, *Pacific Affairs*.

WORK IN PROGRESS: Contribution to a book on ANZUS and Pacific security issues edited by Jacob Bercovitch, for Macmillan (London).

*   *   *

ALEXANDER, Kate
See ARMSTRONG, Tilly

*   *   *

ALPERT, Hollis   1916-
(Robert Carroll)

PERSONAL: Born September 24, 1916, in Herkimer, N.Y.; son of Abraham and Myra (Carroll) Alpert; married Joan O'Leary (a teacher), October 1, 1960. *Education:* Attended New School for Social Research, 1947-48.

ADDRESSES: Home—Box 142, Shelter Island, N.Y. 11964.

CAREER: Book reviewer for *Saturday Review*, New York City, and *New York Times*, New York City, 1947-59; *New Yorker*, New York City, associate fiction editor, 1950-56; *Saturday Review*, New York City, motion picture critic, 1950-72; *Woman's Day*, Greenwich, Conn., film critic, 1953-60, contributing editor, 1956-69; *World*, New York City, managing editor, beginning 1972, film editor and lively arts editor, beginning 1973; *American Film*, Washington, D.C., editor, 1975-80, consulting editor, 1980—. Writing instructor, Division of General Education, New York University, 1948-53. Alger Meadows Distinguished Visiting Professor, Southern Methodist University, 1982. Past director, Edward MacDowell Association. Judge, representing the United States, Berlin Film Festival, 1966. *Military service:* U.S. Army, combat historian, 1943-46; became first lieutenant.

MEMBER: National Society of Film Critics (chairman, 1972-73).

AWARDS, HONORS: Annual award for movie criticism, Screen Directors Guild, 1958.

WRITINGS:

The Summer Lovers, Knopf, 1958.

Some Other Time, Knopf, 1960.

(Under pseudonym Robert Carroll) *Champagne at Dawn*, Dell, 1961.

The Dreams and the Dreamers, Macmillan, 1962.

(Under pseudonym Robert Carroll) *Cruise to the Sun*, Dell, 1962.

For Immediate Release (novel), Doubleday, 1963.

The Barrymores, Dial, 1964.

The Claimant, Dial, 1968.

"The Ski Bum" (screenplay; based on Romain Gary's book of the same title), Avco, 1968.

(Editor with Andrew Sarris) *Film 68/69*, Simon & Schuster, 1969.

The People Eaters, Dial, 1971.

(With Arthur Knight) *Playboy's Sex in Cinema, 1970*, Playboy Press, 1971.

Smash, Dial, 1973.

(With Knight) *Playboy's Sex in Cinema 3*, Playboy Press, 1973.

(With Ira Mothner and Harold Schonberg) *How to Play Double Bogey Golf*, New York Times Co., 1975.

(Under pseudonym Robert Carroll) *A Disappearance*, Dial, 1975.

(Editor) *The Actor's Life: Journals—Charlton Heston*, Dutton, 1979.

(Contributor) *Lana: The Lady, the Legend, the Truth—Lana Turner*, Dutton, 1982.

Burton (biography), Putnam, 1986.

Fellini: A Life (biography), Atheneum, 1986.

Also author of two screenplays, "The Fun Couple" and "Scenes." Contributor of short stories and articles on books, movies, and television to numerous magazines, including *New Yorker, Cosmopolitan*, and *Harper's Bazaar*.

SIDELIGHTS: Although best known as a film critic, Hollis Alpert cultivates many literary fields: novels, biographies, short stories, screenplays, humor, as well as criticism. *The Barrymores*, a biography of the Barrymore family, elicits high praise from several critics, including Charles Dollen who comments in *Best Sellers*, "All the color and drama of the American Theatre of the early twentieth century is brought to life again in this superb volume."

Two of Alpert's more recent biographies, *Burton* and *Fellini: A Life,* have received somewhat mixed critical reviews. In the *Detroit News,* George Bulanda suggests that while Alpert's biography of the legendary actor Richard Burton is a "sympathetic portrayal . . . it often fails to mine the soul of its subject." However, a contributor to *Kirkus Reviews* believes that "Alpert tells Burton's story with great verve . . . dispelling the current prevailing opinion of Burton as a sell-out and hack. . . . [The book is] sound, solid, and constantly intriguing." Similarly, in a review of Alpert's biography of film maker Federico Fellini for the *Los Angeles Times Book Review,* Marsha Kinder acknowledges the difficulty in writing about one who "has mythologized his life with such power that any biography is bound to pale in comparison," but faults Alpert for adopting a "breezy journalistic style rather than scholarly rigor." And although Kinder thinks Alpert is weak on Fellini's finished films, she writes that he is "illuminating on Fellini's collaborative process . . . [and] marvelously detailed on the projects that never made it to the screen." Kinder closes, "Despite its many limitations, his biography is important. . . . Alpert is striving to make a critical intervention—to restore a tottering giant to his rightful place in film history."

BIOGRAPHICAL/CRITICAL SOURCES:

PERIODICALS

Best Sellers, December 15, 1964, April 15, 1968, November 15, 1971.
Detroit News, March 23, 1986.
Kirkus Reviews, December 15, 1985.
Los Angeles Times Book Review, December 7, 1986.
New York Herald Tribune Book Review, July 20, 1958.
New York Times, November 8, 1971.
New York Times Book Review, January 3, 1965, April 28, 1968, November 21, 1971, November 25, 1973.
Saturday Review, August 13, 1960, March 16, 1968, November 20, 1971.
Washington Post Book World, March 23, 1986.

*   *   *

ANDERSEN, Kurt 1954-

PERSONAL: Born August 22, 1954, in Omaha, Neb.; son of Robert Keith (a lawyer) and Jean (Swarr) Andersen; married Anne Kreamer (a marketing executive), May 9, 1981. *Education:* Harvard University, A.B. (magna cum laude), 1976. *Politics:* Democrat. *Religion:* Unitarian-Universalist.

ADDRESSES: Home—343 East Ninth St., New York, N.Y. 10003. *Office—Spy,* 295 Lafayette St., New York, N.Y. 10012.

CAREER: National Broadcasting Co. (NBC-TV), New York City, writer, 1976-81; *Time,* New York City, staff writer, 1981-83, associate editor, 1983-86, architecture critic, 1985—; *Spy,* New York City, co-editor, 1986—.

WRITINGS:

NONFICTION

The Real Thing, Doubleday, 1980.
(With Mark O'Donnell and Roger Parloff) *Tools of Power,* Viking, 1980.
(With Ann Hodgman, Fred Graver, Ellis Weiner, and Peter Cohn) *The Reagan Report,* Doubleday, 1984.
(Editor with Gene Shalit) *Laughing Matters* (American humor anthology), Doubleday, 1987.

OTHER

Writer for "Daytime Television Drama," a comedy special broadcast by WCVB-TV, Boston, May, 1975. Contributor to magazines and newspapers, including *New York Times* and *Vanity Fair.* Past editor of *Harvard Lampoon.*

SIDELIGHTS: The Real Thing is Kurt Andersen's humorous guide to the quintessential attributes and artifacts of American life. He examines a wide range of subjects, including consumer products, weapons, human feelings, art forms, places, and even the animal world. His second book, *Tools of Power,* is a satirical dissection of the corporate ethos and its most ferocious devotees.

BIOGRAPHICAL/CRITICAL SOURCES:

PERIODICALS

Boston Globe, November 26, 1986.
Chicago Tribune Book World, April 11, 1982.
Newsday, October 9, 1986.
New York Daily News, December 18, 1980.
Philadelphia Inquirer, October 3, 1986.
Soho News, November 12, 1980.

*   *   *

ANGUS, Ian
See MACKAY, James (Alexander)

*   *   *

APFEL, Necia H(alpern) 1930-

PERSONAL: Born July 31, 1930, in Mount Vernon, N.Y.; daughter of Simon A. and Sidonia (Frank) Halpern; married Donald A. Apfel (an orthodontist), September 7, 1952; children: Mimi, Steve. *Education:* Tufts University, B.A. (magna cum laude), 1952; graduate study at Harvard University, 1953-54, and Northwestern University, 1963-67.

ADDRESSES: Home and office—3461 University Dr., Highland Park, Ill. 60035. *Agent*—Ray Peekner Literary Agency, 3210 South Seventh St., Milwaukee, Wis. 53215.

CAREER: Worked at miscellaneous jobs in Boston, Mass., 1954-55; Standard Oil Company, Chicago, Ill., research analyst, 1955-57; Adler Planetarium, Chicago, Ill., associate director of Astro-Science Workshop, 1973-79, writer, 1979—. Lecturer in astronomy at elementary and junior high schools, 1973—; conducts classes in astronomy for children at Adler Planetarium.

MEMBER: American Association for the Advancement of Science, Astronomical Society of the Pacific, League of Women Voters (member of board of directors, 1960-62), Phi Beta Kappa.

WRITINGS:

(With J. Allen Hynek) *Astronomy One* (college textbook), W. A. Benjamin, 1973, 2nd edition published as *Architecture of the Universe,* W. A. Benjamin, Cummings, 1979.
It's All Relative: Einstein's Theory of Relativity (juvenile), Lothrop, 1981.
Stars and Galaxies (juvenile), F. Watts, 1982.

The Moon and Its Exploration (juvenile), F. Watts, 1982.
Astronomy and Planetology (young adult), F. Watts, 1984.
Astronomy Projects for Young Scientists, Arco, 1984.
*It's All Elementary: From Atom to the Quantum World of
    Quarks, Leptons, and Gluons,* Lothrop, 1985.
Calendars, F. Watts, 1985.
Space Station, F. Watts, 1987.
Nebulae: The Birth and Death of Stars, Lothrop, 1988.
Space Law, F. Watts, 1988.

Also author of ''Ask Ulysses,'' a monthly column in *Odyssey.*
Contributor to numerous magazines.

SIDELIGHTS: Necia H. Apfel told *CA:* ''After I left Harvard
University Graduate School in 1954, I held miscellaneous jobs
while my husband completed dental school. In 1963 I went
back to school, this time to Northwestern University Graduate
School (astronomy department). This was a field I had always
been interested in since childhood but was discouraged from
pursuing. 'Women don't become astronomers,' I was told. My
decision to return to school came after being given a telescope
for my birthday by my husband. I then took an adult education
class in astronomy and realized how very interested I was in
this subject.

''In 1967 I was appointed a research assistant at Northwestern.
The project that I worked on involved the study of spectro-
scopic binary stars. Dr. J. Allen Hynek was in charge of this
project, and this association eventually led to our co-author-
ship of *Astronomy One,* which was published in 1973.

''From 1979 to 1982 I was busy writing the three juvenile
books now in print. The first one was especially difficult because I wanted to be sure that my explanations of Einstein's
theory could really be understood by a high school (and possibly a very bright junior high school) student. And, of course,
by an adult! I feel it is important for young people to be
exposed to these concepts as early as possible so that they will
be more comfortable with them later on. And I was always
fascinated with the subject, especially when I was told many
years ago that only a handful of people could understand it,
let alone write about it. The book contains no math but has
lots of photos and diagrams. I'm quite proud of it. It is currently being translated into Japanese, but I don't know when
the Japanese edition will be published.

''The other two books are 'First Books' and are meant for
elementary school children. They were fun to write because
both subjects were very familiar to me from my work on the
textbooks and also from my school lectures.

''*Astronomy and Planetology* is a book filled with ideas for
science fair projects in the field of astronomy. It is for high
school students and has information about other science competitions open to this age group.

''At the Adler Planetarium I give courses in astronomy for
children. I particularly like to teach the eight-to-eleven-year-
old group because I find that they are by far the most exciting
and imaginative. It is the same group that I write for in *Odyssey* magazine. My monthly column, ''Ask Ulysses,'' in that
magazine answers readers' questions. Only children can think
up the kind of questions I receive. They are marvelous. Several
times a year I write an article for this same magazine. Some
of my subjects have been black holes, stellar evolution, nebulae, sunspots, comets, sidereal time, galaxies, and relativity.''

ARMSTRONG, Tilly   1927-
(Kate Alexander, Tania Langley)

PERSONAL: Born April 8, 1927, in Sutton, England; daughter
of Alexander Edward (a plumber) and Florence May (Brain)
Armstrong. *Education:* Attended commercial school in Wimbledon, England.

ADDRESSES: Home—23 Leslie Gardens, Sutton, Surrey SM2
6Q4, England. *Agent*—Curtis Brown Ltd., 162-168 Regent
Street, London W1R 5TB, England.

CAREER: World Health Organization, Geneva, Switzerland,
secretary, 1955-58; Glenbow Foundation, Calgary, Alberta,
Canada, assistant archivist, 1959-61; British Steel Corp., London, England, secretary, 1962-72, personnel officer, 1973-81;
writer, 1981—.

MEMBER: Romantic Novelists Association, Society of Authors, International PEN.

WRITINGS:

LIGHT ROMANTIC NOVELS

Lightly Like a Flower, Collins, 1978.
Come Live with Me, Collins, 1979.
Joy Runs High, Collins, 1979, Dell, 1980.
A Limited Engagement, New English Library, 1980.
Summer Tangle, Piatkis Books, 1983.
Small Town Girl, Piatkis Books, 1983.
Pretty Penny, Piatkis Books, 1985.

DRAMATIC NOVELS; UNDER PSEUDONYM KATE ALEXANDER

Fields of Battle, St. Martin's, 1981.
Friends and Enemies, St. Martin's, 1982.
Paths of Peace, Macdonald Publishers (Edinburgh), 1984.
Bright Tomorrows, Macdonald Publishers (Edinburgh), 1985.
Songs of War, Macdonald Publishers (Edinburgh), 1987.

UNDER PSEUDONYM TANIA LANGLEY

Dawn (period novel), Fawcett, 1980 (published in England as
    Mademoiselle Madeleine, Corgi Books, 1981).
London Linnet, Granada Publishing, 1985.
Genevra, Grafton Books, 1987.

SIDELIGHTS: ''Writing started as a hobby,'' Tilly Armstrong
told *CA,* ''became an absorbing interest, and is now my full-
time occupation. I like to vary my writing, alternating light
romantic novels with nineteenth-century period novels and
strongly dramatic books.

''I wrote for at least twenty years, making only occasional
attempts to get published, all unsuccessful. My breakthrough
came when I started sending manuscripts to women's magazines. I had two romantic serials accepted simultaneously by
the sister magazines, *Woman's Weekly* and *Woman and Home.*

''After that I was launched and started getting my novels into
hardback and paperback. At first I expanded my writing into
other types of novels because I was faced with the possibility
of what I still regard as my true career—personnel work—
coming to an end with cutbacks in the steel industry. I became
redundant in November, 1981, and by that time I was well
launched as a writer under my own name and my two pseudonyms.

''I particularly enjoy the research I do before starting to write
a novel. This is mainly in the local public library, paying
particular attention to old newspapers. For my three war nov-

els, written under the name of Kate Alexander, I also consulted the Imperial War Museum in London. All my books are love stories, but I do like them to have an extra dimension, an interesting overseas setting for the lighter romantic novels, for instance. *Dawn* centered round the Franco-Prussian War of 1870-71, *London Linnett* deals with the London Music Hall at the end of the last century, and *Genevra* with early department stores. Three of the Kate Alexander novels are set in World War II, and two in the post-war period. I classify myself as a storyteller rather than a writer with a message, and I try to write novels with a good, strong story line and well-defined characters.''

* * *

ARNDT, Karl John Richard 1903-

PERSONAL: Born September 17, 1903, in St. Paul, Minn.; son of Edward Louis (a professor and founder of Lutheran Church, Missouri Synod, in China) and Maria (Solomon) Arndt; married Rosine Anne Linhorst, 1933 (divorced); married Blanca Hedwig Renner, October 7, 1950; children: Karl Siegfried Norman, Carola Anne Sylvia. *Education:* Undergraduate study at St. John's College, Winfield, Kan., and under father in Hankow, China; Concordia Seminary, St. Louis, Mo., diploma, 1927; Washington University, St. Louis, Mo., A.M., 1928; graduate study at University of Marburg and University of Berlin, 1928-29; Johns Hopkins University, Ph.D., 1933. *Politics:* Conservative Independent.

ADDRESSES: Home—5 Hazelwood Rd., Worcester, Mass. 01610. *Office*—Department of German, Clark University, Worcester, Mass. 01610.

CAREER: Worked with U.S. Mississippi River Survey Service, 1924-25; instructor in German and Greek at Concordia College, Edmonton, Alberta, Canada, 1925-26; instructor in German at University of Missouri—Columbia, 1929-31, and at Goucher College and Johns Hopkins University, both Baltimore, Md., 1931-33; Hartwick College, Oneonta, N.Y., professor of German and Greek, 1933-35; Louisiana State University, Baton Rouge, assistant professor, 1935-42, associate professor of Germanics, 1942-45; staff member of Education and Religious Affairs Division, U.S. Military Government for Germany, 1945-50; Clark University, Worcester, Mass., professor of German, 1950-74, professor emeritus, 1974—, head of department, 1950-69. Sealsfield Lecturer in Germany (at invitation of Sealsfield Gesellschaft), 1964; lecturer on German-American press history at universities in Germany, 1965; delivered Bicentennial lectures in Kansas, Ohio, and Rhode Island, 1976. Director of Harmony Society Papers project. Member of National Advisory Council on Ethnic Heritage Studies of the United States, 1972-75, and of National Historical Publications and Records commission; consultant to Historic New Harmony, Indiana, Inc., 1975-82.

MEMBER: Modern Language Association of America, American Association of Teachers of German, American Antiquarian Society, Sealsfield Gesellschaft (Germany), Gesellschaft fuer deutsche Presseforschung (Bremen; corresponding member), Phi Beta Kappa.

AWARDS, HONORS: Research grants from Social Science Research Council, 1942, from American Philosophical Society, 1953, 1960, 1963, 1966, and 1972-73, from Pabst Foundation, 1965, from Stiftung Volkswagenwerk, 1967, from National Endowment for the Humanities, 1967-68, and from Deutsche Forschungsgemeinschaft, 1974-76; Guggenheim research fellow, 1957-58; Award of Merit from the American Association for State and Local History, 1976; Das Grosse Verdienstkreuz des Verdienstordens der Bundesrepublik Deutschland, 1986; award from the German-American National Congress, 1986.

WRITINGS:

Early German-American Narratives, American Book Co., 1941.
(With May E. Olson) *German-American Newspapers and Periodicals, 1732-1955: History and Bibliography*, Quelle & Meyer (Heidelberg), 1961, 2nd edition, revised with appendix, Johnson Reprint, 1965.
George Rapp's Harmony Society: 1785-1847, University of Pennsylvania Press, 1965, revised edition, Fairleigh Dickinson University Press, 1972.
George Rapp's Successors and Material Heirs, 1847-1916, Fairleigh Dickinson University Press, 1971.
(Editor) *Charles Sealsfields Saemtliche Werke*, twenty-three volumes, Verlag Georg Olms, 1972-81.
The German Language Press of the Americas, Volume I (with May Olson), Verlag Dokumentation, 1976, Volume II, Verlag Dokumentation, 1973, Volume III, K. G. Saur Verlag, 1980.
A Documentary History of the Indiana Decade of the Harmony Society, 1814-1824, Indiana Historical Society, Volume I: *1814-1819*, 1975, Volume II: *1820-1824*, 1977.
The Treaty of Amity and Commerce of 1785 between His Majesty the King of Prussia and the U.S.A., Verlag Heinz Moos, 1977.
The Annotated and Enlarged Edition of Ernst Steiger's Precentennial Bibliography: The Periodical Literature of the United States, Kraus-Thomson, 1979.
George Rapp's Separatists: 1700-1803, Harmony Society, 1980.
Harmony on the Connoquenessing: George Rapp's First American Harmony: 1803-1815, Harmony Society, 1980.
Smolnikars Beziehungen zu Georg Rapps Harmonie Gesellschaft, Acta Neophilologica (Ljubljana, Yugoslavia), 1981.
(Contributor) *Yearbook of German-American Studies*, University of Kansas, Volume XVI, 1981, Volume XVIII, 1983.
Harmony on the Wabash in Transition: 1824-1826, Harmony Society, 1982.
The First German Broadside and Newspaper Printing of the American Declaration of Independence, Pennsylvania Folklife, 1986.
George Rapp's Years of Glory: 1834-1847, Peter Lang, 1987.

Editor of revised edition of Seidensticker's *First Century of German Printing in America*, 1973, and of Harmony Society papers; also editor of *German Prisoners of War Camp Papers Published in the U.S.A. from 1943 to 1946*, 18 reels of microfilm with a bound guide to all reels, for Library of Congress, 1965. Contributor to *Proceedings of the American Antiquarian Society* and other proceedings and yearbooks. Contributor of about fifty articles and reviews to language and history journals in America and Germany, including *The Louisiana Historical Quarterly* and *Comparative Literature*.

WORK IN PROGRESS: Three remaining volumes of *Documentary History of George Rapp's Harmony Society, 1706-1916*, a ten volumes series; revised edition of Seidensticker's *A History and Bibliography of the First Hundred Years of German Printing in America*.

SIDELIGHTS: Karl John Richard Arndt told *CA:* ''I took to publishing not because I consider myself a writer, which I am not, but because I belong to the last of those fortunate German-Americans who grew up bilingually and who treasure their beautiful language and its old classic literature just as much as Anglo-Americans love theirs. We sang the American national anthem in German and English with love and devotion. We did not worship the Kaiser, and we were more American in our loyalties than the Anglo-Americans in World War I who had never cut the umbilical cord from Britain. As Prussian-Americans we were proud of Frederick the Great because he was a friend of the American Revolution and never sent his soldiers to the United States to fight against our Independence. He was so popular with the Americans that there actually was a movement under way to make his brother our 'king' in order to give our wobbly young democracy more stability. Our Declaration of Independence got its first newspaper announcement in German in Heinrich Miller's *Pennsylvanischer Staatsbote,* and that patriotic German-American would have been the first newspaperman to publish the entire text if he had not been delayed by the time it took to translate it into German. As it is, he was the third newspaperman to print it, and the first to present it in the beautiful Gutenberg type headlines it deserved.

"With a justified pride in my Prussian-American heritage, I was insulted and angered that my King-George-loving countrymen had persecuted my loyal German-American countrymen and actually had passed laws making it illegal to teach German in this free nation. So when the same kind of hatred was developing at the start of World War II, I published my first book, *Early German-American Narratives.* It bore a motto from Charles Sealsfield (Karl Postl), celebrated internationally in the 1840s as 'the greatest American author': 'To be a free native American citizen is the highest privilege—the most glorious attribute.'

"My lifelong research into the great contributions of the German-Americans to the building of this powerful nation has resulted in the development of the most extensive private archives and library in this field of American history. I consider it my purpose in life to transcribe, translate, and interpret the German-American record of achievement to all of my countrymen as well as to people abroad. Because I was so fortunate as to have been educated autocratically by devoted teachers, I still learned to read and write the old German script as written by Martin Luther and Goethe. Germans today, unfortunately, have been 're-educated' with a resulting decline in educational performance and values.

"To uphold the honor of my Prussian-American heritage I began to publish, to pay an obligation to all of my fellow Americans. I expect to continue my work as long as I live."

*   *   *

ARNSTEIN, Walter L(eonard) 1930-

PERSONAL: Second syllable of surname rhymes with "fine"; born May 14, 1930, in Stuttgart, Germany (now West Germany); became U.S. citizen, 1944; son of Richard (a wholesale dealer in textiles) and Charlotte (Heymann) Arnstein; married Charlotte Culver Sutphen (a teacher of piano), June 8, 1952; children: Sylvia, Peter. *Education:* City College (now City College of the City University of New York), B.S. in Social Science, 1951; Columbia University, M.A., 1954; University of London, graduate study, 1956-57; Northwestern University, Ph.D., 1961. *Politics:* Independent.

ADDRESSES: Home—804 West Green St., Champaign, Ill. 61820. *Office*—Department of History, 309 Gregory Hall, 810 South Wright St., University of Illinois, Urbana, Ill. 61801.

CAREER: Roosevelt University, Chicago, Ill., assistant professor, 1957-62, associate professor, 1962-66, professor of history and acting dean of graduate division, 1966-67; University of Illinois at Urbana-Champaign, professor of history, 1968—, chairman of department, 1974-78. Visiting associate professor of history, Northwestern University, Evanston, Ill., 1963-64, 1966; visiting lecturer or professor, City College (now City College of the City University of New York), summers, 1954, 1955, University of Illinois, summer, 1964, and University of Chicago, spring, 1965; visiting fellow, Clare Hall, Cambridge University, 1982. Associate, Center for Advanced Study, University of Illinois, fall, 1972. Member, Illinois Humanities Council, 1980-85, vice-chair, 1983-84. *Military service:* U.S. Army, 1951-53; served in Korea.

MEMBER: Historical Association (England), Royal Historical Society (fellow), North American Conference on British Studies (member of executive committee, 1971-76), American Historical Association (chairman, Schuyler Prize committee, 1980-81), Midwest Conference on British Studies (president, 1980-82), Midwest Victorian Studies Association (president, 1977-80), Phi Beta Kappa, Phi Alpha Theta.

AWARDS, HONORS: Fulbright scholarship in England, 1956-57; Roosevelt University faculty research fellowship, 1962; American Council of Learned Societies fellowship, 1967-68; John Gilmary Shea Prize, American Catholic Historical Association, 1982.

WRITINGS:

The Bradlaugh Case: A Study in Late Victorian Opinion and Politics, Clarendon Press, 1965, revised edition published as *The Bradlaugh Case: Atheism, Sex, and Politics among the Late Victorians,* University of Missouri Press, 1984.

A History of England, edited by Lacey B. Smith, Heath, Volume IV: *Britain Yesterday and Today: 1830 to the Present,* 1966, 5th edition, 1988, Volume III: *The Age of Aristocracy, 1688-1830,* 3rd edition (with William B. Willcox; Arnstein was not associated with earlier editions), 1976, 5th edition, 1988.

(Contributor) F. C. Jaher, editor, *The Rich, the Wellborn, and the Powerful,* University of Illinois Press, 1973.

(Contributor) Alan O'Day, editor, *The Edwardian Age: Conflict and Stability, 1900-1914,* Shoe String, 1979.

(Editor) *The Past Speaks: Sources and Problems in British History since 1688,* Heath, 1981.

Protestant Versus Catholic in Mid-Victorian England: Mr. Newdegate and the Nuns, University of Missouri Press, 1982.

(Contributor) Gail Malmgreen, editor, *Religion in the Lives of English Women, 1750-1930,* Croom Helm, 1986.

Also editor of and contributor to *Modern Historians of Britain,* 1987. Contributor to numerous journals, including *Albion, History Today, Irish Historical Studies, Journal of British Studies, Journal of the History of Ideas,* and *Victorian Studies.* Also contributor to newspapers. Advisory board member, *Victorian Studies,* 1966-75; member, board of editors, *The Historian,* 1976—, and *American Historical Review,* 1982-85.

SIDELIGHTS: Walter L. Arnstein, the author of numerous works on British history, explores the roots and political implications of nineteenth-century anti-Catholic sentiment in his book *Protestant Versus Catholic in Mid-Victorian England: Mr. Newdegate and the Nuns.* The book's chief subject, Charles Newdegate, was a long-standing member of Parliament and a primary leader of the English anti-Catholic movement; the title specifically refers to the 1870 House of Commons committee headed by Newdegate to investigate convents and the possibility that women were being lured into a life of enslavement. The book's larger purpose, however, as Edward Norman comments in the *Times Literary Supplement,* is "a study of the penetration of religious issues into Victorian politics." R. W. Davis in the *American Historical Review* likewise notes that "Arnstein has set out to rescue the anti-Catholic factor in nineteenth-century English society and politics from the obscurity that has always enshrouded it. As always, he tells his story well, with style and humor, weaving it around the career of . . . Newdegate." Norman concurs, adding that *Protestant Versus Catholic* "in general is a model of its kind[,] . . . entertainingly written, yet strictly academic in its use of source materials and interests."

BIOGRAPHICAL/CRITICAL SOURCES:

PERIODICALS

American Historical Review, February, 1983.
History, June, 1983.
Times Literary Supplement, November 11, 1965, July 16, 1982.
Yale Review, March, 1966.

＊　　＊　　＊

ASCHER, Sheila
(Ascher/Straus, a joint pseudonym)

PERSONAL: Born in New York, N.Y.; daughter of Arnold (a plumber) and Bessie (Eisenberg) Ascher. *Education:* Received B.A. from Brooklyn College and M.A. from Columbia University.

ADDRESSES: Home—118-07 Newport Ave., Rockaway Park, N.Y. 11694.

CAREER: Writer, 1973—.

AWARDS, HONORS: Experimental fiction prize from *Panache* magazine, 1973, for story "City/Edge"; Pushcart Prize from Pushcart Press, 1978-79, for excerpt from novel titled "Even after a Machine Is Dismantled, It Continues to Operate, with or without Purpose"; New York State Creative Artists Public Service fellowship in fiction, 1981-82; Treacle Press First Novel Prize, 1982, for *The Menaced Assassin.*

WRITINGS:

WITH DENNIS STRAUS, UNDER JOINT PSEUDONYM ASCHER/STRAUS

Letter to an Unknown Woman (story), Treacle Press, 1980.
The Menaced Assassin (novel), Treacle Press, 1982.
Red Moon/Red Lake (novella), Top Stories, 1984.

SPACE NOVELS; WITH STRAUS, UNDER JOINT PSEUDONYM ASCHER/
    STRAUS

"As It Returns," first presented in New York at Contemporary Arts Gallery of New York University, May, 1975, published in *Seventh Assembling,* 1977.
"The Blue Hangar," first presented in New York at Gateway National Recreation Area, August 2-3, 1975, published in *Coda,* April/May, 1976, in *Queen Street T Magazine,* spring, 1977, and in *Interstate,* 1979.
"Twelve Simultaneous Sundays," first presented in New York at Gegenschein Vaudeville Placenter, September 19-December 5, 1976.

CONTRIBUTOR TO ANTHOLOGIES

Pushcart Prize Anthology III, Pushcart Press, 1978-79.

Likely Stories, Treacle Press, 1981.
Chelsea: A Retrospective, Chelsea Associates, 1984.
Chouteau Review: Ten Year Retrospective, Chouteau Review, 1985.

OTHER

Also co-publisher with Straus of "Green Inventory," partially published by Ghost Dance Press, winter, 1975-76, and spring, 1977. Creator of language art gallery installations, including "Language and Structure in North America," Toronto; "Beyond the Page," Philadelphia, "Last Correspondence Show," Sacramento, "First New York Post Card Show," New York, "International Mail Art Exhibition," Northampton, Mass., "TELIC Exhibition," Kansas City, Mo., "Assembling Exhibition," New York. Contributor to journals, including *Chicago Review, Interstate, Exile, Chouteau Review, Sun and Moon, Chelsea, Paris Review, Beyond Baroque, Gallimafry, Panache, Aspen Anthology, Aphra, Tamarisk, Zone, Calyx, Annex, Benzene, Fifth Assembling, Ghost Dance, Neoneo Do-Do, Telephone, Sixth Assembling, Gegenschein Quarterly, Source, Eighth Assembling, Margins,* and *Precisely.*

WORK IN PROGRESS: A multi-volume novel with Straus called *Monica's Chronicle;* a novel "attempting to divine the hidden presence of the future in our midst and to suggest the nature of a kind of sub-population drawn to it."

SIDELIGHTS: "There is no question when you read what they write, you're in the presence of Genius," said Hugh Fox regarding Sheila Ascher and Dennis Straus, the individuals behind the Ascher/Straus pseudonym. Though they sign both names on their writings, Ascher and Straus do not work together, and they write for different reasons.

In order to produce a work, the authors avoid collaborating in the conventional manner. They share experiences, material, and observations, but one writes while the other criticizes and edits. "We're a Collective," Ascher told the *Cumberland Journal.* "We POOL everything. We don't work together. I don't know what he's doing, he doesn't know what I'm doing, then we put it all together. It's very strange." According to Straus, Ascher writes to discover life's guiding principles while he identifies writing with dreaming. "For me reading and writing were like always forms of a dream, a waking dream," he explained. Writing, he continued, is "a matter of finding a way of dreaming—on paper."

Ascher and Straus produce experimental literature. Perhaps the most conventional in appearance, *The Menaced Assassin,* their first novel in book form, takes place on the plane of magic and dreams. In the novel, a woman tries to make herself into the person she wants to be, an individual who reflects the cultural obsessions generated by contemporary media.

Ascher and Straus's other creations are space novels, works that use non-written components, such as photographs or airfields, as well as the written word. Using architecture, "public spaces," or huge edifices to structure these "environmental narratives," the authors bring physical and material elements to the works so that reading a space novel becomes an active, public experience instead of a private pastime. For instance, "Twelve Simultaneous Sundays" is a space novel written publicly on twelve consecutive Sundays. "Each week a new element was installed," explained Ascher, "and there was no way to read the whole book at any one time, you had to keep coming back." Such an innovation, the authors suggested, could change the style of the novel as a genre. "The space novel," they remarked, "might at some point signal the end of the novel as a bastion of art privacy, of private consumerism, of product purchase, relaxation, nest building, and interior decoration.''

Ascher told *CA:* ''My real writing life began with the awareness that writing is artificial. Nothing natural or necessary about it and no privileged equation between it and life. Life is life and writing is writing. This fact is so obvious that the perennial argument between defenders of 'experimental' and 'traditional' writing about what fiction ought to be ('imagination,' 'meta-fiction,' 'deconstruction,' etc. vs. 'imitation of life') has always seemed false to me. Artists have always invented new strategies of reduction and exaggeration to find fresh forms for the inner reality of their visions and for some correspondence, however abstract, mysterious and emblematic, to the outer world. Fiction is great because there is no recipe for it, certainly not 'life' or 'reality' or even 'fiction.' There have been so many dumb things said on that score that, I think, when a writer first discovers that fiction is an artifact, its meaning in its montage, there's a need to make that clear in the fiction. That was true for me and then, gradually, the need wore out.

''In the work (early 'anti-fictions' of the mid-seventies, visual language work, large-scale re-inventions of the fundamental form of the book, over-all structural texts, novels, stories) I've co-published, *not* co-authored, with Dennis Straus (the Ascher/Straus emblem is a sign devised for a collective enterprise that includes all possible mutually helpful writing procedures *except* writing together) I see the evolution of several ideas. Early structuralism opens up to attempt to include traditionally nonfictional elements and to incorporate materials from our life; we try to develop methods of addressing and approaching the reader, exploring the book as a bridge and a barrier; exploration of what might be called theme-oriented montage as the basis of narrative over and above nineteenth century conventions of writing, plot and character development; some rather complex reconstructions in which sets of montaged fictions are related in binary sets; fiction as 'site reading' and 'space novel.'

''In the late seventies we backed off from the space novel idea partly because pursuing it to its next logical stages would have meant further development of performance, plastic and electronic elements at the expense of writing. We both had a hunger for writing's solitariness.

''It's clear to me, but can't be to others because things don't appear when they're written and seldom in the sequence they're written, that everything carries the work done before it. All the earlier formal and conceptual concerns are recycled in some way in the more recent stories and novels (probably why, though they seem relatively straightforward to us, others still label them 'experimental').

''*Monica's Chronicle,* the long project we're doing now (which I was doing in one form or another all along), picks up the thread of fiction as the reading of a place, fiction as a long look rather than a series of quick glances, fiction as a revelation of process, as a direct approach to the reader over a duration capable of entering the reader's life as an element of living (bridging writer and reader through a shared duration), presented as a sequence of novels of panoramic extension. The biography of one person's knowledge of others and of a place.''

BIOGRAPHICAL/CRITICAL SOURCES:

PERIODICALS

Chelsea, Number 36, 1977.

Cumberland Journal, spring, 1981.
Interstate 12, 1979.
Library Journal, October 1, 1981.
Village Voice, October 19, 1982.
Zone, spring/summer, 1981.

* * *

ASCHER/STRAUS
   See ASCHER, Sheila
   and STRAUS, Dennis

* * *

AUSTER, Paul   1947-

PERSONAL: Born February 3, 1947, in Newark, N.J.; married Lydia Davis (a writer); married second wife, Siri Hustuedt, 1981; children: two. *Education:* Columbia University, B.A., 1969, M.A., 1970.

ADDRESSES: Home—458 Third St., Brooklyn, N.Y. 11215.

CAREER: Variously employed as a merchant seaman, a census taker, a tutor, a telephone operator for the Paris bureau of the *New York Times,* and as the caretaker of a farmhouse in Provence, France; translator, critic, poet, novelist. Teacher in creative writing program, Princeton University, 1986—.

AWARDS, HONORS: Poetry grant from Ingram Merrill Foundation, 1975 and 1982; P.E.N. Translation Center grant, 1977; National Endowment for the Arts fellowship for poetry, 1979, and for creative writing, 1985; *City of Glass* was nominated for an Edgar Award for best mystery novel, 1986; *The Locked Room* was nominated for a *Boston Globe* Literary Press Award for fiction.

WRITINGS:

Unearth: Poems, 1970-1972, Living Hand, 1974.
Wall Writing: Poems, 1971-1975, Figures, 1976.
''Eclipse'' (play), first produced in New York City by Artists' Theatre, March, 1977.
Facing the Music, Station Hill, 1980.
White Spaces, Station Hill, 1980.
The Invention of Solitude, SUN, 1982.
In the Country of Last Things, Viking, 1987.

''THE NEW YORK TRILOGY''

City of Glass, Sun & Moon Press, 1985.
Ghosts, Sun & Moon Press, 1986.
The Locked Room, Sun & Moon Press, 1987.

EDITOR

The Random House Book of Twentieth-Century French Poetry, Random House, 1982.
(And translator) Joseph Joubert, *The Notebooks of Joseph Joubert: A Selection,* North Point Press, 1983.

TRANSLATOR

A Little Anthology of Surrealist Poems, Siamese Banana Press, 1972.
Jacques Dupin, *Fits and Starts: Selected Poems of Jacques Dupin,* Living Hand, 1974.
(With Lydia Davis) Saul Friedlander and Mahmoud Hussein, *Arabs and Israelis: A Dialogue,* Holmes & Meier, 1975.
The Uninhabited: Selected Poems of Andre de Bouchet, Living Hand, 1976.

(With L. Davis) Jean-Paul Sartre, *Life Situations*, Pantheon, 1978.
(With L. Davis) Jean Chesneaux, *China: The People's Republic*, Pantheon, 1979.
(With L. Davis) Chesneaux and others, *China from the 1911 Revolution to Liberation*, Pantheon, 1979.
Stephane Mallarme, *A Tomb for Anatole*, North Point Press, 1983.
Maurice Blanchot, *Vicious Circles*, Station Hill, 1985.
Philippe Petit, *On the High Wire*, Random House, 1985.
(With Margit Rowell) Joan Miro, *Selected Writings*, G. K. Hall, 1986.

OTHER

Contributor of articles and translations of poetry to magazines, including *New York Times Book Review*, *Art News*, *Poetry*, *New York Review of Books*, *Harper's* and *Saturday Review*.

WORK IN PROGRESS: A new book of poems.

SIDELIGHTS: Paul Auster has been a published author since the mid-1970s, but it was not until he brought out his "New York Trilogy" in the mid-1980s that he began to attract serious critical attention. Before producing this trio of post-modern detective novels, he had labored in relative obscurity as a poet, essayist, and translator of French literature. Even after completing the first volume, *City of Glass*, Auster was not immediately successful: the grim and intellectually puzzling mystery was rejected by seventeen different publishers. Nevertheless, when Sun & Moon Press finally issued the novel in 1985, it attracted far more notice than Auster's earlier work and generated considerable interest in the remaining two projected volumes. Completed in 1987, the trilogy has raised Auster's visibility and marked him as a talent to watch. From critics such as Toronto *Globe and Mail* contributor Margaret Cannon, he is already evoking the highest praise: "As a novelist, Paul Auster has gone beyond excellence and given the phrase 'experimental fiction' a good name. With these three novels, known as the New York Trilogy, Auster has created bona fide literary works, with all the rigor and intellect demanded of contemporary literature."

Each of the three novels tells a different story, but all share common properties. In addition to their New York setting, the books are linked by style and theme. In one of the books, Auster appears as a character in his own novel, and in all three he intentionally blurs the distinction between author and text. This post-modern device, as Jack Fuller notes in the Chicago *Tribune Books*, raises questions of identity that resonate throughout the series: "Who exactly is the client? Who is the villain? Who is the author? There are dopplegangers and chilling coincidences. And in the less literal sense, there is the identification of the hunter with his quarry."

While instances of confused or mistaken identity are common in the mystery genre, critics say that Auster takes this convention and develops it into a metaphor for contemporary urban life. "In his detectives who degenerate beyond the standard seediness into self-jailing voyeurs and bagpersons in the cramped streets of New York City, he has provided a striking vision of contemporary American stasis," writes *Washington Post Book World* contributor Dennis Drabelle. He labels the novels *"post-existentialist private eye."*

Auster's dark vision emerges in the trilogy's first novel, *City of Glass*. On the surface, it appears to be a clever mystery novel that exploits the conventions of the detective genre. "The real mystery, however, is one of confused character identity," suggests *New York Times Book Review* contributor Toby Olson, "the descent of a writer into a labyrinth in which fact and fiction become increasingly difficult to separate." The novel opens when Quinn, a pseudonymous detective novelist, receives a phone call intended for a real detective (whose name we will later learn is Paul Auster). Lonely and bored, Quinn takes on Auster's identity and accepts the case. His job is to trail a madman named Stillman, recently released from a mental institution to which he had been committed for isolating his son in a locked room for nine years. Stillman, once a brilliant linguist, had segregated his son in hopes of recapturing the primordial human language spoken by Adam and Eve. Now that Stillman has been released, his son's life is in danger. Thus a detective is hired.

Critical response to *City of Glass* has been highly enthusiastic. At the same time that he satisfies mystery readers' appetites for a good story, Auster moves into the realm of serious literature, his supporters say. "'City of Glass' is about the degeneration of language, the shiftings of identity, the struggle to remain human in a great metropolis, when the city itself is cranking on its own falling-apart mechanical life that completely overrides any and every individual," notes *Los Angeles Times Book Review* critic Carolyn See. She deems the book "an experimental novel that wanders and digresses and loses its own narrative thread, but with all that . . . thoughtfully and cleverly draws our attention to these questions of self." The way the novel subtly shifts from a standard mystery story to an existential quest for identity also captures Toby Olson's attention: "Each detail, each small revelation must be attended to as significant. And such attention brings ambiguity, confusion, and paranoia. Is it important that Quinn's dead son has the same name as Stillman? What can it mean that 'Quinn' rhymes with 'twin' and 'sin'?" As Canon puts it, "This is a novel that's full of intellectual puzzles, not all of them resolved." Despite its challenges, Olson believes that "the book is a pleasure to read, full of suspense and action."

In *Ghosts*, the second volume of the trilogy, Auster continues his investigation of lost identity on a more abstract plane. "A client named White hires a detective named Blue to follow a man named Black," Drabelle explains. "Gradually Blue realizes he's been ruined. All he can do is stare at Black, eternally writing a book in the rented room across the street, and draw a weekly paycheck. Black and White are probably the same person, and Blue is 'trapped . . . into doing nothing, into being so inactive as to reduce his life to almost no life at all.'" Auster's choice of names for his protagonists coupled with his coy and knowing tone throughout the book suggest that he is playing mind games with the reader. The real mystery, he implies, is not within the story but "on some higher level," as Rebecca Goldstein observes. "We are not being asked to submerge ourselves in this story, to believe in its reality," Goldstein continues in the *New York Times Book Review*. "We are to stay above it, to read it as, well, metaphor; and our fanatical attention to details and frenetic attempts at deduction (both necessary for reading a mystery novel correctly) are to be directed upward toward the question, what does it all mean?"

Goldstein acknowledges that *Ghosts*, which solves the internal mystery but leaves the larger questions unanswered, does not fit the mold of the traditional detective novel. Nonetheless, she judges the work "nearly perfect." Others are less impressed. Margaret Cannon, citing problems with continuity, concludes that *Ghosts* has "as much weight as any middle-of-three work can have. It provides the history and heft for the next book, but it cannot really stand alone as a mystery with a beginning, a middle, and an end.''

The trilogy's concluding volume, *The Locked Room,* is widely judged to be the richest and by far the most compelling book of the trilogy. Less abstract and more accessible, this story features flesh and blood characters with whom readers can easily identify. Several reviewers suggest that Auster's use of a first-person narrator enhances the book. ''When Auster finally allows himself the luxury of character, what a delicious treat he serves up for the reader!'' Carolyn See writes in the *Los Angeles Times.* Though *The Locked Room* is a mystery like the first two installments, this ''story is told in the first person by a genuine character who feels love and pain and envy.'' Because of the first-person narration ''Mr. Auster's philosophical asides now sound heartfelt instead of stentorian and his descents into semiological *Angst* feel genuinely anguished and near,'' Steven Schiff suggests in the *New York Times Book Review.* He and other critics hypothesize that the nameless narrator represents Auster himself.

The story begins when the narrator is summoned by the wife of an old friend from childhood with whom he has lost touch. Fanshawe, as the friend is called, has disappeared and is presumed dead. A fantastically gifted writer, Fanshawe has left behind some unpublished writings as well as instructions for his friend to see them into print. As time passes, the narrator easily moves into Fanshawe's existence, marrying his wife, publishing his work, and eventually engendering rumors that he is actually Fanshawe or, at least, the man who created the works. When he receives a communication from the real Fanshawe, the narrator is plunged into danger. ''What happens next cannot be revealed,'' See insists in her book review,

''because . . . Auster has created characters so fragile and believable that their privacy should only be broken by a respectful reader who cares enough to buy their book.''

Without revealing the ending, Schiff concludes that ''the novel's most vivid passages conjure up a true dark night of the soul. . . . Mr. Auster puts his finger on the pulsing locus of language and identity. He understands that the detective of the self is trapped, forced to use that clumsiest of tools, language, to ferret out what mere language can never discover. Putting a name on something makes it at once available and all the more elusive. . . . In 'The Locked Room,' Mr. Auster proclaims the urgency of that dilemma, not just for writers but for all those who seek the truth behind the fictions they read and the fictions they live.''

BIOGRAPHICAL/CRITICAL SOURCES:

PERIODICALS

Globe and Mail (Toronto), March 14, 1987.
Los Angeles Times, September 1, 1986, March 2, 1987, June 18, 1987.
Los Angeles Times Book Review, November 17, 1985.
Nation, November 20, 1982.
New Yorker, December 30, 1985.
New York Times Book Review, January 23, 1983, February 27, 1983, January 15, 1984, November 3, 1985, May 25, 1986, June 29, 1986, January 4, 1987, May 17, 1987.
Times Literary Supplement, August 30, 1985.
Tribune Books (Chicago), March 29, 1987.
Washington Post Book World, December 5, 1982, June 15, 1986, March 29, 1987.

—Sketch by Donna Olendorf

B

BABBIE, Earl (Robert) 1938-

PERSONAL: Born January 8, 1938, in Detroit, Mich.; son of Herman Octave (an automobile body mechanic) and Marion (Towle) Babbie; married Sheila Trimble (a project assistant for Erhard Seminars Training), May 17, 1965; children: Aaron Robert. *Education:* Harvard University, A.B. (cum laude), 1960; University of California, Berkeley, M.A., 1966, Ph.D., 1969. *Politics:* "Active, reformist, civil libertarian." *Religion:* None.

ADDRESSES: Office—Department of Sociology, Chapman College, Orange, Calif. 92666.

CAREER: University of California, Berkeley, research sociologist at Survey Research Center, 1966-68, assistant director of center, 1967-68; University of Hawaii, Honolulu, assistant professor, 1968-70, associate professor, 1970-74, professor, 1974-80, affiliate professor of sociology, 1980-87, chairman of department, 1973-74, 1977-79, program director for survey research at Social Science Research Institute, 1968-69, director of Institutional Research Office, 1970, director of Survey Research Office, 1970-73, associate director of Social Science Research Institute, 1972-73; Babbie Enterprises, Mill Valley, Calif., president, 1976—; Chapman College, Orange, Calif., professor of sociology and chairman of department, 1987—. University of California, Berkeley, visiting scholar, 1975, visiting professor, 1980. Partner, Pacific Poll Co., 1968-70; member of Hawaii State Census Tract Committee, 1969-74; president of Save Wawamalu Association, 1971-73; member of research committee of Hawaii Visitors Bureau, 1972-74; vice-president of Hawaii Center for Environmental Education, 1973-74; Erhard Seminars Training of Hawaii, vice-president, 1975-76, member of national advisory board, 1976-80. Member of board of directors of Citizens for Hawaii, 1972-74, Policy Research Institute, 1976-79, and Holiday Project, 1981-83; member of planning committee of University of Hawaii Gerentology Center, 1977-78. Member of research advisory committee of Hawaii Commission on Children and Youth, 1972-74; chairman of advisory council of Hunger Project, 1978-83. *Military service:* U.S. Marine Corps, 1960-66; active duty, 1960-63; became first lieutenant.

MEMBER: American Sociological Association, American Association for Public Opinion Research, American Civil Liberties Union, Zero Population Growth (member of board of directors, 1981-83).

AWARDS, HONORS: Grant from Haas Community Fund, 1973, for the writing of *The Practice of Social Research;* grant from Erhard Seminars Training of Hawaii, 1975.

WRITINGS:

(With Charles Y. Glock and Benjamin B. Ringer) *To Comfort and to Challenge,* University of California Press, 1967.

(With William Nicholls) *Oakland in Transition: A Summary of the 701 Household Survey* (monograph), Survey Research Center, University of California, 1969.

Science and Morality in Medicine, University of California Press, 1970.

A Profile of the Honolulu Model Neighborhoods: 1969 (monograph), Honolulu Model Cities Project, 1970.

Hubris: Hawaii Uniform Bank and Remote Interactive System (monograph), Survey Research Office, University of Hawaii, 1971.

The Maximillion Report (monograph), Citizens for Hawaii, 1972.

Survey Research Methods, with instructor's manual, Wadsworth, 1973.

(Contributor) Glock, editor, *Religion in Sociological Perspective,* Wadsworth, 1973.

The Practice of Social Research, Wadsworth, 1975, 4th edition, 1985.

(With Robert Huitt) *Practicing Social Research* (manual), Wadsworth, 1975, 2nd edition, 1979.

Society by Agreement, Wadsworth, 1977, 2nd edition published as *Sociology: An Introduction,* 1980, 3rd edition, 1983.

Understanding Sociology: A Context for Action, Wadsworth, 1981.

Social Research for Consumers, Wadsworth, 1982.

Apple LOGO for Teachers, Wadsworth, 1984.

You Can Make a Difference: The Heroic Potential within Us All, St. Martin's, 1985.

Also author of *Observing Ourselves,* 1986. Contributor to academic journals, including *Review of Religious Research, Journal for the Scientific Study of Religion, American Sociological Review, Social Forces, American Journal of Correc-*

tion, and *Graduate Review.* Editorial reader for *Sociology of Education,* 1967.

WORK IN PROGRESS: Doorways to Beyond; The Sociological Spirit.

SIDELIGHTS: Earl Babbie writes: "You can make a difference. Indeed, you do and will make a difference—inevitably. A question worth asking yourself is: 'What kind of difference am I making—today, right now?'"

AVOCATIONAL INTERESTS: "Saving the world."

*   *   *

BAKER, Michael H(enry) C(hadwick)   1937-

PERSONAL: Born June 19, 1937, in Croydon, Surrey, England; son of Leonard Chadwick (a chauffeur) and Elsie (a cook; maiden name, Knight) Baker; married Maeve Finucane (a teacher), August 17, 1968; children: William, Daniel, Samuel. *Education:* Attended Croydon Art School, 1958-61; Chelsea Art School, diploma in design, 1962; Liverpool Art College, art teacher's diploma, 1963. *Politics:* "Socialist (member of Labour Party)." *Religion:* Christian.

ADDRESSES: Home—75 Northmoor Way, Wareham, Dorsetshire BH20 4EG, England. *Office*—Swanage Middle School, Swanage, Dorsetshire, England.

CAREER: Newspaper reporter and photographer, 1954-55; industrial and commercial photographer, 1955-58; Southport School of Art, Southport, Lancashire, England, lecturer in photography, 1964-66; art teacher in elementary schools in Huyton, England, 1967-68, and Croydon, England, 1968-73; Oxted County Comprehensive School, Oxted, England, art teacher in secondary school, 1973-77; Purbeck Teachers Centre and Swanage Middle School, Swanage, Dorsetshire, England, art teacher, 1977—. *Military service:* Royal Air Force, senior aircraftsman, 1956-58.

MEMBER: Amnesty International (Poole Group), Great Western Society, Society of Authors, Irish Railway Record Society.

WRITINGS:

Irish Railways since 1919, Ian Allen, 1972.
Journey to Katmandu (travel book), David & Charles, 1974.
Railways of the Republic of Ireland: A Pictorial Survey of the G. S. R. and C. I. E., 1925-1975, D. B. Barton, 1975.
Sussex Villages, R. Hale, 1977.
Sussex Scenes, R. Hale, 1978.
Vintage Train, Great Western Society, 1980.
The Changing London Midland Scene, 1948-83, Ian Allen, 1983.
The Changing Western Scene, 1948-84, Ian Allen, 1984.
Great Western Tribute, Ian Allen, 1985.
Steam Echoes, Silver Link Publishing, 1986.
Waterloo to Weymouth, Patrick Stephens, 1987.

Also author of *The Changing Southern Scene, 1948-1981,* 1981. Contributor to periodicals, including *Railway World, Modern Railways, Railway Magazine,* and *Dorset County Magazine.* Editor of *Heritage Education News* and *Great Western Echo.*

WORK IN PROGRESS: Three children's books; books on the Great Western Railway and on Wessex.

AVOCATIONAL INTERESTS: Travel, Ireland, industrial archaeology, children.

BAN, Joseph D(aniel)   1926-

PERSONAL: Born April 12, 1926, in Homestead, Pa.; son of Joseph (a building contractor) and Suzannah (Petrusan) Ban; married Arline June Chapman (a writer for children), March 31, 1951. *Education:* University of Pittsburgh, B.S. in C.E., 1950; Colgate Rochester Divinity School, B.D., 1953; graduate study at University of Rochester, 1951, and Union Theological Seminary, New York, N.Y., 1956-58; University of Oregon, Ph.D., 1974.

ADDRESSES: Office—Divinity College, McMaster University, Hamilton, Ontario, Canada L8S 4K1.

CAREER: Baptist clergyman. Associate pastor in Rochester, N.Y., 1950-53, and Dayton, Ohio, 1953-56; pastor in New Brunswick, N.J., 1956-58; American Baptist Home Mission Societies, New York, N.Y., and Valley Forge, Pa., program associate in Division of Evangelism, 1958-64; Pennsylvania State University, University Park, executive director of University Christian Association, 1964-66, campus minister, 1967; Linfield College, McMinnville, Ore., associate professor, 1967-74, professor of religious studies and history, 1974-78, chaplain, 1967-73; McMaster University, Divinity College, Hamilton, Ontario, professor of Christian ministry and director, master of religious education programme, 1978—.

MEMBER: American Academy of Religion, American Baptist Historical Society, American Association of University Professors, Association of Professors and Researchers in Religious Education, Canadian Society of Church History.

AWARDS, HONORS: Education for Change was named American Baptist "Best Book of the Year," 1968; Association of Theological Schools in United States and Canada grant, 1982-83; grant from Canadian Society, 1985, for an innovative course, "The Religious Development of Adolescents in Canadian Society"; research award, Arts Research Board of McMaster University, 1985.

WRITINGS:

(Contributor) *The Church's Educational Ministry: A Curriculum Plan,* Bethany Press, 1965.
Education for Change, Judson, 1968.
(Contributor) Charles L. Wallis, editor, *The Minister's Manual for 1970,* Harper, 1969.
Facing Today's Demands, Judson, 1970.
Jesus Confronts Life's Issues, Judson, 1972.
(Editor with Paul R. Dekar) *In the Great Tradition,* Judson, 1982.
E. J. Furcha, editor, *Encounters with Luther,* McGill University, 1984.

WITH WIFE, ARLINE J. BAN

Jesus Makes the Difference, Judson, 1966.
God's Gift of Life, Christian Board of Publication (St. Louis), 1969.
As Wide as the World, Judson, 1971.
The New Disciple, Judson, 1975.
Celebrating God's Gift of Life: Vacation Ventures, Christian Board of Publication, 1982.
Long Journey to Freedom: Old Testament, Christian Board of Publication, 1982.
Living the Word, Christian Board of Publication, 1982.
Long Journey to Freedom: New Testament, Christian Board of Publication, 1982.
The Bible: Who? What? When? Where? Why?, Christian Board of Publication, 1983.

In Jesus' Day, Christian Board of Publication, 1983.

OTHER

Author of Baptist manuals and booklets, one in Spanish. Contributor and consulting editor of "Makers of Modern Thought" series, Judson, 1972. Contributor to *Biographical Dictionary of British Radicals in the Seventeenth Century,* Harvester, 1981, and to *Canadian Baptist History and Polity,* 1982. Contributor of more than one hundred articles, book reviews, and sermons to religious periodicals.

WORK IN PROGRESS: Christian religious education and the nurturing process; editing a book about Christology considered historically; *A Comparative Study of the Development of Baptist Higher Education in Great Britain, Canada, and the United States, 1679-1900,* a monograph; "T. C. Douglas and W. Aberhart: A Comparison of Their Theological Premises and Social Perspectives," a chapter for Acadia University.

SIDELIGHTS: Joseph D. Ban once told *CA:* "Writing, for me, is primarily a means of creative expression. This remains true though much of what has been published of my work is quite practical in nature. Time for writing comes on weekends and days off from a full schedule of classroom and other academic duties. My research has been made possible primarily through the inter-library loan system, a great boon to a serious writer.

"In recent years, much of my time has been spent writing with my wife, Arline. While she, too, has had several books of her own published, we enjoy writing together most of the time. It is a 'we' experience when we co-author a text. It involves numerous conferences, writing individually, editing each other's contributions, more consultation and, finally, a completed product where it is difficult for either of us to recall who wrote exactly which paragraph. We have also benefitted from skilled editors who have made the end result look far better than the raw manuscript."

*   *   *

BANKS, Carolyn   1941-

PERSONAL: Born February 9, 1941, in Pittsburgh, Pa.; daughter of Phillip J. and Victoria (Zbel) Dogonka; married second husband, Robert Rafferty (a writer). *Education:* University of Maryland, B.A. (with high honors), 1968, M.A., 1969.

ADDRESSES: Home—16111 FM 969, Austin, Tex. 78724.

CAREER: Writer. Former instructor in journalism and creative writing at the University of Maryland, Bowie State College, and Piedmont Virginia Community College; instructor in creative writing, Austin Community College, 1983—. Has conducted writing workshops for groups, including the Austin Writers League and the San Antonio Writers Guild.

MEMBER: PEN, Authors League of America, Mystery Writers of America, Authors Guild.

AWARDS, HONORS: Maryland fellowship, 1969.

WRITINGS:

(Editor with Morris Freedman) *American Mix,* Lippincott, 1972.
Mr. Right (novel), Viking, 1979.
The Adventures of Runcible Spoon, Ethos Enterprises, 1979.
The Darkroom (novel), Viking, 1980.
The Girls on the Row (novel), Crown, 1984.
Patchwork (novel), Crown, 1986.

Contributor of book reviews to *Washington Post Book World, New York Times,* and *Houston Post.* Also contributor to periodicals, including *Redbook, New Black Mask Quarterly,* and *Sports Illustrated.*

WORK IN PROGRESS: The Horse Lovers Guide to Texas, a nonfiction book for Texas Monthly Press; *Trophy.*

SIDELIGHTS: "I like the idea of writing within a well-defined genre—suspense in my case—but somehow going beyond the requirements of the genre," novelist Carolyn Banks told *CA.* In her best books, Banks combines elements of the traditional mystery story with a shrewd understanding of human psychology, particularly the darker side of human relationships. For the reader, the effect is terrifying—"like stepping on a Ferris wheel and finding out you're on the roller coaster instead," writes Lisa Siegel Foster in the *Los Angeles Times Book Review.*

Mr. Right, Banks's first novel, is a suspenseful tale about a woman, Lida, and her love affair with Duvivier, an author of sadomasochistic novels who writes under several pseudonyms. As her relationship with the novelist progresses, Lida discovers that Duvivier is not her lover's real name, and, upon investigation, learns his true name and that he was once a college professor. Duvivier has kept his real name hidden, fearing it will link him to the murder of a college coed who was seen with him on the night of her death. Because he cannot recall the events of the evening, Duvivier has led himself to believe he is the killer, though in reality he is not. Afraid that Lida will reveal his identity, Duvivier plots her death. *Mr. Right* has been warmly received by critics. Eve Zibart of the *Washington Post Book World* calls it "devious and delicious" and recommended "a swift second reading is worthwhile just to admire Banks's wiliness."

Banks's second novel, *The Darkroom,* was inspired by the U.S. Central Intelligence Agency's (CIA) disclosure that it tested mind-altering drugs on people without informing them of the personality changes they would suffer, and never explaining the devastating alterations (that sometimes led to suicide) to the families of the victims. *The Darkroom* deals with a seemingly mild-mannered, intelligent man who violently murders his mother, wife, and three children after disfiguring photographs of them. Unaware that he is a victim of CIA drug experimentation, the man, William Thomas Holland, flees into the wilderness and after a time is presumed dead. But a CIA agent continues stalking Holland. When the agent and murderer meet, Holland is found living in a secluded cabin, under a new name, with a divorcee and her two sons. His pastime? Distorting photographs of his new companions.

Commenting on Banks's second book, Stanley Ellin of the *Washington Post Book World* writes: "All this [CIA drug experimentation] is now a matter of public record, and Carolyn Banks has drawn from that record to set forth a story which is the more effective because it is not accusatory. Those who may feel that paranoia, whatever colors drape it, is no substitute for conscience will find in Carolyn Banks' novel the most dramatically telling argument for their increasingly unpopular position."

Banks believes her fourth novel best succeeds in combining a traditional mystery story with psychological insight. "*Patchwork* is a book about a tortured relationship between mother and son rather than just a suspense novel," Banks told *CA.* In this chilling tale, Rachel—a high-strung divorcee who supports herself by selling patchwork—lives in fear of Drew, her emotionally disturbed teenager. Theirs has not been an affectionate relationship, and, in frustration, Rachel has committed Drew to a halfway house in southern Texas and set out for Austin to forge a new life of her own. Just as her prospects are improving, Rachel learns that Drew has escaped and that her former husband has been found brutally murdered, his body wrapped in a patchwork quilt. Fearing for her life, Rachel aimlessly crisscrosses the city, "stumbling about in mixed parental agony and outright victim terror," according to John Katzenbach in the *Washington Post Book World*.

The narrative unfolds in alternate chapters as Drew and Rachel each reveal the hurts and disappointments that have made them enemies: Rachel has always imparted the worst motives to her son's behavior; Drew has never known a mother's unquestioning love. Katzenbach believes that "Banks portrays this emotional highwire act admirably. The memories add immeasurably to the impact of the novel. The characters are fully realized." He also commends Banks's ability to use such descriptions to "further her plot. Banks is delivering suspense in this book, not a treatise on mother-son relations. What she manages, within the structure of the thriller, to impart about the difficulties in raising problem children is relatively sophisticated." Writing in the San Antonio *Express-News*, Judyth Rigler similarly observes: "Banks knows a great deal about the parent-child relationship and its convolutions.... The combination makes for a tight thriller."

BIOGRAPHICAL/CRITICAL SOURCES:

PERIODICALS

Express-News (San Antonio), September 7, 1986.
Los Angeles Times Book Review, November 6, 1983, September 14, 1986.
New York Times Book Review, March 25, 1979.
Washington Post, February 10, 1979, May 12, 1980, May 17, 1986, April 5, 1987.

* * *

BARTH, John (Simmons) 1930-

PERSONAL: Born May 27, 1930, in Cambridge, Md.; son of John Jacob and Georgia (Simmons) Barth; married (Harriette) Anne Strickland, January 11, 1950 (divorced, 1969); married Shelly I. Rosenberg (a teacher), December 27, 1970; children: (first marriage) Christine Anne, John Strickland, Daniel Stephen. *Education:* Attended Juilliard School of Music; Johns Hopkins University, A.B., 1951, M.A., 1952.

ADDRESSES: Home—Baltimore, Md. *Office*—Writing Seminars, Johns Hopkins University, Baltimore, Md. 21218. *Agent*—International Creative Management, 40 West 57th St., New York, N.Y. 10019.

CAREER: Pennsylvania State University, University Park, instructor, 1953-56, assistant professor, 1957-60, associate professor of English, 1960-65; State University of New York at Buffalo, professor of English, 1965-71, Edward H. Butler Professor of English, 1971-73; Johns Hopkins University, Baltimore, Md., Alumni Centennial Professor of English and Creative Writing, 1973—.

MEMBER: American Academy and Institute of Arts and Letters, American Academy of Arts and Sciences.

AWARDS, HONORS: National Book Award nomination, 1956, for *The Floating Opera*, and 1968, for *Lost in the Funhouse*; Brandeis University Creative Arts Award, 1965; Rockefeller

Foundation grant, 1965-66; National Institute of Arts and Letters grant, 1966, for *Giles, Goat-Boy; or, The Revised New Syllabus*; Litt.D., University of Maryland, 1969; National Book Award, 1973, for *Chimera*.

WRITINGS:

NOVELS

The Floating Opera, Appleton-Century-Crofts, 1956, revised edition, Doubleday, 1967, reprinted with new foreword by the author, Doubleday-Anchor, 1988.
The End of the Road, Doubleday, 1958, revised edition, 1967, reprinted with new foreword by the author, Doubleday-Anchor, 1988.
The Sot-Weed Factor, Doubleday, 1960, revised edition, 1967, reprinted with new foreword by the author, Doubleday-Anchor, 1988.
Giles, Goat-Boy; or, The Revised New Syllabus, Doubleday, 1966, reprinted with new foreword by the author, Doubleday-Anchor, 1988.
LETTERS, Putnam, 1979.
Sabbatical: A Romance, Putnam, 1982.
Tidewater Tales: A Novel, Putnam, 1987.

SHORT STORIES

Lost in the Funhouse: Fiction for Print, Tape, Live Voice, Doubleday, 1968, reprinted with new foreword by the author, Doubleday-Anchor, 1988.

NOVELLAS

Chimera, Random House, 1972.

OTHER

(Contributor) Quinn, editor, *The Sense of the 60s*, Free Press, 1968.
(Contributor) Weintraub and Young, editors, *Directions in Literary Criticism*, Pennsylvania State University Press, 1973.
The Literature of Exhaustion, and The Literature of Replenishment (essays), Lord John Press, 1982.
The Friday Book: Essays and Other Nonfiction, Putnam, 1984.
Don't Count on It: A Note on the Number of the 1001 Nights, Lord John Press, 1984.

Contributor to numerous periodicals, including *Atlantic, Hopkins Review, Esquire, Kenyon Review*, and *Johns Hopkins Magazine*.

SIDELIGHTS: Master of contemporary fiction John Barth often defines himself as a "concocter of comic novels," an inventor of universes who is, above all, a lover of storytelling. For almost forty years, the Maryland-born author has displayed his command of many fictional forms, including short experimental fiction, the novella, and both the short and the long novel. Barth has also produced important nonfiction. His essay "The Literature of Exhaustion" is "one of the more influential pieces to come out of an American fiction writer of Barth's generation," Jack Fuller reports in the *Chicago Tribune Book World*. Barth's literary rank is a subject of critical debate, but "in his fascinated commitment to the art—and to the criticism—of storytelling, he has no rival," declares William Pritchard in the *New York Times Book Review*. Noting the author's other characteristics, *John Barth* author E. P. Walkiewicz names the subject of his study a "writer who throughout his career has exhibited great versatility, technical virtuosity, learning, and wit."

Introducing Barth as the "most cerebral of novelists," Curt Suplee goes on to state in the *Washington Post* that Barth has reaped "a madcap eminence (and occasional odium) for huge and bawdy intellectual fables, philosophical vaudeville, [and] rococo parodies of antique literary forms." Barth's first novel, *The Floating Opera*, was second-runner-up for the National Book Award in 1956; *Lost in the Funhouse: Fiction for Print, Tape, Live Voice* was nominated for the same award in 1968, and *Chimera* won it in 1973. In addition, every year on his birthday, the author hears from a nationwide fan club, The Society for the Celebration of Barthomania. "Fortunately for the size of one's ego, there are always at least as many critics telling you to go back to [the] marsh and stick your head in it," Barth remarked to Suplee. The unpredictable author's encyclopedic fictions have baffled some critics and bored others, yet nearly all reviewers recognize his genius even when pronouncing his novels unreadable or tedious. A typically mixed response printed in the *Times Literary Supplement* rates *The Sot-Weed Factor, Giles, Goat-Boy; or, The Revised New Syllabus,* and *Chimera* "easily the best worst in modern fiction." Their author, critics have found, is just as difficult to assess. Efforts to place Barth in a literary category are futile, Walkiewicz explains, due to "the formal complexity, verbal richness, and eclectic content" of the books.

Multiple puns, literary jokes and labyrinthine plots reminiscent of Vladimir Nabokov and Jorge Luis Borges secure Barth's standing with "the great sportsmen of contemporary fiction," to quote *City of Words: American Fiction, 1950-1970* author Tony Tanner. Frank D. McConnell's study, *Four Postwar Novelists: Bellow, Mailer, Barth, and Pynchon,* notes the difference between the pure sport of Nabokov's *Pale Fire* and Barth's fiction, which combines lexical play with "the stuff of history, of change and the dynamic flux of ideas." The heroes in Barth's "preposterous fictions" attempt to find "a philosophical justification for life, search for values and a basis for action in a relativistic cosmos, [and] concern themselves with . . . the question of whether character and external reality are stable or floating phenomena," Gerhard Joseph summarizes in *John Barth.* Furthermore, indicates Walkiewicz, in all the books, Barth "has undermined the foundations of his own authority, and has toyed with a profound skepticism that calls into question . . . all systems of ethics and philosophy." In *The Contemporary Writer,* L. S. Dembo and Cyrena N. Pondrom affirm, "It is appropriate that Barth should refuse to see himself as a part of any intellectual tradition, including nihilism, while remaining one of the best comic-absurdists of his time." The books are not strictly novels of ideas, say critics, who point to an exuberant comic sexuality and a pervasive concern with aesthetics as the dominating features of Barth's work.

Notions about the theory and practice of fiction figure prominently in Barth's canon. One of these ideas, expressed in "The Literature of Exhaustion," is the difficulty of achieving originality in the twentieth century after so many narrative possibilities have been used by other storytellers. Barth's preoccupation, as he told Annie Le Rebeller in a *Caliban* interview, is to "keep a foot in two doors," to be original, "and, at the same time, explore especially the oldest conventions of the medium for their possible present usefulness." This engagement with the history of fiction binds Barth to "a crucial phase in the evolution of modern literature generally," McConnell reports. Writing in *Twentieth Century Literature,* Manfred Puetz deems Barth's writings "epitomes of contemporary American fiction: they expose some of its key problems and they test representative strategies for solving them."

"Almost all commentators" saw Barth's first novel, *The Floating Opera,* "as a philosophical work," Frank Gado generalized in an interview with Barth published in *First Person: Conversations on Writers and Writing.* Barth admitted he was engrossed in certain problems, particularly suicide and nihilism (the view that all beliefs and values are relative and that life is meaningless). He planned to write a comic "philosophical minstrel show" informed by memories of a showboat he had seen as a child. "The plan grew;. . . I decided to write three novels, all dealing with the problem of nihilism." For the first one, he told Gado, "my notion was to take a man who . . . decides to commit suicide" for "ostensibly logical" reasons. The narrator-protagonist Todd Andrews realizes that if there are no absolutes, one's own version of reality amounts to only one of numerous other possibilities; even one's own identity is not certifiable in such a world. On the other hand, shifts in philosophical positions do nothing to alleviate the arbitrariness and finality of biological facts such as his own potentially fatal heart condition. Finding no way to overcome such facts, and seeing no ultimate justification for any action, Andrews decides to blow up the Floating Opera with himself aboard during one of its performances. "*The Floating Opera* is not merely an account of Todd's Hamlet-like musings," *Dictionary of Literary Biography* contributor Arthur D. Casciato relates. Citing Andrews from within the narrative, Casciato elaborates, "the story is 'fraught with curiosities, melodrama, spectacle, instruction, and entertainment.' Its digressive plot includes a grisly World War I foxhole scene in which Todd bayonets a German soldier, an adulterous *menage a trois,* and a hilariously complicated legal dispute complete with seventeen wills and 129 jars of human excrement." By the end of the story, Andrews "comes to the conclusion, by the same operation of reason, that there's no more reason to kill himself than not to kill himself; that indeed, there's no reason to do anything," Barth told Gado.

The End of the Road, as the second novel to treat nihilism according to Barth's plan, "would begin with the conclusion of the first as its premise but come to completely different conclusions—horrifying conclusions, where people who shouldn't die do die, where people are destroyed by their own and other people's ideas," the author explained to Gado. Andrews of *The Floating Opera* "reveals that he has only been able to move and act at all by adopting a series of masks," and he recognizes that the people in his life are equally inauthentic, notes Tanner. Jacob Horner of *The End of the Road* promotes these views to Rennie, the wife of Joe Morgan, "a fanatical ideologue whose philosophical wrestling match" against Horner "ends disastrously," Joseph reports. Morgan, who has married Rennie because he can make her a disciple of his ethical system, deliberately introduces her to Horner "as an ethical experiment," to quote from the novel. Horner undermines Rennie's faith in her husband's authenticity, then sleeps with her. She conceives a child who may be either Morgan's or Horner's, then decides to have an abortion. Barth's all-pervasive humor dismisses "the ordinary moral and psychological implications" of these events, says Beverly Gross in the *Chicago Review.* But then, the novel "repudiates itself, or rather it repudiates what would seem to be its glib ability to deal with, and therefore dismiss, ugliness, pain, and despair" when Rennie chokes to death on her own vomit during the abortion. "Rennie's hemorrhaging corpse cannot be transformed into comedy, nor does Barth try. That is the second stage of undercutting: having reduced everything to comedy," Barth exposes humor's inadequacy, maintains Gross. Barth repeats this strategy in other books, "working steadily against an initial premise or turning a literary tradition against itself,'' Gado notes.

The premise destroyed at the end of *The Sot-Weed Factor* is the radical innocence of the seventeenth-century poet Ebenezer Cooke. At the outset of this mock-epic, Cooke determines to remain a virgin but later finds that he must consummate his marriage to a whore and contract her social disease if he is to regain his estate from her in the morally and politically corrupt colony of Maryland. Cooke's tutor and ethical opposite, Henry Burlingame, promotes an unbridled sexuality and radical cynicism perhaps no more viable than the virgin poet's innocence, remarks *Saturday Review* contributor Granville Hicks, who relates that Burlingame's impotence is one of many ironies in the book. In *Forum-Service*, Leslie Fiedler notes that Barth ''distorts the recognitions and reversals of popular literature, first in the direction of travesty and then of nightmare: brother and sister recognize each other on the verge of rape; Indian and white man find they possess a common father when they confess a common genital inadequacy; the tomahawked and drowned corpses in one chapter revive in the next. Yet somehow the parody remains utterly serious, the farce and melodrama evoke terror and pity, and the flagrant mockery of a happy ending constricts the heart. And all the while one *laughs,* at a pitch somewhere between hysteria and sheer delight. The book is a joke book, an endless series of gags. But the biggest joke of all is that Barth seems finally to have written something closer to the 'Great American Novel' than any other book of the last decade.'' In a *Book Week* poll, two hundred literary professionals confirmed this estimate by listing *The Sot-Weed Factor* among the twenty best novels written between 1945 and 1965.

Among the book's achievements is a plot deliberately more complicated and more completely resolved than that of *Tom Jones,* many critics observe. Moreover, as Joseph Featherstone quips in a *New Republic* review, Barth ''pinch[es] the behind of Bawd history.'' Others remark that he proves himself a competent pasticheur of eighteenth-century literature from *Don Quixote* and *Candide* to *Tristram Shandy* and *Fanny Hill.* In Fiedler's view, *The Sot-Weed Factor* is ''no mere pastiche, but a piece of ingenius linguistic play, a joyous series of raids on half-forgotten resources of the language, largely obscene.'' ''At one point in the book,'' Tanner says, ''two women exchange terms of sexual abuse for seven pages. Ludicrous as a piece of history, this minor verbal gesture reflects a major mood of the book, namely the dominance of words over things. . . . Like these good ladies, or rather the author behind them, you can call each fact a hundred names—indeed, you can proliferate names quite independently of facts. . . . The substantiality of fact melts away as we watch him at his brilliant rhetorical play.''

Surely, ''the notion of any serious historical inquiry is undermined'' in *The Sot-Weed Factor,* Tanner maintains; the book reminds us that American history is the result of ''storytelling,'' one of ''our attempts to name and control the world around us,'' McConnell concurs. Furthermore, ''for Heide Ziegler, *The Sot-Weed Factor* is, 'a, or even *the,* decisive landmark in the development of postmodern fiction,' since it marks a 'shift in commitment from the realm of reality to the realm of the imagination,''' *Contemporary Authors Bibliographical Series* contributor Joseph Weixlmann writes in a commentary on Ziegler's *Amerikastudien* essay. ''Ziegler insists that, by treating both fictional and 'historical' events as *stories,* Barth deconstructs the traditional notion of reality and provides for its reconstruction on his own terms.''

Barth indeed reinvents the universe, making it a University, in *Giles, Goat-Boy; or, The Revised New Syllabus.* With it, he ''became a key figure in what was seen by many critics as a revolt against realism in the . . . American novel of the 1960's,'' David Lodge indicates in the *Times Literary Supplement.* This revolt, says Gado, is ''the most fundamental revolution in fiction in the last two hundred years.'' In a *Wisconsin Studies* interview with John Enck, Barth said he set out to write a ''comic Old Testament,'' or ''souped-up Bible'' after reviewers had alerted him to parallels between Ebenezer Cooke and the archetypical hero of world mythology. In preparation, Barth studied the works of comparative mythologists who had seen certain events and conditions recur in the life stories of many ritual heroes. These events include a period of testing and a descent into the dark underworld to achieve immortality for oneself and sometimes for others—a sequence symbolic of the stages of development common to every human life, Campbell suggests. *Giles* ''was for better or worse the conscious and ironic orchestration'' of this archetype, the author discloses in *Chimera,* which would further exploit ritual hero myths.

In this ''wildly rambunctious'' novel, as *New York Times Book Review* contributor Guy Davenport describes it, George Giles, raised as the goat Billy Bockfuss, sets out to become the savior, or Grand Tutor, of his world. ''The narrative requires Giles to work out a viable ethical position for himself and his potential tutees'' and to descend into the belly of the computer that controls the University to either Pass or Fail, Robert Scholes sums up in the *New York Times Book Review.* ''[Giles] first tries the two extremes of ethical absolutism, maintaining on one tour of the campus that good and evil are totally separate, and on another that they are indistinguishable. When both of these doctrines have disastrous results, he is forced to a third position, in which he sees the problem as too subtle for formulation,'' says Scholes in his synopsis. Along the way, Barth supplies ''sometimes sacrilegious imitations and distortions of . . . demigod heroes from Dionysius and Oedipus to Moses and Christ,'' McConnell notes. Tanner suggests that ''it is perhaps another of Barth's ironies that it has taken over 700 pages to bring his hero to a realization that truth lies beyond terms.''

If Barth debunks all orthodoxies and academic guideposts in *Giles,* as Scholes's study *The Fabulators* states, he also undercuts his own authority by enclosing the text in a frame of introductory publisher's and author's disclaimers, and several endnotes that question the testament's validity. Tanner comments, ''We become aware of a writer going to perverse lengths . . . not only to demonstrate what he can invent—and that is prodigious—but to demonstrate how he can equivocate about, trivialize, and undermine his own inventions.'' The book's point, Gross speculates, is ''to expose the fraudulence of [narrative] art.''

Giles was Barth's first commercial success. Sales of his ''souped-up Bible'' doubled and redoubled the combined sales of previous books, which had brought him critical acclaim and a largely academic underground following, but only modest financial rewards. The widespread popularity of *Giles* seemed to generate a tidal wave of good fortune for Barth, who received a formal recognition for achievement in fiction from Brandeis University's Creative Arts Commission and a $2,500 grant from the National Institute of Arts and Letters. Doubleday capitalized on the new momentum and reissued Barth's complete works to date, but not before their author had trimmed and polished *The End of the Road* and *The Sot-Weed Factor* and restored the ending of *The Floating Opera*. Back in 1955, the young author had rewritten the ending of the manuscript to satisfy an editor in order to see the book published, but the amendment had displeased the critics. The 1967 edition contains the ending as it was originally conceived.

"The Literature of Exhaustion," also published in 1967, increased Barth's fame. The seminal essay, first printed in the *Atlantic,* has been "reprinted, quoted, and 'explained' by any number of critics and teachers anxious to clarify and celebrate the fiction, not only of Barth, but of his contemporaries," McConnell reports. It was often misunderstood, claims Barth in a later essay, "The Literature of Replenishment." Perceived as another "death of the novel" treatise akin to the statements of Louis D. Rubin, Susan Sontag, and others, it was actually a state-of-the-art message that proposed various keys to the novel's survival in the face of exhausted possibilities. The misread essay, Barth goes on, "was really about . . . the effective 'exhaustion' not of language or literature, but of the aesthetic of high modernism: that admirable, not-to-be-repudiated, but essentially completed 'program'" that had produced masterpieces of erudition and technique such as James Joyce's *Ulysses*. Speaking to Phyllis Meras of the *New York Times Book Review,* Barth explained, "the old masters of 20th-century fiction—especially [James] Joyce and [Franz] Kafka in their various ways—brought prose narrative to a kind of ultimacy." The next generation had not yet produced the work that would be the next stage in the genre's history, and critics had begun to talk of the art form's death. But "a few people—like Beckett and the Argentinian, Borges, and Nabokov, for example—have been able to turn this ultimacy against itself in order to produce new work," Barth told Meras. This view puts the novelist "in competition with the accumulated best of human history," and one response to this problem, Barth later remarked to Gado, "is to ignore it." Barth has instead found a number of ways to meet this challenge.

One way is "to write a novel about it," Barth's 1967 essay states. "Fiction" that aspires to become "part of the history of fiction," as Barth demonstrates in *The Friday Book,* "is almost always about itself," whatever else may be its concerns. Another way to go beyond the achievements of past novelists without repudiating their accomplishments is to parody them. "Far from disowning a received way of doing something difficult, [parody] is meant to show rather that it can be done easily and for sport," Richard Poirier explains in his study of postmodern fiction, *The Performing Self*. The writer can also move out of realism (which has been outdone by cinema and electronic media) into irrealism, to bring fiction up to date with "painting, music, and . . . the age," Joe David Bellamy notes in *The New Fiction: Interviews with Innovative American Writers*. Another way to extend the life of the novel is to seize upon one of the last resources of originality left to the modern artist, "the voice, the authorial instrument that shapes the retelling," in Joseph's words; or, as Paul Gray of *Time* magazine puts it, "to exalt artifice and make the telling the subject of the tale." Such writing must be "comic about its own self-consciousness" to be interesting, Barth expressed to Bellamy in a *New American Review* interview. A writer can also revive an exhausted genre by going, as Barth often says, "back to the roots" of a tradition, or to the roots of storytelling itself, to discover unused possibilities or received stories that may be reshaped to fit his own purpose.

Barth's characters dramatize these solutions in *Lost in the Funhouse* and *Chimera,* two collections of shorter fiction that explore "the oral narrative tradition from which printed fiction evolved," according to his article, "Getting Oriented" in *The New York Times Book Review*. McConnell points out that "neither book is, finally, a 'collection.' Both are a series of tales which, in their order of telling and their explicit comments upon each other, are something like novels." When seen as novels, their "plot" is "what happens to the storyteller himself as he moves through the series" of related short stories and novellas.

The stories in *Funhouse* depict characters lost in the mazes of refracting and distorting mirrors and echo chambers; their confusions express "the condition of *disorientation*" that Barth identifies in "Getting Oriented" as his own "fictionary stock in trade. Intellectual and spiritual disorientation is the family disease of all my main characters—a disease usually complicated by ontological disorientation, since knowing where you're at is often contingent upon knowing who you are." Puetz relates this concern to contemporary views on personality. "The novel of the sixties has celebrated . . . the second coming of Proteus, the archetypal shape-shifter. . . . If change itself is the defining feature of human existence, the argument goes, then why not . . . become a whole spectrum of varying selves?" This shape-shifting, Tanner feels, brings Barth to an "impasse" in which the author "can no longer get hold of any 'reality' at all; everything he touches turns into fictions," or the sound of his own voice. "To find an exit from a world of self-generated fictions . . . demands an intense effort," Puetz writes. "The feasibility and the formal implications of such an effort as much as the increasing worries about the exit from the maze of fiction prove to be the opening themes of . . . *Funhouse* and *Chimera*."

Chimera contains three novellas, the retellings of three myths whose heroes, like Barth, are in the process of reorientation to discern their future: Bellerophon, who learns that one does not become a hero by merely imitating heroes; Dunyazade, who, after witnessing countless permutations of narrative and sexual expression while stationed at the foot of her sister Scheherazade's bed, must make her future out of whatever is left; and Perseus, whose walk into the future takes him past the scenes of his life so far, depicted on the walls of his temple, which is shaped like a nautilus shell. Unlike a closed circle, the temple spirals outward, allowing Perseus to move forward by retracing his own history. Barth explained in the *Caliban* interview how the image further relates to his oeuvre: "When the chambered nautilus adds a new chamber to itself, that chamber is determined somewhat by its predecessors, but it's where the beast is living presently, and he's a larger animal for it." Each new room is a gnomon, "something you can *add* to an already existing figure to change its size without changing its basic shape." This structural principle, "and logarithmic spirals in general, winds through the *Chimera* novellas," says Barth, who points out in *The Friday Book* that the length of each novella is proportioned to the next one according to logarithmic measurements. This structure replicates "the way I like to think about my past, present, and future work," he says in the interview; in other words, each new novel will be his endeavor "to see what new changes I can ring around some old concerns without falling into complete self-parody." Though many reviewers see *Funhouse* and *Chimera* as proof that Barth has been swallowed up by his own self-conscious obsession, others concur with McConnell that the author's attempt "to write himself out of a corner" generally succeeds. Subsequent books, they maintain, demonstrate Barth's ability to invent new work by recycling traditional literature, and his own.

LETTERS—larger and more complex than its predecessors, "brilliant, witty . . . and damn near unreadable as well," to quote Peter S. Prescott of *Newsweek*—rehearses Barth's literary past in letters he ostensibly receives from characters in previous novels. At the same time, scholars note, it carries the author beyond the "impasse" of predominantly aesthetic concerns into the world of public events. *LETTERS* sums up the decade of the seventies along with Barth's collected works, observes Frederick R. Karl in his *American Fictions, 1940-1980: A Comprehensive History and Critical Evaluation.* Because the book "put[s] the weight of the past on every present activity" and offers the War of 1812 as "the major clue to American history," Karl deems it "invaluable" as a cultural document despite complexities that bar a general readership. Writing in the *Washington Post Book World*, Tanner praises a plot that intertwines plots from the lives of his previous characters with plots brought forward from the American Revolution, further braided with plots "which are active in contemporary America" relevant to "a 'second revolution.'" *LETTERS*, says Benjamin De Mott in an *Atlantic* review "is by turns a brain-buster, a marathon, an exasperation, a frustration, a provocation to earnest thought. Barth is preaching, wittily but with total conviction, on the limits of our kind, on the sanity of doubting that we know where, in our lives, fiction stops."

"A condensed overview cannot begin to suggest the wealth of stories and word play, the complications and correspondences that 'Letters' affords," claims Prescott, who lists among the book's embellishments "all manner of alphabetical, anagrammatical, and numerological games." For example, as Thomas R. Edwards notes in the *New York Times Book Review*, the first letters of the book's epistles, when arranged on a calendar for the dates on which they were composed, "spell out the story's secret subtitle . . . in a shape that itself spells out 'LETTERS'!" Such devices, claims Karl, disclose "the anagrammatic quality not only of a given work but of an entire career," an intricate pattern from which the author struggles to break free. "He announces that he would like to . . . re-establish the cordial relations once enjoyed between the novel and 'reality,' whether psychologically, sexually, socially, or politically understood. The book is really about mid-life crisis," McConnell concludes in a *Books & Arts* review, "the mid-life crisis of literature itself, of Western (particularly American) civilization, and of John Barth, middle-aged novelist." McConnell believes that "this self-confrontation at mid-career may be the single finest achievement of this exceptionally fine, very important book." Many other reviews were not as complimentary. *LETTERS* "received a very poor press," reports Karl, who esteems it "with all its excesses, an uncanny fiction, a capping of Barth's career and the entire postwar era."

The Friday Book: Essays and Other Nonfiction is "required reading for any serious student of Barth's canon," Weixlmann notes. Its contents constitute "a resume of my Stories" from *The Floating Opera* to *The Tidewater Tales: A Novel* "and an account of what I believe I have been up to in writing them," Barth says in the introduction to one of its pieces. The book begins with "Some Reasons Why I Tell the Stories I Tell . . .", an essay that reveals the elements of his personal history that have become part of his unique aesthetic. His books "tend to come in pairs" because he was born an opposite-sex twin. "In myth, twins signified whatever dualisms a culture entertained: . . . good / evil, creation / destruction, what had they." For Western culture, he explains, they signify the divided or alienated self in search of the missing half. Thus he is a writer

"in part because I no longer have my twin to be wordless with." And since twins share "a language before . . . and beyond speech," they acquire language primarily for "dealing with the outsiders," a factor that explains why Barth is "perhaps unnaturally conscious" of language, "forever at it, tinkering, foregrounding it." If being a twin underscored life's dualities, living in the landscape of tidewater Maryland where borders are always shifting blurred the distinctions between them. Barth remarks, "Your web-foot amphibious marsh-nurtured writer will likely by mere reflex regard many conventional boundaries and distinctions as arbitrary, fluid, negotiable: form versus content, realism versus irrealism, fact versus fiction, life versus art." The unimpeded flatness of the marshland, he claims, partly accounts for his drive to become distinguished at something.

As a young man with this goal in mind, Barth went to the Juilliard School of Music in New York to become a famous jazz arranger. Instead, he found himself a talented amateur among professionals, and "went home to think of some other way to become distinguished." There he discovered he had won a scholarship to Johns Hopkins University and accepted it. As an undergraduate, he filed books in the Classics Department and the stacks of the Oriental seminary, and became enchanted with the tenth-century Sanskrit *Ocean of Story* and Richard Burton's annotated *Arabian Nights*—two reservoirs of frame-tale literature that were to inspire him throughout his career. Barth is particularly moved by Scheherazade, whose tales told at night to her misogynist ruler prevented him from executing her in the morning. She is, he says in "Getting Oriented," a fit metaphor for "the condition of narrative artists in general and of artists who work on University campuses in particular," who must literally "publish or perish." Her example also suggested to him several ways to survive twentieth-century pressures on the novel, and a justification for writing self-reflexive fiction. As he reasons in *The Friday Book*, "We tell stories and listen to them because we live stories and live in them. Narrative equals language equals life: To cease to narrate . . . is to die. . . . If this is true, then not only is all fiction fiction about fiction, but all fiction about fiction is in fact fiction about life."

Barth graduated with a commitment to become a writer and meanwhile earn a living by teaching, a choice he came to by means of "passionate default or heartfelt lack of alternatives." He has taught at Pennsylvania State University, the State University of New York at Buffalo, and at his alma mater. Partly due to these affiliations, Barth has been called an academic writer. Though he resisted this label at first, his mid-life orientation brought him to recognize, as he says in "Getting Oriented," that all of his novels are about education—or rather, "imperfect or misfired education." In *Harper's*, he writes, "There is chalk dust on the sleeve of my soul. . . . I have never been away from classrooms for longer than a few months. . . . I believe I know my strengths and limitations as a teacher the way I know them as a writer: doubtful of my accomplishments in both metiers, I am not doubtful at all that they *are* my metiers, for good or ill." However, Barth remains an arranger at heart, as he says in *The Friday Book*, and his "chief pleasure is to take a received melody—an old narrative poem, a classical myth, a shopworn literary convention . . .—and, improvising like a jazzman within its contraints, reorchestrating it to its present purpose."

With *Sabbatical: A Romance*, Barth "resume[s] a romance with realism," he intimates to Suplee. Shorter than previous novels and less obsessed with comments on his craft, the book stresses certain apocalyptic elements that Barth has carried from the beginning. "Todd Andrews in 'The Floating Opera' (and again in 'Letters') wonders sentence by sentence whether his heart will carry him from subject to predicate; in 'Sabbatical,' set on Chesapeake Bay in 1980, the background question is whether the world will end before the novel does," Barth states in the *New York Times Book Review*. On their sabbatical, narrator-protagonists Fenwick Turner and Susan Seckler cruise to the Caribbean and return to Chesapeake Bay. The possibly CIA-related death of Fenwick's twin brother is one of several mysteries they encounter along the way, and "the story fills up with the rough contemporary world," Michael Wood relates in the *New York Times Book Review*. In fact, the book "was occasioned" by the mysterious death of ex-CIA official John Paisley, whose corpse was found in Barth's "home waters" in 1978, as he told Suplee. Suplee notes, "This literal intrusion of the real world becomes a ditto in the novel: Barth simply reprints 20 pages of Paisley stories from The Baltimore Sun."

Sabbatical nonetheless retains some familiar Barth trademarks, notes Charles Trueheart in a *Washington Post Book World* review. It "is the record of its own composition" and "Fenn and Susan argue incessantly about the proper way to tell the story . . . and remind one another of the literary traditions into which their narrative falls." John W. Aldridge, also writing in the *Washington Post Book World*, approves Barth's new tack toward realism: "While to be sure the story does contain elements indicating that the familiar temporizing mind of John Barth is still hard at work, they are effectively subordinated to the strong realistic thrust of the narrative and so provide the book with an agreeable controlled complexity instead of burying it beneath the old fog-bank of endless equivocation."

By design, *Tidewater Tales: A Novel* was to be "a sort of opposite-sex twin to *Sabbatical*," featuring a married couple afloat on the same bay, whose situation, Barth reveals in *The Friday Book*, was to be "rather the reverse of Fenwick's and Susan's." Whereas Susan of *Sabbatical* wonders how she can bring children into the world at this late hour and aborts twins, Katharine Sagamore of *Tidewater Tales* happily carries and delivers twins, not fully knowing what to make of the fact that people still desire to procreate in a threatened world. Again, two lines of interest develop: one, a plot entangled with the problematical real world on the verge of apocalypse; and the other, related to stories from classical literature that parallel the Sagamore's voyage. Toronto *Globe & Mail* reviewer Douglas Hill praises the book's "dizzying . . . manipulations of literary forms and traditions." Aldridge concurs that it is "the richest, most ebullient and technically daring" of Barth's canon to date, "crowded" as it is "with grand virtuosic effects that seem to have nothing to do with the action except to interrupt it, . . . offered simply because they are such fun." The stories of Odysseus, Don Quixote, Sheherazade, Huck Finn, and more resurface here, their retelling facilitated by events in the realistic narrative. Some reviewers find the tales improved in the retelling while others, such as *New York Times Book Review* contributor William Pritchard, are less enamored. Pritchard qualifies his opinion by saying that "Barth gives ample food to please or displease everyone's taste." Moved by the book's "richness as a love story—marital, filial, domestic— and also its love of a place, of a country, even as place and country are scarred by human depredations," Pritchard leaves it to the reader to decide "whether the novel's ending—or its various coves and shallows sailed into along the way—give us something more rich and strange than a funhouse."

"Barth has now written the same novel twice," using materials already employed in previous works, notes *Los Angeles Times Book Review* contributor Richard Lehan, who wonders what kind of work can follow. More nonfiction, perhaps; or fiction that investigates "the way that evil comes into being and how we best cope with it," a theme suggested in *Sabbatical* and *Tidewater Tales*. Barth speculated to Israel Shenker for the *New York Times Book Review*, "Maybe when I'm 90 I'll be as grave as Sophocles at 90. More likely, Zeus willing, I'll be writing comedy in my 80's as Thomas Mann did, and die laughing."

In any case, Barth has parlayed his talents into a permanent place in literary history; commentary proliferates in the wake of each new offering from Barth, and criticism of his entire oeuvre shows no signs of abatement, according to a *Mississippi Quarterly* overview by Charles B. Harris. As of 1986, writes Walkiewicz, "Barth's 'significance,' his place in the tradition remain, of course, matters very much under consideration or open to debate." Poirier explains why that place is not clear; he allows that Barth is "perhaps more intellectually attuned, . . . and surely more philosophically adroit than all but a few of the exclusively literary critics now writing in America or Europe." At the same time, however, Poirier goes on to observe, "admiration for [his] thinking about literature must very often contend with the experience of reading [his] novels. . . . We sit in a favorite chair . . . and we open, let us say, *Giles, Goat-Boy*. Several days later we're probably no longer infatuated with repeated illustrations that literary and philosophical structures are really put-ons, and that what we are doing is kind of silly."

"While there are those who, as always, are of the opinion that [Barth] has reduced the art of fiction to the chronicling 'of minstrel misery,' there are also many who are willing to affirm that he has added a number of 'minstrel masterpieces' . . . to the treasury," Walkiewicz notes. He adds that "if Barth has earned the high praise he . . . has received from some, if he deserves to be called the 'best writer of fiction we have at present, and one of the best we have ever had,' it is because he has given form and substance to a body of work that is traditional, contemporary, and trail-blazing, consistent and evolutionary, self-affirming and self-questioning, that acknowledges contradictions and contrarieties and enlists them in the service of art and humanity." Weixlmann comments, "Barth has, on various occasions, indicated that the true measure of his authorial success will not be taken for decades, even centuries; that his attempt, as a writer, is to rival Shakespeare and Cervantes rather than his contemporaries. In this context, Barth scholarship is in its infancy, despite the fact that much serious critical attention has already been focused on his work." Barth criticism has itself become the subject of several compendiums, including *Critical Essays on John Barth* by Joseph J. Waldmeir. In one essay collected by Waldmeir, Richard W. Noland concludes that Barth's "most interesting and important achievement [as of 1966] is the embodiment of philosophical ideas in a form both tragic and comic. . . . He considers each of the ways in which Western man has attempted to fill his life with value after the death of the old gods . . . only to find all of them inadequate." All inadequate, perhaps, except for storytelling, Josephine Hendin contends in *Harper's*. Her survey of Barth's work as far as *Chimera* distills Barth's message that "storytelling is life's means and only prize. And no one has written more glitteringly than John Barth of the worthlessness of the heart, or the great munificence of language in bestowing so much grandeur, so much richness, so many pearly epigrams on all us swine.''

Barth's manuscripts reside in the Library of Congress, and the libraries of Pennsylvania State and Johns Hopkins Universities.

MEDIA ADAPTATIONS: The End of the Road was made into a film.

BIOGRAPHICAL/CRITICAL SOURCES:

BOOKS

Adams, Robert Martin, *After Joyce: Studies in Fiction after "Ulysses"*, Oxford University Press, 1977.
Allen, Mary, *The Necessary Blankness: Women in Major American Fiction of the Sixties*, University of Illinois Press, 1976.
Authors in the News, Gale, Volume I and II, 1976.
Baldwin, Kenneth H. and David K. Kirby, editors, *Individual and Community: Variations on a Theme in American Fiction*, Duke University Press, 1975.
Barth, John, *The Floating Opera*, Appleton-Century-Crofts, 1956, revised edition, Doubleday, 1967, reprinted with a new foreword by the author, Doubleday-Anchor, 1988.
Barth, John, *The End of the Road*, Doubleday, 1958, revised edition, 1967, reprinted with a new foreword by the author, Doubleday-Anchor, 1988.
Barth, John, *The Sot-Weed Factor*, Doubleday, 1960, revised edition, 1967, reprinted with a new foreword by the author, Doubleday-Anchor, 1988.
Barth, John, *Lost in the Funhouse: Fiction for Print, Tape, Live Voice*, Doubleday, 1968, reprinted with new forward by the author, Doubleday-Anchor, 1988.
Barth, John, *Chimera*, Random House, 1972.
Barth, John, *LETTERS*, Putnam, 1979.
Barth, John, *The Friday Book: Essays and Other Nonfiction*, Putnam, 1984.
Bellamy, Joe David, *The New Fiction: Interviews with Innovative American Writers*, University of Illinois Press, 1974.
Bergonzi, Bernard, *The Situation of the Novel*, University of Pittsburgh Press, 1970.
Bryant, Jerry, *The Open Decision: The Contemporary American Novel and its Intellectual Background*, Free Press, 1970.
Caramello, Charles, *Silverless Mirrors: Self and Postmodern American Fiction*, University Presses of Florida, 1983.
Contemporary Authors Bibliographical Series, Volume I: *American Novelists*, Gale, 1986.
Contemporary Literary Criticism, Gale, Volume I, 1973, Volume II, 1974, Volume III, 1975, Volume V, 1976, Volume VII, 1977, Volume IX, 1978, Volume X, 1979, Volume XIV, 1980, Volume XXVII, 1984.
Dembo, L. S. and Cyrena N. Pondrom, editors, *The Contemporary Writer*, University of Wisconsin Press, 1972.
D'Haen, Theo, *Text to Reader: a Communicative Approach to Fowles, Barth, Cortazar, and Boon*, John Benjamins, 1983.
Dictionary of Literary Biography, Volume II: *American Novelists since World War II*, Gale, 1978.
Gado, Frank, *First Person: Conversations on Writers and Writing*, Union College Press, 1973.
Gardner, John, *On Moral Fiction*, Basic Books, 1978.
Harris, Charles B., *Contemporary American Novelists of the Absurd*, College and University Press, 1971.
Harris, Charles B., *Passionate Virtuosity: The Fiction of John Barth*, University of Illinois Press, 1983.

Hassan, Ihab, *The Dismemberment of Orpheus*, Oxford University Press, 1971.
Hauck, Richard Boyd, *A Cheerful Nihilism: Confidence and "The Absurd" in American Humorous Fiction*, Indiana University Press, 1971.
Hergt, Tobias, *Das Motiv der Hochschule im Romanwerk van Bernard Malamud und John Barth*, Lang, 1979.
Hipkiss, Robert A., *The American Absurd: Pynchon, Vonnegut, and Barth*, Associated Faculty Press, 1984.
Hyman, Stanley Edgar, *Standards: A Chronicle of Books for Our Time*, Horizon, 1966.
Joseph, Gerhard, *John Barth*, University of Minnesota Press, 1970.
Karl, Frederick R., *American Fictions, 1940-1980: A Comprehensive History and Critical Evaluation*, Harper, 1983.
Kennard, Jean E., *Number and Nightmare*, Archon, 1975.
Klinkowitz, Jerome, *Literary Disruptions: The Making of a Post-Contemporary American Fiction*, University of Illinois Press, 1975.
Klinkowitz, Jerome, *Literary Subversions: New American Fiction and the Practice of Criticism*, Southern Illinois University Press, 1985.
Kostelanetz, Richard, editor, *American Writing Today*, Forum Books / Voice of America Editions, 1982.
Kostelanetz, Richard, editor, *On Contemporary Literature*, Avon, 1964.
Lehan, Richard, *A Dangerous Crossing*, Southern Illinois University Press, 1973.
McConnell, Frank D., *Four Postwar American Novelists: Bellow, Mailer, Barth, and Pynchon*, University of Chicago Press, 1976.
Morrell, David, *John Barth: An Introduction*, Pennsylvania State University Press, 1976.
Olderman, Raymond M., *Beyond the Waste Land: A Study of the American Novel in the Nineteen-Sixties*, Yale University Press, 1972.
Poirier, Richard, *The Performing Self*, Oxford University Press, 1971.
Porush, David, *The Soft Machine: Cybernetic Fiction*, Methuen, 1985.
Raban, Jonathan, *The Technique of Modern Fiction*, Edward Arnold, 1966.
Scholes, Robert, *The Fabulators*, Oxford University Press, 1967.
Schulz, Max F., *Black Humor Fiction of the Sixties: A Pluralistic Definition of Man and His World*, Ohio University Press, 1973.
Stark, John O., *The Literature of Exhaustion: Borges, Nabokov, Barth*, Duke University Press, 1974.
Tanner, Tony, *City of Words: American Fiction, 1950-1970*, Harper, 1971.
Tharpe, Jac, *John Barth: The Comic Sublimity of Paradox*, Southern Illinois University Press, 1974.
Tilton, John W., *Cosmic Satire in the Contemporary Novel*, Bucknell University Press, 1977.
Vidal, Gore, *Matters of Fact and Fiction: Essays, 1973-1976*, Random House, 1977.
Vine, Richard Allan, *John Barth: An Annotated Bibliography*, Scarecrow, 1977.
Waldmeir, Joseph J., editor, *Critical Essays on John Barth*, G. K. Hall, 1980.
Walkiewicz, E. P., *John Barth*, G. K. Hall, 1986.
Walsh, Thomas P. and Cameron Northouse, *John Barth, Jerzy Kosinski, and Thomas Pynchon: A Reference Guide*, G. K. Hall, 1977.

Weixlmann, Joseph, *John Barth: A Bibliography*, Garland Publishing, 1976.

Werner, Craig Hansen, *Paradoxical Resolutions: American Fiction since Joyce*, University of Illinois Press, 1982.

Ziegler, Heide and Christopher Bigsby, editors, *The Radical Imagination and the Liberal Tradition: Interviews with English and American Novelists*, Junction, 1982.

PERIODICALS

America, September 17, 1966, November 26, 1966, October 7, 1972, November 18, 1972.

Amerikastudien, Volume XXV, number 2, 1980.

Antioch Review, spring, 1980, fall, 1982.

Atlantic, August, 1967, July 1968, October, 1968, October, 1972, November, 1979, June, 1982.

Best Sellers, October 1, 1966, October 15, 1968, November 1, 1973.

Booklist, November 15, 1966, November 15, 1972.

Books & Arts, October 26, 1979.

Books and Bookmen, April, 1967, November, 1968.

Book Week, September 26, 1965, August 7, 1966.

Buffalo Courier Express Magazine, September 12, 1976.

Caliban, Volume XII, 1975

Canadian Review of Contemporary Literature, June, 1982.

Chicago Review, winter-spring, 1959, November, 1968.

Chicago Tribune, August 21, 1960, September 15, 1968, June 7, 1987.

Chicago Tribune Book World, November 11, 1979, May 30, 1982, January 13, 1985.

Christian Century, September 21, 1966.

Commentary, October, 1966.

Commonweal, October 21, 1966, December 2, 1966.

Contemporary Literature, winter, 1971, winter, 1981.

Criticism, winter, 1970.

Critique, fall, 1963, winter, 1965-66, Volume IX, number 1, 1966, Volume XIII, number 3, 1972, Volume XVII, number 1, 1975, Volume XVIII, number 2, 1976.

Detroit News, September 17, 1972, September 30, 1979.

Encounter, June, 1967.

Esquire, October, 1979.

Falcon, spring, 1972.

Forum-Service, January 7, 1961.

Georgia Review, summer, 1974.

Globe & Mail (Toronto), September 3, 1966, January 26, 1985, July 4, 1987.

Guardian, October 13, 1961.

Harper's, September, 1972, September, 1973, November, 1986.

Harrisburg Patriot (Pennsylvania), March 30, 1965.

Horizon, January, 1963.

Hudson Review, autumn, 1967, spring, 1969, winter, 1972-73.

Illustrated London News, April 8, 1967.

Journal of Narrative Technique, winter, 1978, winter, 1981.

Kenyon Review, winter, 1961.

Life, August 12, 1966, October 18, 1968, October 6, 1972.

Listener, March 30, 1967, October 3, 1968, September 18, 1969.

London Magazine, May, 1967, December, 1969.

Los Angeles Times Book Review, November 18, 1984, June 28, 1987.

Massachusetts Review, May, 1960.

Mississippi Quarterly, spring, 1979.

Modern Fiction Studies, winter, 1968-69, spring, 1973, autumn, 1974, summer, 1976, summer, 1979.

MOSAIC: A Journal for the Study of Literature and Ideas, Volume III, number 2, 1970, fall, 1974.

Nation, November 19, 1960, September 5, 1966, October 28, 1968, December 18, 1972, October 13, 1979.

National Observer, August 1, 1966, August 29, 1966, September 16, 1968, February 23, 1970, October 7, 1972.

National Review, December 3, 1968, October 13, 1972.

New American Review, April, 1972.

New Leader, February 13, 1961, March 2, 1964, April 12, 1965.

New Republic, September 3, 1966, November 23, 1968, December 1, 1979.

New Statesman, October 13, 1961, March 31, 1967, September 19, 1969, July 19, 1974.

Newsweek, August 8, 1966, December 19, 1966, September 30, 1968, February 16, 1970, October 9, 1972, January 1, 1973, October 1, 1979, May 24, 1982.

New Yorker, December 10, 1966, September 30, 1972, December 31, 1979, June 7, 1982.

New York Herald Tribune Book Review, July 20, 1958, September 26, 1965.

New York Review of Books, August 18, 1966, October 19, 1972, July 15, 1976, December 20, 1979, June 10, 1982.

New York Times, August 3, 1966, November 21, 1967, October 16, 1968, February 9, 1969, February 11, 1970, March 18, 1970, November 21, 1970, September 20, 1972, October 1, 1979, May 27, 1982, June 28, 1982.

New York Times Book Review, August 21, 1960, June 6, 1965, May 8, 1966, August 7, 1966, October 20, 1968, September 24, 1972, December 3, 1972, April 1, 1979, July 15, 1979, September 30, 1979, May 9, 1982, June 20, 1982, September 16, 1984, November 18, 1984, January 5, 1986, June 28, 1987.

Novel: A Forum on Fiction, October 20, 1968, winter, 1971, September 24, 1972, December 3, 1972, July 15, 1979, September 30, 1979.

Observer, October 10, 1965, April 2, 1967, September 29, 1968, September 14, 1969, July 21, 1974, May 29, 1977.

Partisan Review, winter, 1967, summer, 1968, spring, 1969, summer 1983.

Philadelphia Inquirer, February 22, 1976.

Playboy, March, 1967.

Prairie Schooner, summer, 1969.

Prism, spring, 1968.

Psychology Today, January, 1973.

Publishers Weekly, October 22, 1979.

Punch, April 5, 1967, October 2, 1968.

Saturday Review, November 26, 1960, July 3, 1965, August 6, 1966, September 30, 1967, September 28, 1978, October 13, 1979.

South Atlantic Quarterly, summer, 1969.

Spectator, March 31, 1967, September 20, 1969, July 20, 1974, May 10, 1980, August 7, 1982.

Studies in Short Fiction, fall, 1973, fall, 1974, summer, 1975.

Time, July 21, 1958, September 5, 1960, February 12, 1965, May 17, 1967, September 27, 1968, February 23, 1970, October 2, 1972, October 8, 1979, May 31, 1982.

Times Literary Supplement, October 27, 1961, March 30, 1967, October 10, 1968, September 18, 1969, July 26, 1974, May 30, 1980, July 23, 1982.

Tri-Quarterly, winter, 1967, winter, 1968, spring, 1975, fall, 1981.

Twentieth Century Literature, April, 1973, December, 1975, December, 1976.

Village Voice, October 6, 1966, September 17, 1979, November 19, 1979.

Virginia Quarterly Review, autumn, 1969, winter, 1972.

Voice Literary Supplement, May, 1982.

Washington Post, June 17, 1966, September 26, 1968, June 17, 1982.

Washington Post Book World, September 17, 1967, September 15, 1968, May 18, 1969, August 6, 1972, November 18, 1973, September 30, 1979, May 23, 1982, November 18, 1984, June 7, 1987.

Washington Post Potomac, September 3, 1967.

Wisconsin Studies in Contemporary Literature, winter-spring, 1965, autumn, 1966.

Yale Review, spring, 1973.

—*Sketch by Marilyn K. Basel*

* * *

BARZINI, Luigi (Giorgio, Jr.) 1908-1984
(Louis Smith)

PERSONAL: Born December 21, 1908, in Milan, Italy; died of lung cancer, March 31, 1984, in Rome, Italy; buried in Orvieto, Italy; son of Luigi (a journalist) and Mantica (Pesavento) Barzini; married Giannalisa Feltrinelli, April 12, 1940 (divorced); married Paola Gadola, September 12, 1949 (divorced); children: (first marriage) Ludovica, Benedetta; (second marriage) Luigi, Andrea, Francesca. *Education:* Columbia University, B.Litt., 1930. *Politics:* Partito Liberale Italiano. *Religion:* Catholic.

ADDRESSES: Home—1055 Via Cassia, Tomba di Nerone, Rome, Italy.

CAREER: Journalist, politician, nonfiction writer. Worked for a small newspaper in Long Island, N.Y., under pen name Louis Smith; *Corriere della Sera*, Milan, Italy, roving correspondent, 1931-40, special writer, 1954-61, columnist, beginning 1978; exiled by Mussolini as "a dangerous enemy of the Fascist regime," 1940-44; *Il Globo*, Rome, Italy, editor and publisher, 1944-47. Elected member of Italian Parliament, 1958, re-elected, 1963 and 1968. Writer in residence, Wesleyan University, Middletown, Conn., 1964.

AWARDS, HONORS: Bagutta Tripoli Prize, 1940, for *Evasione in Mongolia*.

WRITINGS:

IN ITALIAN

Nuova York, G. Agnelli (Milan), 1931.

Gli americani sono soli al mondo, Mondadori (Milan), 1952, English translation by the author published as *Americans Are Alone in the World*, Random House, 1953, reprinted, Penguin, 1985.

I communisti non hanno vinto, Mondadori, 1955.

(Editor) *Avventure in Oriente*, Mondadori, 1959.

Mosca, Mosca, Mondadori, 1960, 3rd edition, 1961.

L'Europa domani mattina, Longanesi & Co., 1964.

Le Paure d'iere, Reporter (Rome), 1968.

L'Antropometro italiano, Mondadori, 1973.

Also author of nonfiction book *Evasione in Mongolia*, 1940, and of play "I Disarmati," produced in Rome, 1957. Columnist for Milan weekly magazine *L'Europeo*.

IN ENGLISH

The Italians, Atheneum, 1964, reprinted, Hamish Hamilton, 1987.

From Caesar to the Mafia: Sketches of Italian Life, Library Press, 1971.

O America: When You and I Were Young, Harper, 1977 (published in England as *O America: A Memoir of the Twenties*, Hamish Hamilton, 1977).

The Europeans, Simon & Schuster, 1983 (published in England as *The Impossible Europeans*, Weidenfeld & Nicolson, 1984).

Memories of Mistresses: Reflections from a Life, Collier/Macmillan, 1986.

Contributor to *Encounter, Harper's, Preuves, Der Monat, New York Review of Books, Life*, and other magazines.

SIDELIGHTS: Italian-born, American-educated journalist Luigi Barzini was regarded as one of the world's foremost authorities on Italian culture and politics. His reputation stemmed largely from *The Italians*, an international bestseller that Barzini published first in English and then in his native Italian. Written with charm, wit, and an intimate knowledge of Italy, the 1964 guidebook intrigued American readers, but rankled many of Barzini's countrymen who bristled at his portrayal of a frustrated, incompetent nation that had fallen victim to its own grandiose illusions. Barzini, who served three terms as a member of the Italian Parliament, attributed his outlook to the years he spent as a student in the United States. "I had the advantage of being both inside and outside my subject, of knowing Italy like an Italian and seeing it like a foreigner," he told Sanche de Gramont in *Book Week*. Throughout his journalistic career Barzini continued to travel widely, crisscrossing the Atlantic to report news and gather material for his celebrated geopolitical essays. But his constant rambling left Barzini philosophically ungrounded in any culture. He compared himself to an ocean liner that regularly sailed back and forth between Europe and America but was not at home on either shore. "My natural habitat was between the two continents," he once said, as reported in the *Los Angeles Times*.

Barzini first traveled to the United States in 1925, when he was sixteen years old. His father, one of Italy's most distinguished journalists, had been offered the editorship of a new Italian-language newspaper in New York City, and the elder Barzini regarded the position as a respite from his constant travels and an opportunity to introduce his family to a more egalitarian way of life. "I wanted my children to grow up where their future depended not on family connections, political factions, powerful friends, intrigue or camarillas, but on their talent, capacity for hard work, and real worth," the father said, as reported in the *Washington Post Book World*.

The young Barzini enrolled in journalism courses at Columbia University and began to prepare for his own newspaper career. To improve his fluency in English, he enrolled in Latin classes. "Latin forced me to translate a language substantially like my own into contemporary English," Barzini wrote in his memoir of this period, *O America: When You and I Were Young*. "I owe my knowledge of written English to that training." After graduation, Barzini worked as a cub reporter for a Long Island newspaper under the pen name Louis Smith. The Anglicized pseudonym did not prevent Barzini's colleagues from teasing him about his ethnic origins; they called him "Mr. Smith-a" and "Lou the Wop." These and other incidents of racial stereotyping convinced Barzini that he would never be allowed to reach his full potential as a journalist in America. In 1930 he returned to Italy and hired on as a roving correspondent for the Milan daily where his father had worked, *Corriere della Sera*.

Assigned to the London office, the young journalist soon found himself at odds with Italian dictator Benito Mussolini, whose fascist policies Barzini had endorsed for a short time. "The very first instructions I received were, 'Do not mention the world economic crisis,'" Barzini recalled in *The Italians.* "They were Mussolini's own words relayed to all journalists. I remember asking myself what would have happened if the Italian press had stopped mentioning the Atlantic Ocean: would Italians have drowned trying to go to New York on bicycles?" Barzini's frank criticism incited Mussolini's displeasure, and ten years later, when World War II broke out, Barzini found himself denounced as "a dangerous enemy of the Fascist regime" and exiled to the coast of Tuscany. After the war ended, Barzini returned to journalism and settled in Rome.

Barzini became a journalist of international stature during the 1950s and also published *Americans Are Alone in the World,* his first important book. Written in Italian in 1952 and translated into English the next year by Barzini, the publication sketched a critical, though sympathetic, view of America's role in world affairs. The work drew sharp criticism from *New York Times* contributor Henry Steele Commager, who wrote, "To say of the nation that saw the real issues of the war . . . that it does not know what it is doing or where it is going is to confess a deep misunderstanding." The book attracted more favorable notice from Atheneum editor Simon Michael Bessie, who liked it so much that he asked Barzini to write a book about Italy for American tourists. That project evolved into *The Italians,* Barzini's tour de force that took almost ten years to complete.

Conceived in the early 1950s, *The Italians* was not published until 1964 for several reasons. First of all, Barzini was extremely active in newspaper work requiring international travel; then, in 1958, he was elected as a Liberal party member to the lower house of the Italian Parliament and his free time was further curtailed. Barzini's priorities did not change until 1960, when he suffered a serious heart attack from which he never expected to fully recover. Facing what he thought would be his death, the author poured all his energies into *The Italians.*

Originally written in English for an American audience, *The Italians* attempted to capture the spirit of Italian life and the essence of her people. Unlike the standard tour guides, Barzini's did not characterize the population as fun-loving or extol the pleasures of la dolce vita. Rather, he attacked Italians as "a frustrated, incompetent race who have over the centuries become the victims of their own cleverness and their own machinations," according to Robert Neville in the *New York Times Book Review.* "In essence, the author believes that the Italians have developed a fatal flaw of character that prevents them from achieving real national greatness and which causes them habitually to generate poor governments and successive tyrannies."

That flaw, as Barzini saw it, was the Italian emphasis on appearance over reality. He argued that everywhere in Italy substance was subservient to style. Fashionable clothing was more important than having enough food to eat. The architectural splendor of a church was more important than its suitability for parishioners engaged in prayer. In the political arena, empty propaganda and slogans were substituted for solid social reforms. In Italy, "everyone is nearly always putting on a theatrical performance, and bitter historical experiences have persuaded him to escape into shallow pleasures and distraction," remarked Denis Mack Smith in the *New York Review*

of Books. "Public and private life therefore are both governed by a reliance on make-believe and flattery. Nothing in Italy is quite what it seems. Even the passions of anger and love are often calculated."

Barzini found the effects of this hypocrisy chilling. By living in what he called "a penumbra of half-truths," the Italians had lost their ability to distinguish between what was really worthwhile and what was only of superficial importance. This lack of values helped make them dupes for political mountebanks such as Mussolini, whose Fascist policies merely appeared to make Italy strong. "Instead of producing responsible, educated statesmen able to come to grips with major problems, these flaws in the national character tend to throw up tyrants who strengthen these popular defects and usually lead the country to disaster," Neville explained.

In reviewing the book, several critics charged Barzini with the same penchant for exaggeration and deception that he denounced in his countrymen. "If dissembling is the essence, if Italians above all 'consider lying about their unfortunate country a sacred duty,' may not Mr. Barzini still be deceiving us out of ingrained habit?" asked Smith. Still, he conceded that Barzini's "theme is brilliantly argued" and acknowledged that "his book is like good talk, witty, unpretentious, escaping from logical difficulties in laughter, often instructive, never for one moment a bore. . . . Even where it is hard to agree with him about Italians, one can be fascinated by the author himself." Neville reached a similar conclusion: "It is hardly necessary to agree on every turning of Mr. Barzini's reasoning to recognize the brilliance of his thesis. . . . This is a quite remarkable performance." Concluded the *New Yorker* critic: "Mr. Barzini has written an invaluable and astringent guidebook to his country. He is obviously in earnest, and he just as obviously does not expect to be taken altogether seriously."

Turning from the Italy of his adulthood to the America of his youth, Barzini narrowed his focus to a more personal account in *O America: When You and I Were Young.* This memoir of his formative years in the United States drew evocative parallels between Barzini's callow optimism and that of 1920s America. "Barzini's point is that his youthful innocence and self-confidence precisely coincided with the last years of America's," wrote *Newsweek*'s Peter Prescott. "From this premise he has spun a modestly engaging book that is part memoir and part essay on our national condition." While there was nothing particularly unique about Barzini's coming of age, the book has special value because of the insight it sheds on Barzini's outlook, according to some critics. Barzini retreated to Europe in search of better job opportunities; "the irony was that, in spite of it all, I could not leave America behind. Something in me was forever American," he allowed.

Barzini drew on his experience as a journalist and world traveler in the last book he published in his lifetime, *The Europeans.* A polemic on cultural influence in politics, the book evolved from the "national personality" theory of history the author had developed in earlier writings. "The way a nation, and its politicians, act is—he seems to argue—fatally conditioned by the 'national personality,' which is itself the collective expression of individual idiosyncracies," *Times Literary Supplement* contributor Stanley Johnson explained. As Barzini surveyed the so-called "imperturbable" British, the "mutable" Germans, the "careful" Dutch, and others whom he tagged with a label, he demonstrated how their national pride and cultural diversity hindered any real progress toward a politically unified Europe.

Critical consensus was that the vivaciousness and sophistication of Barzini's arguments helped compensate for their logistic shortcomings. As Richard Rodriguez put it in the *Los Angeles Times Book Review:* "Reducing entire nations and their histories to single adjectives is, of course, an outrage. We let Barzini get away with it because he is Italian. There is humor and wit in these pages. . . . In deeper ways, too, he impresses. While history seems a matter of memorization for Americans, it is personal memory for Barzini. . . . His is an intellect without specific borders. He carries with him several languages, knowledge of several cultures. . . . The prose (in clear English) is evidence of an international man." In a similar vein, *New York Times Book Review* contributor Mavis Gallant noted that "his asides and comments are a pleasure. Very often, it is like being at dinner with a fascinating and knowledgeable *causeur.* . . . He speaks with a specific and special voice—elegant, erudite, humane, disenchanted and alarmed, conservative, Latin and Catholic." Concluded *Atlantic* contributor Phoebe-Lou Adams: "This is a stimulating and informative book. It is also a pleasure to read."

MEDIA ADAPTATIONS: The Italians was adapted for television and presented as an NBC News special.

BIOGRAPHICAL/CRITICAL SOURCES:

BOOKS

Barzini, Luigi, *The Italians,* Atheneum, 1964, reprinted, Hamish Hamilton, 1987.
Barzini, Luigi, *O America: When You and I Were Young,* Harper, 1977.
Barzini, Luigi, *The Europeans,* Simon & Schuster, 1983.

PERIODICALS

Book Week, August 23, 1964, May 16, 1965.
Book World, May 30, 1971.
Chicago Tribune Book World, July 31, 1983.
Commonweal, December 18, 1964.
Los Angeles Times, April 1, 1984.
Los Angeles Times Book Review, July 24, 1983, January 25, 1987.
Newsweek, April 4, 1977.
New Yorker, September 12, 1964, June 27, 1983.
New York Review of Books, September 10, 1964, August 18, 1983.
New York Times, January 3, 1954, April 12, 1977, March 23, 1978, April 22, 1983, December 23, 1986.
New York Times Book Review, August 23, 1964, April 3, 1977, May 15, 1983.
Saturday Review, May 29, 1971, May 14, 1977.
Time, September 25, 1964, July 4, 1977, July 11, 1983.
Times Literary Supplement, October 22, 1964, August 19, 1983.
Washington Post Book World, April 17, 1977, May 8, 1983.
Yale Review, March, 1965.

OBITUARIES:

PERIODICALS

Chicago Tribune, April 3, 1984.
Los Angeles Times, April 1, 1984.
Newsweek, April 9, 1984.
New York Times, April 1, 1984.

Time, April 9, 1984.
Times (London), April 3, 1984.
Washington Post, April 1, 1984.†

—*Sketch by Donna Olendorf*

* * *

BEER, John B(ernard) 1926-

PERSONAL: Born March 31, 1926, in Watford, Hertfordshire, England; son of John Bateman (a civil servant) and Eva (Chilton) Beer; married Gillian Patricia Kempster Thomas (a university teacher), July 7, 1962; children: three sons. *Education:* St. John's College, Cambridge, B.A., 1950, M.A., 1955, Ph.D., 1957.

ADDRESSES: Home—6 Belvoir Ter., Cambridge CB2 2AA, England. *Office*—Peterhouse, Cambridge University, Cambridge CB2 1RD, England.

CAREER: Cambridge University, St. John's College, Cambridge, England, research fellow, 1955-58; University of Manchester, Manchester, England, lecturer in department of English, 1958-64; Cambridge University, fellow of Peterhouse, 1964—, university lecturer, 1964-78, reader, 1978-87, professor of English literature, 1987—. Coleridge Bicentenary Lecturer at Christ's Hospital and Highgate, 1972; visiting professor, University of Virginia, 1975; visiting lecturer in India, 1978-79, and in Korea, 1985. *Military service:* Royal Air Force, 1946-48.

WRITINGS:

Coleridge, the Visionary, Chatto & Windus, 1959, Collier Books, 1962, reprinted, Greenwood Press, 1978.
The Achievement of E. M. Forster, Chatto & Windus, 1962, Barnes & Noble, 1963.
(Editor) Samuel Taylor Coleridge, *Poems,* Dutton, 1963, reprinted, Dent, 1986.
Milton, Lost and Regained, British Academy, 1964.
Blake's Humanism, Barnes & Noble, 1968.
Blake's Visionary Universe, Barnes & Noble, 1969.
(Editor and contributor) *Coleridge's Variety: Bicentenary Studies,* Macmillan, 1974.
Coleridge's Poetic Intelligence, Barnes & Noble, 1977.
Wordsworth and the Human Heart, Columbia University Press, 1978.
Wordsworth in Time, Faber, 1979.
(Editor with G. K. Das and contributor) *E. M. Forster, a Human Exploration: Centenary Essays,* New York University Press, 1979.
(Compiler with wife, Gillian Beer) *Heroes and Victims: Poems,* Macdonald Educational, 1979.
(Compiler with G. Beer) *Magic and Mystery: Poems,* Macdonald Educational, 1979.
(Compiler with G. Beer) *Taking a Closer Look: Poems,* Macdonald Educational, 1979.
(Compiler with G. Beer) *Telling a Story: Poems,* Macdonald Educational, 1979.
William Blake, 1757-1827, Profile Books, 1982.
(Compiler with G. Beer) *Delights and Warnings: A New Anthology of Poems,* Macdonald, 1984.
(Editor and contributor) *A Passage to India: Essays in Interpretation,* Barnes & Noble, 1986.

CONTRIBUTOR

H. S. Davies and G. Watson, editors, *The English Mind,* Cambridge University Press, 1964.

R. L. Brett, editor, *S. T. Coleridge,* Bell, 1971.

A. E. Dyson, editor, *English Poetry: Select Bibliographical Guides,* Oxford University Press, 1971.

M. D. Paley and M. Phillips, editors, *William Blake: Essays in Honour of Sir Geoffrey Keynes,* Oxford University Press, 1973.

Phillips, editor, *Interpreting Blake,* Cambridge University Press, 1979.

W. Crawford, editor, *Reading Coleridge,* Cornell University Press, 1979.

D. Sultana, editor, *Coleridge: Biographical and Critical Essays,* Vision Press, 1981.

V. A. Shahane, editor, *Approaches to E. M. Forster,* Heinemann, 1981.

Judith Herz and Robert K. Martin, editors, *Forster Centenary Essays,* Macmillan, 1981.

J. Pipkin, editor, *English and German Romanticism: Cross Currents and Controversies,* Carl Winter, 1985.

R. L. Snyder, editor, *Thomas de Quincey: Bicentenary Studies,* University of Oklahoma Press, 1985.

R. Gravil, L. Newly, and N. Roe, editors, *Coleridge's Imagination,* Cambridge University Press, 1985.

D. Jasper, *The Interpretation of Belief,* Macmillan, 1986.

G. Salgado and G. K. Das, editors, *The Spirit of D. H. Lawrence,* Macmillan, 1987.

OTHER

Contributor to *Encyclopaedia Britannica.* Contributor of articles to journals, including *Blake Newsletter, Cambridge Review, Journal of English and Germanic Philology, Modern Language Review, New Statesman, Spectator, Review of English Studies, Times Higher Education Supplement,* and *Times Literary Supplement.*

WORK IN PROGRESS: Research on nineteenth-century authors for a book on the idea of the unconscious, *The Hidden Self;* an edition of Coleridge's *Aids to Reflection* for "The Collected Coleridge"; two further books on Coleridge and Wordsworth, *Coleridge's Play of Mind* and *Wordsworth and Coleridge: The Critical Dialogue;* editing the Romantic period volume in the *Cambridge History of Literary Criticism;* general editor of a collection of Coleridge's writings organized by theme.

SIDELIGHTS: John B. Beer told *CA:* "In recent years I have been particularly interested in two related themes, which formed the topics of my twin books on Wordsworth. It is sometimes assumed that the unconscious was 'discovered' by Freud, but close study of Romantic and nineteenth-century literature shows that the phenomena which he was investigating had been a subject of deep interest for at least a century. Since analytic tools were not available, however, writers were forced to deal with it through their own art, concentrating on the creative powers of the psyche rather than on its functions of adaptation. Alongside this interest there persisted a belief in the power of the 'heart,' developed out of the eighteenth-century cult of sensibility and adopted as a counterweight to mechanistic interpretations of the world. To many modern readers the latter is simply embarrassing, but without an understanding of and allowance for it, we misread a good deal of nineteenth-century literature. The two books I am preparing will trace these topics, respectively, through a number of writers, including the early Romantics, Keats, De Quincey, Dickens, Ruskin, George Eliot, Forster and Lawrence. In several cases the same writer will figure strongly in both books.

"I am also interested in the interrelation of forms and energies as a theme both in the subject matter and in the creative work of the same period."

AVOCATIONAL INTERESTS: Travel, music, and walking in town and country.

*   *   *

BELDEN, Wilanne Schneider   1925-

PERSONAL: Born October 14, 1925, in Pittsburgh, Pa.; daughter of W. J. (a salesman) and Ida Mary (a teacher; maiden name, Hood) Schneider; married Robert Adams Belden (a business consultant and college lecturer), August 14, 1948; children: Leigh Schneider. *Education:* State University of Iowa, B.F.A., 1946; San Diego State College (now San Diego State University), teacher's certificate, 1958; California Western University (now United States International University), M.A., 1963; further graduate study at various universities. *Politics:* Republican. *Religion:* Episcopalian.

ADDRESSES: Home and office—1029 Santa Barbara St., San Diego, Calif. 92107.

CAREER: Erie Playhouse, Erie, Pa., director of children's theatre, 1948; San Diego Chamber of Commerce, San Diego, Calif., corresponding secretary, 1955-58; San Diego Unified School District, San Diego, teacher, 1958-86; lecturer. Teacher of animated filmmaking at University of California Extension, San Diego, 1973; staff teacher in filmmaking at La Jolla Museum of Contemporary Art, La Jolla, Calif., 1973; supervisor of student teachers. Founding member and performer, Old Globe Consort, 1955; founding director of San Diego Gilbert & Sullivan Repertory Company, 1970. Consultant to San Diego City Schools G.A.T.E. program.

MEMBER: Authors League of America, Authors Guild, California Association for the Gifted, Association of San Diego Educators of the Gifted.

WRITINGS:

Mind-Call (modern fantasy; juvenile), Atheneum, 1981.
Rescue of Ranor (juvenile), Atheneum, 1983.
Mind-Hold (fantasy; juvenile), Harcourt, 1987.
Frankie! (fantasy; juvenile), Harcourt, 1987.
(Contributor) Andre Norton, editor, *Tales of the Witch World,* Pinnacle Books, 1987.
Mind-Find (fantasy; juvenile), Harcourt, 1988.

WORK IN PROGRESS: Shanna and the Piper; Martin and the Wrizzle; Jerith; a sequel to *Frankie!;* three titles in the *Mind* series; a variety of other works for adults and young readers.

SIDELIGHTS: The writings of Wilanne Schneider Belden form an integral part of her larger concern, the nurturing and guidance of highly intelligent children. As Belden told *CA:* "Somehow, to be different in this way is to be other-than-human. The kids I teach have to face this. And they aren't nonhuman. They are the best the human race has yet developed. I want other children to meet such young people, to accept that having intellectual gifts makes a person only as different from others as all others are from each other."

Belden's *Mind* group of books were written in response to the shortage she perceived in literature that "faced squarely and without equivocation the almost insurmountable problem of being very highly intelligent." She continued: "I write what my editor calls science fiction and what I call modern fantasy because I read it and always have. The most interesting, exciting, mind-stretching books I read as a child and young person were in those categories.'' Belden named MacDonald, Tolkien, Lang, Norton, Bradbury, Burroughs, and Le Guin among those who influenced her writing.

Underlying Belden's personal philosophy is a belief that every child is gifted in some way. She summed up her views on the writer's craft by saying: ''While a story is written with a specific target audience in mind, the book is enjoyed by people of all ages who retain the attributes of childhood—the ability to wonder, to explore, to greet each new thing with delight.''

AVOCATIONAL INTERESTS: Drama, dance, photography, music, gardening, handcrafts, travel.

* * *

BENNETT, James Thomas 1942-

PERSONAL: Born October 19, 1942, in Memphis, Tenn.; son of Louie Edward (a surgeon) and Carrie (a dancer; maiden name, Tunnell) Bennett; married Sara Ellen Dorman (an executive), September 2, 1967. *Education:* Case Institute of Technology (now Case Western Reserve University), B.S., 1964, M.S., 1966, Ph.D., 1970. *Politics:* Libertarian. *Religion:* Presbyterian.

ADDRESSES: Home—5011 Gadsen Dr., Fairfax, Va. 22032. *Office*—Department of Economics, George Mason University, Fairfax, Va. 22030.

CAREER: Ford Motor Co., Dearborn, Mich., operations research analyst on finance central staff, 1964-65; Cleveland State University, Cleveland, Ohio, assistant professor of industrial management, 1967-70; George Washington University, Washington, D.C., began as assistant professor, became associate professor of economics, 1970-75; George Mason University, Fairfax, Va., professor of economics, 1975—, senior staff scientist with program in logistics. Research fellow at Federal Reserve Bank, Cleveland, 1969-70; member of board of trustees of Ohio Epsilon Corp.; consultant to Chesapeake & Ohio Railway and Cleveland Transit System.

MEMBER: American Economic Association, American Statistical Association, Contemporary Economics and Business Association, Econometric Society, Phi Kappa Psi, Tau Beta Pi.

WRITINGS:

(With Manuel H. Johnson) *The Political Economy of Federal Government Growth, 1959-1978,* Texas A & M University Press, 1980.
Deregulating Labor Relations, Fisher Institute, 1981.
Better Government at Half the Price, Caroline House, 1981.
Underground Government: The Off-Budget Public Sector, Cato Institute, 1984.
(With Thomas J. DiLorenzo) *Destroying Democracy: How Government Funds Partisan Politics,* Cato Institute, 1985.

Editor of *Journal of Labor Research.*

WORK IN PROGRESS: Unfair Competition: The Profits of Nonprofits.

SIDELIGHTS: James Thomas Bennett suggests in his survey co-authored with Thomas J. DiLorenzo, *Destroying Democracy: How Government Funds Partisan Politics,* that ''there is a network of tax-exempt organizations that ostensibly pursue acceptable (that is, politically neutral) goals, but are up to no good,'' explains Ernest Van den Haag in the *New York Times Book Review.* Van den Haag notes that much of the money received by such organizations, on both sides of political center, is ''diverted to lobbying and organizing for partisan causes.'' And while he concurs with Bennett and DiLorenzo's opposition to such public funding of ''rightist as well as leftist political activity,'' he also wishes the authors had shown the amounts of money involved annually and ''the porous Government procedures that allow tax money to be used for partisan politics.'' A *Kirkus Reviews* contributor believes that Bennett and DiLorenzo ''do a sound job of maintaining an evenhanded reporting of their research, which brings out in the open a problem easily obscured by the daily headlines.''

BIOGRAPHICAL/CRITICAL SOURCES:

PERIODICALS

Kirkus Reviews, October 15, 1985.
New York Times Book Review, December 22, 1985.

* * *

BENTLEY, Judith (McBride) 1945-

PERSONAL: Born April 8, 1945, in Indianapolis, Ind.; daughter of Robert Edward (a college president) and Luella (Hart) McBride; married Allen Bentley (an attorney), June 6, 1970; children: Anne, Peter. *Education:* Oberlin College, B.A., 1967; New York University, M.A. (history of American civilization), 1969, M.A. (educational psychology), 1975. *Religion:* Congregational.

ADDRESSES: Home and office—4747 132nd Ave. S.E., Bellevue, Wash. 98006.

CAREER: Saturday Review, New York City, editorial assistant, 1970-71, assistant editor, 1972; Newsweek Books, New York City, copy editor, 1973-74; New York City Community College, Brooklyn, N.Y., adjunct instructor in reading skills, 1975-77; Dalton School, New York City, preceptor, 1977-79; writer and editor, 1979—; adult high school teacher, 1982—.

MEMBER: Pacific Northwest Writers Conference.

WRITINGS:

FOR YOUNG PEOPLE

State Government, F. Watts, 1978.
The National Health Care Controversy, F. Watts, 1981.
American Immigration Today: Pressures, Problems, Policies, Messner, 1981.
Busing: The Continuing Controversy, F. Watts, 1982.
Justice O'Connor, Messner, 1983.
The Nuclear Freeze Movement, F. Watts, 1984.
Refugees Search for a Haven, Messner, 1986.
Archbishop Desmond Tutu, Enslow, 1988.

OTHER

Contributor to magazines, including *Family Health* and *Back-Packer.*

WORK IN PROGRESS: ''Inquiry Units in Washington State History,'' with a grant from Seattle Community College District.

SIDELIGHTS: Judith Bentley once told *CA:* ''After working in various publishing jobs and then teaching, I began writing a few years ago when my first child was born. I have found it an ideal way to combine parenting with the satisfaciton that comes from a more widely recognized profession. I write mainly nonfiction for junior high and high school students. My main interests are contemporary issues, American history, and women's issues.''

More recently, Bentley explained how those interests developed: ''When I was growing up, I loved to read those orange, hard-cover historical biographies with silhouette illustrations. I now realize that many of them were as much fiction as fact, with likely thoughts and feelings put into the heads and hearts of the heroes and heroines. Yet they were lively, and they recreated history in a way my textbooks could not.

''I also realize now that some people were missing in books for children and young adults. Daniel Boone and Clara Barton were fine subjects, partly because their rough edges were sanded and their radical ideas didn't sound radical a hundred years later. Mother Jones and Gandhi were closer in history and more threatening in thought or action.

''My goal is to write the kind of biographies that bring historical and contemporary leaders to life for young people and to tell their stories with the rough edges intact and the conflicts of history unsoftened. I would like to provide new models to supplement the ones I grew up on. Fortunately, there are more women now to choose as subjects and young people have a greater awareness of international leaders, too.''

*   *   *

BETTELHEIM, Bruno   1903-

PERSONAL: Born August 28, 1903, in Vienna, Austria; came to United States in 1939, naturalized citizen in 1944; son of Anton and Paula (Seidler) Bettelheim; married Gertrud Weinfeld (a teacher and researcher), May 14, 1941; children: Ruth, Naomi, Eric. *Education:* University of Vienna, Ph.D., 1938. *Politics:* Democrat. *Religion:* Jewish.

ADDRESSES: Home—718 Adelaide Pl., Santa Monica, Calif. 90402.

CAREER: Progressive Education Association, Chicago, Ill., research associate, 1939-41; Rockford College, Rockford, Ill., associate professor of psychology, 1942-44; University of Chicago, Chicago, Ill., assistant professor, 1944-47, associate professor, 1947-52, professor of educational psychology, 1952-73, Stella M. Rowley Distinguished Service Professor of Education, and professor of psychology and psychiatry, 1963-73, head of Sonia Shankman Orthogenic School, 1944-73; writer, 1973—. Diplomate of American Psychological Association. Fellow of Center for Advanced Studies in the Behavioral Sciences, 1971-72. Former member of Chicago Council for Child Psychology.

MEMBER: American Psychological Association (fellow), American Orthopsychiatric Association (fellow), American Philosophical Association, American Association of University Professors, American Sociological Association, American Academy of Education (founding member), American Academy of Arts and Sciences, Chicago Psychoanalytical Society, Quadrangle Club.

AWARDS, HONORS: D.H.L. from Cornell University; National Book Award and National Book Critics Circle Award, both 1977, both for *The Uses of Enchantment: The Meaning and Importance of Fairy Tales; Los Angeles Times* current interest prize nominee, 1983, for *Freud and Man's Soul.*

WRITINGS:

(With Morris Janowitz) *Dynamics of Prejudice: A Psychological and Sociological Study of Veterans,* Harper, 1950.

Love Is Not Enough: The Treatment of Emotionally Disturbed Children, Free Press, 1950.
Overcoming Prejudice (booklet), Science Research Associates, 1953.
Symbolic Wounds: Puberty Rites and the Envious Male, Free Press, 1954, revised edition, Collier Books, 1962.
Truants from Life: The Rehabilitation of Emotionally Disturbed Children, Free Press, 1955.
The Informed Heart: Autonomy in a Mass Age, Free Press, 1960.
Paul and Mary: Two Case Histories from "Truants from Life," Doubleday-Anchor, 1961.
(With others) *Youth: Change and Challenge* (proceedings of the American Academy of Arts and Sciences), American Academy of Arts and Sciences, 1961.
Dialogues with Mothers, Free Press, 1962.
Child Guidance, a Community Responsibility: An Address, with a Summary of Public Provisions for Child Guidance Services to Michigan Communities, Institute for Community Development and Services, Continuing Education Service, Michigan State University, 1962.
(With Janowitz) *Social Change and Prejudice: Including Dynamics of Prejudice,* Free Press, 1964.
Art: As the Measure of Man, Museum of Modern Art, 1964.
The Empty Fortress: Infantile Autism and the Birth of the Self, Free Press, 1967.
Mental Health in the Slums: Preliminary Draft, Center of Policy Study, University of Chicago, 1968.
The Children of the Dream, Macmillan, 1969, reprinted as *The Children of the Dream: Communal Childrearing and American Education,* Avon, 1970, published in England as *The Children of the Dream: Communal Child-Rearing and Its Implications for Society,* Paladin, 1971.
Food to Nurture the Mind, Children's Foundation (Washington, D.C.), 1970.
Obsolete Youth: Toward a Psychograph of Adolescent Rebellion, San Francisco Press, 1970.
(With others) *Moral Education: Five Lectures,* Harvard University Press, 1970.
A Home for the Heart, Knopf, 1974.
The Uses of Enchantment: The Meaning and Importance of Fairy Tales, Knopf, 1976.
Surviving, and Other Essays, Knopf, 1979, reprinted with a new introduction as *Surviving the Holocaust,* Flamingo, 1986.
(With Karen Zelan) *On Learning to Read: The Child's Fascination with Meaning,* Knopf, 1982.
Freud and Man's Soul, Knopf, 1982.
A Good Enough Parent: A Book on Child Rearing, Knopf, 1987.

Columnist for *Ladies' Home Journal.* Contributor to professional and popular journals, including *New Yorker* and *New York Times Book Review.*

SIDELIGHTS: Bruno Bettelheim is a world authority on the treatment of childhood emotional disorders, especially autism and juvenile psychosis. Himself a survivor of debilitating experiences in concentration camps at Dachau and Buchenwald, Bettelheim brings to his work firsthand knowledge of the acute anxiety engendered by extreme situations; his efforts with mentally ill children reflect his sensitivity to their often-unarticulated fears. Bettelheim's writings have found an audience beyond the psychoanalytic community, as he seeks to explain psychological phenomena without resorting to professional jargon. In books such as *Love Is Not Enough: The Treatment of*

Emotionally Disturbed Children, Truants from Life: The Rehabilitation of Emotionally Disturbed Children, and *The Empty Fortress: Infantile Autism and the Birth of the Self,* he describes the pioneering efforts of staff at the Sonia Shankman Orthogenic School of the University of Chicago, where he presided from 1944 until 1973. He has also written two penetrating works on the Nazi death camps, *The Informed Heart: Autonomy in a Mass Age* and *Surviving, and Other Essays,* both of which explore the psychological legacy of the camp experience. Since his retirement from the University of Chicago, Bettelheim has undertaken other projects aimed at specialists and general readers alike. He sounds a call for childhood intellectual stimulation in *The Uses of Enchantment: The Meaning and Importance of Fairy Tales* and *On Learning to Read: The Child's Fascination with Meaning,* and he discusses the implications of mistranslation in *Freud and Man's Soul.* *Spectator* contributor Anthony Storr believes that Bettelheim's writings bear witness to a "long and fruitful life" celebrating "the fact that the human spirit can sometimes triumph over Hell itself."

New York Times Book Review correspondent Paul Roazen observes that Bettelheim "stands as one of Freud's genuine heirs in our time. Fearlessly independent and yet working within Freud's great discoveries, Bettelheim has sought to think through all of human psychology for himself." To a certain extent, Bettelheim's life parallels that of the "father of psychoanalysis." Both Bettelheim and Freud grew up in Vienna; both chose to work and live there until Nazi atrocities forced them to go elsewhere. As a young student forty seven years Freud's junior, Bettelheim was strongly influenced by psychoanalytic theory and was frankly awed by Freud's accomplishments. In a piece for the *New York Times Book Review,* Bettelheim recalls passing the apartment building where Freud lived and worked: "I used to walk on this street, more often than not choosing to use this hilly, unattractive way to get where I was going only because Freud lived there." Having received a Ph.D. in psychology from the University of Vienna in 1938—and having undergone psychoanalysis—Bettelheim set himself on a career dedicated to "a distinctive vein of Freudian orthodoxy, free of the scholasticism that has settled like dust over psychoanalytic literature," according to Joseph Featherstone in *The New Republic.* Like Freud, Bettelheim undertook clinical work that had lasting implications for his writings. Featherstone claims: "In his hands, orthodox concepts are metaphors for real experiences, not abstractions leading bloodless lives of their own."

The Nazis annexed Austria in 1938, just after Bettelheim had finished his degree requirements. Later that same year, Bettelheim, a Jew, was arrested and sent first to Dachau and then to Buchenwald. He endured the camps for one year, and when he was released, he drew upon his harrowing experiences there to form his professional positions. Storr notes that, while incarcerated, Bettelheim "was able to use his psychoanalytic experience and insight to distance himself from the impact of what surrounded him, [and] that made it possible for him to come through. Bettelheim was not only able to survive, but also to make positive use of his experience." In fact, Bettelheim conducted research in the camps and observed the impact of the life-threatening and dehumanizing environment on numerous individuals. After being freed and moving to the United States, he summarized these observations in a landmark article, "Individual and Mass Behavior in Extreme Situations." Ironically, the article, which was the first by a scholar to detail the Nazis' methods, was rejected by numerous periodicals un-

til 1943, when it appeared in *The Journal of Abnormal and Social Psychology.* As the death camps were liberated, revealing Bettelheim's assertions and conclusions to be true, his article gained worldwide renown and became required reading for all officers in the United States military service.

Bettelheim's camp experiences are explored in more depth in *The Informed Heart* and *Surviving, and Other Essays.* "Although Bettelheim's contribution to our understanding of psychotic children is important," Storr writes, "it is by his account of the concentration camps that he will be remembered. . . . *The Informed Heart* has long been famous. . . . What he has to say is of such signal importance to our understanding of human nature that it cannot be too often repeated." *New York Review of Books* contributor Charles Rycroft describes *The Informed Heart* as "largely an analysis of what decided whether a person lived or died in a concentration camp. In it [Bettelheim] was concerned not so much with the physical capacity to survive brutality and torture as with the psychological factors determining whether a person will be able to resist demoralization in a setting in which he has ceased to be in any way a free agent—a setting, moreover, which is designed to reduce him to a nonentity and, indeed, has no wish that he should go on living." Critics have found much to praise in *The Informed Heart.* In his *New York Times Book Review* assessment, Franz Alexander remarks: "This is a dignified book, convincing because it is not derived from textbook knowledge, but from insights gained in the laboratory of the author's own life. In it reason and life experiences are closely integrated." *New Statesman* essayist Maurice Richardson contends that the book "gives you the impression of being lit from within by a humanist glow. [Bettelheim's] clinical but by no means cold detachment from the horrors, both factual and social of the camps is moving and impressive."

Almost twenty years separate the publication dates of *The Informed Heart* and *Surviving, and Other Essays.* The latter work represents Bettelheim's retrospective attempts to understand not only the burden of experience he bears, but also the lasting legacy of guilt and commitment borne by all survivors. "The experience had to be confronted," Clara Claiborne Park declares in the *Nation,* "not because it could be denied or left behind . . . but because only by confronting it, not once but over and over again, could meaning be found. The full heroism of that early objectivity [in *The Informed Heart*] can be measured only after reading the later essays." In a *New York Times Book Review* assessment of *Surviving, and Other Essays,* Paul Robinson writes: "Among Bettelheim's many virtues are intellectual humility, analytic skill and unfailing clarity of expression. He is altogether compelling when he recounts his experiences as a camp inmate and survivor. He's not merely persuasive, but moving when he tells that he was able to retain his identity within the camps because, in his earlier life, he had cultivated the powers of observation and analysis. . . . In his survival, one witnesses the triumph of civilization, of mind, of inner culture against almost impossible odds, and the prospect is exhilarating." *New York Review of Books* essayist Rosemary Dinnage adds that the collection exposes Bettelheim's two great strengths: "his totally realistic acceptance of the satanic in human beings and of the gross disintegrations of personality this can impose on others, and his simultaneous unshaken confidence in order and mutuality and reconstruction." Claiborne Park similarly concludes that in *Surviving, and Other Essays,* "it is finally to the humanity of society that Bettelheim has survived to bear witness."

According to Richard Rhodes in the *Chicago Tribune Book*

World, Bettelheim's identity as a psychologist and teacher is closely linked to his identity as a survivor of the Holocaust. Bettelheim's experimental approach at the Orthogenic School "was directly a result of his camp experience," Rhodes states. "He saw at Dachau that a total environment is a far more powerful instrument of personality change than the partial environment of classical psychoanalysis. . . . He realized that camp victims and psychotic children have much in common—that both became what they became by adapting to extreme situations. He designed his school, then, as a total environment that might reverse in the direction of healing and of hope the total environments of extremity that he had experienced and studied. By design and by the sheer force of its director's compassion, the school has salvaged and restored to function children of whom all other agencies had despaired, which for Bettelheim must be a profoundly gratifying experience of humane revenge." Indeed, Elsa First reports in the *New York Review of Books* that Bettelheim was driven "to create a therapeutic environment which in each detail of everyday life would create an existence that he envisioned as the exact opposite of the dehumanization so systematically engineered by the camps." Choosing his staff and even the decor with great care, Bettelheim created "probably the most remarkable mental institution in the country," in the words of a *New Yorker* reviewer. The Orthogenic School, with its humane, deinstitutionalized approach, has had an unprecedented eighty-five per cent cure rate among children thought to be far beyond help.

Love Is Not Enough, Truants from Life, The Empty Fortress, and *A Home for the Heart* all document events at the Orthogenic School and outline Bettelheim's educational and therapeutic philosophy. In *The Empty Fortress,* for instance, Bettelheim advances his theory of autism and reviews the case histories of three autistic children who were patients at the school. Central to Bettelheim's treatment approach is the belief that autistic behavior occurs when a child perceives that none of his acts have any effect on the outside world. Therapy therefore must have as its goal the development of autonomy in the child's social perception. A *Scientific American* reviewer of *The Empty Fortress* finds Bettelheim's strategy in the clinic even more convincing than his theories: "The pragmatic argument of successful therapy is generally powerful in medicine, but the humanity, intelligence, self-sacrifice and endurance of the therapy given by Dr. Bettelheim and his devoted staff seem to outweigh the specific content of any theory." *New Republic* contributor Robert Coles feels that the author is "modest, sensible and unpretentious when he tries to specify the particulars that make for autism." Bettelheim's 1974 overview of his professional stance, *A Home for the Heart,* has also received critical acclaim. Elsa First writes: "Bettelheim's myth of the embattled child served to inspire a powerful amount of goodness within the fortress of his school. His clinical intuitiveness and resourcefulness and the unfailing respect he showed his psychotic children were remarkable. . . . There are many useful lessons to be learned from Bettelheim's retrospective look at his life's work." Elizabeth Janeway expresses a similar view in the *New York Times Book Review:* "Bettelheim combines a capacity for lucid speech with a mind of rare strength and subtlety, as his readers well know. He is a natural parabolist, capable of seeing the universe in a grain of sand and passing the vision on. . . . Those who get most from Bettelheim will be those who read him with eyes open and minds alert to the nuances and vistas of this thought."

During the 1970s and 1980s, Bettelheim has focused much of his attention on improving the nurture of healthy children. In

The Children of the Dream: Communal Child-Rearing and American Education he discusses the ramifications of a childhood spent in an Israeli kibbutz. Both *The Uses of Enchantment* and *On Learning to Read* offer strident calls for reform in American early childhood education through the use of traditional fairy tales and other more stimulating reading matter. Bettelheim believes that fantasy—even violent fantasy—is necessary for children and that fairy tales often offer healthy outlets for subconscious wishes and anxieties. As Richard Todd notes in an *Atlantic* review of *The Uses of Enchantment,* Bettelheim "makes plain that the [fairy] tales are supple, many-layered things, and that different children may find in the same story quite different, even contradictory, forms of psychic comfort. . . . He is sincere in his urgency about the irreplaceableness of these traditional tales, so many of which are now effectively forgotten, or adulterated into Disneyesque good cheer." *New York Review of Books* essayist Harold Bloom calls *The Uses of Enchantment* "a splendid achievement, brimming with useful ideas, with insights into how young children read and understand, and most of all overflowing with a realistic optimism and with an experienced and therapeutic good will." In his *New York Times Book Review* assessment of *The Uses of Enchantment,* John Updike hails the work as "a charming book about enchantment, a profound book about fairy tales. . . . What is new, and exciting, is the warmth, humane and urgent, with which Bettelheim expounds fairy tales as aids to the child's growth."

In 1982 Bettelheim published his controversial book *Freud and Man's Soul,* a short study of how standard English translations of Freud misrepresent Freud's intentions. Storr explains in the *New Republic:* "[Bettelheim] believes that the effect of the English translation of Freud's ideas was to make them into an abstract intellectual system, something that might be applied to the understanding of others in a cerebral fashion, but that was not easily applicable to the study of one's own unconscious." *Los Angeles Times Book Review* contributor Harvey Mindess further contends that Bettelheim sees the results of these expositional misrepresentations as having produced "an impression of Freud as far more impersonal than he was, and to define psychoanalysis as a medical specialty when its founder intended it to be 'a part of psychology' and an inquiry into the nature of the soul." Opinions on the validity of Bettelheim's thesis vary widely. *Voice Literary Supplement* reviewer Walter Kendrick asserts that Bettelheim's "desire to make Freud sweet and cuddly has caused him to write a stupid, dangerous little book." Frank Kermode likewise notes in the *New York Times Book Review* that it is "salutary to have instruction in what we have lost [through translation]. But on the evidence here presented, Bettelheim has treated rather harshly a huge labor of translation, carried out with devotion and skill, and has unfairly visited the failings of American psychoanalytic practice on that translation." Storr, on the other hand, finds Bettelheim's concern "to resuscitate Freud as a humanist . . . an understandable aspiration," and in the London *Times,* A. S. Byatt concludes: "We need books like Bettelheim's to keep us alert and supple, to remind us of the complex nature of language and translation, culture and history, the limitations of their power, the power of their limitations."

Both Bettelheim's clinical accomplishments and his body of writing reflect a half century's devotion to improving the human condition. *New York Times* correspondent James Atlas suggests that life itself "has provided Professor Bettelheim with ample opportunities to witness human behavior in all its terrifying variety, and to nurture what is valuable in it while remorselessly condemning what is dangerous.'' To *Washington Post Book World* critic William McPherson, Bettelheim is "renowned in his field and acclaimed throughout the world" because he is "a survivor who bears witness" not only to the disintegration of the personality but also to the resurgence and resilience of the human spirit. Rosemary Dinnage also contends that Bettelheim's experiences have strengthened, not shaken, his faith in cooperation between individuals. "Bettelheim's achievement," Dinnage concludes, "is that while his professional life *has* been concerned with the distress of others, he has also been able to teach us through the writings—objective rather than passionate—that are based on his own distresses and endurance. Those experiences are the basis of his special understanding both of the growth and the destruction of what makes a person human.''

BIOGRAPHICAL/CRITICAL SOURCES:

BOOKS

Bettelheim, Bruno, *The Informed Heart: Autonomy in a Mass Age,* Free Press, 1960.
Bettelheim, Bruno, *A Home for the Heart,* Knopf, 1974.
Bettelheim, Bruno, *Surviving, and Other Essays,* Knopf, 1979, reprinted with a new introduction as *Surviving the Holocaust,* Flamingo, 1986.

PERIODICALS

America, August 7, 1976.
American Academy of Political and Social Science: Annals, July, 1950, November, 1950, September, 1961.
American Journal of Sociology, May, 1961, July, 1969.
American Political Science Review, June, 1961.
American Sociological Review, August, 1950, October, 1955, June, 1961.
Atlantic, June, 1976.
Book World, April 27, 1969.
Chicago Sunday Tribune, July 16, 1950.
Chicago Tribune Book World, April 29, 1979, February 21, 1982.
Choice, October, 1967, October, 1974, October, 1976.
Christian Century, December 6, 1967, June 23-30, 1976.
Critic, October-December, 1974.
Harper's, June, 1976.
Harvard Educational Review, fall, 1967.
Journal of Home Economics, October, 1955, November, 1962.
Los Angeles Times, October 16, 1983, October 12, 1986.
Los Angeles Times Book Review, January 23, 1983.
Nation, June 24, 1950, July 30, 1955, April 1, 1961, May 12, 1979, February 12, 1983.
National Review, May 10, 1974, August 20, 1976.
New Leader, March 31, 1969.
New Republic, May 22, 1961, March 4, 1967, May 24, 1969, April 20, 1974, May 29, 1976, December 31, 1982.
New Statesman, March 17, 1961, September 26, 1969, June 7, 1974.
Newsweek, January 10, 1983.
New Yorker, April 22, 1974, January 25, 1982.
New York Review of Books, May 4, 1967, May 30, 1974, July 15, 1976, April 19, 1979, April 1, 1982.
New York Times, February 12, 1950, September 17, 1950, May 29, 1955, March 24, 1969, August 15, 1979, December 21, 1982.
New York Times Book Review, October 8, 1961, February 26, 1967, April 6, 1969, March 17, 1974, May 23, 1976, January 2, 1977, April 29, 1979, January 31, 1982, February 6, 1983.

San Francisco Chronicle, March 26, 1950, July 16, 1950.
Saturday Review, July 8, 1961, June 9, 1962, May 17, 1969, May 15, 1976.
Scientific American, July, 1967.
Spectator, October 23, 1976, April 1, 1978, August 11, 1979, March 20, 1982.
Time, May 3, 1976.
Times (London), December 22, 1983.
Times Literary Supplement, October 9, 1969, August 2, 1974, October 1, 1976, July 29, 1983, August 15, 1986.
Voice Literary Supplement, February, 1983, December, 1985.
Washington Post Book World, June 13, 1976, May 13, 1979, January 3, 1982.

—*Sketch by Anne Janette Johnson*

*   *   *

BICKHAM, Jack M(iles)   1930-
(Jeff Clinton, John Miles, George Shaw)

PERSONAL: Born September 2, 1930, in Columbus, Ohio; son of John Robert (a manufacturing executive) and Helen E. (Miles) Bickham; married Janie R. Wallace, November 23, 1952; children: Robert, Daniel, Stephen, Lise. *Education:* Ohio State University, B.A., 1952; University of Oklahoma, M.A., 1960. *Politics:* Democrat. *Religion:* Roman Catholic.

ADDRESSES: Home—2113 Bois de Arc, Norman, Okla. 73071. *Office*—School of Journalism, University of Oklahoma, Norman, Okla. 73019. *Agent*—Andrea Cirillo, Jane Rotrosen Agency, 226 East 32nd St., New York, N.Y. 10016.

CAREER: Norman Transcript, Norman, Okla., reporter, 1956-60; Oklahoma Publishing Co., Oklahoma City, Okla., assistant Sunday editor on *Daily Oklahoman* (newspaper), 1960-66; *Oklahoma Courier* (newspaper), Oklahoma City, managing editor, 1966-69; University of Oklahoma, School of Journalism, Norman, 1969—, began as assistant professor, became professor of journalism. Oklahoma City University, part-time teacher of journalism, 1963-66. *Military service:* U.S. Air Force, 1952-54; became first lieutenant.

MEMBER: Authors League of America, Authors Guild, Western Writers of America.

AWARDS, HONORS: Editor of the Year, Sigma Delta Chi, 1969; trophy for best novel, Oklahoma Writers Federation, 1969, 1971, 1973; Oklahoma writing award, 1971; named outstanding professor, University of Oklahoma, 1972; Florence Roberts Head Memorial Award, 1984, for *I Still Dream about Columbus.*

WRITINGS:

Gunman's Gamble, Ace Books, 1958.
Feud Fury, Ace Books, 1959.
Killer's Paradise, Ace Books, 1959.
The Useless Gun, Ace Books, 1960.
(Under pseudonym John Miles) *Dally with a Deadly Doll,* Ace Books, 1960.
Hangman's Territory, Ace Books, 1960.
Gunmen Can't Hide, Ace Books, 1961.
(Under pseudonym John Miles) *Trouble Trails,* Bouregy, 1963.
Trip Home to Hell, Berkley Publishing, 1965.
The Padre Must Die, Doubleday, 1967.
The War on Charity Ross, Doubleday, 1967.
The Shadowed Faith, Doubleday, 1968.
Target: Charity Ross, Doubleday, 1968.

Decker's Campaign, Doubleday, 1970.
The Apple Dumpling Gang, Doubleday, 1970.
Jilly's Canal, Doubleday, 1972.
Goin', Paperback Library, 1972.
Dopey Dan, Doubleday, 1972.
Katie, Kelly and Heck, Doubleday, 1973.
Baker's Hawk (Reader's Digest Condensed Book selection), Doubleday, 1973.
(Under pseudonym John Miles) *The Night Hunters*, Bobbs-Merrill, 1973.
Emerald Canyon, Doubleday, 1974.
The Silver Bullet Gang, Bobbs-Merrill, 1974.
The Blackmailer, Bobbs-Merrill, 1974.
A Boat Named Death, Doubleday, 1975.
Showdown at Emerald Canyon, Doubleday, 1975.
Operation Nightfall, Bobbs-Merrill, 1975.
Twister, Doubleday, 1977.
The Winemakers, Doubleday, 1977.
The Excalibur Disaster, Doubleday, 1978.
A Question of Ethics, Pocket Books, 1979.
Dinah, Blow Your Horn, Doubleday, 1979.
The Regensburg Legacy, Doubleday, 1980.
All the Days Were Summer, Doubleday, 1981.
I Still Dream about Columbus, St. Martin's, 1982.
Ariel, St. Martin's, 1984.

UNDER PSEUDONYM JEFF CLINTON

The Fighting Buckaroo, Berkley Publishing, 1961.
Range Killer, Berkley Publishing, 1962.
Wildcat's Rampage, Berkley Publishing, 1962.
Wildcat against the House, Berkley Publishing, 1963.
Wildcat's Revenge, Berkley Publishing, 1964.
Killer's Choice, Berkley Publishing, 1964.
Wildcat Takes His Medicine, Berkley Publishing, 1966.
Wanted: Wildcat O'Shea, Berkley Publishing, 1967.
Wildcat on the Loose, Berkley Publishing, 1967.
Watch Out for Wildcat, Berkley Publishing, 1968.
Kane's Odyssey, Laser Books, 1976.

Also author of other "Wildcat" books.

OTHER

Also author of *Halls of Dishonor*, 1980, and *Miracleworker*, 1987. Contributor of short stories and articles to *Journalism Quarterly, Sporting News, Explicator, Sports Illustrated, Time, Life*, and *Official Detective*.

SIDELIGHTS: Jack M. Bickham, a licensed private pilot, told *CA*, "People who say they lack time to write amuse me." He adds that his writing emphasis is changing from westerns to mystery and contemporary comedy.

MEDIA ADAPTATIONS: Several of Bickham's books have been made into motion pictures, including *The Apple Dumpling Gang*, produced by Walt Disney Productions, *Baker's Hawk, Katie, Kelly and Heck*, and *Dinah, Blow Your Horn*.

AVOCATIONAL INTERESTS: Amateur radio, organic gardening, playing guitar.

BIOGRAPHICAL/CRITICAL SOURCES:

PERIODICALS

New York Times Book Review, August 11, 1968, May 11, 1980.
Washington Post Book World, April 20, 1980.

BIDERMAN, Albert D. 1923-

PERSONAL: Born July 10, 1923, in Paterson, N.J.; son of Isaac and Celia (Silberstein) Biderman; married Sumiko Fujii, November 9, 1951; children: David Taro, Joseph Shiro, Paula Kei. *Education:* New York University, A.B., 1947; University of Chicago, M.A., 1952, Ph.D., 1964.

ADDRESSES: Home—6247 North Kensington St., McLean, Va. *Office*—American University, Massachusetts and Nebraska Aves. N.W., Washington, D.C. 20016.

CAREER: Illinois Institute of Technology, Chicago, instructor in sociology, 1948-52; U.S. Air Force, Maxwell Air Force Base, Ala., research social psychologist, 1952-57; Bureau of Social Science Research, Washington, D.C., senior research associate, 1957-86; American University, Washington, D.C., research professor of justice, 1986—. Consultant to advisory committees to Secretary of Defense on Prisoners of War, 1954, Agency for International Development, 1960, 1966-68, President's Commission on Law Enforcement and Administration of Justice, 1965-67, Bureau of Census, 1969-76, and President's Commission on Federal Statistics, 1971. Active in community, civic, and recreational organizations. *Military service:* U.S. Army, 1943-45.

MEMBER: American Sociological Association, American Association for Public Opinion Research, Society for the Study of Social Problems, District of Columbia Sociological Society (president, 1965-66).

AWARDS, HONORS: Research fellowships, Human Ecology Fund, 1957-58, American Association for the Advancement of Science, 1981, American Statistical Association, 1985; Stewart A. Rice Merit Award, District of Columbia Sociological Society, 1985.

WRITINGS:

(Editor with Herbert Zimmer) *The Manipulation of Human Behavior*, Wiley, 1961.
March to Calumny: The Story of American POW's in the Korean War, Macmillan, 1963, reprinted, Arno, 1979.
(Co-editor) *Mass Behavior in Battle and Captivity: The Communist Soldier in the Korean War*, University of Chicago Press, 1968.
(With Elisabeth T. Crawford) *The Political Economics of Social Research: The Case of Sociology*, Bureau of Social Science Research, 1968.
(Compiler with Crawford) *Social Scientists and International Affairs: A Case for a Sociology of Social Science*, Wiley, 1969.
(Editor with Thomas F. Drury) *Measuring Work Quality for Social Reporting*, Halsted, 1976.
(With Albert J. Reiss) *Data Sources on White-Collar Law Breaking*, U.S. National Institute of Justice, 1980.

CONTRIBUTOR

Morris Janowitz, editor, *The New Military: Changing Patterns of Organization*, Russell Sage Foundation, 1964.
George H. Grosser and others, editors, *The Threat of Impending Disaster: Contributions to the Psychology of Stress*, MIT Press, 1964.
Raymond A. Bauer, editor, *Social Indicators*, MIT Press, 1966.
Mortimer Appley and Richard Trumbull, editors, *Psychological Stress*, Appleton-Century-Crofts, 1966.
Sol Tax, editor, *The Draft: A Handbook of Facts and Alternatives*, University of Chicago Press, 1967.

Byron P. Rourke, editor, *Explorations in the Psychology of Stress and Anxiety,* Longman, 1969.
N. A. B. Wilson, editor, *Manpower Research,* English Universities Press, 1969.
Roger W. Little, editor, *Handbook of Military Institutions,* Sage Publications, 1971.
Sam C. Sarkesian, editor, *The Military-Industrial Complex: A Reassessment,* Sage Publications, 1972.
Robert L. Clewett and Jerry C. Olson, editors, *Social Indicators and Marketing,* American Marketing Association, 1974.
Israel Drapkin and Emilio Viano, editors, *Victimology: A New Focus,* Lexington Books, 1975.
Crawford and Stein Rokkan, editors, *Sociological Praxis,* Sage Publications, 1976.
H. Wallace Sinaiko and Laurie A. Broedling, editors, *Perspectives on Attitude Assessment: Surveys and Their Alternatives,* Pendleton Publications, 1976.
Rokkan, editor, *A Quarter Century of International Social Science,* Concept Publishing (New Delhi), 1979.

OTHER

Also author of numerous research papers on indoctrination of American prisoners of war, coercive interrogation, and captivity situations published by the U.S. Air Force. Also contributor to *International Encyclopedia of the Social Sciences.* Contributor of articles to professional journals.

WORK IN PROGRESS: "Internment and Custody," for the *International Encyclopedia of the Social Sciences.*

*   *   *

BIENENFELD, Florence L(ucille) 1929-

PERSONAL: Born December 29, 1929, in Los Angeles, Calif.; daughter of Jack and Gertrude (Lewis) Gottlieb; married Milton Bienenfeld (a business executive), September 7, 1952; children: Ruth Bienenfeld Barrett, Joel, Daniel. *Education:* California State University, B.A., 1950; University of California, Los Angeles, M.A., 1968; doctoral study at University of Southern California, 1972-73; Columbia Pacific University, Ph.D., 1981. *Politics:* Democrat. *Religion:* Jewish.

ADDRESSES: Home—Marina del Rey, Calif.

CAREER: Elementary school teacher, 1949-51; educational therapist and private practitioner in marriage and family counseling, 1968-74; Conciliation Court of Los Angeles County, Santa Monica, Calif., senior marriage and family counselor, 1974-76; Superior Court of Los Angeles County, Los Angeles, Calif., child custody investigator, 1977; Conciliation Court of Los Angeles County, senior marriage and family counselor, 1977-85; marriage and family counselor and mediator. Workshop leader; lecturer; guest on radio and television programs.

MEMBER: American Association for Marriage and Family Therapy (clinical member), Association of Family Conciliation Courts.

AWARDS, HONORS: Award of merit from Association of Family Conciliation Courts, 1980, for outstanding service to children of divorce, their families, and to A.F.C.C.

WRITINGS:

My Mom and Dad Are Getting a Divorce (juvenile), EMC Corp., 1980.
Child Custody Mediation, Science & Behavior Books, 1983.

Making a Magnificent Marriage, Pine Mountain Press, 1985.
Helping Your Child Succeed after Divorce, Hunter House, 1987.
Diet for Health Cookbook, Royal Publishing, 1987.

Also author of *The Intimate Couple, Parenting with Love, Mothers: The Greatest Jugglers on Earth,* and *Making Peace with the Past,* all unpublished.

SIDELIGHTS: Florence Bienenfeld told *CA:* "I want to ease tension and pain for children involved in marital or post-marital conflicts. Most children take divorce very hard, and they take custody battles even harder. Children can recover from the divorce when their parents allow them to heal. Regrettably, some parents continue to argue and fight after the separation and divorce. The children become the focal point for their arguments and bitterness. Parental hostility often escalates and never ends. For some children there is no relief from parental conflict throughout their entire childhood. When these children grow up many of them carry unhappy memories of this experience into adulthood, and this can ruin their lives.

"In an age of much violence and harshness throughout the world, there are small inroads being made toward humanizing life for children. In some birth centers and hospitals newborns are being placed in a warm bath to soothe their entrance to the world. There is much talk and action being taken to protect children from physical and sexual abuse. One very important inroad is divorce counseling and mediation for parents as a measure for protecting children from the abuse of divorce."

*   *   *

BIERS, William Richard 1938-

PERSONAL: Born October 29, 1938, in Brussels, Belgium; American citizen born abroad; son of Howard (an engineer) and Constance (Britain) Biers; married Jane Carol Chitty (a museum curator), 1966; children: Katherine Laura. *Education:* Brown University, A.B., 1961; University of Pennsylvania, Ph.D., 1968.

ADDRESSES: Home—2310 Fairmont, Columbia, Mo. 65203. *Office*—Department of Art History and Archaeology, University of Missouri, Pickard Hall, Columbia, Mo. 65211.

CAREER: American School of Classical Studies, Athens, Greece, secretary, 1964-68; University of Missouri—Columbia, assistant professor, 1968-72, associate professor, 1972-81, professor of classical archaeology, 1981—, chairman of department, 1973-75, 1977-80. Member of managing committee of American School of Classical Studies, Athens.

MEMBER: Archaeological Institute of America (member of governing board), College Art Association, Midwest Art History Society, University Club (New York), Athenaeum (London).

WRITINGS:

The Archaeology of Greece: An Introduction, Cornell University Press, 1980, revised edition, 1987.
(Associate editor) *Corinthiaca: Studies in Honor of Darrell A. Amyx,* University of Missouri Press, 1986.
Mirobriga, British Archaeological Reports Ltd., 1987.

Contributor to archaeology journals.

WORK IN PROGRESS: Archaeological projects in Greece and Portugal; studies of ancient Greek ceramics.

BLAKE, Stephanie
 See PEARL, Jacques Bain

* * *

BODART, Joni
 See BODART-TALBOT, Joni

* * *

BODART-TALBOT, Joni 1947-
 (Joni Bodart)

PERSONAL: Surname is pronounced Bo-*dar;* born December 16, 1947, in Winchester, Va.; daughter of Albin J. J. (an income tax consultant) and Frances (a high school English teacher; maiden name, Higginbotham) Bodart; married Lou Bodart-Talbot, April 17, 1987. *Education:* Texas Woman's University, B.A. and B.S., both 1969, M.L.S., 1971, M.A., 1983, Ph.D., 1985. *Politics:* Democrat. *Religion:* Presbyterian.

ADDRESSES: Home—704 Riverview Cr., Emporia, Kan. 66801. *Office*—Department of Library/Information Management, Emporia State University, Emporia, Kan. 66801.

CAREER: Albuquerque Public Library, Albuquerque, N.M., children's librarian and assistant branch head, 1969-70; Santa Rosa-Sonoma County Public Library, Santa Rosa, Calif., young adult and reference librarian, 1971-73; Alameda County Public Library, Fremont Main Library, Fremont, Calif., young adult librarian, 1973-78; Stanislaus County Free Library, Modesto, Calif., young adult coordinator, 1978-79; writer, 1979—, Pergamon Press, Elmsford, N.Y., library consultant, 1981-82; Survival House, Krum, Tex., business manager/therapist, 1982-83; Emporia State University School of Library and Information Management, Emporia, Kan., assistant professor, 1983—. Gives workshops and lectures.

MEMBER: American Library Association (chairperson of Young Adult Services Division best books committee, 1980-81), Bay Area Young Adult Librarians (past president), convenor, Booktalking Discussion Group, 1983—.

WRITINGS:

Booktalk!: Booktalking and School Visiting for Young Adults, H. W. Wilson, 1980.
Booktalk! 2: Booktalking for All Ages and Audiences, H. W. Wilson, 1985.

Reviewer for "Adult Books for Young Adults," a column in *School Library Journal,* 1971-76; author of "Book You!" column in *Voice of Youth Advocates,* 1984—. Editor, *Top of the News/Journal of Youth Services in Libraries,* 1985—.

WORK IN PROGRESS: Booktalk! 3, completion expected in 1988; research on systems theory approach to libraries, communication patterns, and relationship patterns in libraries, research on the effects of booktalking.

SIDELIGHTS: Joni Bodart-Talbot wrote: "Being a teenager was not easy for me, and I want to use my talents as a librarian and therapist to help others work through their problems as successfully as possible. In addition, I enjoyed my years as a YA [young adult] librarian so much that now I enjoy encouraging others to enter the field through teaching. I would suggest that novices get involved. Don't hesitate to work for your professional organizations, to ask questions, take risks, and care about the people you work with. If you are open with teenagers, they will open up to you—the rewards are worth the work and the risk!"

AVOCATIONAL INTERESTS: Reading (especially mystery and science fiction), writing, traveling, movies, music, Oriental cuisine, sport cars, collecting antiques, cookbooks, wine, and unique kitchen gadgets.

* * *

BODO, Murray 1937-

PERSONAL: Born June 10, 1937, in Gallup, N.M.; son of Louis John (a politician) and Pauline (Bonan) Bodo. *Education:* Duns Scotus College, B.A., 1960; Xavier University, M.A., 1967. *Politics:* Democrat.

ADDRESSES: Home and office—1723 Pleasant St., Cincinnati, Ohio 45210.

CAREER: Ordained Roman Catholic priest of Franciscan Order (O.F.M.), 1964; St. Francis Seminary, Cincinnati, Ohio, teacher of English, beginning 1965, spiritual director, beginning 1966, head of department of English, beginning 1970, vice-rector, 1972; member of the board, Franciscan Province of St. John, 1977-79; Duns Scotus College, Southfield, Mich., chairman of English department and spiritual director, 1978-79; Chatfield College, St. Martin, Ohio, instructor in English, 1979—; St. Anthony Messenger Press, Cincinnati, Ohio, member of staff, 1979—. Guest lecturer, Cincinnati School for the Creative and Performing Arts, 1987—. Summer staff member, International Franciscan Study Pilgrimage in Assisi, Italy, 1976—.

MEMBER: International Academy of Franciscan Studies (Perugia, Italy; fellow).

AWARDS, HONORS: Cincinnati Editors Award, 1980, for *Clare;* third prize, National Catholic Press Association, 1983, for poem "Good Friday."

WRITINGS:

PUBLISHED BY ST. ANTHONY MESSENGER PRESS

Francis: The Journey and the Dream, 1972.
Walk in Beauty: Meditations from the Desert, 1974.
Song of the Sparrow, 1976.
Clare: A Light in the Garden, 1979.
Sing Pilgrimage and Exile, 1980.
Letters from Pleasant Street, 1981.
Juniper: Friend of Francis, Food of God, 1983.
Jesus, a Disciple's Search, 1986.

PUBLISHED BY DOUBLEDAY

The Way of St. Francis, 1984.
Through the Year with St. Francis, 1987.

RECORDINGS

(With Susan Saint Sing) "The Song of St. Francis," 1980.
(With Sing) "Seasons," 1981.
(With Sing) "The Desert Speaks," 1984.
"A Mosaic of Francis," 1986.
"Francis: The Journey and the Dream" (adaptation of his book of the same title), St. Anthony Messenger Press, 1987.

OTHER

Contributor of poems to *St. Anthony Messenger.*

WORK IN PROGRESS: The Verse King, a novel; *Crossing the Divide,* short stories and poems.

SIDELIGHTS: Murray Bodo grew up in Gallup, N.M., the closest town to the Navajo Reservation. As a Franciscan, he spent summers working at St. Michaels, central mission for the Navajo apostolate. His second book describes, with the aid of photographs, the Navajo country and the people who live there.

Bodo told *CA:* "Priest and poet? Perhaps I can say it best this way: In this constant craft / This trying, over and over again / to make words sing, / I find redemption. / The word becomes flesh / in the word multiplied / and juxtaposed and edited / and erased and rejected / and sometimes dying / and rising from the tomb. / The page is my parish / and words my people. / At times we break into song."

Bodo's work has been translated into Japanese, French, Danish, Italian, and Spanish.

*   *   *

BONATTI, Walter 1930-

PERSONAL: Born June 22, 1930, in Bergamo, Italy; son of Angelo and Agostina (Appiani) Bonatti; married (separated). *Religion:* Christian.

ADDRESSES: Home—Via Gentilino 9/A, Milan, Italy 20136.

CAREER: Epoca (weekly magazine), Milan, Italy, journalist and correspondent, 1965-79; writer, 1979—. *Military service:* Corpo Militare Alpini, 1951-52.

AWARDS, HONORS: Gold, silver, and bronze medals from the Italian Republic for civil valor; French Legion of Honor; gold medal from the Consiglio d'Europa; grand prize from the Sports Academy of Paris; gold medal for sports valor; Argosy Giant of Adventure Award, 1971.

WRITINGS:

(Also photographer) *Le mie montagne,* Zanichelli, 1961, revised edition, Rizzoli, 1983, translation by Lovett F. Edwards published as *On the Heights,* Hart-Davis, 1964.
I giorni grandi, preface by Dino Buzzati, A. Mondadori, 1971, Zanichelli, 1978, translation by Geoffrey Sutton published as *The Great Days,* Gollancz, 1974.
Ho vissuto tra gli animali selvaggi, Zanichelli, 1980.
Avventura, Rizzoli, 1984.
Magia del Monte Bianco, Massimo Baldini Editore, 1984, translation by Sutton published as *Magic of Mount Blanc,* Gollancz, 1985.
Processo al K2, Massimo Baldini Editore, 1985.
La mia Patagonia, Massimo Baldini Editore, 1986.

BIOGRAPHICAL/CRITICAL SOURCES:

PERIODICALS

Esquire, November, 1965.
Guardian Weekly, December 21, 1974.
Reader's Digest, September, 1965.
Times Literary Supplement, March 28, 1975.

*   *   *

BOSWORTH, R(ichard) J(ames) B(oon) 1943-

PERSONAL: Born December 7, 1943, in Sydney, Australia; son of Richard C. L. (a professor of chemistry) and Thelma H. E. (Boon) Bosworth; married Michal Gwyn Newell (a writer), September 23, 1965; children: Edmund R. F., Mary F. *Education:* University of Sydney, B.A. (with honors), 1965,

M.A. (with honors), 1967; Cambridge University, Ph.D., 1971. *Politics:* Australian Labor Party. *Religion:* None.

ADDRESSES: Home—40 Robert St., Como, 6152 Western Australia. *Office*—Department of History, University of Western Australia, 6009 W.A.

CAREER: University of Sydney, Sydney, Australia, lecturer, 1969-73, senior lecturer, 1974-81, associate professor of history, 1981-86; University of Western Australia, professor of history, 1987—. Deputy director of F. May Foundation for Italian Studies.

MEMBER: Australasian Association for European History (president), Australian Historical Association.

WRITINGS:

Benito Mussolini and the Fascist Destruction of Liberal Italy, Rigby (Adelaide, Australia), 1973.
Italy, the Least of the Great Powers: Italian Foreign Policy before the First World War, Cambridge University Press, 1979.
(With J. K. Wilton) *Italy and the Approach of the First World War,* Macmillan, 1983.
Old Worlds and New Australia: The Post-War Migrant Experience, Penguin, 1984, 3rd edition, 1987.
La Politica estera dell' Italia giolittiana, Riuniti (Rome), 1986.

EDITOR

(With Gianfranco Cresciani) *Altro Polo: A Volume of Italian Studies,* F. May Foundation (Sydney, Australia), 1979.
(With G. Rizzo) *Altro Polo: Intellectuals and Their Ideas in Contemporary Italy,* Sydney, 1983.

CONTRIBUTOR

Marian Kent, editor, *The Great Powers and the Downfall of the Ottoman Empire,* Allen & Unwin, 1982.
M. M. Guidetti, editor, *Corso di storia d'Italia e d'Europa: Communita e popoli* (title means "Introductory Textbook to the History of Italy and Europe: Community and People"), Volume VII, Jaca Books, 1982.
R. Langhorne, editor, *Diplomacy and Intelligence in the Second World War,* Cambridge University Press, 1985.

OTHER

Editor of *Teaching History,* 1971-79.

SIDELIGHTS: R. J. B. Bosworth told *CA:* "My interest in Italian history is accidental; my being an Australian is accidental. I would like to be an enemy of all nationalisms, but once committed to Italy (or Australia), I don't see how one can change. This means that my critical interpretation of Italian foreign policy as managed by its ruling elite from 1860 to 1945, or of Australian immigration policy since the Second World War, tends to place me on the left politically. At the same time I remain enough of a liberal to be almost as skeptical of the ideologizing of some Marxist or other radical historians. But, safely enclosed in the cozy nook of Australia, beyond what one Australian novelist has called 'the rage of history,' one can afford the luxury of being soft-centered."

*   *   *

BOTTNER, Barbara 1943-

PERSONAL: Born May 25, 1943, in New York, N.Y.; daughter of Irving (a business executive) and Elaine (Schiff) Bottner. *Education:* Attended Boston University, 1961-62, and Ecole des Beaux Arts, 1963-64; University of Wisconsin, B.S., 1965; University of California, Santa Barbara, M.A., 1966.

ADDRESSES: Home—848 North Detroit St., Los Angeles, Calif. 90046.

CAREER: Free-lance writer. Actress, kindergarten teacher, animation producer, writer, and artist; Parsons School of Design, New York, N.Y., instructor, beginning 1973; instructor at Otis Art Institute of Los Angeles County. Work has been represented in film festivals in London, Melbourne, Ottawa, and New York City.

AWARDS, HONORS: Best Film for Television award from International Animation Festival, Annecy, France, 1973, for "Goat in a Boat"; Cine Golden Eagle for animated film "Later That Night."

WRITINGS:

JUVENILE

What Would You Do with a Giant?, Putnam, 1972.
Fun House, Prentice-Hall, 1975.
Eek, a Monster, Macmillan, 1975.
The Box, Macmillan, 1975.
What Grandma Did on Her Birthday, Macmillan, 1975.
Big Boss! Little Boss!, Pantheon, 1978.
Jungle Day, Delacorte, 1978.
There Was Nobody There, Macmillan, 1978.
Messy, Delacorte, 1979.
Dumb Old Casey Is a Fat Tree, Harper, 1979.
Myra, Macmillan, 1979.
Horrible Hannah, Crown, 1980.
Mean Maxine, Pantheon, 1980.
The World's Greatest Expert on Absolutely Everything—Is Crying, Harper, 1985.
Nothing in Common, Harper, 1986.
Zoo Song, Scholastic Inc., 1987.
M. K. Price (teen novel), Harper, 1988.

OTHER

Author of films "Goat in a Boat" and "Later That Night." Contributor of children's book reviews to the *New York Times Book Review;* contributor of editorial illustrations to the *New York Times, Ms., Viva,* and *Intellectual Digest;* contributor of cartoons to *Viva* and *Penthouse;* also contributor to *Los Angeles Times, Cosmopolitan,* and *Playgirl.*

WORK IN PROGRESS: Various screenplays and teleplays.

AVOCATIONAL INTERESTS: Dancing, cooking, jogging, travel.

BIOGRAPHICAL/CRITICAL SOURCES:

FILMS

"All about Time and No Time," New York University, 1974.

*   *   *

BRADBROOK, M(uriel) C(lara) 1909-

PERSONAL: Born April 27, 1909, in England; daughter of Samuel (a superintendent in His Majesty's waterguard) and Annie Wilson (Harvey) Bradbrook. *Education:* Girton College, Cambridge, B.A., 1930, M.A. and Ph.D., 1933, Litt.D., 1955. *Religion:* Church of England.

ADDRESSES: Home—Girton College, Cambridge, England.

CAREER: Cambridge University, Cambridge, England, research fellow of Girton College, 1932-35, staff fellow, 1936-62, university lecturer, 1945-62, reader, 1962-65, professor of English, 1965-76, vice-principal, 1961-66, principal of Girton College, 1968-76. Principal officer of Industries and Manufactures Departments two and three, Board of Trade, London, 1941-45. Resident, Folger Shakespeare Library, Washington, D.C., and Huntington Library, California, 1958-59; trustee, Shakespeare's Birthplace, 1967. Visiting professor, University of California, Santa Cruz, 1966, Kuwait University, 1969, Kenyon College, 1977, and National Humanities Center, 1979, 1981. Fellow, Rhodes University, South Africa, 1979, 1984. Visiting scholar, Japanese Society for Promotion of Science (Tokyo), 1985, Fudan University (Shanghai), 1985.

MEMBER: Royal Society of Literature (fellow), Norwegian Academy of Arts and Sciences.

AWARDS, HONORS: Harness prize, 1931, for *Elizabethan Stage Conditions;* Allen scholar, Cambridge University, 1935; Litt.D., University of Liverpool, 1964, University of Sussex, 1972, University of London, 1973, and Kenyon College, 1977; LL.D., Smith College, 1965; Ph.D., Gottenburg, 1975.

WRITINGS:

Elizabethan Stage Conditions: A Study of Their Place in the Interpretation of Shakespeare's Plays, Cambridge University Press, 1932, reprinted, 1968.
Themes and Conventions of Elizabethan Tragedy (also see below), Cambridge University Press, 1934, 2nd edition, 1980.
The School of Night: A Study in the Literary Relationships of Sir Walter Raleigh, Cambridge University Press, 1936, Russell, 1965.
(With M. G. Lloyd Thomas) *Andrew Marvell*, Cambridge University Press, 1940.
Joseph Conrad: Poland's English Genius, Cambridge University Press, 1941, Russell, 1965.
Ibsen the Norwegian: A Revaluation, Chatto & Windus, 1946, revised edition, Shoe String, 1966.
T. S. Eliot, Longmans, Green, 1950, revised edition, 1968.
Shakespeare and Elizabethan Poetry: A Study of His Earlier Work in Relation to the Poetry of the Time (also see below), Chatto & Windus, 1951, Oxford University Press, 1952, reprinted, R. West, 1978.
(Compiler) *The Queen's Garland: Verses Made by Her Subjects for Elizabeth I, Now Collected in Honour of Her Majesty Queen Elizabeth II*, Oxford University Press, 1953, Longwood, 1983.
The Growth and Structure of Elizabethan Comedy (also see below), Chatto & Windus, 1955, new edition, Chatto & Windus, 1973.
Sir Thomas Malory, Longmans, Green, 1958, 2nd edition, 1967.
The Rise of the Common Player: A Study of Actor and Society in Shakespeare's England (also see below), Harvard University Press, 1962, reprinted, Cambridge University Press, 1979.
English Dramatic Form: A History of Its Development, Barnes & Noble, 1965.
Shakespeare's Primitive Art, British Academy, 1965.
The Tragic Pageant of "Timon of Athens": An Inaugural Lecture, Cambridge University Press, 1966.
That Infidel Place: A Short History of Girton College, 1869-1969, Chatto & Windus, 1969.

Shakespeare the Craftsman (also see below), Barnes & Noble, 1969.

(Contributor) *Tributes in Prose and Verse to Shotaro Oshima, President of the Yeats Society of Japan,* Hokuseido Press (Tokyo), 1970.

T. S. Eliot: The Making of "The Waste Land," Longman for the British Council, 1972.

Literature in Action: Studies in Continental and Commonwealth Society, Barnes & Noble, 1972.

Malcolm Lowry: His Art and Early Life, Cambridge University Press, 1974.

The Living Monument: Shakespeare and the Theatre of His Time (also see below), Cambridge University Press, 1976.

(Contributor) Ronald Kayman, editor, *My Cambridge,* Robson Books, 1977.

(Contributor) Ian Scott Kilvent, editor, *George Chapman,* Longman for the British Council, 1977.

Shakespeare: The Poet in His World, Columbia University Press, 1978.

A History of Elizabethan Drama, Cambridge University Press, 1979, Volume I: *Themes and Conventions of Elizabethan Tragedy,* Volume II: *The Growth and Structure of Elizabethan Comedy,* Volume III: *The Rise of the Common Player: A Study of Actor and Society in Shakespeare's England,* Volume IV: *Shakespeare and the Elizabethan Poetry: A Study of His Earlier Work in Relation to the Poetry of the Time,* Volume V: *Shakespeare the Craftsman,* Volume VI: *The Living Monument: Shakespeare and the Theatre of His Time.*

John Webster: Citizen and Dramatist, Columbia University Press, 1980.

The Collected Papers of Muriel Bradbrook, Barnes & Noble, Volume I: *Artist and Society in Shakespeare's England,* 1982, Volume II: *Women and Literature: 1779-1982,* 1983, Volume III: *Aspects of Dramatic Form in the English and the Irish Renaissance,* 1983.

Also editor with Nevill Coghill of *British Writers and Their Work,* Volume I: *Geoffrey Chaucer and Sir Thomas Malory.* Contributor of articles and reviews to *Sunday Telegraph* (London), *New Statesman, Modern Language Review,* and other periodicals and newspapers.

SIDELIGHTS: Writing in the *New York Review of Books,* Frank Kermode comments: "Muriel Bradbrook . . . has produced over the years a large body of writing, learned but accessible and occasionally adventurous, in the Elizabethan and Shakespearian fields." Citing Bradbrook's "thorough knowledge of Elizabethan society," T. J. Remington of *Library Journal* calls *Shakespeare: The Poet in His World* of "great value overall as a critical interpretation of the Shakespearean canon." Speaking of Bradbrook's *The Living Monument,* a study of Shakespearean drama as it has been presented at different times, the *Economist* critic finds that "Bradbrook amply proves the aptness of her title, for this book is in many ways a worthy salute to a 'living monument'."

"Muriel Bradbrook has taught us so much about certain aspects of Elizabethan drama and poetry that she richly deserves the accolade implicit in the publication of her collected papers," remarks Charles Martindale in the *Times Literary Supplement* about *The Artist and Society in Shakespeare's England.* According to Martindale, the essays in this volume offer "a combination of textual exegesis and old fashioned literary history" and include biographical as well as various literary and cultural influences. "She has always brought to

the task an enviable breadth of knowledge, and her work well stands the test of time."

Bradbrook recently told *CA:* "I am still learning from Shakespeare and am planning a new study. In 1985, I made my first visit to China to meet Shakespeareans."

BIOGRAPHICAL/CRITICAL SOURCES:

BOOKS

Axton, Marie and Raymond Williams, editors, *English Drama: Forms and Development; Essays in Honour of Muriel Clara Bradbrook,* Cambridge University Press, 1968.

PERIODICALS

Books and Bookmen, May, 1979.
Economist, December 18, 1976.
Encounter, July, 1977.
Library Journal, January 15, 1979.
New Statesman, July 19, 1974, December 17, 1976.
New York Review of Books, November 5, 1970.
Spectator, March 21, 1969.
Times Literary Supplement, January 1, 1970, February 11, 1977, April 17, 1981, October 22, 1982.
Virginia Quarterly Review, spring, 1979.
Yale Review, spring, 1979.

*   *   *

BRANDEWYNE, (Mary) Rebecca (Wadsworth) 1955-

PERSONAL: Born March 4, 1955, in Knoxville, Tenn.; daughter of Gayle Bryan (a nuclear physicist and metallurgist) and Beverly Harris (in sales and promotion; maiden name, Stamps) Wadsworth. *Education:* Wichita State University, B.A. (cum laude), 1975, M.A., 1979.

ADDRESSES: Home and office—P.O. Box 780036, Wichita, Kan. 67206.

CAREER: National Dental Warranty (dental insurance firm), Wichita, Kan., director of public relations and editor of *Dental Warranty News,* 1974-76; International Business Machines Corp., Data Processing Division, Wichita, executive secretary to branch manager, 1976-77; Alliance Corp. (life insurance firm), Wichita, office manager and executive secretary, 1977-80; Glaves, Weil & Evans (attorneys), Wichita, legal secretary, 1980; free-lance writer, 1980—. Guest on radio and television programs throughout the United States.

MEMBER: Mensa, National Writers Club, Romance Writers of America (charter member), Western Writers of America, Society of Professional Journalists, Women in Communications, Affaire de Coeur, National Organization of Mid-Eastern Artists and Dancers, Wichita State University Alumni Association.

AWARDS, HONORS: Certificate of appreciation from Society of Professional Journalists, 1974; certificate of appreciation from Women in Communications, 1974, presidential plaque, 1975; outstanding merit citation from Going-Out Adventure Club of New York, 1982; Silver Pen Award, 1986, 1987, and Golden Certificate, 1987, from Affaire de Coeur; Reviewer's Choice Award, 1986, from *Romantic Times.*

WRITINGS:

No Gentle Love (historical romance), Warner Books, 1980.
Forever My Love (historical romance), Warner Books, 1982.

Love, Cherish Me (historical romance), Warner Books, 1983.
Rose of Rapture (historical romance), Warner Books, 1984.
And Gold Was Ours (historical romance), Warner Books, 1984.
The Outlaw Hearts (historical romance), Warner Books, 1986.
Desire in Disguise (historical romance), Warner Books, 1987.
Passion Moon Rising (science fiction), Pocket Books, 1988.
Upon a Moon-Dark Moor (gothic saga), Warner Books, 1988.

Contributor to magazines and newspapers, including *Philadelphia Style*, *UNIVERCity*, and *Sunflower*.

WORK IN PROGRESS: Two gothic sagas entitled *Across a Star-Strewn Sea* and *Beneath a Sun-Washed Sky*.

SIDELIGHTS: Rebecca Brandewyne told *CA:* "I was a very solitary child who began reading at the age of three. My mother took me to the library once a week when I was growing up, and sometimes, I read as many as twenty books a week. When I was about seven or eight, I read a book called *Nine Coaches Waiting* by Mary Stewart, my favorite author, and fell desperately in love with her tall dark hero, Raoul de Valmy. This love affair continued through the years, until I decided to create my own tall dark heroes. I started writing primarily because I hated working nine-to-five, and I wanted to be my own boss. It was a case of 'beginners luck.' The first book I ever wrote, *No Gentle Love,* sold to Warner Books in 1978, and my career as an entrepreneurial woman was launched. I have since discovered that writing has become a passion with me.

"I guess you would say I am your typical moody, temperamental, creative artist. When my work goes well, I am ecstatic; when it falters, I am equally depressed. I want each novel to be better than the last, and I strive relentlessly to make each so. Though outwardly a realist, inwardly I am a romantic at heart, which is why I write historical romance novels. I get particularly angry when people sneer at the romance genre. Don't they realize they are scoffing at such greats as Margaret Mitchell, Kathleen Winsor, Daphne du Maurier, Rafael Sabatini, Sir Walter Scott, and Charles Dickens? This is sad. I often think those who jeer do so because they are lacking romance in their own lives. This is why I put so much work into the relationships between my heroes and heroines. I want my readers to see my characters' strengths and weaknesses and the manner in which they communicate to overcome the difficulties between them.

"I think communication is extremely important in any relationship, but most especially between lovers. Having studied under one of the foremost authorities in the field of interpersonal communication and having taught interpersonal communication for two years, I know how hard it is for people to communicate with each other. This is especially true of lovers, who perhaps fear rejection most deeply. In addition, most people lack the knowledge and insight necessary to deal with the feelings generated at a highly intimate level. I try to show this in my books—in the way in which my heroes and heroines clash in the beginning, then gradually learn to trust, understand, and communicate openly and honestly with each other. When they have reached this intimate and fulfilling level of communication, physically, mentally, emotionally, and spiritually, then they neither need, nor want, more than one such relationship in their lives. That is what I write about. That is what I call love.''

AVOCATIONAL INTERESTS: Art, astrology and the occult, belly dancing, chess, musical composition and performance (singing and playing the guitar), embroidery, needlepoint, boating, fencing, horseback riding, racquetball, shooting, tennis.

BIOGRAPHICAL/CRITICAL SOURCES:

BOOKS

Biederman, Jerry, and Tom Silberkleit, editors, *My First Real Romance,* Stein & Day, 1985.
Falk, Kathryn, *Love's Leading Ladies,* Pinnacle, 1982.
Guiley, Rosemary, *Love Lines,* Facts on File, 1983.

PERIODICALS

Houston Chronicle, October 26, 1980.
Newsweek, May 10, 1982.
New York Times Book Review, January 17, 1982.

*   *   *

BRANDT, Leslie F. 1919-

PERSONAL: Born February 12, 1919, in Morris, Minn.; son of Elmer F. and Clara (Johnson) Brandt; married Edith Tokle (a junior high school teacher), August 30, 1942; children: Sonia Marie, Daniel Leslie, Donald Mark. *Education:* Augsburg College, B.A., 1941; further study at Lutheran Bible Institute, Minneapolis, Minn., 1941-42, Augsburg Theological Seminary, 1942-45, College of Chinese Studies, Peking, China, 1947-48, and American Institute of Family Relations, 1959-61.

ADDRESSES: Home—2255 Cottage Way, Vista, Calif. 92083.

CAREER: Ordained to ministry of American Lutheran Church, 1945; pastor in Pukwana, S.D., 1945-46; missionary in Peking and Shanghai, China, 1946-48; evacuated from Shanghai during Communist takeover, 1948; pastor in Minneapolis, Minn., 1949-51; service pastor (as civilian) in Taiwan and Japan, 1951-54, establishing service centers and acting as auxiliary chaplain on Navy ships in port; pastor in Williston, N.D., 1954-58, Westminster, Calif., 1958-63, and Los Angeles, Calif., 1963-67; Valley Lutheran Church, North Hollywood, Calif., pastor, 1967-73; Trinity Lutheran Church, Victorville, Calif., pastor, 1973-77.

WRITINGS:

Good Lord, Where Are You?, Concordia, 1967.
Great God, Here I Am, Concordia, 1969.
God Is Here: Let's Celebrate!, Concordia, 1969.
Contemporary Introits and Collects for the Twentieth Century, C.S.S. Publishing, 1970.
Can I Forgive God?, Concordia, 1970.
The Lord Rules: Let Us Serve Him, Concordia, 1971.
Meditations of a Radical Christianity, C.S.S. Publishing, 1973.
Psalms/Now, Concordia, 1973.
Living through Loving: Reflections on Letters of the New Testament, Concordia, 1974.
Book of Christian Prayer, Augsburg, 1974, revised edition, 1980.
(With wife, Edith Brandt) *Growing Together: Prayers for Married People,* Augsburg, 1975.
Contemporary Introits for the Revised Church Calendar, Concordia, 1975.
Epistles/Now, Concordia, 1976.
Why Did This Happen to Me?, Concordia, 1978.
Jesus/Now, Concordia, 1978.
Prophets/Now, Concordia, 1979.
Christ in Your Life: What God's News Can Do for You, Concordia, 1980.

A Battle Manual for Christian Survival, Concordia, 1980.
Meditations on a Loving God, Concordia, 1983.
Bible Readings for the Retired, Augsburg, 1984.
Bible Readings for Troubled Times, Augsburg, 1985.
Meditations on the Journey of Faith, Concordia, 1986.
Two Minutes with God, Augsburg, 1988.

Contributor to religion publications. Former weekly newspaper columnist in Williston, N.D., and Westminster, Calif.

* * *

BRASCH, Walter Milton   1945-

PERSONAL: Born March 2, 1945, in San Diego, Calif.; son of Milton and Helen (Haskin) Brasch; married Ila Wales (a journalist-linguist), September 30, 1970 (divorced, March, 1977); married Vivian Fluck, June 14, 1980 (divorced, September, 1983); married Rosemary Renn, December, 1983. *Education:* Attended University of California, 1962-64, and LaVerne College, 1964; San Diego State College (now University), A.B., 1966; Ball State University, M.A., 1969; Ohio University, Ph.D., 1974. *Politics:* Independent Democrat. *Religion:* Jewish.

ADDRESSES: Office—Department of English, Bloomsburg University, Bloomsburg, Pa. 17815.

CAREER: Employed as sports editor, city editor, features writer, and investigative reporter for daily newspapers in California, Indiana, Iowa, and Ohio, 1965-72; MID Productions, Athens, Ohio, writer and executive director, 1972-74; Temple University, Philadelphia, Pa., assistant professor of journalism and mass communications, 1974-76; Brasch & Brasch Publishers, Ontario, Calif., editor-in-chief, 1976-80; Bloomsburg University, Bloomsburg, Pa., assistant professor, 1980-82, associate professor, 1982-87, professor of journalism, 1987—, director of graduate program in communication, 1980-83. Freelance advertising-publicity writer and consultant, 1964—. Writer and producer for United Screen Artists, 1976-80. Commonwealth Speaker, Pennsylvania Humanities Council, 1981-85. Member of Iowa Governor's Committee for the Employment of the Handicapped, 1971-73, and of Ohio Governor's Committee for the Dictionary of American Regional English, 1973-74; member of U.S. Coast Guard Auxiliary.

MEMBER: Newspaper Guild, Writers Guild, Authors League of America, American Dialect Society, Association for Education in Journalism, Society of Professional Journalists, Association of Pennsylvania State College and University Faculty (secretary, 1983-85), Phi Kappa Phi (president of Bloomsburg chapter, 1983-84), Kappa Tau Alpha, Pi Gamma Mu, Alpha Kappa Delta.

AWARDS, HONORS: Certificate of Outstanding Service from Alpha Phi Omega, 1966; Certificate of Appreciation from U.S. Department of Commerce, 1970; Certificate of Merit from Gordon Wiseman Conference on Interpersonal Communication, 1973; Creative Teaching Award, 1981, and Creative Arts Award, 1983, both from Bloomsburg University; *Scribendum Libros* award, Alpha Kappa Delta, 1985; also recipient of writing awards from Press Club of Southern California and Pacific Coast Press Club, and of several research grants.

WRITINGS:

(With Ila Wales) *A Comprehensive Annotated Bibliography of American Black English,* Louisiana State University Press, 1974.

Black English and the Mass Media, University of Massachusetts Press, 1981, revised edition, University Press of America, 1984.
Columbia County Place Names, Columbia County Historical Society, 1982.
Cartoon Monickers, Popular Press, 1983.
The Press and the State, University Press of America, 1986.
ZIM, Associated University Presses, 1987.

Also author of *The Unionization of the Journalist,* 1988.

PLAYS

"Answer Me Not in Mournful Numbers," first produced in Waterloo, Iowa at Theatre Seventies, 1969.
"Sand Creek," first produced at Theatre Seventies, 1972.

OTHER

Also author of multimedia shows, including "In the Beginning . . . (the Indian)," 1972, "A Language and Culture Happening," 1972, "Songs of the Battle," 1972, "Songs of the Civil War," 1973, and "Sounds of Protest," 1982. Author of television scripts. Contributor of over 250 articles to general interest magazines and academic journals. Editor-in-chief of *Spectrum* magazine, 1986—.

WORK IN PROGRESS: A TV documentary; a multimedia show; a series of short stories; a novel; two nonfiction books.

SIDELIGHTS: Walter Brasch writes: "I'm a journalist, a writer who looks at society and tries to understand, then analyze and explain its many complex parts as they relate to an organic whole. For that reason, my writings—both popular as well as academic—can't really be pigeon-holed; the writings are, in reality, about people; the process is journalism. I became a writer-journalist because I did it better than anything else I ever did, and because I found that writing well, with the ability to understand people and their society, and trying to help people understand their part of the world, is one of the most challenging things a person can do. I write from the gut, and for the heart; I write because I enjoy it, and because it has been good to me. I write about what I'm interested in, and go from topic to topic, and issue to issue, as my needs change."

AVOCATIONAL INTERESTS: Music (especially country, bluegrass, dixieland), theatre, political public relations, popular culture, "and just about anything that happens to tickle my fancy at the moment."

* * *

BRISBANE, Katharine   1932-

PERSONAL: Born January 7, 1932, in Singapore; daughter of David William (a civil engineer) and Myra Gladys Brisbane; married Philip Edward Parsons (a lecturer), 1960. *Education:* University of Western Australia, B.A., 1953. *Religion:* Anglican.

ADDRESSES: Home and office—Currency Press, 330 Oxford Street, Paddington, Sydney, New South Wales 2021, Australia.

CAREER: West Australian (newspaper), Perth, Western Australia, Australia, theatre critic, 1959-61 and 1962-65; *Australian* (newspaper), Sydney, New South Wales, Australia, national critic, 1967-74; Currency Press, Paddington, Sydney, founder and publisher, 1971—; *National Times,* Sydney, national theatre writer, 1981-82; Griffin Theatre, Sydney, vice-chairman, 1985.

MEMBER: Australian National Playwrights Conference (chairman, 1977, 1984—).

AWARDS, HONORS: Dorothy Crawford Award, Australian Writers' Guild, 1985, for contribution to Australian theatre.

WRITINGS:

EDITOR

Entertaining Australians, Currency Press, 1988.
The Performing Arts in Australia, Currency Press and Cambridge University Press, Volume I: *A Companion to Theatre in Australia,* 1988, Volume II: *A Companion to Australian Film Radio and Television,* 1988, Volume III: *A Companion to Music in Australia,* in press.

CONTRIBUTOR

Geoffrey Dutton, editor, *The Literature of Australia,* Penguin, 1976.
Contemporary Dramatists, St. James Press, 1977, revised edition, 1987.
Allardyce Nicoll, editor, *World Drama,* Harrap, 1977.
(With Manning Clark and David Malouf) *New Currents in Australian Writing,* Angus & Robertson, 1978.
Peter Holloway, editor, *Contemporary Australian Drama: Perspectives Since 1955,* Currency Press, 1981, revised edition, 1987.

AUTHOR OF INTRODUCTION; ALL PUBLISHED BY CURRENCY PRESS

Alexander Buzo, *Three Plays* (contains "Rooted," "Roy Murphy," and "Norm and Ahmed"), 1973.
Peter Kenna, *A Hard God,* 1974.
K. S. Prichard, *Brumby Innes,* 1974.
Prichard, *Bid Me to Love,* 1974.
Jim McNeil, *How Does Your Garden Grow?,* 1975.
John Romeril, *The Floating World,* 1975.
Ray Lawler, *Summer of the Seventeenth Doll,* 1978.
Patrick White, *Big Toys,* 1979.
Kenna, *Furtive Love,* 1980.
White, *Collected Plays,* Volume I, 1985.
David Williamson, *Collected Plays,* Volume I, 1986.
World Encyclopaedia of Contemporary Theatre, York University (Ontario) for the International Theatre Institute, in press.

SIDELIGHTS: Katharine Brisbane told *CA:* "Having now been a press theatre critic for twenty years and a publisher of the Australian playwright for sixteen, I suppose what is distinctive about my writing as a critic is in always approaching the theatre as an expression of a country's history and character (the vast cultural changes in Australia during these years have largely contributed to this); and the business of criticism as requiring a close understanding of the theatre profession, its changing conditions, and its people."

*   *   *

BRODY, Jane E(llen) 1941-

PERSONAL: Born May 19, 1941, in Brooklyn, N.Y.; daughter of Sidney (an attorney and civil servant) and Lillian (a teacher; maiden name, Kellner) Brody; married Richard Engquist (a lyricist), October 2, 1966; children: Lee Erik and Lorin Michael (twins). *Education:* Cornell University, B.S., 1962; University of Wisconsin (now University of Wisconsin—Madison), M.S., 1963. *Religion:* Jewish.

ADDRESSES: Home—Brooklyn, N.Y. *Office*—New York *Times,* 229 West 43rd St., New York, N.Y. 10036. *Agent*—Wendy Weil Agency, Inc., 747 Third Ave., New York, N.Y. 10017.

CAREER: Minneapolis Tribune, Minneapolis, Minn., reporter, 1963-65; *New York Times,* New York, N.Y., science writer, 1965—, author of column, "Personal Health," 1976—; lecturer on health and nutrition, 1979—; star of "Good Health from Jane Brody's Kitchen" television series for Public Broadcasting Service (PBS-TV).

AWARDS, HONORS: Howard Blakeslee Award, American Heart Association, 1971; Science Writers' Award, American Dental Association, 1971, 1978; J. C. Penney-University of Missouri journalism award, 1978; Lifeline Award, American Health Foundation, 1978; Ph.D., Princeton University, 1987.

WRITINGS:

(With husband, Richard Engquist) *Secrets of Good Health,* Popular Library, 1970.
(With Arthur Holleb) *You Can Fight Cancer and Win,* Quadrangle, 1978.
Jane Brody's Nutrition Book, Norton, 1981.
Jane Brody's The New York Times Guide to Personal Health, Times Books, 1982.
Jane Brody's Good Food Book: Living the High Carbohydrate Way, Norton, 1985.

SIDELIGHTS: Thanks to the popularity of her widely syndicated weekly newspaper column "Personal Health," Jane E. Brody has come to be closely associated with sensible health habits. Brody initially trained for a career in biochemistry but became disillusioned with the limited scope offered in lab work. She had always enjoyed her work as editor of her college literary magazine, and so she decided to combine her two enthusiasms—science and writing—to pursue work as a science writer.

Brody had been working as a general reporter for the *Minneapolis Tribune* for only two years when she was hired as a full-time science writer for the *New York Times.* For several years she specialized in stories on medicine and biology, but she told *Publishers Weekly* interviewer Sybil Steinberg, "My feeling from the day I was hired was that the *Times* needed to do more popular medicine: to help people to understand how their bodies worked. I felt that people needed to know not just how to recognize disease but how to stay well."

These aims led Brody to establish her "Personal Health" column in 1976. In it, she discusses in layman's terms an almost limitless variety of topics, including nutrition, diseases, medication, exercise, and health-related news stories. Ideas for articles come from her frequent study of medical journals as well as from reader suggestions. Response to Brody's column is "enormous and gratifying," reports Steinberg. "Most letters are in the nature of thanks for clarifying matters about illnesses that the writers say are insufficiently explained by doctors."

Brody's special interest in nutrition was sparked by her own weight problem and her concern for her sons' diets, as well as by her study of worldwide disease and diet patterns. Her research convinced her that most Americans, including herself, needed to cut their intake of fat and sugar while increasing their level of complex carbohydrates, as found in foods such as pasta, breads, and potatoes. Brody collected her findings in *Jane Brody's Nutrition Book,* which became a best-seller.

In 1985 she published *Jane Brody's Good Food Book* as a companion volume to her *Nutrition Book*. *Good Food* shows how to put the principles of the *Nutrition Book* into practice. Richard Wolff calls *Jane Brody's Good Food Book* a unique source in his *Washington Post Book World* review: "It is simultaneously a book on nutrition and weight loss; a 'how to' equip a kitchen, shop for food, stock a larder, cook and eat out; and a recipe book." Brody emphasized her conviction that good nutrition need not be unpleasant in her interview with Steinberg: "I wrote *Jane Brody's Good Food Book* for the average American who likes to *eat* and likes to *live*. . . . I don't like to feel deprived any more than the next person."

Brody summarizes her total health philosophy as one of simple moderation—a concept foreign to many Americans. "There's a feeling of entitlement in the American character," she told Steinberg. "It's the idea: 'I was good all week so I can pig out on Haagen Dazs on the weekend.' Americans really don't want to give up their special passions. I say it is okay to indulge them now and then if you lead a healthy life the rest of the time."

CA INTERVIEW

CA interviewed Jane Brody by telephone on December 1, 1986, at her home in Brooklyn, New York.

CA: It's been said that you get more mail from readers, in response to your "Personal Health" column, than any other writer for the New York Times. *Your books and magazine articles undoubtedly add to that mail. Do the letters indicate that your writing has helped a great many people to make healthy changes in their lives?*

BRODY: Absolutely. It's been the most rewarding aspect of my work. This is why I read readers' letters, and I answer most of them. Some people are referred to my column by their doctors, which is especially encouraging. The doctors who do that look upon my column as an adjunct to their jobs and as an aid that saves them time and can explain things in language that they would have difficulty doing themselves. As far as the letters in response to the books are concerned, they're off the wall. It's so wonderful that, if I had the time and energy, I'd write a book every year.

CA: The simplicity of explanation that causes doctors to refer patients to your column is one of the most distingushed aspects of your work, I think. You take material from pertinent sources and present it in a usable way. Was this one of your goals when you began adding journalism courses to the science courses in college?

BRODY: I have to admit that my initial instinct was a totally selfish one: I loved learning about science. I got a big kick out of the fact that I could have a job in which I was constantly learning. And of course the discovery that I helped people by conveying this information to the lay public gave me an added incentive that became my primary focus ultimately. By the time I got to graduate school, actually, I already saw signs of leaning toward the kind of writing that helps people live better and understand things better and know how to cope better.

CA: The companion volumes Jane Brody's Nutrition Book *(1981) and* Jane Brody's Good Food Book *(1985) continue to sell very well, so they're obviously being read and heeded. Is a third book on food growing out of response to these?*

BRODY: What will eventually come out of them is a second *Good Food* book, because I've invited readers to send me recipes. I get on the average three letters a day on the book, and quite a number of those people who write send recipes. Some send only one recipe, and some send a whole bunch of recipes. And some say, "Do you still want more recipes?"

CA: And you'll have to test all those recipes in your own kitchen?

BRODY: Yes. Obviously I'll have to preselect; I'm not going to test every single one of them, because they don't all sound good. But presumably people are sending me recipes that they like, so they've already been through one tasting session. One of the most interesting things about getting the recipes is seeing what people think of as being healthy recipes. Some of them have a lot more fat in them, for example, than I would ever use—not most, but some. You can see how difficult it is to drag oneself away from the old ways of doing things. If you look at old recipes, you'll see that they have huge amounts of sugar in comparison to current recipes for the same foods. People are gradually weaning themselves away from the dependence on an overkill of fat and sugar and salt. Some of the recipes I get go back a long way. People say they've reduced the amount of sugar; well, it still could get cut in half and you probably would have a better product.

CA: Are there sources that you read regularly for new developments in medicine and health?

BRODY: Yes. About thirty different publications come across my desk every week that I look at. They run the gamut from first-run journals like the *New England Journal of Medicine*, the *Journal of the American Medical Association*, and the *Annals of Internal Medicine* to some of the specialty journals in obstetrics and gynecology and pediatrics to what we call the medical throwaways, things like *Patient Care Magazine*, *Hospital Practice*, *Contemporary Pediatrics*, *Drug Therapy*, and other such publications that are written by experts in their special fields and are very useful background information, for kind of an overview of those fields.

CA: There are a lot of books written on health now, some of them obviously more useful than others. Do you feel compelled to look at them all in the course of your work?

BRODY: So many come in that it's become prohibitive to peruse most of them carefully. I just look for certain hallmark signs. If I come across a book that's touting megadoses of this, that, or the other thing, it automatically goes to the throwaway file because there just isn't evidence to substantiate that kind of practice, and why waste my time? But there are many books that are good. I'm flabbergasted at how many books are published each year, most of which just collect dust, but some of them are excellent.

CA: You've repeatedly given your family credit for their tremendous support in your work, and you and your husband co-authored the first book, Secrets of Good Health. *How did the collaboration come about, and how did it work in the actual research and writing?*

BRODY: That little book was done on a commission. It had a very specific purpose: it was designed to help young couples who were just getting going to establish healthy living habits and good medical practice so that they wouldn't end up spending a lot of money on doctor bills. My husband was an editor for many years, and originally this was going to be an editing project. It turned into a writing project. I supplied the material and the direction, and he put it together. I was pregnant at the time, and I couldn't stay awake for much of it! It's seen kicking around somewhere every so often, but it is not in print.

As far as the other books are concerned, I've written them wholly by myself, and the family support has mainly come in mechanical ways. When I'm working on a book, my husband takes over most of my share of the household chores. The boys had to wash most of the dishes when I was cooking those recipes for the last book. And they all had to taste everything! I had lots and lots of tasting parties. I'm kind of a do-it-yourselfer; I don't usually hire people to do these things. So basically what it amounts to is that my husband would get the mechanical end of the thing together: we had to have forms prepared and pencils attached to them, and the tables had to be set in certain ways and all the different foods labeled. It wasn't difficult, but it was fairly complicated getting it all coordinated—and getting the food made also—and making sure that everybody filled out the forms properly so that they would be useful.

CA: You've proven by your own example that we can change our eating habits and be healthier for it. Do you think we've become much wiser eaters in this country with the increase of good information on nutrition?

BRODY: I think some people have become wiser eaters. A lot of people *think* they've become wiser eaters, which means that some of the time they eat wisely and the rest of the time they throw caution to the wind. There are several trends. One is certainly showing that we're eating fewer eggs and less red meat; the decline in eating red meat has been dramatic. We're eating more low-fat and skimmed dairy products and less of the whole-fat dairy products. This includes cottage cheese, yogurt, and milk. We're eating more chicken, probably because it's remained a cheap food and very accessible. We're eating slightly more fish, but mostly in the restaurant market and not at home. The most discouraging trend in overall consumption patterns is that cheese continues to go up, and cheese is a very, very poor food from a nutritional standpoint because it's so high in saturated fat and cholesterol. I say it's a poor choice particularly when you hold it up against lean red meat. The other discouraging thing is the I-deserve-it attitude that I see prevailing throughout the country; I've eaten a spartan appetizer or two appetizers and a salad or a skimpy dinner, and now I can have my double chocolate Haagen-Dazs. This dessert pattern is very noticeable in restaurants, and I'm sure it's happening also in people's homes. I'm not saying that one can never have ice cream. I certainly do, and I wouldn't want to be told I couldn't. But it's the pattern that I'm concerned about.

CA: What do you consider our greatest health problems?

BRODY: Certainly from a nutritional point of view, the single greatest problem is obesity. We have forty percent of the population twenty or more pounds above ideal body weight. That is a lot of fat people, and many of those people, even in their forties, already have signs of problems in their entire bodies from poor living habits.

CA: Do your articles ever provoke controversy among readers?

BRODY: Yes. Recently I've gotten a slew of letters on an article I did on how to help babies sleep. I heard from some parents who were kind of La Leche League parents who called to my attention a book on nighttime problems with babies that recommends exactly the opposite of what my column did. We're printing a whole lot of those letters. The controversy involved the very fundamental difference between letting your baby cry and feeding your baby every time it opens its mouth.

CA: Through syndication, the "Personal Health" columns reach many readers besides New York Times *ones. Do you seem to have a different audience altogether for the writing you've done for* Family Circle *and other magazines aimed primarily at women?*

BRODY: Not entirely, because the *Times* column appears in so many papers that are very un-*Times*y, and they would include many of the same kinds of readers that you'd find reading *Family Circle*. But that is a specialized audience, which is why I've continued to do the column for *Family Circle*. I think every little thing makes a difference, and the more exposure people have to these ideas, the more they are going to make changes in the societal norm. And once there's a societal norm, then people adopt it; they just follow the leader, and that's a perfectly good way to go as long as the leader is doing the right thing.

CA: I was amused to read in Len Albin's article on you in Fifty Plus *that your lecture spots have included a "Chocolate Weekend" at the Mohonk Mountain House in the Catskills. What kind of audiences are more usual for the lectures?*

BRODY: It runs the gamut from medical-center-sponsored health days and women's health programs to spouse programs at corporate meetings. Invariably the spouses say, "My husband should have heard you. He should hear it from you instead of from me." That's the most common type of meeting I speak to.

CA: Recently you've been doing a series of cooking shows on public television. Are there plans to continue that?

BRODY: They're very interested in seeking funding for another ten-part series, and they've already asked me if I want to do it, so it's a real possibility. But public television is solely dependent on contributions from people like you and me. I enjoyed doing the series. I was working with a very intelligent group of people who did not sacrifice information for the sake of television, which is very important. I'd do it again in a minute. I just got good at it when we finished the show; I need another crack at it.

CA: One of the ways you stay fit and keep up your energy for all the work is by getting regular exercise, and plenty of it. What would you recommend people do when the weather is truly too awful to get outside and they don't belong to a health club?

BRODY: You can put on an exercise tape or just some nice music and do basic stretching. You can do running or jogging in place in a circumscribed area in your house, or jumping rope if your knees can take it—and your neighbors. If you can afford a piece of equipment, something like a rowing machine or an exercise bicycle or a ski-track would be an excellent piece of equipment to have at home for those days that it's pouring or pitch dark or whatever.

CA: What do you think of the health clubs, generally?

BRODY: A lot of them are not well supervised, and the people who show you how to use the equipment don't know what they're doing and don't watch carefully enough. But many of them are excellent. You have to check out what the facility offers; how much it costs; if it's under construction, when it's going to be finished—things of that sort. The most important thing is the credentials of the trainer. Also, I'm a swimmer, and I would not join a health club that didn't have a good lap pool.

CA: Stress has been named as one of the main causes of poor health. Do you think large cities are particularly stressful?

BRODY: It's the pace of life that makes large cities stressful, but not all cities are stressful. Maybe they're more stressful than rural areas, but when I go out of New York City and into almost every other large city, things seem to move at a much healthier pace.

CA: So it's New York that's especially stressful?

BRODY: It's a city *like* New York, where everybody is trying to get his or her oar in, trying to get there first. The hugeness and density of the population is not conducive to a warm, cordial feeling when you meet somebody in New York.

CA: The thinking on alcohol now generally seems to be that a little is a good thing for us. How can people best determine what's right for them individually, what's a beneficial or safe level of alcohol?

BRODY: Basically it's one—at most two—drinks a day. And a drink is defined as a jigger of hard alcohol, which is an ounce and a half, about four ounces of wine or three ounces of sherry, one ounce of liqueur, twelve ounces of beer. Any of these is one drink. If you see somebody who's drinking two drinks, you don't want your kids in the car with that person.

CA: By all accounts of your lifestyle, you're an early riser and a very hard worker. What kind of writing and lecturing schedule do you keep now?

BRODY: The lecturing is totally at the mercy of seasons. There's a very big season in the fall and another big season in the spring. Things are really quiet between Thanksgiving and New Year's. It's a great relief. But in the fall I give huge numbers of lectures. In one three-week period I gave eight lectures, and that's too many—it takes a lot of time.

CA: I imagine the traveling isn't easy either.

BRODY: I find it hardest when I haven't been on the road for a while. But I have learned ways of making it easier. I carry on my luggage; I have a little wheeled cart that I put it all on so I don't have to carry it by hand until I get inside the airplane. When I'm not certain about what I'm going to be fed and when, I take a sandwich with me that contains healthy food. I have my running clothes all packed and ready to go and my cosmetic bag all packed and ready to go; it's just a matter of throwing it all in the suitcase. But I find that the travel time is an excellent and productive time for me. It's a sort of white noise that I don't have to pay any attention to, and I carry a little computer that weighs about four pounds. I write on it, and everything is stored in its memory.

CA: Do you normally write every day?

BRODY: No. There has to be a day when I read and make phone calls, so I don't write every day. But I write every week.

CA: You've recently done some writing about aging. Will there be more?

BRODY: We have as the fastest growing segment of our population people over sixty-five, who, incidentally, are growing sicker faster than they are growing older. This means that the proportion of people over sixty-five who are sick at any one time is growing. So aging will be, I would guess, a continuing topic. Most of the people now in this over-sixty-five generation grew up in an era when patients were encouraged to be ignorant about their health, so they've got to learn to pay attention to their health, because their lives may depend on it.

CA: Beyond the recipes coming in now that may become another cook book, are there special projects you know you'll be doing?

BRODY: No. I'm really trying to use this year as a recoupment time. My children are seniors in high school and they're applying to colleges now. I feel that I've got another eight or nine months with them before they're gone. I realize they'll come back on many vacations and I'll probably be sick of them after a while, but I would like not to get too heavily involved in any specific thing, any ongoing work, until they're off to college.

CA: You've never had any regrets about deciding against full-time lab work in science?

BRODY: Never. Most people have to pay to get an education. As I said earlier, I get paid to be educated, and I can't think of anything more fun.

BIOGRAPHICAL/CRITICAL SOURCES:

PERIODICALS

Chicago Tribune, November 14, 1985.
Fifty Plus, March, 1984.
New York Review of Books, June 9, 1977.
New York Times, August 5, 1977, July 10, 1981.
Publishers Weekly, October 18, 1985.
Washington Post, September 27, 1982.
Washington Post Book World, June 12, 1977, October 27, 1985.

—*Interview by Jean W. Ross*

*   *   *

BROKHOFF, John R(udolph) 1913-

PERSONAL: Born December 19, 1913, in Pottsville, Pa.; son of John H. (a businessman) and Gertrude (Heiser) Brokhoff; married Barbara Barnett (a minister), June 9, 1972. *Education:* Muhlenberg College, A.B., 1935; University of Pennsylvania, M.A., 1938; Lutheran Theological Seminary, Philadelphia, Pa., B.D., 1938.

ADDRESSES: Home—119 Harborage Ct., Clearwater, Fla. 33515.

CAREER: Ordained minister of Lutheran Church in America, 1938; assistant pastor in Richmond, Va., 1938-40; pastor in Marion, Va., 1940-42, Roanoke, Va., 1942-45, Atlanta, Ga.,

1945-55, Charlotte, N.C., 1955-62, and Lanadale, Pa., 1962-65; Emory University, Candler School of Theology, Atlanta, professor of homiletics, 1965-79. Guest professor, Emory University, 1950-54; lecturer, Gammon Theological Seminary, 1966. Chairman, United Lutheran Radio Committee, 1948-54; moderator of youth program, Radio WSB, Atlanta, 1953-54, Radio WBT, Charlotte, 1955-56, and WSOC-TV, Charlotte, 1957-59; member of answer panel, "Pastors Face Your Questions," WBTV, Charlotte, 1956-62. Member of executive committee, Lutheran Synod of North Carolina, 1959-62; member of executive board, North Carolina Council of Churches, 1962. Member of board of trustees, Lutheran Children's Home of the South, 1951-54; secretary of board of trustees, Protestant Radio Center, Inc., 1959-62; member of board of directors, Academy of Preachers, Philadelphia Lutheran Seminary, 1984-85. Councillor, National Lutheran Council, 1951-55; member of advisory board, Juvenile Court, Atlanta, 1954; member of consulting committee, United Lutheran Church Department of Architecture, 1956-62.

MEMBER: Evangelical Ministers Association of Atlanta (president, 1948), Atlanta Christian Council (president, 1950-52), Atlanta Lutheran Pastors' Association (president, 1953), Mecklenburg Christian Ministers' Association (president, 1960), Charlotte Lutheran Pastors' Association (president, 1957-59), Omicron Delta Kappa, Tau Kappa Alpha, Alpha Kappa Alpha.

AWARDS, HONORS: George Washington Medal from Freedoms Foundation for sermon, "Human Rights or Duties?"; D.D., Muhlenberg College, 1951.

WRITINGS:

Read and Live: A Study Dealing with How to Use the Bible, Muhlenberg Press, 1953.
This Is Life, Revell, 1959.
This Is the Church, Lutheran Church Press, 1964.
Defending My Faith, two volumes, Lutheran Church Press, 1966.
Table My Faith, two volumes, Lutheran Church Press, 1966.
Table for Lovers, C.S.S. Publishing, 1974.
(Contributor) Charles L. Wallis, compiler, *Eighty-Eight Evangelistic Sermons,* Baker Book, 1974.
If Your Dearest Should Die, C.S.S. Publishing, 1975.
Wrinkled Wrappings, C.S.S. Publishing, 1975.
Lectionary Preaching Workbook, Series C, C.S.S. Publishing, 1979.
Lectionary Preaching Workbook, Series A, C.S.S. Publishing, 1980.
Lectionary Preaching Workbook, Series B, C.S.S. Publishing, 1981.
The Case of the Missing Body, C.S.S. Publishing, 1982.
Luther Lives, C.S.S. Publishing, 1982.
Preaching the Parables, Series B, C.S.S. Publishing, 1987.
This You Can Believe, C.S.S. Publishing, 1987.

Also author of *Youth's World, Christ in the Gospels, Why?,* and *Christian Strategy,* published by Lutheran Church Press; contributor to *Notable Sermons from Protestant Pulpits* and *Preaching the Nativity.* Contributor of articles to *Christian Century Pulpit, Pulpit Digest, Lutheran,* and *Good News.*

*   *   *

BRONK, William 1918-

PERSONAL: Born February 17, 1918, in Fort Edward, N.Y.; son of William M. and Ethel (Funston) Bronk.

ADDRESSES: Home—57 Pearl St., Hudson Falls, N.Y. 12839.

CAREER: Poet and essayist. *Military service:* U.S. Army, 1941-45; became lieutenant.

AWARDS, HONORS: American Book Award for poetry, 1982, for *Life Supports.*

WRITINGS:

POETRY

Light and Dark, Origin Press, 1956, 2nd edition, Elizabeth Press, 1975.
The World, the Worldless, New Directions, 1964.
The Empty Hands, Elizabeth Press, 1969.
That Tantalus, Elizabeth Press, 1971.
Utterances: The Loss of Grass, Trees, Water: The Unbecoming of Wanted and Wanter, Burning Deck, 1972.
To Praise the Music, Elizabeth Press, 1972.
Looking at It, Sceptre Press, 1973.
A Partial Glossary: Two Essays, Elizabeth Press, 1974.
The Stance, Graywolf Press, 1975.
Silence and Metaphor, Elizabeth Press, 1975.
Finding Losses, Elizabeth Press, 1976.
The Meantime, Elizabeth Press, 1976.
My Father Photographed with Friends and Other Pictures, Elizabeth Press, 1976.
Twelve Losses Found, Grosseteste, 1976.
That Beauty Still, Burning Deck, 1978.
Life Supports, North Point, 1982.
Light in a Dark Sky, William Ewert, 1982.
Careless Love and Its Apostrophes, Red Ozier Press, 1985.
Manifest; And Furthermore, North Point, 1987.

ESSAYS

The New World, Elizabeth Press, 1974.
The Brother in Elysium, Elizabeth Press, 1980.
Vectors and Smoothable Curves, North Point, 1983.

SIDELIGHTS: In poems that have often been compared to those of Wallace Stevens, William Bronk investigates the nature of consciousness, time and space, and the poetic fictions that will suffice in an age of disbelief and uncertainty. As Michael Heller remarks in the *New York Times Book Review,* Bronk's poetry "offers another way of looking at our common humanity, not in some imagined concurrence of shared knowledge, but in our need to construct and reconstruct worlds, in our attempts to appease a common metaphysical hunger." Many critics also note that his meditative and experimental poems use a language stripped of ornament, imagery, and metaphor. "His poetry of statement," comments *Saturday Review* contributor Robert D. Spector, "impresses with its clarity and precision of language; it manages to make metaphysics a subject of human emotion rather than a grand abstraction."

Both Felix Stefanile and Richard Elman have called Bronk one of the best, if uncelebrated, of America's poets. In his *Parnassus: Poetry in Review* discussion of Bronk's approach to time and human history, Stefanile observes: "[For] Bronk ancient mountains and modern cities coexist in the flux of time in which man is trapped. That is why his startling connections are always so utterly contemporary, and personally relevant. Man is not man-in-history, or man-as-savage, but *man.* No other poet in the United States is quite like this." And though his poetry describes the anguish and uncertainty of modern life, it does not succumb to despair. Instead, as Spector points out, "it recognizes our need 'to make / a world for survival . . . ,' since 'One is nothing with no world.'" His poems instruct us, Heller remarks: "that the worlds we seem to share are created worlds; 'like pieces of music, they are composed, oh wholly and well composed.'"

Bronk's poetry considers the limits of human knowledge. "The natural world, Bronk would insist, is a world we can never know," explains Heller. Consequently, Heller noted, Bronk's work suggests that the recognition of this basic estrangement between man and nature "illuminates and clarifies the human situation." To address this understanding and the need for "well-composed" worlds, Bronk searches for the appropriate form, style, and language. Elman declares in the *New York Times Book Review:* "Every new volume of his poems is engraved with terse statement, a high seriousness and strong uncluttered feeling. With each new volume he seems to be determined to make his utterance all the more specific, determined and quiet, as if he wrote his poems in the voice and with the mind in which we all truly sometimes think, beautifully and sublimely, through our perceptions." Heller also applauds Bronk's attempt to find a suitable language for describing human perception and its limits; he notes that Bronk seeks to discover "the exacting and naked process of realization."

Bronk has occasionally turned to the essay form to address many of the same topics that preoccupy him in his poetry. In *Vectors and Smoothable Curves,* a collection of essays written over a period of forty years, the author discusses subjects as varied as the Inca and Maya civilizations of the Americas, nineteenth-century American literature, and the nature of time and space. Fred Moramarco characterizes Bronk's essays as "exhilarating reading" in the *Los Angeles Times,* and *New York Times Book Review* contributor Andrea Barnet remarks that Bronk's "unusual sensibility and expressiveness at times raise his essays to the narrative pitch of poetry."

BIOGRAPHICAL/CRITICAL SOURCES:

BOOKS

Contemporary Literary Criticism, Volume X, Gale, 1979.

PERIODICALS

Contemporary Literature, fall, 1982.
Grosseteste Review, spring, 1972.
Hudson Review, winter, 1976-77, September, 1984.
Los Angeles Times, January 26, 1984.
New York Times Book Review, March 9, 1975, September 18, 1977, December 13, 1981, January 1, 1984.
Parnassus: Poetry in Review, spring-summer, 1977.
Saturday Review, February 13, 1965, July 8, 1978.

*   *   *

BROUGHTON, T(homas) Alan   1936-

PERSONAL: Born June 9, 1936, in Bryn Mawr, Pa.; son of T. Robert S. and Annie Leigh (Hobson) Broughton; married Susan Becker (divorced, 1962); married Lenore Follansbee (divorced, 1969); married Mary Twitchell (divorced, 1975); married Laurel Ginter, 1982; children: (first marriage) Shannon Leigh; (second marriage) John Camm; (fourth marriage) Travers Nathaniel. *Education:* Attended Harvard University, 1954-57, and Juilliard School of Music, 1957-59; Swarthmore College, B.A. (with honors), 1962; University of Washington, Seattle, M.A., 1964.

ADDRESSES: Home—406 South Winooski Ave., Burlington, Vt. 05401. *Office*—Department of English, University of Vermont, 315 Old Mill, Burlington, Vt. 05401.

CAREER: Private piano teacher, 1959-62; Sweet Briar College, Sweet Briar, Va., instructor in English, 1964-66; University of Vermont, Burlington, assistant professor, 1966-70, associate professor, 1970-74, professor of English, 1974—, director of writer's workshop. Speaker and lecturer at many universities in the United States and abroad.

MEMBER: Authors Guild, Authors League of America, PEN, Poetry Society of America, American Academy of Poets, Phi Beta Kappa.

AWARDS, HONORS: Chicago Review Fiction Contest honorable mention, 1969; *Yankee* Annual Poetry Award, 1971, 1973, 1975; Borestone Awards, 1972, 1973, 1974; *Virginia Quarterly Review* Emily Balch Award, 1974; National Endowment for the Arts fellowship in fiction, 1976-77; Guggenheim fellowship in fiction, 1982-83.

WRITINGS:

The Skin and All (poems), George Little Press, 1972.
In the Face of Descent (poems), Carnegie-Mellon University Press, 1975.
Adam's Dream (poems), Northeast/Juniper, 1975.
A Family Gathering (Book-of-the-Month Club alternate selection), Dutton, 1977.
Far from Home (poems), Carnegie-Mellon University Press, 1979.
The Man on the Moon (stories and poems), Barlenmir House, 1979.
The Others We Are (poems), Northeast/Juniper, 1979.
Winter Journey (novel), Dutton, 1980.
The Horsemaster (novel), Dutton, 1981.
Dreams before Sleep (poems), Carnegie-Mellon University Press, 1982.
Hob's Daughter (novel), Morrow, 1984.
Preparing to Be Happy, Carnegie-Mellon University Press, 1988.

CONTRIBUTOR TO ANTHOLOGIES

Best Poems of 1972: Borestone Mountain Poetry Awards 1973, Pacific Books, 1973.
Best Poems of 1973: Borestone Mountain Poetry Awards 1974, Pacific Books, 1974.
Best Poems of 1974: Borestone Mountain Poetry Awards 1975, Pacific Books, 1975.
Michael McMahon, editor, *Flowering after Frost: The Anthology of Contemporary New England Poetry,* Branden Press, 1975.
Alan F. Pater, editor, *Anthology of Magazine Verse and Yearbook of American Poetry: 1980 Edition,* Monitor Book, 1981.
Pater, editor, *Anthology of Magazine Verse and Yearbook of American Poetry, 1981,* Monitor Book, 1981.
Gerald Costanzo, editor, *Three Rivers, Ten Years: An Anthology of Poems from Three Rivers Poetry Journal,* Carnegie-Mellon University Press, 1983.
Pater, editor, *Anthology of Magazine Verse and Yearbook of American Poetry for 1984,* Monitor Book, 1984.
DeWitt Henry, editor, *Ploughshares Reader: New Fiction for the Eighties,* Pushcart, 1985.
Available Press/PEN Short Story Collection, Ballantine, 1985.

OTHER

Contributor of short stories and poems to literary magazines, including *American Weave, Beloit Poetry Journal, Common-*

weal, Prairie Schooner, Yankee, Cimarron, Poetry, and *Cosmopolitan.*

WORK IN PROGRESS: Novels, poems, novellas, and short stories.

SIDELIGHTS: "By all odds," notes Susan Wood in the *Washington Post Book World,* "*Winter Journey* should not be a particularly successful novel. Its plot and characters are, on the surface anyway, fairly standard, if not trite. . . . Yet, thanks to T. Alan Broughton's considerable talent, these stock elements combine into a moving, finely crafted novel, full of real people about whom the reader comes to care deeply."

Wood's comments are characteristic of critical reaction to Broughton's works. *New York Times* reviewer John Leonard describes *Winter Journey* as the story of a young man, an aspiring pianist, whose mother takes him to Rome after her marriage breaks up. Their journey is one of self-discovery, of maturing, a story which, as Leonard states, "has been written before and will be written again, although probably not as well as T. Alan Broughton has written this time. . . . Not the least of Mr. Broughton's accomplishments is to seize material we had thought to be worn out, used up, discarded, replaced—by a newer model of antistory, the ironic grimace—and make it somehow lyrical all over again."

In the *New York Times Book Review* John Casey echoes the opinions of both Wood and Leonard; for him, "the effect of [*Winter Journey*] is that of intimate personal narration. There is a sense (historically accurate and well-rendered) that the characters are bound in by politeness and good taste from being open and easily familiar with each other." He adds that such consideration has gone out of fashion in recent literature: "This theme is most often treated comically or bitterly and ironically, so it is a pleasure to find that [Broughton] treats it lyrically and romantically."

Broughton's *The Horsemaster* is a novel about a young woman's search for her biological father and her impact on his life and the lives of those around him. Although *Washington Post* reviewer Matthew Schudel calls it "an approachable and well-written novel," he nonetheless regards *The Horsemaster* as "a somewhat uneven accomplishment. In style and theme, Broughton resembles, say, Wallace Stegner and Frederick Busch in the way he depicts the unexpected or unexamined complexities in the lives of ordinary people in the overlooked corners of America. Unfortunately, Broughton presents too little of their daily working lives and too much of their memories, brooding and dreaming to convince us of their ordinariness. The result is an overly psychological picture of people whose primary concerns are probably much more humdrum than Broughton allows them to be."

Ralph B. Sipper, writing for the *Los Angeles Times Book Review,* offers a different assessment; he feels that "one of Broughton's graces is to have written a psychological novel that does not psychologize or employ clinical jargon. Feelings, dreams and memories are precisely catalogued, not diluted by superficial analysis." Similarly, Alexandra Johnson writes in the *Chicago Tribune Book World* that *The Horsemaster* is "a rich and intricate story of how two strangers, grappling with their own private needs, gradually assume responsibility for the other. . . . It's a novel of intense affirmation, a hauntingly poignant study of a man growing up."

T. Alan Broughton had this to say about his feelings on his own work: "This dream begins in my childhood. I sleep and in my sleeping mind, deep in that area close to oblivion, I

hear the sound of a tone. Sometimes that tone will be accompanied by a visual counterpart in the form of perfectly arranged objects that scatter into disorder, then reform. The sound is a clear, perfectly tuned, unbroken note. But in its very perfection resides a dread since I know it must break. It does, and as it disintegrates I am lost in terror—a chaos beyond all light and joy. But in the noise that tone has become, I find relief since I know it must turn back to order, and it does. A dream of paradoxes; music and the dissolution from which it rises. Unbearable joy, ecstatic terror. This is the rhythm of death and rebirth, the dream that forms everything I write."

AVOCATIONAL INTERESTS: Music.

BIOGRAPHICAL/CRITICAL SOURCES:

PERODICALS

Chicago Tribune Book World, March 23, 1980, November 8, 1981.
Los Angeles Times, January 17, 1980.
Los Angeles Times Book Review, October 18, 1981.
New York Times, January 11, 1980.
New York Times Book Review, May 15, 1977, October 14, 1984.
Washington Post, October 31, 1981.
Washington Post Book World, February 3, 1980.

*   *   *

BROWN, Cassie   1919-1986

PERSONAL: Born January 10, 1919, in Rose Blanche, Newfoundland, Canada; died December 30, 1986; daughter of Wilson Gordon and Caroline (Hillier) Horwood; married Donald Frank Brown (a consultant), September 10, 1945; children: Derek, Christine. *Education:* Attended schools in Newfoundland. *Religion:* Protestant.

ADDRESSES: Home—P.O. Box 5806, St. John's, Newfoundland, Canada.

CAREER: Stenographer, journalist, playwright, radio worker; free-lance writer. President of Karwood Ltd., 1966-86.

AWARDS, HONORS: Arts and Letters awards from the government of Newfoundland, annually, 1953-57, for short stories and radio plays.

WRITINGS:

Death on the Ice, Doubleday, 1972.
A Winter's Tale, Doubleday, 1976.
Standing into Danger, Doubleday, 1979.

Also author of plays, including "Wreckers" and "Down by the Sea," and adaptations, documentaries, and commentaries for Newfoundland Regional Network of Canadian Broadcasting Corp. Work represented in anthologies, including *The Book of Newfoundland,* edited by J. R. Smallwood, Newfoundland Book Publishers, 1975. Author of weekly column, "The Inside Track," *Daily News,* St. John's, Newfoundland, 1959-66. Contributor to *Atlantic Advocate* and other periodicals. Editor and publisher of *Newfoundland Woman,* 1962-65.

*   *   *

BRUNING, Nancy P(auline)   1948-

PERSONAL: Born November 7, 1948, in New York; daughter of Nicholas Cornelius and Anne Marie (Liebenberg) Bruning;

married Michael Ross (a writer and musician), December 12, 1981. *Education:* Pratt Institute, B.A., 1969.

ADDRESSES: Home—980 Bush, Apt. 503, San Francisco, Calif. 94109. *Agent*—Susan Ann Protter, 110 West 40th St., New York, N.Y. 10018.

CAREER: McCall's Needlework and Crafts, New York City, writer and crafts designer, 1971-73; Tree Communications, Inc., New York City, editor and project director, 1974-77; free-lance writer, 1977—; Krames Communications, Inc., San Francisco, Calif., conceptual editor/writer, 1986—.

MEMBER: Authors Guild, Authors League of America.

WRITINGS:

(Editor with Robert Levine) *The Cold Weather Catalog: Learning to Love Winter,* Doubleday, 1977.
(Editor) Sylvia Rosenthal, *Cosmetic Surgery: A Consumer's Guide,* Lippincott, 1977.
(Contributor) Maggie Oster, editor, *The Green Pages,* Ballantine, 1977.
Lady's Luck Companion (on gambling), Harper, 1979.
The Beach Book, Houghton, 1981.
(With Jane Katz) *Total Fitness through Swimming,* Doubleday, 1981.
A Consumer Guide to Contact Lenses, Dial, 1982.
Coping with Chemotherapy, Doubleday, 1985.
(With Elliott Seligman) *Consultation with Your Psychotherapist,* Simon & Schuster, 1986.
(With Shari Lieberman) *Design Your Own Vitamin and Mineral Program,* Doubleday, 1987.

Contributor to *Family Creative Workshop.* Contributor to magazines and newspapers, including *Travel and Leisure, McCall's,* and *Social Issues and Health Review.*

SIDELIGHTS: Nancy P. Bruning told *CA:* "I write and edit illustrated books and booklets as an extension of my degree in visual communication. No matter what the subject matter, one of my goals is to combine word and pictures in order to communicate most effectively. I always try to inform entertainingly and entertain informatively.

"The age of video-computer communications will no doubt change the face of publishing. I find this exciting, not frightening. Besides, nothing can ever take the place of curling up under a shady tree with a good book that has real pages to turn."

*   *   *

BRUTON, Eric (Moore) 1915-

PERSONAL: Born in 1915, in London, England; son of James Eli (a headmaster) and Flora (Moore) Bruton; married Anne Valerie Britton (a novelist; died, 1976). *Education:* Attended private schools and college.

ADDRESSES: Home—Bentley Old Hall, Bentley, Ipswich, Suffolk IP8 3JX, England. *Agent*—Elaine Greene Ltd., 31 Newington Green, Islington London N16 9PU, England.

CAREER: Writer, jeweller, teacher. Publisher of *Retail Jeweller;* director, N.A.G. Press, 1962—; publisher, Northwood Publications, 1967—. Founder and director of Diamond Boutique Ltd., and Things and Ideas Ltd.; former director of riding school. Freeman of City of London. Visiting lecturer, Sir John Cass College, London. *Military service:* Royal Air Force, senior technical officer, 1940-46.

MEMBER: Gemmological Association of Great Britain (fellow), British Horological Institute (fellow), Worshipful Company of Clockmakers (liveryman), Worshipful Company of Turners (liveryman), Worshipful Company of Goldsmiths (honorary freeman), Antiquarian Horological Society.

AWARDS, HONORS: Special award, American Watchmakers Institute, for contributions to the science of horology; Hanneman Award, for outstanding contribution to gemmological literature.

WRITINGS:

NONFICTION

The True Book about Clocks (juvenile), Muller, 1957.
The True Book about Diamonds (juvenile), Muller, 1961.
Automation (juvenile), Muller, 1962, 2nd edition, English Language Society, 1964.
Dictionary of Clocks and Watches, Arco, 1962.
The Longcase Clock, Arco, 1964, 2nd edition, Granada, 1977.
Clocks and Watches 1400-1900, Praeger, 1967.
Clocks and Watches, Paul Hamlyn, 1968.
Diamonds, N.A.G. Press, 1970, Chilton, 1971, 2nd edition, 1978.
Hallmarks and Date Letters on Gold and Silver, revised edition, N.A.G. Press, 1970.
Antique Clocks and Clock Collecting, Paul Hamlyn, 1974.
The History of Clocks and Watches, Orbis, 1979.
The Wetherfield Collection: A Guide to Dating English Antique Clocks, N.A.G. Press, 1981.
Legendary Gems, Chilton, 1984.

FICTION

Death in Ten Point Bold, Jenkins, 1957.
Die Darling Die, T. V. Boardman, 1959.
Violent Brothers, T. V. Boardman, 1960.
The Hold Out, T. V. Boardman, 1961.
King Diamond, T. V. Boardman, 1961.
The Devil's Pawn, T. V. Boardman, 1962.

"INSPECTOR GEORGE JUDD" SERIES

The Laughing Policeman, T. V. Boardman, 1963.
The Finsbury Mob, T. V. Boardman, 1964.
The Smithfield Slayer, T. V. Boardman, 1965.
The Wicked Saint: A City of London Police Novel, T. V. Boardman, 1965.
The Fire Bug: A City of London Police Novel, T. V. Boardman, 1967.

OTHER

(Contributor) Herbert Harris, editor, *John Creasey's Mystery Bedside Book,* Hodder & Stoughton, 1966.

Contributor of articles on engineering and antiquarian subjects to periodicals. Editor of *Travel, Goldsmiths Journal, Horological Journal, Gemmologist, Industrial Diamond Review,* and other publications.

SIDELIGHTS: Eric Bruton's book *Diamonds* has been translated into Spanish.

WORK IN PROGRESS: Dictionary of Clocks and Watches; History of the English Clock and Watch Industry.

AVOCATIONAL INTERESTS: Foreign travel to visit gem mining areas and to see ancient clocks; gardening; "learning about off-beat subjects."

BULLARD, Oral 1922-

PERSONAL: Born January 24, 1922, in Vassar, Kan.; son of Elvin Lee and Lois Marcia (Howland) Bullard; married Suzanne Stapleford, February 16, 1946; children: Randall, Tracy, Eric Lee. *Politics:* Independent. *Religion:* "I believe in God."

ADDRESSES: Home—294 Southwest Fifth, Beaverton, Ore. 97005. *Office*—Touchstone Press, 6775 Southwest 111th, Beaverton, Ore. 97005.

CAREER: Arcady Press, Portland, Ore., vice-president, 1956-64, president, 1964-66; Irwin-Hodson Co. (printers), Portland, vice-president, 1966-70; Touchstone Press, Beaverton, Ore., founder and president, 1965—. Honorary president, Oregon Printing Industry, 1965. *Military service:* 383rd AAA (AW) Bn., 1943-45; served in United States, Australia, New Guinea, Moluccas, and Philippines.

WRITINGS:

Crisis on the Columbia, Touchstone, 1968.
Short Trips and Trails: The Columbia Gorge, Touchstone, 1974.
The Second Parting, Lochan Experience, 1980.
Lancaster's Road: The Historic Columbia River Scenic Highway, T.M.S. Book Service, 1982.
Konapee's Eden, Historic and Scenic Handbook, Columbia River Gorge, T.M.S. Book Service, 1985.

Contributor to magazines and newspapers.

WORK IN PROGRESS: A novel centered in eastern Oregon.

SIDELIGHTS: Oral Bullard told *CA:* "My writing career started at age twelve or thirteen when I won a statewide contest in my native Kansas. At age seventeen," Bullard wrote, he graduated from high school and became "general reporter and sportswriter" in a southeast Kansas town. "I 'rode a hot fighter' through the Kansas City Golden Gloves and all the way to Chicago, hobnobbing along the way with the likes of Ernie Mehl, sports columnist for the *Kansas City Star,* and Arch Ward of the *Chicago Tribune.* The spring I was eighteen I began to get published in pulp magazines.

"I dabbled in fiction for a number of years, with small results and then wrote *Crisis on the Columbia* in 1968. Encouraged by [an] *Audubon* magazine review, [I] continued with nonfiction for a number of years, publishing many articles in West Coast publications and producing three more books on the Columbia Gorge and a collection of some of these articles plus some short stories and poems.

"My advice to aspiring writers is WRITE. In my capacity as a regional publisher I encounter many persons who *talk about writing* but don't produce much if anything at all.

"I view the current national writing scene with some misgivings because of the influence of television on book writers. I think this is to the detriment of good fiction as some national editors have told me they want writing to be visual, so it can easily be adapted to television or the big screen. On the other hand, this opens up possibilities for publishing regional fiction and I am interested in that both as a publisher and as a writer."

AVOCATIONAL INTERESTS: Travel, conservation, the human potential movement.

*   *   *

BURG, Dale R(onda) 1942-

PERSONAL: Born April 27, 1942, in Valley Stream, New York; daughter of Sylvan A. (an attorney) and Miriam (an actress and writer; maiden name, Layn) Burg; married Richard Nusser; children: Alden Fitzpatrick. *Education:* Brown University, A.B., 1962; Cornell University, M.A., 1964.

ADDRESSES: Office—130 West 57th St., New York, N.Y. 10019.

CAREER: Television production assistant, Leo Burnett, 1964; member of press and promotion department, Columbia Artists Management, 1964-67; administration assistant, Gimbels Theatre Club, 1967; administration assistant, APA-Phoenix Repertory Co., 1967-70; publicist, Abby Hirsch Public Relations, 1970-72; Columbia Pictures Industries, New York, N.Y., manager of corporate communications, 1972-83, and director of television writers' workshop; free-lance writer, 1983—. Instructor at New York University, 1979-81, and at The New School, 1984.

MEMBER: Writers Guild of America (East), Women in Film.

WRITINGS:

(With Abby Hirsch) *The Great Carmen Miranda Look-Alike Contest & Other Bold-Faced Lies* (nonfiction), St. Martin's, 1974.
(With Mary Ellen Pinkham) *Mary Ellen's Help Yourself Diet Plan,* St. Martin's, 1974.
How to Help the One You Love Stop Drinking, Putnam, 1986.

Writer for Columbia Broadcasting System (CBS) and National Broadcasting Co. (NBC). Author of columns with Mary Ellen Pinkham, "Mary Ellen," in *Star,* weekly, 1983—, and "From Mary Ellen's Kitchen," in *Family Circle,* monthly, 1984—. Contributor to periodicals, including *Working Woman, Cosmopolitan, Glamour, Woman's Day, Ladies Home Journal,* and *Village Voice.*

WORK IN PROGRESS: Writing nonfiction.

SIDELIGHTS: Dale R. Burg told *CA:* "Through years of public relations work in the entertainment field (much of it prior to my long association with Columbia Pictures), I met editors who commissioned my earliest and very occasional pieces—generally humorous, first-person essays. When I observed someone reading—and laughing aloud at—my first published piece in the *Village Voice,* I had a wonderful sense of accomplishment, and I prefer writing light pieces though most of the time the words don't come easily.

"Ghost-writing for Mary Ellen Pinkham, the helpful hints expert who sold millions of her reference books, proved a breakthrough in my career. Sometimes it's odd ghost-writing humor (I wonder how many others have such a job!), but I love the chance to do humorous essays on a regular basis (as in the *Star*).

"I think humorists are observers of life, unlike fiction writers, who are *storytellers,* and I envy people who can spin a good yarn, while I appreciate being able to 'get the laugh' (and I enjoy collaborating with storytellers in script form). My greatest moments in front of the word processor are the ones when a joke comes so suddenly and unexpectedly it makes *me* laugh out loud. There are a very few consistently good humor writers out there, conspicuously Nora Ephron, Anna Quirdlen, Dan Jenkins."

*   *   *

BURKE, David 1927-

PERSONAL: Born May 17, 1927, in Melbourne, Australia;

son of John William (an accountant) and Gertrude Olive (an opera singer; maiden name, Davies) Burke; married Helen Patricia Wane (a journalist), March 5, 1957; children: Mary, Anne, Margaret, Jane, Julia. *Education:* Attended school in South Brisbane, Queensland, Australia.

ADDRESSES: Home—Sydney, Australia. *Office*—P.O. Box 82, Mosman, New South Wales 2088, Australia. *Agent*—Curtis Brown Ltd., William St., Paddington, New South Wales, Australia.

CAREER: Worked as radio scriptwriter and production assistant, Melbourne, Australia, 1948-50; *Melbourne Herald-Sun,* Melbourne, reporter, feature writer, and sub-editor, 1950-56; *Sydney Morning Sun-Herald,* Sydney, Australia, reporter and feature writer, 1956-62; free-lance author, 1965—; has also worked for Victorian Railways and in public relations.

MEMBER: Royal Australian Historical Society, Australian Railway Historical Society, Rail Transport Museum, Australian Society of Authors.

WRITINGS:

(With C. C. Singleton) *Railways of Australia,* Angus & Robertson, 1963.
Monday at McMurdo (novel), Muller, 1967.
Come Midnight Monday (juvenile), illustrations by J. Mare, Methuen, 1976.
Great Steam Trains of Australia, Rigby, 1978.
Darknight (novel), Methuen, 1979.
Observer's Book of Steam Locomotives of Australia, Methuen, 1979.
Full Steam across the Mountains, illustrations by Phil Belbin, Methuen, 1981.
Changing Trains, Methuen, 1982.
Rings of the Iron Horse (biography), Methuen, 1985.
"Mary Ward, Then and Now" (30-minute video program), Loreto, Kirribilli (Australia), 1985.
Man of Steam (biography), Iron Horse Press (Australia), 1986.

WORK IN PROGRESS: A history of "the politics, planning and construction of the Trans-Australian Railway, 1912-17, as the first great work of the Federation."

SIDELIGHTS: David Burke told *CA:* "I regard myself as a general free-lance writer, but my lifelong interest in railroads has led me to study the history of various Australian railways and their impact on the social and economic development of Australia. I tend to alternate between fact and fiction in my writing. I am almost constantly doing research at national and state libraries, archives, etc., and I maintain comprehensive files."

MEDIA ADAPTATIONS: Come Midnight Monday was adapted for television and produced as a seven-episode serial by the Australian Broadcasting Commission, first broadcast in 1982.

*   *   *

BURLAND, Brian (Berkeley) 1931-

PERSONAL: Given name is pronounced "*Bree*-on"; born April 23, 1931, in Bermuda; son of Gordon Hamilton (a yacht builder) and Honor Alice Croydon (Gosling) Burland; married Edwina Ann Trentham, July 7, 1962; children: Susan, Anne, William,

Benjamin. *Education:* Attended University of Western Ontario.

ADDRESSES: Home—Book Hill Rd., Essex, Conn. 06426. *Agent*—Carol E. Rinzler, Rembar & Curtis, 19 West 44th St., New York, N.Y. 10036; Murray Pollinger, 4 Garrick St., London WC2E 9BH, England.

CAREER: Company director of family business in Bermuda, 1951-55; full-time professional writer. Writer-in-residence, Southern Seminary (Buena Vista, Va.), 1973. Teacher of seminars on his own novels at Washington and Lee University, Southern Seminary, and American School, London. Principal instructor, Bermuda Writer's Conference, 1978. Instructor at University of Hartford, 1981-82; guest fellow at Yale University, 1982-83. Broadcasts his own stories and poems on British Broadcasting Corp. (BBC) Radio 3, 1968—. *Wartime service:* British Merchant Marine, 1944.

MEMBER: Authors League of America, Poetry Society of America, PEN American Center, Writers Guild, Royal Bermuda Yacht Club.

AWARDS, HONORS: A Fall from Aloft nominated for an American Academy of Arts and Letters award for excellence; fellow, Royal Society of Literature, 1979; Individual Artists grant, Connecticut Commission on Arts, 1984.

WRITINGS:

NOVELS

Undertow, Barrie & Rockliff, 1971.
The Sailor and the Fox, Farrar, Straus, 1973.
Surprise, Harper, 1974.
Stephen Decatur, the Devil, and the Endymion, Allen & Unwin, 1975.
The Flight of the Cavalier, W. H. Allen, 1980.

"THE BERMUDIANS" NOVEL SERIES

A Fall from Aloft, Barrie & Rockliff, 1968, Random House, 1969.
A Few Flowers for St. George, Barrie & Rockliff, 1970.
Love Is a Durable Fire, Norton, 1986.
Whatwanderwith, Norton, 1987.

OTHER

St. Nicholas and the Tub (juvenile), Holiday House, 1964.

Also author of *Latitude Unknown.* Author of two screenplays. Contributor of poems to literary journals in the United States, Canada, and England since 1967, including *Vogue* (London). Assistant editor, *Bermudian,* 1957-58.

WORK IN PROGRESS: Additional novels for "The Bermudians" series, which Burland says will eventually be a sextet; a series of poems to be titled *My Life: A Poem;* three books of poetry entitled *Lovesongs, Lays and Bawdies; Songs More Somber;* and *Heroes* are waiting for publishers; narrative poem about Bermuda from 1609-1959.

SIDELIGHTS: Brian Burland's *A Fall from Aloft* relates one boy's progress through adolescence while working on a freighter. Janice Elliott of the *New Statesman* admires Burland's "eye for detail and the relentless conviction of his writing." Describing Burland's prose as "tautly poetic," Elliott remarks that the author "knows how to peg allegory to the ground with realism.'' The *Saturday Review*'s R. E. Long concurs with several of Elliott's observations. Calling *A Fall from Aloft* ''a brilliant depiction of a thirteen-year-old boy's traumatic coming of age,'' Long notes that it will ''inevitably be compared with [Golding's] *Lord of the Flies* and [Hughes's] *A High Wind in Jamaica*.''

Burland told *CA:* ''*A Fall from Aloft* and *A Few Flowers for St. George* are required reading at many universities in the United States, Great Britain, Canada, and Holland. Just before his death, Dr. Mark Van Doren nominated *A Fall from Aloft* for an award for excellence to the American Acadmey of Arts and Letters.''

Burland can ''reproduce by voice, nineteen dialects/accents of the English language'' and adds that most of his ancestors for the past 350 years have been half American and half British. Burland has ''lived for lengthy periods in London, New England, Bermuda, Eire [Ireland], and Canada'' and has traveled extensively in the United States, Britain, Ireland, the West Indies, Canada, Greece, and Spain.

MEDIA ADAPTATIONS: Burland has sold thirteen film options; QM (Quinn-Martin) Productions purchased movie rights to *The Sailor and the Fox,* for which Dean Riesner has written the screenplay.

AVOCATIONAL INTERESTS: World War I, classical and modern Greece, American Indians, Afro-American history, slavery, classical music, movies, ships and the sea, sailing, boxing, cricket.

BIOGRAPHICAL/CRITICAL SOURCES:

PERIODICALS

Los Angeles Times, March 31, 1986.
New Statesman, October 25, 1968.
Newsweek, February 5, 1973.
New York Times Book Review, November 1, 1964, January 4, 1970, January 12, 1975, April 26, 1987.
Saturday Review, January 10, 1970.
Times Literary Supplement, November 28, 1968, September 14, 1973.

C

CALAIS, Jean
See RODEFER, Stephen

*   *   *

CALDER, Jason
See DUNMORE, John

*   *   *

CALVIN, Henry
See HANLEY, Clifford

*   *   *

CALVINO, Italo   1923-1985

PERSONAL: Born October 15, 1923, in Santiago de Las Vegas, Cuba; grew up in San Remo, Italy; died following a cerebral hemorrhage, September 19, 1985, in Siena, Italy; son of Mario (a botanist) and Eva (a botanist; maiden name, Mameli) Calvino; married Chichita Singer (a translator), February 19, 1964; children: Giovanna. *Education:* University of Turin, graduated, 1947.

ADDRESSES: Home—Rome, Italy (winters); Castiglione della Pescaia, Siena, Italy (summers). *Agent*—Agenzia Letteraria Internazionale, 41 via Manzoni, 20121 Milan, Italy.

CAREER: Writer. Member of editorial staff of Giulio Einaudi Editore, 1947-83; lecturer. *Military service:* Italian Resistance, 1943-45.

AWARDS, HONORS: Viareggio Prize, 1957; Bagutta Prize, 1959, for *I racconti;* Veillon Prize, 1963; Premio Feltrinelli per la Narrativa, 1972; honorary member of the American Academy and Institute of Arts and Letters, 1975; Oesterreichiches Staatspreis fuer Europaeische Literatur, 1976; *Italian Folktales* was included on the American Library Association's Notable Book List for 1980; Grande Aigle d'Or du Festival du Livre de Nice (France), 1982; honorary degree from Mt. Holyoke College, 1984; Premio Riccione (Italy), for *Il sentiero dei nidi de ragno.*

WRITINGS:

FICTION

Il sentiero dei nidi di ragno, Einaudi (Turin, Italy), 1947, translation by Archibald Colquhoun published as *The Path to the Nest of Spiders,* Collins, 1956, Beacon Press, 1957, reprinted, Ecco Press, 1976.

Ultimo viene il corvo (short stories; title means "Last Comes the Crow"; also see below), Einaudi, 1949.

Il visconte dimezzato (novel; title means "The Cloven Viscount"; also see below), Einaudi, 1952.

L'entrata en guerra (short stories; title means "Entering the War"), Einaudi, 1954.

Il barone rampante (novel; also see below), Enaudi, 1957, translation by Colquhoun published as *The Baron in the Trees,* Random House, 1959, original Italian text published under original title with introduction, notes and vocabulary by J. R. Woodhouse, Manchester University Press, 1970.

Il cavaliere inesistente (novel; title means "The Nonexistent Knight"; also see below), Einaudi, 1959.

La giornata d'uno scutatore (novella; title means "The Watcher"; also see below), Einaudi, 1963.

La speculazione edilizia (novella; title means "A Plunge into Real Estate"; also see below), Einaudi, 1963.

Ti con zero (stories), Einaudi, 1967, translation by William Weaver published as *T Zero,* Harcourt, 1969 (published in England as *Time and the Hunter,* J. Cape, 1970).

Le cosmicomiche (stories), Einaudi, translation by Weaver published as *Cosmicomics,* Harcourt, 1968.

La memoria del mondo (stories; title means "Memory of the World"), Einaudi, 1968.

(Contributor) *Tarocchi,* F. M. Ricci (Parma), 1969, translation by Weaver published as *Tarots: The Viscount Pack in Bergamo and New York* (limited edition), F. M. Ricci, 1975.

La citta invisibili (novel), Einaudi, 1972, translation by Weaver published as *Invisible Cities,* Harcourt, 1974.

Il castello dei destini incrociati (includes text originally published in *Tarocchi*), Einaudi, 1973, translation by Weaver published as *The Castle of Crossed Destinies,* Harcourt, 1976.

Marcovaldo ovvero le stagioni in citta, Einaudi, 1973, translation by Weaver published as *Marcovaldo: or, The Seasons in the City,* Harcourt, 1983.

Se una notte d'inverno un viaggiatore (novel), 1979, translation by Weaver published as *If on a winter's night a traveler,* Harcourt, 1981.

Palomar (novel), Einaudi, 1983, translation by Weaver published as *Mr. Palomar,* Harcourt, 1985.

Cosmicomiche vecchie e nuove (title means "Cosmicomics Old and New"), Garzanti, 1984.

Sotto il sole giaguaro (stories), Garzanti, 1986.

OMNIBUS VOLUMES

Adam, One Afternoon and Other Stories (contains translation by Colquhoun and Peggy White of stories in *Ultimo viene il corvo* and "La formica argentina"; also see below), Collins, 1957, reprinted, Secker & Warburg, 1980.

I racconti (title means "Stories"; includes "La nuvola de smog" and "La formica argentina"; also see below), Einaudi, 1958.

I nostri antenati (contains *Il cavaliere inesistente, Il visconte dimezzato,* and *Il barone rampante;* also see below), Einaudi, 1960, reprinted, 1982, translation by Colquhoun with new introduction by the author published as *Our Ancestors,* Secker & Warburg, 1980.

The Nonexistent Knight and The Cloven Viscount: Two Short Novels (contains translation by Colquhoun of *Il visconte dimezzato* and *Il cavaliere inesistente*), Random House, 1962.

La nuvola de smog e La formica argentina (also see below), Einaudi, 1965.

Gli amore dificile (contains stories originally published in *Ultimo viene il corvo* and *I racconti*), Einaudi, 1970, translation by Weaver, Colquhoun, and Wright published as *Difficult Loves,* Harcourt, 1984, translation by Weaver and D. C. Carne-Ross published with their translations of "La nuvola de smog" and *La speculazione edilizia* under same title (also see below), Secker & Warburg.

The Watcher and Other Stories (contains translations by Weaver, Colquhoun, and Wright of *La giornata d'uno scutatore,* "La nuvola de smog," and "La formica argentina"), Harcourt, 1971.

EDITOR OR CO-EDITOR

Cesare Pavese, *La letteratura americana e altri saggi,* Einaudi, 1951.

(And reteller) *Fiabe italiane: Raccolte della tradizione popolare durante gli ultimi cento anni e transcritte in lingua dai vari dialetti,* Einaudi, 1956, translation by Louis Brigante of selections published as *Italian Fables,* Orion Press, 1959, translation by George Martin of complete text published as *Italian Folktales,* Harcourt, 1980.

Pavese, *Poesie edite e inedite,* Einaudi, 1962.

Pavese, *Lettere* (with Lorenzo Mondo and Davide Lajolo) Volume I: *1924-1944,* (sole editor) Volume II: *1945-1950,* Einaudi, 1966.

Vittorini: Progettazione e letteratura, All'insegno del pesce d'oro, 1968.

(And reteller) Ludovico Ariosto, *Orlando furioso,* Einaudi, 1970.

Jakob Ludwig Karl Grimm and Wilhelm Karl Grimm, *Fiabe,* Einaudi, 1970.

L'uccel belverde e altre fiabe italiane, Einaudi, 1972, translation by Sylvia Mulcahy of selections published as *Italian Folk Tales,* Dent (London), 1975.

Il principe granchio e altre fiabe italiane, Einaudi, 1974.

Racconti fantastici dell'Ottocento, Mondadori (Milan), 1983.

Also editor of fiction series "Cento Pagi" for Einaudi.

OTHER

Collezione di sabbia: Emblemi bizzarri e inquietanti del nostro passato e del nostro futuro gli og getti raccontano il mondo (articles), Garzanti, 1984.

Una pietra sopra: Discorsi di letteratura e societa (essays), Einaudi, 1980, translation by Patrick Creagh published as *The Uses of Literature: Essays,* Harcourt, 1986.

Co-editor with Elio Vittorini of literary magazine, *Il Menabo,* 1959-66.

SIDELIGHTS: Italian novelist and short story writer Italo Calvino was famous for the monumental collection of Italian fables he edited as well as for the fables he wrote. Commenting in the *New York Times Book Review,* for example, novelist John Gardner called Calvino "one of the world's best fabulists." Although he wrote in what Patchy Wheatley referred to in the *Listener* as a "dazzling variety of fictional styles," his stories and novels were all fables for adults. Gore Vidal noted in a *New York Review of Books* essay that because Calvino both edited and wrote fables he was "someone who reached not only primary school children . . . but, at one time or another, everyone who reads."

Calvino's theory of literature, established very early in his career, dictated his use of the fable. For Calvino, to write any narrative was to write a fable. In *Guide to Contemporary Italian Literature: From Futurism to Neorealism,* Sergio Pacifico quoted a portion of Calvino's 1955 essay "Il midollo del leone" ("The Lion's Marrow") in which the novelist wrote: "The mold of the most ancient fables: the child abandoned in the woods or the knight who must survive encounters with beasts and enchantments remains the irreplaceable scheme of all human stories."

To understand Calvino, therefore, one must first understand the fable. Calvino "portrayed the world around him," Sara Maria Adler noted in *Calvino: The Writer as Fablemaker,* "in the same way it is portrayed in the traditional fable. In all his works, the nature of his narrative coincides with those ingredients which constitute the underlying structure of the genre."

A traditional fable, Adler explained, is told from a child's point of view and usually has a young protagonist. Although not all of Calvino's protagonists or narrators are young, John Gatt-Rutter mantained in the *Journal of European Studies,* "The childlike psychology is characteristic of all [of them], whatever their supposed age." The presence of such a youthful narrator/protagonist in Calvino's work lent a fanciful touch to his fiction because, according to Pacifici, "only a youngster possesses a real sense of enchantment with nature, a sense of tranquility and discovery of the mysteries of life."

Another aspect of the fable is what Adler called "the basic theme of tension between character and environment." A typical tale might have a child lost in the woods, for example. Such tension is also a constant in Calvino's fiction. Adler noted, "No matter what the nature of the author's fantasy may be, in every case his characters are faced with a hostile, challenging environment [over] which they are expected to triumph." In "The Argentine Ant," for instance, a family moves to a house in the country only to find it inhabited by thousands of ants. In a more comic example from *Mr. Palomar,* the title character must decide how to walk by a sunbather who has removed her bathing suit top—without appearing either too interested or too indifferent.

Calvino began his career as a fabulist in the late 1940s while still under the influence of the leading writers of postwar Italy.

These authors, who had been kept from writing about the world around them by government censorship, now turned wholeheartedly to their everyday life for themes and action for their narratives. Together they formed the neorealist literary movement and, according to Nicholas A. DeMara in the *Italian Quarterly*, drew "material directly from life and . . . reproduce[d] faithfully real situations through traditional methods."

Conceived in this milieu, Calvino's first novel, *The Path to the Nest of Spiders*, and his short story collections, *Adam, One Afternoon* and *L'entrata in guerra* ("Entering the War"), are all realistic. A *Times Literary Supplement* reviewer noted, for example, that the narratives were "sometimes based on autobiography, and mainly set against the background of recent Italian history and politics." But even while the three works portrayed the realities of war, Calvino's imagination was the dominant element.

The Italian novelist Cesare Pavese was one of the first to note the appearance of fantasy in Calvino's work. Adler reported that, in a 1947 review of *The Path to the Nest of Spiders*, Pavese praised the book's originality, noting "the shrewdness of Calvino, squirrel of the pen, has been this, to climb upon the plants, more in play than out of fear, and to observe . . . life like a fable of the forest, noisy, multi-colored, [and] 'different'."

Following the standard form of a fable, *The Path to the Nest of Spiders* has a young protagonist, an adolescent boy named Pin. According to critics DeMara and Adler, Calvino's choice of Pin as his protagonist allowed the novelist to add fanciful elements to an otherwise realistic story. "In [*The Path to the Nest of Spiders*]," DeMara stated, "Calvino portray[ed] an essentially realistic world, but through the use of the adolescent figure he [was] frequently able to inject into the work a sense of fantasy." Pin is nearly a child, and he describes his world as many children do, using a combination of real and imaginary elements. A fable-like quality is added to the novel, Adler observed, because "seen through the boy's own eyes . . . [everything] is thus infused with a fanciful and spirited attitude toward life. . . . The countryside may be as lyrical as an animated cartoon, while at other times it may assume the proportions of a nightmare."

Calvino's childlike imagination and sense of playfulness filled his work with fantasy but also served another purpose. According to J. R. Woodhouse in *Italo Calvino: A Reappraissal and Appreciation of the Trilogy*, "Calvino's description of child-like candour is often a very telling way of pointing to an anomaly, a stupidity in society, as well as providing a new and refreshing outlook on often well-worn themes." In this way Calvino added another fable-like dimension to his work, that of moral instruction.

Young people play prominent roles in all three of the novels in Calvino's *Our Ancestors* trilogy: *The Cloven Viscount*, *The Baron in the Trees*, and *The Nonexistent Knight*. The "tension between character and environment" and the moral intent are also clear in the three works. They demonstrate the reasoning behind JoAnn Cannon's assertion in *Modern Fiction Studies* that "the fantastic in Calvino is not a form of escapism, but is grounded in a persistent sociopolitical concern."

The narrator of *The Baron in the Trees*, for instance, is the younger brother of the twelve-year-old baron of the title who ascends into the trees to avoid eating snail soup. In *Books Abroad*, Pacifici noted that *The Baron in the Trees* stands for man who, by choosing and acting an extraordinarily eccentric

role, tries to fulfill a certain aspiration of diversity apparently denied to man in our age." And in his introduction to *Our Ancestors*, Calvino explained the meaning of *The Cloven Viscount*, a narrative about a soldier split in half by a cannonball during a crusade: "Mutilated, incomplete, an enemy to himself is modern man; Marx called him 'alienated,' Freud 'repressed'; a state of ancient harmony is lost, [and] a new state of completeness aspired to."

Calvino's ability to fuse reality and fantasy captured the imagination of critics on both sides of the Atlantic. For example, in the *New York Times Book Review* Alan Cheuse wrote about Calvino's "talent for transforming the mundane into the marvelous," and in the *London Review of Books* Salman Rushdie referred to Calvino's "effortless ability of seeing the miraculous in the quotidian." According to *New York Times* reviewer Anatole Broyard, the books in which Calvino perfected this tendency were three later works: *Cosmicomics*, *Invisible Cities*, and *If on a winter's night a traveler*. With their juxtaposition of fantasy and reality these books led critics such as John Updike and John Gardner to compare Calvino with two other master storytellers noted for using the same technique in their fiction: Jorge Luis Borges and Gabriel Garcia Marquez.

The stories in *Cosmicomics*—as well as most of the stories in *T Zero* and *La memoria del mondo* (*Memory of the World*)—chronicle the adventures of Qfwfq, a strange, chameleon-like creature who was present at the beginning of the universe, the formation of the stars, and the disappearance of the dinosaurs. In a playful scene typical of Calvino—and reminiscent of the comic episodes of Garcia Marquez's *One Hundred Years of Solitude*—Qfwfq describes how time began: According to his story, all the universe was contained in a single point until the day one of the inhabitants of the point, Mrs. Ph(i)Nko, decided to make pasta for everyone. Rushdie explained, "The explosion of the universe outwards . . . is precipitated by the first generous impulse, the first-ever 'true outburst of general love,' when . . . Mrs. Ph(i)Nko cries out: 'Oh, if I only had some room, how I'd love to make some noodles for you boys.'"

Even as his fiction became more and more fantastic in the Qfwfq stories, Calvino continued to maintain the moral and social overtones present in his earlier work. In *Science-Fiction Studies*, Teresa de Lauretis observed that while Calvino's fiction acquired a science-fiction quality during the 1960s and 1970s due to its emphasis on scientific and technological themes, it was still based on specific human concerns. "The works," she commented, "were all highly imaginative, scientifically informed, funny and inspired meditations on one insistent question: What does it mean to be human, to live and die, to reproduce and to create, to desire and to be?"

In a *New Yorker* review Updike made a similar observation about the seriousness underlying Calvino's fantasies. Updike wrote: "Calvino is . . . curious about the human truth as it becomes embedded in its animal, vegetable, historical, and comic contexts; all his investigations spiral in upon the central question of *How shall we live?*"

Invisible Cities was the book which Calvino called his "most finished and perfect" in a *Saturday Review* interview with Alexander Stille. It was also, according to Lorna Sage in the *Observer*, "the book that first brought him large-scale international acclaim."

Invisible Cities relates an imaginary conversation between the thirteenth-century explorer Marco Polo and the emperor Kublai Khan in which Polo describes fifty-five different cities within the emperor's kingdom. Critics applauded the book for the beauty of Calvino's descriptions. In the *New Republic,* for instance, Albert H. Carter III called it "a sensuous delight, a sophisticated literary puzzle," while in the *Chicago Tribune* Constance Markey judged it "a fragile tapestry of mood pieces." Perhaps the most generous praise came from *Times Literary Supplement* contributor Paul Bailey, who observed, "This most beautiful of [Calvino's] books throws up ideas, allusions, and breathtaking imaginative insights on almost every page."

Invisible Cities is another fable with a youthful Marco Polo and a moral to be pondered. Adler explained: "Polo's task is that of teaching the aging Kublai Khan to give a new meaning to his life by challenging the evil forces in his domain and by insuring the safety of whatever is just. . . . [Polo's] observations . . . are a general explanation of the world—a panoramic view where rich and poor, the living and the dead, young and old, are challenged by the complex battles of existence."

In the *Hudson Review,* Dean Flower compared *Invisible Cities* with one of Calvino's later novels, *The Castle of Crossed Destinies,* calling them both "less novels than meditations on the mysteries of fictive structures." This statement could also be applied to Calvino's most experimental novel, *If on a winter's night a traveler. The Castle of Crossed Destinies,* like *The Nonexistent Knight,* is a chivalric tale filled with knights and adventure. *If on a winter's night a traveler,* however, is not only different from Calvino's previous work, it is also marked by a complexity that makes it his least fable-like book.

In *If on a winter's night a traveler,* Calvino parodied modern fictional styles in a complicated novel-within-a-novel format. But even this novel included at least one element of the fable. In *Newsweek* Jim Miller noted that in Calvino's introduction to *Italian Folktales* the novelist wrote, "There must be present [in the . . . tale] the infinite possibilities of mutation, the unifying element in everything: men, beasts, plants, things." While the fable explores mutation in nature, in *If on a winter's night a traveler* Calvino explored the "infinite possibilities of mutation" within the novel.

Calvino's childlike imagination allowed him to leave the tenets of neorealism behind and opened up infinite possibilities for his fiction. He imaginatively used the traditional fable form to write non-traditional fiction. Although he was a fabulist, according to Pacifici in *A Guide to Modern Italian Literature,* Calvino's works were "not . . . flights from reality but [came] from the bitter reality of our twentieth century. They are the means—perhaps the only means left to a writer tired of a photographic obsession with modern life—to re-create a world where people can still be people—that is, where people can still dream and yet understand."

AVOCATIONAL INTERESTS: Movies, especially American ones.

BIOGRAPHICAL/CRITICAL SOURCES:

BOOKS

Adler, Sara Maria, *Calvino: The Writer as Fablemaker,* Ediciones Jose Porrua Turanzas, 1979.
Contemporary Literary Criticism, Gale, Volume V, 1976, Volume VIII, 1978, Volume XI, 1979, Volume XXII, 1982, Volume XXX, 1984, Volume XXXIX, 1986.
Gatt-Rutter, John, *Writers and Politics in Modern Italy,* Holmes & Meier, 1978.
Mandel, Siegfried, editor, *Contemporary European Novelists,* Southern Illinois University Press, 1986.
Pacifici, Sergio, *A Guide to Contemporary Italian Literature: From Futurism to Neorealism,* World, 1962.
Woodhouse, J. R., *Italo Calvino: A Reappraisal and an Appreciation of the Trilogy,* University of Hull, 1968.

PERIODICALS

Atlantic, March, 1977.
Chicago Tribune, November 10, 1985.
Commonweal, November 8, 1957, June 19, 1981.
Globe and Mail (Toronto), July 7, 1984, January 25, 1986.
Hudson Review, summer, 1984.
Italian Quarterly, winter, 1971.
Journal of European Studies, December, 1975.
Listener, February 20, 1975, March 17, 1983, September 26, 1985.
London Review of Books, September 30, 1981.
Los Angeles Times Book Review, November 27, 1983, October 6, 1985, October 20, 1985.
Modern Fiction Studies, spring, 1978.
Nation, February 19, 1977, May 23, 1981, December 29, 1984-January 5, 1985.
New Criterion, December, 1985.
Newsweek, February 14, 1977, November 17, 1980, June 8, 1981, November 28, 1983, October 8, 1984, October 21, 1985.
New Yorker, February 24, 1975, April 18, 1977, February 23, 1981, August 3, 1981, September 10, 1984, October 28, 1985, November 18, 1985.
New York Review of Books, November 21, 1968, January 29, 1970, May 30, 1974, May 12, 1977, June 25, 1981, December 6, 1984, November 21, 1985.
New York Times, October 11, 1959, August 6, 1968, January 13, 1971, May 5, 1981, November 9, 1983, September 25, 1984, November 26, 1984, September 26, 1985.
New York Times Book Review, November 8, 1959, August 5, 1962, August 12, 1968, August 25, 1968, October 12, 1969, February 7, 1971, November 17, 1974, April 10, 1977, October 12, 1980, June 21, 1981, January 22, 1984, October 7, 1984.
New York Times Magazine, July 10, 1983.
Observer, September 22, 1985.
PMLA, May, 1975.
Saturday Review, December 6, 1959, November 15, 1969, May, 1981, March/April, 1985.
Science-Fiction Studies, March, 1986.
Spectator, February 22, 1975, May 14, 1977, August 15, 1981, September 24, 1983.
Time, January 31, 1977, October 6, 1980, May 25, 1981, October 1, 1984, September 23, 1985.
Times (London), July 9, 1981, September 1, 1983, October 3, 1985.
Times Literary Supplement, April 24, 1959, February 23, 1962, September 8, 1966, April 18, 1968, February 9, 1973, December 14, 1973, February 21, 1975, January 9, 1981, July 10, 1981, September 2, 1983, July 12, 1985, September 26, 1986.
Village Voice, December 16, 1981.
Voice Literary Supplement, October, 1986.
Washington Post, January 13, 1984.
Washington Post Book World, April 25, 1971, October 12, 1980, June 7, 1981, November 18, 1984, September 22, 1985, November 16, 1986.

OBITUARIES:

PERIODICALS

Chicago Tribune, September 21, 1985.

Detroit Free Press, September 20, 1985.
Los Angeles Times, September 21, 1985.
New York Times, September 20, 1985.
Times (London), September 20, 1985.
Washington Post, September 20, 1985.†

—*Sketch by Marian Gonsior*

*   *   *

CANETTI, Elias 1905-

PERSONAL: Born July 25, 1905, in Russe, Bulgaria; son of Jacques (a businessman) and Mathilde (Arditti) Canetti; married Venetia Taubner-Calderon, February 26, 1934 (died May 1, 1963); married; wife's name Hera; children: (second marriage) Johanna. *Education:* Attended schools in England, Austria, Switzerland, and Germany; University of Vienna, Dr. Philosophy, 1929. *Religion:* Jewish.

ADDRESSES: Home—London, England, and Zurich, Switzerland. *Office*—c/o Farrar, Straus & Giroux, 19 Union Sq. West, New York, N.Y. 10003.

CAREER: Writer and lecturer, 1931—.

AWARDS, HONORS: Prix International (Paris), 1949, for *Die Blendung;* Deutscher der Stadt (Vienna), 1966; Deutscher Kritikerpreis (Berlin), 1967; Grosser Oesterreichischer Staatspreis (Vienna), 1968; George Buechner Prize (Darmstadt), 1972; Franz Nabl Prize (Graz), 1975; Nelly Sachs Prize (Dortmund), 1975; Gottfried Keller Preis (Zurich), 1977; Order Pour le merito (Bonn), 1979; Johann Peter Hebel Preis, 1980; Premio Europa Prato (Italy), 1980; Kafka Prize and Nobel Prize for literature, both 1981; Order of Merit, Federal Republic of Germany; D.Litt., University of Manchester; Dr. Philosophy, University of Munich.

WRITINGS:

Hochzeit (play; first produced in Braunschweig, West Germany, February 6, 1965), [Berlin], 1932, reprinted, Hanser Verlag, 1981, English translation by Gitta Honegger published as *The Wedding,* PAJ Publications, 1986.
Die Blendung (novel; title means "The Deception"), H. Reichner, 1935, English translation, under the personal supervision of Canetti, by C. V. Wedgwood published as *Auto-da-fe,* J. Cape, 1946, published as *The Tower of Babel,* Knopf, 1947, reprint published as *Auto-da-fe,* Stein & Day, 1964, reprinted, Seabury, 1979.
Fritz Wotruba (criticism), Brueder Rosenbaum, 1955.
Masse und Macht (nonfiction), Claassen Verlag, 1960, English translation by Carol Stewart published as *Crowds and Power,* Viking, 1962, reprinted, Seabury, 1978.
Welt im Kopf, edited and with an introduction by Erich Fried, Stiasny Verlag, 1962.
Komoedie der Eitelkeit (three-part play, written 1933-34; first produced in Braunschweig, November 3, 1965), Hanser Verlag, 1964, Sessler (Munich), 1976, English translation by Honegger published as *Comedy of Vanity and Life-Terms,* PAJ Publications, 1983.
The Numbered (play; first produced at Oxford Playhouse, Oxford, England, November 5, 1956), published as *Die Befristeten,* Hanser Verlag, 1964, published as *The Numbered,* Marion Boyars, 1984.
Dramen (contains *Hochzeit, Komoedie der Eitelkeit,* and *Die Befristeten*), Hanser Verlag, 1964.
Aufzeichnungen, 1942-1948 (notebooks), Hanser Verlag, 1965.

Die Stimmen von Marrakesch (travel), Hanser Verlag, 1968, English translation by J. A. Underwood published as *The Voices of Marrakesh: A Record of a Visit,* Seabury, 1978.
Der Andere Prozess, Neue Rundschau, 1968, English translation by Christopher Middleton published as *Kafka's Other Trial: The Letters to Felice,* Schocken, 1974.
Macht und Ueberleben: Drei Essays, Literarische Colloquium, 1972.
Die Gespaltene Zukunft: Aufsaetz und Gesppraeche, Hanser Verlag, 1972.
Die Provinz des Menschen: Aufzeichnungen 1942-1972, Hanser Verlag, 1973, English translation by Joachim Neugroschel published as *The Human Province,* Seabury, 1978.
(Author of commentary) Alfred Hrdlicka, *Graphik,* Propylaeen (Berlin), 1973.
Der Ohrenzeuge: 50 Charaktere, Hanser Verlag, 1974, English translation by Neugroschel published as *Earwitness: Fifty Characters,* Seabury, 1979.
Das Gewissen der Worte: Essays, Hanser Verlag, 1975, English translation by Neugroschel published as *The Conscience of Words,* Seabury, 1979.
Die Gerettete Zunge: Geschichte einer Jugend (autobiography), Hanser Verlag, 1977, English translation by Neugroschel published as *The Tongue Set Free: Remembrance of a European Childhood,* Seabury, 1979.
Die Fackel im Ohr: Lebensgeschichte 1921-1931 (autobiography), Hanser Verlag, 1980, English translation by Neugroschel published as *The Torch in My Ear,* Farrar, Straus, 1982.
Das Augenspiel: Lebensgeschichte 1931-1937 (autobiography), Hanser Verlag, 1985, English translation by Ralph Manheim published as *The Play of the Eyes,* Farrar, Straus, 1986.

SIDELIGHTS: Nobel Prize-winner Elias Canetti has achieved a considerable literary reputation primarily on the strength of two works—his 1935 novel *Die Blendung* (published in English as *Auto-da-fe* and *The Tower of Babel*) and his 1960 psycho-sociological study of crowd behavior, *Masse und Macht* (translated as *Crowds and Power*). These two books established Canetti's position "among the most distinguished writers in contemporary German literature," according to Sidney Rosenfeld in *World Literature Today.* Long admired as a profound thinker in Europe, Canetti was largely overlooked in English-speaking countries until he won the Nobel Prize in 1981. As Susan Sontag notes in the *New York Review of Books,* Canetti's work "has never lacked admirers, and yet aside from scattered reviews he has not been much written about." A recent and aggressive translation program has brought English readers access to most of Canetti's writing, thereby extending his audience beyond the bounds of the literary establishment. Sontag feels that the author's effort "has been to stand apart from other writers and he has succeeded. Shunning the modern means by which a writer gains an audience, he long ago decided that he would, he must, live long enough for his audience to come to him. Canetti is, both literally and by his own ambitions, a writer in exile."

The literal exile to which Sontag alludes began early in Canetti's childhood. Born in Bulgaria to parents whose Jewish forebears were driven from Spain by the Inquisition, Canetti has lived in Austria, Switzerland, Germany, and England. Nazi anti-Semitism compelled him to move to England in 1939, and it was in that country—writing in German—that he composed most of his works. *New Yorker* contributor George Steiner suggests that the "wild hazards" of Canetti's own fate have produced "the stoic force that gives to his writings their compelling edge." Although as Rosenfeld notes, Canetti is a writer "whose sensibilities are keenly attuned to the most critical problems of the modern epoch," Sontag and others credit Canetti with a sophisticated perception of the human psyche that transcends the twentieth century and even the modern age. "Canetti is not Eurocentric—one of his large achievements as a mind," writes Sontag. "Conversant with Chinese as well as with European thought, with Buddhism and Islam as with Christianity, Canetti enjoys a remarkable freedom from reductive habits of thinking. He seems incapable of using psychological knowledge in a reductive way."

Several essential ideas have intrigued Canetti throughout his working career. His novel *Auto-da-fe* explores one of these, "the destructiveness of paranoia. His great theme is the fascism of the soul, the tendency of the human mind to fortify itself with aggressive power plays," in the words of *Voice Literary Supplement* contributor Gary Giddins. *Chicago Review* essayist Ian Watson contends that in *Auto-da-fe* Canetti uses the minutiae of lunatic delusions to expose "the obsessions and fantasies of everyday life, raised to a new pitch of intensity, where they possess the exaggerated savagery of a cartoon strip." In the *Times Literary Supplement*, Idris Parry comments that Canetti is "a specialist in the observation of fixed ideas. . . . He is fascinated by the delusions of people who live in capsules." Canetti is also associated with a strident rejection of death and an energetic support of life and intellectual growth. Sontag notes: "Canetti insists that death is really unacceptable; unassimilable, because it is what is outside life; unjust, because it limits ambition and insults it." She continues: "Canetti does not justify his yearning for longevity with any appeal to its greater scope for good works. So large is the value of the mind that it alone is used to oppose death."

The theme most closely associated with Canetti, however, is that of the psychology of crowd phenomena, a study that consumed the author for more than thirty years. According to Giddins, Canetti's "fidelity to the study of crowd behavior, . . . surely constitutes one of the most stubborn devotions in contemporary scholarship." In *Crowds and Power*, which he considers his "life's work," Canetti exhaustively explores crowd pathology from historical, psychological, and even biological perspectives, locating its impetus—"the yearning for power—in the very mitosis and cellular colonization from which life derives," to quote Giddins.

Through these and other provocative reflections, Canetti has stimulated his own thought and has offered his readers intense challenges. *Spectator* correspondent Iris Murdoch claims that Canetti's work produces "that rare sense of being 'let out' into an entirely new region of thought. Canetti has done what philosophers ought to do, and what they used to do: he has provided us with new concepts." In *Modern Austrian Literature*, Marion E. Wiley offers similar praise. Wiley writes: "[The] critic accustomed to the desperate confusion reflected in the literature of the later twentieth century may be moved to note that the reflective writing of Canetti is a stimulating and complementary addition to contemporary prose. It is stimulating to share ideas with an author who verbalizes his thoughts with clarity, frequent wit, and appropriate compassion. It is also encouraging to encounter the refutation of inevitability and the advocacy of spirited inquiry. In this respect Canetti is the antipode to the writer who records primarily the spiritual malnutrition of contemporary society and the resulting loss of illusions. Canetti possesses a view of life which impels him to search for alternative approaches to existence."

Much is known about Canetti's early life by virtue of his three autobiographical volumes, translated from the original German as *The Tongue Set Free: Remembrance of a European Childhood, The Torch in My Ear,* and *The Play of the Eyes*. In these works covering the first third of his life, Canetti recounts the many influences on his emotional and intellectual growth— the polyglot culture into which he was born, the demands of his exacting mother, and the inspiration offered by teachers and European literati. Canetti was born in Russe, Bulgaria, a Danube port city where it was common to hear seven or eight languages spoken every day. In his home, his parents addressed him in Ladino, a Spanish dialect of Sephardic exiles; the servants spoke Bulgarian. Additionally, Canetti's parents used German to communicate private thoughts to one another, "and from this association with secrecy the language seemed to him a vehicle of magical incantation," according to Parry. Sontag also notes that Canetti's family example "and the velocity of his childhood all facilitated an avid relation to language." By the time he turned ten, Canetti knew four languages, including the English he learned during a year his family spent in Manchester. It was German, however, that captured his imagination, even though his mother's methods of teaching it were particularly severe. "I was reborn under my mother's influence to the German language, and the spasm of that birth produced the passion tying me to both the language and my mother," Canetti claims in *The Tongue Set Free*. "Without these two, basically one and the same, the further course of my life would have been senseless and incomprehensible."

From 1913 to 1921, Canetti attended school in Vienna and Zurich, pursuing his greatest interests, literature and writing. His father had died and his mother was consumed with concern that a literary bent would cause her son to become "soft." Determined to expose Canetti to harsh reality, she moved him from Zurich to Frankfurt, a city struggling with the ravages of World War I. Canetti finished his secondary schooling there in 1924 and returned to Vienna to study chemistry—at his mother's insistence—even though he was determined to be a writer. Although chemistry held little appeal for him, he obtained a doctorate in the subject from the University of Vienna in 1929. Canetti's college years in Vienna were made more pivotal by his interest in the work of Viennese satirist Karl Kraus, a sensational orator, critic, and author of the journal *Die Fackel (The Torch)*. *New York Review of Books* contributor S. S. Prawer suggests that Kraus's public readings left a "profound and lasting impression" on the young Canetti. During that period Canetti also met Bertolt Brecht, Geroge Grosz, and Isaac Babel, and he especially enjoyed a productive working relationship with Babel.

In *The Torch in My Ear*, Canetti describes the "most crucial day" in his life, July 15, 1927. On that day he was enveloped by and "dissolved" into a crowd of irate workers who burned down Vienna's Palace of Justice in protest over a controversial verdict. In that experience, contends Parry, Canetti "found both theme and image for his life's work. . . . From that moment he resolved to dedicate his energies to the study of crowds and mass phenomena." An idea for fiction also came to Canetti in 1927, according to Parry, but the novel was influenced more by Canetti's impressions of paintings—most notably Rembrandt's "The Blinding of Samson" and Breughel's "The Triumph of Death"—as well as his fascination with the grotesque and the power of the fixed idea. At the age of twenty-four, Canetti began to write what he thought would be the first of eight novel-length sketches of monomaniac characters—his tale of the "Book Man's" descent into self-immolation, *Auto-da-fe*.

First published in 1935 as *Die Blendung*, the novel *Auto-da-fe* took on "the monumentality of a classic" almost overnight in Germany, according to Steiner. Its popularity was short-lived, however, because Nazi censors removed it from circulation. After the Second World War, the book slowly began to draw more readers; it was reissued in Germany and an authorized English translation by C. V. Wedgwood appeared in 1946. Modern critics are generous in their praise of the work; some consider it one of the most important novels of the twentieth century. Steiner contends that *Auto-da-fe* "remains a classic study of the violence subtly but steadily present in abstract thought, of the pathological element in pure scholarship." Calling it "uncompromising and brilliant," *Critique* contributor Mark Sacharoff finds the novel the most "obsessional portrayal of obsessive characters in all of literature. . . . *Auto-da-fe*, long buried by a combination of unfavorable circumstances, has again come to light and now has a chance to be re-evaluated."

In *Harper's*, Jeffrey Burke writes that *Auto-da-fe* "describes the descent into madness of a world-renowned but reclusive sinologist whose scholarly life disintegrates at the hands of three vulgar, brutish characters. . . . It is the professor who dominates the novel. Canetti creates him out of the quirks and compulsions of a strong mind steeped in erudition." Sacharoff suggests that all of the four major characters are "driven from minute to minute by a central preoccupation and by all the speculations which radiate from it. . . . Thus, if we are to speak of Canetti's originality, a good starting-point would be the singularity and unswerving purpose with which he has pursued his characters' warped preoccupations." *Spectator* reviewer Kate O'Brien cites the work for its agonizingly slow detail and its sophisticated method: "With dessicated, pedantic caution, [Canetti] reflects fantasy against fact, merges nightmare with routine, cupidity with fanatical innocence, and so establishes his forces as one great hell. . . . All in a curiously dry writing, where no detail is spared, and while asking the most detached patience for phantasmagoria beyond comparable echo. . . . There is no light. Only vileness enthroned, and reason nobly flying to its own obliteration. A mad, magnificent work which we are not able to endure, which perhaps we are right not to accept, but of which we dare not deny the genius or the justification."

In Steiner's view of *Auto-da-fe*, "the holocaust to come somehow cast its hungry shadow on the entire fable." Parry likewise contends that "the destructive fires of history and the ritual fires of mythology" seem to converge in the novel. Parry adds that in the fate of Kien, the central character, "we sense both a timeless human declension into death and a contemporary reference to individuality lost in the forest of flags and figures at Nuremburg, that ordered system of savagery." Whether or not the book prefigured the rise of European fascism, its author certainly foresaw the destruction to come in Germany. Canetti left for Paris in 1938 and moved to England in 1939. Nazism and its extreme measures strengthened Canetti's resolve to delve into the psychology of crowds; however, he retained a loyalty to German culture and continued to write in German, attuned, in Sontag's words, to "the higher cosmopolitanism. . . . With this decision, not the one made by most Jewish intellectuals who were refugees from Hitler, Canetti chose to remain unsullied by hatred, a grateful son of German culture who wants to help make it what one can continue to admire. And he has."

Masse und Macht, translated as *Crowds and Power*, is the culmination of more than thirty years' work for Canetti. According to Bruce Cook in the *Washington Post Book World*, the book "astonished the intellectual world—not just with its scholarship, some of it from the most recondite sources, but also with its insights, which are packed into gnomic essays . . . that can be read independently but stand as building blocks of the whole work." Cook adds: "It is a book that is not easily summarized, ranging as it does over the whole of human history to examine every conceivable aspect of mass psychology. . . . Its style, anecdotal and accessible, slyly implies the author's attitude of skepticism toward human institutions and his contempt for the men whom historians hold great. *Crowds and Power* is the nearest thing to a book of wisdom we are likely to get in the 20th century." Murdoch feels that to deal adequately with the work, "one would have to be, like its author, a mixture of historian, sociologist, psychologist, philosopher and poet. One is certainly confronted here with something large and important: an extremely imaginative, original and massively documented theory of the psychology of crowds."

When evaluating *Crowds and Power*, critics stress its unique blend of historical/psychological discourse and poetic anecdotage. In an essay for *MOSAIC: A Journal for the Comparative Study of Literature and Ideas*, Dagmar Barnouw suggests that Canetti "does not judge crowds directly . . . from a particularly 'elitist' position, or indirectly like the stoical Freud who finds them frighteningly alien and therefore keeps them at bay. He demonstrates their destructive potential, their deadly interaction with systems of power whose operators know, as Hitler for instance showed very clearly, that the member of a mass society which is, of course, a hierarchically structured group of a great number of individuals, is willing to forget the sting of death . . . if he can rid himself, through temporary immersion in the crowd, of the sting of isolation." Burke notes: "Having made the uncommon choice of so common a fact of life as crowds, [Canetti] then supplies his own definitions, arrives at conclusions, and supports his findings with references from decades of reading in world literature, myth, history, and anthropology. In doing so, he arrives at a level of discourse that is less convincing than it is cerebrally poetic." Despite this objection, Burke claims that *Crowds and Power* "is capable of engaging a willing mind." Murdoch calls the book "marvelously rewarding . . . even if one were to read it without any theoretical interests at all. It is written in a simple, authoritative prose, . . . and it is radiant with imagination and humor. . . . We need and we shall always need the visions of great imaginers and solitary men of genius."

"Since the publication of *Crowds and Power*, Canetti has written several . . . works that encircle the major works like satellites," writes Giddins. "But taken together they also suggest a new and less isolated stage in Canetti's devotion to writing." Canetti's other publications include volumes of essays and aphorisms, plays, criticism, a travelogue, a highly regarded study of a portion of Franz Kafka's letters, and the three volumes of autobiography. Cook feels that as each piece of Canetti's work receives translation, the author "is more clearly defined as the important figure in European literature that he certainly is." Giddins sees a common thread that unites all of Canetti's disparate works. The critic comments: "As novelist, philosopher, and autobiographer, Canetti, the intransigent moral witness, offers no moral codes, utopian dreams, or escape hatches for 'our monstrous century.' The only code to which he adheres absolutely—a writer's code—is to stand in undaunted opposition to his time. . . . At 60, Canetti was essentially a two-book writer. His subsequent work can be read as an attempt to integrate the writer into the vision, to demonstrate that 'the representative writer of this age' can personally exemplify the virtues—diligence, disaffection, scholarship, realism—that make grace possible in an insane world.''

Canetti eschewed the publicity surrounding his choice as a Nobel Prize recipient, and he continues to live and write far from the public eye. As William Gass observes in *New Republic,* Canetti "has now achieved such fame as to be unknown all over the world. His obscurity is a part of his character, and is a credit to him, for he might be more widely recognized if his thought were sly and riddling, got up in a seductive lingo all its own so as to seem complex and problematic, not simply, plainly, and vertiginously deep.'' *Spectator* contributor Paul Theroux offers concurrent praise. "Canetti's reputation has been so formidable as to be off-putting;'' Theroux contends, "and the less a person like Canetti is read the more grotesque he seems, until at last he becomes merely a terrifying presence. . . . The strange thing is that Canetti sometimes seems so original as to be an invented figure, yet no single mind could have invented this man, unless it were Canetti himself. . . . My feeling is that Canetti has been associated (unfairly) with gloom—long lugubrious tomes written at the Wailing Wall. That is such an unfair impression of a mind so nimble, imaginative and humane.'' According to Marion E. Wiley, Canetti's reflective prose "attests to the success of his intellectual exploration. In respect to this achievement his prose is a unique contribution to contemporary writing, and his belated reception . . . is a noteworthy entry for a history of German literary reception.''

AVOCATIONAL INTERESTS: Canetti gave *CA* the following list: anthropology, history, psychiatry, history of religions, philosophy, sociology, psychology, and the civilizations of Egypt, Sumer, Greece, Rome, Persia, India, China, Japan, Mexico, Maya, Inca. He added: "It is ridiculous to have so many; but they are all equally important to me and have cost me years and decades of study.''

BIOGRAPHICAL/CRITICAL SOURCES:

BOOKS

Best, Alan and Hans Wolfschuetz, *Modern Austrian Writing: Literature and Society after 1945,* B & N Imports, 1980.
Canetti, Elias, *Die Gerettete Zunge: Geschichte einer Jugend,* Hanser Verlag, 1977, English translation by Joachim Neugroschel published as *The Tongue Set Free: Remembrance of a European Childhood,* Seabury, 1979.
Canetti, Elias, *Die Fackel im Ohr: Lebensgeschichte 1921-1931,* Hanser Verlag, 1980, English translation by Neugroschel published as *The Torch in My Ear,* Farrar, Straus, 1982.
Canetti, Elias, *Das Augenspiel: Lebensgeschichte 1931-1937,* Hanser Verlag, 1985, English translation by Ralph Manheim published as *The Play of the Eyes,* Farrar, Straus, 1986.
Contemporary Literary Criticism, Gale, Volume III, 1975, Volume XIV, 1980, Volume XXV, 1983.
Elias Canetti, R. Boorberg (Stuttgart), 1970.
Schultz, Uwe, editor, *Das Tagebuch und der Moderne Autor,* Hanser Verlag, 1965.
Sontag, Susan, *Under the Sign of Saturn,* Farrar, Straus, 1980.

PERIODICALS

Books Abroad, autumn, 1965.

Book Week, May 29, 1966.
Canadian Forum, April, 1947.
Chicago Review, May, 1969.
Chicago Tribune Book World, January 6, 1980.
Critique: Studies in Modern Fiction, Volume XIV, number 1, 1972.
Globe and Mail (Toronto), October 4, 1986.
Harper's, January, 1980.
Los Angeles Times Book Review, June 6, 1982, October 3, 1982, August 31, 1986.
Manchester Guardian, May 10, 1946.
Modern Austrian Literature, Volume XII, number 2, 1979.
MOSAIC: A Journal for the Comparative Study of Literature and Ideas, winter, 1974.
New Republic, November 8, 1982.
Newsweek, October 26, 1981.
New Yorker, May 19, 1980, November 22, 1982.
New York Herald Tribune Book Review, February 23, 1947.
New York Review of Books, September 25, 1980, February 4, 1982, November 4, 1982, July 17, 1986.
New York Times, October 16, 1981, February 27, 1982, March 20, 1982, September 17, 1982, July 1, 1986, August 10, 1986.
New York Times Book Review, April 29, 1979, September 19, 1982.
Publishers Weekly, October 31, 1981.
San Francisco Chronicle, March 9, 1947.
Saturday Review, December, 1978.
Saturday Review of Literature, March 8, 1947.
Spectator, May 24, 1946, September 7, 1962, November 30, 1985, April 19, 1986.
Sunday Times (London), August 15, 1982.
Time, October 26, 1981.
Times (London), February 18, 1982.
Times Literary Supplement, July 8, 1965, October 31, 1968, January 15, 1971, January 25, 1974, January 10, 1975, February 28, 1975, December 22, 1975, January 9, 1981, October 23, 1981, July 26, 1985.
Voice Literary Supplement, March, 1982, October, 1982.
Washington Post, October 16, 1981.
Washington Post Book World, September 26, 1982.
World Literature Today, winter, 1978, spring, 1979, autumn, 1979, spring, 1981, winter, 1985, May 20, 1984.

—*Sketch by Anne Janette Johnson*

*   *   *

CAREY, Omer L. 1929-

PERSONAL: Born January 24, 1929, in Ellsworth, Ill.; son of George Franklin (a railroad telegrapher) and Nola (Thompson) Carey; married Carol Grant, June 20, 1954; children: Gayle, Craig, Dale, Bryan, Grant. *Education:* Illinois Wesleyan University, B.A., 1954; additional study for teaching certificate at Illinois State University, 1955-56; graduate study at Southern Illinois University, 1957-59, and University of Illinois, 1957; Indiana University, M.B.A., 1960, D.B.A., 1962. *Politics:* Republican. *Religion:* Methodist.

ADDRESSES: Home—7625 Island Dr., Anchorage, Alaska 99504. *Office*—Department of Business Administration, Anchorage Senior College, University of Alaska, Anchorage, Alaska 99504.

CAREER: State Farm Mutual Automobile Insurance Co., Bloomington, Ill., staff member in accounting department, 1947-49, 1952-55; Illinois Power Co., Havana, accountant,

1949-52, 1955; high school teacher in Bethalto, Ill., 1956-59; Indiana University at Bloomington, teaching assistant in business, 1959-62; Idaho State University, Pocatello, assistant professor of business administration and assistant director of Bureau of Business Research, 1962-64; Washington State University, College of Economics and Business, Pullman, 1964-73, began as assistant professor, became professor of business administration, chairman of department, 1968-73; University of Alaska, Anchorage, professor of business administration, 1973-86, Harold T. Caven Professorship in Business and Finance, 1977-86, professor emeritus, 1986—, associate dean, 1977-79, dean of School of Business and Public Administration, 1979-80, graduate program director, 1980-82. Visiting assistant professor of finance, University of Washington, Seattle, summer, 1966; visiting professor of management science and assistant director of Center for Entrepreneurship and Pacific Development, Alaska Pacific University, 1986-87; Fulbright fellow, Managing Development Centre, University of Waikato, New Zealand. Expert witness, business appraiser, and business consultant. Active at local, state, and national levels of Association for Retarded Citizens.

MEMBER: National Education Association, Financial Management Association, Phi Kappa Phi, Beta Gamma Sigma, Blue Key.

WRITINGS:

(With Frank Seelye, Harold White, and Donald Carrell) *Personnel Policies of Small Business*, Small Business Administration and Idaho State University, 1964.

(Contributor) *Trends in Distribution, Services and Transportation*, Bureau of Economic and Business Research, Washington State University, 1966.

(Editor) *Military-Industrial Complex and United States Foreign Policy*, Washington State University, 1969.

(Contributor) *Management and Public Policy*, School of Management, State University of New York at Buffalo, 1971.

(Contributor) Johnson and Weisbrod, editors, *The Daily Economist*, Prentice-Hall, 1973.

(With Green) *Bristol Bay: Its Potential and Development*, State of Alaska, Department of Commerce and Economic Development, 1976.

(Contributor with Dean Olson) Karl Vesper, editor, *The Pacific Northwest: Small Business and Entrepreneurship in Region Ten*, University of Oregon, 1979.

(With Olson) *Financial Tools for Small Businesses*, Reston, 1982.

(With Olson) *Opportunity Management: Strategic Planning for Smaller Business*, Reston, 1985.

Contributor to journals.

*   *   *

CARLINSKY, Dan 1944-

PERSONAL: Born March 9, 1944, in Holyoke, Mass.; son of Louis H. and Ethel (Mag) Carlinsky; married Nancy Cooperstein, August 25, 1972. *Education:* Columbia University, B.A., 1965, M.S., 1966.

ADDRESSES: Home and office—301 East 78th St., New York, N.Y. 10021.

CAREER: Freelance writer and journalist.

WRITINGS:

(With Edwin Goodgold) *Trivia* (also see below), Dell, 1966.

(With Goodgold) *More Trivial Trivia* (also see below), Dell, 1966.

(With Goodgold) *Rock 'n' Roll Trivia*, Popular Library, 1970.

(Compiler) *A Century of College Humor*, Random House, 1971.

(With David Heim) *Bicycle Tours in and around New York*, Hagstrom, 1975, revised edition published as *Twenty Bicycle Tours in and around New York City*, Backcountry, 1984.

(With Goodgold) *The Compleat Beatles Quiz Book*, Warner Books, 1975.

(With Goodgold) *The World's Greatest Monster Quiz*, Berkley Publishing, 1975.

(With Goodgold) *Trivia and More Trivia* (contains *Trivia* and *More Trivial Trivia*), Castle Books, 1975.

The Complete Bible Quiz Book, Berkley Publishing, 1976.

Typewriter Art, Price, Stern, 1977.

The Great 1960's Quiz, Harper, 1978.

The Jewish Quiz Book, Doubleday, 1979.

Do You Know Your Husband?, Price, Stern, 1979.

Do You Know Your Wife?, Price, Stern, 1979.

The Great Bogart Trivia Book, Fawcett, 1980.

Are You Compatible?, Price, Stern, 1981.

Do You Know Your Mother?, Price, Stern, 1981.

Do You Know Your Father?, Price, Stern, 1981.

Celebrity Yearbook, Price, Stern, 1982.

College Humor, Harper, 1982.

Do You Know Your Boss?, Price, Stern, 1983.

(With Goodgold) *The Status Game*, New American Library, 1986.

Stop Snoring Now!, St. Martin's, 1987.

OTHER

Author of syndicated newspaper column, "It's on the Tip of My Tongue." Contributor to periodicals, including *New York Times, Travel and Leisure, Playboy, Redbook, Woman's Day,* and *T.V. Guide.*

BIOGRAPHICAL/CRITICAL SOURCES:

PERIODICALS

Chicago Tribune Book World, December 19, 1982.

*   *   *

CARROLL, John Millar 1925-

PERSONAL: Born December 6, 1925, in Philadelphia, Pa.; son of William (an engineer) and Mary Ann (Millar) Carroll; married Beryl Lois Skuce, October 28, 1944; children: William James, John, Jr., William Kingsley, Robert Loren, Richard Alan, Sandra Joy, Robert Alexander. *Education:* Lehigh University, B.S., 1950; Hofstra University, M.A., 1955; New York University, D.Eng.Sc., 1968.

ADDRESSES: Office—Department of Computer Science, University of Western Ontario, London, Ontario, Canada N6A 5B7.

CAREER: National Bureau of Standards, Washington, D.C., and White Sands, N.M., radio engineering aide, 1947-48; *Electronics*, New York, N.Y., assistant editor, 1952-54, associate editor, 1954-57, managing editor, 1957-64; Lehigh University, Bethlehem, Pa., associate professor of industrial engineering, 1964-68; University of Western Ontario, London, Ontario, professor of computer science, 1968—. Secretary of field-test panel, National Stereophonic Radio Committee, 1959-60; member of commitee on information handling, Engineering Service Library, 1964-68; trustee of Engineering

Index, 1968-71; computer scientist, Naval Research Laboratory, 1982-83. Consultant to Canadian Privacy and Computer Task Force, 1971, and to Canadian Security and Intelligence Service, 1984; advisor on computer security to Royal Canadian Mounted Police, 1975-76. *Military service:* U.S. Navy, 1944-47, 1950-52; became ensign.

MEMBER: Institute of Electrical and Electronics Engineers (senior member, chairman of symbols committee, 1962-64, vice-chairman, information retrieval committee, 1964—, executive vice-chairman, engineering societies library committee on information handling), Tau Beta Pi, Alpha Pi Mu, Pi Tau Sigma, Sigma Pi Sigma, Pi Delta Epsilon.

WRITINGS:

Mechanical Design for Electronics Production, McGraw, 1956.
Electron Devices and Circuits, McGraw, 1962.
Careers and Opportunities in Electronics, Dutton, 1963.
The Story of the Laser, Dutton, 1964, revised edition, 1970.
Secrets of Electronic Espionage, Dutton, 1966.
Careers and Opportunities in Computer Science, Dutton, 1967.
The Third Listener: Personal Electronic Espionage, Dutton, 1969.
Confidential Information Sources: Public and Private, Security World Publishing, 1975.
Data Base and Computer Systems Security, edited by Robert M. Curtice, Q.E.D. Information Sciences, 1976.
Computer Security, Butterworth, 1977, revised edition, 1987.
Controlling White Collar Crime: Design and Audit for Systems Security, Butterworth, 1982.
Managing Risk: A Computer-Aided Strategy, Butterworth, 1984.
Simulation Using Personal Computers, Prentice-Hall, 1987.

EDITOR

Transistor Circuits and Applications, McGraw, 1957.
Modern Transistor Circuits, McGraw, 1959.
Design Manual for Transistor Circuits, McGraw, 1961.
Tunnel-Diode and Semi-conductor Circuits, McGraw, 1963.
Microelectronic Circuits and Applications, McGraw, 1965.
(With Donald G. Fink) *Standard Handbook for Electrical Engineers*, 10th edition, 1968.
Computer Simulation in Energy Planning, Society for Computer Simulation, 1983.
Emergency Planning, Society for Computer Simulation, 1985.

OTHER

Also contributor to *McGraw-Hill Science and Technology Yearbook*.

SIDELIGHTS: "I wrote *Computer Security* to unify the diverse disciplines of a very complex field," John Millar Carroll told *CA*. The professor of computer science at the University of Western Ontario in London, Ontario, since 1968 wrote that a "desire to peek into secret places" partly accounts for his interest in his career. With his books on electronic espionage and computer security systems design, Carroll hopes to "put decision making on a logical well-informed basis." His first writing, he noted, was "Boy Scout news for the *Farmington Post*," and he credits Hemingway's short sentences as an influence. When asked to describe his writing habits, he said, "[I] ride my horse until I get a good idea, then type the idea into my word processor." His advice to aspiring writers is "Don't do it unless you enjoy it."

Carroll's books are used in college and university courses and have been translated into French, Spanish, Italian, German, Japanese, Chinese, Urdu, Hindi, Arabic, Serbo-Croation, and other languages.

*   *   *

CARROLL, Robert
See ALPERT, Hollis

*   *   *

CARTER, Nick
See SMITH, Martin Cruz

*   *   *

CARTWRIGHT, Vanessa
See PRESTON, Harry

*   *   *

CASEY, John (Dudley) 1939-

PERSONAL: Born January 18, 1939, in Worcester, Mass.; son of Joseph Edward (a lawyer) and Constance (Dudley) Casey; married Jane Barnes (a writer), June 17, 1967 (divorced); married Rosamond Pinchot Pittman (an artist and calligrapher), 1982; children: (first marriage) Maud Innis, Eleanor Dudley. *Education:* Harvard University, B.A., 1962, LL.B., 1965; University of Iowa, M.F.A., 1968.

ADDRESSES: Office—Department of English, Wilson Hall, University of Virginia, Charlottesville, Va. 22904. *Agent*—Brandt & Brandt, 1501 Broadway, New York, N.Y. 10036.

CAREER: University of Virginia, Charlottesville, associate professor of English, 1972—. Admitted to Washington, D.C., Bar, 1966. *Military service:* U.S. Army Reserve, active duty, 1959-60.

AWARDS, HONORS: Runner-up, Ernest Hemingway Award, 1978; Guggenheim fellowship, 1979-80; Friends of American Writers award, 1980, for *Testimony and Demeanor;* National Endowment for the Arts fellowship, 1982-83.

WRITINGS:

An American Romance (novel), Atheneum, 1977.
Testimony and Demeanor (short stories and novella), Knopf, 1979.
(Author of afterword) *The Stories of Breece D'J Pancake*, Little, Brown, 1983.
South Country (novel), Knopf, 1988.

Contributor to magazines, including *New Yorker, Sports Illustrated, Harper's, Esquire, Ploughshares,* and *Shenandoah,* and to newspapers.

SIDELIGHTS: John Casey's first novel, *An American Romance,* drew some admiring notices from critics like John Leonard of the *New York Times,* who says that this satire on a love affair among intellectuals "is witty and savage on university life at Radcliffe, in Chicago and Iowa City. It allows pushers and dropouts, failed poets and owners of cattle a human dimension. It is in love wth the theater, from Ben Jonson to [Eugene] Ionesco. . . . But it is principally a love story onto which theories of sensuality, of perception, of ceremony and of need—for sanctuary, approval, forgiveness—have been grafted or glossed. It respects its characters. It swims in the language."

Testimony and Demeanor, Casey's next book, is a collection of three short stories and a novella. These pieces were seen in a mixed light by some critics. Their general consensus is that the title story is the book's best work—"a brilliant piece of writing about a young lawyer plugging away in a New York firm," as John Halperin remarks in a *Los Angeles Times Book Review* article. But the other three entries, he continues, "commit the one fault Henry James declared that no piece of fiction can afford: They bore." *Washington Post* reviewer Dennis Drabelle sees "a pattern . . . emerging from Casey's stories. They center on the initiation of a gifted and cosseted young man into rougher, more compromising circles. This, of course, is a hoary theme, but Casey refreshes it with his attention to nuance." And to Leonard, who assesses the book in a *New York Times* review, the author's "eye for color, texture, earth and sky is in superb working order. His ear hears every nuance. His wit stings. Academic politics, the nature of friendship, social insecurity, adolescent sexuality, literary criticism and art itself are explored with a passionate sophistication."

BIOGRAPHICAL/CRITICAL SOURCES:

PERIODICALS

Chicago Tribune Book World, July 29, 1979.
Los Angeles Times Book Review, July 15, 1979.
New York Times, April 26, 1977, June 15, 1979.
New York Times Book Review, June 24, 1979.
Washington Post, June 18, 1979.

*   *   *

CHANDLER, Linda S(mith)   1929-

PERSONAL: Born February 4, 1929, in Wadesboro, N.C.; daughter of Clinton Ashe and Emma (Sikes) Smith; married Gordon Yearby Chandler (a pressman), October 17, 1948; children: Gordon Lee, Judi Chandler Crouse, Linda Ann Horne. *Education:* Attended Croft Secretarial School, 1947-48, and Duke University. *Politics:* Democrat. *Religion:* Southern Baptist.

ADDRESSES: Home—2208 Tampa Ave., Durham, N.C. 27705. *Office*—Chapel, Duke University, Durham, N.C. 27706.

CAREER: Held part-time secretarial positions in Durham, N.C., 1957-75; Duke University, Durham, hostess at university chapel, 1975—. Taught at Ridgecrest and Glorieta conference centers. Curriculum writer for Southern Baptist Convention Sunday School Board. Member of Durham County Board of Health, 1972-83, Durham County Board of Education, 1976—, North Carolina Interagency Council on Community Schools, 1979-84, board of trustees of North Carolina Baptist Homes, 1981-83, board of directors of North Carolina School Board Association, 1982-86, advisory committee of Child Abuse and Prevention of Parental Stress (CAPPS), Durham Citizens' Safety Council, Durham Democratic Women, and advisory board of Parents Involved in Preschool Education (PIPE).

MEMBER: Society of Children's Book Writers, National Writers Club, North Carolina Poetry Society, North Carolina Community Education Association, Durham County Association for Childhood Education, Delta Kappa Gamma.

WRITINGS:

FOR CHILDREN

My Family Loves Me, Convention Press, 1978.

Hello, My Church, Broadman, 1980.
Uncle Ike, Broadman, 1981.
David Asks, "Why?," Broadman, 1981.
Dr. Harms, the Helper, WMU Press, 1984.
When I Talk to God, Broadman, 1984.

Also author of series "Parents, Enjoy Your Children," in *Living with Preschoolers,* 1984—. Contributor to magazines, including *Christian Advocate, Child Life, Biblical Recorder, Look and Listen, Living With Teenagers, The State Magazine of North Carolina,* and *Church Administration.*

WORK IN PROGRESS: A book about the basic needs of children and a just for fun book about a cat that lived in a Gothic cathedral.

SIDELIGHTS: Linda S. Chandler commented: "Writing for children has been an important part of my life. I have made two child-study trips abroad, visiting schools in Italy, Israel, Switzerland, and England. I am also involved in conducting book fairs in different parts of the country and enjoy going into classrooms to talk to children about writing, books, and the importance of self-expression. I believe we should do everything we can to help children learn to love books and think of them as friends.

"I believe we should encourage children to write—if they have an interest—not for the sake of publication, as fine as that is, but for the sake of expression and sharing. Writing one's thoughts, ideas, hopes, fears, and moments of joy, provides insight for others who may care deeply to know the individual."

BIOGRAPHICAL/CRITICAL SOURCES:

PERIODICALS

Durham Herald, April 20, 1980, October 11, 1981.
Raleigh News and Observer, January 31, 1982.

*   *   *

CHANDONNET, Ann F.   1943-

PERSONAL: Surname is pronounced Shan-doe-*nay;* born February 7, 1943, in Lowell, Mass.; daughter of Leighton D. (a farmer) and Barbara (Cloutman) Fox; married Fernand Chandonnet (a radio announcer), June 11, 1966; children: Yves, Alexdre Jules. *Education:* Lowell State College, B.S. (magna cum laude), 1964; University of Wisconsin, M.S., 1965; graduate study at Boston University, 1967.

ADDRESSES: Home—6552 Lakeway Dr., Anchorage, Alaska 99502.

CAREER: Dog-walker, housepainter, secretary; high school English teacher in the public schools of Kodiak, Alaska, 1965-66; Lowell State College, Lowell, Mass., instructor in English, 1966-69; Security National Bank, Oakland, Calif., secretary to manager, 1970-71; First Enterprise Bank, Oakland, administrative assistant to president, 1971-72; *Anchorage Daily News,* Anchorage, Alaska, food editor, beginning 1975, children's book reviewer, 1979-83; *Anchorage Times,* Anchorage, feature writer, 1982—; free-lance writer.

MEMBER: Literary Artists Guild of Alaska, Alaska Press Women, Mayflower Descendants in the State of Alaska.

AWARDS, HONORS: First place award from Alaska Press Women, 1975, for a feature article, "Keeping an Ancient Art Alive," a profile of one of the last surviving Aleut basketweavers.

WRITINGS:

Incunabula (poems), Quixote Press, 1967.
The Complete Fruit Cookbook, 101 Productions, 1972.
The Cheese Guide and Cookbook, Nitty Gritty Productions, 1973.
The Wife & Other Poems, privately printed, 1977, 2nd edition, 1980.
The Wife: Part 2 (poems), privately printed, 1979.
(Self-illustrated) *The Once & Future Village of Ikluat-Eklutna*, privately printed, 1979.
At the Fruit-Tree's Mossy Root, Wings Press, 1980.
Ptarmigan Valley (poems), Lightning Tree, 1980.
Auras, Tendrils (poems), Penumbra Press, 1984.

Also author of *On the Trail of Eklutna*, 1986. Contributor to *California Girl, Venus, Early American Life, Anchorage Daily News, Great Lander, Women's Circle: Home Cooking, Christian Science Monitor,* and *Alaska Journal.* Food editor, *Diablo Valley Voice,* 1971-72.

WORK IN PROGRESS: *All that Words Can Say,* poems.

AVOCATIONAL INTERESTS: Conducting living history interviews, skindiving, backpacking, sewing, gardening.

*   *   *

CHEKKI, Dan(esh) A(yyappa)   1935-

PERSONAL: Born February 5, 1935, in Haveri, Karnatak, India; son of Virappa C. (a pleader) and Chenabasavva Yagati; married Sheela D. Leelavati Metgud, May 8, 1966; children: Mahantesh, Chenaviresh. *Education:* Karnatak University, B.A., 1956, Ph.D., 1966; University of Bombay, M.A., 1958, LL.B., 1959, D.Lib., 1960.

ADDRESSES: *Home*—38 Fitzgerald Crescent, Winnipeg, Manitoba, Canada R3R IN8. *Office*—Department of Sociology, University of Winnipeg, 515 Portage Ave., Winnipeg, Manitoba, Canada R3B 2E9.

CAREER: University of Bombay, Government Law College, Bombay, India, lecturer in sociology, 1958-61; Karnatak University, Dharwar, India, lecturer in sociology, 1961-66; University of Winnipeg, Winnipeg, Manitoba, assistant professor, 1968-71, associate professor, 1971-78, professor of sociology, 1979—, Institute of Urban Studies, faculty associate, 1983—. Reader at Karnatak University, 1967-72. Member of board of directors of Family Bureau of Greater Winnipeg, 1970-74, and Family Services of Winnipeg, 1976-81.

MEMBER: International Sociological Association (secretary, Community Research Committee, 1984—), Canadian Association of South Asian Studies, National Council of Family Relations, Academy of Research (president), American Sociological Association, Indian Sociological Society, Policy Studies Organization, American Academy of Political and Social Science, World Future Society, Hindu Society of Manitoba (member of board of directors, 1981-82).

AWARDS, HONORS: Research grants from Karnatak University, 1967-68, and from University of Winnipeg, 1970-78.

WRITINGS:

Social Aspects of Ornaments (translation from Kannada language), Karnatak University, 1967.
(Contributor) *The Family in India*, Mouton, 1974.
Modernization and Kin Network, E. J. Brill, 1974.

The Social System and Culture of Modern India, Garland Publishing, 1975.
(Contributor) G. R. Gupta, editor, *Main Currents in Indian Sociology*, Carolina Academic Press, 1976.
The Sociology of Contemporary India, South Asia Books, 1978.
Community Development: Theory and Method of Planned Change, Vikas Publishing House (India), 1980.
Participatory Democracy in Action: International Profiles of Community Development, Vikas Publishing House, 1980.
(Contributor) *Structured Inequality in Canada*, Prentice-Hall, 1980.
Organized Interest Groups and the Urban Policy Process, Institute of Urban Studies, 1985.
Citizen Attitudes toward City Services and Taxes, Institute of Urban Studies and Institute for Economic and Social Research, 1985.
Guru, Bless Me with Your Grace, University of Winnipeg, 1986.
Contemporary Community: Change and Challenge, Garland Publishing, 1988.
Contemporary Community: Dynamics and Issues, JAI Press, 1988.

Also author of *The Hegemony of American Sociology.* Editor of sociology series in Reference Library of Social Sciences, 1980—. Contributor to journals. Assistant editor of *International Journal of Comparative Sociology,* 1964; associate editor of *Journal of Comparative Family Studies,* 1970—, and *Contributions to Asian Studies,* 1971-74; advisory editor, *Indian Journal of Social Research,* 1982—, and *Journal of Sociological Studies.*

WORK IN PROGRESS: *Urban Policy in Canada; Native Youth in the Urban Context.*

SIDELIGHTS: Dan Chekki told *CA:* "Writing books based on social research has been a stimulating and challenging task aimed at understanding and interpreting social reality and discovering the unknown."

AVOCATIONAL INTERESTS: Photography, art collecting.

*   *   *

CHENEY, Ted
See CHENEY, Theodore Albert

*   *   *

CHENEY, Theodore A. Rees
See CHENEY, Theodore Albert

*   *   *

CHENEY, Theodore Albert   1928-
(Ted Cheney, Theodore A. Rees Cheney)

PERSONAL: Born January 1, 1928, in Milton, Mass.; son of Ralph Albert and Ruth (Rees) Cheney; married Dorothy Catherine Bates, September 3, 1949; children: Glenn Alan, Ralph Hunter, Bonnie Bates, Burke Adams. *Education:* Boston University, A.B., 1951, M.A. (geography), 1952; Fairfield University, M.A. (communication), 1973. *Politics:* "Progressive Conservative." *Religion:* Protestant.

ADDRESSES: *Home*—399 Round Hill Rd., Fairfield, Conn. 06430. *Office*—Graduate School of Corporate and Political Communication, Fairfield University, Fairfield, Conn. 06430.

CAREER: Photogrammetrist for Park Aerial Surveys, Inc., 1952-54; Cornell University, Ithaca, N.Y., assistant professor of photogrammetry, 1954-58; Geotechnics & Resources, Inc., White Plains, N.Y., vice-president, 1958-64; Dunlap & Associates ("think tank"), Darien, Conn., senior scientist, 1964-69; Fairfield University, Fairfield, Conn., associate professor of communication and English and director of professional writing program, 1969—, acting dean, 1981, 1982. *Military service:* U.S. Navy, 1945-47.

WRITINGS:

(Editor) *Burma: Landforms, Forestry, Geology,* Cornell University Press, 1956.
Fort Churchill, Manitoba, Canada: An Environmental Analysis, Cornell University Press, 1957.
(Under name Ted Cheney) *Land of the Hibernating Rivers* (juvenile), Harcourt, 1968.
Camping by Backpack and Canoe, Harper, 1970.
(Editor) Howard Smith and Paul Brourer, *Performance Appraisal and Human Development,* Addison, 1980.
(Under name Theodore A. Rees Cheney) *Day of Fate* (novel), Ace Books, 1981.
Getting the Words Right: How to Revise, Edit, and Rewrite, Writer's Digest, 1983.
Writing Creative Nonfiction, Writer's Digest, 1987.
Living in Polar Regions, Watts, 1987.

SIDELIGHTS: Theodore Albert Cheney volunteered to go to Little America, Antarctica, at the age of seventeen while in the U.S. Navy. This led to a life-long interest in polar matters and his book *Land of the Hibernating Rivers.* He told *CA:* "Life around the circumpolar world is so different twenty years after *Land of the Hibernating Rivers,* I just felt I had to update it, so I wrote *Living in Polar Regions.*"

*   *   *

CHEYNEY, Arnold B.   1926-

PERSONAL: Born February 23, 1926, in Massillon, Ohio; son of Ray A. and Viola May (Zurcher) Cheyney; married Jeanne Smith, September 3, 1948; children: Steven, Timothy. *Education:* Kent State University, B.S., 1944, M.Ed., 1951; Ohio State University, Ph.D. 1964. *Religion:* Baptist.

ADDRESSES: Home—5861 Southwest 51st Terr., Miami, Fla. 33155. *Office*—School of Education, University of Miami, Coral Gables, Fla. 33124.

CAREER: Elementary teacher in public schools of Suffield, Ohio, 1949-50, and Canton, Ohio, 1950-55; elementary principal in Canton, 1955-58, supervisor of elementary education, 1958-61; Ohio State University, Columbus, instructor in education, 1961-64; University of Miami, Coral Gables, Fla., 1964—, began as associate professor, currently professor of elementary education. *Military service:* U.S. Marine Corps., 1944-46; served in South Pacific, Okinawa, and China; received Purple Heart.

MEMBER: International Reading Association, National Council of Teachers of English, National Education Association (life member).

AWARDS, HONORS: American Library Association Outstanding Academic Book award, 1973, for *The Ripe Harvest;* Educator of the Year Award, Miami Chapter of Phi Delta Kappa, 1987.

WRITINGS:

Teaching Culturally Disadvantaged in the Elementary School: A Language Approach, C. E. Merrill, 1967, 2nd edition published as *Teaching Children of Different Cultures in the Classroom: A Language Approach,* 1976.
Teaching Reading Skills through the Newspaper, International Reading Association, 1971.
(Editor) *The Ripe Harvest: Educating Migrant Children,* University of Miami Press, 1972.
Puppet Enrichment Program, Ideal School Supply Company, 1973.
Curriculum for Grades Two and Three, Baptist Publications, 1973.
Press: A Handbook Showing the Use of Newspaper in the Elementary Classroom, Educational Service, 1978.
The Writing Corner, Scott, Forseman, 1979.
Video: A Handbook Showing the Use of Television in the Elementary Classroom, Educational Service, 1980.
The Poetry Corner, Scott, Foresman, 1982.
The Map Corner, Scott, Foresman, 1983.
The Spelling Corner, Scott, Foresman, 1985.
I Know How! Following Directions, Scott, Foresman, 1987.
One, Two, Buckle My Shoe: Rhymes for Reading Readiness, Scott, Foresman, 1987.
Narration, DLM, Inc., in press.
Exposition, DLM, Inc., in press.
Description, DLM, Inc., in press.
Comparison and Contrast, DLM, Inc., in press.
Persuasion, DLM, Inc., in press.

Author of monthly column for NIE Information Service, 1984—. Contributor of over 200 articles to periodicals.

*   *   *

CLIFFORD, Margaret Cort   1929-
(Peggy Clifford, M. C. Cort, Margaret Cort)

PERSONAL: Born September 20, 1929, in Cincinnati, Ohio; daughter of George Edward (an executive) and Margaret Barrington (Mackoy) Clifford. *Education:* Chatham College, Pittsburgh, Pa., B.A., 1951.

ADDRESSES: Home—Philadelphia, Pa.

CAREER: Before moving to Aspen, Colo., was engaged in newspaper, publicity, and advertising work in Pittsburgh, Pa., and New York, N.Y.; *Aspen Times,* Aspen, Colo., managing editor, 1956-59, columnist, 1965—, writing "Vagrant Dialogues" and "Talk of the Times."

AWARDS, HONORS: Aspen Times received Parkhurst Award in 1958 for ten-part symposium on education which Clifford wrote.

WRITINGS:

(Under name Margaret Cort) *Little Oleg,* Carolrhoda, 1971.

UNDER NAME PEGGY CLIFFORD

Elliott (juvenile), illustrations by J. Chwast, Houghton, 1967.
(With J. M. Smith) *Aspen: Dreams and Dilemmas,* Swallow Press, 1970.
The Gnu and the Guru Go behind the Beyond (juvenile), illustrations by Eric Von Schmidt, Houghton, 1970.
To Aspen and Back: An American Journey, St. Martin's, 1980.

OTHER

Also author of *Taking Things Hard,* 1976. Author of a documentary series on American environments and search for community, 1972-74, and of filmscript, "Captain of a Huckleberry Party, Henry Thoreau," for Public Broadcast Service, 1972. Contributor to magazines and newspapers. Editor of *Aspen Flyer,* 1954-59, and of *Junior Reviewers* magazine, 1958-59.

SIDELIGHTS: Margaret Cort Clifford once told *CA:* "I write because I have to write and write all the time. No hobbies. No avocations. . . . In my writing I attempt to pierce the dark and unravel the mystery which surrounds us. But, ultimately, the most important question is not what . . . but WHY?"

BIOGRAPHICAL/CRITICAL SOURCES:

PERIODICALS

New York Times Book Review, November 2, 1980.†

*   *   *

CLIFFORD, Peggy
    See CLIFFORD, Margaret Cort

*   *   *

CLINTON, Jeff
    See BICKHAM, Jack M(iles)

*   *   *

CLINTON, Richard Lee   1938-

PERSONAL: Born September 20, 1938, in Cookeville, Tenn.; son of Howard C. (a salesman) and Nelva Dee (Webb) Clinton; married Susan Jeffries, September 17, 1964 (divorced, 1985); married Rosalie Clapp Norwood, November 1, 1986; children: (first marriage) Lara, Lisa. *Education:* Vanderbilt University, B.A., 1960, M.A. (history) and M.A. (Latin American studies), both 1964; attended Instituto Tecnologico y de Estudios Superiores de Monterrey, summer, 1960, Universidad Nacional Mayor de San Marcos, summer, 1961, and Goethe Institute, summer, 1963; University of North Carolina, Ph.D., 1971. *Politics:* "Democratic (for want of a better alternative)." *Religion:* "Pantheism."

ADDRESSES: Home—2951 Northwest Hayes Ave., Corvallis, Ore. 97330. *Office*—Department of Political Science, Oregon State University, Corvallis, Ore. 97331.

CAREER: First National City Bank of New York, loan officer in Overseas Division, 1964-68; University of North Carolina at Chapel Hill, assistant professor of political science and research associate of Carolina Population Center, 1971-76, member of faculty of graduate curriculum in ecology, 1974-76; Oregon State University, Corvallis, assistant professor, 1976-77, associate professor, 1978-85, professor of political science, 1985—, assistant dean for research and faculty development, 1976-77, associate dean of College of Liberal Arts, 1978-82. Referee for Burgess Publishing Co., Cambridge University Press, Harper & Row Publishers, Inc., and W. H. Freeman & Co. Has participated in numerous scholarly and civic conferences. Member of advisory board, United Campus Ministry, Oregon State University, 1978—; consultant to numerous governmental and private agencies, including Ford Foundation, International Planned Parenthood Federation, United Nations Education, Cultural and Scientific Organization, National Institute of Child Health and Human Development, U.S. Department of State, and Smithsonian Institution.

MEMBER: International Population Policy Consortium (coordinator, 1971-72; executive secretary, 1972-75), American Political Science Association, American Association for Higher Education, Latin American Studies Association, American Civil Liberties Union, Environmental Defense Fund, Common Cause, Public Citizen, Pacific Coast Council on Latin American Studies.

AWARDS, HONORS: National Institute of Health Centers grant, 1974-77; National Institute of Child Health and Human Development grant, 1976-79; Oregon Committee for the Humanities grant, 1978-79; Association of American Colleges Project QUILL grant, 1980-81; Fulbright senior lectureship, Lima, Peru, 1982-83; visiting scholar grant, Stanford University, 1984; Alpha Lambda Delta Outstanding Teacher Award, Oregon State University, 1985.

WRITINGS:

Problems of Population Policy Formation in Peru, Carolina Population Center, University of North Carolina, 1971.
(Editor with William S. Flash and R. Kenneth Godwin) *Political Science in Population Studies,* Heath, 1972.
(Editor with Godwin) *Research in the Politics of Population,* Heath, 1973.
(Editor) *Population and Politics: New Directions in Political Science Research,* Heath, 1973.
Poblacion y desarrollo en el Peru, University of Lima, 1985.

CONTRIBUTOR

Lewis Hanke, editor, *History of Latin American Civilization: Sources and Interpretations,* revised edition, Little, Brown, 1973.
Se-Jin Kim, editor, *Afro-Asian World in Transition,* North Carolina Central University, 1974.
Terry McCoy, editor, *The Dynamics of Population Policy in Latin America,* Ballinger, 1974.
Godwin, editor, *Comparative Policy Analysis: The Study of Population Policy Determinants in Developing Countries,* Heath, 1975.
David W. Orr and Marvin S. Soroos, editors, *The Global Predicament: Ecological Perspectives on World Order,* University of North Carolina Press, 1979.
Wes Jackson, editor, *Man and the Environment,* 3rd edition, W. C. Brown, 1979.
(With Godwin) John D. Martz and Lars Schoultz, editors, *Latin America, the United States, and the Inter-American System,* Westview Press, 1980.

OTHER

Contributor of articles and reviews to numerous professional journals, including *Perspective, American Political Science Review, Library Journal, World Affairs, Bulletin of Atomic Scientists,* and *Inter-American Economic Affairs.* Referee for numerous professional journals, including *Journal of Developing Areas, Latin American Research Review, Social Science Quarterly, Western Political Quarterly, American Political Science Review,* and *Demography.*

WORK IN PROGRESS: Research on the concept of eco-development and on political implications of demographic and ecological realities.

SIDELIGHTS: Richard Lee Clinton once told *CA:* "My studies have convinced me that the current predicament of mankind is unprecedented and desperate, that the next few generations will quite certainly experience a steady deterioration in their quality of life, and that the survival of civilization and perhaps of our species is becoming increasingly unlikely. Man's technological cleverness has far outrun his wisdom and ability to cope with human and social problems. Present values and institutions—such things as capitalism, materialism, individualism, nationalism, bureaucratic organization, and reliance on continuous growth—must undergo radical alteration if the future is to hold any promise whatever."

In 1987, seven years after making that statement, Clinton writes, "I find I was overly optimistic in assuming several subsequent generations. The problems I alluded to have worsened even more rapidly than I had expected, and the degree of public ignorance, apathy, and manipulability has reached unbelievable proportions. The consequence has been a lawless, ideologically blinded administration that has squandered opportunities for peace—or at least for lessening tensions and reducing the ecocidal arms race between us and the Soviets—and for preparing for the transition from a consumer society to a sustainable one."

*   *   *

CLOUDSLEY-THOMPSON, J(ohn) L(eonard) 1921-

PERSONAL: Born May 23, 1921, in Murree, British India (now Pakistan); son of A.G.G. (a medical doctor) and M.E. (Griffiths) Thompson; married J. Anne Cloudsley (a physiotherapist), 1944; children: John Hugh, Timothy, Peter Leslie. *Education:* Pembroke College, Cambridge, B.A., 1946, M.A., 1948, Ph.D., 1950. *Religion:* Church of England.

ADDRESSES: Home—4 Craven Hill, London W2 3D5, England; and Little Clarkes, Little Sampford, Saffron Walden, Essex CB10 2SA, England. *Office*—Department of Zoology, University College, University of London, Gower St., London WC1E 6BT, England.

CAREER: University of London, King's College, London, England, lecturer in zoology, 1950-60; University of Khartoum, Khartoum, Sudan, professor of zoology and keeper of Sudan Natural History Museum, 1960-71; University of London, Birkbeck College, professor of zoology, 1972-85, University College, professor emeritus, 1985—. Visiting professor, University of Kuwait, 1978 and 1983, University of Nigeria, 1981, University of Qatar, 1986, and Australian National University, 1987. Member of expeditions to Iceland, 1947, southern Tunisia, 1954, and various parts of central Africa, 1960-73. Delegate to international congresses on entomology, zoology, herpetology, biological rhythms, and bioclimatology. *Military service:* British Army, 1940-44; wounded in Libya, 1942, but rejoined regiment for D-Day offensive in Normandy; became captain.

MEMBER: World Academy of Art and Science (fellow), Institute of Biology (fellow), Linnean Society (London; fellow; vice-president, 1975-76, and 1977-78), Royal Entomological Society (London; fellow), British Arachnological Society (president, 1982-85; vice-president, 1985-86), British Herpetological Society (honorary member), British Naturalists' Association (chairman, 1974-83; vice-president, 1985—), Biological Council (chairman, 1977-82), British Society for Chronobiology (chairman, 1985-87), Zoological Society (London; fellow), Freemen of the City of London (honorary captain), Worshipful Company of Skinners, (liveryman).

AWARDS, HONORS: D.Sc., University of London, 1960; Royal African Society Medal, 1969; National Science Foundation fellow, University of New Mexico, 1969; Silver Jubilee gold medal and D.Sc., University of Khartoum, both 1981; Institute of Biology KSS Charter Award, 1981; Biological Council Medal, 1985; J. H. Grundy Medal, Royal Army Medical College, 1987; Leverhulme emeritus fellowship, 1987-89.

WRITINGS:

(Editor) *Biology of Deserts,* Institute of Biology, 1954.
Spiders, Scorpions, Centipedes, and Mites, Pergamon, 1958.
Animal Behaviour, Oliver & Boyd, 1960, Macmillan, 1961.
(With John Sankey) *Land Invertebrates,* Methuen, 1961.
Rhythmic Activity in Animal Physiology and Behaviour, Academic Press, 1961.
(With Michael J. Chadwick) *Life in Deserts,* Dufour, 1964.
Animal Conflict and Adaptation, Dufour, 1965.
Desert Life, Pergamon, 1965.
Animal Twilight: Man and Game in Eastern Africa, Dufour, 1967.
Microecology, St. Martin's, 1967.
The Zoology of Tropical Africa, Norton, 1969.
Animals of the Desert, Bodley Head, 1969, McGraw, 1971.
(With F. T. Abushama) *A Guide to the Physiology of Terrestrial Arthropoda,* Khartoum University Press, 1970.
The Temperature and Water Relations of Reptiles, Merrow, 1971.
Spiders and Scorpions, Bodley Head, 1973, McGraw, 1974.
Desert Life, Danbury, 1974.
Bees and Wasps, Bodley Head, 1974, McGraw, 1976.
Terrestrial Environments, Halsted, 1975.
Insects and History, Weidenfeld & Nicolson, 1975, St. Martin's, 1976.
Crocodiles and Alligators (juvenile), Bodley Head, 1975, McGraw, 1977.
The Ecology of Oases, Merrow, 1975.
Tortoises and Turtles, Bodley Head, 1976.
(Co-editor) *Environmental Physiology of Animals,* Blackwell, 1976.
Evolutionary Trends in the Mating of Arthropoda, Meadowfield Press, 1976.
Man and the Biology of Arid Zones, E. J. Arnold, 1977.
The Desert, Putnam, 1977.
Dietary Adaptations in Animals, Meadowfield Press, 1977.
The Size of Animals, Meadowfield Press, 1977.
The Water and Temperature Relations of Woodlice, Meadowfield Press, 1977.
Animal Migration, Putnam, 1978.
Why the Dinosaurs Became Extinct, Meadowfield Press, 1978.
Wildlife of the Desert, Hamlyn, 1979.
Biological Clocks: Their Functions in Nature, Weidenfeld & Nicolson, 1980.
Tooth and Claw: Defensive Strategies in the Animal World, Dent, 1980.
(Contributor) David M. Burn, editor, *The Complete Encyclopedia of the Animal World,* Octopus, 1980.
Form and Function in Animals, Meadowfield Press, 1980.
Camels (juvenile), Wayland, 1980.
Seals and Sea Lions (juvenile), Wayland, 1981.
Vultures (juvenile), Wayland, 1981.
(With D. G. Applin) *Biological Periodicities: A New Interpretation,* Meadowfield Press, 1982.
(Editor) *Sahara Desert,* Pergamon, 1984.
Just Look at . . . Living in the Desert (juvenile), MacDonald Educational, 1984.
Guide to Woodlands, Crowood, 1985.
Evolution and Adaption of Terrestrial Arthropods, Springer-Verlag, 1988.

Also author of monographs. Contributor to reference works, including *Encyclopaedia Britannica* and *Encyclopedia Americana.* Contributor to science journals. Editor of *Journal of Arid Environments;* member of editorial board of *Environmental Research, Journal of Herpetology, Journal of Interdisciplinary Cycle Research, Comparative Physiology and Ecology,* and *International Journal of Biometeorology.*

WORK IN PROGRESS: Research on the ecology and physiology of desert animals, thermal physiology, and biological rhythms; editing "Adaptions of Desert Organisms," a book series for Springer-Verlag.

SIDELIGHTS: J. L. Cloudsley-Thompson told *CA:* "The only real justification for writing, research, or any other creative endeavour is that it is interesting and fun. If the work helps others, or gives them pleasure, so much the better, but these are merely 'spin offs.'"

Cloudsley-Thompson's philosophy that research and writing should be "interesting and fun" has been noted by reviewers. They praise the author for his easily understood prose written for the non-specialist. Commenting on one of Cloudsley-Thompson's books about animal life, David Graber states in the *Los Angeles Times: "Animal Migration* is a solid, challenging book, far from dry. All the 'gee wow' anybody could need is provided by [photographs of the] animals themselves, while the author simply tells it, straight and true." John R. Krebs, in a *Nature* review of *Tooth and Claw: Defensive Strategies in the Animal World,* observes: "The book touches on some issues without trying to discuss them in ... full.... However, it would be churlish to criticize a popular book for not exploring recondite details. The main aim of Cloudsley-Thompson's book is to entertain and stimulate the reader. In this it succeeds."

AVOCATIONAL INTERESTS: Music (particularly opera), travel, photography.

BIOGRAPHICAL/CRITICAL SOURCES:

PERIODICALS

Los Angeles Times, December 22, 1978.
Nature, November 6, 1980.
Times Literary Supplement, September 19, 1980.

*   *   *

CLUN, Arthur
    See POLSBY, Nelson W(oolf)

*   *   *

COHEN, (Stephen) Marshall   1929-

PERSONAL: Born September 27, 1929, in New York, N.Y.; son of Harry (an investment broker) and Fanny (Marshall) Cohen; married Margaret Dennes, February 15, 1964; children: Matthew, Megan. *Education:* Dartmouth College, B.A., 1951; Harvard University, M.A., 1953; Magdalen College, Oxford, graduate study, 1953-54.

ADDRESSES: Home—10218 Autumn Leaf Cir., Los Angeles, Calif. 90077. *Office*—University of Southern California, Los Angeles, Calif. 90089.

CAREER: Harvard University, Cambridge, Mass., assistant professor of philosophy and general education, 1958-62; University of Chicago, Chicago, Ill., assistant professor, 1962-

63, associate professor of philosophy, 1964-67, acting chairman of college philosophy department, 1965-66; Rockefeller University, New York City, associate professor of philosophy, 1967-70; City University of New York, New York City, professor of philosophy at College of Staten Island and Graduate School and University Center, 1970-83, executive officer, program in philosophy at Graduate School and University Center, 1975-83; University of Southern California, Los Angeles, professor of philosophy and law, and dean of humanities, 1983—.

Visiting associate professor at University of California, Los Angeles, summer, 1963, University of Minnesota, fall, 1966, Yale University, 1968-69, 1972-73, University of California, Berkeley, summer, 1971, and Harvard University, summer, 1972. Visiting professor of philosophy at New School for Social Research, 1973-74, Barnard College, 1979-81, and United States Military Academy, 1982. Lecturer at Lowell Institute, 1957-58, Princeton University, 1964-65, and Yale College, 1975; Phi Beta Kappa visiting scholar, 1975-76; New York Council for the Humanities lecturer, 1982-83. Senior fellow in law, Yale University, 1964-65; fellow of Trumbull College, 1968-73, New York Institute for the Humanities, 1979-82, and the Humanities Institute, 1984—; visiting fellow, All Souls College, Oxford, 1976-77. Ralph Waldo Emerson prize committee, member, 1971-74, chairman, 1972-74. Principal investigator, Project on Professional Ethics, Andrew W. Mellon Foundation, 1981-83. Member of committee for the study of incarceration (Goodell Committee), 1971-75. Member of Institute for Advanced Study, 1981-82.

MEMBER: American Philosophical Association, American Society for Political and Legal Philosophy, Society for Philosophy and Public Policy (member of executive committee, 1969-70), Amintaphil, Phi Beta Kappa.

AWARDS, HONORS: Harvard University, Sheldon travelling fellowship, 1953-54, Society of Fellows, 1955-58, Santayana fellowship, fall, 1962; grant from National Endowment for the Humanities, 1975; Guggenheim fellowship, 1976-77; Rockefeller Foundation Humanities fellowship, 1977.

WRITINGS:

(Editor and author of introduction) *The Philosophy of John Stuart Mill,* Modern Library, 1961.
(Contributor) Marvin Levich, editor, *Aesthetics and the Philosophy of Criticism,* Random House, 1964.
(Contributor) Max Black, editor, *Philosophy in America,* Cornell University Press, 1965.
(Contributor) J. R. Burr and L. M. Goldinger, editors, *Philosophy and Contemporary Issues,* Macmillan, 1967.
(Contributor) F. A. Tillman and S. M. Cahn, editors, *Philosophy of Art and Aesthetics,* Harper, 1969.
(Contributor) R. Poirier and Frank Kermode, editors, *An Oxford Reader: Varieties of Contemporary Discourse,* Oxford University Press, 1971.
(Contributor) R. M. Hutchins and M. J. Adler, editors, *The Great Ideas Today: 1971,* Encyclopaedia Britannica, 1971.
(Editor with Gerald Mast) *Film Theory and Criticism: Introductory Readings,* Oxford University Press, 1974, 3rd edition, 1985.
(Editor with T. Nagel and T. Scanlon) *War and Moral Responsibility,* Princeton University Press, 1974.
(Editor with Nagel and Scanlon) *The Rights and Wrongs of Abortion,* Princeton University Press, 1974.

(Contributor) V. Held, S. Morgenbesser, and Nagel, editors, *Philosophy, Morality, and International Conflict,* Oxford University Press, 1974.

(With others) *Doing Justice,* Hill & Wang, 1976.

(Editor with Nagel and Scanlon) *Equality and Preferential Treatment,* Princeton University Press, 1977.

(Editor with Nagel and Scanlon) *Marx, Justice, and History,* Princeton University Press, 1980.

(Contributor) Gerald Myers and Gordon Fancher, editors, *Philosophical Essays on Dance,* Dance Horizon, 1981.

(Editor with Nagel and Scanlon) *Medicine and Moral Philosophy,* Princeton University Press, 1982.

(Editor with Roger Copeland) *What Is Dance?: Readings in Theory and Criticism,* Oxford University Press, 1983.

(Editor and author of preface) *Ronald Dworkin and Contemporary Jurisprudence,* Rowman & Allanheld, 1983.

(Contributor) D. MacLean and C. Mills, editors, *Liberalism Reconsidered,* Rowman & Allanheld, 1983.

(Editor with C. Beitz, Scanlon, and A. J. Simmons) *International Ethics,* Princeton University Press, 1985.

Editor of "Philosophy and Society" series, Rowman & Littlefield, 1977-82, and "Ethical, Legal, and Political Philosophy" series, Princeton University Press, 1983—. Contributor to *Encyclopedia of Philosophy.* Contributor of articles and reviews to *Kenyon Review, Journal of Philosophy, New York Review of Books, Yale Law Journal, Partisan Review,* and *Massachusetts Review.* Editor, *Philosophy and Public Affairs,* 1971—.

*   *   *

COLEN, B. D.   1946-

PERSONAL: Born August 23, 1946, in New York, N.Y.; son of Donald J. (a public relations director) and Marcia (a writer; maiden name, Sufrin) Colen; married Sara Hannan (an artist), December 11, 1971; children: Benjamin Donald. *Education:* George Washington University, B.A., 1973. *Politics:* "Liberal conservative/conservative liberal."

ADDRESSES: Agent—Edward J. Acton, Inc., 928 Broadway, Suite 301, New York, N.Y. 10010.

CAREER: Washington Post, Washington, D.C., staff writer, specializing in medicine, health, and medical ethics, beginning 1970; currently science editor of *Newsday,* Long Island, N.Y. Lecturer in journalism at George Washington University.

WRITINGS:

Karen Ann Quinlan: Dying in the Age of Eternal Life, Nash Publishing, 1976.

Born at Risk, photographs by Linda Wheeler, St. Martin's, 1981.

The Family Medical Diary, Dell, 1982.

The Diabetic's 365-Day Medical Diary, New American Library, 1983.

The COPD Medical Diary—365 Days of Better Breathing: Chronic Obstructive Pulmonary Disease, New American Library, 1983.

Take Care: Patients' Guide to Personal Health, Quill, 1984.

Hard Choices: Mixed Blessings of Modern Medical Technology, Putnam, 1986.

Health and medicine columnist for *Gentlemen's Quarterly.*

SIDELIGHTS: Journalist B. D. Colen is the author of several books that explore the ethical questions physicians face be-

cause of technological advances such as respirators, artificial hearts, and incubators. In *Karen Ann Quinlan: Dying in the Age of Eternal Life,* for example, Colen discusses the impact of life-prolonging techniques that allow patients like Quinlan to remain in vegetative states for lengthy amounts of time. His second book, *Born at Risk,* is concerned with advances in neonatology that enable physicians to save the lives of premature infants who, despite the advanced technology, frequently sustain neurological damage.

Colen probes similar issues in *Hard Choices: Mixed Blessings of Modern Medical Technology.* In this book Colen describes the case studies of seven critically ill patients, who range in age from toddlers to the elderly. Their stories, writes Robin Marantz Henig in the *Washington Post,* "highlight just how complex our choices have become amid the technological wizardry so common in modern hospitals. The choices all basically boil down to this: When should no effort be spared to save a life, no matter what the consequences, and when should the medical heroics cease?" Colen's opinion, according to Henig, is that aggressive technological intervention should not be used "if it means prolonging death instead of life."

A *Publishers Weekly* critic calls *Hard Choices* "an uncomfortable book, a significant book," and while *Chicago Tribune* reviewer Jeff Lyon observes that "there are few new thoughts here," he adds: "Colen's strength is in explaining, for the layman, the tangle of issues surrounding the new technologies." Henig believes that in choosing his case studies "Colen seems to opt for the unusual over the ordinary," and that "this dilutes the book's true power." Henig concludes: "Hard choices are not confined to families dealt a medical oddity through some bitter twist of fate. Hard choices are, for most of us, in our very own futures."

BIOGRAPHICAL/CRITICAL SOURCES:

PERIODICALS

Chicago Tribune, August 19, 1986.
New York Times Book Review, September 7, 1986.
Publishers Weekly, July 4, 1986.
Washington Post, February 13, 1981, August 12, 1986.
Washington Post Book World, October 17, 1976.

*   *   *

CONDON, Richard (Thomas)   1915-

PERSONAL: Born March 18, 1915, in New York, N.Y.; son of Richard Aloysius and Martha Irene (Pickering) Condon; married Evelyn Hunt, January 14, 1938; children: Deborah Weldon, Wendy Jackson. *Education:* Attended schools in New York.

ADDRESSES: Home—3436 Asbury, Dallas, Tex. 75205. *Agent*—Harold Matson, 276 Fifth Ave., New York, N.Y. 10001.

CAREER: Publicist in New York, N.Y., and Hollywood, Calif., for Walt Disney Productions, 1936-41, Twentieth Century-Fox Film Corp., 1941-45, Richard Condon, Inc., 1945-48, and Paramount Pictures Corp., 1948-53, and in Europe and Great Britain for United Artists Corp., 1953-57; novelist. Producer, with Jose Ferrer, of Broadway shows "Twentieth Century" and "Stalag 17," 1951-52.

MEMBER: International Confederation of Book Actors (honorary life president), Dramatists Guild, Authors Guild, Authors League of America.

AWARDS, HONORS: Writers Guild of America award, 1986, and Bafta Award from British Academy of Film and Television Sciences, both for screen adaptation of *Prizzi's Honor.*

WRITINGS:

And Then We Moved to Rossenarra; or, The Art of Emigrating, Dial, 1973.
(With daughter, Wendy Jackson) *The Mexican Stove: What to Put on It and in It,* Doubleday, 1973, reprinted, Taylor Publishing, 1988.

NOVELS

The Oldest Confession (Book-of-the-Month Club alternate selection), Appleton-Century-Crofts, 1958.
The Manchurian Candidate, McGraw, 1959.
Some Angry Angel: A Mid-Century Faerie Tale, McGraw, 1960.
A Talent for Loving; or, The Great Cowboy Race, McGraw, 1961.
An Infinity of Mirrors, Random House, 1964.
Any God Will Do, Random House, 1965.
The Ecstasy Business, Dial, 1967.
Mile High (Literary Guild alternate selection), Dial, 1968.
The Vertical Smile (Literary Guild selection), Dial, 1971.
Arigato, Dial, 1972.
Winter Kills, Dial, 1974.
The Star Spangled Crunch, Bantam, 1974.
Money Is Love, Dial, 1975.
The Whisper of the Axe, Dial, 1976.
The Abandoned Woman: A Tragedy of Manners, Dial, 1977.
Bandicoot, Dial, 1978.
Death of a Politician, Richard Marek, 1978.
The Entwining, Richard Marek, 1980.
Prizzi's Honor (second novel in trilogy; Book-of-the-Month Club joint main selection; also see below), Coward, McCann & Geoghegan, 1982.
A Trembling upon Rome, Putnam, 1983.
Prizzi's Family (first novel in trilogy; Literary Guild joint main selection), Putnam, 1986.
Prizzi's Glory (third novel in trilogy), Dutton, 1988.

SCREENPLAYS

(With Janet Roach) ''Prizzi's Honor'' (adaptation), Twentieth Century-Fox Film Corp., 1985.

Also author of ''The Summer Music.''

OTHER

Also author of a play ''Men of Distinction,'' produced on Broadway, 1953. Contributor to *Holiday, Nation, Vogue, Harper's, Gourmet, Esquire, Travel and Leisure,* and *Sunday Times Magazine.* Condon's novels have been published in twenty-two languages and in braille.

WORK IN PROGRESS: Screenplays based on *Arigato* and *Bandicoot.*

SIDELIGHTS: Since he began writing at age forty-two following a successful career as a movie publicist, novelist Richard Condon ''has proved original, prolific, and profitable, possibly in that order,'' writes *Los Angeles Times* arts editor Charles Champlin. Condon's reputation as a writer of what Richard Lingeman describes in the *New York Times* as ''cynical, hip political thrillers that contain [a unique] extravagance of invention'' was secured with his first two novels, *The Oldest Confession* and *The Manchurian Candidate.* Condon's body of work includes over twenty novels, two nonfiction books, a handful of plays and screenplays, and numerous articles on

his twin passions, food and travel. This output has netted him an income of about two and a half million dollars, which Condon told *Publishers Weekly* interviewer John F. Baker ''sounds like a lot, but it's only about what someone in middle management would have made over the same period in salary. The difference—and it's an important one—is that I've lived wherever I wanted to, and I didn't have to drive to the office every day.''

Condon has taken full advantage of his freedom as a writer. Although he now resides in the United States, for nineteen years Condon and his family lived in countries such as France, Spain, Switzerland, and Ireland. Condon's focus in his novels, however, usually reflects his concerns about American society, particularly the United States government. Condon commented to Herbert Mitgang in the *New York Times:* ''Every book I've ever written has been about abuse of power. I feel very strongly about that. I'd like people to know how deeply their politicians are wronging them.''

Condon's preoccupation with examining abuses of power has made him into a cult figure of sorts to readers who share his convictions. *New York Times Book Review* contributor Leo Braudy describes Condon's writing as ''paranoid surrealism,'' fiction that draws ''equally on the facts of national life and the cliches of popular fiction to create a world where technology, politics and history [have] run wild and the only possible humanism [is] gallows humor.'' Other novelists who have written in this genre include Joseph Heller, William Burroughs, Norman Mailer, Thomas Berger, Ken Kesey, and Thomas Pynchon. Braudy declares that Condon is ''one of the most distinguished members of this group and through the controlled corrosiveness of his two great early novels—'The Manchurian Candidate' (1959) and 'Some Angry Angel' (1960)—has some claim to being a founder.''

As Braudy indicates, Condon's novels are entertaining, despite their underlying seriousness. This assessment is compatible with Condon's personal goals as a writer, which he discusses in a *People* magazine interview with Anne Maier. ''I have never written for any other reason than to earn a living. This is certainly true of other writers, but some poor souls get mightily confused with art. I am a public entertainer who sees his first duty as the need to entertain himself.'' Most reviewers share Condon's candid view of his writing. A *New York Times Book Review* contributor, for example, writes: ''Despite the cult that has grown up around Condon, he is not really a great novelist, and certainly makes no pretensions about the value of his work. But as a practitioner of the fiction of information, no one else comes close to him.'' Since Condon's novels entertainingly mirror the concerns of readers, they fulfill what *Washington Post Book World* contributor Roderick MacLeish describes as the primary obligations of the thriller novel: ''To tell a good story and to reflect the fears and fantasies of [the author's] time.'' Condon, in MacLeish's estimation, ''is one of the living masters of [this] genre.''

Most of the material for Condon's personal blend of reality and bizarre invention—called ''mythologized fact'' by one reviewer—has come from ''the dirty linen closets of politics and money,'' according to a *New York Review of Books* critic. ''His view—it might be called Condon's Law—is that when you don't know the whole truth, the worst you can imagine is bound to be close. . . . [He] isn't an analyst but an exploiter of our need to believe the worst. He does it skillfully, but his books would be less fun than they are if one didn't suspect that he believes the worst too, that his pictures of a world of fools eternally at the mercy of knaves are also pictures of what, with anger and disgust, he takes to be the case.''

The ''mythologized fact'' of Condon's second novel, *The Manchurian Candidate,* ''touched a nerve that made America jump,'' according to a *Newsweek* reviewer. Published in 1959, *The Manchurian Candidate* remains Condon's most highly acclaimed novel, one that critics frequently cite as a basis of comparison to his later works. The title of the book refers to the main character, Raymond Shaw, a soldier who becomes a prisoner of war in Korea and is unknowingly brainwashed into committing crimes for his former captors *after* he returns to the United States. Commenting on this novel as well as on Condon's first novel, *The Oldest Confession, New Yorker* critic Whitney Baillett writes that they both ''are brilliant, highly individualistic, and hopelessly unfashionable demonstrations of how to write stylishly, tell fascinating stories, assemble plots that suggest the peerless mazes of Wilkie Collins, be very funny, make acute social observations, and ram home digestible morals. They demonstrate, in short, a good many of the things that were expected of the novel before the creative-writing courses got its practitioners brooding in their mirrors.'' A *Chicago Sunday Tribune* reviewer describes *The Manchurian Candidate* as ''a novel of today, crammed with suspense, humor, horror, satire, sex, and intrigue. . . . Fitting all [the] sidelines of the plot into a whole was a monumental writing task, and few authors could have succeeded as admirably as Condon. The result is an exciting, brilliantly told story, peopled with characters symbolic of our times.''

Although other reviewers express similarly enthusiastic opinions about the novel, they distinguish carefully between Condon's novel and literature. A *New Statesman* critic, for example, comments that *The Manchurian Candidate* is ''so well written, and so ingeniously constructed, that [it] command[s] the highest admiration without ever being considered, or even asking to be considered, as 'literature.' '' A *New York Herald Tribune Book Review* critic calls the novel ''a smooth and palatable pousse-cafe of political satire, psychological speculation, pleasantly risque antics a la Thorne Smith, and espionage maneuvering. . . . The basic assumptions of the plot do not withstand close examination. Happily, however, such examination is not necessary: this is a diversion, and a good one.'' After recommending a place for it on a ''Ten Best Bad Novels'' list—''books whose artistic flaws are mountainous but whose merits, like Loreleis on the rocks above, keep on luring readers''—a *Time* reviewer notes: ''The book carries a superstructure of plot that would capsize Hawaii, and badly insufficient philosophical ballast. Yet Condon distributes his sour, malicious humor with such vigor and impartiality that the novel is certain to be read and enjoyed.''

Although Condon followed *The Manchurian Candidate* with several relatively successful novels, some reviewers were disappointed by his post-1964 efforts. A few became increasingly annoyed by Condon's mania for trivia and for what they perceived to be thinly veiled didacticism masquerading as satire. Others cited his lack of restraint as a major problem, claiming that it led him to portray scenes that are in bad taste or far too exaggerated to be anywhere near believable. In a review of *The Ecstasy Business,* for example, a *Christian Century* reviewer writes: ''Condon's fans will find all the old razzmatazz here—the gimmicky language . . . and a cast of larger-than-life zanies. . . . [But] like Condon's fourth novel, *A Talent for Loving,* this, his seventh, is a pointlessly funny 'entertainment,' a white rather than a black comedy. . . . [*The Ecstasy Business*] is an immoral waste of Condon's talent. Most damn-

ing of all: even the humor rests on shaky topical sands; the next generation will need scholarly footnotes to know why they should have laughed at Condon's parting shot.''

Reviews of *An Infinity of Mirrors* (1964), and *The Vertical Smile* (1971) revealed similarly disillusioned opinions. In a review of *The Vertical Smile,* a *Time* critic declares: ''Since the foaming manias of [his first two novels], Condon's fine, random wrath has aged until it is nothing more than irritability. Once he could have picked up the Republican and Democratic parties by their tails and swung them around his head like a couple of dead cats. . . . Now he can't manage it.'' Reed Whittemore speculates in the *New Republic:* ''My guess is that Condon has had it with the genre itself, and this is his way of moving on—to what and where I wouldn't know. A large talent in limbo.'' Reviewing *An Infinity of Mirrors* in *Newsweek,* the critic concludes: ''Condon, who seems to be equipped to write sound, pertinent, appealing stories in the almost vacant territory between the literary drive-ins of Robbins and Wallace and the transcendental realm of pure literature, has suffered here, one hopes, a temporary setback.''

Critics' hopes for Condon's recovery were realized with the publication of his 1974 novel *Winter Kills.* Condon's most enthusiastically received novel since *The Manchurian Candidate,* *Winter Kills* closely parallels the lives of members of the Kennedy family. The main character, Nick Thirkield, is the half brother of John F. Kennedy analogue Tim Kegan, a young, liberal Irish president who is assassinated by a lone maniac. The assassin is caught and charged with the murder, but when Thirkield learns that another man may also have been involved, he has the case reopened.

Several reviewers found themselves pleasantly surprised by *Winter Kills. New York Times Book Review* contributor Leo Braudy, for example, comments that *Winter Kills* is ''a triumph of satire and knowledge, with a delicacy of style and a command of tone that puts Condon once again into the first rank of American novelists.'' Braudy explains, '' 'Winter Kills' succeeds so brilliantly because the Kennedy assassination furnished Condon with a familiar mythic landscape through which his Gulliver-like hero can wander, simultaneously prey to Lilliputian politics, Brobdingnagian physicality, Laputan science, and Houyhnhnm moralism.'' Christopher Lehmann-Haupt expresses a like opinion in the *New York Times.* ''By the time I reached the end of the novel's incredibly complex plot and had followed Nick Thirkield through the many blind alleys and trapdoors that eventually bring him face to face with the person behind his brother's assassination, I was a Richard Condon fan once more.''

Extrapolation contributor Joe Sanders once observed: ''In Condon's novels, politics determines the shape of society, but politics is not a voluntary, cooperative activity, entered into for some common end; it is a device by which a few clever people manipulate many others to gain their selfish ends.'' Sanders's comment is particularly relevant to *Winter Kills,* for the novel's conclusion reveals that the person responsible for arranging Kegan's assassination is none other than his own father, a likeness of Joseph Kennedy. Discussing the similarities between his novel and historical events, Condon told *Washington Post* reporter Joseph McLellan: ''It doesn't really matter who killed Kennedy or who killed Abe Lincoln—they're dead. What matters is that the manipulators are so powerful they can have someone like that killed because he's bad for business.''

Time reviewer John Skow finds Condon's paranoia simplistic. He writes, "Condon has unraveled. The world's villainy simply does not work so simply. To pretend that it does is mindless mischief." Braudy, on the other hand, describes *Winter Kills* as "a paranoid novel that does not leave us trapped inside its world, but functions instead as a liberation, exposing through the gentler orders of fiction the way we have been programmed to believe anything in print." A *Spectator* contributor comments that Condon's ending, intended to surprise the reader, is really quite traditional. "The novel falls apart into scraps of received phraseology and it is so bound by the conventional laws of fiction that the conventionally surprising ending can be guessed a third of the way through—on the antique, statistical principle of bad crime fiction that the guilty party is always the one who is least suspected." And while Lehmann-Haupt also expresses disappointment because he "caught on too early what the ultimate outcome would be," he finds the novel's conclusion satisfying. He writes: "It may not be true that America is run by a small, conspiring oligarchy. It may not be true that things happen in the White House at the whim of movie stars and labor leaders, of courtesans and generals. But the possibilities are no longer inconceivable."

Winter Kills was made into a critically acclaimed but briefly run film of the same title. Although Condon was not directly involved in the making of "Winter Kills," the film's quality drew his attention and support. "When my other books were made into movies, I would see them once and then forget about them," he commented to McLellan. "But this one I have seen twice, and my total satisfaction is based on the fact that the producers go for broke. They didn't evade the opportunity to malign authority. The movie goes several steps beyond my novel, and it's the first movie I've seen that really deals with the American culture of money and manipulation. It's a hard, dirty, sinister book and movie."

In a lengthy article for *Harper's* magazine entitled "Who Killed *Winter Kills*?," in which he discusses the novel and its transformation into film, Condon writes: "I wrote *Winter Kills* to reflect, in parable form, on the confusing trail of events that had followed the murder of John Kennedy. . . . The novel worked outward from the core of the real event—the assassination—advancing through mazes of American myth and nightmare, and using the motley cast this country provided: a blinkered presidential commission, the media, . . . revealed oligarchs, and labor leaders. The trail led . . . [to] that small community of people who run the United States and who had decided that the president should be murdered because he was not 'cooperating' with them. The father, an active member of the group, was chosen to carry out the deed, because only he could get close enough."

After two years of filming for which most of the cast and crew were never paid, "Winter Kills" opened in New York in 1979 to favorable reviews. The film's three-week run in showcase theaters was followed by what Condon calls "the Great and Mysterious Disappearance." This disappearance, Condon adds in *Harper's*, "began to offer a feast for the paranoid among us." Condon's paranoia was further incited by the murder of one of the producers shortly after the film's opening; two years later the second producer was sentenced to forty years in prison on a drug charge.

The movie was briefly re-released in 1982 and 1983. *Publishers Weekly* reporter John F. Baker observes: "Recently ['Winter Kills'] resurfaced briefly to equal enthusiasm and disappeared again. It seems to be currently in limbo—and is meanwhile on the way to becoming a sort of cult classic. Condon hints darkly that his theme, that a presidential assassination is in the interests of many of the world's most powerful people, may be behind the movie's strangely checkered career to date." *Los Angeles Times* arts editor Charles Champlin offers this view: "Why a film succeeds or fails is seldom absolutely knowable. It may have been, may still be, too early for a black comedy drawn from a national tragedy, even if there are lingering uncertainties about the tragedy, that the film, at least in parable, seems to be addressing."

Condon's novel *Prizzi's Honor* deals with a similarly sensitive milieu: organized crime. Although this setting has been exploited by several other authors, notably Mario Puzo, reviewers believe that Condon's novel offers a fresh outlook. Champlin observes in the *Los Angeles Times Book Review:* "Condon, once again accepting the perceived reality as police leaks, newspaper exposes and Puzo have given it to us—complete with Sicilian litany of *consiglieri, capiregimes, sottocapos, soldati,* and a godfather with a lethal wheeze and a mind Machiavelli might envy—steps over it to present an outrageous and original love story. . . ." *New York Times Book Review* editor Robert Asahina notes: "Richard Condon is not Mario Puzo; suspense, not the family saga, is his forte. And he winds the mainspring of the plot so tight that the surprise ending will knock your reading glasses off. Yet 'Prizzi's Honor' is also a sendup of the prevailing sentimental picture of the underworld. To Mr. Condon, there *is* honor among these thieves—but it is precisely in the name of *omerta* that the *fratellanza* has been willing to 'cheat, corrupt, scam, and murder anybody who stands between them and a buck.'"

The novel's love interest involves Charley Partanna, a gourmet cook, compulsive house cleaner, and hit man for the Prizzi family, and Irene Walker, a tax consultant and free-lance killer for hire. "It is something of a challenge to a novelist to create a love interest in a story that pairs two ruthless murderers," observes *Times Literary Supplement* critic Alan Bold. "Irene is presented as a colder fish than Charley—she has risen to the top of her profession on account of her ability to murder without remorse. She is as sound a psychopath as Charley. Condon suggests, however, that such creatures are capable of a great passion and Charley, for one, is sure that his love is the real thing." *New York Times* reviewer Susan Bolotin likewise comments on the originality of this pairing: "If boy-meets-girl/boy-gets-girl love stories seem poisonously tiresome to you, Richard Condon's boisterous new novel may prove the perfect antidote. It's true that 'Prizzi's Honor' starts off with a familiar melody . . . , but the book soon turns into a fugue with variations so intricate that the genre may never recover."

Despite opposition from Charley's father, Charley and Irene are wed. Condon takes the couple through a convoluted plot that includes "a kidnapping, international financial intrigue, a gangland war, police on the take, the power struggle within the family, contract killings, [and] lots of jolly sex," writes Bolotin. According to several reviewers, Condon's exploration of the seamier side of organized crime is distressing. *Best Sellers* contributor Tony Bednarczyk writes: "There is solid storytelling, but the subject raises disturbing questions about morals, and-or the lack thereof. It is a fast-paced, very readable story, but one feels a bit guilty for being interested in what comes next." A *Washington Post Book World* reviewer finds it unrealistic for Condon to expect readers to care about his psychopathic characters simply because he gives them "a few homey attributes." The reviewer adds that Charley's cooking and cleaning compulsions are ''supposed to endear him to us, despite the fact that he goes for the slow kill, described in lavish detail. We're to laugh while his wife [Irene], plotting kidnapping and murder, at the same time dazzles as a hostess.''

While *Time* critic Michael Demarest also believes that *Prizzi's Honor,* ''like most of [Condon's] books, comes sometimes too close to the truth for comfort,'' he nevertheless concludes: ''Condon's stylish prose and rich comedic gift once again spice a moral sensibility that has animated 16 novels since *The Manchurian Candidate* appeared in 1962. If wit and irony could somehow neutralize villainy, the novelist would make a fine FBI director.'' Other reviewers express similarly laudatory views. Champlin writes: ''Condon is once again the story-telling satirist with a sharp eye and a high velocity typewriter. 'Prizzi's Honor' may not be his best work but it ranks well up in the canon.'' Concludes Asahina: ''Twenty years after 'The Manchurian Candidate,' it's nice to know that Mr. Condon is still up to his sly tricks. In his case, at least, it's a pleasure that—as he tells us an old Sicilian proverb has it—'The less things change, the more they remain the same.'''

Prizzi's Honor was also made into a successful film of the same title, with Jack Nicholson and Kathleen Turner playing the roles of Charley Partanna and Irene Walker. The film was nominated for several Academy Awards, and the screenplay, adapted by Condon and co-author Janet Roach, received awards from the Writers Guild of America and the British Academy of Film and Television Sciences. The project was initiated and eventually directed by John Huston, who was attracted to the material by ''that wonderful hyperbole and extravagance mixed with grandeur that Richard [Condon] has in all his best books—I thought this one epitomized that,'' he told *New York Times* reporter Janet Maslin. Huston added that he was also drawn to the book's ''outstandingly jaundiced view of American enterprise and the ethics of the business world.''

Huston and movie critics alike believe that ''Prizzi's Honor'' is faithful to the novel, a feat they attribute to Condon and Roach's skillfully adapted screenplay. Huston commented to Maslin: '' 'Prizzi's Honor' . . . has the same quality as the book—it walks a very narrow tightrope, it can turn funny and then turn serious. This, I hope, is the unique quality of the picture: the ability to be not just one thing.'' *New York Times* critic Vincent Canby notes: ''Admirers of Mr. Condon may be glad to know that great chunks of the original Condon dialogue are as alive on screen as on the page.'' Paul Attanasio writes in the *Washington Post:* ''Richard Condon has nicely adapted the screenplay (along with Janet Roach) by cutting and splicing his own novel—it's a cornucopia of quirks, homely maxims, bits of mob jargon and odd arcana about everything from interior decorating to hormonal secretions. Condon and Roach have an acute feel for the elaborate rhythms of Brooklynese; and they succeed elegantly at making the lives of the hoodlums seem completely normal, at making murder as routine as taking out the garbage.''

''Prizzi's Honor'' received unequivocal praise from many reviewers; some describe the film as the year's finest. Canby writes: '' 'Prizzi's Honor' delivers a kind of high most commonly associated with controlled substances, or with works of art of liberating imagination. From start to finish, this exhilarating adaptation of Richard Condon's phantasmagorical and witty novel—set inside the world of the Mafia—ascends, plunges and races around hairpin curves, only to shoot up again and dive over another precipice.'' *Chicago Tribune* reviewer Gene Siskel describes ''Prizzi's Honor'' as ''a classic piece of moviemaking,'' and *Los Angeles Times* film critic Sheila Benson notes, ''To say the film is the treaure of the year would be to bad-mouth it in this disastrous season. 'Prizzi's Honor' would be the vastly original centerpiece of a *great* year.'' Benson concludes: ''In its dangerous mix of love and murder, Huston is traversing terrain that he (and certainly 'The Manchurian Candidate' author Condon) blazed decades ago. This '80s-version denouement may distress the squeamish, but it's right in keeping with Prizzi honor.''

MEDIA ADAPTATIONS: The Oldest Confession and *The Manchurian Candidate* were both filmed by United Artists Corp., the former in 1961 as ''The Happy Thieves'' and the latter in 1962. *A Talent for Loving* was adapted into a film. *Winter Kills* was filmed by Avco Embassy Pictures in 1979.

CA INTERVIEW

CA interviewed Richard Condon by telephone on October 3, 1986, at his home in Dallas, Texas.

CA: You were a publicist for movie studios for twenty-two years before you became a writer. How did you make the switch?

CONDON: There wasn't very much choice. I had developed three duodenal ulcers, and my wife said I just had to get out of that work, so I decided to try to write a novel. I was working for United Artists at the time. When I went in to tell my friend and boss, Max Youngstein, that I had to leave because of the ulcers and that I was going to write, he said, ''Well, come back and we'll see if we have a contract in the files.'' When I came back at two o'clock, lo and behold, he had ''found'' a six-months' severance pay contract. So I was able to complete the book. It was accepted by Appleton-Century-Crofts, and they sold the paperback rights instantly and then the film rights were sold straight off. I never had to look back. I was very lucky all the way.

CA: Had you done any fiction writing before that, or thought about doing any?

CONDON: No. I had written some magazine things in the line of duty when I was in the advertising business in the 1930s. About 1934, when I returned from being a waiter on a cruise liner, I wrote a piece for *Esquire* on Mickey Finns. One of the ad agency's clients was Chile. I wrote a piece called ''Midsummer Skiing in Chile,'' and the closest I'd been to a pair of skis was getting off a bus in front of Abercrombie & Fitch in New York. That's the extent of any writing I had done.

CA: What had you learned in your work with the studios that proved to be valuable in the writing?

CONDON: We had to look at the films of all of our competitors, which meant seeing eight films a week for twenty-two years. Most of them were, shall we say, average, but they all had one thing in common: they all knew how to tell a story. I learned beginning, middle, and ending for scenes—and, come to think of it, beginning, middle, and ending for sentences—and characters and exits and entrances. This was all unconsciously washing over me for twenty-two years.

CA: You'd been with people a great deal, I would imagine, in the earlier work. Was it hard to get used to the solitary hours of writing?

CONDON: Oh no. I detested publicity work. I was born to sit quietly in a cool room and type. The idea of my former life is grotesque. I would get to the office about nine in the morning. At five o'clock a whole drove of directors and actors would come in from California, and they would have to be entertained. They would be entertained in the theater and in nightclubs until one or two o'clock in the morning. And constantly talk, talk, talk, talk, talk. It was something that had been inculcated in me from when I was about twenty-two, I guess, so it sort of came naturally, but the day it stopped was cause for celebration.

CA: The subject of United States politics has provided the material for some of your best-known books, including The Manchurian Candidate, Death of a Politician, *and* Winter Kills. *Were you an early student of the political scene?*

CONDON: No. Italians have their opera and we have our politics. I have a great cultural interest in politics, not so much informational or governmental. It's a form of high entertainment and low comedy. It has everything: it's melodramatic, it's sinister, and it has wonderful villains. It's the villains that make good literature, because they're the only ones in the story who know what they want.

CA: And it's hard to imagine anything better than politics for providing a story that would be unbelievable if you made it up from scratch.

CONDON: Exactly. No question about it.

CA: Has the resemblance of some of your political characters to real people ever gotten you into trouble?

CONDON: No—not that I know of, anyway. You know, I had that film "Winter Kills." I lived in Ireland at the time. The film was on a twelve-week schedule. At nine and a half weeks they ran out of money, and they were four years in refinancing it. When they finally finished it, it opened in what they call showcase houses, about fourteen of them in the U.S., before going on into the circuit. Well, the reviews were absolutely staggeringly great. The *New York Times* was abject in its admiration, and the *New Yorker* went on for page after page. The film played for three weeks, and instead of going on into the circuit, it disappeared. It disappeared for three or four years. When the director, out of frustration, scraped together the money to buy the exhibition rights, he started all over again and it disappeared again.

CA: That was in 1983, I believe. Has anything happened since?

CONDON: No. The reason it disappeared was that the Kennedy family didn't want it played. I thought hard about what I would do in the same situation. The company that distributed the film did 890 million dollars a year with the defense department in arms procurement. All you have to do is have the senator's third assistant call and say that the senator is very unhappy about this film. It just vanished.

CA: That's terrible.

CONDON: No, it's not terrible. I'd do the same thing myself. Ted Kennedy was offended for his father—his father being one of the most offensive men we've had in this century. But that's the only time I can think of when there was a direct negative response.

CA: Your books often begin with skepticism, the deep-seated belief that information is being concealed and/or manipulated, which seems to have a large basis in real life. Do you think people have gotten any smarter about the official line since Watergate?

CONDON: We are taught in civics class that we should take these things very seriously and that we should try for better and better government. But actually, people look at it as opera. It's another form of entertainment. When you have to get the children to the dentist during the day, you have to pay your bookmaker, you have to do the shopping, and you have to bowl with the boys at night, there could be as many as 103 decisions to be made in a single day. You don't have time even to read the newspaper—not that that's a yardstick against the conduct of politicians. So, since they flood the television with this entertaining information about these rascals, it's accepted completely by the entire populace of the United States, except the American Civil Liberties Union, to be entertainment.

CA: It doesn't seem to relate to us directly sometimes.

CONDON: Do you know of anybody in Switzerland who would regard politics this way? Believe me, we lived in Switzerland and there was a question of raising the price of milk by two centimes. Now, it was impossible to raise the price of milk by two centimes unless that was put to a referendum in the canton. It was put to a referendum and the people decided yes, the milk company had to get the two centimes, so they voted it. That's democracy at its most elemental, and it requires a very small population, among other things. We're taught over and over again that we are living in the greatest democracy in the world, and it's a mockery. I don't know what it is. It isn't fascism, it isn't communism, but it certainly damn well isn't a democracy, because the people themselves have been steadily stultified by this absolute avalanche of constant political information into extreme indifference and they have a sense of hopelessness about what they can do about anything individually.

CA: The research for A Trembling upon Rome *must have been a massive job. How had the idea for the book developed?*

CONDON: The idea for the book came from reading something in the British press that I hadn't known about. There had been three popes in the world who had been sitting simultaneously. I started looking into it just to satisfy my curiosity about the political tension that would have resulted from this kind of situation, and of course I got into the Middle Ages, the economics of the Medicis, and the whole banking system and its relationship with the church. The dominating force of Europe, which was then Christendom, was ostensibly the church, but actually it was the owners of Christendom—the bankers, the weavers, etc.—who were in control. And the first among these shall be the Medicis.

CA: "Prizzi's Honor" wowed just about everybody. Vincent Canby said it best when he wrote that it "does to 'The Godfather' what Henry Fielding's 'Joseph Andrews' did to Samuel Richardson's 'Pamela.' " Did you and Janet Roach write the movie script with Jack Nicholson and Kathleen Turner and Anjelica Huston in mind?

CONDON: Janet and I never collaborated. I wrote three or four drafts, and then I got something called an aneurysm of the abdominal aorta, which is a grand thing not to get. That required intricate surgery and long recuperation. In any event, John Huston, the director, felt that he had to have a final polish job, and he brought Janet in. I hadn't met Janet. We weren't collaborators; we just both signed the same script. But back to your question, I must start by saying that Nicholson's performance was nonpareil. It was so distinguished as to be hallowed. But I resisted the idea of Nicholson because he seemed to me to be more a German American than a Sicilian American. That only goes to show that novelists don't know anything about making films. Huston, who is one of the most splendid, gifted cinematic storytellers of all time, knows what he wants and he makes it work.

CA: You were surely one of the earliest users of a word processor for writing books, so you've probably gone through several major improvements in the system.

CONDON: Yes. Incidentally, the first novelist to use a word processor was John Hersey, who borrowed the word processor at Yale University, where he is some sort of an officer. I was in Ireland, and I bought one from Olivetti and went to school in Kent, England, for about four days. Adept I'm not. It was sixty days before I could type my name on the thing. Now I have what they call a dedicated word processor, which only means it's not a computer which you program with word processing; that's all it does. It can do about 310 moves, of which I can do about sixty.

CA: Your plots are sometimes rather maze-like. Do you just start out and let a story go in whatever direction it seems to take, or is there some careful planning at the beginning?

CONDON: I don't know how careful the planning is, except that I have to know the end and then to work my way backward to the middle. When I wrote *The Manchurian Candidate,* I actually wrote it from the ending forward to the beginning. The lines of supply for character and plot are then known; when you are working backwards from the terminal it all has to come true. But if I know the ending and the middle, sure, I let it go free.

CA: Many writers say they get bored if they have something outlined too carefully, and sometimes can't even stand to finish it.

CONDON: Not only that, but I think if you have any interest at all in writing character, you can start out with a blueprint of where the characters are going to go but then they become like people and they want to do other things and you go off the track. And if you're lucky, you allow that to happen, providing that as you go over the top of the middle, you can now begin to herd them toward the ending of the story, which you know in advance.

CA: Besides the fiction, you've done a lot of writing about food and travel. Tell me first about the food. Are you a cook yourself?

CONDON: No, not at all. I haven't got the patience to be a cook. I think if you ever try to reduce any writing to its absolute element, it's the five senses. They are all put in a background of pathos or melodrama or documentary or whatever, but it's still the five senses. That's the common link between the writer and the reader; that's what you know you share. So

I write about food just to hone my ability to write about sight, taste, smell, and texture.

CA: You've talked a bit about living in Switzerland and Ireland. Do you have a favorite place outside this country?

CONDON: My favorite place, including this country, is Switzerland. We were there again this summer. I try to write at least one article on Switzerland every summer. We lived in seven foreign countries in twenty-seven years. My older girl speaks five languages, my younger speaks three, my wife speaks three, and they have friends all over. My factory is just as big as the typewriter; I can hold it on my lap.

CA: Does knowing you're going to be writing about a place in any way lessen your enjoyment in traveling there?

CONDON: No, but I think the most important thing in a novel, including plot and character, is place. The reader has to feel the security of where he is while he's reading. It's absolutely essential that you lock in the surroundings of this new—you hope—world that he's about to enter by giving him a sure footing in it. So I try to go to a lot of places to get a feeling about them.

CA: How long have you lived in Dallas?

CONDON: Six years. My younger daughter, Wendy, has two children now, so we came over to watch them for a while. We live in a part of town that's about half a block from Southern Methodist University, and it's like the Metro lot in the old days when they did the Andy Hardy pictures, little houses and lots of trees and that kind of stuff.

CA: What do you enjoy reading?

CONDON: Tom Keneally's work, absolutely. And there are others, but I read mostly nonfiction because I crib a lot from it. I read books just for general information, and I have these yellow markers that I mark things with as I go along. Four years later, when I'm dealing with a specific subject, I can go back and flip through to the yellow markers and crib stuff.

CA: The second Prizzi book, Prizzi's Family, *is just recently out. Will the Prizzis go on beyond this?*

CONDON: The Prizzi thing is a trilogy. The whole theme of it is that money, no matter where it comes from, demands respectability if there's enough of it. *Prizzi's Family* is really the first book in the sequence. *Prizzi's Honor* is the second, and the third will be called *Prizzi's Glory.* It tells of the ultimate rise of the surviving members of the Prizzi family—as the robber barons rose in the 1860s and '70s: the Harrimans, the Rockefellers, the Vanderbilts, who were in their day excoriated as criminals and are today the leaders of our society. We could go back to the Magna Carta, when those ruffian barons said to the king, "Sign here." It's always been, throughout history, that while cheap labor was coming in at the bottom to support the economy, the very rich who had once been cheap labor are now, after six or seven generations, up at the top; they are the dominant forces in society socially, financially, and culturally. And that's where this will end. Charley Partanna will be made Ambassador to the Court of St. James.

BIOGRAPHICAL/CRITICAL SOURCES:

BOOKS

Condon, Richard, *Death of a Politician*, Richard Marek, 1978.
Contemporary Authors Autobiography Series, Volume I, Gale, 1984.
Contemporary Literary Criticism, Gale, Volume IV, 1975, Volume VI, 1976, Volume VIII, 1978, Volume X, 1979, Volume XLIV, 1987.
Newquist, Roy, *Conversations*, Volume I, Rand McNally, 1967.

PERIODICALS

America, September 12, 1964.
Atlantic, September, 1969.
Best Sellers, September 15, 1964, September 1, 1969, June, 1982, December, 1986.
Books and Bookmen, December, 1969, August, 1982.
Book Week, September 13, 1964.
Book World, October 24, 1967, August 17, 1969, October 31, 1971.
Chicago Sunday Tribune, March 1, 1958, May 31, 1959.
Chicago Tribune, June 14, 1985.
Chicago Tribune Book World, June 6, 1982.
Christian Century, September 16, 1964, February 21, 1968, October 1, 1969.
Christian Science Monitor, September 11, 1969.
Detroit News, October 9, 1983.
Extrapolation, summer, 1984.
Globe & Mail (Toronto), December 6, 1986.
Harper's, September, 1977, May, 1983.
Los Angeles Times, February 19, 1983, June 14, 1985, August 16, 1987.
Los Angeles Times Book Review, April 25, 1982.
Nation, February 3, 1962.
New Republic, October 16, 1971.
New Statesman, November 8, 1968, October 10, 1969, September 5, 1975, August 13, 1976.
Newsweek, September 14, 1964, June 9, 1975.
New Yorker, June 21, 1958, May 30, 1959, April 2, 1960, July 22, 1961, August 25, 1975, December 11, 1978.
New York Herald Tribune Book Review, June 1, 1958, June 28, 1959, May 1, 1960.
New York Herald Tribune Books, August 27, 1961.
New York Review of Books, February 8, 1979.
New York Times, June 22, 1958, April 26, 1959, May 24, 1974, May 21, 1976, April 20, 1982, June 9, 1985, June 14, 1985, October 29, 1986.
New York Times Book Review, March 20, 1960, July 23, 1961, September 13, 1964, October 29, 1967, August 31, 1969, October 10, 1971, May 26, 1974, May 25, 1975, May 23, 1976, April 18, 1982, September 4, 1983, September 28, 1986.
New York Times Magazine, September 2, 1979.
People, December 8, 1986.
Publishers Weekly, June 24, 1983.
Saturday Review, June 14, 1958, April 2, 1960, November 28, 1964, September 6, 1969.
Spectator, April 22, 1972, September 21, 1974.
Time, July 6, 1959, July 21, 1961, March 22, 1968, September 5, 1969, October 4, 1971, June 24, 1974, June 2, 1975, May 17, 1982, June 10, 1985, September 22, 1986.
Times (London), October 25, 1985, January 15, 1987.
Times Literary Supplement, October 5, 1967, October 16, 1969, April 28, 1972, September 20, 1974, June 11, 1982.
Village Voice, October 9, 1969.
Washington Post, November 10, 1978, May 10, 1979, September 13, 1980.
Washington Post Book World, May 30, 1976, April 4, 1982, June 14, 1985, August 24, 1986.

—*Sketch by Melissa Gaiownik*
—*Interview by Jean W. Ross*

*   *   *

COOK, Chris(topher)   1945-

PERSONAL: Born June 20, 1945, in Leicester, England; son of William and Kathleen (Chatterton) Cook. *Education:* St. Catharine's College, Cambridge, B.A., 1967, M.A., 1970; Oriel College and Nuffield College, Oxford, D.Phil., 1974. *Politics:* Liberal. *Religion:* Anglican.

ADDRESSES: Home—Wimbledon, England. *Agent*—Hilary Rubinstein, A. P. Watt and Co., 26-28 Bedford Row, London WC1R 4HL, England. *Office*—Department of History, Polytechnic of North London, Prince of Wales Rd., Kentish Town, London N.W.5, England.

CAREER: Oxford University, Magdalen College, Oxford, England, lecturer in politics, 1969-70; University of London, London School of Economics and Political Science, London, England, senior research officer, 1970-80; Polytechnic of North London, London, head of department of history, 1980—.

WRITINGS:

(Editor with David McKie) *Election '70: The "Guardian"/Panther Guide to the General Election*, Panther, 1970.
(Editor with McKie) *The Decade of Disillusion: British Politics in the Sixties*, Macmillan, 1972.
(Editor with John Ramsden) *By-Elections in British Politics*, Macmillan, 1973.
(Editor with McKie) *The "Guardian"/Quartet Election Guide*, Quartet Books, 1974.
The Age of Alignment: Electoral Politics in Britain, 1922-1929, Macmillan, 1975.
(With Brendan Keith) *British Historical Facts, 1830-1900*, Macmillan, 1975.
(With John Paxton) *European Political Facts, 1918-1973*, Macmillan, 1975.
(Editor with Gillian Peele) *The Politics of Reappraisal, 1918-1939*, Macmillan, 1975.
(With Philip Jones, Josephine Sinclair, and Jeffrey Weeks) *Sources in British Political History, 1900-1951*, Macmillan, Volume I: *A Guide to the Archives of Selected Organisations and Societies*, 1975, Volume II: *A Guide to the Private Papers of Selected Public Servants*, 1975, Volume III: *A Guide to the Private Papers of Members of Parliament, A-K*, 1977, Volume IV: *A Guide to the Private Papers of Members of Parliament, L-Z*, 1977, Volume V: *A Guide to the Private Papers of Selected Writers, Intellectuals and Publicists*, 1978, Volume VI (first consolidated supplement), 1985.
(Editor with Alan Sked) *Crisis and Controversy: Essays in Honour of A. J. P. Taylor*, Macmillan, 1976.
A Short History of the Liberal Party, Macmillan, 1976, 2nd edition, 1984.
(Editor with Mary Barker) *Pears Encyclopaedia of Myths and Legends*, Pelham, Volume I: *The Ancient Near and Middle East; Classical Greece and Rome*, 1976, Volume II: *Northern Europe, Southern and Central Africa*, 1977, Volume III: *The Orient*, 1977, Volume IV: *Oceania and Australia, the Americas*, 1978.

(With Ken Powell) *English Historical Facts, 1485-1603*, Macmillan, 1977.

A History of the Great Trains, Weidenfeld & Nicholson, 1977.

(With John Stevenson) *The Slump: Society and Politics during the Depression*, J. Cape, 1977.

(With Stevenson) *The Atlas of Modern Warfare*, Weidenfeld & Nicholson, 1978.

(With Paxton) *European Political Facts, 1848-1918*, Macmillan, 1978.

(With McKie and Melanie Phillips) *The "Guardian"/Quartet Election Guide*, Quartet Books, 1978.

(With Stevenson) *Longman Atlas of Modern British History: A Visual Guide to British Society and Politics, 1700-1970*, Longman, 1978.

(Editor with Ramsden) *Trends in British Politics since 1945*, Macmillan, 1978.

The Guinness Book of Winners and Champions, Guinness Superlatives, 1979, 2nd edition, 1981.

(With Paxton) *Commonwealth Political Facts*, Macmillan, 1979.

(With Mary Francis) *The First European Elections: A Handbook and Guide*, Macmillan, 1979.

(Editor with W. Awdry) *A Guide to the Steam Railways of Great Britain*, Pelham, 1979.

(With Edward Blishen) *Pears Guide to Today's World*, Pelham, 1979.

(With Sked) *Post-War Britain: A Political History*, Harvester, 1979, 2nd edition, Penguin, 1984.

(With Stevenson) *British Historical Facts, 1760-1830*, Macmillan, 1980.

(With John Wroughton) *English Historical Facts, 1603-1688*, Macmillan, 1980.

(Editor with Ian Taylor) *The Labour Party: An Introduction to Its History, Structure and Politics*, Longman, 1980.

(With Paxton) *European Political Facts, 1789-1848*, Macmillan, 1981.

(Editor) Simon James, *Pears Guide to Money and Investment*, Pelham, 1982.

(Editor with Ben Pimlott) *Trade Unions in British Politics*, Longman, 1982.

(With David Killingray) *African Political Facts since 1945*, Macmillan, 1983.

Dictionary of Historical Terms: A Guide to the Main Themes, Events, Cliques, and Innuendoes of Over One Thousand Years of World History, Macmillan, 1983, published as *Dictionary of Historical Terms: A Guide to Names and Events of Over One Thousand Years of World History*, Peter Bedrick, 1984.

(With Stevenson) *The Longman Handbook of Modern British History, 1714-1980*, Longman, 1983.

(With Paxton) *European Political Facts, 1918-1984*, new edition, Facts on File, 1986.

Also author with Geoff Pugh of *Sources in European Political History*, 1986. Editor of *Pears Cyclopaedia: A Book of Background Information and Reference for Everyday Use*, Pelham, 1974—.

BIOGRAPHICAL/CRITICAL SOURCES:

PERIODICALS

Times Literary Supplement, April 6, 1984, November 9, 1984, April 26, 1985.

*   *   *

COOK, Fred J(ames)   1911-

PERSONAL: Born March 8, 1911, in Point Pleasant, N.J.; son of Frederick P. (a hardware store employee and tax collector) and Huldah (Compton) Cook; married Julia Barbara Simpson, June 5, 1936 (died, 1974); married Irene H. Line, June 22, 1976; children: (first marriage) Frederick P. II, Barbara Jane (Mrs. Richard Shibla). *Education:* Rutgers University, B.Litt., 1932. *Politics:* "Mugwump, New Dealish."

ADDRESSES: Home—722 Fernmere Ave., Interlaken, N.J. 07712. *Agent*—Peter Shepherd, Harold Ober Associates, Inc., 40 East 49th St., New York, N.Y. 10017.

CAREER: Asbury Park Press, Asbury Park, N.J., reporter, 1933-36, assistant editor, then city editor, 1938-44; *New Jersey Courier*, Toms River, editor, 1936-37; *New York World Telegram and Sun*, New York, N.Y., rewrite man, 1944-59; free-lance writer, 1959—.

MEMBER: Authors League of America.

AWARDS, HONORS: New York Newspaper Guild Page One Award for best city reporting, 1958, best magazine feature, for "The FBI," 1959, best magazine reporting, for "The Shame of New York," 1960, and for crusading journalism, for series on the energy crisis in the *Nation*, 1980; Sidney Hillman Award, 1960, for magazine article in the *Nation*, "Gambling, Inc."

WRITINGS:

The Girl in the Death Cell (on the Snyder Gray case), Gold Medal Books, 1953.

The Girl on the Lonely Beach (on the Starr Faithful case), Fawcett, 1954.

(With Robert Hendrickson) *Youth in Danger*, Harcourt, 1956.

The Unfinished Story of Alger Hiss, Morrow, 1958.

What Manner of Men: Forgotten Heroes of the Revolution, Morrow, 1959.

(Editor) Bruce Lancaster, *The Golden Book of the American Revolution* (young adult), introduction by Bruce Catton, Golden Press, 1959.

(Editor) *The Second World War* (juvenile), Golden Press, 1960.

Rallying a Free People: Theodore Roosevelt, Kingston House, 1961.

A Two-Dollar Bet Means Murder, Dial, 1961.

John Marshall: Fighting for Justice, Kingston House, 1961.

Entertaining the World: P. T. Barnum, Encyclopaedia Britannica, 1962.

The Warfare State, foreword by Bertrand Russell, Macmillan, 1962.

Building the House of Labor: Walter Reuther, Encyclopaedia Britannica, 1963.

The FBI Nobody Knows, Macmillan, 1964.

Barry Goldwater: Extremist of the Right, Grove, 1964.

The Corrupted Land: The Social Morality of Modern Americans, Macmillan, 1966.

The Secret Rulers: Criminal Syndicates and How They Control the U.S. Underworld, Duell, Sloan & Pearce, 1966.

The Plot against the Patient, Prentice-Hall, 1967.

What So Proudly We Hailed, Prentice-Hall, 1968.

Franklin D. Roosevelt: Valiant Leader (juvenile), Putnam, 1968.

The New Jersey Colony (juvenile), Collier, 1969.

The Nightmare Decade: The Life and Times of Senator Joe McCarthy, Random House, 1971.

The Army-McCarthy Hearings, April-June, 1954: A Senator Creates a Sensation Hunting Communists, F. Watts, 1971.

The Rise of American Political Parties, F. Watts, 1971.

The Cuban Missile Crisis, October, 1962: The U.S. and Russia Face a Nuclear Showdown, F. Watts, 1972.

The Demagogues (juvenile), Macmillan, 1972.

The Muckrakers: Crusading Journalists Who Changed America, Doubleday, 1972.
Dawn over Saratoga: The Turning Point of the Revolutionary War, Doubleday, 1973.
Mafia, Fawcett, 1973.
American Political Bosses and Machines, F. Watts, 1973.
Lobbying in American Politics, F. Watts, 1976.
Privateers of '76, illustrated by William L. Verrill, Jr., Bobbs-Merrill, 1976.
Julia's Story: The Tragedy of an Unnecessary Death, Holt, 1976.
Mob, Inc., F. Watts, 1977.
Storm before Dawn (novel), Condor, 1978.
City Cop (juvenile), Doubleday, 1979.
The Ku Klux Klan: America's Recurring Nightmare, Messner, 1980.
The Crimes of Watergate, F. Watts, 1981.
The Great Energy Scam: Private Billions vs. Public Good, Macmillan, 1982.
Maverick: Fifty Years of Investigative Reporting (autobiography), introduction by Studs Terkel, Putnam, 1984.

Contributor to *Reader's Digest, American Heritage, Saturday Review, Nation, New York Times, True Detective*, and other publications.

SIDELIGHTS: Fred J. Cook "is by profession a muckraker," writes Peter S. Prescott in *Newsweek*. Though Cook began as a cub reporter for the local New Jersey newspaper *Asbury Park Press* and then worked for fifteen years as a rewrite man for the *New York World Telegram and Sun*, he has since gained recognition for tackling high-level corruption in a tough-minded way. In more than forty adult and juvenile books, some of which were run serially in the *Nation*, Cook has championed the victims of injustice and has delved deep into a number of heretofore "untouchable" organizations such as the CIA. As a result of his unrelenting devotion to getting at the "hows" and "whys" of existing conditions, Cook has won several journalism awards, including a number of Page One Awards from the New York Newspaper Guild and the 1960 Sidney Hillman Award.

During his stint as a rewrite man for the *New York World Telegram and Sun*, Cook became "pretty well disenchanted with the distortions" he encountered, notes *Nation* contributor Blair Clark. As a result, Cook began submitting his exposes to the *Nation*, a journal he found to be more aligned with his own goals. Although Clark believes Cook "created himself as a great investigative journalist," he is also convinced that Carey McWilliams, the editor of *Nation* at that time, personally encouraged Cook to tap his as yet unused talents. To date, Cook has defended such controversial newsmakers as Alger Hiss and Sacco and Vanzetti, and he has investigated several organizations, including the FBI, the CIA, the Mafia, and the Ku Klux Klan.

One of Cook's most impassioned accounts evolved out of the death of his first wife, Julia, whom Cook believes suffered fatally from improper monitoring following successful heart surgery. In *Julia's Story: The Tragedy of an Unnecessary Death*, Cook argues that there is "little excuse for the fragmentation of care, the lack of communication between members of the medical team, the failure to inform the patient or the patient's family properly, the treatment of parts of a patient (according to the physician's particular specialty) instead of a whole human being, the too ready dismissal of a patient's symptoms as 'imaginary' or inconsequential," according to Jane E. Brody in the *New York Times*. In the opinion of *New York Times Book Review* contributor William A. Nolen, himself a surgeon, "Cook tells his story poignantly, and he makes his case forcefully and lucidly. Medicine is too fragmented; partly, at least, as a result of the tremendous growth in scientific knowledge that has taken place in the last few years. . . . Till we can devise a fail-safe program, tragedies like that of Julia Cook will occur." However, Brody makes the assertion that "it is books like this that could help to instigate change in the system."

As an advocate of the underdog, Cook has met with considerable critical acclaim. *Nation* critic Sean Cronin finds *What So Proudly We Hailed*, Cook's bitter assessment of Lyndon B. Johnson's Great Society, "a lively, provocative but, above all, a relevant book. [Cook's] insight is sharp, his comment always to the point. He is a great one to prick bubble reputations and explode myths." Writing on *The Nightmare Decade: The Life and Times of Senator Joe McCarthy*, *Saturday Review* contributor Fred Darwin believes "Cook combines abundant detail—thoroughly documented—with an engrossing narrative. [The] *Nightmare Decade* reads like an adventure tale, though it is an all too accurate account of a nation's misadventure."

On the other hand, there are those who take issue with Cook's style and approach. In his *Newsweek* review of *The Nightmare Decade*, Prescott describes Cook as "a dreadful writer[,] . . . far too fond of secondary sources—is there no one who knew McCarthy well whom he might have interviewed at length?" Robert Yoakum makes a similar observation about *The Corrupted Land: The Social Morality of Modern Americans* noting in the *New Republic* that there is little indication the author conducted his own interviews. Regarding Cook's charge that America's ethics revolve around corporate "bigness" and greed, Yoakum points out that Cook fails to take into account any of America's strengths. Additionally, writes the reviewer, Cook "repeats himself too often, stays pitched at the same level of indignation too long, ignores too much contradictory and inconvenient evidence, is sloppy about sources, and weighs down perfectly good stories with a heavy-handed insistence that all of them serve as proof of total ethical collapse." According to a *Times Literary Supplement* critique of *The Corrupted Land*, "Cook is one of the most active and censorious observers of the American scene. He has produced entertaining and useful books, but he has the habit of overplaying the censorial role."

The reviews of Cook's autobiography, *Maverick: Fifty Years of Investigative Reporting*, are also mixed. Carolyn See of the *Los Angeles Times* claims that "obviously, one is supposed to love this book. Here's a man, Fred J. Cook, a Don Quixote of journalism, championing the underdog for an entire lifetime, his phone tapped by the FBI, double-crossed repeatedly by philistine editors and publishers." In spite of all of this, See remarks, "I still don't like [*Maverick*]. . . . The taint of self-congratulations is just too strong, too embarrassingly, outrageously strong here. This is a book about how wonderful Fred J. Cook is, and it's written by Fred J. Cook." In contrast, Melinda Stivers Leach writes in *Library Journal* that as a result of Cook's lengthy descriptions on how he performs his research, "this is an excellent journalism textbook as well as an enlightening chronicle of modern history." And, from Clark's viewpoint, "there must be young journalists out there still who chafe against the restraints of homogenized establishment organs and wish they could break the mold and do something serious on their own. They would find a model in this book on the life and work of Fred J. Cook."

AVOCATIONAL INTERESTS: Reading, fishing, swimming, big league baseball, and the fortunes of the Rutgers football team.

CA INTERVIEW

CA interviewed Fred J. Cook by telephone on March 30, 1987, at his home in Interlaken, New Jersey.

CA: As Studs Terkel said in his introduction to Maverick, *your autobiography, you wouldn't have been happy settling in as a newspaper editor, however well-paid and respected, because you had "a natural antipathy toward heavyweights ganging up on featherweights, in the name of Americanism," and you wanted to go after them as an investigative reporter. Where did the hatred of injustice begin?*

COOK: It began when I was a cub reporter down in Ocean County, New Jersey, and I saw the way the very strong political machine trampled on the average person. If the little guy's interests conflicted with their desires or some of their payoffs, he really got shafted. I saw the crookedness; I saw the payoffs that were rampant at that time. That early experience, when I was still a little wet behind the ears as a reporter, stimulated my maverick tendencies, my desire to find out what was going on, what was wrong, and to try and correct it if I could.

CA: You decided when you were fifteen that you wanted to be a writer because you loved books. Who were your favorites among the authors you read early?

COOK: When I was quite young, *Treasure Island* and *Robinson Crusoe* were two of my favorites. Later I read James Fenimore Cooper's *Leatherstocking Tales;* my dad had a set of those. And Sir Walter Scott. We had a set of his novels in the house, and I read several of those. I read a lot of Zane Grey, and H. Rider Haggard: *She, Allan Quartermain, King Solomon's Mines.* Later I read quite a lot of Dickens and Thackeray. From the time I was in grammar school I loved reading and I loved books. I wanted to write. In the very simplistic way of a young man, I figured that if I wanted to learn to write, one of the ways of doing it was to be a reporter. That's why I got into the newspaper business.

CA: I imagine the real training in journalism came after *the four years at Rutgers University. How well prepared did you feel when you first encountered the raw material of your work, things like the deeply ingrained political corruption?*

COOK: I had read about political corruption—Boss Tweed and so forth—but I don't think you realize what it is and what damage it can do and how ruthless it can be unless you see it for yourself, get your nose rubbed in it. While I was prepared for it intellectually, realistically on a personal and emotional level I wasn't prepared for it.

CA: Were there older, experienced newsmen who gave advice and served as models?

COOK: Yes. Early on, I got a lesson in journalistic courage. My teacher was the editor of a small weekly newspaper in New Jersey. In his seventies when I met him, William H. Fischer was embarked on a crusade against a mob-run gambling boat and official protection that reeked of bribery. His blunt charges of corruption stirred up a political hurricane and led to his indictment for criminally libeling the entire Republican organization of the county. How do you libel an entire organization? It was patently ridiculous, and the prosecution, taking a shellacking, offered all kinds of deals; but Fischer, this doughty little vibrant editor, in effect told them to go to hell. He was still fighting when he died.

CA: You've always taken on the tough guys—organized crime, corrupt politicians, the oil companies, the FBI, the medical profession. You described in Maverick *the harassment you got while you were investigating the Alger Hiss case. Have you often felt in physical danger?*

COOK: No, I haven't—at least I haven't worried about it. I just figured I would do what I had to do, what I set out to do, and let the chips fall where they may. I've had reports that there were people who didn't like me and would like to see things happen to me, but I've never been threatened directly.

CA: What sort of minimum components does a story have to have in order to get you hooked?

COOK: I get hooked on a story when I see what seems to be injustice. I've described such cases in *Maverick:* the William Remington case, which I thought was a judicial horror; the Alger Hiss case, which I thought was a frame; and a couple of military injustice cases, Marion Denton's and Joseph Patrick Kauffman's—guys in the military who went through a horrible experience in the military courts in which the proper processes were absolutely ignored in order to uphold the brass. These kinds of things trigger my interest.

CA: In Julia's Story, *1976, the very sad and shocking account of your first wife's unnecessary death, you showed the "splintered American medical system" at its incompetent worst. You had dealt with the medical system earlier in* The Plot against the Patient, *published in 1967. Do you feel the books have had any influence on the system?*

COOK: *Julia's Story* had at least a temporary influence: a couple of doctors got shifted around. Whether it actually made any deep change in the system or not I don't know. I know the book itself caused a lot of reader attention. I got more calls and letters and reaction from it than I had had from anything I had written before, because people go through this kind of experience; I recounted in *Julia's Story* some of the stories that came in to me from the time I wrote the first magazine article that led to the book. People who have suffered as I suffered from medical incompetence want and need an outlet, and a lot of them came to me for advice. So I felt that maybe I did some good in warning people of what to look out for. A lot of people put sort of a blind trust in the ones who are supposed to be the great experts—I guess I did. Maybe it helps to tell them not to be so blindly trusting when they are facing a problem of their own.

CA: Did you ever hear personally from the Great Doctor, as you called him in Julia's Story?

COOK: No, I never did. *New York* magazine ran the first account of what became *Julia's Story,* and I heard later that you couldn't get a copy of that issue anywhere in this immediate area. I was told that the Great Doctor's colleagues at the hospital had purchased every copy on the racks.

CA: At the end of Julia's Story *you wrote about Dr. Lawrence L. Weed and his Problem Oriented Medical Information System (PROMIS), based on the use of computers to record and check a patient's medical history and thus do away with the fragmentation of records and treatment. What has happened with PROMIS?*

COOK: I haven't been in touch with Dr. Weed for some years now. I went up to Burlington, Vermont, to talk to him and to see his system, and I was quite impressed with it, as I indicated in the book. But whether he managed to break through the medical wall or not, I really don't know.

CA: You're known to be a thoroughgoing, determined researcher. What stories have been the hardest to get at the facts for?

COOK: One of the hardest stories was the one that gave me my reputation in some circles, the Alger Hiss case. I really went through a lot of brain cudgeling and soul searching on that one, because it was not as clear-cut as the Remington case, which I think was a horrible example of legal injustice. Hiss's case is too, but it's more complicated and a lot more involved, with more shady elements in it. I came to the conclusion in the long run that the Hiss case didn't hang together, and of course the subsequent discoveries through the Freedom of Information Act, I think, just about blow the prosecution's case. That was one that I really wrestled with.

CA: Are there stories you'd like to go back to and do follow-up articles or books on?

COOK: I don't know. I'm seventy-six, and I've reached a point where I really don't feel like going back and doing the kind of digging that you have to do to put together a solid piece of work. The research and writing that go into something like this seem daunting at the present moment.

CA: It must be wearing emotionally as well as physically.

COOK: Oh, it is.

CA: When you started out as a reporter, newspapers weren't competing with television. Beyond or in addition to financial considerations, how do you feel the papers have been affected by the subsequent development and popularity of television?

COOK: Certainly the evening newspaper has almost gone out of existence in a lot of areas. The morning papers have managed to survive because they can hit the readers earlier in the day and give a more complete wrap-up of what has happened the day before. But the evening papers have been just about eliminated, and television news, I think, has had a lot to do with it. On television and radio you have a minute-by-minute, hour-by-hour rendering of the news; the evening papers are just not able to keep up. And if the reader wanted a complete wrap-up of the news that was breaking during the day, he got it in his next morning paper.

CA: Do you think the competition has put pressure on the papers to approach their reporting any differently?

COOK: I don't think it has changed reporting much. When something like the Watergate scandal breaks, or something like the Iran scandal that we have today, I think the reporting is much the same kind of digging, investigative work that was

always done—for example, in Teapot Dome and other headline cases. That kind of reporting hasn't changed. It's just a question of whether you have the resources and the will to go and do it. A lot of papers don't anymore; a lot of them don't feel like getting involved. That was the story on Watergate. The *Washington Post* and the *New York Times*—the *Post* primarily—did the job. A lot of papers just sat on their hands and carried routine wire service stories and let it go at that.

CA: In an ideal world, how do you think television and the print news media should work together in imparting the news?

COOK: I doubt that television and print media can ever work very well together. They are just two different, competing mediums. Television is so hair-trigger, so episodic; it has to get its pictures, its snatches of interviews, into the station in the next minute. The print media have more time and opportunity to develop a story in more explicit detail; and, if both TV and print are covering the same event, the time-pressed TV reporters with their shouted questions and their photographers yelling for one more shot can turn the whole thing into chaos. The mediums are so different I see little chance for smooth working relationships.

CA: You described in Maverick *how you often saw the news distorted through laziness, whim, or outside influences. Do you think the newspaper industry today does an adequate job of setting standards for itself and enforcing them?*

COOK: What I was referring to in *Maverick* was mainly a political bias in the coverage of our particular paper in New York, which was very strongly Republican. The guys who handled the political reporting were chosen for the safety of their beliefs. I haven't had personal experience in dealing with City Desk since 1959, so I don't know exactly how pervasive that kind of thing is. When I was in the business, the attitude of the front office, the political preference of the front office, seeped down and determined a lot of the character of the reporting, especially on political affairs. Whether that's still true or not, I don't know; I haven't had recent personal experience with it. But I would suspect that probably it is.

CA: It's a great problem to know whether you're getting the whole story on something in the news. Maybe it always has been a problem.

COOK: Yes. What I ran into many a time when I had a story that I felt should be used, and should be developed in detail, was that the powers above me didn't want to do it. Sometimes it was killed.

CA: Your association with the Nation *must have been a tremendous help in those cases; some of the stories found an outlet there.*

COOK: Yes. The *Nation* was my safety valve. When a story was killed at the paper and it was a good story, I could go to Carey McWilliams at the *Nation* and he would use it. Of course that didn't make me very popular at my own office!

CA: Among your many books are several written specifically for young readers, such as The Golden Book of the American Revolution, The Demagogues, *and* City Cop. *What do you consider most important in writing for that audience? Are there special goals?*

COOK: One thing, of course, is to make sure that your language is clear enough and simple enough to be understandable. You have to change gears a little bit and not be too wordy or involved. In writing many of the books I did for young people, I wrote on much the same themes—the Mob, political corruption, things of that kind as well as straight historical books. It's a question of making your writing very simple, very clear, and having it move.

CA: There's a novel among your credits, the 1978 book Storm before Dawn. *Was it a nice change of pace doing something you didn't have to dig up facts for?*

COOK: Yes. It was something I'd been rocking around in my head for some years, and I wanted to do it. Finally, with the Bicentennial celebration coming up, I figured it was time for me to write it, and I did. But I couldn't get a publisher for it. It was a historical novel laid in the backwaters of New Jersey during the Revolution. At the time I wrote it, I ran into several kinds of opposition. For one thing, this was just at the time that the women romance writers were taking charge, especially in the paperback field. I was told, you can't write a book with the man as the central figure; the woman has to be the central figure. In my innocence, I had made a privateer the central figure! Of course it didn't work. I finally got it published, but with an obscure publishing house. They had no distribution, and the thing died. It was something I wanted to do, but it was a financial loss, and it's best forgotten.

CA: You wrote about American social morality in A Corrupted Land, *published in 1966. How do you feel about us twenty years later? What are your greatest concerns?*

COOK: Well, look at Wall Street today. I think one of the things that runs through our society is enormous greed. We're so greedy, so money-conscious; we judge success by the amount of money people accumulate. The people involved in this latest scandal on Wall Street are people who had everything in the world that anybody could want in the way of income, and yet they had to go beyond the law and cut all kinds of ethical corners and everything else to get more. I think the title *A Corrupted Land* is still apt today.

BIOGRAPHICAL/CRITICAL SOURCES:

BOOKS

Cook, Fred J., *Maverick: Fifty Years of Investigative Reporting* (autobiography), introduction by Studs Terkel, Putnam, 1984.

PERIODICALS

Library Journal, September 1, 1984.
Los Angeles Times, October 18, 1984.
Nation, September 2, 1968, December 29, 1984-January 5, 1985.
New Republic, April 2, 1966, April 20, 1967.
Newsweek, June 14, 1971.
New York Times, January 12, 1967, June 29, 1976.
New York Times Book Review, January 29, 1967, August 15, 1976, March 27, 1983, September 30, 1984.
Saturday Review, January 14, 1967, July 13, 1968, September 18, 1971.
Times Literary Supplement, May 27, 1965.

—*Sketch by Cheryl Gottler*

—*Interview by Jean W. Ross*

COOK, Stephani 1944-

PERSONAL: Born October 19, 1944, in Chicago, Ill.; divorced; children: Alexandra Siegel, Zachary Siegel. *Education:* Barnard College, B.A., 1966; Columbia University, M.A., 1972.

ADDRESSES: Home—Pound Ridge, N.Y. *Agent*—Ned Leavitt, William Morris Agency, 1350 6th Ave., New York, N.Y. 10019.

CAREER: Eileen Ford Agency, New York City, model, 1964-70; private practice of psychotherapy and sex therapy in New York City, 1971-78; Young & Rubicam (advertising agency), New York City, research executive, 1983-84; D.Y.R., New York City, creative planning manager, 1984-86; Television Bureau of Advertising, New York City, director of retail marketing, 1986—. Family Counseling host on television talk show, 1976-77; developed and presented self-image seminars for *Glamour*, 1977-78; writer.

WRITINGS:

Second Life (autobiography; Literary Guild dual main selection; Young Parents Book Club alternate selection), Simon & Schuster, 1981.
(With Richard Lumiere) *Healthy Sex—and Keeping It That Way: A Complete Guide to Sexual Infections*, Simon & Schuster, 1983.
(With R. Stein) *Set Free*, Simon & Schuster, 1987.

Also contributor of articles to numerous periodicals, including *Family Weekly*, *Gentleman's Quarterly*, *Glamour*, and *Mademoiselle*.

SIDELIGHTS: Stephani Cook's autobiographical *Second Life*, which describes the author's experience wth patronizing doctors who consistently misdiagnosed her life-threatening illness, is "a medical horror story," according to *Newsweek*'s Walter Clemons. When Cook, a former cover girl and model, began to experience sporadic chest pains, her doctors dismissed them as postpartum hysteria brought on by the birth of her second child. When the pains persisted, Cook underwent a D&C (a surgical procedure in which tissue is scraped from the wall of the uterus), and she was administered periodic doses of antibiotics. When subsequent tests revealed blood clots in her venal system, Cook was subjected to a radical hysterectomy because her doctors believed that her ovarian veins were producing the dangerous emboli. Following the surgery, however, Cook's pain increased and she began to exhibit new symptoms.

Open-heart surgery came next because her doctors suspected that a tumor on her heart might be causing the clots. Cook underwent the procedure only to find out later that the clots were actually fragments of a rare placental cancer that could have been readily diagnosed two years earlier with a simple urinalysis and that neither the hysterectomy nor the heart surgery had been necessary. Cook eventually recovered after extensive treatment with chemotherapy.

Washington Post critic Laurel Lee praised Cook's account of her ordeal, noting that the author's "skill with the written word . . . makes vivid her physical and mental sufferings. Her language," Lee continued, "is rich with insights and imagery." Clemons, who admitted that he hadn't wanted to read *Second Life*, reported that he "was fascinated and shaken by it," and commended the book as "a salutary manual of hard-earned rage."

Cook told *CA:* "My book is really much more about a woman's search for self than about cancer, which only supplies the overriding metaphor and the narrative trajectory."

Vivian Castleberry of the *Dallas Times Herald* agreed, praising *Second Life* as "the best feminist book of this decade—maybe ever—and it is all the more powerful because it isn't meant to be a feminist book at all. . . . [It] is a feminist book because it portrays in absolute candor the psychology of women, how they feel, what they think, how they perceive, what they dream."

BIOGRAPHICAL/CRITICAL SOURCES:

PERIODICALS

Dallas Times Herald, November 4, 1981.
Newsweek, November 2, 1982.
People, December 14, 1981.
Washington Post, September 12, 1981.

*   *   *

COOMBS, Philip H(all) 1915-

PERSONAL: Born August 15, 1915, in Holyoke, Mass.; son of Charles Gilmore and Nellie (Hall) Coombs; married Helena Brooks, October 18, 1941; children: Peter Brooks, Helena Hall. *Education:* Amherst College, B.A., 1937; graduate study at University of Chicago, 1937-39, and Brookings Institution, 1939-40. *Politics:* Democrat.

ADDRESSES: Home—River Road, Essex, Conn. 06426. *Office*—International Council for Educational Development, P.O. Box 217, Essex, Conn. 06426.

CAREER: Williams College, Williamstown, Mass., instructor in economics, 1939, 1940-41; U.S. government, Washington, D.C., economist in Office of Price Administration, 1941-42, economic adviser in Office of Economic Stabilization, 1945-46; Amherst College, Amherst, Mass., professor of economics, 1947-49; President's Materials Policy Commission (Paley Commission), Washington, D.C., executive director, 1950-52; Ford Foundation, New York, N.Y., program director for education, and director of research, Fund for the Advancement of Education, 1952-60; U.S. Department of State, Washington, D.C., assistant secretary of state for international educational and cultural affairs, 1961-62; International Institute for Educational Planning, Paris, France, director, 1963-68, director of research, 1969-70; International Council for Educational Development, Essex, Conn., vice-chairman, 1970—. Chairman of U.S. delegation to UNESCO Conferences on Economic Growth and Educational Development in Addis Ababa, 1961, and Santiago, 1962; chairman of Organization for Economic Co-operation and Development Conference on Educational Investment and Economic Growth, Washington, D.C., 1962. Consultant on education and economic planning to governments of India, 1953-55 and 1986, Turkey, 1957, and Spain, 1967-71 and 1987. Visiting lecturer, Harvard University, Graduate School of Education, 1969; visiting professor, Yale University, Institute of Social Science, 1970-71. Cofounder, Center for Educational Enquiry, 1970. *Military service:* U.S. Army, Office of Strategic Services, 1943-45; received Legion of Merit.

MEMBER: International Society for Public Administration, American Economic Association, Council on Foreign Relations, Phi Beta Kappa, Century Association (New York).

AWARDS, HONORS: L.H.D., Amherst College, 1962; LL.D., Brandeis University and Monmouth College, 1962; Council on Foreign Relations fellowship, 1962-63; Brookings Institution guest fellow, 1963.

WRITINGS:

The Fourth Dimension of Foreign Policy—Educational and Cultural Affairs, Council on Foreign Relations and Harper, 1964.
Education and Foreign Aid, Harvard University Press, 1965.
The New Media: Memo to Educational Planners, UNESCO, 1967.
The World Educational Crisis: A Systems Analysis, Oxford University Press, 1968.
What Is Educational Planning?, UNESCO, 1970.
Managing Educational Costs, Oxford University Press, 1972.
New Paths to Learning for Rural Children and Youth, International Council for Educational Development, 1973.
Attacking Rural Poverty: How Nonformal Education Can Help, Johns Hopkins Press, 1974.
(Editor) *Education for Rural Development: Case Studies for Planners,* Praeger, 1975.
(Editor) *Meeting the Basic Needs of the Rural Poor: The Integrated, Community-Based Approach,* Pergamon, 1980.
Future Critical World Issues in Education: A Provisional Report of Findings, International Council for Educational Development, 1981.
New Strategies for Improving Rural Family Life, International Council for Educational Development, 1981.
The World Crisis in Education: The View from the Eighties, Oxford University Press, 1985.
Cost Analysis: A Tool for Educational Policy and Planning, World Bank/Oxford University Press, 1987.

Contributor to journals.

SIDELIGHTS: Philip H. Coombs told *CA:* "Most of my books and shorter pieces are addressed to a wide diversity of present and future policy-makers and practitioners of social, economic, and educational development, especially in developing countries. The aim is to communicate to them significant findings of our highly interdisciplinary field research in the hope that it will help them do a better job.

"For such communication to succeed, the author must put himself (or herself) in the skin of his (or her) audience and address them in a clear, jargon-free, efficient, and interesting manner, using practical examples to which they can readily relate. Such writing is the hardest work I do. It usually means throwing away the first several pages of each chapter until I finally discover what it is I want to say and how to say it as clearly and briefly as possible. I know I have succeeded—though it also bugs me—when some reader (often an academic who writes turgid articles for professional journals) exclaims, 'I wish I could write as easily, clearly, and interestingly as you do!' No doubt he could, but it would take a lot more thought and effort."

Coombs noted that his writings "have been published in numerous foreign languages and reached interested practitioners in remote parts of Africa, Asia, Latin America and the Caribbean. They are also widely used in universities and foreign aid organizations."

AVOCATIONAL INTERESTS: Sailing, fishing, swimming, touring, reading, house repairs, community service.

COOVER, James B(urrell) 1925-
(C. B. James)

PERSONAL: Born June 3, 1925, in Jacksonville, Ill.; son of James V. (a printer) and F. Elizabeth (Burrell) Coover; married Georgena Walker (a childhood specialist), September 28, 1945; children: Christopher, Mauri, Regan. *Education:* Northern Colorado University, B.A., 1949, MA., 1950; University of Denver, M.A., 1953.

ADDRESSES: Home—111 Marjann Ter., Tonawanda, N.Y. 14223. *Office*—Department of Music, State University of New York, Buffalo, N.Y. 14214.

CAREER: Bibliographical Center for Research, Denver, Colo., assistant director, 1950-53; Vassar College, George Sherman Dickinson Library, director, 1953-67; State University of New York at Buffalo, professor of music, 1967—, Ziegele Professor, 1981—. Manager and player with Hudson Valley Philharmonic Orchestra, 1959-67. New York State Council on the Arts, member, 1964-65, consultant, 1965-68; member of Mayor's Commission on the Arts, Poughkeepsie, N.Y., 1965-67. *Military service:* U.S. Army, 1943-45; served in European theater.

MEMBER: Association Internationale des bibliotheques musicales, Dictionary Society of North America, American Association of University Professors, Music Library Association (president, 1959-60).

WRITINGS:

Photoduplication Services: A Survey, 1951, Bibliographical Center for Research, 1951.
(Compiler) *A Bibliography of Music Dictionaries,* Bibliographical Center for Research, 1952, 3rd edition published as *Music Lexicography,* Carlisle Books, 1971.
Music Lexicography Including a Study of Lacunae: 1500-1700, Bibliographical Center for Research, 1958.
(Editor) *The 'Rainbeau' Catalog,* Distant Press, 1962.
(Author of appendix) Johannes Tinctoris, *Terminorum musicae diffinitorium* (title means "Dictionary of Musical Terms"), Free Press, 1963.
(With Richard Colvig) *Medieval and Renaissance Music on Long-Playing Records,* Information Coordinators, 1964.
(Contributor) C. J. Bradley, editor, *Manual of Music Librarianship,* Music Library Association, 1966.
Gesamtausgaben: A Checklist, Distant Press, 1970.
(With Colvig) *Medieval and Renaissance Music on Long-Playing Records: Supplement, 1962-1971,* Information Coordinators, 1973.
(Contributor) Bradley, editor, *Reader in Music Librarianship,* Microcard Editions, 1974.
(Author of preface) Guy A. Marco, *Information on Music,* Kent State University Press, 1974.
(Under pseudonym C. B. James) *Up to the Hilt!: An Index to an Unwritten Chronicle of the Hardcore,* Leftover Press, 1975.
(Contributor) *New Grove Dictionary of Music and Musicians,* 6th edition, Macmillan, 1980.
Musical Instrument Collections, Information Coordinators, 1981.
Music Publishing, Copyright, and Piracy in Victorian England, Mansell, 1985.
(Editor with Bradley) *Richard S. Hill: Tributes from Friends,* 1987.
Music at Auction: Putlick and Simpson (of London), 1794-1971, Information Coordinators, 1988.

Contributor of articles and reviews to music and library journals.

SIDELIGHTS: James B. Coover told *CA:* "The appellation 'author' is probably a bit exalted for a person whose work has been mostly bibliographic. But it's heady, and I like it!"

*   *   *

CORBETT, Scott 1913-

PERSONAL: Born July 27, 1913, in Kansas City, Mo.; son of Edward Roy and Hazel Marie (Emanuelson) Corbett; married Elizabeth Grosvenor Pierce, 1940; children: Florence Lee. *Education:* Kansas City Junior College, A.A., 1932; University of Missouri—Columbia, B.J., 1934. *Religion:* Episcopalian.

ADDRESSES: Home—149 Benefit St., Providence, R.I. 02903. *Agent*—Curtis Brown Ltd., 10 Astor Place, New York, N.Y. 10003.

CAREER: Writer. Moses Brown School, Providence, R.I., English teacher, 1957-65. *Military service:* U.S. Army 42nd (Rainbow) Infantry Division, 1943-46; became sergeant; army correspondent and final editor, continental edition, *Yank.*

MEMBER: Authors Guild, Authors League of America.

AWARDS, HONORS: Edgar Allan Poe Award, Mystery Writers of America, 1963, for *Cutlass Island;* Mark Twain Award, Missouri Library Association, 1976, and Golden Archer Award, University of Wisconsin, 1978, both for *The Home Run Trick.*

WRITINGS:

The Relucant Landlord, illustrated by Paul Galdone, Crowell, 1950.
Sauce for the Gander (Book-of-the-Month Club alternate selection), illustrated by Don Freeman, Crowell, 1951.
We Chose Cape Cod, Crowell, 1953.
Cape Cod's Way: An Informal History (nonfiction), Crowell, 1955.
(With Manuel Zora) *The Sea Fox: The Aventures of Cape Cod's Most Colorful Rumrunner,* Crowell, 1956.

JUVENILES

Susie Sneakers, illustrated by Leonard Shortall, Crowell, 1956.
Midshipman Cruise, Atlantic-Little, Brown, 1957.
Tree House Island (Junior Literary Guild selection), illustrated by Gordon Hansen, Atlantic-Little, Brown, 1959.
Dead Man's Light, illustrated by Shortall, Atlantic-Little, Brown, 1960.
Danger Point: The Wreck of the Birkenhead, Atlantic-Little, Brown, 1962.
Cutlass Island (Junior Literary Guild selection), illustrated by Shortall, Atlantic-Little, Brown, 1962.
What Makes a Car Go? (nonfiction), illustrated by Leonard Darwin, Atlantic-Little, Brown, 1963.
One by Sea (Junior Literary Guild selection), illustrated by Victor Mays, Atlantic-Little, Brown, 1965.
What Makes TV Work? (nonfiction), illustrated by Darwin, Atlantic-Little, Brown, 1965.
The Cave above Delphi, illustrated by Gioia Fiammenghi, Holt, 1965.
What Makes a Light Go On? (nonfiction; Junior Literary Guild selection), illustrated by Darwin, Atlantic-Little, Brown, 1966.
Pippa Passes, illustrated by Judith Gwyn Brown, Holt, 1966.

The Case of the Gone Goose, illustrated by Paul Frame, Atlantic-Little, Brown, 1966.

Diamonds Are Trouble, Holt, 1967, revised edition published as *The Trouble with Diamonds,* illustrated by Bert Dodson, Dutton, 1985.

What Makes a Plane Fly? (nonfiction), illustrated by Darwin, Atlantic-Little, Brown, 1967.

Cop's Kid, illustrated by Jo Polseno, Atlantic-Little, Brown, 1968.

The Case of the Fugitive Firebug, illustrated by Frame, Atlantic-Little, Brown, 1969.

Ever Ride a Dinosaur?, illustrated by Mircea Vasiliu, Holt, 1969.

Diamonds Are More Trouble, Holt, 1969.

Rhode Island (nonfiction), Coward, 1969.

The Baseball Bargain, illustrated by Wallace Tripp, Atlantic-Little, Brown, 1970.

What Makes a Boat Float? (nonfiction), illustrated by Mays, Atlantic-Little, Brown, 1970.

The Mystery Man, illustrated by Nathan Goldstein, Atlantic-Little, Brown, 1970.

Steady, Freddie! (Junior Literary Guild selection), illustrated by Lawrence Beall Smith, Dutton, 1970.

The Case of the Ticklish Tooth, illustrated by Frame, Atlantic-Little, Brown, 1971.

The Red Room Riddle: A Ghost Story, illustrated by Geff Gerlach, Atlantic-Little, Brown, 1972.

Dead before Docking, illustrated by Frame, Atlantic-Little, Brown, 1972.

The Big Joke Game (Junior Literary Guild selection), illustrated by Vasiliu, Dutton, 1972.

Run for the Money, illustrated by Dodson, Atlantic-Little, Brown, 1973.

Dr. Merlin's Magic Shop, illustrated by Joe Mathieu, Atlantic-Little, Brown, 1973.

What about the Wankel Engine? (nonfiction), illustrated by Jerome Kuehl, Four Winds Press, 1974.

Here Lies the Body, illustrated by Gerlach, Atlantic-Little, Brown, 1974.

The Case of the Silver Skull, illustrated by Frame, Atlantic-Little, Brown, 1974.

The Great Custard Pie Panic, illustrated by Mathieu, Atlantic-Little, Brown, 1974.

Take a Number, Dutton, 1974.

The Case of the Burgled Blessing Box, illustrated by Frame, Atlantic-Little, Brown, 1975.

The Boy with Will Power, illustrated by Ed Parker, Atlantic-Little, Brown, 1975.

The Boy Who Walked on Air, illustrated by Parker, Atlantic-Little, Brown, 1975.

Captain Butcher's Body, illustrated by Gerlach, Atlantic-Little, Brown, 1976.

The Hockey Girls, Dutton, 1976.

The Foolish Dinosaur Fiasco, illustrated by Jon McIntosh, Atlantic-Little, Brown, 1978.

Bridges (nonfiction; ALA Notable Book), illustrated by Richard Rosenblum, Four Winds Press, 1978.

The Discontented Ghost, Dutton, 1978.

The Mysterious Zetabet (Junior Literary Guild selection), illustrated by McIntosh, Atlantic-Little, Brown, 1979.

The Donkey Planet, illustrated by Troy Howell, Dutton, 1979.

Jokes to Read in the Dark (nonfiction), illustrated by Annie Gusman, Dutton, 1980.

Home Computers: A Simple and Informative Guide (nonfiction), Atlantic-Little, Brown, 1980.

The Deadly Hoax, Dutton, 1981.

Grave Doubts, Atlantic-Little, Brown, 1982.

Jokes to Tell Your Worst Enemy (nonfiction), illustrated by Gusman, Dutton, 1984.

Down with Wimps!, illustrated by Larry Ross, Dutton, 1984.

Witch Hunt, edited by Melanie Kroupa, Atlantic-Little, Brown, 1985.

"TRICK" SERIES; ILLUSTRATED BY GALDONE

The Lemonade Trick (Junior Literary Guild selection), Atlantic-Little, Brown, 1960.

The Mailbox Trick, Atlantic-Little, Brown, 1961.

The Disappearing Dog Trick, Atlantic-Little, Brown, 1963.

The Limerick Trick (Junior Literary Guild selection), Atlantic-Little, Brown, 1964.

The Baseball Trick, Atlantic-Little, Brown, 1965.

The Turnabout Trick, Atlantic-Little, Brown, 1967.

The Hairy Horror Trick, Atlantic-Little, Brown, 1969.

The Hateful Plateful Trick, Atlantic-Little, Brown, 1971.

The Home Run Trick, Atlantic-Little, Brown, 1973.

The Hockey Trick, Atlantic-Little, Brown, 1974.

The Black Mask Trick, Atlantic-Little, Brown, 1976.

The Hangman's Ghost Trick, Atlantic-Little, Brown, 1977.

"THE GREAT McGONIGGLE" SERIES; ILLUSTRATED BY BILL OGDEN

The Great McGoniggle's Gray Ghost, Atlantic-Little, Brown, 1975.

The Great McGoniggle's Key Play, Atlantic-Little, Brown, 1976.

The Great McGoniggle Rides Shotgun, Atlantic-Little, Brown, 1977.

The Great McGoniggle Switches Pitches, Atlantic-Little, Brown, 1980.

OTHER

Contributor to periodicals, including *Saturday Evening Post,* *Atlantic,* and *Good Housekeeping.*

SIDELIGHTS: "My parents ruined my chances of ever being a great novelist by giving me a happy childhood. Everybody knows that's no way to become another Dickens," wrote Scott Corbett in his contribution to *Something about the Author Autobiography Series.* But Corbett has been writing successfully since the fifties, giving his young readers an abundance of nonfiction, and mystery and adventure tales, including his well-known "Trick" series. Corbett prides himself on the fact that he is one of a few hundred authors in America who earn a living solely on their writing. He has written more than seventy books, some of them while at sea.

Corbett did not originally write for children. He maintains that his "lowly" beginning as a writer revolved around his obsession with jokes. During his two years of junior college in Kansas City, Missouri, Corbett perused jokebook after jokebook, and consequently learned the technique behind successful joke writing. He eventually sent some of his own jokes to pulp magazines and found himself "staring in ecstasy at a two-dollar check. That was the standard rate," wrote Corbett in the *SATA Autobiography Series.* When the humor page of the *Saturday Evening Post* began accepting his jokes, Corbett realized he had "broke[n] into the big time."

Corbett received his degree in journalism from the University of Missouri but never worked for a newspaper. His interest was in free-lance work, and though various opportunities arose whereby Corbett could have bettered his income, he believes he has a guardian angel who has kept him from writing for anyone but himself. Corbett stayed with free-lance writing and succeeded.

Corbett's first book, an adult novel written in 1950 entitled *The Reluctant Landlord,* was inspired by the experiences he and his wife had as landlords of a Manhattan brownstone. The book was bought by Twentieth Century-Fox for $17,500 and was made into the movie "Love Nest." Although Corbett had reservations about portraying his tenants realistically, he says in his autobiographical essay that "people don't care what you write about them if you write it with affection. [My tenants] were instantly my best publicity agents. They would go into bookstores, stealthily push a best-seller display aside, and put *The Reluctant Landlord* in its place."

Corbett wrote more adult fiction and also nonfiction, but in the mid-1950s, when he could not make his publisher's idea for a book work, he wrote a children's book instead and realized he had found his niche as a writer at last. Several of his children's books are Junior Literary Guild selections, and his 1962 work entitled *Cutlass Island* was granted the Edgar Allan Poe Award from Mystery Writers of America. *The Lemonade Trick* from Corbett's "Trick" series has sold nearly a million copies since its appearance in 1960.

In *The Lemonade Trick,* young Kerby Maxwell and a friend discover that after adding a chemical solution to some lemonade, whoever drinks the special concoction becomes *good.* According to Corbett in the *SATA Autobiography Series,* the first pages of *The Lemonade Trick* are autobiographical, and "then comes the zany 'What if . . .?'" For Corbett, "'What if . . .?' is what makes a story. I start with an everyday situation, and then think, 'What if, instead of the expected, the unexpected happens?'" Corbett says his entire "trick" series evolved from this manner of thinking, and so, too, did his book *The Red Room Riddle: A Ghost Story.*

Corbett and his wife have traveled throughout the world, mostly on freighters. Corbett once wrote to *CA* regarding his days at sea: "We have been at sea a total of over three years. This has been possible because I find I can get as much productive work done at sea as I do at home, and *productive* work (this fact is sometimes overlooked by busy-work experts) is the work that really matters."

Corbett's manuscripts are included in the de Grummond Collection at the University of Southern Mississippi and the Kerlan Collection at the University of Minnesota.

MEDIA ADAPTATIONS: The Reluctant Landlord was made into a movie entitled "Love Nest" by Twentieth Century-Fox, 1950, starring June Haver and Bill Lundigan, and featuring Marilyn Monroe; *The Red Room Riddle* was made into a movie for ABC-TV, 1983, with screenplay by Stephen Manes; *The Great McGoniggle's Gray Ghost* was made into a recording for Listening Library, 1980.

AVOCATIONAL INTERESTS: Walking, reading, travel, tennis, chess, fishing, boats, islands, the sea, and New England fishing villages.

BIOGRAPHICAL/CRITICAL SOURCES:

BOOKS

Books for Children: 1960-1965, American Library Association, 1966.
Children's Literature in the Elementary School, Holt, 1961.
Children's Literature Review, Volume I, Gale, 1976.
Larrick, Nancy, *A Parent's Guide to Children's Reading,* 3rd edition, Doubleday, 1969.
Something about the Author Autobiography Series, Volume II, Gale, 1986.

* * *

CORMIER, Robert (Edmund) 1925-
(John Fitch IV)

PERSONAL: Born January 17, 1925, in Leominster, Mass.; son of Lucien Joseph (a factory worker) and Irma (Collins) Cormier; married Constance B. Senay, November 6, 1948; children: Roberta S., Peter J., Christine J., Renee E. *Education:* Attended Fitchburg State College, one year.

ADDRESSES: Home—1177 Main St., Leominster, Mass. 01453.

CAREER: Radio WTAG, Worcester, Mass., writer, 1946-48; *Telegram & Gazette,* Worcester, reporter, 1948-55; *Fitchburg Sentinel,* Fitchburg, Mass., reporter, 1955-59, wire editor, 1959-66, became associate editor, 1966; free-lance writer, 1978—. Writing consultant to the *Telegram & Gazette.*

MEMBER: L'Union St. Jean Baptiste d'Amerique.

AWARDS, HONORS: Best human interest story of the year, Associated Press in New England, 1959 and 1973; best newspaper column, K. R. Thomson Newspapers, Inc., 1974; "Outstanding Book of the Year" awards, *New York Times,* 1974, for *The Chocolate War,* 1977, for *I Am the Cheese,* and 1979, for *After the First Death;* "Best Book for Young Adults" citations, American Library Association, 1974, for *The Chocolate War,* 1977, for *I Am the Cheese,* 1979, for *After the First Death,* and 1983, for *The Bumblebee Flies Anyway;* Maxi Award, *Media and Methods,* 1976; Doctor of Letters, Fitchburg State College, 1977; Woodward School Annual Book Award, 1978, for *I Am the Cheese;* Lewis Carroll Shelf Award, 1979, for *The Chocolate War;* "Notable Children's Trade Book in the Field of Social Studies" citation, National Council for Social Studies and Children's Book Council, 1980, for *Eight Plus One;* Assembly on Literature for Adolescents (ALAN) Award, National Council of Teachers of English, 1982; "Best of the Best Books, 1970-1983" citations, American Library Association, for *The Chocolate War, I Am the Cheese,* and *After the First Death;* "Best Books of 1983" citation, *School Library Journal,* for *The Bumblebee Flies Anyway;* "Honor List" citation, *Horn Book,* 1986, for *Beyond the Chocolate War.*

WRITINGS:

FICTION

Now and at the Hour, (novel), Coward, 1960.
A Little Raw on Monday Mornings (novel), Sheed, 1963.
Take Me Where the Good Times Are (novel), Macmillan, 1965.
The Chocolate War (novel), Pantheon, 1974, with teacher's guide by Lou Willett Stanek, Dell, 1975.
I Am the Cheese (novel), Pantheon, 1977, with teacher's guide by Stanek, Dell, 1978.
After the First Death (novel), Pantheon, 1979.
Eight Plus One (short stories), Pantheon, 1980.
The Bumblebee Flies Anyway (novel), Pantheon, 1983.
Beyond the Chocolate War (novel), Knopf, 1985.

Also author of *The Rumple Country* and *In the Midst of Winter,* both unpublished novels.

CONTRIBUTOR

Betsy Hearne and Marilyn Kay, editors, *Celebrating Children's Books: Essays in Honor of Zena Sutherland*, Lothrop, 1981.

Sixteen: Short Stories by Outstanding Writers for Young Adults, Delacorte, 1984.

Mark I. West, editor, *Trust Your Children: Voices against Censorship in Children's Literature*, Neal-Schuman, 1987.

OTHER

Fitchburg Sentinel, author of book review column, "The Sentinel Bookman," 1964-78, and of human interest column under pseudonym John Fitch IV, 1969-78; also author of monthly human interest column, "1177 Main Street," for *St. Anthony Messenger*, 1972-82. Contributor of articles and short stories to periodicals, including *Catholic Library World, McCall's, Redbook, Saturday Evening Post, Sign,* and *Woman's Day*.

WORK IN PROGRESS: Another novel.

SIDELIGHTS: With his 1974 novel *The Chocolate War* and the string of acclaimed works that followed, Robert Cormier has secured a position as one of today's foremost authors writing for adolescents. Tony Schwartz in *Newsweek* calls Cormier young adult literature's "best-selling heavyweight writer, an equivalent to Saul Bellow or William Styron." Cormier's much-discussed—and, in some circles, controversial—novels explore themes uncommon to young adult fiction, such as the relationship between good and evil, the struggle of individuals with institutions, and the abuse of power and authority. His novels involve teenage protagonists faced with difficult, uncompromising situations: Jerry Renault in *The Chocolate War*, brutalized by an entire school for his decision to boycott a fund-raising campaign; Ben in *After the First Death*, betrayed by his own father in order to protect a secret government project; and Kate, also in *After the First Death*, killed by a terrorist to whom she had expressed compassion and understanding. "Cormier seems to believe that teenagers are more idealistic today than in years past," writes Joe Stines in the *Dictionary of Literary Biography*, "and he affords them respect and responsibility in his writing while simultaneously awakening them to the harsh realities of life in contemporary America." While some reviewers and educators have criticized Cormier's work for portraying too bleak a view of reality for adolescents—his work has been nearly banned from some school libraries—a larger number recognize the value and contribution of his fiction to the corpus of young adult literature. W. Geiger Ellis in the *ALAN Review* praises Cormier for characters that have "stepped boldly and independently into the world of adolescent literature where most characters finally got their first bra, reached a decision about having intercourse, chose to have an abortion or a baby, kicked a drug habit or adjusted to a single-parent home. . . . It took the good sense of [Cormier] to have a larger view and see the much greater problems that young people face."

Cormier has commented on how he finds the trials that face adolescents both meaningful and inspiring. "An adult is in charge of his own life, while teen-agers face . . . tests every day and yet they're held down," he told Merri Rosenberg in the *New York Times Book Review*. "They don't have the freedom that adults have. . . . Kids that age want to be independent and free, and they think they are, but they're the most conformist group in the world. . . . It's a wonderfully dramatic time to write about." Cormier's understanding of adolescent issues and his ability to communicate to adolescents is evident in the large number who have been compelled to either write or call Cormier directly with questions or comments about his books. Cormier has found that his young readers are generally untroubled by the messages of his novels. "They don't get upset," he told Rosenberg, "They might say to me, 'Gee I wish Jerry Renault . . . hadn't lost in the end,' but they're not upset about the world I portray because they're in that world every day and they know it's war, psychological war. I seldom get a young person taking me to task for being too brutal." Cormier maintains that he writes novels with young adults as characters, and not young adult novels, although he acknowledges the fact that adolescents are his most avid readers. "I've aimed for the intelligent reader," he explains in his *CA* interview, "and have often found that that reader is fourteen years old." Questioned about the possible role models he may be providing teenagers, Cormier told Anita Silvey in *Horn Book Magazine*, "I'm not worrying about corrupting youth. I'm worrying about writing realistically and truthfully to affect the reader. . . . What I worry about is good taste and getting my message across by whatever means I can."

Cormier had three moderately successful "adult" novels to his credit—*Now and at the Hour, A Little Raw on Monday Mornings,* and *Take Me Where the Good Times Are,* in addition to numerous short stories—yet Stine notes that the best-selling and critically acclaimed *The Chocolate War* has emerged as the "cornerstone of his writing career." Extending from a personal experience in which Cormier's son refused to sell chocolates for a high school fund-raiser, *The Chocolate War*, according to Theodore Weesner in the *New York Times Book Review*, is "a story with a highly serious message not only about the usurpation and misuse of power but about power's inevitable staying." In the novel, Jerry Renault, a perplexed freshman at a Catholic boys school, is caught in a power play between Archie Costello, leader of the school's gang-like secret society, and Brother Leon, the school's headmaster and organizer of the fund-raiser. The headmaster secretly enlists the gang to help sell the chocolates; at the same time Archie, the leader, challenges Jerry to boycott the sale for ten days. Jerry complies; however, when the ten days are over, he decides (for reasons he's not sure of) to continue the boycott. When Jerry's stand begins to catch on with other students, the fund-raiser is threatened. Archie proceeds to focus the gang's activities on ensuring the success of the chocolate sale. Under their influence, which includes blackmail and physical force, sales increase dramatically and the fund-raiser becomes very popular. Jerry, however, continues to hold out and becomes the scorn of the school. In the novel's final scene, Archie rigs a fight in which Jerry is nearly beaten to death by the gang leader's subordinates. "Do I dare disturb the universe?"—the motto Jerry has posted in his locker—takes on special meaning. "Worse than the physical and official brutality is Jerry's moral breakdown," observes Hazel Rochman in the *New York Times Book Review*. "He discovers his own pleasure in violence, and in his defeat whispers to the friend who betrayed him: 'play ball. . . . Don't disturb the universe.'"

The Chocolate War created a sensation among critics, the majority of whom found its messages both powerful and disturbing. A number of reviewers focused on the fine line drawn between good and evil. "*The Chocolate War* . . . is a tour de force, and a tour de force of realism," writes Peter Hunt in the *Times Literary Supplement*. "With a pace and terror reminiscent of [Arthur Miller's] *The Crucible*, we see growing up as the realization that the world is rotten; that good and evil are barely distinguishable—both show weakness, fear, and selfishness.'' Margery Fisher echoes this view, stating in *Growing Point* that *The Chocolate War* ''ends in doubt—one might say in an inglorious draw. Presumably [Cormier] was not evading an ending but honestly intended to suggest that no decision between Good and Evil was really possible.'' The novel also makes a strong case against complacency, however. ''Cormier underscores the fact that good guys do not always win,'' writes Stines, ''[and] indicts those who remain indifferent in the face of evil or wrongdoing, pointing out that anyone who takes the risk of challenging evil can be destroyed both physically and psychologically.'' Patricia Campbell concurs, pointing out in her book *Presenting Robert Cormier* that *The Chocolate War* stresses the importance of standing up for one's convictions and supporting those who take initiative. ''Only by making that gesture can we hold on to our humanity, even when defeat is inevitable.... When the agents of evil are other human beings, perhaps good can win if enough people have the courage to take a stand together.''

The Chocolate War also addresses the pressures and dangers of conformity. In *The Marble in the Water: Essays on Contemporary Writers of Fiction for Children and Young Adults*, David Rees notes that ''on the surface . . . [the novel] is about power, power structures, corruption—about how absolute power corrupts absolutely. But, more subtly, beneath the surface, it is about compromise and the choice between hunting with the pack or searching for strength as an individual: about the toughness needed in the struggle to be a successful outsider.... The desire to be accepted is a major weakness which can easily be exploited by the wicked.'' Weesner finds that the novel's message regarding conformity and power offers a potentially important learning tool. ''Presenting as it does a philosophical plateau between childhood and adulthood, [*The Chocolate War*] seems an ideal study for the high school classroom. The characters . . . are accurate and touch close enough to raise questions of identification, questions of one's location within an arena of power, and also provide some hard recognition of the functions of power within a society.''

Although *The Chocolate War* received extensive praise from numerous critics and garnered a number of literary awards, some reviewers questioned the book's suitability for young audiences. Comments range from labeling the novel ''not appropriate for young people because it presents a distorted view of reality and because it lacks hope'' (Norma Bagnell, *Top of the News*) to ''there is no place on the shelves of a children's library for such a delight in the destruction of innocence'' (*Junior Bookshelf*). The book was nearly banned from some school libraries on the basis that its themes were disturbing and inappropriate for young readers. ''The book always triumphed, but even when you won, you lost,'' Cormier told Laurel Graeber in a *Publishers Weekly* profile. ''They'd say, 'Well, okay, but we'll put a mark on it indicating there's special permission needed to read it, or we'll put it in a special section.' And the narrowness of the victories always bother me—a three-to-two committee vote isn't any resounding triumph. And I'm just a minor part of it all, when you consider the great books that are being attacked.''

Response to negative criticism of *The Chocolate War* was both extensive and direct. Betty Carter and Karen Harris write in *Top of the News* that ''Robert Cormier does not leave his readers without hope, but he does deliver a warning: they may not plead innocence, ignorance, or prior commitments when the threat of tyranny confronts them. He does not imply that resistance is easy, but he insists it is mandatory.'' Commenting in *Signal*, Pelorus responds to those critics who claim that the

realism in the novel is too attractive and that the ending is hopeless: ''I would argue, and I fancy Cormier would too, that the real point of his book is to cause young readers to see the result of certain kinds of behavior and to opt not for the hopeless end that the logically worked-out image presents, but just for the opposite.'' In *American Libraries*, Richard Peck called *The Chocolate War* ''surely the most uncompromising novel ever directed to the '12 and up reader'—and very likely the most necessary. It depicts the mass psychology behind the looming menace of the gangs that have never been more omnipotent than now.... Anyone banning this book for its locker-room-realistic language is committing a crime against the young.''

Cormier's next novel, *I Am the Cheese*, is one of psychological suspense and deception, ''a horrifying tale of government corruption, espionage, and counter espionage told by an innocent young victim,'' writes S. L. Kennerly in *School Library Journal*. The victim is fourteen-year-old Adam Farmer, the son of a man with a hidden past: a government witness living under a false identity. One part of the book is told by Adam; another part, running concurrently, is a series of taped conversations between Adam and a psychiatrist pretending to help him, but really a government agent trying to determine what he knows. Bit by bit, Adam discovers (as does the reader) that no one around him is what they seem—and neither is he. Rather, notes Newgate Callendar in the *New York Times Book Review*, Adam is ''indeed the cheese—the bait around which the rats gather. Little he can do about it, except react the way God and Freud have provided. The ending is grim indeed.'' Anne Scott MacLeod in *Children's Literature in Education* describes *I Am the Cheese* as Cormier's ''most Kafka-esque'' novel, writing that ''the narrative technique, combined with a nearly overwhelming sense of loneliness, helplessness, and hopelessness give . . . a surreal quality.... It is as though [Adam] were alone in a computer room where every machine is programmed to cancel him out.''

Several critics commented on similarities between *I Am the Cheese* and *The Chocolate War*. Paul Heins of *Horn Book* believes that in both books, ''Mr. Cormier is actually writing about human integrity; and in the course of doing so, he cogently uncovers the lacerations that evil often inflicts upon the innocent.'' Lance Salway of the *Times Literary Supplement* states that the theme dominating the two novels is one ''of innocence and morality destroyed by the ruthless ambition of the masters of a corrupt society.'' He also notes, however, that *I Am the Cheese* extends into more disturbing territory. ''The hero is an unwilling, uncomprehending and truly innocent victim of a greater, more hideous conspiracy; the corrupt society is our own, and the innocent victim must be completely destroyed in order to sustain it.'' Rees echoes this aspect: ''There is little obvious compromise in *I Am the Cheese*, for political power and corruption are not illustrated in this book through the world of school life, but by the power of the government itself, and Cormier's message here is much more bleak: that the stand of one or two individuals against the whole apparatus of government is hopeless.''

A number of reviewers singled out the structure and writing technique of *I Am the Cheese* as important to its impact. ''The genius of the novel is that it is both a logical puzzle and exciting thriller, that it engenders detachment and involvement at the same time,'' writes Perry Nodelman in *Children's Literature in Education*. ''Cormier achieves that paradoxical combination by focusing our attention on the past—making us think about what might have happened, as mysteries do—

while at the same time keeping us ignorant of the present that mysterious past led to.'' Adam's bike ride through the New England countryside—the significance of which the reader gradually realizes—exemplifies this technique. ''As in dreams real emotions are translated into fantasy people and events,'' writes Campbell, ''so as the bike ride progresses Adam's hidden awareness of the menace all around him begins to come to the forefront of his mind and take on personification, shape, and form.'' This effect ultimately accentuates the novel's message. ''The book is more than just a good thriller,'' notes Salway. ''Cormier has written a chilling study of a mind on the verge of disintegration, and presented us with a view of our society that is too dire to contemplate.'' Charles Michener, in a 1977 issue of *Newsweek,* proclaimed *I Am the Cheese* ''simply one of the best novels written for any age group this year,'' adding that ''Cormier's style is swift and sure; his sense of place and people is . . . colorful . . . ; his denouement is truly shattering, explosive with paranoia and compassion.''

Cormier's next novel, *After the First Death,* is another psychological thriller which further explores the themes of fear, betrayal, and the abuses of power, while charting new territory. An account of terrorists hijacking a busload of schoolchildren in Massachusetts, *After the First Death* moves deeply into the minds of three teenage protagonists: Miro, one of the terrorist hijackers, Kate, the driver of the bus, and Ben, son of an Army general in negotiation with the terrorists. Amelia M. Bell in the *ALAN Review* notes a similarity among these three characters in that their ''lives are irrevocably changed by events beyond their control,'' and that they share a ''quest for the knowledge and experience that mark the closing of the gap between childhood and adulthood.'' However, Dominic Hibberd observes in the *Times Literary Supplement* that this knowledge and experience develop in ''a bleak world, in which understanding is corrupted into manipulation and love into destruction.'' As in other Cormier novels, an adult world is implicated. Ellin writes that ''the adults in whose orbits [the young adults] move . . . have their own desperate needs, and no matter what side they are on and no matter how fervently they believe that they act only to create a world fit for their children, it is their children that they sacrifice to the process.'' Barbara F. Harrison echoes both these points in *Horn Book Magazine:* ''On one level the book is about the nature of individual and collective identity. On another, it is about the victimization of innocence.''

MacLeod calls these first three young adult novels of Cormier ''at bottom, political.'' Accordingly, Cormier is distinguished as a novelist for adolescents in that he ''is far more interested in the systems by which a society operates than he is in individuals. His novels center on the interplay between individuals and their context, between the needs and demands of the system and the needs and rights of individuals—in other words, on the political context in which his characters, like all of us, must live.'' In line with the two previous novels, *After the First Death* ''shows privileged position and privileged information used to manipulate the weak and the unwary,'' MacLeod continues; it is particularly similar to *I Am the Cheese* in that, ''the discussion of political evil is cast in fiercely contemporary terms, and the shadow of statism stretches long over the narrative.'' Cormier likewise presents a warning in *After the First Death* ''that political innocence is a dangerous quality, that it can be a kind of collaboration with evil, that innocence is often acquiescence through moral neutrality in the abuse of power by the powerful, and in the sacrifice of the individual to the political organization.'' Campbell clarifies the roots of

this struggle. ''The 'enemy' . . . is not necessarily evil. The unifying characteristic in all these manifestations of the concept can be neatly pinned down with the word 'implacable'. . . . What fascinates Cormier, the eternal question that draws him back again and again, is 'How can we confront the utterly Implacable and still remain human?' His emotion centers on the individual made powerless, cut off from all recourse.''

Cormier's sequel, *Beyond the Chocolate War,* together with these first three young adult novels, ''form a tetralogy of political statement and are undoubtedly Cormier's mature masterpieces,'' writes Campbell. The four are connected by ''the brilliant and complex structure, the intricate wordplay and subtlety of thought, and above all the power and conviction of theme [that] are unequaled by anything of his that came before or has yet come after.'' *Beyond the Chocolate War* was largely written at the urgings of numerous readers who pressed Cormier for knowledge of the original characters' fates, something in which Cormier was also interested. While reviewers detect the presence of traditional Cormier themes in the sequel, some have remarked that the novel focuses on character development at the expense of thematic development. Rochman comments that *Beyond the Chocolate War* is ''not as starkly dramatic as its predecessor,'' noting that ''it relies too much on . . . explication, and there is less action and more emphasis on the internal lives of many characters.'' Roger Sutton concurs, writing in the *School Library Journal* that ''Cormier continues his exploration into good and evil . . . [yet] intensifies and explicates what was powerfully implicit in the first book. While the sequel can be read independently, [new] readers . . . may be puzzled by what is essentially a string of thematic reverberations.'' Nonetheless, Sarah Hayes maintains in the *Times Literary Supplement* that Cormier ''excels in his juxtaposition of the horrific and the ordinary; of the sinister and the explicable.'' As in his other novels, Cormier is interested in ''the flashpoint at which violence can suddenly erupt, and as suddenly turn tragedy into farce.''

Cormier's 1983 novel, *The Bumblebee Flies Anyway,* is distinct from his other young adult writings. ''Balancing on the fine line between realism and fantasy, [the novel] finds joy and even triumph in the grimmest circumstances,'' writes John Knowles in the *New York Times Book Review*. *The Bumblebee Flies Anyway* takes place in the ''Complex,'' an experimental hospital for the incurably ill, where the resident patients have volunteered to be subjects for testing drugs that may help cure people in the future. One of the patients, Barney, comes up with the idea of providing his friend Mazzo, another patient, the thrill of a lifetime. Barney leads a group of the residents on a project that involves disassembling a wooden mock-up sports car from a neighboring junkyard and reassembling it into a vehicle that will fly them into space. ''The last ride of this car,'' remarks Knowles, ''is to be apocalyptic, a defiance of gravity, just as the flight of the bumblebee, aerodynamically implausible, seems to be.'' There is an implication that a suicide pact is being made among the friends; however, the broader implication is, as Campbell notes, the realization of ''free choice'' outside ''the terrible, implacable fact of impending death,'' and that ''suicide is irreconcilable with an act of faith.'' Barney's building of the car represents the attainment of ''that humanizing gesture against the Implacable that is so central in Cormier's cosmos.'' The action of the story is played out in an almost dreamlike state that mixes hope with tragedy. Zena Sutherland remarks in *Bulletin of the Center for Children's Books* that ''it moves, with relentless inevitability . . . to the requiem of hopeless despair that, for each patient, still holds some passion for an affirmative act of life.''

Despite its serious and grim subject matter, *The Bumblebee Flies Anyway* impressed reviewers with its resilience. Anthony Horowitz writes in the *Times Literary Supplement* that although ''[the novel] raises some profound questions about medical ethics, about manipulation and about the attitudes to death of the dying and those closest to them[,]. . . even more enduring . . . are the final images of the book where, despite everything, a mood of magnificent optimism prevails, soaring from the terrible mundanity of pain and suffering to the inspiring and poetic victory of the unbroken human spirit.'' Similarly, Knowles detects a sense of triumph in the book's ending: ''Into the doomed, compartmentalized, infected world of the Complex there comes a kind of hope, of a flight defying the laws of the universe, of 'breaking through the grayness and the loneliness . . . out into the stars and the planets and beyond.'''

Reflecting on what is most important to him as a writer, Cormier has stated that expressing both the truth and the emotional content of his artistic vision are utmost, a commitment that many reviewers feel contributes to making Cormier's work unique within the scope of young adult literature. ''[The] novels of Robert Cormier have consistently transcended the limitations of the genre,'' writes Geraldine DeLuca in the *Lion and the Unicorn*. ''He has avoided the thin characterizations and glib language that are so familiar . . . perhaps because he is faithful to his own vision, writing more truly for himself than many other writers.'' In an interview with Paul Janezco of *English Journal*, Cormier talks about the particular importance that emotions play: ''[An] emotion sparks my impulse to write and I find myself at the typewriter trying to get the emotion and its impact down on paper. . . . The thing I'm trying to do is communicate with the reader—communicate the emotion I want him to feel. I sacrifice everything to do that. I want to hit the reader with whatever emotion I want to portray, or whatever action will make it vivid.'' In the *Proceedings of the Eighth Annual Conference of the Children's Literature Association*, Millicent Lenz describes Cormier as a ''romantic ironist'' and states that he is ''to be thanked for his unflinching artistic presentation of evil, for by it we may rediscover the vision of the good.'' Lenz cites lines from a passage in *After the First Death* describing the character Kate: ''She caught her breath, pondering a new thought: the possibility that hope comes out of hopelessness and that the opposites of things carry the seeds of birth—love out of hate, good out of evil. Didn't flowers grow out of dirt?''

CA INTERVIEW

CA interviewed Robert Cormier by telephone on April 13, 1987, at his home in Leominster, Massachusetts.

CA: After three novels and many short stories for adults, The Chocolate War *was a resounding success and placed you solidly as a writer for young adults. It wasn't a label you'd consciously sought. How do you feel about it now, and how much does it influence the actual writing?*

CORMIER: Sometimes I'm of two minds about it. On the one hand, this label has gained me a terrific audience of young people, and I know the success of my career has turned on that audience. I hear from them all the time, letters and phone calls, and I do a lot of speaking at schools and libraries, which

I enjoy very much doing. So it has been very good. The only qualm I do have is that I think the label does limit my audience. I really don't feel that I write young adult books, and I think a lot of adults who might read them stay away from them because of the label. But that is the only detrimental effect I can come up with.

In terms of my own writing, the beautiful part of it is that I can still write and have this audience and yet not limit my plots or my subtleties. I don't have to simplify stories. I write as if the audience didn't exist, really. I've aimed for the intelligent reader and have often found that that reader is fourteen years old.

CA: You told Victoria Irwin for the Christian Science Monitor *that you enjoy writing about young people because you feel an affinity for them. Did that come primarily from having your own children?*

CORMIER: Yes, I think it definitely did. First of all, it comes from memories of my own teenage years. If I have total recall of anything, it's not facts and figures but the way those years were, and not ever wanting to go through them again. Then when my own children became teenagers, I saw them going through the same things that I'd gone through and realized that they were universal and timeless. Seeing my own children renewing those adolescent years did lead me to start writing about them—but not for them. The short stories prior to *The Chocolate War* in which I dealt with young people were inspired by that same combination of my children's experiences and my memories of my own.

CA: Yes. You explained in the introductions to the stories collected in Eight Plus One *how things that happened to your children played a part in your writing, and* The Chocolate War *grew out of an experience your son Peter had. How have your children responded to your books?*

CORMIER: They're very supportive. One thing that makes a parent feel good is doing something that makes his children proud of him. They've all been avid readers, so my having achieved a reputation as a writer has made them very proud. And it's always been a family affair anyway. While they were growing up, I was writing all the time. They shared the bad times, the rejections, as well as the good times when a sale would come along and we'd go out and have a family dinner to celebrate, or go shopping and buy gifts. They've always been very much a part of the writing.

CA: And you've more than once spoken of the support your wife has given.

CORMIER: Oh yes. In fact, I've always thought my wife would have made a great editor, because she has a very discerning eye. She reads my work before anyone else sees it. It's terrific to have a built-in editor, and someone that you trust. She does the final manuscript typing, and then I usually circulate it among my children prior to publication.

CA: In what ways have you found your newspaper work helpful in writing fiction?

CORMIER: The main thing, I think, is the discipline it establishes. In newspaper work you write to a deadline; you write every day, when you don't feel like writing. You have to write economically, and sometimes to order. You may cover a lengthy story and then be told to cut it down to two pages. I think a lifetime of doing that carries over to my own work. I find that discipline seems to be such a problem, not only with myself, but with other people. I know a lot of talented people who never seem to get around to writing something. I have always been able to do this on weekends and nights. Besides the discipline I've gotten from the newspaper work, there's that direct journalistic style, which I still use to some extent. I use a lot of similes and metaphors, figures of speech, but essentially my style is very direct, and I strive for clarity. I think that comes out of my newspaper work, making the story real to the reader without any embellishment. In fiction, though, you can embellish somewhat and be more creative.

CA: The subconscious plays a great part in your writing, as you've described it. Are there ways you can aid and abet that faculty so that it can keep working at its best for you?

CORMIER: I think why I like novel writing in contrast to short story writing is that your characters are developed, and then they're sort of with you all the time, the way friends would be with you. And sometimes the best idea of what a character should do in the plot comes when I'm driving the car downtown or something like that. In terms of a schedule, I don't think of what I have to write on a given day. For instance, when I sat down this morning at the typewriter, I wasn't thinking in terms of having to write five pages or ten pages, but of what the characters were going to do. That's how they become real and stay with you.

I think the subconscious works in another way. I usually look at the writing late at night before I go to bed and begin writing again in the morning. I have a feeling something happens while I sleep. This night-morning habit sets up a continuity and a momentum, and I'm sure the subconscious has a part in that. It's hard to trace it, but I know that if I'm away from the work for a while, like on an extended trip, it's harder getting back in the swing of things, because the characters start fading in my mind.

CA: In an interview with Paul Janeczko for English Journal *you said that you write to communicate the emotions of your characters. How emotionally involved with them do you become in the writing?*

CORMIER: Very emotionally involved, really. Often things happen to them that upset me, that I don't want to happen. I was greatly affected by Kate's death in *After the First Death,* and the death of the little boy, Raymond. When I realized that the situation was set up so that a child would have to be murdered in cold blood, I really was aghast that I'd written myself into that kind of corner. Knowing what had to happen when I saw Kate's fate developing, knowing that she would ultimately and ironically do something that would cause her death, really bothered me. You do get involved with your characters, which is sometimes a hard thing for people who don't write to understand. I've said this at symposiums, and people look at me strangely. It doesn't bother me as much as if real people die, not to that extent. But it does affect me.

CA: Is your own emotion during the writing a measure of how well a story is working?

CORMIER: Yes, definitely. In fact, I abandoned a novel a couple of years ago because of that. I thought it was a very clever plot, and I still think it's a very clever plot, with a

couple of great psychological twists. My protagonist was a middle-aged man, and frankly I was not emotionally involved with him. So he began to bore me, and I just abandoned the novel. Because I wasn't emotionally involved with the character in that novel, it was more or less hack work, being clever. I think writing is more than that.

CA: I Am the Cheese is a difficult book not only emotionally, but also in terms of plot. Patricia J. Campbell discussed it quite intelligently in Presenting Robert Cormier. *Do readers have a hard time with it?*

CORMIER: Yes, they do. I receive an awful lot of mail, and a good deal of it concerns *I Am the Cheese.* A typical letter from a fourteen-year-old might say, "Dear Mr. Cormier: I just read *I Am the Cheese.* I read it twice. Will you please answer the following questions . . ." Then there's a long list of questions. And it's difficult for adults as well. There is a degree of ambiguity in it in the first place; all the questions aren't answered in the story. It's a funny thing about the writing. I wonder sometimes how I might have written a book if I had known the effect it would have on people. Writing is so private; even though you're writing for publication, at the time you're doing it you're not thinking of people reacting in a certain way. So when I see these questions come in, I wonder whether I might have clarified it a bit more. I'm not sure whether I would or not.

CA: What do you hope readers will get from the books?

CORMIER: I really try to affect them emotionally, to get some kind of reaction. I hope a book will linger with the reader. I'm not writing to make people feel good, and I think indifference would be the worst of all. I'd rather have a critical review than no review. I'm happy to have people put down the book and say, "Yes, that's the way it could happen. I don't *like* what happened, but that's the way it *could* happen."

CA: There's so much dishonesty between adults and young people, as you've said yourself. Adults like to say, "These are the happiest years of your life," and that's usually not true.

CORMIER: Yes. Kids are told that all the time. I was told that. I thought, something's got to be wrong, because these are terrible years. They had their peaks and pits, but there were so many pits! And you're not in control of your life. There's no perspective. They tell you they want you to be responsible people, and then they tell you to be in at eleven o'clock. There are all these dichotomies at work. I think some of the dishonesty comes from adults wanting to protect their children from certain realities, to sugar-coat what's going on. I used to be told, "You won't remember this on your wedding day." It didn't help at the moment, when I was really lacerated by something.

CA: No. And once you begin to get smart, you just think you're being lied to a lot.

CORMIER: Yes. I think kids are being lied to so much. In fact, they become accustomed to the lies, like the television lie that the good guy wins at the end of the program, the heroes of "Miami Vice" go on forever. They're even lied to in the commercials. Everybody knows that buying the right deodorant is not going to win you love. There's a continual lying going on, and they're adjusting to that. So when they read a realistic book, they cling to it and think, here's someone telling the truth. This is reflected in the letters I get from young people. So many readers say, "You tell it the way it is." That's very gratifying, because I get so many complaints from adult would-be censors.

CA: Speaking of television, one criticism that's made constantly of young people is that they watch television instead of reading. Do you consider television a competitor with your books?

CORMIER: It is such a visual world, it's so hard to avoid it. But somebody's reading out there, because kids are reacting. I know a lot of my books are in the classroom, so kids are getting them from teachers. I'd say yes, obviously the kids are watching television, and they can't be reading a book at the same time. We are creating a visual need. On MTV, they're aiming for an attention span of about three minutes. It is having an effect. But thank goodness there are still young people who love to pick up a good book at the library and rush home with it. And there are a number of them around, according to the mail I get.

CA: Do troubled young people call or write for help?

CORMIER: Not very often. When it does happen, it really shakes me up emotionally. I received a phone call last year from a girl in a psychiatric clinic in Connecticut who got a great deal of comfort out of *I Am the Cheese* because she felt that she was without identity, much like Adam, in a world she hadn't made. We spoke for probably a half-hour. Occasionally I'll go into a school and someone will mention a problem. But it's rare. Most of the letters I get are from kids who just want to touch base, and probably want to be writers, so they don't bring up problems. They may say there's a situation in their school something like one I've written about, but they really don't ask my advice about personal problems.

CA: You were reluctant to do a sequel to The Chocolate War, *but* Beyond the Chocolate War *apparently kept tugging at you. After the second book, do you feel through with the characters and the story?*

CORMIER: I thought I was! I wrote *Beyond the Chocolate War* after being badgered by young people for years and years asking what happened to the characters from *The Chocolate War*, and I wanted to find out. I thought I had closed the door on them; by the time I had finished the second book, I was kind of weary of Archie Costello and company. But again they're asking questions. And I'm kind of intrigued with Archie; I sometimes wonder what he would be like a few years into the future—say at twenty-eight. And Jerry Renault still intrigues me. He seemed to develop more for me in the sequel than he did in the original book. It's been on my mind. Who knows? It took me ten years to get around to *Beyond the Chocolate War*. I have no immediate plans for another book on the topic, but I must say those characters are pretty much alive to me. But then some of the characters from the other books are alive to me even now, and I haven't felt any compulsion to write about them.

CA: Maybe that's just a sign that they're good characters, they're real.

CORMIER: I hope so. There was a very minor character in *The Chocolate War*, Tubs Casper, who appeared for one scene. The kids invariably asked about him and what happened to him, almost to the point of being angry with me for introducing

him and not bringing him back. And in a way, even though I felt bad that I hadn't brought him back, it delighted me that the character became so real from that one simple scene. It's great when your characters really have life.

CA: How do you feel about Anne Scott MacLeod's definition, in Children's Literature in Education, *of your novels as "at bottom, political," because you are "far more interested in the systems by which society operates than . . . in individuals"?*

CORMIER: First of all, I'm always conscious of being a storyteller, and stories turn on creating real characters. I have themes or issues that I'm interested in as an individual, and if I can bring them into play, fine. Even writing about a chocolate sale in high school, I suddenly realized that I was exploring the abuse of power, intimidation, things like that. But those aren't my primary concerns. I'm always most concerned with the story itself and the people, creating people who really live and affect the reader. A story doesn't work at all unless the characters are real. I don't think of myself as a thematic writer or as writing primarily to explore current issues or to expose things going on in the world. This is secondary. And while I hope it's there on a secondary level and can be explored and communicated, I think of myself primarily as a storyteller.

CA: Do you think criticism in the field of young adult literature is generally good?

CORMIER: I think there are some very good things being done now. The Twayne series of biographies of young adult writers, of which mine is one, I think is a good step ahead. The *ALAN Review*, which concentrates on young adult books, has some great articles. *VOYA (Voice of Youth Advocates)* does a fine job. Slowly but surely, I think, the critical writing is becoming much more widespread and better than it was a few years ago. I think the best critical writing is the kind that illuminates the work for the subject. Patricia Campbell did that in her Twayne book; she made some links that surprised me. That kind of criticism is valid, but sometimes I read something I'm very puzzled about, because it wasn't anything that I had in mind. Often critics look for symbolism in things that really don't exist. And yet I think there are some subconscious things that get into the books that I'm probably not even aware of.

CA: Much of the critical writing on your work has dealt with its bleakness, and you have countered the criticism in various ways, depending on the specific circumstances. How would you respond to the charge now, considering the body of your work at this point?

CORMIER: I guess my attitude hasn't changed. I've never let the criticism affect my writing. I think there are values in my work that go beyond the bleakness. I'm so used to hearing that criticism, I really don't give it much thought. If I feel I'm doing my job honestly, being faulted for other things doesn't bother me. And I didn't set out to explore a whole bleak landscape in a body of work. When I wrote *The Chocolate War*, I wasn't aware that I was going to write *I Am the Cheese*. I didn't feel the books were that similar when I was writing them. The thing I've always been afraid of is rewriting the same novel; that's why I hesitated to do a sequel to *The Chocolate War*. That's one of the reasons why Jerry was such a problem: I didn't want to bring him back to Trinity, because I thought then I would just be writing *The Chocolate War* all over again. So I've been careful about that, even though people have looked at my writing as a body of work and seen similarities. I try to make each novel as different as possible. But maybe I haven't. It's always how the reader sees it.

The novel that I'm now working on is different from the work that is recent, at least. It's not because I was trying to strike out in any particular direction; it's something that took hold of me emotionally at a particular time in my life. I just go to the typewriter every day, and characters come to life for me to write about.

MEDIA ADAPTATIONS: "I Am the Cheese," a motion picture adapted from Cormier's novel of the same name, was released in 1983 by the Almi Group, starring Robert Wagner, Hope Lange, Robert Macnaughton, and featuring Cormier in the role of Mr. Hertz; "The Chocolate War," "I Am the Cheese," and "After the First Death," were all released as records and cassettes by Miller Brody in 1982.

BIOGRAPHICAL/CRITICAL SOURCES:

BOOKS

Campbell, Patricia J., *Presenting Robert Cormier*, Twayne, 1985.
Children's Literature Review, Volume XII, Gale, 1987.
Contemporary Literary Criticism, Gale, Volume XII, 1980, Volume XXX, 1984.
Cormier, Robert, *The Chocolate War*, Pantheon, 1974.
Cormier, Robert, *After the First Death*, Pantheon, 1979.
Cormier, Robert, *Eight Plus One*, Pantheon, 1980.
Cormier, Robert, *The Bumblebee Flies Anyway*, Pantheon, 1983.
Dictionary of Literary Biography, Volume LII: *American Writers for Children since 1960: Fiction*, Gale, 1986.
Inglis, Fred, *The Promise of Happiness: Value and Meaning in Children's Fiction*, Cambridge University Press, 1981.
Rees, David, *The Marble in the Water: Essays on Contemporary Writers of Fiction for Children and Young Adults*, Horn Book, 1980.

PERIODICALS

ALAN Review, fall, 1981, winter, 1985.
America, May 15, 1965.
American Libraries, October, 1974.
Atlantic, September, 1960.
Best Sellers, October 1, 1963, April 15, 1974, November, 1980.
Booklist, July 1, 1974, September 15, 1980, September 1, 1983, March 15, 1985.
Books for Keeps, September, 1985.
Boston Globe Magazine, November 16, 1980.
Bulletin of the Center for Children's Books, December, 1980, September, 1983.
Catholic World, December, 1960.
Children's Literature Association Quarterly, spring, 1986.
Children's Literature in Education, summer, 1981, summer, 1983.
Christian Science Monitor, June 1, 1979, May 20, 1980.
Commonweal, July 2, 1965.
English Journal, September, 1975, September, 1977.
Fitchburg Sentinel, August 2, 1960.
Growing Point, July, 1975.
Horn Book, August, 1977, April, 1979.
Horn Book Magazine, December, 1983, March-April, 1985, July-August, 1985.
Junior Bookshelf, June, 1975, August, 1979, December, 1985.
Kirkus Reviews, June 1, 1960.
Leominster Daily Enterprise, July 28, 1960.

Lion and the Unicorn, fall, 1978, winter, 1979-80.
Manchester Guardian, June 22, 1979.
Media and Methods, May-June, 1978.
Newsweek, December 19, 1977, July 16, 1979.
New York Herald Tribune Book Review, July 31, 1960.
New York Times, November 11, 1983.
New York Times Book Review, April 25, 1965, May 5, 1974, May 1, 1977, April 29, 1979, November 9, 1980, November 13, 1983, May 5, 1985.
Proceedings of the Eighth Annual Conference of the Children's Literature Association, March, 1981.
Publishers Weekly, October 7, 1983, July 24, 1987.
School Library Journal, May, 1977, March, 1979, September, 1980, November, 1982, April, 1985.
Signal, September, 1975.
Time, August 1, 1960.
Times (London), November 14, 1985.
Times Educational Supplement, November 18, 1977, January 13, 1984.
Times Literary Supplement, April 4, 1975, December 2, 1977, December 14, 1979, November 25, 1983, November 29, 1985.
Top of the News, spring, 1980, winter, 1980.
Voice of Youth Advocates, December, 1980.
Washington Post Book World, May 13, 1979, November 6, 1983, June 9, 1985.
World of Children's Books, fall, 1977.

—*Sketch by Michael E. Mueller*
—*Interview by Jean W. Ross*

*   *   *

CORT, M. C.
   See CLIFFORD, Margaret Cort

*   *   *

CORT, Margaret
   See CLIFFORD, Margaret Cort

*   *   *

CORWIN, Ronald G(ary) 1932-

PERSONAL: Born June 14, 1932, in Waterloo, Iowa; son of Leonard John and Beuhlah (Morris) Corwin; married Bonnie Titus, June 20, 1954; children: Cheryl, Marcia, Blair. *Education:* Iowa State Teachers College (now University of Northern Iowa), B.A. (with high honors), 1954; University of Iowa, graduate study, 1956; University of Minnesota, M.A., 1958, Ph.D., 1960.

ADDRESSES: Home—859 Old Woods Rd., Worthington, Ohio 43085. *Office*—Department of Sociology, Ohio State University, Columbus, Ohio 43210.

CAREER: University of Minnesota, Minneapolis, instructor in sociology, research fellow, and project director, 1959-60, assistant professor of education and research associate in sociology, 1960-61; Ohio State University, Columbus, assistant professor, 1961-65, associate professor, 1965-69, professor of sociology, 1969—. Visiting summer lecturer, Columbia University, 1965. Acting branch chief, Bureau of Research, U.S. Office of Education, 1966-67. Consultant, National Education Association, 1968-81, Abt Associates, Inc., 1973—, Center for Educational Policy and Management, University of Oregon, 1975-80, U.S. Office of Education Teacher Corps, 1975-

80, Research for Better Schools, Inc., 1976-80, and Center for Vocational Education, Ohio State University, 1984. *Military service:* U.S. Army, served in Japan, 1954-56; became sergeant.

MEMBER: American Educational Research Association (vice-president, 1969-71), American Sociological Association (fellow), North Central Sociological Association.

AWARDS, HONORS: U.S. Public Health Service grant, 1960-61; U.S. Office of Education grant, 1962-68; *Foundations of Administration* was selected by Alpha Lamda Delta as one of the year's ten significant books in education, 1967; Wright Award for service to organized student activities and development of student leadership, Ohio State University, 1967; Ford Foundation and National Education Association grant, 1968-73; selected as fifth among fourteen individuals for the greatest contribution to the field of sociology of education during the past twenty-five years, University of Nebraska, 1974.

WRITINGS:

(With M. J. Taves and J. Eugene Haas) *Role Conception and Success and Satisfaction,* Bureau of Business Research, Ohio State University, 1963.

A Sociology of Education: Emerging Patterns of Class, Status and Power in the Public Schools, Appleton-Century-Crofts, 1965.

(With Williard Lane and William Monahan) *Foundations of Administration in Education: A Behavioral Analysis,* Macmillan, 1966, revised edition, 1967.

Militant Professionalism: A Study of Conflict in High Schools, Appleton-Century-Crofts, 1970.

(Editor wth Saad Z. Nagi) *The Social Contexts of Research,* Wiley, 1972.

Reform and Organizational Survival: The Teacher Corps as an Instrument of Educational Change, foreword by Melvin Tumin, Wiley, 1973.

Education in Crisis: A Sociological Analysis of Schools and Universities in Transition, Wiley, 1974.

(With Roy Edelfelt and Elizabeth Hanna) *Lessons from the Teacher Corps,* National Education Association, 1974.

(Editor and contributor with Edelfelt) *Perspectives on Organizations,* American Association of Colleges for Teacher Education, Volume I: *Viewpoints for Teachers,* 1976, Volume II: *The School as a Social Organization,* 1977, Volume III: *Schools in the Larger Social Order,* 1978.

(Editor and contributor) *Sociology of Education and Socialization,* JAI Press, Volume I, 1980, Volume II, 1982.

(Author of foreword) Sam Sieber, *Fatal Remedies: The Ironies of Social Intervention,* Plenum, 1981.

(Editor) *Research in Sociology of Education and Socialization,* JAI Press, Volume II: (and contributor and author of foreword) *Research on Educational Organizations,* 1981, Volume III: *Policy Research,* 1982.

The Entrepreneurial Bureaucracy: Biographies of Two Federal Programs in Education, JAI Press, 1983.

The Organization-Society Nexus: A Critical Review of Models and Metaphors, Greenwood Press, 1987.

CONTRIBUTOR

(With Taves) Howard Freeman and others, editors, *Handbook of Medical Sociology,* Prentice-Hall, 1963.

Haas, *Role Conception and Group Consensus,* Ohio State University, 1964.

James Skipper and Robert Leonard, editors, *Social Interaction and Patient Care,* Lippincott, 1965.

Donald Hansen, editor, *Counseling in Society,* Houghton, 1966.

Hansen and Joel Gerst, editors, *On Education: Sociological Perspectives,* Wiley, 1967.

Stanley M. Elam, Myron Lieberman, and Michael H. Moskow, editors, *Readings on Collective Negotiations in Public Education,* Rand McNally, 1967.

Bruce Eckland, editor, *Perspectives on Human Deprivation,* National Child Health Institute, U.S. Public Health Service, Department of Health, Education and Welfare, 1968.

R. J. Havighurst, editor, *Readings,* Allyn & Bacon, 1968.

Harold I. Goodwin and Patrick W. Carlson, editors, *The Collective Dilemma: Negotiations in Education,* Charles Jones Publishing, 1969.

Hansen, editor, *Explorations in the Sociology of Counseling,* Houghton, 1969.

Fred D. Carver and Thomas J. Sergiovanni, editors, *Organizations and Human Behavior: Focus on Schools,* McGraw, 1969.

J. Belasco and M. Milstein, editors, *Behavioral Science and Educational Administration,* Allyn & Bacon, 1970.

Simon Marcson, *Decentralization and Community Control in Urban Areas,* Rutgers University, 1971.

Encyclopedia of Education, Macmillan, 1971.

Ronald Pavalko, editor, *Sociological Perspectives on Organizations,* F. E. Peacock, 1972.

Alfred Lightfoot, editor, *Inquiries into the Social Foundations of Education,* Rand McNally, 1972.

Jerald T. Hage and Koya Azumi, editors, *Sociological Study of Organizations,* Heath, 1972.

Rudolph Moos and Paul Insel, editors, *Issues in Social Ecology,* National Press, 1973.

Sieber and David Wilder, editors, *The School in Society: Studies in the Sociology of Education,* Free Press, 1973.

Jack Culbertson and others, *Social Science Content for Preparing Educational Leaders,* C. E. Merrill, 1973.

Controversy in American Education: An Anthology of Crucial Issues, Macmillan, 1973.

F. Kast and J. Rosenweig, editors, *Organization and Management,* 2nd edition, McGraw, 1974.

Donald Gerwin, editor, *The Employment of Teachers: Some Analytical Views,* McCutchan, 1974.

Fred N. Kerlinger and John Carroll, editors, *Review of Research in Education 2, 1974,* F. E. Peacock, 1974.

Monahan, editor, *Theoretical Dimensions of Educational Administration,* Macmillan, 1975.

J. Cistone, editor, *Understanding School Boards: Problems and Prospects,* Heath, 1975.

Peter Schmidt, editor, *Innovation: Diffusion Von Neuerungen im Sozialen Bereich,* Hoffman and Compe Verlag, 1975.

K. Ryan, editor, *Teacher Education,* National Society for the Study of Education, 1975.

M. Jacobs, editor, *Flexible Education for the Health Professions,* Wiley, 1976.

M. Martinez, Jr. and J. M. Weston, editors, *School and Community: Issues and Alternatives,* Kendall/Hunt, 1976.

Mary Jane Ward and M. E. Fetler, editors, *Instruments for Use in Nursing Education Research,* Western Interstate Commission for Higher Education, 1978.

Edward Sagarin, editor, *Sociology: The Basic Concepts,* Holt, 1978.

Edelfelt, editor, *Staff Development for School Improvement,* National Center for Teaching and Learning, Eastern Michigan University, 1983.

Kathryn Borman and Jane Reisman, editors, *Becoming a Worker,* Ablex Publishing, 1985.

Also contributor to H. D. Gideonse, R. Koff, and J. Schwab, editors, *Values, Inquiry and Education,* 1981, and Norman J. Boyan, editor, *The Handbook of Research on Educational Administration,* 1987.

OTHER

Contributor to numerous journals, including *American Sociological Review, American Journal of Sociology, Contemporary Sociology, Social Forces, Sociology of Education, Journal of Applied and Behavioral Science, Internatioanl Review of Education,* and *Administrative Science Quarterly.* Associate editor of *Sociology of Education,* 1970-74 and 1980-84.

SIDELIGHTS: Ronald G. Corwin is a distinguished scholar in the field of sociology; his major contributions to the discipline have helped define the field of educational sociology and have earned him an international reputation. Reviewing his highly esteemed textbook *A Sociology of Education* for *Social Forces,* Bruce K. Eckland suggests that "Corwin provides us with something more than simply a framework by which to understand the organization of the school system. Throughout his work, new ideas crystallize, ideas which give a notably different perspective, at times, on some of the broader issues confronting society, particularly in the areas of social stratification and complex organizations." Calling Corwin's tone "consistently analytical and critical," Edgar Z. Friedenberg concludes in *Administrative Science Quarterly* that the book is "clearly written, comprehensive, and so extensively and precisely annotated as to provide a reliable index of the literature of educational sociology up to its date of publication, and in a conveniently accessible form."

Corwin examines the relationship between professionalism and bureaucracy in *Militant Professionalism,* which Paul A. Paschke calls an "interesting, informative book" in *Administrative Science Quarterly.* "By observing the day-to-day conflicts of teachers and administrators, [Corwin] provides valuable evidence of the growth of professionalism and the forms it takes when it occurs in a highly bureaucratic setting." Paschke concludes that "not only does [Corwin's] analysis point out the organizational nature of conflict generated over professionalization, but it also points to serious deficiencies in our scientific conceptualization of organizations and organizational change." Reviewing *Militant Professionalism* for *American Sociological Review,* Marvin Bressler believes that "Corwin's closely reasoned and generously documented inquiry places all sociologists of education in his debt."

Corwin's *Reform and Organizational Survival: The Teacher Corps as an Instrument of Change* served as the subject of a 1974 symposium by the U.S. Office of Education and inspired a volume of related essays, *The Federal Role in School Reform,* edited by T. G. Fox. In the latter Melvin Tumin writes that "Corwin's sociological analysis of the strategies of organizational survival stands out as a luminous clarification of the meaning of complex systems and their interlocking networks of entrenched opposing forces and interests, and the deeply habituated resistance to change that virtually define such systems." Explaining in *Administrative Science Quarterly* that the Teacher Corps was initially a field experiment sponsored by the federal government to improve educational opportunities for disadvantaged youth, Donald J. McCarty says that "Corwin's well-measured analysis [in *Reform and Organizational Survival*] points out that the structural features in the organization life of the public schools were deeply rooted and difficult to alter." Finding the book "well written and stimulating," McCarty feels that it offers "intriguing new ideas

about the complexities of organizational change." And in the foreword to Corwin's book, Tumin concludes: "Corwin's work describes, analyzes, and clarifies certain basic necessities in the field of education that must be recognized if we are to find the freedom to alter things to approximate more closely the visions we all share of equal quality education for all."

BIOGRAPHICAL/CRITICAL SOURCES:

BOOKS

Corwin, Ronald G., *Reform and Organizational Survival: The Teacher Corps as an Instrument of Change,* Wiley, 1973.
Fox, T. G., editor, *The Federal Role in School Reform,* Teacher Corps, U.S. Office of Education, 1975.

PERIODICALS

Administrative Science Quarterly, June, 1966, September, 1971, September, 1974.
American Educational Research Journal, fall, 1974.
American Sociological Review, December, 1971.
Contemporary Sociology, July, 1975.
Social Forces, December, 1966, September, 1975.
Sociology, July, 1975.

*   *   *

COTTRELL, Jack (Warren) 1938-

PERSONAL: Born April 30, 1938, in Georgetown, Ky.; son of Major Franklin and Jewell May (Mitchell) Cottrell; married Barbara Agnes Gordin, May 30, 1959; children: Russell Warren, Cathleen Beth, Susan Lynn. *Education:* Cincinnati Bible Seminary, A.B., 1959, Th.B., 1960; University of Cincinnati, A.B., 1962; Westminster Theological Seminary, M.Div., 1965; Princeton Theological Seminary, Ph.D., 1971.

ADDRESSES: Home—2828 Lehman Road, Cincinnati, Ohio 45204. *Office*—2700 Glenway Ave., Cincinnati, Ohio 45204.

CAREER: Ordained minister of Christian church, 1956; minister in Florence, Ind., 1956-58, Albany, Ky., 1958-59, Goshen, Ohio, 1959-62; Cincinnati Christian Seminary, Cincinnati, Ohio, professor of theology, 1967—. Former owner of Christian Used Book Exchange.

MEMBER: Evangelical Theological Society.

WRITINGS:

His Way, Standard Publishing, 1973.
(Contributor) U. Gabler and E. Herkenrath, editors, *Heinrich Bullinger 1504-1575,* Theologischer Verlag, 1975.
(Contributor) Clark Pinnock, editor, *Grace Unlimited,* Bethany Fellowship, 1976.
Being Good Isn't Good Enough: God's Wonderful Grace, edited by Nancy Borton, Standard Publishing, 1976.
Solid!: The Authority of God's Word, Standard Publishing, 1978, published as *The Authority of the Bible,* Baker Book, 1979.
His Truth, Standard Publishing, 1980.
The Bible Says, Standard Publishing, 1982, reprinted as Volume II of *Tough Questions, Biblical Answers,* College Press, 1986.
What the Bible Says about God the Creator, College Press, 1983.
What the Bible Says about God the Ruler, College Press, 1984.
Tough Questions, Biblical Answers, College Press, Volume I, 1985, Volume II, 1986.

What the Bible Says about God the Redeemer, College Press, 1987.

(Contributor) C. Pinnock, editor, *Grace Abounding*, Zondervan, 1988.

Contributor of articles to periodicals, including *Christianity Today, Christian Standard, Lookout, Restoration Herald*, and *Seminary Review*. Editor, *Seminary Review*, beginning 1973.

* * *

COURTNEY, (John) Richard 1927-

PERSONAL: Born June 4, 1927, in Newmarket, England; son of Arthur John (a teacher) and Celia Annie Courtney; married Rosemary Gale (a writer and editor); children: Anne, John. *Education:* University of Leeds, B.A., 1951, diploma in education, 1952.

ADDRESSES: Home—Jackson's Point, Ontario, Canada L0E 1L0. *Office*—Ontario Institute for Studies in Education, 252 Bloor St. W., Toronto, Ontario, Canada M5S 1V6.

CAREER: Teacher at primary school in Dalham, England, 1948; teacher of drama at high schools in Leeds, England, 1952-55, and Colne Valley, England, 1955-59; University of London, Institute of Education, London, England, senior lecturer in drama at Trent Park College, 1959-67, warden of Sir Phillip Sassoon Hall, 1961-64; University of Victoria, Victoria, British Columbia, associate professor of theatre, 1968-71; University of Calgary, Calgary, Alberta, professor of drama, 1971-74, head of Developmental Drama Summer School, 1970-72; professor of arts and education at Ontario Institute for Studies in Education, Toronto, and University of Toronto, Graduate Centre of Drama, both 1974—.

Lecturer at Goldsmith's College, London, summers, 1973-74; visiting fellow at Melbourne State College, 1979; visiting instructor at University of Western Ontario, 1980; lecturer at universities in England, Australia, the United States, and Hong Kong. Actor with British Broadcasting Corp. Northern Repertory Company, 1954-64, and English Theatre Guild; performed in repertory, music halls, and amateur productions; director of Proscenium Players, Leeds, and educational theatre productions; founder of Four Valleys Youth Theatre, 1955; co-founder of Enfield Youth Theatre, 1961; life patron of North Hertfordshire Youth Theatre. Artist, with exhibitions of paintings. Chairman of task force on arts and education in Canada, 1975-79, and national inquiry into arts and education in Canada, 1979; guest on television programs in Canada, United States, Hong Kong, and Australia; consultant to Canada Council, Design Canada, and Ontario Arts Council. *Military service:* Royal Air Force, 1945-48.

MEMBER: Canadian Conference of the Arts (member of board of governors, 1970; member of executive committee, 1971; vice-president, 1972; national president, 1973-76), Canadian Child and Youth Drama Association (member of board of directors, 1968-69; president, 1969-72), Creative Education Foundation, Educational Drama Association, Society for Teachers of Speech and Drama, Folklore Society, Royal Society of Arts (fellow), Canadian Society for Aesthetics, British Society for Aesthetics, British Children's Theatre Association, British Society of Dramatherapy, American Councils of the Arts (governor, 1974-77), American Theatre Association (member of Theatre Education Commission, 1979-81), American Society for Aesthetics.

AWARDS, HONORS: Alberta Achievement Award from government of Alberta, 1973, for services to arts and education; Canadian Silver Jubilee Medal from governor-general of Canada, 1977; fortieth anniversary award, Canadian Conference of the Arts, 1985; research awards from Social Sciences and Humanities Research Council of Canada, Design Canada, Ontario Arts Council, and Ontario Ministry of Education.

WRITINGS:

Wild Eyed Girl (poems), Stockwell, 1948.
Producing a Play, Union Publishing, 1958.
Drama for Youth, Pitman, 1964.
(Editor) *College Drama Space*, Institute of Education, University of London, 1964.
Teaching Drama, Cassell, 1965.
The School Play, Cassell, 1966.
The Drama Studio, Pitman, 1967.
Play, Drama, and Thought: The Intellectual Background to Dramatic Education, Cassell, 1968, 3rd edition, Drama Book Specialists, 1974.
Teaching and the Arts: Arts Education in Australia, with Specific Reference to Drama Education in Victoria, Melbourne State College, 1979.
(Editor) *The Face of the Future: The Report of the National Inquiry into Arts and Education in Canada*, Canadian Conference of the Arts, 1979.
The Dramatic Curriculum, Drama Book Specialists, 1980.
(With Paul Park) *Learning in the Arts*, Ministry of Education, Ontario, 1980.
(Editor with Gertrud Schattner) *Drama in Therapy*, Volume I: *Children*, Volume II: *Adults*, Drama Book Specialists, 1981.
History of British Drama, Littlefield, Adams, 1982.
Re-Play: Studies of Human Drama in Education, Ontario Institute for Studies in Education Press, 1982.
The Rarest Dream: Play, Drama and Thought Re-Visited, National Association for the Teaching of Drama (London), 1984.
(With David Booth, John Emerson, and Natalie Kuzmich) *Teacher Education in the Arts*, Bison Books, 1985.
The Quest: Research and Inquiry in Arts Education, University Press of America, 1986.
Dictionary of Developmental Drama, C. C Thomas, 1987.

CONTRIBUTOR

Lawrence Hayes, editor, *Education and the Arts*, Australian National University, 1971.
John Hodgson and Martin Banham, editors, *Drama in Education*, Pitman, Volume I, 1973, Volume II, 1974, Volume III, 1975.
Nellie McCaslin, editor, *Theatre for Young Audiences*, Longman, 1978.
Leslie J. Kaslof, editor, *Whoiistic Dimensions in Healing*, Doubleday, 1978.
Martin Engel and Jerome Hausman, editors, *Fourth Yearbook on Research in Arts and Aesthetic Education*, Central Midwest Regional Educational Laboratory, 1981.
Judith Kase-Polisini, editor, *Creative Drama in a Developmental Context*, University Press of America, 1985.
Anton Wagner, editor, *Contemporary Canadian Theatre: New World Visions*, Simon & Pierre, 1985.

OTHER

Editor of monograph series ''Discussions in Developmental Drama,'' University of Calgary, 1971-74. Contributor of more than one hundred articles, stories, poems, and reviews to scholarly journals, popular magazines, and newspapers, including *Gryphon, Players, Connecticut Review, Queen's Quarterly, Children's Theatre Review,* and *Youth Theatre Journal.* Contributing editor to *Curriculum Inquiry,* 1975-78.

WORK IN PROGRESS: The Practical Knowledge of Arts Teachers: Elementary, for the Ontario Ministry of Education; *Secret Spirits: Possession and Performance of Canadian Indians on Vancouver Island; The Dancing Priest: Ritual Origins of Greek Tragedy; The Birth of God: The Ritual Drama of Ancient Israel; On Theatre: The Theory of Drama in Performance; Acts of Mind; The Comic World of Carlo Goldoni; Play: From Pre-History to Post-Structuralism.*

SIDELIGHTS: Richard Courtney told *CA:* "I have always been concerned with the drama of existence. Human drama commences in the first months of life—we make sense out of the world by creating a dramatic relationship with it—and theatre is simply the tip of the iceberg of human existence.

"In a recent 'Sunrise Semester' series on CBS-TV, I explained that in order to understand this process, we have to examine it from the inside out and from the outside in. How can we understand ourselves or other people unless we do both things at the same time? Our inner world (the 'me') creates a drama between itself and other people and things. Yet, at the same time, the outer world (our society and culture) is made up of other people who are also creating their own dramas; this opens up some possibilities to us, but closes off others. This accounts for two types of my writing: studies in children's play, maturation, and education (the drama of the inner), and studies of ceremonialism and ritual (the drama of the outer).

"Yet, a play in a theatre provides human beings with models as to how to live their lives—how to relate the inner to the outer—and that is what makes theatre so significant as an art form. This accounts for my third type of writing: studies of plays and the theatre."

BIOGRAPHICAL/CRITICAL SOURCES:

PERIODICALS

Cambridge Daily News, April 18, 1968.
Canadian Theatre Review, October, 1982.
Children's Theatre Review, fall, 1981, fall, 1982.
Communication Education, 1982.
Educational Theatre Journal, March, 1976.
Journal of Creative Behavior, spring, 1970.
L'Expression, November, 1981.
Theatre Design and Technology, October, 1968.
Theatre News, fall, 1982.
Times Educational Supplement, April 8, 1983.
Times Literary Supplement, November 11, 1964, March 31, 1967, May 31, 1968.
Victoria Daily Times, January 20, 1968, July 20, 1968, May 23, 1970.

*   *   *

CRANKSHAW, Edward 1909-1984

PERSONAL: Born January 3, 1909, in Woodford, Essex, England; died November 30, 1984, of cancer in London, England; son of Arthur B. and Amy (Bishop) Crankshaw; married Clare Chesterton Carr, 1931. *Education:* Attended Bishop's Stortford College.

CAREER: Observer, London, England, correspondent on Soviet affairs, 1947-68; broadcaster on Soviet affairs for British Broadcasting Corp. *Military service:* Territorial Army, 1939-46; became lieutenant colonel; intelligence officer stationed with the British Military Mission in Moscow, 1941-43.

AWARDS, HONORS: Ehrenkreuz fuer Wissenschaft und Kunst, 1st class, from Austria, 1964; *Yorkshire Post* Award, 1976, and Heinemann Award, 1977, both for *The Shadow of the Winter Palace: The Drift to Revolution, 1825-1917;* Whitbread Prize, 1982, for *Bismarck.*

WRITINGS:

Joseph Conrad: Some Aspects of the Art of the Novel, John Lane, 1936, Russell, 1963, reprinted, Macmillan, 1976.
Vienna: The Image of a Culture in Decline, Macmillan, 1938, reprinted, 1976.
Russia and Britain, Collins, 1944.
Russia and the Russians, Macmillan (London), 1947, Viking, 1948.
Cracks in the Kremlin Wall, Viking, 1951 (published in England as *Russia by Daylight,* M. Joseph, 1951).
The Forsaken Idea: A Study of Viscount Milner, Longmans, Green, 1952, reprinted, Greenwood, 1974.
Gestapo: Instrument of Tyranny, Viking, 1956, published as *Gestapo,* Pyramid Books, 1957.
Russia without Stalin: The Emerging Pattern, Viking, 1956.
Khrushchev's Russia, Penguin, 1959, 2nd edition, 1963.
(Editor and author of introduction) Artur Schnadel, *My Life and Music,* Longmans, Green, 1961.
The Fall of the House of Habsburg, Viking, 1963.
The New Cold War: Moscow vs. Peking, Penguin, 1963.
Khrushchev: A Career, Viking, 1966 (published in England as *Khrushchev: A Biography,* Collins, 1966).
Maria Theresa, Viking, 1970.
(Author of introduction and commentary) *Khrushchev Remembers,* Little, Brown, 1970.
The Habsburgs: Portrait of a Dynasty, Viking, 1971.
Tolstoy: The Making of a Novelist, Viking, 1974.
The Shadow of the Winter Palace: Russia's Drift to Revolution (Book-of-the-Month Club selection), Viking, 1976 (published in England as *The Shadow of the Winter Palace: The Drift to Revolution, 1825-1917,* Macmillan [London], 1976).
Bismarck, Viking, 1981.
(Editor) Sergei Aksakov, *A Russian Gentleman,* Oxford University Press, 1982.
Putting up with the Russians: Commentary and Criticism, 1947-84, Viking, 1984.

Contributor to *Atlantic, Encounter,* and other periodicals.

NOVELS

Nina Lessing, Macmillan, 1938.
The Creedy Case, M. Joseph, 1954.

TRANSLATOR

Hans Chlumberg, *Miracle at Verden,* Gollancz, 1932.
Ernst Toller, *Blind Goddess* (five-act play), John Lane, 1934.
Toller, *I Was a German,* Morrow, 1934, 2nd edition published as *Learn from My Youth,* Farrar & Rinehart, 1936.
Toller, *Transfiguration,* John Lane, 1935.
Toller, *Draw the Fires* (play), John Lane, 1935.
Hermann Kesten, *Happy Man!,* John Lane, 1935.
(With W. H. Auden) Toller, *No More Peace,* Farrar & Rinehart, 1937.

Kesten, *Spanish Fire: The Story of Ferdinand and Isabella*, Hutchinson, 1937.

Rene Behaine, *Survivors*, with preface by Ford Madox Ford, Houghton, 1938.

Behaine, *Conquest of a Life*, George Allen, 1939.

SIDELIGHTS: Edward Crankshaw was for many years a leading British authority on Soviet affairs. In his books, articles, and essays on the Soviet Union—and during his twenty-one years with the *Observer* newspaper—Crankshaw presented what many commentators believed was a balanced and sensible view of Soviet policy. Richard Davy, writing in the London *Times*, observed that Crankshaw's "sense of the reality and tragedy of Russia . . . made his political and historical writings among the most distinguished in Britain." Writing in the *New York Times*, Wolfgang Saxon described Crankshaw as "Britain's premier journalistic expert on Soviet politics," while the London *Times* called him "one of England's most original and most perceptive writers on Russia and on eastern and central Europe."

Crankshaw's fundamental argument was that, despite the dictatorial nature of the Soviet government and the dangers of its recurring crises with the Western powers, it was necessary for the West to coexist with the Soviet Union. Those who feared that the Soviets were intent on conquering the world were simply wrong. Crankshaw saw Soviet expansionism as nothing but a logical updating of traditional czarist imperialism. He advocated a firm and calm opposition to it. At the same time, he saw detente as a naive attempt at accommodation and found much of the Western peace movement to be ignorant of Soviet realities. "Crankshaw," Abraham Brumberg wrote in the *New Republic*, "was not given to illusions, either of the left or of the right, and his judgments have the force not of revealed, or of comforting, but of observable truth."

The Second World War dramatically changed the course of Crankshaw's life. During the 1930s he had worked as a journalist in London and Vienna and had translated a number of books into English. With the outbreak of war, however, Crankshaw entered the army. He was soon posted in Moscow as an intelligence officer with the British Military Mission. His contact with the Russian people—for whom he developed a lifelong fondness—led Crankshaw in 1944 to publish *Russia and Britain*, a history of diplomatic relations between the two countries. The reviewer of the book for the *Spectator* noted "Crankshaw's obvious affection for the Russians" and his "reservations about some aspects of the present regime." Following the war Crankshaw became the *Observer*'s correspondent on Soviet affairs, a post he was to hold until 1968.

During the years he reported on Soviet affairs, Crankshaw chronicled the evolution of Soviet society from the bloody dictatorship of Joseph Stalin to the bureaucratic machine of Leonid Brezhnev. Among his many books on the Soviet Union were two studies of 1950s Soviet society, *Cracks in the Kremlin Wall* and *Russia without Stalin: The Emerging Pattern*, a biography of Soviet leader Nikita Khrushchev and the introduction and notes for Khrushchev's memoirs, the historical study *The Shadow of the Winter Palace: Russia's Drift to Revolution*, and the collection *Putting up with the Russians: Commentary and Criticism, 1947-1984.*

In all his writings Crankshaw consistently emphasized the historical continuity of Russian society from the centuries of czarist rule to the present communist regime. In the book *Cracks in the Kremlin Wall*, he argued that under Stalin the last traces of Marxism had been eliminated from Soviet life and a tra-ditional, nationalistic dictatorship—similar to that of the czars—had been established. In an essay published in *Putting up with the Russians* Crankshaw wrote: "The Soviet Union is not a brand-new realm. Under entirely new management it is still Eternal Russia." As a writer for the *Chicago Tribune* noted, Crankshaw believed "that communist Russia could be understood only as an extension of centuries of dictatorship."

This premise is argued forcefully in *The Shadow of the Winter Palace*, a history of the political upheavals which led to the Russian Revolution of 1917 and the creation of the Soviet Union. Crankshaw shows that "there seems to be a Czarist precedent for almost every post-Czarist policy," as the *New Yorker* critic observed. The communist practice of sending dissidents to psychiatric hospitals was first conceived by Czar Nicholas I; the czarist press was heavily censored, as is the Soviet press; and the czarist suppression of minorities and imperialist expansion abroad are still the policies of the Soviets today. Richard Pipes of the *New York Times Book Review* wrote that "the parallels with the Soviet regime are not explicitly made, but often hinted at, and a perceptive reader will have no difficulty drawing his own conclusions." Fay Willey of *Newsweek* concluded that the Russians had "succumbed to rulers in many ways indistinguishable from the czars." Critical reaction to *The Shadow of the Winter Palace* was generally favorable. The *Economist* reviewer believed it to be a "beautifully written and immensely readable chronicle of Russia," while Neal Ascherson of *New Statesman* found it "comprehensive, marvellously and scrupulously written, full of wit and coloured at times with passionate sarcasm." The book received the *Yorkshire Post* Award and the Heinemann Award.

A selection of Crankshaw's short pieces about Soviet life are gathered together in *Putting up with the Russians*. It is "a splendid microcosmic survey of the historical, cultural, political and social complexities of post-revolutionary Russia," as Beaufort Cranford of the *Detroit News* described the book. "Each piece [in the collection]," Brumberg wrote, "is a gem, as fresh, enlightening, and pertinent today as when it was written." Although the pieces were written over the course of several decades, Crankshaw's approach remained consistent. As Davy commented, Crankshaw "has long had a record of keeping his head, largely because he has always had his feet firmly planted in Soviet reality." Similarly, Cranford admitted that he could not "vouch for the accuracy of Crankshaw's conclusions," but found that "he does speak with the clear voice of reason to laymen like me." Timothy Garton Ash, writing in the *Spectator*, called Crankshaw "trenchant, stylish, honest and brief."

"Difficult to place politically," as Saxon maintained, Crankshaw counseled against Western fears of a "communist menace" while calling for strong measures against Soviet expansionism. His skepticism about East-West detente and his genuine concern for the Russian people served to further obscure his position on the political spectrum. The London *Times* noted that Crankshaw's "view was . . . very different from others, uncluttered by fashionable theories that were going the rounds. . . . More often than not it was his view that was later seen to have been the right one." Brumberg explained that Crankshaw possessed a "penchant for clear thinking and [a] distaste for simplistic generalizations and sanctimonious cant." Because of Crankshaw's belief in the necessity for coexistence between East and West, Saxon called him "a conservative dedicated to the survival of European civilization."

BIOGRAPHICAL/CRITICAL SOURCES:

BOOKS

Crankshaw, Edward, *Putting up with the Russians: Commentary and Criticism, 1947-84*, Viking, 1984.

PERIODICALS

American Spectator, October, 1982.
Canadian Forum, February, 1967.
Chicago Tribune, December 5, 1984.
Christian Science Monitor, October 12, 1963, May 20, 1970.
Detroit News, November 25, 1984.
Economist, September 11, 1976.
New Republic, April 15, 1985.
New Statesman, October 4, 1963, July 16, 1976.
Newsweek, August 16, 1976.
New Yorker, October 4, 1976.
New York Times, October 7, 1956, March 7, 1970, November 17, 1981.
New York Times Book Review, September 5, 1976.
Saturday Review, October 27, 1956, June 25, 1966.
Spectator, May 19, 1944, November 21, 1981, August 25, 1984.
Times (London), December 17, 1981, January 7, 1984, July 26, 1984.
Times Literary Supplement, June 10, 1944, July 27, 1984.

OBITUARIES:

PERIODICALS

AB Bookman's Weekly, January 21, 1985.
Chicago Tribune, December 5, 1984.
Los Angeles Times, December 8, 1984.
New York Times, December 5, 1984.
Time, December 17, 1984.
Times (London), December 3, 1984.
Washington Post, December 4, 1984.†

—Sketch by Thomas Wiloch

*   *   *

CRAWFORD, Iain (Padruig)   1922-

PERSONAL: Born January 21, 1922, in Inverness, Scotland; son of Peter and Joan (Macdonald) Crawford; married Nora Laidlaw; children: Michael, Francesca, Douglas, Neil. *Education:* Attended public schools in Inverness and Glasgow, Scotland. *Politics:* Liberal.

CAREER: Clan Line Steamers Ltd., cadet, 1939-42; Scotsman Publications, Edinburgh, Scotland, reporter, sub-editor, and drama critic, 1947-50; *Bulletin*, Glasgow, Scotland, leader writer, 1950; British Broadcasting Co., publicity officer in Soctland, 1950-54; affiliated with *Scottish Daily Express*, 1958-59; *Evening Standard*, London, England, columnist, 1959-61; full-time writer, 1961—. *Military service:* Royal Navy, 1942-46; became lieutenant; mentioned in dispatches.

MEMBER: Society of Authors, Circle of Wine Writers (founder), London Scottish Rugby Football Club, Arts Theatre Club.

WRITINGS:

The Burning Sea, Cassell, 1959.
What about Wine?, Greenlys, 1962.
(Editor) Francis Chichester, *London Man*, Chichester, 1962, revised edition, 1965.

The Cafe Royal Story, Hutchison, 1963.
The Profumo Affair: A Crisis in Contemporary Society, White Lodge, 1963.
The Sinclair Exclusive, Macdonald, 1964.
Gateway to Wine, Grants, 1964.
Wine on a Budget, Hamlyn, 1964.
Scare the Gentle Citizen, Hammond, 1965.
Make Me a Wine Connoisseur, Dickens Press, 1969.
Havana Cigar, Hunters & Frankau, 1983.

Also author of plays, "Broomstick over Badenoch," and "Under the Light," and of scripts for radio, television, and films. Travel correspondent, *Sunday Express* and *House and Garden;* film and drama critic, *Scottish Field*. Contributor of articles to newspapers and magazines. Travel editor, *This Week*.

WORK IN PROGRESS: A second novel in thriller series begun with *Scare the Gentle Citizen;* a travel book on Rumania.

AVOCATIONAL INTERESTS: "Music, wine, cricket, golf, rugby, the theater, argument, women, and travel."†

*   *   *

CRAWFORD, Linda   1938-

PERSONAL: Born August 2, 1938, in Detroit, Mich.; daughter of Arthur R. (a foundry owner) and Mary E. (a weaver; maiden name, Forshar) Crawford; lives with author Sandra Scoppettone. *Education:* University of Michigan, B.A., 1960, M.A., 1961.

ADDRESSES: Home—131 Prince St./3 Fl., New York, N.Y. 10012. *Agent*—Warren Bayless, 156 East 52nd St., New York, N.Y. 10022.

CAREER: Chicago Tribune, New York Bureau, New York, N.Y., feature writer, 1961-67. Writer.

AWARDS, HONORS: Grant from Ludwig Vogelstein Foundation, 1975.

WRITINGS:

NOVELS

In a Class by Herself, Scribner, 1976.
Something to Make Us Happy, Simon & Schuster, 1978.
Vanishing Acts, Putnam, 1983.
Ghost of a Chance, Arbor House, 1985.

SIDELIGHTS: Linda Crawford's novel *Ghost of a Chance* chronicles a year in the lives of two women: Kate Wiley, a frustrated novelist who makes her living as a ghostwriter, and Beryl Swarr, a nondescript bank teller. The women's lives are intertwined when Kate is hired to write a book about Beryl's recent ordeal as hostage to a homicidal maniac. The book, "Captive Courageous," becomes a bestseller, and Beryl is transformed into a zealous advocate for other hostage victims. Susan Dooley comments in the *Washington Post Book World* that "as the spirit of the messiah transforms Beryl, Kate . . . finds herself mired in Beryl's life as the one-time captive turns captor."

Laura Furman describes *Ghost of a Chance* in the *Los Angeles Times Book Review* as "a pleasure to read, witty and well worked out. . . . [Crawford] writes convincingly about the complex, insoluble troubles of a grown-up heroine." *New York Times Book Review* contributor Ellen Pall observes that although Crawford's narrative shifts uneasily from "canny satire [to] gentle introspection," the novel "is nevertheless a frequently very delightful book.'' Furman concludes: "By the end of 'Ghost of a Chance,' one feels that Kate is indeed a captive courageous, one who might break loose at any time.''

BIOGRAPHICAL/CRITICAL SOURCES:

PERIODICALS

Globe and Mail (Toronto), November 16, 1985.
Los Angeles Times Book Review, August 25, 1985.
New York Times, October 15, 1976.
New York Times Book Review, October 24, 1976, July 28, 1985.
Washington Post Book World, July 7, 1985.

*   *   *

CREELEY, Robert (White) 1926-

PERSONAL: Born May 21, 1926, in Arlington, Mass.; son of Oscar Slade (a physician) and Genevieve (Jules) Creeley; married Ann McKinnon, 1946 (divorced, 1955); married Bobbie Louise Hawkins, January 27, 1957 (divorced, 1976); married Penelope Highton, 1977; children: (first marriage) David, Thomas, Charlotte; (second marriage) Kirsten (stepdaughter), Leslie (stepdaughter; deceased), Sarah, Katherine; (third marriage) William, Hannah. *Education:* Attended Harvard University, 1943-44 and 1945-46; Black Mountain College, B.A., 1955; University of New Mexico, M.A., 1960.

ADDRESSES: Office—Department of English, State University of New York, Buffalo, N.Y. 14260.

CAREER: Poet, novelist, short story writer, essayist, and editor. Divers Press, Palma, Mallorca, Spain, founder and publisher, 1950-54; Black Mountain College, Black Mountain, N.C., instructor in English, 1954-55; instructor at school for young boys, Albuquerque, N.M., beginning 1956; University of New Mexico, Albuquerque, instructor in English, 1961-62; University of British Columbia, Vancouver, instructor in English, 1962-63; University of New Mexico, lecturer in English, 1963-65; State University of New York at Buffalo, visiting professor, 1965-66, professor of English, 1967—, David Gray Professor of Poetry and Letters, 1978—. Participated in numerous poetry readings and writers' conferences. With American Field Service, India and Burma, 1945-46.

MEMBER: American Academy and Institute of Arts and Letters.

AWARDS, HONORS: Levinson Prize, 1960, for group of ten poems published in *Poetry;* D. H. Lawrence fellowship (for summer writing), University of New Mexico, 1960; National Book Award nomination, 1962, for *For Love;* Leviton-Blumenthal Prize, 1964, for group of thirteen poems published in *Poetry;* Guggenheim fellowship in poetry, 1964-65, and 1971; Rockefeller Foundation grant, 1966; Union League Civic and Arts Foundation Prize, 1967; Shelley Award, 1981, and Frost Medal, 1987, both from Poetry Society of America; National Endowment for the Arts grant, 1982; Deutsche Auftauschdienst Programme (DADD) providing residency in Berlin, 1983, 1987; Leone d'Oro Premio Speziale, Venice, 1985.

WRITINGS:

POETRY

Le Fou, Golden Goose Press, 1952.
The Kind of Act Of, Divers Press (Palma, Mallorca, Spain), 1953.
The Immoral Proposition, Jonathan Williams, 1953.

A Snarling Garland of Xmas Verse (published anonymously), Divers Press, 1954.
All That Is Lovely in Men, Jonathan Williams, 1955.
(With others) *Ferrin and Others,* Gerhardt (Germany), 1955.
If You, Porpoise Bookshop, 1956.
The Whip, Migrant Books, 1957.
A Form of Women, Jargon Books, 1959.
For Love: Poems 1950-1960, Scribner, 1962.
Distance, Terrence Williams, 1964.
Two Poems, Oyez, 1964.
Hi There!, Finial Press, 1965.
Words (eight poems), Perishable Press, 1965.
Poems 1950-1965, Calder & Boyars, 1966.
About Women, Gemini, 1966.
For Joel, Perishable Press, 1966.
A Sight, Cape Coliard Press, 1967.
Words (eighty-four poems), Scribner, 1967.
Robert Creeley Reads (with recording), Turret Books, 1967.
The Finger, Black Sparrow Press, 1968, enlarged edition published as *The Finger Poems, 1966-1969,* Calder & Boyars, 1970.
5 Numbers (five poems), Poets Press, 1968, published as *Numbers* (text in English and German), translation by Klaus Reichert, Galerie Schmela (Dusseldorf, Germany), 1968.
The Charm: Early and Collected Poems, Perishable Press, 1968, expanded edition published as *The Charm,* Four Seasons Foundation, 1969.
Divisions and Other Early Poems, Perishable Press, 1968.
Pieces (fourteen poems), Black Sparrow Press, 1968.
The Boy (poem poster), Gallery Upstairs Press, 1968.
Mazatlan: Sea, Poets Press, 1969.
Pieces (seventy-two poems), Scribner, 1969.
Hero, Indianakatz, 1969.
A Wall, Bouwerie Editions, 1969.
For Betsy and Tom, Alternative Press, 1970.
For Benny and Sabrina, Samuel Charters, 1970.
America, Press of the Black Flag, 1970.
Christmas: May 10, 1970, Lockwood Memorial Library, State University of New York at Buffalo, 1970.
St. Martin's, Black Sparrow Press, 1971.
1-2-3-4-5-6-7-8-9-0, illustrated wth drawings by Arthur Okamura, Shambala, 1971.
Sea, Cranium Press, 1971.
For the Graduation, Cranium Press, 1971.
Change, Hermes Free Press, 1972.
One Day After Another, Alternative Press, 1972.
For My Mother: Genevieve Jules Creeley, 8 April 1887-7 October 1972 (limited edition), Sceptre Press, 1973.
His Idea, Coach House Press, 1973.
Kitchen, Wine Press, 1973.
Sitting Here, University of Connecticut Library, 1974.
Thirty Things, Black Sparrow Press, 1974.
Backwards, Sceptre Press, 1975.
Hello, Hawk Press, 1976, expanded edition published as *Hello: A Journal, February 29-May 3, 1976,* New Directions, 1978.
Away, Black Sparrow Press, 1976.
Presences (also see below), Scribner, 1976.
Selected Poems, Scribner, 1976.
Myself, Sceptre Press, 1977.
Later, Toothpaste, 1978, expanded edition, New Directions, 1979.
The Collected Poems of Robert Creeley, 1945-1975, University of California Press, 1982.
Echoes, Toothpaste, 1982.

Mirrors, New Directions, 1983.
Memories, Pog Press, 1984.
Memory Gardens, New Directions, 1986.
The Company, Burning Deck, 1988.

EDITOR

Charles Olson, *Mayan Letters,* Divers Press, 1953, Grossman, 1968.
(With Donald M. Allen, and contributor) *New American Story,* Grove, 1965.
(And author of introduction) Olson, *Selected Writings,* New Directions, 1966.
(With Allen, and contributor) *The New Writing in the U.S.A.,* Penguin, 1967.
Whitman, Penguin, 1973.

CONTRIBUTOR TO ANTHOLOGIES

A New Folder; Americans: Poems and Drawings, edited by Daisy Aldan, Folder Editions, 1959.
The New American Poetry: 1945-1960, edited by Allen, Grove, 1960.
The Beat Scene, edited by Elias Wilentz, Corinth, 1960.
Short Story 3, Scribner, 1960.
Contemporary American Poetry, revised and enlarged edition, edited by Allen, Penguin, 1962.
The Moderns: An Anthology of New Writing, edited by LeRoi Jones, Cornith, 1963.
Contemporary American Poetry, revised edition, edited by Donald Hall, Penguin, 1963.
American Poems: A Contemporary Collection, edited by Jascha Kessler, Southern Illinois University Press, 1964.
Today's Poets: American and British Poetry since the 1930s, edited by Chad Walsh, Scribner, 1964.
A Critical Anthology of English and American Poems, edited by Karl Kroeber and John O. Lyons, Harper, 1965.
American Poetry, edited by Gay Wilson, Walter B. Rideout, and James K. Robinson, Harper, 1965.
A Controversy of Poets, edited by Paris Leary and Robert Kelly, Doubleday, 1965.
A Poetry Reading against the Vietnam War, edited by Robert Bly and David Ray, The American Writers against the Vietnam War, 1966.
Where Is Vietnam? American Poets Respond, edited by Walter Lowenfels, Doubleday, 1967.
Introduction to Poetry, edited by Louis Simpson, St. Martin's, 1967.
The New Modern Poetry: British and American Poetry since World War II, edited by M. L. Rosenthal, Macmillan, 1967.
War Poems, edited by Diana Di Prima, Poets Press, 1968.
100 Postwar Poems: British and American, edited by Rosenthal, Macmillan, 1968.
Naked Poetry: Recent American Poetry in Open Forms, edited by Stephen Berg and Robert Mezey, Bobbs-Merrill, 1969.
Norton Anthology of Modern Poetry, edited by Richard Ellmann and Robert O'Clair, Norton, 1973.
The New Oxford Book of American Verse, edited by Ellmann, Oxford University Press, 1976.

Also contributor to other anthologies.

OTHER

The Gold Diggers (short stories), Divers Press, 1954, expanded edition published as *The Gold Diggers and Other Stories,* J. Calder, 1965, reprinted, Marion Boyars, 1980.

The Island (novel), Scribner, 1963, reprinted, Marion Boyars, 1980.
(Author of preface) George Bowering, *Sticks and Bones,* Tishbooks, 1963.
An American Sense (essay), Sigma Press, 1965.
(Author of preface) David Franks, *Touch,* Red Wheelbarrow Press, 1965.
(Author of introduction) Fielding Dawson, *Krazy Kat/The Unveiling and Other Stories,* Black Sparrow Press, 1969.
A Quick Graph: Collected Notes and Essays, edited by Donald M. Allen, Four Seasons Foundation, 1970.
Notebook, Bouwerie Editions, 1972.
Listen (play; produced in London, 1972), Black Sparrow Press, 1972.
A Sense of Measure (essays), Calder & Boyars, 1972.
A Day Book (poems and prose; also see below), Scribner, 1972.
(Author of introduction) Bob Doerr, *Song of the Maize: A Mosaic of Mayan Cosmology,* Ganesh Press, 1972.
Inside Out (lecture), Black Sparrow Press, 1973.
Contexts of Poetry: Interviews 1961-1971, Four Seasons Foundation, 1973.
The Creative (lecture), Black Sparrow Press, 1973.
Mabel: A Story, and Other Prose (includes *A Day Book* and *Presences*), Calder & Boyars, 1976.
Was That a Real Poem and Other Essays, Four Seasons Foundation, 1979.
Charles Olson and Robert Creeley: The Complete Correspondence, edited by George Butterick, Black Sparrow Press, Volumes I-II, 1980, Volume III, 1981.
(Contributor with Jim Dine and Martin Friedman) *Jim Dine* (catalog), edited by W. J. Beal, Abbeville Press, 1984.
Collected Prose, Marion Boyars, 1984, corrected edition, University of California Press, c. 1987.
Collected Essays, University of California Press, in press.

Contributor to literary periodicals, including *Paris Review, Nation, Black Mountain Review, Origin, Yugen,* and *Big Table.* Founder and editor, *Black Mountain Review,* 1954-57.

WORK IN PROGRESS: Editing *The Essential Burns* for Ecco Press.

SIDELIGHTS: Once known primarily for his association with the group called the "Black Mountain Poets," Robert Creeley has become an important and influential literary figure in his own right. Creeley was born in Arlington, Massachusetts, and raised in a rural New England setting. His father, Oscar Slade Creeley, was a physician in Watertown, Massachusetts, and shortly before his death, when Robert was only four, moved the family to a small farm in West Acton. His father's premature death left his mother, Genevieve Jules Creeley, the sole support of Robert and his older sister, Helen. Creeley attended Holderness School in Plymouth, New Hampshire, on a scholarship and soon began to develop his writing talents. His articles and stories appeared regularly in the school's literary magazine, and in his senior year he became its editor in chief. Creeley was admitted to Harvard in 1943, but his academic life was disrupted when he served as an ambulance driver for the American Field Service in 1944 and 1945.

Creeley returned to Harvard after the war and became associated with the literary crowd there, a group that included writers John Hawkes, Mitchell Goodman, and Kenneth Koch. He married Ann McKinnon in 1946, and the couple moved to Truro, Massachusetts, where they lived for a year before moving to a small farm near Littleton, New Hampshire, to begin raising a family. Creeley continued writing during these years and began corresponding with Cid Corman and Charles Olson, two poets who were to have a substantial influence on the direction of his future work. Excited especially by Olson's ideas about literature, Creeley began to develop a distinctive and unique poetic style.

Throughout the 1950s he was associated with the ''Black Mountain Poets,'' a group of writers including Denise Levertov, Ed Dorn, Fielding Dawson, and others who had some connection with Black Mountain College, an experimental, communal college in North Carolina that was a haven for many innovative writers and artists of the period. Creeley edited the *Black Mountain Review* and developed a close and lasting relationship with Olson, who was the rector of the college. The two engaged in a lengthy, intensive correspondence about literary matters that has been collected and published as *Charles Olson & Robert Creeley: The Complete Correspondence*. Olson and Creeley together developed the concept of ''projective verse,'' a kind of poetry that abandoned traditional forms in favor of a freely constructed verse that took shape as the process of composing it was underway. Olson called this process ''composition by field,'' and his famous essay on the subject, ''Projective Verse,'' was as important for the poets of the emerging generation of the 1950s as T. S. Eliot's ''Tradition and the Individual Talent'' was to the poets of the previous generation. Olson credited Creeley with formulating one of the basic principles of this new poetry: the idea that ''form is never more than an extension of content.''

According to Cynthia Edelberg in *Robert Creeley's Poetry: A Critical Introduction*, another important influence on Creeley's work at this time was Paul Valery, whose book *Monsieur Teste* ''was Creeley's bible from the late forties until he rejected it in the sixties.'' In this work Valery contends that the most significant subject for any writer is the operation of his own mind and its interaction with the world. Creeley's emphasis on charting his impressions of an immediate experience may well have been derived from his reading of Valery. But it was shaped as well by the poetic climate of the 1950s and early 1960s, which made the ''chronicle of the moment'' a characteristic poetic form, from the *Lunch Poems* of Frank O'Hara to the Whitmanesque catalogues of Allen Ginsberg and the harrowing confessional exposes of Sylvia Plath and Robert Lowell.

Creeley was a leader in the generational shift that veered away from history and tradition as primary poetic sources and gave new prominence to the ongoing experiences of an individual's life. Because of this emphasis, the major events of his life loom large in his literary work. Creeley's marriage to Ann ended in divorce in 1955. The break up of that relationship is chronicled in fictional form in his only novel, *The Island*, which drew upon his experiences on the island of Mallorca, off the coast of Spain, where he lived with Ann and their three children (David, Tom, and Charlotte) in 1953 and 1954. After the divorce Creeley returned to Black Mountain College for a brief time before moving west to make a new life. He was in San Francisco during the flowering of the ''San Francisco Poetry Renaissance'' and became associated for a time with the writers of the Beat Generation: Allen Ginsberg, Jack Kerouac, Michael McClure, and others. His work appeared in the influential ''beat'' anthology, *The New American Poetry: 1945-1960*, edited by Donald Allen.

In 1956 he accepted a teaching position at a boys' school in Albuquerque, New Mexico, where he met his second wife,

Bobbie Louise Hawkins. Bobbie and her two daughters from a previous marriage, Kirsten and Leslie, formed his new family; two additional daughters, Sarah and Katherine, were born in the late 1950s. The Creeleys spent two winters in Guatemala before returning to Albuquerque where he received an M.A. degree. In 1961 his stepdaughter Leslie was killed in an accident. This event is the subject of one of his most moving poems, ''For Leslie.'' Creeley taught for a time at the University of New Mexico and the University of British Columbia before establishing a long-term residence in Placitas, a small town north of Albuquerque. During the early 1960s as his work became well known he participated in many poetry readings and writers' conferences and won both Guggenheim and Rockefeller grants. Since 1966 he has been on the faculty of the State University of New York at Buffalo, and, in 1978, he was appointed David Gray Professor of Poetry and Letters there.

Though Creeley published poetry and fiction throughout the 1950s and 1960s and had even established his own imprint, the Divers Press, in 1952, his work did not receive important national recognition until Scribner published his first major collection, *For Love: Poems 1950-1960*, in 1962. This book collected work that he had been issuing in small editions and little magazines during the previous decade.

At this point in his career, his distinctive poetic voice gathered large numbers of followers and imitators. It was a voice that conveyed, as William Spanos declared in *Boundary*'s Creeley issue, ''a music from the edge'' that epitomized the poetry revolution of the period. Along with Allen Ginsberg, Lawrence Ferlinghetti, Paul Blackburn, Gary Snyder, and other poets who were intent on linking poetry and performance, Creeley awakened a sense of new rhythmical possibilities for the spoken word. The unforgettable sound of his voice reading poetry typified Olson's famous dictum that poetry needed to put into itself ''the breathing of the man who writes.'' Creeley's mentors were Ezra Pound, William Carlos Williams, Louis Zukofsky, and Olson, and the odd, off-center sound of his work when he reads it aloud is an amalgam of those influences. As he writes, in *A Sense of Measure*, ''Williams showed me early on that rhythm was a very subtle experience, and that words might share equivalent duration even though 'formally' they seemed in no way to do so. Pound said, 'LISTEN to the sound that it makes,' and Olson . . . made it evident that we could only go 'By ear.' Finally, there was and is the fact of, what it was one had to say—in Louis Zukofsky's sense, 'Out of deep need . . . !' ''

The very first poem in *For Love*, ''Hart Crane,'' with its unorthodox, Williams-like line breaks, its nearly hidden internal rhymes, its subtle assonance and sibilance, announces the Creeley style:

> He had been stuttering, by the edge
> of the street, one foot still
> on the sidewalk, and the other
> in the gutter . . .
> like a bird, say, wired to flight, the
> wings, pinned to their motion, stuffed.

That style can be defined by an intense concentration on the sounds and rhythms of language as well as the placement of the words on the page. This intensity produces a kind of minimal poetry, which seeks to extract the bare linguistic bones from ongoing life experiences. In his introduction to *The New Writing in the U.S.A.*, Creeley cites approvingly Herman Melville's definition of ''visible truth''—''the apprehension of the absolute condition of present things''—and supplements it with William Burroughs's famous statement from *Naked Lunch* about the writer's task: ''There is only one thing a writer can write about: what is in front of his senses at the moment of writing. . . . I am a recording instrument . . . I do not presume to impose 'story' 'plot' 'continuity'. . . .''

Applying Burroughs's assertion to poetry meant not imposing on the work lyricism, metaphor, paradox, irony, closure, or any other conventional elements of poetry. Creeley's most memorable early poems nearly always adopted this antipoetic stance toward both language and experience. They avoided traditional poetic devices in favor of a keen attentiveness to experience and to the ways in which a writer struggles to articulate consciousness. Characteristically, the reader is plunged into a middle of an ongoing occurrence by means of a snatch of conversation, or more usually, by an internal monologue that recreates the feeling of a fleeting moment, a sudden awareness, or a traumatic event. The poems are built around Creeley's perception of the event and the ''visible truth'' he garners from it. That is, he seems to be searching constantly for an absolute truth in a fleeting moment. This pattern is true of almost all of the most frequently anthologized poems, such as ''I Know a Man'' (''As I sd to my / friend, because I am / always talking—John, I / sd . . .''), ''The Whip'' (''I spent a night turning in bed, / my love was a feather, / a flat / sleeping thing . . .''), ''The Warning'' (''For love—I would / split open your head and put / a candle in / behind the eyes''), and ''A Wicker Basket'' (''Comes the time when it's later / and onto your table the headwaiter / puts the bill . . .'').

Creeley sharpened and developed this style throughout the 1960s and 1970s in a series of books that seemed almost designed to exemplify the principles of projective verse and the ideas about poetry he proposed in a number of critical essays and talks. A poem called ''Waiting'' from *Words,* Creeley's second major collection, characterize the problems a writer encounters transforming experience into poetry. His typical stance, described in this poem, is that of a poet struggling to bring a poem into being with no resources other than the heightened attention he brings to the task. He ''pushes behind the words,'' giving his emotions and experiences the formal contours that embody their meaning. Creeley's fear is that the words will quit coming:

> What if it all stops.
> Then silence
> is as silence was
> again.
>
> What if the last time
> he was moved to touch,
> work out in his own mind,
> such limits was the last—
>
> and then a quiet, a dull
> space of hanging actions, all
> depending on some time
> has come and gone.

For Creeley, without the words that emanate from experience, life seems ''a dull space of hanging actions''; the relations between things become severed and a sense of utter formlessness prevails. By discovering the appropriate form for the transitory emotional states he *needs* to write about, Creeley has always *used* poetry to take stock of both the world around him and the state of his being at any particular moment. In addition, he has always tried to write about his experiences without

the stale viewpoint of habitual thought. As he puts it in a poem called ''The Mountains in the Desert'':

> Tonight let me go
> at last out of whatever
> mind I thought to have,
> and all the habits of it.

These lines are not a longing for insanity but rather a call for a clarity of vision unencumbered by preconceptions. It is Creeley's version of the advice Ezra Pound gave to all creative artists, ''Make it New.''

In *Pieces, A Day Book, Thirty Things,* and *Hello: A Journal, February 29-May 3, 1976,* books published between 1968 and 1978, Creeley attempted to break down the concept of a ''single poem'' by offering his readers sequential, associated fragments of poems with indeterminate beginnings and endings. All of these works are energized by the same heightened attention to the present that characterizes Creeley's earlier work; but in *Hello,* a book written as journal entries over a five week period while Creeley travelled in the Orient and South Pacific, he speculates on the possibility of using memory rather than the present as a poetic source. Considering his hometown in Massachusetts, he asks

> May I let this be
> West Acton, and
> myself six? No,
> I don't travel that way
>
> ,despite memories
> all the dear or awful
> passages apparently
> I've gone through.
>
> Back to the weather
> and dripping nose
> I truly wanted to forget here,
> but haven't—

The poetry remains stubbornly rooted in the present despite the insistent intrusion of memories, both recent and long past. This poem, as well as many others in *Hello,* refers to the last days of Creeley's relationship with his second wife, Bobbie. That marriage ended in divorce in 1976, the same year he met Penelope Highton, his third wife, on this trip while travelling in New Zealand. In this sense, the book may be described in much the same terms as Sherman Paul in his book, *The Lost America of Love,* describes *For Love,* ''Poems of two marriages, the breakup of one, the beginning of another.'' For all of Creeley's experimentation, he has always been in some ways an exceedingly domestic poet; his mother, children, wives, and close friends are the subjects of his very best work. Because Creeley's second marriage lasted nearly twenty years, the sense of a major chunk of his life drifting away from him is very strong in *Hello.* Creeley here conveys the traumatic emotional state that almost always accompanies the break up of long term relationships. En route to Perth, he writes:

> Sitting here in limbo, there are
> people walking through my head.

In Singapore he remarks on his tenuous hold on things:

> Getting fainter, in the world,
> fearing something's fading,
> deadened, tentative responses—
> go hours without eating,

scared without someone to be
with me. These empty days.

And in Manila he fights feelings of desperation:

Each time *sick loss*
feeling starts to hit me,
think of *more* than that,
more that ''I'' thought of.

Although *Hello* is superficially a record of Creeley's travels, the poems are not really about the countries he has visited, but rather about the landscape of mind he has brought with him.

It is not until Creeley's next major collection, *Later,* published by New Directions in 1979, that the poetry seems to shift into a new phase characterized by a greater emphasis on memory, a new sense of life's discrete phases, and an intense preoccupation with aging. In ''Myself,'' the first poem in *Later,* he writes:

What, younger felt
was possible, now knows
is not—but still
not changed enough—

. . . . . .

I want, if older,
still to know
why, human, men
and women are

so torn, so lost
why hopes cannot
find better world
than this.

This futile but deeply human quest captures the spirit of Creeley's later work. It embodies a commonly shared realization: one becomes older but still knows very little about essential aspects of life, particularly the mysteries of human relationships. And as Alan Williamson observes in his *New York Times Book Review* assessment of *Later,* ''In general, the stronger the note of elegaic bafflement and rage (the past utterly gone, the compensating wisdom not forthcoming), the better the writing.''

In one of several poems in *Later* called ''For Pen''—the title echoing his vocation as well as referring more apparently to the nickname of his third wife, Penelope—Creeley finds little difference between the desires of youth and age, except that age conspires with physical decline to make a mockery of desire:

I want the world,
I did always,

. . . . . .

But to have it
be echo, feeling
that was years ago—
now my hands are

wrinkled and my hair
goes grey—seems
ugly burden
and mistake of it.

So sing this
weather, passing

grey and blue
together, rain and sun.

The contraries expressed in the final stanza suggest a resolution of a civil war within the soul of the aging speaker, a coming to terms with the inevitability of aging.

This tone of resigned acceptance characterizes many of the poems in *Later.* These are in fact ''later'' poems, that phase of Creeley's life and career has arrived. He realizes, in ''After,'' that

I'll not write again
things a young man
thinks, not the words
of that feeling.

But there are other words he can and does make poetry of— the words of present feelings that both incorporate and reflect upon the past. These words are the ''measure'' of a life—what one is and has been capable of. ''Measure is my testament,'' Creeley writes in *A Sense of Measure.* ''What uses me is what I use and in that complex measure is the issue. I cannot cut down trees with my bare hand, which is measure of both tree and hand. In that way I feel that poetry, in the very subtlety of its relation to image and rhythm, offers an intensely various record of such things. It is equally one of them.'' Creeley continues to adhere to this testament in *Later,* where the poems seem to be a part of his continuing effort to discover the measure of things—the worth of any of life's singular episodes to the whole of that life.

This effort culminates in the ten part title poem, ''Later,'' written over a period of ten days in September of 1977. The poem presents a kaleidoscopic view of various times and events important to Creeley's life, beginning with the evocation of a lost youth:

Shan't be winding
back in blue
gone time ridiculous
nor lonely

anymore. Gone,
gone—wee thin
delights, . . .

Once again, as in ''For Pen,'' the color blue, with its suggestion of vast expanses of sky as well as loneliness, sadness, and pain evokes the young Creeley who materializes through the ''grey mist'' (suggestive of age) in the second section of the poem. Youth, in later life, can only become a palpable part of the present through the evocative power of memory: an image of the young man preparing for school one winter morning comes sharply into focus:

You won't want to be early
for passage of grey mist
now rising from the faint

river alongside the childhood fields. . . .

. . . . . .

That's mother sitting there,
a father dead in heaven,
a dog barks, steam of
drying mittens on the stove,
blue hands, two doughnuts
on a plate.

How odd, of all the diverse events of childhood, that memory seizes these particulars: the steaming mittens on the stove, the barking dog, the two doughnuts. The next section of the poem comments on how certain empirical sensations are repositories of memory, like Marcel Proust's madeleine cakes. A taste, a smell, a touch, can evoke a lost world:

> sudden
>
> smell of burning
> leaves makes
> place in time
>
> these days
> (these days)
> passing,
>
> common
> to one
> and all.

The parenthetical "these days" refers to the days of the past encapsulated in the present through the recollection of certain images and physical sensations. "Later" continues to present a flood of childhood memories: a lost childhood dog that Creeley fantasizes running into again after all these years; memories of his mother and West Acton friends and neighbors; sights and sounds of his early days all evoked and made a part of the poetry he is composing in an attic room in Buffalo, September 1977:

> There's more always here
>
> than just me, in this room,
> this attic, apartment,
>
> this house, this world,
> can't escape.

The poem's final lines reveal the most affirmative and optimistic aspects of Creeley's later work:

> . . . the wonder of life is
>
> that *it is* at all,
> this sticky sentimental
>
> warm enclosure,
> feels place in the physical
>
> with others,
> lets mind wander
>
> to wondering thought,
> then lets go of itself,
>
> finds a home
> on earth.

This acceptance of things as they are is tempered in the later work by a nostalgia for things as they were. One feels, in *Later,* a longing for the excitement and turmoil of the Black Mountain-Beat Generation days when poetry seemed much more central to American life and culture than it does in the technology-dominated society of the later twentieth century. Sometimes in these poems the present seems less something to express wonderment about than a great decline. In "Place," Creeley writes:

> I need the oldtime density,
> the dirt, the cold,
> the noise through the floor—
> my love in company

In the work produced after the material included in his *Collected Poems, 1945-1975* there is an increasing tendency to

derive poetry from what the English Romantic poet William Wordsworth called "emotion recollected in tranquility." It is a poetry that remembers and reflects and seems much less tied to the exigencies of the present than the earlier work.

In *Mirrors,* published in 1984, the commitment to identifying and reconstructing those moments from the past that have most shaped his life deepens. The collection bears an epigraph from Francis Bacon: "In Mirrors, there is the like / Angle of Incidence, from the Object / to the Glasse, and from the Glasse / to the Eye." Poetry, in this sense, is the mirror which deflects the memory of past experience into our awareness in the present. Creeley reaches into early childhood in a poem called "Memory 1930" to illuminate the moment he learned of his father's death at a time when he was obviously too young to comprehend the impact it would have on his entire life. Here he presents it as a major fissure in his early life, viewed from an "angle of incidence" over fifty years later. He creates a picture of himself as a child, witnessing what appears as a surreal scene:

> I sit, intent, fat
>
> the youngest of the suddenly
> disjunct family, whose father is
>
> being then driven in an ambulance
> across the lawn, in the snow, to die.

The slowness of the final line with its two caesurae causes the image of the departing ambulance to appear as if in slow motion. It is as if Creeley, who has written about the death of his father more obliquely in earlier work, can now bring that momentous event clearly into focus so that he observes the impact it had on his young self, who sits intently observing its occurrence. The older Creeley watches the young Creeley watching his father being driven away in an ambulance to die.

This poem and others in *Mirrors* are attempts at recovering those pieces of the past that best reflect Creeley's life. Although memory is the source of many of these poems, Creeley is after an evocation of the experience itself, not merely its memory. But in language, experience can be recreated only through the reflective medium of words. The poems here give us pieces of the mirror, the whole of which contains an image of Creeley's life. In poem after poem there are echoes of Ezra Pound's *"dove sta memora,"* that major theme of lost memories in the *Pisan Cantos,* a poem Pound wrote at age sixty, determined to perpetuate the things that meant most to him. "What thou lovest well remains," he wrote in that poem's most famous lines, "the rest is dross, / What thou lov'st well shall not be reft from thee / What thou lov'st well is thy true heritage." And "Pull down thy vanity, it is not man / Made courage, or made order, or made grace, / Pull down thy vanity, I say pull down." Creeley concludes a poem called "Song" with a similar sentiment:

> . . . All vanity, all mind flies
> but love remains, love, nor dies
> even without me. Never dies.

Mirrors reveals how much a part of our characters memories become with each passing year, so that as we age we accumulate the mannerisms of our parents and reexperience past situations. In "Mother's Voice," Creeley not only hears his mother's voice, but makes it a part of his own:

> In these few years
> since her death I hear

mother's voice say
under my own, I won't

want any more of that.
My cheekbones resonate
with her emphasis.

This theme of the present incorporating the past is most literal in "Prospect," one of the most memorable poems in *Mirrors*. It is an atypical Creeley poem because it utilizes conventional elements of poetry—symbolism, metaphor, and imagery—in a surprisingly traditional manner. In fact, the poem has a remarkably unique resonance because Creeley's physical description of nature conveys both present and past psychological states. It takes no deep looking into the poem to see the landscape as emblematic of the state of Creeley's later life, invigorated by a new marriage and the birth of a new child, his son William:

Green's the predominant color here,
but in tones so various, and muted

. . . .

it seems a subtle echo of itself.
It is the color of life itself,

it used to be. Not blood red,
or sun yellow—but this green,

echoing hills, echoing meadows,
childhood summers blowsiness, a youngness
one remembers hopefully forever.

There is a purposeful ambiguity in that "hopefully." One remembers such a landscape charged with hope, and one will hopefully continue to remember it. It is, in its current manifestation, a landscape filled with echoes and repetitions. Green, the color of life and vitality dominates, "but in tones so various, and muted . . . it seems a subtle echo of itself." Though the prospect described here is lovely and calm, it lacks the passion and energy of previous times ("not blood red, / or sun yellow"). The poem concludes with the reflections awakened by a contemplation of this landscape:

It is thoughtful, provokes here

quiet reflections, settles the self
down to waiting now apart

from time, which is done,
this green space, faintly painful.

That final phrase surprises, coming at the end of an otherwise tranquil and nearly celebratory poem. It reminds the reader that although embarking on a new life can create the illusion that it is possible to exist in an Edenic landscape apart from time, in reality the past remains an integral part of the present. "Faintly painful," with its echoing first syllable rhyme is exactly right to convey the contrary feelings of both relief and regret that the poem ultimately leaves the reader with—relief that the thoughtfulness the landscape provokes is not more painful, regret that there is any pain at all.

But pain has been one of the most constant elements in Creeley's work, and this later poetry continues to search for words to express it with sensitivity and exactness and without the sometimes maudlin excesses of "confessional" verse. Though these poems are more rooted in memory than the earlier work,

Creeley remains committed to the poetic task of getting things exactly right. This has been the task of his writing throughout his career, and as readers look into the "mirror" of Creeley's work, they can see not only his aging, but their own.

BIOGRAPHICAL/CRITICAL SOURCES:

BOOKS

Allen, Donald, editor, *The New American Poetry: 1945-1960*, Grove, 1960.
Allen, Donald, editor, *Robert Creeley, Contexts of Poetry: Interviews, 1961-1971*, Four Seasons Foundation, 1973.
Allen, Donald and Warren Tallman, editors, *The Poetics of the New American Poetry*, Grove, 1973.
Butterick, George F., editor, *Charles Olson and Robert Creeley: The Complete Correspondence*, Black Sparrow Press, 1980.
Carroll, Paul, *The Poem in Its Skin*, Follett, 1968.
Charters, Samuel, *Some Poems/Poets: Studies in American Underground Poetry since 1945*, Oyez, 1971.
Contemporary Literary Criticism, Gale, Volume I, 1973, Volume II, 1974, Volume IV, 1975, Volume VIII, 1978, Volume IX, 1978, Volume XV, 1980, Volume XXXVI, 1986.
Cook, Albert, *Prisms: Studies in Modern Literature*, Indiana University Press, 1967.
Cook, Bruce, *The Beat Generation*, Scribner, 1971.
Corman, Cid, editor, *The Gist of Origin*, Viking, 1975.
Creeley, Robert, *For Love: Poems 1950-1960*, Scribner, 1962.
Creeley, Robert, *Words*, Perishable Press, 1965.
Creeley, Robert, *A Sense of Measure*, Calder & Boyars, 1972.
Creeley, Robert, *Hello*, Hawk Press, 1976, expanded edition published as *Hello: A Journal, February 29-May 3, 1976*, New Directions, 1978.
Creeley, Robert, *Later*, Toothpaste, 1978, expanded edition, New Directions, 1979.
Creeley, Robert, *Was That a Real Poem and Other Essays*, edited by Allen, Four Seasons Foundation, 1979.
Creeley, Robert, *The Collected Poems of Robert Creeley, 1945-1975*, University of California Press, 1982.
Creeley, Robert, *Mirrors*, New Directions, 1983.
Creeley, Robert and Donald Allen, editors, *New American Story*, Grove, 1965.
Creeley, Robert and Donald Allen, editors, *The New Writing in the U.S.A.*, Penguin, 1967.
Dembo, L. S., *Conceptions of Reality in Modern American Poetry*, University of California Press, 1966.
Dictionary of Literary Biography, Gale, Volume V: *American Poets since World War II*, 1980, Volume XVI: *The Beats: Literary Bohemians in Postwar America*, 1983.
Duberman, Martin, *Black Mountain: An Exploration in Community*, Anchor Books, 1972.
Edelberg, Cynthia Dubin, *Robert Creeley's Poetry: A Critical Introduction*, University of New Mexico Press, 1978.
Faas, Ekbert, *Towards a New American Poetics: Essays and Interviews*, Black Sparrow Press, 1979.
Ford, Arthur L., *Robert Creeley*, Twayne, 1978.
Hamburger, Michael, *The Truth of Poetry Tensions in Modern Poetry from Baudelaire to the 1960's*, Weidenfeld & Nicolson, 1969.
Hass, Robert, *Twentieth Century Pleasures*, Ecco Press, 1984.
Howard, Richard, *Alone with America: Essays on the Art of Poetry in the United States since 1950*, Atheneum, 1969.
Mariani, Paul, *A Usable Past*, University of Massachusetts Press, 1984.
Norman, Charles, editor, *Poets on Poetry*, Free Press, 1962.

Novik, Mary, *Robert Creeley: An Inventory, 1945-70,* Kent State University Press, 1973.

Olson, Charles, *Mayan Letters,* edited by Robert Creeley, Divers Press, 1953, Grossman, 1968.

Olson, Charles, *The Human Universe,* Auerhan, 1965.

Paul, Sherman, *The Lost America of Love,* Louisiana State University Press, 1981.

Rosenthal, M. L., *The New Poets: American and British Poetry since World War II,* Oxford University Press, 1967.

Sheffler, Ronald Anthony, *The Development of Robert Creeley's Poetry,* University of Massachusetts, 1971.

Smith, Barbara Herrnstein, *Poetic Closure: A Study of How Poems End,* University of Chicago Press, 1968.

Stepanchev, Stephen, *American Poetry since 1945,* Harper, 1965.

Sukenik, Ron, *Down and In,* Morrow, 1987.

Tallman, Warren, *Three Essays on Creeley,* Coach House Press, 1973.

Vendler, Helen, *A Part of Nature, A Part of Us,* Harvard University Press, 1980.

Wilson, John, editor, *Robert Creeley's Life and Work: A Sense of Increment,* University of Michigan Press, 1987.

PERIODICALS

American Book Review, May/June, 1984.

American Poetry Review, November/December, 1976.

Atlantic, November, 1962, February, 1968, October, 1977.

Books Abroad, autumn, 1967.

Book Week, June 4, 1967.

Boundary 2, spring, 1975, spring and fall (special two volume issue on Creeley), 1978.

Cambridge Quarterly, summer, 1969.

Canadian Forum, August, 1967, September, 1970.

Christian Science Monitor, October 9, 1969.

Commonweal, December 10, 1965.

Contemporary Literature, spring, 1972.

Critique, spring, 1964.

Encounter, February, 1969.

Fifties, Volume II, 1959.

Harpers, August, 1967, September, 1983.

Hudson Review, summer, 1963, summer, 1967, spring, 1970, summer, 1977.

Iowa Review, spring, 1982.

Kenyon Review, spring, 1970.

Kulchur, Number 3, 1961.

Library Journal, September 1, 1979.

Listener, March 23, 1967.

London Magazine, June/July, 1973.

Los Angeles Times Book Review, April 17, 1983, October 30, 1983, March 4, 1984, June 24, 1984.

Minnesota Review, Volume VIII, number 2, 1986, Volume IX, number 1, 1969.

Modern Poetry Studies, winter, 1977.

Nation, August 25, 1962.

National Observer, October 30, 1967.

National Review, November 19, 1960.

New Leader, October 27, 1969.

New Republic, October 11, 1969, December 18, 1976.

New Statesman, August 6, 1965, March 10, 1987.

New York Review of Books, January 20, 1966, August 1, 1968.

New York Times, June 27, 1967.

New York Times Book Review, November 4, 1962, September 22, 1963, November 19, 1967, October 27, 1968, January 7, 1973, May 1, 1977, March 9, 1980, August 7, 1983, June 24, 1984, September 23, 1984.

Observer, September 6, 1970.

Open Letter, winter, 1976-77.

Paris Review, fall, 1968.

Parnassus, fall/winter, 1984.

Partisan Review, summer, 1968.

Poetry, March, 1954, May, 1958, September, 1958, March, 1963, April, 1964, August, 1966, January, 1968, March, 1968, August, 1968, May, 1970, December, 1970, September, 1984.

Publishers Weekly, March 18, 1968.

Sagetreib, Volume I, number 3, winter, 1982, Volume III, number 2, fall, 1984.

Saturday Review, August 4, 1962, December 11, 1965, June 3, 1967.

Sewanee Review, winter, 1961.

Southwest Review, winter, 1964.

Time, July 12, 1971.

Times Literary Supplement, March 16, 1967, August 7, 1970, November 12, 1970, December 11, 1970, May 20, 1977, May 30, 1980, February 20, 1981, November 4, 1983.

Village Voice, October 22, 1958, December 10, 1979, November 25, 1981.

Virginia Quarterly Review, summer, 1968, winter, 1972, spring, 1973.

Western Humanities Review, spring, 1970.

World Literature Today, autumn, 1984.

Yale Review, October, 1962, December, 1969, spring, 1970.

—*Sidelights by Fred Moramarco*

*　　*　　*

CROSS, Gilbert B. (Jon Winters)

PERSONAL: Born in Walkden, near Manchester, England; son of Gilbert Edward Cross; married; children: two. *Education:* Manchester University, B.A., 1961; University of London, post-graduate certificate in education, 1962; University of Louisville, M.A., 1965; University of Michigan, Ph.D., 1971.

ADDRESSES: Home—1244 Ferdon, Ann Arbor, Mich. 48104. *Office*—Department of English Language and Literature, Eastern Michigan University, Ypsilanti, Mich. 48197.

CAREER: Eastern Michigan University, Ypsilanti, 1967—, currently professor of English language and literature. Writer.

WRITINGS:

(Co-editor with Alfred Nelson) *Drury Lane Journal: Selections from James Winston's Diaries, 1819-1827,* Society Theatre Research, London, 1974.

Next Week East Lynne: Domestic Drama in Performance, Bucknell University Press, 1976.

(Co-editor with Atelia Clarkson) *World Folktales: A Scribners Resource Collection,* Scribners, 1980.

JUVENILE

A Hanging at Tyburn, Atheneum, 1983.

Mystery at Loon Lake, Atheneum, 1986.

Terror Train, Atheneum, 1987.

UNDER PSEUDONYM JON WINTERS

The Drakov Memoranda, Avon, 1979.

The Catenary Exchange, Avon, 1983.

Berlin Fugue, Avon, 1985.

CROUCH, Marcus 1913-

PERSONAL: Born February 12, 1913, in Tottenham, Middlesex, England. *Education:* University of London, B.A., 1934.

ADDRESSES: Home—Tyn Llidiart, Pentre Celyn, Ruthin, Clwyd, Wales.

CAREER: Branch librarian, Tonbridge, Kent, England, 1939-48; Kent County Library, Maidstone, England, deputy county librarian, 1948-77; full-time writer, 1977—.

MEMBER: Library Association (fellow), Society of Authors.

WRITINGS:

(Editor) *Chosen for Children: An Account of the Books Which Have Been Awarded the Library Association's Carnegie Medal, 1936-1957,* Library Association, 1957, revised edition, 1977.
Beatrix Potter, Bodley Head, 1960, Walck, 1961.
Treasure Seekers and Borrowers: Children's Books in Britain 1900-1960, Library Association, 1962.
Britain in Trust: England and Wales, International Publications Service, 1963.
(Editor) *Books about Children's Literature,* Library Association, 1963, revised edition, 1966.
Rivers of England and Wales, Constable, 1965.
Kent, Hastings House, 1966, 2nd edition, Batsford, 1967.
Fingerprints of History, Longmans, Green, 1968.
Heritage of Sussex, Macdonald & Evans, 1969.
Heritage of Essex, Hastings House, 1969.
Canterbury, Longmans, Green, 1970.
Detective in the Landscape of Southeast England, Longman, 1972.
The Nesbit Tradition: Children's Novels 1945-1970, Rowman & Littlefield, 1973.
Cream of Kent, Cassell, 1973.
(With Winnifred F. Bergess) *Victorian and Edwardian Kent,* Batsford, 1974.
The Home Counties, R. Hale, 1975.
(Editor) *Book of Kent,* P. Norbury Publications, 1976.
(Editor) *Brer Rabbit,* Pelham Books, 1977.
(Adaptor; illustrated by William Stobbs) *Six against the World, and Other Stories of the Brothers Grimm,* Pelham Books, 1978.
Walks in West Kent, Shire Publications, 1978.
(Adaptor; illustrated by Stobbs) *The Ivory City, and Other Stories from India and Pakistan,* Pelham Books, 1980.
(Illustrated by Stobbs) *Rainbow Warrior's Bride,* Pelham Books, 1981.
The Whole World Storybook, Oxford University Press, 1983.
Rich Man, Poor Man, Beggarman, Thief: Folk Tales from Around the World, Oxford University Press, 1985.

WORK IN PROGRESS: A book of Russian tales built around the archetypal peasant character, Ivan.

SIDELIGHTS: Marcus Crouch writes: "From early childhood I was convinced that I would be a writer, especially a poet. This dream faded during the War and, after my return from army service overseas, I destroyed all my poems. In 1948, however, I began reviewing books (an activity which has continued unbroken to the present day), and from this came a series of commissions to write books reflecting my principal interests: children and the books they read for pleasure and the history and present state of the English countryside.

"Since my retirement from my occupation as a librarian, the direction of my work has changed. Thanks to the encourage-

ment of the distinguished illustrator William Stobbs, I have found a new outlet in the retelling of traditional folk-tales. I have tried to get back to the oral origins of these tales, excising all sophistication and literary devices and telling the stories as they might have been if the march of urban civilization had not destroyed the conditions in which they flourished. The results may have had no great commercial success, but they have given the writer considerable satisfaction."

BIOGRAPHICAL/CRITICAL SOURCES:

PERIODICALS

Observer Review, November 29, 1970.
Times Literary Supplement, October 16, 1969, October 30, 1970.

*   *   *

CRYSTAL, David 1941-

PERSONAL: Born July 6, 1941, in Lisburn, County Antrim, Northern Ireland; son of Samuel Cyril and Mary (Morris) Crystal; married Molly Stack, April 1, 1964 (deceased, 1976); married Hilary Norman, September 18, 1976; children: (first marriage) Steven David, Susan Mary, Timothy Joseph, Lucy Alexandra; (second marriage) Benjamin Peter. *Education:* University College, London, B.A., 1962, Ph.D., 1966, F.C.S.T., 1983. *Politics:* None. *Religion:* Roman Catholic.

ADDRESSES: Home—Akaroa, Gors Ave., Holyhead, Gwynedd LL65 1PB, Wales. *Office*—P.O. Box 5, Holyhead, Gwynedd LL65 1RG, Wales.

CAREER: University of London, University College, London, England, research assistant, 1962-63; University of Wales, University College of North Wales, Bangor, assistant lecturer in linguistics, 1963-65; University of Reading, Reading, England, lecturer, 1965-69, reader, 1969-75, professor of linguistics, 1975-85; University of Wales, University College of North Wales, honorary professor of linguistics, 1986—.

MEMBER: International Phonetic Association, Linguistics Association of Great Britain, British Association of Applied Linguistics, Royal Society of Arts (fellow), Philological Society, Linguistic Society of America.

WRITINGS:

(With R. Quirk) *Systems of Prosodic and Paralinguistic Features in English,* Mouton & Co., 1964.
Linguistics, Language and Religion, Hawthorn, 1965.
What Is Linguistics?, Edward Arnold, 1968, 5th edition, 1985.
(With D. Davy) *Investigating English Style,* Longmans, Green, 1969.
Prosodic Systems and Intonation in English, Cambridge University Press, 1969.
(Editor with W. Bolton) *The English Language,* Cambridge University Press, 1969.
Linguistics, Penguin, 1971, 2nd edition, 1985.
The English Tone of Voice, Edward Arnold, 1975.
(With Davy) *Advanced Conversational English,* Longman, 1975.
(With J. Bevington) *Skylarks,* Nelson, 1975.
(With P. Fletcher and M. Garman) *The Grammatical Analysis of Language Disability,* Edward Arnold, 1976.
Child Language, Learning and Linguistics, Edward Arnold, 1976, 2nd edition, 1987.
(Contributor) *The Library of Modern Knowledge,* Readers Digest Press, 1978.

(Contributor) A. Bullock, editor, *A Dictionary of Modern Thought*, John M. Fontana, 1978, 2nd edition, 1987.
Working with LARSP, Edward Arnold, 1979.
(With J. Foster) *Databank Reading Series*, Edward Arnold, 1979.
(Editor) *Eric Partridge: In His Own Words*, Deutsch, 1980.
A First Dictionary of Linguistics and Phonetics, Deutsch, 1980, 2nd edition published as *Dictionary of Linguistics and Phonetics*, 1985.
Introduction to Language Pathology, Edward Arnold, 1980.
Clinical Linguistics, Springer, 1981, revised edition, Edward Arnold, 1987.
Directions in Applied Linguistics, Academic Press, 1981.
(Editor) *Linguistic Controversies*, Edward Arnold, 1982.
Profiling Linguistic Disability, Edward Arnold, 1982.
Who Cares about English Usage?, Penguin, 1984.
Linguistic Encounters with Language Handicap, Basil Blackwell, 1984.
(Contributor) *Readers Digest Book of Facts*, Readers Digest Press, 1985.
Listen to Your Child, Penguin, 1986.
(Editor with Boltan) *The English Language*, Sphere, 1987.
(Editor) *Cambridge Encyclopedia of Language*, Oxford University Press, 1987.
Rediscover Grammar, Longman, 1988.
English Language Companion, Penguin, 1988.

Also editor, *The Language Library*, Deutsch, and *Applied Language Studies*, Academic Press. Editor, *Journal of Child Language*, 1973-85.

SIDELIGHTS: John Ross of the *Times Literary Supplement* comments about David Crystal's *A First Dictionary of Linguistics and Phonetics*, "What we have here are definitions and explanations covering the main areas of twentieth-century linguistic thought, presented in a language as clear and elegant as one could hope for." Ross continues, "For all the author's claims about the limitations of the work, it covers an impressive range of subjects." Observing that "Crystal maintains remarkable objectivity," Ross concludes, "probably the work's most outstanding quality—certainly the one most useful to its readers—is its resolute fair-mindedness."

AVOCATIONAL INTERESTS: Music (in all forms), cinema, book collecting.

BIOGRAPHICAL/CRITICAL SOURCES:

PERIODICALS

New York Times Book Review, May 10, 1981.
Times Literary Supplement, February 27, 1981, March 20, 1981.

* * *

CUNNINGHAM, Laura 1947-

PERSONAL: Born January 25, 1947, in New York, N.Y.; daughter of Laurence Moore (an aviator) and Rose Weiss; married Barry Cunningham (a journalist), December 4, 1966. *Education:* New York University, B.A., 1966.

ADDRESSES: Home—New York, New York. *Agent*—Owen Laster, William Morris Agency, 1350 Avenue of the Americas, New York, N.Y. 10019.

CAREER: Author.

MEMBER: Authors League of America, Dramatists Guild, Authors Guild, Writers Guild of America, Girl Scouts of America, Poets and Writers, New Dramatists, Writer's Community.

WRITINGS:

NOVELS

Sweet Nothings, Doubleday, 1977.
Third Parties, Coward, 1980.
Sleeping Arrangements, Knopf, 1988.

PLAYS

"Bang," first produced in Chicago, Ill., at Steppenwolf Theatre Company, 1986.
"Beautiful Bodies," first produced in Montclair, N.J., at Whole Theatre Company, 1987.

Also author of two related one-act plays, "Where She Went, What She Did" and "The Man At the Door," and "Cruising Close to Crazy," as yet unpublished.

OTHER

Contributor of articles and reviews to periodicals, including the *New York Times, Atlantic, Vogue*, and *Newsday*.

SIDELIGHTS: Laura Cunningham describes the problems faced by descendants of the very rich in her humorous novel *Third Parties*. The novel is set in Darton's Wood, an extravagant playground built by turn-of-the-century robber barons. Their third-generation descendants struggle to maintain the grand estates in spite of twentieth-century maintenance costs. Into this scene moves Isaac Katcher, a songwriter from the Bronx who finds peace in the beauty of Darton's Wood. When a corporation threatens to transform the country retreat to modern developments, Katcher, "in a hilarious show of strength, . . . musters an army of ex-wives and social misfits who share his views and, in a brilliantly engineered filibuster, literally bores the opposition into surrender," relates Elizabeth Forsythe Hailey in the *New York Times Book Review*. *Los Angeles Times Book Review* contributor Joan Reardon rates *Third Parties* "definitely one of a kind," and further calls it "a wonderful blend of fantasy and funk, . . . a just-right blend of snappy and sassy satire."

Cunningham once wrote *CA:* "I have a typical writer's personal history, that is: atypical. I am of Jewish-Southern Baptist descent, was orphaned at age eight, and raised by two unmarried uncles (both writers). I'm a third-generation author: my grandparents also wrote stories and books. Motivation? I didn't know there was anything else to be. Had I known, I would have been a ballerina."

BIOGRAPHICAL/CRITICAL SOURCES:

PERIODICALS

Chicago Magazine, December, 1986.
Los Angeles Times Book Review, October 12, 1980.
New York Times Book Review, October 26, 1980.

D

DABBERDT, Walter F. 1942-

PERSONAL: Born October 12, 1942, in New York, N.Y.; son of Richard and Marie (Thaeter) Dabberdt; married wife, Meredith, August, 1967; children: Jennifer, Geoffrey. *Education:* State University of New York Maritime College, B.S., 1964; University of Wisconsin—Madison, M.S., 1966, Ph.D., 1969.

ADDRESSES: Office—National Center for Atmospheric Research, P.O. Box 3000, Boulder, Co. 80307-3000.

CAREER: U.S. Army, Natick Laboratories, Natick, Mass., visiting scientist, 1969-70; SRI International, Menlo Park, Calif., associate director of Atmospheric Science Center, 1970-85; National Center for Atmospheric Research, Boulder, Co., research scientist, 1985—. Member of advisory council of Bay Area Air Quality Management District, 1980-85.

MEMBER: Air Pollution Control Association, American Meteorological Society.

AWARDS, HONORS: National Research Council fellowship, 1969-70; Fellow of Alexander von Humboldt Foundation at University of Munich, 1977-78.

WRITINGS:

Whole Air Weather Guide, Solstice Publications, 1976.
Weather for Outdoorsmen, Scribner, 1981.
(Editor) *Atmospheric Dispersion of Hazardous/Toxic Materials from Transport Accidents,* Elsevier, 1984.

Contributor of twenty-five articles to scientific journals, and an eight-article series on weather and boating to *Motorboat,* 1977-78.

SIDELIGHTS: Walter F. Dabberdt told *CA:* "The focus of my popular writings has been to communicate scientific knowledge and information concerning weather to the lay audience and especially [to] those segments that work and recreate outdoors."

AVOCATIONAL INTERESTS: Sailing, skiing, tennis, photography, viniculture ("and of course the effect of weather on these activities").

DANIELS, Roger 1927-

PERSONAL: Born December 1, 1927, in New York, N.Y.; son of George Roger (an author) and Eleanor (Lustig) Daniels; married Judith Marcia Mandel, October 2, 1960; children: Richard John, Sarah Elizabeth. *Education:* University of Houston, B.A., 1957; University of California, Los Angeles, M.S., 1958, Ph.D., 1961.

ADDRESSES: Office—Department of History, University of Cincinnati, Cincinnati, Ohio.

CAREER: Wisconsin State College and Institute of Technology, Platteville (now University of Wisconsin—Platteville), assistant professor, 1961-62, associate professor of history, 1962-63; University of California, Los Angeles, assistant professor of history, 1963-68; University of Wyoming, Laramie, associate professor, 1968-71, professor of history, 1971; State University of New York College at Fredonia, professor of history, 1971-76; University of Cincinnati, Cincinnati, Ohio, professor of history, 1976—. *Military service:* U.S. Army, 1952-54; became sergeant.

MEMBER: American Historical Association, Economic History Association, Organization of American Historians, American Association of University Professors.

WRITINGS:

The Politics of Prejudice: The Anti-Japanese Movement in California and the Struggle for Japanese Exclusion, University of California Press, 1962, 2nd edition, 1977.
(With Harry H. L. Kitano) *American Racism: Exploration of the Nature of Prejudice,* Prentice-Hall, 1969.
Concentration Camps USA: Japanese Americans and World War II, Holt, 1971.
The Bonus March: An Episode of the Great Depression, Greenwood Press, 1971.
(Compiler with Spencer C. Olin, Jr.) *Racism in California: A Reader in the History of Oppression,* Macmillan, 1972.
The Decision to Relocate the Japanese Americans, Harper, 1975, 2nd edition, Krieger, 1986.
(Editor) *Three Short Works on Japanese Americans,* Arno, 1978.
Anti-Chinese Violence in North America: An Original Anthology, Arno, 1979.
(Editor) *Two Monographs on Japanese Canadians,* Arno, 1979.

Concentration Camps, North America: Japanese in the United States and Canada during World War II, Krieger, 1981.

(Editor with Sandra C. Taylor and Harry H. L. Kitano) *Japanese Americans: From Relocation to Redress,* University of Utah Press, 1986.

(With Kitano) *Asian Americans,* Prentice-Hall, 1987.

Asian America: Chinese and Japanese in the United States since 1850, University of Washington Press, 1988.

Contributor to history journals.

*   *   *

DANIELSSON, Bengt (Emmerik) 1921-

PERSONAL: Born July 6, 1921, in Krokek, Sweden; son of Emmerik D. and Greta (Kaellgren) Danielsson; married Marie-Therese Sailley, April 22, 1948; children: Maruia, Matuanui. *Education:* University of Uppsala, Ph.D., 1955.

ADDRESSES: Home—Papehue, Paea, 19 KM Tahiti, French Polynesia.

CAREER: Anthropologist and writer. Member of field research expedition among Jibaro Indians, Upper Amazons, 1946-47; member of Kon-Tiki expedition, 1947; field work in and member of Pacific Science Board Atoll Research expedition to Tuamotu Islands; French Polynesia, 1949-52; associate anthropologist, Bernice P. Bishop Museum, Honolulu, Hawaii, 1952; field work in Australia, 1955-56; leader of George Vanderbilt tichtyological expedition to Society Islands, 1957; field work in Polynesia, 1958-62; Swedish Consul in French Polynesia, 1960-78; National Museum of Ethnography, Stockholm, Sweden, director, 1967-71; producer and writer. Technical adviser, "Mutiny on the Bounty," 1961; leader of Swedish Television expedition to South Seas, 1962. Organizer of Gauguin exhibitions in the University Museum, Philadelphia, 1969, the National Museum of Art, Stockholm, 1970, and Louisiana Museum, Denmark, 1982.

WRITINGS:

Den lyckliga oen, Forum (Stockholm), 1951, translation by F. H. Lyon published as *The Happy Island,* Allen & Unwin, 1952, published as *Raroia: Happy Island of the South Seas,* Rand McNally, 1953.

Soederhavets gloemda oear: Reseskildring fran Marquesasoearna, Saxon & Lindstrom (Stockholm), 1952, translation by Lyon published as *Forgotten Islands of the South Seas,* Adventurers Club, 1956.

Soederhavskaerlek: En skildring av polynesiernas sexualliv och familjefoerhaallanden, Forum, 1954, translation by Lyon published as *Love in the South Seas,* Reynal, 1956.

Work and Life on Raroia: An Acculturation Study from the Tuamotu Group, French Oceania, Almqvist & Wiksells (Uppsala), 1955, Macmillan, 1956.

Bumerang, Forum, 1956.

Villervalle i Soederhavet (juvenile), Saxon & Lindstrom, 1957, translation by Reginald Spink published as *Terry in the South Seas* (illustrated by Pierre Heyman), Allen & Unwin, 1959.

Villervalles okenaventyr (juvenile), Saxon & Lindstrom, 1958, translation by Spink published as *Terry in Australia,* Allen & Unwin, 1959.

Det stora vaagspelet: Tahiti Nui-expeditionen, photographs by Alain Brun and A. Sylvain, Saxon & Lindstrom, 1959, translation by Lyon published as *From Raft to Raft,* Doubleday, 1960.

(With Rolf du Rietz) *Med Bounty till Soederhavet,* Saxon & Lindstroem, 1962, translation by Alan Tapsell published as *What Happened on the Bounty,* Allen & Unwin, 1962, Rand McNally, 1964.

Aloha: Resare-Bengt beraettar, Tidens, 1962.

Kapten Villervalle (juvenile), illustrations by Liliane and Paul Risch, Saxon & Lindstrom, 1963, translation by Roy Duffel published as *Terry's Kon-Tiki Adventure,* Verry, 1965.

(Author of preface) A. Sylvain, *Nus de Tahiti,* Prisma (Paris), 1963.

Gauguin soederhavsaar, Forum, 1964, translation by Spink published as *Gauguin in the South Seas,* Allen & Unwin, 1965, Doubleday, 1966.

(With Patrick O'Reilly) *Gaugin journaliste a Tahiti et ses articles des "Guepes"* (collection of articles), Societe des oceanistes (Paris), 1966.

(With wife, Marie-Therese Danielsson) *Moruroa, mon amour,* Stock (Paris), 1974, translation published as *Moruroa, mon amour: The French Nuclear Tests in the Pacific,* Penguin, 1977, reprinted as *Poisoned Reign: French Nuclear Colonialism in the Pacific,* 1986.

Tahiti: Circle Island Tour Guide, Les Editions du Pacifique, 1976.

Le Memorial polynesien (history of French Polynesia), six volumes, Editions Hibiscus (Papeete), 1978-80.

Tahiti Autrefois, Editions Hibiscus (Papeete), 1981.

Exploring the Pacific Way, Allen & Unwin, 1988.

Contributor of articles to professional journals, including *Journal of Polynesian Society* and *Atoll Research Bulletin,* and to travel books.

BIOGRAPHICAL/CRITICAL SOURCES:

PERIODICALS

Christian Science Monitor, July 7, 1966.

Manchester Guardian, July 8, 1960.

New Statesman, June 21, 1966.

New York Herald Tribune Book Review, November 22, 1953, July 8, 1956.

New York Herald Tribune Lively Arts, March 26, 1961.

New York Review of Books, July 1, 1966.

New York Times Book Review, November 22, 1953, August 5, 1956, January 1, 1961, May 29, 1966.

Reporter, August 11, 1966.

Spectator, March 2, 1956, July 15, 1960.

Time, May 6, 1966.

Times Literary Supplement, December 19, 1952, March 16, 1956, August 12, 1960, January 6, 1966.

*   *   *

DAVENPORT, Guy (Mattison, Jr.) 1927-
(Max Montgomery)

PERSONAL: Born November 23, 1927, in Anderson, S.C.; son of Guy Mattison (an express agent) and Marie (Fant) Davenport. *Education:* Duke University, B.A., 1948; Merton College, Oxford, B.Litt., 1950; Harvard University, Ph.D., 1961. *Politics:* "Democrat and Conservative." *Religion:* Baptist.

ADDRESSES: Home—621 Sayre Ave., Lexington, Ky. 40508. *Office*—Department of English, University of Kentucky, Lexington, Ky. 40506.

CAREER: Washington University, St. Louis, Mo., instructor in English, 1952-55; Haverford College, Haverford, Pa., assistant professor of English, 1961-63; University of Kentucky,

Lexington, professor of English, 1963—. Lecturer, University of Toronto, 1984, and Washington and Lee University, 1985. State secretary, Rhodes Scholarship Selection Committee. *Military service:* U.S. Army, Airborne Corps, 1950-52.

AWARDS, HONORS: Rhodes scholarship, Merton College, Oxford, 1948-50; Anne Flexner Creative Writing Award, 1948; Blumenthal-Leviton Prize for Poetry, 1967; Kentucky Research Award, 1976; University of Kentucky Arts and Sciences Distinguished Professor citation, 1977; Morton Dauwen Zabel Award from the American Academy and Institute of Arts and Letters, 1981, for fiction; American Book Award nominations, 1981, for translation of *Archilochos, Sappho, Alkman,* and 1982, for *The Geography of the Imagination: Forty Essays;* National Book Critics Circle Award nomination, 1982, for *The Geography of the Imagination: Forty Essays;* University of Kentucky Alumni Distinguished Professor citation, 1983; Thomas Carter Award, *Shenandoah,* 1986, for literary criticism.

WRITINGS:

(Editor and author of introduction and notes) *The Intelligence of Louis Agassiz: A Specimen Book of Scientific Writings,* Beacon Press, 1963, reprinted, Greenwood Press, 1983.

(Translator) *Carmina Archilochi: The Fragments of Archilochos,* University of California Press, 1964.

(Translator and author of introduction) *Sappho: Songs and Fragments,* University of Michigan Press, 1965.

Flowers and Leaves: Poema vel sonata, carmina autumni primaeque veris transformationum, Jargon Society, 1966.

Cydonia Florentia, Lowell-Adams House Printers, 1966.

Pennant Key-Indexed Guide to Homer's "Iliad," Educational Research Associates, 1967.

Pennant Key-Indexed Guide to Homer's "Odyssey," Educational Research Associates, 1967.

Do You Have a Poem Book on E. E. Cummings?, Jargon Society, 1969.

(Author of introduction) *An Ear in Bartram's Tree: Selected Poems of Jonathan Williams, 1957-67,* University of North Carolina Press, 1969.

(Author of introduction) Ronald Johnson, *Valley of the Many-Colored Grasses,* Norton, 1969.

Jonathan Williams, Poet, Asphodel Book Shop, 1969.

Tatlin! (short fiction), Scribner, 1974.

(Author of preface) William Benton, translator, *L'Apres-midi d'un faune,* Pyramid Editions, 1976.

(Author of introduction) Ronald Johnson, *Radi Os,* Sand Dollar, 1977.

(Also illustrator) *Da Vinci's Bicycle: Ten Stories by Guy Davenport* (short fiction), Johns Hopkins University Press, 1979.

(Author of introduction) Jonathan Williams, *Elite/Elate: Poems, 1971-1975,* Jargon Society, 1979.

Herakleitos and Diogenes, Grey Fox, 1979, revised edition, 1981.

(Translator) *Archilochos, Sappho, Alkman,* University of California Press, 1981.

Eclogues: Eight Stories by Guy Davenport (short fiction), North Point Press, 1981.

The Geography of the Imagination: Forty Essays, North Point Press, 1981.

The Mimes of Herondas, Grey Fox Press, 1981.

Trois Caprices (short fiction), Pace Trust, 1982.

The Resurrection in Cookham Churchyard, Jordan Davies, 1982.

(Author of introduction) Vladimir Nabokov, *Lectures of Don Quixote,* Harcourt, 1983.

(Author of introduction) Montaigne, *Travel Journal,* North Point Press, 1983.

Goldfinch Thistle Star, Red Ozier Press, 1983.

Cities on Hills: A Study of I-XXX of Ezra Pound's Cantos, UMI Research Press, 1983.

Maxims of the Ancient Egyptians, Pace Trust, 1983.

The Bowmen of Shu, Grenfell Press, 1983.

(Also illustrator) *Apples and Pears and Other Stories* (short fiction), North Point Press, 1984.

The Bicycle Rider, Red Ozier Press, 1985.

Thasos and Ohio: Poems and Translations, 1950-1980, North Point Press, 1986.

Jonah, Nadja Press, 1986.

August, Close Grip Press, 1986.

Every Force Evolves a Form, North Point Press, 1987.

The Jules Verne Steam Balloon, North Point Press, 1987.

ILLUSTRATOR

Hugh Kenner, *The Stoic Comedians,* Beacon Press, 1964.

Hugh Kenner, *The Counterfeiters,* Indiana University Press, 1968.

Ronald Johnson, *The Spirit Walks, the Rocks Will Talk,* Jargon Society, 1969.

Allen Mandelbaum, *The "Aeneid" of Virgil,* University of California Press, 1972.

CONTRIBUTOR

Lewis Leary, editor, *Method and Motive in "The Cantos" of Ezra Pound,* Columbia University Press, 1954.

Dominique de Roux, editor, *Les Cahiers de l'Herne: Ezra Pound,* [Paris], 1965.

Eva Hesse, editor, *Ezra Pound: 22 Versuche ueber einer Dichter,* Athenaeum Verlag, 1967.

Ezra's "Bowmen of Shu," Adams House, 1967.

Jonathan Williams, *Sharp Tools for Catullan Gardens,* Indiana University, 1967.

Hesse, editor, *New Approaches to Ezra Pound,* Faber, 1969.

Peter Jay, editor, *The Greek Anthology,* Oxford University Press, 1973.

Madeira and Toasts for Basil Bunting, Jargon Society, 1977.

Charles Tomlinson, editor, *The Oxford Book of Verse in English Translation,* Oxford University Press, 1980.

OTHER

Also author of libretti for Lukas Foss's "Carmina Archilochi" and Richard Swift's "Songs of Archilochos." Contributor of short stories to *Hudson Review* and of essays, reviews under pseudonym, Max Montgomery, and articles to *Virginia Quarterly Review, National Review, New York Times Book Review, Life,* and other publications. Contributing editor, *National Review,* 1962—. Illustrator for *Arion,* 1964—, and *Paideuma,* 1972—.

SIDELIGHTS: An immensely learned scholar, Guy Davenport has published essays, translations, fiction, poetry, and illustrations, all to critical acclaim. *New Yorker* contributor George Steiner notes that Davenport "is among the very few truly original, truly autonomous voices now audible in American letters. . . . A Davenport sentence or short paragraph . . . is instantaneously recognizable." The author is perhaps best known for his "excellent and original feel for fictional forms" that demonstrates a "high ability to evoke cerebral excitement," according to Curtis Johnson in the *Chicago Review.* Indeed, Davenport's creative prose works are often sets of imaginative exercises, or in his own words, "assemblages of history and necessary fiction" that bear little resemblance to the conventional short story form. As George Kearns explains in the *Hudson Review,* none of the "usual senses for 'story' suggests the combination of audacious invention, sentence-by-sentence surprise, playfulness and archaic wonder of the world Davenport . . . continues to explore." In his fiction and nonfiction alike, Davenport seeks to demonstrate the vital propinquity of the archaic through a poetic language rich in levels of meaning. His goal, writes Walter Sullivan in the *Sewanee Review,* is "to establish new connections between old and new, to discover further dimensions in the continuum of human history, and, by explaining to us a past that we do not understand, to afford us a measure of hope for our tawdry present, our seemingly hopeless future."

"Nothing attracts Guy Davenport like a world almost impossible to imagine, requiring reconstitution atom by atom," declares Hugh Kenner in the *National Review.* Davenport's aesthetic is essentially modernist; critics feel he is indebted to Ezra Pound, although he is by no means an imitator of that noted poet. Steiner observes that Davenport "is faithful to Ezra Pound's injunction that prose ought to be at least as well crafted as verse. He is a master of subtle pace." Steiner feels likewise that the author's "esoteric lusts of learning" place him within a tradition that Pound embraced. "Indeed," writes Steiner, "Pound and Davenport seem to represent a cultural omnivorousness, an attempt at making a complete inventory of the world's aesthetic-poet loot." Bob Halliday elaborates in the *Washington Post Book World:* "Davenport is at his best when discussing highly allusive art like the poetry of Pound and [Louis] Zukofsky, and it is of these writers that one is reminded when turning from his criticism to his fiction. The art of allusion, of adding layers of meaning and context to a fictional world through a system of references and quotations, has been near the center of all of Davenport's fiction to date. . . . Unusual demands are made on the reader's knowledge of literary history, philosophy, art and language, especially as they relate to the modernist eruptions which took place during the early part of this century." *New York Times Book Review* contributor Hilton Kramer concludes: "Far from finding the sheer range of Pound's linguistic, historical and esthetic interests in any way daunting, [Davenport] has addressed himself to a similar variety of challenges with an impressive energy and application. . . . Davenport is an exceptionally able reader of difficult modern texts and is often wonderfully alert to the sort of unlikely connections that illuminate a whole literary landscape."

In his *Georgia Review* essay on *Tatlin!,* Richard Wertime provides a description of Davenport's fiction that applies as well to the author's other collections—*Da Vinci's Bicycle, Eclogues: Eight Stories,* and *Apples and Pears and Other Stories.* The works, contends Wertime, are not "short fiction" in the customary sense, but rather are "tales full of essaying, imaginative renditions of historical facts, revolving meditations on the philosophic problems that have most vexed our century. Davenport has virtually contrived a new genre to house the breadth of his interests. Happily, . . . his work is still fictive in essence. In fact, its most striking attribute is not the intelligent commentary on the human condition—and there is plenty of that—nor yet the dazzle of its language, . . . it is, rather, the keenness of the eye which observes." According to Kramer, Davenport's conception of the short-story form "is remarkable. He has given it some of the intellectual density of the learned essay, some of the lyric concision of the modern poem—some of its difficulty too—and a structure that often resembles a film documentary. The result is a tour de force

that adds something new to the art of fiction." Davenport employs collage and montage to course across centuries; his "characters" include Gertrude Stein, Franz Kafka, Leonardo da Vinci, Richard Nixon, and a host of philosophers, inventors, explorers and other seminal thinkers from history. *Village Voice* contributor Darryl Pinckney claims that Davenport's stories "exhibit a formidable range of learning and an appealing audacity of language. . . . Much of his lavish display depends on appropriations of history, remote subjects, and an overwhelming flow of words."

Davenport draws upon vast learning to produce his fiction; the levels of allusion central to his work demand a knowledgeable reader. *New York Times Book Review* contributor Andrew C. J. Bergman notes that a Davenport work "manifests the poet's concentration on resonant verbal texture, the specialist's reverent, if not rapturous, familiarity with classical civilization and intellectual history, and the abstruse density of the difficult academic essay. Davenport's immense erudition courses through the book like a current in a river that takes us through some exotic, alluring terrain. But it's an outing that requires some special enthusiasm and equipment; he makes few . . . concessions to comfort." Sam Tanenhaus claims in the *Village Voice* that Davenport is "a bona fide polymath, steeped in languages, the arts, and science: sometimes he crystallizes diverse ingredients into vivid Cubist portraits, full of arresting planes; but often, snared in his own learning, he muddles his collages with showy erudition and promiscuous name-dropping." *Saturday Review* correspondent Jack Sullivan likewise contends that Davenport's collages "are often impressive in their cleverness and intricacy, but sometimes wearying in their self-conscious erudition."

Bearing in mind Davenport's intended audience, a majority of the critics share Hilton Kramer's view that the author's stories prove "an absolute delight to the literary connoisseur." In the *Washington Post Book World,* Jerome Klinkowitz writes that the fiction is appealing "because deep down it reflects the way our imaginations create a world. . . . Fine writing and fresh perceptions are the mutually shared joys of Guy Davenport's fiction. Reading it is a lifetime experience." Steiner offers a concurrent opinion: "It is Davenport's genius to bring together a Byzantine high literacy and a profoundly American at-homeness on the earth. This interplay gives his whole work its offbeat freshness, its irreverent piety." Curtis Johnson concludes: "Davenport's whole achievement is unique. By tapping an immense erudition and by combining traditional and avant-garde techniques and forms to write about actual persons and events, he has created a vast flowing poetry celebrating the mind of man."

Davenport has also authored numerous essays and reviews. Forty of these are collected in *The Geography of the Imagination,* published in 1981. Halliday calls the book a "superb collection," doubly beguiling in its "stylistic wit and . . . the acumen demonstrated in its arguments." *Times Literary Supplement* reviewer Adam Mars-Jones notes that Davenport is "a master of the learned essay, but a quirky one," whose ". . . sheer range of reference and experience is exhilarating." Mars-Jones continues: "Guy Davenport incarnates a blithe Greek appetite for pleasure and knowledge. His retrieval of the past is a series of *tours de force.* . . . Yet what makes him distinctive is not his obsession with the transmission of culture, but his confidence in that transmission." In a *New Leader* essay on *The Geography of the Imagination,* William C. Watterson writes: "Rich in wit and insight, these essays on history, literature and art eschew the systematic rigor of academic discourse in favor of a critical idiom that is bold and exploratory. . . . Each effort aims to invigorate, not embalm.''

Davenport, who teaches at the University of Kentucky, told the Toronto *Globe and Mail* that he ''blundered into academic life.'' As a Rhodes scholar with a doctorate from Harvard, he is perhaps more ambitious than this modest assertion suggests. He brings an equally modest attitude to his evaluation of his fiction. In a *New York Times Book Review* essay, he claims that he was urged toward fiction by the knowledge ''that I would get everything wrong, every detail, every emotion, every image. I would create by moving from mistake to mistake, so that the result would be a perfect blank if you compared it to reality (which can't be done) or to that official fiction, history.'' He adds some thoughts on art and literature: ''A meaningless world is intolerable, corrosive, depressing. Our understanding of the world is largely secret, limited to our kin and friends, and evaporates in the winds of time. The artist's understanding of the world is public, available to all, and can become a long-lasting resource. . . . Two people attentive to a detail of the world make a society, and the object they find significant has crossed over from meaninglessness to symbol. Art is always the replacing of indifference by attention.'' He concludes: ''I am a minor—an amateur—writer working at the edge of the community of writers. I could not write at all until I had found a way to exhaust, in my small way and to the best of my ability, the subject I'd chosen.''

Davenport told *CA:* ''Primarily a teacher, I consider all my writing as extensions of the classroom. The translations (Heraclitus, Alkman, Menander, Sappho, Archilochos) are meant to serve the Greekless, as my stories are lessons in history. My poems are lessons in aesthetics. There is room enough for self-expression in even the most rigorously scholarly writing, and thus I have avoided all temptations to use writing for personal expression. Language is the one social bond, and should be objective, useful, instructive.''

BIOGRAPHICAL/CRITICAL SOURCES:

BOOKS

Contemporary Literary Criticism, Gale, Volume VI, 1976, Volume XIV, 1980, Volume XXXVIII, 1986.

PERIODICALS

Chicago Review, Volume XXVI, number 4, 1975.
Critique, March, 1981.
Georgia Review, winter, 1975.
Globe and Mail (Toronto), November 17, 1984.
Harper's, August, 1981.
Hudson Review, spring, 1975, autumn, 1980.
Los Angeles Times, December 12, 1984.
National Review, September 28, 1979, November 13, 1981.
New Leader, June 29, 1981.
New Literary History, autumn, 1977.
New Yorker, November 30, 1981.
New York Review of Books, March 3, 1966, December 12, 1974.
New York Times, August 26, 1974.
New York Times Book Review, October 20, 1974, June 17, 1979, September 6, 1981, April 4, 1982.
Prairie Schooner, summer, 1975.
Review of Contemporary Fiction, spring, 1986.
Saturday Review, July 7, 1979.
Sewanee Review, summer, 1975.
Times Literary Supplement, April 24, 1981, March 8, 1985.

Village Voice, January 14, 1980, December 23, 1981, December 18, 1984.
Vort, Volume III, number 3, 1976.
Washington Post Book World, August 11, 1974, July 15, 1979, September 6, 1981, January 20, 1985.

—*Sketch by Anne Janette Johnson*

*   *   *

DAVIDSON, Cathy Notari   1949-

PERSONAL: Born June 21, 1949, in Chicago, Ill.; daughter of Paul C. (an executive in solar energy) and Leeann Ripes (a caseworker; maiden name, Behnke) Notari; married Arnold E. Davidson (a college teacher); children: Charles R. *Education:* Elmhurst College, B.A., 1970; State University of New York at Binghamton, M.A., 1973, Ph.D., 1974; postdoctoral study at University of Chicago, 1975-76.

ADDRESSES: Office—Department of English, Morrill Hall, Michigan State University, East Lansing, Mich. 48824.

CAREER: Elmhurst College, Elmhurst, Ill., instructor in English, 1973-74; St. Bonaventure University, St. Bonaventure, N.Y., instructor in English, 1974-75; Michigan State University, East Lansing, assistant professor, 1976-82, associate professor of English, 1982—. Visiting professor at Kobe College, Nishinomiya, Japan, 1980-81 and 1987-88.

MEMBER: Modern Language Association of America, Women's Caucus on Modern Languages, College English Association, Women's Studies Association, Midwest Modern Language Association (chairperson of Late Nineteenth-Century American Literature Division, 1982).

AWARDS, HONORS: Irving J. Lee Memorial Award from International Society for General Semantics, 1974, for dissertation, ''The Poetics of Perception: A Semantic Analysis of the Fiction of Ambrose Bierce''; fellow at Newberry Library, 1976; Michigan State University Teacher-Scholar Award, 1979; grant from National Endowment for the Humanities, 1980; Canadian Embassy Faculty Enrichment fellowship, 1984; American Antiquarian Society's Peterson fellow, 1984; grant-in-aid, American Council of Learned Societies, 1986; John Simon Guggenheim Foundation fellowship, 1986; Distinguished Faculty Award, Michigan State University, 1987.

WRITINGS:

(Editor with E. M. Broner) *The Lost Tradition: Mothers and Daughters in Literature,* Ungar, 1980.
(Editor with husband, Arnold E. Davidson) *The Art of Margaret Atwood: Essays in Criticism,* House of Anansi Press, 1981.
(Editor) *Critical Essays on Ambrose Bierce,* G. K. Hall, 1982.
(Editor) *The Complete Short Stories of Ambrose Bierce,* University of Nebraska Press, 1984.
The Experimental Fictions of Ambrose Bierce: Structuring the Ineffable, University of Nebraska Press, 1984.
(Editor) Susanna Rawson, *Charlotte Temple,* Oxford University Press, 1986.
(Editor) Hannah Foster, *The Coquette,* Oxford University Press, 1986.
Revolution and the Word: The Rise of the Novel in America, Oxford University Press, 1986.
Reading America: Essays on the History of Culture and Literacy in America, Johns Hopkins University Press, 1987.

Contributor to literature journals. Contributor of articles to *Ms.* and *Vogue*. Contributing editor of *Women's Studies Newsletter*.

SIDELIGHTS: Cathy Notari Davidson commented: "I am interested in relationships between social and political activities and the creative arts, particularly fiction. Right now my principal focus is the relationship between what happened after the American Revolution (the various radical and reactionary stances) and the first novels written in America. It's a 'pure' way to study the impact of society on literature, and literature on society, since both American culture and American fiction were being defined as 'American' for the first time."

*   *   *

DAVIS, Robert Con 1948-

PERSONAL: Born July 4, 1948, in Phoenix, Ariz.; son of Hugh G. and Elva Covene (Wood) Davis. *Education:* California State University, Hayward, B.A., 1972; University of California, Davis, M.A., 1974, Ph.D., 1979.

ADDRESSES: *Home*—1507 Westbrook Ter., Norman, Okla. *Office*—Department of English, University of Oklahoma, Norman, Okla. 73019.

CAREER: University of Pisa, Pisa, Italy, lecturer in American literature, 1974-75; University of California, Davis, visiting assistant professor of English and comparative literature, 1979-80; University of Oklahoma, Norman, associate professor of English, 1980—. Co-director of Oklahoma Project for Discourse and Theory.

MEMBER: Modern Language Association of America, Semiotics Society of America.

AWARDS, HONORS: Fulbright fellowship for Italy, 1974-75; University of Oklahoma summer fellowship, 1981, 1984.

WRITINGS:

(Editor) *The Fictional Father: Lacanian Readings of the Text,* University of Massachusetts Press, 1981.
(Editor) *Twentieth-Century Interpretations of "The Grapes of Wrath,"* Prentice-Hall, 1982.
(Editor) *Lacan and Narration,* Johns Hopkins University Press, 1984.
(Co-editor) *Rhetoric and Form,* University of Oklahoma Press, 1985.
(Editor) *Contemporary Literary Criticism,* Longman, 1986.
(Co-editor) *White on White,* Johns Hopkins University Press, 1988.

Contributor of articles and reviews to literature journals. Guest editor of *Arizona Quarterly,* spring, 1980; book review editor of *Genre*.

WORK IN PROGRESS: *The Paternal Romance: The Father in Fiction*, a study of authority and narrative structure in Anglo-American fiction, Lacanian in orientation.

SIDELIGHTS: Robert Con Davis once told *CA:* "I am glad the study of American literature has become more sophisticated in its critical methodology. For too long American critics have worked in isolation from the philosophical and critical developments in the rest of the world. I think a critic should work from intensely personal interests, but then find access to communal and cultural discourse of his/her time. The dialogue between American and French critics in the last twenty years is a healthy sign that a viable cultural discourse is today taking place. The current generation of American scholar/critics, I think, will build on this work and will continue to reconcile American scholarship with European theoretical speculation. The day may come soon when being American will no longer be synonymous with being anti-intellectual and anti-theoretical."

*   *   *

DAVIS, (Benton) Vincent (Jr.) 1930-

PERSONAL: Born May 3, 1930, in Chattanooga, Tenn.; son of Benton Vincent (a businessman) and Mildred Elizabeth (Jackson) Davis; married Anne Watts DePierri, March 16, 1957; children: Gail Borden, Benton Vincent III, Jackson Beecher. *Education:* Vanderbilt University, B.A. (cum laude), 1952; Princeton University, M.P.A., 1959, M.A., 1960, Ph.D., 1961.

ADDRESSES: *Home*—3533 Gloucester Dr., Westmorland, Lexington, Ky. 40510. *Office*—1665 Patterson Tower, University of Kentucky, Lexington, Ky. 40506-0027.

CAREER: Princeton University, Princeton, N.J., instructor in political science and research assistant, Center of International Studies, 1959-61; Dartmouth College, Hanover, N.H., assistant professor of government, 1961-62; University of Denver, Denver, Colo., associate professor in Graduate School of International Studies and research associate of Social Science Foundation, 1962-71; University of Kentucky, Lexington, Patterson Professor of International Studies and director of Patterson School of Diplomacy and International Commerce, 1971—. Visiting research associate, Center for International Studies, Princeton University, 1969-70; Visiting Nimitz Chair Professor of Foreign Affairs, U.S. Naval War College, 1970-71; guest lecturer at colleges, universities, professional and research organizations, and businesses and at U.S. government agencies, including departments of State, Defense, Education, and Agriculture and National Security Council.

President, Littleton Council for Human Relations, 1965-66; member of U.S. District Export Council, 1977-81, of Council on Foreign Relations Committee on International Affairs fellowship program, 1979-82, and of Inter-University Seminar on Armed Forces and Society. Has presented papers and chaired panels at national and international conventions; has given testimony before U.S. congressional committees. Consultant and advisor on international affairs and international commerce to numerous organizations, including United States Information Agency (USIA), Agency for International Development (AID), Institute for Defense Analysis (IDA), and Rand Capital Corporation (RAND). *Military service:* U.S. Naval Reserve, active duty, 1952-56, primarily as dive-bomber with carrier squadrons in Caribbean and Mediterranean; became captain.

MEMBER: International Institute of Strategic Studies (London), International Studies Association (executive director, 1964-70; president, 1976-77), Amerian Academy of International Business, American Political Science Association, American Association for Advancement of Science, U.S. Naval Institute, Naval Historical Foundation, Southern Political Science Association.

WRITINGS:

Postwar Defense Policy and the U.S. Navy, 1943-46, University of North Carolina Press, 1966.
The Admirals Lobby, University of North Carolina Press, 1967.
The Politics of Innovation: Patterns in Navy Cases, Graduate School of International Studies, University of Denver, 1967.

The Department of Defense (special report), Institute for Defense Analyses, 1968.

Research on American Foreign Policy: A Conference Report, Graduate School of International Studies, University of Denver, 1970.

Henry Kissinger and Bureaucratic Politics: A Personal Appraisal, Institute of International Studies, University of South Carolina, 1979.

EDITOR

(With Arthur N. Gilbert, and contributor) *Basic Courses in International Relations,* Sage Publications, 1968.

(With James N. Rosenau and Maurice A. East, and contributor) *The Analysis of International Politics,* Free Press, 1971.

(And contributor) *The Post-Imperial Presidency,* Transaction Books, 1980.

(With Robert J. Art and Samuel P. Huntington) *Reorganizing America's Defense: Leadership in War and Peace,* Pergamon-Brassey's, 1985.

Founding editor, "Monograph Series in World Affairs," Graduate School of International Studies, University of Denver, 1964-68; founding editor and then co-editor with Maurice A. East, "Sage Professional Papers in International Studies" series, Sage Publications, 1971-77; founding editor, "'Third Century' Books" series, University Press of Kentucky, 1975—. Also general editor of "Anthology of Syllabi" series, five volumes, Sage Publications.

CONTRIBUTOR

Keith Clark and Laurence J. Legere, editors, *The President and the Management of National Security,* Praeger, 1969.

James A. Barber, Jr. and Stephen E. Ambrose, editors, *The Military and American Society: Essays and Readings,* Free Press, 1972.

Morton H. Halperin and Arnold Kanter, editors, *Readings in American Foreign Policy: A Bureaucratic Perspective,* Little, Brown, 1973.

Richard G. Head and Ervin J. Rokke, editors, *American Defense Policy,* 3rd edition (Davis was not associated with earlier editions), Johns Hopkins University Press, 1973, 4th edition, John E. Endicott and Roy W. Stafford, Jr. editors, 1977.

To Use the Sea: Readings in Seapower and Maritime Affairs, Naval Institute Press, 1973.

John P. Lovell and Philip S. Kronenberg, editors, *New Civil-Military Relations: The Agonies of Adjustment to Post-Vietnam Realities,* Transaction Books, 1974.

International Encyclopedia of the Social Sciences, Free Press, 1979.

Sam C. Sarkesian, editor, *Defense Policy and the Presidency: Carter's First Years,* Westview, 1979.

Sarkesian, editor, *Presidential Leadership and National Security: Styles, Institutions and Politics,* Westview, 1984.

Stephen J. Cimbala, editor, *National Security Strategy: Choices and Limits,* Praeger, 1984.

Cimbala, editor, *The Reagan Defense Program: The First Four Years,* Scholarly Resources, 1986.

George K. Osborn, Asa Clark and others, editors, *Vietnam: Did It Make a Difference?,* Johns Hopkins University Press, 1987.

Joseph Kruzel, editor, *The American Defense Annual 1987-88,* Heath, 1987.

OTHER

Author of papers for the state of Kentucky. Occasional columnist for *Christian Science Monitor.* Contributor of articles and reviews to scholarly and professional journals and to newspapers, including *Political Science Review, American Behavioral Scientist, International Studies Notes, American Political Science Review, International Studies Quarterly,* and *SAIS Review.*

WORK IN PROGRESS: Articles on U.S. foreign policy and defense policy.

SIDELIGHTS: Vincent Davis told *CA:* "My research and writing are key components of my professional career as a specialist on foreign policy, defense policy, and international relations in general. Given the continuing crises in world affairs in my lifetime, my hope is that my writings will light a few small candles in this darkness."

*　　*　　*

DAVIS, William C(harles)　1946-

PERSONAL: Born September 28, 1946, in Kansas City, Mo.; son of Eual Edward (a salesman) and Martha (an accountant; maiden name, Joan) Davis; married Pamela S. McIntyre, July 22, 1969 (divorced); children: M. Jefferson, Rebecca M. *Education:* Sonoma State College (now University), A.B., 1968, M.A., 1969. *Politics:* Democrat.

ADDRESSES: Home and office—240 Gettysburg Rd., Mechanicsburg, Pa.

CAREER: Historical Times, Inc., Harrisburg, Pa., editorial assistant, 1969-72; National Historical Society, Gettysburg, Pa., editor of *American History Illustrated* and *Civil War Times Illustrated,* 1972-76, president, 1976-82; Historical Times, Inc., executive director, 1982-84, corporate editorial director, 1984-85, president of Museum Editions, Ltd., 1986—; writer. Consultant for numerous Civil War television movie and documentary productions, including "The Blue and the Gray" eight-hour mini-series for Columbia Pictures, 1982, and a Florentine Production documentary for Public Broadcasting Service. Consultant for History Book Club, Easton Press Library of Military History, U.S. Intelligence Historical Society, and Eastern National Park and Monument Association for the National Park Service.

MEMBER: Manuscript Society, Southern Historical Association.

AWARDS, HONORS: Breckinridge: Statesman, Soldier, Symbol received Jules F. Landry Award from Louisiana State University Press, 1974, for the best book on Southern history, literature, and biography, Phi Alpha Theta Award, 1975, for best work in history, and the Jefferson Davis Award from Museum of the Confederacy and the Confederate Memorial Literary Society, 1975, for the best book on Confederate history; Pulitzer Prize nomination, 1975, for *Breckinridge: Statesman, Soldier, Symbol,* and 1978, for *Battle at Bull Run;* fellow, U.S. Army Military History Institute, 1975, for contributions to the study of American military history; honorary doctor of humane letters, Lincoln Memorial University, 1976; Fletcher Pratt Award, 1977; fellow, Royal Photographic Society, 1985, for "The Image of War" series.

WRITINGS:

(Author of introduction) Ed Porter Thompson, *History of the Orphan Brigade,* Morningside Press, 1974.

Breckinridge: Statesman, Soldier, Symbol, Louisiana State University Press, 1974.

The Battle of New Market (Military Book Club selection), Doubleday, 1975.

Duel between the First Ironclads (Military Book Club selection), Doubleday, 1975.

Battle at Bull Run (Military Book Club and History Book Club selections), Doubleday, 1977.

The Orphan Brigade: The Kentucky Confederates Who Couldn't Go Home (History Book Club selection), Doubleday, 1980.

The Image of War (History Book Club and Literary Guild selections), Doubleday, Volume I: *Shadows of the Storm,* 1981, Volume II: *The Guns of '62,* 1982, Volume III: *The Embattled Confederacy,* 1982, Volume IV: *Fighting for Time,* 1983, Volume V: *The South Besieged,* 1983, Volume VI: *The End of an Era,* 1984.

The Imperiled Union (History Book Club selection), Doubleday, Volume I: *The Deep Waters of the Proud,* 1982, Volume II: *Stand in the Day of Battle,* 1983.

Brother against Brother, Time-Life, 1983.

First Blood, Time-Life, 1983.

Gettysburg: The Story behind the Scenery, KC Publications, 1983.

Civil War Parks: The Story behind the Scenery, KC Publications, 1984.

Touched by Fire: A Photographic Portrait of the Civil War (History Book Club selection), Little, Brown, Volume I, 1985, Volume II, 1986.

Death in the Trenches, Time-Life, 1986.

CONTRIBUTOR

Encyclopedia of Southern History, Louisiana State University Press, 1979.

Dictionary of American Military Biography, Greenwood Press, 1984.

Rebels Resurgent, Time-Life, 1985.

Above and Beyond: The Congressional Medal of Honor, Boston Publishing, 1985.

Historical Times Illustrated Encyclopedia of the Civil War, Harper, 1986.

The Cavalry (part of "The Wars of America" series), Boston Publishing, 1987.

OTHER

Ghost writer of *Tenting Tonight,* Time-Life, 1985; author without by-line of *Spies, Scouts, and Raiders,* Time-Life, 1986. Contributor to journals, such as *American Heritage, American History Illustrated, British Heritage, Civil War Times,* and *Smithsonian.*

WORK IN PROGRESS: A Mighty Fortress: Fort Sumter in the Civil War for University of South Carolina Press; two volumes on the Civil War for "The Wars of America" series for Boston Publishing; Volume III of *The Imperiled Union* for Doubleday.

SIDELIGHTS: William C. Davis's *The Orphan Brigade: The Kentucky Confederates Who Couldn't Go Home* chronicles the Civil War activities of the those Kentucky soldiers who, unlike most of their fellow Kentuckians, elected to side with the Confederacy. Robert Kirsch of the *Los Angeles Times* notes that "Davis's intimate account captures the pride and loyalty of the regiments, brings individuals alive, draws heavily on the records and narratives left by the brigade under encouragement by Capt. Ed Porter Thompson, an amateur historian." Rory Quirk writes in the *Washington Post* that "the battles are rich with detail," yet criticizes the book's lack of

maps: "This absence of detailed maps is a regrettable omission in an otherwise informative, comprehensive and colorful account."

BIOGRAPHICAL/CRITICAL SOURCES:

PERIODICALS

Los Angeles Times, April 18, 1980.
Washington Post, May 30, 1980.

*   *   *

DAVIS, William Virgil 1940-

PERSONAL: Born May 26, 1940, in Canton, Ohio; son of Virgil Sanor and Anna Bertha (Orth) Davis; married Carol Ann Demske (an English teacher), July 17, 1971; children: William Lawrence. *Education:* Ohio University, A.B., 1962, M.A., 1965, Ph.D., 1967; Pittsburgh Theological Seminary, M.Div., 1965.

ADDRESSES: Home—2633 Lake Oaks Rd., Waco, Tex. 76710. *Office*—Department of English, Baylor University, Waco, Tex. 76798.

CAREER: Ordained Presbyterian minister, 1970; Ohio University, Athens, assistant professor of English, 1967-68; Central Connecticut State University, New Britain, assistant professor of English, 1968-71; Tunxis Community College, Farmington, Conn., assistant professor of English, 1971-72; University of Illinois at Chicago, assistant professor of English, 1972-77; Baylor University, Waco, Tex., associate professor, 1977-79, professor of English and writer-in-residence, 1979—. Guest professor of English and American literature at the University of Vienna, 1979-80; writer in residence at the University of Montana, 1983; guest professor of American Studies at the University of Copenhagen, 1984. Gives poetry readings and lectures nationally and internationally.

MEMBER: International Association of University Professors (IAUPE), PEN, Academy of American Poets, Modern Language Association of America, SCMLA, RMMLA, MMLA, Poetry Society of America, Poets and Writers, Texas Institute of Letters, Texas Association of Creative Writing Teachers, Ohio University Board of Visitors, Phi Kappa Phi, Tau Kappa Alpha.

AWARDS, HONORS: Bread Loaf Writers' Conference scholar in poetry, 1970, and fellow in poetry, 1980; graduate faculty fellow in creative writing at the University of Illinois, 1974; faculty fellow in poetry at Baylor University, 1979; Yale Series of Younger Poets award, 1979, for *One Way to Reconstruct the Scene;* Fulbright grant for guest professorship at University of Vienna, 1979-80 and at the University of Copenhagen, Denmark, 1984; Lilly Foundation grant, 1979-80; Distinguished Humanities Lecturer, Southwest Conference Humanities Consortium, 1981-82; Calliope Press Chapbook Prize, 1984, for *The Dark Hours.*

WRITINGS:

(Editor and author of introduction) *George Whitefield's Journals, 1737-1741,* Scholar's Facsimiles & Reprints, 1969.

(Contributor) James Richard McLeod, editor, *Theodore Roethke: A Bibliography,* Kent State University Press, 1973.

(Contributor) *Encyclopedia of World Literature in the Twentieth Century,* Ungar, 1975, revised edition, 1986.

One Way to Reconstruct the Scene (poems), Yale University Press, 1980.

The Dark Hours (poems), Calliope Press, 1984.
Understanding Robert Bly, University of South Carolina Press, 1988.

Contributor of more than sixty-five articles to journals, including *James Joyce Quarterly, Studies in Short Fiction, Wallace Stevens Journal,* and *Modern Poetry Studies;* of more than 650 poems to more than one hundred journals, including *Poetry, Atlantic Monthly, North American Review, The Hudson Review,* and *Poetry Northwest;* and of short stories to *Northeast, U.S. Catholic, Malahat Review, New Orleans Review,* and other journals. Also author of numerous reviews of poetry, fiction, and scholarly books.

WORK IN PROGRESS: A collection of poems, *Winter Light;* several articles on contemporary American and British poetry.

AVOCATIONAL INTERESTS: Painting, travel.

*　　*　　*　　*

DAY, A(rthur) Grove　1904-

PERSONAL: Born April 29, 1904, in Philadelphia, Pa.; son of Arthur Sinclair (a salesman) and Clara Tomlinson (Hogeland) Day; married Virginia T. Molina (a college instructor), July 2, 1928. *Education:* Stanford University, A.B., 1926, M.A., 1942, Ph.D., 1944.

ADDRESSES: Home—1434 Punahou St., Apt. 1223, Honolulu, Hawaii 96822. *Agent*—John Hawkins & Associates, 71 West 23rd St., New York, N.Y. 10010.

CAREER: Columbia University, New York, N.Y., research assistant at Institute of Educational Research, 1926-27; freelance writer, 1927-30; Stanford University, Stanford, Calif., research assistant, 1932-36, assistant director of engineering, science, and management war training, 1943-44; University of Hawaii, Honolulu, assistant professor, 1944-46, associate professor, 1946-50, professor, 1950-61, senior professor of English, 1961-69, professor emeritus, 1969—, chairman of department, 1948-53. Proprietor, White Knight Press (private press), 1940—. Fulbright senior research fellow in Australia, 1955; Smith-Mundt Visiting Professor of American Studies, University of Barcelona, 1957-58; Fulbright visiting professor of American studies, University of Madrid, 1961-62. Chairman of publications committee, Tenth Pacific Science Congress, 1977. Occasional lecturer aboard cruise ships.

MEMBER: Authors Guild, Authors League of America, Modern Language Association of America, Phi Beta Kappa, Phi Kappa Phi, Elks, Adventurers' Club of Honolulu.

AWARDS, HONORS: Hawaii State Award for Literature, 1980.

WRITINGS:

Tommy Dane of Sonora (juvenile fiction), Century, 1929.
(With Fred J. Buenzle) *Bluejacket: An Autobiography,* Norton, 1939, reprinted, U.S. Naval Institute, 1986.
Coronado's Quest: The Discovery of the Southwestern States, University of California Press, 1940, revised edition, 1982.
(With Ralph S. Kuykendall) *Hawaii: A History,* Prentice-Hall, 1948, revised edition, 1978.
The Sky Clears: Poetry of the American Indians, Macmillan, 1951, new edition, 1964.
Hawaii and Its People, Duell, Sloan & Pearce, 1955, revised edition, 1969.
(With James A. Michener) *Rascals in Paradise,* Random House, 1957.

Hawaii, Fiftieth Star, Duell, Sloan & Pearce, 1960, 2nd edition, Meredith, 1969.
The Story of Australia, Random House, 1960.
James A. Michener, Twayne, 1964, revised edition, 1977.
They Peopled the Pacific, Duell, Sloan & Pearce, 1964.
Louis Becke, Twayne, 1966.
Explorers of the Pacific, Duell, Sloan & Pearce, 1966.
Coronado and the Discovery of the Southwest, Meredith, 1967.
Pirates of the Pacific, Meredith, 1968.
Adventurers of the Pacific, with foreword by James A. Michener, Meredith, 1969.
Jack London in the South Seas, Four Winds Press, 1971.
Pacific Islands Literature: One Hundred Basic Books, University Press of Hawaii, 1971.
(With Edgar C. Knowlton, Jr.) *V. Blasco Ibanez,* Twayne, 1972.
What Did I Do Right? (auto-bibliography), privately printed, 1974.
Robert D. Fitzgerald, Twayne, 1974.
Kamehameha, First King of Hawaii, edited by Dorothy Hazama, Hogarth Press, 1974.
Eleanor Dark, Twayne, 1976.
Books about Hawaii: Fifty Basic Authors, University Press of Hawaii, 1977.
Captain Cook and Hawaii, Hogarth Press, 1977.
(With Amos P. Leib) *Hawaiian Legends in English: An Annotated Bibliography,* University Press of Hawaii, 1979.
Mad about Islands: Novelists of a Vanished Pacific, Mutual of Honolulu, 1987.

EDITOR

Fernando Cortes: Despatches from Mexico (Spanish textbook), American Book Co., 1935.
(With Carl Stroven) *The Spell of the Pacific: An Anthology of Its Literature,* Macmillan, 1949.
(With William F. Bauer) *The Greatest American Short Stories,* McGraw, 1953, published as *The Greatest American Short Stories: Twenty Classics of Our Heritage,* 1970.
(With Stroven) *A Hawaiian Reader,* with introduction by James A. Michener, Appleton, 1959.
(With Stroven) *Best South Sea Stories,* Appleton, 1964.
Jack London, *Stories of Hawaii,* Appleton, 1965.
Mark Twain's Letters from Hawaii, Appleton, 1966.
(With Stroven) *True Tales of the South Seas,* Appleton, 1966.
Louis Becke, *South Sea Supercargo,* University Press of Hawaii, 1967.
(With Stroven) *The Spell of Hawaii,* Meredith, 1968.
(And author of introduction) *Melville's South Seas: An Anthology,* Hawthorn, 1970.
The Art of Narration: The Novella, McGraw, 1971.
The Art of Narration: The Short Story, McGraw, 1971.
(And author of introduction) Robert L. Stevenson, *Travels in Hawaii,* University Press of Hawaii, 1973.
Modern Australian Prose, 1901-1975, Gale, 1980.
(With Bacil F. Kirtley) *Horror in Paradise,* Mutual of Honolulu, 1986.
The Lure of Tahiti, Mutual of Honolulu, 1986.

OTHER

Contributor to *Encyclopedia of Poetry and Poetics,* 1965, and *Encyclopaedia Britannica,* 1968; also contributor of short stories and articles to national magazines. Editor-in-chief, *Pacific Science,* 1947-48.

SIDELIGHTS: A. Grove Day told *CA:* "I do not remember any time when I did not wish to publish books. [I am] especially interested in history and biography of Hawaii and Pacific region; James A. Michener has termed me 'the world's foremost authority on Pacific literature.' [I] retired from [the] university in 1969 but still write every morning.''

AVOCATIONAL INTERESTS: Travel, swimming.

BIOGRAPHICAL/CRITICAL SOURCES:

PERIODICALS

New Statesman, June 23, 1967.

*   *   *

de BLIJ, Harm J(an)   1935-

PERSONAL: Surname is pronounced *duh-Blay;* born October 9, 1935, in Schiedam, Netherlands; son of Hendrik and Nelly (Erwich) de Blij; married Katherine Powers (divorced, 1971); married Bonnie Doughty, 1977. *Education:* University of the Witwatersrand, B.Sc., 1955; Northwestern University, M.A., 1957, Ph.D., 1959.

ADDRESSES: Home—Three Grove Isle Dr., Coconut Grove, Fla. *Office*—Department of Geography, University of Miami, Coral Gables, Fla. 33124.

CAREER: University of Natal, Pietermaritzburg, South Africa, lecturer in geology and geography, 1959-60; Michigan State University, East Lansing, assistant professor, 1961-63, associate professor, 1964-67, professor of geography, 1967-69, associate director of African Studies Center, 1964-69; University of Miami, Coral Gables, Fla., chairman of geography department, 1969-76, associate dean of College of Arts and Sciences, 1976-78, professor of geography, 1978—. Northwestern University, visiting lecturer, spring, 1959, visiting assistant professor, 1960-61, visiting associate professor, 1963-64; visiting professor of geography, Institute for Shipboard Education, University of Colorado, autumn, 1978, and University of Hawaii, autumn, 1979; Presidential Professor, Colorado School of Mines, 1981-82. Visiting geographical scientist, Association of American Geographers, 1967-70. Representative for Miami University to board of directors, Organization for Tropical Studies. Founder of Miami Geographical Society. Consultant to Encyclopaedia Britannica Films, Inc., 1963-65, Bobbs-Merrill Reprint Series in Geography, 1966-72, and Encyclopaedia Britannica Educational Corp., 1980—; member of editorial advisory board, John Wiley & Sons, Inc. (publishers), 1968-72 and 1975-78, and Hamilton Publishing Co., 1972-75; member of editorial advisory board for cartography, Hammond, Inc. (publishers), 1974—; consultant on African maps and text, Atlas project, National Geographic Society, 1979-80. Member of wine tasting panel, *Miami Herald,* 1980-84.

MEMBER: Association of American Geographers (councillor, 1970-72; member of steering committee, Southeastern Division, 1970-73; secretary, 1972-75), National Council for Geographic Education (member of executive board, 1970-74), National Geographic Society, Royal African Society, American Geographical Society, African Studies Association, American Association of University Professors, Florida Society of Geographers, Society of Wine Educators, Phi Kappa Phi, Sigma Xi, Gamma Theta Upsilon.

AWARDS, HONORS: Grants from Ford Foundation, 1962 and 1966; grant from Midwest Consortium for International Assistance, 1967; grant from Association of American Geogra-

phers, 1975; Presidential Scholar, University of Miami; Prix d'Honneur, 1984, Organisation Internationale Vinicole, Paris.

WRITINGS:

Africa South, Northwestern University Press, 1962.
(Contributor) O. Williams and N. Hurvitz, editors, *Economic Framework of South Africa,* Shuter and Shooter (Pietermaritzburg, South Africa), 1962.
Subsaharan Africa, Michigan State University Continuing Education Service, 1963.
Dar Es Salaam: A Study in Urban Geography, Northwestern University Press, 1963.
A Geography of Subsaharan Africa, Rand McNally, 1964.
Political Geography, University of the Air, Michigan State University, 1965.
Systematic Political Geography, Wiley, 1967, 3rd edition, with Martin Ira Glassner, 1981.
A Guide to Subsaharan Africa, Michigan State University Continuing Education Service, 1968.
Mombasa: An African City, Northwestern University Press, 1968.
(Contributor) J. Kritzeck and W. H. Lewis, editors, *Islam in Africa,* Van Nostrand, 1969.
Geography: Regions and Concepts, Wiley, 1971, 5th edition, with Peter O. Muller, 1988.
Essentials of Geography, Wiley, 1973.
Man Shapes the Earth, Hamilton Publishing, 1974.
(Contributor) C. G. Knight and J. L. Newman, editors, *Contemporary Africa,* Prentice-Hall, 1976.
(Contributor) *CBS News Almanac,* Hammond, 1977.
(With Alan C. G. Best) *African Survey,* Wiley, 1977.
(With David Greenland) *The Earth in Profile: A Physical Geography,* Canfield Press, 1977.
Human Geography: Culture, Society, and Space, Wiley, 1977, 3rd edition, with Muller, 1986.
(Contributor) P. E. James and G. J. Martin, editors, *The Association of American Geographers: The First Seventy-five Years,* Association of American Geographers, 1979.
The Earth: A Topical Geography, Wiley, 1980.
Geography of Viticulture, Miami Geographical Society, 1981.
(Editor, with Esmond Bradley Martin, and contributor) *African Perspectives: An Exchange of Essays on the Economic Geography of Nine African States,* Methuen, 1981.
Wine: A Geographic Appreciation, Littlefield, 1983.
Wine Regions of the Southern Hemisphere, Rowman & Allanheld, 1985.
The Earth: A Physical and Human Geography, Wiley, 1988.

Also author of television series, "Subsaharan Africa," for Michigan State University Continuing Education Service, 1963, and "Political Geography," for University of the Air, Michigan State University, 1964. Columnist for *Focus,* American Geographical Society, 1985—. Contributor to *Encyclopaedia Britannica,* 1974; also contributor to *Proceedings of the Second University of Manitoba Conference on Commonwealth Affairs,* 1962. Contributor of articles and reviews to professional journals, including *Economic Geography, Canadian Journal of African Studies, Professional Geographer, South African Journal of Science,* and *Journal of Geography;* contributor of articles to *Miami News* and *Museum.* Member of editorial board, *Comparative Urban Research,* 1972-74; member of editorial committee, *Southeastern Geographer,* 1980-84; member of editorial board, *Annals of the Association of American Geographers,* 1985—; editor, *Journal of Geography,* 1970-74; editor, *National Geographic Research,* 1984—.

WORK IN PROGRESS: Wine Regions and Districts of North America.

SIDELIGHTS: Harm J. de Blij spent ten years in Africa and has continued research there at intervals since leaving. He visited the Soviet Union in 1964 and the People's Republic of China in 1981. De Blij is fluent in Afrikaans, Dutch, and German. A generalist by temperament, he is also interested in the arts. De Blij is a sometime professional violinist.

* * *

DEBREU, Gerard 1921-

PERSONAL: Born July 4, 1921, in Calais, France; son of Camille and Fernande (Decharne) Debreu; married Francoise Bled, June 14, 1945; children: Chantal (Mrs. Paul Teller), Florence (Mrs. Gilles Tetrault). *Education:* Attended Ecole Normale Superieure, Paris, 1941-44; University of Paris, Agrege de l'Universite, 1946, D.Sc., 1956.

ADDRESSES: Office—Department of Economics, University of California, Berkeley, Calif. 94720.

CAREER: Centre National de la Recherche Scientifique, Paris, France, research associate, 1946-48; University of Chicago, Chicago, Ill., research associate of Cowles Commission for Research in Economics, 1950-55; Yale University, New Haven, Conn., Cowles Foundation associate professor of economics, 1955-61; University of California, Berkeley, professor of economics, 1962—, professor of mathematics, 1975, faculty research lecturer, 1984-85, university professor, 1985—. Yale University, visiting professor of economics, fall, 1961, visiting professor at Cowles Foundation for Research in Economics, fall, 1976; visiting professor at Center for Operations Research and Econometrics, University of Louvain, fall, 1971, winter, 1972, University of Canterbury, Christchurch, summer, 1973, and University of Sydney, summer, 1987. Erskine fellow, University of Canterbury, June, 1987. *Military service:* French Army, 1944-45.

MEMBER: Econometric Society (president, 1971), National Academy of Sciences, American Academy of Arts and Sciences (fellow), American Philosophical Society, American Association for the Advancement of Science (fellow), Associe Etranger de l'Academie des Sciences de L'Institut de France.

AWARDS, HONORS: Rockefeller fellow in United States, Sweden, and Norway, 1948-50; Center for Advanced Study in the Behavioral Sciences fellow, 1960-61; Guggenheim fellow, 1968-69; Erskine fellow at University of Canterbury, summer, 1969; Churchill College overseas fellow, 1972; Senior U.S. Scientist Award, Alexander von Humboldt Foundation, University of Bonn, 1977; Dr.rer.pol.h.c., University of Bonn, 1977; Docteur en Sciences Economiques h.c., University of Lausanne, 1980; Doctor of Science h.c., Northwestern University, 1981; Distinguished Fellow of the American Economic Association, 1982; Nobel Memorial Prize in Economic Sciences, Royal Swedish Academy of Sciences, 1983; Docteur h.c. de l'Universite des Sciences Sociales de Toulouse, 1984; Commandeur de l'Ordre National du Merite, 1984; doctor of social science h.c., Yale University, 1987.

WRITINGS:

Theory of Value, Wiley, 1959, new edition, Yale University Press, 1971.
Mathematical Economics: Twenty Papers of Gerard Debreu, Cambridge University Press, 1983.

Contributor to economics journals. Former associate editor of *International Economic Review.* Member of editorial board of *Journal of Economic Theory;* member of adivsory board of *Journal of Mathematical Economics.*

SIDELIGHTS: Gerard Debreu, a French-born economist and professor at the University of California at Berkeley, received the 1983 Nobel Prize in economics for his research demonstrating mathematical proof of the classic theory of supply and demand. Debreu received the award eleven years after his research partner, Kenneth J. Arrow of Harvard University, won the prize in 1972. Prior to winning the Nobel Prize, Debreu was well-known in economics circles for his 1959 work, *Theory of Value,* considered a classic of modern economic thought. Debreu describes his approach to economics as follows: "I seek to set up abstract models, couched in mathematical terms, to give an account of the way the many agents of which an economy is composed make decisions and how those decisions are consistent with each other." Computer models based on Debreu's work are routinely used by the World Bank and similar agencies for analyzing trends in national economies and world markets. In awarding the Nobel Prize, the Royal Swedish Academy of Sciences commended Debreu on work which has had a "profound and unsurpassed effect on the choice of methods and analytic techniques in economics."

BIOGRAPHICAL/CRITICAL SOURCES:

PERIODICALS

Chicago Tribune, October 18, 1983.
New York Times, October 18, 1983.
Washington Post, October 19, 1983.

* * *

DEGENHARDT, Henry W(illiam) 1910-

PERSONAL: Born March 24, 1910, in Osnabrueck, Germany; son of August (a high school teacher) and Jane B.T. (a teacher; maiden name, Macdonald) Degenhardt; married Almuth Brecht, May 28, 1943; children: Donald W. *Education:* Attended University of Freiburg, 1928-29, University of Munich, 1929, University of Berlin, 1929-30, and University of Marburg, 1930-33.

ADDRESSES: Home—3 Horsecombe Brow, Bath BA2 5QY, England.

CAREER: Free-lance teacher and translator, 1933-51; College of Careers (Pty.) Ltd. (publisher of study aids), Cape Town, South Africa, managing director, 1951-62; writer for *Keesing's Contemporary Archives,* 1962-81.

WRITINGS:

Treaties and Alliances of the World, Keesing's, 1968, 4th edition, Longman/Gale, 1986.
(With Alan J. Day) *Political Parties of the World,* Longman, 1980, 2nd edition, Longman/Gale, 1984.
(Contributor) Day, editor, *Border and Territorial Disputes,* Longman, 1982, 2nd edition, 1987.
Political Dissent, Longman/Gale, 1983, (contributor) 2nd edition published as *Revolutionary and Dissident Movements,* Longman, 1987.
Maritime Affairs: A World Handbook, Longman/Gale, 1985.

* * *

DEKKER, Carl
See LAFFIN, John (Alfred Charles)

DEMARIS, Ovid
See DESMARAIS, Ovid E.

*   *   *

DeSALVO, Louise A(nita)   1942-

PERSONAL: Born September 27, 1942, in Jersey City, N.J.; daughter of Louis B. (a machinist) and Mildred (Calabrese) Sciacchetano; married Ernest J. DeSalvo (a physician), December 21, 1963; children: Jason, Justin. *Education:* Rutgers University, B.A., 1963; New York University, M.A., 1972, Ph.D., 1977.

ADDRESSES: Home—1045 Oakland Court, Teaneck, N.J. 07666; Stoney Ridge, Sag Harbor, N.Y. *Office*—Department of English, Hunter College of the City University of New York, 695 Park Ave., New York, N.Y. 10021.

CAREER: High school English teacher in Wood-Ridge, N.J., 1963-67; Fairleigh Dickinson University, Teaneck, N.J., coordinator of English education, 1977-83; Hunter College of the City University of New York, New York, N.Y., professor of English and women's studies, 1983—.

MEMBER: Modern Language Association of America, National Council of Teachers of English, Assembly on Literature for Adolescents, Bronte Society, Virginia Woolf Society, Women's Ink, Northeast Victorian Studies Association.

AWARDS, HONORS: National Endowment for the Humanities grant, 1980; seal from Committee on Scholarly Editions from Modern Language Association of America, 1980, for *Melymbrosia: Early Version of "The Voyage Out"*; distinguished achievement award from Educational Press Association of America, 1980, for "Writers at Work"; President's Award for scholarship from Hunter College, 1986.

WRITINGS:

Virginia Woolf's First Voyage: A Novel in the Making, Rowman & Littlefield, 1980.
Melymbrosia: Early Version of "The Voyage Out," New York Public Library, 1980.
(With Carol Ascher and Sara Ruddick) *Between Women*, Beacon Press, 1984.
(Editor with Mitchell A. Leaska) *The Letters of Vita Sackville-West to Virginia Woolf*, Morrow, 1984.
Nathaniel Hawthorne: A Feminist Reading, Harvester, 1987.
"Children Never Forget": Virginia Woolf on Childhood, Adolescence, and Young Adulthood, Beacon Press, 1988.
Casting Off: A Novel, Harvester, 1988.

Contributor to literature journals.

WORK IN PROGRESS: A collection of short stories by Irish women writers with Kathleen D'Arcy and Katherine Hogan.

SIDELIGHTS: Louise DeSalvo wrote: "Reconstructing the earlier version of Virginia Woolf's first novel was extremely exciting. Knowing that I would be making an earlier version of a novel available that no one but Virginia Woolf herself might have seen carried me through the years that the work was in progress.

"Virginia Woolf is an endlessly fascinating subject for research. I have been working on Woolf for over fifteen years and believe that I have just begun to scratch the surface. There

is now an enormous amount of interest in the reasons why Woolf developed the views she did. Researchers such as Jane Marcus are looking at the earlier political views of her family members—people like Sir James Fitzjames Stephen, who was one of the great codifiers of English law.

"We are beginning to look at the intellectual climate in which Woolf moved and we are learning that she did not develop her feminist views, her pacifist views, in a vacuum but instead in response to views held by members of her very own family. Unlike many of us, she was not protesting the way *society* thought about issues such as women's rights; she was revising views held by her very own forebears.

"I have spent some time reconstructing Woolf's life at fifteen and I was amazed to learn that in that year Woolf read no less than fifty weighty volumes and even at that early age she was concerned with matters of English history. I am beginning to think that Woolf was primarily a historian of English manners and morals who happened to write fiction. When I began my research, I had believed that she was simply a storyteller. And I believe that the direction that I have taken is the direction that many contemporary critics of Woolf are now taking—we are now interested in seeing how this woman connected with the most important issues of her time; we no longer see her as a dreamer spinning self-indulgent fictions."

DeSalvo added: "Writing my own first novel was an exciting enterprise after spending so many years researching someone else's creativity."

BIOGRAPHICAL/CRITICAL SOURCES:

PERIODICALS

Globe and Mail (Toronto), January 5, 1985.
Los Angeles Times Book Review, December 23, 1984.
Times (London), December 20, 1984.
Times Literary Supplement, December 21, 1984.

*   *   *

DESMARAIS, Ovid E.   1919-
(Ovid Demaris)

PERSONAL: Born September 6, 1919, in Biddeford, Me.; son of Ernest J. and Aurore (Casavant) Desmarais; married Inez E. Frakes, May 15, 1942; children: Linda Lee, Peggy Ann. *Education:* College of Idaho, A.B. 1948; Syracuse University, law student; Boston University, M.S., 1950.

ADDRESSES: Home—P.O. Box 6071, Santa Barbara, Calif. 93111.

CAREER: Quincy Patriot Ledger, Quincy, Mass., reporter, 1949-50; United Press, Boston, Mass., reporter, 1950-52; *Los Angeles Times*, Los Angeles, Calif., advertising copy chief, 1953-59; free-lance writer, 1959—. *Military service:* U.S. Army Air Forces, five years; became warrant officer.

WRITINGS—Under name Ovid Demaris:

Ride the Gold Mare, Gold Medal, 1957.
The Hoods Take Over, Gold Medal, 1957.
The Lusting Drive, Gold Medal, 1958.
The Slasher, Gold Medal, 1959.
The Long Night, Avon, 1959.
The Extortioners, Gold Medal, 1960.
The Enforcer, Gold Medal, 1960.
Lucky Luciano, Monarch, 1960.
The Gold-Plated Sewer, Avon, 1960.

Candyleg, Gold Medal, 1961.
The Lindbergh Kidnaping Case, Monarch, 1961.
Dillinger Story, Monarch, 1961.
The Parasites, Berkeley, 1962.
(With Ed Reid) *The Green Felt Jungle* (nonfiction), Trident, 1963.
The Organization, Tower, 1964, published as *Fatal Mistake*, 1966, published as *The Contract*, Belmont Books, 1970.
(With Garry Wills) *Jack Ruby*, New American Library, 1968.
Captive City (nonfiction), Lyle Stuart, 1969.
America the Violent, Cowles, 1970.
Poso del Mundo, Little, Brown, 1970.
The Overlord, New American Library, 1972.
Dirty Business: The Corporate-Political Money-Power Game, Harper Magazine Press, 1974.
The Director: An Oral Biography of J. Edgar Hoover, Harper Magazine Press, 1975.
(With Judith Exner) *Judith Exner: My Story* (biography), Grove, 1977.
Brothers in Blood: The International Terrorist Network, Scribner, 1977.
The Last Mafioso: The Treacherous World of Jimmy Fratianno (biography), Times Books, 1981.
The Vegas Legacy (novel), Delacorte, 1983.
The Boardwalk Jungle (nonfiction), Bantam, 1986.

Contributor to *Esquire*, *Popular Mechanics*, and other magazines.

SIDELIGHTS: Ovid E. Desmarais, better known as Ovid Demaris, told *CA:* "For me, writing has always been a learning experience. The subject matter has to intrigue me, something that I want to know more about, and the only way I can [experience] that is to research it to the best of my ability. When I wrote *Poso del Mundo*, I spent seven months snooping around the Mexican border, from Tijuana to Matamoros; for *Brothers in Blood: The International Terrorist Network*, I traveled to foreign countries to interview terrorists and the cops who hunt them; for *The Last Mafioso: The Treacherous World of Jimmy Fratianno*, I got my inside story of Mafia life from the horse's mouth: Jimmy Fratianno; and for my latest nonfiction book, *The Boardwalk Jungle*, I learned all I could about the hotels, the politicians, and the hoods that inhabit that tiny island. The same applies to fiction. *The Vegas Legacy* required researching the history of Nevada politics and gambling, and many of the characters were based on the people who made it happen. This is the way I work, my curiosity is what keeps me going, and since there is so much out there that I want to know more about, I doubt that I will ever run out of writing material."

Demaris's books have been translated and published in twenty-two countries.

AVOCATIONAL INTERESTS: Tennis.

BIOGRAPHICAL/CRITICAL SOURCES:

PERIODICALS

America, May 16, 1970.
Best Sellers, August 1, 1969.
Book World, January 14, 1968.
Los Angeles Times, May 22, 1986.
National Review, April 9, 1968, December 23, 1977, March 3, 1978.
New York Times Book Review, April 12, 1970, October 30, 1977, February 15, 1981.
Saturday Review, August 9, 1969.

Washington Post, May 13, 1986.
Washington Post Book World, February 8, 1981.

*   *   *

DEVANEY, John 1926-

PERSONAL: Born March 15, 1926, in New York, N.Y.; son of John (an engineer) and Delia Devaney; married Barbara Masciocchi (a graphics designer), April 16, 1955; children: John, Luke. *Education:* New York University, B.S., 1949. *Politics:* Democrat. *Religion:* Roman Catholic.

ADDRESSES: Home—P.O. Box 690, Easthampton, N.Y. 11937. *Office*—520 LaGuardia Pl., New York, N.Y. 10012.

CAREER: Science Illustrated, New York City, writer, 1948-50; *Quick*, New York City, medical editor, 1952-54; *Parade*, New York City, sports editor, 1955-61; free-lance writer, 1961—. *Military service:* U.S. Army, 1944-46.

WRITINGS:

Bob Cousy, Putnam, 1965.
The Pro Quarterbacks, Putnam, 1966.
The Great Olympic Champions, Putnam, 1967.
Bart Starr, Scholastic Book Services, 1967.
The Greatest Cardinals of Them All, Putnam, 1968.
Baseball's Youngest Big Leaguers, Holt, 1969.
The Baseball Life of Mickey Mantle, Scholastic Book Services, 1970.
Juan Marichal: Mister Strike, Putnam, 1970.
Super Bowl!, Random House, 1971.
Star Pass Receivers of the NFL, Random House, 1972.
The World Series: A Complete Pictorial History, Rand McNally, 1972.
The Complete Handbook of Pro Football 1972, Lancer Militaria, 1972.
The Complete Handbook of Pro Football 1973, Lancer Militaria, 1973.
Gil Hodges: Baseball Miracle Man, Putnam, 1973.
The Bobby Orr Story, Random House, 1973.
Joe Namath, Scholastic Book Services, 1973.
Tom Seaver, Popular Library, 1974.
O. J. Simpson: Football's Greatest Runner, Paperback Library, 1974.
The Baseball Life of Johnny Bench, Scholastic Book Services, 1974.
(With Burt Goldblatt) *The Stanley Cup: An Illustrated History*, Rand McNally, 1975.
(With Bob Cousy) *The Killer Instinct*, Random House, 1975.
Great Upsets of Stanley Cup Hockey, Garrard, 1976.
(With wife, Barbara Devaney) *The Indianapolis 500*, Rand McNally, 1976.
(With Sonny Grosso) *Murder at the Harlem Mosque*, Crown, 1976.
Adolph Hitler, Mad Dictator of World War II, Putnam, 1977.
(Wth Lawrence T. Lorimer) *The Football Book*, Random House, 1977.
Douglas MacArthur, Something of a Hero, Putnam, 1979.
Superstars of Sports: Today and Yesterday, Woodhill, 1979.
Super Rex, Condor Publishing, 1980.
Blood and Guts: The True Story of General George S. Patton, Messner, 1982.
Secrets of the Super Athletes: Tips for Fans and Players—Soccer, Dell, 1982.
Where Are They Today? Great Sports Stars of Yesteryear, Crown, 1985.

Winners of the Heisman, Walker & Co., 1986.
Lyndon Baines Johnson, President, Walker & Co., 1986.
Franklin D. Roosevelt, President, Walker & Co., 1987.

Also author of *One Thousand and One New Job Opportunities*, Popular Library. Contributor to *Saturday Evening Post, Redbook, Parade, This Week, Sport, Pageant, American Legion, Boy's Life,* and *Catholic Digest.* Editor of *Sport*, 1980-81; also editor of CBS Popular Sports Magazines, 1981-85.

WORK IN PROGRESS: The Self-Made Woman, for Quinlan.

AVOCATIONAL INTERESTS: Collecting records of the jazz and swing orchestras of the 1920-1950 period.

BIOGRAPHICAL/CRITICAL SOURCES:

PERIODICALS

Chicago Tribune Book World, April 13, 1986.

*   *   *

DEVERAUX, Jude
See WHITE, Jude Gilliam

*   *   *

DILLENBERGER, Jane   1916-

PERSONAL: Born February 27, 1916, in Hartford, Wis.; daughter of John Minot Daggett (an automotive sales representative); married John Dillenberger (a professor of historical theology at Graduate Theological Union, Berkeley), July 19, 1962. *Education:* Attended University of Wisconsin, one year, and University of Iowa, one year; University of Chicago, B.A., 1940; Radcliffe College, M.A., 1944; Drew University, additional graduate study, 1958-59.

ADDRESSES: Home and office—1536 Le Roy Ave., Berkeley, Calif. 94708.

CAREER: Art Institute of Chicago, Chicago, Ill., curatorial assistant in department of prints and drawings, 1940-41; Boston Athenaeum, Boston, Mass., head of art department, 1944-45; Newark Museum, Newark, N.J., docent and staff member, 1945-46; Drew Theological Seminary, Madison, N.J., lecturer in Christianity and art, 1950-62; San Francisco Theological Seminary, San Francisco, Calif., lecturer, 1963-65, associate professor of Christianity and the arts, 1965-71; Graduate Theological Union, Berkeley, Calif., associate professor, 1967-76, professor of theology and visual arts, 1976-78, became professor emerita; adjunct faculty member at Hartford Seminary Foundation and adjunct professor of American Studies at Trinity College and the Greater Hartford Consortium for Higher Education. Lecturer in art history, University of California Extension Division, 1963—; adjunct professor at Lone Mountain College, 1974-78, and at Trinity College, 1979-80. Special researcher in charge of catalogue of collection, San Francisco Museum of Art, 1963-65; guest curator at University Art Museum, University of California, Berkeley, 1971-73, at Indianapolis Museum of Art, 1975-77, at National Collection of Fine Arts, 1976-78, and at the Wadsworth Atheneum, 1980.

MEMBER: College Art Association, American Academy of Religion, Society for Art, Religion and Contemporary Society.

AWARDS, HONORS: Grant from Rockefeller Foundation, 1961 and 1970-71, for research on religious art; grant from Lilly Endowment Fund, 1971-72 and 1975-76, for exhibition work; grant from National Endowment for the Humanities, 1973-74, for research in problems of American religious art, 1700-1900; grant from National Endowment for the Arts, 1975-76, for exhibition preparation and research.

WRITINGS:

Style and Content in Christian Art, Abingdon, 1965, reprinted, Crossroad Publishing, 1986.
Secular Art with Sacred Themes, Abingdon, 1969.
(Contributor with husband, John Dillenberger) *Humanities, Religion, and Arts Tomorrow*, Holt, 1971.
(With Joshua C. Taylor) *The Hand and the Spirit: Religious Art in America, 1700-1900*, University Art Museum, 1972.
(With J. Dillenberger) *Perceptions of the Spirit in Twentieth-Century American Art*, Indianapolis Museum of Art, 1977.
(Contributor) T. G. Madsen, editor, *Reflections on Mormonism: Judeo-Christian Parallels*, Brigham Young University Press, 1978.
(With J. C. Taylor, J. Dillenberger, R. Murray, and R. Soria) *Perceptions and Evocations: The Art of Elihu Vedder*, Smithsonian Institution Press, 1979.
(Contributor) *Women, Religion and Social Change*, State University of New York Press, 1983.
(Contributor) D. Apostolos-Cappadona, editor, *Art Creativity and the Sacred*, Crossroads, 1984.
(With J. Dillenberger) *Paul Tillich and the Visual Arts*, Crossroad Publishing, 1987.

Contributor of articles on religious art to various periodicals, including *Drew Gateway, Liturgical Arts Quarterly, Religion and Life,* and *Theology Today.* Member of editorial board of *Studia Mystica.*

SIDELIGHTS: Jane Dillenberger told *CA:* "I write, not as self-expression, but with the hope that I can help readers to *see* works of art, to *study* them, to understand them, to delight in them. My hope is that readers may never, never again make the stupid statement, 'I don't know anything about art, but I know what I like.' Those who don't know anything about art don't know what they like!"

*   *   *

DIOMEDE, John K.
See EFFINGER, George Alec

*   *   *

DIXON, George
See WILLIS, Ted

*   *   *

DOENIM, Susan
See EFFINGER, George Alec

*   *   *

DOSKOCILOVA, Hana   1936-

PERSONAL: Born July 11, 1936, in Jihlava, Czechoslovakia; daughter of Jan (a lawyer) and Maria (Juraskova) Doskocil; married Miroslav Sekyrka (a bookseller), September 21, 1961. *Education:* Attended public schools in Znojmo, Czechoslovakia.

ADDRESSES: Home—Praha 10-Vrsovice, Madridska 4/820, Czechoslovakia. *Office*—Albatros, Na Perstyne 1, Prague 1, Czechoslovakia.

CAREER: Clerk in coal store in Jihlava, Czechoslovakia, 1954-56; Academy of Sciences, Prague, Czechoslovakia, clerk, 1956-59; Albatros (publishers for children and young people), Prague, press editor, 1959-61, proofreader, 1961-64, editor in department for small children, 1964-72; free-lance writer, 1972—.

WRITINGS:

JUVENILES

Pohadky pro deti, mamy a taty (title means "Fairy Tales for Children, Mothers, and Fathers"), Statni Nakladatelstvi Detske Knihy (Prague), 1961, reprinted, Albatros (Prague), 1987.

Psanicko pro tebe—O hrackach (title means "A Letter for You—About Toys"), Statni Nakladatelstvi Detske Knihy, 1964.

Bydlim doma (title means "I Live at Home"), Statni Nakladatelstvi Detske Knihy, 1966.

Kajetan the Magician (translated from the German), Artia (Prague), 1967.

Cervena lodicka (title means "The Little Red Ship"), Mlada fronta (Prague), 1968.

Modern Czech Fairy Tales (English translation from the Czech), Artia, 1969.

Animal Tales, translations from the Czech by Eve Merriam, adapted by William Howard Armstrong, Doubleday, 1970.

Micka z trafiky a kocour Pivoda (title means "Pussy Cat from the Tobacconist's and Tomcat Pivoda"), Albatros, 1971.

Zviratka z celeho sveta (title means "The Animals from the Whole World"), Albatros, 1971.

Kudy chodi maly lev (title means "Where the Little Lion Walks"), Albatros, 1972.

Medvedi pohadky (title means "The Bear Fairy Tales"), Albatros, 1973.

Ukradeny orloj (title means "Rob of Astronomical Clock"), Materidouska (Prague), 1973.

Basama bernardyn a Vendulka (title means "St. Bernard Dog Named Basama and a Girl Vendulka"), Orbis (Prague), 1973.

Zviratka z lesa (title means "The Animals from the Wood"), Albatros, 1974.

Drak Barborak a Ztraceny kral Kulajda (title means "Dragon Barborak and the Lost King Kulajda"), Albatros, 1974.

Posledniho kousne pes: A dalsich ctyriadvacet prislovi v pohadkach (title means "The Last Will Be Bitten by the Dog: Proverbial Fairy Tales"), Albatros, 1974.

Eliska a tata Kral (title means "Elizabeth and Her Father King"), Albatros, 1977.

Dva dedecci z Dlouhe mile (title means "Two Grandfathers from Long Mile"), Albatros, 1978.

Jelen se zlatymi parohy (title means "The Hart with Golden Antlers"), Artia, 1978.

Jak se vychovava papousek (title means "How the Parrot Is Educated"), Albatros, 1979.

Fanek a Vendulka (title means "Small Francis and a Girl Vendulka"), Albatros, 1980.

Pohadky na dobry den (title means "Tales for a Good Day"), Albatros, 1982.

Krtek v sedmem nebi (title means "The Mole in Seventh Heaven"), Albatros, 1982.

Chaloupka z perniku (title means "Little Cottage of Gingerbread"), Artia, 1982.

Chaloupka z marcipanu (title means "Little Cottage of Marzipan"), Artia, 1983.

Diogenes v sudu—a dalsich dvacet znamych pribehu z doby davne a nejdavnejsi (title means "Diogenes in the Barrel and Twenty Other Well-Known Stories"), Albatros, 1985, 2nd edition in German, Swedish and Polish, 1987.

Pet prani: obrazkova knizka (a picture book; title means "Five Aspirations"), Albatros, 1987.

My a Mys (title means "We and the Mouse") Albatros, 1988.

Pejskovani s Polynou (title means "Dog's Games with Poly"), Albatros, 1989.

OTHER

Also author of *Krtek a paraplicko* (title means "The Mole and Little Gamp"), Publishing House Schulfernsehen (Cologne, West Germany). Author of juvenile television scripts, 1963-73, animated cartoons, 1969-71, and of a puppet play. Author of "Povidky o obrazech" (title means "Stories about the Pictures"), a series of twenty-four stories published in *Magazin "Ohnicek,"* 1985-86. Member of editorial council, *Materidouska* (children's monthly), 1966-72.

SIDELIGHTS: Many of Hana Doskocilova's books have been translated into Russian, German, French, Dutch, Japanese, and English.

* * *

DOTY, Carolyn 1941-

PERSONAL: Born July 28, 1941, in Tooele, Utah; daughter of Oran Earl (an engineer) and Dorothy (a teacher; maiden name, Anderson) House; married William Doty (an analyst), February 2, 1963 (divorced, 1981); married Gardner H. Mein (a writer and teacher), June 16, 1986; children: (first marriage) Stuart William, Margaret. *Education:* University of Utah, B.F.A., 1963; University of California, Irvine, M.F.A., 1979.

ADDRESSES: Home—1630 Barker, Lawrence, Kan. 66044. *Agent*—Virginia Barber Literary Agency Inc., 353 West 21st St., New York, N.Y. 10011.

CAREER: School Testing Service, Berkeley, Calif., assistant director, 1965-70; San Francisco State University, San Francisco, Calif., lecturer, 1980; University of California, Irvine, lecturer, 1984-86; University of Kansas, Lawrence, assistant professor, 1986—; writer. Prose director of Squaw Valley Community of Writers. Personnel director of Camping Unlimited for Retarded Children; member of board of directors of Berkeley Day Care Center for the Retarded.

AWARDS, HONORS: Honorable mention from Joseph Henry Jackson Competition of San Francisco Foundation, 1975, for novel in progress; award for excellence from Santa Barbara Writers Conference, 1978.

WRITINGS:

A Day Late (novel), Viking, 1980.
Fly Away Home (novel), Viking, 1982.
What She Told Him (novel), Viking, 1985.

Contributor to *Paris Review, Bay Guardian, Berkeley Gazette,* and *Los Angeles Times.*

WORK IN PROGRESS: Two novels, *With No Kisses* and *A Little Company.*

SIDELIGHTS: Carolyn Doty's first novel, *A Day Late,* focuses on two grief-stricken individuals—Sam, who has recently lost his fifteen-year-old daughter to brain cancer, and Katy, a seventeen-year-old girl abandoned by her lover once he discovers she is pregnant. Sam picks up Katy while she is hitchhiking, and the two spend one day together during which time their common feeling of grief initiates a bond. Anatole Broyard of the *New York Times* believes Doty "is dealing with dangerous material" in *A Day Late*. "Sam's problem, and . . . Doty's problem in this first novel, is to keep his grief from turning into sentimentality, to keep his pity for his daughter pure, safe from self-pity. . . . Almost every novelist wants to play with death, but the subject is surrounded by emotions that all too quickly putrefy." Although Broyard expresses such reservations, *Sunday Denver Post* contributor Rosemarie Stewart believes that even if "the subject matter sounds grim, it doesn't come off that way," and Richard Bradford of the *New York Times Book Review* concurs: "Despite the sadness that surrounds Sam and Katy, 'A Day Late' is in no way depressing. . . . This may be a first novel, but it is the work of a gifted novelist, a writer of intelligence and style who is not afraid to probe into characters too rich and complex for the easy, labeling adjective." Broyard commends Doty for the novel's closing action, emphasizing his belief that "there are no solutions, only gestures. 'A Day Late' is an interesting gesture."

Like *A Day Late*, Doty's subsequent novels are psychological dramas. *Fly Away Home* details Sally Bryan's short-term attempt to free herself from her family burdens—a thirteen-year-old severely retarded son and an indifferent husband. She returns with her precocious eight-year-old daughter to the Sun Valley of her college days as a reprieve from reality. For Evelyn Wilde Mayerson in the *Washington Post Book World*, "Doty, in exploring moral and ethical dilemmas, fulfills the novelist's responsibility to do more than entertain the reader. . . . The strength of [*Fly Away Home*] is the delicacy and thoughtfulness with which the author deals with a startling concept: That the ultimate freedom for women includes the right to detach themselves from not only husband but child, including the severely handicapped child whose care preempts all else." *Los Angeles Times* critic Elaine Kendall, in turn, finds that *Fly Away Home* "is not inspirational, outlining the miracles to be wrought by love and dedication, nor is it a story of triumph over adversity. Such books, heartwarming as they are, cannot afford the luxuries of humor, satire or anger. Those are the novelist's prerogatives, and Doty employs them judiciously in this sensitive and candid book. The subject is an emotional mine field, negotiated without hesitation or a single false step."

Doty's third novel, entitled *What She Told Him*, explores the disturbed psyche of a young man, Cal Newkirk, after he hears rumors that his brave, World War II-hero father may have been a brutal rapist. Because his mother dies before he can establish the facts, Cal sets out in search of his parentage but ends up in jail on fraudulent rape charges. "Muddling through a disastrous marriage, then stumbling into a sexual-assault charge of which he isn't even sure whether he's guilty, Cal is warped from within by fantasies and nightmares that seem to stem from the rapist, his father, whose taint he thinks he carries," surmises Amy E. Schwartz, a *New Republic* reviewer. According to Schwartz, "Doty is at her best when exploring the shadowy areas of Cal's psyche. She goes courageously past the initial questions of rape and violence to more complicated and ambiguous sequences." In the *Los Angeles Times Book Review*, Doris Grumbach expresses dissatisfaction with *What She Told Him* because she is convinced the reader cannot care for Cal nor for his "plodding and listless" search for his roots. "In [Doty's] two earlier novels . . . [she] proved herself capable of skillful, convincing fiction. How then do we account for this toneless meander into a lymphatic mode of storytelling, into a fiction lacking intensity, suspense or, worse, cred-

ibility? My suspicion is that it was a novel born of an idea rather than sprung from character or compelling event, a thesis proposed and then requiring proof." However, for Eleanor Foa Dienstag in the *New York Times Book Review*, Doty "convincingly evokes the bleak terrors of prison, the narrow decencies and patriotism of heartland America, as well as Cal's tormented psyche; and her varied cast of characters drop clues like crumbs that finally lead Cal toward salvation."

Doty told *CA:* "My principal area of interest lies in writing fiction set in the small towns of the western United States, undoubtedly because I grew up in one of them. The characters I write about tend to be those who have experienced some human tragedy or trauma out of the ordinary range of things. I like to take a character who has done something inconceivable to most people—a child molester, for example—and see if I can't go backward from the event and find experiences, events, etc., that make the action more comprehensible. Also, because of my training and interest in painting, I like to create as visual an environment as is possible, again dealing primarily with the mountains, deserts, and small towns of Utah, Nevada, and Montana.

"I also enjoy teaching creative writing in spite of those who maintain it can't be done. What can be given, I believe, is as much knowledge about the tools available, and as much information as one has at one's command about what it takes to be a writer."

BIOGRAPHICAL/CRITICAL SOURCES:

PERIODICALS

Boston Sunday Globe, April 27, 1980.
Christian Science Monitor, July 30, 1980.
Los Angeles Times, April 24, 1980, March 18, 1982.
Los Angeles Times Book Review, February 3, 1985.
New Republic, May 20, 1985.
New York Times, April 16, 1980.
New York Times Book Review, May 4, 1980, February 3, 1985.
Sunday Denver Post, June 8, 1980.
Times Literary Supplement, May 29, 1981.
Washington Post, March 11, 1982.
Washington Post Book World, June 15, 1980.

*   *   *

DRIMMER, Frederick   1916-

PERSONAL: Born August 8, 1916, in Brooklyn, N.Y.; son of John (a restaurant owner) and Mina (Lichtenberg) Drimmer; married Evelyn Laderman (a librarian), August 24, 1940; children: John Andrew, Jean Louisa. *Education:* City College (now City College of the City University of New York), B.A. (magna cum laude), 1938; Columbia University, M.A., 1940; New School for Social Research, additional graduate study, 1947-48.

ADDRESSES: Home—281 Grumman Ave., Norwalk, Conn. 06851.

CAREER: Greenberg (publishing house), New York City, editor-in-chief, 1940-46; Greystone Press, New York City, editor-in-chief, 1946-56; Famous Artists School, Inc., Westport, Conn., editor-in-chief, 1956-72; *Funk and Wagnalls Encyclopedia*, New York City, writer and editor, 1974-78. Instructor in English at City College (now City College of the City University of New York), 1946-47, and at Norwalk Community

College, 1966-67. *Military service:* U.S. Naval Reserve, 1943-46; became ensign.

MEMBER: Phi Beta Kappa.

AWARDS, HONORS: The Elephant Man was named notable juvenile trade book in the field of social sciences by the National Council for the Social Sciences.

WRITINGS:

(Contributor) *Complete Book of Mothercraft*, Greystone, 1952.
Very Special People: The Struggles, Loves, and Triumphs of Human Oddities (nonfiction), Crown, 1973, revised edition, Bell, 1985.
In Search of Eden (nonfiction), C. R. Gibson, 1973.
Daughters of Eve (nonfiction), C. R. Gibson, 1975.
Body Snatchers, Stiffs, and Other Ghoulish Delights (nonfiction), Fawcett, 1981.
The Elephant Man (fiction), Putnam, 1985.
Don't Call Them Freaks! (nonfiction), Atheneum, 1988.

EDITOR

The Knapsack Book (anthology), Greenberg, 1942.
The Animal Kingdom, three volumes, Greystone, 1953.
Scalps and Tomahawks (nonfiction), Coward McCann, 1961, revised edition published as *Captured by the Indians*, Dover, 1985.
A Friend Is Someone Special (anthology), C. R. Gibson, 1975.
Prayer (anthology), C. R. Gibson, 1978.
How to Draw and Paint Landscapes, Cortina, 1983.

OTHER

Also author of film, "Some Call Them Freaks," Home Box Office, 1981.

Contributor to books, including *People's Almanac, Reader's Digest Family Health Guide*, and *You and the Law*, all published by Reader's Digest Press.

SIDELIGHTS: Frederick Drimmer told *CA* that his book *Body Snatchers, Stiffs, and Other Ghoulish Delights* "came about in a most unusual way. I was scheduled to give a series of lectures on human oddities for college audiences, and I needed pictures to illustrate it. I found a showman in North Carolina who owned an enormous collection of these pictures. He also owned two dead bodies that he exhibited around the country, and he suggested there would be considerable interest in a book about 'stiffs,' as he called them. Research led me into the whole fascinating story of body snatching in Britain and the United States as well as such curious incidents as the theft of Charlie Chaplin's body and the bizarre attempt to steal Abraham Lincoln's. I was intrigued by such strange people as Martin Van Butchell, who embalmed his wife and kept her in the parlor, and Elmer McCurdy, the long-dead outlaw who turned up on a movie set. Readers seem to find them just as memorable."

MEDIA ADAPTATIONS: "Journals of the Pioneers," a two-volume audio-cassette by Recorded Books, 1981, was based on Drimmer's book *Scalps and Tomahawks.*

AVOCATIONAL INTERESTS: Travel, music, languages.

BIOGRAPHICAL/CRITICAL SOURCES:

PERIODICALS

Bridgeport Sunday Post, November 24, 1974, September 22, 1985.

Sunday Advocate (Stamford, Conn.), October 25, 1981.
The Hour (Norwalk, Conn.), October 30, 1981, October 5, 1985.

*   *   *

DuBAY, Sandra   1954-

PERSONAL: Born October 6, 1954, in Battle Creek, Mich.; daughter of Harry Andrew (a municipal employee) and Reatha Lenore (Bingham) DuBay. *Education:* Washtenaw Community College, A.A., 1974; University of Michigan, B.A., 1976. *Politics:* Independent. *Religion:* Methodist.

ADDRESSES: Home—801 Bradfield, Bay City, Mich. 48706.

CAREER: The Other Room (crisis intervention center), Bay City, Mich., counselor, 1977-78; free-lance writer, 1978—.

WRITINGS:

HISTORICAL ROMANCE NOVELS

Mistress of the Sun King, Tower, 1980, published as *Crimson Conquest*, Leisure Books, 1984.
Flame of Fidelity, Tower, 1981, Leisure Books, 1986.
The Claverleigh Curse, Zebra Books, 1982.
Fidelity's Flight, Leisure Books, 1982.
Whispers of Passion, Leisure Books, 1984.
In Passion's Shadow, Leisure Books, 1984.
Where Passion Dwells, Leisure Books, 1985.
By Love Beguiled, Leisure Books, 1986.
Burn On Sweet Fire, Leisure Books, 1987.
Scarlet Surrender, Leisure Books, 1987.

WORK IN PROGRESS: Two historical novels and one historical romantic suspense novel.

SIDELIGHTS: Sandra DuBay told *CA:* "At an early age I discovered that it was much easier for me to communicate through writing than verbally. At about the same time I was given a copy of *Forever Amber*, and it started my interest in history and historical fiction.

"I think that the most important part of any novel is an interesting cast of characters since, regardless of how intriguing the plot may be, if the characters are dull or annoying no reader is going to care to follow them through the book. For me the characters often determine whether or not I finish a novel. I have put aside several novels after only a half-dozen chapters simply because I did not find the characters interesting. Conversely, I have occasionally come to a dead stop on a book for weeks because I was at a point where I would have to kill off a character I particularly liked.

"In writing historical novels, research is always a fascinating part of the writing. I love finding old memoirs and biographies from the early to mid-nineteenth century. Today's historians seem intent on presenting only the facts, whereas their counterparts of the past had no qualms about including gossip and rumors that can be of great use to the historical romance novelist.

"As for the actual mechanics of writing, I believe in outlines. In addition to a general outline of the entire book that I made before starting the novel, I outline every chapter. These outlines tend to be very detailed, often running ten to fifteen pages for a fifteen to twenty page chapter. As a result, by the time I sit down to actually write the chapter it comes out in something very nearly its final form. Aside from minor corrections, my finished manuscripts are almost copies of the first drafts."

AVOCATIONAL INTERESTS: Reading, browsing in book stores.

BIOGRAPHICAL/CRITICAL SOURCES:

PERIODICALS

Bay City Times, May 18, 1980, November 19, 1981, September 7, 1986.
Detroit Free Press, June 6, 1982.
Romantic Times, March/April, 1986, February/March, 1987.

* * *

DUKORE, Margaret Mitchell 1950-

PERSONAL: Born September 27, 1950, in Honolulu, Hawaii; daughter of Donald D. (a teacher) and Winifred (a social worker; maiden name, Murfin) Mitchell; married Bernard F. Dukore (a professor), November 13, 1973 (separated); children: Joan. *Education:* Lewis and Clark College, B.S., 1972.

ADDRESSES: Home—3819 Sierra Drive, Honolulu, Hawaii 96816. *Agent*—Bobbe Siegel, 41 West 83rd St., New York, N.Y. 10024.

CAREER: Worked in retailing in Honolulu, Hawaii, 1972-74; actress in Honolulu, 1972-81; editor, *Idea Bank* (a thesaurus for computer software), 1983-85; film reviewer, Honolulu International Film Festivals and East/West Center, Honolulu, Hawaii; writer.

MEMBER: Screen Actors Guild.

AWARDS, HONORS: Maxwell Perkins Award from Scribner, 1982, for *A Novel Called Heritage.*

WRITINGS:

"Move" (two-act play), first produced in Richmond, Va., at Virginia Museum Theatre, 1981.
A Novel Called Heritage, Scribner, 1982.
Bloom (novel), F. Watts, 1985.

Also author of the plays "Family Weekend," "Not Gold," "Marriage Working: A Fantasy," and "No Free Lunch." Author of the screenplays "Jane Doe" and "Busted Wings." Author of screen treatments, "Beauty and the Band" (the Ina Ray Hutton story for Bette Midler), and "Seven Days," both for Cherry Lane Productions.

WORK IN PROGRESS: "Accidental Freedom Ride," a screenplay; *Charlotte Malone,* a novel.

SIDELIGHTS: Margaret Mitchell Dukore told CA: "I was always a raconteur, so I wrote because it was a shame to waste all those good stories on people who would just laugh and then forget them. The writer who has influenced me the most is J. D. Salinger. The writer I most admire is Vladimir Nabokov. I believe a writer should read *everything*—Nabokov, Jacqueline Susann, *New Republic, National Review, Cosmopolitan.* I believe every 'serious' thing I write should have something funny in it, and I believe that every funny thing I write should have something serious in it. If not . . . well, then it wouldn't be at all like life."

Dukore's first novel, *A Novel Called Heritage,* "is about the writing of a novel" but it has "none of the snoremongering qualities typical of that breed," writes James Kaufmann in a *Chicago Tribune Book World* review. Its heroine, the eighteen-year-old Annie Foster, sends chapters of her first novel to a senior editor at a fictional publishing firm; their correspondence, also included between the developing chapters, is the innovative feature of Dukore's book. "The technique offers an inviting double-perspective: What Annie thinks of her life, as revealed in the novel; and what she thinks of the novel as revealed in her letters," observes Curt Suplee of the *Washington Post.* The letters also provide "outrageously funny and frequently all-too-true glimpses of the world of publishing," according to Kaufmann, who feels, on the other hand, that these barbs are not the book's main subject. "The portrayal of Annie's mother . . . anchors this novel," he maintains.

Indeed, the main character of the novel-within-the-novel is Annie's mother Kate, a former actress who had quickly become dissatisfied with domestic life as the wife of a drama professor. With her "marathon bickering," says Suplee, Kate "excoriates her husband for the waste of her talents, and flounces through the house playing the part of a cynical, melodramatic victim. . . . She is determined to pull the rest of the clan into the acrid hell of remorse she can only escape in death." Kate's terrorizing influence on her husband and children is felt even after her suicide, Annie's novel reveals. In supporting roles throughout the book are Annie's father, his ex-wife, and his mistress. When her father suddenly becomes violent, Annie fears more than ever that she must inherit the madness that apparently runs in the family.

"The reader's ample fascination with the characters has to contend against one of the most relentlessly nasty narrative voices in modern memory," Suplee notes, and although he can see Dukore's attempt to let Annie's language reflect Kate's "pathologically ugly view of the world," he defines Annie's ever-present vulgarity and sarcasm as "the prose equivalent of a chain-saw competition hosted by Joan Rivers." He concludes that *A Novel Called Heritage* is nonetheless a remarkable first novel in that it displays "not merely an inventive structure but a comic horror show of painfully memorable characters."

BIOGRAPHICAL/CRITICAL SOURCES:

PERIODICALS

Chicago Tribune Book World, April 25, 1982.
Library Journal, February 1, 1982.
Washington Post, May 7, 1982.

* * *

DUNCAN, Denis (Macdonald) 1920-

PERSONAL: Born January 10, 1920, in Bedlington, England; son of Reginald (a pastor) and Clarice Ethel (Hodgkinson) Duncan; married Henrietta Watson MacKenzie Houston (a secretary), March 21, 1942; children: Carol Louise, Raymond Denis. *Education:* Attended George Watson's College, Edinburgh, 1931-38; University of Edinburgh, M.A., 1940, B.D. (with distinction), 1943.

ADDRESSES: Home—1 Cranbourne Rd., London N10 2BT, England.

CAREER: Ordained minister of Church of Scotland, 1943; St. Margaret's parish, Juniper Green, Edinburgh, Scotland, minister, 1944-50; Trinity Duke Street Parish Church, Glasgow, Scotland, minister, 1950-57; *British Weekly,* London, England, and Edinburgh, managing editor, 1957-70, managing director, 1967-70; Highgate Counselling Centre, London, director, 1969—; Westminster Pastoral Foundation, London, associate director and training supervisor, 1971-79; director, The Churches' Council for Health and Healing, 1982—. Writer and interviewer for television, 1953-57; founder and director of Church of Scotland press, publicity, and information office, 1954-57; broadcaster and scriptwriter for Scottish television, 1963-68; concert promoter for Edinburgh Festival, 1966—; managing director of DPS Publicity Services Ltd., 1967-74; producer, with Benita Kyle, of a concert series, "Communication through the Arts," 1970—; chairman of International Committee of World Association of Pastoral Care and Counselling, 1977-79.

MEMBER: International Biographical Association (fellow), United Nations Association of Scotland (honorary vice-chairman), Institute of Journalists, Institute of Community Service, Institute of Pastoral Education and Counselling, London Arts Club.

WRITINGS:

Here Is My Hand: The Story of Lieutenant Colonel Alida Bosshardt of the Red Light Area, Amsterdam, Hodder & Stoughton, 1977.
A Day at a Time: A Thought and a Prayer for Each Day of the Year, two volumes, Arthur James, 1980.
Creative Silence: Through Inner Silence to the Harvest of the Spirit, Arthur James, 1980.
Love, the Word That Heals, Arthur James, 1981.
The Way of Love: A Thought and a Prayer a Day at a Time, Westminster, 1982.

Also author of *Victorious Living*, Arthur James.

EDITOR

William Barclay, *Through the Year with William Barclay: Devotional Readings for Every Day*, Hodder & Stoughton, 1971, published as *Daily Celebration: Devotional Readings for Every Day of the Year*, Word, Inc., 1973.
John C. Heenan, *Through the Year With Cardinal Heenan: Devotional Readings for Every Day*, Hodder & Stoughton, 1972.
Barclay, *Every Day with William Barclay: Devotional Readings for Every Day*, Hodder & Stoughton, 1973.
(And adapter) Barclay, *Marching Orders: Daily Readings for Younger People* (juvenile), Hodder & Stoughton, 1973.
(And adapter) Barclay, *Marching On: Daily Readings for Younger People* (juvenile), Hodder & Stoughton, 1974, Westminster, 1975.
John B. Phillips, *Through the Year with J. B. Phillips: Devotional Readings for Every Day*, Hodder & Stoughton, 1974, published as *For This Day*, Word, Inc., 1975.

OTHER

Founder and editor of *Rally*, 1956-67.

WORK IN PROGRESS: Research on healing and the Holy Spirit.

SIDELIGHTS: Denis Duncan told *CA:* " 'Deep speaks to deep' is an Old Testament statement about communication. In the Psalms, it is known that encounter takes place at the unconscious level, not the conscious. It is when 'the hidden depths' in one make contact with 'the hidden depths' in another that things begin to happen."

AVOCATIONAL INTERESTS: Badminton, music, literature.

DUNCAN, Lois 1934-
(Lois Kerry)

PERSONAL: Original name, Lois Duncan Steinmetz; born 1934, in Philadelphia, Pa.; daughter of Joseph Janney and Lois (Foley) Steinmetz (both magazine photographers); married second husband, Donald Wayne Arquette (an electrical engineer), July 15, 1965; children: (first marriage) Robin, Kerry, Brett; (second marriage) Donald, Jr., Kaitlyn. *Education:* Attended Duke University; University of New Mexico, B.A. (cum laude), 1977.

ADDRESSES: Home—1112 Dakota N.E., Albuquerque, N.M. 87110. *Agent*—Claire Smith, Harold Ober Associates, 40 East 49th St., New York, N.Y. 10017.

CAREER: Writer of youth books, adult novels, short stories, and magazine articles. Instructor in journalism and magazine photographer, University of New Mexico, 1970-81. Lecturer at writers' conferences.

MEMBER: National League of American Pen Women, Authors Guild, Authors League of America, New Mexico Press Women, Phi Beta Kappa.

AWARDS, HONORS: Three-time winner during high school years of *Seventeen* magazine's annual short story contest; Seventeenth Summer Literary Award, Dodd, Mead & Co., 1958, for *Debutante Hill;* Best Novel Award, National Press Women, 1966, for *Point of Violence;* Special Award, Mystery Writers of America, 1966, for *Ransom*, 1969, for *They Never Came Home*, 1985, for *The Third Eye*, and 1986, for *Locked in Time;* Zia Award, New Mexico Press Women, 1969, for *Major Andre: Brave Enemy;* grand prize winner, *Writer's Digest* Creative Writing Contest, 1970, for short story; Theta Sigma Phi Headliner Award, 1971; *Summer of Fear* won the Dorothy Canfield Fisher Award, 1978, the California Young Reader Medal, 1983, the New Mexico Young Reader Award, the New Mexico Land of Enchantment Award, 1983, and was named an American Library Association Best Book for Young Adults; *Killing Mr. Griffin* was named an American Library Association Best of the Best Books, 1978, was a runner-up for the California Young Reader Medal, won a Massachusetts Children's Book Award, 1982, and won an Alabama Young Readers' Choice Award, 1982-83 and 1986-87.

Stranger with My Face was named a Best Book for Young Readers by the *New York Times*, 1981, an American Library Association Best of the Best Books, 1981, and an American Library Association Best Book for Young Adults, won the Ethical Culture School Book Award, 1981, a Best Novel Award from National League of American Pen Women, 1982, the Zia Award from New Mexico Press Women, 1983, a Massachusetts Children's Book Award, 1983, the South Carolina Young Readers Award, 1984, a California Young Reader Medal, 1984, and the Indiana Young Hoosier Award, 1986, and was named a best book of the year by *English Teachers' Journal* and University of Iowa; *Chapters: My Growth as a Writer* was named an American Library Association Best Book for Young Adults, 1982; OMAR Children of Indiana Book Award, 1983, and Indiana Young Hoosier Award, both for *A Gift of Magic;* Indiana Young Hoosier Award, 1987, for *The Third Eye;* Children's Book Award, National League of American Pen Women, 1987, for *Horses of Dreamland*.

WRITINGS:

Debutante Hill, Dodd, 1958.

The Littlest One in the Family, illustrations by Suzanne K. Larsen, Dodd, 1960.

The Middle Sister, Dodd, 1961.

Game of Danger, Dodd, 1962.

Silly Mother (Junior Literary Guild section), illustrations by Larsen, Dial, 1962.

Giving Away Suzanne, illustrations by Leonard Weisgard, Dodd, 1963.

Season of the Two-Heart, Dodd, 1964.

Ransom, Doubleday, 1966, published as *Five Were Missing,* New American Library, 1972.

Point of Violence, Doubleday, 1966.

They Never Came Home (Junior Literary Guild selection), Doubleday, 1968.

Peggy, Little, Brown, 1970.

Hotel for Dogs, illustrations by Leonard Shortall, Houghton, 1971.

A Gift of Magic, illustrations by Arvis Stewart, Little, Brown, 1971.

I Know What You Did Last Summer, Little, Brown, 1973.

When the Bough Breaks, Doubleday, 1974.

Down a Dark Hall, Little, Brown, 1974.

Summer of Fear (Junior Literary Guild selection), Little, Brown, 1976.

Killing Mr. Griffin, Little, Brown, 1978.

Daughters of Eve, Little, Brown, 1979.

Stranger with My Face, Little, Brown, 1981.

(Self-illustrated) *From Spring to Spring* (poetry), Westminster Press, 1982.

The Terrible Tales of Happy Days School (poetry), illustrations by Friso Henstra, Little, Brown, 1983.

The Third Eye (Junior Literary Guild selection), Little, Brown, 1984, published as *The Eyes of Karen Connors,* Hamish Hamilton, 1985.

Locked in Time (Junior Literary Guild selection), Little, Brown, 1985.

Horses of Dreamland, illustrations by Donna Diamond, Little, Brown, 1985.

The Twisted Window (Junior Literary Guild selection), Delacorte, 1987.

Songs from Dreamland, Random House, 1988.

Wonder Kid Meets the Evil Lunch Snatcher, Little, Brown, 1988.

The Birthday Moon, Viking, in press.

UNDER PSEUDONYM LOIS KERRY

Love Song for Joyce, Funk, 1958.

A Promise for Joyce, Funk, 1959.

NONFICTION

Major Andre: Brave Enemy, Putnam, 1969.

How to Write and Sell Your Personal Experiences, Writer's Digest, 1979.

Chapters: My Growth as a Writer, Little, Brown, 1982.

OTHER

A Visit with Lois Duncan (videotape), RDA Enterprises, 1985.

Songs from Dreamland (audio-cassette of original lullabies), RDA Enterprises, 1987.

Selling Personal Experiences to Magazines (audio-cassette), RDA Enterprises, 1987.

Contributor of articles and short stories to *Good Housekeeping, Redbook, McCall's, Reader's Digest, Saturday Evening Post, Woman's Day, Writer, Ladies' Home Journal,* and other magazines.

WORK IN PROGRESS: Two young adult novels for Delacorte.

SIDELIGHTS: Lois Duncan, a popular author of young adult books, has learned to tailor her work to a generation of teens more familiar with television than books. "Television has had an enormous effect upon youth books," she writes in the *Something about the Author Autobiography Series.* "Few of today's readers are patient enough to wade through slow paced, introductory chapters as I did at their ages to see if a book is eventually going to get interesting. If their interest isn't caught immediately, they want to switch channels." Her methods have succeeded with adults and juveniles alike, according to *Times Literary Supplement* reviewer Jennifer Moody, who writes that Duncan is "popular . . . not only with the soft underbelly of the literary world, the children's book reviewers, but with its most hardened carapace, the teenage library book borrower."

The constant element in Duncan's books is suspense. "The growing sense of unease is Lois Duncan's hallmark . . . ," notes Sarah Hayes in the *Times Literary Supplement.* "She can play the part of the novelist, but at heart she is a spine-chiller." Moody concurs, saying that Duncan possesses "a rare gift for suspense." According to Leigh Dean in the *Children's Book Review Service,* Duncan's readers look for "unconventional characters, and situations steeped in danger, magic, and intrigue."

Duncan started writing stories for magazines as a teenager and progressed to book-length manuscripts as she matured. One of her first efforts was *Debutante Hill,* a love story for teens, that Duncan, then a young housewife, wrote to pass the lonely hours while her husband was attending law school. She entered the book in Dodd, Mead and Company's "Seventeenth Summer Literary Contest." "It was returned for revisions because in it a young man of twenty drank a beer . . . ," Duncan writes in the *Something about the Author Autobiography Series.* "I changed the beer to a Coke and resubmitted the manuscript. It won the contest, and the book was published." Duncan thinks the story "sweet and sticky and pap," but a reviewer for the *Christian Science Monitor* stated at the time of the book's release that Duncan "writes exceptionally well, and has the happy ability to make a reader care what happens to her characters."

When her first marriage ended in divorce, Duncan returned to magazine writing. In 1965, she married Don Arquette, and "now that the financial pressure was off, I also felt free to turn back to my non-lucrative, but immeasurably enjoyable, hobby of writing teenage novels," she recalls in the *Something about the Author Autobiography Series.* In 1968, she wrote *Ransom,* an adventure story that her publisher refused to handle, since it deviated from her former style. Doubleday took it on, and *Ransom* became a runner-up for the Edgar Allan Poe Award. Zena Sutherland, writing for *Bulletin of the Center for Children's Books,* praises *Ransom*'s dramatic suspense; Dorothy M. Broderick says in the *New York Times Book Review* that the character of Glenn Kirtland "makes it something more than another good mystery."

As a child, Duncan liked to create imaginary characters. In the *Something about the Author Autobiography Series* she tells how she used to frighten her younger brother with stories about the "'Moon Fairy', come to deliver the message that the moon was falling toward the earth." As an adult, the delight in fantasy became an interest in the paranormal; she has included ESP, witchcraft, and astral projection in many of her books. In *Stranger with My Face,* seventeen-year-old Laurie discovers not only that she is adopted, but that she has a twin sister. This sister is "the evil version of herself, who travels by astral projection and is determined to inhabit Laurie's body," writes Jean Fritz in the *New York Times Book Review*.

Down a Dark Hall is also a teen Gothic. Through attempting to get it published, Duncan learned "about the newest taboos for youth novels...," she writes in the *Something about the Author Autobiography Series*. "I had assumed I could write about almost anything I wanted to. *Down a Dark Hall* was a strange sort of Gothic about a girl who went off to boarding school and discovered too late that the headmistress was a medium. Ghosts of long dead artists, writers, and composers came flocking back to invade the minds and bodies of the unfortunate students. This book was returned for revisions, not because the plot was so wild, but because the ghosts in the story were male and the victims were female.... I was now told 'Librarians won't touch a book that portrays women as the weaker sex.' When I changed the ghost of a male poet into the ghost of Emily Bronte, the book was accepted."

Daughters of Eve also involves the supernatural. A student with ESP suspects that something is wrong with the faculty adviser who heads a high school girls' club. The adviser leads the group into increasingly more violent acts in the name of feminism. The portrayal of a negative feminist element in *Daughters of Eve* has drawn some strong remarks from critics. "It has an embittered tone of hatred that colors the characterization," suggests Zena Sutherland in *Bulletin of the Center for Children's Books*. Jan M. Goodman thinks along similar lines, writing in the *Interracial Books for Children Bulletin* that Duncan "clearly places a harsh value judgment on violent solutions, and ... she leaves the impression that fighting for women's rights leads to uncontrollable anger and senseless destruction.... The book's deceptive interpretation of feminism plus its dangerous stereotypes make it a harmful distortion of reality." But Natalie Babbitt finds the work "refreshing" and likes the fact that "there are no lessons." In the *New York Times Book Review*, she compares the book to William Golding's *Lord of the Flies* and concludes that *Daughters of Eve* "is strongly evenhanded, for it lets us see that women can be as bloodthirsty as men ever were."

Killing Mr. Griffin also features a dangerous leader, a teenaged boy who guides a group of friends into kidnapping their strict high school teacher and intimidating him into giving less homework. The teacher dies when he misses his angina medication. "Lois Duncan breaks some new ground in a novel without sex, drugs or black leather jackets," comments Richard Peck in the *New York Times Book Review*. "But the taboo she tampers with is far more potent and pervasive: the unleashed fury of the permissively reared against any assault on their egos and authority.... The value of the book lies in the twisted logic of the teenagers and how easily they can justify anything."

While Peck likes the beginning of *Killing Mr. Griffin*, he criticizes the end for descending "into unadulterated melodrama.... The book becomes an 'easy read' when it shouldn't." Duncan again points to her readers to explain the style of her writing. Television "has conditioned its viewers to expect instant entertainment.... Because of this, writers have been forced into utilizing all sorts of TV techniques to hold their readers' attention," she points out in the *Something about the Author Autobiography Series*.

Duncan goes on to say that people continually ask her, "'Are you going to keep writing?' They might as well ask if I plan to continue breathing. I expect to do both just as long as I possibly can.... I'm 'doing my job and having fun.'"

The videotape *A Visit with Lois Duncan* can be obtained through Lois Duncan at her home address.

MEDIA ADAPTATIONS: Summer of Fear was made into a television movie for the National Broadcasting Company (NBC-TV).

BIOGRAPHICAL/CRITICAL SOURCES:

BOOKS

Contemporary Literary Criticism, Volume XXVI, Gale, 1983.
Duncan Lois, *How to Write and Sell Your Personal Experiences*, Writer's Digest, 1979.
Duncan, Lois, *Chapters: My Growth as a Writer*, Little, Brown, 1982.
Something about the Author Autobiography Series, Volume II, Gale, 1986.

PERIODICALS

Alan Review, spring, 1980.
Booklist, September 15, 1976.
Bulletin of the Center for Children's Books, April, 1982.
Chicago Tribune Book World, July 4, 1982.
Children's Book Review Service, spring, 1982.
Christian Science Monitor, February 5, 1959.
Good Housekeeping, September, 1977.
Interracial Books for Children Bulletin, Volume XI, number 6, 1980.
New York Times Book Review, June 5, 1966, December 11, 1966, June 8, 1969, November 10, 1974, March 6, 1977, April 30, 1978, January 27, 1980, February 22, 1981, November 15, 1981, March 26, 1982, February 6, 1983.
Times Literary Supplement, March 27, 1981, March 26, 1982, February 22, 1985, May 9, 1986.
Writer's Digest, December, 1957, December, 1959, May, 1962.

—*Sketch by Jani Prescott*

*   *   *

DUNMORE, John 1923-
(Jason Calder)

PERSONAL: Born August 6, 1923, in Trouville, France; son of William Ernest (a businessman) and Marguerite (Martin) Dunmore; married Joyce Langley (a city councillor); children: Paul Vincent, Patricia Margaret. *Education:* University of London, B.A., 1950; University of New Zealand, Ph.D., 1961. *Politics:* Labour Party. *Religion:* Roman Catholic.

ADDRESSES: Home—35 Oriwa St., Waikanae, New Zealand. *Office*—Massey University, Palmerston North, New Zealand.

CAREER: Worked as school teacher, 1951-57; Massey University, Palmerston North, New Zealand, senior lecturer, 1961-66, professor of French, 1966-84. Managing editor, Heritage Press.

MEMBER: PEN, New Zealand Playwrights' Association (executive member), Australasian Language and Literature Association (president, 1980-82).

AWARDS, HONORS: Sir James Wattie Book of the Year Award, 1969, for *The Fateful Voyage of the St. Jean-Baptiste;* named chevalier of French Legion of Honour, 1977; named officier, Academic Palms, 1986.

WRITINGS:

French Explorers in the Pacific, Oxford University Press, Volume I, 1965, Volume II, 1969.
Le Mystere d'Omboula, Longmans, Paul, 1966.
(Editor) R. R. Milligan, *The Map Drawn by the Chief Tukitahua*, Reeds, 1966.
Aventures dans le Pacifique, Reeds, 1967.
Success at University, Whitcoulls, 1968.
Success at School, Whitcoulls, 1969, reprinted as *Step by Step Exam Success*, Cavanaun Books, 1979.
The Fateful Voyage of the St. Jean-Baptiste, Pegasus Press, 1969.
(Editor) Norman Kirk, *Towards Nationhood*, New Zealand Books, 1969.
Meurtre a Tahiti (title means "Murder in Tahiti"), Longmans, Paul, 1971.
Norman Kirk: A Portrait, New Zealand Books, 1972.
(Editor) *An Anthology of French Scientific Prose*, Hutchinson, 1973.
(Translator) Gabriel Linge, *In Search of the Maori*, New Zealand Books, 1974.
(Translator) Georges Pisier, *Kunie; or, The Isle of Pines*, Noumea, 1978.
The Expedition of the St. Jean-Baptiste: From Journals of Jean de Surville and Guillaume Labe, Hakluyt Society [Cambridge], 1981.
How to Succeed as an Extra-Mural Student, Dunmore Press, 1983.
(Translator) R. Herve, *Chance Discovery of Australia and New Zealand*, Dumore Press, 1983.
Pacific Explorer: The Life of J. F. de la Perouse, Naval Institute Press, 1985.
(Editor) *Le Journal de Laperouse*, two volumes, Imprimerie Nationale (Paris), 1985.

UNDER PSEUDONYM JASON CALDER

The Man Who Shot Rob Muldoon, Dunmore Press, 1976.
A Wreath for the Springboks, Dunmore Press, 1978.
The O'Rourke Affair, Dunmore Press, 1979.
Target Margaret Thatcher, Robert Hale, 1981.

OTHER

Also author of *New Zealand: The North Island* and *New Zealand: The South Island*, both 1987.

WORK IN PROGRESS: The Fabulous Pacific (provisional title), a new history of the Pacific merging Polynesian/Melanesian mythology and history with European exploration and colonization, completion date expected in 1989.

SIDELIGHTS: John Dunmore once told *CA:* "I have always moved freely from scholarly work to the theatre or the adventure thriller. My special field is the Pacific in the eighteenth century, in particular the work of explorers and especially the French. As an academic, I have published what academics are expected to publish; but like many academics, I have found relaxation and useful outlets in drama, thrillers, and politics (but then these three may well be synonymous)."

*　　*　　*

DWIGGINS, Don 1913-

PERSONAL: Born November 15, 1913, in Plainfield, N.J.; son of Clare Victor (a cartoonist) and Betsey (Lindsay) Dwiggins; married Olga Arabsky; children: Don Lindsay, Toni Kay. *Education:* Attended Los Angeles Junior College, 1932-33.

ADDRESSES: Home—3816 Paseo Hidalgo, Malibu, Calif. 90265.

CAREER: Commercial pilot. *Los Angeles Daily News*, Los Angeles, Calif., aviation editor, 1947-54; *Los Angeles Mirror News*, Los Angeles, aviation editor, 1956-62; station KTTV, Los Angeles, news writer, 1964; Disney Studios, Burbank, Calif., editor of "Mickey Mouse Newsreel," 1965; senior editor, *Plane & Pilot* (magazine), 1974-87; free-lance writer. Space technology consultant, Lockheed Aircraft Co., 1964. *Military service:* U.S. Army Air Forces, 1942-43; became master sergeant. Royal Air Force, flight instructor, 1944-47.

MEMBER: Aviation Aerospace Writers Association, Writers Guild of America, West.

AWARDS, HONORS: Award for best California news story of 1960, for coverage of Chessman execution; Aviation Aerospace Writers Association award for best aviation feature in metropolitan newspaper, 1961, and award for best aviation book, 1968, for *Hollywood Pilot; The Eagle Has Landed* was selected as one of the Child Study Association's Books of the Year, 1970.

WRITINGS:

"Frankie" (a biography of Frank Sinatra), Paperback Library, 1961.
The S. O. Bees, New American Library, 1963.
They Flew the Bendix Race, Lippincott, 1965.
The Air Devils, Lippincott, 1966.
Hollywood Pilot, Doubleday, 1967.
The SST: Here It Comes, Ready or Not, Doubleday, 1968.
The Barnstormers, Grosset & Dunlap, 1968.
Space and the Weather, Golden Gate, 1968.
Bailout, Crowell, 1969.
Famous Flyers and the Ships They Flew, Grosset & Dunlap, 1969.
Voices in the Sky, Golden Gate, 1969.
On Silent Wings, Grosset & Dunlap, 1970.
The Eagle Has Landed, Golden Gate, 1970.
Spaceship Earth, Golden Gate, 1970.
Into the Unknown, Golden Gate, 1971.
Robots in the Sky, Golden Gate, 1972.
The Sky Is Yours, Children's Press, 1973.
Riders of the Winds, Hawthorn Books, 1973.
The Search for Energy, Children's Press, 1974.
Build Your Own Sports Plane, Hawthorn Books, 1974.
Restoration of Antique and Classic Planes, TAB Books, 1975.
Aircraft Metal Work, TAB Books, 1976.
Why Airplanes Fly (juvenile), Children's Press, 1976.
The Asteroid War (juvenile), Children's Press, 1978.
Jimmy Fox and the Flying Falcon (juvenile), Children's Press, 1978.
Jimmy Fox and the Mountain Rescue (juvenile), Children's Press, 1979.
Low-Horsepower Fun Aircraft You Can Build, TAB Books, 1979.
Man-Powered Aircraft, TAB Books, 1979.
Thirty-one Practical Ultralight Aircraft You Can Build, TAB Books, 1980.
Flying the Frontiers of Space, Dodd, 1982.
Flying the Space Shuttles, Dodd, 1985.
Hello? Who's Out There?: The Search for Extraterrestrial Life, Dodd, 1987.

Also author of television material. Contributor of more than one thousand articles to numerous periodicals, including *Sat-*

urday Evening Post, Reader's Digest, Collier's, True, Argosy, This Week, and *Parade.*

SIDELIGHTS: Don Dwiggins wrote *CA:* "As a former newspaper reporter/editor and World War II Royal Air Force flight instructor, I have felt a need to tell the exciting and meaningful stories of aerospace in terms that may inspire young readers to seek and perhaps personally explore our frontiers of space. From early biographical studies of noted pilots to today's accounts of space shuttle flights and planetary explorations, I have tried to cover the full spectrum of thrilling adventures in aerospace. I am happy to know that the tragic accident to the Space Shuttle Challenger has not dimmed the enthusiasm of our youth to share the understanding of how and why we seek to expand our knowledge of our universe.

"My *Hello? Who's Out There?: The Search for Extraterrestrial Life* was written to open new horizons of understanding of our place in the vast cosmos. Future books will explore such advanced planned NASA projects as manned visits to Mars and to space stations, and establishment of colonies on the Moon. Once our young folks grasp the vastness of such efforts, they will know that exploration of new frontiers continues."

* * *

DYNES, Russell R(owe) 1923-

PERSONAL: Born October 2, 1923, in Dundalk, Ontario, Canada; son of Oliver Wesley (a college professor) and Carlotta (Rowe) Dynes; married Susan M. Swan, July 25, 1947; children: Russell, Jr., Patrick, Gregory, Jon. *Education:* University of Tennessee, B.A., 1948, M.A., 1950; Ohio State University, Ph.D., 1954. *Politics:* Independent Democrat. *Religion:* Methodist.

ADDRESSES: *Home*—346 South College Ave., Newark, Del. 19711. *Office*—Department of Sociology, University of Delaware, Newark, Del. 19716.

CAREER: University of Tennessee, Knoxville, instructor, 1948-50; Ohio State University, Columbus, associate professor, 1951-65, professor of sociology, 1965-77, chairman of department, 1974-77, co-director of Disaster Research Center, 1964-77; American Sociological Association, Washington, D.C., executive officer, 1977-82; University of Delaware, Newark, professor and chairman of Department of Sociology, 1982—. Visiting professor, University College, Cardiff, Wales, 1985. Senior Fulbright lecturer, Ain Shams University, United Arab Republic, 1964-65; Fulbright lecturer, Center for Advanced Study in Sociology, University of Delhi, 1972; honorary faculty member, Defense Civil Preparedness Staff College, 1973. President, Disaster Research Services, Inc., 1972-77. Wesley Foundation, trustee, 1958—, treasurer, 1961-63; member of staff, Arab State Centre for Education in Community Development, United Arab Republic, 1964-65; member of Mayor's Faculty Commission, Columbus, 1967-68; chairman of Committee on International Disaster Assistance, 1976-79; director of emergency preparedness task force, President's Commis-

sion on the Accident at Three Mile Island, 1979. Member of advisory committee, Committee on International Exchange of Persons, 1970-71; member of special advisory committee on emergency housing, National Research Council-National Academy of Sciences, 1972; consultant to Federal Disaster Assistance Agency, 1978—. *Military service:* U.S. Army, Corps of Engineers, 1942-46; became sergeant.

MEMBER: International Sociological Association, American Sociological Association, American Association for the Advancement of Science, Society for the Scientific Study of Religion (treasurer, 1976-79), Religious Research Association (fellow; treasurer, 1983-86), American Association of University Professors (member of board of directors, Ohio State University chapter, 1970-71), North Central Sociological Society, Ohio Valley Sociological Society (journal editor, 1958-63; vice-president, 1970-71), Ohio Council of Family Relations (journal editor, 1960-63).

WRITINGS:

(With A. Clarke, S. Dinitz, and I. Ishino) *Social Problems: Dissensus and Deviation in an Industrial Society,* Oxford University Press, 1964.
The Functioning of Expanding Organizations in Community Disasters, Office of Civil Defense, 1968.
(Editor with Dinitz and Clarke) *Deviance: Studies in the Process of Stigmatization and Societal Reaction,* Oxford University Press, 1969, 2nd edition, 1975.
Organized Behavior in a Disaster, Heath, 1970.
(With E. L. Quarantelli) *Disruption on the Campuses of Ohio Colleges and Universities, Spring, 1970,* Ohio Council of Churches and Ohio Board, United Ministries in Higher Education, 1970.
(With Dennis E. Wenger) *Environment Crises,* Water Resources Center, Ohio State University, 1971.
(With Wenger) *A Model of Community Problem Solving and Selected Empirical Applications,* Water Resources Center, Ohio State University, 1971.
(With Quarantelli and Gary A. Kreps) *A Perspective on Disaster Planning,* Disaster Research Center, Ohio State University, 1972.
(With Quarantelli and James L. Ross) *Police Perspectives and Behavior in a Campus Disturbance,* Ohio State University Research Foundation, 1972.
(With William A. Anderson) *Social Movements, Violence, and Change: The May Movement in Curacao,* Ohio State University Press, 1975.
(H. Freeman, P. Rossi, and William Foote Whyte) *Applied Sociology,* Jossey-Bass, 1983.
(With Arthur Power Dudden) *The Fulbright Experience: 1946-86,* Transaction Books, 1987.
(With Carlo Pelanda) *The Sociology of Disaster,* Franco Angeli, 1987.

Also author of *Deviance: Definition, Management, Treatment,* 1975, and of a number of shorter works. Associate editor, *Review of Religious Research,* 1968-76.

E

EAGLETON, Terence (Francis) 1943-
(Terry Eagleton)

PERSONAL: Born in 1943, in Salford, England. *Education:* Trinity College, Cambridge, M.A. and Ph.D.

ADDRESSES: Home and office—Wadham College, Oxford University, Oxford, England.

CAREER: Cambridge University, Jesus College, Cambridge, England, fellow, 1964-69; Oxford University, Wadham College, Oxford, England, fellow and tutor in poetry, 1969—. Selector for Poetry Book Society, 1969-71.

WRITINGS:

The New Left Church (essays), Helicon, 1966.
Shakespeare and Society: Critical Studies in Shakespearean Drama, Schocken, 1967.

UNDER NAME TERRY EAGLETON

(Editor) *Directions: Pointers for the Post-Conciliar Church* (essays), Sheed, 1968.
(Editor with Brian Wicker) *From Culture to Revolution: The Slant Symposium, 1967* (essays), Sheed, 1968.
The Body as Language: Outline of a "New Left" Theology, Sheed, 1970.
Exiles and Emigres: Studies in Modern Literature, Schocken, 1970.
Myths of Power: A Marxist Study of the Brontes, Barnes & Noble, 1975.
Marxism and Literary Criticism, University of California Press, 1976.
Criticism and Ideology: A Study in Marxist Literary Theory, Verso, 1976, Schocken, 1978.
Walter Benjamin; or, Towards a Revolutionary Criticism, Schocken, 1981.
The Rape of Clarissa: Writing, Sexuality and Class Struggle in Samuel Richardson, University of Minnesota Press, 1982.
Literary Theory: An Introduction, University of Minnesota Press, 1983.
The Function of Criticism: From the Spectator to Post-Structuralism, Verso, 1984.
(Editor) Laura Brown, *Alexander Pope,* Basil Blackwell, 1985.
(Editor) James Kavanaugh, *Emily Bronte,* Basil Blackwell, 1985.

(Editor) Stan Smith, *W. H. Auden,* Basil Blackwell, 1985.
William Shakespeare, Basil Blackwell, 1986.
Against the Grain: Selected Essays, 1975-1985, Verso, 1986.
Saints and Scholars (novel), Verso, 1987.

OTHER

Contributor to *Slant, Times Literary Supplement, Stand,* and *Commonweal.* Poetry reviewer, *Slant.*

SIDELIGHTS: Terry Eagleton is "widely regarded as the foremost young Marxist literary thinker in England," writes a *Washington Post Book World* contributor. Concerned with the ideologies found in literature, Eagleton examines the role of Marxism in discerning these ideologies. "Always alert to the underside or reversible lining of any intellectual model, Eagleton tracks the cross-currents and strategies of literary criticism with a uniquely agile understanding," states Chris Baldick in the *Times Literary Supplement.* Eagleton's books have not only clarified arcane critical theories of literature for the novice but have also posed provocative questions to the specialists. His polemical expositions in literary theory have generated a spirited critical response, and even those opposed to his stance speak readily about his "accessible" and persuasive prose. "Unlike too many other theorists, Marxist or otherwise," says Steven G. Kellman in *Modern Fiction Studies,* "Eagleton writes with grace, clarity, and force." In *Thought,* Walter Kendrick points also to Eagleton's "sprightly style and . . . lively sense of humor, rare commodities in his field."

Eagleton's brief but concise *Marxism and Literary Criticism* discusses the author of a work as producer, as well as the relationships between literature and history, form and content, and the writer and commitment. As George Woodcock observes in the *Sewanee Review,* Eagleton perceives Marxist criticism to be "part of a larger body of theoretical analysis that aims to understand *ideologies*—the ideas, values and feelings by which men experience their societies at various times. And certain of those ideas, values and feelings are available to us only in literature." Woodcock praises Eagleton's clear and vigorous writing, adding that he is "brisk and specific, and tells us a great deal . . . about the more important continental European Marxist critics, their books, and their theories." Peter Conrad, however, sees a need for more textual examples in *Marxism and Literary Criticism,* and he refers to it in the *Spectator* as "a case of theory talking about itself." Michael

Wilding similarly finds the book "academic and self-referential," suggesting in *Modern Language Review* that Eagleton approaches Marxist literary criticism "as a subject, rather than as an instrument for revealing other subjects." Nevertheless, noting that the book avoids "pseudo-philosophical jargon," R. Berg-Pan maintains in *World Literature Today* that Eagleton "introduces the neophyte to a very complex set of problems with ease and great skill." Moreover, Woodcock says that Eagleton is "one of the few Marxist theoreticians willing to see Marxism itself not as a self-sufficient doctrine but as part of a spectrum of related doctrines."

According to Jonathan Culler in *Poetics Today*, Eagleton's academic best seller, *Literary Theory: An Introduction*, is a "vigorous articulation of what has become a common theme today in the realm of critical theory: the call for criticism and for literary theory to assume a relationship to history, both by confronting the question of their insertion in social and political history and by taking account of their own history." As John Lucas notes in a *Times Literary Supplement* review of *Against the Grain: Selected Essays, 1975-1985*, Eagleton is "one of a number of critics and theorists on the left who have necessarily drawn attention to improper or at least ideologically-based privileging of certain authors and texts." In *Literary Theory*, Eagleton begins with the observation that "literary criticism is by nature a political act, even (or especially) when it eschews direct political engagement," writes Kendrick, and in this volume, Eagleton connects each school of literary study with the ideology of its particular time and place.

Literary Theory is a "remarkable and important book," writes Charles Sugnet in *American Book Review*, adding that it "does what a good introduction should do—it synthesizes tendencies already in the air and makes them widely accessible in clear prose." Culler believes it to be Eagleton's "best work: provocative, efficient, and for the most part well-informed." Praising the stylistic grace and precision with which Eagleton distills complex theories of literature, critics especially address the book's provocative premise. "A Marxist with wit, Terry Eagleton is magisterial in his deployment of a wide range of ideas, but rarely dispassionate . . . ," says Kellman. "After patient scrutiny of the writings of numerous contemporary critics, Eagleton confesses that he has not come to praise theory but to bury it."

"Under cover of writing a primer on current literary criticism," writes Sugnet, ". . . Eagleton dissolves his own field of inquiry by arguing that there is no such thing as 'literature,' and therefore no 'literary theory.'" As Lennard J. Davis explains in *Nation*, "Literature and the cult of the literary are ideologies that exalt high cultural artifacts like novels, poems and plays over other forms of writing and representation." Eagleton would prefer to replace literature, as it is presently being studied, with the more encompassing discipline of rhetoric as it was practiced from Greek and Roman times until the eighteenth century. "Literature would be, of course, only a branch of this study," summarizes Kendrick. "It would share the field with polemics, journalism, and even the labels on beer cans. . . . A rhetorical approach to literary texts would at least acknowledge one important fact about them that all current critical methodologies tend to ignore: that they are modes of persuasion, designed to elicit some response, even if only complacency, in their readers. That response, like the text which provokes it, must be political in the widest sense."

David Forgacs questions Eagleton's proposal of subsuming literature into a wider study and wonders in *Poetics Today*,

"Who is going to supply the methodologies and the courses, and with what claims to expertise in the field." Among other criticisms, Denis Donoghue faults Eagleton in the *New York Review of Books* for failing to adequately define "history" or how it "proves invulnerable to the irony he so relentlessly directs against other ultimate categories." But in *South Atlantic Quarterly*, Wallace Jackson thinks that Eagleton "de-mythologizes the high-cultural pretensions of literary study in the university, recognizes that in fact such study underwrites the practices of state capitalism, and effectively nullifies whatever radical power literature may have as an instrument of social criticism and social change." Kendrick notes in the *New York Times Book Review* that while *Literary Theory* is intended for a nonacademic audience, "academics will be unable to ignore it. . . . Eagleton's expositions render even the most jargon-ridden of contemporary theories accessible to the ordinary educated person, and the questions posed by *Literary Theory* will have to be answered, either by the theoreticians themselves or by those who validate them by accepting their authority." Kellman, who believes that Eagleton successfully assimilates "a motley crowd of structuralists, feminists, hermeneuticians, psychoanalysts, and deconstructionists to his argument that there are no innocent readings, that every literary experience is shaped by ideology," recommends that it "ought to be read with the same blend of enthusiasm and wariness with which it was written, but it ought to be read by anyone concerned with contemporary theory."

Eagleton's *The Function of Criticism: From the Spectator to Post-Structuralism* augments *Literary Theory* in that it traces the history of English literary criticism "from its earliest recognizable appearance around the turn of the eighteenth century to its present institutionalized form," writes Kendrick in the *Voice Literary Supplement*. It is a "polemical history, not of criticism as such," observes Patrick Parrinder in the *London Review of Books*, "but of the 'critical institution' within which it acquired what Eagleton recognises as social significance." And David Montrose points out in the *New Statesman* that Eagleton "seeks to 'recall criticism to its traditional role'— engagement in cultural politics—from what he considers a position of crisis, where it is narrowly preoccupied with literary texts and estranged from social life through confinement to Academe and 'the literary industry.'" "But the heart of this book," says Christopher Norris in *British Book News*, "is clearly to be found in Eagleton's use of the 'public sphere' as a concept to articulate and clarify the relation between criticism and ideology."

Citing Eagleton's greatest strength as "his tenacity in pursuing a contradiction through its every shifting guise and permutation," Baldick adds, "Of all living Marxist critics, he is most emphatically the dialectician . . . and it is the resulting stress upon contradiction which ensures that his historical placings of writers highlight rather than erase their particular features." Norris suggests, however, that at times the polemics are too forceful and reduce his opponents to "so many shadowy figures in a dance-like routine of ingenious argumentation." But understanding the book to concern "all that is wrong with professionalism," Gary Wihl indicates in *South Atlantic Quarterly* that it "enables us to keep in mind its overriding revolutionary point; it attempts to draw us out of our narrowly sanctifying view of literary history and reminds us of our predicament as critics." Baldick believes that in the "urgency and integrity of this view, Terry Eagleton has marked out a position which further discussions of the state of criticism will have to address if they are to take their historical bearings."

Norris concludes in *Southern Humanities Review* that "Eagleton is a stylist of great resource whose arguments derive much of their power from the presently embattled situation of literary theory." And Parrinder suggests that while "one does not go to Eagleton's works for true judgment, by and large, and it is hard to know what contribution he has made to the emancipation of the masses," he nonetheless maintains that "Eagleton remains one of the most spectacular orators in the park, and English criticism would be a good deal less entertaining without his pamphlets."

AVOCATIONAL INTERESTS: Poetry, theatre.

BIOGRAPHICAL/CRITICAL SOURCES:

PERIODICALS

American Book Review, May-June, 1985.
British Book News, February, 1985.
Commentary, March, 1984.
Comparative Literature, fall, 1986.
French Review, March, 1985.
German Quarterly, summer, 1985.
Library Journal, February 15, 1977.
London Review of Books, February 7, 1985.
Modern Fiction Studies, summer, 1984.
Modern Language Review, January, 1979, April, 1985.
Modern Philology, August, 1985.
Nation, December 24, 1983, January 21, 1984.
New Republic, November 10, 1986.
New Statesman, June 3, 1983, October 5, 1984.
New York Review of Books, July 21, 1983, December 8, 1983, November 6, 1986.
New York Times, April 18, 1986.
New York Times Book Review, September 4, 1983.
Observer (London), March 31, 1985.
Poetics Today, Volume 5, number 1, 1984, Volume 5, number 2, 1985, Volume 7, number 1, 1986.
Sewanee Review, fall, 1978.
South Atlantic Quarterly, summer, 1985, spring, 1986.
Southern Humanities Review, summer, 1985.
Spectator, August 21, 1976.
Thought, December, 1984.
Times Literary Supplement, July 13, 1967, January 23, 1969, August 14, 1970, October 23, 1970, May 20, 1977, November 12, 1982, February 4, 1983, June 10, 1983, November 23, 1984, July 4, 1986.
Victorian Studies, summer, 1985.
Washington Post Book World, October 2, 1983.
World Literature Today, winter, 1977.
Voice Literary Supplement, June, 1983, March, 1985.
Yale Review, summer, 1984.

—*Sketch by Sharon Malinowski*

*   *   *

EAGLETON, Terry
    See EAGLETON, Terence (Francis)

*   *   *

EDDISON, John   1916-

PERSONAL: Born September 7, 1916, in Derbyshire, England; son of Frederick William (a clergyman) and Dorothea (Buchanan-Dunlop) Eddison. *Education:* Trinity College, Cambridge, M.A., 1939.

ADDRESSES: Home—Durham Lodge, Crowborough, Sussex, England.

CAREER: Ordained minister in Church of England, 1939; St. John's, Tunbridge Wells, England, curate, 1939-43; Scripture Union, London, England, traveling secretary, 1942-80. Honorary chaplain to Bishop of Rochester, 1947-59. Member of board of directors of school companies.

MEMBER: National Club, Marylebone Cricket Club.

WRITINGS:

Search Party, Scripture Union, 1960.
The Troubled Mind, Scripture Union, 1963, Concordia, 1972.
Christian Answers about Doctrine, Scripture Union, 1966.
Christian Answers to Contemporary Problems, Scripture Union, 1967.
Who Died Why, Scripture Union, 1970.
God's Frontiers, Scripture Union, 1972.
To Tell You the Truth, Scripture Union, 1972.
It's A Great Life, Scripture Union, 1973.
What Makes a Leader, Scripture Union, 1974.
Understandng Bible Topics, Scripture Union, 1977.
Step by Step, Walters, 1977.
Talking to Children, Walters, 1978.
Your Money and Your Life, Walters, 1979.
What Christians Believe, Hodder & Stoughton, 1981.
Towards Confirmation, Marshall, 1982.
(Editor) *Bash: A Study in Spiritual Power,* Marshall, 1983.
The Bible, Scripture Union, 1984.
The Last Lap, Kingsway, 1986.

*   *   *

EFFINGER, George Alec   1947-
    (John K. Diomede, Susan Doenim)

PERSONAL: Born January 10, 1947, in Cleveland, Ohio; son of George Paul and Ruth (Uray) Effinger. *Education:* Attended Yale University, 1965 and 1969, and New York University, 1968. *Politics:* "Intermittent." *Religion:* "A sort of nervous curiosity."

ADDRESSES: Home—P.O. Box 15183, New Orleans, La. 70175. *Agent*—Richard Curtis, 164 East 64th St., New York, N.Y. 10021.

CAREER: Free-lance writer. Marvel Comic Books, New York, N.Y., writer, 1971.

MEMBER: Authors Guild of the Authors League of America, Science Fiction Writers of America, PEN.

AWARDS, HONORS: The stories "All the Last Wars at Once," "The Aliens Who Knew, I Mean, *Everything,*" and "The City on the Sand" were nominated for the World Science Fiction Convention's Hugo Award; *What Entropy Means to Me* was nominated for the Nebula Award, Science Fiction Writers of America, 1973; "The Aliens Who Knew, I Mean, *Everything*" was nominated for the Nebula Award.

WRITINGS:

SCIENCE FICTION

What Entropy Means to Me, Doubleday, 1972.
Relatives, Harper, 1973.
Mixed Feelings (story collection), Harper, 1974.
(With Gardner Dozois) *Nightmare Blue,* Berkley, 1975.
Irrational Numbers (story collection), Doubleday, 1976.

Those Gentle Voices: A Promethean Romance of the Space-ways, Warner, 1976.

Death in Florence, Doubleday, 1978, published as *Utopia Three*, Playboy Press, 1980.

Dirty Tricks (story collection), Doubleday, 1978.

Heroics, Doubleday, 1979.

The Wolves of Memory, Putnam, 1981.

Idle Pleasures (story collection), Berkley, 1982.

The Nick of Time, Doubleday, 1985.

When Gravity Fails, Arbor House, 1986.

The Bird of Time, Doubleday, 1986.

"PLANET OF THE APES" SERIES

Man, the Fugitive, Award Books, 1974.

Escape to Tomorrow, Award Books, 1975.

Journey into Terror, Award Books, 1975.

Lord of the Apes, Award Books, 1976.

OTHER

Felicia (novel), Berkley, 1976.

Blood Pinball (nonfiction), Dell, 1981.

(Contributor) Sharon Jarvis, editor, *Inside Outer Space*, Ungar, 1985.

Contributor, sometimes under pseudonyms, of over 100 stories to anthologies and magazines, including the *Magazine of Fantasy and Science Fiction* and *Fantastic Stories*.

SIDELIGHTS: George Alec Effinger "was something of a prodigy," Mark Owings maintains in the *Science Fiction and Fantasy Book Review*. While still in his early twenties, Effinger attended the Clarion Science Fiction Writers' Workshop, a leading writing program in the science fiction genre. He was soon selling his short stories to major anthologies and magazines; three of his stories appeared in the first of the Clarion Workshop collections. Effinger also wrote scripts for Marvel Comics for a time.

With his first novel, *What Entropy Means to Me*, published when he was twenty-five, Effinger garnered widespread critical attention in the science fiction field. An ambitious, humorous work interweaving four story lines and parodying everything from medieval romances to science fiction movies, *What Entropy Means to Me* "cannot be easily categorized," as Edward A. Sklepowich states in *Extrapolation*. "The impact of this colorful, meaningful book," Theodore Sturgeon explains in the *New York Times Book Review*, "must be experienced to be fully savored. Read it—then challenge yourself to tell someone else what has happened."

The novel is set on the planet of Home and concerns a quest by the eldest son of the ruling family to find his lost father. The son, Dore, follows the course of the planet's River of Life as he searches. Because Dore does not return from his journey, the remaining family members do not know what has befallen him. It is left to the younger son, Seyt, to chronicle the journey his brother has made, a journey that is an unsolved mystery. Seyt borrows from old adventure stories, epics, and fairy tales to construct a plausible account of his brother's fate. Other family members read and criticize the manuscript as it is being written and Seyt revises his story or incorporates their suggestions as he sees fit. His creative efforts eventually displease his family, however. His speculations as to the deeper meanings of Dore's journey raise a religious controversy which leads to Seyt's banishment from the family castle and the beginning of his own journey into the world. Speaking to the *Library Journal* about the novel, Effinger claims that it is "an

attempt to weld successfully the episodic novel with the more organic sort. On another level I have tried to take a classic form—the novel of moral education—and fill it with astoundingly unconventional characters, to see what happens to both morals *and* education."

Critical reaction to the novel focused on Effinger's humorous commentary on artistic creation. "The openly allegorical narrative," Carol M. Ward explains in the *Dictionary of Literary Biography*, "explores the creative process: the artist's experience of reality, the transformation of raw materials through his imagination, the influence of criticism on his work, and the subsequent effect of his artistic creation upon life itself." "In *What Entropy Means to Me*," Sklepowich argues, "[Effinger] parodies the creative act itself and the overworked conventions of the epic tale, fantasy, science fiction, and the comic book, particularly certain character types and plot situations, contriving a fascinating piece of innovative fiction."

Effinger's subsequent books have earned him a growing reputation in the science fiction field. His *Death in Florence*, for example, concerns a utopian project in which a large area of central Europe is emptied of its population so that a select group of colonists can build a new society. The story becomes an ironic examination of religious faith when the colonists grow disillusioned with the project's founder but embrace the ideals that inspire him. Ward praises the "deft characterizations, the allegorical implications of the narrative, the skillful orchestration of the plots, and the use of black humor."

Perhaps the most discussed characteristics of Effinger's work have been his extensive use of allusions and his ever-present irony. In a review of *The Bird of Time* for the *New York Times Book Review*, Gerald Jonas notes that Effinger "has peppered his story with allusions to everything from the poetry of Emily Dickinson to the science fiction of the 1950's, from quantum mechanics to the French deconstructionists." Speaking of "Heartstop," included in the *Idle Pleasures* collection, Alexander Butrym of *Fantasy Review* believes that Effinger's wide-ranging allusions make it into "a rich and multidimensional story." Butrym defines Effinger as "a witty, clever, and interesting writer who communicates his vision with strong irony." Gregory Feeley of the *Washington Post Book World* believes that Effinger is "best known for ironic and witty novels."

Effinger is often labeled a surrealist, a term he does not believe describes him accurately. Speaking to James Gunn in *Fantasy Newsletter*, Effinger explains his approach to writing as "using the traditional materials of science fiction . . . in a manner that is surreal. But beyond that, I have tried to develop an exploration of character, of motivation, and of response to crisis that is beyond the scope of the surreal story." Effinger's stories, a critic for the *New York Times Book Review* comments, "belong to a world that has been shaped not only by Asimov and Heinlein but also by Borges, Pynchon and Barthelme." Sklepowich also sees Effinger's affinity with contemporary experimental writers. He places Effinger in the same company as "Borges, Barth, Barthleme, Coover, and other writers of experimental fiction with an orientation toward fantasy." Ward concludes that Effinger "is one of the most promising and prolific of the new breed of contemporary writers of speculative fiction."

"When I first began to write," Effinger explains to *CA*, "seeing one of my stories in a magazine or one of my books on a shelf in a store was exciting. Unfortunately, that excitement wanes, although the excitement of the creative act itself never diminishes. Now my own gratification must come from somewhere else. I am glad, therefore, that I have many goals yet una-chieved; I cannot imagine being able to write merely for the checks, as if writing were nothing more than a job. Writing is a joy, but the source of the joy is internal, now. The visible results mean less to me: the physical books, the money deposited in the bank, the reviews. I write for fun and for a kind of self-challenge. I dare myself to develop a difficult idea. I do not know about my popularity among critics and readers, but as long as I get a kick out of watching my struggling characters, then I will stay at the typewriter. When that thrill ends, I think I will find something else to do. Maybe I'll be a professional bowler.''

BIOGRAPHICAL/CRITICAL SOURCES:

BOOKS

Dictionary of Literary Biography, Volume VIII: *Twentieth-Century American Science Fiction Writers*, Gale, 1981.

PERIODICALS

Booklist, January 1, 1983.
Extrapolation, May, 1977.
Fantasy Newsletter, January, 1982.
Fantasy Review, May, 1984.
Foundation, March, 1977.
Library Journal, June 15, 1972.
Magazine of Fantasy and Science Fiction, February, 1973.
New Orleans Times-Picayune, August 1, 1982.
New York Times Book Review, September 3, 1972, December 23, 1973, April 25, 1976, November 28, 1976, June 8, 1986.
Science Fiction and Fantasy Book Review, March, 1982.
Science Fiction Review, May, 1980, November, 1981.
Washington Post Book World, January 24, 1982, July 28, 1985, February 22, 1987.

—*Sketch by Thomas Wiloch*

* * *

EGGERT, James Edward   1943-
  (Jim Eggert)

PERSONAL: Born February 3, 1943, in Chicago, Ill.; son of Robert J. (an economist and forecaster) and Elizabeth (Bauer) Eggert; married Patricia Stock (a journalist), May 8, 1971; children: Anthony, Leslie. *Education:* Lawrence University, B.A., 1967; Michigan State University, M.A., 1968. *Religion:* Society of Friends (Quakers).

ADDRESSES: Home—Route 3, Box 264, Colfax, Wis. 54730. *Office*—Department of Social Sciences, University of Wisconsin—Stout, Menomonie, Wis. 54751.

CAREER: U.S. Peace Corps, Washington, D.C., volunteer worker in Kenya, 1964-66; University of Wisconsin—Stout, Menomonie, instructor, 1968-72, assistant professor, 1971-79, associate professor of social sciences, 1980—.

MEMBER: Thoreau Society, Nature Conservancy, Wisconsin Association of Environmental Educators.

WRITINGS—Under name Jim Eggert:

(With wife, Pat Eggert) *The No-Mortgage Home*, Bergamot Press, 1973.
What Is Economics?, William Kaufmann, 1977, revised edition, 1987.
Investigating Microeconomics, William Kaufmann, 1979.

Low-Cost Earth Shelters, Stackpole, 1982.
Invitation to Economics, William Kaufmann, 1984.
Milton Friedman, Thoreau, and Grandfather Pine, Winston-Derek, 1986.

Contributor to magazines, including *Co-Evolution Quarterly, Jump River Review, Craft Connection, Craft Report,* and *School Shop.*

WORK IN PROGRESS: Additional essays and possibly a book bridging economics with ecology.

SIDELIGHTS: In *What Is Economics?*, Jim Eggert explores fundamental economic questions using diagrams, photographs, cartoons, and examples from everyday life. In addition, he presents environmental, political, and social issues that directly relate to basic economic principles. The primer has been adopted for class use in more than one hundred fifty colleges and universities across the country. More recently, in *Milton Friedman, Thoreau, and Grandfather Pine*, Eggert makes his first attempt, through essays and poetry, to bridge standard economic notions with the values of ecology.

AVOCATIONAL INTERESTS: High jumping, music, natural history.

* * *

EGGERT, Jim
  See EGGERT, James Edward

* * *

ELLIOTT, Emory   1942-

PERSONAL: Born October 30, 1942, in Baltimore, Md.; son of Emory Bernard and Virginia Louise (Ulbrick) Elliott; married Georgia Ann Carroll (an English instructor), May 14, 1966; children: Scott, Mark, Matthew, Laura, Constance. *Education:* Loyola College, Baltimore, Md., A.B., 1964; Bowling Green State University, M.A., 1966; University of Illinois, Ph.D., 1972.

ADDRESSES: Home—214 Western Way, Princeton, N.J. 08540. *Office*—Department of English, Princeton University, 22 McCosh, Princeton, N.J. 08540.

CAREER: Cameron State College, Lawton, Okla., part-time instructor in English, 1967; U.S. Military Academy, West Point, N.Y., instructor in English, 1968-69; Princeton University, Princeton, N.J., assistant professor, 1972-77, associate professor, 1977-81, professor of English, 1981—, Richard Stockton Bicentennial Preceptor, 1975-78, director of undergraduate studies in English, and director of American Studies Program, 1977—, master, Lee Butler College, 1982-86, chairman of English department, 1987—. Faculty member, Salzburg Seminar, 1985; visiting lecturer in China, France, Italy, Germany, Brazil, Hungary, and Switzerland. Educational consultant, Western Electric Corp., 1974-79; writing consultant, Bell Laboratories, 1975-79, RCA Corp., 1980-81. *Military service:* U.S. Army, 1966-69; became captain.

MEMBER: Modern Language Association of America, American Studies Association, American Society for Eighteenth-Century Studies.

AWARDS, HONORS: Woodrow Wilson fellowship, 1971-72; American Council of Learned Societies fellowship, summer, 1973; Guggenheim fellowship, 1976-77; fellow, National Humanities Center, 1979-80; senior fellow, National Endowment for the Humanities, 1986-87.

WRITINGS:

Power and the Pulpit in Puritan New England, Princeton University Press, 1975.

(Editor) Puritan Influences in American Literature, University of Illinois Press, 1979.

Revolutionary Writer: Literature and Authority in the New Republic, 1725-1910, Oxford University Press, 1982.

(Editor) Dictionary of Literary Biography, Gale, Volume XXIV: American Colonial Writers, 1606-1734, 1984, Volume XXXI: American Colonial Writers, 1735-1781, 1984, Volume XXXVII: American Writers of the Early Republic, 1985.

General editor of Columbia Literary History of the United States, 1987. Series editor of The American Novel, Cambridge University Press, and Penn Studies in Contemporary American Fiction.

WORK IN PROGRESS: History and Fiction in America.

SIDELIGHTS: Emory Elliott told CA: "The rise of a theoretically informed new historical criticism is a very exciting development for literary study."

*   *   *

EPSTEIN, Leslie   1938-

PERSONAL: Born May 4, 1938, in Los Angeles, Calif.; son of Philip (a screenwriter) and Lillian (Targen) Epstein; married Ilene Gradman, November 1, 1969; children: Anya, Paul and Theo (twins). Education: Yale University, B.A., 1960, graduate study, 1963-65, D.F.A., 1967; Oxford University, diploma, 1962; University of California, Los Angeles, M.A., 1963.

ADDRESSES: Office—Creative Writing Program, College of Liberal Arts, Boston University, 236 Bay State Rd., Boston, Mass. 02215. Agent—Lois Wallace, Wallace, Aitken & Shiel, Inc., 118 East 61st St., New York, N.Y. 10024.

CAREER: Queens College of the City University of New York, Flushing, N.Y., lecturer, 1965-67, assistant professor, 1968-70, associate professor, 1970-75, professor of English, beginning 1976; Boston University, Boston, Mass., currently director of Creative Writing Program.

MEMBER: International PEN.

AWARDS, HONORS: Rhodes scholarship, 1960-62; National Endowment for the Arts grant, 1972; Fulbright fellowship, 1972-73; CAPS grant, 1976-77; Guggenheim fellowship, 1977-78; Most Distinguished Work of Fiction nomination from the National Book Critics Circle, 1979, and American Library Association Notable Book citation, 1980, both for King of the Jews: A Novel of the Holocaust.

WRITINGS:

NOVELS

P. D. Kimerakov, Little, Brown, 1975.
King of the Jews: A Novel of the Holocaust, Coward, 1979.
Regina, Coward, 1982.

SHORT STORIES

The Steinway Quintet Plus Four, Little, Brown, 1976.
Goldkorn Tales, Dutton, 1985.

OTHER

Contributor of stories, articles, and reviews to periodicals, including Atlantic Monthly, Esquire, Nation, Antaeus, Playboy, and Antioch Review.

SIDELIGHTS: "If writers got gold stars for the risks they took, Leslie Epstein would get a handful," writes Katha Pollitt in the New York Times Book Review. Epstein's fiction tackles weighty themes with light humor. His first novel, P. D. Kimerakov, is a satire of Cold War tensions between the U.S.S.R. and the United States. David Bromwich praises the skillful characterizations and elegant style found in P. D. Kimerakov, but finds the humor somewhat forced and therefore unsuccessful. Bromwich notes in the New York Times Book Review that "this defect may be a sign of Leslie Epstein's honesty: he cannot hide the essential grimness of this particular corner of history." The reviewer concludes that while Epstein's tone is at odds with his subject, "one senses in him what is rare enough at any time: the presence of a sly, appealing, grave and humorous talent."

Epstein's next publication was a collection of short fiction, The Steinway Quintet Plus Four. The humor in the story "The Steinway Quintet" comes through the voice of its narrator, Lieb Goldkorn. Called "a truly enchanting character" by the New York Times's Michiko Kakutani, Lieb Goldkorn personifies the dignified Jewish culture that once inhabited New York City's lower east side. He is the pianist in a quintet that plays in the Steinway Restaurant—"once a favorite haunt of Sarah Bernhardt and Einstein, but now the lonely relic of a vanished Jewish community," according to Pollitt. Epstein contrasts that faded culture with New York's contemporary atmosphere of violence when two young street toughs, armed and wired on drugs, terrorize the Steinway Restaurant and hold its customers and employees hostage for a ridiculous ransom. Throughout the ordeal, Goldkorn remains "at once shrewd and wide-eyed, . . . the perpetual optimist," writes Pollitt. Her review highlights the story's deft humor, but Kakutani emphasizes that the author makes a powerful statement on his deeper theme as well: "In its juxtaposition of Old World culture and contemporary violence, ['The Steinway Quintet' is] an organic and wholly complete work of art." Lieb Goldkorn is also featured in a later story collection entitled Goldkorn Tales. Kakutani deems this volume an "energetic, densely patterned" work, one which illuminates "revenge and forgiveness and the stunning tricks that life can play on its victims."

Epstein's most controversial work to date has been his 1979 novel King of the Jews. In it, he examines the role that some European Jews played in betraying their own people to the Nazis. The story focuses on the leader of the Judenrat, or governing council of elders, in the ghetto of a Polish industrial city. The Nazis ordered the establishment of Judenrat to control the population they had forced into the ghettos; the councils' duties eventually included drawing up lists of passengers for the trains to the death camps. Forced to choose between their people and the Nazis, Judenrat leaders knew that if they did not supply the required quotas for the trains, the entire ghetto might be destroyed in one stroke. The ambiguity of this position led at least one Judenrat leader to take his own life.

Epstein's protagonist in King of the Jews is based on Mordecai Chaim Rumkowski, the real-life elder of the ghetto in Lodz, Poland. Rumkowski is notorious for having relished the power of his position. Like him, the fictional Isaiah Chaim Trumpelman eagerly volunteers for the position of council elder. Then he exploits his privileges, riding a limousine or on a white stallion, even having his picture printed on the currency and stamps used in the ghetto. Many critics praise Epstein's characterization of Trumpelman for its depth. The man is depicted in larger-than-life style as someone who enjoyed his role; yet Epstein also shows the Elder's apparently real concern for orphans, his uncertainties, and the rationalizations that allowed him to continue in his position. For example, when the grisly destination of the trains is made clear to him, he justifies his cooperation with the Nazis, saying that by sending ten Jews away, he is saving one hundred others. He even begins to think of himself as a savior—"the King of the Jews."

Robert Alter states in the *New York Times Book Review* that until *King of the Jews* was published, "no work of fiction [had] opened up so fully the unbearable moral dilemma in which the Judenrat members found themselves, governing with a pistol at their heads, administering the processes of death, corrupted of course by their awful power, yet trying to preserve life when there was no real way to preserve it." *Washington Post Book World* contributor Michael Kernan notes the author's original approach to his material: "Writing in the manner of the old Jewish storytellers, Epstein dares to be funny. It is the mordant humor that has always been the visible rage of those who are forbidden to show their rage. . . . History has been turned into, not merely fiction, but myth. . . . A Yiddish folktale."

That approach drew objections from other reviewers. Irving Abrahamson protests in the *Chicago Tribune Book World* that *King of the Jews* treats the Holocaust so lightly as to be offensive: "*King of the Jews* is a one-dimensional piece, failing utterly to explore the complex historical, philosophical, theological implications of the greatest crime in history. The spectacle of a government applying resources and power to annihilate a defenseless, isolated, and abandoned people, the incredible organization of a society and a culture to the mass production of death *demand* greater analysis and imagination than one can find here. . . . *King of the Jews* must be accounted a failure in concept, taste, and execution." Other reviewers,

however, identify the ironic humor in Epstein's writing as part of a classic tradition. Robert Alter calls it "a kind of grim moral fable that often reminds one of the fantastic yet profoundly historical narrative inventions that Kafka produced . . . or Nabokov." Kernan concludes that *King of the Jews* "may prove the most successful of all [novels about the Holocaust] . . . because it manages, incredibly, to place the experience in the context of written Jewish tradition."

King of the Jews has been published in many foreign languages.

BIOGRAPHICAL/CRITICAL SOURCES:

BOOKS

Contemporary Literary Criticism, Volume XXVII, Gale, 1984.

PERIODICALS

Best Sellers, August, 1975.
Chicago Tribune Book World, February 25, 1979.
Commentary, May, 1979.
Los Angeles Times, February 17, 1983, April 23, 1985.
New Republic, March 10, 1979.
Newsweek, January 29, 1979.
New York Times, February 7, 1979, April 3, 1985.
New York Times Book Review, August 10, 1975, December 12, 1976, February 4, 1979, May 5, 1979, October 10, 1982, November 21, 1982, April 7, 1985.
Publishers Weekly, January 8, 1979.
Saturday Review, March 31, 1979.
Village Voice, February 19, 1979, January 18, 1983.
Washington Post, March 11, 1979, January 1, 1983.
Washington Post Book World, March 20, 1985.
Yale Review, October, 1979.†

—Sketch by Joan Goldsworthy

F

FAELTEN, Sharon 1950-

PERSONAL: Born March 16, 1950, in Wilson Borough, Pa.; daughter of Joseph Edward (an engineer) and Marie (a music teacher; maiden name, Sabatine) Policelli; married John Faelten (a survey crew chief), April 13, 1974. *Education:* Grove City College, B.A., 1972; attended Cedar Crest College, 1979-81.

ADDRESSES: Office—Rodale Press, Inc., 33 East Minor St., Emmaus, Pa. 18098.

CAREER: Worked in sales, restaurants, and a health-care agency on Cape Cod, Mass., 1972-77; Rodale Press, Inc., Emmaus, Pa., associate editor, 1977-83, editor, 1983—.

WRITINGS:

Recipes for Natural Slenderness, Rodale Press, 1979.
(With Rebecca Christian, Jim Nechas, and Emrika Padus) *The Prevention Guide to Surgery and Its Alternatives,* Rodale Press, 1980.
The Complete Book of Minerals for Health, Rodale Press, 1981.
The Allergy Self-Help Book, Rodale Press, 1983.
A Lifetime of Beauty, Rodale Press, 1985.
The Complete Book of Stress Reduction, in press.

Contributor to *Prevention, Runner's World, Practical Homeowner, Cosmopolitan, Children,* and *Reader's Digest.*

SIDELIGHTS: Sharon Faelten told *CA:* "Health and fitness are challenging topics for journalists. Medical care is more complex than ever. That can frighten or confuse the public. So I try to write in a compelling yet friendly and humorous manner. Health journalism must be lively as well as clear and accurate, or the reader never goes beyond the first paragraph. I regard my books as links between people in the medical profession and the reading public."

* * *

FANDEL, John 1925-

PERSONAL: Born September 10, 1925, in Yonkers, N.Y.; son of John Peter and Ivy (Ekblom) Fandel. *Education:* Trinity College, Hartford, Conn., A.B., 1948; graduate study at Yale University, 1948-49, and Fordham University, 1951-52; Middlebury College, A.M., 1952. *Religion:* Roman Catholic.

ADDRESSES: Home—609 Palmer Rd., Yonkers, N.Y. 10701. *Office*—Department of English, Manhattan College, Bronx, N.Y. 10471.

CAREER: University of Notre Dame, Notre Dame, Ind., instructor in English, 1949-51; Lawrence College (now University), Appleton, Wis., visiting lecturer in English, 1952-53; Manhattan College, Bronx, N.Y., 1958—, began as lecturer, became professor of English. *Military service:* U.S. Naval Reserve, active duty, 1943-46.

MEMBER: International P.E.N., Poetry Society of America, Phi Beta Kappa.

WRITINGS:

POETRY

The World I Wake, Nordic Press, 1958.
Testament, Sheed, 1959.
Body of Earth, Roth, 1972.
How a Cold Moon Becomes a Rose and Other Transformations, Manhattan College, 1973.
The Deserted Greenhouse, Roth, 1974.
God's Breath in Man, Roth, 1977.
The Small Event, Halfpenny Press, 1977.
Out of Our Blue, Sparrow Press, 1977.
Dry Pumice, Halfpenny Press, 1978.
Bach and a Catbird and Others, Roth, 1978.
A Midnight Question, The Sign Press, 1982.
A Morning After, Forward Movement, 1984.

OTHER

Contributor to magazines. Poetry editor of *Commonweal.*

* * *

FANTE, John (Thomas) 1911-1983

PERSONAL: Born April 8, 1911, in Denver, Colo.; died May 8, 1983, in Woodland Hills, Calif.; son of Nicholas Peter and Mary (Capolungo) Fante; married Joyce H. Smart (a poet), July 31, 1937; children: Nicholas, Daniel, Victoria, James. *Education:* Attended University of Colorado and Long Beach Junior College.

CAREER: Writer. Worked in a cannery, and as a hotel clerk, stevedore, and grocery clerk; worked for Office of War Information during World War II.

AWARDS, HONORS: Academy Award nomination, 1957, for "Full of Life"; National Catholic Theatre Drama Award, 1964.

WRITINGS:

NOVELS

Wait until Spring, Bandini, Stackpole, 1938, reprinted, Black Sparrow Press, 1983.

Ask the Dust, Stackpole, 1939, reprinted, with new preface by Charles Bukowski, Black Sparrow Press, 1980.

Full of Life (also see below), Little, Brown, 1952, reprinted, Black Sparrow Press, 1987.

The Brotherhood of the Grape, Houghton, 1977.

Dreams from Bunker Hill, Black Sparrow Press, 1982.

1933 Was a Bad Year, Black Sparrow Press, 1985.

The Road to Los Angeles, Black Sparrow Press, 1985.

SCREENPLAYS

(With Ross B. Wills) "East of the River," Warner Bros., 1940.

(With Lynn Root and Frank Fenton) "The Golden Fleecing," Metro-Goldwyn-Mayer, 1940.

(With Herbert Kline) "Youth Runs Wild," RKO, 1944.

(With Jack Leonard) "My Man and I," Metro-Goldwyn-Mayer, 1952.

"Full of Life" (based on novel of same title), Columbia, 1957.

(With Daniel Fuchs and Sonya Levien) "Jeanne Eagles," Columbia, 1957.

(With Edmund Morris) "Walk on the Wild Side," Columbia, 1962.

(With Joseph Petracca) "The Reluctant Saint," Davis-Royal Films International, 1962.

(With Joseph Cavelli and William Wood) "My Six Loves," Paramount, 1963.

"Maya," Metro-Goldwyn-Mayer, 1966.

Also author of unproduced screenplays, including "The Roses" and "The Fish Don't Bite."

OTHER

Dago Red (story collection), Viking, 1940.

(With Rudolph Borchert) *Bravo, Burro!* (juvenile), Hawthorn, 1970.

The Wine of Youth: Selected Stories of John Fante, Black Sparrow Press, 1985.

West of Rome (two novellas), Black Sparrow Press, 1986.

Contributor of stories to *American Mercury, Virginia Quarterly Review, Atlantic, Good Housekeeping, Saturday Evening Post, Scribner's, Collier's,* and other publications.

SIDELIGHTS: In a series of four novels published over as many decades, John Fante "chronicled the saga of a young poet moving to professional and personal maturity in the Los Angeles of the 1930s," as Burt A. Folkart wrote in the *Los Angeles Times.* The protagonist of the series, Arturo Bandini, is an Italian-American who dreams of becoming a famous writer. But to achieve this dream, he must transcend his troubled family life. The novels about Bandini's efforts to become a success comprise, Ben Pleasants stated in the *Los Angeles Times Book Review,* "a magnificent family chronicle." Fante was also known for his screenplays, especially "Full of Life," "Jeanne Eagles," "The Reluctant Saint," and "Walk on the Wild Side," and for his many short stories.

Born in Colorado to an immigrant Italian family, Fante left for Los Angeles in the early 1930s, intent on becoming a successful writer. After living in near-poverty for a time, Fante found success with his short stories. His first story was published in 1932 in H. L. Mencken's legendary *American Mercury* magazine. Over the next decade, Mencken encouraged the young writer in his creative efforts and published a number of his stories. Mencken also helped Fante to find a publisher for his first novel and suggested that he try his hand at screenwriting. Because of Mencken's work on his behalf Fante called him, in a letter quoted by Michael Moreau of the *Los Angeles Times Magazine,* "the most vital and inspiring man in my life."

Fante's standing as a writer was greatly enhanced with the appearance of his first novel, *Wait until Spring, Bandini,* published in 1938. In this book Fante began the story of Arturo Bandini, a young Italian-American from Colorado who dreams of becoming a writer. The parallels between Bandini and Fante are many. As Gerald Mangan noted in the *Times Literary Supplement,* Bandini "shares most of the given facts of Fante's own early life. The son of poor Italian-Catholic parents in small-town Colorado, whose burning ambitions lead him to the bright lights of Los Angeles, Bandini is clearly the *alter ego* in what amounts to [an] autobiography." Edward M. White, writing in the *Los Angeles Times Book Review,* described *Wait until Spring, Bandini* as "an affecting and unified book portraying the painful family situation of Arturo Bandini, a young adolescent obviously modeled after the author." Mangan believed that *Wait until Spring, Bandini* was "a lucid and strikingly unsentimental account of a close-knit family struggling, against the odds, to survive hard times with dignity; and its most impressive achievement is the central portrait of [Bandini's] parents." Mangan concluded that the novel "proved to be [Fante's] masterpiece."

Arturo Bandini reappeared the following year in *Ask the Dust,* Fante's second novel. The book recounts Bandini's efforts to earn a living as a writer in Los Angeles, and tells of his unhappy love affair with a Mexican waitress. Mencken also appears in the story, disguised as the character J. C. Hackmuth, a magazine editor who befriends the struggling Bandini. Writing in the *Dictionary of Literary Biography Yearbook,* Michael Mullen listed the book's strongest points as "the wry portrait of Bandini, who believes himself a great but undiscovered writer whose books will one day be found on library shelves, and the portrait of Los Angeles, [which together] make the novel more than just another book about an aspiring writer." Wayne Warga of the *Los Angeles Times* found that "Bandini isn't the only strong character in 'Ask the Dust.' Los Angeles is another, and it is Fante's/Bandini's commentary on this city, its people and its customs which helps to make this such a remarkable book." Iris Barry of *Books* felt that *Ask the Dust* "carries considerable impact and, despite so much that is painful, contemptible, ugly in its subject matter, it leaves the reader in a state of speculation and interest." Although objecting to some of the book's subject matter, H. L. Binsse of *Commonweal* called *Ask the Dust* "quite an extraordinary piece of work."

Ask the Dust sold only a few copies when first published, partly because its publisher, Stackpole, was involved in expensive litigation that year and could not afford to give the book a proper advertising budget. But *Ask the Dust* was the Fante book "around which a cult has formed," as Warga explained. And Pleasants noted that "Carey McWilliams, Charles Bukowski and [Robert] Towne think it one of the greatest novels published in America." The book's cult popularity led in 1980 to its reprinting by Black Sparrow Press, an event which finally brought it to the attention of a much larger audience. Fante was happy with the acclaim his book belatedly received. "What pleases me most," he told Warga, "is to be hearing from so many people and to know the damn thing has stood up to the test of time."

The adventures of Arturo Bandini continued in *Dreams from Bunker Hill*, published in 1982, and in the posthumously published *The Road to Los Angeles*. *Dreams from Bunker Hill* was dictated by Fante to his wife, Joyce. Fante went blind in 1978 due to diabetes and was unable to type the manuscript himself. The book is a loosely plotted novel in which Bandini, now working as a screenwriter, returns home to Colorado for a visit. The frustrations of writing for Hollywood are the novel's special focus. *Dreams from Bunker Hill*, Elaine Kendal of the *Los Angeles Times* believed, "is less structured than the [other Bandini] novels, but suffused with the same idiosyncratic blend of gritty vitality and good-humored irony." The novel's portrait of a disenchanted film writer moved Mangan to write that "its surface wryness does not distract us from the sense that it crystallizes a few decades of frustration."

The Road to Los Angeles deals with an earlier period in Bandini's career when, as White stated, he was "a late adolescent, rebellious and outrageous, just out of school, trying to make it in a Los Angeles that offers no way to reach the American dream." Bandini's delusions of being a great writer are mocked and satirized in the book. "The comedy," Mangan reported, "is Quixotic in the truest sense, but it alternates subtly with the darker side of [Bandini's] megalomania." The first three Bandini novels together form what Kendal described as a "substantial, sensitive and ironic triad." Mangan believed that "Bandini is a magnificent creation."

Among Fante's novels not concerned with the Arturo Bandini character, *Full of Life* was his most successful. It is the story of his wife's first pregnancy and her conversion to Catholicism, and the characters in the novel share the real names of Fante and his wife. The book was first marketed, in fact, as nonfiction. Fante's ability to blend a lighthearted account of the trials and joys of young expectant parents with a more serious religious theme was noted by several reviewers. P. M. Pasinetti of *Saturday Review*, for example, explained that Fante, "as he avoids the horrors of cuteness in dealing with his comic effects, avoids pretentiousness in handling his serious theme." Writing in the *New York Herald Tribune Book Review*, Joanna Spencer was "surprised that the significant religious experience should have been coupled with such a lighthearted, charming account of pregnancy." *Full of Life* was condensed by the *Reader's Digest*, translated into German and Italian, and was filmed in 1957. Fante wrote the screen adaptation of his novel, for which he received an Academy Award nomination.

Fante's work as a screenwriter had begun in 1940 after his first three books proved to be financial failures. As he explained in *Full of Life*, "First book sold 2300 copies. Second book sold 4800 copies. Third book sold 2100 copies. But they don't ask for royalty statements in the picture business. If you have what they want at the moment they pay you, and pay you well." For three decades Fante wrote for the screen, garnering credits for such popular films as "Jeanne Eagles," "The Reluctant Saint," "My Six Loves," and "Walk on the Wild Side." White claimed that Fante had "developed a modest following with his Depression-era novels and stories, although the last years of his life were spent in prosperous obscurity as a screenwriter." But John Martin tells Warga that Fante was respected in the film community. He was, Martin stated, "admired for the fact he's done what most screenwriters would like to do. He's stayed home and written novels. In some professions this would cause envy, but not among screenwriters. From them such a writer elicits praise."

BIOGRAPHICAL/CRITICAL SOURCES:

BOOKS

Dictionary of Literary Biography Yearbook, 1983, Gale, 1984.
Fante, John, *Full of Life*, Little, Brown, 1952, reprinted, Black Sparrow Press, 1987.
Peragallo, Olga, *Italian-American Authors and Their Contributions to American Literature*, S. F. Vanni, 1949.

PERIODICALS

Atlantic, December, 1939.
Books, November 12, 1939.
Common Ground, spring, 1941.
Commonweal, December 1, 1939, May 16, 1952.
Los Angeles Times, March 5, 1980, March 23, 1982.
Los Angeles Times Book Review, July 8, 1979, March 24, 1985, November 17, 1985, March 9, 1986, November 30, 1986.
Los Angeles Times Magazine, April 26, 1987.
New Yorker, November 11, 1939, June 2, 1986.
New York Herald Tribune Book Review, April 27, 1952.
New York Times, November 19, 1939, June 15, 1952.
New York Times Book Review, March 6, 1977.
San Francisco Chronicle, March 9, 1941.
Saturday Review, April 26, 1952.
Saturday Review of Literature, November 25, 1939.
Time, October 7, 1940.
Times Literary Supplement, March 20, 1987.

OBITUARIES:

PERIODICALS

Chicago Tribune, May 14, 1983.
Los Angeles Times, May 12, 1983.
Newsweek, May 23, 1983.
New York Times, May 13, 1983.
Washington Post, May 13, 1983.†

—*Sketch by Thomas Wiloch*

*   *   *

FARRELL, Michael 1944-

PERSONAL: Born May 15, 1944, in County Derry, Northern Ireland; son of Thomas and Helena (O'Reilly) Farrell; married Orla O'Hare, 1964; children: Sean. *Education:* Queen's University, Belfast, Northern Ireland, B.A., 1967; University of Strathclyde, graduate study, 1967-68. *Politics:* "Marxist (Trotskyist)." *Religion:* None.

ADDRESSES: Home—20 Trench Ave., Belfast II, Northern Ireland. *Office*—Connolly Bookshop, Avoca Park, Anderstown, Belfast, Northern Ireland.

CAREER: Belfast College of Technology, Belfast, Northern Ireland, teacher of history and general studies, 1968—. Founding member and member of central committee of Peoples Democracy ("a Marxist group dedicated to achieving a united Socialist Ireland").

WRITINGS:

The Struggle in the North, Pluto Press, 1970.

Northern Ireland, the Orange State (political history from a socialist viewpoint), Urizen, 1976.

The Poor Law and the Workhouse in Belfast, 1838-1948, Public Record Office of Northern Ireland, 1978.

(Editor with Vincent Browne) *The Magill Book of Irish Politics*, Magill Publications, 1981.

Thy Tears Might Cease, Arena Books, 1984.

Sheltering the Fugitive? The Extradition of Irish Political Offenders, Mercier Press, 1985.

Author of political pamphlets. Contributor to magazines. Editor of *Unfree Citizen*, 1976—.

WORK IN PROGRESS: Research on the links between British forces and paramilitary armed gangs during the establishment of Northern Ireland, 1920-25.

SIDELIGHTS: Michael Farrell writes that he was raised in a Roman Catholic family in rural Northern Ireland and studied briefly for the priesthood. He was prominent in the leadership of the civil rights struggle in Northern Ireland between 1968 and 1970. He stood for Parliament against Ian Paisley. He was jailed without benefit of trial in 1971 and again in 1973, but was released after a thirty-five-day hunger strike. He writes: ''I have become steadily more committed to Marxism as I have seen the naked violence used by the world's oldest democracy (Britain) in Northern Ireland. My main interest is the struggle of mankind to be free.''

*   *   *

FEIWEL, George R(ichard) 1929-

PERSONAL: Born July 4, 1929, in Cracow, Poland; son of Herman (a lawyer) and Resia (Wang) Feiwel; married Ida Rieger (a research associate), May 19, 1957. *Education:* McGill University, B.Com., 1955, M.A., 1961, Ph.D., 1963; graduate study at University of California, Berkeley, 1961-62.

ADDRESSES: Home—5507 Holston Hills Rd., Knoxville, Tenn. 37914-5133. *Office*—Department of Economics, University of Tennessee, Knoxville, Tenn. 37916.

CAREER: University of Alberta, Edmonton, associate professor of economics, 1962-66; University of Tennessee, Knoxville, professor, 1966-76, alumni distinguished service professor of economics, 1977—. Visiting faculty member, Cambridge University, 1965, 1969, 1972; research associate, Harvard University, 1966, 1967, 1971, 1975, Clare Hall, Cambridge, England, 1972, University of California, Berkeley, 1976, 1977; visiting professor, Instituto di Studi per lo Sviluppo Economico, 1969, 1970, University of Stockholm, 1973, University of California, Berkeley, 1977, 1979, Harvard University, 1978, 1984, 1985, University of California, Davis, 1982. Chancellor's research scholar, University of Tennessee, 1976. Member of American Economic Association's search committee for editors of *American Economic Review* and *Journal of Economic Literature*, 1977-78.

MEMBER: American Economic Association.

AWARDS, HONORS: Guggenheim fellow, 1968-69; fellowships and grants from American Council of Learned Societies, Social Science Research Council, American Philosophical Society, Canada Council, and National Science Foundation; elected Phi Kappa Phi university lecturer and macebearer, University of Tennessee, 1970-71; the two-volume work *Industrialization and Planning under Polish Socialism* was selected by *Choice* as an outstanding book for 1972.

WRITINGS:

The Economics of a Socialist Enterprise: A Case Study of the Polish Firm, Praeger, 1965.

The Soviet Quest for Economic Efficiency: Issues, Controversies and Reforms, Praeger, 1967, expanded and updated edition, 1972.

New Economic Patterns in Czechoslovakia: The Impact of Growth, Planning, and the Market, Praeger, 1968.

(Editor) *New Currents in Soviet-Type Economies: A Reader*, International Textbook Co., 1968.

(Contributor) G. Franco, editor, *Studi sulle politiche monetarie le creditizie per lo sviluppo economico*, Edizioni Cedam, 1970.

Industrialization and Planning under Polish Socialism, Volume I: *Poland's Industrialization Policy, a Current Analysis: Sources of Economic Growth and Retrogression*, Volume II: *Problems in Polish Economic Planning: Continuity, Change, and Prospects*, Praeger, 1971.

(Contributor) *Recent Developments in the Polish Financial System*, Arms Control and Disarmament Agency, 1971.

(Author of introduction) Michal Kalecki, *The Last Phase in the Transformation of Capitalism*, Monthly Review Press, 1972.

Essays on Planning in Eastern Europe, Instituto di Studi per lo Sviluppo Economico, 1973.

The Intellectual Capital of Michal Kalecki: A Study in Economic Theory and Policy, foreword by Lawrence R. Klein, University of Tennessee Press, 1975.

Growth in a Supply Constrained Economy, Instituto di Studi per lo Sviluppo Economico, 1975.

Growth and Reforms in Centrally Planned Economies: Lessons of Bulgarian Experience, Praeger, 1977.

(Editor and contributor) *Samuelson and Neoclassical Economics*, Kluwer-Nijhoff, 1982.

(Editor and contributor) *Issues in Contemporary Microeconomics and Welfare*, Macmillan, 1985.

(Editor and contributor) *Issues in Contemporary Macroeconomics and Distribution*, Macmillan, 1985.

(Editor and contributor) *Arrow and the Ascent of Modern Economic Theory*, Macmillan, 1986.

(Editor and contributor) *Arrow and the Foundations of the Theory of Economic Policy*, Macmillan, 1986.

Also author of booklet on the meanings of cost. Contributor of articles to *Collier's Encyclopedia, Economia Internazionale, Ricerche Economiche, Indian Economic Journal, Rendiconti, Keio Economic Studies, Soviet Studies, Osteuropa Wirtscahft, Scientia,* and numerous other journals. Member of editorial board, *Journal of Economic Literature*, 1976-78, and *Economia*, 1977—.

WORK IN PROGRESS: Editing and contributing to *The Economics of Imperfect Competition and Employment: Joan Robinson and Beyond*, Macmillan, and *Joan Robinson and Modern Economic Theory*, Macmillan; research on contemporary economic theory, and growth planning and marketing.

SIDELIGHTS: Some of George R. Feiwel's books have been translated into Italian, Japanese, and Spanish.

AVOCATIONAL INTERESTS: Travel.

*   *   *

FERNANDEZ, James William 1930-

PERSONAL: Born November 27, 1930, in Chicago, Ill.; son of James W. and Marian Adeline (McClintock) Fernandez;

married Renate Hellene Lellep, October 28, 1959; children: Lisa O., Lucas O., Andres M. *Education:* Amherst College, B.A., 1952; Northwestern University, Ph.D., 1962.

ADDRESSES: Home—74 Marion Rd. E., Princeton, N.J. 08540. *Office*—Department of Anthropology, University of Chicago, 1126 East 59th St., Chicago, Ill. 60637.

CAREER: Smith College, Northampton, Mass., instructor, 1961-63, assistant professor of anthropology, 1963-64; Dartmouth College, Hanover, N.H., associate professor, 1964-69, professor of anthropology, 1969-75; Princeton University, Princeton, N.J., professor of anthropology, 1975-86; University of Chicago, Chicago, Ill., professor of anthropology, 1986—. Consultant to Foreign Service Institute, U.S. Peace Corps, and Experiment in International Living.

MEMBER: American Anthropological Association (fellow), American Society for the Study of Religion, Society for Spanish and Portuguese Historical Studies, African Studies Association (fellow), Northeast Anthropological Association (president, 1974-75), Society for Applied Anthropology.

AWARDS, HONORS: Ford Foundation fellowship, 1958-61; Social Science Research Council fellowship, 1965-66; National Science Foundation grant, 1970-72.

WRITINGS:

Microcosmogeny and Modernization in Africa, Cahiers d'Etudes Africaines (Paris), 1969.
Fang Architectonics, Institute for the Study of Human Issues, 1976.
Bwiti: An Ethnography of the Religious Imagination in Africa, Princeton University Press, 1982.
Persuasions and Performances: The Play of Tropes in Culture, Indiana University Press, 1986.

WORK IN PROGRESS: Pronouncing Pronouns: The Role of Figurative Statement in Behavior; and two collections, *The Idea of the "Commons" in Spanish Rural Life* and *On Being in One's House in Spain.*

* * *

FICHTER, George S. 1922-
(George Kensinger, Matt Warner, Marc Ziliox)

PERSONAL: Born September 17, 1922, in Hamilton, Ohio; married Nadine K. Warner, February 10, 1945; children: Susan Kay, Thomas Matt, Jane Ann. *Education:* Miami University, Oxford, Ohio, B.A., 1947; North Carolina State College, M.Sc., 1948; graduate study at University of North Carolina.

ADDRESSES: P.O. Box 3280, DeLand, Fla. 32720.

CAREER: Miami University, Oxford, Ohio, instructor in zoology, 1948-50; vice-president and editor in chief, Fisherman's Press, Inc., 1950-55; Sport Fishing Institute, Washington, D.C., assistant executive vice-president, 1956-57; free-lance writer and editor of natural history books, primarily for young people, 1957-63; Western Publishing Co., New York, N.Y., editor of Golden Guides, 1963-67, director of Golden Guides, 1967-68, managing editor of *Golden Bookshelf of Natural History;* free-lance writer and editor, 1968—. Member of national Citizen's Committee for Outdoor Recreation; delegate to White House Conference on Natural Beauty; member, by appointment, of Florida Recreational Trails Conference; president of Dr. Paul Dudley White National Bicycling Foundation, 1967-77. Consultant to Western Publishing Company. *Military service:* U.S. Army Air Forces, 1942-46.

MEMBER: American Entomological Society, American Littoral Society, Izaak Walton League of America (honorary member), Dr. Paul Dudley White Bicycle Club of Homestead (president, 1963-79), Sigma Xi, Phi Kappa Phi.

AWARDS, HONORS: National award, American Youth Hostels, 1967, for developing with wife, Nadine K. Fichter, the Bikeways concept.

WRITINGS:

(With Reuben W. Eschmeyer) *Good Fishing,* Harper, 1959.
(Under pseudonym Matt Warner) *Your World, Your Survival* (Junior Literary Guild selection), Abelard, 1970.
Birds of Florida, E. A. Seemann, 1971.
(Compiler) *The Florida Cookbook,* E. A. Seemann, 1973.
(Co-author) *Fresh and Saltwater Fishes of the World,* Vineyard Books, 1976.
Cats of the World, Bantam, 1976.
(Author and editor) *How to Build an Indian Canoe,* McKay, 1976.
(Ghost co-author) *Inside Bicycling,* Regnery, 1977.
Strangest Creatures in the World, Bantam, 1977.
Dangerous Animals of the Sea, Bantam, 1977.
Bicycles and Bicycling, F. Watts, 1978.
Iraq, F. Watts, 1978.
Pet Amphibians and Reptiles, F. Watts, 1978.
Working Dogs, F. Watts, 1978.
Music the Indians Gave Us, McKay, 1978.
(Co-author) *Bicycle Racing,* Contemporary Books, 1978.
The Future Sea, Sterling, 1978.
Fishing the Four Seasons, Contemporary Books, 1978.
Florida: A Visual Geography, Sterling, 1979.
(Co-author) *Life Science* (junior high text), Prentice-Hall, 1979.
Racquetball, F. Watts, 1979.
Snakes of the World, F. Watts, 1979.
The Plains Indians and How They Lived, McKay, 1980.
The Bulge of Africa, F. Watts, 1981.
Disastrous Fires, F. Watts, 1981.
Space Shuttle, F. Watts, 1981.
Poisonous Snakes of the World, F. Watts, 1981.
Karts and Karting, F. Watts, 1981.
Comets and Meteors, F. Watts, 1982.
Birds, Random House, 1982.
Rocks and Minerals, Random House, 1982.
Wildflowers, Random House, 1982.
Reptiles and Amphibians, Random House, 1982.
Florida Living Cookbook, Pineapple Press, 1985.
Cells, F. Watts, 1986.

PUBLISHED BY GOLDEN PRESS

Reptiles and Their Way of Life, 1960.
Fishes and How They Live, 1960.
Flying Animals, 1961.
(Contributor and managing editor) *Golden Encyclopedia of Natural History,* sixteen volumes, 1962.
Snakes, 1963.
Fishes, 1963.
(Managing editor) *Insects,* 1964.
Reptiles, Questions and Answers, 1965.
(With Phil Francis) *A Guide to Fresh- and Salt-Water Fishing,* 1965.
Insect Pests, 1966 (published in England as *Insect Pests: A Guide to Pests of Houses, Gardens, Farms and Pets,* Hamlyn, 1967).
Rocks, 1966.
(Editor with S. Herbert Zim) *Trees of North America,* 1968.

The Animal Kingdom: An Introduction to the Major Groups of Animals, 1968.
Snakes and Other Reptiles, 1968.
Airborne Animals, 1969.
Exploring Biology, 1970.
Exploring with a Microscope, 1970.
Earth and Ecology, 1972.
(With Keith Kingbay) *Bicycling*, 1972.
Cats, 1973.
Animals, 1973.
(With Taylor R. Alexander) *Ecology*, 1973.
Animals: Mammals from All over the World, 1973.
(Under pseudonym Matt Warner) *Reptiles and Amphibians*, 1974.
Insects, 1975.
Flowers, Trees, and Garden Plants, 1975.
Changing World for Wildlife, 1977.
The Human Body, 1977.

OTHER

Also author of *Fishing*, 1954. Editor of books in the "Golden Guides" series and "Golden Field Guides" series. Contributor to *World Book Encyclopedia, American People's Encyclopedia Yearbook*, and numerous other books. Author of biweekly column "Science World" for Gannett News Service. Contributor of technical articles to professional and scientific journals, and of more than three hundred articles to *Reader's Digest, Coronet, Pageant, Science Digest, National Wildlife, International Wildlife, Boys' Life, Saturday Evening Post*, and numerous other magazines. Also editor of *Florida Outdoors* magazine, 1957-63.

WORK IN PROGRESS: Several books, including *Fishes of Florida, Seashore Life*, and *Underwater Farming*.

SIDELIGHTS: Some of George S. Fichter's books have been translated into French, Spanish, and Portuguese.

*   *   *

FINLAY, William
See MACKAY, James (Alexander)

*   *   *

FIRMIN, Charlotte   1954-

PERSONAL: Born May 2, 1954, in London, England; daughter of Peter (a writer and illustrator) and Joan (a bookbinder; maiden name, Clapham) Firmin; married Robert Herbert (a graphic designer), 1981; children: Olivia, Ruth. *Education:* Attended Hornsey School of Art, 1972-73; Brighton Polytechnic, B.A. (with honors), 1976. *Politics:* Socialist. *Religion:* Agnostic.

ADDRESSES: Home—59 Stone St., Faversham, Kent, England.

CAREER: Author and illustrator of books for young people. Assistant at London Society of Genealogists, 1980-82.

WRITINGS:

JUVENILES; SELF-ILLUSTRATED

Hannah's Great Decision, Macmillan (London), 1978.
Claire's Secret Ambition, Macmillan, 1979.
Eggbert's Balloon, Collins, 1979.
The Eggham Pot of Gold, Collins, 1979.

Egglantine's Party, Collins, 1979.
The Giant Egg Plant, Collins, 1979.

JUVENILES; ILLUSTRATOR

Annabel Farjeon, *The Cock of Round Hill*, Kaye & Ward, 1977.
Terence Deary, *The Custard Kid*, A. & C. Black, 1978.
H. Rice, *The Remarkable Feat of King Caboodle*, A. & C. Black, 1979.
Birthe Alton, *The Magic of Ah*, Kaye & Ward, 1980.
Deary, *Calamity Kate*, A. & C. Black, 1980.
Mary Dickinson, *Alex's Bed*, Deutsch, 1980.
Dickinson, *Alex and Roy*, Deutsch, 1981.
Deary, *The Lambton Worm*, A. & C. Black, 1981.
Dickinson, *Alex and the Baby*, Deutsch, 1982.
Dickinson, *Alex's Outing*, Deutsch, 1983.
Dickinson, *New Clothes for Alex*, Deutsch, 1984.
Maurice Jones, *I'm Going on a Dragon Hunt*, Deutsch, 1987.
Jones, *I'm Going on a Gorilla Hunt*, Deutsch, 1988.

WORK IN PROGRESS: Illustrating *Alex Short Stories* and Evelyn de Jong's *Isn't She Clever*, both for Deutsch.

SIDELIGHTS: Charlotte Firmin told *CA* that her work "is all a matter of luck, observation, persistence, and optimism."

*   *   *

FITCH, John IV
See CORMIER, Robert (Edmund)

*   *   *

FITZHARDINGE, Joan Margaret   1912-
(Joan Phipson)

PERSONAL: Born November 16, 1912, in Warrawee, New South Wales, Australia; married Colin Hardinge Fitzhardinge; children: one daughter, one son. *Education:* Frensham School, Mittagong, New South Wales, Australia.

ADDRESSES: Home—Wongalong, Mandurama, New South Wales 2792, Australia. *Agent*—A. P. Watt & Son, 26/28 Bedford Row, London WC1R 4HL, England.

CAREER: Author of children's books.

MEMBER: Australian Society of Authors.

AWARDS, HONORS: Children's Book Council of Australia Book of the Year Award, 1953, for *Good Luck to the Rider*, and 1963, for *The Family Conspiracy;* Boys' Clubs of America Junior Book Award, 1963, for *The Boundary Riders; New York Herald Tribune* Children's Spring Book Festival Award, 1964, for *The Family Conspiracy;* Honour Book Award from International Board on Books for Young People, 1985, for *The Watcher in the Garden*.

WRITINGS—All under pseudonym Joan Phipson:

Good Luck to the Rider, Angus & Robertson, 1952, Harcourt, 1968.
Six and Silver, Angus & Robertson, 1954.
It Happened One Summer, Angus & Robertson, 1957.
The Boundary Riders, Harcourt, 1962.
The Family Conspiracy, Harcourt, 1962.
Threat to the Barkers, Harcourt, 1963.
Birkin, Lothian, 1965, Harcourt, 1966.
A Lamb in the Family, Hamish Hamilton, 1966.

The Crew of the Merlin, Constable, 1966, published as *Cross Currents,* Harcourt, 1967.
Peter and Butch, Harcourt, 1969.
The Haunted Night, Harcourt, 1970.
Bass and Billy Martin, Macmillan, 1972.
The Way Home, Atheneum, 1973.
Horse with Eight Hands, Atheneum, 1974.
Polly's Tiger, Dutton, 1974.
The Cats, Macmillan, 1976.
Fly into Danger, Atheneum, 1976, published as *The Bird Smugglers,* Methuen, 1979.
When the City Stopped, Atheneum, 1978, published as *Keep Calm,* Macmillan, 1978.
Fly Free, Atheneum, 1979, published as *No Escape,* Macmillan, 1979.
Mr. Pringle and the Prince, Hamish Hamilton, 1979.
A Tide Flowing, Atheneum, 1981.
The Watcher in the Garden, Atheneum, 1982.
Beryl the Rainmaker, Antelope Island, 1984.
The Grannie Season, Antelope Island, 1985.
Dinko, Methuen, 1985.
Hit and Run, Atheneum, 1986.

SIDELIGHTS: Joan Margaret Fitzhardinge, an award-winning children's novelist from Australia who writes as Joan Phipson, recalls for *Something about the Author Autobiography Series* her beginnings as a writer: "As I remember, I gave it no thought at all. I just wrote, and my only guide was what I thought I would have liked to read when I was about nine years old." Phipson also indicates that from the time of her introduction to the Australian countryside, she has needed to write about it, and a contributor to the *Times Literary Supplement* remarks that she "always tells a rousing story in the framework of Australian physical space." *The Cats,* for instance, relates the kidnapping of two teenage brothers who are taken deep into the outback, "where the relationship between criminal and victim begins to change," observes Susan Meyers in the *New York Times Book Review.* Unfamiliar with the hostile terrain of the bush, the kidnappers must rely upon help from their more knowledgeable hostages to escape the pursuing wild cats. "Perhaps most remarkable," says Laura Cecil in the *Times Literary Supplement,* "is [Phipson's] imaginative portrayal of the landscape and weather of the bush, which is never simply descriptive but used as an integral part of the plot and emotional atmosphere."

BIOGRAPHICAL/CRITICAL SOURCES:

BOOKS

Children's Literature Review, Volume V, Gale, 1983.
Something about the Author Autobiography Series, Volume III, Gale, 1986.

PERIODICALS

New York Times Book Review, May 9, 1965, November 21, 1976.
Saturday Review, April 22, 1967.
Times Literary Supplement, June 17, 1965, November 24, 1966, June 26, 1969, September 28, 1973, September 20, 1974, October 1, 1976, September 29, 1978, December 14, 1979, March 28, 1980, March 30, 1984, September 7, 1984.

*   *   *

FOKKEMA, D(ouwe) W(essel)   1931-

PERSONAL: Born May 4, 1931, in Utrecht, Netherlands; son of Dirk and Gijsbertha (Van der Meulen) Fokkema; married Elrud Kunne-Ibsch; children: (previous marriage) Aleide, Diederik. *Education:* State University of Leyden, Chinese studies, 1953-56, Litt.D., 1965; University of Amsterdam, M.A., 1956; University of California, Berkeley, Chinese studies, 1963-64.

ADDRESSES: Office—Institute of Comparative Literature, Ramstraat 31, University of Utrecht, Utrecht, Netherlands.

CAREER: Netherlands Ministry of Foreign Affairs, 1959-68, head of East Asia desk in The Hague, 1965-66, Netherlands Charge d'Affairs in Peking, China, 1966-68; University of Utrecht, Utrecht, Netherlands, beginning 1968, associate professor, 1971-80, professor of comparative literature, 1980—. Erasmus Lecturer on the Civilization of the Netherlands, Harvard University, 1983. *Military service:* Netherlands Air Force, 1956-58; beame first lieutenant.

AWARDS, HONORS: Commonwealth Fund Harkness fellow, 1963-64; Fulbright grant, summer, 1973; Netherlands Institute for Advanced Study in the Humanities and Social Sciences fellow, 1977-78.

WRITINGS:

Rivieren (poetry), Boucher, 1957.
Literary Doctrine in China and Soviet Influence, 1956-60, foreword by S. H. Chen, Mouton, 1965.
Report from Peking: Observations of a Western Diplomat on the Cultural Revolution, C. Hurst, 1971.
Het Chinese Alternatief in Literature en Ideologie, Abeiderspers, 1972.
(Editor with E. Zuercher) *Balans van de Culturele Revolutie,* Arbeiderspers, 1973.
(With wife, Elrud Kunne-Ibsch) *Theories of Literature in the Twentieth Century: Structuralism, Marxism, Aesthetics of Reception, Semiotics,* C. Hurst, 1977, St. Martin's, 1978.
(Editor with W. J. M. Bronzwaer and Kunne-Ibsch) *Teksboek Algemene Literatuurwetenschap,* Ambo, 1977.
(Editor wth Bart Tromp) *China op het breukvlak,* Arbeiderspers, 1981.
Chinees Dagboek, Arbeiderspers, 1981.
(With Kunne-Ibsch) *Het Modernisme in de Europese Letterkunde, 1910-1940,* Arbeiderspers, 1984.
Literary History, Modernism, and Postmodernism, John Benjamins, 1984.
(Editor with Hans Bertens) *Approaching Postmodernism,* John Benjamins, 1986.
(Editor with Matei Calinescu) *Exploring Postmodernism,* John Benjamins, 1987.
(With Kunne-Ibsch) *Modernist Conjectures: A Mainstream in European Literature, 1910-1940,* C. Hurst, 1987.

WORK IN PROGRESS: A study of literary conventions; epistemological issues in the study of literature.

*   *   *

FOLLETT, Robert J(ohn) R(ichard)   1928-

PERSONAL: Born July 4, 1928, in Oak Park, Ill.; son of Dwight W. (an executive) and Mildred (Johnson) Follett; married Nancy L. Crouthamel, December 30, 1950; children: Brian L., Kathryn R., Jean A., Lisa W. *Education:* Brown University, A.B., 1950; Columbia University, graduate study, 1950-51.

ADDRESSES: Home—300 South Euclid Ave., Oak Park, Ill. 60302. *Office*—1000 West Washington Blvd., Chicago, Ill. 60607.

CAREER: Follett Publishing Co., Chicago, Ill., editor, 1951-55, sales manager, 1955-58, general manager of educational division, 1958-68, president, 1968-78, president of Follett International, 1972—, chairman and director of Follett Corp., 1979—. President, Alpine Research Institute, 1968—; member of Illinois Governor's Commission on Schools, 1972, and National Advisory Council on Educational Statistics, 1975-77; chairman, Book Distribution Task Force on the book industry, beginning 1978. Member of board of directors, Community Foundation of Oak Park and River Forest, 1959-86, Fund for Justice, 1974-77, and Fund for Character, 1982—; trustee, Institute for Educational Data Systems, 1965—. Republican State Committeeman, Illinois Seventh Congressional District, 1982—. *Military service:* U.S. Army, Psychological Warfare School, 1951-53.

MEMBER: Association of American Publishers (director, 1972-79), Mid-America Publishers Association (founder), Chicago Publishers Association (president, 1976—), Sierra Club, Cliff Dwellers, River Forest Tennis Club.

WRITINGS:

Your Wonderful Body, Follett, 1962.
How to Keep Score in Business, Follett, 1978.
What to Take Backpacking—And Why, Alpine Guild, 1978.
The Financial Side of Book Publishing, Association of American Publishers, 1982, revised edition, Alpine Guild, 1987.
Financial Feasibility in Book Publishing, Alpine Guild, 1986.
Financial Report Fundamentals, Alpine Guild, 1987.

Contributor to numerous professional journals.

SIDELIGHTS: Robert J. R. Follett wrote *CA:* "All of my books have a single impetus. They were written to help someone learn about something. I get great pleasure from helping people to learn.

"Each book I have written has been sparked by the inquiry of a potential reader. The subjects have been ones in which I already had an interest, of course, but the spark from a potential reader was essential.

"Writing involves making decisions. What shall the topic be? How shall it be organized? In what mode of expression shall it be presented? Where to begin? What sentences should be in the paragraph? In what order? What words shall be chosen for the sentences? How shall they be ordered? Is this a place for a conjunction, a comma, a semicolon? Or should there be a period and another sentence? These and many other choices must constantly be made by writers. The choices are made in terms of the objectives the writer has. For some writers, the primary objective is emotional impact. For others, it is maximum understanding. Other writers have other objectives. Objectives guide choices.

"Some writers make decisions unconsciously. The result is great if they are truly gifted. Most of us have to make the decisions and choices more consciously. I find this process a very satisfying aspect of writing.

"The act of writing is more pleasurable for me than the event of publication. The process gives more joy than the product. When my children grew up and left home I had the time to write. I have tried to use that time and have something in work

constantly. I can't write as well as Will Durant. I hope I can write as long."

AVOCATIONAL INTERESTS: Running, skiing, reading, music, painting, sculpture, and sewing.

* * *

FORD, Betty
    See FORD, Elizabeth Anne Bloomer

* * *

FORD, Elizabeth Anne Bloomer 1918-
(Betty Ford)

PERSONAL: Born April 8, 1918, in Chicago, Ill.; daughter of William Stephenson (a salesman) and Hortense (Neahr) Bloomer; married William C. Warren, 1942 (divorced, 1947); married Gerald R. Ford (a former congressman and the thirty-eighth president of United States), October 15, 1948; children: Michael Gerald, John Garner, Steven Meigs, Susan Elizabeth. *Education:* Attended Bennington College, 1936 and 1937. *Politics:* Republican. *Religion:* Episcopalian.

ADDRESSES: Home and office—Box 927, Rancho Mirage, Calif. 92270.

CAREER: Dance instructor in Grand Rapids, Mich., 1932-39; Martha Graham Concert Group, New York City, dancer, 1939-41; Herpolscheimer's Department Store, Grand Rapids, fashion director, 1943-48; Betty Ford Center at Eisenhower Medical Center (alcohol and drug rehabilitation unit), Rancho Mirage, Calif., co-founder and president, 1982—. Model at John Powers Agency, New York City, 1939-41; Sunday school teacher at Emmanuel on the Hill Episcopal Church, Alexandria, Va., 1961-64. Member of board of directors of League of Republican Women and of The Lambs; member of advisory board of Rosalind Russell Medical Research Fund. Program chairman of Alexandria Cancer Fund; honorary chairman of Palm Springs Desert Museum; chairman of Washington Heart Association's Heart Sunday. Trustee of Nursing Home Advisory and Research Council, Inc.; national trustee of Nation Symphony Orchestra. Member of national committee on observance of International Women's Year, 1977, and of Golden Circle Patrons Center Theatre for Performing Arts; patron of Salvation Army Auxilary annual fashion show luncheon; supporter of National Endowment for the Arts. Association with Childrens Hospital, Washington, D.C.; formerly associated with Cub Scouts of America.

MEMBER: American Red Cross Senate Wives Club (president).

AWARDS, HONORS: Silver Anniversary Humanitarian Award, 1975, from Philadelphia Association of Retarded Children; Rita V. Tishman Human Relations Award, 1975, from Women's Division of the Anti-Defamation League of B'nai B'rith; named distinguished woman of the year, 1975, by National Art Association; named woman of the year, 1975, by *Newsweek,* and 1976, by *Ladies' Home Journal;* Silver Spirit of Life Award, 1976, from Los Angeles City of Hope National Medical Center; Centennial Award, 1976, from *McCall's;* Media Award for Communication of Hope, 1976, from American Cancer Society; Spirit of Independence Award, 1976, from Golden Supper Club; Parson's Award, 1976, from New York Parsons School of Design; LL.D., University of Michigan, 1976; Alfred P. Sloan, Jr., Memorial Award, 1977.

WRITINGS—Under name Betty Ford:

(With Chris Chase) *The Times of My Life* (Book-of-the-Month Club selection), Harper, 1978.
(With Chase) *Betty: A Glad Awakening*, Doubleday, 1987.

SIDELIGHTS: "The point is, I am an ordinary woman who was called onstage at an extraordinary time. I was no different once I became First Lady than I had been before. But through an accident of history, I became interesting to people." Such is the reasoning of Betty Ford, wife of the thirty-eighth president of the United States and author of *The Times of My Life*, an autobiography that, according to A. H. Cain of the *Library Journal*, "reveals why she is one of America's most admired women."

Born in Chicago, Illinois, but raised in Grand Rapids, Michigan, Betty Ford spent her childhood as a tomboy tagging after her older brothers. Like many girls, she took dancing lessons, and she delighted in the surprises her salesman father brought home for her after his trips. By the time she was seventeen, her father had died of accidental carbon monoxide poisoning, and Ford had embarked on a life of her own as a model and a dance instructor.

When she was twenty, Ford met Martha Graham, the renowned dancer and choreographer, at a concert in Ann Arbor, Michigan. "I ran around backstage," Ford recalled, "grabbed Martha's hand and blurted out, 'If I come to New York, can I be at your school?'" Graham agreed and Ford became a member of the dance company's entourage. "[Graham] shaped my whole life. She gave me the ability to stand up to all the things I had to go through, with much more courage than I would have had without her," Ford revealed to *Newsweek*.

In 1941, Ford left Graham's troupe and returned home at her mother's request. She continued to teach dance classes and worked as the fashion coordinator of a department store in Grand Rapids. She dated Bill Warren, whom she remembered as a "blond with curly hair, . . . a good dancer, a good tennis player, he drank and flirted and, unlike some of the men I dated, he wasn't a bit stuffy." Her mother and stepfather, though, "were not enthusiastic about Bill Warren," so he became "all the more alluring" to their child. Ford married Warren in 1942, a union that went "from bloom to bust in five years." "The things that made our dating so amusing," Ford assessed, "were the things that made the marriage difficult. . . . Here I was, ready for a home and children, and Bill was by no means ready to settle down. There was nothing I could do to change him."

Within a year of her divorce, Ford met and married Gerald Ford. She thought she was "marrying a lawyer, and he would practice law until it was time for him to retire, and we would live a quiet life in Grand Rapids." Instead, she became the bride of a politician who arrived "so late for the wedding [because he was campaigning] I almost married the best man." Ford's matron of honor warned her that as a politician's wife she would never "have to worry about other women. Jerry's work will be the other woman." "But I didn't care," Ford insisted, "I was crazy about the man."

As the wife of a congressman, Ford did compete with her husband's work. "My brother and sister-in-law had been right," she reflected. "Work *was* Jerry's mistress. Weekends, when he didn't have any staff in the office, he'd go there anyway, and I'd go, too, and spend the day helping with the filing. I'd putter around, do what simple jobs I could, just to be with him." The congressman worked through vacations, campaigned in Grand Rapids instead of celebrating their wedding anniversaries together, and when he became minority leader of the House of Representatives, Ford's husband spent 258 days per year away from home. By then her children had arrived, and they became her "whole life."

Then problems began for Ford. She suffered a pinched nerve plus spinal arthritis, and she fell into a long-term dependency on medication and alcohol to alleviate the pain. Though she felt neglected and resentful, she refused to admit it to herself. "One night," she remembered, "I rolled over in bed, saw Jerry lying beside me and said, 'What are *you* doing here?'— but mostly I bottled up my misery." Feeling as though she were being taken for granted, Ford needed some of the attention that she was doling out as a wife and mother. "I was so hurt," she wrote, "that I'd think: I'm going to get in the car, and I'm going to drive to the beach, and nobody's going to know where I am. I wanted them to worry about me. I wanted them to say, 'Well, my gosh, Mother is gone, what are we going to do?'"

In 1973, Ford's husband was appointed vice-president of the United States to replace Spiro Agnew, who had resigned the position. Eight months later, when Richard Nixon resigned from the presidency, Ford became the First Lady, a job she did not expect or want. "Jerry did not want this [the presidency]," she recalled. "I certainly did not want it, and neither did our children. But the main point was, it was best for the country." Though she was "scared to death" of her new position, she was committed to it from the beginning, and when her husband took his oath of office, Ford "felt like I was taking that oath, too."

Ford adapted to the role of First Lady well. Though the job entailed many responsibilities and pressures, she reveled in them. "It's her turn now, bless her heart," a friend told the *New York Times*, "and now that she doesn't have to worry about things like whether the beds are made, she's loving it." Friends and family felt that Ford's position as the First Lady was where she belonged. "She's a celebrity in her own right," said her son Michael. "I see *her* on TV and in the newspapers now. All those years Mom did all the dirty work, cleaning up after the four of us, taking us to appointments and fixing our meals, and then when Dad got home we'd be so excited to see him we'd just crawl all over him, ignoring her. I know I was at fault for assuming that's the way things were, and not showing my appreciation for all the love and care she had for us." A friend of the Fords added: "After 26 years in his [President Ford's] shadow, she's in the limelight now." Ford, according to a *New York Times* article, saw even more of her husband once they settled in the White House.

She was expected to be, as her friend maintained in a *Ladies' Home Journal* article, "a lovely First Lady, somewhat shy, but thoroughly nice and totally honest," which she was. With a reputation for candor, Ford won "approval for her charm, honesty, and good humor," reported Laura Berman of the *Miami Herald*. *Newsweek*'s woman of the year in 1975, Ford was the most outspoken First Lady since Eleanor Roosevelt. At her first official public speaking engagement while she was still the vice-president's wife, Ford destroyed her prepared speech because she would "rather say what I want," and she did not hesitate to speak on a variety of sensitive subjects. For example, Ford told a *McCall's* interviewer that reporters had asked her about "everything but how often I sleep with my husband, and if they'd asked me that, I would have told them." When asked, she responded "as often as possible."

In a now famous "60 Minutes" interview, a segment that generated the most mail in the show's history, the First Lady discussed marijuana, equal rights for women, abortion, and the possibility of a premarital affair for her daughter, Susan. Though some individuals, such as W. A. Criswell, the pastor of the world's largest Southern Baptist congregation, and Gordon B. Hinckley, a Mormon elder, were offended by Ford's remarks, most people, including feminist Betty Friedan, were pleased with them. Mary McGrory praised Ford for "getting her information from the real world," and *Newsweek* cited that a 1975 Harris survey "showed overwhelming approval for Betty's plain speaking." Even the president agreed, saying "I'm proud of what Betty had to say." In fact, as *Time* noted, Ford's "husband gives every indication of pride in her enterprise. Hearing about the anti-Betty pickets outside the White House, he responded with a good natured display of liberated gallantry: 'Fine,' he declared. 'Let them demonstrate against you. It takes the heat off me.'"

Ford's appeal, observed Nancy Hawks, chairperson of the National Endowment of the Arts, is that "she's never for a moment pretentious. What she thinks, she says." The household columnist Heloise remarked: "The gals love the way she comes out and says what she thinks. They feel as if she's their next door neighbor, just one of the bunch. She doesn't seem a *bit* stuck up." Ford's priorty is honesty. She is willing to say what she perceives to be true, whether it upsets people or not, and this is what people find engaging. "You're foolish if you try to beat around the bush," the First Lady explained. "You just meet yourself coming around the bush the other way." She's "not afraid to say what's on her mind and she's willing to admit some faults, some personal imperfections," wrote Berman.

Shortly after becoming First Lady, Ford discovered that she had breast cancer and underwent a radical mastectomy and chemotherapy. Because of her frankness in facing cancer, she is credited with encouraging and saving other women from the disease. "I got a lot of credit for having gone public with my mastectomy," wrote Ford, "but if I hadn't been the wife of the President of the United States, the press would not have come racing after my story, so in a way it was fate."

Several years after her cancer ordeal, Ford once again showed great courage when facing personal trauma. Ford's dependency on painkillers became more pronounced after her husband lost the 1976 presidential election and her family returned to private life. An alcoholic, she began overmedicating herself. "At first, I was bitter toward the medical profession," she revealed. "Fourteen years of being advised to take pills, rather than wait for the pain to hit. I had never been without my drugs. I took pills for pain, I took pills to sleep, I took mild tranquilizers. Today things are changing. Doctors are being educated right along with the rest of us, but some of them used to be all too eager to write prescriptions. It was easier to give a woman tranquilizers and get rid of her than sit and listen to her." Ford's stay at the U.S. Naval Hospital in Long Beach, a center for alcohol and drug rehabilitation therapy, was actively covered by the press, and Ford herself was vocal about her addiction and rescue since she was eager to help others in similar states. "I'm not out to rescue anybody who doesn't want to be rescued," she commented. "I just think it's important to say how easy it is to slip into a dependency on pills or alcohol. And how hard it is to admit that dependency."

In her autobiography, Ford narrated her life in detail, and her story, suggested Priscilla Johnson McMullan of the *Chicago Tribune*, is one "for the rest of us to emulate." Although the book was well received, Ford worried about it. She "wasn't so sure she'd done the right thing," stated *Newsweek* reporters. Ford told them: "When I saw my name used at the beginning of an article with a picture of a woman smashed out of sight, I thought, 'Why in the world did I ever open my mouth?' Since then, I've had telegrams and phone calls from people all over the world saying 'Please *don't* stop talking.'"

Encouraged by the public's response to her candor, Ford decided to write a second autobiography, *Betty: A Glad Awakening*. But this time the former First Lady delved deeply into her alcoholism and drug dependency—painful issues she had only superficially addressed before. "It's like taking another inventory," Ford explained to Andrea Chambers in *People* magazine. "The first book was on the outside—about people, places, and things. This book came very much from the inside. I thought I had examined my feelings before, but I really hadn't. I found I had carefully skipped over things. You know, honest self-deception."

Betty: A Glad Awakening, co-authored by the same writer who worked on her first book, chronicles Ford's dawning awareness of and eventual triumph over chemical addiction. It "is really a modest book about one woman's capacity for change: about the daily effort to live uncushioned by pills or liquor; about learning to connect with people once dismissed as pitiable or worse," writes *New York Times Book Review* contributor Marian Sandmaier. Describing it as "a confession marked by candor and salinity," a *Time* reviewer notes, "There are no miracles here, but there is a collective refusal to succumb to the temptations of self-pity or despair."

Publication of *Betty: A Glad Awakening* was timed to coincide with a made-for-TV movie dramatizing Ford's addiction, and she endorsed the project by appearing on the air to discuss chemical dependency after the show. Ford also embarked upon a two-month publicity tour to promote her book. Though she described the tour to Detroit audiences as "a death march with room service" and admitted to Chambers that parts of the TV-movie were "painful for me and my family to watch," Ford cooperated fully in such projects because "I was convinced that it would help thousands of people." All proceeds from the book were donated to the Betty Ford Center, a chemical dependency recovery unit that she helped found and that she discusses at length in the autobiography.

In fact, Ford's enthusiastic endorsement of the Betty Ford Center and her proselytizing about the joys of recovery strike some reviewers as the weak point of the book. "Betty Ford is able to leap over the barrier between the presidency and the common folks, and the connection makes her book a remarkable, at times inspirational document," writes Grace Lichtenstein in the *Washington Post Book World*. "Unfortunately," she continues, "there is almost too much general comment, by Ford and others, about what alcoholism is, how support groups work and how wonderful the Betty Ford Center . . . is for people who can afford its $5,500 treatment. The punch of *Betty: A Glad Awakening* is watered down with a great deal of gushing filler about the new lease on life anyone can buy by cleaning up his or her act."

Sandmaier expresses a similar view, suggesting that the "lengthy treatises" Ford subjects the reader to are "comparable to being stuck at a party with somebody's gabby Aunt Ethel." However, Sandmaier tempers this criticism by acknowledging that her objections are mostly literary—"quibbles of style . . . that are unlikely to make the book any less valuable to Mrs Ford's primary audience: alcohol and drug users who are still in hiding." As Ford herself acknowledged to *Washington Post* reporter Donnie Radcliffe: "I've helped others, and there is nothing more fulfilling than being able to help someone else. And I've been able to do it on my own."

MEDIA ADAPTATIONS: Betty: A Glad Awakening was the basis for a television drama shown on ABC-TV in March, 1987 and starring Gena Rowlands.

AVOCATIONAL INTERESTS: Gardening.

BIOGRAPHICAL/CRITICAL SOURCES:

BOOKS

Feinman, Jeffrey, *Betty Ford*, Award Books, 1976.
Ford, Betty and Chris Chase, *The Times of My Life*, Harper, 1978.
Ford, Betty and Chris Chase, *Betty: A Glad Awakening*, Doubleday, 1987.
McPherson, Myra, *Power Lovers*, Putnam, 1975.
Weidenfeld, Sheila Rabb, *First Lady's Lady: With the Fords at the White House*, Putnam, 1979.

PERIODICALS

Biography News, September, 1974.
Chicago Tribune, November 6, 1978.
Detroit Free Press, February 22, 1987, June 10, 1987.
Detroit News, September 15, 1981.
Esquire, December 19, 1978.
Good Housekeeping, May, 1974, August, 1976, September, 1978.
Ladies' Home Journal, October, 1974, May, 1976, July, 1978, October, 1978, November, 1978.
Library Journal, December 15, 1978.
Los Angeles Times Book Review, March 29, 1987.
McCall's, May, 1974, October, 1974, December, 1974, February, 1975, September, 1975, May, 1976, January, 1977, July, 1978.
Miami Herald, August 9, 1974.
National Review, August 29, 1975.
New Republic, May 26, 1979.
Newsweek, June 2, 1974, June 23, 1974, August 19, 1974, October 7, 1974, October 28, 1974, January 27, 1975, August 18, 1975, December 1, 1975, December 29, 1975, July 4, 1976, August 23, 1976, March 21, 1977, August 1, 1977, December 25, 1978, January 15, 1979.
New York Post, December 15, 1973, August 17, 1974.
New York Times, October 15, 1973, August 5, 1975, January 25, 1977, November 8, 1978, November 10, 1978.
New York Times Book Review, November 26, 1978, September 9, 1979, March 1, 1987.
New York Times Magazine, December 8, 1974.
People, August 26, 1974, October 23, 1978, March 9, 1987.
Progressive, January, 1979.
Redbook, January, 1977.
Saturday Evening Post, September, 1976.
Time, December 17, 1973, May 13, 1974, August 12, 1974, August 26, 1974, September 16, 1974, October 7, 1974, December 30, 1974, March 3, 1975, June 23, 1975, July 28, 1975, August 25, 1975, September 1, 1975, December 1, 1975, January 5, 1976, March 22, 1976, May 3, 1976, July 5, 1976, August 16, 1976, August 30, 1976, January 24, 1977, March 21, 1977, April 24, 1978, October 23, 1978, March 16, 1987.

Times (London), October 15, 1987.
U.S. News and World Report, August 19, 1974, October 7, 1974, December 30, 1974, August 25, 1975, December 15, 1975, December 29, 1975, March 8, 1976, October 18, 1976, June 20, 1977.
Village Voice, November 27, 1978.
Vogue, September, 1974, April, 1975.
Washington Post, November 9, 1978, April 24, 1983.
Washington Post Book World, October 29, 1978, March 1, 1987.
Washington Post Magazine, July 21, 1974.
West Coast Review of Books, January, 1979.†

*   *   *

FOX, Anthony
    See FULLERTON, Alexander (Fergus)

*   *   *

FREEDMAN, Russell (Bruce)   1929-

PERSONAL: Born October 11, 1929, in San Francisco, Calif.; son of Louis N. (a publisher's representative) and Irene (Gordon) Freedman. *Education:* Attended San Jose State College (now University), 1947-49; University of California, Berkeley, B.A., 1951.

ADDRESSES: Home and office—280 Riverside Dr., New York, N.Y. 10025.

CAREER: Associated Press, San Francisco, Calif., newsman, 1953-56; J. Walter Thompson Co. (advertising agency), New York City, television publicity writer, 1956-60; Columbia University Press, New York City, associate staff member, *Columbia Encyclopedia*, 1961-63; Crowell-Collier Educational Corp., New York City, editor, 1964-65; New School for Social Research, New York City, writing workshop instructor, 1969-86. Free-lance writer, particularly for young people. *Military service:* U.S. Army, Counterintelligence Corps, 1951-53.

MEMBER: Authors League of America, American Civil Liberties Union.

AWARDS, HONORS: Immigrant Kids was named a notable children's book of 1980 by the Association for Library Service; *Children of the Wild West* was named a notable children's book of 1983 by the American Library Association; Western Heritage Award from National Cowboy Hall of Fame, 1984, for *Children of the Wild West; Cowboys of the Wild West* was named a notable children's book of 1985 by the American Library Association.

WRITINGS:

BOOKS FOR YOUNG PEOPLE

Thomas Alva Edison, Study-Master, 1966.
How Animals Defend Their Young, Dutton, 1978.
Immigrant Kids, Dutton, 1980.
When Winter Comes, Dutton, 1981.
Animal Superstars, Prentice-Hall, 1981.
Children of the Wild West, Clarion Books, 1984.
Cowboys of the Wild West, Clarion Books, 1985.
Lincoln: A Photobiography, Clarion Books, 1985.

BOOKS FOR YOUNG PEOPLE; PUBLISHED BY HOLIDAY HOUSE

Teenagers Who Made History, 1961.

2000 Years of Space Travel, 1963.
Jules Verne: Portrait of a Prophet, 1965.
Scouting with Baden-Powell, 1967.
(With James E. Morriss) *How Animals Learn,* 1969.
(With Morriss) *Animal Instincts,* 1970.
Animal Architects, 1971.
(With Morriss) *The Brains of Animals and Man,* 1972.
The First Days of Life, 1974.
Growing up Wild: How Young Animals Survive, 1975.
Animal Fathers, 1976.
Animal Games, 1976.
How Birds Fly, 1977.
Hanging On: How Animals Carry Their Young, 1977.
Getting Born, 1978.
Tooth and Claw: A Look at Animal Weapons, 1980.
They Lived with the Dinosaurs, 1980.
Farm Babies, 1981.
Killer Fish, 1982.
Killer Snakes, 1982.
Dinosaurs and Their Young, 1983.
Rattlesnakes, 1984.
Sharks, 1985.
Indian Chiefs, 1987.

OTHER

The First Fifty Years (adult), Holiday House, 1985.

Contributor to *Columbia Encyclopedia,* 3rd edition, and to the *New Book of Knowledge Annual,* 1981—. Also contributor to *Cricket, Ranger Rick,* and other periodicals.

*   *   *

FREEMAN, Howard E(dgar)   1929-

PERSONAL: Born May 28, 1929, in New York, N.Y.; son of Herbert M. (a business executive) and Rose (Herman) Freeman; married Sharon Kleban, August 7, 1953 (divorced, 1973); married Marian A. Solomon, 1978; children: (first marriage) Seth Richard, Lisa Jill. *Education:* New York University, B.A., 1948, M.A., 1950, Ph.D., 1956.

ADDRESSES: Home—7911 Hillside Ave., Los Angeles, Calif. 90046. *Office*—Department of Sociology, 264 Haines Hall, University of California, 405 Hilgard Ave., Los Angeles, Calif. 90024.

CAREER: Brandeis University, Waltham, Mass., associate professor, 1960-63, professor of social research, 1964-69, Morse Professor of Urban Studies, 1969-72, director of research center, 1960-66; Ford Foundation, social science advisor for Mexico, Central America, and the Caribbean, 1972-74; University of California, Los Angeles, professor of sociology, 1974—, chairman of department, 1986—, director of Institute for Social Science Research, 1974-81. Lecturer and research consultant, Boston College, 1957-65; visiting professor of sociology, University of Wisconsin, 1966-67, University of Colorado, summer, 1967. Russell Sage Foundation, sociologist, 1967-72, consulting sociologist, 1974-77. Director, Task Force of Sociology, National Library of Medicine Project, 1966-67.

Research advisor, Demonstration and Grant Program, Social Security Administration, 1961-65, Institute of Nutrition of Central America and Panama of Pan American Health Organization, 1965—; senior research advisor, Robert Wood Johnson Foundation, 1976—. Member of professional advisory committee, Massachusetts Association for Mental Health, Inc.,

1962-65; member of administrative committee, Massachusetts Health Research Institute, 1963-66; member of Panel on Social Indicators, Office of the Secretary, Department of Health, Education and Welfare, 1966-69; member of review committee, State Comprehensive Health Planning Program for Massachusetts, 1968-72. Consultant or research consultant to numerous organizations, including V.A. Hospitals in Boston, Bedford, and Brockton, 1956-65, National Institute of Nutrition, Bogota, Colombia, 1968-79, National Status Offender Program, 1976—, and National Science Foundation, 1977-79. *Military service:* U.S. Air Force Reserve, 1953-62; became captain.

MEMBER: American Sociological Association, American Psychological Association, American Association for Public Opinion Research, National Academy of Sciences (member, Institute of Medicine), National Conference on Social Welfare, U.S.-Mexico Border Health Association, Eastern Sociological Society, Society for the Study of Social Problems, Sociological Research Association.

AWARDS, HONORS: Hofheimer Prize, American Psychiatric Association, 1963, for *The Mental Patient Comes Home.*

WRITINGS:

(With Ozzie G. Simmons) *The Mental Patient Comes Home,* Wiley, 1963.
(Editor with Sol Levine and Leo G. Reeder) *Handbook of Medical Sociology,* Prentice-Hall, 1963, 4th edition, 1988.
(With others) *The Middle-Income Negro Family Faces Urban Renewal,* Housing and Home Finance Agency, 1965.
(With Camille Lambert) *The Clinic Habit,* College and University Press, 1967.
(With Norman R. Kurtz) *America's Troubles: A Casebook on Social Conflict,* Prentice-Hall, 1969, 2nd edition, 1973.
(Editor with others) *The Dying Patient,* Russell Sage, 1970, 2nd edition (editor with Orville G. Brim, Levine, and Norman Scotch), Transaction Books, 1982.
(With Clarence Sherwood) *Social Policy and Social Research,* Prentice-Hall, 1970.
(With Wyatt C. Jones) *Social Problems: Causes and Controls,* Rand McNally, 1970, 3rd edition (with Jones and Lynne G. Zucker), 1979.
(Author of foreword and contributor) Francis G. Caro, editor, *Readings in Evaluation Research,* Russell Sage, 1971, 2nd edition, 1977.
(Editor with others) *The Social Scene,* Winthrop Publishing, 1972.
(With Ilene N. Bernstein) *Academic and Entrepreneurial Research,* Russell Sage, 1975.
(Author of foreword) Thomas Cook, *Sesame Street Revisited,* Russell Sage, 1975.
(Author of foreword) Stephen M. Shortell and William C. Richardson, *Health Program Evaluation,* C. V. Mosley, 1978.
(Editor) *Policy Studies Review Annual II,* Sage Publications, 1978.
(With Peter H. Rossi and Sonia R. Wright) *Evaluation: A Systematic Approach,* Sage Publications, 1979, 3rd edition (with Rossi), 1985.
(Editor with wife, Marian A. Solomon) *Evaluation Studies Review Annual VI,* Sage Publications, 1981.
(Editor with Russell Dynes, Rossi, and William F. Whyte) *Applied Sociology,* Jossey-Bass, 1983.
(Editor with Leigh Burstein and Rossi) *Collecting Evaluation Data: Problems and Solutions,* Sage Publications, 1985.

CONTRIBUTOR

E. Gartley Jaco, editor, *Patients, Physicians, and Illness*, Free Press, 1958.

Dorrian Apple, editor, *Sociological Studies of Health and Sickness*, McGraw, 1959.

Theodore R. Sarbin, editor, *Studies in Behavior Pathology: The Experimental Approach to the Psychology of the Abnormal*, Holt, 1961.

William McPhee and William A. Glaser, editors, *Public Opinion and Congressional Elections*, Free Press, 1962.

William T. Smelser and Neil J. Smelser, editors, *Personality and Social Systems*, Wiley, 1963, reprinted, 1977.

The Social Welfare Forum, Columbia University Press, 1963.

William Gomberg and Arthur Shostak, editors, *Blue Collar World*, Prentice-Hall, 1964.

Stanton Wheeler, editor, *Controlling Delinquents*, Wiley, 1967.

Leigh M. Roberts and others, editors, *Comprehensive Mental Health: The Challenge of Evaluation*, University of Wisconsin Press, 1968.

S. Kirson Weinberg, editor, *The Sociology of Mental Disorders*, Aldine, 1968.

E. Borgatta and R. Evans, editors, *Smoking, Health and Behavior*, Aldine, 1968.

Stephen P. Spitzer and Norman K. Denzin, editors, *The Mental Patient: Studies in the Sociology of Deviance*, McGraw, 1968.

Alvin Winder, editor, *Adolescence: Contemporary Studies*, American Book Co., 1968.

W. A. Many and Frank W. Lanning, editors, *Basic Education for the Adult Learner*, Houghton, 1968.

G. Lindzey and E. Aronson, editors, *Handbook of Social Psychology*, Volume V, 2nd edition, Addison-Wesley, 1969.

William S. Sahakian, editor, *Psychopathology Today*, F. E. Peacock, 1970.

Herbert Schulberg and others, editors, *Program Evaluation in the Health Fields*, Behavioral Publications, 1970.

Morton Levitt and Ben Rubenstein editors, *The Mental Health Field: A Critical Appraisal*, Wayne State University Press, 1971.

Richard O'Toole, editor, *The Organization, Management and Tactics of Social Research*, Schenckman, 1971.

Carol H. Weiss, editor, *Evaluating Action Programs: Readings in Social Action and Education*, Allyn & Bacon, 1972.

James E. Albert and Murry Komioss, editors, *Social Experiments and Social Program Evaluation*, Bollinger Publishing, 1974.

Frank R. Scarpitti and Paul T. McFarland, editors, *Deviance: Action, Reaction, Interaction*, Addison-Wesley, 1975.

Nicholas J. Demerath and others, editors, *Social Policy and Sociology*, Academic Press, 1975.

Gene M. Lyons, editor, *Social Research and Public Policies*, Dartmouth College, 1975.

Stuart S. Nagel, editor, *Policy Studies and the Social Sciences*, Heath, 1975.

Gerald T. Horton, editor, *Readings on Human Services Planning*, Human Services Institute for Children and Families, 1975.

Jack Meslin, editor, *Rehabilitation Medicine and Psychiatry*, C. C Thomas, 1976.

Robert W. Binstock and Ethel Shanas, editors, *Handbook of Aging and the Social Sciences*, Van Nostrand, 1976, 2nd edition, 1986.

Marcia Guttentag, editor, *Evaluation Studies Review Annual II*, Sage Publications, 1977.

Clark C. Abt, editor, *Problems in American Social Policy Research*, Abt Books, 1980.

Erwin S. Solomon, editor, *Evaluating Social Action Projects*, United Nations Educational, Scientific and Cultural Organization (UNESCO), 1980.

Robert A. Levine and others, editors, *Evaluation Research and Practice*, Sage Publications, 1981.

Richard O. Mason and E. Burton Swanson, *Measurement for Management Decision*, Addison-Wesley, 1981.

Allan W. Johnson and others, editors, *Contemporary Health Services: Social Science Perspectives*, Auburn House, 1981.

John W. Reich, editor, *Experimenting in Society: Issues and Examples in Applied Psychology*, Scott, Foresman, 1982.

(With Robert E. Klein, John Townsend, and Aaron Lechtig) *Benchmark Papers in Behavior*, Hutchinson Ross, in press.

OTHER

Editor of Prentice-Hall series in social policy, 1970-76. Contributor to proceedings of Institute on Health Care Needs of the Elderly Patient, 1961, Conference of New England Gerontological Society, 1963, American Statistical Association, 1964, and Council of University Institutes for Urban Affairs, 1970. Contributor to numerous journals, including *American Journal of Sociology, American Sociological Review, American Sociologist, Contemporary Sociology, Journal of Psychology,* and *Public Opinion Quarterly.* Co-editor, *Evaluation Review*, 1976—. Associate editor, *American Sociological Review*, 1962-66, *Social Problems*, 1962-66, and *Sociological Methods and Research*, 1971-76. *Journal of Health and Social Behavior*, associate editor, 1966-69, editor, 1969-72. Consulting editor, *Community Mental Health Journal*, 1964-80. Member of editorial advisory board, *New Directions for Program Evaluation*, 1981—. Member of editorial board, *Values and Ethics in Health Care*, 1977, and *Annals of Public Administration*, 1979—. Referee, *American Journal of Public Health*, 1974—.

*   *   *

FRY, Michael G(raham) 1934-

PERSONAL: Born November 5, 1934, in Brierley, England; son of Cyril Victor (a surveyor) and Margaret Mary (Copley) Fry; married Anna Maria Fulgoni, May, 1957; children: Michael Gareth, Gabriella, Margaret Louise. *Education:* University of London, B.Sc. (with honors), 1956, Ph.D., 1963. *Religion:* Roman Catholic.

ADDRESSES: Home—480 South Orange Grove, Pasadena, Calif. 91105. *Office*—School of International Relations, University of Southern California, Los Angeles, Calif. 90007.

CAREER: University of Toronto, Toronto, Ontario, lecturer in history, 1961-62; University of Saskatchewan, Saskatoon, lecturer, 1962-63, assistant professor of history, 1963-65; Carleton University, Ottawa, Ontario, assistant professor, 1965-66, associate professor, 1966-72, professor of history, 1972-78, associate director of School of International Affairs, 1973-76, director, 1976-77; School of International Affairs, University of Denver, Denver, Colo., dean and professor, 1978-81; School of International Relations, University of Southern California, Los Angeles, director and professor, 1981—. Visiting professor, University of Leningrad, 1976, and Middle East Center, University of Utah, 1979. *Military service:* British Army, 1956-58.

MEMBER: International Studies Association (vice-president, 1977), Royal Historical Society, Canadian Historical Association, American Historical Association, Society for Historians of American Foreign Relations.

AWARDS, HONORS: Canada Council Fellowships, 1966, 1967, 1968, 1973, and 1976; North Atlantic Treaty Organization research fellowship, 1969-70.

WRITINGS:

Illusions of Security: North Atlantic Diplomacy, 1918-1922, University of Toronto Press, 1972.
(Editor) *"Freedom and Change": Essays in Honour of Lester B. Pearson,* McClelland & Stewart, 1975.
Lloyd George and Foreign Policy, Volume I: *The Education of a Statesman, 1890-1916,* McGill-Queen's University Press, 1977.
(With Itamar Rabinovich) *Despatches from Damascus: Gilbert Mackereth and British Policy in the Levant, 1933-39,* Tel Aviv University Press, 1986.

Contributor to history journals, including *Canadian Journal of History, Journal of Modern History,* and *Royal United States Institution Journal.*

WORK IN PROGRESS: Lloyd George and Foreign Policy, Volume II.

SIDELIGHTS: Michael G. Fry told *CA:* "I am a student of international history, the international relations of the great powers in the 20th century, and the functioning of the international system. I am a historian who is attempting to cross disciplinary boundaries and relate to other scholars in the field of international relations. I am also concerned with dissent about foreign and defence policies."

BIOGRAPHICAL/CRITICAL SOURCES:

PERIODICALS

Journal of American History, December, 1972.
Times Literary Supplement, August 19, 1977.

*   *   *

FULLERTON, Alexander (Fergus) 1924-
(Anthony Fox)

PERSONAL: Born September 20, 1924, in Suffolk, England; son of John Skipwith Fullerton; married Priscilla Mary Edelston, 1956; children: John, Simon, Giles. *Education:* Attended Royal Naval College, Dartmouth, England, 1938-41.

ADDRESSES: Home—County Cork, Ireland. *Agent*—John Farquharson Ltd., 162-168 Regent St., London W1R 5TB, England.

CAREER: Writer. Royal Navy, regular officer in Submarine Service and Russian interpreter, 1942-49, became lieutenant; editorial director, Peter Davies Ltd. (publishers), London, England, and Arrow Books Ltd. (paperback division of Hutchinson & Co. Ltd.), London.

AWARDS, HONORS—Military: Mentioned in dispatches, Far East, 1945.

WRITINGS:

Surface!, P. Davies, 1953.
Bury the Past, P. Davies, 1954.
Old Moke, P. Davies, 1954.
No Man's Mistress, P. Davies, 1955.
A Wren Called Smith, P. Davies, 1957.
The White Men Sang, P. Davies, 1958, reprinted, Mayflower Books, 1977.
The Yellow Ford, P. Davies, 1959.
The Waiting Game, Ives Washburn, 1961.
Soldier from the Sea, P. Davies, 1962.
The Thunder and the Flame, Hodder & Stoughton, 1964.
Lionheart, Norton, 1965.
Chief Executive, Cassell, 1969, published in U.S. as *The Executives,* Putnam, 1970.
The Publisher, Putnam, 1971.
Store, Cassell, 1971.
The Escapists, Cassell, 1972.
Other Men's Wives, Cassell, 1973.
Piper's Leave, Cassell, 1974.
(Under pseudonym Anthony Fox) *Threat Warning Red,* M. Joseph, 1979.
(Under pseudonym Anthony Fox) *Kingfisher Scream,* Viking, 1980.
Regenesis, M. Joseph, 1982.
The Aphrodite Cargo, M. Joseph, 1985.
Special Deliverance, Macmillan, 1986.
Special Dynamic, Macmillan, 1987.
Special Deception, Macmillan, 1988.

"EVERARD" SERIES; WORLD WARS I AND II NAVAL ADVENTURE NOVELS

The Blooding of the Guns, M. Joseph, 1976.
Sixty Minutes for St. George, M. Joseph, 1977.
Patrol to the Golden Horn, M. Joseph, 1978.
Storm Force to Narvik, M. Joseph, 1979.
Last Lift from Crete, M. Joseph, 1980.
All the Drowning Seas, M. Joseph, 1981.
A Share of Honour, M. Joseph, 1982.
The Torch Bearers, M. Joseph, 1983.
The Gatecrashers, M. Joseph, 1984.

SIDELIGHTS: Regarding Alexander Fullerton's *The Torch Bearers,* Michael Trend in the *Times Literary Supplement* writes that "Fullerton's novel makes much of how people deceive one another and themselves, both in terms of the progress of the war and in his characters' inner lives; his main theme, though, is courage—especially the courage, or the lack of it, of the individual in the face of danger."

Fullerton's novels *Special Deliverance, Special Dynamic,* and *Special Deception* form a trilogy about the Special Boat Squadron of the Royal Marines. His novel *Store* has been translated into German.

BIOGRAPHICAL/CRITICAL SOURCES:

PERIODICALS

Times Literary Supplement, July 23, 1970, December 23, 1983.

G

GALLICO, Paul (William) 1897-1976

PERSONAL: Born July 26, 1897, in New York, N.Y.; died July 15, 1976, in Monaco; son of Paolo (a concert pianist and music teacher) and Hortense (Erlich) Gallico; married Alva Thoits Taylor, September 5, 1921 (divorced, 1934); married Elaine St. Johns, April 12, 1935 (divorced, 1936); married Pauline Gariboldi, 1939 (divorced); married Virginia von Falz-Fein, July 19, 1963; children: (first marriage) William Taylor, Robert Leston; Ludmila (stepdaughter). *Education:* Columbia University, B.A., 1921.

CAREER: Writer. National Board of Motion Picture Review, New York City, review secretary, 1921; *New York Daily News,* New York City, movie critic, 1922; sports writer, 1923-24, sports editor, columnist, and assistant managing editor, 1924-36; *Cosmopolitan,* New York City, war correspondent in Europe, 1943; Columbia University, New York City, instructor in extension school, 1944. *Military service:* U.S. Navy, gunner, 1918.

MEMBER: Quiet Birdman (international hangar), Fencer's Club (New York); London Fencing Club, Buck's Club, Epee Club (all London).

AWARDS, HONORS: O. Henry Prize, 1941; Academy Award nomination for "Pride of the Yankees," 1942; de Beaumont Sword, British National Epee Team Championship, 1949.

WRITINGS:

Farewell to Sport, Knopf, 1938, reprinted, Holtzman, 1981.

The Adventures of Hiram Holliday, Knopf, 1939, reprinted, Penguin Books, 1967.

The Secret Front, Knopf, 1940.

The Snow Goose (also see below), Knopf, 1941.

Lou Gehrig: Pride of the Yankees (also see below), Grosset, 1942.

Golf Is a Friendly Game, Knopf, 1942.

Confessions of a Story Writer (autobiography and stories), Knopf, 1946.

The Lonely, M. Joseph, 1947, Knopf, 1949.

The Abandoned, Knopf, 1950 (published in England as *Jennie,* M. Joseph, 1950).

The Small Miracle, M. Joseph, 1951, Doubleday, 1952.

Trial by Terror, Knopf, 1952, new edition, Nelson & Sons, 1978.

Snowflake, M. Joseph, 1952, Doubleday, 1953.

The Foolish Immortals, Doubleday, 1953.

Love of Seven Dolls (also see below), Doubleday, 1954.

Ludmila: A Legend of Lichtenstein, M. Joseph, 1955, published in America as *Ludmila,* Doubleday, 1959.

Thomasina: The Cat Who Thought She Was God, Doubleday, 1957, published as *Thomasina,* Avon, 1981.

The Steadfast Man: A Biography of St. Patrick, Doubleday, 1958 (published in England as *The Steadfast Man: A Life of St. Patrick,* M. Joseph, 1958).

Mrs. 'Arris Goes to Paris, Doubleday, 1958 (published in England as *Flowers for Mrs. Harris,* M. Joseph, 1958).

Too Many Ghosts, Doubleday, 1959.

The Hurricane Story, M. Joseph, 1959, Doubleday, 1960.

Mrs. 'Arris Goes to New York, Doubleday, 1960 (published in England as *Mrs. Harris Goes to New York,* M. Joseph, 1960).

Further Confessions of a Story Writer: Stories Old and New, Doubleday, 1961 (published in England as *Confessions of a Story-Teller,* M. Joseph, 1961).

(Author of introduction) Ian Fleming, *Gilt Edged Bonds,* Macmillan, 1961.

Coronation, Doubleday, 1962.

Scruffy: A Diversion, Doubleday, 1962.

Love, Let Me Not Hunger, Doubleday, 1963.

The Day the Guinea Pig Talked, Heinemann, 1963, Doubleday, 1964.

(With Suzanne Szasz) *The Silent Miaow: A Manual for Kittens, Strays, and Homeless Cats,* Crown, 1964.

The Hand of Mary Constable, Doubleday, 1964.

The Day Jean-Pierre Was Pignapped, Heinemann, 1964, Doubleday, 1965.

Three Stories (contains *The Snow Goose, The Small Miracle,* and *Ludmila*), M. Joseph, 1964, published as *Three Legends,* Doubleday, 1966.

Mrs. 'Arris Goes to Parliament, Doubleday, 1965 (published in England as *Mrs. Harris, M.P.,* Heinemann, 1965).

The Golden People (nonfiction), Doubleday, 1965.

The Day Jean-Pierre Went round the World, Heinemann, 1965, published as *The Day Jean-Pierre Went around the World,* Doubleday, 1966.

The Man Who Was Magic: A Fable of Innocence, Doubleday, 1966.

The Revealing Eye: Personalities of the 1920s, Atheneum, 1967.

The Story of Silent Night, Crown, 1967.
Gallico Magic (contains *Mrs. 'Arris Goes to Paris, Mrs. 'Arris Goes to New York, Mrs. 'Arris Goes to Parliament, The Snow Goose, The Small Miracle, Ludmila,* and *Coronation*), Doubleday, 1967.
The Lost Christmas, Street & Zeus, 1968.
Manxmouse, Coward, 1968.
The Poseidon Adventure, Coward, 1969.
The Day Jean-Pierre Joined the Circus, F. Watts, 1969.
Matilda, Coward, 1970.
The Zoo Gang, Coward, 1971.
Honorable Cat, Crown, 1972.
The Boy Who Invented the Bubble Gun: An Odyssey of Innocence, Delacorte, 1974.
Mrs. 'Arris Goes to Moscow, Delacorte, 1974 (published in England as *Mrs. Harris Goes to Moscow*, Heinemann, 1974).
Miracle in the Wilderness: A Christmas Story of Colonial America, Delacorte, 1975 (published in England as *Miracle in the Wilderness: A Story for Christmas*, Heinemann, 1975).
Adventures of Jean-Pierre, Piccolo Books, 1975.
Beyond the Poseidon Adventure, Delacorte, 1978.
The House That Wouldn't Go Away, Delacorte, 1980.

SCREENPLAYS

"No Time to Marry," Columbia, 1937.
"Pride of the Yankees" (based on *Lou Gehrig: Pride of the Yankees*), RKO, 1942.
"Joe Smith, American," Metro-Goldwyn-Mayer, 1942.
"The Clock," Metro-Goldwyn-Mayer, 1945.
"Never Take No for an Answer" (based on *The Small Miracle*), Souvaine Selective, 1951.
"Lili" (based on *Love of Seven Dolls*), Metro-Goldwyn-Mayer, 1953.
"Merry Andrew," Metro-Goldwyn-Mayer, 1957.
"Big Operator," Metro-Goldwyn-Mayer, 1959.
"The Three Lives of Thomasina" (based on *Thomasina: The Cat Who Thought She Was God*), Walt Disney Productions, 1963.
"The Snow Goose" (based on novel of the same title), National Broadcasting Company, 1971.

CONTRIBUTOR

Vogue's First Periodical, Messner, 1942.
Jack A. Goodman, editor, *While You Were Gone: A Report on Wartime Life in the United States*, Simon & Schuster, 1946.
Helen R. Hull, editor, *Writer's Book*, Harper, 1950.
William Targ, editor, *Readers for Writers*, Hermitage, 1951.
Don Congdon, editor, *The Thirties: A Time to Remember*, Simon & Schuster, 1962.
A. S. Burack, editor, *The Writer's Handbook*, Writer, Inc., 1968.

OTHER

Contributor of several hundred stories to *Saturday Evening Post, New Yorker, Argosy, Good Housekeeping, Cosmopolitan,* and other publications.

SIDELIGHTS: Paul Gallico was a popular writer for both adults and children. "I'm a storyteller," he once told Jerome Haltzman of *New York.* "I'm a rotten novelist. I'm not even literary. I just like to tell stories and all my books tell stories." Gallico's forty books and several hundred short stories won him "a large popular following," Boyd Litzinger explained

in the *Dictionary of Literary Biography.* Among his best known works were *The Snow Goose, The Poseidon Adventure,* and the series of books featuring the English cleaning woman Mrs. Harris.

The son of an immigrant concert pianist, Gallico met many of the leading classial musicians of the day during his childhood. But his father's attempt to make a musician of him failed. "He had the good sense to give it up," Gallico told Haltzman. "I simply had no talent for playing." Gallico's talent for sports, however, led him to play football in high school and to captain his college rowing team at Columbia University. The 6-foot, 3-inch Gallico worked his way through college as a longshoreman. After a short stint as a gunner during the First World War, Gallico finally received his degree in 1921 and soon found a job as a sports writer with the *New York Daily News.*

Gallico "burst upon the newspaper scene," Paul Hodge remarked in the *Washington Post,* "by getting Jack Dempsey to box a round with him." The Dempsey fight lasted less than two minutes and ended with Gallico on the mat unconscious. But it provided him with a popular story. He was soon challenging other stars in some three dozen different sports. Gallico swam with Johnny Weissmuller, hit the pitching of Dizzy Dean, and skied an Olympic course. He also raced boats, airplanes and cars. The approach won him a host of readers. During the 1930s, Hodge reported, Gallico was "one of the highest paid sports writers in America."

At the age of thirty-nine, however, Gallico decided to leave the newspaper business in favor of a free-lance writing career. "After thirteen years of looking at every kind of athletic contest," he explained in *Confessions of a Story Writer,* "I had nothing more to say. Better to get out while the getting was good and before the readers made the same discovery I had." Another factor in Gallico's decision was his success at breaking into the slick magazine fiction market. His efforts at fiction writing had finally begun to pay off after nearly twenty years of perseverance. During the 1930s and 1940s, Gallico's stories became a mainstay of the *Saturday Evening Post, Cosmopolitan,* and other magazines.

With the appearance of *The Snow Goose* in 1940, Gallico achieved his only "real critical success," as Marcelle Bernstein commented in the *Dallas News. The Snow Goose* was a popular success as well, hitting the best seller charts. Set during the Dunkirk evacuation of the Second World War, it tells the story of a hunchback's love for a beautiful girl and of the injured snow goose who brings them together. Although it takes place in a contemporary scene, the novel has a myth-like quality noted by several reviewers. "Gallico," Margaret Clark reported in the *Boston Transcript,* "writes skillfully in a cadence identical with that of ancient legend." Robert Van Gelder of the *New York Times* claimed that *The Snow Goose* was "a timely legend that makes use of every timeless appeal that could be crowded into it." Bernstein described the book as Gallico's "tour de force."

The Snow Goose proved to be a model for many of Gallico's later children's novels, which often feature animal characters. In *Thomasina: The Cat Who Thought She Was God,* for example, Gallico wrote of a remarkable cat who seemed to return from the dead. In *Manxmouse,* he invented a hybrid creature with a mouse's body, a rabbit's ears, and monkey's paws. *Matilda* is the story of a boxing kangaroo, while several other books concern Jean-Pierre, an adventurous guinea pig. Animals are also prominent characters in Gallico's more serious stories, such as *The Small Miracle,* the story of a young boy who takes his sick donkey to be healed at a saint's shrine.

Among Gallico's most popular books for adults were those in the lighthearted series about Mrs. Harris. Based on an English cleaning woman once employed by Gallico, Mrs. Harris is a middle-aged woman whose whimsical adventures take her to Paris, New York, Moscow, and even to a seat in the British parliament. The *New Yorker* reviewer described *Mrs. 'Arris Goes to Paris* as "a charming, sweetly scented fairy tale," while the *Kirkus* critic called the novel "one of those enchanting—and enchanted—stories that couldn't possibly happen but that it would be fun to think could happen." Speaking of *Mrs. 'Arris Goes to New York,* Fanny Butcher of the *Chicago Tribune* believed it "light hearted whimsy, or satire, or spoof, or just a sequel. . . . Read it without pretending to believe it and you may well enjoy the fun."

One of Gallico's best-known novels was *The Poseidon Adventure,* the story of an ocean liner capsized by a tidal wave. A handful of survivors must make their way to safety through the upside-down ship before it sinks. The book was a bestseller, was made into a popular motion picture, and helped to spawn a number of other disaster novels in the early 1970s. But critical reaction was more subdued. Martin Levin of the *New York Times Book Review* commented that the characters' personal histories "may be damp with sentimentality as well as brine—but the author's skill as a storyteller invests them with enough suspense to last the desperate journey." Writing in *Best Sellers,* William B. Hill maintained that "this story . . . has too much of the sort of reflection in which fictional characters always indulge during protracted crises; and, as a parable, the tale is either very obscure or else it is saying something quite wild. Yet the characters are intriguing and the incidents—granted that there are too many of them—are interesting."

The success of Gallico's writing career enabled him to indulge one of his greatest passions, "living well," as he once told *CA.* As Bernstein explained, Gallico was "a teller of tales, a dreamer of dreams, a romantic. And for such unfashionable qualities he has always had a vast market, great financial reward and the opportunity to live where and as he wishes." Gallico lived in England, Mexico, San Francisco, Paris, Lichtenstein and, at the time of his death in 1976, in Monaco. Speaking to Haltzman about his long-time residence in Europe, Gallico explained: "I'm not an expatriate. I'm an American who likes to live in Europe. But I've kept my American citizenship and pay full American taxes."

The popularity of his work pleased Gallico, who saw his role as that of a storyteller above all else. Litzinger claimed that "Gallico probably will hold no high rank with contemporary critics who seek virtues other than those he displays. But Gallico saw himself as a competent professional writer and entertainer. . . . Given the limitations and the unquestionable skills implicit in these terms, Paul Gallico has his respectable place." Speaking to Bernstein, Gallico remarked: "In place of great literary fame, I've got millions of people who care about what I write and who like me. What the hell more do I want?"

MEDIA ADAPTATIONS: Trial by Terror was filmed as "Assignment Paris," Columbia, 1952; *The Adventures of Hiram Holliday* was adapted as a television series, National Broadcasting Company, 1956; *Mrs. 'Arris Goes to Paris* was filmed for television in 1958, and adapted as a musical; *The Poseidon Adventure* was filmed by Twentieth Century-Fox, 1972; *The Small Miracle* was filmed for television, National Broadcast-

ing Company, 1973; *The Boy Who Invented the Bubble Gun: An Odyssey of Innocence* was filmed; television rights for *The Zoo Gang* were sold to the National Broadcasting Company.

BIOGRAPHICAL/CRITICAL SOURCES:

BOOKS

Authors in the News, Volume I, Gale, 1976.
Contemporary Literary Criticism, Volume II, Gale, 1974.
Dictionary of Literary Biography, Volume IX: *American Novelists, 1910-1945,* Gale, 1981.
Gallico, Paul, *Confessions of a Story Writer,* Knopf, 1946.
Gallico, Paul, *Further Confessions of a Story Writer: Stories Old and New,* Doubleday, 1961.

PERIODICALS

Best Sellers, September 1, 1969, July 1, 1970.
Books and Bookmen, August, 1970, February, 1972.
Boston Transcript, April 12, 1941.
Chicago Tribune, March 20, 1960.
Editor and Publisher, September 14, 1957.
Kirkus, September 1, 1958.
New Republic, June 29, 1974.
Newsweek, July 9, 1947.
New York, May 6, 1974.
New Yorker, November 22, 1958.
New York Herald Tribune Book Review, April 27, 1952.
New York Times, April 13, 1941.
New York Times Book Review, July 4, 1965, November 7, 1965, November 28, 1965, October 16, 1966, December 10, 1967, June 23, 1968, August 24, 1969, June 23, 1974.
Publishers Weekly, January 22, 1973.
Saturday Evening Post, May 26, 1951.
Saturday Review, November 25, 1967.
Spectator, May 9, 1969.
Times Literary Supplement, April 15, 1965, October 27, 1966, June 16, 1974.
Variety, July 21, 1976.
Wilson Library Bulletin, May, 1964.
Young Readers' Review, September, 1968.

OBITUARIES:

PERIODICALS

AB Bookman's Weekly, October 4, 1976.
Newsweek, July 26, 1976.
New York Times, July 17, 1976.
Publishers Weekly, July 26, 1976.
Washington Post, July 17, 1976.†

—*Sketch by Thomas Wiloch*

*　　　*　　　*

GARDEN, Bruce
　See MACKAY, James (Alexander)

*　　　*　　　*

GEAREY, John 1926-

PERSONAL: Born July 3, 1926, in Montreal, Quebec, Canada; son of John (a clerk) and Frances (Ruttenberg) Gearey; married Dorothy Cameron, September 24, 1955; children: Francis, Mairi. *Education:* McGill University, B.A., 1950; University of Toronto, M.A., 1952; Columbia University, Ph.D., 1960.

ADDRESSES: Home—2600 Netherland Ave., Apt. 3105, Riverdale, N.Y. 10463. *Office*—Department of German, City College of the City University of New York, Convent Ave., New York, N.Y. 10031.

CAREER: Oberlin College, Oberlin, Ohio, instructor in German, 1956-61; Columbia University, New York, N.Y., assistant professor of German, 1961-64; City College of the City University of New York, associate professor, 1964-82, professor of German, 1982—. Consultant, Random House and Oxford University Press. *Military service:* Canadian Army, 1944-45.

MEMBER: North America Goethe Society, Modern Language Association of America, Germanic Society of America, United Federation of Teachers (New York).

AWARDS, HONORS: Bonn Government scholarship; Payne Foundation fellowship.

WRITINGS:

(Editor and contributor) *Einfuhrung in die deutsche Literatur,* Holt, 1964.
(Editor) *Michael Kohlhaus,* Oxford University Press, 1967.
Heinrich von Kleist: A Study in Tragedy and Anxiety, University of Pennsylvania Press, 1968.
Goethe's ''Faust'': The Making of Part One, Yale University Press, 1981.
(Editor) *Goethe's Essays on Art and Literature,* Suhrkamp, 1985.

Consulting editor for *Germanic Review* and *German Quarterly.*

SIDELIGHTS: Gearey's book on Heinrich von Kleist was chosen by the U.S. Information Service for its Overseas Book Exhibit for 1969 and 1970.†

*   *   *

GIROUX, E. X.
See SHANNON, Doris

*   *   *

GLIDEWELL, John Calvin   1919-

PERSONAL: Born November 5, 1919, in Okolona, Miss.; son of Henry Clay and Jessie Kate Glidewell; married Frances Reed, 1941; children: Pamela, Janis. *Education:* University of Chicago, A.M., 1949, Ph.D., 1953.

ADDRESSES: Home—101 Longwood Place, Nashville, Tenn. 37215. *Office*—Department of Psychology and Human Development, Vanderbilt University, Nashville, Tenn. 37203.

CAREER: University of Chicago, Human Dynamics Laboratory, Chicago, Ill., project director, 1948-49; Meridian Public Schools, Meridian, Miss., director of psychological services, 1949-51; U.S. Air Force, Maxwell Air Force Base, Ala., Human Resources Research Institute, project director, 1951-53; St. Louis County Health Department, Clayton, Mo., director of research and development, 1953-67; Washington University, St. Louis, Mo., Medical School, research assistant, 1954-58, research instructor, 1958-64, research assistant professor of medical psychology, 1964-67, Social Science Institute, director of training program for social science research in community mental health, 1958-66, Department of Sociology and Anthropology, associate professor of social psychology, 1963-

65, Graduate Institute of Education, associate professor of educational psychology, 1965-67; University of Chicago, professor of education and behavioral science, beginning 1967, chairman of educational psychology faculty, 1970-73; Vanderbilt University, Nashville, Tenn., professor of psychology, 1981—. Adjunct staff member, National Training Laboratories, National Education Association, 1950—; lecturer in public health, School of Nursing, Washington University, School of Nursing, St. Louis University, and Marilac College, 1957-65. *Military service:* U.S. Army, 1942-46; became captain. U.S. Air Force Reserve, 1946-50; active duty, 1950-52; retired as major.

MEMBER: International Association of Applied Social Scientists (member of board of directors, 1970-73), American Psychological Association (fellow), American Sociological Association (fellow), National Training Laboratories Association (fellow), American Public Health Association (fellow; Mental Health Section, secretary, 1964-66, chairman, 1968), Society for the Psychological Study of Social Issues (fellow), Midwest Psychological Association, Sigma Xi.

WRITINGS:

(Editor and contributor) *Parental Attitudes and Child Behavior,* C. C Thomas, 1961.
(With L. M. Smith and others) *Socialization and Social Organization in Elementary Classrooms,* Social Science Research Council, 1965.
(With Martha M. Brown and others) *Nurses, Patients and Social Systems,* University of Missouri Press, 1968.
(With C. S. Swallow) *The Prevalence of Maladjustment in Elementary Schools,* Joint Commission on the Mental Health of Children, 1968.
Choice Points: The Emotional Problems of Living with People, M.I.T. Press, 1970.
(Editor) *The Social Context of Learning and Development,* Gardner Press, 1977.
(Editor and contributor) *Corporate Cultures: Research Implications for Managers and HRD,* American Society for Training and Development, 1986.

CONTRIBUTOR

Leadership Training for Community Health Promotion, U.S. Public Health Service, 1957.
Dorothy Stock and H. A. Thelen, editors, *Emotional Dynamics and Group Culture,* New York University Press, 1958.
C. Shagass and B. Pasamanick, editors, *Child Development and Child Psychiatry,* American Psychiatric Association, 1960.
W. G. Bennis, K. D. Benne, and R. Chin, editors, *Planning of Change,* Holt, 1961.
C. Mial and D. Mial, editors, *Community Development: Selected Readings,* National Training Laboratories, National Education Association, 1962.
J. R. Newbrough, editor, *Community Mental Health: Individual Adjustment or Social Planning?,* National Institute of Mental Health, 1962.
Mildred B. Kantor, editor, *Mobility and Mental Health,* C. C Thomas, 1965.
(With others) M. L. Hoffman and L. W. Hoffman, editors, *Review of Child Development Research,* Russell Sage, 1966.
E. M. Bower and W. G. Hollister, editors, *Behavioral Science Frontiers in Education,* Wiley, 1967.
R. Williams and L. Ozarin, editors, *Community Mental Health: An International Perspective,* Jossey-Bass, 1967.

(With others) E. L. Cowen, E. A. Garner, and M. Zax, editors, *Emergent Approaches to Mental Health Problems,* Appleton-Century-Crofts, 1967.

J. W. Carter, editor, *Research Contributions from Psychology to Community Mental Health,* Behavioral Publications, 1968.

L. M. Roberts, N. S. Greenfield, and M. H. Miller, editors, *Comprehensive Mental Health: The Challenge of Evaluation,* University of Wisconsin Press, 1968.

S. B. Sells, editor, *The Definition and Measurement of Mental Health,* U.S. Public Health Service, 1968.

J. G. Howells, editor, *Modern Perspectives in International Child Psychiatry,* Oliver & Boyd, 1969.

A. J. Bindman and A. D. Spiegel, editors, *Perspectives in Community Mental Health,* Aldine, 1969.

G. Rosenblum, editor, *Issues in Community Psychology and Preventive Mental Health,* Behavioral Publications, 1971.

M. J. Feldman, editor, *Theory and Research in Community Mental Health,* State University of New York at Buffalo, 1971.

(With J. J. Sherwood) W. W. Burk, editor, *Contemporary Organization Development: Approaches and Interventions,* National Training Laboratories Learning Resources, 1972.

S. E. Golann and C. Eisdorfer, editors, *Handbook of Community Mental Health,* Appleton-Century-Crofts, 1972.

L. Bellak, editor, *The Concise Handbook of Community Psychiatry and Community Mental Health,* Grune, 1974.

K. D. Benne, L. P. Bradford, J. R. Gibb, and R. Lippitt, editors, *The Laboratory Method of Learning and Changing,* Science & Behavior Books, 1975.

A Tribute to Lee Bradford, University of Cincinnati Press, 1976.

I. Iscoe, B. L. Bloom, and C. D. Spielberger, editors, *Community Psychology in Transition,* Hemisphere Publishing, 1977.

D. Bar-Tal and L. Saxe, editors, *Social Psychology of Education: Theory and Research,* Hemisphere Publishing, 1978.

G. Bermant, H. C. Kelman and D. P. Warwick, editors, *The Ethics of Social Intervention,* Hemisphere Publishing, 1978.

(With others) A. Nadler, J. D. Fisher, and B. M. DePaulo, editors, *New Directions in Helping: Applied Research in Help-Seeking and Reactions to Aid,* Volume III, Academic Press, 1983.

R. D. Felner, L. Jason, J. Moritsugo, and S. S. Farber, editors, *Preventive Psychology,* Pergamon Press, 1983.

S. V. Lourenco and J. Smilansky, editors, *A Handbook of Leadership Development,* Jossey-Bass, 1987.

OTHER

Author of numerous research reports for various organizations, including St. Louis County Health Department and Swampscott Conference. Contributor to *Third Year Book* of the American Association of Public Schools, 1955; contributor to proceedings of the Ninth Congress of the Interamerican Society of Psychology, 1962. Contributor to psychiatry, public health, education, and sociology journals, including *Journal of Educational Research, American Journal of Orthopsychiatry, American Journal of Psychiatry, Human Organization, Journal of Social Issues, Human Relations,* and *American Journal of Community Psychology.* Associate editor, *Adult Leadership,* 1958-62; special issue editor, *Journal of Social Issues,* 1959; editor, *American Journal of Community Psychology,* 1976—.

WORK IN PROGRESS: Articles on social organization in elementary schools, corporations, universities, and large banks.

SIDELIGHTS: John Calvin Glidewell told *CA:* ''I try to write because ideas interest me profoundly, and I think that ideas interest everybody else. I enjoy trying to express ideas as clearly and as precisely as can be. In part, the great human capacity to communicate drives my expression, but human communication is never precise. Others' ideas stir my juices, my motives, my feelings, and my thoughts; what I absorb is my reconstruction of what I think I read or heard; it is never exactly what others said. That continuous reconstruction fires the wondrous creativity of the human exchange of thought. In fact, I think that the more precisely accurate communication becomes, the less creative it becomes; the less precisely accurate, the more creative—lots of misses, to be sure, but a few vivid, life-changing hits. That fact makes the quest for truth and love a never-ending, always fascinating quest. My profound interest in ideas, their communication, and their myriad transformations, forces me to try to write, to try to activate my reconstructions and those of others. Another force: I simply enjoy trying to express ideas.''

*   *   *

GLOVER, Michael   1922-

PERSONAL: Born May 20, 1922, in London, England; son of James Alison (a physician) and Katharine (Merriam) Glover; married Daphne Bowring, September 1, 1945; children: Stephanie (died, 1983). *Education:* St. John's College, Cambridge, M.A., 1947. *Religion:* Church of England.

ADDRESSES: Home—Bidcombe, France Lynch near Stroud, Glostershire, England.

CAREER: British Council, London, England, director of educational aids department, 1947-70. Writer. *Military service:* British Army, Sherwood Foresters, 1941-46; served in North Africa and Italy; taken prisoner of war. British Army Reserve, London Rifle Brigade Rangers, 1948-63; became major.

MEMBER: Society for Army Historical Research, Royal United Service Institution.

WRITINGS:

Wellington's Peninsular Victories, Macmillan, 1963.
Wellington as Military Commander, Van Nostrand, 1968.
Britannia Sickens: Sir Arthur Wellesley and the Convention of Cintra, Leo Cooper, 1970.
Legacy of Glory: The Bonaparte Kingdom of Spain, Scribner, 1971.
1815, Cardinal, 1973.
Assemblage of Indian Army Soldiers and Uniforms from the Paintings by the Late Chater Paul Chater, Perpetua Press, 1973.
The Peninsular War: A Concise History, David & Charles, 1974.
Rorke's Drift: A Victorian Epic, Leo Cooper, 1975.
General Burgoyne in Canada and America, Gordon & Cremonesi, 1976.
Wellington's Army in the Peninsula, David & Charles, 1977.
A Very Slippery Fellow: Sir Robert Wilson, 1777-1849, Oxford University Press, 1978.
The Napoleonic Wars: An Illustrated History, Batsford, 1979.
A Gentleman Volunteer: George Hennell, 1812-13, Heinemann, 1979.
Warfare from Waterloo to Mons, BCA Publications, 1980.

Warfare in the Age of Bonaparte, BCA Publications, 1980.
The Velvet Glove: The Decline and Fall of Moderation in War, Hodder & Stoughton, 1982.
The Flight for the Channel Ports: A Study in Confusion, Leo Cooper, 1984.
A New Guide to the Battlefields of Northern France and the Low Countries, M. Joseph, 1987.
An Improvised War: Ethiopia, 1940-41, Leo Cooper, 1987.

Also author of radio scripts. Contributor of articles to *History Today* and *Journal of the Society of Army Historical Research*.

* * *

GOLE, Victor Leslie   1903-

PERSONAL: Born November 4, 1903, in North Fitzroy, Australia; son of Leonard Escott and Sarah (Legassick) Gole; married Eve Bartle Gillard, November 2, 1939; children: Wilma Lee Gole Sturrock, Barton Victor (deceased). *Education:* Attended technical secondary school in Brisbane, Australia. *Religion:* Protestant.

ADDRESSES: Home—72 Canberra Grove, Brighton, Victoria 3187, Australia. *Office*—V. L. Gole Proprietary Ltd., 636 St. Kilda Rd., Melbourne, Victoria 3004, Australia.

CAREER: Associated with MacRobertsons Ltd., A. W. Allen Ltd., Allied Bruce Small Ltd., all in Melbourne, Victoria, Australia, 1924-1953; V. L. Gole Proprietary Ltd., Melbourne, director, 1954—.

MEMBER: Australian Society of Accountants (fellow), Australian Institute of Management (associate fellow), Institute of Chartered Secretaries and Administrators (fellow), Institute of Directors (fellow).

AWARDS, HONORS: M.B.A. from University of Melbourne, 1974.

WRITINGS:

(Editor) *Fitzgerald's Analysis and Interpretation of Financial Statements*, Butterworth, 1966.
Fundamentals of Financial Management in Australia, Butterworth, 1968, 3rd edition, 1980.
Accounting for Businessmen: Australian Proprietary Companies Management Finance and Taxation, Butterworth, 1970.
Valuation of Businesses, Shares, and Property, Butterworth, 1980.
Questions on Finance Management, Butterworth, 1984.
Answers on Finance Management, Butterworth, 1984.

Contributor to accounting journals.

SIDELIGHTS: Victor Leslie Gole wrote: "I have for many years lectured to accountants, company secretaries, managers, and varied audiences on accounting, financial management, and kindred subjects. I have been inclined to record in book form much of the subject matter on which I lecture."

* * *

GOODGOLD, Edwin   1944-

PERSONAL: Born June 12, 1944, in Tel Aviv, Israel; son of Eugene (a factory foreman) and Ahuva Goodgold. *Education:* Columbia University, B.A., 1965; New York University, graduate studies. *Religion:* Jewish.

ADDRESSES: Home—200 West 70th St., New York, N.Y. 10023.

CAREER: Writer-researcher for metropolitan Sunday newspapers, New York, N.Y., 1964—.

WRITINGS:

(With Dan Carlinsky) *Trivia* (also see below), Dell, 1966.
(With Carlinsky) *More Trivial Trivia* (also see below), Dell, 1966.
I Spy: Robert Culp and Bill Cosby, the Swift and Swinging Story of TV's Favorite Spies, Grosset, 1967.
(With Carlinsky) *Rock 'n' Roll Trivia*, Popular Library, 1970.
(Editor with Ken Weiss) *To Be Continued: A Complete Guide to over 220 Motion Picture Serials with Sound Tracks*, Crown, 1972.
(With Carlinsky) *Trivia and More Trivia* (contains *Trivia* and *More Trivial Trivia*), Castle Books, 1975.
(With Carlinsky) *The Compleat Beatles Quiz Book*, Warner Books, 1975.
(With Carlinsky) *World's Greatest Monster Quiz*, Berkley Publishing, 1975.
(With Carlinsky) *The Status Game*, New American Library, 1986.

Contributor to *Playboy, Playbill, Show*, and other magazines.

* * *

GOODMAN, Felicitas D(aniels)   1914-

PERSONAL: Born January 30, 1914, in Budapest, Hungary; came to United States, 1947; naturalized citizen, 1950; daughter of Nikolaus (an industrial manager) and Maria (Uhlig) Daniels; married Glenn H. Goodman (a university professor), March 27, 1937 (divorced, 1967); children: Nicolas D., Frederick K., Susan V. (Mrs. John Josephson), Beatrice Emm. *Education:* University of Heidelberg, diploma (translating and interpreting), 1936; Ohio State University, M.A., 1968, Ph.D., 1971.

ADDRESSES: Home—114 East Duncan St., Columbus, Ohio 43202.

CAREER: Free-lance translator, 1936—; Ohio Wesleyan University, Delaware, visiting lecturer in German, 1947-51; Battelle Memorial Institute, Columbus, Ohio, multi-lingual translator, 1951-58; American Chemical Society, Columbus, multi-lingual abstractor, 1958-64; Ohio State University, Columbus, visiting lecturer in German, 1962-68; Denison University, Granville, Ohio, assistant professor, 1968-75, associate professor of linguistics and anthropology, 1975-79, professor emeritus, 1979—. Founder, Cuyamungue Institute for Teaching and Research in Anthropology. Anthropological field worker in Yucatan, Mexico, 1969—.

MEMBER: American Anthropological Association (fellow), American Association for the Advancement of Science (fellow), Society for the Scientific Study of Religion.

WRITINGS:

Die blaue Bruecke (title means "The Blue Bridge"), Schwerdtfeger, 1947.
Speaking in Tongues: A Cross-Cultural Study of Glossolalia, University of Chicago Press, 1972.
(With Jeannette H. Henney and Esther Pressel) *Trance, Healing, and Hallucination: Three Field Studies in Religious Experience*, Wiley, 1974.
Anneliese Michel und ihre Daemonen: Der Fall Klingenberg in wissenschaftlicher Sicht (nonfiction), Christiana, 1980,

translation by the author published as *The Exorcism of Anneliese Michel*, Doubleday, 1981.

Ecstasy, Ritual, and Alternate Reality: Religion in a Pluralistic World, Cuyamungue Institute, 1986.

TRANSLATOR

(Into German) Washington Irving, *Rip Van Winkle*, Schmidt, 1948.

(Into German) Walter C. Reckless, *Die Kriminalitaet in den USA, und ihre Behandlung* (title means "Crime and Its Treatment in the U.S.A."), de Gruyter, 1964.

(Into English) Hans Peter Duerr, *Dreamtime: Concerning the Boundary between Wilderness and Civilization*, Basil Blackwell, 1985.

CONTRIBUTOR

Kurt Ruediger, editor, *Zyklische Dichtungen der Gegenwart* (title means "Modern Poetry Cycles"), Karslruher Bote, 1965.

Erika Bourguignon, editor, *Religion, Altered States of Consciousness, and Social Change*, Ohio State University, 1973.

Irving I. Zaretsky and Mark P. Leone, editors, *Religious Movements in Contemporary America*, Princeton University Press, 1975.

Agenhananda Bharati, editor, *Ritual, Cults, and Shamanism*, Mouton, 1975.

Carole E. Hill, editor, *Symbols and Society: Essays on Belief Systems in Action*, University of Georgia Press, 1975.

Bourguignon, editor, *A World of Women: Anthropological Studies of Women in the Societies of the World*, Praeger, 1980.

Encyclopedia of Religion, Macmillan, 1985.

OTHER

Contributor of about twenty articles to journals, including *Medikon, Confinia Psychiatrica, Semiotica, Journal for the Scientific Study of Religion, New Society*, and *Psychotherapy and Psychosomatics*.

SIDELIGHTS: Felicitas D. Goodman writes: "Star-War robots and micronauts notwithstanding, most children will still turn with utter abandon to sand, water, even playdough, stuff they can have complete control over. For me, the empty page has signalled the same thrill ever since I first learned to draw a letter. To write a book seemed to me the pinnacle of achievement even before I could read one. By the time I was a teenager, I had decided that I was not going to invent characters. What I would do was to present real people, in real-life situations.

"It is understandable, perhaps, for as a Hungarian-born child growing up in Rumania, a Hungarian-trained schoolgirl living in Germany, a European woman coming to terms with this country, I was not only always the outsider, but also the fascinated observer. Even my first book, although listed as fiction, is really a collection of stories about people I knew— living in the Third Reich, confronting Nazi horror—in the guise of fairytales about tyranny in an oriental kingdom. But it was not until I discovered ethnographic writings when I returned to graduate school in 1965 that I felt I had come into my own. My first model was Oscar Lewis. After reading his books about the Sanchez family and others, and then walking the streets of Mexico City, I had the eerie feeling of being surrounded by houses of glass; I knew how the people lived behind these walls. Although I have written other material, as

the need arose, to compose ethnographic life histories is still what I like to do best."

Goodman is bilingual in German and Hungarian, speaks, reads, and writes French, Spanish, Rumanian, and Maya, and translates all Germanic and Romance languages; she also knows some Russian and Navaho.

*   *   *

GOODWIN, Doris (Helen) Kearns 1943-
(Doris Helen Kearns)

PERSONAL: Born January 4, 1943, in Rockville Centre, N.Y.; daughter of Michael Alouisius (a bank examiner) and Helen Witt (Miller) Kearns; married Richard Goodwin (a writer and political consultant), 1975; children: three sons. *Education:* Colby College, B.A. (magna cum laude), 1964; Harvard University, Ph.D., 1968. *Religion:* Roman Catholic.

ADDRESSES: Home—Concord, Mass.

CAREER: U.S. Government, Washington, D.C., State Department intern, 1963, House of Representatives intern, 1965, Department of Health, Education, and Welfare, research associate, 1966, special assistant to Willard Wirtz, Department of Labor, 1967, special assistant to President Lyndon Johnson, 1968; Harvard University, Cambridge, Mass., assistant professor, 1969-71, associate professor of government, beginning 1972, assistant director of Institute of Politics, beginning 1971, member of faculty council. Special consultant to President Johnson, 1969-73. Hostess of television show, "What's the Big Idea," WGBH-TV, Boston, Mass., 1972; political analyst for news desk, WBZ-TV, Boston. Member of Democratic party platform committee, 1972; member of Women's Political Caucus in Massachusetts (member of steering committee, beginning 1972). Trustee of Wesleyan University, Colby College, and Robert F. Kennedy Foundation.

MEMBER: American Political Science Association, Council on Foreign Relations (member of nominating and reform committees, 1972), Women Involved (chairman and member of board of advisers), Group for Applied Psychoanalysis, Phi Beta Kappa, Phi Sigma Iota, Signet Society.

AWARDS, HONORS: Fulbright fellow, 1966; Outstanding Young Woman of the Year award from Phi Beta Kappa, 1966; White House fellow, 1967.

WRITINGS:

(Under name Doris Helen Kearns) *Lyndon Johnson and the American Dream*, Harper, 1976.

(Contributor) Marc Pachter, editor, *Telling Lives: The Biographer's Art*, New Republic Books, 1979.

The Fitzgeralds and the Kennedys: An American Saga, Simon & Schuster, 1987.

Also contributor of articles to *New Republic*.

SIDELIGHTS: Doris Kearns Goodwin, a former professor of government at Harvard University, is the author of two highly acclaimed biographies. *Lyndon Johnson and the American Dream* is a political and pyschological study of the thirty-sixth president, while *The Fitzgeralds and the Kennedys: An American Saga* examines the life of John F. Kennedy as well as the two generations that preceded him.

The circumstances surrounding the writing of *Lyndon Johnson and the American Dream* are interesting and somewhat unusual. Goodwin first met Johnson at a White House dance in

1967. At the time, she was a White House fellow working as a special assistant to Willard Wirtz. She had recently co-authored an article for *New Republic* entitled "How to Remove LBJ in 1968," in which she was sharply critical of Johnson's foreign policy. Johnson was aware of her feelings when he met her, but instead of arguing with her, he asked her to dance. At the end of the evening, he suggested that she be assigned to work with him in the White House. According to *Nation* reviewer Ronnie Dugger, in befriending Goodwin, Johnson had apparently heeded the advice of John Roche, one of his aides, who told him that having a White House fellow who was critical of the administration would cause him to appear open-minded and unthreatened by the growing anti-war sentiment in America. When Johnson eventually asked Goodwin to help him write his memoirs, she agreed; after his retirement, she traveled to the Johnson ranch in Austin, Texas, on weekends, holidays and vacations to help Johnson write the "official" version of his presidency.

Johnson's choice of Goodwin as his biographer was one many observers found noteworthy. In addition to being critical of his administration, she was, as *New York Times Book Review* contributor David Halberstam notes, "respected in the Eastern intellectual world which Johnson was sure despised him." With Goodwin (as one of their own) telling his story, he believed that the group he felt excluded from would finally, if not accept him, then at least listen to his story. He had, as a writer for the *New Yorker* put it, become "preoccupied wth the verdict of history." He wanted to be remembered as a successful president; he sought out writers who would be friendly in their judgment of him. According to *New Republic* contributor Robert Coles, Johnson is reported to have told Goodwin that she reminded him of his mother, and as he spent more and more time with her, he apparently came to believe that she felt sympathetic towards him and that she would write a flattering portrayal of him.

Published in 1977, four years after Johnson's death, *Lyndon Johnson and the American Dream* met with a good deal of acclaim. Halberstam calls the book "a fascinating and unusual addition to the Johnson shelf." Christopher Lehmann-Haupt of the *New York Times* deems it "the most penetrating, fascinating political biography I have ever read." Reviewers also found favor with Goodwin's writing. In his *Washington Post Book World* review, Horace Busby describes the author's prose as "vivid and sensitive" and her portrait of the ex-president "the most fascinating and absorbing and, yes, sympathetic to appear in contemporary literature." The quality that many critics admired in the book was Goodwin's objectivity. Coles sees her "open-eyed restraint" as one of the book's greatest assets. Similarly, Halberstam describes Goodwin as "a good listener . . . at once intelligent and sympathetic, and yet strong and independent enough to make her story credible."

In *Lyndon Johnson and the American Dream*, Goodwin does more than recount the details of Johnson's personal life and political career; she also offers a probing study of the former president's personality, examining in particular how his early years were integral in making him the politician he became. As Goodwin sees it, Johnson's political ambitions, his quest for power, and his plans for the "Great Society" all stemmed from an effort to free himself from the conflict he felt torn by from birth. His mother was shy, genteel, and dignified; his father was easy-going, flamboyant, and frequently ill-mannered. As *Saturday Review* contributor Larry McMurtry explains, Goodwin "demonstrates again and again how Johnson's youthful need to keep the peace between his parents

affected his style as a politician, a style dependent upon endless and often very subtle personal negotiation." This psycho-biographical approach drew quite a bit of critical attention, most of it positive. In his *Newsweek* review Paul D. Zimmerman praises Goodwin for "producing a sensible, scrupulous compassionate study of the connections between Lyndon Johnson's psychological drives and his political fortunes." He adds, "Other books, pitched at a greater distance from their subject, will undoubtedly offer a more definitive social and political appraisal of the Johnson Presidency. But none is likely to offer a sharper, more intimate portrait of Lyndon Johnson in full psychic undress." Writes McMurtry, "the effort she has made to untangle the psychic knots of his character and relate them to his actions as a leader is . . . extremely loyal, requiring much empathy and a long application of effort and intelligence."

One of the more controversial aspects of the book was Goodwin's analysis of Johnson's dreams; several critics wondered about the validity of these interpretations. "She seems," writes *New York Review of Books* contributor Gary Wills, "insufficiently aware of the fact that dreams told in a persuasive context cannot have the evidentiary value of those discussed in analysis." McMurtry, on the other hand, claims that Goodwin "makes a tentative, fair, never very dogmatic use of the tools of psychoanalysis." James M. Perry writes in the *National Observer* that although Goodwin presents "some pretty heavy character analysis amounting to psychohistory" in her book, "she is honest enough to admit that there are vast empty spaces in what we know about the human mind and human behavior."

In a *New Republic* article, Goodwin wrote that she would rather have waited a number of years before writing *Lyndon Johnson and the American Dream*, so that she could "really understand and convey its human value." But she was a young Harvard professor, and as she said, "I had to publish." In spite of Goodwin's disclaimers, most reviewers tend to side with McMurtry when he calls *Lyndon Johnson and the American Dream* "a triumph—partly [Goodwin's] and partly Lyndon Johnson's" and deems the book "by far the most significant we have of Johnson."

Six months after *Lyndon Johnson and the American Dream* was published, Simon & Schuster contracted Goodwin to write a biography of Johnson's predecessor, John F. Kennedy. Goodwin began work in late 1977 but what she initially envisioned as a three-year project on Kennedy's life evolved into a multi-generational saga of two Irish-American families. As she explained to the *Detroit News:* "As I got into the project, I realized I wanted to do a book about my own heritage, something different than just a biography of Jack. I wanted to look at the whole assimilation of an immigrant group, the Irish, over a period of time, an assimilation that ended up in the most dramatic way by having Kennedy becoming the president of the United States." Divided into three parts and spanning nearly a century, *The Fitzgeralds and the Kennedys: An American Saga* chronicles three generations of Fitzgeralds and Kennedys—from the baptism of John "Honey Fitz" Fitzgerald in 1863 to the inauguration of his grandson and namesake John F. Kennedy in 1961.

The enormous amount of research entailed in a work of such scope was one reason it took Goodwin nearly a decade to complete her second book. Another factor was her decision to spend more time with her family. The birth of her youngest son, Joey, "changed my whole feeling toward the project,"

Goodwin told Judith Michaelson in the *Los Angeles Times*. "When I was writing the Johnson book and was still single, it was probably the most important thing in my life, and I would stay up if I wanted to, until midnight. With this book when I started it, the kids were so little that I could spend only two or three hours on it at the beginning. It was deeper than that. I wasn't panicked about it. It wasn't the thing I was obsessed about. I was obsessed about the kids." Goodwin also sees another fundamental difference between the writing of these two books—her contact with the subjects themselves. In writing the Johnson book, "I was aware of being captive to him," Goodwin told the *Washington Post*. On the other hand, she says of the Fitzgerald-Kennedy book: "these were not people that I knew. I had to recreate them for myself first, in order to render them to the reader. Part of what gave me the confidence to write honestly . . . is that I began to feel I knew them."

Although quite a few books have been written about the Kennedys in recent years, Goodwin was able to add fresh material to her work as a result of her access to two valuable sources. One of these was her husband, Richard, a former speechwriter for and advisor to Lyndon Johnson and Robert and John Kennedy. Having known the Kennedys for over twenty-five years, Richard Goodwin was able to provide his wife with an insider's view of the family. Through her husband's close ties to the Kennedys, Goodwin also came upon a mine of information untapped by previous biographers—one hundred and fifty cartons of Joseph Kennedy's personal correspondence. These letters not only permitted Goodwin to fill in important details concerning Joseph's business dealings, they also allowed her to gain insight into his relationships with his wife and children. Goodwin in turn was able to use the contents of these letters to stimulate the latent memories of Joseph's wife, Rose. In doing so she was able to dispel certain notions about John and his father as well as offer new perspectives on existing knowledge about other family members.

Critical reaction to *The Kennedys and the Fitzgeralds* was enthusiastic, with many critics praising Goodwin's treatment of what has become a rather well-traversed subject. Writes Christopher Lehmann-Haupt of the *New York Times:* "The story is familiar enough. We've read its various parts in at least a dozen books over the past quarter century. . . . Yet rarely has this familiar saga seemed so fresh and dramatic. Rarely have its characters been so alive and individual. Rarely have popular history rung so authentic, or, conversely, fresh scholarship struck us as so captivating." Similarly, *Los Angeles Times Book Review* contributor Robert Dallek notes: "The elevation of the Kennedys to the status of a royal family has led to an outpouring of articles and books on the entire clan. Doris Kearns Goodwin's new study is now the best book on the subject." Goodwin's writing style also met with acclaim. *Washington Post* critic George V. Higgins calls *The Fitzgeralds and the Kennedys* "an anecdotal, thoughtful genealogy" and deems Goodwin "a meticulous and felicitous writer." Geoffrey C. Ward, writing in the *New York Times Book Review* describes Goodwin's portrayal of the book's main characters as "remarkably rich and fully rounded," adding, "her accounts of the events through which they all lived [are] unusually complex and elegantly rendered."

In his *New York Times* review Lehmann-Haupt comments on the tri-generational approach the author employs in *The Fitzgeralds and the Kennedys,* deeming it "deceptively simple," and commends Goodwin on the book's attention to detail and "thematic coherence." What gives *The Fitzgeralds and the*

Kennedys thematic unity is largely its emphasis on the concept of the family. As Goodwin told the *New York Times*, it is through this multigenerational approach that "the reader will, I hope, be able to see more clearly the inescapable impact of family relationships over time, the repeated patterns of behaviour, both enviable and dubious, the same strengths and the same weaknesses that crop up again and again." Ward praises Goodwin for her adherence to such an approach, noting that Goodwin "does not so much excuse the less attractive chapters of the Kennedy saga as attempt to understand them, while providing the kind of informed historical context without which no family's history can ever be understood. She never loses sight of the fact that family *matters,* that what happens within one generation inevitably has its impact on the next."

While *The Fitzgeralds and the Kennedys* was generally well-received, some critics had mixed reactions to the book. Ward, for example, finds fault with Goodwin's rendering of the voices of those she interviewed during her research. He writes: "Ms. Goodwin is a serious, sensitive biographer, and she has clearly mined a good deal of important new material from those with whom she talked. But the impact of much that they told her is vitiated by the artful way in which she seems to have sculptured their memories." He adds, "In *The Fitzgeralds and the Kennedys* it is too frequently true that when key witnesses to important events are heard from, the reader cannot help wondering who is really talking, whose conclusions are being reached." Similarly, though he admires Goodwin's "tact and scholarship," *Time* contributor R. Z. Shepard claims: "The author overextends herself when she tries to occupy high critical ground. She is on much firmer ground when sticking to her own preconception, an alluring vision of history as romance."

Most critics were aware of Goodwin's close personal and political ties to the Kennedy family, and a great many praised Goodwin for her ability to write *The Fitzgeralds and the Kennedys* objectively, or as Dallek puts it, "with compassion and understanding." Commending Goodwin for "deftly eliding the problem implicit in the fact that her husband, Richard Goodwin, has been a Kennedy confidant for about three decades—while employing the advantage of that relationship," Higgins goes on to note: "I think she dealt brilliantly with the potential problem. She has ended her chronicle at JFK's inauguration, in 1961. While I think a stranger to the living family might have employed harsher rhetoric to deliver the moral and ethical estimates she renders, her verdicts are—though mercifully couched—just, complete and unsparing." "Mrs. Goodwin pulls no punches when it comes to the faults and frailties of the Fitzgerald and Kennedy families," writes Lehmann-Haupt, adding, "because Mrs. Goodwin examines their characters so intelligently, and because she places them all in the broader sweep of history, she never appears to be debunking her subjects. . . . In short, the legend remains intact in both its triumphant and tragic aspects. We get the Fitzgeralds and the Kennedys with and without tears. We are permitted to envy them, and yet also to be grateful that most of us, at least, have not been cursed with their radiant gifts and their ambition to reach and grasp the sun."

MEDIA ADAPTATIONS: American Broadcasting Companies, Inc. has purchased the television rights to *The Fitzgeralds and the Kennedys: An American Saga.*

BIOGRAPHICAL/CRITICAL SOURCES:

PERIODICALS

Commentary, August, 1976.

Detroit News, March 27, 1987.
Los Angeles Times, March 4, 1987.
Los Angeles Times Book Review, March 1, 1987.
Nation, September 4, 1976.
National Observer, June 19, 1976.
New Republic, August 7 & 14, 1976, March 23, 1979.
New Statesman, October 8, 1976.
Newsweek, May 31, 1976, February 9, 1987.
New Yorker, June 7, 1976.
New York Review of Books, June 24, 1976.
New York Times, June 7, 1976, February 2, 1987.
New York Times Book Review, June 6, 1976, February 15, 1987.
Saturday Review, June 12, 1976.
Spectator, October 16, 1976.
Time, February 16, 1987.
Times Literary Supplement, December 10, 1976, July 17, 1987.
Washington Post, January 20, 1987.
Washington Post Book World, December 12, 1976.†

—*Sketch by Robert F. Scott*

*   *   *

GREEN, Judith
See RODRIGUEZ, Judith Green

*   *   *

GREENE, Laura 1935-

PERSONAL: Born July 21, 1935, in New York, N.Y.; daughter of Charles (in sales) and Ida (Katz) Offenhartz; married Victor Robert Greene (a professor of American history), February 21, 1957; children: Jessica, Geoffrey. *Education:* Boston University, B.S., 1958; University of Pennsylvania, M.A., 1963; also attended Kansas State University, 1963-72, and University of Wisconsin—Milwaukee, 1984-87.

ADDRESSES: Home and office—4869 North Woodburn St., Milwaukee, Wis. 53217.

CAREER: Junior high school English teacher in Yeadon, Pa., 1961-62; high school English teacher in Haddonfield, N.J., 1962-63; Kansas State University, Manhattan, instructor in English, 1962-73; teacher at religious schools in Milwaukee, Wis., 1973—. Member of teaching staff at University of Bremen, 1981, and University of Wisconsin—Milwaukee, 1982.

MEMBER: Authors League of America, Authors Guild, Society of Children's Book Writers, Council for Wisconsin Writers, Chicago Reading Roundtable.

AWARDS, HONORS: Citation from National Council of the Social Studies, 1979, for *I Am an Orthodox Jew;* Arthur Tofte Memorial Award from Council for Wisconsin Writers, 1981, for *Sign Language;* International Award for Exemplary Teaching, Kohl Foundation, 1985.

WRITINGS:

JUVENILES

I Am an Orthodox Jew, Holt, 1979.
I Am Somebody, Children's Press, 1980.
Change: Geting to Know about Ebb and Flow (illustrations by Gretchen Mayo), Human Sciences Press, 1981.
Help: Getting to Know about Needing and Giving, illustrations by Mayo, Human Sciences Press, 1981.
(With Eva Barash Dicker) *Sign Language: A First Book*, F. Watts, 1981.

Careers in the Computer Industry, F. Watts, 1983.
Computers in Business and Industry, F. Watts, 1984.
Computer Pioneers, F. Watts, 1985.
Sign Language Talk, F. Watts, 1987.

WORK IN PROGRESS: More children's books.

SIDELIGHTS: "Children's egos are very fragile things," Greene wrote to *CA*. "What children think of themselves is an important factor in forming their egos and thus their personalities. One thing that affects children's self-images is the way they perceive their differences and their unique qualities. I write about the differences among people which are often a source of pain and prejudice, but I try to look at these differences as a potential source of pride.

"*I Am an Orthodox Jew* is about what it's like to be a member of a community which is different from that of the majority. *I Am Somebody* concerns a boy who isn't as good at sports as he'd like to be. The characters in both books are proud of what they are, even though they rub against their differences. *Help* and *Change* deal with the idea that we don't always have control over everything in life, yet, despite this, each of us can do significant things. *Sign Language* explains a language with a unique communication base to hearing children. It is my hope that children with hearing disabilities, who read this book, will feel a sense of pride in their own special language. I write about people and their feelings because I care very much about the hurt we inflict upon one another.

"I have strong feelings about the women's movement. I support the Equal Rights Amendment and believe women should have the same opportunities, benefits, and responsibilities as men. Yet, I fear that in the struggle for this cause (which is so right), it is the children who are being hurt, as are the women who choose not to engage in out-of-home employment. I have two full-time jobs: writing and homemaking; I am committed to both with equal fervor."

*   *   *

GRIMM, Reinhold 1931-

PERSONAL: Born May 21, 1931, in Nuremberg, Germany (now West Germany); came to United States in 1967; son of Eugen (a laborer) and Anna (Kaeser) Grimm; married Anneliese E. Schmidt, September 25, 1954; children: Ruth Sabine. *Education:* Attended University of Colorado, 1952-53; Erlangen University, Ph.D., 1956.

ADDRESSES: Home—3983 Plymouth Circle, Madison, Wis. 53705. *Office*—Department of German and Comparative Literature, University of Wisconsin, Madison, Wis. 53706.

CAREER: Erlangen University, Erlangen, West Germany, assistant professor of German literature, 1957-61; Frankfurt University, Frankfurt, West Germany, assistant professor of German literature, 1961-67; University of Wisconsin—Madison, Alexander Hohlfeld Professor of German, 1967-80, Vilas Professor of Comparative Literature and German, 1980—. Visiting professor, New York University and Columbia University, both 1967, University of Florida, 1973, University of Virginia, 1978; distinguished visiting professor, New Mexico State University, 1986.

MEMBER: Modern Language Association of America, American Association of Teachers of German (president, 1974-75).

AWARDS, HONORS: Foerderungspreis der Stadt Nuernberg, 1964; Guggenheim fellow, 1969-70; Institute for Research in the Humanities fellow, 1981.

WRITINGS:

Gottfried Benn: Die farbliche Chiffre in der Dichtung (title means "Gottfried Benn: The Color-Emblem in Literature"), H. Carl (Nuremberg), 1958, 2nd edition, 1962.

Bertolt Brecht: Die Struktur seines Werkes (title means "Bertolt Brecht: The Structure of His Work"), H. Carl, 1959, 6th edition, 1972.

Bertolt Brecht, J. B. Metzler, 1961, 3rd revised edition, 1971.

Bertolt Brecht und die Weltliteratur (title means "Bertolt Brecht and World Literature"), H. Carl, 1961.

(With Heinz Otto Burger) *Evokation und Montage: Drei Beitraege zum Verstaendnis moderner deutscher Lyrik* (title means "Evocation and Montage: Three Contributions towards an Understanding of Modern German Poetry"), Sachse & Pohl, 1961, revised edition, 1967.

Strukturen: Essays zur deutschen Literatur (title means "Structures: Essays on German Literature"), Sachse & Pohl, 1963.

(Author of afterword) Denis Diderot, *Das Paradox ueber den Schauspieler* (title means "The Paradox of the Comedian"), Insel Verlag, 1964.

(With others) *Romanticism Today: Friedrich Schlegel, Novalis, E. T. A. Hoffmann, Ludwig Tieck,* Inter Nationes (Bonn), 1973.

Nach dem Naturalismus: Essays zur modernen Dramatik (title means "Beyond Naturalism: Essays on Modern Drama"), Athenaeum Verlag, 1978.

Brecht und Nietzsche oder Gestandnisse eines Dichters (title means "Brecht and Nietzsche or Confessions of a Poet"), Suhrkamp, 1979.

Von der Armut und vom Regen: Rilkes Antwort auf die soziale Frage (title means "Of Poverty and Rain: Rilke's Answer to the Social Question"), Athenaeum Verlag, 1981.

(With Walter Hinck) *Zwischen Satire und Utopie: Zur Komiktheorie und zur Geschichte der europaeischen Komoedie* (title means "Between Satire and Utopia: On the Theory and History of European Comedy"), Suhrkamp, 1982.

Texturen: Essays und anderes zu Hans Magnus Enzensberger (title means "Textures: Essays and Other Writings on Hans Magnus Enzensberger"), Peter Lang, 1984.

Love, Lust, and Rebellion: New Approaches to Georg Buechner, University of Wisconsin Press, 1985.

EDITOR OR COMPILER

(With Wolf-Dieter Marsch) *Die Kunst im Schatten des Gottes: Fuer und wider Gottfried Benn,* Sachse & Pohl, 1962.

(With Viktor Zmegac) Iwan Goll, *Methusalem oder der ewige Buerger: Ein satirisches Drama* (title means "Methusalah or the Eternal Bourgeois: A Satiric Drama"), de Gruyter, 1966.

Episches Theater (title means "Epic Theater"), Kiepenheuer & Witsch, 1966, 3rd edition, 1987.

Zur Lyrik-Diskussion (title means "Concerning the Lyric"), Wissenschaftliche Buchgesellschaft, 1966, 2nd edition, 1974.

(And author of introduction) *Deutsche Romantheorien: Beitraege zu einer historischen Poetik des Romans in Deutschland* (title means "German Theories of the Novel: Essays towards a Historical Poetics of the Novel in Germany"), Athenaeum Verlag, 1968, 2nd edition, 1974.

Bertolt Brecht: Leben Eduards des Zweiten von England; Vorlage, Texte und Materialien (title means "Bertolt Brecht: The Life of Edward II of England; Sources, Texts and Materials"), Suhrkamp, 1968.

(With Conrad Wiedemann) *Literatur und Geistesgeschichte: Festgabe fuer Heinz Otto Burger* (title means "Literature and History: A Congratulatory Volume for Heinz Otto Burger"), E. Schmidt, 1968.

(With Jost Hermand and author of introduction) *Deutsche Revolutionsdramen* (title means "German Dramas of Revolution"), Suhrkamp, 1969.

(With Henry J. Schmidt) *Brecht Fibel* (title means "Brecht Primer"), Harper, 1970.

(And author of introduction) *Deutsche Dramentheorien: Beitraege zu einer historischen Poetik des Dramas in Deutschland* (title means "German Theories of the Drama: Essays towards a Historical Poetics of the Drama in Germany"), Athenaeum Verlag, 1971, 3rd edition, 1981.

(With Klaus L. Berghahn) *Schiller: Zur Theorie und Praxis der Dramen* (title means "Schiller: Theory and Practice of His Plays"), Wissenschaftliche Buchgesellschaft, 1972, 2nd edition, 1981.

(With Hermand) *Methodenfragen der deutschen Literaturwissenschaft* (title means "Methodological Problems in German Literary Criticism"), Wissenschaftliche Buchgesellschaft, 1973.

(With Helene Scher) Friedrich Duerrenmatt, *Die Ehe des Herrn Mississippi: Eine Komodie* (title means "The Marriage of Mr. Mississippi: A Comedy"), Holt, 1973.

(With Peter Spycher and Richard Zipser) *From Kafka and Dada to Brecht and Beyond,* University of Wisconsin Press, 1982.

Hans Magnus Enzensberger, Suhrkamp, 1984.

Editor, with Jost Hermand, of sixteen volumes sponsored by Deutsche Abtelung of University of Wisconsin, including *Die sogenannten Zwanziger Jahre* (title means "The So-Called Twenties"), Gehlen, 1970, *Die Klassik-Legende* (title means "The Myth of Classicism"), Athenaeum Verlag, 1971, *Exil und innere Emigration* (title means "Exile and Inner Emigration"), Athenaeum Verlag, 1972, and *Blacks and German Culture,* 1986.

OTHER

Also contributor of about 100 essays and scholarly articles to numerous periodicals. Editor or co-editor of yearbooks and journals, mainly on German and comparative literature, including *Monatshefte,* 1967—, *German Studies,* 1969—, *Text und Kontext,* 1978—, and *PMLA,* 1982-85.

WORK IN PROGRESS: A book on the images of the black man in German literature.

*   *   *

GUTHRIE, Donald 1916-

PERSONAL: Born February 21, 1916, in Ipswich, England; son of Malcolm (an engineer) and Maud (Lindeboom) Guthrie; married Mary Freeman, March 2, 1946; children: Eleanor, Alistair, Rosalyn, Anthony, Adrian, Andrew. *Education:* London Bible College, B.D. (with honors), 1949; University of London, M.Th., 1951, Ph.D., 1961. *Religion:* Christian.

CAREER: Employed as an accountant, 1934-46; London Bible College, London, England, senior lecturer in New Testament, 1949—, vice-principal, 1977-82, vice-president, 1985—.

MEMBER: Studiorum Novi Testamenti Societas.

WRITINGS:

The Pastoral Epistles and the Mind of Paul, Tyndale Press, 1956.

The Epistle to the Hebrews in Recent Thought, London Bible College, 1956.

The Pastoral Epistles, Tyndale Press, 1957.

New Testament Introduction, Volume I: *The Pauline Epistles,* Tyndale Press, 1961, 2nd edition, Inter-Varsity Press, 1964, Volume II: *Hebrews to Revelation,* Tyndale Press, 1962, 2nd edition, Inter-Varsity Press, 1964, Volume III: *Gospel and Acts,* Inter-Varsity Press, 1965, 3rd revised edition published in one volume, Tyndale Press, 1970.

Epistles from Prison, Abingdon, 1964.

(Editor) *Galatians,* Thomas Nelson, 1969.

(Editor with J. A. Motyer), *The New Bible Commentary,* 3rd revised edition, Eerdmans, 1970.

A Shorter Life of Christ, Zondervan, 1970.

Jesus the Messiah: An Illustrated Life of Christ, Zondervan, 1972.

(Consulting editor) *Lion Handbook to the Bible,* Lion, 1973.

The Apostles, Zondervan, 1975.

(Consulting editor) *Illustrated Bible Dictionary,* Inter-Varsity Press, 1980.

New Testament Theology, Inter-Varsity Press, 1981.

The Epistle to the Hebrews, Eerdmans, 1983.

The Teaching of the New Testament, Scripture Union, 1983.

Exploring God's Word: Ephesians, Colossians, Philippians, Hodder & Stoughton/Eerdmans, 1984.

Exploring God's Word: John's Gospel, Hodder & Stoughton/Eerdmans, 1986.

Contributor to encyclopedias. Contributor of articles to theology journals.

WORK IN PROGRESS: The Relevance of John's Apocalypse, Paternoster.

SIDELIGHTS: Donald Guthrie told *CA:* "Writing serious textbooks is a demanding business. It lacks the exhilaration of [writing] . . . fiction. It has to find creativity in other ways. This is not difficult when the subject matter affects the writer himself as is the case in all effective theological writing. But the aim must be more than to grapple with issues, whether theoretical or practical. Creativity is achieved, not by the exploration of new ideas as in scientific writing, but in the lucid explanation of important truths to bring out their relevance.

"Because a writer of text-books must be acquainted with what other writers in the same field are saying, there are various ways in which this has an effect on method and style. Where clearly written and interesting accounts already exist, it puts an onus on the writer to do better. In that case he must himself be convinced that there is room for another presentation. In the field of biblical studies, justification for new books is often found in tackling the subject from a different point of view. Much of my own writing has been prompted by the conviction that existing treatments have been approached from presuppositions that I wished to challenge."

AVOCATIONAL INTERESTS: Music, photography, motoring.

H

HALL, Linda B(iesele) 1939-

PERSONAL: Born August 2, 1939, in Cleveland, Ohio; daughter of Rudolph Leopold (an engineer) and Peggy (a writer; maiden name, Soule) Biesele; married James Q. Hall, August 4, 1960 (divorced October, 1975); children: Leslie Elena, Douglas Winfield. *Education:* University of Texas, B.A., 1960; Southern Methodist University, M.A., 1970; Columbia University, M.Phil., 1975, Ph.D., 1976. *Politics:* Democrat. *Religion:* Unitarian-Universalist.

ADDRESSES: Office—Department of History, University of New Mexico, Albuquerque, N.M. 87106.

CAREER: Universidad del Valle, Cali, Colombia, instructor in English, 1962-63; Universidad de los Andes, Bogota, Colombia, instructor in English, 1964-68; Trinity University, San Antonio, Tex., assistant professor, 1976-80, associate professor of history, 1980-86, and chairperson of inter-American studies; affiliated with University of New Mexico, Albuquerque, 1986—. Member of steering committee of National Task Force on Mexico-U.S. Relations and Migration of the Undocumented, 1979-80.

MEMBER: Latin American Studies Association, Association of Borderlands Scholars, American Historical Association.

AWARDS, HONORS: Kent fellow of Danforth Association, 1974-76; Danforth associate, 1977-83; National Endowment for the Humanities grant, 1977, fellow, 1981-82.

WRITINGS:

Alvaro Obregon: Power and Revolution in Mexico, 1911-1920, Texas A & M University Press, 1981.
(With Don M. Coerver) *Texas and the Mexican Revolution,* Trinity University Press, 1984.
(With Coerver) *Revolution on the Border: The United States and Mexico, 1910-1920,* University of New Mexico Press, in press.

Contributor to history journals and *Southwest Review.*

SIDELIGHTS: Linda B. Hall told *CA:* "I am interested in the revolutionary process and its effects on individual lives as well as on social institutions. My book on Obregon was particularly directed toward the effect that one man had on bringing the violence of an especially bloody revolution to a close and to the reestablishment of institutional government. My work on the U.S.-Mexican border addressed the social and economic effects of that same revolution. I have done extensive oral history work with survivors, and find that a fruitful method of historical inquiry. My literary criticism is quite different from my historical writing, and my choice of subjects reflects my enthusiasm for the universal insights of contemporary Latin American authors. All my writing is profoundly influenced by the seven years, 1961 to 1968, that I spent in Colombia.

*　　*　　*

HANDLIN, Oscar 1915-

PERSONAL: Born September 29, 1915, in New York, N.Y.; son of Joseph and Ida (Yanowitz) Handlin; married Mary Flug, September 18, 1937 (died, May, 1976); married Lilian Bombach, June 17, 1977; children: (first marriage) Joanna F., David P., Ruth B. *Education:* Brooklyn College (now Brooklyn College of the City University of New York), B.A., 1934; Harvard University, M.A., 1935, Ph.D., 1940.

ADDRESSES: Home—18 Agassiz St., Cambridge, Mass. 02140. *Office*—Widener 783, Harvard University, Cambridge, Mass. 02138.

CAREER: Brooklyn College (now Brooklyn College of the City University of New York), Brooklyn, N.Y., instructor in history, 1936-38; Harvard University, Cambridge, Mass., instructor, 1939-44, assistant professor of history, 1944-47, assistant professor of social science, 1947-48, associate professor, 1948-54, professor of history, 1954—, Winthrop Professor of History, 1962-65, Charles H. Pforzheimer University Professor, 1970—, director of Center for Study of Liberty in America, 1958-66, director of Charles Warren Center for Studies in American History, 1965-72, director of Harvard University Library, 1979-85. Harmsworth Professor, Oxford University, 1972-73. U.S. Board of Foreign Scholarships, vice-chairman, 1962-65, chairman, 1965-68; fellow, Brandeis University, 1965—; trustee, New York Public Library, 1973-80. Associate of the National Academy of Education. Public lecturer on historical problems and current events.

MEMBER: American Historical Association, National Education Association, American Academy of Arts and Sciences, American Jewish Historical Society (vice-president, 1973—), American Antiquarian Society, Massachusetts Historical Society, Colonial Society of Massachusetts, St. Botolph's Club.

AWARDS, HONORS: Union League Club award for history, 1934; J. H. Dunning Prize, American Historical Association, 1941, for *Boston's Immigrants, 1790-1865: A Study in Acculturation;* Award of Honor, Brooklyn College, 1945; Pulitzer Prize in history, 1951, for *The Uprooted;* Guggenheim fellowship, 1954-55; grants from Social Science Research Council and Clark-Milton Fund of Harvard University; Christopher Award, 1958, for *Al Smith and His America;* LL.D, Colby College, 1962; Litt.D., Hebrew Union College, 1967, Northern Michigan University, 1969, and Lowell University, 1980; H.H.D., Oakland University, 1968; D.H.L., Seton Hall University, 1972, Boston College, 1975; D.Letters, Brooklyn College of the City University of New York, 1972; Robert H. Lord Award, 1972; L.H.D., University of Cincinnati, 1981; Fulbright Distinguished American fellow, 1986.

WRITINGS:

Boston's Immigrants, 1790-1865: A Study in Acculturation, Harvard University Press, 1941, 2nd edition, 1959.
(With first wife, Mary F. Handlin) *Commonwealth: A Study of the Role of Government in the American Economy: Massachusetts 1774-1861,* Harvard University Press, 1947, revised edition, 1969.
The Uprooted, Little, Brown, 1951, revised edition, 1973, 2nd enlarged edition, 1983.
The American People in the Twentieth Century, Harvard University Press, 1954.
Adventure in Freedom: Three Hundred Years of Jewish Life in America, McGraw, 1954.
Chance or Destiny: Turning Points in American History, Little, Brown, 1955.
Race and Nationality in American Life, Little, Brown, 1957.
Al Smith and His America, Little, Brown, 1958.
Newcomers: Negroes and Puerto Ricans in a Changing Metropolis, Harvard University Press, 1959.
John Dewey's Challenge to American Education: Historical Perspectives on the Cultural Context, Harper, 1959.
(With M. F. Handlin) *The Dimensions of Liberty,* Harvard University Press, 1961.
The Americans: A New History of the People of the United States, Atlantic Monthly Press, 1963.
Fire-Bell in the Night: The Crisis in Civil Rights, Atlantic Monthly Press, 1964.
A Continuing Task: The American Jewish Joint Distribution Committee, Random House, 1964.
History of the United States, two volumes, Holt, 1967.
America: A History, Holt, 1968.
(With M. F. Handlin) *Facing Life: Youth and the Family in American History,* Little, Brown, 1971.
Statue of Liberty, Newsweek Books, 1971.
A Pictorial History of Immigration, Crown, 1972.
(With M. F. Handlin) *The Wealth of the American People: A History of American Affluence,* McGraw, 1975.
Truth in History, Harvard University Press, 1979.
(With wife, Lilian Handlin) *Abraham Lincoln and the Union,* Atlantic Monthly Press, 1980.
The Distortion of America, Atlantic Monthly Press, 1981.
(With L. Handlin) *A Restless People: Americans in Rebellion, 1770-1787,* Doubleday, 1982.
(With Bernard Bailyn, Donald Fleming, and Stephen Thernstrom) *Glimpses of the Harvard Past,* Harvard University Press, 1986.
Liberty and Power 1600-1760, Harper, 1986.

EDITOR

This Was America: True Accounts of People, Places, Manners and Customs, as Recorded by European Travelers to the

Western Shore in the Eighteenth, Nineteenth, and Twentieth Centuries, Harvard University Press, 1949.
(With others) *Harvard Guide to American History,* Belknap, 1954.
Readings in American History, Knopf, 1957.
Gerald Mortimer Capers, *Stephen A. Douglas: Defender of the Union,* Little, Brown, 1959.
Immigration as a Factor in American History, Prentice-Hall, 1959.
(With John Clive) Gottlieb Mittelberger, *Journey to Pennsylvania,* Harvard University Press, 1960.
American Principles and Issues, Holt, 1961.
(With J. E. Burchard) *The Historian and the City,* MIT Press, 1963.
H. S. Merrill, *Bourbon Leader,* Little, Brown, 1965.
Children of the Uprooted, Braziller, 1966.
(With M. F. Handlin) *Popular Sources of Political Authority: Documents on the Massachusetts Constitution of 1780,* Harvard University Press, 1966.
Dissent, Democracy, and Foreign Policy, Foreign Policy Association, 1968.
Harvard Encyclopedia of American Ethnic Groups, Harvard University Press, 1980.

OTHER

Also editor of *Library of American Biography,* 1951—. Contributor to Bowers' *Foreign Influences in American Life,* 1944, and to *Atlantic, New York Times Magazine, Commentary, Saturday Review,* and other periodicals.

SIDELIGHTS: A Pulitzer Prize-winning historian, Oscar Handlin is recognized as one of the foremost scholars of his generation. Many of his books are considered pioneering contributions to the fields of American ethnic, social and urban history. Handlin is especially well known for his interpretations of the immigrant experience in America, including *Boston's Immigrants, 1790-1865: A Study in Acculturation,* which won the prestigious Dunning Prize from the American Historical Association, and *The Uprooted,* which won the Pulitzer Prize. As the Charles H. Pforzheimer University Professor at Harvard, Handlin has also taught history and supervised the education of some of the nation's leading university historians. Despite his extensive academic associations, however, Handlin strives to make his books accessible to a general audience. *Dictionary of Literary Biography* contributor Arnold Shankman calls Handlin "one of the most prolific and influential American historians of the twentieth century. . . . Equally adept at writing history aimed at scholars and at the public, Handlin is one of a handful of professional historians whose works are popular with general readers."

Himself the son of Jewish immigrants, Handlin was born and raised in Brooklyn, New York. Even as a youth, he excelled in academics; Shankman notes that by the age of eight Handlin resolved to become a historian "and became a voracious reader who could often be seen reading books as he delivered groceries for his father." He graduated from Brooklyn's New Utrecht High School at the age of sixteen and within three years had earned his bachelor's degree from Brooklyn College. Then he was accepted for graduate work at Harvard, where he made a detailed study of Boston's immigrants in the late eighteenth and early nineteenth centuries for his doctoral dissertation. In 1940, Handlin received his Ph.D., and the following year, *Boston's Immigrants, 1790-1865* was published. According to Shankman, the work "was acclaimed as a model study, and Handlin was praised for creatively making use of census data and other government documents, for his familiarity with sociological concepts to explain assimilation and acculturation, and for his imaginative use of the immigrant press, a hitherto neglected source.... *Boston's Immigrants* ... is still frequently used as a required reading in college courses.''

Even before he earned his doctorate—and well before he turned thirty—Handlin joined the faculty at Harvard. Between 1939, when he began to teach in Cambridge, and 1951, he published three books: *Boston's Immigrants, Commonwealth: A Study of the Role of Government in the American Economy: Massachusetts 1774-1861* (co-authored with his first wife, Mary Handlin), and *The Uprooted.* In the *New Republic,* Jack N. Rakove writes: ''Defying the accepted notion that historians need aging before they do their best work, these three books established Handlin's reputation for originality of thought and subtlety of exposition.... [The] first two books were classic monographs, written for a scholarly audience. In *The Uprooted,* Handlin cut loose from the limiting conventions of academic writing in order to raise the most basic questions about the immigrants' journey between cultures.'' Handlin contends in these works that emigration was a central experience of millions of newcomers to America, and that the immigrants so transplanted had to modify traits developed in their Old World homes, causing them to suffer from culture shock. Rakove writes: ''In seeking what was typical and common in [immigrants'] experiences, Handlin predictably risked glossing over distinctions among and within different groups of immigrants. But at the same time he revealed his keen awareness of a different sort of complexity: the uncertainty, poignancy, and fundamental ambivalence that governed the immigrants' inner lives.''

''By the late 1950s,'' Shankman observes, ''Handlin was publishing nearly a book a year. Few aspects of American history escaped his gaze. Civil rights, ethnicity, urban history, the history of education, and foreign affairs all caught his attention.'' As race relations became an increasingly pertinent issue, the historian published *The Newcomers: Negroes and Puerto Ricans in a Changing Metropolis* and *Fire-Bell in the Night: The Crisis in Civil Rights.* Both books dispute the view that blacks and Hispanics are more prone to criminal activities than other ethnic groups; Handlin stresses the importance of education as the path to assimilation for the racial minorities. Later in the 1960s, Handlin turned his attention to another controversial issue: the burgeoning of college enrollment and the campus unrest sparked by radical students. A supporter of the Vietnam War, the reelection of Richard Nixon, and traditional academic values, Handlin became ''a critic of the go-go mentality of educational expansion'' who ''could hardly applaud the prevailing atmosphere of American universities,'' to quote Rakove. Handlin's *The American College and American Culture* and his works with his first wife, Mary, *Facing Life: Youth and the Family in American History* and *The Wealth of the American People: A History of American Affluence,* aroused controversy for the harsh criticism the historian levels against affluent—and unappreciative—youth. When Handlin turned his attention to the difficulties besetting his academic field—in *Truth in History*—he was equally passionate. That work explores the aims and methods of valid historical research while disparaging careerism, distortion of fact to fit theory, and partisanship in the academic ranks. Rakove calls *Truth in History* ''as carefully conceived an exposition of the craft as any American historian has ever produced,'' but notes nevertheless that the essay collection is ''troubling'' because ''... even

sympathetic readers will wonder whether his oracular judgments represent something more than the evidence itself supports.''

According to Shankman, Handlin ''has not sought to shun controversy. For more than thirty years his views on the origins of slavery, the nature of immigration to America, the work of New Left historians, and the obligations of the student of history have sparked debates and caused the publication of countless articles.... But even his most severe critics have not denied that Oscar Handlin has made lasting contributions as a teacher and scholar.'' As Rakove concludes, Handlin has shown ''how an historian could write for a broader public without compromising his obligation to do justice to the complexity of the past.... His own work [is] an example of how history could be done.''

BIOGRAPHICAL/CRITICAL SOURCES:

BOOKS

Bushman, Richard L., Neil Harris, David Rothman, Barbara Miller Solomon, and Stephan Thernstrom, editors, *Uprooted Americans: Essays to Honor Oscar Handlin,* Little, Brown, 1980.
Cunliffe, Marcus and Robin W. Winks, *Pastmasters: Some Essays on American Historians,* Harper, 1969.
Dictionary of Literary Biography, Volume XVII: *Twentieth Century American Historians,* Gale, 1983.
Handlin, Oscar, *Truth in History,* Harvard University Press, 1979.
Stave, Bruce, editor, *The Making of Urban History,* Sage Publications, 1977.

PERIODICALS

Amerian Jewish History, December, 1980.
Atlantic, April, 1958.
Book World, December 5, 1971.
Current History, May, 1958.
Los Angeles Times, December 12, 1986.
Los Angeles Times Book Review, February 22, 1981, April 18, 1982.
New England Quarterly, September, 1959.
New Republic, February 23, 1980, October 25, 1980.
Newsweek, January 11, 1971.
New York Times, December 30, 1970, November 12, 1971, July 29, 1981.
New York Times Book Review, December 27, 1959, April 2, 1972, February 25, 1978, March 1, 1981, October 18, 1981, March 14, 1982, September 21, 1986.
Saturday Review, August 24, 1963.
Village Voice, October 1, 1980.

—*Sketch by Anne Janette Johnson*

*   *   *

HANLEY, Clifford   1922-
(Henry Calvin)

PERSONAL: Born October 28, 1922, in Glasgow, Scotland; son of Henry and Martha (Griffiths) Hanley; married Anna Easton Clark, January 10, 1948; children: Clifford, Jane, Joanna. *Education:* Attended schools in Glasgow, Scotland.

ADDRESSES: Home—36 Munro Rd., Glasgow, Scotland. *Agent*—Curtis Brown Ltd., 1 Craven Hill, London W2 3EW, England.

CAREER: Scottish Newspaper Services (news agency), Glasgow, reporter, 1941-46; *Daily Record,* Glasgow, columnist, 1946-57; *TV Guide,* Glasgow, columnist, 1957-58; *Evening Citizen,* Glasgow, columnist, 1958-60; *Spectator,* London, England, television critic, 1963. Director, Glasgow Films Ltd., 1957-63. Appears regularly on television in Scotland "as subversive social commentator." Lecturer.

MEMBER: National Union of Journalists, International PEN (member of Glasgow council, 1962—; former Scottish chairman), Glasgow Literary and Philological Society (president, 1962-63), Screenwriters Guild, Scottish Arts Council, Inland Waterways Advisory Council.

AWARDS, HONORS: Academy Award ("Oscar"), Academy of Motion Picture Arts and Sciences, 1960, for "Seawards the Great Ships."

WRITINGS:

Dancing in the Streets (autobiography), Hutchinson, 1958.
Love from Everybody (novel), Hutchinson, 1959, published as *Don't Bother to Knock,* Brown, Watson, 1961.
The Taste of Too Much (novel), Hutchinson, 1960, revised edition, edited by Vincent Whitcombe, Blackie & Son, 1967.
Second Time Round (novel), Houghton, 1964 (published in England as *Nothing but the Best,* Hutchinson, 1964).
A Skinfull of Scotch (novel), Houghton, 1965.
The Hot Month (novel), Houghton, 1967.
The Red-Haired Bitch (novel), Houghton, 1969.
The Burns Country, J. Arthur Dent, 1975.
Prissy (novel), Collins, 1978.
The Biggest Fish in the World, Chambers, 1979.
The Scots, Times Books, 1980.
The Spirit of Scotland, B.B.C. Scotland, 1980.
Another Street, Another Dance (novel), Mainstream, 1983.
(And editor) *Glasgow: A Celebration,* Mainstream, 1984.

PLAYS

"Seawards the Great Ships" (screenplay), Films of Scotland, 1960.
"The Durable Element," first produced in Dundee, 1961.
(With Ian Gourlay) "Saturmacnalia" (musical), first produced at Citizens Theatre, Glasgow, Scotland, 1962.
"Dear Boss" (television play), first produced in England, 1962.
(With Gourlay) "Oh for an Island" (musical), first produced at Citizens Theatre, 1963.
(With Gourlay) "Dick McWhittie" (musical), first produced at Citizens Theatre, 1964.
(And director) "Hero of a Hundred Fights," first produced at the Perth Theatre, 1968.
(With Gourlay) "Oh Glorious Jubilee" (musical), first produced at the Royal Gala Opening of Leeds Playhouse Theatre, December 10, 1970.
"Down Memory Lane," broadcast by STV, 1971.

THRILLERS; UNDER THE PSEUDONYM HENRY CALVIN

The System, Hutchinson, 1962.
It's Different Abroad, Harper, 1963.
The Italian Gadget, Hutchinson, 1966.
The DNA Business, Hutchinson, 1967.
A Nice Friendly Town, Hutchinson, 1967.
Miranda Must Die, Hutchinson, 1968.
Boka Lives!, Harper, 1969.
The Chosen Instrument, Hutchinson, 1969.
The Poison Chasers, Hutchinson, 1971.

Take Two Popes, Hutchinson, 1974.

OTHER

Song lyrics include Scotland's unofficial national anthem, "Scotland the Brave." Contributor of several hundred articles to newspapers in Great Britain.

SIDELIGHTS: The author of a dozen novels under the pseudonym Henry Calvin, humorist and self-described "subversive social commentator" Clifford Hanley is also the author of a dozen books under his own name, beginning with his autobiography, *Dancing in the Streets.* While his books have enjoyed the best critical reception in the United States, Hanley's writings for radio, television and the stage have brought him the most recognition in his homeland. Hanley is perhaps best known there as the author of the lyrics to "Scotland the Brave," now the unofficial Scottish national anthem, and as the maker of "Seawards the Great Ships," a documentary film that won the Oscar for Best Foreign Documentary in 1960.

Hanley was born in 1922 in Scotland's largest city, Glasgow. He defines the city in *Glasgow: A Celebration* as the "grimy swamp of drink and violence, deprivation and anarchy" that is nevertheless worth celebrating because "it is hypnotic." This perhaps explains why the industrial seaport in west central Scotland is a familiar presence in his books. The eighth child of Henry and Martha Griffiths Hanley, whose parents had moved to Glasgow from Dublin and Tiree in the Inner Hebrides, respectively, the author was surrounded by a variety of verbal traditions. "We spoke the King's English without any difficulty at school, a decent grammatical informal Scots in the house, and gutter-Glasgow in the streets," Hanley discloses in his autobiography. Sheila G. Hearn comments in the *Dictionary of Literary Biography: British Novelists since 1960* that this environment facilitated Hanley's "sensitivity to dialogue, and this has stood him in good stead even when dealing with the English-speaking characters who largely populate his fiction."

Hanley's parents were Conservatives of the working class, but he adopted socialism when in his teens and soon became an active member of the Independent Labour Party. During World War II, Hanley was a conscientious objector who wrote news reports for the Scottish newspapers. In those years, he "also developed his interest in staging amateur plays and shows," Hearn relates, adding that Hanley's "success with a radio comedy series established him as an entertainer as well as a journalist." In the years after the war, Hanley wrote "Scotland the Brave," *Dancing in the Streets,* and *Love from Everybody,* the three works for which he is perhaps best known.

Dancing in the Streets, the account of Hanley's childhood in Glasgow's tenements, is "immensely entertaining," Hearn observes. Hanley's novel *Love from Everybody* likewise manifests the writer's inclination to the comic, as several women arrive in Edinburgh to visit the main character, a travel agent who has at various times given each of them a key to his flat. The autobiography's success, especially in the United States, together with the money Hanley received for the film rights to *Love from Everybody,* enabled him to retire from journalism in 1960 to concentrate on fiction writing. Hanley wrote two plays for the stage and one for television, two documentary films, and a pseudonymous thriller in the first year of that retirement, and he has produced, on the average, a book per year ever since. Hanley "has continued to be a prolific columnist and media personality as well," Hearn states.

Hanley's wide experience in theater informs his novel, *The Red-Haired Bitch*. The book "concerns the staging of a play originally intended to debunk the sentimental popular view of Mary Queen of Scots which is turned by a commercially minded theater manager into a musical romance that merely reinforces the accepted image," Hearn summarizes. The life of the production is threatened, as are several marriages, by the antics of the male lead, the director's wife, and a promiscuous supporting actress. "Hanley gives solidity to all of these particulars, and lots of Glaswegian local color," writes Martin Levin in the *New York Times Book Review*. Reviewers of the book maintain differing opinions. Its detractors—among them a *Best Sellers* contributor and Hearn—feel that it raises serious themes without developing them fully; conversely, a *Times Literary Supplement* reviewer appreciates Hanley's "oppressively real" characters.

The most strident criticisms focus on Hanley's use of stereotypes. For example, *A Skinfull of Scotch*, which finds humor in the familiar image of the hard-drinking, bag-pipe-toting, kilted Scot, evokes and perpetuates dangerous and "long-redundant myths," in Hearn's view. Donald Campbell, on the other hand, finds Hanley's "instinct for character cliche" forgivable in light of the seemingly inexhaustible energy of his prose. Campbell makes these remarks in a *British Book News* review of *Another Street, Another Dance*, a book in which characters transcend stereotypes, in his opinion. This novel, published in 1983, returns to the setting of Hanley's first book, Glasgow between the wars. In this novel, the city of the author's childhood has become the home of Meg Macrea, survivor of unlucky love. A peasant widow who loses her second husband because of his drinking, Meg raises five children against the onslaughts of urban life, which include prejudice and poverty. Campbell insists that despite the author's generally "simplistic approach to characterization," the heroine of this "heart-warming tale" is movingly real.

Hanley told *CA*: "I intended to be a writer from childhood, so there is no point in wondering now if it was wise. It is easier than working and it makes a living. When I am writing a novel it comes out at high speed, three to five thousand words a day. If I were not a professional typist I don't think I could stand it.

"In the early days I had ambitions to expand the frontiers of the art, to shine fresh light into obscure corners of the human spirit. It is a great relief to get past all that and accept myself as an entertainer. If one of my books makes a long boring journey quite pleasant, I have won."

AVOCATIONAL INTERESTS: Music and talk, brewing own beer, sailing in self-built boat.

BIOGRAPHICAL/CRITICAL SOURCES:

BOOKS

Dictionary of Literary Biography, Volume XIV: *British Novelists since 1960,* Gale, 1983.
Hanley, Clifford, *Dancing in the Streets,* Hutchinson, 1958.
Hanley, Clifford, *Second Time Round,* Houghton, 1964.
Hanley, Clifford, *A Skinfull of Scotch,* Houghton, 1965.
Hanley, Clifford, *The Hot Month,* Houghton, 1967.
Hanley, Clifford, *The Red-Haired Bitch,* Houghton, 1969.
Hanley, Clifford, *Glasgow: A Celebration,* Mainstream, 1984.

PERIODICALS

Best Sellers, July 15, 1964, August 15, 1969.
Books and Bookmen, May, 1967, September, 1968, June, 1969.
Book Week, August 2, 1964.
British Book News, October, 1983.
New York Herald Tribune Books, May 26, 1963.
New York Times Book Review, August 30, 1964, July 20, 1969.
Punch, March 15, 1969, April 23, 1969, September 3, 1969.
Times Literary Supplement, March 9, 1967, June 29, 1967, September 21, 1967, May 8, 1969.

* * *

HANRIEDER, Wolfram F.   1931-

PERSONAL: Born May 9, 1931, in Munich, Germany; naturalized U.S. citizen; son of Josef and Barbara (Laubmeier) Hanrieder. *Education:* University of Chicago, B.A., 1958, M.A., 1959; University of California, Berkeley, Ph.D., 1963.

ADDRESSES: Home—4812 Winding Way, Santa Barbara, Calif. 93111.

CAREER: Princeton University, Princeton, N.J., research associate, Center of International Studies, 1963-64, assistant professor of political science, 1964-67; University of California, Santa Barbara, associate professor, 1967-71, professor of political science, 1971—. Visiting professor at University of California, Berkeley, 1966, University of Kiel, 1974, School of Advanced International Studies, Johns Hopkins University, 1974, and University of Cologne, 1985. Milton R. Merrill Professor of Political Science, Utah State University, 1973. Fulbright professor, University of Munich and University of Braunschweig, 1969-70. Eric Voegelin professor, University of Munich, 1984, 1986.

AWARDS, HONORS: NATO research fellow; Order of Merit, First Class, Federal Republic of Germany.

WRITINGS:

West German Foreign Policy, 1949-1963: International Pressure and Domestic Response, Stanford University Press, 1967.
(Editor with R. A. Falk and contributor) *International Law and Organization,* Lippincott, 1968.
(Contributor) Roy C. Macridis, editor, *Modern European Governments: Cases in Comparative Policy Making,* Prentice-Hall, 1968.
The Stable Crisis: Two Decades of German Foreign Policy, Harper, 1970.
(Editor and contributor) *Comparative Foreign Policy: Theoretical Essays,* McKay, 1971.
(Editor and contributor) *The United States and Western Europe: Political, Economic and Strategic Perspectives,* Winthrop Publishing, 1974.
(Contributor) W. Link and W. Feld, editors, *The New Nationalism: Implications for Transatlantic Relations,* Pergamon, 1979.
(Contributor) *America's Transformation from Kennedy to Carter,* ICA, 1979.
(With Graeme Auton) *The Foreign Policies of Germany, France, and Britain,* Prentice-Hall, 1979.
(With Larry V. Buel) *Words and Arms: Dictionary and Data of National Security and Defense Policy,* Westview, 1979.
(Editor and contributor) *Arms Control and Security: Current Issues,* Westview, 1979.
(Editor and contributor) *West German Foreign Policy, 1949-1979,* Westview, 1979.
(Editor and contributor) *Economic Issues and the Atlantic Community,* Praeger, 1980.

(Editor and contributor) *Helmut Schmidt: Perspectives on Politics,* Praeger, 1982.
(Editor and contributor) *Technology, Strategy, and Arms Control,* Westview, 1985.
Global Peace and Security: Trends and Challenges, Westview, 1987.
Arms Control, the FRG, and the Future of East-West Relations, Westview, 1987.

Contributor of numerous articles to *Policy Standards Journal, Western Political Quarterly, American Political Science Review, Journal of Common Market Studies,* and other periodicals.

WORK IN PROGRESS: A book on German foreign policy.

* * *

HARCLEROAD, Fred F(arley)   1918-

PERSONAL: First syllable of surname rhymes with "lark"; born November 22, 1918, in Cheyenne, Wyo.; son of Fred F. and Ina Mary (Livermore) Harcleroad; married Moyne Payne, December 20, 1942; children: Patricia Irene, Fred Douglass. *Education:* Colorado State College (now University of Northern Colorado), B.A., 1939, M.A., 1942; Stanford University, Ph.D., 1948.

ADDRESSES: Home—840 Via Linterna, Tucson, Ariz. 85718.

CAREER: High school teacher and principal in Ault, Colo., 1939-43; Menlo Junior College, Menlo Park, Calif., teacher, counselor, and director of dormitory, 1943-46; San Diego State College (now University), San Diego, Calif., 1946-52, began as assistant professor, professor of education, 1951-52, director of audiovisual services, 1947-50, director of secondary education, 1949-51, chairman of Division of Education, 1951-52; San Jose Junior College, San Jose, Calif., dean of instruction, 1952-53; San Jose State College (now University), San Jose, dean of instruction, 1952-57, dean of college, 1957-59; California State University, Hayward, professor of higher education and president, 1959-67; University of Iowa, Iowa City, professor of higher education, 1968-74; University of Arizona, Tucson, professor of higher education, 1974—, director of Center for the Study of Higher Education, 1974-80.

Assistant and acting instructor, Stanford University, summers, 1944, 1945; visiting professor, University of Southern California, summers, 1951, 1958, California State University, San Diego, summer, 1954, Pennsylvania State University, summer, 1956, University of Hawaii, summer, 1961, and University of Washington, summer, 1969. President of American College Testing Program, 1967-74. Member of Committee on Intercultural Education, 1966-69; member of National Commission on Accrediting Study, 1971-72; member of ERIC Clearinghouse on Higher Education, 1973-79; member of Task Force on Interagency Cooperation for Council on Postsecondary Accreditation, 1976-78; National Home Study Council Accrediting Commission, public commissioner, 1976-82, chairman, 1977-81. Education Commission on the States, member of advisory committee on higher education, 1966-68, vice-chairman of advisory committee on higher education, 1967-68, member of planning board, Kellogg In-Service Education Project, 1976-79. Member of State of California advisory committee on real estate education and research, 1956-59; member of advisory panel of Southern California Community College Study, 1971-72; member of advisory board of ERIC Clearinghouse for Junior Colleges, 1973-77. Consultant to

McGraw-Hill Book Co., 1959-63, U.S. Department of Health and Human Services, 1964, 1966-67, 1969, Los Angeles Times-Mirror Corp., 1967, Education Commission of the States, 1972-73, 1977-80, and American Association of State Colleges and Universities Research Center for Planned Change, 1979-80.

MEMBER: National Education Association, American Council on Education (member of Pacific Coast committee), American Association for Higher Education, Association of Professors of Higher Education (member of executive committee, 1973-76; president, 1974-75), American Association of Community and Junior Colleges (president of College and University Section, 1975-76), Association for Educational Communications and Technology, Foundation for Educational Communications and Technology (member of board of directors, 1971-78, 1980-82), Association for the Study of Higher Education, Western College Association (member of board of directors and executive committee, 1963-67), Higher Education Colloquium, Commonwealth Club of California, Pi Kappa Delta, Kappa Delta Pi, Phi Mu Alpha, Phi Kappa Phi, Phi Alpha Theta, Phi Delta Kappa.

AWARDS, HONORS: Trailblazer Award, University of Northern Colorado, 1970.

WRITINGS:

(With William Allen) *Audio-Visual Administration,* W. C. Brown, 1951.
(With James W. Brown and Richard B. Lewis) *Audio-Visual Instruction, Technology, Media and Methods,* McGraw, 1959, 6th revised edition, 1983.
(Editor) *Learning Resources in Colleges and Universities,* U.S. Office of Education, 1964.
Need for Fiscal Authority and Responsibility in the California State Colleges, California State Colleges, 1967.
The Historical Background, Current Status, and Future Plans of the Developing State Colleges and Universities, U.S. Office of Education, 1969.
(Editor) *Issues of the 70s: The Future of Higher Education,* Jossey-Bass, 1970.
(Editor) *New Directions in Higher Education,* American College Testing Program, 1971.
(Editor with Jean H. Cornell) *Assessment of Colleges and Universities,* American College Testing Program, 1971.
(Editor) *Comprehensive Information Systems for Statewide Planning in Higher Education,* American College Testing Program, 1971.
(Editor) *Planning for State Systems of Postsecondary Education,* American College Testing Program, 1971.
(With Robert J. Armstrong) *New Dimensions of Continuing Studies Programs in the Massachusetts State College System,* American College Testing Program, 1972.
(With Frank Dickey) *Educational Auditing and Voluntary Institutional Accrediting,* ERIC, 1975.
Institutional Efficiency in State Systems of Public Higher Education, American Association of State Colleges and Universities, 1975.
Administration of Statewide Systems of Higher Education, American College Testing Program, 1975.
(With C. Theodore Molen, Jr. and Suzanne Van Ort) *The Regional State Colleges and Universities in the Middle 1970s,* American Association of State Colleges and Universities, 1976.
Educational Auditing and Accountability, Council on Postsecondary Accreditation, 1976.

(Editor) *The Study of Higher Education: Some Papers on Administrative Theory and Practice*, Association of Professors of Higher Education, 1976.

(With T. Harry McKinney and S. V. Martorana) *Postsecondary Education in North Dakota: An Agenda for 1977-78*, North Dakota Postsecondary Education Commission, 1977.

(With Brown and Lewis) *Instructor's Manual to Accompany Audio-Visual Instruction: Technology, Media and Methods*, 5th edition, 1977.

(Editor) *Financing Postsecondary Education in the 1980s*, University of Arizona, 1979.

Accreditation: History, Process, and Problems, ERIC, 1980.

Voluntary Organizations in America and the Development of Educational Accreditation, Council on Postsecondary Accreditation, 1980.

(With Enarson and others) *Partners in Quality*, North Dakota Cimmission on Higher Education, 1986.

(With Allan Ostar) *Colleges and Universities for Change: America's Comprehensive Public State Colleges and Universities*, University Press of America, 1987.

Also author of *Audio-Visual Instructional Technology Manual for Independent Study*, with Brown and Lewis, and of *International Education in the Developing State Colleges and Universities*, with Alfred Kilmartin, 1966.

CONTRIBUTOR

Audio-Visual Instructional Materials Manual, McGraw, 1959.

William J. McKeefery, *Parameters of Learning*, Southern Illinois University Press, 1970.

New Horizons in Admissions Excellence, Brigham Young University, 1970.

Target for the 70s, American Association of State College and Universities, 1970.

G. Kerry Smith, editor, *New Teaching, New Learning*, Jossey-Bass, 1971.

Roy Trout, *Exploring Non-Traditional Degree Programs in Higher Education*, American College Testing Program, 1971.

Paul L. Dressel and Frances H. Delisle, *Blueprint for Change: Doctoral Programs for College Teachers*, American College Testing Program, 1972.

Richard M. Millard, *Vocation: Central Aim of Education*, American College Testing Progam, 1973.

Exploring the Case for Low Tuition in Public Higher Education, American College Testing Program, 1974.

Berdahl, *Evaluating Statewide Boards*, Jossey-Bass, 1975.

Community College Staff Development, National Board on Graduate Education, 1975.

Martorana and Eileen Kuhns, *Managing Academic Change*, Jossey-Bass, 1975.

Academic Program Evaluation, Jossey-Bass, 1980.

Jedamus, Peterson and others, *Improving Academic Management: A Handbook of Planning and Institutional Research*, Jossey-Bass, 1980.

Hample and others, *New Directions in Institutional Research*, Jossey-Bass, 1981.

Altbach and Berdahl, *Higher Education and American Society*, Pergamon, 1981.

Young, Kenneth and others, *Understanding Accreditation: A Practical Guide to Self-Regulation in Postsecondary Education*, Jossey-Bass, 1982.

Also contributor to *Academic Program Evaluation, New Directions for Institutional Research*, 1980, and to *The Changing Nature of Rehabilitation Administration and Supervision*, with Amos Sales, 1981.

OTHER

Contributor to *Proceedings* of Northwest Association of Secondary and Higher Schools Annual Convention, 1970, and to *Summer 1970 Philosophic Exchange Annual Proceedings*, 1970. Contributor of articles and reviews to higher education journals. Audiovisual editor of *California Journal of Secondary Education*, 1952-55; member of editorial board, *Audio-Visual Communication Review*, 1959-65.

SIDELIGHTS: Fred F. Harcleroad told *CA:* "As a youth I loved poetry and secretly wrote many poems, but never had the courage to show them to others. And my series of youth adventure books never passed the writing of the first one, at age ten. Likewise the short stories of my university creative writing class never went out, even though the writer who taught the class was encouraging. Thus, my published writing has been professional, and all of it has 'come hard,' on top of full-time work, mostly when other people were sleeping. Most of it comes from a feeling of compulsion, a wondering why I and two others of a dozen friends were the only ones left alive after World War II. There had to be some reason—so I figured I had to leave the world a little bit better, as my friends gave their lives to do, and those of us left had to do the work of three or four. The writing was much easier than my friends dying to keep totalitarianism in any form from ruling the world."

*   *   *

HARDESTY, Nancy A(nn)   1941-

PERSONAL: Born August 22, 1941, in Lima, Ohio; daughter of Byron Tapscott (a tool and die maker) and Ruth Lucille (a bank clerk; maiden name, Parr) Hardesty. *Education:* Wheaton College, Wheaton, Ill., A.B., 1963; Northwestern University, M.S.J., 1964; University of Chicago, Ph.D., 1976. *Politics:* Democrat. *Religion:* Episcopalian.

ADDRESSES: Home—2534 Bradford Sq. N.E., Atlanta, Ga. 30345.

CAREER: Lima News, Lima, Ohio, reporter, 1961-63; *Christian Century*, Chicago, Ill., editorial assistant, 1964-65; *Eternity*, Philadelphia, Pa., assistant editor, 1966-69; Trinity College, Deerfield, Ill., assistant professor of English and sports information director, 1969-73; Emory University, Candler School of Theology, Atlanta, Ga., assistant professor of American church history, 1976-80; Central Gwinnett High School, Lawrenceville, Ga., English teacher, 1980-82; freelance writer/editor, 1982—. Founding member, Evangelical Women's Caucus, Daughters of Sarah.

WRITINGS:

(Contributor) Robert G. Clouse and others, editors, *The Cross and the Flag*, Creation House, 1972.

(With Letha Scanzoni) *All We're Meant to Be: A Biblical Approach to Women's Liberation*, Word Books, 1974, revised edition, Abingdon, 1986.

(Contributor) Gary R. Collins, editor, *It's O.K. to Be Single*, Word Books, 1976.

(Contributor) Helen Gray Crotwell, editor, *Women and the Word*, Fortress, 1978.

(Contributor) Rosemary Ruether and Eleanor McLaughlin, editors, *Women of Spirit*, Simon & Schuster, 1979.

Great Women of Faith, Baker Book, 1980.

(Contributor) Jim Towns, editor, *Solo Flight,* Tyndale, 1980.
(Contributor) Theodore Runyon, editor, *Sanctification and Liberation,* Abingdon, 1981.
(Contributor) Hilah F. Thomas and Rosemary Skinner Keller, *Women in New Worlds,* Abingdon, 1981.
Women Called to Witness, Abingdon, 1984.
Inclusive Language in the Church, John Knox, 1987.

WORK IN PROGRESS: A history of Christianity for junior high children, for Westminster; a study of adult children of fundamentalism; a history of gender relations and sexuality in the Judeo-Christian tradition.

SIDELIGHTS: Nancy A. Hardesty told *CA:* ''I have been reared, educated and employed within a conservative, 'evangelical' Christian context. There I have seen first-hand the discrimination practiced against women and have felt the frustration when such oppression is buttressed with biblical and religious arguments. I decided to fight back. My goal is to learn more about Christian women of the past, their work and their beliefs, and then to communicate their inspiring stories to people today.''

*　　*　　*

HARMON, Robert Bartlett 1932-

PERSONAL: Born November 29, 1932, in Helper, Utah; son of John Harold (a salesman) and Winnie Ethlynn (Bartlett) Harmon; married Merlynn Swensen, August 18, 1961; children: Marriner John, Jane Anne, David Wright, James Bartlett, Nancy Louise. *Education:* Brigham Young University, B.A., 1958, M.A., 1960; Rutgers University, M.L.S., 1962; graduate study at San Jose State University, 1966-68. *Politics:* Republican. *Religion:* Church of Jesus Christ of Latter-day Saints (Mormon).

ADDRESSES: Home—964 Chapel Hill Way, San Jose, Calif. 95122. *Office*—Library, San Jose State University, San Jose, Calif. 95192.

CAREER: San Jose State University, San Jose, Calif., librarian II, 1962-65, senior assistant librarian, 1969-75, associate librarian, 1975—, reference librarian, 1979—, Library Education and Assistance Program lecturer in Graduate School of Librarianship, head of acquisitions department, 1969-79. Editor and publisher, Dibco Press, 1966—; founder and research bibliographer, Bibliographic Research Library, 1970—.

MEMBER: American Library Association (founder and director of Bibliographic Information Center for the Study of Political Science, 1970—), Bibliographical Society of America, American Printing History Association, Hemingway Society, John Steinbeck Society of America, Mormon History Association, California Library Association (college and university section), Kappa Delta Pi.

WRITINGS:

The Cole Family: A Brief Bibliography, privately printed, 1964.
A Preliminary Checklist of Materials on Harman-Harmon Genealogy, privately printed, 1964.
Political Science: A Bibliographical Guide to the Literature, four volumes, Scarecrow, 1965-74.
(With John Ray Harmon) *Descendants of Charles Claymore Bartlett and Annie Katrine Jensen,* Harmonart, 1965.
Sources and Problems of Bibliography in Political Science, Dibco, 1966.

Suggestions for a Basic Political Science Library, Bibliographic Information Center for the Study of Political Science, 1970.
Political Science Seminar Research Methods Manual, Bibliographic Information Center for the Study of Political Science, 1970.
Imperialism as a Concept of Political Science: Essay and Bibliography, Bibliographic Information Center for the Study of Political Science, 1971.
Art and Practice of Diplomacy, Scarecrow, 1971.
Methodology and Research in Political Science: An Annotated Bibliography, Bibliographic Information Center for the Study of Political Science, 1972.
Elementary Cataloging Manual for Small Libraries, Dibco, 1972.
Earthquakes: Toward a Bibliography of Bibliographies, Dibco, 1972.
John Steinbeck: Toward a Bibliography of Bibliographies, Dibco, 1973.
Georgette Heyer: A Preliminary Checklist, Dibco, 1974.
The Ghostly Bibliography, Dibco, 1975.
Selected Guide to Annotated Sources of Information in Political Science, General Learning Press, 1975.
Simplified Cataloging Manual for Small Libraries and Private Collections, Bibliographic Research Library, 1975.
Developing the Library Collection in Political Science, Scarecrow, 1976.
(With Margaert A. Burger) *An Annotated Guide to the Works of Dorothy L. Sayers,* Garland, 1977.
Understanding Ernest Hemingway: A Study and Research Guide, Scarecrow, 1977.
The First Editions of Ernest Hemingway, Hermes House, 1978.
The First Editions of William Faulkner, Hermes House, 1978.
The First Editions of John Steinbeck, Hermes House, 1978.
The First Ediitons of Robinson Jeffers, Hermes House, 1978.
The First Editions of Gertrude Stein, Hermes House, 1978.
The First Editions of F. Scott Fitzgerald, Hermes House, 1978.
Elements of Bibliography: A Simplified Approach, Scarecrow, 1981.
A Collector's Guide to the First Editions of John Steinbeck, Opuscala Press, 1985.
The Collectible John Steinbeck: A Practical Guide, McFarland & Co., 1986.
(Compiler with Robert L. Lauritzen) *Index to the Steinbeck Research Center at San Jose State University: A Descriptive Catalogue,* Steinbeck Research Center, 1987.
Steinbeck Bibliographies: An Annotated Guide, Scarecrow, 1987.

Also author of bibliographies for ''Public Administration and Architecture'' series, Vance Bibliographies, 1974. Editor, *The Steinbeck Collector,* 1979—.

WORK IN PROGRESS: Introductory Guide to the Study of Bibliography; the second edition of *Developing the Library Collection in Political Science; Introductory Guide to the Study of International Relations.*

SIDELIGHTS: Robert Bartlett Harmon wrote *CA:* ''I continue to attempt what seems at times to be the impossible, to compile bibliographic instruments that most users will find valuable in their research endeavors. As bridges to information, bibliographies, if compiled effectively, offer unexcelled opportunities for researchers to uncover gold mines of unsuspected information related to their interests. With the advent of machine-readable databases and means to access them via computers with modems, the use of bibliographic information becomes more widely disseminated and thus more valuable to users at all levels.''

*   *   *

HARTEL, Klaus Dieter
   See VANDENBERG, Philipp

*   *   *

HARVEY, John F(rederick) 1921-

PERSONAL: Born August 21, 1921, in Maryville, Mo.; son of Abraham Frederick and Lois Ernestine (Glenn) Harvey. *Education:* Dartmouth College, A.B., 1943; University of Illinois, B.S., 1944; University of Chicago, Ph.D., 1949.

ADDRESSES: P.O. Box 122, Lyndonville, Vt. 05851.

CAREER: John Crerar Library, Chicago, Ill., assistant cataloger, 1944-45, assistant medical reference librarian, 1945-47; University of Chicago Library, Chicago, administrative assistant, 1949-50; Parsons College, Fairfield, Iowa, librarian and professor of library science, 1950-53; Kansas State Teachers College of Pittsburg (now Pittsburg State University), Pittsburg, professor, head librarian, and chairman of department of library science, 1953-58; Drexel Institute of Technology (now Drexel University), Philadelphia, Pa., director of libraries, 1958-63, Graduate School of Library Science, dean and professor, 1958-67; University of Tehran, Tehran, Iran, professor of library sciences, 1967-71, chairman of department, 1967-68; Iranian Documentation Centre and Tehran Book Processing Centre, Tehran, founder, technical director, 1968-71; University of New Mexico, Albuquerque, dean of Library Services, 1972-74; Hofstra University, Hempstead, N.Y., dean of Library Services, 1974-76; writer, editor, and consultant, 1976-78; visiting professor at Mottahedin University, Tehran, 1978-80. Pennsylvania director, National Library Week, 1960-62. Consultant to organizations, including World Health Organization. *Military service:* U.S. Army, 1942-43.

MEMBER: American Library Association, American Association of University Professors, American Society of Information Science, Association of College and Research Libraries, Church and Synagogue Library Association, Library Administration and Management Association, American Institute of Iranian Studies, British Institute of Persian Studies, Institute of Information Scientists (London), Iranian Library Association, Middle East Librarians Association, New England Association of Schools and Colleges, Library Public Relations Association of Philadelphia, Phi Kappa Phi, Melvil Dui Chowder and Marching Association (New York), La Societe des Amities Francaises (Tehran), Archons of Colophon (New York), Brothers Three of Moriarity (Santa Fe).

AWARDS, HONORS: Library Binding Institute Silver Book Award, 1965; Fulbright grant, 1967-71.

WRITINGS:

Action Manual for Library Recruiters (monograph), Joint Committee on Library Work as a Career, 1956.
The Librarian's Career: A Study of Mobility, University of Rochester Press, for Association of College and Research Libraries, 1957.
(Compiler with Phillips Temple) *A Directory of Library Periodicals in the Continental United States,* State College Library (Pittsburg, Kan.), 1957.

(With Louis Shores and Robert Jordan) *The Library College,* Drexel, 1964.
Data Processing in College and Public Libraries, Drexel, 1966.
Report to Chancellor Torab Mehra Covering Recommendations for the Development of Jundi Shapur University Library Services, University of Tehran, 1968.
Iranian Senior College Library Standards, Educational Resources Information Center, 1971.
Toward a Definition of International and Comparative Library Science, Educational Resources Information Center, 1972.
Comparative and International Library Science, Scarecrow, 1977.
Church and Synagogue Libraries, Scarecrow, 1980.
(With Elizabeth Dickinson) *Affirmative Action in Libraries,* Scarecrow, 1982.
(Editor with Peter Spyers-Duran) *Austerity Management in Academic Libraries,* Scarecrow, 1983.
(Editor with Frances Laverne Carroll) *Internationalizing Library Education,* Greenwood Press, 1987.

Editor, ''Drexel Library School'' series, 1960-67 and ''Drexel Information Science'' series, Spartan Press, 1964-67; editor, *Library Journal* ''Recruitment'' series, 1962. Contributor to *Encyclopedia Americana,* 1963, *Bowker Library Annual,* 1963, *American Educator Encyclopedia* of United Educators, and proceedings of the Southwest Asian Documentation Centre Conference, 1970. Contributor of articles and reviews to professional journals. Honorary contributing consultant, *International Library Review,* 1969—; editor of various newsletters.

SIDELIGHTS: Toward a Definition of International and Comparative Library Science has been translated into Chinese.

*   *   *

HASTINGS, Adrian 1929-

PERSONAL: Born June 23, 1929, in Kuala Lumpur, Malaya; son of William George (a barrister) and Hazel Mary (Daunais) Hastings; married Elizabeth Ann Spence, 1979. *Education:* Oxford University, B.A., 1949, M.A., 1953; Propaganda Fide, Rome, Italy, D.D., 1958; Cambridge University, postgraduate certificate of education, 1958. *Politics:* Liberal.

ADDRESSES: Home—3 Hollin Hill House, 219 Oakwood Ln., Leeds LS8 2PE, England.

CAREER: Ordained Roman Catholic priest, Rome, Italy, 1955; worked in Africa, principally Uganda, Tanzania, and Zambia, 1958-72; University of London, School of Oriental and African Studies, London, England, research officer and fellow of St. Edmund's House, 1973-76; University of Aberdeen, Aberdeen, Scotland, lecturer, 1976-80, reader, 1980-82; University of Zimbabwe, Harare, professor of religious studies, 1982-85; University of Leeds, Leeds, England, professor of theology and head of department of theology and religious studies, 1985—. Visiting professor of theology, University of Lovanium (now Universite Nationale du Zaire), Kinshasa, Zaire, 1963-64. Editor of *The Journal of Religion in Africa,* 1985—.

WRITINGS:

Prophet and Witness in Jerusalem, Helicon, 1958.
(Editor) *The Church and the Nations,* Sheed, 1959.
One and Apostolic, Sheed, 1963.
The World Mission of the Church, Paulist Press, 1964.
Church and Mission in Modern Africa, Fordham University Press, 1967.

A Guide to Vatican II, two volumes, Darton, Longman, and Todd, 1968-69.
Mission and Ministry, Sheed, 1971.
Church and Ministry, Gaba, 1972.
Christian Marriage in Africa, S.P.C.K., 1973.
Wiriyamu, Orbis, 1974.
The Faces of God, Orbis, 1976.
African Christianity, Seabury, 1976.
(Editor) *Bishops and Writers: Aspects of the Evolution of Modern English Catholicism*, Anthony Clarke, 1977.
In Filial Disobedience, Mayhew-McCrimmon, 1978.
A History of African Christianity, 1950-1975, Cambridge University Press, 1979.
In the Hurricane, Collins, 1986.
A History of English Christianity 1920-1985, Collins, 1986.

WORK IN PROGRESS: A history of the churches in Africa from the fifteenth to the twentieth century.

* * *

HEALEY, Brooks
See ALBERT, Burton, Jr.

* * *

HEFTER, Richard 1942-

PERSONAL: Born March 20, 1942, in New York, N.Y.; son of Joseph (a translator) and Pauline (a bookkeeper; maiden name, Cohen) Hefter; married Olivia McLaren (vice-president of Optimum Resource, Inc.), October 23, 1967; children: Christopher, Nicholas, Gillian, Johnathan. *Education:* Pratt Institute, B.F.A., 1964.

ADDRESSES: Home—Emmons Lane, East Canaan, Conn. 06024. *Office*—c/o Optimum Resource, Inc., Station Place, Norfolk, Conn. 06058.

CAREER: Painter, printmaker, graphic designer, publisher, author. One Strawberry, Inc. (publishing company), New City, N.Y., president, 1975—; Euphrosyne, Inc. (licensing and publishing firm), Norfolk, Conn., vice-president, 1977—; Hefter, Johnson & Associates (*WOW Magazine*), Princeton, N.J., partner, 1977-81; Optimum Resource, Inc. (computer software), Norfolk, Conn., president, 1980—.

MEMBER: Authors Guild, Authors League of America.

AWARDS, HONORS: Fulbright fellowship, 1965; American Institute of Graphic Arts Children's Book Show selection, 1971-72, for excellence in graphic design in *Everything: An Alphabet, Number, Reading, Counting, and Color Identification Book*; Parents' Choice Award for excellence in media for children, 1983, 1984, 1985, 1986, for *Stickybear ABC, Stickybear Numbers, Stickybear Bop, Stickybear Basketbounce, Stickybear Opposites, Stickybear Shapes, Stickybear Town Builder*, and *Car Builder*; Software Showcase Award at Consumer Electronics Show, 1983-84, for *Stickybear ABC, Chivalry*, and *Stickybear Opposites*, 1985, for *Stickybear Math*; Software's Greatest Hits from American Library Association, 1984, for *Stickybear ABC* and *Stickybear Numbers*, 1985, for *Stickybear Typing* and *Stickybear Town Builder*; 1984 Outstanding Software Award and Gold Medal for Education from *Creative Computing*, for *Stickybear Opposites*; Best of the Best Award from Electronic Learning, 1985, for *Stickybear Reading*; Educator's Pick from *Evanston Educators' Newsletter*, 1986, for *Stickybear Printer*; Second Annual A+ Readers' Choice Award,

from *A+ Magazine*, 1986, for *Stickybear ABC*; Critics' Choice Award for Best Educational Software of 1986 from *Family Computing*, for *Stickybear Town Builder* and *Car Builder*; Nibble Software Excellence Award from *Nibble: The Reference for Apple Computing*, 1987, for "Stickybear" Series; Best Software of 1987 for Apple II Computers from *A+ Magazine*, for *Stickybear ABC*; Evanston Educators' Award for Excellence from *Evanston Educators' Newsletter*, for *Stickybear ABC, Stickybear Numbers, Chivalry, Stickybear Basketbounce, Stickybear Opposites, Stickybear Shapes, Stickybear Math, Stickybear Reading, Stickybear Town Builder*, and *Stickybear Printer*; *Stickybear ABC* and *Stickybear Numbers* were chosen Best Software of the Year by *Learning*; *Old Ironsides* was granted a certificate of merit from Electronic Fun with Computers and Games.

WRITINGS:

(Editor) *The Strawberry Mother Goose* (verse), illustrated by Lawrence Di Fiori, One Strawberry, 1975.
(Editor with Ruth Lerner Perle and Jacquelyn Reinach, and illustrator) *Sweet Pickles Dictionary*, sixteen volumes, Time-Life, 1982.

JUVENILES; SELF-ILLUSTRATED

(With Martin Moskof) *A Shufflebook* (story in phrases on cards), Western Publishing, 1970.
(With Moskof) *An Animal Shufflebook* (story in phrases on cards), Western Publishing, 1971.
(With Moskof) *Everything: An Alphabet, Number, Reading, Counting, and Color Identification Book*, Parents' Magazine Press, 1971.
(With Moskof) *Christopher's Parade*, Parents' Magazine Press, 1972.
(With Moskof) *The Great Big Alphabet Picture Book with Lots of Words*, Grosset, 1972.
A B C Coloring Book, Dover Books, 1973.
(With Phillip Johnson) *The Great Wow Toy Book*, Scholastic, 1982.
(With Johnson) *The Great Wow Game Book*, Scholastic, 1982.
Bears at Work, Optimum Resource, 1983.
The Stickybear Book of Weather, Optimum Resource, 1983.
Jobs for Bears, Optimum Resource, 1983.
Watch Out! The Stickybear Book of Safety, Optimum Resource, 1983.
Lots of Little Bears, Optimum Resource, 1983.
Bears Away from Home, Optimum Resource, 1983.
Where Is the Bear?, Optimum Resource, 1983.
Neat Feet, Optimum Resource, 1983.
Babysitter Bears, Optimum Resource, 1983.
Fast Food, Optimum Resource, 1983.
The Stickybear's Scary Night, Optimum Resource, 1984.

"STRAWBERRY BOOK" SERIES; SELF-ILLUSTRATED

An Animal Alphabet, One Strawberry, 1974.
A Noise in the Closet, One Strawberry, 1974.
Noses and Toes, One Strawberry, 1974.
One White Crocodile Smile, One Strawberry, 1974.
The Strawberry Picture Dictionary, One Strawberry, 1974.
The Strawberry Word Book, One Strawberry, 1974.
The Strawberry Book of Colors, One Strawberry, 1975.
Things That Go, One Strawberry, 1975.
Yes and No: A Book of Opposites, One Strawberry, 1975.
The Strawberry Book of Shapes, One Strawberry, 1976.
One Bear Two Bears: The Strawberry Number Book Strawberry/McGraw, 1980.

The Strawberry Look Book, Strawberry/McGraw, 1980.

"SWEET PICKLES" SERIES; SELF-ILLUSTRATED

Hippo Jogs for Health, Holt, 1977.
Lion Is Down in the Dumps, Holt, 1977.
Moody Moose Buttons, Holt, 1977.
Stork Spills the Beans, Holt, 1977.
Very Worried Walrus, Holt, 1977.
Yakety Yak Yak Yak, Holt, 1977.
Zip Goes Zebra, Holt, 1977.
Kiss Me—I'm Vulture, Holt, 1978.
No Kicks for Dog, Holt, 1978.
Pig Thinks Pink, Holt, 1978.
Turtle Throws a Tantrum, Holt, 1978.
Who Can Trust You—Kangaroo?, Holt, 1978.
Xerus Won't Allow It, Holt, 1978.
The Great Race, Euphrosyne, 1981.
Quick Lunch Munch, Euphrosyne, 1981.
Robot S.P.3, Euphrosyne, 1981.
Wet All Over, Euphrosyne, 1981.
The Secret Club, Euphrosyne, 1981.
Some Friend, Euphrosyne, 1981.

ILLUSTRATOR

Fred Rogers, adapter, *The Elves, the Shoemaker, and the Shoemaker's Wife: A Retold Tale*, Small World Enterprises, 1973.
Speedy Delivery: A Story from Mister Rogers' Neighborhood, Small World Enterprises, 1973.
Kathleen N. Daly, editor, *Bruno Bear's Bedtime Book* (poems), One Strawberry, 1976.
Judy Freudberg, *Some More Most*, One Strawberry, 1976.
Joan Lamport, *The Wordship Activity Book*, Arista Corporation, 1976.
Perle, *The Grand Prize*, Euphrosyne, 1981.
Elaine P. Wonsavage, *Preschool Program*, Volumes I-VIII, Weekly Reader Books, 1981.
Wonsavage, *Preschool Program*, Volumes IX-XVI, Weekly Reader Books, 1982.
Wonsavage, *Preschool Program*, Volumes XVII-XXXVI, Weekly Reader Books, 1982.
Goof-Off Goose's Dinner Party, Random House, 1982.
Edith Adams, *The Scaredy Book*, Random House, 1983.
Adams, *The Noisy Book*, Random House, 1983.
Ellen Weiss, *The Angry Book*, Random House, 1983.
Weiss, *The Messy Book*, Random House, 1983.

ILLUSTRATOR; "SWEET PICKLES" SERIES; WRITTEN BY REINACH

Elephant Eats the Profits, Holt, 1977.
Fish and Flips, Holt, 1977.
Fixed by Camel, Holt, 1977.
Goose Goofs Off, Holt, 1977.
Me Too Iguana, Holt, 1977.
Quail Can't Decide, Holt, 1977.
Rest Rabbit Rest, Holt, 1977.
Who Stole Alligator's Shoe, Holt, 1977.
Happy Birthday Unicorn, Holt, 1978.
Jackal Wants Everything, Holt, 1978.
Nuts to Nightingale, Holt, 1978.
Octopus Protests, Holt, 1978.
Scaredy Bear, Holt, 1978.
A Bad Break, Euphrosyne, 1980.
Rainy Day Parade, Euphrosyne, 1980.
Wait Wait Wait, Euphrosyne, 1980.
What a Mess, Euphrosyne, 1980.

What's So Great about Nice?, Euphrosyne, 1980.
Ice Cream Dreams, Euphrosyne, 1981.
Wet Paint, Euphrosyne, 1981.
Sweet Pickles A through Z, Cherry Lane, 1985.
Songs with Giggles and Tickles and Pickles, Cherry Lane, 1985.

SOFTWARE; CO-AUTHOR, ILLUSTRATOR, AND DESIGNER; PUBLISHED BY OPTIMUM RESOURCE

(With Jane Worthington, Steve Worthington, and Spencer K. Howe), *Stickybear ABC*, 1982.
(With J. Worthington and S. Worthington) *Stickybear Numbers*, 1982.
(With Jack Rice) *Old Ironsides*, 1982.
(With Rice) *Stickybear Bop*, 1982.
(With S. Worthington) *Chivalry*, 1983.
(With S. Worthington) *Stickybear Basketbounce*, 1983.
(With J. Worthington and S. Worthington) *Stickybear Opposites*, 1983.
(With J. Worthington and S. Worthington) *Stickybear Shapes*, 1983.
(With S. Worthington) *Fat City*, 1983.
(With Susan Dubicki) *Beach Landing*, 1984.
(with S. Worthington) *Run for It*, 1984.
(With Dubicki) *Stickybear Math*, 1984.
(With S. Worthington) *Stickybear Reading*, 1984.
(With S. Worthington) *Stickybear Spellgrabber*, 1984.
(With Dave Lusby) *Stickybear Town Builder*, 1984.
(With Dubicki) *Stickybear Typing*, 1984.
(With Dubicki) *Stickybear Math 2*, 1985.
(With Dave Cunningham) *Car Builder*, 1985.
(With Cunningham and Dubicki) *Codes and Cyphers*, 1985.
(With Lusby) *Stickybear Printer*, 1985.
(With Cunningham) *Stickybear Drawing*, 1986.
(With V. R. Swami) *Math Word Problems*, 1986.
(With S. Worthington) *Stickybear Basic*, 1986.
(With Lusby) *Stickybear Music*, 1986.
(With S. Worthington) *Stickybear Reading Comphrehension*, 1986.
(With Swami) *Map Skills*, 1987.
(With Swami) *Stickybear Word Problems*, 1987.
(With Gary Doody) *Reading Comprehension*, 1987.
(With Cunningham and Dubicki) *Stickybear Parts of Speech*, 1987.
(With Doody) *Spelling Rules*, 1988.
(With Dubicki) *Vocabulary Development*, 1988.
(With Dubicki) *Punctuation Rules*, 1988.
(With Dubicki) *Stickybear Math 3*, 1988.
(With Swami) *Problems with Fractions and Decimals*, 1988.
(With S. Worthington) *Stickybear Writer*, 1988.

OTHER

Editor, art director, and creator of *WOW Magazine*.

SIDELIGHTS: Richard Hefter wrote to *CA* that he thoroughly enjoys his role as writer, illustrator, and software designer: "My company, Optimum Resource, has been an industry leader in bringing quality educational programming to children and adults throughout the world. The 'Sweet Pickles' books have appeared in three languages, the 'Strawberry Book' series in more than seven, and two of the 'Stickybear' [software] programs have been released in French. Absolute delight in the work that I do attends every day, and I am grateful to [be] able to reach so many children."

MEDIA ADAPTATIONS: "Colors" (filmstrip with guide and records or cassettes; based on *The Strawberry Book of Colors*), Miller-Brody Productions, 1976; "Noses and Toes" (filmstrip with guide and records or cassettes), Miller-Brody Productions, 1976; "One White Crocodile Smile" (filmstrip with guide and records or cassettes), Miller-Brody Productions, 1976; "Yes and No" (filmstrip with guide and records or cassettes), Miller-Brody, 1976.

BIOGRAPHICAL/CRITICAL SOURCES:

PERIODICALS

Publishers Weekly, July 22, 1983.

* * *

HEINBERG, Paul (Julius) 1924-

PERSONAL: Born August 25, 1924, in Birmingham, Ala.; son of Benjamin Fries and Juliette Helen (Isaacs) Heinberg; married Joyce Suwal, July 8, 1945; children: Juliette Caye Anson. *Education:* Columbia University, B.S., 1949, M.A., 1950; University of Iowa, Ph.D., 1956. *Politics:* Democrat. *Religion:* Jewish.

ADDRESSES: Home—1530 Ahuawa Loop, Honolulu, Hawaii 96816. *Office*—Department of Communication, Grg. 343, University of Hawaii at Manoa, 2500 Campus Rd., Honolulu, Hawaii 96822. *Agent*—Bertha Klausner International Literary Agency Inc., 71 Park Ave., New York, N.Y. 10016.

CAREER: Texas Woman's University, Denton, instructor in speech and drama, 1950-52; Oklahoma State University, Stillwater, assistant professor of speech, 1952-57; University of Iowa, Iowa City, assistant professor of speech and dramatic art, 1957-65; University of Hawaii at Manoa, Honolulu, associate professor, 1965-69, professor of communication, 1969—, director of Speech-Communication Center, 1965-70. Vice-president, International Learning Systems, Honolulu, 1967—; president, PEP Associates (learning system development), Honolulu, 1971-74. Member of the board of directors of Honolulu Rapid Transit, 1971-74. Consultant, AT&T, 1957-66, Hawaii Telephone, 1970-76, and Institute of Educational Research, 1958-62. *Military service:* U.S. Army Air Forces, 1941-47; bomber pilot; became first lieutenant; received Air Medal with four oak leaf clusters.

MEMBER: International Communication Association, Society for General Systems Research, Acoustical Society of America, Speech Communication Association of America, American Psychological Association, National Society for Programmed Instruction, Teachers of English to Speakers of Other Languages.

AWARDS, HONORS: First Prize in verse play from California Olympiad of the Arts, 1964, for "Man Unmanned"; recipient of grants from Oklahoma Research Foundation, 1959, University of Iowa Research Foundation, 1962, AT&T, 1963, and FAA, 1980.

WRITINGS:

Voice Training, Ronald, 1964.
"Man Unmanned" (play), first produced in Iowa City, Iowa, 1965.
Speech-Communication Learning System, Volumes I and II, University of Hawaii Speech-Communication Center, 1968, revised edition, 1969.
Rx for Education, Human Development, Ltd., 1975.

Contributor to *Pacific Speech, Speech Teacher, New York Times, Journal of Educational Research,* and *Speech Monographs.* Editor of *Pacific Speech,* 1966-69.

WORK IN PROGRESS: New Communication, a trade book.

* * *

HEISLER, Martin O. 1938-

PERSONAL: Born April 5, 1938, in Budapest, Hungary; U.S. citizen; son of Steven I. (a businessman) and Magdolna (Stern) Heisler; married Elizabeth Trudie Jacobs (a clerk), September 11, 1960; children: Laura Magdolna, Diana Alice. *Education:* University of California, Los Angeles, B.A., 1960, M.A., 1962, Ph.D., 1969.

ADDRESSES: Home—1801 Republic Rd., Silver Spring, Md. 20902. *Office*—Department of Government and Politics, University of Maryland, College Park, Md. 20742.

CAREER: University of Illinois, Urbana, instructor of political science, 1964-66; University of Maryland, College Park, currently member of faculty in department of government and politics, 1967. Visiting professor, University of Kentucky, summer, 1967.

MEMBER: American Sociological Association, American Political Science Association, Caucus for a New Political Science (member of executive committee, 1971-72), International Studies Association.

AWARDS, HONORS: Woodrow Wilson fellow, 1960; grant from General Research Board, 1971.

WRITINGS:

(Editor and contributor) *Politics in Europe: Structures and Processes in Some Postindustrial Democracies,* McKay, 1974.
(Editor with Richard D. Lambert) *Ethnic Conflict in the World Today,* American Academy of Political and Social Science, 1977.
(Editor with Robert M. Lawrence) *International Energy Policy,* Lexington Books, 1980.
(With Barbara S. Heisler) *From Foreign Workers to Settlers? Transnational Migration and the Emergence of New Minorities,* Sage Publications, 1986.

Editor of series, "Comparative Studies of Political Life," McKay. Editor of *Bulletin of Comparative Interdisciplinary Studies,* 1970-73.

WORK IN PROGRESS: The Comparative Study of Political Life; a book on Brussels, for University of California Press.

SIDELIGHTS: Martin O. Heisler speaks French and Flemish, as well as his native Hungarian, and reads Spanish, Italian, and Serbo-Croatian.

AVOCATIONAL INTERESTS: Photography, travel.†

* * *

HENDRICK, George 1929-

PERSONAL: Born March 30, 1929, in Stephenville, Tex.; son of Hoyt (a rancher) and Bessie Lea (Sears) Hendrick; married Willene Lowery, January 23, 1955. *Education:* Texas Christian University, B.A., 1948, M.A., 1950; University of Texas, Ph.D., 1954.

ADDRESSES: Office—Department of English, University of Illinois at Urbana-Champaign, Urbana, Ill. 61810.

CAREER: Southwest Texas State Teachers College (now Southwest Texas State University), San Marcos, assistant professor of English, 1954-56; University of Colorado, Boulder, member of English department faculty, 1956-60; Johann Wolfgang Goethe-Universitat (University of Frankfurt), Frankfurt am Main, West Germany, professor of American literature and culture, 1960-65, co-director of English seminar, and director of Amerika-Institut; University of Illinois at Chicago Circle, professor of English, 1965-67; University of Illinois at Urbana-Champaign, professor of English, 1967—, head of department, 1971-76, associate dean of graduate college, 1967-71. Visiting professor, University of Illinois, Chicago Undergraduate Division (now University of Illinois at Chicago Circle), 1964-65.

MEMBER: Modern Language Association of America, Midwest Modern Language Association.

WRITINGS:

(With Donna Gerstenberger) *Directory of Periodicals Publishing Articles in English and American Language and Literature,* A. Swallow, 1959, 4th edition, 1974.
(Editor) *1785 Bhagavad-Gita,* translation by Charles Wilkins, Scholars' Facsimiles, 1959.
(With Gerstenberger) *The American Novel: A Checklist of Twentieth Century Criticism,* A. Swallow, 1960.
Katherine Anne Porter, Twayne, 1965, revised edition (with wife, Willene Hendrick), in press.
Mazo de la Roche, Twayne, 1970.
A Checklist of American Literary Manuscripts in Australia, Canada, India, Israel, Japan and New Zealand, Bull Publishing, 1972.
(With Lynn Altenbernd) *The Sandburg Roots,* University of Illinois Library Friends, 1976.
Henry Salt, Humanitarian Reformer and Man of Letters, University of Illinois Press, 1977.
(With J. A. Robbins and others) *American Literary Manuscripts,* University of Georgia Press, 1977.
Remembrances of Concord and the Thoreaus: Letters of Horace Hosmer to Dr. S. A. Jones, University of Illinois Press, 1977.
(Editor with Fritz Oehlschlaeger) *Toward the Making of Thoreau's Modern Reputation: Selected Correspondence of S. A. Jones, A. W. Hosmer, H. S. Salt, H. G. O. Blake and D. Ricketson,* University of Illinois Press, 1979.
(Editor with W. Hendrick) *On the Illinois Frontier: Dr. Hiram Rutherford, 1840-1848,* Southern Illinois University Press, 1981.
Thoreau amongst Friends and Philistines and Other Thoreauviana by Dr. S. A. Jones, Ohio University Press, 1983.
(Editor with Margaret Sandburg) *Ever the Winds of Chance,* University of Illinois Press, 1983.
The Selected Letters of Mark Van Doren, Louisiana State University Press, 1986.
Sandburg's "Fables, Foibles, and Foobles," University of Illinois Press, in press.

WORK IN PROGRESS: By the Author of "Cousin Sally Dilliard," with Willene Hendrick; *Homeopathy and Literature in Nineteenth-Century America;* an edition of the letters of James Jones.

SIDELIGHTS: George Hendrick told *CA:* "In recent years I have concentrated on publishing, with appropriate introduc-

tions and annotations, unknown or little-known works by and about American writers—the letters and humorous articles by a pioneer Illinois physician, the unfinished volume of Sandburg's memoirs, the Thoreauvian works of the homeopathic physician Dr. S. A. Jones—and I have also been editing the letters of American writers. This work continues, often with collaborators, and I am presently editing the humorous writings of Hamilton C. Jones (author of "Cousin Sally Dilliard") and the letters of James Jones, author of *From Here to Eternity* and other novels. I am attempting to make available to the reading public some important documents concerning our literary and cultural heritage."

*   *   *

HERBERT, Gilbert   1924-

PERSONAL: Born June 22, 1924, in Johannesburg, South Africa; son of Benjamin (a merchant) and Sophia (a musician; maiden name, Miller) Herbert; married Valerie Ryan (a teacher), June 18, 1953; children: Barry (deceased), Margaret. *Education:* University of the Witwatersrand, B.Arch., 1947, Diploma in Town Planning, 1951, M.Arch., 1955; University of South Africa, D.Litt. et Phil., 1969. *Religion:* Jewish.

ADDRESSES: Home—8 Eder St., Haifa, Israel 34752. *Office*—Faculty of Architecture, and Town Planning, Technion: Israel Institute of Technology, Haifa, Israel.

CAREER: University of the Witwatersrand, Johannesburg, South Africa, lecturer in architecture, 1947-61; University of Adelaide, Adelaide, Australia, reader in architecture and town planning, 1961-68; Technion: Israel Institute of Technology, Haifa, associate professor, 1968-72, professor of architecture, 1972-74, Mary Hill Swope Professor of Architecture, 1974—, dean of faculty of architecture and town planning, 1973-74. Adjunct professor at Bezalel Academy of Art and Design, 1970-72, 1976-78. Architectural consultant, 1947-68.

MEMBER: Israel Institute of Engineers and Architects, South African Institute of Architects, Royal Australian Institute of Architects (fellow), Royal Institute of British Architects (fellow), Society of Architectural Historians.

AWARDS, HONORS: Architectural Critics and Writers Award from Institute of South African Architects, 1980, for outstanding contribution in the fields of architectural history and criticism, and for *Martienssen and the International Style;* Joseph H. Hazen Award for Literature of Twentieth Century Art from Israel Museum, 1982, for "Gropius, Hirsch, and the Saga of the Copper Houses" and "The Packaged House: Dream and Reality"; D.Arch., University of the Witwatersrand, 1986.

WRITINGS:

The Synthetic Vision of Walter Gropius, Witwatersrand University Press, 1959.
Martienssen and the International Style, Balkema, 1975.
Pioneers of Prefabrication, Johns Hopkins University Press, 1978.
The Dream of the Factory-Made House: Walter Gropius and Konrad Wachsmann, MIT Press, 1984.

CONTRIBUTOR

Gershon Von Schwarze, editor, *Dialogue in Development,* Association of Engineers and Architects in Israel, 1970.
Don Soen, editor, *New Trends in Urban Planning,* Pergamon, 1979.

R. F. Ericson, editor, *Improving the Human Condition: Quality and Stability in Social Systems,* Springer-Verlag, 1979.

Muriel Emanuel, editor, *Contemporary Architects,* Macmillan, 1980.

Marvin Kranzberg, editor, *Ethics in an Age of Pervasive Technology,* Westview, 1980.

Warren Sanderson, editor, *International Handbook of Contemporary Developments in Architecture,* Greenwood Press, 1981.

N. Pressman, editor, *Creating Livable Cities,* Contact, 1981.

E. Schiller, editor, *Haifa and Her Sites,* Ariel Press, 1985.

OTHER

Contributor to *Encyclopedia of Building Technology,* edited by H. J. Cowan, and *Encyclopaedia of Modern Architecture.* Contributor to architecture journals in England, the United States, Australia, Canada, Israel, and South Africa. Associate editor of *South African Architectural Record,* 1949-60; corresponding editor of *Australian Planning Institute Journal,* 1965-68; editorial advisory committee, *Architectural Science Review,* 1977—; review board, *Plan SA,* 1986—; chairman of editorial advisory committee, *Documentation Unit Publications,* 1987—.

WORK IN PROGRESS: Erich Mendelsohn in Palestine, with Ita Heinze-Greenberg.

SIDELIGHTS: Gilbert Herbert told *CA:* "First and foremost I am a teacher, and my writing deals with theories, and the facts uncovered by historical research. It tends, therefore, to be didactic in purpose, and, at times, didactic in tone. When a critic complained of one of my early articles that it was heavy going, he was rapped over the knuckles by Walter Gropius who said: 'Gilbert Herbert is a serious scholar, and his work is not intended to be merely entertaining.' Nevertheless, I took the criticism to heart, for there is no need for scholarship to be dull, obscure, or pretentious. Least of all, a work of architectural history.

"The cultural historian is, in his own way, something of a detective. In his attempt at reconstructing a true mosaic of past events, he searches for clues, for fragments of information, and for logical connections, cohesive patterns. He is guided as much by intuition as knowledge. He is baffled by obscure facts, frustrated by missing evidence; and sometimes he is rewarded by flashes of insight, revelations of the truth, which must be later substantiated by evidence, and properly documented. The pursuit of historical knowledge is therefore charged, as is a detective story, with an underlying element of tension, with the excitement of the chase, with the drama of the denouement. Moreover, a study of architectural history deals not only with artifacts, physical objects, sticks and stones, not only with dry dates and chronologies—important as these may be—but with a rich cast of characters, whose complex personalities must be understood, whose motivations, ambitions and dreams are vital to an interpretation of events. Then, there is the broad sweep of historical context: cultural and technological change, ideologies and politics, the inexorable pressures of economics. The broad panorama, the human drama, the piquant incident, are all germane to the writing of history, as is the hard core of solid fact."

BIOGRAPHICAL/CRITICAL SOURCES:

PERIODICALS

Times Literary Supplement, June 21, 1985.

HIEATT, Constance B(artlett)   1928-

PERSONAL: Born February 11, 1928, in Boston, Mass.; daughter of Arthur Charles and Eleonora (Very) Bartlett; married Allen Kent Hieatt (a college professor and writer), October 25, 1958. *Education:* Attended Smith College, 1945-47; Hunter College (now Hunter College of the City University of New York), A.B., 1953, M.A., 1957; Yale University, Ph.D., 1959. *Religion:* Episcopalian.

ADDRESSES: Office—University of Western Ontario, London, Ontario, Canada N6A 3K7.

CAREER: Held various positions of a secretarial or editorial nature in publishing and teaching, 1948-57; City College (now City College of the City University of New York), New York, N.Y., lecturer in English, 1959-60; Queensborough Community College of the City University of New York, Bayside, N.Y., assistant professor, 1960-64, associate professor of English, 1964-65; St. John's University, Jamaica, N.Y., associate professor, 1965-67, professor of English, 1967-69; University of Western Ontario, London, professor of English, 1969—.

MEMBER: International Society of Anglo-Saxonists, International Arthurian Society, International Saga Society, Society for the Advancement of Scandinavian Studies, Children's Literature Association, Mediaevel Academy of America, Modern Language Association of America, Association of Canadian University Teachers of English, Royal Society of Canada (fellow).

WRITINGS:

(Editor and translator with husband, A. Kent Hieatt) *The Canterbury Tales by Geoffrey Chaucer,* Bantam, 1964, 2nd edition, 1981.

(Translator) *Beowulf, and Other Old English Poems,* introduction by A. K. Hieatt, Odyssey Press, 1967, revised edition, Bantam, 1983.

The Realism of Dream Visions: The Poetic Exploitation of the Dream-Experience in Chaucer and His Contemporaries, Mouton, 1967.

Essentials of Old English: Readings with Keyed Grammar and Vocabulary, Crowell, 1968.

(Editor) *The Miller's Tale of Geoffrey Chaucer,* Odyssey Press, 1970.

(Editor with A. K. Hieatt) *Edmund Spenser: Selected Poetry,* Appleton-Century-Crofts, 1970.

(Translator) *Karlamagnus Saga: The Saga of Charlemagne and His Heroes,* Pontifical Institute of Medieval Studies, Volume I, 1975, Volume II, 1975, Volume III, 1980.

(With Sharon Butler) *Pleyn Delit: Medieval Cookery for Modern Cooks,* University of Toronto Press, 1976, revised edition, 1979.

(Editor with Butler) *Curye on Inglysch: English Culinary Manuscripts of the 14th Century,* Oxford University Press for the Early English Text Society, 1985.

An Ordinance of Pottage: 15th-Century English Culinary Specialties, Prospect Books, in press.

JUVENILES; ADAPTER

(With A. K. Hieatt) *The Canterbury Tales of Geoffrey Chaucer,* Golden Press, 1961.

Sir Gawain and the Green Knight, illustrated by Walter Lorraine, Crowell, 1967.

The Knight of the Lion, illustrated by Joseph Low, Crowell, 1968.

The Knight of the Cart, illustrated by John Gretzer, Crowell, 1969.

The Joy of the Court, illustrated by Pauline Baynes, Crowell, 1971.

The Sword and the Grail, illustrated by David Palladini, Crowell, 1972.

The Castle of Ladies, illustrated by Norman Laliberte, Crowell, 1973.

The Minstrel Knight, illustrated by James Barkley, Crowell, 1974.

WORK IN PROGRESS: A translation, with Minette Grunmann-Gaudet, of *Guillaume de Marchaut's Dit de l'Alerion.*

SIDELIGHTS: A scholar of medieval language and literature, Constance B. Hieatt is noted for her adaptations of Arthurian legends for children, many of which have been praised for their authenticity and readability. Regarding her work for *The Sword and the Grail,* Feenie Ziner writes in the *New York Times Book Review* that Hieatt has created "a lucid moving story from a lode of jumbled sources" and commends the version for being "accessible to readers too young to cope with complexities of versions by Andrew Lang, James Knowles, or Howard Pyle." Furthermore, Ziner notes that Hieatt's adaptation, which presents the famous Grail as a mysteriously magical bestower of food instead of a chalice with special powers derived from bearing Christ's blood, displays "a pre-Christian symbolism . . . far more comprehensible than the religious one." Regarding another of Hieatt's adaptations, *The Knight and the Lion,* Doris Orgel in the *New York Times Book Review* writes that Hieatt's retelling of the twelfth-century romance "make[s] a once-upon-a-time world come glowingly alive, . . . [and] is clearly the work of a scholar, yet . . . highly readable throughout."

More recently, Hieatt has turned her scholarly interests towards medieval culinary texts. Her 1985 book, *Curye on Inglysch: English Culinary Manuscripts of the 14th Century,* co-edited with Sharon Butler, contains some of the earliest known recipe collections in the English language, some of which have never before been published. In a review for the *London Review of Books,* Christopher Driver comments that Hieatt and Butler's "own understanding of both modern and ancient culinary processes matches their familiarity with Medieval English" and calls their work "beyond praise."

BIOGRAPHICAL/CRITICAL SOURCES:

PERIODICALS

Book Week, May 7, 1972.
Commonweal, November 21, 1969.
London Review of Books, June 19, 1986.
New York Times Book Review, April 16, 1967, October 20, 1968, August 20, 1972.
Times Literary Supplement, May 13, 1977.

*   *   *

HILL, Denise   1919-

PERSONAL: Born August 1, 1919, in London, England; daughter of Harry (a company secretary) and Marie-Louise (Arrault) Dixon; married Patrick John Hill (a scientific assistant), May 17, 1946; children: Peter Nicholas, Frances Elisabeth. *Education:* Attended secondary school in England, 1932-35.

ADDRESSES: Home—Anchorage, Avenue Rd., North Hayling Island, Hampshire PO11 0LX, England.

CAREER: Writer. Home Office, London, England, civil servant, 1939-47; Hayling Island, Hampshire, England, librarian, 1956-64; Hampshire County Council, school secretary in Havant, Hampshire, 1964-72, social worker for the blind in Portsmouth, Hampshire, 1974-79.

WRITINGS:

JUVENILES

The Clever Car (illustrated by Robert Hales), Methuen, 1965.
A Pony for Two, Collins, 1965.
Coco the Gift Horse, Collins, 1966.
The Helicopter Children (illustrated by Ferelith Eccles-Williams), Methuen, 1967.
The Witch at Lundy Cottage (illustrated by Paul Wright), Hamish Hamilton, 1975.
The Castle Grey Pony (illustrated by Trevor Ridley), Hamish Hamilton, 1976.
No Friends for Simon (illustrated by Doreen Caldwell), Hamish Hamilton, 1977.
William and the Mutt (illustrated by Jane Paton), Hamish Hamilton, 1977.
The Birthday Surprise (illustrated by Maureen Bradley), Hamish Hamilton, 1978.
The Wrong Side of the Bed (illustrated by Caldwell), Hamish Hamilton, 1981.
Counterplot in Riot City, Marshall Pickering, 1984.
The Secret Sign (sequel to *Counterplot in Riot City*), Marshall Pickering, 1985.
The Enemy Sea, Marshall Pickering, in press.

Also author of *Misti.*

WORK IN PROGRESS: "I am planning a children's book, again with a Christian background, possibly set in Britain in the first century A.D."

SIDELIGHTS: Denise Hill told *CA:* "I was born in 1919, so I have become what is known as a senior citizen. I started writing with adult short stories. I had some success with these in magazines, and three of them were broadcast on the 'BBC Morning Story' around 1960. I turned to writing for children in the early 1960's and was lucky enough to have two books about horses accepted. I must say that in my teens I was madly horsey, and was able to transfer some of this enthusiasm onto paper."

Hill says that her positions as a librarian and school secretary were useful and of "tremendous value in writing for children, particularly the one as a school secretary. It is a unique position in that a school secretary can be approached and yet has no responsibility for discipline—the pupils tended to talk among themselves as if I were invisible, and dialogue was presented to me on a plate!"

Hill also told *CA:* "I might add that 'retirement' is a laughable word—it just means that I have given up the job for which I was paid! I shall continue to write, and write, and write, and hope publishers will appreciate my efforts. I would very much like to feel that children in America will read my books."

*   *   *

HILLS, C(harles) A(lbert) R(eis)   1955-
(David Welsh)

PERSONAL: Born August 21, 1955, in London, England; son

of Arthur Ernest and Maria Jose (Reis) Hills. *Education:* Hertford College, Oxford, B.A., 1976; University of Sussex, M.A., 1977; doctoral research at St. Antony's College, Oxford, 1977-78. *Politics:* "Non-aligned."

ADDRESSES: Home and office—3 Lucas House, Albion Ave., London S.W.8, England.

CAREER: Stonehart Publications, London, England, editorial/production assistant, 1978-79; free-lance writer and editor, 1979-81; IPC Business Press, Sutton, England, news reporter for *Electrical and Radio Trading,* 1981-85; *Encyclopaedia Britannica,* editorial assistant, 1985-86; free-lance writer and journalist, 1986—.

WRITINGS:

The Rhine (juvenile), Wayland, 1979.
The Danube (juvenile), Wayland, 1979.
The Fascist Dictatorships (textbook), Batsford, 1979.
The Hitler File (textbook), Batsford, 1980.
World Trade (textbook), Batsford, 1981.
The Seine (juvenile), Wayland, 1981.
Modern Industry (textbook), Batsford, 1982.
Growing up in the 1950's, Batsford, 1983.
Law and Order, Batsford, 1983.
Living through History: The Second World War, Batsford, 1985.
The Destruction of Pompeii and Herculaneum, Dryad, 1987.

CONTRIBUTOR

John Gaisford, editor, *Atlas of Man,* Marshall Cavendish, 1978.
J. P. Kenyon, editor, *A Dictionary of British History,* Secker & Warburg, 1981.
Guide to Historic Britain, Nicholson Guides, 1982.
PEN New Fiction II, Quartet, 1987.

SIDELIGHTS: C. A. R. Hills told *CA:* "Until recently I have been largely an author of educational books for schools and of contributions to reference books. But I wished eventually to branch out into other types of writing, especially fiction, and that then I would give up educational writing to 'leave my time and mind free.' That time has come. I have now published seven project books for schools and I am proud of these books, but I do not intend to write more, at least for some time. My writing interests now are two: fiction and literary journalism/writing. I began writing short stories when I was twenty-nine, and have so far completed six short stories and a novella. I think that thirty-two is a good age to begin writing a novel, and accordingly I shall start soon."

*   *   *

HINDLE, Brooke   1918-

PERSONAL: Born September 28, 1918, in Drexel Hill, Pa.; son of Howard Brooke and Marion (Manchester) Hindle; married Helen Morris, August 21, 1943; children: Margaret Joan (Mrs. Robert M. Hazen), Donald Morris. *Education:* Attended Massachusetts Institute of Technology, 1936-38; Brown University, A.B. (magna cum laude), 1940; University of Pennsylvania, M.A., 1942, Ph.D., 1949.

ADDRESSES: Home—5114 Dalecarlia Dr., Bethesda, Md. 20816.

CAREER: Institute of Early American History and Culture, Williamsburg, Va., research associate, 1948-50; New York University, New York, N.Y., associate professor, 1950-61,

professor of history, 1961-74, chairman of University College department of history, 1965-67, dean of University College, 1967-69, head of university department of history, 1970-74; Smithsonian Institution, National Museum of American History, Washington, D.C., director, 1974-78, senior historian, 1978-85, historian emeritus, 1985—. Lecturer in history at College of William and Mary, 1948-50, and Northwestern University, summer, 1950; Spahr Lecturer, Dickinson College, 1951; special lecturer, Polytechnic Institute of Brooklyn, 1964; National Defense Education Act (NDEA) lecturer, North Carolina State University, summer, 1967; Killian Visiting Professor, Massachusetts Institute of Technology, 1971-72; Anson G. Phelps Lecturer, New York University, 1979; lecturer, New York State Historical Society, summer, 1980; visiting professor, University of Central Florida, winter, 1981; distinguished visiting professor, University of Delaware, 1982. Eleutherian Mills-Hagley Foundation, senior resident scholar, 1969-70, member of advisory committee, 1971-74, member of board of trustees, 1974-85; member of board of directors, George Sarton Memorial Foundation, 1958-64; member of council, Institute of Early American History and Culture, 1964-67. Member of numerous visiting and advisory committees for various universities, including Yale University and Harvard University. *Military service:* U.S. Naval Reserve, Midshipman's School, 1942-43, instructor in engineering. U.S. Navy, radar maintenance officer, 1943-45; became lieutenant; served on U.S.S. Chenango; received Pacific Asiatic Medal with seven stars, Philippine Liberation Medal with one star, and Navy Unit Commendation.

MEMBER: International Academy of History of Sciences (corresponding member), American Historical Association, Society of American Historians, Organization of American Historians, American Antiquarian Society, American Council of Learned Societies (member of secretaries' conference, 1959-60), American Association for the Advancement of Science (fellow; member of council, 1973-74; chairman of Section L executive committee, 1980-81), American Philosophical Society, History of Science Society (member of council, 1955-58, 1962-65; secretary, 1958-60), Society for the History of Technology (member of advisory council, 1965-70; member of executive council, 1970-73; vice-president, 1977-80; president, 1981—), Society for Industrial Archeology, Royal Society of Arts (fellow), Pilgrim Society (fellow), Association for Living Historical Farms, Massachusetts Historical Society (corresponding member), Colonial Society of Massachusetts, Phi Beta Kappa (president of New York branch, 1965-67).

AWARDS, HONORS: Book selection, American History Publication Society, 1956, for *The Pursuit of Science in Revolutionary America;* National Science Foundation grant, 1959; American Philosophical Society grant, 1961; Guggenheim fellowship, 1964-65; Secretary's Award for Exceptional Services, Smithsonian Institution, 1976; Fellows Award Medal, Early American Industries Association, 1983; Leonardo da Vinci Medal, Society for the History of Technology, 1984.

WRITINGS:

The Pursuit of Science in Revolutionary America, University of North Carolina Press, 1956, reprinted, Norton, 1974.
David Rittenhouse, Princeton University Press, 1964, reprinted, Arno, 1980.
Technology in Early America: Needs and Opportunities for Study, University of North Carolina Press, 1966.
Emulation and Invention, New York University Press, 1981.

(With Steven Lubar) *Engines of Change*, Smithsonian Institution Press, 1986.

EDITOR

America's Wooden Age: Aspects of Its Early Technology, Sleepy Hollow Restorations (Tarrytown, N.Y.), 1975.
Early American Science, Science History Publications, 1976.
The Scientific Writings of David Rittenhouse, Arno, 1980.
Material Culture of the Wooden Age, Sleepy Hollow Restorations, 1981.
(With Edgar P. Richardson and Lillian B. Miller) *Charles Wilson Peale and His World*, Abrams, 1984.
(With Margaret Latimer and Melvin Kranzberg) *Bridge to the Future*, New York Academy of Sciences, 1984.

AUTHOR OF INTRODUCTION

The Narrative of Ethan Allen, [New York, N.Y.], 1961.
Barbara E. Benson, editor, *Benjamin Henry Latrobe and Mocure Robinson: The Engineer as Agent of Technological Transfer*, Eleutherian Mills Historical Library, 1975.
Charles E. Peterson, editor, *Building Early America*, [Radnor, Pa.], 1976.
Cyril S. Smith, *From Art to Science*, [Cambridge, Mass.], 1980.
Neil L. York, *Mechanical Metamorphosis*, Greenwood Press, 1985.
John M. Staudenmaier, *Technology's Storytellers*, Massachusetts Institute of Technology Press, 1985.

CONTRIBUTOR

John and Mary's College; The Boyd Lee Spahr Lectures, 1951-56, [Carlisle, Pa.], 1956.
Marshall W. Fishwick, editor, *American Studies in Transition*, [Philadelphia, Pa.], 1964.
H. Trevor Colbourn, editor, *The Colonial Experience*, Houghton, 1966.
Lucius F. Ellsworth and Maureen A. O'Brian, editors, *Material Culture*, [Philadelphia], 1969.
Early Scientific Books in Schaffer Library, Union College, [Schenectady, N.Y.], 1971.
James Kirby Martin, editor, *Interpreting Colonial America*, [New York], 1973.
Philip C. Rittenbush, editor, *Technology as Institutionally Related to Human Values*, [Washington, D.C.], 1974.
Alexandra Oleson and Sanborn C. Brown, editors, *The Pursuit of Knowledge in the Early American Republic*, [Baltimore, Md.], 1976.
Visiting Our Past: America's Historylands, [Washington, D.C.], 1977.
Ian M. G. Quimby, editor, *Material Culture and the Study of American Life*, [New York], 1978.
Technology and Its Impact on Society, [Stockholm], 1979.
Carroll W. Pursell, Jr., editor, *Technology in America: A History of Individuals and Ideas*, [Washington, D.C.], 1979.
Randolph S. Klein, *Science and Society in Early America*, American Philosophical Society, 1986.

OTHER

Member of board of editors, "Three Centuries of Science in America" series, Arno, 1978-80. Also contributor to *Dictionary of Scientific Biography*, 1970-77, *Dictionary of Notable American Women*, 1971, and *Encyclopedia of American Biography*, 1974; also contributor to proceedings of Congres International d'Histoire des Sciences, Barcelona, 1960, Warsaw, 1968, American Philosophical Society, 1964, and International Congress of the History of Science, Paris, 1964, Tokyo, 1975; also contributor to conferences of the Burndy Library, 1976, and the Congress for Creative America, 1977. Contributor of articles and reviews to professional journals, including *Isis, American Historical Review, Journal of American History, New England Quarterly, Science*, and *Technology and Culture*. Member of board of editors, *William and Mary Quarterly*, 1964-66.

WORK IN PROGRESS: Lucky Lady and the Navy Mystique, a book about "life aboard a warship."

SIDELIGHTS: Brooke Hindle told *CA:* "My writing is that of a historian, trained in the belief that good history rests entirely upon good writing. The objective is to communicate effectively my feeling and understanding derived from careful research. The need is to contribute to the influential historical publications that constitute our social memory.

"My work began with the study of early American science and technology and the publication of the insights that came to me. After moving primarily into the history of technology, I became increasingly conscious of the fundamental importance of visual or spatial thinking in technology and of the necessity of integrating that mode of thought into my publications. That led me to move from New York University to the National Museum of American History. The key requirement was to gain the feel for spatial thought, but it became clear I could not communicate that understanding by words alone—any more than art historians can publish most of their writings without accompanying pictures. More to the point, my recent publications include drawings and photographs that are much more fundamental than mere illustrations. They are a central part of the publication, although their meaning has to be conveyed through the written word. For me, this became a new sort of writing that I am still seeking to make more effective."

BIOGRAPHICAL/CRITICAL SOURCES:

PERIODICALS

Washington Post Book World, February 9, 1986.

*   *   *

HJELTE, George   1893-1979

PERSONAL: Surname is pronounced Jelt-*ay;* born July 4, 1893, in San Francisco, Calif.; died January 4, 1979; son of Anton and Augusta (Pihlgren) Hjelte; married Frances Smith, June 12, 1920; children: George S., Helen Anne (Mrs. Woody Grey), Dorothy Virginia (Mrs. Harvey John Meyer). *Education:* University of California, Berkeley, B.S., 1917; Cambridge University, graduate study, 1917. *Politics:* Republican. *Religion:* Protestant.

ADDRESSES: Home—4468 Dundee Dr., Los Angeles, Calif. 90027.

CAREER: State of California, assistant supervisor of physical education, 1919-21; City of Berkeley, Calif., superintendent of recreation, 1921-26; City of Los Angeles, Calif., general manager, department of playgrounds and recreation, 1926-30; County of Westchester, N.Y., superintendent of recreation, 1930-33; City of Los Angeles, general manager, department of recreation and parks, 1933-62. Consultant on parks and recreation, 1962-78, including consultant to National Recreation and Park Association on master study for New York City, 1965-66, and special consultant to Recreation and Youth

Services Council of Los Angeles, 1966-67. Director of Civil Defense, Los Angeles, 1941-45. *Military service:* U.S. Army, Infantry, 1917-18; served in France; became captain; received Belgian Croix de Guerre. U.S. Navy, Special Services, 1937-41; became lieutenant commander.

MEMBER: American Recreation Society (fellow; president, 1937-41), National Recreation and Park Association (fellow), American Academy of Physical Education, California Recreation and Park Association, Phi Delta Kappa, Lambda Alpha, Pi Sigma Epsilon.

WRITINGS:

Administration of Public Recreation, Macmillan, 1942, reprinted, 1971.
(Contributor) *Sports and Recreation Facilities for School and Community,* Prentice-Hall, 1958.
(With Jay S. Shivers) *Public Administration of Park and Recreational Services,* Macmillan, 1963.
(With Shivers) *Planning Recreational Places,* Fairleigh Dickinson University Press, 1971.
(With Shivers) *Public Administration of Recreational Services,* foreword by Robert W. Crawford, Lea & Febiger, 1972, 2nd edition, foreword by Joseph Halper, 1978.
Footprints in the Parks, illustrated by Sue Hjelte, Public Service Publications, 1977.

Also author of *The Development of a City's Public Recreation Service: 1904-1963,* Public Service Publications. Contributor to yearbook of American Association for Health, Physical Education and Recreation, 1951.†

*   *   *

HOBAN, Lillian   1925-

PERSONAL: Former surname, Aberman; born May 18, 1925, in Philadelphia, Pa.; married Russell Hoban (an author and artist), January 31, 1944 (divorced, 1975); children: Phoebe, Abrom, Esme, Julia. *Education:* Attended Philadelphia Museum School of Art, 1942-44, and the Hanya Holm School of Dance.

ADDRESSES: Home—Wilton, Conn.

CAREER: Illustrator of books for children. Has also worked in a slenderizing salon and as a modern dance instructor in New York and Connecticut.

AWARDS, HONORS: Christopher Award, Children's Book Category, 1971, for *Emmet Otter's Jug-Band Christmas* (written by Russell Hoban).

WRITINGS:

SELF-ILLUSTRATED

(With Russell Hoban) *London Men and English Men,* Harper, 1962.
(With R. Hoban) *Some Snow Said Hello,* Harper, 1963.
(With R. Hoban) *Save My Place,* Norton, 1967.
Arthur's Christmas Cookies, Harper, 1972, reprinted, 1986.
The Sugar Snow Spring, Harper, 1973.
Arthur's Honey Bear, Harper, 1974, reprinted, 1986.
Arthur's Pen Pal, Harper, 1976.
Mr. Pig and Sonny Too, Harper, 1976.
Stick-in-the-Mud Turtle, Greenwillow, 1977.
I Met a Traveller, Harper, 1977.
Arthur's Prize Reader, Harper, 1978.
Turtle Spring, Greenwillow, 1978.

Harry's Song, Greenwillow, 1980.
Mr. Pig and Family, Harper, 1980.
Arthur's Funny Money, Harper, 1981.
No, No, Sammy Crow, Greenwillow, 1981.
It's Really Christmas, Greenwillow, 1982.
(With daughter Phoebe Hoban) *Ready-Set-Robot!,* Harper, 1982.
(With P. Hoban) *The Laziest Robot in Zone One,* Harper, 1983.
Arthur's Halloween Costume, Harper, 1984.
Grandparents' Houses, Greenwillow, 1984.
Arthur's Loose Tooth, Harper, 1985.
The Case of the Two Masked Robbers, Harper, 1985.
Silly Tilly and the Easter Bunny, Harper, 1987.

ILLUSTRATOR

R. Hoban, *Herman the Loser,* Harper, 1961.
R. Hoban, *The Song in My Drum,* Harper, 1961.
R. Hoban, *The Sorely Trying Day,* Harper, 1964.
R. Hoban, *Nothing to Do,* Harper, 1964.
R. Hoban, *Bread and Jam for Frances,* Harper, 1964, reprinted, 1986.
R. Hoban, *A Baby Sister for Frances,* Harper, 1964.
Robert P. Smith, *When I Am Big,* Harper, 1965.
R. Hoban, *What Happened When Jack and Daisy Tried to Fool with the Tooth Fairies,* Scholastic Book Services, 1965.
R. Hoban, *The Story of Hester Mouse Who Became a Writer and Saved Most of Her Sisters and Brothers and Some of Her Aunts and Uncles from the Owl,* Norton, 1965.
R. Hoban, *Tom and the Two Handles,* Harper, 1965, reprinted, 1984.
Felice Holman, *Victoria's Castle,* Norton, 1966.
Carl Memling, *A Gift-Bear for the King,* Dutton, 1966.
Mitchell F. Jayne, *The Forest in the Wind,* Bobbs-Merrill, 1966.
R. Hoban, *The Little Brute Family,* Macmillan, 1966.
R. Hoban, *Goodnight* (verse), Norton, 1966.
R. Hoban, *Henry and the Monstrous Din,* Harper, 1966.
Miriam Cohen, *Will I Have a Friend?,* Macmillan, 1967.
R. Hoban, *Charlie the Tramp,* Four Winds, 1967, (book and record) Scholastic Book Services, 1970.
R. Hoban, *The Mouse and His Child* (novel), Harper, 1967, reprinted, Avon, 1986.
R. Hoban, *The Stone Doll of Sister Brute,* Macmillan, 1968.
R. Hoban, *A Birthday for Frances,* Harper, 1968.
R. Hoban, *The Pedaling Man, and Other Poems,* Norton, 1968.
R. Hoban, *Ugly Bird,* Macmillan, 1969.
Jan Wahl, *A Wolf of My Own,* Macmillan, 1969.
R. Hoban, *Harvey's Hideout,* Parents' Magazine Press, 1969.
R. Hoban, *The Mole Family's Christmas,* Parents' Magazine Press, 1969, reprinted, Scholastic, Inc., 1986.
R. Hoban, *Best Friends for Frances,* Harper, 1969.
Aileen T. Fisher, *In One Door and Out the Other: A Book of Poems,* Crowell, 1969.
R. Hoban, *A Bargain for Frances,* Harper, 1970.
Alma M. Whitney, *Just Awful,* Addison-Wesley, 1971, reprinted, Harper, 1986.
Ellen Parsons, *Rainy Day Together,* Harper, 1971.
Meindert De Jong, *Easter Cat,* Macmillan, 1971.
R. Hoban, *Emmet Otter's Jug-Band Christmas,* Parents' Magazine Press, 1971.
M. Cohen, *Best Friends,* Macmillan, 1971.
R. Hoban, *Egg Thoughts, and Other Frances Songs,* Harper, 1972.

M. Cohen, *The New Teacher*, Macmillan, 1972.
Marjorie Weinman Sharmat, *Sophie and Gussie*, Macmillan, 1973.
M. Cohen, *Tough Jim*, Macmillan, 1974.
William Cole, *What's Good for a Three-Year-Old?*, Holt, 1974.
Crescent Dragonwagon, *Strawberry Dress Escape*, Scribner, 1975.
Janet Schulman, *The Big Hello*, Greenwillow, 1976.
Diane Wolkstein, *Squirrel's Song: A Hopi Indian Tale*, Knopf, 1976.
M. Cohen, *"Bee My Valentine!,"* Greenwillow, 1978.
T. Zagone, *No Nap for Me*, Dutton, 1978.
Sue Alexander, *Seymour the Prince*, Pantheon, 1979.
M. Cohen, *Lost in the Museum*, Greenwillow, 1979.
Paula Kurzband Feder, *Where Does the Teacher Live?*, Dutton, 1979.
Ron Roy, *Awful Thursday*, Pantheon, 1979.
J. Schulman, *The Great Big Dummy*, Greenwillow, 1979.
M. W. Sharmat, *Say Hello, Vanessa*, Holiday House, 1979.
Nancy Willard, *Papa's Panda*, Harcourt, 1979.
M. Cohen, *First Grade Takes a Test*, Greenwillow, 1980.
M. Cohen, *No Good in Art*, Greenwillow, 1980.
Dorotha Ruthstrom, *The Big Kite Contest*, Pantheon, 1980.
M. Cohen, *Jim Meets the Thing*, Greenwillow, 1981.
Bernice Rabe, *The Balancing Girl*, Dutton, 1981.
M. Cohen, *So What?*, Greenwillow, 1982.
M. Cohen, *See You Tomorrow, Charles*, Greenwillow, 1983.
Judy Delton, *I'm Telling You Now*, Dutton, 1983.
Johanna Hurwitz, *Rip-Roaring Russell*, Morrow, 1983.
M. Cohen, *Jim's Dog Muffins*, Greenwillow, 1984.
James Howe, *The Day the Teacher Went Bananas*, Dutton, 1984.
M. W. Sharmat, *The Story of Bentley Beaver*, Harper, 1984.
M. Cohen, *Liar, Liar, Pants on Fire!*, Greenwillow, 1985.
M. Cohen, *Starring First Grade*, Greenwillow, 1985.
M. W. Sharmat, *Attila the Angry*, Holiday House, 1985.
J. Hurwitz, *Russell Rides Again*, Morrow, 1985.

SIDELIGHTS: Lillian Hoban always wanted to be an illustrator, but gave it up for a while after her marriage to author Russell Hoban in order to study dance professionally. After the birth of her third child, she began illustrating her husband's books for children, as well as the writings of other authors, and eventually wrote and illustrated her own books. Hoban finds drawing completely satisfying and her illustrations are described by a *New York Times Book Review* contributor as having a "cozy charm." She usually works in black and white or in two colors. In addition to pencil illustrations, such as those in *Bread and Jam for Frances* and several other books, Hoban also uses a pen and ink wash. Her crayon, tempera, and chalk illustrations for a recent book of poetry, *Grandparents' Houses*, are in "clear, vibrant colors," writes Kathie Meizner in *School Library Journal,* and exhibit a "dramatic and expressive quality . . . done in a variety of styles."

MEDIA ADAPTATIONS: Filmstrips entitled the "Frances Series" have been distributed by BFA Educational Media, and "Will I Have a Friend," by Macmillan in 1974.

BIOGRAPHICAL/CRITICAL SOURCES:

PERIODICALS

New York Times Book Review, April 15, 1973.
School Library Journal, February, 1985.
Times Literary Supplement, September 20, 1974.†

HOBAN, Russell (Conwell) 1925-

PERSONAL: Born February 4, 1925, in Lansdale, Pa.; son of Abram T. (an advertising manager for the *Jewish Daily Forward*) and Jeanette (Dimmerman) Hoban; married Lillian Aberman (an illustrator), January 31, 1944 (divorced, 1975); married Gundula Ahl (a bookseller), 1975; children: (first marriage) Phoebe, Abrom, Esme, Julia; (second marriage) Jachin Boaz, Wieland, Benjamin. *Education:* Attended Philadelphia Museum School of Industrial Art, 1941-43.

ADDRESSES: Home and office—Fulham, London, England. *Agent*—David Higham Associates Ltd., 5-8 Lower John St., Golden Sq., London W1R 4HA, England.

CAREER: Artist and illustrator for magazine and advertising studios, New York City, 1945-51; Fletcher Smith Film Studio, New York City, story board artist and character designer, 1951; Batten, Barton, Durstine & Osborn, Inc., New York City, television art director, 1952-57; J. Walter Thompson Co., New York City, television art director, 1956; free-lance illustrator for advertising agencies and magazines, including *Time, Life, Fortune, Saturday Evening Post, True*, 1957-65; Doyle, Dane, Bernbach, New York City, copywriter, 1965-67. Art instructor at the Famous Artists Schools, Westport, Conn., and School of Visual Arts, New York City. Writer. *Military service:* U.S. Army, Infantry, 1943-45; served in Italian campaign; received Bronze Star.

MEMBER: Authors Guild, Authors League of America, Society of Authors, PEN.

AWARDS, HONORS: The Sorely Trying Day, The Mouse and His Child, How Tom Beat Captain Najork and His Hired Sportsmen, and *Dinner at Alberta's* have all been named notable books by the American Library Association; *Bread and Jam for Frances* was selected as a Library of Congress Children's book, 1964; Boys' Club Junior Book Award, 1968, for *Charlie the Tramp; Emmet Otter's Jug-Band Christmas* was selected as one of *School Library Journal*'s Best Books, 1971, and received the Lewis Carroll Shelf Award and the Christopher Award, both 1972; Whitbread Literary Award, 1974, and International Board on Books for Young People Honor List, 1976, both for *How Tom Beat Captain Najork and His Hired Sportsmen; A Near Thing for Captain Najork* was selected as one of the best illustrated children's books of the year by the *New York Times*, 1976; *Riddley Walker* received John W. Campbell Memorial Award for the best science fiction novel of the year by Science Fiction Research Association, 1981, and was nominated as the most distinguished book of fiction by National Book Critics Circle and for the Nebula Award by Science Fiction Writers of America, both 1982; Recognition of Merit, George G. Stone Center for Children's Books, 1982, for his contributions to books for younger children.

WRITINGS:

NOVELS

The Lion of Boaz-Jachin and Jachin-Boaz, Stein & Day, 1973.
Kleinzeit: A Novel, Viking, 1974.
Turtle Diary, J. Cape, 1975, Random House, 1976.
Riddley Walker, J. Cape, 1980, Summit Books, 1981.
Pilgermann, Summit Books, 1983.
The Medusa Frequency, Atlantic Monthly, 1987.

JUVENILES

What Does It Do and How Does It Work?: Power Shovel, Dump Truck, and Other Heavy Machines, illustrations by the author, Harper, 1959.

The Atomic Submarine: A Practice Combat Patrol under the Sea, illustrations by the author, Harper, 1960.

Bedtime for Frances, illustrations by Garth Williams, Harper, 1960, reprinted, 1976.

Herman the Loser, illustrations by Lillian Hoban, Harper, 1961.

The Song in My Drum, illustrations by L. Hoban, Harper, 1961.

(With L. Hoban) *London Men and English Men*, Harper, 1962.

(With L. Hoban) *Some Snow Said Hello*, Harper, 1963.

The Sorely Trying Day, illustrations by L. Hoban, Harper, 1964.

A Baby Sister for Frances, illustrations by L. Hoban, Harper, 1964.

Nothing to Do, illustrations by L. Hoban, Harper, 1964.

Bread and Jam for Frances, illustrations by L. Hoban, Harper, 1964, reprinted, 1986.

Tom and the Two Handles, illustrations by L. Hoban, Harper, 1965, reprinted, 1984.

The Story of Hester Mouse Who Became a Writer and Saved Most of Her Sisters and Brothers and Some of Her Aunts and Uncles from the Owl, illustrations by L. Hoban, Norton, 1965.

What Happened When Jack and Daisy Tried to Fool the Tooth Fairies, illustrations by L. Hoban, Scholastic Book Services, 1965.

Henry and the Monstrous Din, illustrations by L. Hoban, Harper, 1966.

The Little Brute Family, illustrations by L. Hoban, Macmillan, 1966.

Goodnight (verse), illustrations by L. Hoban, Norton, 1966.

(With L. Hoban) *Save My Place*, Norton, 1967.

Charlie the Tramp, illustrations by L. Hoban, Four Winds, 1967, (book and record) Scholastic Book Services, 1970.

The Mouse and His Child (novel), illustrations by L. Hoban, Harper, 1967, reprinted, Avon, 1986.

A Birthday for Frances, illustrations by L. Hoban, Harper, 1968.

The Pedaling Man, and Other Poems, illustrations by L. Hoban, Norton, 1968.

The Stone Doll of Sister Brute, illustrations by L. Hoban, Macmillan, 1968.

Harvey's Hideout, illustrations by L. Hoban, Parents' Magazine Press, 1969.

Best Friends for Frances, illustrations by L. Hoban, Harper, 1969.

Ugly Bird, illustrations by L. Hoban, Macmillan, 1969.

The Mole Family's Christmas, illustrations by L. Hoban, Parents' Magazine Press, 1969, reprinted, Scholastic, Inc., 1986.

A Bargain for Frances, illustrations by L. Hoban, Harper, 1970.

Emmet Otter's Jug-Band Christmas, illustrations by L. Hoban, Parents' Magazine Press, 1971.

Egg Thoughts, and Other Frances Songs, illustrations by L. Hoban, Harper, 1972.

The Sea-Thing Child, illustrations by son, Abrom Hoban, Harper, 1972.

Letitia Rabbit's String Song (Junior Literary Guild selection), illustrations by Mary Chalmers, Coward, 1973.

How Tom Beat Captain Najork and His Hired Sportsmen, illustrations by Quentin Blake, Atheneum, 1974.

Ten What?: A Mystery Counting Book, illustrations by Sylvie Selig, J. Cape, 1974, Scribner, 1975.

Crocodile and Pierrot: A See the Story Book, illustrations by S. Selig, J. Cape, 1975, Scribner, 1977.

A Near Thing for Captain Najork, illustrations by Q. Blake, J. Cape, 1975, Atheneum, 1976.

Arthur's New Power, illustrations by Byron Barton, Crowell, 1978.

The Twenty-Elephant Restaurant, illustrations by Emily Arnold McCully, Atheneum, 1978, published in England with illustrations by Q. Blake, J. Cape, 1980.

La Corona and the Tin Frog (originally published in *Puffin Annual*, 1974), illustrations by Nicola Bayley, J. Cape, 1978, Merrimack Book Service, 1981.

The Dancing Tigers, illustrations by David Gentlemen, J. Cape, 1979, Merrimack Book Service, 1981.

Flat Cat, illustrations by Clive Scruton, Philomel, 1980.

Ace Dragon Ltd., illustrations by Q. Blake, J. Cape, 1980, Merrimack Book Service, 1981.

They Came from Aargh!, illustrations by Colin McNaughton, Philomel, 1981.

The Serpent Tower, illustrations by David Scott, Methuen/Walker, 1981.

The Great Fruit Gum Robbery, illustrations by C. McNaughton, Methuen, 1981, published as *The Great Gum Drop Robbery*, Philomel, 1982.

The Battle of Zormla, illustrations by C. McNaughton, Philomel, 1982.

The Flight of Bembel Rudzuk, illustrations by C. McNaughton, Philomel, 1982.

Big John Turkle, illustrations by Martin Baynton, Walker Books, 1983, Holt, 1984.

Jim Frog, illustrations by M. Baynton, Walker Books, 1983, Holt, 1984.

Lavinia Bat, illustrations by M. Baynton, Holt, 1984.

Charlie Meadows, illustrations by M. Baynton, Holt, 1984.

The Rain Door, J. Cape, 1986.

The Marzipan Pig, J. Cape, 1986.

OTHER

(Illustrator) W. R. Burnett, *The Roar of the Crowd: Conversations with an Ex-Big-Leaguer*, C. N. Potter, 1964.

(Contributor) Edward Blishen, editor, *The Thorny Paradise: Writers on Writing for Children*, Kestrel, 1975.

Also contributor of articles to *Holiday*.

SIDELIGHTS: "Russell Hoban is a writer whose genius is expressed with equal brilliance in books both for children and for adults," writes Alida Allison in the *Dictionary of Literary Biography*. Peter S. Prescott reports in *Newsweek* that in England, where Hoban's work is particularly successful, he shows signs of becoming a cult writer, and "like other cult writers . . . he writes about ordinary decent people making life-affirming gestures in a world that threatens to dissolve in madness; like them, he writes a prose that is often fresh and funny, occasionally precious." Largely self-educated, Hoban has moved masterfully from artist and illustrator to the author of children's fables and adult allegorical fiction. Praising his "unerring ear for dialogue," his "memorable depiction of scenes," and his "wise and warm stories notable for delightful plots and originality of language," Allison considers Hoban to be "much more than just a clever and observant writer. His works are permeated with an honest, often painful, and always uncompromising urge toward self-identity." Noting that "this theme of identity becomes more apparent, more complex as Hoban's works have become longer and more penetrating," Allison states, "Indeed, Hoban's writing has leaped and bounded—paralleling upheavals in his own life."

Although Hoban has originated several well-known characters in children's literature, including Charlie the Tramp, Emmet Otter, the Mouse and his Child, and Manny Rat, he is especially recognized for a series of bedtime books about an anthropomorphic badger named Frances. Reviewers generally concur that these stories depict ordinary family life with much humor, wit, and style. Benjamin DeMott suggests in the *Atlantic* that "these books are unique, first, because the adults in their pages are usually humorous, precise of speech, and understandingly conversant with general life, and second, because the author confronts—not unfancifully but without kinky secret garden stuff—problems with which ordinary parents and children have to cope." *Bedtime for Frances,* for instance, concerns nighttime fears and is regarded by many as a classic in children's literature. A contributor to *Junior Bookshelf* thinks that Hoban tells this tale with "beautiful economy," adding that "this is the rarest kind of picture-book text, rhythmic, natural, unalterable." And according to a *Saturday Review* contributor, "The exasperated humor of this book could only derive from actual parental experience, and no doubt parents will enjoy it."

"Hoban has established himself as a writer with a rare understanding of childhood (and parental) psychology, sensitively and humorously portrayed in familiar family situations," writes Allison. He and his first wife, Lillian, also an illustrator and author of books for children, collaborated on many successful works, including several in the Frances series. Allison notes that although their work together was usually well-received, "there were pans as well as paeans." While some books have been faulted for "excessive coziness, for sentimentality, and for stereotyped male-female roles," Allison adds that a more general criticism of their work together is that "it tends toward repetition." However, in their *Children and Books,* May Hill Arbuthnot and Zena Sutherland find that all of Hoban's stories about Frances show "affection for and understanding of children" as well as "contribute to a small child's understanding of himself, his relationships with other people, and the fulfillment of his emotional needs." Further, they say, "These characters are indeed ourselves in fur." Yet as a *Times Literary Supplement* contributor observes, "Excellent as [the Frances books] are, they give no hint that the author had in him such a blockbuster of a book as *The Mouse and His Child.*"

Revered in England as a modern children's classic, *The Mouse and His Child* is described in the *New York Times Book Review* by Barbara Wersba as a story about two wind-up toy mice who are discarded from a toyshop and are then "buffeted from place to place as they seek the lost paradise of their first home—a doll house—and their first 'family,' a toy elephant and seal." Ill-equipped for the baffling, threatening world into which they are tossed, the mouse and his child innocently confront the unknown and its inherent treachery and violence, as well as their own fears. The book explores not only the transience and inconstancy of life but the struggle to persevere also. "Helpless when they are not wound up, unable to stop when they *are,* [the mice] are fated like all mechanical things to breakage, rust and disintegration as humans are to death," writes Margaret Blount in her *Animal Land: The Creatures of Children's Fiction.* "As an adult," says Blount, "it is impossible to read [the book] unmoved." Distressed, however, by the "continuing images of cruelty and decay," Penelope Farmer remarks in *Children's Literature in Education* that *The Mouse and His Child* is "like Beckett for children." But assessing whatever cruelty and decay there is in the novel as the "artful rendering of the facts of life," Allison affirms, "If there is betrayal,

there is also self-sacrifice. If there is loss, there is also love. If there is homelessness, there is also destination. The mouse child gets his family in the end; children's literature gets a masterpiece."

"Like the best of books, [*The Mouse and the Child*] is a book from which one can peel layer after layer of meaning," says the *Times Literary Supplement* contributor. Some critics, however, wonder whether it is a children's book at all. Wersba, for instance, feels that "it is the mouse, his child and their search we care about—not metaphysics—and the intellectual trappings of this story are unnecessary." Hoban responds to such assessments in an essay for *Books for Your Children:* "When I wrote [*The Mouse and the Child*] I didn't think it was [a children's book]. I was writing as much book as I was capable of at the time. No concessions were made in style or content. It was my first novel and . . . it was the fullest response I could make to being alive and in the world." Believing the book reveals "an absolute respect for its subject—which means its readers as well," Isabel Quigley adds in the *Spectator,* "I'm still not sure just who is going to read it but that hardly seems to matter. . . . It will last." Hoban feels that within its limitations, the book is suitable for children, though. "Its heroes and heroines found out what they were and it wasn't enough, so they found out how to be more," he says in his essay. "That's not a bad thought to be going with."

Hoban moved to England in 1969 and continues to reside there with his family from a second marriage. Some critics conjecture about the emotional impact that the dissolution of Hoban's first marriage, as well as subsequent estrangements from his children, may have had upon his work, particularly since it was during this period of time that he began to write for an adult audience. Steven Rattner, who interviewed Hoban for the *New York Times,* indicates that because of the extensive publicity that this subject has generated, Hoban declines to discuss it further, stating, "I no longer want to see anything in print about my saying this or that about my first marriage." However, in a *Publishers Weekly* interview, Hoban relates to Barbara A. Bannon that frequent discussions with an analyst about his writing have afforded him an opportunity to become "good friends" with his head. Consequently, Hoban's children's fables have evolved into works that probe beneath the surface of ordinary experience and ponder questions of psychology, philosophy, and theology. Allison thinks that "the presence in Hoban's novels of that impersonal, vast, and random power—call it the mindless flow of birth and death and circumstance—reveals itself in images which seem drawn from depth psychology, from a genius who has traveled through his own muck confronting the fact of his helplessness."

The Lion of Boaz-Jachin and Jachin-Boaz, his first novel for an adult audience, is the "most autobiographical novel I've written," Hoban acknowledges to Bannon. It is described by Allison as the story of a mapmaker who promises his son a master map in which everything that the father has learned and that the son will ever need to know is revealed. However, because of the father's quest for a more meaningful life, he deserts his family and takes the map with him instead. The son follows in anger, and from his own imagination, materializes an extinct lion. "Hoban excels in the clash of the physical and metaphysical," says a *Times Literary Supplement* contributor; and although Noel Perrin feels that "where the book is fabulous, it tends to work," he adds in the *New York Times Book Review* that "the magic simply does not fit into the modern world [Hoban] insists on interpenetrating." Nevertheless, Perrin suggests that the book seems to "celebrate a release from the kinds of constraints a writer of books for small children—even a distinguished one like . . . Hoban—must work under. Everything he couldn't do in [the Frances books] he does here. If those books were innocent, here he delights in being raunchy. If they were simple, these are complex. . . . The one thing that carries over is a vein of fantasy.''

Departing, however, from fantasy as well as autobiography in his *Turtle Diary,* Hoban writes about a man and woman who meet through their pursuit of a common goal to release captive turtles into the sea. The story unfolds simultaneously from the diaries of the two somewhat reclusive individuals; and according to Paul Gray in *Time,* these alternating diary entries ''crackle with witty detail, mordant intelligence and self-deprecating irony.'' Gillian McMahon-Hill considers ''*Turtle Diary,* in some ways Hoban's finest writing yet,'' in that it ''provides the best marriage of his concise, poetic and rhythmic expression with his dry, witty observation,'' and continues in *Children's Literature in Education* that ''stylistically the novel is more ambitious and more accomplished than anything previously written.''

Suggesting that in *Turtle Diary,* Hoban is ''fighting free of the 'lie' at the heart of his past work,'' Edmund White explains in the *New York Times Book Review:* ''No affection is wasted on the turtles. They are chillingly unhuman, mere shells for living instinct. . . . Nor are the people especially endearing. Hoban is at pains to make them unappetizing.'' Gray thinks that Hoban ''argues gently but profoundly that human lives are really composed of details as mysterious in their power as the force that tugs the turtles.'' Prescott feels that the novel is about the ''recovery of life''; but, ''unlike the humans,'' notes Gray, ''the creatures know where they must go and venture without questioning.'' White believes, however, that not only are [Hoban's] characters dim, but the thematic underpinnings of the book seem flimsy.'' Yet Perrin maintains that Hoban's early books are ''best regarded as part of the learning process by which . . . Hoban prepared himself to write 'Riddley Walker.' And that is a book so shimmering with power, a fantasy so darkly perfect, as to excuse any little errors its author may have made en route.''

Nominated as the most distinguished book of fiction by the National Book Critics Circle, and for the Nebula Award by the Science Fiction Writers of America, *Riddley Walker* received the John W. Campbell Memorial Award from the Science Fiction Research Association as the year's best science fiction novel. *Riddley Walker* imagines a world and civilization decades after a nuclear holocaust; the story of what remains is narrated in a fragmented, phonetical English by a twelve-year-old boy struggling to comprehend the past so that its magnificence might be recaptured. ''Set in a remote future and composed in an English nobody ever spoke or wrote,'' writes DeMott in the *New York Times Book Review,* ''this short, swiftly paced tale juxtaposes preliterate fable and Beckettian wit, Boschian monstrosities and a hero with Huck Finn's heart and charm, lighting by El Greco and jokes by Punch and Judy. It is a wrenchingly vivid report on the texture of life after Doomsday.''

Detecting similarities in *Riddley Walker* to other contemporary works such as Anthony Burgess's *The Clockwork Orange,* John Gardner's *Grendel,* and the complete works of William Golding, DeMott believes that ''in vision and execution, this is an exceptionally original work, and Russell Hoban is actually his own best source.'' *Riddley Walker* ''is not 'like' anything,'' concurs Victoria Glendinning in the *Listener.* As

A. Alverez expresses in the *New York Review of Books,* Hoban has ''transformed what might have been just another fantasy of the future into a novel of exceptional depth and originality.'' And according to Joel Conarroe in the *New York Times Book Review,* ''There were critics, including myself, who thought . . . Hoban had produced the year's most distinguished fiction.''

Critically lauded and especially popular in England, *Riddley Walker* has been particularly commended for its inventive language, which Alverez thinks ''reflects with extraordinary precision both the narrator's understanding and the desolate landscape he moves through.'' Reviewing the novel in *Time,* Gray finds that the book's narrative generates its own suspense— ''the fascination of watching a strange world evolve out of unfamiliar words.'' Similarly, in the *Washington Post Book World,* Michael Dirda believes that ''what is marvelous in all this is the way Hoban makes us experience the uncanny familiarity of this world, while also making it a strange and animistic place, where words almost have a life of their own.'' ''What Hoban has done,'' suggests Bannon, ''is to invent a world and a language to go with it, and in doing both he remains a storyteller, which is the most significant achievement of 'Riddley Walker.' ''

Alverez calls *Riddley Walker* an ''artistic *tour de force* in every possible way,'' but Natalie Maynor and Richard F. Patteson suggest in *Critique* that even more than that, it is ''perhaps the most sophisticated work of fiction ever to speculate about man's future on earth and the implications for a potentially destructive technology.'' Eliot Fremont-Smith maintains in the *Village Voice* that ''the reality of the human situation now is so horrendous and bizarre that to get a hold on it requires all our faculties, including the imaginative. We can't do it through plain fact and arms controllers' reasoning alone. . . . Read *Riddley,* too.'' Although Kelly Cherry refers to the novel in the *Chicago Tribune Book World* as a ''philosophical essay in fictional drag,'' Philip Howard writes in the London *Times* that *Riddley Walker* is a ''powerful vision and a true fiction, in that it tells us something about ourselves and the indomitable spirit of man.'' Similarly, DeMott thinks that Hoban's focus on what has been lost in civilization ''summons the reader to dwell anew on that within civilization which is separate from, opposite to, power and its appurtenances, ravages, triumphs.'' *Riddley Walker,* says DeMott, is ''haunting and fiercely imagined and—this matters most—intensely ponderable.''

According to a *Harper's* contributor, *Riddley Walker* apparently left Hoban ''in a place where there was further action pending and this further action was waiting for the element that would precipitate it into the time and place of its own story.'' *Pilgermann* was precipitated by a night spent ''under the stars'' in Galilee, says the *Harper's* contributor, who deems the novel ''both *Riddley Walker*'s complement and mirror image.'' Set in the eleventh century, *Pilgermann* is narrated by a ''young European Jew who, made a eunuch by Christian peasants, decides his going to Jerusalem may keep God from leaving the world,'' writes Thomas LeClair in the *Washington Post Book World.* Pilgermann, from the German for pilgrim, is what the narrator calls himself, but his pilgrimage is one that he does not complete. As Michiko Kakutani explains in the *New York Times,* ''Killed during the siege of Antioch in 1098, he is now a disembodied spirit—'a whispering out of the dust'—who speaks with the patchy, retrospective knowledge of history.'' ''Reduced to 'waves and particles,' [the narrator] nonetheless survives as a sentient memory,'' notes Francis King in a *Spectator* review of the novel. King discusses *Pilgermann*'s "mystical disquisitions, often difficult to follow, on such subjects as predestination or the nature of good and evil, or of symbolical events." Finding the book "dense with mythic allusions and metaphysical speculation," Kakutani observes that "between the rather portentous theorizings, there are clever, philosophical pranks and strangely brilliant passages of description that have the visual impact of paintings glimpsed in a museum."

"Like everything that Russell Hoban writes, 'Pilgermann' is striking and strange," remarks Anthony Thwaite in the London *Observer,* adding that it also suggests a parody of Bunyan—"a series of dark sayings." While Conarroe thinks the novel borrows from several literary genres, including pilgrimage narrative, allegory, and historical fiction, he maintains that "what we have here is not so much a tale of adventure as a meditation on history, loss and grief, a dark treatise on the mysterious nature of things narrated by a 'microscopic chip in that vast circuitry in which are recorded all the variations and permutations thus far.' The novel is a network of small interlocking essays on matters no less significant than mutability and mortality." In his interview with Rattner, Hoban discusses the religious theme of *Pilgermann,* pointing also to the religious aspects of *Riddley Walker,* whose narrator, "confused in a continually wondering way," similarly attempts "to get to the heart of the matter . . . where God is in one form or another." *Pilgermann,* Hoban continues, is comprised of "answers to that question, many of which are contradictory." And although Gray finds the theological aspects of the novel tedious, he considers that "the quality of [Hoban's] ideas is less important than the restless energy of the mind that forms them. He is trying to grasp what cannot be known." "Hoban is a writer who, in his idiosyncratic boldness, never overreaches himself," states King. "One would no more call this book an easy read than one would call an ascent of Mont Blanc an easy walk; but in each case the views are magnificent."

Some critics examine the scholarly and profusely footnoted *Pilgermann* in the shadow of the overwhelmingly successful *Riddley Walker.* Thwaite, for instance, thinks that as powerful as *Pilgermann* is, it lacks the "total rightness of Hoban's best work" and suggests that "some of the effects seem too willed, some of the messages too incoherent, as if he had grabbed too eagerly for a dream that was fading even as he tried to set it down." However, Gray does not believe that it was Hoban's purpose to "pursue a single train of logic or evidence" but rather "to make sense of the universe that contains him. He is not a thinker but an artist." Conarroe, who finds *Riddley Walker* "more consistently riveting" than *Pilgermann,* nevertheless concludes: "To say, though, that . . . Hoban's novel does not measure up to its predecessor is not to suggest that it is an unworthy work of art. 'Riddley Walker,' after all, is miraculous: 'Pilgermann' is merely remarkable."

Hoban, whose papers are included in the Kerlan Collection at the University of Minnesota, is the author of nearly sixty books; although most are for children, for whom he continues to write, adults have found much in his books to appreciate as well. The world that Hoban often explores may be a child's world, but it is a world seen in its complexity. "In my books there aren't characters who are simply bad or simply good," Hoban tells Fred Hauptfuhrer in *People.* "Nothing in life is that simple." Writing for adults has added both breadth and depth to Hoban's work; and as his work has grown in complexity, he has commented upon the process by which an idea evolves into a book. In his interview with Rattner, for example, Hoban recalls: "In all the novels I've written, something I see gets

me started. Usually that starting element is a nucleus that gathers other things to itself." And as he explains further to Bannon: "There always seems to be something in my mind waiting to put something together with some primary thought I will encounter. It's like looking out of the window and listening to the radio at the same time. I am committed to what comes to me, however it links up."

In an essay appearing in *The Thorny Paradise: Writers on Writing for Children,* Hoban addresses what appears to be an intrinsic characteristic of his writing for both children and adults: "If in my meandering I have seemed to offer tangled thinking more than worked-out thoughts, it has not been through self-indulgence; I have wanted to join the action of my being with that of my readers in a collective being. Collectively we must possess and be repossessed by the past that we alter with our present, must surrender the vanity of personal identity to something more valuable." More recently, in the Rattner interview, Hoban expresses what he understands to be his function as a writer—"to offer what I hope will be a fruitful confusion"—adding that "all kinds of stupid people are offering sterile clarity. What needs to be recognized is the confusion." Underlying the most powerful of Hoban's works, according to Allison, is the idea that "we must struggle for meaning and identity and place against the random element of loss in the attempt to gain 'self-winding.'" She considers Hoban a "great writer because he makes unsentimental reality into art."

MEDIA ADAPTATIONS: The Mouse and His Child was made into a feature-length animated film by Fario-Lockhart-Sanrio Productions in 1977 and starred the voices of Cloris Leachman, Andy Devine, and Peter Ustinov (who also read an abridged version of the novel for a Caedmon recording in 1977); *Turtle Diary* was adapted for the screen by United British Artists/Brittanic in 1986, featuring a screenplay by Harold Pinter and starring Glenda Jackson and Ben Kingsley.

Glynnis Johns recorded selections from *Bedtime for Frances, A Baby Sister for Frances, Bread and Jam for Frances,* and *A Birthday for Frances* in a sound recording entitled "Frances," as well as selections from *A Bargain for Frances, Best Friends for Frances,* and *Egg Thoughts, and Other Frances Songs* in a sound recording entitled "A Bargain for Frances and Other Stories," both by Caedmon in 1977.

BIOGRAPHICAL/CRITICAL SOURCES:

BOOKS

Arbuthnot, May Hill and Zena Sutherland, *Children and Books,* 4th edition, Scott, Foresman, 1972.
Blishen, Edward, editor, *The Thorny Paradise: Writers on Writing for Children,* Kestrel, 1975.
Blount, Margaret, *Animal Land: The Creatures of Children's Fiction,* Morrow, 1974.
Children's Literature Review, Volume III, Gale, 1978.
Contemporary Literary Criticism, Gale, Volume VII, 1977, Volume XXV, 1983.
Dictionary of Literary Biography, Volume LII: *American Writers for Children since 1960,* Gale, 1986.

PERIODICALS

American Artist, October, 1961.
Antioch Review, summer, 1982.
Atlantic, August, 1976, December, 1983.
Books for Your Children, winter, 1976.
Chicago Tribune Book World, July 12, 1981.
Children's Literature in Education, March, 1972, spring, 1976.

Critique, fall, 1984.
Educational Foundation for Nuclear Science, June, 1982.
Encounter, June, 1981.
Globe and Mail (Toronto), March 29, 1986.
Harper's, April, 1983.
Junior Bookshelf, July, 1963.
Listener, October 30, 1980.
Los Angeles Times, February 14, 1986.
New Statesman, May 25, 1973, April 11, 1975.
Newsweek, March 1, 1976, June 29, 1981, December 7, 1981, May 30, 1983, February 17, 1986.
New Yorker, March 22, 1976, July 20, 1981, August 8, 1983.
New York Review of Books, November 19, 1981.
New York Times, June 26, 1981, November 1, 1981, June 20, 1983, February 14, 1986.
New York Times Book Review, February 4, 1968, March 21, 1976, June 28, 1981, June 6, 1982, May 29, 1983, November 27, 1983.
Observer (London), March 13, 1983.
People, August 10, 1981.
Publishers Weekly, May 15, 1981.
Saturday Review, May 7, 1960, May 1, 1976, December, 1981.
Spectator, May 16, 1969, April 5, 1975, March 12, 1983.
Time, February 16, 1976, June 22, 1981, May 16, 1983.
Times (London), January 7, 1982, March 24, 1983.
Times Literary Supplement, April 3, 1969, March 16, 1973, March 29, 1974, October 31, 1980, March 7, 1986, April 3, 1987, September 4, 1987.
Village Voice, June 15, 1982.
Washington Post, February 28, 1986.
Washington Post Book World, June 7, 1981, June 27, 1982, May 29, 1983, July 12, 1987.
Wilton Bulletin (Wilton, Conn.), September 26, 1962.†

—*Sketch by Sharon Malinowski*

*   *   *

HOBAN, Tana

PERSONAL: Born in Philadelphia, Pa.; daughter of Abram T. (an advertising manager for the *Jewish Daily Forward*) and Jeanette (Dimmerman) Hoban; married Edward E. Gallob (a photographer), 1939 (divorced, 1982), married John G. Morris (a journalist), 1983; children: Miela. *Education:* Graduate of School of Design for Women (now Moore College of Art), 1938.

ADDRESSES: Home—56, Rue des Tournelles, 75003 Paris, France.

CAREER: Writer and artist. Worked as photographer; instructor in photography, University of Pennsylvania, 1966-69. Visiting lecturer at numerous schools throughout the United States, 1974-84; conducted children's photography workshop, Avioriaz, France, 1984. Photographs have been exhibited in one-woman shows at Neikrug Gallery, New York City, 1980, Photographs Unlimited, New York City, 1982, and Galerie Agathe Gaillard, Paris, 1985; work has also been included in exhibitions with that of Margaret Bourke-White, Esther Bubley, Dorothea Lange, and Helen Levitt, 1949, and in the "Family of Man" exhibition at the Museum of Modern Art, New York City, 1955, as well as in other group shows, including the White House Conference on Children and Youth, Washington, D.C., 1960, "What Is Man?" at the Museum of the Philadelphia Civic Center, 1966, and "Les Enfants" at Galerie Agathe Gaillard, 1984.

AWARDS, HONORS: John Frederick Lewis fellowship, 1938; Gold Medal from Chicago Art Directors, 1958, from New York Art Directors, 1962 and 1963, and from Philadelphia Art Directors, 1962 and 1964; named one of ten top women photographers by Professional Photographers of America, 1959; Golden Eagle Award, Council on International Nontheatrical Events (CINE), 1967, for "Catsup"; Children's Book Showcase title, 1972, for *Look Again!*, and 1973, for *Count and See;* second place in Fourth Annual Children's Science Competition, 1975, for *Circles, Triangles, and Squares*; *Dig, Drill, Dump, Fill* named notable children's trade book in field of social studies, 1975; *Big Ones, Little Ones* named an outstanding science trade book, 1976; *Is It Red? Is It Yellow? Is It Blue?* named an American Library Association notable book and an International Reading Association-Children's Book Council children's choice, 1979; *Take Another Look* named an American Library Association notable book, 1981; *More Than One* named an outstanding science trade book, 1981; Washington Children's Book Guild Nonfiction Award, 1982; *Round and Round and Round* named an American Library Association notable book, 1983; Drexel Citation, Drexel University, 1983, for body of creative work; New York Academy of Science Award honorable mention, 1984, for *Is It Rough? Is It Smooth? Is It Shiny?*, 1986, for *Is It Larger? Is It Smaller?*, and 1987, for *Shapes, Shapes, Shapes*; Boston Globe/Horn Book Special Award, 1985, for *One, Two, Three*, which was also named an American Library Association notable book, 1985, and was named to *Horn Book*'s Fanfare List, 1986; *A Children's Zoo* and *Is It Larger? Is It Smaller?* named outstanding science trade books, 1985; George C. Stone Recognition of Merit Award, 1986, for entire body of work; Annual Book Award, Please Touch Museum (Philadelphia), 1986, for *Is It Larger? Is It Smaller?;* Special International Award (Geneva, Switzerland), 1987, for entire body of work.

WRITINGS:

JUVENILES; SELF-ILLUSTRATED

Shapes and Things, Macmillan, 1970.
Look Again!, Macmillan, 1971.
Count and See, Macmillan, 1972.
Push, Pull, Empty, Full: A Book of Opposites, Macmillan, 1972.
Over, Under, and Through, and Other Spatial Concepts, Macmillan, 1973.
Where Is It?, Macmillan, 1974.
Circles, Triangles, and Squares, Macmillan, 1974.
Dig, Drill, Dump, Fill, Greenwillow, 1975.
Big Ones, Little Ones, Greenwillow, 1976.
Is It Red? Is It Yellow? Is It Blue?, Greenwillow, 1978.
One Little Kitten, Greenwillow, 1979.
Take Another Look, Greenwillow, 1981.
More Than One, Greenwillow, 1981.
A, B, See!, Greenwillow, 1982.
Round and Round and Round, Greenwillow, 1983.
I Read Signs, Greenwillow, 1983.
I Read Symbols, Greenwillow, 1984.
I Walk and Read, Greenwillow, 1984.
Is It Rough? Is It Smooth? Is It Shiny?, Greenwillow, 1984.
One, Two, Three, Greenwillow, 1984.
What Is It?, Greenwillow, 1985.
Is It Larger? Is It Smaller?, Greenwillow, 1985.
A Children's Zoo, Greenwillow, 1985.
Panda, Panda, Greenwillow, 1986.
Red, Blue, Yellow Shoe, Greenwillow, 1986.
Shapes, Shapes, Shapes, Greenwillow, 1986.

Twenty-six Letters and Ninety-nine Cents, Greenwillow, 1986.
Dots, Spots, Speckles and Stripes, Greenwillow, 1987.
Look, Look, Look, Greenwillow, in press.

OTHER

How to Photograph Your Child (self-illustrated), Crown, 1953.
(Contributor) "Famous Photographers Tell How" (sound recording), Candid Recordings, 1958.
(Illustrator) Edna Bennett, *Photographing Youth*, Amphoto, 1961.
(Contributor) *Encyclopedia of Photography*, Greystone Press, 1963.
(Illustrator) Edith Baer, *The Wonder of Hands*, Parents' Magazine Press, 1970.

Also producer of film "Catsup," 1967, and of other films based on books of the same title, including "Where Is It?," "One Little Kitten," "Panda, Panda," and "Dancing Zoo Zebra." Also photographer of film strips entitled "Beginning Concepts," Scholastic, Inc.

SIDELIGHTS: Called a "gifted photographer" in *Scientific American*, Tana Hoban has received particular praise for her creative and well-designed photographic concept books for young children. With little or no text, these books of attractive photographs help youngsters identify, explore, and comprehend their world; they frequently offer adults an altered perspective of a child's world as well. Michael Dirda of the *Washington Post Book World* believes that Hoban "recognizes instinctively what will appeal to very young children."

Noted for their clarity and vibrance, Hoban's photographs distinctively reflect a child's experience. For instance, images of such familiar items as bowls, drinking cups, spoons, and socks comprise the infant's book *What Is It?*, which a *New York Times Book Review* contributor commends for "wit in the selection of objects and art in the design." And in *I Walk and Read*, images of various signs and symbols, from neon advertisements to directional signals not only "heighten children's visual awareness of the words they first encounter in the urban out-of-doors," writes Carol Brightman in the *New York Times Book Review*, but encourage them "to explore a larger world that they can touch and smell and see." Further, because the book also indicates for adults "some important subliminal facts about language," Brightman concludes: "No wonder, then, that it often takes a writer or a poet who is privileged with the sensory intelligence of a child to repossess the concreteness of language for the rest of us."

BIOGRAPHICAL/CRITICAL SOURCES:

BOOKS

Children's Literature Review, Volume XIII, Gale, 1987.

PERIODICALS

Los Angeles Times Book Review, March 16, 1986.
New York Times Book Review, May 2, 1971, April 8, 1984, April 14, 1985.
Saturday Review, November 14, 1970.
School Library Journal, April, 1985.
Scientific American, December, 1984.
Washington Post Book World, January 8, 1984, August 11, 1985, March 8, 1987.

*   *   *

HOCHSTEIN, Rolaine

PERSONAL: Born in Yonkers, N.Y.; daughter of Martin R.

(an accountant) and Sara (Weinberger) Abrahams; married Morton H. Hochstein (a writer), August 12, 1951; children: Eric, Kate, Bess. *Education:* Syracuse University, B.A., 1951; Columbia University, M.F.A., 1985.

ADDRESSES: *Agent*—Emilie Jacobson, Curtis Brown Ltd., 10 Astor Pl., New York, N.Y. 10003.

CAREER: Worked as an office clerk, copywriter, assistant editor, and publicist, 1951-55. Teacher in New Jersey State Council for the Arts writer-in-the-schools program, and former teacher at Hampshire College and Tenafly Community School.

MEMBER: PEN, National Writers Union.

WRITINGS:

(With Daniel A. Sugarman) *Seven Stories for Growth*, Pitman, 1965.
(With Sugarman) *The Seventeen Guide to Knowing Yourself*, Macmillan, 1967.
(With Sugarman) *The Seventeen Guide to You and Other People*, Macmillan, 1972.
Stepping Out (novel), Norton, 1977.
Table 47 (novel), Doubleday, 1983.

Short stories have appeared in numerous magazines and anthologies, including *O. Henry Prize Stories*, 1974, 1985.

Contributor of articles and humorous essays to magazines and newspapers, including *Washington Post*, *Los Angeles Times*, *Ms.*, *Good Housekeeping*, *Family Circle*, and *New York Times Magazine*.

WORK IN PROGRESS: *Shipwreck*, a novel.

*   *   *

HODGETTS, Richard M(ichael)   1942-

PERSONAL: Born March 10, 1942, in Bronx, N.Y.; son of Harold Thomas (a postal employee) and Regina (McDermott) Hodgetts; married Sara J. Fontana, August 1, 1970; children: Steven Michael, Jennifer Anne. *Education:* New York University, B.S., 1963; Indiana University, M.B.A., 1964; University of Oklahoma, Ph.D., 1968.

ADDRESSES: *Home*—3930 Durango, Coral Gables, Fla. 33134. *Office*—College of Business, Management Department, Florida International University, Miami, Fla. 33199.

CAREER: University of Nebraska, Lincoln, assistant professor, 1968-70, associate professor, 1970-73, professor of management, 1973-75; Texas Tech University, Lubbock, visiting professor of management, 1975-76; Florida International University, Miami, professor of management, 1976—. Management consultant to businesses and hospitals.

MEMBER: Academy of Management (fellow; secretary of History of Management Division), Academy of International Business, Southern Management Association.

WRITINGS:

Top Management Simulation, D. H. Mark, 1970.
(With Fred Luthans and Kenneth A. Thompson) *Social Issues in Business*, Macmillan, 1972, 5th edition, 1987.
Readings on the Current Social Issues in Business: Poverty, Civil Rights, Ecology, and Consumerism, Macmillan, 1972.
(With Henry Albers) *Cases and Incidents on the Basic Concepts of Management*, Wiley, 1972.
(With Luthans) *Study Guide to Accompany Organizational Behavior*, McGraw, 1973, 2nd edition, 1977.

Management: Theory, Process and Practice, Saunders, 1975, 4th edition, Academic Press, 1986.

(With Richard L. Howe and Ronald Greenwood) *Study Guide to Accompany Management: Theory, Process and Practice,* Saunders, 1975, 3rd edition, Dryden, 1982.

(Editor with A. Thomas Hollingsworth) *Readings in Basic Management,* Saunders, 1975.

(With Max S. Wortman) *Administrative Policy: Text and Cases in the Policy Sciences,* Wiley, 1975, 2nd edition, 1980.

American Business: Social Challenge, Social Response, Saunders, 1977.

(With Terry Smart) *The American Free Enterprise System,* Addison-Wesley, 1978.

(With Steve Altman) *Readings in Organizational Behavior,* Saunders, 1979.

(With Altman) *Organizational Behavior,* Saunders, 1979.

(With C. Edward Cavert) *Study Guide to Accompany Organizational Behavior,* Saunders, 1979.

Human Relations, Dryden, 1980, 3rd edition, 1987.

(With Ruth de Bliek) *Study Guide to Accompany Human Relations,* Dryden, 1980.

Introduction to Business, 2nd edition (Hodgetts was not associated with previous edition), Addison-Wesley, 1980, 3rd edition, 1984.

(With Charles Beavins and Karen Brinkman) *Study Guide to Accompany Introduction to Business,* 2nd edition, Addison-Wesley, 1980.

(With Pamela Keel) *Topics in Small Business Management,* Kendall/Hunt, 1980.

Introduction to Management, Dryden, 1981.

(With Regina and R. Greenwood) *Management Fundamentals: Study Guide,* Dryden, 1981.

(With Smart) *Economics and the Free Enterprise System,* Addison-Wesley, 1982, revised edition, 1987.

Effective Small Business Management, Academic Press, 1982, 2nd edition, 1986.

(With Dorothy Cascio) *Modern Health Care Administration,* Academic Press, 1983.

Personal Finance, Addison-Wesley, 1983.

Management, Academic Press, 1985.

Effective Supervision, McGraw, 1987.

CONTRIBUTOR

Luthans, editor, *Cases, Readings and Review Guide for Principles of Management,* Wiley, 1969.

Business Games Handbook, American Management Association, 1969.

William H. Klein and Darrel C. Murphy, editors, *Policy: Concepts in Organizational Guidance,* Little, Brown, 1973.

Fremtiden Er Naermere End Vi Tror!, Danish Marketing Association (Copenhagen), 1976.

Donald D. White and H. William Vroman, editors, *Action in Organizations: Cases and Experiences in Organizational Behavior,* 2nd edition, Holbrook, 1977.

OTHER

Consulting editor of management series for Academic Press, 1979-85, and for management series for Burgess Communication, 1985-86. Contributor to *Academy of Management Proceedings,* 1973, 1976, and 1978, and to *Proceedings of the Second National ABSEL Conference,* 1975. Author of weekly business column "Minding Your Business," published in *Fort Lauderdale News and Sun Sentinel.* Contributor of articles and reviews to numerous management and business journals and periodicals, including *Business Inquiry, Personnel Journal,*

Management Horizons, Accounting Review, Simulation, and *Personnel Psychology.* Member of review board of *Journal of Management, Research, American Journal of Small Business, Business Research, Strategy and Executive Action,* and *Academy of Management Executive.*

SIDELIGHTS: Richard M. Hodgetts once told *CA:* "I write because I believe knowledge should be conveyed in an up-to-date, interesting fashion; and what field changes more than business? So there is always a new development to be related and the challenge of trying to do this in an entertaining, yet substantive, manner. Too much of business literature is dull and dry. I like to think that every now and then I am able to convey business-related ideas the way they are actually brought to fruition in the 'real' world: excitingly, interestingly, factually, pragmatically, and—when the occasion merits—humorously."

*   *   *

HOEST, Bill
    See HOEST, William P.

*   *   *

HOEST, William P.   1926-
    (Bill Hoest)

PERSONAL: Born February 7, 1926, in Newark, N.J.; son of Earl Sevem and Dorothea (an artist; maiden name, Gamble) Hoest Whittinghill; married Madeline Mezz Jungreis, November 4, 1973; children: Elizabeth, Suzanne, John, Charles, Sharon, Molly, Patricia, William, Julie. *Education:* Graduated from Cooper Union, 1949.

ADDRESSES: Office—c/o King Features Syndicate, 235 East 45th St., New York, N.Y. 10017.

CAREER: Norcross, New York, N.Y., artist, 1948-51; freelance cartoonist, 1955—. Creator of "The Lockhorns," 1968, a Sunday and daily feature comic with more than four hundred outlets in newspapers worldwide, "Agatha Crumm," 1977, a comic strip appearing internationally in more than two hundred newspapers, and "What a Guy," a comic strip originated in 1987, all syndicated by King Features. Also creator of "Bumper Snickers," a weekly cartoon panel in the *National Enquirer,* and "Howard Huge," a weekly cartoon panel appearing in more than one hundred and thirty-five newspapers as one of *Parade Magazine's* "Laugh Parade" columns. *Military service:* U.S. Navy, 1944-47.

MEMBER: National Cartoonists Society, Cartoonists Guild, Comics Council.

AWARDS, HONORS: Reuben Award for best syndicated panel cartoonist of the year from National Cartoonists Society, 1976, for "The Lockhorns," 1977, for magazine panel, and 1980, for "The Lockhorns."

WRITINGS—All under name Bill Hoest:

A Taste of Carrot, Atheneum, 1967.
Howard Huge, Lyle Stuart, 1982.

"THE LOCKHORNS" SERIES

The Lockhorns: What's the Garbage Doing on the Stove?, New American Library, 1975.
The Lockhorns, Number Two: Loretta, the Meat Loaf Is Moving, New American Library, 1976.

The Lockhorns, Number Three: Who Made the Caesar Salad—Brutus?, New American Library, 1977.

The Lockhorns, Number Four: Is This the Steak or the Charcoal?, New American Library, 1979.

The Lockhorns, Number Five: I See You Burned the Cold Cuts Again, New American Library, 1981.

The Lockhorns, Number Six: Of Course I Love You . . . What Do I Know?, New American Library, 1981.

The Lockhorns, Number Seven: Let's Go for a Walk . . . And Bring Your Wallet, New American Library, 1982.

The Lockhorns, Number Eight: I Could Live without These Meals . . . Probably Longer, New American Library, 1982.

The Lockhorns, Number Nine: You Name It . . . I'm Guilty, New American Library, 1982.

Lockhorns I, Tor Books, 1983.

The Lockhorns, Number Two: What Do You Mean You Weren't Listening? I Didn't Say Anything, Tor Books, 1983.

Lockhorns Giant, Number Three, Tor Books, 1984.

"AGATHA CRUMM" SERIES

Agatha Crumm, New American Library, 1980.

The Return of Agatha Crumm, New American Library, 1982.

Agatha Crumm, Number Three: Too Much Is Never Enough, New American Library, 1983.

"BUMPER SNICKERS" SERIES

Bumper Snickers, New American Library, 1976.

More Bumper Snickers, New American Library, 1979.

Even More Bumper Snickers, New American Library, 1982.

Bumper Snickers: Even More Bumper Snickers, Number Three, New American Library, 1982.

OTHER

Also author of *Hoest Toasties*, Grossett & Dunlap.

WORK IN PROGRESS: "Branching out into television and children's books."

SIDELIGHTS: William P. Hoest, whose middle-aged, big-nosed and foreshortened Lockhorns squabble daily to the delight of newspaper readers worldwide, remarked in an interview in *Cartoonist Profiles:* "I was able to gradually, throughout the years, work up a style of drawing that I was comfortable with. I tried my hardest to be loose and free like some of the cartoonists I admired, Saxon, Dedini, Lorenz; but to no avail. My work came out messy. Apparently I am compelled to make lines meet, tidy up the ends, use backgrounds to a minimum and objects only when absolutely necessary. In short, my artwork satisfies me when it is neat, clean, simple, and uncluttered. Perhaps what I am trying to do is somehow, some way, make order out of a harried and complicated life."

Prolific in his cartooning, Hoest described his work habits: "My working day varies with the weather. If the sun is out, I play tennis first and hit the drawing board second. I have no regular working schedule, but I am not lazy. I love my work and have a real need to get to the drawing board. I also have a deep sense of responsibility and always get my work out on time, if not sooner." Hoest told *CA:* "Each week I do twelve daily 'Agatha Crum' strips or four Sundays, twelve daily 'Lockhorns' and two Sundays consisting of four panels, six roughs for 'Bumper Snickers,' one 'Howard Huge,' and two general interest cartoons for 'Laugh Parade' for *Parade Magazine*, and cartoons for the monthly magazines. This does not include time on new books or what I call 'Research and Development' for new features in magazines or for syndication. I don't keep a rigid schedule, but obviously I spend a lot of time at the drawing board, sometimes all night long, to get the work out."

Hoest added: "Fortunately, I love what I'm doing and I'd be doing it anyway. Spare time is a real problem. I've had to be very self-disciplined and organized because I have lots of hobbies that take time such as gardening, woodworking, tennis, and motorcycling.

"Not incidentally, I have a wife and nine children and time with them is precious to me, too. Time is one commodity I have to guard carefully.

"Humor is one of humanity's greatest gifts. It's a pleasure for me as a cartoonist to be able to share a laugh with a fellow human being.

"Life has been good to me and I'm very grateful."

BIOGRAPHICAL/CRITICAL SOURCES:

PERIODICALS

Cartoonist Profiles, December, 1976.

* * *

HOFFMAN, Adeline M(ildred)   1908-1979

PERSONAL: Born May 13, 1908, in Richmond Hill, N.Y.; died October 24, 1979; daughter of Francis (a building specialties dealer) and Helena (Schimmer) Hoffman. *Education:* Trenton State College, diploma, 1928; University of Missouri, B.S., 1930; Columbia University, M.A., 1935; Pennsylvania State University, Ph.D., 1956. *Politics:* Republican. *Religion:* Presbyterian.

ADDRESSES: Home—7 Gilmore Ct., Iowa City, Iowa 52240.

CAREER: High school teacher of home economics in Bel Air, Md., 1930-35, and Freehold, N.J., 1935-36; University of Maryland Co-op Extension Service, Westminster, county home demonstration agent, 1936-43; New York State Emergency Food Commission, New York City, senior nutritionist, 1943-45; University of Delaware Cooperative Extension Service, Newark, specialist in clothing, textiles, and home furnishings, 1945-49; University of Connecticut, Storrs, assistant professor of textiles and clothing, 1949-53; U.S. Department of Health, Education, and Welfare, Washington, D.C., clothing specialist with Defense Welfare Services, 1956-57, special consultant in clothing resources, beginning 1963; Southern Illinois University, Carbondale, professor of textiles and clothing and chairman of department, 1957-61; University of Iowa, Iowa City, professor in charge of teaching and research in textiles and clothing, department of home economics, 1962-76, professor emeritus, 1976-79. Visiting professor, University of Maryland, 1968, 1969. Affiliate staff member, Institute of Gerontology, beginning 1962. Member of board of directors, Christian Retirement Services, Inc., Iowa City; member of women's committee, Japan International Christian University; member of Mid-West Council on Social Research in Aging, and of American Council of Consumer Interests.

MEMBER: International Home Economics Federation, International Platform Association, International Graphoanalysis Society (life member), American Gerontological Society, American Home Economists Association (life member), American Association of University Professors, American Association of University Women, American Dietetic Association, American Association of Textile Chemists and Colorists, Fashion Group, Inc., National League of American Pen Women (national fourth vice-president), University of Missouri Home Economics Alumnae Association (president), Phi Upsilon Omicron, Omicron Nu, Phi Kappa Phi, Pi Lambda Theta, Delta Kappa Gamma, Soroptimist International.

AWARDS, HONORS: Recipient of certificate from Teaching and Education Office of Federal Civil Defense Administration, 1956, and from New Jersey Department of Defense, Division of Civil Defense and Disaster Control, 1957, for outstanding service; University of Missouri, Women's Centennial Award, 1967, citation of merit and Gold Medal Award, both 1970.

WRITINGS:

A Study of Clothing Expenditures of Women Students at Southern Illinois University (booklet), Southern Illinois University, 1960.
(With Iva M. Bader) *Social Science Aspects of Clothing for Older Women: An Annotated Bibliography,* Department of Home Economics and Institute of Gerontology, University of Iowa, 1964.
(Contributor) W. W. Morris and H. Lee Jacobs, editors, *Nursing and Retirement Home Administration,* Iowa State University Press, 1966.
(Editor) *The Daily Needs and Interests of Older People,* C. C Thomas, 1970, 2nd edition edited by Woodrow W. Morris and Bader, 1983.
Clothing for the Handicapped, the Aged, and Other People with Special Needs, illustrated by Lonnie M. Kennedy, foreword by Morris, C. C Thomas, 1979.

Contributor to professional journals.

SIDELIGHTS: Adeline M. Hoffman once told *CA:* "It was my doctoral dissertation that phased in my serious professional writing, but lesser writing started with my high school paper, quarterly and yearbook. At the time, I couldn't afford to subscribe to the high school publications and the pressure of 'school spirit' dictated that I do something to express my school spirit. So, I went out and got ads for the school paper, and as a reward for having brought in the most ad money, I was given a place on the editorial staff. From then on, I have never stopped writing." Believing in the importance of good writing, she added, "I have concentrated on establishing writing awards to help focus attention on excellence in writing among university students."

BIOGRAPHICAL/CRITICAL SOURCES:

PERIODICALS

Aging, March, 1980.
Journal of Home Economics, September, 1970, spring, 1980.†

* * *

HOFFMAN, Richard L(ester) 1937-1981

PERSONAL: Born February 28, 1937, in Philadelphia, Pa.; died December 13, 1981; son of Lester Samuel (a machinist) and Helena (Forrest) Hoffman; married Marie Aileen Regina Golden, July 5, 1968. *Education:* University of Pennsylvania, A.B., 1959; Princeton University, A.M., 1961, Ph.D., 1964.

ADDRESSES: Office—Department of English, Virginia Polytechnic Institute and State University, Blacksburg, Va. 24061.

CAREER: University of Pennsylvania, Philadelphia, instructor, 1963-65, assistant professor of English, 1965-68; Queens College of the City University of New York, Flushing, N.Y., associate professor of English, 1968-71; Virginia Polytechnic

Institute and State University, Blacksburg, Va., professor of English, 1971-81.

MEMBER: Modern Language Association of America, Modern Humanities Research Association, Mediaeval Academy of America, Early English Text Society, Phi Beta Kappa, Eta Sigma Phi.

AWARDS, HONORS: Woodrow Wilson fellow, 1959-60; Danforth fellow, 1959-63; Scribner fellow at Princeton University, 1960-62.

WRITINGS:

Ovid and the Canterbury Tales, University of Pennsylvania Press, 1967, reprinted, University Microfilms, 1985.
(Editor) *History of the English Language: Selected Texts and Exercises,* Little, Brown, 1968, 2nd edition (with Louis McCorry Myers) published as *The Roots of Modern English: Selected Texts and Exercises,* 1971, 2nd edition, 1979.
(Editor with Paul W. Elledge) *Romantic and Victorian: Studies in Memory of William H. Marshall,* Fairleigh Dickinson University Press, 1971.
(With L. M. Myers) *Companion to the Roots of Modern English,* Little, Brown, 1972, 2nd edition, 1979.
(Editor with Maxwell S. Luria) *Middle English Lyrics,* Norton, 1975.

CONTRIBUTOR

Shirley E. Marshall, editor, *A Young American's Treasury of English Poetry,* Washington Square, 1967.
Beryl Rowland, editor, *A Companion to Chaucer Studies,* Oxford University Press, 1968.
R. M. Lumiansky and Herschel Baker, editors, *Critical Approaches to Six Major English Works,* University of Pennsylvania Press, 1968.

OTHER

Contributor of more than twenty articles to language journals, including *Journal of English and German Philology.*

WORK IN PROGRESS: A new edition of *The Tale of Beryn,* for Early English Text Society (Oxford); two "Norton Critical Editions" of Middle English poetry (romances, drama), for Norton with M. S. Luria; *The Tale of Melibee* for the University of Oklahoma Press; *The Variorum Chaucer.*†

* * *

HOLMES, Marjorie (Rose) 1910-

PERSONAL: Born September 22, 1910, in Storm Lake, Iowa; daughter of Samuel Arthur and Rosa (Griffith) Holmes; married Lynn Burton Mighell, April 9, 1932 (deceased); married George P. Schmieler (a physician), July 4, 1981; children: (first marriage) Marjorie Mighell Croner, Mark, Mallory, Melanie Mighell Dimopoulos. *Education:* Attended Buena Vista College, 1927-29; Cornell College, B.A., 1931.

ADDRESSES: Home and office—637 East McMurray Rd., McMurray, Pa. 15317. *Agent*—Edward J. Acton, 928 Broadway, New York, N.Y. 10010.

CAREER: Free-lance writer, columnist, and teacher. Author of bi-weekly column, "Love and Laughter," Washington, D.C. *Star,* 1959-73, also appeared in syndication; author of monthly column, "A Woman's Conversation with God," 1971-77. Teacher of writing, Georgetown University Summer Writers

Conference, 1959-81, Catholic University, 1964-65, University of Maryland, 1967-68, Philadelphia Writers Conference, and Cape Cod Writers Conference. Member of board of directors, Foundation for Christian Living, 1975—. Served as writer and commentator for radio shows, including ''Alexander's Mediation Board'' for the Mutual Network. Lecturer at universities.

MEMBER: Children's Book Guild, American Newpaper Women's Club, Washington National Press Club, Virginia Press Women, Delta Phi Beta.

AWARDS, HONORS: Alumni Achievement Award, Cornell College, 1963; Award for Literature, American Association for Social Psychiatry, 1964; Honor Iowans Award, Buena Vista College, 1966; Woman of Achievement award, National Federation of Press Women, 1972; Scholarship Celebrity Award, Ft. Worth Women in Communications, 1975; Woman of Achievement, McLean, Va., Business and Professional Women, 1976; D.Litt., Buena Vista College, 1976; Freedom Foundation of Valley Forge award, 1977; Distinguished Service Award, Buena Vista College, 1978; Certificate of Merit, Catholic Library Association, 1983, for contribution to high school libraries.

WRITINGS:

World by the Tail, Lippincott, 1943.
Ten o'Clock Scholar, Lippincott, 1947.
Saturday Night (Junior Literary Guild selection), Westminster, 1959.
Cherry Blossom Princess, Westminster, 1960.
Follow Your Dream, Westminster, 1961.
Senior Trip, Westminster, 1962.
Love Is a Hopscotch Thing, Westminster, 1963, published as *Sunday Morning*, Dell, 1982.
Love and Laughter, Doubleday, 1967.
Wanted: Someone to Talk To, Epworth Press, 1967.
I've Got to Talk to Somebody, God: A Woman's Conversation with God, illustrated by Betty Fraser, Doubleday, 1969.
Writing the Creative Article, Writer, Inc., 1969.
Who Am I, God?, Doubleday, 1971.
To Treasure Our Days, Hallmark, 1971.
Two from Galilee (first book in trilogy; also see below), Revell, 1972.
Nobody Else Will Listen, Doubleday, 1973.
You and I and Yesterday, illustrated by Bob Brunson, Morrow, 1973.
As Tall as My Heart, EPM Publications, 1974.
How Can I Find You, God?, Doubleday, 1975.
Beauty in Your Own Back Yard, EPM Publications, 1976.
Hold Me up a Little Longer, Lord, illustrated by Patricia Mighell, Doubleday, 1977.
Lord, Let Me Love, Doubleday, 1978.
God and Vitamins: How Exercise, Diet, and Faith Can Change Your Life, Doubleday, 1980.
To Help You through the Hurting, Doubleday, 1983.
Three from Galilee: The Young Man from Nazareth (second book in trilogy; Literary Guild, Doubleday Book Club, and Guideposts Book Club selection), Harper, 1985.

Also author of filmscript for ''The General Comes Home,'' produced by Metro-Goldwyn-Mayer, and a film adaptation of her book *Two from Galilee*. Contributor of short stories, articles, and poetry to magazines, including *Ladies' Home Journal, Reader's Digest, McCall's,* and *Family Circle*.

WORK IN PROGRESS: The Messiah, the third book in trilogy.

SIDELIGHTS: Marjorie Holmes's book *Two from Galilee* is a love story of the biblical figures Mary and Joseph. Published in 1972, *Two from Galilee* appeared on the *New York Times* bestseller list and was one of the ten best-selling novels of that year. Holmes explained to *Dallas News* writer Kay Crosby Ellis that her intention in writing the novel was to take Mary and Joseph ''out of the art galleries and take away the gold frames and halos which create a barrier for us. I wanted to show them as two people confronted with the great honor but also the great responsibility of serving as the earthly parents of the Christ child.'' She also told Ellis that *Two from Galilee* ''means more to me than anything else I have ever written. If I had never written anything else besides this book, I would still feel like I had accomplished something.''

BIOGRAPHICAL/CRITICAL SOURCES:

BOOKS

Authors in the News, Volume I, Gale, 1976.

PERIODICALS

Catholic Library World, July/August, 1983.
Dallas News, April 6, 1974.
Ladies' Home Journal, December, 1969.
Writer, December, 1979.

*   *   *

HOMBERGER, Eric (Ross) 1942-

PERSONAL: Born May 30, 1942, in Philadelphia, Pa.; son of Alexander and Marilyn (Glick) Homberger; married Judy Jones, June 2, 1967; children: Martin Joshua, Margaret Alissa, Charles Michael. *Education:* University of California, Berkeley, B.A., 1964; University of Chicago, M.A., 1965; Cambridge University, Ph.D., 1972. *Politics:* Socialist. *Religion:* None.

ADDRESSES: Home—74 Clarendon Rd., Norwich NR2 2PN, England.

CAREER: University of Exeter, Exeter, England, temporary lecturer in American literature, 1969-70; University of East Anglia, Norwich, England, lecturer in American literature, 1970—. Visiting member of faculty at University of Minnesota, 1977-78.

MEMBER: British Association for American Studies.

AWARDS, HONORS: Leverhulme fellowship in European studies, 1978-79.

WRITINGS:

(Editor with William Janeway and Simon Schama) *The Cambridge Mind: Ninety Years of the ''Cambridge Review,'' 1879-1969*, Little, Brown, 1970.
(Editor) *Ezra Pound: The Critical Heritage*, Routledge & Kegan Paul, 1972.
The Art of the Real: Poetry in England and America since 1939, Rowman & Littlefield, 1977.
(Co-author) *The Novel and the Second World War*, Macmillan, 1983.
John le Carre, Methuen, 1986.
American Writers and Radical Politics, 1900-1939: Equivocal Commitments, Macmillan, 1987.
Lost New Yorkers: Scenes from the Life of a City, Weidenfeld & Nicolson, 1987.
(Editor with John Charmley) *The Troubled Face of Biography*, Macmillan, 1987.

Contributor to magazines and newspapers, including *Times Literary Supplement, Nation, Economist,* and *Journal of American Studies.*

SIDELIGHTS: Eric Homberger told *CA:* "Living in England since 1965 has enabled me to confront the historical experience of my family (as emigrants, within living memory, from Europe) and of America itself. It has been hard to wave the flag; and I haven't really tried to do so. In partial consequence, I have become interested in fugitive areas of experience, of alienated sensibilities, whether ethnic or political, whose experience may in some way stand for the larger tendency of a society and a way of life.

"I would like to write the kind of literary criticism which is on the brink of becoming history, with its confident and unthinking grasp of the real. Criticism now has almost wholly surrendered that ambition, to its impoverishment, I think; it has the willingness to address a non-specialist reading public. In England fifteen years ago critics still hoped to speak to such an audience. But that has mostly gone and has been replaced by a more vigorous hunger for theorization. The end result: critics only able to speak to each other, inmates, really, in a crumbling and neglected ward, trying to persuade each other that the discipline advances. I want to write a stronger, more political sort of thing. Maybe the form ought to be different. In *Lost New Yorkers* I have tried to combine biography, social history, and some techniques of literary criticism in studies of figures, largely forgotten, who were in their day—nineteenth century—scandalous. I can imagine writing, quite consciously, to reach a wider audience, or at least a different one; the only problem is that the audience I would like to address may no longer exist."

*   *   *

HOURANI, George F(adlo)   1913-1984

PERSONAL: Born June 3, 1913, in Manchester, England; came to United States in 1950, naturalized in 1956; died, 1984; son of Fadlo and Somaya (Racy) Hourani; married Celeste Habib, June 15, 1940. *Education:* Oxford University, B.A. (honors), 1936; Princeton University, Ph.D., 1939.

ADDRESSES: Home—105 Troy Del Way, Williamsville, N.Y. 14221. *Office*—Department of Philosophy, State University of New York at Buffalo, Buffalo, N.Y. 14260.

CAREER: Government Arab College, Jerusalem, lecturer in philosophy and classics, 1939-48; University of Michigan, Ann Arbor, assistant professor, 1950-55, associate professor, 1955-60, professor of Arabic studies, 1960-64, professor of Islamic history and philosophy, 1964-67; State University of New York at Buffalo, professor of philosophy, 1967-84, chairman of the department, 1976-80. Visiting professor of philosophy, University of California, Los Angeles, 1979. Member of editorial board, State University of New York Press, 1972-77.

MEMBER: American Philosophical Association, American Oriental Society (president, 1978-79), Middle East Institute, Middle East Studies Association (president, 1968), Royal Institute of Philosophy.

AWARDS, HONORS: Ford Foundation research fellowship, Egypt, 1956-57; Guggenheim Foundation fellowship, Middle East, 1963-64.

WRITINGS:

Arab Seafaring in the Indian Ocean in Ancient and Early Medieval Times, Princeton University Press, 1951.

Ethical Value, University of Michigan Press, 1956.
Ibn Rushd (Averroes): Kitab fasl al-maqal (a critical edition of the Arabic text), E. J. Brill, 1959.
Averroes on the Harmony of Religion and Philosophy, Luzac Co., for E. J. W. Gibb Memorial Series and UNESCO, 1961.
(Contributor) Ralph Lerner and Muhsin Muhdi, editors, *Medieval Political Philosophy,* Free Press, 1963.
(Contributor) Arthur Hyman and James T. Walsh, editors, *Philosophy in the Middle Ages,* Harper, 1967.
Islamic Rationalism: The Ethics of 'Abd-al-Jabbar, Clarendon Press, 1971.
(Editor) *Essays in Islamic Philosophy and Science,* State University of New York Press, 1975.
Reason and Tradition in Islamic Ethics, Cambridge University Press, 1985.

Contributor to honorary volumes and to *Encyclopedia Americana* and *Encyclopedia International.* Contributor of about thirty articles to professional journals, including *Muslim World, Humanist, Journal of the American Oriental Society, Middle East Journal, Literature East and West,* and *Studia Islamica.* Associate editor of *Journal of the American Oriental Society,* 1964-70.

BIOGRAPHICAL/CRITICAL SOURCES:

BOOKS

Marmura, Michael E., editor, *Islamic Theology and Philosophy: Studies in Honor of George F. Hourani,* State University of New York Press, 1984.

PERIODICALS

Times Literary Supplement, June 11, 1971, April 30, 1976.

OBITUARIES:

PERIODICALS

Journal of the American Oriental Society, January/March, 1985.
Muslim World, July/October, 1984.†

*   *   *

HOUSE, Ernest R(obert)   1937-

PERSONAL: Born August 7, 1937, in Alton, Ill.; married Donna Brown (a nurse), February 1, 1964; children: Kristin, Colby. *Education:* Washington University, St. Louis, Mo., A.B., 1959; Southern Illinois University, M.S., 1964; University of Illinois, Ed.D., 1968.

ADDRESSES: Office—University of Colorado, School of Education, Boulder, Colo. 80309.

CAREER: Junior high school English teacher in Roxana, Ill., 1960-64; University of Illinois at Urbana-Champaign, University High School, Urbana, consultant to Illinois Demonstration Project and English Curriculum Project, 1964-65; Cooperative Educational Research Laboratory, Northfield, Ill., manager of project for evaluation of Illinois gifted, 1967-68, manager of evaluation role development program, 1968-69; University of Illinois at Urbana-Champaign, director of Illinois gifted program evaluation and educational specialist at Center for Instructional Research and Curriculum Evaluation, 1969-71, assistant professor, 1971-75, associate professor, 1975-79, professor of education, 1979-85; University of Colorado, Boulder, professor of education and director of laboratory for policy studies, 1985—. Member of research staffs of political figures Adlai Stevenson III, 1970, and Paul Simon, 1972.

MEMBER: Phi Beta Kappa, Phi Delta Kappa, Kappa Delta Pi.

AWARDS, HONORS: Travel Study Grant, Ford Foundation, 1975.

WRITINGS:

(Editor) *School Evaluation: The Politics and Process,* McCutchan, 1973.
The Politics of Educational Innovation, McCutchan, 1974.
The Logic of Evaluative Argument, Center for the Study of Evaluation, 1977.
(With Stephen D. Lapan) *Survival in the Classroom,* Allyn & Bacon, 1978.
Evaluating with Validity, Sage Publications, 1980.
(Editor with Sandra Mathison and others) *Evaluation Studies Review Annual,* Volume 7, Sage, 1982.
(Editor) *Philosophy of Evaluation,* Jossey-Bass, 1983.
(Editor and author of introduction) *New Directions in Educational Evaluation,* Falmer Press, 1986.
Jesse Jackson's PUSH for Excellence, Greenwood Press, 1988.

Also author of *The Modern Theory of Evaluation,* and of technical reports. Contributor of over one hundred articles and reviews to education journals.

* * *

HUEY, F. B., Jr. 1925-

PERSONAL: Born January 12, 1925, in Denton, Tex.; son of F. B. (in insurance) and Gwendolyn (Chambers) Huey; married Nonna Turner, December 22, 1950; children: Mary Anne, Linda Kaye, William David. *Education:* University of Texas, B.B.A., 1945; Southwestern Baptist Theological Seminary, M.Div., 1958, Th.D., 1961; Ph.D., 1979.

ADDRESSES: Home—6128 Whitman, Fort Worth, Tex. 76133. *Office*—Department of Old Testament, Southwestern Baptist Theological Seminary, 2001 West Seminary, Fort Worth, Tex. 76122.

CAREER: Ordained Baptist minister, 1956; Security National Life Insurance Co., Denton, Tex., accountant, 1947-55; pastor of Baptist churches in Bolivar, Texas., 1956-61; Southern Baptist Convention, Foreign Mission Board, Richmond, Va., missionary in Rio de Janeiro, Brazil, 1961-66; professor of Old Testament at South Brazil Baptist Theological Seminary, 1961-66; Southwestern Baptist Theological Seminary, Fort Worth, Tex., professor of Old Testament, 1965—, associate dean for Ph.D. degree.

MEMBER: National Association of Baptist Professors of Religion, Society of Biblical Studies, Theta Xi, Delta Sigma Pi, Beta Gamma Sigma.

WRITINGS:

(Contributor) C. W. Scudder, editor, *Crises in Morality,* Broadman, 1964.
Exodus: A Study Guide Commentary, Zondervan, 1977.
Yesterday's Prophets for Today's World, Broadman, 1980.
Jeremiah: Bible Study Commentary, Zondervan, 1981.
Numbers: Bible Study Commentary, Zondervan, 1981.
Ezekiel-Daniel, Broadman, 1983.
(Co-author) *A Student's Dictionary for Biblical and Theological Studies,* Zondervan, 1983.
(Contributor) Ron Youngblood, editor, *The Genesis Debate,* Nelson, 1986.

(Contributor) *The Expositor's Bible Commentary,* Zondervan, in press.

Co-translator of *New American Standard Bible.* Contributor to *Pictorial Encyclopedia of the Bible* and *Mighty Works of Grace.* Contributor to theology journals.

WORK IN PROGRESS: Contributions to *Disciple's Study Bible* and *Layman's Bible Dictionary,* for Holman, *Illustrated Guide to the Bible,* for Marshall Pickering Publishing, and *Mercer Dictionary of the Bible,* for Mercer Press.

* * *

HUGHES, Monica (Ince) 1925-

PERSONAL: Born November 3, 1925, in Liverpool, England; daughter of Edward Lindsay (a mathematician) and Phyllis (Fry) Ince; married Glen Hughes, April 22, 1957; children: Elizabeth, Adrienne, Russell, Thomas. *Education:* Educated privately in England and Scotland.

ADDRESSES: Home—13816 110-A Ave., Edmonton, Alberta, Canada T5M 2M9.

CAREER: Dress designer in London, England, 1948-49, and Bulawayo, Rhodesia (now Zimbabwe), 1950; bank clerk in Umtali, Rhodesia, 1951; National Research Council, Ottawa, Ontario, laboratory technician, 1952-57; full-time writer, 1975—. *Military service:* Women's Royal Naval Service, 1943-46.

MEMBER: Writers Union of Canada, Canadian Society of Children's Authors, Illustrators, and Performers, Writers Guild of Alberta, Science Writers of America.

AWARDS, HONORS: Beaver Award, 1980; Vicky Metcalf Award, 1981; Alberta Culture juvenile novel award, 1981; Canada Council prize for children's literature, 1981, 1982; IBBY certificate of honour, 1982; Vicky Metcalf short story award, 1983; Saskatchewan Library Association young adult novel award, 1983; Alberta R. Ross Annett Award, Writers Guild of Alberta, 1983, 1984, 1986.

WRITINGS—All juveniles:

NOVELS

Gold-Fever Trail: A Klondike Adventure, John LeBel, 1974.
Crisis on Conshelf Ten, Copp, 1975, Atheneum, 1977.
Earthdark, Hamish Hamilton, 1977.
Ghost Dance Caper, Hamish Hamilton, 1978.
The Tomorrow City, Hamish Hamilton, 1978.
Beyond the Dark River, Atheneum, 1979.
Hunter in the Dark, Atheneum, 1982.
Ring-Rise, Ring-Set, MacRae, 1982.
The Beckoning Lights, LeBel, 1982.
The Treasure of the Long Sault, LeBel, 1982.
Space Trap, MacRae, 1983.
My Name Is Paula Popowich, Lorimer, 1983.
Devil on My Back, MacRae, 1984.
Sand Writer, MacRae, 1985.
Dream Catcher, MacRae, 1986.
Blaine's Way, Irwin, 1986.
Log Jam, Irwin, 1987.

"ISIS" TRILOGY

The Keeper of the Isis Light, Atheneum, 1980.
The Guardian of Isis, Atheneum, 1981.
The Isis Pedlar, Atheneum, 1982.

CONTRIBUTOR

Magook, McClelland & Stewart, 1977.
Out of Time, Bodley Head, 1984, Harper, 1985.
Dragons and Dreams, Harper, 1985.
The Windows of Dreams, Methuen, 1986.

SIDELIGHTS: Monica Hughes is respected as one of Canada's finest writers for young adults—"a writer of rare integrity and great narrative powers," according to Marcus Crouch in *Junior Bookshelf*. Prolific in many genres, she is best known for her science fiction. Like her other work, it is often praised for its lively plotting, well-rounded characterizations, and sensitive exploration of moral issues. Sarah Ellis adds in *Horn Book* magazine that "a documentary flair is also a factor in one of Monica Hughes's great strengths as a science fiction writer— her technical neatness. She always manages to give the essential scientific background economically, without becoming bogged down in hardware."

Hughes travelled the world for many years before settling in Canada and beginning to write seriously. Most of her novels are set in Canada or in an alien world very like it. Her first published work was a Canadian historical adventure entitled *Gold-Fever Trail: A Klondike Adventure*. Thanks to Hughes's extensive research, the setting is made vividly real, and "the reader becomes completely engrossed" in the author's evocation of Canada's Gold Rush, writes Marion Pape in the *World of Children's Books*. Marion Brown notes in *In Review: Canadian Books for Children* that "Ms. Hughes's prose style is straightforward, lucid and extremely readable, and her characters are believable flesh and blood people.... I only wish that the author had spent twice as much time and effort to make the book twice as long." *Gold-Fever Trail* was used as a supplemental history text in the schools of Alberta, Canada.

Hughes moved into science fiction with her second novel, *Crisis on Conshelf Ten*. Like much of her work in this genre, it is set in the near future and involves a logical projection of present-day events on Earth. In *Crisis on Conshelf Ten*, the exploitation of Third World countries has been extended to lunar and undersea colonies. Outlaw bands of settlers strike back against the greedy corporations that oppress them by sabotaging oil and fishery plants. While some reviewers find Hughes's political message somewhat overstated, most praise her for a fast-moving story and a fascinating portrayal of undersea living.

Themes of ecological and cultural harmony also dominate *Beyond the Dark River*. The story takes place some time after a Canadian nuclear holocaust. City dwellers have become savage mutants; only the inhabitants of certain isolated communities have survived unharmed. Groups who have always been self-sufficient, such as the Cree Indians and the German Hutterites, have suffered little from the collapse of the great urban centers, but when a mysterious plague begins to claim the small children of these communities, two young people—an Indian girl and a Hutterite boy, aged fifteen and sixteen—join forces to brave the urban mutants in their search for effective medicine. Once again Hughes was praised for her enlightening portrait of both the Cree and Hutterite cultures, as well as her "vividly realised post-apocalypse Canada," as Neil Philip describes it in the *Times Educational Supplement*. The author's message about the importance of living in harmony with the earth never overpowers her story, believes Patrick Verrour; he writes in *In Review: Canadian Books for Children* that *Beyond the Dark River* proves "that [Hughes] can write fast-moving

narrative without neglecting to touch on some deep concerns she has about technology's threat to individual freedom."

Hughes's most acclaimed work is her "Isis" trilogy: *The Keeper of the Isis Light, The Guardian of Isis*, and *The Isis Pedlar*. The trilogy embraces many of its author's favorite themes, including moral growth through struggle, survival in alien environments, and the integration of cultures. Deep in space and far in the future, the planet Isis has been settled only by a scientist couple from Earth and their child, born on Isis. At the opening of *The Keeper of the Isis Light*, however, the planet is inhabited only by an extraordinarily intelligent robot, The Guardian, and Olwen Pendennis, a sixteen-year-old girl. Olwen has no memory of her life before the age of five, when her parents were killed. The Guardian saved Olwen and surgically altered her body to ensure her survival in Isis's atmosphere. When a new party of settlers arrives, Olwen cannot understand why they are repulsed by her leathery green-gold skin and huge nostrils. They offer to take her in if she will submit to more surgical alterations—alterations which would make her physically acceptable to the colonists, but also dependent on their life-support systems. Olwen eventually decides to remain free, although that means she must accept her aloneness as well. Thoughtful and absorbing, *The Keeper of the Isis Light* "reverberates in the reader's mind long after . . . the last word," declares *In Review: Canadian Books for Children* contributor Irma McDonough.

The Guardian of Isis and *The Isis Pedlar* follow the descendants of the planet's second settlers as they quickly regress to a primitive superstitious state. The Guardian has come to be worshipped as a god; the unnaturally long-lived Olwen is regarded as a witch. Together they manage to set the budding society of Isis on the right course. "It is a long time since I was so impressed by a book about the future," writes Crouch in a *Junior Bookshelf* review of *The Guardian of Isis*. "Monica Hughes tells a grand story; she is also a serious anthropologist and philosopher and she knows how the human mind works. . . . [She] brings before us the strange world of Isis in all its beauty and integrates setting and action and character in exemplary fashion. Her book is an excellent 'read,' a tract on society and a relevant commentary on the history of our own times."

In an essay for *Canadian Children's Literature: A Journal of Criticism and Review*, Hughes shares some of her thoughts about writing for young adults: "I think Science Fiction is very, very good for young people—particularly today, when they are facing so many difficult choices in life, and we don't even know what kind of choices in their future. Becoming familiar with Science Fiction, I think, helps us reach out fearlessly into that many-branched future and take control perhaps, of our destiny. . . . I think my chief criterion for a story for children . . . is that one should write as truthfully as possible, even if it isn't easy or painless. One faces oneself in the darkest places of one's memory and one's subconscious, and out of that comes both joy and sorrow. But always—and I think again this is perhaps the second crucial thing for children—always there must come hope."

AVOCATIONAL INTERESTS: Swimming, walking, beachcombing ("very difficult on the prairies"), weaving.

BIOGRAPHICAL/CRITICAL SOURCES:

BOOKS

Children's Literature Review, Volume IX, Gale, 1985.
Signal Review 1: A Selective Guide to Children's Books, Thimble Press, 1983.

PERIODICALS

Booklist, April 15, 1977, June 1, 1985.
Books in Canada, December, 1982, December, 1983, March, 1984.
Bulletin of the Center for Children's Books, April, 1985.
Canadian Children's Literature: A Journal of Criticism and Review, Number 17, 1980, Number 26, 1982.
Christian Science Monitor, October 5, 1984.
Globe and Mail (Toronto), May 2, 1987.
Growing Point, March, 1976, November, 1978, November, 1979, September, 1982, January, 1984, September, 1984.
Horn Book, June, 1982, September/October, 1984, May/June, 1985.
In Review: Canadian Books for Children, summer, 1976, June, 1979, August, 1979, April, 1980, February, 1981, April, 1982, Number 33, 1984.
Junior Bookshelf, June, 1977, October, 1978, December, 1978, June, 1980, October, 1981, August, 1982, December, 1983, October, 1984.
Language Arts, May, 1982, January, 1984.
Maclean's Magazine, June 28, 1982.
Quill and Quire, April, 1982, February, 1983, March, 1983, November, 1983.
School Librarian, September, 1980, December, 1983, September, 1984.
Science Fiction and Fantasy Book Review, March, 1982, July/August, 1982.
Times Educational Supplement, August 18, 1978, February 15, 1980, June 5, 1981, November 19, 1982, June 8, 1984.
Times Literary Supplement, March 28, 1980, September 18, 1981, July 23, 1982.
World of Children's Books, spring, 1988.

—*Sketch by Joan Goldsworthy*

*   *   *

HUMPHREY, James H(arry)   1911-

PERSONAL: Born February 26, 1911, in Marietta, Ohio; son of Harry and Nellie (Pugh) Humphrey; married Frances Drokopil, March 29, 1945; children: Joy Nell. *Education:* Denison University, B.S., 1933; Western Reserve University (now Case Western Reserve University), M.S., 1946; Boston University, Ph.D., 1951. *Religion:* Protestant.

ADDRESSES: Home—9108 St. Andrews Place, College Park, Md. 20740. *Office*—Department of Physical Education, University of Maryland, College Park, Md. 20740.

CAREER: Bedford Board of Education, Bedford, Ohio, director of health and physical education, 1937-49; Michigan State University, East Lansing, assistant professor of health and physical education, 1951-53; University of Maryland, College Park, associate professor, 1953-56, professor of physical education and health, 1956—. Distinguished visiting scholar, University of Delaware, 1965; distinguished visiting professor, Texas A & M University, 1971; lecturer to learned societies and educational groups. Member, International Compendium of Eminent People in the Field of Exceptional Education, 1973. *Military service:* U.S. Naval Reserve, 1943-45.

MEMBER: American Academy of Physical Education, American Alliance for Health, Physical Education, and Recreation,

American School Health Association (fellow; past chairman of research council), Society for Research in Child Development (fellow), Society of Children's Book Writers, Science for the Handicapped Association, Association for Anthropological Study of Play.

AWARDS, HONORS: American Alliance for Health, Physical Education, Recreation National Honor Award, 1972, and R. Tait McKenzie Award, 1976.

WRITINGS:

(With Harris F. Beeman) *Intramural Sports: A Text and Study Guide,* W. C. Brown, 1954, 3rd edition, Princeton Book, 1980.
(With Leslie W. Irwin) *Principles and Techniques of Supervision in Physical Education,* Mosby, 1954, 3rd edition, Princeton Book, 1980.
(With Irwin and Warren R. Johnson) *Methods and Materials in School Health Education,* Mosby, 1956.
(With W. R. Johnson and Granville Bradley Johnson) *Your Career in Physical Education: An Introduction to the Profession for Young Men and Women,* Harper, 1957.
Elementary School Physical Education: With Emphasis upon Its Integration in Other Curriculum Areas, Harper, 1958.
(Editor with Edwina Jones and Martha J. Haverstick) *Readings in Physical Education for the Elementary School,* National Press, 1958, 2nd edition, 1960.
(With W. R. Johnson and Virginia D. Moore) *Elementary School Health Education: Curriculum, Methods, Integration,* Harper, 1962.
(With W. R. Johnson and others) *Health Concepts for College Students,* Ronald, 1962.
(Compiler with Doris E. Terry and Howard S. Slusher) *Readings in Health Education: A Collection of Selected Articles for Use in Personal Health and Health Education Courses,* W. C. Brown, 1964.
Child Learning through Elementary School Physical Education, W. C. Brown, 1966, 2nd edition (with daughter, Joy N. Humphrey), 1974.
(With Anne Gayle Ingram) *Introduction to Physical Education for College Students,* Holbrook, 1969.
(With Dorothy D. Sullivan) *Teaching Slow Learners through Active Games,* C. C Thomas, 1970.
(With Sullivan) *Teaching Reading through Motor Learning,* C. C Thomas, 1973.
(With J. N. Humphrey) *Learning to Listen and Read through Movement,* Kimbo Educational, 1974.
(Contributor) Loyda M. Shears and Eli M. Bower, editors, *Games in Education and Development,* C. C Thomas, 1974.
Teaching Elementary School Science through Motor Learning, C. C Thomas, 1975.
Education of Children through Motor Activity, C. C Thomas, 1975.
(With others) *Health Teaching in Elementary Schools,* C. C Thomas, 1975.
(With R. B. Ashlock) *Teaching Elementary School Mathematics through Motor Learning,* C. C Thomas, 1976.
Improving Learning Ability through Compensatory Physical Education, C. C Thomas, 1976.
Physical Education as a Career, C. C Thomas, 1978.
(With J. N. Humphrey) *Help Your Child Learn the 3 R's through Active Play,* C. C Thomas, 1980.
(With J. N. Humphrey) *Sports Skills for Boys and Girls,* C. C Thomas, 1980.

(With J. N. Humphrey) *How Teachers Can Cope with Stress,* [College Park, Md.], 1980.
Child Development through Physical Education, C. C Thomas, 1980.
(With J. N. Humphrey) *Reducing Stress in Children through Creative Relaxation,* C. C Thomas, 1981.
A Textbook of Stress, C. C Thomas, 1982.
(Contributor) Hans Selye, editor, *Selye's Guide to Stress Research,* Volume III, Van Nostrand, 1983.
Profiles in Stress, AMS Press, 1986.
Stress in Coaching, C. C Thomas, 1988.

RECORDINGS; ALL PRODUCED BY KIMBO EDUCATIONAL

"Teaching Children Mathematics through Games, Rhythms and Stunts," 1968.
"Stunts and Tumbling for Elementary School Children," 1969.
(With others) "Teaching Reading through Creative Movement," 1969.
(With J. N. Humphrey) "Helping Children Understand about Stress," 1980.

OTHER

Author, with Moore, of "Read and Play" series, six books, Muller, 1965. Contributor to proceedings of professional organizations, including International Reading Association, International Seminar on Play, and National Science Teachers Association. Contributor to professional journals, including *Stress, Perceptual and Motor Skills, Research Quarterly,* and *Academic Therapy.* Member of board of associate editors, *Research Quarterly,* 1954-59 and 1960-63; research editor, *Journal of School Health,* 1962-65.

*   *   *

HUNTER, Joan
    See YARDE, Jeanne Betty Frances

*   *   *

HUNTING, Constance   1925-

PERSONAL: Born October 15, 1925, in Providence, R.I.; daughter of Walter Donald (a civil engineer) and Mildred (Farrill) Coulter; married Robert Stilwell Hunting (a professor of English), August 28, 1948; children: Robert Samuel Coulter, Miranda Willson Goulden. *Education:* Brown University, B.A. (cum laude), 1947; studied piano at New England Conservatory, 1950.

ADDRESSES: Office—Puckerbrush Press, 76 Main St., Orono, Me. 04473.

CAREER: Purdue University, West Lafayette, Ind., instructor in English, 1954-55; University of Maine at Orono, CED instructor in English, 1969—, writer in residence, 1979; Puckerbrush Press, Orono, founder, publisher, and editor, 1970—. Conducted TV interviews with young poets of Maine, 1973; affiliated with public radio show, "Small Press Notes," 1979—. Coordinator of NESPA in Maine, 1975-80. Participant in Poet in Schools Program, 1979, and Poet in Library Program, 1985. Fellow of MacDowell Colony, 1973. Member of board of directors, Bangor Symphony Orchestra, 1971—; member of literature panel, Maine Commission on Arts and Humanities, 1975-80.

MEMBER: American Academy of Poets, Virginia Woolf Society (founding member), Maine Writers and Publishers Alliance (president, 1978-79), Friends of Charleston.

AWARDS, HONORS: Recipient of Sesquicentennial Poetry Prize of Indiana, 1968; Indiana University Writers Prize, 1970, for *After the Stravinsky Concert;* named "Woman of the Year" by TV, Press, and Radio Women of Maine, 1972.

WRITINGS:

POETRY

After the Stravinsky Concert, Scribner, 1969.
Cimmerian, Puckerbrush Press, 1972.
Beyond the Summerhouse, Puckerbrush Press, 1976.
Nightwalk, University of Maine Press, 1979.
Dream Cities, Puckerbrush Press/ECW Press, 1982.
Collected Poems, 1969-1982, National Poetry Foundation, University of Maine at Orono, 1983.
A Day at the Shore, Theodore Press (Bangor, Maine), 1983.
Looking Glass Days, Theodore Press, 1985.
Between the Worlds, Theodore Press, 1987.

EDITOR

Lee Sharkey, *Farmwife,* Puckerbrush Press, 1977.
Douglas Young, *Between Sundays,* Puckerbrush Press, 1978.
Christopher Fahy, *Greengroundtown,* Puckerbrush Press, 1978.
Anne Hazlewood-Brady, *One to the Many,* Puckerbrush Press, 1979.
May Sarton, *Writings on Writing,* Puckerbrush Press, 1980.
Thelma C. Nason, *A Stranger Here, Myself,* Puckerbrush Press, 1980.
Michael McMahon, *Dead of Winter,* Puckerbrush Press, 1982.
Sanford Phippen, *The Police Know Everything: And Other Maine Stories,* Puckerbrush Press, 1982.
May Sarton: Woman and Poet, National Poetry Foundation, University of Maine at Orono, 1982.
(With Virgil Bisset) *In a Dark Time,* Puckerbrush Press, 1983.
Roberta Chester, *Light Years,* Puckerbrush Press, 1983.
Muriel Young, *My Life as a Maine-iac,* Puckerbursh Press, 1984.
Sonya Dorman, *Palace of Earth,* Puckerbrush Press, 1984.
Jonathan Aldrich, *Death of Michelangelo,* Puckerbrush Press, 1985.
Lotus Snow, *One Little Room an Everywhere: The Novels of Barbara Pym,* Puckerbrush Press, 1986.
Mabel E. Sarton, *Letters to May, 1917-1948,* Puckerbrush Press, 1986.
Muska Nagel, *Things that Surround Us,* Puckerbrush Press, 1987.

Also editor of *New Maine Writing Anthology,* 1977, 1979.

OTHER

Contributor to *Poetry, Western Humanities Review, University of Massachusetts Quarterly, New York Times,* and *Christian Century.* Editor of *Puckerbrush Review,* 1978—.

WORK IN PROGRESS: Translating *Le Roman Psychologique de Virginia Woolf,* by Floris Delattre.

SIDELIGHTS: Christian Science Monitor reviewer Victor Howes says of Constance Hunting's first book of poetry, *After the Stravinsky Concert:* "She writes with a fine fragility. Her people are the ghosts and the near ghosts of memory. . . . What she has given us in her best poems is a family album raised to the nth power, the power of imagination.''

BIOGRAPHICAL/CRITICAL SOURCES:

PERIODICALS

Christian Science Monitor, August 7, 1969.

*   *   *

HURT, James (Riggins) 1934-

PERSONAL: Born May 22, 1934, in Ashland, Ky.; son of Joe (a farmer) and Martha Clay (Riggins) Hurt; married Phyllis Tilton (a professor of music), June 5, 1958; children: Christopher, Ross, Matthew. *Education:* University of Kentucky, A.B., 1956, M.A., 1957; Indiana University, Ph.D., 1965.

ADDRESSES: Home—1001 West William, Champaign, Ill. 61820. *Office*—325 English Bldg., 608 South Wright St., University of Illinois at Urbana-Champaign, Urbana, Ill. 61801.

CAREER: University of Ilinois at Urbana-Champaign, assistant professor, 1966-69, associate professor, 1969-73, professor of English, 1973—. Member of Great American People Show, Illinois State Historical Society. *Military service:* U.S. Army, 1957-59.

AWARDS, HONORS: Illinois Center for Advanced Study fellow, 1979-80, 1986-87.

WRITINGS:

Aelfric, Twayne, 1972.
Catiline's Dream: An Essay on Ibsen's Plays, University of Illinois Press, 1972.
(Editor) *Focus on Film and Theatre,* Prentice-Hall, 1974.
(Editor with Brian Wilkie) *Literature of the Western World,* Volume I: *The Ancient World through the Renaissance,* Volume II: *Neoclassicism through the Modern Period,* Macmillan, 1984, 2nd edition, in press.

Also author of plays, *Angel Band, Walden: A Ceremony,* and *Abraham Lincoln Walks at Midnight,* 1980.

I

ING, Dean 1931-

PERSONAL: Born June 17, 1931, in Austin, Tex.; son of Dean Emory (a personnel specialist) and Louise (a linotype operator; maiden name, Hardin) Ing; married Geneva Baker (a broadcaster), August 21, 1959; children: Diana Capri, Laura Victoire, Dina Valerie, Dana Christie. *Education:* Fresno State University, B.A., 1956; San Jose State University, M.A., 1970; University of Oregon, Ph.D., 1974.

ADDRESSES: Agent—Eleanor Wood, 432 Park Ave. S., Suite 1205, New York, N.Y. 10016.

CAREER: Aerojet-General, Sacramento, Calif., engineer, 1957-62; Lockhead & United Technologies, San Jose, Calif., senior engineer, 1962-70; Missouri State University, Maryville, assistant professor of speech, psycholinguistics, and media, 1974-77; full-time writer, 1977—. *Military service:* U.S. Air Force, 1951-55; became airman first class.

MEMBER: Science Fiction Writers of America.

WRITINGS:

SCIENCE FICTION NOVELS

Soft Targets, Ace Books, 1979.
Anasazi, Ace Books, 1980.
Systemic Shock, Ace Books, 1981.
High Tension, Ace Books, 1982.
Pulling Through, Ace Books, 1982.
Single Combat, TOR Books, 1983.
Wild Country, TOR Books, 1985.

NOVELS

Blood of Eagles (thriller), TOR Books, 1987.
Firefight 2000, Baen Books, 1987.
The Big Lifters, TOR Books, 1987.

NONFICTION

(With Jerry Pournelle) *Mutual Assured Survival,* Baen Books, 1984.
(With Leik Myrabo) *The Future of Flight,* Baen Books, 1985.
The Chernobyl Syndrome, Baen Books, in press.

OTHER

Contributor of stories to magazines.

WORK IN PROGRESS: Continuing research on urban survival.

SIDELIGHTS: Dean Ing told *CA:* "Since I deplore the voracious appetite of the public for entertainment-for-entertainment's sake, most of my work has a clear didactic element. You may expect ninety percent entertainment and ten percent message from me. I believe that Jefferson's ideal of the independent yeoman farmer should be familiar to every generation because I mistrust a technological society in which most members are thoroughly incompetent to maintain the hardware or the software."

BIOGRAPHICAL/CRITICAL SOURCES:

PERIODICALS

New York Times, February 26, 1985.

*   *   *

INGLIS, Brian (St. John) 1916-

PERSONAL: Born July 31, 1916, in Dublin, Ireland; son of Claude Cavendish (an engineer) and Vera (Blood) Inglis; married Ruth Langdon (a journalist), December 23, 1958 (divorced, 1972); children: Diana Eleanor, Neil Langdon. *Education:* Magdalen College, Oxford, B.A. (with honors), 1939; University of Dublin, Ph.D., 1950.

ADDRESSES: Home—Garden Flat, 23 Lambolle Rd., London N.W. 3, England. *Agent*—Curtis Brown Ltd., 162 Regent St., London W1R 5TA, England.

CAREER: Irish Times, Dublin, Ireland, columnist, 1946-48, Parliamentary correspondent, 1950-53; University of Dublin, Trinity College, Dublin, assistant to professor of modern history, 1949-53, lecturer in economics, 1951-53; *Spectator,* London, England, assistant editor, 1954-59, editor, 1959-62, director, 1962—. Television commentator on a number of programs, including "What the Papers Say," 1956—, and "All Our Yesterdays," 1961-73. *Military service:* Royal Air Force, 1940-46; became squadron leader; mentioned in dispatches.

WRITINGS:

The Freedom of the Press in Ireland, Faber, 1954.
The Story of Ireland, Faber, 1956.

Emotional Stress and Your Health, Criterion, 1958 (published in England as *Revolution in Medicine,* Hutchinson, 1958).
West Briton, Faber, 1962.
The Case for Unorthodox Medicine, Putnam, 1964 (published in England as *Fringe Medicine,* Faber, 1964.
Private Conscience, Public Morality, Deutsch, 1964.
A History of Medicine, Weidenfeld & Nicolson, 1965.
Doctors, Drugs and Disease, Deutsch, 1965.
Abdication, Macmillan, 1966.
Men of Conscience, Macmillan, 1971 (published in England as *Poverty and the Industrial Revolution,* Hodder & Stoughton, 1971).
Roger Casement, Harcourt, 1974.
The Forbidden Game, Scribner, 1975.
The Opium War, Hodder & Stoughton, 1976.
Natural and Supernatural, Hodder & Stoughton, 1978.
Natural Medicine, Collins, 1979.
The Diseases of Civilisation, Hodder & Stoughton, 1981.
Science and Parascience: A History of the Paranormal, 1914-1939, Hodder & Stoughton, 1984.
The Paranormal, Granada Publishing, 1985.
The Hidden Power, J. Cape, 1986.
The Unknown Guest, Chatto & Windus, 1987.
The Power of Dreams, Grafton Books, 1987.

BIOGRAPHICAL/CRITICAL SOURCES:

PERIODICALS

Times, March 22, 1984.

*   *   *

INGOLD, Gerard (Antoine Hubert)   1922-

PERSONAL: Born September 22, 1922, in Agadir, Morocco; son of Francois Joseph Jean (a general and author) and Marie-Antoinette (Didierjean) Ingold; married Jacqueline Valentin, June 28, 1946; children: Francois-Rodolphe, Charles. *Education:* University of Paris, degree in law, 1946. *Religion:* Catholic.

ADDRESSES: Home—Villa L'Ancrage, Deauville 14, France.

CAREER: Worked in colonial administration in Brazzaville, Middle Congo (now People's Republic of the Congo), 1946-48; Cristalleries de Saint-Louis, Paris, France, head of commercial department, 1949-51, office director, 1951-57, sales manager, 1957—. Sales consultant, 1961—. *Military service:* Second French Armored Division, 1939-45; received Croix de Guerre, Order of Merit, and chevalier of Legion of Honor.

MEMBER: Sons of the American Revolution (France).

AWARDS, HONORS: History prize from Academie d'Alsace, 1969, for *Un Matin bien rempli;* history prize from French Academy, 1986.

WRITINGS:

IN ENGLISH

The Art of the Paperweight: Saint Louis, Paperweight Press, 1981.
From Glass to Crystal, Denoce (France), 1986.

IN FRENCH

St. Louis (history of the Saint Louis Co.), Synergic, 1957.
Un Matin bien rempli; ou, La Vie d' un pilote de chasse de la France libre, 1921-1941, preface by Charles de Gaulle, Charles-Lavauzelle, 1969.

Boulez, Presse papicas sulfures, Herme (France), 1985.

WORK IN PROGRESS: Researching the history of glass and crystal in Europe and the United States.

SIDELIGHTS: Gerard Ingold told *CA:* "I came to write a book about paperweights because of requests from American friends and collectors and because I work in a glass company (one of the most ancient in France). Since the mid-nineteenth century my mother's family has headed the St. Louis Crystal Company. I speak and write English and German."

*   *   *

ITALIAANDER, Rolf (Bruno Maximilian)   1913-

PERSONAL: Born February 20, 1913, in Leipzig, Germany (now East Germany; a Dutch citizen by birth); son of Kurt and Charlotte Italiaander. *Education:* Studied in Leipzig, Berlin, Paris, London, Oxford, and Rome.

ADDRESSES: Home—St. Benedictstrasse 29, Hamburg 13, Federal Republic of Germany.

CAREER: Writer, ethnologist, and explorer in Africa and Asia. Visiting professor of African history and civilization at colleges and universities, including Michigan State University, Kalamazoo College, schools of the United Negro College Fund, and Hope College. Co-founder and honorary secretary of Free Academy of Art, Hamburg, 1948-69; founder of Museum of Naive Art in Hamburg-Rade (now Museum Rade am Schloss Reinbeck). German Translator's Union, founder, 1954, currently honorary president. Honorary Consul to Senegal 1964.

MEMBER: International Africa Institut (London), Frobenius Institut (Frankfurt), Societe des Africanistes (Paris), Michigan Academy of Science, Arts, and Letters, American Academy of Political and Social Science, American Committee on Africa, New York Academy of Sciences, Austrian Explorers Society, Rissho kosei-kai (honorary), Brighter Society Movement, Heinrich Barth Society (honorary president), Gesellschaft zur Erforschung der Naturvoelker, Islam Institute, Phi Alpha Theta.

AWARDS, HONORS: Hans Henny Jahnn Prize for literary work and efforts toward the betterment of race relations; officer, Order of the Senegal; Distinguished Achievement Award from Hope College, 1976; member, Great Order of Merit of the Republic of Austria; member (first class), Order of Merit of the Federal Republic of Germany; honorable member of Green Flag of Europe Union; honorary member of several international institutions.

WRITINGS:

So lernte ich segelfliegen, Orell Fuessli, 1931.
Hallo! Boys!, Haupt, 1932.
Mein Fahrrad und ich, Weiss, 1935.
Lennart und Faber, Weiss, 1935.
Segelflug in aller Welt, Reclam, 1936.
Erlebnisse beim Segelflug, Reclam, 1936.
Gebrueder Lenz auf Tipelfahrt, Oxford University Press, 1937.
Manfred Freiherr von Richthofen, Weichert, 1938.
Goetz von Berlichingen, Weichert, 1939.
Spiel und Lebensziel, G. Weise, 1939.
Wegbereiter deutscher Luftgeltung, Gutenburg, 1941.
Werkpilot Steffens, Franckh, 1942.
Italo Balbo, Knorr & Hirth, 1942.
Banzai!, [Riga], 1943.
Besiegeltes Leben, Volksbuecherei-Verlag, 1949.

Nordafrika heute, Zsolnay, 1952.

Land der Kontraste, Broschek, 1953.

Wann reist du ab, weisser Mann?, Broschek, 1954.

Door Het Oerwoud Naar de Woestijn, Donker, 1955.

Vom Urwald in die Wueste, Broschek, 1955.

In het Land van Albert Schweitzer, Donker, 1955.

Geliebte Tiere, Westermann, 1957.

De Blanke Oganga: Albert Schweitzer, Donker, 1957.

Neue Kunst in Afrika, Bibliographisches Institut, 1957.

Menschen in Africa, Bibliographisches Institut, 1957.

Mubange: Der Junge aus dem Urwald, C. Ueberreuter, 1957.

Hedendaagse Negerkunst uit Centraal-Afrika [Amsterdam], 1957, translation published as *Contemporary Negro Painting and Graphic Art from Central Africa: The Collection of Rolf Italiaander*, Hope College, 1962.

Der ruhelose Kontinent, Econ-Verlag, 1958.

Im Lande Albert Schweitzers, Broschek, 1958.

Taenzer, Tiere und Daemonen, Wancura, 1960.

Tanz in Afrika: Ein Phaenomen in Leben der Neger, Rembrandt-Verlag, 1960.

Die neuen Maenner Afrikas: Ihr Leben, ihre Taten, ihre Ziele, Econ-Verlag, 1960, translation published as *The New Leaders of Africa*, Prentice-Hall, 1961.

Moebange, de Jongen in het Oerwould, Broekman & DeMeris, 1961.

Tausendundeine Weisheit, Wancura, 1961.

Africana: Selected Bibliography of Readings in African History and Civilization, History Department, Hope College, 1961.

Schwarze Haut im roten Griff, Econ-Verlag, 1962.

Hans and Jean: A Reader for Colleges and Universities, Hope College Press, 1962.

Afrika in Opkomst: Geschiedenis en economische ontwikkeling van alle staten, Broekman & DeMeris, 1962.

Immer wenn ich unterwegs bin: Verse und kleine Prosa, Mundusverlag, 1962.

Der Buehnenbildner Karl Groening, [Hamburg], 1962.

Brueder der Verdammten: Menschliche Entwicklungshilfe in Afrika, Amerika, Asien, Signum, 1963, published as *Neue Hoffnung fuer Aussaetzige*, Mission, 1971.

Die neuen Maenner Asiens, Econ-Verlag, 1964.

Die Friedensmacher: Drei Neger erhielten den Friedens-Nobelpreis (R. Bunche, Martin Luther King, Albert John Luthuli), Oncken, 1965.

Im Namen des Herrn im Kongo: Geschnisse, Erlegnisse, Ergebnisse, foreword by St. C. Neill, Oncken, 1965.

Burg Pyrmont in des Eifel, Pillig/Eifel, 1965.

Bingo und Bongo vom Kongo, illustrations by Stefan Lemke and Marie-Luise Pricken, Agentur des Rauhen Hauses, 1967.

Karl May, Editions Quebec, 1967.

Lebensentscheidung fuer Israel, foreword by Ahser Ben-Natan, J. Fink, 1967.

Gedanken ueber Albert Schweitzer, Freie Akademie der Kuenste, 1968.

Richard N. Coudenhove-Kalergi: Begruender der Pancuropa-Bewegung, afterword by Pierre Gregoire, Eurobuch-Verlag, 1969.

Terra dolorosa: Wandlungen in Lateinamerika, introduction by Rudolf Grossmann, afterword by Gilberto Freyre, Brockhaus, 1969.

Hallelujas, Christians, 1970.

Denn man beruehrt uns nicht, Mission, 1971.

Profile und Perspektiven: Christen in der Dritten Welt, Evangelisch-Lutherische Mission, 1971.

Wird Europa untergehen?, Industrie und Handelskammer, 1971.

Juden in Latein-America, Olamenu (Tel-Aviv), 1971.

Die neuen Herren der alten Welt, Econ-Verlag, 1972.

Das Elefanten-Maedchen, Bitter, 1972.

Partisanen und Profeten, Evangelisch-Lutherische Mission, 1972.

SokaGakkai: Japans neue Buddhisten, Evangelisch-Lutherische Mission, 1973.

Spass an der Freud: Laienmaler und naive Maler an 99 Beispielen dargestellt, Christians, 1974.

Kiri, Geister der Suedsee: Phantastische Geschichten, E. Klopp, 1975.

(With Klaus Gundermann and Joachim Buechner) *Geld in der Kunst: Geld und Geldeswert in Skulptur, Graphik und Malerei*, Steinbock-Verlag, 1976.

(With others) *Buecherrevision: Zwischen Erfolgen und Niederlagen*, Christians, 1977.

Naive Kunst und Folklore, Edition Museum Rade, 1977.

(With Neiz Pentzlin) *Bei Wempe gehn die Uhren anders: Chronik ein mittelstaend*, Christians, 1978.

Jack London, Colloquium-Verlag, 1978.

Wer seinen Bruder nicht liebt . . . : Begegnungen und Erfahrungen in Asien, Evangelisch-Lutherische Mission, 1978.

Harmonie mit dem Universum: Zwiegespraech zwischen Europa und Japan, foreword by Werner Kohler, Aurum-Verlag, 1978.

Afrika hat viele Gesichter: Ein humanist Lesebuch (afterword by Mobyem M. K. Mikanza), Droste-Verlag, 1979.

(With Klaus W. Schoettler) *Fietes Wochenende in Hamburg*, Brigg, 1979.

Die Suedsee, auch eine Herausforderung: Tagebuecher ein Individualisten aus Indonesien und Papua-Niugini, Droste-Verlag, 1979.

(With Arnold Bauer and Herbert Krafft) *Berlins Stunde Null: 1945*, Droste-Verlag, 1979.

(With Martin Gosebruch and Reinhardt Guldager) *Afrikanische Impressionen: Kunst, Kult, Architektur*, Droste-Verlag, 1980.

Xocolatl: Ein suesses Kapitel unserer Kulturgeschichte, Droste-Verlag, 1980.

Mein afrikanisches Foto-Album, Brigg, 1981.

Speise der Goetter: Eine Kulturgeschichte der Xocolatl in Bildern, Droste-Verlag, 1983.

Lichter im Norden: Erinnertes und Bedachtes, Husum, 1983.

Durchschrittene Raeume, Husum, 1983.

Anfang mit Zuversicht: Kultur in Hamburg nach dem Krieg, Asmus, 1984.

Besinnung auf Werte: Persoenlichkeiten in Hamburg nach dem Krieg, Asmus, 1984.

Mut, Fantasie und Hoffnung: Nachkriegsjahre in Hamburg, Asmus, 1985.

Kunstsammler, glueckliche Menschen, Droste-Verlag, 1985.

Vielvoelkerstadt, Hambug und seine Nationalitaeten, Droste-Verlag, 1986.

EDITOR

Joachim Christian Nettelbeck, *Mein Leben*, Sporn, 1938.

Englische Perspektiven, Laatzen, 1948.

Frank Theiss, Krueger, 1950.

Henry Benrath in Memoriam, Deutsche Verlags-Anstalt, 1954.

Nordafrika: Marokko, Algerien, Tunesien, Libyen, Reich, 1956.

Herrliches Hamburg, Broschek, 1957.

(With Willy Haas) *Berliner Cocktail*, Zsolnay, 1957.

Ivo Hauptmann, Freie Akademie der Kuenste, 1957.

Schwarze Weisheiten: Negersprichwoerter, Klemm, 1958, published as *Schwarze Weisheiten: Sprichwoerter, Anekdoten und Meditationen aus Afrika*, Droste-Verlag, 1978.

Hans Leip: Leben und Werk, Freie Akademie der Kuenste, 1958.

Teenagers, Broschek, 1958.

Hans Henny Jahnn, *Aufzeichnungen eines Einzelgaengers*, List, 1959.

Kongo: Bilder und Verse, Bertelsmann, 1959.

Fritz Kronenberg, Freie Akademie der Kuenste, 1960.

Jahnn, *Buck der Freunde*, Freie Akademie der Kuenste, 1960.

Herder-Blaetter: Faksimile-Ausgabe zum 70; Geburtstag von Willy Haas, Freie Akademie der Kuenste, 1962.

Karl Groening, Freie Akademie der Kuenste, 1962.

Pariser Cocktail, foreword by Andre Maurois, Zsolnay, 1963.

Koenig Leopolds Kongo: Dokumente und Pamphlete von Mark Twain, Edmund D. Morel, Roger Casement, Ruetten & Loening, 1964.

Umbestaendliche und eigentliche Beschreibung von Africa 1668, Steingrueben (Stuttgart), 1964.

Peter Martin Lampel, Freie Akademie der Kuenste, 1964.

Gleise und Nebengleise des O. H. Strohmeyer, Freie Akademie der Kuenste, 1964.

Internationaler Kongress Literarischer Uebersetzer, Athenaeum-Verlag, 1965.

Die Herausforderung des Islam, Musterschmidt-Verlag, 1965.

Mutter Courage und ihr Theater: Ida Ehre und die Hamburger Kammerspiele, Freie Akademie der Kuenste, 1965.

In der Palmweinschenke, Erdmann, 1966.

Frieden in der Welt, aber wie? Gedanken des Friedens-Nobelpreistraeger, foreword by Carl Friedrich von Weizsaecker, J. Fink, 1967.

Heinrich Barth, *Im Sattel durch Nord-und Zentralafrika: Reisen und Entdeckung in den Jahren 1849-1855*, Brockhaus, 1967.

Weder Krankheit noch Verbrechen, Gala-Verlag, 1969.

Kultur ohne Wirtschaftswunder, Delp, 1970.

Akzente eines Lebens, afterword by Peter Jokostra, C. Schuenemann, 1970.

Ade, Madame Muh! Bauersleute dichten heute, afterwords by Karl Krolow and Heinz Haushofer, Pandion, 1970.

Albanien: Vorposten China, Delp, 1970.

Er schloss uns einen Weltteil auf, Pandion, 1970.

Diktaturen im Nacken, Delp, 1971.

Argumente kritischer Christen: Warum wir nicht aus der Kirche austreten, Echter-Verlag, 1971.

Moral—wozu? Ein Symposium, Delp, 1972.

Eine Religion fuer den Frieden: Die Rissho Kosei-Kai: Japanische Buddhisten fuer die Oekumene der Religionen, foreword by Werner Kohler, Evangelisch-Lutherische Mission, 1973.

Heisses Land Nuigini, Evangelisch-Lutherische Mission, 1974.

Im Lande Albert Schweitzers: Zum 100; Geburtststag des Urwaldarztes, Claudius Verlag, 1974.

Indonesiens verantwortliche Gelleschaft, Evangelisch-Lutherische Mission, 1974.

Hugo Eckener, *Im Luftschiff ueber Laender und Meere: Erlebnisse und Erinnerungen*, Heyne, 1979.

Schleswig-Holstein: Zwei Meere, ein Land, Weidling, 1979.

Hugo Eckener: Ein Moderner Columbus, Stadler, 1979.

Hugo Eckener: Die Weltschau eines Luftschiffers, Husum, 1980.

Ferdinand Graf von Zeppelin: Reitergeneral, Diplomat, Luftschiffpionier; Bilder und Dokumente, Stadler, 1980.

Ich bin ein Berliner, Weidling, 1980.

Jenseits der Deutsch-Deutschen Grenze, Weidling, 1981.

Ein Deutscher Namens Eckener, Stadler, 1981.

Die grosse Zeit der deutschen Hanse, Husum, 1981.

Wir erlebten das Ende der Weimarer Republik, Droste-Verlag, 1982.

Nikkyo Niwano, *Ein Mann kaempft fuer den Frieden*, Aurum, 1982.

Der Fall Oscar Wilde: Triumph und Tragoedie eines Dichterlebens, Eremitten-Presse, 1982.

Mehr als Schwarze Magie, Aurum, 1983.

Geh hin zu den Menschen: Ein neuhumanistisches Lesebuch, Droste-Verlag, 1983.

Scripta: Aus der Autographen-Sammlung Rolf Italiaander, Edition Museum Rade, 1984.

SIDELIGHTS: Rolf Italiaander, a Dutch citizen by birth, is the prolific author and editor of books in German. Also an ethnologist who has traveled widely in Africa and Asia to examine folk art, Italiaander founded the Museum of Naive Art in Hamburg-Rade, West Germany, which is now called the Museum Rade am Schloss Reinbeck. The specialist in African history and civilization has often been a visiting professor in the United States. Italiaander's contribution to the 32nd International Congress for Asian and North African Studies declares, ''When citizens with any sense of international obligation for other peoples take a critical look at and analyze the present evolution of mankind, they cannot help being very deeply concerned. Of course, there is a great deal of discussion about the urgency of international understanding but in practice far less is accomplished. [The fact that the world has seen] well over 150 'local wars' since 1945 do[es] not sound exactly promising. Where are those leaders with a moral sense of responsibility, who possess the strength and wisdom to put an end to worldwide crime? Where are the scientists who do not devote themselves exclusively to their own particular field—no doubt valuable in itself—but apply their specialist knowledge to the creation of a highly ethical society which is conscious of the fact that we have entered a disastrous technological civilization, designed without any creative ideals and hence without responsibility? All scientists should never cease to consider this macabre situation afresh with the aim of eliminating deplorable and insupportable conditions. The development of any form of science is futile if humanity is going to destroy itself. T. S. Eliot warned us decades ago of a humanity in the future without human fellow feelings.'' Italiaander delivered this challenge to scientists and world leaders in Hamburg, West Germany in August, 1986.

BIOGRAPHICAL/CRITICAL SOURCES:

BOOKS

Kirchhof, Regina, editor, *Rolf Italiaander*, Christians, 1977.

J

JACOBSEN, Josephine 1908-

PERSONAL: Born August 19, 1908, in Cobourg, Ontario, Canada; daughter of Joseph Edward (a doctor) and Octavia (Winder) Boylan; married Eric Jacobsen, March 17, 1932; children: Erlend Ericsen. *Education:* Educated by private tutors and at Roland Park Country School, 1915-18. *Politics:* Democrat. *Religion:* Roman Catholic.

ADDRESSES: Home—Mt. View Rd., Whitefield, N.H. 03598 (summer); 220 Stony Ford Rd., Baltimore, Md. 21210 (winter). *Agent*—McIntosh & Otis Inc., 475 Fifth Ave., New York, N.Y. 10017. *Office*—Poetry Office, Library of Congress, Washington, D.C. 20540.

CAREER: Library of Congress, Washington, D.C., poetry consultant, 1971-73, honorary consultant in American letters, 1973-79. Lecturer for the American Writers Program annual meeting, Savannah, Georgia, 1984. Member of the literature panel, National Endowment for the Arts, 1979-83.

MEMBER: Poetry Society of America (vice-president, 1978-79), Baltimore Citizens' Planning and Housing Association, Baltimore Center Stage Association, Baltimore Museum of Art, Walters Art Gallery, Hamilton Street Club.

AWARDS, HONORS: The Shade-Seller: New and Selected Poems, was nominated for a National Book Award; *A Walk with Raschid and Other Stories* was selected one of the Fifty Distinguished Books of the Year by *Library Journal;* recipient of award from the American Academy and Institute of Arts and Letters for Service to Literature; received fellowships from Yaddo, the Millay Colony for the Arts, and the MacDowell Colony; Doctor of Humane Letters from Towson State University, Goucher College, and College of Notre Dame of Maryland; Literary Lion, New York Public Library, 1985.

WRITINGS:

POETRY

For the Unlost, Contemporary Poetry, 1946.
The Human Climate, Contemporary Poetry, 1953.
The Animal Inside, Ohio University Press, 1966.
(Editor) *From Anne to Marianne: Some American Women Poets,* Library of Congress, 1972.
The Instant of Knowing, Library of Congress, 1974.
The Shade-Seller: New and Selected Poems, Doubleday, 1974.

One Poet's Poetry, Agnes Scott College, 1975.
The Chinese Insomniacs: New Poems, University of Pennsylvania Press, 1981.
Adios, Mr. Moxley, Jackpine, 1986.
The Sisters: New and Selected Poems, Bench Press, 1987.

OTHER

(With William R. Mueller) *The Testament of Samuel Beckett* (dramatic criticism), Hill & Wang, 1964.
(With Mueller) *Ionesco and Genet: Playwrights of Silence* (dramatic criticism), Hill & Wang, 1968.
A Walk with Raschid and Other Stories (short stories), Jackpine, 1978.
(Contributor) *The Way We Live Now,* Ontario Press, 1986.
Substance of Things Hoped For, Doubleday, 1987.

Work represented in anthologies, including *Best American Short Stories,* 1966, *O. Henry Prize Stories,* 1967, 1971, 1973, 1976, and 1985, *Fifty Years of the American Short Story,* 1970, *A Geography of Poets,* edited by William Field, *A Treasury of American Poetry,* edited by Nancy Sullivan, *Night Walks: Short Stories,* edited by Joyce Carol Oates, *A Treasury of American Short Stories,* edited by Sullivan, *Pushcart Prizes Six,* and *Belles Lettres,* 1986.

SIDELIGHTS: Josephine Jacobsen is "extremely interested" in the theatre, and has acted with the Vagabond Players in Baltimore. Equally interested in travel, she has visited Mexico, Guatemala, Venezuela, the Caribbean Islands, France, Italy, Greece, Morocco, Kenya, Tanzania, Portugal, Madeira, Spain, and Canada.

MEDIA ADAPTATIONS: Three poems from *The Chinese Insomniacs: New Poems* were set to Jean Eigelberger Ivey's composition "Notes toward Time," March, 1984; the poem "The Monosyllable" from *The Chinese Insomniacs* was performed at the Baltimore Musem of Art, Baltimore, Maryland, 1987.

BIOGRAPHICAL/CRITICAL SOURCES:

PERIODICALS

New York Times Book Review, April 4, 1982.
Poetry, March, 1983.

JACOBSON, Nolan Pliny 1909-

PERSONAL: Born March 27, 1909, in Hudson, Wis.; son of Jacob Albert and Lena (Engen) Jacobson; married Grace Webb (a teacher), November 24, 1939; children: Albert Page, Susan Faye. *Education:* Attended University of Wisconsin, 1930-32; Emory University, A.B., 1940, B.D., 1942; University of Chicago, Ph.D., 1946.

ADDRESSES: Home—812 South Laurel Ave., Adel, Ga. 31620.

CAREER: Huntingdon College, Montgomery, Ala., professor of philosophy, 1946-49; University of Oregon, Eugene, interim head of department of religion, 1949-51; University of Florida, Gainesville, associate professor of religion, 1951-54; Winthrop College, Rock Hill, S.C., professor of philosophy, 1954-74, distinguished professor, 1962-63, chairman of department, 1954-74. Summer visiting professor at Emory University, 1948, and University of Denver, 1975; lecturer at University of Florida, 1961; visiting professor, Queens College, Charlotte, N.C., 1974-79; lecturer at University of Tokyo, Nihon University, Waseda University, and International Christian University, Tokyo. *Military service:* U.S. Navy, chaplain, 1943-46; participated in invasion of Okinawa.

MEMBER: International Association of Buddhist Studies, Association for Asian Studies, American Philosophical Association, Society for Asian and Comparative Philosophy, Societe Europeenne de Culture, Philosophy of Education Society (past president, Southeastern region), Southern Society for Philosophy of Religion (past president), South Carolina Philosophy Society (past president), South Carolina Committee for Non-Western Studies (chairman), Phi Kappa Phi, Phi Sigma Tau.

AWARDS, HONORS: Ford Foundation grant for research at International Institute for Advanced Buddhistic Studies, Rangoon, Burma, 1961-62; Swearinger grant for study in Japan, 1972.

WRITINGS:

(Contributor) John Nordskog, editor, *Social Change*, University of Southern California Press and McGraw, 1960.
Buddhism: The Religion of Analysis, Allen & Unwin, 1966, Southern Illinois University Press, 1970.
(Contributor) Nicholas Steneck, editor, *Science and Society: Past, Present and Future*, University of Michigan Press, 1975.
Nihon-do: The Japan Way, Risosha (Tokyo), 1977.
Life Sciences in an Oriental Culture, Kyoritsu-Shuppan (Tokyo), 1977.
Buddhism in the Contemporary World: Change and Self-Correction, Southern Illinois University Press, 1983.
(Editor and contributor; with Kenneth K. Inada) *Buddhism and American Thinkers*, State University of New York Press, 1984.
Understanding Buddhism, Southern Illinois University Press, 1986.
The Heart of Buddhist Philosophy, Southern Illinois University Press, 1988.

Contributor of essay to souvenir volume presented to President Radhakrishnan of India on his sixty-seventh birthday, 1965. Contributor to professional journals in India, France, Mexico, England, the United States, and Japan.

WORK IN PROGRESS: The American Alternative.

SIDELIGHTS: Nolan Pliny Jacobson told *CA:* "Civilizations are under threat everywhere on earth. Their greatest peril has its origin in the failure of large-scale cultural forms to give individual men and women a feeling of being in direct contact with life.

"American thinking is as slow to change as the weathering of rock. The Japanese are more flexible, leaning out of their own culture to learn other options from the community of humankind."

*   *   *

JAGER, Okke 1928-

PERSONAL: Born April 23, 1928, in Delft, The Netherlands; son of Johann Coenraad (a surveyor) and Anna Wouterina (Wingerden) Jager; married Antje Lagerwerf, October 1, 1952; children: Ruth, Judith, Job. *Education:* Free University of Amsterdam, D.D., 1962. *Religion:* Reformed Church.

ADDRESSES: Home—Jacob Catsstraat 433, Kampen, The Netherlands.

CAREER: Clergyman in The Netherlands, in Vrouwenpolder, 1952-56, Almelo, 1956-60, and Haarlem, 1960-65; broadcaster of religious radio and television, Hilversum, The Netherlands, 1965-73; Theological University, Kampen, The Netherlands, teacher, 1973—.

MEMBER: Society of Dutch Literature.

WRITINGS:

Poezie en religie (title means "Poetry and Religion"), Zomer & Keuning (Wageningen, The Netherlands), 1952.
Feest op feest (title means "Feast after Feast"), Zomer & Keuning, 1956.
Interview met de tijdgeest (title means "Interview of the Spirit of the Times"), J. H. Kok (Kampen, The Netherlands), 1956.
Worden als een kind (title means "To Become Like a Child"), J. H. Kok, 1956.
Jeugd en evangelie (title means "Youth and Gospel"), Zomer & Keuning, 1957.
Op de man af (title means "Straight from the Shoulder"), J. H. Kok, 1958.
De humor van de Bijbel in het Christelijk leven (title means "The Humor of the Bible"), J. H. Kok, 1958.
Uw wil geschiede, Bosch & Keuning, 1958, translation by M. E. Osterhaven published as *What Does God Want, Anyway?*, Judson, 1972.
Kom haastig! Gedichten over de wederkomst van Jezus (poetry; title means "The Come-back of Jesus"), J. H. Kok, 1959.
Zegen u zelf: Tien radio-spreken (sermons; title means "Bless Yourself"), J. H. Kok, 1959.
Parade of paradijs (title means "Parade or Paradise"), J. H. Kok, 1960.
Wij mogen van geluk spreken (title means "Happiness for Us"), Zomer & Keuning, 1961.
Het eeuwige leven: Met name in verband met de verhouding van tijd en eeuwigheid (title means "The Everlasting Life: Time and Eternity"), J. H. Kok, 1962.
Achter een glimlach (title means "Behind a Smile"), J. H. Kok, 1964.
Een groene pasen (title means "Green Easter"), Zomer & Keuning, 1964.
Geloven na kerktijd: Een nieuwe bundel televisie-dagsluitingen (title means "Belief After Church Hours"), Zomer & Keuning, 1965.

Daglicht: Bijbels dagboek (title means "Daylight: Exegesis"), J. H. Kok, 1967.

Eigentijdse verkondiging: Beschouwingen over de vertolking van het Evangelie in het taaleigen van der moderne mens (title means "Timely Preaching of the Gospel for Modern Man"), J. H. Kok, 1967.

Een witte kerst (title means "White Christmas"), Zomer & Keuning, 1968.

Het klagen wordt gezang (title means "Topics of the Church"), J. H. Kok, 1969.

Land van Jahwe (title means "Land of Jahwe"), Zomer & Keuning, 1969.

Om razend te worden (title means "It's Enough to Drive You Mad"), J. H. Kok, 1969.

Liefde doet wonderen (title means "Love Does Wonders"), Zomer & Keuning, 1970.

Hoedjes met voetjes (title means "Ironical Stories"), J. H. Kok, 1970.

Verkondiging en massamedia (title means "Preaching and Mass Media"), J. H. Kok, 1971.

Binnenpretjen om buitenbeentjes (title means "Personalities of Television"), J. H. Kok, 1971.

Kruisweg (title means "Via Dolorosa"), Zomer & Keuning, 1972.

Baas boven buis (title means "Television: Theory and Practice"), J. H. Kok, 1973.

Bevrijde tijd (title means "To a Culture of Leisure"), Zomer & Keuning, 1974.

Schrale troost in magere jaren: Theologische kritiek in maatschappelijke krises, Ten Have (Baarn, The Netherlands), 1976.

Een tijd van twifel: Preken over levensvargen, J. H. Kok, 1977.

Wij zijn niet machteloos: Een tijdsbeeld met tegenwicht, Ten Have, 1978.

Opklaring: Bijbellezen met verbeelding skracht, Zomer & Keuning (Ede, The Netherlands), 1980.

Het andere in het eendere: Over het denken van Cornelis Verhoeven, Ambo (Baarn), 1982.

Hier scheiden onze wegen, Zomer & Keuning, 1983.

De dood in zijn ware gedaante, Ten Have, 1984.

Liever langer leven, Ten Have, 1984.

Verademing, Zomer & Keuning, 1986.

Geloven wordt onwenning: Naareen tweede primitiviteit?, Ten Have, 1987.

Contributor to journals and periodicals.

*   *   *

JAMES, C. B.
See COOVER, James B(urrell)

*   *   *

JANIS, Irving L(ester) 1918-

PERSONAL: Born May 26, 1918, in Buffalo, N.Y.; son of M. Martin (in shoe business) and Etta (Goldstein) Janis; married Marjorie Graham (a research associate in child psychology), September 5, 1939; children: Cathy Janis Wheeler, Charlotte Janis Mervin. *Education:* University of Chicago, B.S., 1939, graduate study, 1939-40; Columbia University, Ph.D., 1948; New York Psychoanalytic Institute, postdoctoral study, 1948-53.

ADDRESSES: Home—627 Scotland Dr., Santa Rosa, Calif. 95405. *Office*—Department of Psychology, University of California, Berkeley, Calif. 94720.

CAREER: Library of Congress, Washington, D.C., research assistant, 1941; U.S. Department of Justice, Washington, D.C., senior social science analyst, 1941-43; Social Science Research Council, New York, N.Y., research associate, 1945-46, research fellow, 1946-47; Yale University, New Haven, Conn., assistant professor, 1947-51, associate professor, 1951-60, professor of psychology, 1960-85, professor emeritus, 1985—; University of California, Berkeley, adjunct professor of psychology, 1985—. Participant in research panels of the National Science Foundation and National Institute of Mental Health. Research consultant, RAND Corp., 1948-60; member of Surgeon General's Scientific Advisory Committee on the Social Effects of Technology, 1969-72. *Military service:* U.S. Army, Research Branch, 1943-45.

MEMBER: American Psychological Association (fellow; chairman of committee on psychology in national and international affairs, 1965-66), American Association for the Advancement of Science (representative on council, 1965-70), American Academy of Arts and Sciences, Academy of Behavioral Medicine Research.

AWARDS, HONORS: Ford Foundation research grant, 1956; Fulbright research award to University of Oslo, 1957-58; Hofheimer Prize, American Psychiatric Association, 1959, for outstanding contribution in field of psychiatry and mental hygiene; faculty fellowships from Yale University and Social Science Research Council, 1961-62 and 1966-67, for research at Tavistock Clinic and Institute, London, England, and from Social Science Research Council, 1966-67, for research at La Jolla, Calif.; Socio-Psychological Prize, American Association for the Advancement of Science, 1967; Guggenheim fellow, 1973-74; Center for Advanced Study in the Behavioral Sciences fellow, 1973-74; Distingushed Scientific Contributions Award, American Psychological Association, 1981; Netherlands Institute for Advanced Study fellow, 1981-82; Kurt Levin Memorial Award, for research in social psychology, Society for the Psychological Study of Social Issues of the American Psychological Association.

WRITINGS:

Air War and Emotional Stress: Psychological Studies of Bombing and Civilian Defense, McGraw, 1951.

(With C. I. Hovland and H. H. Kelley) *Communication and Persuasion: Psychological Studies of Opinion Change,* Yale University Press, 1953.

Psychological Effects of Atomic Disasters, Industrial College of the Armed Forces, 1954.

Psychological Stress, Wiley, 1958.

(Editor with Hovland) *Personality and Persuasibility,* Yale University Press, 1959.

(Editor) *Personality: Dynamics, Development, and Assessment,* Harcourt, 1969.

Stress and Frustration, Harcourt, 1971.

Victims of Groupthink: A Psychological Study of Foreign Policy Decisions and Fiascoes, Houghton, 1972, 2nd edition published as *Groupthink: Psychological Studies of Policy Decisions and Fiascoes,* 1983.

(With L. Mann) *Decision-Making: A Psychological Analysis of Conflict, Choice, and Commitment,* Free Press, 1977.

(Editor) *Current Trends in Psychology: Readings from American Scientist,* William Kaufmann, 1977.

(With D. Wheeler) *A Practical Guide for Making Decisions*, Free Press, 1980.

(With others) *Counseling on Personal Decisions: Theory and Research on Short-Term Helping Relationships*, Yale University Press, 1982.

Stress, Attitudes, and Decisions: Selected Papers, Praeger, 1982.

Short-Term Counseling: Guidelines Based on Recent Research, Yale University Press, 1983.

CONTRIBUTOR

S. Stouffer and others, editors, *The American Soldier: Combat and Its Aftermath*, Princeton University Press, 1949.

Harold D. Lasswell and N. C. Leites, editors, *Language of Politics: Studies in Quantitative Semantics*, George W. Stewart, 1949.

D. Katz and others, editors, *Public Opinion and Propaganda: A Book of Readings*, Dryden, 1954.

(With R. L. Feierabend) Hovland, editor, *The Order of Presentation in Persuasion*, Yale University Press, 1957.

E. E. Maccoby, T. M. Newcomb, and E. L. Hartley, editors, *Readings in Social Psychology*, 3rd edition (Janis was not associated with earlier editions), Holt, 1958.

W. Muensterberger and S. Axelrad, editors, *Psychoanalysis and the Social Sciences*, Volume V, International Universities, 1958.

G. Lindzey, editor, *Assessment of Human Motives*, Holt, 1958.

M. R. Jones, editor, *Nebraska Symposium on Motivation*, University of Nebraska Press, 1959.

D. Chapman and G. Baker, editors, *Man and Society in Disaster*, Basic Books, 1962.

W. Schramm, editor, *The Science of Human Communications*, Basic Books, 1963.

(With others) J. Yudkin and J. McKenzie, editors, *Changing Food Habits*, MacGibbon & Kee, 1964.

(With H. Leventhal) B. Wolman, editor, *Handbook of Clinical Psychology*, McGraw, 1965.

S. Klausner, editor, *The Quest for Self-Control*, Free Press, 1965.

(With M. B. Smith) H. Kelman, editor, *International Behavior*, Holt, 1965.

(With Leventhal) E. Borgatta and W. W. Lambert, editors, *Handbook of Personality Theory and Research*, Rand McNally, 1967.

L. Berkowitz, editor, *Advances in Experimental Social Psychology*, Academic Press, 1967.

D. Cartwright and A. Zander, editors, *Group Dynamics: Research and Theory*, 3rd edition (Janis was not associated with earlier editions), Harper, 1968.

R. P. Abelson and others, editors, *Theories of Cognitive Consistency: A Sourcebook*, Rand McNally, 1968.

(With L. Mann) A. Greenwald, T. Brock, and T. Ostrom, editors, *Psychological Foundations of Attitudes*, Academic Press, 1968.

F. Redlich, editor, *Social Psychiatry*, Association for Research in Nervous and Mental Disease (New York), 1969.

N. Sanford and C. Comstock, editors, *Sanctions for Evil: Sources of Destructiveness*, Jossey-Bass, 1971.

D. A. Hamburg and C. V. Coelho, editors, *Coping and Adaptation*, Academic Press, 1974.

M. Deutsch and H. Hornstein, editors, *Problems of Applying Social Psychology*, Erlbaum (Hillsdale, N.J.), 1975.

R. S. Lazurus, editor, *Clues to the Riddle of Man*, Prentice-Hall, 1975.

S. S. Nagel, editor, *Policy Studies and the Social Sciences*, Heath, 1975.

J. Howard and A. Strauss, editors, *Humanizing Health Care*, Wiley, 1976.

(With J. Rodin) G. C. Stone, F. Cohen, and N. E. Adler, editors, *Health Psychology*, Jossey-Bass, 1979.

R. I. Evans, *The Making of Social Psychology: Discussions with Creative Contributors*, Gardner Press, 1980.

T. F. Gieryn, editor, *Science and Social Structure: A Festschrift for Robert K. Merton*, New York Academy of Sciences, 1980.

H. Brandstetter, J. Davis, and C. Stocker-Kreichgauer, editors, *Group Decision Making*, Academic Press, 1981.

L. Goldberger and S. Breznitz, editors, *Handbook of Stress*, Free Press, 1982.

(With Mann) N. Feather, editor, *Expectations and Action: Expectancy-Value Models in Psychology*, Erlbaum, 1982.

(With Rodin) H. S. Friedman and M. R. DiMatteo, editors, *Interpersonal Issues and Health Care*, Academic Press, 1982.

Breznitz, editor, *The Denial of Stress*, International University Press, 1983.

D. Meichenbaum and M. Jaremko, editors, *Stress Reduction and Prevention*, Plenum, 1983.

H. H. Blumberg and P. Hare, editors, *Small Groups*, Wiley, 1983.

(With P. Grossman and P. Defares) H. Selye, editor, *Selye's Guide to Stress Research*, Volume III, Van Nostrand, 1983.

(With Mann) D. Johnson and D. Tjosvold, editors, *Conflicts in Organizations*, Irvington, 1983.

D. Gentry, editor, *Handbook of Behavioral Medicine*, Guilford, 1984.

Defares, C. Spielberger, and I. Sarason, editors, *Stress and Anxiety*, Volume IX, Hemisphere Publishing, 1985.

S. Oskamp, editor, *International Conflict and National Public Policy Issues*, Sage Publications, 1985.

J. M. Pennings, editor, *Organizational Strategy and Change*, Jossey-Bass, 1985.

R. K. White, editor, *Psychology and the Prevention of Nuclear War*, New York University Press, 1986.

OTHER

Also author of seven government reports on social psychological surveys. Contributor to proceedings of XV International Congress of Psychology, Amsterdam, 1957, and of XVIII International Congress of Psychology, Moscow, 1966; contributor to *International Encyclopedia of the Social Sciences*, Macmillan, 1968. Contributor of more than fifty articles and research papers to professional journals, including *Journal of Experimental Psychology*, *Public Opinion Quarterly*, *Psychometrika*, *Psychiatry*, *Journal of Personality*, and *Journal of Nervous and Mental Diseases*. Former member of editorial board, *American Scientist;* associate editor, *Sociometry*, 1955-58; consulting editor, *Journal of Abnormal and Social Psychology*, 1955-65, *Journal of Experimental Social Psychology*, 1966-70, and *Journal of Behavioral Medicine;* chairman of editorial board, *Journal of Conflict Resolution*.

WORK IN PROGRESS: The Making of Vital Policy Decisions; Crisis Decisions in the Nuclear Age.

BIOGRAPHICAL/CRITICAL SOURCES:

PERIODICALS

American Psychologist, January, 1982.

JERVELL, Jacob 1925-

PERSONAL: Born May 21, 1925, in Fauske, Norway; son of Sverre (a pastor) and Thora (Mejdell) Jervell; married Kari Lange (a librarian); children: Stephen. *Education:* Attended Lund University, 1950; Oslo University, B.D., 1951, D.D., 1959; graduate study at Heidelberg University, 1953, and Goettingen University, 1954-55. *Religion:* Lutheran.

ADDRESSES: Home—Seterstoea, 2150 Aarnes, Norway. *Office*—Oslo University, Blindern, Oslo 3, Norway.

CAREER: Oslo University, Oslo, Norway, lecturer, 1955-59, professor of biblical theology, 1960—, dean of faculty of theology, 1975-76, vice-chancellor, 1977-80. Visiting professor, Lund University, 1964, Yale University, 1970, and Aarhus University, 1973. Chairman of Norwegian Christian Student Movement, 1958-65.

MEMBER: Norwegian Academy of Science and Letters, Studiorum Novi Testamenti Societas, Norwegian Bible Society (member of board, 1966—), Societe Royale des Lettres de Lund.

AWARDS, HONORS: D.D.h.c., Aarhus University, 1978.

WRITINGS:

Imago Dei (title means "The Image of God"), Vandenhoeck & Ruprecht, 1960.
The Historical Jesus, Forlaget Land og Kirke, 1962, 3rd revised edition, 1978.
Ikke bare ruiner (title means "Not Only Ruins"), Forlaget Land og Kirke, 1967.
Da fremtiden begynte (title means "When the Future Began"), Forlaget Land og Kirke, 1967, 2nd revised edition, 1976.
Studien zu den Testamenten der 12 Patriarchen (title means "Studies in the Testaments of the 12 Patriarchs"), A. Toepelmann, 1969.
Luke and the People of God, Augsburg, 1972, 2nd edition, 1979.
Gud og hans fiender (title means "God and His Enemies"), Oslo University Press, 1973, 2nd edition, 1978.
". . . bare all makt" (title means ". . . Only All Power"), Gyldendal, 1975.
(Editor) *God's Christ and His People,* Universitetsforlaget, 1977.
Ingen har stoerre kjaelighet (title means "Greater Love Has No Man"), Universitetsforlaget, 1979.
Jesus in the Gospel of John, Augsburg, 1984.
The Unknown Paul, Augsburg, 1985.

Contributor to theology journals and periodicals.

WORK IN PROGRESS: Die Apostelgeschichte, for Vandenhoeck & Ruprecht; *History of Early Christianity.*

*   *   *

JESSEL, Camilla (Ruth) 1937-

PERSONAL: Born December 7, 1937, in Bearsted, Kent, England; daughter of Richard Frederick (a naval officer) and Winifred May (Levy) Jessel; married Andrzej Panufnik (a symphonic composer), November 27, 1963; children: Roxanna Anna, Jeremy James. *Education:* Sorbonne, University of Paris, degre superieur, 1959.

ADDRESSES: Home—Riverside House, Twickenham TW1 3DJ, England. *Agent*—David Higham Associates Ltd., 5-8 Lower John St., London W1R 4HA, England.

CAREER: Free-lance photographer and writer. Work shown in group and one-man photographic exhibitions at Royal Festival Hall, Arts Theatre Club, Photographers Gallery, and Royal Photographic Society. Former vice-chairman of Home Welfare Committee; member of United Kingdom Child Care Committee of Save the Children (vice-chairman, 1969-84). School governor, Cranborne Chase School, Wiltshire, England. Council member, Park Lane Group (for young musicians).

MEMBER: Royal Photographic Society (fellow), Performing Rights Society, Society of Authors.

AWARDS, HONORS: Grant from Nuffield Foundation, 1972; Royal Photographic Society fellowship, 1980.

WRITINGS:

JUVENILES; ALL ILLUSTRATED WITH OWN PHOTOS

Manuela Lives in Portugal, Hastings, House, 1967.
Paul in Hospital, Methuen Children's Books (London), 1972.
Mark's Wheelchair Adventures, Methuen Children's Books, 1975.
Life at the Royal Ballet School, Methuen (New York), 1979.
The Puppy Book, Methuen (New York), 1980.
The New Baby, Methuen Children's Books, 1981.
Moving House, Methuen Children's Books, 1981.
Going to the Doctor, Methuen Children's Books, 1981.
Away for the Night, Methuen Children's Books, 1981.
Lost and Found, Methuen Children's Books, 1983.
At Playgroup, Methuen Children's Books, 1983.
Going to Hospital, Methuen Children's Books, 1983.
The Baby-sitter, Methuen Children's Books, 1983.
Learner Bird, Methuen Children's Books, 1983.

"BABYDAYS" SERIES; ALL ILLUSTRATED WITH OWN PHOTOS

Baby's Day, Methuen Children's Books, 1985.
Baby's Toys, Methuen Children's Books, 1985.
Baby's Bedtime, Methuen Children's Books, 1985.
Baby's Clothes, Methuen Children's Books, 1985.
Baby's Food, Methuen Children's Books, 1986.
Where Is Baby?, Methuen Children's Books, 1986.

LYRICS FOR CANTATAS BY HUSBAND, ANDREJ PANUFNIK

Thames Pageant (for children), Boosey & Hawkes, 1969.
Winter Solstice, Boosey & Hawkes, 1972.

PHOTOGRAPHER

Dorothy Shuttlesworth, *Tower of London,* Hastings House, 1970.
Susan Harvey, *Play in Hospital,* Faber, 1972.
David Watkins, *Complete Method for the Harp,* Boosey & Hawkes, 1972.
Penelope Leach, *Baby and Child,* Knopf, 1978.
Sheila Kitzinger, *Pregnancy and Childbirth,* Knopf, 1980.
David Moore, *Multi-Cultural Britain* (booklet), Save the Children, 1980.
Miriam Stoppard, *50 Plus Life Guide,* Dorling & Kindersley, 1983.
Esther Rantzen and Desmond Wilcox, *Baby Love,* Rainbird, 1985.

OTHER

The Joy of Birth: A Book for Parents and Children, Methuen Children's Books, 1982, Dutton, 1983.

Catching the Moment: Photographing Your Child, Dutton, 1985.

Contributor of photographs to newspapers.

WORK IN PROGRESS: A music book for children, publication by Methuen expected in 1988; a book for parents on child development, publication by Dorling & Kindersley, 1988; more children's books for Methuen.

SIDELIGHTS: Camilla Jessel told *CA:* "As a teenager I lived for eighteen months with my parents in a community in South India. I lived a year in Paris, studying French literature and civilization. At the age of twenty I went to America with about one hundred dollars and had twenty-six different temporary secretarial jobs in six cities in one year (Princeton, Washington, New York, New Orleans, Dallas, and San Francisco). I have traveled extensively as a photographer (Africa and Europe) and as the wife of an internationally known conductor and composer (including South America, but not Eastern Europe as my husband is a political refugee).

"I bring up a family and work as my husband's business manager. I enjoy being domestic, cooking, dressmaking, as well as having a career. I believe it's possible to be both liberated and a dedicated wife and mother.

"My motivation is my interest in children and my wish to use photography to combat prejudice and fear, such as the prejudice against the disabled or members of other races; I also want to use photography to educate children and to educate adults to be of more use to children. There is also my sheer enjoyment of photography and an attempt to heighten my own aesthetic standards.

"I started by working with children and was pushed into photography by the press officer of Save the Children, who liked the amateur shots I'd done of the organization's work. These fund-raising photos were followed by lots of hard work and lucky breaks. I worked free-lance, including photographic articles for the *Times Educational Supplement*. My first book was commissioned on the strength of two photographs that appeared in the *Guardian*. Doing color slides for a lecture on the psychology of play of children in the hospital, I got the idea of doing a photographic book to overcome children's fears of the hospital. Then I received a grant for a similar book about disabled children. I continued over the years to work with disadvantaged children, but also worked on other subjects, including the book on birth and the facts of life for children."

Jessel also told *CA*, "Some books have just 'happened,' such as *The Puppy Book* when our labrador had nine puppies, and *Learner Bird*, the story of a baby thrush rescued by my eleven-year-old son." The author and photographer's book for adults, a manual for photographing children, was prompted by circumstances, too, she explains. "While photographing innumerable children for my various books and projects, I was always being asked by parents and child care people for photographic advice, so wrote my book on photography, *Catching the Moment: Photographing Your Child*."

AVOCATIONAL INTERESTS: Music, theatre, art, ballet, literature, international politics.

BIOGRAPHICAL/CRITICAL SOURCES:

PERIODICALS

Daily Telegraph, August 24, 1979.

Guardian, August 24, 1979.
Times Literary Supplement, August 2, 1985.

*   *   *

JOHNSON, Brian (Martin)   1925-

PERSONAL: Born December 5, 1925, in Liverpool, England; son of Reginald (an engineer) and Gladys (Johnson) Johnson; married Sybil Temperton, February 1, 1949; children: Christine, Hilary, Caroline Barbara. *Education:* Attended high school in Birkenhead, England.

ADDRESSES: Home—10 California Lane, Bushey Heath, Watford, Hertfordshire WD2 1EY, England. *Office*—BBC Enterprises, Woodlands, 80 Wood Lane, London W12 0TT, England. *Agent*—Sheila Watson, Watson & Little, Suite 8, 26 Charing Cross Rd., London WC2H 0DG, England.

CAREER: British Broadcasting Corp. (BBC), London, England, radio engineer, 1942-44, studio manager in radio drama department, 1947-51, sound technician for Television Service film unit, 1951-56, camera operator for film unit, 1956-58, assistant producer of documentaries, 1958-63, producer of remote broadcasts on music and sports, 1963-73, producer of science features and editor of weekly science television program, "Tomorrow's World," 1973-76, senior producer of science television documentaries, 1976-86. *Military service:* British Army, Royal Electrical and Mechanical Engineers, 1944-47; served in the Middle East; became sergeant.

WRITINGS:

The Secret War (nonfiction; based on six-part television series of the same name; also see below), Methuen, 1978.
Fly Navy: A History of Maritime Aviation, Morrow, 1981.
A Most Secret Place, Jane's, 1982.
(With H. I. Cozens) *Bombers*, Thames-Methuen, 1982.
Test Pilot (also see below), BBC Publications, 1987.

DOCUMENTARY SCRIPTS FOR TELEVISION

"The Crowded Sky," British Broadcasting Corp. (BBC-TV), April 11, 1978.
"Bombers," BBC-TV, June 12, 1979.
"The Flying Machines of Ken Wallis," BBC-TV, May 13, 1980.
"Sir Frank Whittle, Jet Pioneer," BBC-TV, May 12, 1981.
"Jump Jet," BBC-TV, July 7, 1981.
"Faster than the Sun," BBC-TV, 1984.
(And director) "Supercharged" (science series), BBC-TV, 1984.
"The Long Watch," BBC-TV, 1984.
(And producer and director) "Test Pilot" (six-part series), BBC-TV, 1986.

Contributor to BBC-TV series "Tomorrow's World" and "The Secret War."

OTHER

Contributor to magazines, including *Aeroplane Monthly*, *Shortwave*, and *Radio Times*.

WORK IN PROGRESS: Currently researching a book on the wartime experiences of well-known people; adapting former television work to video; a video on Westminster Abbey.

SIDELIGHTS: Brian Johnson told *CA:* "After many years in BBC-TV, writing, producing, and directing programs as diverse as sports and music, I became fascinated by the archives of the Imperial War Museum, in particular a very large quantity of captured German footage dealing mainly with the experimental work on V2 rockets at Peenemunde, Germany. This material—it was the equivalent of about eighty full-length feature films—was uncataloged and had been released as a consequence of the 'Thirty Year Rule,' which was making available a very large amount of classified material pertaining to World War II.

"The quality of the archive film enabled me to produce six fifty-minute television documentary programs under the general title of 'The Secret War.' The series was very successful in TV terms, and I was asked to write a book on the subject. This book, I am pleased to say, became a best-seller. The success of the book led me to write others, so that now my leisure time is almost totally taken up with writing. Thus, largely by accident, I have become involved in the history of World War II—a war in which I played a distinctly minor role.

"I try, whenever possible, to work from primary sources: it is pleasing to discover some hitherto overlooked fact of history, however small, and, I must confess, to handle and read the documents that once were closely guarded state secrets is a unique experience. There is a strong sense of anticipation when a folder of such documents is before one for the first time: what will it contain? Seldom is there a feeling of disappointment. Archives like the Public Record Office in London might seem to the uninitiated to be dull, dry places. I have not found them so.

"It seems to me that the task of a historian writing for the general reader is to try to convey the excitement of the affairs of the recent past in a way that retains the feeling of being present at, for example, a tense meeting of the war cabinet under Winston Churchill, who was considering intelligence reports of German long-range rockets or the meaning of mysterious radio signals thought to be guiding Luftwaffe night bombers to targets in England and reading the reports of eminent scientists as they considered countermeasures. One mistake by them and over a thousand people could die in a single air raid (as indeed happened on the night of the German attack on Coventry). Henry Ford is reported once to have said, 'History is bunk.' Not so!"

Johnson's *The Secret War* has been translated into German and Dutch.

*   *   *

JOHNSON, Lyndon Baines   1908-1973

PERSONAL: Born August 27, 1908, in Stonewall, Tex.; died January 22, 1973, of a heart attack, in Stonewall, Tex.; buried in Stonewall, Tex.; son of Samuel Ealy, Jr. (a farmer and state legislator), and Rebekah (a teacher of elocution; maiden name, Baines) Johnson; married Claudia Alta (better known as Lady Bird) Taylor, November 17, 1934; children: Lynda Bird (Mrs. Charles S. Robb), Luci Baines. *Education:* Southwest Texas State Teachers College (now Southwest Texas State University), B.S., 1930; Georgetown University, graduate study, 1935-36.

CAREER: Thirty-sixth president of the United States. Spent several years between high school and college doing odd jobs in California and working on road crew in Texas; teacher in public schools of Cotulla, Tex., 1928-29, and Houston, Tex., 1930-31; went to Washington, D.C., as secretary to Congressman Richard Kleberg, 1931-35; Texas state director of Na-

tional Youth Administration, 1935-37; won election to U.S. House of Representatives, 1937-38, filling unexpired term of Congressman James B. Buchanan; U.S. Representative, 1938-48; lost race for vacant U.S. Senate seat in special election, 1941; U.S. Senator, 1949-61, serving as Democratic Party floor leader, 1953-61; made bid for Democratic Party presidential nomination, 1960, and was picked for vice-presidential post by the successful candidate, John F. Kennedy; as vice-president, 1961-63, headed National Aeronautics and Space Council, President's Committee on Equal Employment Opportunity, and Peace Corps Advisory Council; succeeded the assassinated Kennedy to presidency, November 22, 1963; elected president, 1964; retired, 1968, to his Texas ranch and oversaw construction of the Johnson Library on University of Texas campus. *Military service:* U.S. Naval Reserve, active duty, 1941-42; served as special presidential emissary in Australia and New Zealand; became commander; received Silver Star; resigned commission, 1964.

AWARDS, HONORS: LL.D., Southwestern University, 1943, Howard Payne University, 1957, Brown University, 1959, Bethany College, 1959, University of Hawaii, 1961, University of the Philippines, 1961, East Kentucky State College, 1961, William Jewel College, 1961, Gallaudet College, 1961, Elon College, 1962, Wayne State University, 1963, Jacksonville University, 1963, McMurray College, 1963, Tufts University, 1963, University of Maryland, 1963, University of California, 1964, Georgetown University, 1964, University of Texas, 1964, Swarthmore College, 1964, Catholic University of America, 1965, University of Kentucky, 1965, Baylor University, 1965, and Howard University, 1965; L.H.D., Oklahoma City College, 1960, Yeshiva University, 1961, and Florida Atlantic University, 1964; D.Litt., St. Mary's College of California, 1962; D.C.L., Holy Cross College, 1964, and University of Michigan, 1964; D.Polit. Sci., Chulalongkorn University, Thailand, 1966; also received degrees from Princeton University, Texas Christian University, and Southwest Texas State University.

WRITINGS:

(With Robert C. Weaver, Joseph P. Lyford, and John Cogley) *The Negro as an American,* Center for the Study of Democratic Institutions, 1963.

My Hope for America, Random House, 1964.

The President Speaks: On Prosperity and Poverty, Civil Rights, Nuclear War, Communism, Your Future, Dell, 1964.

A Time for Action: A Selection from the Speeches and Writings of Lyndon B. Johnson, 1953-64, with an introduction by Adlai E. Stevenson, Atheneum, 1964.

President Johnson's Design for a "Great Society" (speeches), Congressional Quarterly, 1965.

Lyndon B. Johnson on Conservation, five volumes, U.S. Department of the Interior, 1965.

Public Papers of the President of the United States, Lyndon B. Johnson, Containing the Public Messages, Speeches, and Statements of the President, 1963/64-1967, eight volumes, U.S. Government Printing Office, 1965-68.

The Promise of the New Asia: United States Policy in the Far East as Stated by President Johnson on His Pacific Journey, U.S. Government Printing Office, 1966.

This America, Random House, 1966.

To Heal and to Build: The Programs of Lyndon B. Johnson, edited by James MacGregor Burns, McGraw, 1968.

(Author of introductory message) Robert A. Goldwin, editor, *A Nation of Cities: Essays on American Urban Problems,* Rand McNally, 1968.

The Choices We Face, Bantam, 1969.

(Author of foreword) Eugene R. Black, *Alternative in Southeast Asia,* Praeger, 1969.

The Vantage Point: Perspectives of the Presidency, 1963-1969 (Book-of-the-Month Club selection), Holt, 1971.

The Johnson Presidential Press Conferences, Earl M. Coleman, 1978.

BOOKS OF QUOTATIONS

The Johnson Wit, edited by Frances Spatz Leighton, Citadel, 1965.

The Johnson Humor, edited by Bill Adler, Simon & Schuster, 1965.

Quotations from Chairman LBJ, Simon & Schuster, 1968.

The Quotable Lyndon B. Johnson, edited by Sarah H. Hayes and the staff of *Quote,* Droke, 1968.

OTHER

Also author of numerous published speeches and addresses.

SIDELIGHTS: When President John F. Kennedy was assassinated on November 22, 1963, Vice-President Lyndon Baines Johnson assumed the presidency, a position he was to hold until January of 1969. His administration was marked by the sweeping social legislation of the Great Society, by domestic turmoil, and by an ever-increasing involvement in the Vietnam War. As David Halberstam wrote in the *New York Times Book Review,* Johnson's "life spanned vast and volatile political and social change, and he ruled at a time of shattering events." A commentator for the *Times Literary Supplement* admitted that "Johnson faced an array of problems, internal and external, more complicated than those history has presented any President since Franklin Roosevelt."

Johnson's rise to the presidency came after a long political career as a U.S. Representative and Senator. The Johnson family had been active in politics for many years. His grandfather, as Robert Coles explained in the *New Republic,* had been "a populist; he fought for the hardpressed farmers and laborers of the South and the Opening West." Johnson's father, wrote Paul D. Zimmerman in *Newsweek,* was "a small-town politician who instilled in his boy the merciless machismo of the West." After working for a time as a teacher in his native Texas, Johnson entered politics in the early 1930s as the secretary to Congressman Richard Kleberg.

In 1937 Johnson was elected to the U.S. House of Representatives as a candidate of the Democratic Party. The elder Texas Representative, Sam Rayburn, one of the most influential members of the House during the 1930s and 1940s, took the freshman congressman under his wing. As the Speaker of the House, Rayburn saw to it that his protege was introduced to the right people in Washington, sat on the most advantageous committees, and was taught the behind-the-scenes machinations required to push a bill through Congress. Garry Wills, writing in the *New York Review of Books,* remarked that Johnson "had risen as the client of Sam Rayburn."

In 1948 Johnson was elected to the U.S. Senate where, in the course of the next twelve years, he became one of the most powerful men in Congress. "Johnson acquired power," Zimmerman explained, "by stealth rather than confrontation, accepting control of relatively powerless organizations like the Democratic Policy Committee, which he quietly converted into the powerful scheduling arm for all Senate legislation." Writing in the *New York Review of Books,* William Appleman Williams commented on "Johnson's knowledge of how to move

the system," which Williams attributed to "his white southern experience: if they will not let you run it from the top, then learn how to control it from the side."

Because of his prominent congressional position, Johnson was a leading contender for the Democratic Party's presidential nomination in 1960. But he lost his bid for the nomination to John Kennedy, a Massachusetts senator; Johnson became the Democrats' vice-presidential candidate instead. Their subsequent campaign against the Republican candidate Richard Nixon was a hard-fought contest. Nixon had served as vice-president under former President Dwight D. Eisenhower and was a nationally known political figure. Kennedy and Johnson were relative unknowns on the national scene. But the Kennedy-Johnson ticket won the 1960 election, by a margin of less than one percent of the vote.

Kennedy's administration lasted for less than three years, but it was marked by a series of major foreign crises. Most of the crises, his critics charged, were manufactured by the self-aggrandizing Kennedy himself. In his book *The Kennedy Promise: The Politics of Expectation,* Henry Fairlie argued that foreign crises were occasions for Kennedy to show "a spectacular display of his power in a situation of maximum peril." When a crisis was announced, Fairlie continued, "all over Washington men would rise early to answer the bidding to crisis and to greatness, and the still slumbering public would awake in the morning to find that they had been summoned to meet danger once more, and once more to be rescued from it." The failed Bay of Pigs invasion of Cuba, the Cuban missile crisis, standoffs with the Soviet Union over nuclear arms and the Berlin Wall, and covert operations and assassinations in Vietnam and other countries were among the foreign crises faced by the Kennedy Administration.

At home, Kennedy proposed sweeping changes under what he termed the New Frontier, including civil rights legislation, a massive increase in government social spending, and an aggressive space program. But Kennedy was never to realize his domestic goals. His assassination in Dallas in November of 1963 came before he could institute his New Frontier legislation. It was left to Johnson to complete what Kennedy had begun.

The transition from one president to the next was difficult. Kennedy and Johnson had different political styles: Kennedy was the young, wealthy, Northern liberal who enjoyed confrontation, while Johnson was the Southern, slow-speaking master of congressional compromise. Johnson, a *Times Literary Supplement* writer observed, "was a tough, proud, intelligent man; an American original. But the stage on to which he walked on November 22, 1963, was not set for that type of leading man. The scenario called for a smooth, witty, superficially cultured glamour boy. Johnson was miscast."

Still, Johnson was able to push the domestic programs suggested by the Kennedy Administration through a resistant Congress. "He cashed in on the martyrdom of John F. Kennedy," Larry L. King commented in the *Nation,* "to crash the Civil Rights Act through a foot-dragging Congress." Other legislation—meant to build what Johnson termed the Great Society—covered federal support for education and public housing, a war on poverty, the model cities program, and Medicare. Johnson, John Kenneth Galbraith wrote in the *Saturday Review,* had "a superb sense of priority—of the urgency of the problems of race, the cities, education, medical care, and the poor. He was far better than Kennedy (and I think than Roosevelt) in winning the requisite response from the Congress."

William L. O'Neill, writing in the *New Republic,* spoke of "the political genius" necessary for Johnson to enact "all those memorable bills, even from the reluctant Congress that had frustrated President Kennedy."

Johnson's success at enacting his domestic legislation was not matched in his foreign policy objectives. His overriding failure in foreign policy was the Vietnam War, a war that Johnson inherited from the Kennedy Administration. Kennedy had increased American involvement in Vietnam by sending many new military advisers to the South Vietnamese army. He had also created the Green Berets, an elite military unit for Vietnam duty. Johnson also inherited Kennedy's foreign policy advisers, who argued for increased American military involvement in Vietnam. Reviewing Johnson's book *The Vantage Point: Perspectives of the Presidency, 1963-1969,* the *Times Literary Supplement* critic noted that Johnson's rationale for sending American combat troops to Southeast Asia was accepted by those "with far greater international experience than he.... Many of them had been members of the Kennedy Administration." Galbraith argued that Johnson "was excellent on the problems of which he was personally in command and that included, in particular, anything having to do with the United States. He failed when he had to rely on advisors. Until he became Vice President he had not seriously bothered his mind with most problems of foreign policy. So here he relied not on himself but on the Cold War civilians and the military, and this was fatal." Halberstam also blamed Johnson's advisers for the nation's entry into the Vietnam War. "Poorly advised and served by a group of inherited national security managers," Halberstam wrote, "[Johnson] made the fatal decision to go to war in Vietnam with combat troops."

Once committed to the war, Johnson was reluctant to withdraw troops for fear of appearing weak or to openly declare war for fear of the vastly increased number of casualties that would entail. Johnson's *The Vantage Point* "gives the impression that, from the outset, Johnson wavered between timidity and ruthlessness," the *Times Literary Supplement* critic reported. He chose neither withdrawal nor full-scale war, settling instead for gradual escalation of troop levels at a slow, steady pace. But by late 1967, O'Neill wrote, "Johnson was losing his faith in victory."

The Tet offensive of 1968, a massive series of Viet Cong attacks which were repelled by American troops, gave Johnson a reason for withdrawing from Vietnam. He argued that because Tet had not brought down the South Vietnamese government, the battle had been a victory for American troops. And with this victory, Johnson could safely reduce troop levels while negotiating a peace settlement with the weakened Viet Cong. Though some observers questioned the validity of this appraisal, Johnson began to bring American forces back home.

But domestic opposition to the Vietnam War had damaged Johnson's political effectiveness. Many congressional leaders were critical of his conduct of the war, while public demonstrations protested American involvement. In addition, the expectations raised by Johnson's Great Society programs had not been fulfilled. The resulting frustration and anger, particularly among the nation's blacks, exploded in a series of riots in many large cities. Because of these continuing problems, Johnson announced in April of 1968 that he would not seek another term as president.

Johnson's own story of his years as president was told in *The Vantage Point.* As he explained in the book's introduction: "I make no pretense of having written a complete and definitive history of my Presidency. I have tried, rather, to review that period from a President's point of view." Many reviewers of the book, however, thought that Johnson had other motives for writing it. *The Vantage Point,* Ronnie Dugger maintained in the *Washington Post Book World,* "is Johnson's claim to historic greatness, and I cannot think of any argument for it he has left out. His purpose is less to educate than to convince, less to enlighten than to overwhelm." Halberstam claimed that "the real story of the Johnsonian Presidency is not to be found in this book.... It is all tidied up, antiseptic, ordered, very calm."

Evaluations of Johnson's career ranked him as a major president, despite the difficulties of his administration. O'Neill found him to be "a giant among Presidents, and we live in his shadow still, a place too dark to see exactly where we have been, much less where we are going." Coles described Johnson as "a restless, extravagantly self-centered, brutishly expansive, manipulative, teasing and sly man, but he was also genuinely, passionately interested in making life easier and more honorable for millions of terribly hard-pressed working class men and women." "He was," Halberstam said of Johnson, "a politician and a force the like of which I doubt we shall see again in this country.... The texture of his life is far more interesting than that of either Kennedy, both of whom were comets who flashed before us, filled with light and promise, quickly extinguished. Johnson was real; his highs were higher and his lows were lower than any major figure in recent time."

BIOGRAPHICAL/CRITICAL SOURCES:

BOOKS

Bornet, Vaughn D., *The Presidency of Lyndon B. Johnson,* University Press of Kansas, 1983.
Caro, Robert A., *The Path to Power: The Years of Lyndon Johnson,* Knopf, 1982.
Divine, Robert A., editor, *Exploring the Johnson Years,* University of Texas Press, 1981.
Dugger, Ronnie, *The Politician: The Life and Times of Lyndon Johnson,* Norton, 1982.
Fairlie, Henry, *The Kennedy Promise: The Politics of Expectation,* Doubleday, 1973.
Furer, Howard B., editor, *Lyndon B. Johnson, 1908—; Chronology—Documents—Bibliographical Aids,* Oceania, 1971.
Johnson, Hanes and Richard Harwood, editors, *Lyndon: A Washington Post Pictorial Biography,* Praeger, 1973.
Johnson, Lyndon Baines, *The Vantage Point: Perspectives of the Presidency, 1963-1969,* Holt, 1971.
Kahl, Mary, *Ballot Box Thirteen: How Lyndon Johnson Won His 1948 Senate Race by 87 Contested Votes,* McFarland & Co., 1983.
Kearns, Doris, *Lyndon Johnson and the American Dream,* Harper, 1976.
Mooney, Booth, *The Lyndon Johnson Story,* Bodley Head, 1964.
Mooney, Booth, *LBJ: An Irreverent Chronicle,* Crowell, 1976.
Provence, Harry, *Lyndon B. Johnson,* Fleet, 1964.

PERIODICALS

Book World, November 21, 1971.
Life, November 12, 1971.
Nation, October 25, 1965.
New Republic, November 13, 1971, August 7-14, 1976.
Newsweek, May 31, 1976.
New Yorker, November 13, 1971.

New York Review of Books, December 16, 1971, June 24, 1976.
New York Times, November 2, 1971.
New York Times Book Review, October 31, 1971, June 6, 1976.
Saturday Review, November 6, 1971, June 12, 1976.
Times Literary Supplement, January 21, 1972.

OBITUARIES:

PERIODICALS

L'Express, January 29-February 4, 1973.
Newsweek, February 5, 1973.
New York Times, January 23, 1973.
Time, February, 5, 1973.
Washington Post, January 23, 1973.†

—*Sketch by Thomas Wiloch*

*   *   *

JONAS, Hans 1903-

PERSONAL: Born May 10, 1903, in Moenchengladbach, Germany (now West Germany); came to the United States, 1955; naturalized citizen, 1960; son of Gustav and Rosa (Horowitz) Jonas; married Elenore Weiner, October 6, 1943; children: Ayalah, Jonathan, Gabrielle. *Education:* Attended University of Freiburg, 1921, 1923-24, University of Berlin, 1921-23, and University of Heidelberg, 1926; University of Marburg, Ph.D. (summa cum laude), 1928; postdoctoral study at University of Heidelberg, 1929.

ADDRESSES: Home—9 Meadow Lane, New Rochelle, N.Y. 10805. *Office*—Department of Philosophy, New School for Social Research, 66 West 12th Street, New York, N.Y. 10011.

CAREER: Hebrew University, Jerusalem, Palestine (now Israel), guest lecturer in philosophy, 1938-39, 1946-48; British Council School of Higher Studies, Jerusalem, lecturer in ancient history, 1946-48; McGill University, Montreal, Quebec, teaching fellow in philosophy, 1949-50; Carleton University, Ottawa, Ontario, visiting professor, 1950-51, associate professor of philosophy, 1951-54; New School for Social Research, New York, N.Y., professor of philosophy, 1955-66, Alvin Johnson Professor of Philosophy, 1966-76, Alvin Johnson Professor of Philosophy Emeritus, 1976—, chairman of department, 1956-63 and 1972-75. Visiting professor at Princeton University, 1958, Columbia University, 1961 and 1966-67, Princeton Theological Seminary, 1961-62, Hunter College (now of the City University of New York), 1963-64, and Union Theological Seminary, 1966-76; Ingersoll Lecturer, Harvard University, 1961; Regents Lecturer, University of California, Riverside, 1977; Terry Lecturer, Yale University, 1980; Eric Voegelin Professor, University of Munich, 1982-83. Honorary president, International Colloquium on Gnosticism, Stockholm, Sweden, 1973. Member of Committee on Social Thought, University of Chicago, 1968, 1969, and 1970. *Military service:* British Army, Royal Artillery, 1940-45. Israeli Army Artillery, 1948-49; became first lieutenant.

MEMBER: International Society for Neoplatonic Studies, American Philosophical Association, American Society for the Study of Religion, American Academy of Arts and Sciences (fellow), Institute of Society, Ethics, and the Life Sciences (The Hastings Center), American Association for the Advancement of Science.

AWARDS, HONORS: Lady Davis Foundation fellow, 1949-50; Rockefeller Foundation fellow, 1959-60; D.H.L., Hebrew Union College-Jewish Institute of Religion, 1962; fellow of Center for Advanced Studies, Wesleyan University, 1964-65; National Endowment for the Humanities grant, 1973-74; Rockefeller Foundation grant, 1974-75; D.L.L., New School for Social Research, 1976; D.Theol., University of Marburg, 1976; Henry Knowles Beecher Award, The Hastings Center, 1978; Dr. Leopold Lucas Prize, University of Tuebingen, 1984; Peace Prize of the German Book Trade, 1987, for *The Imperative of Responsibility.*

WRITINGS:

IN ENGLISH

The Gnostic Religion: The Message of the Alien God and the Beginnings of Christianity, Beacon, 1958, 2nd enlarged edition, 1963.
The Phenomenon of Life: Towards a Philosophical Biology, Harper, 1966, reprinted, University of Chicago Press, 1982.
Philosophical Essays: From Ancient Creed to Technological Man, Prentice-Hall, 1974.
The Imperative of Responsibility: In Search of an Ethics for the Technological Age, University of Chicago Press, 1984.

IN ENGLISH; CONTRIBUTOR

Arthur A. Cohen and Marvin Halverson, editors, *A Handbook of Christian Theology,* Meridian Books, 1958.
M. Natanson, editor, *Philosophy of the Social Sciences,* Random House, 1963.
J. P. Hyatt, editor, *The Bible in Modern Scholarship,* Abingdon, 1965.
A. H. Friedlander, editor, *Out of the Whirlwind,* Union of American Hebrew Congregations, 1968.
Francis Oakley and Daniel O'Connor, editors, *Creation: The Impact of an Idea,* Scribner, 1969.
R. L. Heilbroner, editor, *Economic Means and Social Ends,* Prentice-Hall, 1969.
Stuart F. Spicker, editor, *The Philosophy of the Body,* Quadrangle Books, 1970.
Eleanor Kuykendall, editor, *Philosophy in an Age of Crisis,* Harper, 1970.
Paul Freund, editor, *Experimentation with Human Subjects,* Braziller, 1970.
James M. Robinson, editor, *Future of Our Religious Past: Essays in Honor of Rudolph Bultmann,* Harper, 1971.
C. Mitcham and R. Mackey, editors, *Philosophy and Technology,* Free Press, 1972.
J. M. Humber and R. F. Almeder, editors, *Biomedical Ethics and the Law,* Plenum Press, 1976.
H. T. Engelhardt and Spicker, editors, *Philosophical Dimensions of the Neuro-Medical Sciences,* D. Reidel, 1976.
Biomedical Research and the Public, U.S. Government Printing Office, 1977.
G. Widengren, editor, *Proceedings of the International Colloquium on Gnosticism,* E. J. Brill, 1977.
Engelhardt and D. Callahan, editors, *Knowledge, Value, and Belief,* Hastings Center, 1977.
T. L. Beauchamp and LeRoy Walters, editors, *Contemporary Issues in Bioethics,* Dickenson, 1978.
Beauchamp and S. Perlin, editors, *Ethical Issues in Death and Dying,* Prentice-Hall, 1978.
John Richards, editor, *Recombinant DNA: Science, Ethics, and Politics,* Academic Press, 1978.
Engelhardt and Callahan, editors, *Knowing and Valuing: The Search for Common Roots,* Hastings Center, 1980.
M. Kranzberg, editor, *Ethics in an Age of Pervasive Technology,* Westview Press, 1980.

Bentley Layton, editor, *The Rediscovery of Gnosticism I*, E. J. Brill, 1980.

Richard Kennington, editor, *The Philosophy of Baruch Spinoza*, Catholic University of America Press, 1980.

T. A. Shannon, editor, *Bioethics*, Paulist Press, 1981.

E. Partridge, editor, *Responsibilities to Future Generations*, Prometheus Books, 1981.

T. A. Mappels and J. S. Zembati, editors, *Biomedical Ethics*, McGraw, 1981.

L. Hickman and A. al-Hibri, editors, *Technology and Human Affairs*, Mosby, 1981.

Callahan and Engelhardt, editors, *The Roots of Ethics*, Plenum Press, 1982.

J. H. Schaub and S. K. Dickison, editors, *Engineering and Humanities*, Wiley, 1982.

Schaub and K. Pavlovik, editors, *Engineering, Professionalism and Ethics*, Wiley, 1983.

E. C. Hobbs, editor, *Bultmann, Retrospect and Prospect*, Fortress, 1985.

IN GERMAN

Augustin und das paulinische Freiheitsproblem: Eine philosophische Studie zum pelagianischen Streit, Vandenhoeck & Ruprecht, 1930, 2nd revised edition, 1965.

Gnosis und spaetantiker Geist, Vandenhoeck & Ruprecht, Volume I: *Die mythologische Gnosis*, 1934, 3rd revised edition, 1964, Volume II: *Von der Mythologie zur mystischen Philosophie*, 1954, 2nd edition, 1966.

(Contributor) F. L. Cross, editor, *Texte und Untersuchungen zur Geschichte der altchristlichen Literatur*, Akademie-Verlag, 1962.

(Contributor) A. Dempf, H. Arendt, and F. Engel-Janosi, editors, *Politische Ordnung und menschliche Existens. Festgabe fuer Eric Voegelin zum 60. Geburtstag*, C. H. Beck, 1962.

Zwischen Nichts und Ewigkeit: Zur Lehre vom Menschen, Vandenhoeck-Reihe, 1963.

(Contributor) E. Wiedmann, editor, *Epimeleia. Die Sorge der Philosophie um den Menschen*, A. Pustet, 1964.

(Contributor) G. Nolles, editor, *Heidegger und die Theologie*, Chr. Kaieser, 1967.

(Contributor) V. Klosstermann, editor, *Durchblicke. Martin Heidegger zum 80. Geburtstag*, Vittorio Klostermann, 1970.

Wandel und Bestand: Vom Grunde der Verstehbarkeit des Geschichtlichen, Vittorio Klostermann, 1970.

Organismus und Freiheit; Ansaetze zu einer philosophischen Biologie, Vandenhoeck & Ruprecht, 1973.

(Contributor) K. Rudolph, editor, *Gnosis und Gnostizismus*, Wissenschaftliche Buchgesellschaft, 1975.

(Contributor) D. Kaiser, editor, *Gedenken an Rudolph Bultmann*, J. C. B. Mohr, 1977.

Das Prinzip Verantwortung: Versuch einer Ethik fuer die technologische Zivilisation, Insel Verlag, 1979.

Macht oder Ohnmacht der Subjektivitaet?: Das Leib-Seele-Problem im Vorfeld des Prinzips Verantwortung, Insel Verlag, 1981.

(Contributor) Oskar Schatz, editor, *Brauchen wir eine andere Wissenschaft?*, Styria, 1981.

(Contributor) R. Lowe, P. Koslowski, and P. H. Kreuzer, editors, *Fortschritt ohne Mass?*, R. Piper, 1981.

(Contributor) W. Doerr, W. Jacob, and A. Laufs, editors, *Recht und Ethik in der Medizin*, Springer-Verlag, 1982.

(Contributor) D. Roessler and E. Lindenlaub, editors, *Moeglichkeiten und Grenzen der technischen Kultur*, F. K. Schattauer, 1982.

(Contributor) K. H. Delschen and J. Gieraths, editors, *Philosophie der Technik*, M. Diesterweg, 1982.

(With D. Mieth) *Was fuer morgen lebenswichtig ist. Unentdeckte Zukunftswerte*, Herder, 1983.

(With F. Stern) *Reflexionen finsterer Zeit*, J. C. B. Mohr, 1984.

Technik, Medizin und Ethik. Zur Praxis des Prinzips Verantwortung, Insel Verlag, 1985.

(Contributor) H. Daeubler-Gmelin and W. Adlerstein, editors, *Menschengerecht. 6. Rechstpolitischer Kongress der S. P. D.*, C. F. Mueller, 1986.

IN OTHER LANGUAGES

(Contributor) Ugo Bianchi, editor, *Le Origine dello Gnosticismo* (in Italian), E. J. Brill, 1967.

(Contributor) *Le Neoplatonisme* (in French), Centre National de la Recherche Scientifique, 1971.

OTHER

Contributor to *Encyclopedia Hebraica* and *Encyclopedia of Philosophy*. Contributor to numerous periodicals, including *Journal of the History of Philosophy*, *International Philosophical Quarterly*, and *Journal of Religion* (all in English), and *Theologische Zeitschrift*, *Zeitschrift fuer philosophische Forschung*, *Gnomon*, *Merkur*, and *Scheidewege* (all in German).

*   *   *

JONES, Charles Edwin   1932-

PERSONAL: Born June 1, 1932, in Kansas City, Mo.; son of Dess Dain (a streetcar and bus operator) and Dove (Barnwell) Jones; married Beverly Anne Lundy (a librarian), May 30, 1956; children: Karl Laurence. *Education:* Bethany-Peniel College, B.A., 1954; University of Oklahoma, summer graduate study, 1954; University of Michigan, M.A.L.S., 1955; University of Wisconsin, M.S., 1960, Ph.D., 1968; additional study, Episcopal Divinity School, 1975-76. *Politics:* Democrat. *Religion:* Episcopalian.

ADDRESSES: Home—12300 Springwood Dr., Oklahoma City, Okla. 73120.

CAREER: Bethany Nazarene College, Bethany, Okla., reference librarian, 1955-56; Nazarene Theological Seminary, Kansas City, Mo., head librarian, 1958-59; Park College, Parkville, Mo., head librarian, 1961-63; University of Michigan, Ann Arbor, manuscript curator of Michigan Historical Collections, 1965-69; Houghton College, Houghton, N.Y., associate professor of history, 1969-71; Brown University, Providence, R.I., catalog librarian, 1971-76. Visiting professor at Tuskegee Institute, 1968-69, and at Clarion State College, 1979. Consultant for Billy Graham Evangelistic Association, 1972. *Military service:* U.S. Army, 1956-58.

MEMBER: Canadian Church Historical Society, American Theological Library Association.

WRITINGS:

Jonathan Edwards and Politics, 1727-1750, University of Wisconsin, 1960.

Perfectionist Persuasion: The Holiness Movement and American Methodism, 1867-1936, Scarecrow, 1974.

A Guide to the Study of the Holiness Movement, Scarecrow, 1974.

A Guide to the Study of the Pentecostal Movement, two volumes, Scarecrow, 1983.

Also author of *Black Holiness,* 1987.

CONTRIBUTOR

W. J. Scheick, editor, *Critical Essays on Jonathan Edwards,* G. K. Hall, 1980.

R. E. Richey and K. E. Rowe, editors, *Rethinking Methodist History,* Kingswood, 1985.

C. H. Lippy, editor, *Religious Periodicals of the United States,* Greenwood, 1986.

OTHER

Contributor to *Journal of Church and State, Inland Seas, Detroit Historical Society Bulletin, Journal of the Canadian Church Historical Society, Missouri Historical Review, New England Quarterly,* and *North Dakota Quarterly.*

WORK IN PROGRESS: A book on the charismatic movement.

*   *   *

JUNGLE DOCTOR
    See WHITE, Paul Hamilton Hume

K

KABDEBO, Tamas
See KABDEBO, Thomas

* * *

KABDEBO, Thomas 1934-
(Tamas Kabdebo)

PERSONAL: First name is sometimes listed as Tamas; born February 5, 1934, in Budapest, Hungary; naturalized British citizen, 1963; son of Bela and Klara (Kelen) Kabdebo; married Agnes Wohl (an architect), July 27, 1959; children: Lilian Claire, Andrea Mary. *Education:* Attended University of Budapest, 1952-56; University of Wales, B.A., 1960; University of London, Dip. Lib., 1962, M.Phil., 1969. *Religion:* Roman Catholic.

ADDRESSES: Home and office—St. Patrick's College, Maynooth, Ireland.

CAREER: University of London, University College, London, England, assistant librarian, 1961-69; University of Guyana, Georgetown, Guyana, university librarian, 1969-72; City of London Polytechnic, London, librarian, 1973-74; University of Manchester, Manchester, England, social sciences librarian, 1974-82; St. Patrick's College, Maynooth, Ireland, university librarian, 1983—.

MEMBER: P.E.N., Library Association (London).

AWARDS, HONORS: World Poetry Society Award, 1968, for *Hungarian Love Poems of the Twentieth Century;* short story award, 1976.

WRITINGS:

(With Glynn Mills Ashton) *Gemau Hwngaria* (Hungarian short stories in Welsh; title means "Treasures of Hungary"), Gee & Sons (Denbigh, N. Wales), 1962.
Fortified Princecriptions on Poetry (poetry satires), privately printed, 1965.
Erettsegi (novel; title means "Maturity"), Feher Hollo (London), 1971.
Two-Hearted (poems in English and Hungarian), Poetry Seminary Workshop, University College, London, 1973.
Magyar Odisszeuszok (short stories in Hungarian; title means "Odysseus Pannonius"), Dario Detti (Rome), 1974.
Hundred Hungarian Poems, Albion Editions, 1976.

Minden idok (novel; title means "Of All Times"), Griff Verlag, 1978.
Diplomat in Exile (historical monograph), Columbia University Press, 1979.
Hungary, Clio Press, 1980.
Istener (title means "The Gods"), Griff Verlag, 1983.

Also author of *A Guide to the Literature of the Amerindians of Guyana.*

EDITOR

(And translator) Attila Jozsef, *Poems,* Danubia, 1966.
(And contributor) *University College Poetry,* Poetry Seminary Workshop, University College, London, 1967, 1969, 1973.
(With Paul Tabori, and translator) *A Tribute to Gyula Illyes: Poems,* Occidental Press, 1968.
(And translator) *Selected Poems of Gyula Illyes,* Chatto & Windus, 1971.
One Hundred Hungarian Poems, Albion Editions, 1976.

Also editor of anthologies, *Hungarian Love Poems of the Twentieth Century,* 1967, and *British Poets,* 1969, published as special issues of *Poet* magazine (Madras).

TRANSLATOR OF BOOKS FOR CHILDREN

Eva Janikovsky, *Basil and Barnabas,* Chatto & Windus, 1971.
Ferenc Mora, *The Chimney-Sweep Giraffes,* Chatto & Windus, 1971.

OTHER

Contributor of articles or translations to periodicals, including *justforallthat, New Hungarian Quarterly, Image, Poetry Singapore,* and *Resurgence.* Editor of *justforallthat,* 1969-72.

WORK IN PROGRESS: The Poetry of Hungary, with Adam Makkai and Paul Tabori; *The Anthology of Hungarian Poetry in English, 1300-1970.*

SIDELIGHTS: Because he tried to cross the Hungarian-Czech frontier, Thomas Kabdebo was imprisoned for six months on political charges in 1955. After his release from prison, he worked for six months in a coal mine. A member of the National Guard and a newspaper reporter during the 1956 Hungarian Revolution, he finally immigrated to England when the revolution was crushed.

Kabdebo told *CA:* "My travels have taken me around Europe, North and South America, Australia, and a good many islands where I have tried to fish above and under the water. In some capacity or another—refugee, research worker, conference delegate, reporter, interpreter, guide, tourist or fisherman—I have been to thirty-nine countries. My urban relaxation is trying out as many swimming pools as I can (I used to be a swimming international) and looking at as many good pictures as I can find. Apart from my native language Hungarian, and my adopted tongue English, I used to be able to cope with Russian and still can do Italian."

*   *   *

KACHRU, Braj B(ehari) 1932-

PERSONAL: Born May 15, 1932, in Srinagar, Kashmir, India; came to United States in 1963; son of Shyam Lal (an educator) and Tulsidevi (Tutu) Kachru; married Yamuna Keskar (a professor), January 22, 1965; children: Amita, Shamit. *Education:* Jammu and Kashmir University, B.A. (with honors), 1952; Allahabad University, M.A., 1955; University of Edinburgh, Ph.D., 1961. *Religion:* Hindu.

ADDRESSES: Home—2016 Cureton Dr., Urbana, Ill. 61801. *Office*—Department of Linguistics, University of Illinois at Urbana-Champaign, Urbana, Ill. 61801.

CAREER: Deccan College Research Institute, Poona, India, fellow in linguistics, 1957-58; Lucknow University, Lucknow, India, assistant professor of English, in charge of linguistics program, 1962-63; University of Illinois at Urbana-Champaign, research associate, 1963-64, assistant professor, 1964-67, associate professor, 1967-70, professor of linguistics, 1970—, head of department, 1969-79, associate of Center for Advanced Study, 1971-72, and 1979-80, coordinator of Division of Applied Linguistics, 1976—, director of Division of English as a Second Language, 1985—. Visiting professor, National University of Singapore, 1984. Visiting faculty member, Department of Education, Halifax, Nova Scotia, 1967, and East-West Center, Honolulu, Hawaii, 1983; fellow, East-West Center, 1982, 1984, and 1985. Member of South Asian study committees; co-director of summer program in South Asian study, 1967; member of board of trustees, American Institute of Indian Studies, 1980-82; chairman, International Committee for South Asian Languages and Linguistics, 1980—; chairman of seminars in linguistics. Lecturer and keynote speaker at various seminars, including Seminar on Varieties of English, SEAMEO Regional Language Center, Singapore, 1981, Seminar on Stylistics, Regional Language Center, Patiala, India, 1982, Conference on Progress in English Studies, London, 1984, Eighth World Congress of Applied Linguistics, Sydney, Australia, 1987, and Georgetown University Round Table on Languages and Linguistics, Georgetown University, Washington, D.C., 1987. Consultant to American Institute of Indian Studies, 1972, and to Ford Foundation, 1974.

MEMBER: International P.E.N., Dictionary Society of North America, British Association of Applied Linguistics, Linguistic Society of America (director of Linguistic Institute, 1978), American Oriental Society, Linguistic Society of India (life member), Linguistic Association of Canada and the United States, American Association for Applied Linguistics (vice-president, 1983, president, 1984), Teachers of English to Speakers of Other Languages (TESOL).

AWARDS, HONORS: Grants from U.S. Department of Health, Education and Welfare's Institute of International Affairs, 1965-72, for *A Reference Grammar of Kashmiri,* and 1970-72, for *An Introduction to Spoken Kashmiri;* faculty research fellow of American Institute of Indian Studies, New Delhi, India, 1967-68, 1971-72, and 1982.

WRITINGS:

(Editor with wife, Yamuna Kachru) *Studies in Hindi Linguistics,* American Institute of Indian Studies (New Delhi), 1968.

A Reference Grammar of Kashmiri, University of Illinois Press, 1969.

(Author of introduction with Henry Kahane and Charles Kisseberth) *Studies Presented to Robert B. Lees by His Students,* Linguistic Research, Inc. (Edmonton), 1970.

(Editor with Herbert W. Stahlke) *Current Trends in Stylistics,* Linguistic Research, Inc., 1972.

(Editor with R. B. Lees, S. Saporta, A. Pietrangeli, and Y. Malkiel, and contributor) *Issues in Linguistics: Papers in Honor of Henry and Renee Kahane,* University of Illinois Press, 1973.

An Introduction to Spoken Kashmiri, two parts, University of Illinois Press, 1973.

(Editor and contributor) *Papers in South Asian Linguistics,* University of Illinois Press, 1973.

(Editor and contributor) *Dimensions of Bilingualism: Theory and Case Studies,* University of Illinois Press, 1976.

(Editor with S. N. Sridhar) *Aspects of Sociolinguistics in South Asia,* Mouton, 1978.

Kashmiri Literature (monograph), Otto Harrassowitz (Weisbaden), 1981.

(Editor and contributor) *The Other Tongue: English across Cultures,* University of Illinois Press, 1982.

The Indianization of English: The English Language in India, Oxford University Press, 1983.

(Editor and contributor) *Studies in Language Variation: Non-Western Case Studies,* University of Illinois Press, 1983.

(Author of foreword) P. R. Mehendiratta, *University Administration in India and the USA,* [New Delhi], 1984.

(Author of foreword) V. Prakasam and A. Abbi, *Semantic Theories and Language Teaching,* Allied Publishers (New Delhi), 1986.

The Alchemy of English: The Spread, Functions and Forms of English in Non-Native Contexts, Pergamon, 1986.

CONTRIBUTOR

C. E. Bazell, J. C. Catford, M. A. K. Halliday, and R. H. Robins, editors, *In Memory of J. R. Firth,* Longmans, Green, 1966.

John W. M. Verhaar, editor, *Foundations of Language,* Part III, Volume VIII, D. Reidel (Dordrecht, Netherlands), 1968.

Thomas Sebeok, editor, *Current Trends in Linguistics,* Mouton, 1969.

K. L. Goodwin, editor, *National Identity: Proceedings of the Brisbane (Australia) Conference of the Association of Commonwealth Literature and Language,* Heinemann, 1970.

Melvin J. Fox, editor, *Language and Development: A Retrospective Survey of Ford Foundation Language Projects, 1952-1974,* Ford Foundation, 1975.

(With Y. Kachru and T. K. Bhatia) M. K. Verma, editor, *The Notion Subject in South Asian Languages,* University of Wisconsin Press, 1976.

J. E. Alatis, editor, *International Dimensions of Bilingual Education,* Georgetown University Press, 1978.

Joshua Fishman, editor, *Advances in the Study of Societal Multilingualism,* Mouton, 1978.

I. Rauch and G. F. Carr, editors, *Linguistic Method: Papers in Honor of H. Penzl,* Mouton, 1979.

Ladislav Zgusta, editor, *Theory and Method in Lexicography: Western and Non-Western Perspective,* Hornbeam Press, 1980.

Larry E. Smith, editor, *English for Cross-Cultural Communication,* Macmillan (London), 1981.

Charles Ferguson and Shirley B. Heath, editors, *Language in the U.S.A.,* Cambridge University Press, 1981.

R. Kaplan, editor, *Annual Review of Applied Linguistics 1980,* Newbury House, 1981.

Beverley S. Hartford, Albert Valdman, and Charles R. Foster, editors, *Issues in International Bilingual Education: The Role of the Vernacular,* Plenum, 1982.

R. W. Bailey and Manfred Goerlach, editors, *English as a World Language,* University of Michigan Press, 1982.

N. Aggarwal, *English in South Asia: A Bibliographical Survey of Resources,* Indian Documentation Service, 1982.

Annual Review of Applied Linguistics, 1981, Newbury House, 1982.

J. Cobarrubias and Fishman, editors, *Progress in Language Planning,* Mouton, 1983.

Richard B. Noss, editor, *Varieties of English in Southeast Asia,* Regional Language Center (Singapore), 1983.

Edith Bedard and Jacques Maurais, editors, *La Norme Linguistique,* Conseil de la Langue Francaise (Quebec), 1983.

M. Berns and S. J. Savignon, editors, *Initiatives in Communicative Language Teaching,* Addison-Wesley, 1983.

(And author of foreword) Sidney Greenbaum, editor, *The English Language Today,* Pergamon, 1984.

Cheris Kramarae, Muriel Schulz, and William O'Barr, editors, *Language and Power,* Sage Publications, 1984.

Randolph Quirk and Henry Widdowson, editors, *English in the World,* Cambridge University Press, 1985.

Annual Review of Applied Linguistics, 1984, Newbury House, 1985.

Annual Review of Applied Linguistics, 1985, Newbury House, 1986.

R. Carter and C. Brumfit, editors, *Literature and Language Teaching,* Oxford University Press, 1986.

Oxford Guide to the English Language, Oxford University Press, 1986.

Fishman and others, editors, *Festschrift for Charles Ferguson,* Mouton, 1986.

Also contributor to *Theoretical Foundations of Bilingualism,* edited by Henry Tureba.

OTHER

Editor of series "English in the International Context," Pergamon. Contributor of articles and reviews to language, education, and Oriental studies journals, including *Illinois Journal of Education, International Journal of the Sociology of Language, Studies in Linguistic Sciences, Lingua, Journal of the American Oriental Society,* and *Journal of Asian Studies.* Co-editor, *English World-Wide: A Journal of Varieties of English,* 1980-84, *Annual Review of Applied Linguistics,* 1980—, *Language and Development: An International Perspective,* 1982—, and *World Englishes: Journal of English as an International and Intranational Language,* 1984—. Guest editor, South Asian issues of *International Journal of the Sociology of Language* and *Studies in the Linguistic Sciences.* Member of editorial board, *Studies in the Linguistic Sciences,* 1971—, *Papers in Linguistics,* 1972-83, *International Journal of the Sociology*

of Language, 1974—, *Studies in Language Learning,* 1976-77, *TESOL Quarterly,* 1979-83, *Journal of South Asian Literatures,* 1980—, *Journal of Applied Language Study,* 1981—, *Studies in Second Language Acquisition,* 1985—, and *IDEAL: Issues and Developments in English and Applied Linguistics,* 1986—. Consultant to *Random House Dictionary of the English Language,* 1965-66, and *The International Dictionary of English Pronunciation.*

WORK IN PROGRESS: Continuing research on non-native varieties of English, and on Kashmiri language and literature; sociolinguistics and bilingualism.

* * *

KANE, Robert S. 1925-

PERSONAL: Born April 19, 1925, in Albany, N.Y.; son of Samuel Charles and Stella (Weiss) Kane. *Education:* Syracuse University, B.S., 1947; graduate study at University of Southampton, 1948.

ADDRESSES: Home and office—311 East 72nd St., New York, N.Y. 10021. *Agent*—Anita Diamant, 310 Madison Ave., New York, N.Y. 10017.

CAREER: Started as reporter for *Daily Tribune,* Great Bend, Kan., later worked in New York City for *Staten Island Daily Advance* and *New York Herald Tribune,* then for *New York World-Telegram and Sun,* 1954-59; *Playbill,* New York City, travel editor, 1961-63; *Cue,* New York City, travel editor, 1963-73; *50 Plus,* New York City, travel editor, 1982-85. Working-party member, President Johnson's Task Force on Travel, 1968. *Military service:* U.S. Navy, World War II; served in Pacific.

MEMBER: Society of American Travel Writers (regional secretary, 1962-63; national secretary, 1963-64; national president, 1968-69; chairman of board, 1970), National Press Club, P.E.N., American Society of Journalists and Authors, Authors Guild, New York Travel Writers' Association (president, 1977-79), Society of Professional Journalists, Sigma Delta Chi.

AWARDS, HONORS: Hedman Award, 1967; Austrian Gold Medal of Touristic Merit, 1969; Best Travel Book of the Year Award, Society of American Travel Writers, 1981.

WRITINGS:

PUBLISHED BY DOUBLEDAY

Africa A to Z: A Guide for Travelers—Armchair and Actual, 1961, 2nd edition, 1972.
South America A to Z, 1962, revised edition, 1971.
Asia A to Z, 1963.
Canada A to Z, 1964, revised edition, 1976.
South Pacific A to Z, 1966.
Eastern Europe A to Z, 1968.
(Contributor) *Around the World with the Experts,* 1969.
Grand Tour A to Z: The Capitals of Europe, 1972.
London A to Z, 1974.
Paris A to Z, 1974.
Hawaii A to Z, 1975, revised edition, 1981.
Italy A to Z: A Grand Tour of the Classic Cities, 1977.

PUBLISHED BY RAND McNALLY

Germany A to Z Guide, 1980.
Spain A to Z Guide, 1980.
Great Britain A to Z Guide, 1982.

"WORLD AT ITS BEST" SERIES; PUBLISHED BY PASSPORT BOOKS

Germany at Its Best, 1985.
Italy . . . , 1985.
Spain . . . , 1985.
Hawaii . . . , 1985.
Britain . . . , 1986.
France . . . , 1986.
London . . . , 1987.
Paris . . . , 1987.
Switzerland . . . , 1987.
Holland . . . , 1987.

OTHER

Contributor to periodicals, including *Atlantic, Saturday Review, Newsweek, Family Circle, New York Times, Globe and Mail* (Toronto), and *Los Angeles Times.*

SIDELIGHTS: Robert S. Kane has visited well over one hundred countries on six continents and frequently discusses the travel scene on television and radio talk shows.

BIOGRAPHICAL/CRITICAL SOURCES:

New York Times Book Review, June 1, 1986.

*   *   *

KEARNS, Doris Helen
   See GOODWIN, Doris (Helen) Kearns

*   *   *

KELLEY, True (Adelaide)   1946-

PERSONAL: Born February 25, 1946, in Cambridge, Mass.; daughter of Mark E. (an illustrator) and Adelaide (an artist; maiden name, True) Kelley; married Steven Lindblom (a writer and illustrator); children: Jada Winter Lindblom. *Education:* University of New Hampshire, B.A., 1968; attended Rhode Island School of Design, 1968-71.

ADDRESSES: Home and office—Old Denny Hill, Warner, N.H. 03278.

CAREER: Free-lance illustrator, 1971—; writer, 1978—.

MEMBER: Audubon Society, Warner Raconteur's Association, Warner Women's Softball.

AWARDS, HONORS: "Children's Choice," International Reading Association, 1982, for *A Valentine for Fuzzboom;* "Outstanding Science and Trade Book for Children," National Science Teachers Association, 1987, for *What the Moon Is Like.*

WRITINGS:

JUVENILES; SELF-ILLUSTRATED

(With husband, Steven Lindblom) *The Mouses' Terrible Christmas,* Lothrop, 1978.
(With Lindblom) *The Mouses' Terrible Halloween,* Lothrop, 1980.
A Valentine for Fuzzboom, Houghton, 1981.
Buggly Bear's Hiccup Cure, Parents' Magazine Press, 1982.
(With Lindblom) *Let's Give Kitty a Bath,* Addison-Wesley, 1982.
The Mystery of the Stranger in the Barn, Dodd, 1986.
Look, Baby! Listen, Baby! Do, Baby!, Dutton, 1987.

JUVENILES; ILLUSTRATOR

Ann Cole, Carolyn Haas, Faith Bushnell, and Betty Weinberger, *I Saw a Purple Cow,* Little, Brown, 1972.
Franklyn Branley, *Sun Dogs and Shooting Stars: A Skywatcher's Calendar,* Houghton, 1980.
Michael Pellowski, *Clara Joins the Circus,* Parents Magazine Press, 1981.
Cole, Haas, and Weinberger, *Purple Cow to the Rescue,* Little, Brown, 1982.
Branley, *Water for the World,* Crowell, 1982.
Gilda Berger and Melven Berger, *The Whole World of Hands,* Houghton, 1982.
Joanne Oppenheim, *James Will Never Die* (Junior Literary Guild selection), Dodd, 1982.
Branley, *Shivers and Goose Bumps: How We Keep Warm,* Crowell, 1984.
Joyce S. Mitchell, *My Mommy Makes Money,* Little, Brown, 1984.
Joanna Cole, *Cuts, Breaks, Bruises, and Burns: How Your Body Heals,* Harper, 1985.
Eric Arnold and Jeff Loeb, *Lights Out!: Kids Talk about Summer Camp,* Little, Brown, 1986.
Branley, *What the Moon Is Like,* Crowell, 1987.
Patricia Lauber, *Get Ready for Robots,* Crowell, 1987.
Riki Levinson, *Touch! Touch!,* Dutton, 1987.
Branley, *It's Raining Cats and Dogs,* Houghton, 1987.

Also illustrator of numerous textbooks.

*   *   *

KENNEDY, Michael   1926-

PERSONAL: Born February 19, 1926, in Manchester, England; son of Hew Gilbert and Marion Florence (Sinclair) Kennedy; married Eslyn May Durdle, May 16, 1947. *Education:* Attended Berkhamsted School, 1939-41. *Politics:* Conservative. *Religion:* Church of England.

ADDRESSES: Home—3 Moorwood Dr., Sale, Cheshire, England.

CAREER: Daily Telegraph, London, England, member of editorial staff, Manchester office, 1941—, staff music critic, 1951—, northern editor, 1960-86, associate northern editor, 1986—. Royal Manchester College of Music, member of council, honorary member, 1971; Royal Northern College of Music, member of council, 1972—, fellow, 1981. *Military service:* Royal Navy, 1943-46.

MEMBER: Institute of Journalists (fellow), Lancashire County Cricket Club.

AWARDS, HONORS: Order of the British Empire, 1981.

WRITINGS:

The Halle Tradition: A Century of Music, Manchester University Press, 1960.
The Works of Ralph Vaughan Williams, Oxford University Press, 1964.
Portrait of Elgar, Oxford University Press, 1968.
Portrait of Manchester, R. Hale, 1970.
Elgar Orchestral Works, BBC Publications, 1970.
History of Royal Manchester College of Music, Manchester University Press, 1971.
Barbirolli: Conductor Laureate, MacGibbon & Kee, 1971.
(Editor) *Autobiography of Charles Halle,* Elek, 1973.
Mahler, Dent, 1974.

Richard Strauss, Dent, 1976.

(Editor) *Concise Oxford Dictionary of Music*, Oxford University Press, 1980.

Britten, Dent, 1981.

The Halle: 1858-1983, Manchester University Press, 1983.

Strauss Tone Poems, BBC Publications, 1984.

(Editor) *The Oxford Dictionary of Music*, Oxford University Press, 1985.

Adrian Boult, Hamish Hamilton, 1987.

Contributor to *Musical Times*, *Listener*, and *Halle Magazine*.

*   *   *

KENNY, Anthony
See KENNY, Anthony John Patrick

*   *   *

KENNY, Anthony John Patrick   1931-
(Anthony Kenny)

PERSONAL: Born March 16, 1931, in Liverpool, England; son of John and Margaret (Jones) Kenny; married Nancy Caroline Gayley, 1966; children: two sons. *Education:* Attended Gregorian University and St. Benet's Hall, Oxford.

ADDRESSES: Office—Balliol College, Oxford University, Oxford OX1 3BJ, England.

CAREER: Ordained Roman Catholic priest, 1955; curate of Roman Catholic church in Liverpool, England, 1959-63; returned to lay state, 1963; Oxford University, Oxford, England, lecturer at Exeter College and Trinity College, 1963-64, tutor at Balliol College, 1964, fellow, 1964-78, Wilde Lecturer in Natural and Comparative Religion, 1969-72, senior tutor at Balliol College, 1971-72 and 1976-77, master, 1978—. Pro-Vice-Chancellor of Oxford University, 1985—. Assistant lecturer at University of Liverpool, 1961-63; Joint Gifford Lecturer at University of Edinburgh, 1972-73; visiting professor at Stanford University, Rockefeller University, University of Chicago, University of Washington, University of Michigan, and Cornell University.

MEMBER: British Academy (vice-president).

WRITINGS:

Action, Emotion, and Will, Routledge & Kegan Paul, 1963.

(Translator; also author of notes and introduction) St. Thomas Aquinas, *Summa Theologiae*, Volume XXII: *Dispositions for Human Acts* (in Latin and English), edited by Thomas Gilby and others, McGraw, 1964.

Descartes: A Study of His Philosophy, Random House, 1968, Garland Publishing, 1987.

The Five Ways: Saint Thomas Aquinas' Proofs of God's Existence, Routledge & Kegan Paul, 1969.

Wittgenstein, Allen Lane, 1973.

The Nature of the Mind, Edinburgh University Press, 1973.

The Anatomy of the Soul: Historical Essays in the Philosophy of Mind, Basil Blackwell, 1974.

The Development of Mind, Edinburgh University Press, 1974.

Will, Freedom, and Power, Basil Blackwell, 1976.

The Aristotelian Ethics: A Study of the Relationship Between the "Eudemian Ethics" and "Nichomachean Ethics" of Aristotle, Clarendon Press, 1979.

The God of the Philosophers, Clarendon Press, 1979.

Aristotle's Theory of the Will, Duckworth, 1979.

Freewill and Responsibility, Routledge & Kegan Paul, 1979.

Aquinas, Oxford University Press, 1980.

The Computation of Style: An Introduction to Statistics for Students of Literature and Humanities, Pergamon Press, 1982.

Faith and Reason, Columbia University Press, 1983.

Thomas More, Oxford University Press, 1983.

The Legacy of Wittgenstein, Oxford University Press, 1984.

Wyclif, Oxford University Press, 1985.

(Translator) John Wyclif, *Tractatus de Universalibus*, Oxford University Press, 1985.

The Ivory Tower: Essays in Philosophy and Public Policy, Basil Blackwell, 1985.

The Logic of Deterrence, University of Chicago Press, 1985.

A Path from Rome: An Autobiography, Sidgwick & Jackson, 1985, Oxford University Press, 1986.

The Road to Hillsborough: The Shaping of the Anglo-Irish Agreement, Pergamon Press, 1986.

A Stylometric Study of the New Testament, Oxford University Press, 1986.

Reason and Religion: Essays in Philosophical Theology, Basil Blackwell, 1987.

EDITOR

The Responsa Scholarum of the English College, Rome, two volumes, Publications of the Catholic Record Society, 1962-63.

(Also contributor) *Aquinas: A Collection of Critical Essays*, Anchor Books, 1969.

(Also translator) Rene Descartes, *Philosophical Letters*, Clarendon Press, 1971.

Arthur Norman Prior, *Objects of Thought*, Clarendon Press, 1971.

Ludwig Wittgenstein, *Philosophical Grammar*, Basil Blackwell, 1974.

Prior, *The Doctrine of Propositions and Terms*, Duckworth, 1976.

Prior, *Papers in Logic and Ethics*, Duckworth, 1976.

(Also author of introduction) *Rationalism, Empiricism, and Idealism*, Oxford University Press, 1986.

Wyclif in His Times, Clarendon Press, 1986.

OTHER

Editor of *Oxford*, 1972-73.

SIDELIGHTS: A former Catholic priest and the current master of Balliol College at Oxford University, Anthony John Patrick Kenny writes on a variety of philosophical topics, from discussions of current political and public policy issues to assessments of various philosophical thinkers of the past. *Wyclif*, a study of the fourteenth-century English religious reformer and former master of Balliol whose radical doctrines on the Christian Church inspired numerous heresies, "has helped to bring greater justice to one of [Kenny's]... most influential and, later, turbulent predecessors," writes Gordon Leff in the *Times Literary Supplement*, "as well as to redirect attention to too-long neglected matters." Regarding *The Legacy of Wittgenstein*, an evaulation of the controversial twentieth-century master of linguistic analysis, Gordon Baker in the *Times Literary Supplement* notes that Kenny "develops a persuasive case for viewing Wittgenstein as the most important philosopher of the twentieth century [and]... shows that Wittgenstein's ideas have the power to flatten some of the houses of cards that clutter up the landscape in linguistics, psychology and neurophysiology."

Most recently Kenny has written on public policy issues, such as nuclear deterrence in both *The Logic of Deterrence* and *The Ivory Tower: Essays in Philosophy and Public Policy*. In doing so, he has integrated aspects of his religious training while maintaining a distinct intellectual independence, according to some reviewers. John Keegan notes in the *Times Literary Supplement* that *The Logic of Deterrence* "concerns, in the best tradition of Catholic moral philosophy, an acutely immediate issue, [and] is deeply informed by traditional Catholic thinking, but juxtaposes Christian and humanist values in a way that exactly reflects [Kenny's] . . . own intellectual evolution." Kenny's 1985 autobiography, *A Path from Rome*, chronicles this evolution, explaining how he "migrated from the life of a Catholic parish priest to that of an Oxford philosophy don, shedding his religious beliefs in the process while retaining the moral preoccupations that had originally drawn him into the priestly life," adds Keegan. "This he does with transparent frankness and humility," remarks A. N. Wilson in the *Times Literary Supplement*, ". . . [without] the slightest whiff of intellectual superiority in his descriptions of his former teachers and colleagues at the various seminaries he attended."

Kenny is also the author of *The Computation of Style: An Introduction to Statistics for Students of Literature and Humanities*, which covers the field of stylometry, or using statistics to make judgments on literary style. A. Q. Morton notes in the *Times Literary Supplement* that Kenny's introductory book "is the best . . . available on this subject at this level."

BIOGRAPHICAL/CRITICAL SOURCES:

PERIODICALS

Times Literary Supplement, January 25, 1980, May 9, 1980, November 26, 1982, June 14, 1985, July 5, 1985, August 9, 1985, November 15, 1985, February 7, 1986.

*   *   *

KENSINGER, George
    See FICHTER, George S.

*   *   *

KERRY, Lois
    See DUNCAN, Lois

*   *   *

KETCHUM, Robert Glenn   1947-

PERSONAL: Born December 1, 1947, in Los Angeles, Calif.; son of Jack Burson (in business) and Virginia (Moorhead) Ketchum. *Education:* University of California, Los Angeles, B.A. (cum laude), 1970; attended Brooks Institute, 1971; California Institute of the Arts, M.F.A., 1974.

ADDRESSES: Home—696 Stone Canyon Rd., Los Angeles, Calif. 90077. *Office*—National Park Foundation, P.O. Box 57473, Washington, D.C. 20037.

CAREER: Sun Valley Center for the Arts and Humanities, Sun Valley, Idaho, teacher, 1971-73; Los Angeles Center for Photographic Studies, Los Angeles, Calif., member of board of directors, 1975-81, president, 1979; National Park Foundation, Washington, D.C., curator, 1980—. Consultant to Appalachian Environmental Arts Center.

MEMBER: Friends of Photography, Greenpeace, Expedition Research, Phi Delta Theta.

AWARDS, HONORS: Grants from National Park Foundation, 1978, 1979, and Ciba-Geigy Corp., 1979; architecture, planning and design grant, New York State Council on the Arts, 1985.

WRITINGS:

(With Robert Cahn) *American Photographers and the National Parks*, Viking, 1981.
The Hudson River and the Highlands, Aperture, 1985.
(With Carey D. Ketchum) *The Tongass: Alaska's Vanishing Rain Forest*, Aperture, 1987.

Contributor of articles and photographs to more than two hundred magazines and newspapers.

SIDELIGHTS: Robert Glenn Ketchum wrote: "I am actually a working artist who has had the good fortune to get ideas well published. As an artist I am widely published and exhibited. My books arise from my mutual interest in photography and the environment. I travel extensively, both nationally and internationally, and my work is represented by fine galleries around the country. All of my work is directed toward the environment and I am very involved with the politics of the environment. I am also a skilled backpacker and winter mountaineer and have traveled on foot and skis through most of the mountains of North America."

BIOGRAPHICAL/CRITICAL SOURCES:

PERIODICALS

Los Angeles Times Book Review, November 24, 1985.
Popular Photography, March, 1980.
Sun Valley, winter, 1979.
Westways, November 11, 1981.

*   *   *

KISMARIC, Carole   1942-

PERSONAL: Born April 28, 1942, in Orange, N.J.; daughter of John Joseph and Alice (Gruskos) Kismaric; married Charles Mikolaycak (a book illustrator and designer), October 1, 1970. *Education:* Pennsylvania State University, B.F.A., 1964.

ADDRESSES: Home—64 East 91st St., New York, N.Y. 10128.

CAREER: Time-Life, Inc., New York, N.Y., picture editor, 1969-73, associate editor, 1973-75; Photo-200 (photo project to document United States bicentennial), assistant director, 1975-76; *Aperture*, Millerton, N.Y., managing editor, 1976-80, editorial director, 1980-86; Institute for Art and Urban Resources, Inc., Long Island, N.Y., director of publications, 1985—.

WRITINGS:

(Editor) Fred Freeman, *Duel of the Ironclads* (juvenile), Time-Life, 1968.
(Adapter with husband, Charles Mikolaycak, from Norwegian folktale) *The Boy Who Tried to Cheat Death* (juvenile), Doubleday, 1971.
On Leadership, edited and designed by Mikolaycak, I.B.M., 1974.
(Editor with Norman Snyder) *The Photography Catalogue*, Harper, 1976.
(Author of introduction) *Exposure: Ten Photographers' Work* (Creative Artists Public Service Exposure Project), Creative Artists Public Service, 1976.

(Author of introduction) George Krause, *Saints and Martyrs,* Photopia Gallery, 1976.

(Author of introduction) Andre Kertesz, *Andre Kertesz,* Aperture, 1977.

(Editor) Ray Metzker, *Sand Creatures,* Aperture, 1979.

(Editor) Phillip Lopate, *Lisette Model,* Aperture, 1979.

(Editor) *Eugene Atget,* Aperture, 1980.

(Editor) *Man Ray,* Aperture, 1980.

Forced Out: Refugees on the Move, Fund for Free Expression, 1988.

(Adapter) *The Rumor of Pavel and Paali* (juvenile), illustrated by Mikolaycak, Harper, 1988.

(Adapter) *A Gift from Saint Nicholas* (juvenile), illustrated by Mikolaycak, Holiday House, 1988.

(With Marvin Heiferman) *The Picture Library of Everyday Life* (juvenile), Random, 1988.

Also author, with Heiferman, of *Talking Pictures,* 1988. Picture editor, "Time-Life Photography" series, "Time-Life Old West" series, and "Human Behavior" series. Contributor to *Camera* and *du Magazine* (Switzerland).

* * *

KITCHEN, Helen (Angell)

PERSONAL: Born in Fossil, Ore.; daughter of Lloyd Steiwer and Hilda (Miller) Angell; married Jeffrey C. Kitchen, August 12, 1944 (divorced, 1985); children: Jeffrey Coleman, Jr., Erik, Lynn. *Education:* University of Oregon, B.A. (honors), 1942.

ADDRESSES: Home—4309 Embassy Park Dr. N.W., Washington, D.C. 20016. *Office*—Director of African Studies, Center for Strategic and International Studies, Suite 400, 1800 K St. N.W., Washington, D.C. 20006.

CAREER: Reader's Digest, Pleasantville, N.Y., member of editorial staff, 1942-44; political researcher in Cairo, Egypt, 1944-47; *Middle East Journal,* Washington, D.C., assistant editor, 1948; U.S. Department of State, Washington, D.C., special assistant to director of research for Africa, Middle East, and South Asia, 1951-58; *Africa Report,* Washington, D.C., editor-in-chief, 1960-68; director, Africa Area Study, Commission on Critical Choices for Americans, 1974-76; executive director, United States-South Africa Leader Exchange Program, 1978-81; Center for Strategic and International Studies, Washington, D.C., director of African studies, 1981—. Member of board of public advisers, U.S. Department of State, African Bureau, 1963-70; member of Ford Foundation Study Group on South Africa, 1984—; member of board of African Development Foundation 1985—; consultant to Secretary of State's Advisory Committee on South Africa, 1986-87. Consultant to RAND Corp., 1962-68.

MEMBER: Council on Foreign Relations, African Studies Association of United States (trustee, 1964-67), Phi Beta Kappa.

AWARDS, HONORS: Outstanding service award, U.S. Secretary of State, 1957.

WRITINGS:

The Press in Africa, Ruth Sloan Associates, 1956.

Africa: Images and Realities, UNESCO, 1962.

(Editor) *The Educated Africa: A Country-by-Country Survey of Educational Development in Africa,* Praeger, 1962.

(Editor) *A Handbook of African Affairs,* Praeger, 1964.

(Editor) *Footnotes to the Congo Story: An Africa Report Anthology,* Walker & Co., 1967.

Africa: From Mystery to Maze, Lexington Books, 1976.

Where Is South Africa Headed?, Seven Springs Center, 1978.

(Editor) *Options for U.S. Policy toward Africa,* American Enterprise Institute for Public Policy Research, 1979.

U.S. Interests in Africa, Praeger/Center for Strategic and International Studies, 1983.

The United States and South Africa: Realities and Red Herrings, Center for Strategic and International Studies, 1984.

Southern Africa: A Handbook of Political and Economic Analyses, Praeger, 1987.

Contributor to magazines and journals. Editor of fortnightly news analysis, *African Index,* 1978-82; editor of briefing paper series for *CSIS Africa Notes,* 1982—.

* * *

KNIGHT, Etheridge 1931-

PERSONAL: Born April 19, 1931, in Corinth, Miss.; son of Bushie and Belzora (Cozart) Knight; married Sonia Sanchez (divorced); married Mary Ann McAnally, June 11, 1973 (divorced); married Charlene Blackburn; children: (second marriage) Mary Tandiwe, Etheridge Bambata; (third marriage) Isaac Bushie. *Education:* Attended high school for two years; self-educated at "various prisons, jails." *Politics:* "Freedom." *Religion:* "Freedom."

ADDRESSES: Home—2126 North Dexter St., Indianapolis, Ind. 46202.

CAREER: Poet. Writer-in-residence, University of Pittsburgh, Pittsburgh, Pa., 1968-69, and University of Hartford, Hartford, Conn., 1969-70; Lincoln University, Jefferson City, Mo., poet-in-residence, 1972. Inmate at Indiana State Prison, Michigan City, 1960-68. *Military service:* U.S. Army, 1947-51.

AWARDS, HONORS: National Endowment for the Arts grants, 1972 and 1980; National Book Award and Pulitzer Prize nominations, both 1973, for *Belly Song and Other Poems;* Self-Development through the Arts grant, for local workshops, 1974; Guggenheim fellowship, 1974.

WRITINGS:

(Contributor) *For Malcolm,* Broadside Press, 1967.

Poems from Prison, preface by Gwendolyn Brooks, Broadside Press, 1968.

(With others) *Voce Negre dal Carcere* (anthology), [Laterza, Italy], 1968, original English edition published as *Black Voices from Prison,* introduction by Roberto Giammanco, Pathfinder Press, 1970.

A Poem for Brother/Man (after His Recovery from an O.D.), Broadside Press, 1972.

Belly Song and Other Poems, Broadside Press, 1973.

Born of a Woman: New and Selected Poems, Houghton, 1980.

The Essential Etheridge Knight, University of Pittsburgh Press, 1986.

Work represented in many anthologies, including *Norton Anthology of American Poets, Black Poets, A Broadside Treasury, Broadside Poet, Dices and Black Bones,* and *A Comprehensive Anthology of Black Poets.* Contributor of poems and articles to many magazines and journals, including *Black Digest, Essence, Motive, American Report,* and *American Poetry.* Poetry editor, *Motive,* 1969-71; contributing editor, *New Letters,* 1974.

WORK IN PROGRESS: A historical novel on the life of Dermark Vesey.

SIDELIGHTS: Etheridge Knight began writing poetry while an inmate at the Indiana State Prison and published his first collection, *Poems from Prison,* in 1968. "His work was hailed by black writers and critics as another excellent example of the powerful truth of blackness in art," writes Shirley Lumpkin in the *Dictionary of Literary Biography.* "His work became important in Afro-American poetry and poetics and in the strain of Anglo-American poetry descended from Walt Whitman." Since then, Knight has attained recognition as a major poet, earning both Pulitzer Prize and National Book Award nominations for *Belly Song and Other Poems,* as well as the acclaim of such fellow practitioners as Gwendolyn Brooks, Robert Bly, and Galway Kinnell.

When Knight entered prison, he was already an accomplished reciter of "toasts"—long, memorized, narrative poems, often in rhymed couplets, in which "sexual exploits, drug activities, and violent aggressive conflicts involving a cast of familiar folk . . . are related . . . using street slang, drug and other specialized argot, and often obscenities," explains Lumpkin. Toast-reciting at Indiana State Prison not only refined Knight's expertise in this traditional Afro-American art form but also, according to Lumpkin, gave him a sense of identity and an understanding of the possibilities of poetry. "Since toast-telling brought him into genuine communion with others, he felt that poetry could simultaneously show him who he was and connect him with other people." In an article for the *Detroit Free Press* about Dudley Randall, the founder of Broadside Press, Suzanne Dolezal indicates that Randall was impressed with Knight and visited him frequently at the prison: "In a small room reserved for consultations with death row inmates, with iron doors slamming and prisoners shouting in the background, Randall convinced a hesitant Knight of his talent." And says Dolezal, Randall feels that because Knight was from the streets, "He may be a deeper poet than many of the others because he has felt more anguish."

Much of Knight's prison poetry, according to Patricia Liggins Hill in *Black American Literature Forum,* focuses on imprisonment as a form of contemporary enslavement and looks for ways in which one can be free despite incarceration. Time and space are significant in the concept of imprisonment, and Hill indicates that "specifically, what Knight relies on for his prison poetry are various temporal/spatial elements which allow him to merge his personal consciousness with the consciousness of Black people." Hill believes that this merging of consciousness "sets him apart from the other new Black poets . . . [who] see themselves as poets/priests. . . . Knight sees himself as being one with Black people." Randall observes in *Broadside Memories: Poets I Have Known* that "Knight does not objure rime like many contemporary poets. He says the average Black man in the streets defines poetry as something that rimes, and Knight appeals to the folk by riming." Randall notes that while Knight's poetry is "influenced by the folk," it is also "prized by other poets."

Knight's *Born of a Woman: New and Selected Poems* includes work from *Poems from Prison, Black Voices from Prison,* and *Belly Song and Other Poems.* Although David Pinckney states in *Parnassus: Poetry in Review* that the "new poems do not indicate much artistic growth," a *Virginia Quarterly Review* contributor writes that Knight "has distinguished his voice and craftsmanship among contemporary poets, and he deserves a large, serious audience for his work." Moreover, H. Bruce Franklin suggests in the *Village Voice* that with *Born of a Woman,* "Knight has finally attained recognition as a major poet." Further, Franklin credits Knight's leadership "in de-

veloping a powerful literary mode based on the rhythms of black street talk, blues, ballads, and 'toasts.' "

Reviewing *Born of a Woman* for *Black American Literature Forum,* Hill describes Knight as a "masterful blues singer, a singer whose life has been 'full of trouble' and thus whose songs resound a variety of blues moods, feelings, and experiences and later take on the specific form of a blues musical composition." Lumpkin suggests that an "awareness of the significance of form governed Knight's arrangement of the poems in the volume as well as his revisions. . . . He put them in clusters or groupings under titles which are musical variations on the book's essential theme—life inside and outside prison." Calling this structure a "jazz composition mode," Lumpkin also notes that it was once used by Langston Hughes in an arrangement of his poetry. Craig Werner observes in *Obsidian: Black Literature in Review:* "Technically, Knight merges musical rhythms with traditional metrical devices, reflecting the assertion of an Afro-American cultural identity within a Euro-American context. Thematically, he denies that the figures of the singer . . . and the warrior . . . are or can be separate." Lumpkin finds that "despite the pain and evil described and attacked, a celebration and an affirmation of life run through the volume." And in the *Los Angeles Times Book Review,* Peter Clothier considers the poems to be "tools for self-discovery and discovery of the world—a loud announcement of the truths they pry loose."

Lumpkin points out that "some critics find Knight's use of . . . [language] objectionable and unpoetic and think he does not use verse forms well," and some believe that he "maintains an outmoded, strident black power rhetoric from the 1960s." However, Lumpkin concludes: "Those with reservations and those who admire his work all agree . . . upon his vital language and the range of his subject matter. They all agree that he brings a needed freshness to poetry, particularly in his extraordinary ability to move an audience. . . . A number of poets, Gwendolyn Brooks, Robert Bly, and Galway Kinnell among them . . . consider him a major Afro-American poet because of his human subject matter, his combination of traditional techniques wth an expertise in using rhythmic and oral speech patterns, and his ability to feel and to project his feelings into a poetic structure that moves others."

Knight told *CA* he believes a definition of art and aesthetics assumes that "every man is the master of his own destiny and comes to grips with the society by his own efforts. The 'true' artist is supposed to examine his own experience of this process as a reflection of his self, his ego." Knight feels "white society denies art, because art unifies rather than separates; it brings people together instead of alienating them." The western/European aesthetic dictates that "the artist speak only of the beautiful (himself and what *he* sees); his task is to edify the listener, to make him see *beauty* of the world." Black artists must stay away from this because "the red of this aesthetic rose got its color from the blood of black slaves, exterminated Indians, napalmed Vietnamese children." According to Knight, the black artist must "perceive and conceptualize the collective aspirations, the collective vision of black people, and through his art form give back to the people the truth that he has gotten from them. He must sing to them of their own deeds, and misdeeds."

BIOGRAPHICAL/CRITICAL SOURCES:

BOOKS

Contemporary Literary Criticism, Volume XL, Gale, 1986.

Dictionary of Literary Biography, Volume XLI: *Afro-American Poets since 1955*, Gale, 1985.
Knight, Etheridge, *Poems from Prison*, Broadside Press, 1968.
Randall, Dudley, *Broadside Memories: Poets I Have Known*, Broadside Press, 1975.

PERIODICALS

Black American Literature Forum, fall, 1980, summer, 1981.
Black World, September, 1970, September, 1974.
Detroit Free Press, April 11, 1982.
Hollins Critic, December, 1981.
Los Angeles Times Book Review, August 10, 1980.
Negro Digest, January, 1968, July, 1968.
Obsidian: Black Literature in Review, summer and winter, 1981.
Parnassus: Poetry in Review, spring-summer, 1981.
Village Voice, July 27, 1982.
Virginia Quarterly Review, winter, 1981.

—*Sketch by Sharon Malinowski*

*   *   *

KOVEL, Ralph

PERSONAL: Surname is pronounced Cove-*el;* born in Milwaukee, Wis.; son of Lester (a clothing manufacturer) and Dorothy (Bernstein) Kovel; married Terry Horvitz (a writer), June 27, 1950; children: Lee Ralph, Kim (daughter). *Education:* Attended Ohio State University, 1939.

ADDRESSES: Home—22000 Shaker Blvd., Shaker Heights, Ohio 44122.

CAREER: Writer on antiques, in collaboration with wife, 1952—; Ralph M. Kovel & Associates (food brokers), Cleveland, Ohio, president, beginning 1958; Sar-a-Lee (salad dressing manufacturer), Cleveland, president, 1974—. Short course instructor in American decorative arts, Cleveland College, Western Reserve University (now Case Western Reserve University), 1958-63. Co-host and producer, with wife, of syndicated commercial television spots, "Kovels on Collecting," 1981; co-host, with wife, of thirteen half-hour shows, "Kovels on Collecting," broadcast by Public Broadcast Service (PBS-TV), 1987. President, East End Neighborhood House, Cleveland, 1962-63.

MEMBER: Union League Club of Chicago, Oakwood Club, Whitehall Club.

AWARDS, HONORS: Cleveland Area Television Academy Award, 1971; National Antiques Show Annual Award, 1974; Louis S. Peirce Award for outstanding community service.

WRITINGS:

WITH WIFE, TERRY KOVEL; PUBLISHED BY CROWN

Dictionary of Marks: Pottery and Porcelain, 1953.
Directory of American Silver, Pewter and Silver Plate, 1961.
American Country Furniture, 1965.
Kovels' Know Your Antiques (Book-of-the-Month Club selection), 1967, 3rd edition, 1981.
The Kovels' Collector's Guide to Limited Editions, 1974.
The Kovels' Collector's Guide to American Art Pottery, 1974.
Kovels' Price Guide for Collector Plates, Figurines, Paperweights and Other Limited Editions, 1978.
Kovels' Organizer for Collectors, 1978, revised edition, 1983.
Kovels' Illustrated Price Guide to Royal Doulton, 1980, 2nd edition, 1984.

Kovels' Illustrated Price Guide to Depression Glass and American Dinnerware, 1980, 2nd revised edition, 1983.
Kovels' Know Your Collectibles (Book-of-the-Month Club selection), 1981.
Kovels' Book of Antique Labels, 1981.
Kovels' Collectors' Source Book, 1983.
Kovels' New Dictionary of Marks: Pottery and Porcelain, 1850 to Present, 1986.
Kovels' Advertising Collectibles Price List, 1986.
Kovels' How to Sell Your Antiques, 1987.

Also author of *Kovels' Antiques Price List*, 1968-81, published as *Kovels' Antiques and Collectibles Price List*, 1982—, and of *Kovels' Bottle Price List*, published biannually since 1971.

OTHER

Also author, with T. Kovel, of monthly newsletter, "Kovels on Antiques and Collectibles," 1974—, and of monthly columns, "Know Your Antiques," in Features Syndicate, New York, 1954—, and "Your Collectibles," *House Beautiful*, 1979—. Contributor to magazines, including *Family Circle*, *Woman's Day*, *Redbook*, *House Beautiful*, and *Town and Country*.

SIDELIGHTS: In 1950 Ralph and Terry Kovel were paying monthly installments on a $15 music box, their first antique. Today, according to a *New York Times Book Review* critic, their books on antiques and collectibles are regarded "as bibles in their field" and have sold more than one million copies. "There was an explosion in antiques in the 1950s," Ralph Kovel's wife and co-author Terry Kovel said in a *Publishers Weekly* interview with Robert Dahlin. "The United States was finally old enough to have a history and to have something to look back on."

Many of the Kovels' books are price guides—compilations of current prices for antiques and collectibles. Their first book, however, was an alphabetical listing of the marks on the bottom of glassware and pottery. "Terry was in New York with her parents, so I decided to put all the A's and B's [of the pottery marks] together in straight alphabetical order," Ralph Kovel told *Smithsonian* reporter Scott Eyman. "When my wife and her father came home and I showed them my work, he looked at me in disbelief and asked, 'Is that the best way you can spend a weekend of your time?'" The book, *Dictionary of Marks: Pottery and Porcelain*, is now in its thirty-second printing.

The Kovels and their staff of twelve gather information on prices quoted for items throughout the country and feed them into a computer. "We don't write books, we report prices," Ralph Kovel said in *Publishers Weekly*. Terry Kovel agrees. In *Smithsonian* she commented: "We are reporters and researchers; we never make value judgements. A lot of what we do is like biology, devising categories and subcategories for things that have never been categorized before. As far as prices go, we just tell people what's being asked and gotten; prices obviously out of line, we don't use."

The Kovels are themselves avid antique collectors. The basement of their home has been turned into a "country store" museum, writes Eyman, and their house is "furnished in a profusion of heavy styles that should, theoretically, clash [but instead] is a perfect representation of their personalities. Its air of lived in comfort is typical of the unpretentiousness familiar to anyone who has ever seen [the Kovels] on television." Terry Kovel remarked in *Publishers Weekly:* "Any antique dishes that can't go through my dish washer, I can't live with."

The most valuable item they own is an eighteenth-century sil-ver sugar castor made by Paul Revere's father. The Kovels bought it at a house sale for $12; it is actually worth close to $10,000, Ralph Kovel said.

"If you are destined to own an antique, it will wait for you," Ralph Kovel commented in *Smithsonian*. "It's really almost mystical, the sense of union you experience when you first see the antique you've been looking and waiting for. That satisfaction is very, very special. It's what makes all the hard work—the tramping through the woods and dirty shops—more than worthwhile. It's all part of the search for something forgotten and wonderful."

BIOGRAPHICAL/CRITICAL SOURCES:

PERIODICALS

New York Times Book Review, January 25, 1981.
Publishers Weekly, September 25, 1981.
Smithsonian, November, 1980.

*   *   *

KOVEL, Terry   1928-

PERSONAL: Surname is pronounced Cove-*el;* born October 27, 1928, in Cleveland, Ohio; daughter of Isadore (a publisher) and Rix (Osteryoung) Horvitz; married Ralph Kovel (a writer and businessman), June 27, 1950; children: Lee Ralph, Kim (daughter). *Education:* Wellesley College, B.A., 1950; University of Illinois, graduate study, 1961.

ADDRESSES: Home—22000 Shaker Blvd., Shaker Heights, Ohio 44122.

CAREER: Writer on antiques, in collaboration with husband, 1952—; part-time teacher in Lyndhurst, Ohio, 1959-72. Short course instructor in American decorative arts, Cleveland College, Western Reserve University (now Case Western Reserve University), 1958-63. Co-host and producer, with husband, of syndicated commercial television spots, "Kovels on Collecting," 1981; co-host, with husband, of thirteen half-hour shows, "Kovels on Collecting," broadcast by Public Broadcast Service (PBS-TV), 1987.

MEMBER: Ohio Newspaper Women's Association.

WRITINGS:

WITH HUSBAND, RALPH KOVEL; PUBLISHED BY CROWN

Dictionary of Marks: Pottery and Porcelain, 1953.
Directory of American Silver, Pewter and Silver Plate, 1961.
American Country Furniture, 1965.
Kovels' Know Your Antiques (Book-of-the-Month Club selection), 1967, 3rd edition, 1981.
The Kovels' Collector's Guide to Limited Editions, 1974.
The Kovels' Collector's Guide to American Art Pottery, 1974.
Kovels' Price Guide for Collector Plates, Figurines, Paperweights and Other Limited Editions, 1978.
Kovels' Organizer for Collectors, 1978, revised edition, 1983.
Kovels' Illustrated Price Guide to Royal Doulton, 1980, 2nd edition, 1984.
Kovels' Illustrated Price Guide to Depression Glass and American Dinnerware, 1980, 2nd revised edition, 1983.
Kovels' Know Your Collectibles (Book-of-the-Month Club selection), 1981.
Kovels' Book of Antique Labels, 1981.
Kovels' Collectors' Source Book, 1983.

Kovels' New Dictionary of Marks: Pottery and Porcelain, 1850 to Present, 1986.
Kovels' Advertising Collectibles Price List, 1986.
Kovels' How to Sell Your Antiques, 1987.

Also author of *Kovels' Antiques Price List*, 1968-81, published as *Kovels' Antiques and Collectibles Price List*, 1982—, and of *Kovels' Bottle Price List*, published biannually since 1971.

OTHER

Also author, with R. Kovel, of monthly newsletter, "Kovels on Antiques and Collectibles," 1974—, and of monthly columns, "Know Your Antiques," King Features Syndicate, New York, 1954—, and "Your Collectibles," *House Beautiful*, 1979—. Contributor to magazines, including *Family Circle, Woman's Day, Redbook, House Beautiful*, and *Town and Country*.

SIDELIGHTS: See *CA* entry for Ralph Kovel, in this volume.

*   *   *

KREMENTZ, Jill   1940-

PERSONAL: Born February 19, 1940, in New York, N.Y.; daughter of Walter and Virginia (Hyde) Krementz; married Kurt Vonnegut, Jr., November, 1979; children: Lily. *Education:* Attended Drew University, 1958-59, Columbia University, and Art Students League.

ADDRESSES: Home—228 East 48th St., New York, N.Y. 10017.

CAREER: Free-lance photographer and writer. *Harper's Bazaar*, New York City, secretary, 1959-60; *Glamour*, New York City, assistant to the features editor, 1960-61; Indian Industries Fair, New Delhi, India, public relations representative, 1961; *Show*, New York City, reporter and columnist, 1962-64; *New York Herald Tribune*, New York City, staff photographer (first woman to hold this position with a New York City newspaper since World War II), 1964-65; free-lance photographer in Vietnam, 1965-66; *Status and Diplomat*, New York City, associate editor with status of staff photographer, 1966-67; *New York* (magazine), New York City, contributing editor, 1967-68; Time-Life, Inc., New York City, correspondent, 1969-70; *People* (magazine), Chicago, Ill., contributing photographer, 1975—. Work has been exhibited at Madison Art Center (Wisconsin), Morris Museum, University of Massachusetts, Delaware Arts Museum, Newark Museum, Central Falls Gallery in New York, and in permanent collection at Museum of Modern Art and the Library of Congress. Chosen to take the official photographs of four members of the U.S. Cabinet, 1978.

MEMBER: American Society of Magazine Photographers, P.E.N., Women's Forum.

AWARDS, HONORS: A Very Young Dancer was named to American Institute of Graphic Artists Fifty Books of the Year, *School Library Journal* Best Books of the Year List, and the *New York Times* Best Seller List of Children's Books, all 1976; Garden State Children's Book Award, 1980; *A Very Young Rider* and *A Very Young Gymnast* were named to the *School Library Journal* Best Books of the Year List, 1978; *Washington Post*/Children's Book Guild Nonfiction Award, 1984.

WRITINGS:

The Face of South Vietnam (a book of photographs, with text by Dean Brelis), Houghton, 1968.

Sweet Pea: A Black Girl Growing up in the Rural South (a book of photographs with accompanying text), foreword by Margaret Mead, Harcourt, 1969.

Words and Their Masters (a book of photographs, with text by Israel Shenker), Doubleday, 1973.

The Writers Image: Literary Portraits, David Godine, 1980.

(Editor and compiler) *Happy Birthday, Kurt Vonnegut*, Delacorte, 1982.

The Fun of Cooking, Knopf, 1985.

Benjy Goes to a Restaurant (juvenile), Crown, 1986.

Taryn Goes to the Dentist (juvenile), Crown, 1986.

A Visit to Washington, D.C., Scholastic Books, 1987.

"A VERY YOUNG" SERIES; PUBLISHED BY KNOPF

A Very Young Dancer, 1976.

. . . Rider, 1977.

. . . Gymnast, 1978.

. . . Circus Flyer, 1979.

. . . Skater, 1979.

"HOW IT FEELS" SERIES; PUBLISHED BY KNOPF

How It Feels When a Parent Dies, 1981.

. . . to Be Adopted, 1982.

. . . When Parents Divorce, 1984.

"GREAT BIG BOARD BOOKS" SERIES; PUBLISHED BY RANDOM HOUSE

Jack Goes to the Beach, 1986.

Jamie Goes on an Airplane, 1986.

Katherine Goes to Nursery School, 1986.

Lily Goes to the Playground, 1986.

"TOUGH ENOUGH BOOKS" SERIES; PUBLISHED BY RANDOM HOUSE

Holly's Farm Animals, 1986.

Zachary Goes to the Zoo, 1986.

OTHER

Contributor to national and international magazines and newspapers, including *Vogue, Newsweek, Esquire, Holiday, Time, Life*, and *New York Times Book Review*.

SIDELIGHTS: Jill Krementz is generally considered to be one of the most talented and gifted women photojournalists of the day. Whether it be in her portraits of literary figures, her profiles of young people as they pursue such dreams as dancing, gymnastics, circus performing, and skating, or her sensitive exploration into children's emotions when they experience such tragedies as a death or divorce, Krementz captures in text and pictures the true person exposing his or her innermost feelings. "Krementz's photographs are eye-catching and appealing," writes William Jaspershohn in the *Christian Science Monitor*. "She has an uncanny gift for bringing out the best in all her subjects."

While she began her photography career as a free-lance photographer, Krementz soon became the youngest full-time (and the first female) staff photographer at the *New York Herald Tribune*. After spending eighteen months covering a variety of assignments from riots in Harlem to fashion, baseball, and football, Krementz journeyed to Vietnam to chronicle the devastating effects of the war on its land and people. A year later Krementz returned and published her first book, *The Face of South Vietnam*. Lawrence Mahoney of the *Miami Herald* describes *The Face of South Vietnam* as "an understated book,

but one that eloquently conveys the tragedy and beauty of Southeast Asia."

A year after publishing *The Face of South Vietnam*, Krementz wrote *Sweet Pea: A Black Girl Growing up in the Rural South*. In preparation for this book Krementz spent the better part of a year living in Alabama with a poor black family, documenting the life of the 10-year-old daughter. Merrilee Anderson states in *School Library Journal* that "Krementz's clear black-and-white photographs portray the poverty conditions, but they also show a lively girl as she goes to an all-black school and church, works and plays at home, and mixes with friends and relatives; as in all families, there are both humorous and somber moments." And Masha Kabakow Rudman remarks in *Children's Literature: An Issues Approach* that *Sweet Pea* "graphically demonstrates the poverty level of many rural black families. It conveys the idea that this family works hard, enjoys what is enjoyable, and cares very much for each family member and each member of the community. None is self-pitying; none is defeated. . . . The family will endure."

In 1970 Krementz began photographing writers after she learned that publishers often asked authors to supply their own snapshots for the dust jackets of their books. She soon became internationally known for her literary portraits, and now her photographs appear in most of the major national magazines and newspapers, including *Newsweek, Life, Time*, the *New York Times*, and *People*. Elaine Kendall comments in the *Los Angeles Times Book Review* that "Krementz has made a speciality of photographing contemporary writers. She combines an informed sensitivity with a careful use of costume and setting to convey her subject's literary style as well as that person's physical image."

When asked why she began photographing authors, Krementz remarked to Judy Klemesrud of the *New York Times*, "I thought I'd like to carve out a little niche for myself. And I like to read. That's the most important thing." Krementz went on to explain to Mahoney in the *Miami Herald*: "A lot of people think of me as a portrait photographer or portraitist because I photograph so many writers, but I really think of myself more as a documentary photographer because I am basically documenting the lives of all these writers. The portraits are published with reviews and articles about the writers, but my real dream is that all of these photographs will one day be part of a university's archive available to anybody who wants to know how any of these writers lived."

Krementz has also been praised for her books about young people who deal with various challenges, from demanding physical regimes to coping with emotional crises. In Krementz's *A Very Young Dancer, A Very Young Rider, A Very Young Gymnast, A Very Young Circus Flyer*, and *A Very Young Skater*, the reader is introduced to several extraordinary children who dedicated their lives to achieving excellence in their chosen field of competition. "Krementz—well-known for her photographs of writers—also has a documentary eye," writes Clive Barnes in an article on *A Very Young Dancer* published in the *New York Times Book Review*. "She catches the atmosphere of classrooms and locker rooms, of rehearsals and . . . performances. It is a world of make-believe and ritual. Of sweat and effort. Of tinsel and spotlights."

In a review of *A Very Young Gymnast* for the *Bulletin of the Center for Children's Books*, Zena Sutherland comments: "As her followers already know, Krementz is an excellent photographer, and, in following the format of the texts of *A Very Young Dancer* and *A Very Young Rider*, she has again achieved the casual intimacy of a child's conversation. . . . The quality of the book is such that many readers will feel a sense of gratification that someone they know has made it.''

In 1981 Krementz published the first book in her ''How It Feels'' series. The three books that make up this series, *How It Feels When a Parent Dies*, *How It Feels to Be Adopted*, and *How It Feels When Parents Divorce*, concentrate on how children cope with separation and loss.

Carolyn S. Lembeck writes in *Best Sellers* of *How It Feels When a Parent Dies*: ''I read Jill Krementz's *How It Feels When a Parent Dies* with a wonder of recognition, the relief of affirmation, and the serenity of acceptance. Now there is room in the world for the mourning of the young. The book is both evidence and model of our own maturity in dealing with death. . . . This book is a helping book; for the bereaved, their families, their friends, and for all who would share this moment with children.''

''It is obvious that children mourn in many of the ways that adults do, and this lovely book has relevance for readers of all ages,'' states Hilma Wolitzer of *How It Feels When a Parent Dies*. Wolitzer continues in the *New York Times Book Review* that this book ''should offer particular solace and reassurance to those young people who cannot articulate their grief and who are confused and terrified by what has befallen them.''

In her review of Krementz's second book in this series, *How It Feels to Be Adopted*, Alice Digilio remarks in the *Washington Post Book World*: ''There is strong stuff in these pages about what adoption means. Krementz, in her choice of candid and sensitive children to speak their minds on the subject, demands that her readers face important issues—especially the issue of biological parents and the possibility that they or the child might one day want to search for each other. . . . *How It Feels to Be Adopted* is a beautiful book and an honest one. In her photographs Krementz makes sure these children look real, not precious, and what they say rings with sincerity.''

Finally, Susan Hopkins writes in *Voice of Youth Advocates* of the third book in the ''How It Feels'' series, *How It Feels When Parents Divorce*: ''The interviews are candid and revealing, as they tell about the time before the divorce, for some a terrible time, and the first feelings of a changed family. . . . The interviews are enhanced by heartwarming photographs. And the stories provide honest, revealing, and sometimes comforting insights of divorce, for kids, parents and professionals too.''

CA INTERVIEW

CA interviewed Jill Krementz by telephone on January 12, 1987, at her home in New York, New York.

CA: You were known first as a photographer, and now you have a growing reputation as a writer of books for and about children. As both writer and photographer you cast a very special kind of light on your young subjects; you make them the stars. How do you go about creating the sort of trust that must be necessary for a child to talk about very personal feelings?

KREMENTZ: I think the most important aspect of my work is that I do establish trust. I do it by assuring the children on every level that this is a true collaboration between themselves and me, that they will be able to go over the finished copy and make any changes before their parents see it, and that if they change their minds—even after I've done the interview, as long as it's before we've gone to press—they have the option of staying out of the book.

CA: Are they ever shy about being photographed?

KREMENTZ: I don't think so. As long as you aren't trying to photograph your own children, you don't have a big problem. Also, after they've talked about either losing a parent or being adopted or going through a divorce, having their picture taken is the easy part.

CA: You've indicated in talking about your work that both the photography and the writing grew out of an initial journalistic impulse. Does that go back to a very early age?

KREMENTZ: No, but it certainly goes back to my first book, which was called *Sweet Pea*, in which I chronicled the life of a young black girl in the rural South. She was nine at the time. She's about twenty-two now. She and I have children roughly the same age; she has a little boy who's two, and I have a little girl who's four. I've always been curious as to what goes on in other kinds of lives than my own. Being a journalist is, in a way, a license to go backstage to see how things work. I've always been the type of person who wants to know what's going on. If I'm walking down the street and I see a lot of policemen gathered, I'm not the type who can walk on by. It's even more wonderful when all you have to do is flash a police card and they let you in and actually help you *see* what's going on.

CA: Sweet Pea *and another early book of yours,* The Face of South Vietnam, *are very hard to find now. Do you think they'll ever go into new editions?*

KREMENTZ: No, I don't, because I think we've moved into a new kind of publishing which is very bottom-line oriented. I don't think I could get either of those books published in today's market. And even if I published them myself, I don't think I could get bookstores to distribute them.

CA: That's a shame.

KREMENTZ: I think it is too. A lot of people have asked me about *Sweet Pea* in particular because they were hoping I might even do an updated version to show how Sweet Pea's life has changed.

CA: You've credited several people for helping you to become a photographer: Henry Wolf of Show *magazine for loading your first Nikon camera, Ben Price of the* New York Herald Tribune, *Ira Rosenberg at the* Tribune, *Margaret Mead for teaching you the importance of persistence. What about camera technique itself? Was that entirely self-taught?*

KREMENTZ: Yes, more or less. Certainly Ira Rosenberg taught me a lot of technique. He taught me how to pre-set my Leica camera; he taught me how to figure out my depth-of-field and how to work the range-finder on the Leica. But the most important things he taught me were more philosophical than anything else, which is what I think is the difference between making it or not making it. He taught me, as I was admiring one of my pictures on the front page of the paper, that people were already wrapping their fish in it and I'd better think about what I was going to do tomorrow.

Ben Price, who was picture editor at the *Herald Tribune,* had enough faith in me to hire me as a photographer for the paper when I was only twenty-four, and the only woman they ever hired in their history. But basically he made me feel confident that when I was covering a news event, I could go around to the back door, that the front door was always being covered by the wire services. I knew that he would never pick up tomorrow morning's *New York Times* or the *Daily News* and say, "Why didn't you get those pictures?" If those papers had that picture, we wanted something different. The wire services were there to take the ordinary picture, and I could go around to the back door, which is really just a metaphor, I think, for what I like to say when I talk to young photographers about developing their peripheral vision. I think most of my best photographs have been taken in that way. Photographers today get so intent on preconceived ideas of what they're going to photograph. If you go to one of the political conventions, you'll see three hundred photographers standing in line to get their credentials so that they can get a pass to go on the floor, where there are five hundred other photographers working. None of them has the courage to just wander around the edge of the convention floor and look for something a little different.

CA: In her introduction to The Writer's Image, *Trudy Butner Krisher quoted you as saying, "I come from a painting background. I love light and like to use a Vermeer kind of lighting." How else do you feel the art background has influenced the photography?*

KREMENTZ: I've been influenced mainly by the way the artists use light, and certainly by Vermeer, who is one of my favorite artists. I go to museums all the time. I was at the Metropolitan on Sunday looking at the new acquisitions. I would say that I have always drawn my inspiration, and continue to draw my inspiration, from painters rather than from other photographers. I've studied art all my life, really. I was an art major all through school and then went on to study at the Art Students League in New York.

CA: Is it ever hard to hit a balance between artistic considerations, which probably become subconscious at some point, and the desire to get the story, to capture the real person in a journalistic sense?

KREMENTZ: I like to think I bring both elements to bear in my photography. I think it's important. You can't really forget about either one of them. For instance, my picture of E. B. White writing in his boathouse in Maine. That satisfies me, anyway, and I would assume quite a few other people by virtue of the fact that a lot of people want to buy that photograph from me. It satisfies me aesthetically on an artistic level, and journalistically it tells more about E. B. White than any other picture I've ever seen of him.

CA: You've said elsewhere that, of the writers you've photographed, E. B. White was the most exciting prospect and Truman Capote was the most fun to photograph.

KREMENTZ: And Eudora Welty was wonderful.

CA: Yes. There's that fine picture you took of her with the armoire in the foreground.

KREMENTZ: Yes. The armoire that's written about in *The Optimist's Daughter.* I spent the night at her house in Jackson, Mississippi.

CA: Have you had subjects who were difficult in some way to photograph?

KREMENTZ: Usually my subjects aren't difficult because I'm not a paparazzi kind of photographer. It's not as though I'm lurking outside their homes ready to catch them when they walk out. When I arrive to photograph them, they've agreed to be photographed, so I think they try their best. Also, I try not to overstay my welcome. An average sitting lasts less than an hour. I think a lot of photographers don't know when to stop. And I'm happy to show them the pictures. For me it's always been a collaborative process—whether I'm photographing or interviewing.

CA: You won the 1984 Washington Post/*Children's Book Guild Nonfiction Award for your total contribution to "creatively produced books, works that make a difference." Did you gravitate rather spontaneously to working more with children, or was it a deliberate effort to do something new?*

KREMENTZ: I've always loved children, and I think I realize now—sort of retroactively, if you will—that probably it satisfied me on several levels. On one, I enjoyed the work in itself. But I think that on another level it gave me a chance to almost have children of my own, to be involved with them on a very intimate level with enduring relationships. And it was probably the only way I could combine having children in my life and continuing to work professionally and be as involved in my career as I was. Now, of course, I have my own daughter, and it's wonderful. But I don't think I could have handled it much before I did. And I think it's sad in a way. I don't think women should have to wait until they're forty-three and at the top of their profession and making enough money and being able to have totally flexible work hours in order to be a parent. And yet for women who really want to work and who are ambitious, I think it's hard to have children in your early thirties when you're scrambling just to get someplace. I see people having a hard time doing that, and having a hard time keeping their marriages together as a result. Something has to give, and they can't give up the children and don't want to give up their jobs. Some of them now *are* giving up their jobs. That's very unfortunate. I don't like to see women losing economic equity. The average woman who is going to have children and work part-time is going to make very little money. The other alternative, of course, is for them to get divorced and this, too, is unfortunate. I recently did a book called *How It Feels When Parents Divorce* and my feeling is that the kids I talked with suffered even more than those interviewed for *How It Feels When a Parent Dies.* And I think we're going to see even more divorce in the years to come. The two-parent family is already the exception. I pray it won't become obsolete.

CA: In the series of books that began with A Very Young Dancer, *you've shown children seriously engaged in pursuits that involve a lot of hard work and commitment and discipline. Do all the children featured in the series have similarities in their backgrounds that might account for their dedication to their work?*

KREMENTZ: They all had very supportive parents.

CA: Those books are beautiful, and it's tempting to think they were a delight to photograph. But there must have been a lot of hard work involved.

KREMENTZ: Well, they're a delight to look *back* on, sure. But in order to do *A Very Young Dancer* I had to photograph all the rehearsals plus twenty-two consecutive performances of the "Nutcracker." And when I was halfway through the book Stephanie, the young dancer, hurt her leg and for a while we didn't know if she'd be able to dance the role of Marie. For *A Very Young Rider* I had to get up at 4:00 A.M. to go to all the horse shows with Vivi. And as anyone will tell you, watching a horse show can be very tedious. With *A Very Young Skater* I almost froze. You're out on the ice and your hands turn blue. It's cold enough if you're skating, but it's a lot colder if you're not skating. *A Very Young Circus Flyer* was so bizarre that it was kind of fun, but aside from being "The Greatest Show on Earth," it's probably the longest! On Saturdays and Sundays I sat through *three* shows. For *A Very Young Gymnast* I went with the gym team to Germany, so I ended up being the chaperone for a dozen little ten-year-olds who were all homesick! Also the gymnastic book was very hard to do technically, because I had to photograph kids moving at the speed of bullets. So each of those books had its problems. They've all just come out in paperback, by the way.

CA: Do you maintain contact with any of the children who were in How It Feels When a Parent Dies, How It Feels to Be Adopted, *and* How It Feels When Parents Divorce?

KREMENTZ: Yes, I keep in touch with the children in *all* of my books, which would not total over a hundred kids. For example, I just saw Lulu the other night, who was in the divorce book. She's the one whose motto is "Proud to Be Weird." My daughter Lily is in love with her. I've had the longest relationship with Sweet Pea, who has visited us off and on for the past thirteen years. She's grown up to be a beautiful young woman. I have a special relationship with all the kids in *How It Feels to Be Adopted* because after I finished that book we adopted Lily, and they figured I must have a pretty high opinion of them if I'd go out and adopt my own child.

CA: Are the "How It Feels" books being used by adults who work with children? Are they used by therapists?

KREMENTZ: Yes, they are. And I find the adoption book is used by a lot of people who just plain want to adopt children and want to learn how these children are going to feel.

CA: What prompted The Fun of Cooking, *with its enchanting children pictured making such things as "Teddy Bear Bread" and "Doggie Biscuits," with the doggie helping to clean the bowl?*

KREMENTZ: That's really one of my favorites. I liked doing it because, in doing the "A Very Young" series, I'd seen children being put on the fast track at a very early age. As I told Cindy Horchem for the *Topeka Capital-Journal* when *The Fun of Cooking* came out, cooking is not so self-absorbed, not so competitive. I thought it would be nice to do a book showing children doing something that is family oriented and involves sharing. Jason, the child making the dog biscuits, is my brother's little boy and Jessica, on the cover, is his sister. My editor's daughter has a chapter on her pumpkin pie. The best part of doing this book is that my own family got to eat for about a year because I brought home delicious samples.

CA: The series of books that included Lily Goes to the Playground, *starring your daughter, was definitely begun to fill a gap, as you told Jean Mercier for* Publishers Weekly. *What kind of response have those books brought?*

KREMENTZ: My friends whose children own these books tell me that their kids love them, that with some kids it's like a security blanket: they won't go anywhere without *Jack Goes to the Beach* or *Lily Goes to the Playground.* I'm sorry in a way that I did them as mass-market instead of regular trade books, because you don't get any review attention on a mass-market book. I liked the idea of my books being sold in places like K-Mart and Caldors, but the people who shop there aren't really looking for books. The only mass-market books that really do well enough to justify the much lower royalty you get are *really* mass-market, and that means licensed characters. The people who go in the bookstores will spend money on more expensive hard-cover books. As a result the bookstores don't want to waste their limited shelf space on books that only cost $3.95, because if they sell a twelve-dollar book, they're going to get forty percent of twelve dollars, and if they sell a $3.95 book, they're getting forty percent of that. So it's hard to get my lower-priced toddler and preschool books into regular bookstores. I doubt that I'll do mass-market books in the future.

CA: Your husband, the writer Kurt Vonnegut, works on the top floor of your house in New York, as he explained in a preface to The Writer's Image, *and you work on the bottom floor. Do you aid and abet each other in the writing, or rather keep your books to yourselves until they're finished?*

KREMENTZ: We pretty much keep them to ourselves.

CA: You seem to be working mostly with children now. Do you miss the writer photographs, or any of the other things you were doing earlier?

KREMENTZ: I still do photograph writers from time to time as well as other "grownups." I'm going down to Washington very early tomorrow to do some official portraits for Tom Downey, the Congressman from Long Island, and his family. I recently photographed William Paley, the founder of CBS, and Larry Tisch, the new president. I continue to work for various magazines. And I photograph a lot of families on private commission. It's a nice mix—which is what I love about my profession. And I have a new book being published by Scholastic in April. It's called *A Visit to Washington, D.C.* It's similar in format to my "Very Young" books in that I follow one child, six-year-old Matt Wilson, throughout the book and he tells in his own words what he loves to see and do in our nation's capital.

CA: Will you likely stick with children's books for a while, or do you envision your work taking a completely new direction?

KREMENTZ: I think I will continue to do children's books because I am committed to the idea of children *reading* instead of sitting in front of a TV set. I'd like to do a book now getting back more to the genre of the "How It Feels" books, called *How It Feels to Fight for Your Life,* a book about children faced with life-threatening illnesses and how they cope with this on an emotional level. And I might expand *A Visit to Washington, D.C.* into a series.

AVOCATIONAL INTERESTS: Reading, tennis.

BIOGRAPHICAL/CRITICAL SOURCES:

BOOKS

Authors in the News, Gale, Volume I, 1976, Volume II, 1976.
Children's Literature: An Issues Approach, Heath, 1976.
Children's Literature Review, Volume V, Gale, 1983.

PERIODICALS

Best Sellers, January, 1978, August, 1981.
Booklist, December 15, 1979, September 1, 1981.
Boston Sunday Globe, December 28, 1967.
Bulletin of the Center for Children's Books, May, 1978, February, 1979.
Chicago Tribune, April 7, 1985.
Christian Science Monitor, December 4, 1978, April 26, 1979.
Detroit Free Press, December 25, 1974.
Los Angeles Times, June 4, 1981.
Los Angeles Times Book Review, December 21, 1980, December 5, 1982, May 4, 1986.
Miami Herald, April 4, 1975.
Modern Photography, January, 1976.
New Republic, December 13, 1980.
Newsweek, February 5, 1968.
New Yorker, December 23, 1974.
New York Photo District News, June, 1981.
New York Times, January 14, 1977, November 14, 1982.
New York Times Book Review, November 9, 1969, December 26, 1976, December 10, 1978, November 30, 1980, July 19, 1981.
Popular Photography, April, 1975.
Publishers Weekly, October 18, 1976, November 15, 1976, July 26, 1985.
Saturday Review, February 17, 1968, May 9, 1970.
School Library Journal, September, 1970, December, 1977, December, 1978, September, 1981.
Village Voice, December 10, 1980.
Voice of Youth Advocates, June, 1985.
Washington Post Book World, January 9, 1983, November 11, 1984.

—Sketch by Margaret Mazurkiewicz
—Interview by Jean W. Ross

*   *   *

KUZMA, Kay 1941-

PERSONAL: Born April 25, 1941, in Ogallala, Neb.; daughter of Willard J. (in real estate) and Irene (a manager; maiden name, Helm) Humpal; married Jan W. Kuzma (a biostatistician), September 1, 1963; children: Kimberly Kay, Karlene Michelle, Kevin Clark. *Education:* Loma Linda University, B.S., 1962; Michigan State University, M.A., 1963; University of California, Los Angeles, Ed.D., 1970.

ADDRESSES: Office—Parent Scene, Inc., Box 2222, Redland, Calif. 92373.

CAREER: Loma Linda University, Loma Linda, Calif., assistant professor, 1967-73, associate professor of health sciences, 1973—. President, Parent Scene, Inc. (publishing company), 1982—.

WRITINGS:

Child Study through Observation and Participation, R & E Research Associates, 1978.
Guidelines for Child Care Centers, Education Department, Seventh-Day Adventist General Conference, 1978.

My Unforgettable Parents, Pacific Press, 1978.
(With Clare Cherry and Barbara Harkness) *Nursery School and Day Care Center Management Guide*, Fearon, 1978.
The Kim, Kari, and Kevin Storybook (juvenile), Pacific Press, 1979.
Don't Step on the Pansies (poetry), Review & Herald, 1979.
Prime Time Parenting, Rawson Wade, 1980.
Teaching Your Own Preschool Children, Doubleday, 1980.
Working Mothers: How You Can Have a Career and Be a Good Parent, Too, Stratford Press, 1981.
Filling Your Love Cup, Parent Scene, 1982.
Living With God's Kids, Parent Scene, 1983.
The Kim, Kari, and Kevin Storybook #2 (juvenile), Parent Scene, 1984.
To Understand Your Child, Parent Scene, 1985.

Editor of *Parent Scene Newsletter*, 1982—.

WORK IN PROGRESS: A Hug and a Kiss and a Kick in the Pants.

SIDELIGHTS: Kay Kuzma told *CA:* "I never planned to be a working mother. I only wanted to be a good parent. But before I knew it, I was doing both and liking it.

"I believe rearing healthy, happy, competent children is the most important task anyone can be called on to perform. And I feel blessed to have had the opportunity to receive academic training in child development which has allowed me to put good theory into successful practice. How can I share this expertise with other parents who are not as fortunate as I? Teaching and presenting seminars is one way, and I have continued to do this, but it does take time away from home. Writing has provided a wider audience while the children can be playing next to me in my own living room.

"I believe God has a special work for each of us to do, and he can find ways and means of preparing us for that work. That's what he has done for me. I didn't start out a good writer. But with my husband's ideas, critiques, encouragement, and editing and with Esther Glaser's creative writing classes, my skills have developed. Writing has allowed me to have my career and be a good parent, too."

*   *   *

KWITNY, Jonathan 1941-

PERSONAL: Born March 23, 1941, in Indianapolis, Ind.; son of I. J. (a physician) and Julia (Goldberger) Kwitny; married Martha Kaplan (a lawyer), June 2, 1968 (died June 19, 1978); children: Carolyn Ann, Susanna Lynn. *Education:* University of Missouri, B.J., 1962; New York University, M.A., 1964.

ADDRESSES: Office—Wall Street Journal, 200 Liberty St., New York, N.Y. 10281.

CAREER: News Tribune, Perth Amboy, N.J., reporter, 1963-64 and 1967-69; *New York Post*, New York City, reporter, 1969; *Wall Street Journal*, New York City, reporter and staff writer, 1971—. U.S. Peace Corps volunteer in Benin City, Nigeria, 1965-66.

AWARDS, HONORS: First prize for distinguished public service, New Jersey Press Association, 1964 and 1967; honor medal for career achievement, University of Missouri School of Journalism; runner-up for Pulitzer Prize in general nonfiction, 1985, for *Endless Enemies: The Making of an Unfriendly World*.

WRITINGS:

NONFICTION

The Fountain Pen Conspiracy, Knopf, 1973.
The Mullendore Murder Case, Farrar, Straus, 1974.
Vicious Circles: The Mafia in the Marketplace, Norton, 1979.
Endless Enemies: The Making of an Unfriendly World, Congdon & Weed, 1984.
The Crimes of Patriots: A True Tale of Dope, Dirty Money, and the CIA, Norton, 1987.

FICTION

Shakedown (novel), Putnam, 1977.

SIDELIGHTS: An investigative reporter and staff writer for the *Wall Street Journal*, Jonathan Kwitny has also authored several books in which he documents domestic and international corruption within American business while examining the government's role in allowing such corruption to thrive. Kwitny's targets are diverse, ranging from complacent judicial and business officials who help bolster the illegal activities of the Mafia, to U.S. foreign policymakers and American corporate henchmen who encourage corruption within various international sectors. Kwitny's accounts, which offer an array of hard-hitting factual details, have been praised for their thorough and comprehensive research, as well as for their social concern regarding the issues and problems being discussed. A world traveller and former Peace Corps volunteer, Kwitny demonstrates "an instinctive feel for how life is really lived away from the headlines," comments John F. Baker in a profile of the author for *Publishers Weekly*. Kwitny's experiences around the world, which have included interviews with a broad cross-section of people, likewise allow him to focus on the essence of the problems and issues he illuminates. Christopher Lehmann-Haupt in the *New York Times* describes Kwitny as "a liberal with a heart that doesn't bleed easily."

Kwitny first attracted major attention with his 1979 expose entitled *Vicious Circles: The Mafia in the Marketplace*, which reported on Mafia dominance in American industries such as meat and cheese processing, banking and investments, and various labor unions. As with an earlier book, *The Fountain Pen Conspiracy*, which told how investment swindlers work, *Vicious Circles* was praised for its comprehensive accumulation of supporting evidence. "There is not a page that doesn't impress you with how energetically the author has pursued his prey, how deep he has dug for all his facts," comments Lehmann-Haupt. Via tape recordings of underworld figures, police reports, trial transcripts, and personal interviews, *Vicious Circles* "marshals a convincing body of evidence to demonstrate that the Mafia does indeed exist, and that it has penetrated the American business system," notes Joseph P. Parker in *America*. Kwitny's numerous case studies include an account of the Mafia's hold on the New York City meat industry, where processors are virtually obligated to work with the underworld to have their products distributed and sold, in addition to an examination of fraudulent business set-ups and manipulation of labor unions. Kwitny's intent in all of this, as Thomas Powers remarks in the *New York Times Book Review*, is to make understood that "there is no such thing as a 'legitimate' Mafia business; every last one of them is fixed, and the rest of us foot the bill." The Mafia makes "victims . . . [out of] ordinary people," Powers continues, "consumers who must pay the cost of Mafia bribery and extortion in the meat they buy; retired truck drivers cheated out of Teamster pensions; ordinary businessmen who pay for Mafia arson through high insurance premiums."

Regarding the illegal nature of the Mafia, Powers states that another major point of *Vicious Circles* is to show "that the Mafia gets away with it because we let them." Kwitny devotes a large portion of his book to documenting lenient criminal sentencing of convicted Mafia officials and to criticizing the lawyers who often represent Mafia clients because of the more lucrative fees involved. Kwitny proposes a solution to the latter problem, envisioning "a just system in which the best professional debaters do *not* claim an ethical obligation to hire themselves out to whoever has the most money, to defend any argument, no matter how vile, that the person with the most money wants defended." Robert Sherrill in the *Washington Post Book World* comments that "most Americans will find [Kwitny's argument] . . . extremely refreshing, if probably hopeless," adding that "Washington lawyers, with their revolving-door ideology and price-tag sense of justice, will doubtless find [it] . . . naive."

Sherrill praises *Vicious Circles* as "a marvelous piece of grotesque art. It is like an enormous mural by Hieronymus Bosch in which hundreds of strange evil creatures perform their perversions against a background of tangled underbrush." Lehmann-Haupt, however, criticizes this aspect of the book, stating that "where we ought to be impressed by detail, we are simply numbed, because . . . Kwitny tells essentially the same story over and over again, . . . fail[ing] to bring a single incident or character to life." Sherrill, on the other hand, finds a strength in the book's repetitiousness, pointing out that "in isolating details one actually loses the sense of *Vicious Circles*. Its emphasis is on the genre: the unconscionable corporation, the unreal judge, the hermaphroditic (ethically speaking) lawyer. Above all, *Vicious Circles* addresses itself to the most pressing moral questions of our time," that is, the obligation of American corporations and legal representatives to work with clientele they know are associated with the Mafia.

Kwitny's next two books, *Endless Enemies: The Making of an Unfriendly World* and *The Crimes of Patriots: A True Tale of Dope, Dirty Money, and the CIA*, both raise disturbing questions that also touch upon moral issues. This time, Kwitny exposes the corrupt practices of certain international businesses which allegedly operate with the encouragement of government agencies under misguided interpretations of U.S. foreign policy. *Endless Enemies* gathered considerable critical attention in 1984 and is regarded as one of the foremost books on current U.S. foreign policy. Its thesis, reports Baker, is "that the U.S., under the influence of business interests and a seemingly pathological reluctance to let small countries shape their own destiny, has in fact made the world far more difficult and dangerous for itself than it need be." Largely responsible for this situation, Kwitny contends, is a U.S. foreign policy that often views countries in terms of communism versus democracy, and at times indiscriminately supports anti-communist forces who manipulate the politics and economies of their countries for their own profit. "Most tellingly," comments Lenny Glynn in *Maclean's*, "Kwitny reveals how a relatively small, tightly knit web of bankers, oilmen and arms merchants has played on anti-Communist paranoia to advance their own interests through manipulation of U.S. foreign policy." As a result of American support of such groups, the U.S. "keeps obstructing the free play of developing economies," notes Lehmann-Haupt, ". . . reduc[ing] them to corruption and poverty or . . . forc[ing] them to embrace the alternative of socialism." Kwitny draws heavily on his experiences as a world traveller, especially his familiarity with the country of Zaire, to present numerous cases where this has occurred: Angola, Cuba, Ethiopia, Iran, the Philippines, Nicaragua, and Chile, to name a few. "Kwitny takes them all," writes Lehmann-Haupt, ". . . and attempts to show how, ever since the end of World War II, our foreign policy has mainly succeeded in producing precisely the opposite of what would be desirable for us."

Critical reception of *Endless Enemies* was widely enthusiastic and often focused on the meaningful and urgent message expressed by Kwitny. "Jonathan Kwitny is angry about American foreign policy," notes Martin F. Nolan in the *New York Times Book Review*, "[and] he writes about it with immense energy, eloquence, indignation and an appetite for documentation that will stupefy opponents of his arguments." Critics also remarked on the ideals of free trade that permeate Kwitny's account, even in the most severe instances of its abuse. "Almost as striking as this catalogue of outrage is the tone of aggrieved patriotism in which Kwitny recites [it]," comments George Scialabba in the *Voice Literary Supplement*. "After narrating each atrocious episode, he shakes his head, amazed and indignant that American foreign policy has departed so far from the libertarian and free-market principles that made this country great." Kwitny himself gives insight into the principles behind such indignation, telling Baker that "the way you spread our way of life around is by living it—living the principles we profess, not by ignoring them once you're away from home." Critics have praised Kwitny's book for the consistent and balanced approach it takes. "Of all the polemics against our foreign policy that have appeared in the past few decades, 'Endless Enemies' stands out because it is principled and free of ideological cant," writes Nolan. "For destabilizing governments and economies and reckless arms sales and unsound bank loans, . . . Kwitny indicts the malicious and the well-meaning with equal ferocity."

In his latest book, *The Crimes of Patriots: A True Tale of Dope, Dirty Money, and the CIA*, Kwitny further explores the relationship between the way U.S. foreign policy is conducted and corruption in international sectors. Specifically, *The Crimes of Patriots* focuses on the operations of Nugan Hand Bank of Australia, an international investment firm whose 1980 collapse—in which some investors lost their life savings—was connected to numerous allegations of criminal activity, and whose associates and staff were made up of a large number of people with ties to the U.S. military and the CIA. "With remarkable patience and industry," writes a reviewer for *Publishers Weekly*, "Kwitny has pieced together the whole sordid story, involving an institution clearly designed to facilitate the laundering and rapid movement of dubious money." While *The Crimes of Patriots* is, according to Harold Blum in the *New York Times Book Review*, "a case study of how . . . Nugan Hand Bank functioned as, in [Kwitny's] words, 'a giant theft machine,' moving billions illegally around the world, engaged in financing the heroin trade [and] tax fraud," it is also much more. As with *Endless Enemies*, Kwitny levels a larger indictment which, according to Blum, emerges as "a gung-ho foreign policy that allows a mob of military and intelligence veterans to storm about the globe breaking laws and making money in pursuit of an extra-constitutional conception of the national interest." Michael R. Beschloss in the *Chicago Tribune* sees *The Crimes of Patriots* as not only an important but a timely contribution to literature on American foreign

policy. "In the 1980s," he writes, "especially in the wake of the Iran-Contra affair, we are gaining a sense of the degree to which the CIA has tried to mobilize private businessmen with private motives in the service of political aims and how these operations sometimes have spun out of control." Blum concurs, observing that "the Nugan Hand Bank's activities [are] . . . another chilling episode, according to Mr. Kwitny, in the twisted policy that holds that international business is a continuation of international politics by other means." Kwitny, according to Beschloss, "has brought us the complex and mysterious story of the Nugan Hand Bank . . . and its real and symbolic place in the world of American covert operations and diplomacy."

In the opening chapter of *The Crimes of Patriots*, Kwitny writes that "this is not a book for people who must have their mysteries solved. It begins with unanswered questions, and it will end with them." Blum finds a particular strength in this aspect of the book, stating: "These mysteries only help to reinforce one's admiration for Mr. Kwitny's reporting and the clues he uncovered. The unanswered questions—and their implications about the conduct of this country's foreign policy—are as resonant as the ones he does answer." On the book's dustjacket blurbs, Seymour Hersh and Peter Maas express a similar view. "It is unusual to commend a book of investigative journalism that leaves some questions unanswered," writes Hersh, "but Jonathan Kwitny's account of the Nugan Hand affair transcends ordinary journalism. *The Crimes of Patriots* is the story of a reporter at work trying to balance issues of criminality and national security." Maas adds that "Jonathan Kwitny is a peerless investigative reporter."

BIOGRAPHICAL/CRITICAL SOURCES:

BOOKS

Kwitny, Jonathan, *Vicious Circles: The Mafia in the Marketplace*, Norton, 1979.
Kwitny, Jonathan, *Endless Enemies: The Making of an Unfriendly World*, Congdon & Weed, 1984.
Kwitny, Jonathan, *The Crimes of Patriots: A True Tale of Dope, Dirty Money, and the CIA*, Norton, 1987.

PERIODICALS

America, May 5, 1979.
Best Sellers, July, 1979.
Chicago Tribune, August 30, 1987.
Los Angeles Times, September 11, 1984.
Los Angeles Times Book Review, October 5, 1986, September 13, 1987.
Maclean's, August 6, 1984.
Nation, December 22, 1984.
New Leader, September 3, 1984.
Newsweek, December 23, 1974, August 27, 1984.
New Yorker, September 3, 1984.
New York Times, April 5, 1979, July 17, 1984.
New York Times Book Review, April 15, 1979, July 29, 1984, September 6, 1987.
Publishers Weekly, August 27, 1973, October 7, 1974, April 25, 1977, May 11, 1984, Augsut 7, 1987.
Voice Literary Supplement, September, 1984.
Washington Post Book World, May 13, 1979, June 24, 1984.

—*Sketch by Michael E. Mueller*

L

LACY, Norris J(oiner)   1940-

PERSONAL: Born March 8, 1940, in Hopkinsville, Ky.; son of Edwin Vemont (a cook) and Lillian (Joiner) Lacy; married Susan Houston (a teacher), January 6, 1984. *Education:* Murray State University, A.B., 1962; Middlebury College, graduate study, summer, 1962; Indiana University, M.A., 1963, Ph.D., 1967.

ADDRESSES: Home—1904 Countryside Lane, Lawrence, Kan. 66044. *Office*—Department of French, University of Kansas, Lawrence, Kan. 66045.

CAREER: Indiana University at Bloomington, lecturer in French, 1965-66; University of Kansas, Lawrence, assistant professor, 1966-70, associate professor, 1970-75, professor of French language and literature, 1975—, assistant chairman of French and Italian, 1969-72, chairman of French and Italian, 1978-87. Visiting professor at University of California, Los Angeles, 1975-76. Has worked as jazz musician and music teacher.

MEMBER: International Courtly Literature Society, International Arthurian Society (president, 1984-87), Mediaeval Academy of America, Modern Language Association of America, American Association of Teachers of French, Societe Rencesvals.

AWARDS, HONORS: Woodrow Wilson fellowship, 1962-63; grants from American Philosophical Society, 1969, American Council of Learned Societies, 1973, 1985, and National Endowment for the Humanities, 1975.

WRITINGS:

(Editor and contributor) *A Medieval French Miscellany,* University of Kansas, 1972.
(Editor and author of introduction) J. N. Carman, translator, *From Camelot to Joyous Guard: The Old French "La Mort le Roi Artu,"* University Press of Kansas, 1974.
(Editor) *26 Chansons d'amour de la Renaissance* (title means "26 Renaissance Love Songs"), University Press of Kansas, 1975.
(Editor and contributor) *The Comic Spirit in Medieval France,* Soler (Valencia), 1976.
The Craft of Chretien de Troyes: An Essay on Narrative Art, E. J. Brill (Leiden), 1980.
(Co-editor and contributor) *Essays in Early French Literature,* French Literature Publishing Co. (York, S.C.), 1982.

(Editor) *L'Istoyre de Jehan Coquault,* French Literature Publishing Co., 1982.
(Editor and contributor) *The Arthurian Encyclopedia,* Garland Publishing, 1986.
(Co-author) *The Arthurian Handbook,* Garland Publishing, 1987.
(Co-editor and contributor) *The Legacy of Chretien de Troyes,* Rodopi (Amsterdam), 1987.

Contributor to language and literature journals.

WORK IN PROGRESS: An edition of Beroul's *Tristan;* a translation of *La Mort Artu.*

AVOCATIONAL INTERESTS: Photography, music.

*   *   *

LAFFIN, John (Alfred Charles)   1922-
(Carl Dekker, Mark Napier, Dirk Sabre)

PERSONAL: Born September 21, 1922, in Sydney, Australia; son of Charles George and Nellie (a nursing sister; maiden name, Pike) Laffin; married Hazelle Gloria Stonham (her husband's assistant), October 6, 1943; children: Bronwen Diane, Craig Antony, Pirenne Debra. *Education:* University of London, M.A., 1961. *Politics:* "Completely uncommitted." *Religion:* "Humanist Christian."

ADDRESSES: Home—Oxford House, Church St., Knighton, Powys LD7 1AG, Wales.

CAREER: Associated Newspapers, Sydney, Australia, associate editor, 1945-51; York Editing Service, Sydney, managing director, 1951-56; International Correspondence Schools, Sydney, chief instructor and examiner in creative journalism and short story writing, 1951-56; Mayfield College, Sussex, England, head of the departments of English, geography, and sociology, 1959-69; full-time writer, 1969—. Chairman of Sussex branch of British Legion, 1967-69. *Military service:* Australian Army, Infantry, 1940-45; served in New Guinea.

MEMBER: Royal Geographical Society (fellow), Royal Historical Society (fellow), Society for Army Historical Research, Society of Authors, Military History Society of Ireland, Society of Antiquaries of Scotland, Royal United Service Institute.

AWARDS, HONORS: Brantridge College, Sussex, D.Litt., 1972; La Croix du Capitan Michel, 1981.

WRITINGS:

NONFICTION

Return to Glory, Angus & Robertson, 1956.

One Man's War, Angus & Robertson, 1957.

Middle East Journey, Angus & Robertson, 1958.

Digger: The Story of the Australian Soldier, Cassell, 1959, revised edition published as *Digger: The Legend of the Australian Soldier,* Macmillan, 1986.

Scotland the Brave: The Story of the Scottish Soldier, Cassell, 1963.

The Face of War: The Evolution of Weapons and Tactics and Their Use in Ten Famous Battles, Abelard-Schuman, 1963.

Swifter than Eagles: The Biography of Marshal of the Royal Air Force Sir John Maitland Salmond, W. Blackwood, 1964.

Codes and Ciphers: Secret Writing through the Ages (Junior Literary Guild selection), illustrated by C. De La Nougarede, Abelard-Schuman, 1964.

British Campaign Medals, Abelard-Schuman, 1964.

Anzacs at War: The Story of Australian and New Zealand Battles, Abelard-Schuman, 1965, revised edition, Horwitz-Grahame, 1982.

Jackboot: The Story of the German Soldier, Cassell, 1965, 2nd edition, 1966.

Links of Leadership: Thirty Centuries of Command, Harrapp, 1966, published as *Links of Leadership: Thirty Centuries of Military Command,* Abelard-Schuman, 1970.

Tommy Atkins: The Story of the English Soldier, Cassell, 1966.

The Hunger to Come, Abelard-Schuman, 1966, revised and enlarged edition, 1971.

Boys in Battle, Abelard-Schuman, 1967.

Women in Battle, Abelard-Schuman, 1967.

New Geography, 1966-67, Abelard-Schuman, 1967.

The Anatomy of Captivity, Abelard-Schuman, 1968.

New Geography, 1968-69, Abelard-Schuman, 1969.

Jack Tar: The Story of the British Sailor, Cassell, 1969.

Surgeons in the Field, Dent, 1970.

New Geography, 1970-71, Abelard-Schuman, 1971.

(Editor) *Letters from the Front, 1914-1918,* Dent, 1973.

Fedayeen: The Arab-Israeli Dilemma, Free Press, 1973.

Americans in Battle, Crown, 1973.

The French Foreign Legion, Crown, 1974.

The Arab Mind Considered: A Need for Understanding, Taplinger, 1975 (published in England as *The Arab Mind: A Need for Understanding,* Cassell, 1975), published as *Rhetoric and Reality: The Arab Mind Considered,* 1978.

The Israeli Mind, Cassell, 1979.

The Dagger of Islam, Sphere, 1979, Bantam, 1980.

Damn the Dardanelles!, Osprey Publishing, 1980.

The Australian Army at War, 1899-1975, Osprey Publishing, 1982.

The Israeli Army in the Middle East Wars, 1948-73, Osprey Publishing, 1982.

The Arab Armies of the Middle East Wars, 1948-73, Osprey Publishing, 1982.

The PLO Connections, Corgi, 1982.

Fight for the Falklands!, St. Martin's, 1982.

The Man the Nazis Couldn't Catch, Sutton Publishing, 1984.

The War of Desperation: Lebanon, 1982-85, Osprey Publishing, 1985.

On the Western Front: Soldier's Stories from France and Flanders, 1914-1918, Sutton Publishing, 1985.

Know the Middle East (an A-Z reference), Sutton Publishing, 1985.

Brassey's Battles: 3,500 Years of Conflict, Campaigns and Wars from A-Z, Brassey's Defence Publishers, 1986.

War Annual, Brassey's Defence Publishers, Volume I, 1986, Volume II, 1987.

Battlefield Archaeology, Ian Allan, 1987.

Holy War: Islam Fights, Grenada, 1987.

FICTION

(Contributor) *Tales by Australians,* British Authors Press, 1937.

(Under pseudonym Carl Dekker) *Silence So Deadly,* Calvert, 1953.

(Under pseudonym Carl Dekker) *Don't Bother to Knock,* Calvert, 1954.

Death by Ballot, King Books, 1954.

Jungle Manhunt, Horwitz, 1955, 2nd edition, 1958.

Murder on Flight 354, King Books, 1956.

Death Has My Number, Horwitz, 1957.

I'll Die Tonight, Horwitz, 1957.

My Brother's Executioner, Horwitz, 1957.

They Voted Me to Die, Horwitz, 1957.

Crime on My Hands, Horwitz, 1958.

The Dancer of San Jose, Horwitz, 1958.

The Devil's Emissary, Horwitz, 1958.

(Under pseudonym Dirk Sabre) *Murder by Bamboo,* Hammond, Hammond, 1958.

Murder in Paradise, Horwitz, 1958.

Temptress on Trial, Horwitz, 1958.

The Walking Wounded, Amalgamated Press, 1963.

(Under pseudonym Mark Napier) *Doorways to Danger,* Abelard-Schuman, 1966.

Devil's Goad, Dent, 1970.

OTHER

Also author of *The Arabs as Master Slaves,* 1982, and of radio programs for the British Broadcasting Corp. Contributor to *International Year Book,* Caxton. Regular contributor to *Spectator, British Army Review, Daily Telegraph* (London), and *International Herald-Tribune* (Paris); also contributor of articles and short stories to periodicals in the United States, Great Britain, and Australia.

SIDELIGHTS: When John Laffin was only fifteen, his first adult short story was published and another story was included in an Australian national anthology, *Tales by Australians.* Much of Laffin's work since then has been in the area of war and military history, largely because of his personal involvement in World War II.

Laffin also writes extensively on the Middle East and its related themes, such as Islam, terrorism, and Arab hostility to Israel and the West. However, he regards himself "at least by temperament and taste," as much a novelist and poet as a military historian and current affairs analyst. Laffin notes, "I would like to spend five years writing serious fiction, though war would come into at least one novel."

Laffin and his wife, Hazelle, delight in independent travel, but it must have a purpose, he says, because all their holidays are working holidays. "Every morning increases my desire for more and more achievement. With my wife's constant help, I really do work very hard, not just because I have to earn a living but because I have always been determined not to sink without trace."

LANGE, Oliver [a pseudonym] 1927-

PERSONAL: Born December 14, 1927, in New York, N.Y.; married Nancy Henderson (a writer), July 20, 1979; children: Johanna, Jennifer, Jason, Thaddeus, Cassandra, Joshua. *Education:* Columbia University, B.S., 1956. *Politics:* None. *Religion:* None.

ADDRESSES: Home and office—2014 Northwest Bayshore Dr., Waldport, Ore. 97394. *Agent*—JET Literary Associates, Inc., 124 East 84th St., Suite 4A, New York, N.Y. 10028.

CAREER: Associated with *New Yorker* in New York City, beginning 1956; writer, 1956—; worked as a carpenter, handyman, night watchman, and psychiatric social worker. *Military service:* U.S. Army, 1945-51.

WRITINGS:

NOVELS

Vandenberg, Stein & Day, 1971.
Incident at La Junta, Stein & Day, 1973.
Red Snow, Seaview, 1978.
Next of Kin, Seaview, 1980.
The Land of the Long Shadow, Seaview, 1981.
Defiance: An American Novel, Stein & Day, 1981.
Pas de Deux, Seaview, 1982.
The Devil at Home, Stein & Day, 1986.

WORK IN PROGRESS: A novel with the working title of *Tracy's Arena.*

SIDELIGHTS: Distinguishing himself from historic, journalistic, and pedantic writers, Oliver Lange wishes to be known as a storyteller. Characterization is the heart of his stories; he develops a cast of characters and then, as he words it, "steps aside and watches what kind of mischief they'll get into."

Lange's knack for storytelling has been praised by numerous critics. His first novel, *Vandenberg,* is a story about a man's escape from a detention center in a Russian-controlled United States and the escapee's subsequent fight to destroy the center. Peter Sourian of the *New York Times Book Review* wrote of *Vandenberg:* "The author draws his characters with a melodramatic flair, yet he does not generally sacrifice psychological verisimilitudes. [When he] stops to dabble in ideas themselves, he maintains an enviably hard-nosed sense of just how long he can afford to do so, never missing the train of his narrative." William Decker of *Saturday Review* postulated: "In his narrative writing, Mr. Lange is in the class of Hemingway of *For Whom the Bell Tolls.* His style is admirably taut."

Perseverance is a key characteristic of Oliver Lange. He wrote his novel *The Land of the Long Shadow* and then continuously revised it for nineteen years before it was finally accepted for publication. Lange also exhibits determination in his writing habits. When involved in the composition process, he writes as long as eighteen hours per day, breaking only occasionally for food or a nap. He maintains such a pace for weeks, but explains, "This is how books get written."

BIOGRAPHICAL/CRITICAL SOURCES:

PERIODICALS

Best Sellers, March 1, 1971, August 15, 1973.
Detroit News, March 9, 1980.
Los Angeles Times Book Review, August 30, 1981.
New Republic, March 13, 1973.

New York Times Book Review, February 28, 1971, August 12, 1973.
Philadelphia Inquirer, September 5, 1982.
Saturday Review, March 13, 1971.
Washington Post Book World, March 2, 1980.

*   *   *

LANGLEY, Tania
See ARMSTRONG, Tilly

*   *   *

LAQUEUR, Walter (Ze'ev) 1921-

PERSONAL: Born May 26, 1921, in Breslau, Germany (now Wroclaw, Poland); son of Fritz and Else (Berliner) Laqueur; married Barbara Koch, May 29, 1941; children: Sylvia, Shlomit. *Education:* Attended Hebrew University, 1938-39.

ADDRESSES: Office—Center for Strategic and International Studies, Georgetown University, 1800 K Street N.W., Washington, D.C. 20006.

CAREER: Agricultural worker in Palestine (now Israel), 1940-44; newspaper correspondent and freelance writer, 1944-55; *Survey* (quarterly journal), London, England, founder and editor, 1955-67; Institute of Contemporary History and Wiener Library, London, England, director, 1964—; Brandeis University, Waltham, Mass., professor of history of ideas and politics, 1967-72; Georgetown University, Washington, D.C., chairman of international research council of Center for Strategic and International Studies, 1973—, university professor of government, 1977—. Visiting professor at Johns Hopkins University and research fellow at Harvard University, 1957; visiting professor at University of Chicago, 1958, and University of Tel Aviv, 1970—.

AWARDS, HONORS: Distinguished Writer's award from Center for Strategic and International Studies, 1969; Inter Nationes Award, 1985.

WRITINGS:

Communism and Nationalism in the Middle East, Routledge & Kegan Paul, 1956.
(Editor) *The Middle East in Transition: Studies in Contemporary History,* Routledge & Kegan Paul, 1958, reprinted, Books for Libraries Press, 1971.
The Soviet Union and the Middle East, Routledge & Kegan Paul, 1959.
Young Germany, Routledge & Kegan Paul, 1962.
(Editor with Leopold Labedz) *Polycentrism, the New Factor in International Communism* (first published in England as a special issue of *Survey,* 1962), Praeger, 1962.
Russia and Germany: A Century of Conflict, Little, Brown, 1965.
(Editor with Labedz) *The State of Soviet Studies* (essays first published in January and April, 1964, issues of *Survey*), MIT Press, 1965.
(Editor with George L. Mosse) *International Fascism, 1920-1945,* Harper, 1966.
(Editor with Mosse) *The Left-Wing Intellectuals between the Wars, 1919-1939,* Harper, 1966.
(Compiler with Mosse) *1914: The Coming of the First World War* (essays originally published in *Journal of Contemporary History,* Volume I, numbers 3 and 4, 1966), Harper, 1966.

The Fate of the Revolution: Interpretations of Soviet History, Macmillan, 1967, new edition, 1987.

(Editor) *Education and Social Structure in the Twentieth Century*, Harper, 1967.

(Editor) *Literature and Politics in the Twentieth Century*, Harper, 1967.

(Editor with Mosse) *The New History*, Harper, 1967.

The Road to Jerusalem: The Origins of the Arab-Israeli Conflict, 1967, Macmillan, 1968 (published in England as *The Road to War*, Weidenfeld & Nicolson, 1968).

(Editor) *Reappraisals: A New Look at History*, Weidenfeld & Nicolson, 1968.

(Editor) *The Israeli-Arab Reader: A Documentary History of the Middle East Conflict*, Citadel, 1969, revised edition, Penguin Books, 1970, third revised edition, Bantam, 1976.

The Struggle for the Middle East: The Soviet Union in the Mediterranean 1958-1968, Macmillan, 1969 (published in England as *The Struggle for the Middle East: The Soviet Union and the Middle East, 1958-1968*, Routledge & Kegan Paul, 1969), revised edition published as *The Struggle for the Middle East: The Soviet Union and the Middle East 1958-1970*, Penguin Books, 1972.

Europe since Hitler, Weidenfeld & Nicolson, 1970.

The Rebirth of Europe: A History of the Years since the Fall of Hitler, Holt, 1970, revised edition published as *Europe since Hitler: The Rebirth of Europe*, Penguin Books, 1982.

Out of the Ruins of Europe, Library Press, 1971.

(Editor with Evelyn Anderson and others) *A Dictionary of Politics*, Free Press, 1971, revised edition, 1974.

Neo-Isolationism and the World of the Seventies, Library Press, 1972.

A History of Zionism, Holt, 1972.

(With Bernard Krikler) *A Reader's Guide to Contemporary History*, Quadrangle, 1972.

(Editor with George Mosse) *Historians in Politics*, Sage Publications, 1974.

Weimar: A Cultural History, 1918-1933, Putnam, 1974.

Confrontation: The Middle East and World Politics, New York Times Book Company, 1974.

Guerrilla: A Historical and Critical Study, Little, Brown, 1976.

(Editor) *Fascism: A Reader's Guide—Analyses, Interpretations, Bibliography*, University of California Press, 1976.

(Editor) *The Guerrilla Reader: A Historical Anthology*, New American Library, 1977.

Terrorism, Little, Brown, 1977, published as *The Age of Terrorism*, 1987.

(Editor) *The Terrorism Reader: A Historical Anthology*, New American Library, 1978, new edition, 1987.

A Continent Astray: Europe, 1970-1978, Oxford University Press, 1979.

(Editor with Barry Rubin) *The Human Rights Reader*, Temple University Press, 1979.

The Missing Years: A Novel, Little, Brown, 1980.

The Political Psychology of Appeasement: Finlandization and Other Unpopular Essays, Transaction Books, 1980.

The Terrible Secret: An Investigation into the Suppression of Information about Hitler's "Final Solution," Little, Brown, 1980.

Farewell to Europe (novel), Little, Brown, 1981.

(Editor) *The Second World War*, Sage Publications, 1982.

America, Europe, and the Soviet Union, Transaction Books, 1983.

(Editor) *The Pattern of Soviet Conduct in the Third World*, Praeger, 1983.

(Editor) *Looking Forward, Looking Back*, Praeger, 1983.

(Editor) *European Peace Movements and the Future of the Western Alliance*, Transaction Books, 1985.

Germany Today: A Personal Report, Little, Brown, 1985.

A World of Secrets: The Uses and Limits of Intelligence, Basic Books, 1985.

(With Richard Breitman) *Breaking the Silence*, Simon & Schuster, 1986.

Contributor to periodicals, including *Commentary* and *New York Times Magazine*. Founder and co-editor, *Journal of Contemporary History*, 1966—; founder and editor, *Washington Papers*, 1972—; founder and co-editor, *Washington Quarterly of Strategic and International Studies*, 1977—.

SIDELIGHTS: Historian Walter Laqueur has written numerous books on some of the most complex problems of contemporary history—Arab-Israeli relations and the Middle East's influence on world politics, terrorism and guerrilla warfare, Europe since the end of World War II, and the mass murder of Jews in Hitler's devastating "Final Solution." As chairman of the international research board of the Center for Strategic and International Studies at Georgetown University, Laqueur serves as an academic consultant on world affairs to governments around the globe. He is better known, however, as a writer whose "shrewd and well-balanced blend of reportage and analysis . . . sets recent developments in perspective, and provides a good deal of unfamiliar and often intriguing information in the process," in the words of a *New York Times Book Review* contributor. Laqueur is himself a Jew who left Hitler's Germany for Palestine (now Israel) before his twentieth birthday, and he injects his works with analyses drawn from personal experience. A *Times Literary Supplement* reviewer notes that the historian makes use of his commitments in his writings "not to satisfy a moral imperative but as an aid to understanding the twentieth century." In the *New Republic*, Stanley Karnow praises Laqueur for his ability to describe historical events "against the background of a broader global scene. The result is both a microcosmic and macrocosmic view of the world in crisis during a particular period."

"Few men are as qualified to write about Germany as Walter Laqueur, who is both outsider and insider to German society," writes *Detroit News* correspondent Jack Lessenberry. "Though born in what was then Germany (but now a part of Poland as a result of World War II), Laqueur, a Jew, would be dead had he not fled to Palestine. . . . He never went home to stay, and is now [working in] an office just blocks from the White House." Terrence Des Pres elaborates in the *New Republic*: "Rootless and without professional training, [Laqueur] entered the postwar world as a journalist, an editor, and a political analyst, becoming in the process one of the foremost students of our century. . . . While the theorists delivered powerful overviews, Laqueur stayed at the immediate historical level, making modest sense of events, trying the experience of men and nations close-up, bringing small but steady understanding to bear upon problems that could never, except in theory, be wholly grasped or resolved. Unlike those who replaced homelessness with ideas, Laqueur has turned his condition of exile to the pursuit of practical knowledge, with the fortitude of a mind that knows its job to be endless and knows, as theorists do not, that the last word can never be spoken."

Politically, writes Flora Lewis in the *New York Times Book Review*, Laqueur is "a card-carrying member of the postwar academic establishment that organized the intellectual arsenal to see Western Eurpoe through reconstruction, cold war, unprecedented prosperity and the beginnings of detente. He is certainly no dove, but neither is he a hawk, nor is he typical of the other denizens of the political aviary—parrot, ostrich, albatross.'' *New York Times Book Review* contributor Francis Hope calls Laqueur ''a learned defender of the not-so-bad (America and Western Europe) against the manifestly horrible. His main interests have not shifted from his shattered heritage: all things German, Jewish, Russian still concern him, and he thinks they should concern us.'' In recent years Laqueur has even drawn upon this ''shattered heritage'' to produce fiction. His novels *The Missing Years* and *Farewell to Europe* explore the life of an aging Jewish survivor of Hitler's Germany. ''As social history expressed through fiction,'' concludes *New York Review of Books* essayist Neal Ascherson, ''Laqueur's *The Missing Years* is the shrewdest and most observant study of German Jewry I have read.'' Des Pres contends that the fictive form allows Laqueur to ''bring urgency and force to bear upon facts in ways that transform details and events into the units of a language that addresses, through the novel's 'voice,' the human heart.''

As a student, a kibbutz worker, and a journalist, Laqueur witnessed the beginnings of the nation of Israel and many of its subsequent trials and victories. He brings extensive authority to his books on the Middle East, including *The Middle East in Transition: Studies in Contemporary History*, *The Road to Jerusalem: The Origins of the Arab-Israeli Conflict*, *The Israeli-Arab Reader: A Documentary History of the Middle East*, *A History of Zionism*, and *Confrontation: The Middle East War and World Politics*. *Spectator* essayist Donald Watt observes that Laqueur writes of the region ''both as a Jew of the Diaspora and as one of the most able of the younger contemporary historians.'' In a *Book World* review of *The Road to Jerusalem*, Ronald Steel praises the author's objectivity: ''While partial to the Israelis, like most Anglo-American writers on the subject, Laqueur shows considerable sympathy and understanding for the Arabs, and his eminently readable book offers penetrating insight into the [1967] war's origins.'' *Punch* correspondent Jon Kimche likewise calls the work an ''outstandingly admirable and illuminating book on the origins of the Arab-Israeli conflict,'' that is ''so ably and objectively documented . . . that the reader is able to consider the evidence for himself and reach his own conclusions for the time being. He is greatly helped in this by the balanced and objective presentation of the relevant facts.'' According to Chaim Potok in the *New York Times Book Review*, *The Road to Jerusalem* offers ''the best account . . . of the diplomatic maneuverings, the nightmarish dilemmas, the bizarre, almost mindless gambit that took place in the weeks prior to the war. As such, it enables us to see quite clearly the stage upon which the astonishing victory took place.''

Laqueur's *A History of Zionism* places the Jewish presence in the Middle East in broader historical perspective. ''By a large margin this history of Zionism from the early nineteenth century to 1948 is superior in quality to its few predecessors,'' writes a *Times Literary Supplement* reviewer. ''Walter Laqueur . . . has brought to his task both professional knowledge of the history of European and Middle Eastern diplomacy and personal experience of Palestine during some of its most trying years. His book, admirably lucid and readable, is at its best when summarizing the arguments about Jewish destiny put forward by both Zionist and non-Zionist Jewish writers, and in several evocative personal vignettes.'' According to Howard M. Sachar in the *New York Times Book Review*, the author's insights are both good and valid. ''Little that is important in the history of Zionism is neglected in this splendid volume,'' claims Sachar. ''Laqueur's clarity of exposition is not to be confused with mere fluency. It bespeaks rather a lucidity of understanding that should dispel the myth that convolution of structure or style are necessarily synonymous with profundity. More than any other quality, however, it is the author's rigorous objectivity that elevates 'A History of Zionism' light years above its predecessors in this field.''

Laqueur has never limited himself to works on the Middle East. He is also a keen observer of twentieth century European and Soviet affairs. Books such as *The Rebirth of Europe: A History of the Years since the Fall of Hitler* (republished as *Europe since Hitler: The Rebirth of Europe*), *A Continent Astray: Europe 1970-1978*, *Weimar: A Cultural History 1918-1933*, and *The Fate of the Revolution: Interpretations of Soviet History* examine the historical trends that continue to influence economic and cultural development in Europe and the Soviet Union. *New York Times Book Review* contributor David Caute notes that a major theme of *The Rebirth of Europe* is ''the withering away of the more pernicious, and potentially vicious, passions and particularisms of prewar Europe. But the core of Mr. Laqueur's story is this: how a Continent physically and morally shattered by Hitler's war recovered its skills, its creativity and self-confidence with a speed exceeding even the most optimistic predictions. . . . As a general history, 'The Rebirth of Europe' has many virtues; sensibly organized, thoroughly researched, painstakingly accurate and well-written, it displays to advantage the author's already well-proven gift for bringing order to a wide range of material.'' Adam B. Ulam offers similar praise in a *Commentary* assessment of *The Fate of the Revolution*: ''The general reader as well as the harassed college teacher will feel grateful for this reliable guide to what to read about the [Bolshevik] Revolution and its great figures, what to reject as historical fantasy, and what aspects of even the most renowned books on the subject are to be treated with caution or skepticism. . . . Mr. Laqueur's book is . . . an admirable plea for balance in the treatment of the most tangled and controversial events of [modern history].''

Another controversial event—the slow Allied response to information about the Nazi concentration camps during the Second World War—forms the subject of *The Terrible Secret: An Investigation into the Suppression of Information about Hitler's ''Final Solution.''* In a *New Republic* review of the book, Des Pres comments that Laqueur ''is not out to blame or indict; he wants to chart the general response to news of the Final Solution in order to understand why the terrible secret so long remained—and in part still remains—a secret.'' The resulting work, according to the critic, is ''close to a landmark study, not of the Holocaust directly but of the way in which people at every level of involvement responded to incoming information about the massacres and death camps.'' *Times Literary Supplement* correspondent Bernard Wasserstein believes that Laqueur ''is at his lucid best in discussing why it was that so many people, including Jews, could not believe the news even in the face of proofs.'' David Schoenbaum in the *Chicago Tribune Book World* praises Laqueur for exhaustively charting the political, military, and psychological reasons for Allied reluctance to confront and divert the ''Final Solution.'' *The Terrible Secret*, concludes Schoenbaum, ''reaffirms the tenacity, lucidity, and moral seriousness of one of the most important political commentators, strategic analysts, and contemporary historians of our time.''

In order to convey other, more personal thoughts on the legacy of the Holocaust, Laqueur has turned to fiction. *The Missing Years*, published in 1980, and *Farewell to Europe*, published the following year, present the life of a Jewish man "who would be called average but for the fact that he is among the handful of those who actually survived the Nazis," in the words of *New York Times* commentator Christopher Lehmann-Haupt. In *The Missing Years*, the aging Dr. Lasson reflects on his life in Berlin during the Second World War and on his sons' attempts to escape the Nazi terror. *Farewell to Europe* takes Lasson into modern America and Israel, where his sons and grandchildren grapple with their own stresses. *Times Literary Supplement* reviewer Abraham Brumberg finds *The Missing Years* "an engrossing tale, skilfully constructed, its leisurely narrative interspersed with the author's comments and observations, which are always pertinent, frequently sage.... Laqueur has succeeded in making Dr. Lasson a singularly credible and effective witness to a harrowing chapter of modern history." Lehmann-Haupt likewise observes that *The Missing Years* "is not the blockbuster that a more flamboyant dramatist might have flogged from this material, [but] it has a quiet ring of authenticity that only the best of historical writing achieves." In a *Times Literary Supplement* piece on *Farewell to Europe*, S. S. Prawer suggests that Laqueur "is not very good at conveying the feel of a landscape or the physical appearance of his characters—but when it comes to the presentation of political or social argument, not dispassionately but from within a life and a life-style, his novel becomes vivid and absorbing.... Walter Laqueur has given us a novel-sequence which, for all its defects, worthily supplements his distinguished historical, political and sociological analyses of our twentieth-century world."

Laqueur has also tackled an issue of increasing pertinence to modern society—terrorism. After completing two works on guerrilla warfare, *Guerrilla: A Historical and Critical Study* and *The Guerrilla Reader: A Historical Anthology,* he turned to an overview of terrorist acts in *Terrorism* and its companion volume *The Terrorism Reader: A Historical Anthology.* In the *New Republic,* Michael Walzer calls *Terrorism* "a modest and balanced survey by a writer of great skill, who knows foreign languages and can range widely over world history" as well as "an admirable introduction to the central forms of contemporary violence." *Washington Post Book World* reviewer Leonard Bushkoff notes that *Terrorism* "helps to provide depth and substance to a subject usually drowning in sensationalism.... The background [Laqueur] supplies is rich, the arguments systematic, the conclusions convincing." According to James M. Markham in the *New York Times Book Review,* Laqueur's "dispassionate treatment of the emotional subject of terrorism is a healthy antidote to the fearful, overheated atmosphere . . . that can overtake pluralist societies when a small band, grandiloquently styling itself an 'army,' and issuing its 'communiques,' strikes." Hugh Thomas offers a practical suggestion in the *Times Literary Supplement:* "It would undoubtedly be a good thing if Walter Laqueur's fine comparative study of the history of terrorism were to be read in police stations, airport security rooms, army barracks and above all television producers' offices, up and down the world."

In his 1971 book *Out of the Ruins of Europe,* Laqueur states that he resolved to study contemporary history while on guard duty in a kibbutz in 1942. "It occurred to me," he remembers, "that I was very fortunate to be simply alive at a time when so many of my friends and European contemporaries had already perished." Out of this determination to understand the world in which he lives arose the desire to explain his conclusions to others—academic and general reader alike. A *Times Literary Supplement* essayist welcomes Laqueur to the band of "unemotional political thinkers" who, through their scholarship, provide "the salt of the intellectual earth in Western Europe, and particularly in Britain and the United States: the real defenders of free thought, unimpressed by facile pragmatism, basically uninterested in historical tradition of the popular sort, but fanatically devoted to the concept of freedom which we still admire in the West and which they have seen destroyed . . . in their countries of origin." Des Pres feels that all of Laqueur's books have concerned subjects that "turned out to be prime movers of global policy." And in every case, concludes Des Pres, Laqueur "has combined the journalist's sixth sense with the scholar's diligence, and by now he must know as much about our time as anyone on earth."

BIOGRAPHICAL/CRITICAL SOURCES:

BOOKS

Laqueur, Walter, *Out of the Ruins of Europe,* Library Press, 1971.
Laqueur, Walter, *A History of Zionism,* Holt, 1972.
Laqueur, Walter, *Germany Today: A Personal Report,* Little, Brown, 1985.
Walter Laqueur, Inter Nationes (Bonn), 1985.
Walter Laqueur: A Bibliography of His Work, Center for Strategic and International Studies, 1986.

PERIODICALS

Antioch Review, winter, 1967.
Book World, June 23, 1968.
Chicago Tribune Book World, June 15, 1980, January 18, 1981, July 5, 1981.
Commentary, February, 1968, April, 1971.
Detroit News, July 7, 1985.
Globe and Mail (Toronto), June 7, 1986.
Jewish Quarterly, autumn, 1968.
Listener, May 2, 1968.
Los Angeles Times, February 2, 1981, November 29, 1985.
Nation, January 10, 1966, October 28, 1968.
National Review, July 1, 1969.
New Republic, June 1, 1974, June 18, 1977, January 14, 1978, June 30, 1979, May 10, 1980, January 31, 1981, September 2, 1985, September 15, 1986.
New Statesman, June 19, 1970.
New Yorker, September 2, 1985, September 15, 1986.
New York Review of Books, March 3, 1966, August 1, 1968, June 12, 1980, October 22, 1981.
New York Times, January 27, 1975, December 31, 1977, April 11, 1980, June 14, 1985.
New York Times Book Review, December 5, 1965, November 26, 1967, June 2, 1968, January 11, 1970, November 22, 1970, October 17, 1971, November 12, 1972, January 26, 1975, January 23, 1977, October 30, 1977, August 5, 1979, February 1, 1981, May 17, 1981, June 14, 1985, July 28, 1985, November 10, 1985, June 22, 1986.
Partisan Review, summer, 1982.
Punch, April 3, 1968.
Saturday Review, November 13, 1965, July 20, 1968, February 15, 1969, October 28, 1972, January, 1981.
Spectator, March 22, 1968, December 6, 1969, January 29, 1977, April 19, 1980.
Time, January 31, 1977, March 2, 1981.
Times (London), February 14, 1985.
Times Literary Supplement, September 28, 1967, February 3, 1968, July 4, 1968, September 4, 1969, February 5, 1970, June 4, 1970, April 23, 1971, December 22, 1972, January 12, 1973, July 12, 1974, October 25, 1974, March

7, 1975, March 18, 1977, November 18, 1977, May 5, 1978, December 14, 1979, July 4, 1980, November 14, 1980, March 13, 1981, April 16, 1981, March 15, 1985, September 26, 1986, January 30, 1987.

Washington Post, July 16, 1979, March 18, 1980, May 10, 1986.

Washington Post Book World, October 17, 1977, August 25, 1985.

—*Sketch by Anne Janette Johnson*

*   *   *

LASSEN-WILLEMS, James
See WILLEMS, J. Rutherford

*   *   *

LAVER, Michael   1949-

PERSONAL: Born August 3, 1949, in London, England; son of Murray and Kathleen (Blythe) Laver; married Brid Goretti O'Connor, July 28, 1976; children: Conor Murray, Katharine Rose. *Education:* Essex University, B.A., 1970, M.A., 1971; University of Liverpool, Ph.D., 1981. *Politics:* Revolutionary "Cynic." *Religion:* "None of the supernatural variety."

ADDRESSES: Office—Department of Political Science and Sociology, University College, Galway, Ireland.

CAREER: Queens University, Belfast, Northern Ireland, lecturer in politics, 1972-73; University of Liverpool, Liverpool, England, lecturer, 1973-81, senior lecturer in politics, 1981-83; University College, Galway, Ireland, professor and head of Department of Political Science and Sociology, 1983—. Visiting professor of government at University of Texas.

WRITINGS:

(With R. J. Lawrence and Sydney Elliott) *The Northern Ireland Elections of 1973,* H.M.S.O., 1975.
Playing Politics: Seven Games That Bring Out the Politician in Us All, Viking, 1979.
The Politics of Private Desires, Viking, 1981.
The Crime Game, Martin Robertson, 1982.
Invitation to Politics, Martin Robertson, 1983.
Social Choice and Public Policy, Basil Blackwell, 1986.
(Editor) *How Ireland Voted,* Popular Press, 1987.

Contributor to periodicals, including *Political Studies, New Society, Contemporary Review, Parliamentary Affairs, British Journal of Political Science,* and *European Journal of Political Science.* Founding editor of *Irish Political Studies.*

WORK IN PROGRESS: "Three books on various aspects of coalition bargaining. After this, another breakout will be long overdue."

SIDELIGHTS: Michael Laver's *Playing Politics: Seven Games That Bring Out the Politician in Us All* offers seven games in which players learn to despair about the political process. *Chicago Tribune Book World*'s Clarence Peterson notes, "The reader soon catches on that they're not games at all but the real thing, as it might be described by a modern Machiavelli." He calls Laver "an authority on bluffing, lying, and cheating among other political arts."

Laver told *CA:* "I'm a gamesman delighting in complicated trivia—a pathetic excuse for someone who hasn't the nerve to be a real live desperado. *The Crime Game* is a do-it-yourself manual on how to maximize profits when extorting, kidnap-

ping, blackmailing, hijacking, and generally having a good time. After clearing off various commissions and 'serious' books, the time is fast approaching for something that will be more fun to write—a mythology of modern politics."

BIOGRAPHICAL/CRITICAL SOURCES:

PERIODICALS

Chicago Tribune Book World, February 8, 1981.

*   *   *

LESTER, Julius (Bernard)   1939-

PERSONAL: Born January 27, 1939, in St. Louis, Mo.; son of W. D. (a minister) and Julia (Smith) Lester; married Joan Steinau (a researcher), 1962 (divorced, 1970); married Alida Carolyn Fechner, March 21, 1979; children: (first marriage) Jody Simone, Malcolm Coltrane; (second marriage) Elena Milad (stepdaughter), David Julius. *Education:* Fisk University, B.A., 1960.

ADDRESSES: Office—University of Massachusetts—Amherst, Amherst, Mass. 01002.

CAREER: Professional musician and singer, recorded with Vanguard Records; Newport Folk Festival, Newport, R.I., director, 1966-68; WBAI-FM, New York City, producer and host of live radio show, 1968-75; University of Massachusetts—Amherst, professor of Afro-American studies, 1971—, professor of Near Eastern and Judaic Studies, 1982—, acting director and associate director of Institute for Advanced Studies in Humanities, 1982-84. Lecturer at New School for Social Research, New York City, 1968-70; writer-in-residence,Vanderbilt University, 1985. Host of live television show, "Free Time," WNET-TV, New York City, 1971-73.

AWARDS, HONORS: Distinguished Teacher's Award, 1983-84; Faculty Fellowship Award for Distinguished Research and Scholarship, 1985; National Professor of the Year Silver Medal Award, from Council for Advancement and Support of Education, 1985; Massachusetts State Professor of the Year and Gold Medal Award for National Professor of the Year, both from Council for Advancement and Support of Education, both 1986; chosen distinguished faculty lecturer, 1986-87; *To Be a Slave* was nominated for the Newberry Award; *The Long Journey Home: Stories from Black History* was a National Book Award finalist.

WRITINGS:

(With Pete Seeger) *The 12-String Guitar as Played by Leadbelly,* Oak, 1965.
Look out Whitey! Black Power's Gon' Get Your Mama!, Dial, 1968.
To Be a Slave, Dial, 1969.
Black Folktales, Baron, 1969.
Search for the New Land: History as Subjective Experience, Dial, 1969.
Revolutionary Notes, Baron, 1969.
(Editor) *The Seventh Son: The Thoughts and Writings of W.E.B. Du Bois,* two volumes, Random House, 1971.
(Compiler with Rae Pace Alexander) *Young and Black in America,* Random House, 1971.
The Long Journey Home: Stories from Black History, Dial, 1972.
The Knee-High Man and Other Tales, Dial, 1972.
Two Love Stories, Dial, 1972.

(Editor) Stanley Couch, *Ain't No Ambulances for No Nigguhs Tonight* (poems), Baron, 1972.
Who I Am (poems), Dial, 1974.
All Is Well: An Autobiography, Morrow, 1976.
This Strange New Feeling, Dial, 1982.
Do Lord Remember Me (novel), Holt, 1984.
The Tales of Uncle Remus (four-volume series in progress), Dial, Volume I: *The Adventures of Brer Rabbit,* 1987, Volume II: *The Further Adventures of Brer Rabbit,* 1988.
Lovesong: Becoming a Jew (autobiographical), Holt, 1988.

Contributor of essays and reviews to numerous magazines and newspapers, including *New York Times Book Review, New York Times, Nation, Katallagete, Democracy,* and *Village Voice.* Associate editor, *Sing Out,* 1964-70; contributing editor, *Broadside of New York,* 1964-70.

SIDELIGHTS: Julius Lester is "foremost among young black writers who produce their work from a position of historical strength," writes critic John A. Williams in the *New York Times Book Review.* Drawing on old documents and folktales, Lester fashions stories that proclaim the heritage of black Americans and "attempt to recreate the social life of the past," note Eric and Naomi Foner in the *New York Review of Books.* Though historically accurate, Lester's tales are more than simple reportage. Their purpose, as the Foners point out, is "not merely to impart historical information, but to teach moral and political lessons." Because he feels that the history of minority groups has been largely ignored, Lester intends to furnish his young readers with what he calls "a usable past" and with what the Foners call "a sense of history which will help shape their lives and politics."

Lester's characters fall into two categories: those drawn from Afro-American folklore and those drawn from black history. The former are imaginary creatures, or sometimes animals, such as *The Knee-High Man*'s Mr. Bear and Mr. Rabbit; the latter are real people, "ordinary men and women who might appear only in . . . a neglected manuscript at the Library of Congress," according to William Loren Katz in the *Washington Post Book World.* Critics find that Lester uses both types of characters to reveal the black individual's struggle against slavery.

Black Folktales, Lester's first collection of folk stories, features larger-than-life heroes (including a cigar-smoking black God), shrewd animals, and cunning human beings. While some of the characters are taken from African legends and others from American slave tales, they all demonstrate that "black resistance to white oppression is as old as the confrontation between the two groups," says Williams. Most reviewers applaud Lester's view of Afro-American folklore and praise his storytelling skills, but a few object to what they perceive as the anti-white tone of the book. Zena Sutherland, writing in *Bulletin of the Center for Children's Books,* calls *Black Folktales* "a vehicle for hostility. . . . There is no story that concerns white people in which they are not pictured as venal or stupid or both."

Lester also deals with white oppression in his second collection of folktales, *The Knee-High Man and Other Tales.* Although these six animal stories are funny, *New York Times Book Review* critic Ethel Richards suggests that "powerfully important lessons ride the humor. In 'The Farmer and the Snake,' the lesson is that kindness will not change the nature of a thing—in this case, the nature of a poisonous snake to bite." A *Junior Bookshelf* reviewer points out that this story—as well as others in the book—reflects the relationship between owner and slave.

While pursuing the same theme, Lester moves into the realm of nonfiction with *The Long Journey Home: Stories from Black History,* a documentary collection of slave narratives, and *To Be a Slave,* a collection of six stories based on historical fact. Both books showcase ordinary people in adverse circumstances and provide the reader with a look at what Lester calls "history from the bottom up." *Black like Me* author John Howard Griffin, writing in the *New York Times Book Review,* commends Lester's approach, saying that the stories "help destroy the delusion that black men did not suffer as another man would in similar circumstances," and the Foners applaud the fact that "Lester does not feel it is necessary to make every black man and woman a super-hero." *New York Times Book Review* contributor Rosalind K. Goddard recommends Lester's writing as both lesson and entertainment: "These stories point the way for young blacks to find their roots, so important to the realization of their identities, as well as offer a stimulating and informative experience for all."

Lester's books have been translated into seven languages. His photographs of the 1960s civil rights movement have been exhibited at the Smithsonian Institution and are on permanent display at Howard University.

BIOGRAPHICAL/CRITICAL SOURCES:

BOOKS

Children's Literature Review, Volume II, Gale, 1976.
Krim, Seymour, *You and Me,* Holt, 1972.
Lester, Julius, *All Is Well: An Autobiography,* Morrow, 1976.

PERIODICALS

Bulletin of the Center for Children's Books, February, 1970.
Junior Bookshelf, February, 1975.
Nation, June 22, 1970.
New York Review of Books, April 20, 1972.
New York Times Book Review, November 3, 1968, November 9, 1969, July 23, 1972, February 4, 1973, September 5, 1982, February 17, 1985.
Times Literary Supplement, April 3, 1987.
Washington Post, March 12, 1985.
Washington Post Book World, September 3, 1972.

*   *   *

LeTOURNEAU, Richard (Howard) 1925-

PERSONAL: Surname is pronounced "Leh-*ter*-know"; born January 3, 1925, in Stockton, Calif.; son of Robert F. (a manufacturer) and Evelyn (Peterson) LeTourneau; married Louise Marion Jensen, February 8, 1947; children: Robert Gilmour, Caleb Roy, Linda Louise, Liela Lynn. *Education:* Attended Wheaton College, 1946, and Le Tourneau College, 1956; Texas A&M University, B.S., 1958, M.S., 1961; Oklahoma State University, Ph.D., 1970. *Politics:* Republican. *Religion:* Protestant-Evangelical.

ADDRESSES: Home—1307 Briarmeade Dr., Duncanville, Tex. 75137. *Office*—Dallas Baptist University, 7777 West Kiest Blvd., Dallas, Tex. 75227.

CAREER: R. G. LeTourneau, Inc., Longview, Tex., general manager of Mississippi division, 1949-52, vice-president of production, 1952-57, executive vice-president, 1966, president, 1966-71; Le Tourneau College, Longview, administrative vice-president, 1958-62, president, 1962-68, 1975-86; Marathon Manufacturing Co., Houston, Tex., senior vice-president, 1971-72; Mosley Machinery Co., Waco, Tex., president, 1972-73; Le Tourneau Foundation, Longview, vice-president, 1973-75; Dallas Baptist University, Dallas, Texas, provost, 1987—. Member of Texas Industrial Commission, 1959-66; chairman of board of Industrial Arts Commission, Texas Department of Education, 1971—. Member of board of trustees, Toccoa Falls Institute, 1954-75, and Simpson College, 1974-77; chairman of board of trustees, Le Tourneau College, 1968-75, and International Linguistic Center, 1979-86; member of board of directors, Marathon Manufacturing Co., 1971-76, Wycliff Bible Translators, U.S. Home Division, 1973, and Child Evangelism Fellowship, 1986—; member of board of managers, Christian and Missionary Alliance. *Military service:* U.S. Army, 1944-46; served in Pacific Theater.

MEMBER: Society of Automotive Engineers, American Institute of Industrial Engineers, American Society for Engineering Education, Tau Beta Pi, Phi Kappa Phi, Alpha Pi Mu, Sigma Xi.

WRITINGS:

Management Plus: The Spiritual Dimension in Leadership, Zondervan, 1973.
Keeping Your Cool in a World of Tension, Zondervan, 1975.
Success without Succeeding, Zondervan, 1976.
Success without Compromise, Victor Books, 1977.
Democracy in Trouble, LeTourneau Press, 1985.
More than Knowledge, LeTourneau Press, 1985.
Laws of Success for Christians, Le Tourneau Press, 1985.
Finding Your Niche in Life (autobiography), LeTourneau Press, 1985.
Latch Key, LeTourneau Press, 1986.

Also contributor to *Now.*

WORK IN PROGRESS: Research on the relationships between business, Christianity, and education.

*   *   *

LEVENSON, Jordan 1936-
(Jordan O'Levenson)

PERSONAL: Born 1936, in Los Angeles, Calif.; son of Max (a woodturner) and Hilda (a librarian; maiden name, Rothstein) Levenson. *Education:* California State College at Los Angeles (now California State University, Los Angeles), B.S., 1966; University of Southern California, M.B.A., 1970. *Politics:* "Middle of the road."

ADDRESSES: Home—Los Angeles, Calif. *Office*—Levenson Press, P.O. Box 19606, Los Angeles, Calif. 90019.

CAREER: Publisher and writer. Has worked as salesman, manufacturer's representative, decorator, and motion picture construction laborer; professional musician in Los Angeles, Calif., 1951-76; Los Angeles County Department of Public Social Services, Los Angeles, eligibility worker, 1972—. Instructor, University of Southern California Experimental College, 1971-72. Holds one U.S. patent. *Military service:* U.S. Army Reserve, 1959-65.

MEMBER: International Association for Near-Death Studies (IANDS).

WRITINGS:

Retail Fruit Species: Your Shopper's Guide to Their Best Varieties, Levenson, 1972, 2nd edition, 1979.

The Back Lot: Motion Picture Studio Laborer's Craft Described by a Hollywood Laborer, Levenson, 1972.
Abilities of Refracting Telescope Optics: A "Non-Mathematical" Understanding for Buyers and Users, Levenson, 1973.
Vitamins: A Systems Analysis Solution to the Doctor vs. Health Faddist Controversy, Levenson, 1974.
Underlying Concepts of Room Lighting for the Intelligent Layman, Levenson, 1974.
Underlying Concepts of Room Acoustical Control for the Intelligent Layman, Levenson, 1976, revised edition, 1979.
Poor Man's Route to Rich Man's Stock Market Wealth, Levenson, 1980.
How to Buy and Understand Refracting Telescopes, Levenson, 1981.
Your First Trip to Europe: Where, What and How, Volume I, Levenson, 1985.

EDITOR

(Under pseudonym Jordan O'Levenson) *Irish In-Memoriam Poetry: The Book of Tears,* Levenson, 1983.

OTHER

Contributor to *Journal of Irreproducible Results.*

WORK IN PROGRESS: Your First Trip to Euorpe, Volume II; a book in the automotive area.

SIDELIGHTS: Jordan Levenson wrote *CA:* "Levenson Press is a short run publisher of void-filling literature. Short press runs result in higher unit costs. However, the benefit is that specialized audiences will be able to obtain high-quality information that otherwise would not be available because of lack of mass market appeal and therefore lack of major publisher interest."

In a later letter, Levenson explained the origin of his book *Irish In-Memoriam Poetry: The Book of Tears.* "The Irish have a mourning custom in that obituary notices published in newspapers over the years often contain specialized poetry. The death notices are published under the heading 'In Memoriam'. [*Irish In-Memoriam Poetry: The Book of Tears*] is the 'archival' work on this mourning custom and the only book in its specific field of Irish culture. It is, between one set of covers, a collection of over four hundred of these specialized poems. The book also contains text by the editor, who has been in Ireland three times to date.

"There are a few lessons to be learned here. The subject of this book, a practice that is now going out of style, is a part of Irish national culture, and the book should have been created and published by an Irish press. But it wasn't. Why? Either the Irish didn't recognize what they had, or didn't care about it, or publishing poetry isn't profitable. The Irish do care about poetry and publishing it was profitable for the newspapers. But poetry books do not sell well, and this one would not sell in Ireland to the Irish people because they already know the poetry. However, you'd think that a university press would have created the book because the book could have been sold to tourists and to libraries, domestic and foreign. Irish culture sells. The first lesson is the well-known one that foreigners to anywhere will see value and potential in things overlooked by the locals. There was value in *In Memoriam* notices.

"The title of the book, though clearly descriptive for the Irish, is ambiguous for Americans. It could be taken several ways. What is memoriam poetry anyway? Often a listing of the title is the only thing available to communicate the nature of the book. The lesson here is that the title used did not serve the book as it should have. It didn't communicate significantly to American book buyers.

"The third lesson is that the quite clever pen name of the editor, catchy as it is, is more than offset by the failure to make use of the years of effort to gain recognition for the name of this small press author. Levenson watchers, and there seem to be a few, will never know this book has been published because in the author listings (which also list editors by the last name) this book will be listed over O (for O'Levenson) instead of L."

AVOCATIONAL INTERESTS: Trade shows, reading trade journals of various industries, international travel, the stock market.

*   *   *

LEVINSON, Nancy Smiler   1938-

PERSONAL: Born November 5, 1938, in Minneapolis, Minn.; daughter of Paul (an attorney) and Minnie (Meleck) Smiler; married Irwin Levinson (a cardiologist), June 1, 1966; children: Matthew, Danny. *Education:* University of Minnesota, B.A., 1960. *Politics:* Democrat. *Religion:* Jewish.

ADDRESSES: Home and office—1139 Coldwater Canyon Dr., Beverly Hills, Calif. 90210.

CAREER: Port Chester Daily Item, Westchester, N.Y., reporter, 1960-61; Language Laboratory, Columbia University, office worker, 1961-62; *Time* magazine, researcher, 1962-63; Bantam Books, Inc., New York, N.Y., associate editor, 1963-66; teacher in head-start program in Los Angeles, Calif., 1967-68; free-lance writer and editor, 1974—. Tutor of handicapped children.

MEMBER: Society of Children's Book Writers, Southern California Council on Literature for Children and Young People.

AWARDS, HONORS: The Southern California Council on Literature for Children and Young People named *I Lift My Lamp— Emma Lazarus and the Statue of Liberty* a distinguished work of nonfiction in 1986.

WRITINGS:

Contributions of Women: Business (juvenile biography), Dillon, 1981.
World of Her Own (juvenile novel), Harvey House, 1981.
Silent Fear (juvenile novel), Crestwood, 1981.
The First Women Who Spoke Out (juvenile biography), Dillon, 1982.
Make a Wish (novel), Scholastic Book Services, 1983.
The Ruthie Greene Show (juvenile novel), Lodestar, 1985.
(Co-author) *Getting High in Natural Ways* (nonfiction), Hunter House, 1986.
I Lift My Lamp—Emma Lazarus and the Statue of Liberty (juvenile biography), Lodestar, 1986.
The Man Who Broke the Sound Barrier (juvenile biography), Walker & Co., 1988.

Contributor of articles and stories to adult and children's magazines and newspapers, including *Seventeen, American Girl, Highlights for Children, Writer's Digest, Confrontation, Teen, Newsday, Los Angeles Times,* and *Los Angeles Herald Examiner.*

WORK IN PROGRESS: A history story for Lodestar.

SIDELIGHTS: Nancy Smiler Levinson told *CA:* "I have always felt for the one who is different, left out, and that feeling is reflected in much of my fiction. My first published novel, *World of Her Own,* is about a deaf girl being mainstreamed into a public high school. The research was moving; the writing, exciting. It is my hope that the book's readers will become sensitive to the pain and problems of the lone young person across the classroom—and reach out.''

*   *   *

L'HEUREUX, John (Clarke)   1934-

PERSONAL: Born October 26, 1934, in South Hadley, Mass.; son of Wilfred (a civil engineer and artist) and Mildred (an artist; maiden name, Clarke) L'Heureux; married Joan Polston, June 26, 1971. *Education:* Attended National Academy of Theatre Arts, 1952, and College of the Holy Cross, 1952-54; Boston College, A.B., 1959, M.A. (philosophy), 1960, M.A. (English), 1963; Woodstock College, S.T.L., 1967; Harvard University, M.A. (English), 1968.

ADDRESSES: Office—Department of English, Stanford University, Stanford, Calif. 94305.

CAREER: Entered Society of Jesus (Jesuits), 1954; ordained priest, 1965; laicized, 1971. Writer-in-residence, Georgetown University, Washington, D.C., 1964-65, Regis College, Weston, Mass., 1968-69; *Atlantic,* Washington, D.C., staff editor, 1968-69, contributing editor, 1969—; Stanford University, Stanford, Calif., assistant professor, 1973-79, associate professor, 1979-81, professor of English, 1981—, director of creative writing program, 1977—, Lane Professor of Humanities, 1984—. Visiting professor of American literature, Hamline University, 1971, and Tufts College, 1971-73; visiting assistant professor, Harvard University, 1973.

AWARDS, HONORS: Creative writing fellowships from National Endowment for the Arts, 1981, 1986.

WRITINGS:

NOVELS

Tight White Collar, Doubleday, 1972.
The Clang Birds, Macmillan, 1972.
Jessica Fayer, Macmillan, 1976.
A Woman Run Mad, Viking, 1987.

SHORT STORIES

Family Affairs, Doubleday, 1974.
Desires, Holt, 1981.

POETRY

Quick as Dandelions, Doubleday, 1964.
Rubrics for a Revolution, Macmillan, 1967.
One Eye and a Measuring Rod, Macmillan, 1968.
No Place for Hiding, Macmillan, 1971.

OTHER

Picnic in Babylon: A Jesuit Priest's Journal, 1963-67 (autobiography), Macmillan, 1967.

SIDELIGHTS: John L'Heureux has successfully published poetry, novels, and short stories. His short story collection *Desires* receives high praise from Carolyn See in the *Los Angeles Times.* She characterizes L'Heureux's fictional world as a mysterious, otherworldly place. "The functions of American art, religion and philosophy are what L'Heureux is concerned about,'' she notes. ''He seems to be saying, isn't our 20th-Century insistence on the perfectly realized, 'realistic' external detail just essentially and eternally boring? Wouldn't it be better, for our art if not for our own individual lives, if we recognized other, larger grids on which to play out our dramas; wouldn't it make sense to postulate a supernatural good, an ecstatic Absolute, and then order our own lives as if those things existed? It would be more exciting, that way, more 'meaningful,' more elegant.'' *New York Times Book Review* contributor Johanna Kaplan concurs with See that ''the desire for transcendence is the preeminent desire in Mr. L'Heureux's fiction.'' Kaplan also points out that L'Heureux's depiction of everyday life is very bleak—''a landscape of hopelessness and disillusion, a cruel and unforgiving place in which any commonplace pursuit . . . is a doomed and foolish hoax.'' L'Heureux's style is called by Kaplan ''spare, witty, and elegant.'' His stories are often difficult, finds See, but ''their demands are refreshing. They are the opposite of a 'good read.' They are difficult, cranky, beautiful works of art.'' In response to See, L'Heureux told *CA:* ''I have hopes that my . . . book, *A Woman Run Mad*, will take me out of the nice but limiting category of 'being the opposite of a good read,' elegant though that is.''

L'Heureux is competent in French and Latin, and reads Italian and Greek.

AVOCATIONAL INTERESTS: Painting.

BIOGRAPHICAL/CRITICAL SOURCES:

PERIODICALS

Chicago Tribune Book World, April 5, 1981.
Los Angeles Times, April 28, 1981.
New York Times Book Review, April 12, 1981.

*   *   *

LINDBLOM, Steven (Winther)   1946-

PERSONAL: Born March 29, 1946, in Minneapolis, Minn.; son of Charles Edward (a professor of political science and writer) and Rose Catherine Lindblom; married True (Adelaide) Kelley (a writer and illustrator); children: Jada Winter Lindblom. *Education:* Attended St. John's College, Annapolis, Md., 1964-65; Rhode Island School of Design, B.F.A., 1972.

ADDRESSES: Home—Old Denny Hill, Warner, N.H. 03278.

CAREER: Free-lance illustrator and writer.

AWARDS, HONORS: ''Best Books on Science for Children,'' New York Academy of Science, 1982, for *Messing around with Water Pumps and Siphons: A Children's Museum Activity Book;* ''Outstanding Science and Trade Book for Children,'' National Science Teachers Association, 1982, for *The Internal Combustion Engine;* ''Best Books of the Year'' list, Bank Street College of Education, 1985, for *How to Build a Robot.*

WRITINGS:

JUVENILES

(With wife, True Kelley) *The Mouses' Terrible Christmas*, illustrated by Kelley, Lothrop, 1978.
The Fantastic Bicycles Book, Houghton, 1979.
(With Kelley) *The Mouses' Terrible Halloween*, illustrated by Kelley, Lothrop, 1980.
(With Kelley) *Let's Give Kitty a Bath*, illustrated by Kelley, Addison-Wesley, 1982.

How to Build a Robot, Crowell Junior Book, 1985.
Let's Go Shopping, Western Publishing, 1988.
Tiny Dinosaurs, Western Publishing, 1988.

JUVENILES; ILLUSTRATOR

Bernie Zubrowski, *Messing around with Water Pumps and Siphons: A Children's Museum Activity Book*, Little, Brown, 1981.
Ross Olney, *The Internal Combustion Engine*, Lippincott, 1982.
Seymour Simon, *Computer Sense, Computer Nonsense*, Lippincott, 1984.

WORK IN PROGRESS: Juvenile books about flying and dinosaurs.

SIDELIGHTS: Steven Lindblom told *CA:* ''While I have written more fiction than nonfiction at this point, nonfiction writing is my first love.

''I think there are two very negative forces at work on our children today. One is television, which is turning children into drones who are only observers, and who have been convinced that experiences seen on television are somehow as valid as the real thing. (I think a child who neither read nor watched television might be happier and more constructive than one who did both!) The other is that modern technology has become so complex and remote that we begin to see ourselves as its victims rather than its masters and cease accepting any responsibility for the future.

''There are two things good children's nonfiction can do about this: encourage kids to get out and do things for themselves and reduce the world that surrounds them to manageable terms, restoring to them the feeling that they can comprehend it, and therefore control it.

''It's important that kids realize that whenever someone tells them, 'It's too complicated for you to understand,' the person probably is just covering up his own lack of understanding.''

AVOCATIONAL INTERESTS: Old bicycles and machinery, flying, designing and building his ''solar-gothik'' home.

*   *   *

LIPSEY, Richard A(llan)   1930-

PERSONAL: Born July 19, 1930, in Chicago, Ill.; son of David Herbert (a wholesale distributor) and Hilda (Salzberg) Lipsey; married Jill Frisch, April 11, 1964 (divorced January, 1974); married Annette Triestman (a jeweler), June 30, 1977; children: Richard A., Jr. *Education:* University of Pennsylvania, B.S., 1952; University of Chicago, M.B.A., 1962. *Religion:* Jewish.

ADDRESSES: Home—901 Blue Spring Rd., Princeton, N.J. 08540. *Office*—NPD Group, 900 West Side Rd., Port Washington, N.Y. 11050.

CAREER: Motorola, Inc., Chicago, Ill., in marketing, 1957-60; Helene Curtis Industries, Chicago, director of marketing research, 1961-65; Liggett & Myers, New York City, director of marketing research and brand management, 1965-69; V. P. Audits and Surveys, Inc., New York City, director of Leisure Times Research Division, 1970-79; NPD Group, Inc., Port Washington, N.Y., director of sports research, 1984—. *Military service:* U.S. Air Force, 1952-54; became first lieutenant.

WRITINGS:

Sportsguide Master Reference, Sportsguide, 1981, 2nd edition, 1983.
Sportsguide's Pro Sports Directory, Sportsguide, 1983.
Sports Market Place, Sportsguide, 1987.

SIDELIGHTS: Richard A. Lipsey told *CA:* "My writing and editing goal is to provide sports business executives with sources of contacts and information covering all facets of sports—professional and amateur—and to assist those responsible behind-the-scenes in the business of sports."

* * *

LOCHTE, Dick
See LOCHTE, Richard S(amuel)

* * *

LOCHTE, Richard S(amuel)   1944-
(Dick Lochte)

PERSONAL: Born October 19, 1944, in New Orleans, La.; son of Richard Samuel (an insurance investigator) and Eileen (a musician; maiden name, Carbine) Lochte. *Education:* Tulane University, B.A., 1966.

ADDRESSES: Home and office—P.O. Box 5413, Santa Monica, Calif. 90405. *Agent*—William Morris Agency, 1350 Avenue of the Americas, New York, N.Y. 10019.

CAREER: Playboy, Chicago, Ill., publicist and writer, 1966-73; free-lance writer, 1973—. *Military service:* U.S. Coast Guard Reserve, 1962-69; became lieutenant commander.

MEMBER: International PEN, Writers Guild of America, Mystery Writers of America, National Book Critics Circle, Private Eye Writers of America, Authors League of America, American Theater Critics Association, Los Angeles Drama Critics Circle.

AWARDS, HONORS: Nero Wolfe Award, from Rex Stout Society, and special award, from Mystery Writers of America, both 1985, both for *Sleeping Dog.*

WRITINGS:

The Playboy Writer (nonfiction), HMH Publications, 1968.
Death Mask (mystery novel), Sherbourne, 1971.
(Co-author) "Escape to Athena" (screenplay), ITC/Associated Film Distribution, 1979.
(Under name Dick Lochte) *Sleeping Dog* (mystery novel), Arbor House, 1985.
(Under name Dick Lochte) "Philip Strange" (screenplay), Michael Laughlin Productions, 1985.
(Under name Dick Lochte) *Laughing Dog* (sequel to *Sleeping Dog*), Arbor House, 1987.
(Under name Dick Lochte) *Dancing Dog* (sequel to *Sleeping Dog*), Arbor House, 1988.

Also author of the screenplay "Sleeping Dog." Theatre critic for *Los Angeles,* 1974—; columnist for *Los Angeles Times,* 1975-85.

WORK IN PROGRESS: A screenplay entitled "Hot Bodies."

SIDELIGHTS: Richard S. Lochte commented: "It has been said that young writers today are interested in writing The Great American Film instead of The Great American Novel. If true, it is because they are unfamiliar with the differences—

make that perils—the two media hold for the writer. As a novelist, the writer is in total control of the material and as such is responsible for research, accuracy, clarity of thought, and so on. As a screenwriter, he or she prepares a blueprint and thereafter is responsible only for cashing the check for services rendered.

"Writing pulled me through schools and college. If I hadn't been interested in it, I'd probably still be stuck back there trying to figure out why $E=mc^2$. When I didn't know an answer, which was often, I made one up. I did some of my most creative writing in college. Later, it was a way of getting away from a nine to five job. What I got away to, of course, was a nine to nine job. Still, work that you like is easy work. The only easier work I can think of is owning a parking lot, because there you can read on the job and you don't have to change typewriter ribbons."

BIOGRAPHICAL/CRITICAL SOURCES:

PERIODICALS

Los Angeles Times Book Review, November 24, 1985.
New York Times Book Review, November 17, 1985.

* * *

LOGAN, Jake
See PEARL, Jacques Bain
and SMITH, Martin Cruz

* * *

LOPEZ, Barry Holstun   1945-

PERSONAL: Born January 6, 1945, in Port Chester, N.Y.; son of Adrian Bernard and Mary (Holstun) Lopez; married Sandra Landers (a bookwright), June 10, 1967. *Education:* University of Notre Dame, A.B. (cum laude), 1966, M.A.T., 1968; University of Oregon, graduate study, 1969-70.

CAREER: Full-time writer, 1970—. Associate at Gannett Center for Media Studies, Columbia University, 1985—; Distinguished Visiting Writer, Eastern Washington University, 1985; Ida Beam Visiting Professor, University of Iowa, 1985; Distinguished Visiting Naturalist, Carleton College, 1986.

AWARDS, HONORS: John Burroughs Medal for distinguished natural history writing, Christopher Medal for humanitarian writing, and Pacific Northwest Booksellers award for excellence in nonfiction, all 1979, and American Book Award nomination, 1980, all for *Of Wolves and Men;* Distinguished Recognition Award, Friends of American Writers, 1981, for *Winter Count;* National Book Award in nonfiction (formerly American Book Award), Christopher Book Award, Pacific Northwest Booksellers award, National Book Critics Circle award nomination, *Los Angeles Times* book award nomination, American Library Association notable book citation, *New York Times Book Review* "Best Books" listing, and American Library Association "Best Books for Young Adults" citation, all 1986, and Francis Fuller Victor Award in nonfiction from Oregon Institute of Literary Arts, 1987, all for *Arctic Dreams: Imagination and Desire in a Northern Landscape;* Award in Literature from American Academy and Institute of Arts and Letters, 1986, for body of work; Guggenheim fellow, 1987.

WRITINGS:

Desert Notes: Reflections in the Eye of a Raven (fictional narratives), Andrews & McMeel, 1976.

Giving Birth to Thunder, Sleeping with His Daughter: Coyote Builds North America (native American trickster stories), Andrews & McMeel, 1978.

Of Wolves and Men (nonfiction), Scribner, 1978.

River Notes: The Dance of Herons (fictional narratives), Andrews & McMeel, 1979.

Desert Reservation (chapbook), Copper Canyon Press, 1980.

Winter Count (fiction), Scribner, 1981.

Arctic Dreams: Imagination and Desire in a Northern Landscape (nonfiction), Scribner, 1986.

Crossing Open Ground (essays), Scribner, 1988.

CONTRIBUTOR TO ANTHOLOGIES

Thomas Cooley, editor, *The Norton Sampler,* Norton, 1979, new edition, 1985.

Mary Van Derventer, editor, *Earthworks: Ten Years on the Environmental Front,* Friends of the Earth, 1980.

Dewitt Jones, editor, *Visions of Wilderness,* Graphic Arts Center, 1980.

Johnathan Cott and Mary Gimbel, editors, *Wonders: Writings and Drawings for the Child in Us All,* Rolling Stone Press, 1980.

Joseph Trimmer and Maxine Hairston, editors, *The Riverside Reader,* Houghton, new edition, 1985.

Charles Erdoes and Alfonso Ortiz, *American Indian Myths and Legends,* Pantheon, 1985.

James Hepworth and Gregory McNamee, editors, *Resist Much, Obey Little: Some Notes on Edward Abbey,* Dream Garden, 1985.

D. L. Emblen and Arnold Solkov, editors, *Before and After: The Shape and Shaping of Prose,* Random House, 1986.

A. M. Rosenthal, Arthur Gelb, and others, editors, *The Sophisticated Traveler: Enchanting Places and How to Find Them,* Villard Books, 1986.

Rich Ives, editor, *From Timberline to Tidepool: Contemporary Fiction from the Northwest,* Owl Creek Press, 1986.

Richard Haswell and others, editors, *The HBJ Reader,* Harcourt, 1987.

Daniel Halpern, editor, *On Nature,* North Point Press, 1987.

Alexander Blackburn, editor, *The Interior Country: Stories of the Modern West,* Swallow Press/Ohio University Press, 1987.

Robley Wilson, Jr., editor, *Four-Minute Fictions: Fifty Short-Short Stories from The North American Review,* Word Beat Press, 1987.

Also contributor to *Best American Essays 1987,* in press.

OTHER

Contributor of articles, essays, and short fiction to numerous periodicals including *Harper's, North American Review, New York Times, Orion Nature Quarterly, Antaeus, National Geographic,* and *Outside.* Contributing editor, *North American Review,* 1977—, and *Harper's,* 1981-82 and 1984—; guest editor of special section, "The American Indian Mind," for *Quest,* September/October, 1978; correspondent, *Outside,* 1982—; advisory editor, *Antaeus,* autumn, 1986.

WORK IN PROGRESS: A work of fiction, set on the northern plains in the eighteenth century; a work of nonfiction about landscapes remote from North America; essays, articles, and short fiction for magazines.

SIDELIGHTS: Barry Holstun Lopez's early magazine articles and books established his reputation as an authoritative writer on the subjects of natural history and the environment. He has been favorably compared to such distinguished naturalist/authors as Edward Hoagland, Peter Matthiessen, Edward Abbey, Sally Carrighar, and Loren Eiseley. Lopez's more recent works are praised for their philosophical content as well, for in *Of Wolves and Men* and *Arctic Dreams: Imagination and Desire in a Northern Landscape,* the author uses natural history as a metaphor for discussing some larger moral issues. "A writer has a certain handful of questions," he explained to Nick O'Connell in a *Seattle Review* interview. "Mine seem to be the issues of tolerance and dignity. You can't sit down and write directly about those things, but if they are on your mind and if you're a writer, they're going to come out in one form or another. The form I feel most comfortable with, where I do a lot of reading and aimless thinking, is in natural history."

Lopez spent most of his first ten years in Southern California— "before it became a caricature of itself," he told *Western American Literature* interviewer Jim Aton. By the time the family moved back to Lopez's birthplace, New York, he had formed a strong emotional attachment to the West Coast, and so he returned to live there when he was twenty-three years old. His graduate studies in folklore led him to write his first book, a retelling of American Indian stories featuring the coyote as a trickster figure. It was published some time later as *Giving Birth to Thunder, Sleeping with His Daughter: Coyote Builds North America.* Deciding that life as a writer was preferable to life as a scholar, Lopez left the university in 1970, settled with his wife on the McKenzie River in western Oregon, and devoted himself to writing full time.

A 1974 magazine assignment for *Smithsonian* magazine led to Lopez's first major book, *Of Wolves and Men.* His research for that article "catalyzed a lot of thinking about human and animal relationships which had been going on in a vague way in my mind for several years," he said in a *CA* interview. "I realized that if I focused on this one animal, I might be able to say something sharp and clear." In his book, Lopez attempts to present a complete portrait of the wolf. He includes not only scientific information, but also wolf lore from aboriginal societies and an overview of the animal's role in literature, folklore and superstition.

The result, say many critics, is a book that succeeds on several levels. First of all, Lopez has gathered "an extraordinary amount of material," writes a contributor to *The New York Review of Books,* making *Of Wolves and Men* one of the most comprehensive sources of information on these animals ever published. Secondly, in showing readers the many diverse images of the wolf, the author reveals how man "creates" animals by projecting aspects of his own personality on them. Thirdly, Lopez illustrates how undeserved is Western civilization's depiction of the wolf as a ruthless killer. His observations showed him that the Eskimos' conception of the wolf is much closer to the truth; among them, wolves are respected and emulated for their intelligence and strong sense of loyalty. What we think about the wolf may reveal something about ourselves, concludes Lopez, for while Western man has reviled the wolf as a wanton killer, he himself has brutally and pointlessly driven many animals to extinction. Whitley Streiber of the *Washington Post* believes that *Of Wolves and Men* is "a very important book by a man who has thought much on his subject. Above all he has listened to many people who claim to know about wolves. In coming to terms with the difference between what we know and what we imagine about the wolf, Lopez has shed light on some painful truths about the human experience. By laying no blame while facing the tragedy for what it is, he has made what we have done to the wolf a source of new knowledge about man."

Lopez found that he was strongly drawn to the Arctic even after *Of Wolves and Men* was completed. Over the next four years he made several more trips there, and in 1986 he published an account of his travels, entitled *Arctic Dreams: Imagination and Desire in a Northern Landscape.* While the book provides a wealth of factual information about the Arctic region, it is, says the *New York Times*'s Michiko Kakutani, ''a book about the Arctic North in the way that 'Moby-Dick' is a novel about whales.'' Lopez in *Arctic Dreams* restates the deeper themes found in *Of Wolves and Men,* but while *Of Wolves and Men* focused tightly on man's relationship with a specific animal, *Arctic Dreams*'s scope is wider, exploring man's relationship with what Lopez refers to as ''the landscape.'' He explained to Jim Aton, ''By landscape I mean the complete lay of the land—the animals that are there, the trees, the vegetation, the quality of soils, the drainage pattern of water, the annual cycles of temperature, the kinds of precipitation, the sounds common to the region.''

Arctic Dreams drew many favorable reviews, both for its vivid descriptions of the North and for the questions it raises about man's place in nature. ''The writing, at times, is luminous, powerful and musical. Lopez infuses each sentence with grace,'' asserts George Tombs in the Toronto *Globe & Mail.* ''It is a lyrical geography and natural history, an account of Eskimo life, and a history of northern explorations,'' finds *Los Angeles Times Book Review* contributor Richard Eder. ''But mainly, it is a . . . reflection about the meaning of mankind's encounter with the planet. . . . Its question, starting as ecology and working into metaphysics, is whether civilization can find a way of adapting itself to the natural world, before its predilection for adapting the natural world to itself destroys self and world, both.'' Lopez elaborated on the feelings that prompted him to write *Arctic Dreams* in his interview with Aton: ''I think if you can really see the land, if you can lose your sense of wishing it to be what you want it to be, if you can strip yourself of the desire to order and to name and see the land entirely for itself, you see in the relationship of all its elements the face of God. And that's why I say the landscape has an authority.''

Man's interactions with ''the landscape'' are often highlighted in Lopez's fiction as well as in his nonfiction. His short story collections are praised by many reviewers. For example, in a *Detroit News* review of *River Notes: The Dance of Herons,* David Graber writes: ''Lopez delicately surveys the terrain of shared experience between a man and a place, in this case a river in the Pacific Northwest. . . . [The author] has an unsentimental naturalist's knowledge combined with profound love-of-land. . . . [His] writing has a dreamlike quality; the sensuality of his words, his . . . playful choice of simile serve as counterpoint to his precisely accurate portrayals of salmon spawning and herons fishing, of Douglas fir falling to the chainsaw and willow crowding the riverbank.'' Edith Hamilton of the *Miami Herald* says that in *River Notes* ''Lopez transmogrifies the physical characteristics of the river—the bend, the falls, the shallows, the rapids—into human experience: the bend as a man seriously ill for a long time who suddenly, for no reason as the river bends for no reason, decides he will recover. The falls is a strangely gothic convolution of the original fall from grace, brought up to date by a vagabond with mythic yearnings who ends his search at the high brink of the river's falls. . . . Lopez's nice shallows become deep reflecting mirrors, their images multiplying beyond ease. . . . Not since Ken Kesey's drastically different novel, *Sometimes a Great Notion,* has a writer so caught and pinned

the mossy melancholy of Oregon.'' In his *Progressive* review, David Miller makes the point that, despite the book's deceptively simple title, it is no mere study of herons. He writes that *River Notes* ''is about a small world of relationships among people, herons, salmon, cottonwoods—and all creatures drawn to this rushing, tumbling, powerful, and endangered emblem of natural life, the river. . . . [The book] is a thing of beauty in itself, as tantalizingly real and yet as otherworldly as your own reflection on a river's surface. . . . It is a rare achievement; perhaps—I've never said this before and know that only time will tell—it is a work of genius.''

Saturday Review writer Alan Cheuse believes that *Winter Count,* another collection of short fiction, is the book that will win for Lopez ''recognition as a writer who like, say, Peter Matthiessen or Edward Hoagland, goes to the wilderness in order to clarify a great deal about civilization.'' Cheuse commends Lopez for weaving ''a style reminiscent of some important contemporary Latin American magical realists'' and for turning ''the sentiments of a decade's worth of ecology lovers into a deeply felt and unnervingly powerful picture of reality.'' *Los Angeles Times* reviewer Elaine Kendall writes: ''There's a boundary, no wider than a pinstripe, where fact and fiction barely touch. With so much room on either side and assorted areas where overlap is expected, few writers choose to confine themselves to that fine line where the two simply meet. Lopez is one of those few. He makes that delicate border his entire territory. *Winter Count* is a small and perfectly crafted collection of just such encounters between imagination and reality. . . . Lopez's observations are so acute the stories expand of their own accord, lingering in the mind the way intense light lingers on the retina.'' Finally, David Quammen, in a *New York Times Book Review* article, says that *Winter Count* is ''full of solid, quiet, telling short works. Each of the stories . . . is as economical in design, as painstakingly crafted and as resonant as a good classical guitar.'' Quammen concludes that Lopez's fiction ''is as spare, as pared down and elemental as the lives it describes, the values it celebrates. One of his characters says, 'I've thrown away everything that is no good,' and this perilously righteous algorithm seems a key part of the author's own epic.''

Discussing his fiction work with Aton, Lopez commented: ''My interest in a story is to illuminate a set of circumstances that bring some understanding of human life, enough at least so that a reader can identify with it and draw some vague sense of hope or sustenance or deep feeling and in some way be revived. . . . It's important to me . . . to go into a story with a capacity for wonder, where I know I can derive something 'wonder-full' and then bring this into the story so that a reader can feel it and say, 'I am an adult. I have a family, I pay bills, I live in a world of chicanery and subterfuge and atomic weaponry and inhumanity and round-heeled politicians and garrulous, insipid television personalities, but still I have wonder. I have been brought to a state of wonder by contact with something in a story.'''

Lopez's books have been translated into French, German, Swedish, Japanese, Dutch, and Italian.

CA INTERVIEW

CA interviewed Barry Lopez by telephone on January 15, 1987, at his home in Oregon.

CA: Your feeling of kinship with nature and with the other animals is at the heart of your writing. When did it begin?

LOPEZ: A long time ago. I was mesmerized by animals and the other-than-obvious dimension of the natural world when I was a child. I grew up in a rural part of California, and I was around animals from the time I was very young—horses, and I raised pigeons and had dogs. Animals were very special to me, although there was probably less order and cause-and-effect to it than I remember. Then there was a kind of hiatus. We moved from California to New York City. I went to prep school in the city and lost contact with that world of my childhood. It wasn't until I got out of college and moved back West that I was able to renew and deepen those ties.

CA: In both your fiction and nonfiction, the prose is remarkably poetic. Did you come to writing by way of poetry?

LOPEZ: No. I've always found poetry a very difficult, very challenging form to work in, and I've had very little success with it. But certainly the *reading* of poetry, which I did intensely in my teens and twenties, played a part.

CA: When did you actually begin to write?

LOPEZ: In high school. My first short stories and book reviews appeared when I was a junior in college. But I never thought I would be able to make a living as a writer, so I determined toward the end of my undergraduate years that I would probably be a teacher and would write, like everyone else did, on the side. The way it turned out, I was able to make my living writing. But it's a funny thing; you never expect something like that is going to happen, so you prepare to do something else.

CA: There's often a stillness about your writing that seems very much in keeping with its setting. Is that something that you work consciously at, something you hear in the writing as you're doing it?

LOPEZ: I don't think so. I'm often trying to act as an intermediary in my work between particular situations and the reader. I find clarity in stillness—which is probably why I'm more attracted to deserts and places like the Arctic than to the woods, where there's more visual chaos. Probably at work here, too, is a feeling for the connection between stillness and mystery, stillness and prayer. I'm conscious of trying to clarify, to make the language work beautifully, and of the reader's needs—how easy is it going to be for the reader to follow, or how can the reader be brought into the scene without violating the scene or violating the reader? By violating the reader I mean making the reader feel like an outsider, choosing a kind of vocabulary or a tone of voice that makes the reader feel uncomfortable or unwelcome. I always mean for a reader to feel welcome in a place. I'm more aware of these things when I'm writing than of trying consciously to create a stillness.

CA: It's interesting that you think of yourself as an intermediary, because in so much of the writing, you seem to disappear; you remove even yourself from being a possible obstacle between the reader and the setting.

LOPEZ: I try. It's a curious thing to do, in a way. When the reader comes to a writer's work, he or she should sense, very quickly I think, the presence of a distinct personality, someone with a certain ethical, moral, and artistic dimension. And insofar as that writer is a worthy illuminator of the world for the reader, he or she continues to read the writer's work. Writing is really an extraordinary act of self-assertion. You put down on paper the way you understand the world. But, for me, there must be a point where the reader loses sight of the writer, where he gains another understanding, a vision of what lies before the writer; so that by the time the reader finishes a book or an essay, he's really thinking about his own thoughts with regard to that subject, or that place, or that set of events, and not so much about the writer's. The initial step is an act of ego, the next step a loss of ego, a sort of disappearance.

I think this is an old ideal among writers; writers pretty consistently agree among themselves, in my experience, that they are conduits, some sort of lightning rod, an instrument through which something else is passed. That doesn't mean that you're completely passive as a writer. What it means, to me, is that you bring the skills you have to bear—your insight and command of language, your ability to research, whatever your talents might be—to shape something that is moving through you. I think I take more of my direction in this from aboriginal cultures than from contemporary cultures. In aboriginal cultures there is a certain weight of responsibility on the storyteller. The storyteller is a member of the community, but not necessarily a wise man or a wise woman. The storyteller's work is to create an atmosphere in which wisdom can reveal itself. In doing so, he makes the reader feel a part of something. The reader walks away from the story not thinking that the writer is a great artist, but feeling the wisdom, the power, the life blood if you will, of whatever the reader and the writer were involved in together. For me that's very important.

I try to think of phrases to describe a writer's obligation, not necessarily for myself but because people ask me about this and it's frustrating not to have an answer. I end up saying things like "You give yourself over to the place" or "You make yourself open to the place." Or I say that "the place tutors you." What I mean is that there is something going on here, a purpose in life much larger than the individual artist's vision. I operate with a sense that I'm participating in something much larger than my own ability to see or comprehend. Because I believe that, when I go to a place, or when I'm interviewing a person, I'm always aware that there is more here than ever I could comprehend, and that the best way to pass on what is valuable to a reader is to make myself vulnerable or open to the moment or to the event or to the place.

This works a bit differently sometimes with people; people can take advantage of you. But in my experience a place won't. It can take advantage of your inability to survive, but it does not actively deceive. You don't run the same risk in making yourself vulnerable to a place as you do in making yourself vulnerable to another person. This is all very esoteric, but the heart of it is that, as a writer, you make yourself vulnerable, and then you turn around and speak as though you were somebody, hoping that when you speak you'll be able to pass on some of what it was you saw, because you've trained yourself to see. And the reason you want to pass it on is because you believe these things make people healthy. You believe the story, whether it's nonfiction or fiction, has a power to elevate or to heal or to illuminate, to provide hope, to in some way give an individual life greater dimension. Those are all community obligations.

CA: Of Wolves and Men, your first book to get major attention, including several awards, had its beginning in an article you did for Smithsonian. *Were you already very interested in wolves when you began to research that article?*

LOPEZ: No, no more so than in any other animal. When I went to work on the article it gradually became clear to me that a lot of what I had been thinking about wild animals—what they are, how we define them—was becoming more concrete. So the work with wolves, in 1974, actually catalyzed a lot of thinking about human and animal relationships which had been going on in a vague way in my mind for several years, and I realized that if I focused on this one animal, I might be able to say something sharp and clear about the way we treat all animals, and about how we relate to the natural world in the latter part of the twentieth century. I think at that point I came to understand that the animal is construed in quite different ways by different people, and that no one way should be "the best"; each understanding should provide the reader with a certain illumination. So I laid out the scientific view as carefully as I could and then added to that something that I had grown to understand was just as important, an aboriginal view of animals.

Things get a bit difficult here; you can get drawn off into aboriginal romance if you're not careful. But among the hunting peoples still extant in the world—in Australia, the Kalahari Desert, the Arctic, sub-Arctic Canada—there is a rigorous and intelligent and extremely perceptive understanding of animals. It seemed to me, on the face of it, just plain dumb not to ask these people what they thought, because they obviously had a tremendous storehouse of knowledge. And you have to *ask*—it is not in them to proselytize, they aren't going to come and tell us what they think. I would see things like this all the time. In fact, just a couple of months ago I opened a recent issue of a journal called *Arctic,* and there was a wonderful story by two ornithologists who'd made the first discovery of a breeding ground for dovekies in Canada—it could have been "discovered" years earlier, by just asking the hunters in a village called Clyde. Things turn up like this all the time about where animals are, or something unusual they've done.

In writing the wolf book, I thought it would be good to set this forth, that there is another set of field notes if you will, as well as another kind of understanding about the relationship between human beings and wild animals, a tradition we have drifted away from since Mesopotamian times, since we first began to domesticate animals and to raise grain crops, pulling back farther and farther from our own Paleolithic existence in Europe. What we have set aside is still alive among some aboriginal people. I thought it would be good to look this material over. If it did nothing else, it would make the wolf a fuller animal, a more profound mystery.

The next thing, obvious but difficult, was to look at what Western man has done to the wolf—which, at every turn, has been to try to kill it, because it was a competitor for food or because it carried a lot of emotional baggage, which it didn't deserve, about being a force of darkness. The latter part of the book allowed me to look at the wolf in literature, at its role in folklore, and at werewolves and wolf children. Little Red Riding Hood, of course, is very revealing about our attitudes toward wolves, and there's a reason why it suited Rome to have Romulus and Remus suckled by wolves. This idea of the wolf warrior emerges not only in the structure of the Roman army, but much later among the Cheyenne in North America. Toward the end of the book, then, a literary, social, and psychological understanding of the wolf comes into play.

The wolf, the animal itself, riveted my imagination all the time I was working on the book. I became deeply fond of wolves, and I think much of what I learned came as a direct result of paying attention to them as real, individual entities. They simply made me more aware than I had ever been of the world animals inhabit. I wasn't as eager to be a champion of wolves, however, as I was to understand what was going on between us and animals. I wanted to look at that question, to make structures of prejudice and tolerance apparent, to suggest the validity of different ways of knowing.

CA: Did Arctic Dreams *begin with your work in Alaska researching* Of Wolves and Men?

LOPEZ: Yes. I can even tell you the date. It was in June of 1978. I had finished all the work on the wolf book and gone with a friend up into the Brooks Range, partly to clear my mind of that long period of work with wolves. I had no set goal; I just wanted to go back to places I'd been very moved by, and do it without having to think almost always in terms of how it looked to wolves or how wolves were involved. That period during the solstice in 1978 was when I had the first glimmering of an understanding of what *Arctic Dreams* would be all about. And of course the scope of that book is much larger. Instead of focusing on an animal, it's focusing on a place and the animals it contains. It's a much broader inquiry. But in some way the books are related, in the sense that the query is still: What is the relationship between the human imagination and the physical landscape?

I think many writers have the same questions in their minds from the beginning. As you grow older, God willing, you understand them better or how to make them clearer, both for yourself and for the reader. This last year or so since I finished the Arctic work, I've been in Japan and the Galapagos and I'm getting ready to go to Africa. I'm beginning to realize that I want to look into some of these questions that have been on my mind in still more different terms than I have in the past.

CA: Have those two big books appealed to readers you might not have thought they'd appeal to?

LOPEZ: Yes, but I don't think of the reader as someone who is attracted to a *subject* as much as he or she is attracted to an idea, or to a good story. In fact, beyond trying to be clear and trying to tell the story well and not making things up, the obligations I spoke of earlier, I don't think about the reader in specific terms. I'm sometimes surprised, I guess, by letters from people who have no interest, per se, in wolves or icebergs or the Inuit but who say that what you have written is very meaningful to them. But writers work with metaphors. Mine are natural history, anthropology, geography. If a reader says these metaphors worked for him, and his own metaphorical universe is theology or medicine or cattle ranching, well, there's little more that you could hope to accomplish as a writer than to bridge that space between two different ways of comprehending.

CA: In a Publishers Weekly *interview, you told Trish Todd that the Alaskan landscape pulls you "up and out of yourself, and you feel yourself extending into the landscape." Is that feeling of reverence, awe, being in harmony with the universe—whatever it should be called—possible to maintain at all when you come back into the normal routines of life?*

LOPEZ: It's a bit like being in love. When you're in the presence of the beloved, you can't imagine any other moment. But then day-to-day life impinges, the person you love recedes, and you find yourself concentrating on something utterly different. But there is still this very strong attachment in the heart which has to do with memory and longing. I don't think a sense of awe or respect for a particular place diminishes as much as it becomes an isolated memory. Part of the function of literature for me is to rekindle memory and make it part of the present, to compress time. There is a certain amount of ordinary chaos in the human spirit, inside the human mind. I think literature helps to clear that chaos. An example would be if you went off on an extraordinary trip to the American West when you were fifteen years old and then you remember at the age of thirty or forty that it was wonderful but you can't remember why. You long to do it again. Then you pick up a book, and you say, This is why. What I'm reading here is what I felt when *I* was there. The sense of exhilaration is there again. I think what happens after that is that you lead a better life, because your sense of proportion, of your purpose in life, is renewed. The trip that you took when you were a child or when you were on a honeymoon or whatever is brought to life again, and you come to life again with it. The same is true for me. I experience it when I read other people's books or if I go up north and sit around in the night with friends I've traveled with and we remember one story after another. When I go to bed, I feel just as good as I did when we were out in those places creating those stories.

CA: Your talking about stories reminds me of Giving Birth to Thunder. *How did you happen to do that book?*

LOPEZ: That was the second book of mine to be published, but it was the first book I wrote. I wrote it when I was in graduate school at the University of Oregon. I became fascinated with this figure in human legend, the trickster, who, of course, is very much apparent in the folklore of virtually every human society. That character is still on my mind. In fact, this fall I'm going to work with a group of musicians and actors to create a theatrical presentation of those stories, which they will take on tour.

CA: What will you be looking for in Africa?

LOPEZ: I'm not sure. I really can't imagine. Part of being a writer is learning to leave the door open. I will go to Africa with certain questions, but, to be open to Africa, I've got to remind myself when I get off the plane that I have never been there. I really don't know anything. I don't mean I just go off someplace with no plans. I'm not that loosely organized; I tend to be careful about research beforehand and so on. But with the kind of work I do, I'm always aware of having to put myself in the position of someone who knows very little. If I begin to think I know a lot about what's going on, then I won't hear half of what I need to hear. In Eskimo villages, I would always ask the stupid question. And Eskimos are not at all kind about taking advantage of you in a situation like that. But if I didn't ask, all I'd come away with would be the delusion that I had fooled them into thinking that I was knowledgeable or adept. I would have had nothing for the reader. I wouldn't have done my job. I would have to return to my community and say, Well, I went there and I talked a lot, and as a consequence I didn't learn anything.

BIOGRAPHICAL/CRITICAL SOURCES:

BOOKS

Lopez, Barry, *Arctic Dreams: Imagination and Desire in a Northern Landscape* (nonfiction), Scribner, 1986.

PERIODICALS

Chicago Tribune, November 5, 1978, March 30, 1986.
Chicago Tribune Book World, November 23, 1979.
Christian Science Monitor, February 12, 1979.
Detroit News, November 4, 1979.
Globe & Mail (Toronto), May 31, 1986.
Harper's, December, 1984.
Los Angeles Times, November 12, 1978, May 9, 1981.
Los Angeles Times Book Review, March 2, 1986.
Miami Herald, September 30, 1979, March 29, 1986.
Nation, November 11, 1978.
New Republic, June 30, 1979.
Newsweek, October 16, 1978.
New Yorker, February 26, 1979, March 17, 1986.
New York Times, January 4, 1979, February 12, 1986, March 29, 1986.
New York Times Book Review, November 19, 1978, June 14, 1981, February 16, 1986.
Observer, June 24, 1979.
Pacific Northwest, March/April, 1980.
Progressive, May, 1980.
Saturday Review, April, 1981.
Seattle Review, fall, 1985.
Time, March 10, 1986.
Times Literary Supplement, December 7, 1979, August 8, 1986.
Washington Post, November 27, 1978, November 18, 1986, November 24, 1986.
Washington Post Book Review, March 9, 1986.
Western American Literature, spring, 1986.

—*Sketch by Joan Goldsworthy*
—*Interview by Jean W. Ross*

*   *   *

LOURIE, Helen
    See STORR, Catherine (Cole)

*   *   *

LUEKER, Erwin L(ouis) 1914-

PERSONAL: Born December 15, 1914, near Dover, Ark.; son of Charles H. (a farmer) and Louise (Harms) Lueker; married Anna Marie Schick, May 2, 1942 (died, 1973); married Margaret A. Reimann, July 19, 1980; children: (first marriage) Erwin, Jr., Lisette, George, Jonathan. *Education:* Attended St. Paul's College, 1933-35; Concordia Seminary, B.D., 1939; Washington University, M.A., 1940, Ph.D., 1942.

ADDRESSES: Home—7201 Waterman, University City, Mo. 63130.

CAREER: Ordained Lutheran minister, 1939; pastor in Richmond Heights, Mo., 1943-46; Concordia Seminary, St. Louis, Mo., instructor, 1945-46; St. Paul's College, Concordia, Mo., associate professor of languages and humanities, 1946-55; Concordia Seminary, professor of theology and philosophy, 1955-74, director of Correspondence School, 1957-73, acting director of graduate studies, 1965-66; Christ Seminary—Seminex, St. Louis, professor, 1974-80. Adjunct professor, St. Louis University and Eden Theological Seminary, 1974—.

MEMBER: American Philological Association.

WRITINGS:

(Editor) *Lutheran Cyclopedia,* Concordia, 1954, revised edition, 1975.

(With O. E. Feucht, P. Hansen, and F. Kramer) *Engagement and Marriage,* Concordia, 1959.

The Concordia Bible Dictionary, Concordia, 1963.

(With Carl S. Meyer and others) *Moving Frontiers,* Concordia, 1964.

(With Richard Caemmerer) *Church and Ministry in Transition,* Concordia, 1964.

Structured Musings of EL, nine volumes, privately printed, 1968-87.

Change and the Church, Concordia, 1969.

Development-Tension-Crisis: A Study of Interaction of Event and Thought in the Missouri Synod with Documents, privately printed, 1980.

Chapel Musings, privately printed, 1981.

Gospel Declared and Confirmed, privately printed, 1982.

Insights from Quotations in Luke, John, Acts: Supplement I to Gospel Declared and Confirmed, privately printed, 1984.

Insights from Quotations in New Testament Epistles: Supplement II, privately printed, 1985.

The Seer and His Sources: Quotations and Allusions in Revelation, privately printed, 1986.

Heavens Declare, privately printed, 1986.

(Translator) F. Mildenberger, *Theology of the Lutheran Confessions,* Fortress, 1986.

Also author of numerous essays on religious subjects.

Contributor of poetry and of articles to reference works and journals. Former member of editorial board, *Lutheran Witness.*

WORK IN PROGRESS: Study of synoptic problems and New Testament manuscripts; revisions of reference books; poetry.

SIDELIGHTS: Erwin L. Lueker told *CA:* "Religious language is symbolic language, and the deepest religious perceptions are expressed poetically." The author also added that he "plans to make the study of poetry, classics, philosophy, and theology [my] avocation during retirement. [I am] particularly interested in their interrelationships."

M

MacDONALD, Charles B(rown) 1922-

PERSONAL: Born November 23, 1922, in Little Rock, S.C.; son of K. L. and Mary (MacQueen) MacDonald. *Education:* Presbyterian College, A.B., 1942; graduate study at Columbia University, 1946, McGill University, 1947, University of Missouri, 1947, and George Washington University, 1948.

ADDRESSES: Home—5300 Columbia Pike, Arlington, Va. 22204. *Agent*—Brandt & Brandt Literary Agents, Inc., 1501 Broadway, New York, N.Y. 10036.

CAREER: Presbyterian College, Clinton, S.C., instructor in English, 1946-47; Department of the Army, Office of Chief of Military History, Washington, D.C., historian, 1948-52, chief of European section, 1952-56, chief of general history branch, 1956-67, deputy chief historian, 1967-80. *Military service:* U.S. Army, 1942-46; became captain; received Purple Heart, Bronze Star, Silver Star. U.S. Army Reserve, 1946-76; retired as colonel.

AWARDS, HONORS: Secretary of the Army research and study fellowship in military history, 1957-58; Litt.D., Presbyterian College, 1967; Doctor of Humanities, Francis Marion College, 1985.

WRITINGS:

Company Commander, Infantry Journal Press, 1947, illustrated edition, Bantam, 1978.
(With Sidney T. Mathews) *Three Battles: Arnaville, Altuzzo, and Schmidt*, U.S. Government Printing Office, 1952.
The Siegfried Line Campaign, Office of Chief of Military History, Department of the Army, 1963.
The Battle of the Huertgen Forest, Lippincott, 1963.
The Mighty Endeavor: American Armed Forces in the European Theater in World War II, Oxford University Press, 1969, revised edition, Quill, 1985.
Airborne, Ballantine, 1970 (published in England as *By Air to Battle*, Macdonald & Co., 1970).
The Last Offensive, U.S. Government Printing Office, 1973.
(Editor with Anthony Cave Brown) *The Secret History of the Atomic Bomb*, Dial, 1977.
(With Brown) *On a Field of Red: The Communist International and the Coming of World War II*, Putnam, 1981.
A Time for Trumpets: The Untold Story of the Battle of the Bulge, Morrow, 1984 (published in England as *The Battle of the Bulge: The Definitive Account*, Weidenfeld & Nicolson, 1984).

CONTRIBUTOR

Kent R. Greenfield, editor, *Command Decisions*, Harcourt, 1961.
History of the Second World War, Purnell Books, 1966.
Maurice Matloff, editor, *American Military History*, U.S. Government Printing Office, 1969.
Ray Bonds, editor, *The Encyclopedia of Land Warfare*, Salamander, 1976.
Thomas Parrish, editor, *The Encyclopedia of World War II*, Simon & Schuster, 1978.
Bonds, editor, *The Vietnam War: The Illustrated History of the Conflict in Southeast Asia*, Salamander, 1979.

OTHER

Contributor of articles on military subjects to *Encyclopedia Americana, Encyclopaedia Britannica, Grolier Encyclopedia, World Book Encyclopaedia, New York Times Magazine*, and various Army publications.

SIDELIGHTS: Charles B. MacDonald, former deputy chief historian of the U.S. Army, served as a rifle company commander in Europe during World War II. At twenty-two, he fought against the German Army in its final offensive, the Battle of the Bulge. MacDonald recorded his battle experiences in *Company Commander*, the first of many volumes he would publish on the Second World War. As he told *CA:* "*Company Commander*, which has been called 'the infantry classic of World War II' and is still in print after first publication in 1947, brought me into the business of military history. I find it an intriguing field, for however deplorable war is, we must admit that mankind spends a considerable amount of time and endeavor at it, and it behooves an enlightened public to understand it."

When *Company Commander* appeared in 1947, *New York Times* reviewer H. A. DeWeerd called it "an impressive first book." In the *Saturday Review of Literature*, A. C. Fields praised its sincerity: "This is a simple story, told in simple language, of a tough war, and of all the zany and horrible things that went into making it the greatest war in history. There will probably be books which will do a more craftsmanlike literary job in describing World War II; there may even be more lucid explanations of the strategies employed and the problems confronted in this last global battle; but nowhere, I venture to say, will there be a more honest, unassuming portrayal of the hopes and dreams and fears of a young infantry captain than is found here.''

A Time for Trumpets: The Untold Story of the Battle of the Bulge also recounts the eleven-day battle described in *Company Commander*, but instead of giving a single narrative, it relates the conflict from many points of view. ''It is a mosaic of the personal accounts and recorded actions of the commanders and men who actually fought the battle,'' writes William Jackson in the London *Times*. *A Time for Trumpets* focuses as well on the importance of decisions made by commanders struggling with short supplies, little ammunition, and the difficulty of withdrawing from the conflict. ''MacDonald's book brings out with stark clarity the problems which face commanders at all levels in such an operation,'' says Michael Carver of *Times Literary Supplement*.

MacDonald used an enormous amount of technical data and personal information in compiling *A Time for Trumpets*. He combined five years worth of interviews with selected data from American, British, and German records to produce a definitive work. But the juxtaposition of geographical information with military details, including an indiscriminate listing of muster rolls from both sides, results in sensory overload for one reviewer. ''The shortcoming of the author's chosen approach,'' notes Correlli Barnett in the *Washington Post Book World*, ''is that he gives equal weight to a battalion fight for a bridge as to major command decisions or the overall operations of whole divisions. Even though he does interlard this fine-grain narrative with occasional resumes of the overall strategic situation, the ultimate effect is like a close look at a high magnification of a half-tone plate—all dots and no picture.''

But other critics have found *A Time for Trumpets* well-balanced. Linda Charlton, writing in the *New York Times Book Review* says it ''combines a historian's detachment and precision with the personal feeling of a man who was there and cares about his subject.'' Jackson expresses a similar view, noting ''the drabness of the official histories is given colour, and yet the exaggeration, to which personal reminiscences are so often prone, is toned down by cross-reference to official records.'' Carver also finds the work well-composed: ''MacDonald succeeds in achieving a near-perfect balance between detail and the overall picture. His narrative is as clear and well-judged in describing and discussing the decisions, actions and personalities of the commanders . . . as it is in its account of events at the level of the front-line soldier.'' He concludes that the ''book is as valuable to the historian as it is to students of war and to anybody interested in what the war was like.''

MacDonald's works have been published in Argentina, Egypt, France, Israel, Italy, Japan, the Soviet Union, and Sweden.

AVOCATIONAL INTERESTS: Skiing.

BIOGRAPHICAL/CRITICAL SOURCES:

PERIODICALS

Christian Science Monitor, November 29, 1969.
National Observer, January 12, 1970.
National Review, December 2, 1969.
New York Times, November 16, 1947.
New York Times Book Review, December 14, 1969, March 3, 1985.

Saturday Review of Literature, November 1, 1947.
Times (London), November 22, 1984.
Times Literary Supplement, July 23, 1982, December 28, 1984.
Virginia Quarterly Review, spring, 1985.
Washington Post Book World, May 24, 1981, April 14, 1985.

*   *   *

MACE, David Robert   1907-

PERSONAL: Born June 21, 1907, in Montrose, Scotland; came to United States in 1949; retains British citizenship; son of Joseph (a minister) and Josephine (Reid) Mace; married Vera Chapman, July 26, 1933; children: Sheila Mace Runge, Fiona Mace Patterson. *Education:* University of London, B.Sc., 1927; Cambridge University, B.A., 1930, M.A., 1932; graduate study at University of Bristol, 1934; University of Manchester, Ph.D., 1942. *Religion:* Society of Friends.

ADDRESSES: Home—Highland Farms, Black Mountain, N.C. 28711.

CAREER: Methodist minister in England, 1930-40; National Marriage Guidance Council of Great Britain, Rugby, England, executive director, 1942-49, honorary vice-president, 1949—; Drew University, Madison, N.J., professor of human relations, 1949-59; University of Pennsylvania, School of Medicine, Philadelphia, associate professor of family study, 1959-60; American Association of Marriage and Family Therapists, Washington, D.C., executive director, 1960-67; Wake Forest University, Bowman Gray School of Medicine, Winston-Salem, N.C., professor of family sociology, 1967-77. Visiting professor, University of Witwatersrand, Johannesburg, 1954. Leader of seminars and conferences for the World Council of Churches in Southeast Asia, 1954 and in Fiji Islands, 1967-68; leader of seminars in India, 1957-58 and 1966-67, Thailand, 1958, the Caribbean, 1960-64, and Kenya, 1967; participant in various conferences on marriage and the family in Ghana and Nigeria, 1957; leader of team of specialists on good-will mission to South America, 1963; founder of national Family Life Council, Nigeria, 1967. Groves Conference on Marriage and the Family, founding member, secretary treasurer, 1968-71; founding scholar, Groves Academy for Distinguished Family Life Specialists, 1981. Has made study trips to Ghana and Nigeria, 1957, and to Ceylon, 1958; has made other study trips for the World Council of Churches to the Caribbean, 1960-64, and to selected islands of the South Pacific, 1966-67; made study trip for the International Union of Family Organizations to eight Asian countries, 1964. Consultant to Parents without Partners, Inc., 1946-80, World Council of Churches, 1957-71, National Council of Churches, 1958-70, Marriage Council of Philadelphia, 1959-60, and North Carolina Family Life Council, 1970—; consultant to governments of Australia and New Zealand, 1956, 1967-68, and India, 1967-68; consultant in East Africa, 1966-67, Ghana, 1967, and Samoa, Tahiti, and Mexico, 1967-68.

MEMBER: International Union of Family Organizations (Paris; chairman of standing international committee on marriage and marriage guidance, 1953-70; vice-president, 1963-70), American Association of Marriage and Family Therapists, American College of Obstetricians and Gynecologists, National Council on Family Relations (president, 1961-62), Association of Couples for Marriage Enrichment (co-founder; president, 1973-81), Sex Information and Educational Council of the U.S. (president, 1966-68), American Association of Sex Educators and Counselors, Society for the Scientific Study of Sex (charter member).

AWARDS, HONORS: Award from Merrill-Palmer Institute, 1968, for contributions to the field of human development and family life; Distinguished Service Awards from Sex Information and Education Council of the U.S., 1968, American Association of Sex Educators and Counselors, 1972, Association of Couples for Marriage Enrichment, 1976, and Baptist General Convention of Texas, 1983; Distinguished Contribution Award from American Association of Marriage and Family Counselors, 1975; citation for special merit, 1975, and Irwin V. Sperry Award, 1983, both from North Carolina Family Life Council; Distinguished Services to Families Award from National Council on Family Relations, 1975; Man of the Year Award from Forsyth County Mental Health Association (N.C.), 1975; Doctor of Humane Letters from Alma College and Doctor of Social Science, Brigham Young University, both 1977; Richard B. Boren Whole Person Award, 1981; First Annual Award, National Symposium on Family Strength, 1983; Leadership Award, American Association for Marriage and Family Therapy, 1984; Award from the Governor of Kansas, 1986.

WRITINGS:

Does Sex Morality Matter?, Rich & Cowan, 1943.
Marriage Counseling, J. & A. Churchill, 1948.
Marriage Crisis, Delisle, 1948.
Marriage: The Art of Lasting Love, Doubleday, 1952 (published in England as *Marriage: The Art of Lasting Happiness*, Hodder & Stoughton, 1952).
Hebrew Marriage: A Sociological Study, Philosophical Library, 1953.
Whom God Hath Joined: A Book of Christian Marriage, Westminster, 1953, revised edition, 1973.
Success in Marriage, Abingdon, 1958.
The Christian Family in East Asia, World Council of Churches, 1958.
Youth Looks toward Marriage, Finlayson, 1958.
(With Evelyn Duval and Paul Popenoe) *The Churches Look at Family Life*, Broadman, 1964.
(Translator) Robert Grimm, *Love and Sexuality*, Association Press, 1964.
Sex, Love, and Marriage in the Caribbean, World Council of Churches, 1965.
Youth Considers Marriage, Thomas Nelson, 1966.
(Contributor) Jules Saltman, compiler, *Love, Sex, and Marriage*, Grosset, 1968.
Sex, Marriage, and the Family in the Pacific, World Council of Churches, 1969.
The Christian Response to the Sexual Revolution, Abingdon, 1970.
Getting Ready for Marriage, Abingdon, 1972.
Abortion: The Agonizing Decision, Abingdon, 1972.
Sexual Difficulties in Marriage, Fortress Press, 1972.
Love and Anger in Marriage, Zondervan, 1981.
Close Companions: The Marriage Enrichment Handbook, Continuum, 1982.
Prevention in Family Services: Approaches to Family Wellness, Sage Publications, 1983.

WITH WIFE, VERA MACE

Marriage: East and West, Doubleday, 1960.
The Soviet Family, Doubleday, 1963.
We Can Have Better Marriages: If We Really Want Them, Abingdon, 1974.
Men, Women, and God, John Knox, 1975.
Marriage Enrichment in the Church, Broadman, 1976.

How to Have a Happy Marriage, Abingdon, 1979.
What's Happening to Clergy Marriages?, Abingdon, 1981.
Letters to a Retired Couple: Marriage in the Later Years, Judson, 1984.
In the Presence of God: Readings for Christian Marriage, Westminster, 1985.
The Sacred Fire: Christian Marriage through the Ages, Abingdon, 1986.

OTHER

Contributor of more than two thousand articles to professional and popular journals and newspapers. Member of editorial board, *Journal of Marriage and the Family*, 1962-69.

SIDELIGHTS: David Robert Mace told *CA:* "All of my writing has been in the field of sex, marriage, and the family. I have used writing as a means of communicating my opinions, beliefs, and convictions about the field to which I have devoted most of my professional life."

Mace's travels have taken him to seventy-six countries and five times around the world. He spent the summer of 1960 in the Soviet Union collecting material for his book *The Soviet Family* with full cooperation of Soviet authorities.

Among Mace's many achievements as executive director of the National Guidance Council of Great Britain was the initiation and development of Britain's first marriage counseling services—over 100 centers. Mace later told *CA* that he has since "developed marriage counseling services on a national basis in the U.S.A., in South Africa, in Australia, and in New Zealand."

BIOGRAPHICAL/CRITICAL SOURCES:

PERIODICALS

Los Angeles Times, March 9, 1983.

*   *   *

MACE, Elisabeth 1933-

PERSONAL: Born April 16, 1933, in London, England; daughter of Arthur (an engineer) and Ivy (Harvey) Cox; married David Mace (a teacher of creative studies), July 28, 1956; children: Anna Victoria, Simon Harvey. *Education:* University of Reading, B.A. (with honors), 1956. *Politics:* "Not interested."

ADDRESSES: Home—23 Foxglove Ave., Leeds 9, West Yorkshire, England. *Agent*—David Higham Associates Ltd., 5-8 Lower John St., Golden Sq., London W1R 4HA, England.

CAREER: Teacher of elementary and preschool children in Cheltenham, and Boston Spa, England, 1970-81; teacher at Braim Wood Middle School, Leeds, England, 1981—.

WRITINGS:

JUVENILE

Ransome Revisited (science fiction), Deutsch, 1975, published as *Out There*, Greenwillow, 1978.
Travelling Man (science fiction), Deutsch, 1976.
The Ghost Diviners (fantasy), Thomas Nelson, 1977.
The Rushton Inheritance (fantasy), Deutsch, 1978.
The Freedom Cage (fantasy), Deutsch, 1980.

YOUNG ADULT

Brother Enemy (history), Deutsch, 1979, Beaufort Books, 1981.
The Goodall Family Games, Deutsch, 1983.

Boxes, Deutsch, 1984.
Beware the Edge, Deutsch, 1986.

WORK IN PROGRESS: A fantasy novel for young adults.

SIDELIGHTS: Elisabeth Mace told *CA:* "I have always been interested in children's literature, and what children themselves choose to read, or reject or dislike. Science fiction for this age range is a subject which excites but often disappoints its readers. Science fiction, to me, is far more than space opera. Similarly, there's more to ghosts than visitations from the dead!"

AVOCATIONAL INTERESTS: Music (especially choral singing), dolls' costumes, dress designing, and dressmaking.

BIOGRAPHICAL/CRITICAL SOURCES:

PERIODICALS

Times Literary Supplement, September 19, 1980.

*　　*　　*

MACER-STORY, E(ugenia) 1945-

PERSONAL: Born January 20, 1945, in Minneapolis, Minn.; daughter of Dan J. (a hospital director) and Eugenia L. (a dietician; maiden name, Andrews) Macer; married Leon A. Story (a computer systems analyst), October 3, 1970 (divorced October 31, 1975); children: Ezra Arthur. *Education:* Northwestern University, B.S., 1965; Columbia University, M.F.A., 1968. *Politics:* "No strong affiliation." *Religion:* Transcendental.

ADDRESSES: Office—P.O. Box 854, Woodstock, N.Y. 12498.

CAREER: City of New York, N.Y., worked in social service in foster homes for elderly, 1969; *Fond du Lac Commonwealth Reporter,* Fond du Lac, Wis., features reporter, 1970; teacher for art groups such as Polyarts and Joy of Movement in Boston, Mass., 1970-75; Magik Mirror, Salem, Mass., proprietor, 1975-76; Shin Psychic Center, Boston, teacher and psychic, 1976-77; playwright, psychic, and teacher of occult philosophy in New York City, 1977—.

MEMBER: Society for the Investigation of the Unexplained, Dramatists Guild, Theosophical Society, American Association for the Advancement of Science.

AWARDS, HONORS: Shubert fellowship from Columbia University, 1968.

WRITINGS:

Congratulations: The UFO Reality, Crescent Press, 1978.
Angels of Time: Astrological Magick, Regency, 1981.

PLAYS

"The Little Old Hermit of the Northwest Woods" (two-act musical), first produced at Hamilton-Kirkland College, 1972.
"Handsel and Gretal Meet the Ghost of J. Edgar Hoover" (one-act musical), first produced in Boston, Mass., at Fanuiel Hall, 1972.
"Fetching the Tree" (one-act musical), first produced in Boston, at Polyarts, 1973.
"Lady Video & the Econsensor," first produced in Boston at Commonwealth Armory, 1974.
"Visiting Momma" (one-act), first produced in Boston at Theosophical Society, 1975.

"New Day" (one-act musical), first produced in Boston at Shin Psychic Center, 1976.
"The Blues Deduction" (three-act), first produced in Boston at Playwrights Platform, 1976.
"The Autobiography of Morgan Lefay" (one-act musical), first produced in New York City at Americana Hotel, 1978.
"Desiderata" (three-act), first produced in New York City at Theater for the New City, 1978.
"Aphrodite/The Witch Play" (two-act), first produced in New York City at Theater for the New City, 1979.
"Red Riding Hood's Revenge" (one-act musical), first produced in New York City at Inferno Disco, 1980.
"Radish" (one-act musical), first produced in New York City at 18th Street Theater, 1981.
"The Observation Chamber" (one-act), first produced in New York City at 18th Street Theater, 1981.
"The UFO Show" (multi-media documentary), first produced in New York City at Westbeth Arts Center, 1981.
"The Sky Moth Project at Location 30" (three-act), first produced in New York City at Warehouse Theatre, 1982.
"Six Way Time Play," first produced in Woodstock at Channel 6, 1983.
"Eternal Flowers of Ghost Mountain," first produced in New York City at Westside Community Garden, 1984.
"Robin Hood's Nightgown," first produced in New York City at UMC Theater, 1985.
"Canceled and Interrupted Performances," first produced in New York City at Alchemical Space Theater, 1985.
"All Soul's Banquet," first produced at Alchemical Space Theater, 1985.
"Poems with Percussion and Sun Songs," first produced at UMC Theater, 1985.

Also author of plays "Double or Nothing," "Archeological Politics," "Rehearsing on a Polished Floor," "The Crystal Healer," and "Strange Inquiries."

OTHER

Contributor to periodicals, including *TriQuarterly, Shadows, Witches Annual, Woodstock Times, Omni, Pursuit, Frontiers of Science, Mufon UFO Journal, Manhattan Poetry Review,* and *Psychic Guide.*

WORK IN PROGRESS: Poems and plays; research on unidentified flying objects and psychokinesis.

SIDELIGHTS: E. Macer-Story told *CA:* "I think it is true that any author expresses most effectively whatever aspect has affected his or her personality personally. I did not reach my stride as a writer until I discovered how 'psychic' I was—in 1972. Previous to this, I could write the English language, but I had nothing new to say using words. Most psychics are not 'literary' and I think my major interest is simply that I am expressing some things which have not yet been expressed verbally within the Western culture. The Eastern idiom has 'names' for supernatural occurrences, but in the West we must rediscover and re-name the experiences in a way which is comprehensible."

BIOGRAPHICAL/CRITICAL SOURCES:

PERIODICALS

Frontiers of Science, March/April, 1981.
Pursuit, summer, 1979.
Woodstock Times, June 18, 1987.

MACKAY, James (Alexander) 1936-
(Ian Angus, William Finlay, Bruce Garden, Peter Whittington)

PERSONAL: Born November 21, 1936, in Inverness, Scotland; son of William James (an engineer) and Minnie (Matheson) Mackay; married Mary Jackson, September 24, 1960 (divorced April 16, 1973); married Joyce Greaves (a secretary and researcher), October 8, 1973; children: (first marriage) Fiona Elizabeth, Alastair Andrew. *Education:* University of Glasgow, M.A. (with honors), 1958.

ADDRESSES: Home and office—11 Newall Terrace, Dumfries DG1 1LN, Scotland.

CAREER: British Museum, London, England, assistant keeper, 1961-71; full-time writer, 1971—. Member of board of directors, Philatelic Publishers Ltd., 1966-72; antiques advisory editor, Ward, Lock, 1972—. *Military service:* British Army, 1958-61; became lieutenant.

MEMBER: Postal History Society, British Postmark Society, Burns Federation.

AWARDS, HONORS: Silver Medals for philatelic literature at international exhibitions in Leipzig, 1965, Vienna, 1965, Amsterdam, 1967, Sofia, 1969, Prague, 1970, and Poznan, 1973; Silver-gilt medal, Cardinal Spellman Foundation, 1983.

WRITINGS:

A Guide to the Uists, British War Office, 1961, 3rd edition, 1966.
St. Kilda, Scottish Postmark Group, 1963.
The Tapling Collection, British Museum, 1964.
The World of Stamps, Christopher Johnson, 1964.
One Hundred Leaves, British Museum, 1965.
Commonwealth Stamp Design, 1840-1965, British Museum, 1965.
The Story of Malta and Her Stamps, Philatelic Publishers, 1966.
The Story of Great Britain and Her Stamps, Philatelic Publishers, 1967.
Money in Stamps, Lindquist, 1967.
The Story of Eire and Her Stamps, Philatelic Publishers, 1968.
Value in Coins and Medals, Christopher Johnson, 1968.
Cover Collecting, Philatelic Publishers, 1968.
The Story of East Africa and Its Stamps, Philatelic Publishers, 1970.
An Introduction to Small Antiques, Garnstone Press, 1970.
Antiques of the Future, Universe Books, 1970.
Airmails, 1870-1970, Batsford, 1970.
Commemorative Pottery and Porcelain, Garnstone Press, 1970.
Commemorative Medals, Arthur Barker, 1970.
Greek and Roman Coins, Arthur Barker, 1971.
Coin Collecting for Grown-Up Beginners, Garnstone Press, 1971.
The World of Classic Stamps, Putnam, 1972.
The Dictionary of Stamps, Macmillan, 1973.
The Animaliers, Dutton, 1973.
Glass Paperweights, Viking, 1973.
Source Book of Stamps, Ward, Lock, 1974.
Robert Bruce, King of Scots, R. Hale, 1974.
Turn of the Century Antiques: An Encyclopedia, Dutton, 1974.
Collecting Famous Faces, Ward, Lock, 1975.
Encyclopedia of Small Antiques, Harper, 1975.
The Price Guide to Collectable Antiques, Chancery Press, 1975.
Rural Crafts in Scotland, R. Hale, 1976.

Encyclopedia of World Stamps, 1945-1975, McGraw, 1976.
Childhood Antiques, Taplinger, 1976.
Encyclopedia of Isle of Man Coins and Tokens, Pobjoy Mint, 1976.
Banknotes at War, Gibbons, 1977.
The Dictionary of Western Sculptors in Bronze, Chancery Press, 1977.
Yesterday's Junk, Tomorrow's Antiques, Macdonald & Jane's, 1977.
Railway Antiques, Ward, Lock, 1978.
Collectables, Macdonald & Jane's, 1979.
The Price Guide to More Collectable Antiques, Chancery Press, 1980.
Antique Market Values, Link House, 1980-82.
Stamp Collecting, St. Michael, 1980, Van Nostrand, 1983.
Cheque Collecting, Gibbons, 1981.
Key Definitions in Numismatics, Frederick Mueller, 1981.
Antique Collector's Companion, Chancery Press, 1981.
Stamp Facts and Feats, Guinness Superlatives, 1982.
History of Modern English Coinage, 1485-1985, Longman, 1984.
Collecting Local History, Longman, 1984.
The Burns Federation, 1885-1985, Burns Federation, 1985.
British Stamps, Longman, 1985.
(Editor) *The Complete Works of Robert Burns*, Alloway, 1986.
Philatelic Terms Illustrated, Stanley Gibbons, 1987.
(Editor) *The Complete Letters of Robert Burns*, Alloway, 1987.

PRIVATELY PRINTED

(With George F. Crabb) *Tristan da Cunha: Its Posts and Philately*, 1965.
Churchill on Stamps, 1966.
The Circular Name Stamps of Scotland, 1977.
Scottish Postmarks from 1693 to the Present Time, 1978.
The Skeleton Postmarks of Scotland, 1978.
Islands Postal History Series, eleven volumes, 1978-80.
The Floating Post Offices of the Clyde, 1979.
English and Welsh Postmarks since 1840, 1980.
Postal History of the Isle of Wight, 1981.
Telegraphic Codes of the British Isles, 1981.
Post Office Numbers, 1924-1969, 1981.
The Parcel Post of the British Isles, 1982.
Irish Postmarks since 1840, 1982.
Scottish Twin-Arc Postmarks, 1982.
Registered Mail of the British Isles, 1983.
Postal History of Glasgow, 1984.
Irish Slogan Postmarks, 1984.
Official Mail of the British Isles, 1984.
Surcharged Mail of the British Isles, 1985.
Sub Office Rubber Datestamps, four volumes, 1985-86.
Postal History of Dumfries, 1986.
Machine Cancellations of Scotland, 1987.
Number Postmarks of Scotland, 1987.
English Provincial Krag Cancellations, 1987.

UNDER PSEUDONYM IAN ANGUS

Collecting Antiques, Ward, Lock, 1971.
Stamps, Posts and Postmarks, Ward, Lock, 1972.
Coins and Money Tokens, Ward, Lock, 1972.
Medals and Decorations, Ward, Lock, 1973.
Paper Money, Ward, Lock, 1974.
History of Pitney Bowes Ltd., Pitney Bowes, 1975.

UNDER PSEUDONYM WILLIAM FINLAY

(Translator) Dmitri Kandaouroff, *Collecting Postal History*, Eurobook, 1973.

Stamp Design, Peter Lowe, 1974.

UNDER PSEUDONYM BRUCE GARDEN

Make Money with Stamps, Philatelic Publishers, 1967.
Learn about Stamps, Philatelic Publishers, 1968.

UNDER PSEUDONYM PETER WHITTINGTON

Undiscovered Antiques, Garnstone Press, 1971, Scribner, 1972.
Kitchen Antiques, Garnstone Press, 1975.

OTHER

Editor-in-chief, *International Encyclopedia of Stamps,* 1969-72; English language editor, *New World Encyclopedia,* Ward, Lock, 1973. Columnist, *New Daily,* 1962-66, and *Financial Times,* 1967—; feature writer, *British Post Office,* 1970-72, 1986—. Contributor to *Stamp Magazine, Gibbons Stamp Monthly, Investing Professional, Coin and Medal News, Coin Monthly, Antique Dealer and Collectors' Guide,* and *Stamps.* Editor, *The Burns Chronicle,* 1977—, *Postal History Annual,* 1979—, *Pobjoy Collectors' Newsletter,* 1984—, and *Burnsian,* 1986—. Associate, *Scottish National Directory,* 1987—. Consultant, *Longman's Dictionary,* 1979-82.

WORK IN PROGRESS: Research on the memorials, art, and artifacts associated with Robert Burns for an encyclopedia of Burnsiana, to be published in 1988; a social history of the post office.

SIDELIGHTS: James Mackay told *CA:* "A highly developed acquisitive instinct made me an inveterate magpie. When I realized the futility of collecting everything, I was impelled to explore the collectable potential in all manner of objects and what made people collect them.

"My first book was actually a guidebook commissioned by the British War Office in 1961, but prior to that I had written articles for various newspapers and magazines about the Outer Hebrides. During my employment at the British Museum, I was encouraged to write two books on philately. This led to more regular newspaper work which, in turn, attracted the attention of publishers who commissioned books on philately. In 1967 I began writing about collectables in the broadest sense for the *Financial Times,* and my first books on antiques and other aspects of the applied and decorative arts were spin-offs from these weekly articles. Since 1971 I have worked full-time in authorship and journalism.

"I started out with the aim of publicizing stamp collecting, not so much preaching to the converted but propagating the gospel to the layman. Later, as people acquired greater affluence and increased leisure time, I realized that there was a need for books which would help the growing army of antique collectors. In this area, however, I have preferred to explore the newer collectables and the more off-beat subjects, linking them to socio-economic and historic factors. Currently I have gotten deeply involved in aspects of communications and transport history and, specifically, am working on a series of projects dealing with the postal history of the British Isles.

"Since 1978 my wife, Joyce, has been busy publishing books on postal history, and working on the line drawings to illustrate these books has encouraged me to broaden my interests in this medium. For *Antique Market Values* I had to produce some seven hundred line drawings as well as the text, and this is an aspect of my work which I hope to develop. Apart from the books which we have published ourselves, all of the books I have had published since 1961 were commissioned by publishers who made the first approach to me. I have many ideas for books which I should like to write, but have always been kept fully occupied, coping with commissioned work."

Some of Mackay's books have been published in Spanish, Swedish, German, French, Danish, Finnish, Dutch, and Serbo-Croatian.

AVOCATIONAL INTERESTS: Applied and decorative arts, languages (reads most European languages), and offbeat aspects of social history, biography, and travel.

*   *   *

MacMAHON, Bryan (Michael) 1909-

PERSONAL: Born September 29, 1909, in Listowel, County Kerry, Ireland; son of Patric Mary (a land clerk) and Joanna (a teacher; maiden name, Caughlin) MacMahon; married Kathleen Ryan, November 4, 1936; children: Patrick Gerald, James, Bryan, Maurice, Eoin. *Education:* Attended St. Michael's College, Listowel, 1921-28, and St. Patrick's College, Drumcondra, 1928-30; qualified as national teacher, 1930. *Politics:* Eclectic. *Religion:* Roman Catholic.

ADDRESSES: Home and office—38 Church St., Listowel, County Kerry, Ireland. *Agent*—Curtis Brown Ltd., 575 Madison Ave., New York, N.Y. 10022; and A. P. Watt & Son, 26-28 Bedford Row, London WC1R 4HL, England.

CAREER: Writer, folklorist, and lecturer; teacher at parochial primary school in Dublin, Ireland, 1930-31; Scoil Realta na Maidine 2 (name in English, Morning Star School No. 2), Listowel, County Kerry, Ireland, 1942-75, began as teacher, became principal teacher. With his wife ran a bookstore for a time; producer as well as author of plays and pageants, and shareholder (appointed) of Abbey Theatre; initiated series, "The Balladmaker's Saturday Night," for Radio Eireann and has done other broadcasting for Radio Eireann, British Broadcasting Corp., Channel Four Brittain, Yugoslav TV, and various stations on the West Coast in the United States. Represented Ireland in the humanities at Harvard International Seminar, 1963; lectured at Writers' Workshop at University of Iowa, 1965; opening speaker at National Council of Teachers of English conference in Colorado Springs, Colo., 1968; founded first Irish Short Story Workshop, in conjunction with Writers' Week in Listowel, 1972; also has lectured in Germany and throughout Ireland.

MEMBER: Irish Academy of Letters, Irish PEN (president, 1972), Aosdana (Irish Arts Council), Listowel Drama Group (founding member).

AWARDS, HONORS: Bell Award for best short story published in the magazine, 1945; Catholic Press Award for best short story in a Catholic magazine in the United States, 1961, and runner-up (to Flannery O'Connor), 1962; LL.D., National University of Ireland, 1972, for services to Irish literature.

WRITINGS:

The Lion Tamer and Other Stories, Macmillan (London), 1948, Dutton, 1949.
Jackomoora and the King of Ireland's Son (juvenile), Dutton, 1950.
Children of the Rainbow (novel), Dutton, 1952.
The Red Petticoat and Other Stories, Dutton, 1955.
The Honey Spike (novel), Dutton, 1967.
Brendan of Ireland (juvenile), photographs by W. Suschitzky, Hastings House, 1967.
Pasty-O and His Wonderful Pets (juvenile), Dutton, 1970.

Here's Ireland (nonfiction), Dutton, 1971.
(Translator from the Irish) Peig Sayers, *Peig,* Syracuse University Press, 1973.
The End of the World and Other Stories, Poolbeg (Dublin), 1976.
The Sound of Hooves and Other Stories, Bodley Head, 1985.

PLAYS

"The Bugle in the Blood," first produced in Dublin at Abbey Theatre, March, 1949, and still widely performed.
"Song of the Anvil" (first produced in Dublin at Abbey Theatre for International Theatre Festival, 1960; later produced in California by Ria Mooney of Abbey Theatre), published in *Seven Irish Plays, 1946-1964,* edited by Robert Hogan, University of Minnesota Press, 1967.
"The Honey Spike," first produced in Dublin at Abbey Theatre, 1961.
"The Gap of Life," first produced in Dublin at Peacock Theatre by Society of Irish Playwrights, October, 1972.

Author of other plays for Listowel Drama Group and of historical pageants for national occasions in Ireland, including "Seachtar Fear, Seacht La," first produced in Croke Park, Dublin, in commemoration of the 1916 Easter Rebellion and later televised. Also author of "The Master," broadcast on Radio Eireann and produced at the Belltable Theatre in Limerick. Writer of radio and television plays for children and adults.

WORK IN PROGRESS: Short stories, national pageants and a longer untitled experimental work.

SIDELIGHTS: Initial recognition of Bryan MacMahon's work came in the magazine *The Bell,* where he was welcomed as a poet of merit by Frank O'Connor and as a short story writer by editor Sean O'Faolain. His first published collection, *The Lion Tamer and Other Stories,* received a cover note in the *Saturday Review* and such a cordial reception from American critics that it quickly went through four printings. When *Children of the Rainbow* appeared, Henry Seidel Canby called it "the richest and raciest book that has come out of Ireland for many years." Serialized for radio-television presentation, the novel was also published in England and, like many of his stories, it has been translated into German. MacMahon's stories and poems have been published in magazines in Ireland, England, the United States, and Germany, and are included in most anthologies of modern Irish writing. Some of his work has also appeared under undivulged pseudonyms.

MacMahon likes "people, people, people," and lives in a small town because it affords him an unique opportunity of meeting neighbors in all their moods. He credits the tradesmen of the town for his most valuable education and "reckons a visit to the saddler's shop essential in every day."

A life-long collector of native music, MacMahon's work on the Radio Eireann series, "The Balladmaker's Saturday Night," helped pave the way for the current revival of native balladry. As a relief from serious work, he "often writes ballads which are published in his native town by his friend the printer and are sung later in the pubs of Ireland." He is a "fluent speaker of Irish" and says that he "draw[s] much sustenance from a Gaelic background." One of the few "outsiders" who can speak Shelta, the secret language of the Irish traveling people, he considers these people the "final free" and the "outer palisades of human liberty." An article by him on the lives of the Irish travelers appeared in *Natural History* and *Merian* (Germany).

According to MacMahon, Ireland is one of the last places where a human being is valued and is an excellent place to return to after a stint of lecturing in America. He prefers to read short stories and novels in translation from other languages and cultures, chiefly those of Africa, the Philippines, and South America. He finds life exciting and the day too short for his many interests and activities, which include beagling, fishing, and wandering in Ireland.

MEDIA ADAPTATIONS: MacMahon's novel *Children of the Rainbow* and his translation of *Peig* by Peig Sayers have been serialized by Radio Eireann.

BIOGRAPHICAL/CRITICAL SOURCES:

BOOKS

Journal of Irish Literature, Proscenium Press, 1971.

PERIODICALS

Atlantic, May, 1952.
Best Sellers, March 1, 1967.
Library Journal, January 1, 1952, January 1, 1955, January 1, 1967.
New Statesman, September 15, 1967.
New Yorker, March 15, 1952, March 12, 1955.
New York Times, January 30, 1955, February 26, 1967.
Saturday Review, March 25, 1967.
Times (London), May 2, 1985.
Times Literary Supplement, May 23, 1952.

*   *   *

MAESTRO, Betsy C.   1944-

PERSONAL: Surname is pronounced Ma-*es*-troh; born January 5, 1944, in New York, N.Y.; daughter of Harlan R. (a design consultant) and Norma (in education; maiden name, Sherman) Crippen; married second husband, Giulio Maestro (a free-lance writer and book illustrator), December 16, 1972; children: (second marriage) Daniela Marisa, Marco Claudio. *Education:* Southern Connecticut State College, B.S., 1964, M.S., 1970. *Politics:* Democrat.

ADDRESSES: Home and office—74 Mile Creek Rd., Old Lyme, Conn. 06371.

CAREER: Writer. Deer Run School, East Haven, Conn., kindergarten teacher, 1964-75.

MEMBER: National Education Association, Connecticut Education Association.

AWARDS, HONORS: Notable Book Award, American Library Association, 1981, for *Traffic: A Book of Opposites.*

WRITINGS:

JUVENILE PICTURE BOOKS; ILLUSTRATED BY HUSBAND, GIULIO MAESTRO

A Wise Monkey Tale, Crown, 1975.
Where Is My Friend?, Crown, 1976.
Fat Polka-Dot Cat and Other Haiku, Dutton, 1976.
In My Boat, Crowell, 1976.
Harriet Goes to the Circus, Crown, 1977.
Busy Day: A Book of Action Words, Crown, 1978.
Lambs for Dinner, Crown, 1978.
On the Go: A Book of Adjectives, Crown, 1979.
Harriet Reads Signs and More Signs, Crown, 1981.
Traffic: A Book of Opposites, Crown, 1981.

The Key to the Kingdom, Harcourt, 1982.
On the Town: A Book of Clothing Words, Crown, 1983.
The Guessing Game, Grosset & Dunlap, 1983.
(With Ellen DelVecchio) *Big City Port,* Four Winds, 1983.
Around the Clock with Harriet, Crown, 1984.
Harriet at School, Harriet at Play, Harriet at Work, Harriet at Home (four board books), Crown, 1984.
Through the Year with Harriet, Crown, 1985.
Camping Out, Crown, 1985.
Ferryboat, Crowell, 1986.
The Story of the Statue of Liberty, Lothrop, 1986.
The Grab Bag Party, Golden Press, 1986.
The Pandas Take a Vacation, Golden Press, 1986.
The Perfect Picnic, Golden Press, 1987.
The Travels of Freddie and Frannie Frog, Golden Press, 1987.
A More Perfect Union: The Story of Our Constitution, Lothrop, 1987.

WORK IN PROGRESS: *Dollars and Cents for Harriet,* for Crown; *Discovery of the Americas,* for Lothrop; *Temperature,* for Dutton; *Snow Day,* for Scholastic Inc.; *Taxi,* for Clarion Books.

SIDELIGHTS: Betsy C. Maestro, a former kindergarten teacher, and Giulio Maestro, a former advertising designer, have been creating concept books for young children since 1975. The Maestro's books have been praised for their simplicity, clarity, and colorful graphics. Reviewing *On the Town: A Book of Clothing Words,* a *School Library Journal* contributor writes: "Readers familiar with the Maestro style will recognize the fresh, good-natured approach and the resourcefulness which make *On the Town* click."

Betsy C. Maestro once told *CA:* "When you work on picture books for young children, it is impossible to think of the story or concept separately from the illustration. The two are one. I have been very lucky in that, since Giulio and I work together most of the time, we both have a lot of input in each area and give each other suggestions and advice. I loved books as a child (and still do!) and enjoy sharing the ones I write with all the children we know."

AVOCATIONAL INTERESTS: Reading, cooking, gardening, photography, travel, art, antiques.

BIOGRAPHICAL/CRITICAL SOURCES:

PERIODICALS

School Library Journal, November, 1983.

*   *   *

MAESTRO, Giulio 1942-

PERSONAL: Given name is pronounced *Jool*-yoh, and surname, Ma-*es*-troh; born May 6, 1942, in New York, N.Y.; son of Marcello (a writer) and Edna (Ten Eyck) Maestro; married Betsy Crippen (a kindergarten teacher and writer), December 16, 1972; children: Daniela Marisa, Marco Claudio. *Education:* Cooper Union, B.F.A., 1964; further study in printmaking at Pratt Graphics Center.

ADDRESSES: *Home and office*—74 Mile Creek Rd., Old Lyme, Conn. 06371.

CAREER: Design Organization, Inc. (advertising design), New York City, assistant to art director, 1965-66; Warren A. Kass Graphics, Inc. (advertising design), New York City, assistant art director, 1966-69; free-lance writer and book illustrator, 1969—.

AWARDS, HONORS: Two books have been included in American Institute of Graphic Arts Children's Book Shows, *The Tortoise's Tug of War* in the 1971-72 show and *Three Kittens* in the 1973-74 show; artwork from *The Remarkable Plant in Apartment 4* was exhibited in the Society of Illustrators Show, New York, 1974; *Two Good Friends* was chosen an American Library Association Notable Book, 1974; Merit Award from Art Directors Club of New York, 1978, for *Harriet Goes to the Circus*; artwork from *The Tortoise's Tug of War* was included in the 14th Exhibition of Original Pictures of International Children's Books, Japan, 1979; Notable Book Award, American Library Association, 1981, for *Traffic: A Book of Opposites.*

WRITINGS:

SELF-ILLUSTRATED

The Tortoise's Tug of War, Bradbury, 1971.
The Remarkable Plant in Apartment 4, Bradbury, 1973.
One More and One Less (Junior Literary Guild selection), Crown, 1974.
Leopard Is Sick, Greenwillow, 1978.
Leopard and the Noisy Monkeys, Greenwillow, 1979.
A Raft of Riddles, Dutton, 1982.
Halloween Howls, Dutton, 1983.
Riddle Romp, Clarion Books, 1983.
Just Enough Rosie, Grosset & Dunlap, 1983.
What's a Frank Frank? Tasty Homograph Riddles, Clarion Books, 1984.
Razzle Dazzle Riddles, Clarion Books, 1985.
What's Mite Might? Homophone Riddles to Boost Your Word Power, Clarion Books, 1986.

ILLUSTRATOR; JUVENILE PICTURE BOOKS BY WIFE, BETSY C. MAESTRO

A Wise Monkey Tale, Crown, 1975.
Where Is My Friend?, Crown, 1976.
Fat Polka-Dot Cat and Other Haiku, Dutton, 1976.
In My Boat, Crowell, 1976.
Harriet Goes to the Circus, Crown, 1977.
Busy Day: A Book of Action Words, Crown, 1978.
Lambs for Dinner, Crown, 1978.
On the Go: A Book of Adjectives, Crown, 1979.
Harriet Reads Signs and More Signs, Crown, 1981.
Traffic: A Book of Opposites, Crown, 1981.
The Key to the Kingdom, Harcourt, 1982.
On the Town: A Book of Clothing Words, Crown, 1983.
The Guessing Game, Grosset & Dunlap, 1983.
(And Ellen DelVecchio) *Big City Port,* Four Winds, 1983.
Around the Clock with Harriet, Crown, 1984.
Harriet at School, Harriet at Play, Harriet at Work, Harriet at Home (four board books), Crown, 1984.
Through the Year with Harriet, Crown, 1985.
Camping Out, Crown, 1985.
Ferryboat, Crowell, 1986.
The Story of the Statue of Liberty, Lothrop, 1986.
The Grab Bag Party, Golden Press, 1986.
The Pandas Take a Vacation, Golden Press, 1986.
The Perfect Picnic, Golden Press, 1987.
The Travels of Freddie and Frannie Frog, Golden Press, 1987.
A More Perfect Union: The Story of Our Constitution, Lothrop, 1987.

ILLUSTRATOR; JUVENILE PICTURE BOOKS

Millie McWhirter, *A Magic Morning with Uncle Al,* Collins & World, 1969.

Rudyard Kipling, *The Beginning of the Armadillos*, St. Martin's, 1970.

Mirra Ginsburg, *What Kind of Bird Is That?*, Crown, 1973.

Ginsburg, *Three Kittens* (Junior Literary Guild selection), Crown, 1973.

Vicki Kimmel Artis, *Gray Duck Catches a Friend*, Putnam, 1974.

Tony Johnston, *Fig Tale*, Putnam, 1974.

Judy Delton, *Two Good Friends* (Junior Literary Guild selection), Crown, 1974.

Harry Milgrom, *Egg-Ventures* (Junior Literary Guild selection), Dutton, 1974.

Eva Ibbotson, *The Great Ghost Rescue*, Walck, 1975.

Maria Polushkin, *Who Said Meow?* (Junior Literary Guild selection), Crown, 1975.

William R. Gerler, *A Pack of Riddles*, Dutton, 1975.

Delton, *Two Is Company*, Crown, 1976.

Delton, *Three Friends Find Spring*, Crown, 1977.

Delton, *Penny-Wise, Fun-Foolish*, Crown, 1977.

Ruth Lerner Perle and Susan Horowitz, adapters, *Little Red Riding Hood with Benjy and Bubbles*, Holt, 1979.

Perle and Horowitz, adapters, *The Fisherman and His Wife with Benjy and Bubbles*, Holt, 1979.

Perle and Horowitz, adapters, *Rumpelstiltskin with Benjy and Bubbles*, Holt, 1979.

Perle and Horowitz, adapters, *Sleeping Beauty with Benjy and Bubbles*, Holt, 1979.

Ginsburg, *Kitten from One to Ten*, 1980.

Delton, *Groundhog's Day at the Doctor*, Parents Magazine Press, 1980.

Mike Thaler, *Moonkey*, Harper, 1981.

Marvin Terban, *Eight Ate: A Feast of Homonym Riddles*, Clarion Books, 1981.

Terban, *In a Pickle*, Clarion Books, 1983.

Terban, *I Think I Thought*, Clarion Books, 1984.

Terban, *Too Hot to Hoot*, Clarion Books, 1985.

Terban, *Your Foot's on My Feet*, Clarion Books, 1986.

ILLUSTRATOR

Katherine Cutler, *From Petals to Pinecones*, Lothrop, 1969.

Cutler, *Creative Shellcraft*, Lothrop, 1971.

(With others) Richard Shaw, editor, *The Fox Book*, Warner, 1971.

Elyse Sommer, *The Bread Dough Craft Book*, Lothrop, 1972.

Franklyn Branley, *The Beginning of the Earth*, Crowell, 1972.

Jo Phillips, *Right Angles: Paper-Folding Geometry*, Crowell, 1972.

Sommer, *Designing with Cutouts: The Art of Decoupage*, Lothrop, 1973.

Sommer, *Make It With Burlap*, Lothrop, 1973.

(With others) Shaw, editor, *The Cat Book*, Warner, 1973.

Roma Gans, *Millions and Millions of Crystals*, Crowell, 1973.

Mannis Charosh, *Number Ideas through Pictures*, Crowell, 1974.

Carolyn Meyer, *Milk, Butter and Cheese: The Story of Dairy Products*, Morrow, 1974.

Sarah Riedman, *Trees Alive*, Lothrop, 1974.

Melvin Berger, *The New Air Book*, Crowell, 1974.

(With others) Shaw, editor, *The Bird Book*, Warner, 1974.

Gans, *Oil: The Buried Treasure*, Crowell, 1975.

John Trivett, *Building Tables on Tables: A Book about Multiplication*, Crowell, 1975.

Elyse Sommer and Joellen Sommer, *A Patchwork, Applique, and Quilting Primer*, Lothrop, 1975.

(With others) Shaw, editor, *The Mouse Book*, Warner, 1975.

Sigmund Kalina, *How to Make a Dinosaur*, Lothrop, 1976.

Gans, *Caves*, Crowell, 1976.

Berger, *Energy from the Sun*, Crowell, 1976.

Eve Barwell, *Make Your Pet a Present*, Lothrop, 1977.

Caroline Anne Levine, *Knockout Knock Knocks*, Dutton, 1978.

Gail Kay Haines, *Natural and Synthetic Poisons*, Morrow, 1978.

John Trivett and Daphne Trivett, *Time for Clocks*, Crowell, 1979.

Vicki Cobb, *More Science Experiments You Can Eat*, Lippincott, 1979.

Joanne E. Bernstein, *Fiddle with a Riddle: How to Write Riddles*, Dutton, 1979.

Isaac Asimov, *Saturn and Beyond*, Lothrop, 1979.

Boris Arnov, *Water: Experiments to Understand It*, Lothrop, 1980.

Andrea G. Zimmerman, *The Riddle Zoo*, Dutton, 1981.

Branley, *Comets*, Crowell, 1984.

Helen Roney Sattler, *Fish Facts and Bird Brains: Animal Intelligence*, Lodestar, 1984.

Seymour Simon, *Dinosaurs Are the Biggest Animals that Ever Lived*, Lippincott, 1984.

Sattler, *Trainwhistles*, Lothrop, 1985.

Branley, *Sunshine Makes the Seasons*, revised edition, Crowell, 1985.

Branley, *Hurricane Watch*, Crowell, 1986.

Branley, *Rockets and Satellites*, Crowell, 1987.

Branley, *The Beginning of the Earth*, revised edition, Crowell, 1987.

SIDELIGHTS: Giulio Maestro once told *CA:* "I was born in New York City and lived in Greenwich Village most of my life. My family owned a house on Charlton Street, and I attended the Little Red School House from kindergarten through grade six. I started drawing and painting before I even went to school."

Some of Maestro's work has been published in Germany, England, and Japan.

See entry for Betsy C. Maestro, in this volume.

AVOCATIONAL INTERESTS: Reading, painting, gardening, travel.

*   *   *

MAGEE, Wes 1939-

PERSONAL: Born July 20, 1939, in Greenock, Scotland; son of Albert (a minister) and Noreen (Middleton) Magee; married Janet Parkhouse (a teacher), August, 1968; children: Kingsley, Miranda. *Education:* Goldsmiths' College, London, Teachers' Certificate, 1967.

ADDRESSES: Home—Santone House, Low St., Sancton, Near York, England.

CAREER: Brough County Primary School, Brough, England, headmaster, 1981—. Tutor with Arvon Foundation and Poetry Society of Great Britain Critical Service. Lecturer; conducts workshops; adjudicates for poetry writing competitions. *Military service:* British Army, Intelligence, 1960-62.

MEMBER: Poetry Society of Great Britain, National Association of Head Teachers.

AWARDS, HONORS: New Poets Award from Leeds University, 1973, for poetry collection *Urban Gorilla;* Poetry Book Society recommendation, 1978, for *No Man's Land.*

WRITINGS:

No Man's Land (poems), Blackstaff Press, 1978.
The Real Spirit of Christmas (one-act play for children; first produced in Swindon, England, at Park North School Theatre, December 10, 1978), Samuel French, 1978.
Oliver, the Daring Birdman (juvenile), Longman, 1978.
The Space Beasts (juvenile), Kent County Libraries, 1979.
A Dark Age (poems), Blackstaff Press, 1981.
All the Day Through (anthology of poems), Evans Brothers, 1982.
Dragon's Smoke (anthology of poems), Blackwell, 1985.
A Shooting Star (anthology of poems), Blackwell, 1985.
A Calendar of Poems (anthology of poems), Unwin Hyman, 1986.
A Christmas Stocking (anthology of poems), Royce, 1987.
Don't Do That! (stories; juvenile), Ginn, 1987.

Also author of poetry collection, *Urban Gorilla.* Managing editor of the literary magazine *Prism,* 1964-67.

BIOGRAPHICAL/CRITICAL SOURCES:

PERIODICALS

Times Literary Supplement, September 17, 1982, September 24, 1982.

*   *   *

MAGGS, Peter B(lount)   1936-

PERSONAL: Born July 24, 1936, in Durham, N.C.; son of Douglas B. (a professor of law) and Dorothy (Mackay) Maggs; married Barbara Widenor, February 27, 1959; children: Bruce, Gregory, Stephanie, Katherine. *Education:* Harvard University, A.B., 1957, J.D., 1961; Leningrad State University, exchange student, 1961-62.

ADDRESSES: Home—2011 Silver Ct. East, Urbana, Ill. 61801.

CAREER: University of Illinois at Urbana-Champaign, Urbana, College of Law, assistant professor, 1964-67, associate professor, 1967-69, professor of law, 1969—.

MEMBER: American Association for the Advancement of Slavic Studies, American Law Institute.

AWARDS, HONORS: Medal of Merit, U.S. Information Agency. 1959, for services at American Exhibition in Moscow; Fulbright Lecturer on U.S. Law, Moscow State University, spring, 1977.

WRITINGS:

(With Harold J. Berman) *Disarmament Inspection under Soviet Law,* Oceana, 1967.
(With John Hazard and Issac Shapiro) *The Soviet Legal System,* 2nd edition (Maggs was not associated with earlier edition), Oceana, 1969, 3rd edition (with Hazard and William Butler), 1977.
(With Donald Barry, F. J. M. Feldbrugge, and George Ginsburgs) *Soviet Law after Stalin,* Volume I, Sijthoff (Leiden), 1977, Volume II, Sijthoff & Noordhoff International, 1978, Volume III, Sijthoff & Noordhoff International, 1979.
(Translator) Piers Beirne and Robert Sharlet, editors, *Pashukanis: Selected Writings on Marxism and Law,* Academic Press, 1979.
(With Gordon Smith and Ginsburgs) *Soviet and East European Law and the Scientific and Technical Revolution,* Pergamon, 1981.

(With Smith and Ginsburgs) *Law and Economic Development in the Soviet Union,* Westview, 1982.
(With S. Chesterfield Oppenheim, Glen E. Weston, and Roger Schechter) *Unfair Trade Practices and Consumer Protection, Cases and Comments,* 4th edition (Maggs was not associated with earlier editions), West Publishing, 1983.
(With Hazard and William E. Butler) *The Soviet Legal System: The Law in the 1980's,* Oceana, 1984.
(With Oppenheim, Weston, and Schechter) *1986 Supplement to Unfair Trade Practices and Consumer Protection,* West Publishing, 1986.
(Contributor) *Communist Parties and the Law,* Martinus Nijhoff, 1986.
(With James Sprowl) *Computer Applications in the Law,* West Publishing, 1987.

WORK IN PROGRESS: The Soviet Economy: A Legal Analysis.

*   *   *

MAGNUSSON, Magnus   1929-

PERSONAL: Born October 12, 1929, in Reykjavik, Iceland; son of Sigursteinn (Icelandic Counsul-General for Scotland) and Ingibjorg (Sigurdardottir) Magnusson; married Mamie Baird (a journalist), June 30, 1954; children: Sally, Margaret, Anna, Siggy (died, 1973), Jon. *Education:* Jesus College, Oxford, M.A. (with honors), 1951.

ADDRESSES: Home—Blairskaith House, Balmore-Torrance, Glasgow G64 4AX, Scotland. *Agent*—Deborah Rogers, 49 Blenheim Crescent, London W11 2EF, England.

CAREER: Scottish Daily Express, Glasgow, Scotland, reporter and assistant editor, 1953-61; *Scotsman,* Edinburgh, Scotland, chief feature writer and assistant editor, 1961-68; free-lance writer and broadcaster, 1968—; translator; host of British Broadcasting Corp. (BBC) programs, including ''Mastermind,'' ''China,'' ''B.C.: The Archaeology of the Bible Lands,'' ''Chronicle,'' ''Vikings!,'' and ''Living Legends.'' Lord Rector, Edinburgh University, 1975-78. Stewards chairman of York Archaeological Trust, 1975-83, chairman of Scottish Youth Theatre, 1977-78, Scottish Churches Architectural Heritage Trust, 1978-85, and Ancient Monuments Board for Scotland, 1981—. Trustee, National Museums of Scotland.

MEMBER: Royal Society of Edinburgh (fellow), Royal Society of Antiquaries of Scotland (fellow).

AWARDS, HONORS: Times Educational Supplement Information Book Award, 1972, for *Introducing Archaeology;* named Scottish television personality of the year, 1974; Knight of Order of the Falcon (Iceland), 1975, Knight Commander, 1986; Queen's Silver Jubilee Medal, 1977; honorary doctorate from Edinburgh University, 1978, and York University, 1981; Iceland Media Award, 1985.

WRITINGS:

Introducing Archaeology, Walck, 1972.
Viking Expansion Westwards, Walck, 1973.
The Clacken and the Slate: The Story of the Edinburgh Academy, 1824-1874, Collins, 1974.
Hammer of the North, Orbis, 1976, 2nd edition, Viking, 1979.
B.C.: The Archaeology of the Bible Lands, Bodley Head, 1977, published as *Archaeology of the Bible,* Simon & Schuster, 1978.

Landlord or Tenant?: A View of Irish History, Bodley Head, 1978.
Iceland, photographs by John Chang McCurdy, Almenna Bokafelagid, 1979.
Vikings!, Dutton, 1980.
Magnus on the Move, Macdonald, 1980.
Treasures of Scotland, Weidenfeld & Nicolson, 1981.
Lindisfarne, the Cradle Island, Oriel Press, 1984.
Iceland Saga, Bodley Head, 1987.

AUTHOR OF INTRODUCTION

William Watson, *Ancient China*, BBC Publications, 1974.
William L. McKinlay, *Karluk: The Great Untold Story of Arctic Exploration*, Weidenfeld & Nicolson, 1976.
Jeffrey Iverson, *More Lives Than One?: Evidence of the Remarkable Bloxham Tapes*, Souvenir, 1976.
Emrys Jones, editor, *The Atlas of World Geography*, Sundial, 1977.
Peter Jennings, *Face to Face with the Turin Shroud*, Mowbray, 1978.
Yohanan Aharoni and Michael Avi-Yonah, editors, *Modern Bible Atlas*, Allen & Unwin, 1979.
Richard Barber, *Living Legends*, BBC Publications, 1980.
Great Books for Today, Reader's Digest, 1981.
Michael S. Rohan and Allan J. Scott, *The Hammer and the Cross*, Alder, 1981.
James Kennaway, *Household Ghosts*, Mainstream, 1981.
Michael Ingram, *The Voyage of Odin's Raven*, Clearwater Press, 1982.
Robert Burns, *Bawdy Verse and Folksongs*, Papermac, 1982.
Mastermind Four, BBC Publications, 1982.
Alan Boucher, *Northern Voices: Five Contemporary Icelandic Poets*, Wilfion Books, 1984.
Anna Magnusson, *The Village: A History of Quarrier's*, Quarrier's Homes, 1985.

CONTRIBUTOR

The Glorious Privilege: The History of the "Scotsman," Thomas Nelson, 1967.
Ian Grimble and Derick S. Thomson, *The Future of the Highlands*, Routledge & Kegan Paul, 1968.
The "Reader's Digest" Book of Strange Stories, Amazing Facts, Reader's Digest Press, 1975.
Robin Prentice, editor, *The National Trust for Scotland Guide*, J. Cape, 1976.
Ray Sutcliffe, editor, *Chronicle*, BBC Publications, 1978.
Brian Walker, editor, *Pass the Port*, Christian Brann, 1978.
Joseph J. Thorndyke, Jr., editor, *Discovery of Lost Worlds*, American Heritage, 1979.

TRANSLATOR

(With Herman Palsson) *Njal's Saga*, Penguin, 1960.
Halldor Laxness, *The Atom Station*, Methuen, 1961.
Laxness, *Paradise Reclaimed*, Methuen, 1962.
(With Palsson) *The Vinland Sagas: The Norse Discovery of America*, Penguin, 1965.
Laxness, *The Fish Can Sing*, Methuen, 1966.
(With Palsson) Snorri Sturluson, *King Harald's Saga: Harald Hardradi of Norway*, Penguin, 1966.
Samivel, *Golden Iceland*, Almenna Bokafelagid, 1967.
Laxness, *World Light*, University of Wisconsin Press, 1969.
(With Palsson) *Laxdaela Saga*, Penguin, 1969.
Laxness, *Christianity under Glacier*, Helgafell, 1973.

OTHER

Editor of "The Bodley Head Archaeologies," 1970-80, *Echoes*

in Stone, 1983, and consulting editor of *Reader's Digest Book of Facts*, 1985. Founder and editor of *Popular Archaeology*, 1979-80.

WORK IN PROGRESS: Research for a *Dictionary of Norse Mythology*, for Blackwell.

SIDELIGHTS: Magnus Magnusson lists his recreations as "digging and delving," which result from his work as a reporter—not only of the current scene but also of the world of archaeology. Says Magnusson, "Archaeological reports are the news stories of the past—and luckily, you can't libel the dead!"

Magnusson commented that he considers man-made artifacts unearthed by excavators to be time machines to transport a person into the past. Much of his recent work has been concerned with bringing the past to life again through history and archaeology.

* * *

MAINSTONE, Rowland J(ohnson) 1923-

PERSONAL: Born July 27, 1923; son of Rowland (an accountant) and Elizabeth (Johnson) Mainstone; married Madeleine Francoise Rozendaal, June 5, 1954 (died October 30, 1979); married Rhoda Mary Thicknesse, September 22, 1982; children: Rowland Robert, Anita Francesca, Marion Margery. *Education:* University of Liverpool, B.Eng. (with first class honors), 1943, M.Eng., 1946, D.Eng., 1974.

ADDRESSES: Home—20 Fishpool St., St. Albans, Hertfordshire AL3 4RT, England.

CAREER: Worked for Building Research Establishment, Garston, England, 1948-79. Consultant and visiting professor at Bartlett School of Architecture and Planning, University College, London, 1979—; Hoffman Wood professor of architecture, University of Leeds, 1985-86.

MEMBER: Institute of Civil Engineers, Institution of Structural Engineers (fellow), Society of Antiquaries (fellow), Royal Society of Arts (fellow), Royal Institute of British Architects (honorary fellow), American Society of Architectural Historians, Architectural Association, Accademia Pontaniana (fellow), Architecture Club, Baconian Club.

AWARDS, HONORS: Sir Banister Fletcher Prize from Authors Club of the United Kingdom, 1977, for *Developments in Structural Form*.

WRITINGS:

(Contributor) David Billington and Robert Mark, editors, *Civil Engineering: History, Heritage, and the Humanities*, Volume II, Princeton University Press, 1970.
Developments in Structural Form, MIT Press, 1975.
(Contributor) Trevor Williams, editor, *A History of Technology*, Volume VII: *The Twentieth Century*, Oxford University Press, 1978.
(Contributor and co-editor) *Tall Buildings: Criteria and Loading*, American Society of Civil Engineers, 1980.
(Contributor) Patrick Nuttgens, editor, *The World's Great Architecture*, Hamlyn, 1980.
(With first wife, Madeleine Mainstone) *The Seventeenth Century*, Cambridge University Press, 1981.
(Contributor) A. W. Skempton, editor, *John Smeaton, F.R.S.*, Thomas Telford, 1981.
(Contributor) Bernard Feilden, editor, *Conservation of Historic Buildings*, Butterworth & Co., 1982.

(Contributor) A. R. Collins, editor, *Structural Engineering: Two Centuries of British Achievement*, Tarot, 1983.
Repair and Strengthening of Historical Monuments and Buildings in Urban Nuclei, United Nations Industrial Development Organization, 1984.
(Contributor) John Musgrove, editor, *Sir Banister Fletcher's History of Architecture*, 19th edition, Butterworth & Co., 1987.
Hagia Sophia: Architecture, Structure and Liturgy of Justinian's Great Church, Thames & Hudson, 1988.

Contributor to *Macmillan Encyclopedia of Architecture and Technological Change* and *Macmillan Encyclopedia of Architects*. Contributor of about one hundred articles and reviews to architecture journals and technical publications.

WORK IN PROGRESS: Research on the history of several major domed buildings, on the historical development of design procedures, and on the structural conservation of historic buildings.

SIDELIGHTS: Rowland J. Mainstone wrote: "My central research interest is in the creative process, particularly in the areas of architectural and structural design. Even today I see the conception and realization of new forms as necessarily rooted in what has been done already. Hence I also have a strong interest in the history of past achievements. But I realize that architectural and structural design are more constrained than most arts by practical necessities of many kinds, including the wishes and whims of those who provide the drive and the money. In writing for a general readership, I attempt to show how particular buildings came to be as they are and for what purpose. In writing for fellow professionals, I attempt to look more deeply into the 'how' in ways that are relevant to present practice.

"This central interest spills out, on the one hand, into other arts, particularly painting and sculpture, which I practice a little as a pure amateur, and on the other hand, into more philosophical interests and a wider interest in other aspects of history. My first wife was a professional art historian, one daughter has followed her, and the other has trained as a sculptor.

"In my research, I am a great believer in drawing my own conclusions from the primary evidence—whether this is a building or a document. Hence I have traveled widely, inspected in great detail many outstanding buildings and other structures, and tried to read in the original any relevant documents. Partly to try out new ideas, I have also lectured widely in Britain, continental Europe, and the United States and less widely elsewhere.

"I see writing as another not entirely dissimilar art. Lazy by nature, I do not produce successive drafts to discover what I want to say. I ruminate on the subject until I think I 'know' before turning to the typewriter—or, more recently, the word processor. The test is in what emerges. I know that I have ruminated enough if what I want to say seems to write itself in the only possible way. I recognize my thoughts in it. But the pattern of words takes shape only on the page or the screen.

"Since suitable photographs and drawings can often assist greatly in illuminating my subjects, I also make full use of them, integrating them closely with the text and usually taking or preparing them myself."

MAITLAND, Derek 1943-

PERSONAL: Born April 17, 1943, in Chelmsford, Essex, England; son of James and Constance (Smallridge) Maitland. *Education:* Attended secondary schools in England and Australia. *Politics:* Liberal socialist. *Religion:* Christian.

CAREER: Script writer, reporter, and subeditor for television stations in Sydney, Australia, prior to 1965; employed with Australian Broadcasting Commission, 1965; reporter for *South China Morning Post*, Hong Kong, newscaster for Rediffusion Television, Hong Kong, and feature editor for *Bangkok Post*, Bangkok, Thailand, 1965-68; Copley News Service, San Diego, Calif., staff correspondent in Saigon, 1968; British Broadcasting Corp., London, England, subeditor and script writer, 1970; free-lance correspondent in Beirut, Lebanon, for Copley News Service, *San Francisco Chronicle*, and *Toronto Daily Star*, 1971—.

WRITINGS:

The Only War We've Got, Morrow, 1970.
T-Minus Tower, MacGibbon & Kee, 1971.
The Alpha Experience, W. H. Allen, 1974.
Breaking Out, St. Martin's, 1979.
The Firecracker Suite: Comic Tales of a Cultural Collision, CFW Publications (Hong Kong), 1980.
(Editor) Saul Lockhart, *Manila by Night*, CFW Publications, 1981.
Setting Sails: A Tribute to the Chinese Junk, photographs by Nik Wheeler, Publications Division, South China Morning Post, 1981.
This Is China, Hamlyn, 1982.
(With Jacki Passmore) *5000 Years of Tea: A Pictorial Companion*, CFW Publications, 1982.
Hong Kong in Focus, CFW Publications, 1984.

WORK IN PROGRESS: The Sheik, a novel based on the life of a Bedouin sheik in Jordan's Wadi Rum who is trying to protect his corrupted tribe from modern civilization.

SIDELIGHTS: Derek Maitland once told *CA* that his writing has been influenced by a variety of experiences. "Hemingway and Salinger provided the emotional element, and [my] first expedition in 1965 to Southeast Asia provided the material," he said. "Vietnam itself added fear, anger, new political awareness and motivation for *The Only War We've Got*. Since my twelve months there I have been fascinated, almost obsessed, by man's capacity for violence, his own obsession with war and the thin red line of mentality that separates warrior from peacenik. During the three years I spent in London after Saigon, this old horror returned over a three-month period covering the Northern Ireland crisis for the BBC. In my third expedition, covering the Middle East from Beirut, the Arab-Israeli conflict has shown me the ridiculous lengths to which men will go to prove they are men."

BIOGRAPHICAL/CRITICAL SOURCES:

PERIODICALS

Time, November 16, 1970.
Times Literary Supplement, May 14, 1970.†

* * *

MALVEAUX, Julianne M(arie) 1953-

PERSONAL: Born September 22, 1953, in San Francisco, Calif.; daughter of Proteone Alexandria Malveaux (a social worker).

Education: Boston College, A.B., 1974, M.A., 1975; Massachusetts Institute of Technology, Ph.D., 1980.

ADDRESSES: Home—226 Kingston St., San Francisco, Calif. 94110.

CAREER: WFAA-TV, Dallas, Tex., media intern, summer, 1975; White House Council of Economic Advisers, Washington, D.C., junior staff economist, 1977-78; Rockefeller Foundation, New York City, research fellow, 1978-80; New School for Social Research, New York City, assistant professor of economics, 1980-81; San Francisco State University, San Francisco, Calif., assistant professor of economics, 1981-85; University of California, Berkeley, research associate, 1985—, also visiting professor. Member of board of directors of National Child Labor Committee.

MEMBER: American Economic Association, National Economic Association, Bay Area Association of Black Journalists, Delta Sigma Theta.

WRITINGS:

(With Phyllis A. Wallace and Linda P. Datcher) *Black Women in the Labor Force,* MIT Press, 1980.
(Editor with Margaret Simms) *Slipping through the Cracks: The Status of Black Women,* Transaction Books, 1986.

Also author of *No Images: Contemporary Black Women in the Workplace.* Weekly columnist for the *San Francisco Sun Reporter,* 1981—; guest columnist for *USA Today.* Contributor of more than one hundred articles to magazines, including *Essence, Black Enterprise, Working Woman,* and *Black Scholar.* Contributing editor to *Essence,* 1984—.

WORK IN PROGRESS: A set of essays on progressive coalitions and a novel tentatively titled, *Other People's Things.*

SIDELIGHTS: Julianne M. Malveaux commented: "I like to describe myself as a poet/writer/economist. My academic training has been in economics, and I have written about my research both for fellow academics and for broader audiences. But I have also been writing poetry since I was sixteen, and have written for a variety of magazines about subjects that include, but are not limited to, money issues. Because I consider myself a 'renaissance person' and have a variety of interests, I finish projects by immersing myself in them for two- or three-day periods at a time. I also maintain the writing habit by keeping a journal, though this is difficult on long vacations.

"My research has often been infuriating—only by viewing detailed occupational data can the extent of occupational segregation be understood. While many of the overt barriers against women's mobility in the workplace have been removed, the more subtle barriers that remain are difficult to act on. So even though women have made some headway, more than half of all women still work in clerical and service jobs, and another quarter work in other female-stratified jobs. This situation does not change considerably for young (twenty-five to thirty-four years old) women.

"Not only is the pace of social change exceedingly slow, but the backlash in terms of the new racism, sexism, and classism are incredibly frustrating. I cherish the privilege to write about these things and to have my work published, but I also struggle with the roles I try to combine: writer, economist, activist. I have role models for my efforts though, and when I feel especially overwhelmed I like to think of myself as someone who is following in the footsteps of W.E.B. DuBois, a scholar/activist and very lyrical writer."

MANVELL, (Arnold) Roger   1909-

PERSONAL: Born October 10, 1909, in Leicester, England; son of Arnold and Gertrude (Baines) Manvell. *Education:* Attended University of Leicester; University of London, B.A. (first class honours in English language and literature), 1930, Ph.D., 1936.

ADDRESSES: Home—15 Above Town, Dartmouth, Devonshire, England. *Office*—College of Communication, Boston University, 640 Commonwealth Ave., Boston, Mass. 02215. *Agent*—Margaret Hanbury, 27 Walcot Square, London SE11 4UB, England.

CAREER: University of Bristol, Department of Extra-Mural Studies, Bristol, England, lecturer in literature and drama, 1937-40; wartime officer, Government of Great Britain, Ministry of Information, Films Department, 1940-45; research officer and lecturer, British Film Institute, 1945-47; British Film Academy, London, England, director, 1947-59; consultant to Society of Film and Television Arts, 1959-75; Boston University, Boston, Mass., visiting professor of film, 1975-81, professor of film, 1981—. Visiting fellow, University of Sussex; Bingham Professor of Humanities, University of Louisville, 1973. Governor, London Film School, 1966-74; vice-chairman, National Panel for Film Festivals, 1974-78. Has served on juries of international film festivals, appeared on television in many countries, and lectured widely.

MEMBER: Radio-writers Association (chairman, 1962-64), Society of Authors (member of committee of management, 1954-57, 1965-68), Society of Lecturers (chairman, 1959-61), Screen and Television Writers Association.

AWARDS, HONORS: Commander of Order of Merit of the Italian Republic, 1970; Order of Merit (First Class) of Federal Republic of Germany, 1971; D.Litt. from University of Sussex, 1971, and University of Louisville, 1979; D.F.A., New England College, 1974.

WRITINGS:

Film, Pelican, 1944.
(Contributor) *Twenty Years of British Film,* Grey Walls Press, 1947.
(Editor) *Experiment in the Film,* Grey Walls Press, 1948, reprinted, Arno, 1970.
(With Rachael Low) *The History of the British Film,* Volume I: *1896-1906,* Allen & Unwin, 1948.
(With Paul Rotha) *Movie Parade, 1888-1949,* Studio Publications, 1950.
(Editor) *Three British Screenplays,* Methuen, 1950.
A Seat at the Cinema, Evans Brothers, 1951.
(Editor with R. K. N. Baxter) *Cinema,* Penguin, 1952, reprinted, Arno, 1978.
On the Air, Deutsch, 1953.
The Animated Film, Sylvan, 1954.
The Film and the Public, Pelican, 1955.
(With John Huntley) *The Technique of Film Music,* Focal Press, 1957, 2nd edition, 1976.
The Dreamers (novel), Simon & Schuster, 1957.
(With John Halas) *The Technique of Film Animation,* Focal Press, 1959, 4th edition, 1976.
The Passion (novel), Heinemann, 1960.
(With Heinrich Fraenkel) *Doctor Goebbels: His Life and Death,* Simon & Schuster, 1960, revised edition published as *Dr. Goebbels,* New English Library, 1968.

The Living Screen, Harrap, 1961.

(Author, with Louise Manvell, of commentary) *The Country Life of Sailing Boats*, Country Life, 1962.

(With Halas) *Design in Motion*, Studio Publications, 1962.

(With Fraenkel) *Goering*, Simon & Schuster, 1962 (published in England as *Hermann Goering*, Heinemann, 1962).

(With Fraenkel) *The Man Who Tried to Kill Hitler*, Coward, 1964 (published in England as *The July Plot: The Attempt in 1944 on Hitler's Life and the Men Behind It* [also see below], Bodley Head, 1964).

(With Fraenkel) *Himmler*, Putnam, 1965 (published in England as *Heinrich Himmler*, Heinemann, 1965).

What Is a Film?, William Macdonald, 1965.

The July Plot: A Play for Television, Blackie & Son, 1966.

New Cinema in Europe, Dutton, 1966.

This Age of Communication, Blackie & Son, 1966.

(Editor with A. William Bluem) *Television: The Creative Experience*, Hastings House, 1967 (published in England as *The Progress of Television*, Focal Press, 1967).

(With Fraenkel) *The Incomparable Crime: Mass Extermination in the Twentieth Century; the Legacy of Guilt*, Putnam, 1967.

New Cinema in the USA, Dutton, 1968.

Ellen Terry, Putnam, 1968.

New Cinema in Britain, Dutton, 1969.

(With Fraenkel) *The Canaris Conspiracy: The Secret Resistance to Hitler in the German Army*, McKay, 1969.

S.S. and Gestapo: Rule by Terror, Ballantine, 1970.

Sarah Siddons, Putnam, 1970.

(With Halas) *Art in Movement*, Hastings House, 1970.

(With Fraenkel) *The German Cinema*, Praeger, 1971.

The Conspirators: 20 July 1944, Ballantine, 1971.

Shakespeare and the Film, Praeger, 1971, revised edition, A. S. Barnes, 1979.

(With Fraenkel) *Hess: A Biography*, MacGibbon & Kee, 1971.

(Editor) *International Encyclopedia of Film*, Crown, 1972.

Goering, Ballantine, 1972.

(Author of introduction) *Masterworks of the German Cinema*, Harper, 1974.

Charles Chaplin, Little, Brown, 1974.

(With Fraenkel) *The Hundred Days to Hitler*, St. Martin's, 1974 (published in England as *Seizure of Power: One Hundred Days to Hitler*, Dent, 1974).

Films and the Second World War, A. S. Barnes, 1975.

Love Goddesses of the Movies, Crescent, 1975.

(With Fraenkel) *Inside Adolph Hitler*, Pinnacle Books, 1975, revised edition published as *Hitler: The Man and the Myth*, 1977.

The Trial of Annie Besant and Charles Brodlaugh, Horizon Press, 1976.

Theater and Film: A Comparative Study of the Two Forms of Dramatic Art, and of the Problems of Adaptation of Stage Plays into Films, Farleigh Dickinson University Press, 1979.

Ingmar Bergman, Arno, 1980.

Art and Animation: The Story of Halas and Batchelor Animation Studio, 1940-1980, Hastings House, 1980.

(With Michael Fleming) *Images of Madness: On Portrayal of Insanity in the Feature Film*, Farleigh Dickinson University Press, 1985.

Elizabeth Inchbald: England's Principal Woman Dramatist in Eighteenth-Century London, University Press of America, 1987.

(Editor and author of introduction) *Selected Comedies of Elizabeth Inchbald*, University Press of America, 1987.

Editor, "National Cinema" series, Grey Walls Press, 1948-53. Contributor of articles to *Encyclopaedia Britannica* and film journals. Editor, *Penguin Film Review*, 1946-49, and Society of Film and Television Arts *Journal*, 1959-75; associate editor, *New Humanist*, 1967-75.

SIDELIGHTS: Roger Manvell's work encompasses two distinct fields: film and theater and the history of the Third Reich. In both areas, Manvell receives critical praise. A *Times Literary Supplement* critic finds that *Ellen Terry*, a biography of the Victorian actress, "will probably be the standard work on Ellen Terry for a long time. . . . [Manvell] has made a useful contribution to the history of the English theatre and to our understanding of one of the greatest of our actresses." *The Canaris Conspiracy*, a study of German opposition to Nazi rule "is a competent and admirably-written account, historical journalism of the best kind," comments another *Times Literary Supplement* reviewer.

BIOGRAPHICAL/CRITICAL SOURCES:

PERIODICALS

Best Sellers, July 1, 1968, July 15, 1969, February 15, 1971.

National Observer, May 27, 1968.

Newsweek, May 27, 1968.

New York Times Book Review, May 26, 1968.

Times Literary Supplement, April 13, 1967, August 10, 1967, May 9, 1968, July 17, 1969.

*   *   *

MARKS, Alfred H(arding) 1920-

PERSONAL: Born July 18, 1920, in Farmingdale, N.Y.; son of Theodore Augustus (a merchant and farmer) and Greta (Boettiger) Marks; married Herta Mattler, December 20, 1942; children: Thea Welch, Christina Haley, Stuart. *Education:* Potsdam State College (now State University of New York College at Potsdam), student, 1936-39, B.Ed., 1946; Syracuse University, M.A., 1949, Ph.D., 1953. *Politics:* Democrat. *Religion:* Dutch Reformed.

ADDRESSES: Home—10 Bruce St., New Paltz, N.Y. 12561. *Office*—State University of New York College at New Paltz, New Paltz, N.Y. 12561.

CAREER: U.S. Department of Defense, Washington, D.C., research analyst, 1946-47; Syracuse University, Syracuse, N.Y., instructor, 1949-53; Ohio State University, Columbus, instructor, 1953-56; Ball State Teachers College (now Ball State University), Muncie, Ind., began as assistant professor, became associate professor of English, 1956-63; State University of New York College at New Paltz, professor of English, 1963-85, emeritus professor of American literature, 1985—. Director, Carl Carmer Center for Catskill Mountain and Hudson River Studies, 1975-85. President, John Burroughs Association, Inc., 1985—. Senior Fulbright lecturer, Kanazawa University, Japan, 1965-66; visiting professor, University of Hawaii, 1973-74; participant, National Endowment for the Humanities Institute on Japanese Literature, Princeton University, summer, 1979. *Military service:* U.S. Army, 1942-46; became first lieutenant.

MEMBER: Modern Language Association of America, Japan Society, Association of Teachers of Japanese, Haiku Society of America, American Federation of Teachers.

WRITINGS:

(Translator) Yukio Mishima, *Forbidden Colors,* Knopf, 1968, reprinted, Putnam, 1981.

(Translator) Mishima, *Thirst for Love,* Knopf, 1969, reprinted, Putnam, 1981.

(With Barry D. Bort) *Guide to Japanese Prose,* G. K. Hall, 1975, 2nd edition, 1984.

(Translator with Thomas Kondo) Ihara Saikaku, *Tales of Japanese Justice,* University of Hawaii Press, 1979.

(With Edythe Polster) *Surimono: Prints by Elbow,* Lovejoy Press, 1981.

(Compiler) *What Shall I Read on Japan: An Introductory Guide,* 12th edition (Marks not associated with earlier editions), Japan Society, 1982.

Also author of *Literature of the Mid-Hudson Valley,* 1974. Contributor to journals, including *American Literature* and *PMLA.* Editor, *Literature East & West,* 1961-66, editor-in-chief, 1966—; editor, *John Burroughs Review,* 1985—.

*   *   *

MARKS, Elaine   1930-

PERSONAL: Born November 13, 1930, in New York, N.Y.; daughter of Harry and Ruth (Elin) Marks. *Education:* Bryn Mawr, A.B. (magna cum laude), 1952; University of Pennsylvania, M.A., 1953; New York University, Ph.D., 1958.

ADDRESSES: Home—2040 Field St., Madison, Wis. 53713. *Office*—Department of French and Women's Studies Program, University of Wisconsin, Madison, Wis.

CAREER: New York University, New York, N.Y., instructor, 1957-60, assistant professor of French, 1960-62; University of Wisconsin—Milwaukee, associate professor of French, 1963-65; University of Massachusetts—Amherst, professor of French, 1965-66, 1971-73; University of Wisconsin—Madison, lecturer, 1977, professor of French and women's studies, 1980—, director of Women's Studies Research Center, 1978-85, chair of Women's Studies Program, 1979-82. Herbert F. Johnson Postdoctoral Fellow at the Institute for Research in the Humanities, University of Wisconsin—Madison, 1962-63. Panelist, National Endowment for the Humanities, 1973—; member of Graduate Record Examination Committee of Examiners for the Advanced Test in French, 1978—. Keynote speaker for Workshop on Women-Related Issues and Library Services, University of Wisconsin—Parkside, 1978; speaker at Forum on International Femnist Criticism, Modern Language Association, San Francisco and at Second Sex Conference on Feminist Theory, New York Institute for the Humanities, both 1979; has also presented papers and lectures at numerous universities, including University of Wisconsin—Milwaukee, Marquette University, Northwestern University, University of Rochester, Barnard College, University of Arizona, and University of Iowa. Manuscript reader for several publishers.

MEMBER: Modern Language Association of America (member of executive committee of Division on Women's Studies in Language and Literature, 1977-81; member of executive council, 1984-87), American Association of Teachers of French, National Women's Studies Association, Midwest Modern Language Association (member of executive committee, 1978-81).

AWARDS, HONORS: Fulbright fellowship, Paris, 1956-57; Alumnae Pin for Scholarship, New York University, 1958; grants from Ford Foundation, Johnson Foundation, Stackner Family Foundation, and Evjue Foundation for Women's Studies Research Center, 1979-84.

WRITINGS:

Colette (a critical study), Rutgers University Press, 1960, reprinted, Greenwood Press, 1981.

(Editor and author of introduction) *French Poetry from Baudelaire to the Present: With English Prose Translations* (anthology), Dell, 1962.

(Editor) *Gigi and Other Stories,* New American Library, 1963.

(Editor with Richard Tedeschi) Andre Gide, *L'Immoraliste,* Macmillan, 1963.

(Editor with Charles Carlut) *Recits de nos jours,* Macmillan, 1964.

Encounters with Death: An Essay on the Sensibility of Simone de Beauvoir, Rutgers University Press, 1973.

(Contributor) *Twentieth Century French Fiction: Essays for Germaine Bree,* Rutgers University Press, 1975.

(Contributor) Sidonie Cassirer, editor, *Teaching about Women in the Foreign Languages: French, Spanish, German, Russian,* Feminist Press, 1975.

(Editor with George Stambolian and contributor) *Homosexualities and French Literature* (anthology), Cornell University Press, 1979.

(Contributor) Richard A. Brooks, general editor, *Critical Bibliography of French Literature,* Volume VI: *The Twentieth Century,* Syracuse University Press, 1980.

(Contributor) Jean-Albert Bede and William Edgerton, editors, *Columbia Dictionary of Modern European Literature,* 2nd edition (Marks was not associated with earlier edition), Columbia University Press, 1980.

(Editor with Isabelle de Courtivron) *New French Feminisms* (anthology), University of Massachusetts Press, 1980.

(Author of preface) Eisinger and McCarty, editors, *Colette: The Woman, the Writer,* Pennsylvania State University Press, 1981.

(Author of preface) Paula Gilberg Lewis, editor, *Traditionalism, Nationalism, and Feminism: Women Writers of Quebec,* Greenwood Press, 1985.

(Contributor) Schusterand Van Dyne, editor, *Women's Place in the Academy,* Rowman & Allenheld, 1985.

Critical Essays on Simone de Beauvoir, G. K. Hall, 1987.

Author of radio script "Colette a cent ans," WCFR-Radio, University of Massachusetts, 1973; author with Edward T. Gargan of talk "Jean-Paul Sartre," WHA-Radio, Madison, Wisconsin, May 26, 1980. Contributor to *Encyclopedia Americana, Encyclopedia of World Literature in the Twentieth Century,* and *Columbia Dictionary of European Literature.* Also contributor of essay on Simone de Beauvoir to *Dictionary of Literary Biography,* Gale, and of articles and book reviews to journals, including *French Review, Modern Language Journal, Romanic Review, New York Times Book Review,* and *Voyages.* Member of editorial board of *Signs: Journal of Women in Culture and Society.*

WORK IN PROGRESS: Research for *The Body in Decline: Discourses on Aging and Sexuality; 1929 Litterature Feminine* by Jean Larnac for the *Harvard History of French Literature; Sappho 1900* for the Yale French series *The Politics of Tradition: Placing Women in French Literature;* a two-volume study of Claire Lechat de Kersaint, Madame de Duras, 1778-1828; continued study of contemporary critical theory with particular emphasis on questions relating to autobiographical and biographical texts and to new definitions of humanism and feminism; continued reading of French women writers for articles, talks, and teaching.

* * *

MARTIN, Graham Dunstan 1932-

PERSONAL: Born October 21, 1932, in Leeds, England; son of Edward Dunstan (a schoolmaster) and Margaret (Lightbody) Martin; married Ryllis Daniel, August 21, 1954 (divorced); married Anne Moone Crombie (a social worker), June 14, 1969; children: Jonathan, Stefan, Juliet, Lewis, Aidan. *Education:* Oriel College, Oxford, B.A., 1954; Victoria University of Manchester, graduate certificate, 1955; Linacre House, Oxford, B.Litt., 1965.

ADDRESSES: Office—Department of French, University of Edinburgh, 4 Buccleuch Pl., Edinburgh 8, Scotland.

CAREER: Writer. Worked as teacher of French and English in secondary schools in England, 1956-65; University of Edinburgh, Edinburgh, Scotland, lecturer in French, 1965—. Lecturer in English at University of Paris, 1976-77.

MEMBER: British Society of Aesthetics.

WRITINGS:

(Translator; with John H. Scott) *In the Year of the Strike* (poetry), Rapp & Whiting, 1968.
(Editor and translator) Paul Valery, *Le Cimetiere marin,* Edinburgh University Press, 1971.
(Translator; with Scott) *Love & Protest* (poetry), Harper, 1972.
(Editor and translator) *Anthology of Contemporary French Poetry,* Edinburgh University Press, 1972.
(Translator) Peter Sharratt, editor, Louise Labe, *Sonnets,* Edinburgh University Press, 1973.
Language, Truth, and Poetry: Notes towards a Philosophy of Literature, Edinburgh University Press, 1975.
(Translator with others) Jean-Claude Renard, *Selected Poems,* Oasis Press, 1978.
Giftwish (novel), Allen & Unwin, 1980, Houghton, 1981.
The Architecture of Experience: The Role of Language and Literature in the Construction of the World, Edinburgh University Press, 1981.
Catchfire (novel), Allen & Unwin, 1981, Houghton, 1982.
The Soul Master (novel), Allen & Unwin, 1984.
Time-Slip (novel), Allen & Unwin, 1986.
The Dream Wall (novel), Allen & Unwin, 1987.

WORK IN PROGRESS: A fairy tale for adults; a work of literary philosophy.

SIDELIGHTS: Graham Dunstan Martin told *CA:* "My academic work is based on a love of poetry, a love of teaching, a detestation of 'conventional wisdom,' and a belief in the relevance of literature to life. Nor is anything more relevant than fantasy, my essays in this genre having arisen out of reading fairy tales to my small sons. I have on two occasions spent a year working in France (my favorite place, along with Scotland), and of course speak French (a physical pleasure, like food or folksinging)."

* * *

MATHESON, John Ross 1917-

PERSONAL: Born November 14, 1917, in Arundel, Quebec, Canada; son of Alexander Dawson (a minister) and Gertrude (McCuaig) Matheson; married Edith May Bickley, August 4, 1945; children: Duncan, Wendy Simpson, Jill Perry, Donald, Roderick, Murdoch. *Education:* Queen's University, Kingston, Ontario, B.A., 1940; Osgoode Hall Law School, Barrister-at-Law, 1948; University of Western Ontario, LL.M., 1954; Mount Allison University, M.A., 1975. *Religion:* United Church of Canada.

ADDRESSES: Home—Rideau Ferry, Ontario, Canada K0G 1W0. *Office*—Court House, Perth, Ontario, Canada K7H 1G1.

CAREER: Called to the Bar of Ontario, 1948; Matheson, Henderson & Hart (law firm), Brockville, Ontario, attorney, 1949-68; created Queen's Counsel, 1967; Judicial District of Ottawa-Carleton, Ontario, judge, 1968-78; County Court of Lanark, Ontario, judge, 1978-84; District Court of Ontario, judge, 1985—. Member of Canadian House of Commons for Leeds, 1961-68, chairman of standing committee on external affairs, 1963-65, parliamentary secretary to prime minister, 1966-68. Life member of council of Queen's University, Kingston, Ontario. Member of United Services Institute of Canada. *Military service:* Canadian Army, Royal Canadian Horse Artillery, 1940-44; received Canadian Forces Decoration, 1975; appointed honorary colonel, 1977.

MEMBER: United Empire Loyalists Association of Canada (honorary vice-president, 1974—), Canadian Amateur Boxing Association (honorary secretary, 1972—), Canadian Bible Society (life governor), Canadian Bar Association (life member), Canadian Economic Association (life member), Canadian Olympic Association, Royal Canadian Artillery Association (life member), Canadian Corps of Commissionaires (life member), Heraldry Society of Canada (fellow), Royal Economic Association (fellow), Society of Antiquaries of Scotland (fellow), National Trust for Scotland (life member), Royal Order of Scotland, Order of St. John (genealogist of Priory of Canada), Phi Delta Phi, Masons (Scottish Rite 33), Rotary International.

AWARDS, HONORS: Armigerous by Lyon Court, 1959, and College of Arms, 1972; knight of justice of Order of St. John, 1974; knight commander of merit of Order of St. Lazarus, 1975; companion of Most Honourable Order of Meritorious Heritage, 1976; distinguished service award from Queen's University, 1977; essay prize from Commonwealth Heraldry Board, 1980, for "The Beley Lecture"; Montreal Medal from Queen's University Alumni, 1981; LL.D. honoris causa, 1984.

WRITINGS:

Canada's Flag: A Search for a Country, G. K. Hall, 1980, revised edition, Mika, 1986.
Sinews of the Heart, Lancelot Press (Nova Scotia), 1982.

WORK IN PROGRESS: The Order of Canada: The Search for Merit.

SIDELIGHTS: "In 1943," John Ross Matheson told *CA,* "when I was a forward observation officer of artillery with the British Eighth Army in Italy, a German shell burst over my head and put fragments of steel through my helmet into my skull. I changed from a young athlete to a traumatic epileptic, an amnesiac, a partial paraplegic, and partial hemiplegic. There was a long period of recovery, a happy marriage, six great children, and now grandchildren. My ambitions have always exceeded my real ability. I believe I recognize my limitations now, and am discovering new avenues for challenge. While I serve daily as a judge, I hope and pray I am growing wiser and am by no means through."

Matheson's books were motivated, at least in part, by his own involvement in the research and development that led to Canada's flag and the establishment of the Order of Canada.

* * *

McCAULEY, Martin 1934-

PERSONAL: Born October 18, 1934, in Omagh, Northern Ireland; son of Isaac Edmund (a farmer) and Levenna (Anderson) McCauley; married Marta Kring, August 26, 1966; children: John Hugh. *Education:* University of London, B.A., 1966, Ph.D., 1973; also attended Sorbonne, University of Paris, 1961, University of Perugia, 1962, and Timiryazev Agricultural Academy, Moscow, U.S.S.R., 1969. *Religion:* Presbyterian.

ADDRESSES: Home—10 Greenway, Totteridge, London N20 8ED, England. *Office*—London School of Slavonic and East European Studies, University of London, Senate House, Malet St., London WC1E 7HU, England.

CAREER: Engaged in building industry, 1955-61; University of London, London School of Slavonic and East European Studies, London, England, lecturer in Russian and Soviet institutions, 1968-85, senior lecturer in Soviet and East European studies, 1985—.

MEMBER: Association of University Teachers, Royal Institution of Chartered Surveyors (professional associate), National Association of Soviet and East European Studies (chairman, 1985-88).

WRITINGS:

(Editor and translator) *The Russian Revolution and the Soviet State, 1917-1921: Documents,* Macmillan, 1975, revised edition, 1979.
Khrushchev and the Development of Soviet Agriculture: The Virgin Land Programme, 1953-1964, Macmillan, 1976.
(Editor and contributor) *Communist Power in Europe, 1944-1949,* Macmillan, 1977.
Marxism-Leninism in the German Democratic Republic: The Socialist Unity Party (SED), Macmillan, 1979.
The Stalin File, Batsford, 1979.
The Soviet Union since 1917, Longman, 1981.
Stalin and Stalinism, Longman, 1983.
(Editor and contributor) *The Soviet Union in the 1980's,* Heinemann, 1983.
The Origins of the Cold War, Longman, 1983.
East Germany since 1945, Macmillan, 1983.
Octobrists to Bolsheviks: Imperial Russia, 1905-1917, Edward Arnold, 1984.
(Editor with Stephen Carter) *Leadership and Succession in the Soviet Union, Eastern Europe, and China,* Macmillan, 1986.
(Editor and contributor) *Khrushchev and Khrushchevism,* Macmillan, 1987.
(Editor and contributor) *The Soviet Union under Gorbachev,* Macmillan, 1987.

SIDELIGHTS: Martin McCauley told *CA:* "Since my subjects are Soviet politics and contemporary history, I have a great interest in East-West relations and the problems of world peace. I have traveled extensively in the Soviet Union. Another area of interest is German affairs, and I visit West Germany every year and East Germany when I can.

"The arrival of Mikhail Gorbachev was a watershed in Soviet politics. Convinced that the Soviet system is in crisis, he has boldly outlined fundamental changes in the traditional methods of running the country. As a Leninist, he wishes to maintain the hegemony of the Communist Party. This means that all key decisions will continue to be taken at the centre by a small elite. Since the mid-1970s, the economy has stagnated and the Soviet Union is failing to catch up with the United States and the rest of the West. The basic flaw is that the command economy—one in which enterprises fulfill orders handed down from above and have little autonomy—is not capable of coping with the demands of the modern world. Prices are determined at the centre and they do not reflect relative scarcity. As the economy has grown, a vast bureaucracy has come into being to regulate administratively economic activity. Gorbachev has perceived that this command model—the Stalinist model—has outlived its usefulness. He is trying to replace the administratively run economy by an economically run system. By 1991, a new economic order has to be in place, one which will permit dynamic growth, especially in areas of high technology. The standing of the Soviet Union depends on this as well as its military security.

"In order to effect an economic revolution, Gorbachev has launched *glasnost* (openness) and democratisation which, if allowed to flower, will amount to the beginning of a political revolution. The Soviet Union has become a vast experimental laboratory with great risks being taken by Gorbachev personally. Some power will have to flow from the centre to the periphery, but how much? Will the Party and government officials, who will lose some of their power to enterprises, be able to delay or sabotage the new economic order? Will the revolution of rising expectations, set in motion by Gorbachev, lead to social unrest should living standards fail to rise significantly?

"There are many tensions in the economic, social, and political reforms being proposed by Gorbachev. The possibility exists that the centre may feel that control is slipping away from it and immediately seek to reimpose authority. The Soviet Union is attempting to do something which has never succeeded in a socialist society, achieve the economic dynamism of capitalism within a socialist framework. Gorbachev's political future will depend on his achieving success in this bold venture."

* * *

McCONNOR, Vincent

ADDRESSES: Agent—Jane Jordan Browne, Multimedia Development, Inc., 410 South Michigan Ave., Room 828, Chicago, Ill. 60605.

CAREER: Writer, editor, and producer in New York, N.Y.; worked in radio, 1935-49, and in television, 1949-63; novelist, 1965—.

WRITINGS:

The French Doll, Hill & Wang, 1965.
The Provence Puzzle: An Inspector Damiot Mystery, Macmillan, 1980.
The Riviera Puzzle: An Inspector Damiot Mystery, Macmillan, 1981.
The Paris Puzzle: An Inspector Damiot Mystery, Macmillan, 1982.
I Am Vidocq, Dodd, 1985.
(Contributor) *Murder in Los Angeles,* Morrow, 1987.
Limbo, Mysterious Press, 1987.
The World's Oldest Eye, Tor Books, 1988.

Contributor of more than thirty short stories to periodicals, including *Esquire, MD, Alfred Hitchcock Mystery Magazine,* and *Ellery Queen Mystery Magazine.*

WORK IN PROGRESS: Another novel.

BIOGRAPHICAL/CRITICAL SOURCES:

PERIODICALS

Globe and Mail (Toronto), November 23, 1985.
Los Angeles Times Book Review, July 18, 1982, November 24, 1985, February 2, 1986.
New York Times Book Review, May 2, 1965, May 16, 1982.
Saturday Review, May 25, 1968, June, 1986.
Washington Post Book World, March 21, 1982.

*   *   *

McDONNELL, Christine   1949-

PERSONAL: Born July 3, 1949, in Southampton, N.Y.; daughter of Peter Joseph and Margaret (Doyle) McDonnell; married Terry Shaneyfelt, December 8, 1979; children: Garth (stepson), Soo Ae, Joseph Doo Wook. *Education:* Barnard College, B.A., 1972; Columbia University, M.L.S., 1973; graduate study at Simmons College, 1979-81.

ADDRESSES: Home—117 Pembroke St., Boston, Mass. 02118.

CAREER: New York Public Library, New York, N.Y., children's librarian, 1972-75; junior high school librarian in Arlington, Mass., 1976-79; Simmons College, Boston, Mass., director of community programs at Center for the Study of Children's Literature, 1979-81; teacher in Brookline, Mass., 1982—.

WRITINGS:

CHILDREN'S FICTION

Don't Be Mad, Ivy, Dial, 1981.
Toad Food and Measle Soup, Dial, 1982.
Lucky Charms and Birthday Wishes, Viking, 1984.
Count Me In, Viking, 1986.
Just for the Summer, Viking, 1987.

OTHER

Contributor of articles and reviews to magazines and newspapers, including *Horn Book.*

SIDELIGHTS: Christine McDonnell wrote: "For the past fifteen years I have been involved with children's books as a librarian, a reviewer, and a teacher. I began to write fiction in 1978, starting with adult short stories and working my way down through adolescent characters until I found the Ivy stories deep in my memory. Ivy is about six or seven. Several of her escapades—various chapters in *Don't Be Mad, Ivy*—are based on my own memories of 'The Birthday Present,' 'The Swimming Pool,' and 'The Borrowed Bear.' Others have developed from her fictional character and from the personality of her friend, Leo.

"In *Toad Food and Measle Soup, Lucky Charms and Birthday Wishes,* and *Just for the Summer,* the same group of children have adventures. Each book features one child as the central character, always someone who was a minor character in the book before. Thus, Leo, who was a character in *Don't Be Mad, Ivy,* is the main character in *Toad Food and Measle Soup.* Then Emily Mott, a classmate of Ivy and Leo's, is the main character in *Lucky Charms and Birthday Wishes.* In *Just*

for the Summer, Lydia, who visited briefly in *Lucky Charms,* returns to spend the summer in the house next door to Emily's. Each book builds on the last, although they are not a series that must be read in sequence. By staying with this cast of characters, I have at my disposal a group of distinct individuals that I already know well. I like them, and it's nice not to have to say goodbye to them at the end of a book.

"*Count Me In* is not part of the series. A novel for older children, it concerns fourteen-year-old Katie, whose mother Maddie has recently remarried and is now expecting a baby. Katie's feelings of isolation and her fantasies about living with her father come to a head during the summer and the fall of her first year in high school. It is a book about new shapes of families, and the struggle that all of us have in finding a place for ourselves within our family."

*   *   *

McSHERRY, Frank D(avid), Jr.   1927-

PERSONAL: Born December 18, 1927, in McAlester, Okla.; son of Frank D. (an attorney) and Mary (a teacher; maiden name, Clinton) McSherry. *Education:* Attended Texas A & M University, 1946, University of Oklahoma, 1947-48 and 1949-53, and University of Santo Tomas, 1948.

ADDRESSES: Home—314 West Jackson, McAlester, Okla. 74501.

CAREER: Commercial artist, 1953-74. Member of McAlester Arts and Humanities Council; president of McAlester Friends of the Library, 1981-82. *Military service:* U.S. Army Air Forces, 1945-47.

MEMBER: McAlester Writers Guild (past president), Baker Street Irregulars (honorary member).

WRITINGS:

(Editor with Martin Greenberg and Charles G. Waugh) *Baseball Three Thousand,* Elsevier/Nelson, 1981.
(Editor with Greenberg and Waugh) *A Treasury of American Horror Stories,* Crown/Bonanza, 1985.
(Editor with Greenberg and Waugh) *Detectives A-Z,* Crown/Bonanza, 1985.
(Editor with Greenberg and Waugh and author of introduction) *Strange Maine,* Tapley, 1986.
(Editor with Greenberg and Waugh and author of introduction) *Darkness in Dixie,* August House, 1987.
(Author of introduction) Greenberg and Waugh, editors, *Best Horror Fiction of A. Conan Doyle,* Academy Chicago, 1987.
(Editor with Greenberg and Waugh and author of introduction) *Murder and Mystery in Boston,* Dembner, 1987.
(Editor with Greenberg and Waugh and author of introduction) *Sunshine Crimes,* Rutledge, 1987.
Studies in Scarlet (critical articles on the detective story), Borgo, 1987.
Blink of an Eye (psychoanalytical interpretation of science fiction theme), Borgo, 1987.

Also author of *A Study in Black,* and *William F. Nolan: Profile of a Multi-Media Writer,* edited by Jeffrey Elliott, Borgo. Contributor to anthologies, including *Popular Culture and the Expanding Consciousness,* edited by Ray B. Browne, Wiley, *A Mystery Reader,* edited by Nancy Ellen Talburt and Lyna Lee Montgomery, Scribner, and *Villains, Detectives, and Heroes,* edited by Michael L. Cook, Greenwood Press. Contributor of articles and stories to magazines, including *Armchair Detective, Mike Shayne Mystery, Zane Grey Western, The Mystery Fancier,* and *Mystery Reader's Newsletter.*

WORK IN PROGRESS: A Study in War, a psychoanalytic study of war and analysis of battle tactics by means of mass psychology; reference books on mystery, film, and science fiction (with Greenberg and Waugh), for Garland Publishing.

SIDELIGHTS: Frank D. McSherry, Jr., once told *CA:* "I am extremely interested in the use of psychoanalysis as a basis for the formation of an overall theory of both criminal behavior and military tactics. I hope the theory formed will explain past and future criminal behavior and permit prediction of the future and explanation of past military tactical actions. The basic theme of my writing is that intelligent use of the scientific method will solve our problems."

* * *

MEAD, Sidney Moko 1927-

PERSONAL: Born January 8, 1927, in Wairoa, New Zealand; son of Sidney Montague (a contractor) and Paranihia Mead; married June Te Rina (a teacher), October 22, 1950. *Education:* University of Auckland, B.A., 1964, M.A., 1965; University of Southern Ilinois, Ph.D., 1968. *Politics:* Mana Motuhake (Independence Party). *Religion:* Anglican.

ADDRESSES: Home—10 Spiers St., Karori, Wellington N.2, New Zealand. *Office*—Department of Maori, Victoria University of Wellington, Private Bag, Wellington, New Zealand.

CAREER: Art and craft specialist, 1947-51; head teacher at schools in New Zealand, 1951-70; University of Auckland, Auckland, New Zealand, lecturer in Maori studies, 1970-71; McMaster University, Hamilton, Ontario, associate professor of anthropology, 1971-72 and 1973-77; Victoria University of Wellington, Wellington, New Zealand, professor of Maori, 1977—. Member of board of directors of Ngati Awa Trust.

MEMBER: Pacific Arts Association (president), Ki-Poneke Marae Society, Polynesian Society.

AWARDS, HONORS: Canadian Commonwealth research fellowship for University of British Columbia, Vancouver, Canada, 1972-73; Elsdon Best Memorial Medal, 1983; Pacific Arts Association Frigate Bird Award, 1984.

WRITINGS:

Taniko Weaving, A. H. & A. W. Reed (Wellington, New Zealand), 1952.

We Speak Maori, A. H. & A. W. Reed, 1959.

(Editor with Bruce Biggs and Patrick Hohepa) *Selected Readings in Maori,* A. H. & A. W. Reed, 1959, 2nd revised edition with illustrations by Mead, 1967.

The Art of Taniko Weaving: A Study of Its Context, Technique, Style, and Developments, A. H. & A. W. Reed, 1968.

Traditional Maori Clothing: A Study of Technological and Functional Change, A. H. & A. W. Reed, 1969.

(Translator into modern text with G. C. Petersen) *Portraits of the New Zealand Maori Painted in 1844 by George French Angas,* A. H. & A. W. Reed, 1972.

Material Culture and Art in the Star Harbour Region, Eastern Solomons (monograph), Royal Ontario Museum, 1973.

(With L. Birks, H. Birks, and E. Shaw) *The Lapita Pottery Style of Fiji and Its Associations,* Polynesian Society, 1975.

Exploring the Visual Art of Oceania, University Press of Hawaii, 1979.

(Editor) *Te Maori: Maori Art from New Zealand Collections,* Abrams, 1984.

Magnificent Te Maori: Te Maori Whakahirahira, Heinemann (Auckland, New Zealand), 1986.

Te Toi Whakairo: The Art of Maori Carving, Reed Methuen, 1986.

Also author of *The Costume Styles of Classical Maori in New Zealand,* 1969.

IN MAORI

Ko Te Tahae Nei ko Tawhaki (title means "This Fellow Tawhaki"), A. H. & A. W. Reed, 1960.

(Editor with Biggs) *He Kohikohinga Aronui* (title means "A Collection of Valuable Texts"), A. H. & A. W. Reed, 1964.

Nga Taonga Tuki Iho a Ngati Awa: The Writings of Hamiora Tumutara Te Tihi-o-whenua Pio, 1885-87, A. H. & A. W. Reed, 1981.

SIDELIGHTS: Sidney Moko Mead wrote *CA:* "I am concerned with Maori rights in New Zealand, with the cultural renaissance that is happening, with the Treaty of Wailangi and other issues of pressing moment, but my main contribution to our people is through knowledge and the power of the written word."

* * *

MEHTA, Ved (Parkash) 1934-

PERSONAL: Born March 21, 1934, in Lahore, India (now Pakistan); naturalized U.S. citizen, 1975; son of Amolak Ram (a doctor and health official) and Shanti (Mehra) Mehta; married Linn Cary (an assistant program officer at Ford Foundation), 1983; children: Sage, Natasha. *Education:* Pomona College, B.A., 1956; Balliol College, Oxford, B.A. (with honors), 1959; Harvard University, M.A., 1961.

ADDRESSES: Office—*New Yorker,* 25 West 43rd St., New York, N.Y. 10036. *Agent*—Georges Borchardt Inc., 136 East 57th St., New York, N.Y. 10022.

CAREER: New Yorker magazine, New York, N.Y., staff writer, 1961—. Professor of literature, Bard College, Annandale-on-Hudson, N.Y., 1985, 1986.

MEMBER: Phi Beta Kappa.

AWARDS, HONORS: Hazen fellowship, 1956-59; Secondary Education Board Annual Book Award, 1958; Harvard Prize fellowship, 1959-60; Ford Foundation travel and study grants, 1971-76; Guggenheim fellowships, 1971-72 and 1977-78; D.Litt., Pomona College, 1972, Bard College, 1982, and Williams College, 1986; Dupont Columbia Award for excellence in broadcast journalism, 1977-78, for documentary film "Chachaji, My Poor Relation"; Association of Indians in America Award, 1978; Ford Foundation Public Policy grant, 1979-82; John D. and Catherine T. MacArthur Foundation fellowship, 1982-87; Distinguished Service Award, Asian/Pacific Americans Liberty Association, 1986; New York City Mayor's Liberty Medal, 1986.

WRITINGS:

Face to Face: An Autobiography, Atlantic-Little, Brown, 1957.

Walking the Indian Streets (travel; first appeared in the *New Yorker*), Atlantic-Little, Brown, 1960, 3rd revised edition, Penguin (Middlesex), 1975.

Fly and the Fly-Bottle: Encounters with British Intellectuals, (first appeared in the *New Yorker*), Atlantic-Little, Brown, 1963, 2nd edition, Columbia University Press, 1983.

The New Theologian (first appeared in the *New Yorker*), Harper, 1966.

Delinquent Chacha (novel; first appeared in the *New Yorker*), Harper, 1976.

Portrait of India, Farrar, Straus, 1970.

John Is Easy to Please: Encounters with the Written and the Spoken Word, Farrar, Straus, 1971.

Daddyji (autobiographical; also see below), Farrar, Straus, 1972.

Mahatma Gandhi and His Apostles (first appeared in the *New Yorker*), Viking, 1977.

The New India (first appeared in the *New Yorker*), Viking, 1978.

Mamaji (autobiographical; also see below), Oxford University Press, 1979.

The Photographs of Chachaji: The Making of a Documentary Film (first appeared in the *New Yorker; also see below*), Oxford University Press, 1980.

A Family Affair: India under Three Prime Ministers (sequel to *The New India;* first appeared in the *New Yorker*), Oxford University Press, 1982.

Vedi (autobiographical), Oxford University Press, 1982.

The Ledge between the Streams (autobiographical), Norton, 1984.

Daddyji/Mamaji (combined edition of *Daddyji* and *Mamaji*), Picador, Pan Books, 1984.

Sound-Shadows of the New World (autobiographical), Norton, 1986.

Three Stories of the Raj (fiction), Scolar, 1986.

CONTRIBUTOR TO ANTHOLOGIES

Henry I. Christs and Herbert Potell, editors, *Adventures in Living,* Harcourt, 1962, 1968.

Leo Kneer, editor, *Perspectives,* Scott, Foresman, 1963.

K. L. Knickerbocker and H. W. Reninger, *Interpreting Literature,* Holt, 1965, 1969.

Norman Cousins, editor, *Profiles of Nehru,* Indian Book Company (Delhi), 1966.

George Arms, William M. Gibson, and Louis G. Locke, editors, *Readings for Liberal Education,* Holt, 1967.

Walter Havighurst, Arno Jewett, Josephine Lowery, and Philip McFarland, editors, *Exploring Literature,* Houghton, 1968.

Nicholas P. Barker, editor, *Purpose and Function in Prose,* Knopf, 1969.

Mary V. Gaver, editor, *Background Readings in Building Library Collections,* Scarecrow, 1969.

Cousins, editor, *Profiles of Gandhi,* Indian Book Company, 1969.

Jerome W. Archer and Joseph Schwartz, editors, *A Reader for Writers: A Critical Anthology of Prose Readings,* McGraw, 1971.

T. Sadasivan, editor, *Rajaji-93 Souvenir,* T. Sadasivan, 1971.

Margaret Cormack and Kiki Skagen, editors, *Voices from India,* Praeger, 1971.

John F. Savage, editor, *Linguistics for Teachers,* Science Research Associates, 1973.

Albert R. Kitzhaber, editor, *Style and Synthesis,* Holt, 1974.

Anne Fremantle, editor, *A Primer of Linguistics,* St. Martin's, 1974.

Donald J. Johnson and Jean E. Johnson, editors, *Through Indian Eyes,* Praeger, 1974.

Havighurst, Jewett, Lowrey, and McFarland, editors, *Houghton Mifflin Literature Series, Grade 8,* Houghton, 1978.

Robert E. Beck, editor, *Experiencing Biography,* Hayden Book, 1978.

Ganesh Bagchi, editor, *ISCE English Language Test Papers,* Oxford University Press (New Delhi), 1982.

Irving Kenneth Zola, editor, *Ordinary Lives,* Apple-Wood, 1983.

Dean W. Tuttle, editor, *Self-Esteem and Adjusting with Blindness: The Process of Responding to Life's Demands,* C. C Thomas, 1984.

1985 Medical and Health Annual, Encyclopaedia Britannica, 1984.

India: A Teacher's Guide, Asia Society, 1985.

OTHER

Writer and commentator of documentary film "Chachaji, My Poor Relation," the filming of which is recounted in his book *The Photographs of Chachaji: The Making of a Documentary Film.* Contributor of articles and stories to American, British, and Indian newspapers and magazines, including *Atlantic, Saturday Review, New York Times Book Review, Village Voice, World, Political Science Quarterly, Hindustan Times* (New Delhi), *Asian Post,* and *Debonaire* (Bombay).

SIDELIGHTS: Ved Mehta was born in India and returns there often—in his writings. From his first book to his most recent, Mehta has made this country of contradictions his backdrop, whether his description is political or personal. According to Maureen Dowd in the *New York Times Magazine,* William Shawn, Mehta's editor at the *New Yorker* (where Mehta is presently a staff writer), believes that "more than any other writer Mehta has educated Americans about India, illuminating that country with an insider's sensibility and an outsider's objectivity."

As natives of Lahore, India, which is now Pakistan, Mehta's own parents typified the split in India between West and East, between new technology and ancient tradition. Mehta's father was educated in medicine in England and became an important figure in India's public health service. Mehta's mother, uneducated, is a woman of superstition, confident in the powers of faith healers. When Mehta lost his sight at age four from a bout with meningitis, his mother was convinced his blindness was only a temporary form of punishment and followed a Muslim's advice, applying antimony to Mehta's eyes and flogging him with twigs, among other things. Mehta's more progressive-minded father believed an education would be the only way for his son to avoid the typical life of a blind person in India—alms beggar or chair caner. At age five, Mehta was sent to Bombay's Dadar School for the Blind, an American mission school so lacking in sanitation that this once-healthy boy suffered from numerous infections, including ringworm, typhoid fever, malaria, and bronchitis. At age fifteen, after experiencing the upheaval that accompanied the 1947 partition of India, he travelled alone to the United States to study at the only American school that would accept him, the Arkansas School for the Blind in Little Rock. From there, Mehta went on to excel at Pomona College in California, at Balliol College in Oxford, England, and finally at Harvard University. In 1961, at the age of twenty-six, he became a staff writer for the *New Yorker* magazine. All but one of his books have appeared first in installments in the *New Yorker.*

Whereas Mehta's first book, *Face to Face: An Autobiography,* addresses his blindness, most of his subsequent works skirt this topic. In fact, for a while Mehta demanded that his publishers avoid any reference to his blindness on his book jackets. Writing in the *New York Times Book Review* in 1960,

Herbert L. Matthews noted that "Mehta plays an extraordinary trick on his prospective readers and on anyone who does not know about him or has not read his previous book, *Face to Face.* . . . He has written [*Walking the Indian Streets*] about his return to India after ten years' absence as if he had normal vision."

Many of Mehta's books contain elaborate visual imagery, and reviewers refer to him as the blind man who can see better than the rest of us. Carolyn See explains in the *Los Angeles Times:* "When Mehta shows us the building of a dam; hundreds of brightly clad peasants carrying just a few bricks at a time; when in 'Mahatma Gandhi and His Apostles,' Mehta conjures up the evenings when the movement was still young, when the fragrance of blossoms was everywhere and Gandhi's followers stayed up late, out of doors, laughing, rubbing each other's backs—a whole world is given to us, and of course the kicker in all this is that . . . Mehta is blind." It was not until *Daddyji,* Mehta's biography of his father, that Mehta made reference to his blindness once again, and it was not until a later autobiographical work, *Vedi,* that he wrote "from the perspective of total blindness," according to Janet Malcom in the *New York Review of Books.* "[*Vedi*] is entirely without visual descriptions. We follow the blind child into the orphanage, and, like him, we never learn what the place or any of the people in it looked like. We hear, we feel, but we see nothing. . . . As the child misses the familiar persons and things of home, so the reader misses the customary visual clues of literature. . . . Not the least of *Vedi*'s originality is this very stylistic denial, which amounts to an approximation of the experience of blindness."

Although Mehta has written nonfiction, a novel, essays, and even a documentary script, highest critical regard has been for his contributions to the autobiographical genre. *Face to Face,* written when Mehta was in his early twenties, chronicles Mehta's early life, from his childhood in India to his three-year stay at the Arkansas School for the Blind where, among other things, he first encountered racism—"I wondered how dark I was, how much I looked like a Negro," Peter Ackroyd quotes Mehta in the London *Times.* Commenting in the *New York Herald Tribune Book Review,* Gerald W. Johnson observes: "It is extraordinary when a man at twenty-three has the material for an autobiography that deserves the serious attention of the intelligent, and still more extraordinary when a man so young can present his material in an arresting fashion. . . . Mehta has both material and ability."

Three years after *Face to Face* came *Walking the Indian Streets,* Mehta's memoir of his month-long visit to India afer a ten-year absence. Dowd records how Mehta had idealized his native country during those years by listening to Indian music and dreaming about an arranged marriage to a beautiful Punjabi girl. The India Mehta encountered, however, disturbed him and shattered his idealistic vision. "Everywhere I went, I was assaulted by putrid odors rising from the streets, by flies relentlessly swarming around my face, by the octopus-like hands of a hundred scabrous, deformed beggars clutching at my hands and feet. My time in the West had spoiled me and I could now hardly wait to get back," Mehta wrote of his experience, as Dowd reports.

While he wrote numerous books on the politics and culture of a changing India during the twelve years following the 1960 publication of *Walking the Indian Streets,* Mehta eventually turned once more to the autobiographical form and began disclosing his life in very small chunks, expanding the years of his earlier autobiography *Face to Face* into several volumes and then proceeding to cover new ground. Indeed, Mehta's biographical/autobiographical *Daddyji* and *Mamaji* describe many years in his parents' lives before he was even born. Both books are noted for their adept presentations of the middle-class family in India. "[*Daddyji*'s] value," writes P. K. Sundara Rajan in the *Saturday Review,* "lies in the fact that . . . Mehta transforms an individual experience into one that is universal." And in his *New York Times Book Review* assessment of *Mamaji,* Clark Blaise feels "family is the tidiest metaphor for the vastness of India. To understand its compelling and often terrible hold is to possess a special understanding of the culture. . . . Mehta patiently delivers that understanding and courageously presents it without interpretation, limiting even its expected 'warmth' in the service of a sharper clarity." It is also with these two books that "Mehta draws a sharp contrast between his rational, decisive, tough-minded, Western-educated, physician father and his superstitious, backward, uneducated, childish, tender-hearted mother," remarks Malcolm.

The author followed the portraits of his parents with *Vedi,* which begins with Mehta boarding a train for the Bombay school for the blind, located approximately a thousand miles from his home. Mehta recounts his years at the Dadar School from age five to nine. In a London *Times* article, Howard states that "without sentimentality or self-pity [Mehta] recreates that vanished and alien world in one of the richest works of memory of our century." Though Mehta was frequently fighting disease, reviewers comment on how effectively this well-to-do boy adapted to his slum-like surroundings. Blaise notes in the *New York Times Book Review* that *Vedi* "is clearly a mature work. . . . Readers of the two earlier volumes of family biography [*Daddyji* and *Mamaji*] will find less of the overt 'India experience' in 'Vedi,' and more of the dreamlike landscape of childhood. The touch and smell of parents, the test of wills, nightmares, pets."

"Now I want to proclaim this autobiography as nothing less than a literary masterpiece," declares *Times Literary Supplement* contributor R. K. Narayan of Mehta's memoir *The Ledge between the Streams.* In *The Ledge between the Streams,* London *Times* reviewer Howard says, "nothing much happens; except the most important thing in the world, a child growing up to accept life and enjoy the world." *The Ledge between the Streams* encompasses Mehta's years from age nine to fifteen. *New York Times* critic Michiko Kakutani capsulizes the Mehta described in this memoir as a "clumsy blind boy, plucky but hopelessly gauche when it came to participating in . . . fun and games—flying kites, riding bicycles and ponies, playing hide-and-seek. . . . In any case, having spent the first half of 'The Ledge' documenting the innocent world of his youth, . . . Mehta then goes on to show how that world was destroyed by the 1947 partition of the Indian subcontinent into India and Pakistan," an event that "turned many families, including . . . Mehta's own, into political and religious refugees. It is this depiction of the partition, as filtered through the sensibility of a 12-year-old boy, that distinguishes 'The Ledge' as a memoir." What reviewers also find successful about *The Ledge between the Streams* is the fact that the reader forgets his author is blind, a condition which is precisely in line with Mehta's long-time philosophy.

Mehta moves into his adolescent years with *Sound-Shadows of the New World,* the account of his first three years in the United States at the Arkansas School for the Blind. According to Mary Lutyens in the *Spectator,* "the vivid, detailed descriptions of this homesick boy's gradual adaptation to an alien culture are uplifting and enthralling,'' while Ackroyd believes ''the single most important quality of the young . . . Mehta was his courage; *Sound-Shadows of the New World* is a record of that courage.'' This autobiography reveals how the boy who did not know how to eat with a fork and knife when he first arrived in America eventually became president of the student senate and editor of the school newspaper, an experience that convinced him of his desire to become a journalist. More volumes of Mehta's memoirs are expected to appear in the years to come, a prospect that pleases critics who find his works fascinating and dismays those who feel he has already written enough about himself. Yet as Philip Howard observes in the London *Times,* Mehta's ''very special kind of autobiography . . . is clearly going to run for as long as he lives.''

From 1970 to 1982, Mehta authored four nonfiction books aimed at disclosing the social and political milieu of modern-day India. According to Dowd, Mehta's ''reports include vivid descriptions of Indian politics, dinner parties given by the viceroy, the assault of the industrial revolution, the attempts at birth control. His work explores the conflict between East and West in the Indian culture and its mixture of grace and vulgarity.'' Dowd further records professor of modern Indian literature at Columbia University Robin Lewis's estimation that ''in a very quiet way, . . . Mehta is breaking the Western stereotypes and getting America to look at India as something other than a grandiose stage setting. He's taking the raw material of his personal experience and combining it with some of the pains, crises and historical dislocations that India has gone through.''

Mehta's *Portrait of India,* published in 1970, ''seems as vast as India'' to Stephen Spender in the *New York Times Book Review;* ''it is immensely readable, and the reader not only has the sense of immersion in the sights, scents and sounds of India, he also meets representative people from high and low walks of life.'' While a *Times Literary Supplement* reviewer feels Mehta has failed to produce a portrait of his native land, the *New York Times*'s Thomas Lask believes that if the reader can get through the first seventy-five pages, ''you will find yourself in a first-class book. . . . It is surprising how, by the end of the book, the Indian continent has managed to assume a knowledgeable shape and how the problems begin to make sense in terms of the people and the land.''

Of Mehta's political books, his 1977 account entitled *Mahatma Gandhi and His Apostles* has received the most attention. Though reviewers stress that some four hundred biographies have been written about the ''acclaimed father of India,'' Mehta's tactics have been singled out as unique. As Mehta states in the preface to his book, his desire is ''both to demythologize Gandhi and to capture something of the nature of this influence on his followers and . . . their interpretations of his life on India.'' To do this, Mehta travelled to India and England to speak directly with a number of the remaining disciples of Gandhi, something no other biographer had thought to do. As *New York Times* contributor Paul Grimes remarks, ''the interviews make it clear that Gandhi-ism did not survive with them. Some profess to be still propagating the Mahatma's cause, but it is obvious that over the years their interpretations of it have become warped—if they ever were otherwise.''

Grimes finds Mehta's account of Gandhi ''much more than a biography'' and ''a remarkable examination of the life and work of a human being who has been extolled around the world as one of the greatest souls of all time.'' Other reviewers

criticize Mehta for concentrating too heavily on Gandhi's personal life. *Times Literary Supplement* reviewer Eric Stokes feels that Mehta who is ''busy destroying old myths . . . is silently weaving a new one of his own. . . . The ultimate distortion in Mehta's picture of the Mahatma is . . . that it allows almost no place for the politician.'' Leonard A. Gordon in the *Nation* likewise senses that ''Mehta has spent so much time with the private Gandhi, fascinated like his subject with food, sex and hygiene, that we learn almost nothing about the man's great appeal and political skills.'' Nevertheless, Stokes believes ''Mehta's highly readable book may mark the beginning of a phase when Gandhi is eventually rescued from the hagiographers and given a juster appraisal by his countrymen.'' In Dowd's interview with Mehta, Mehta mentions his hope that Mahatma's idealism be restored in his native country: ''Gandhi had the right vision for a poor country. . . . What people in India need basically is fertilizer, clean water, good seed, good storage facilities . . . , and proper sanitation. Those are the priorities. That's what Gandhi taught.''

While most of Mehta's books have been published in India, it is as a staff writer for the *New Yorker* that Mehta is best known in the United States and England. And though to some he may be an easy man to classify, he said to Dowd: ''I don't belong to any single tradition. I am an amalgam of five cultures— Indian, British, American, blind and [the *New Yorker*].'' *Publishers Weekly* contributor Stella Dong records Mehta's life-long literary intentions: ''I'm not just slavishly following a chronological framework or trying to interpret India or blindness or any of that. All I'm trying to do is to tell a story of not one life, but many lives—and through those stories, to try to say something that's universal.''

Several of Mehta's books have been translated into Dutch, Finnish, French, Greek, Gujarati, Hindi, Italian, Japanese, Marathi, Spanish, and Urdu.

BIOGRAPHICAL/CRITICAL SOURCES:

BOOKS

Contemporary Literary Criticism, Volume XXXVII, Gale, 1986.
Cousins, Norman, *Present Tense: An American Editor's Odyssey,* McGraw, 1967.
Mehta, Ved, *Face to Face: An Autobiography,* Atlantic-Little, Brown, 1957.
Mehta, Ved, *Daddyji,* Farrar, Straus, 1972.
Mehta, Ved, *Mahatma Gandhi and His Apostles,* Viking, 1977.
Mehta, Ved, *Mamaji,* Oxford University Press, 1979.
Mehta, Ved, *Vedi,* Oxford University Press, 1982.
Mehta, Ved, *The Ledge between the Streams,* Norton, 1984.
Mehta, Ved, *Sound-Shadows of the New World,* Norton, 1986.
Weeks, Edward, *In Friendly Candor,* Little, Brown, 1959 (published in England as *In Friendly Candour,* Hutchinson, 1960).

PERIODICALS

Atlantic, November, 1963.
Book World, May 10, 1970.
Chicago Tribune Book World, May 10, 1970.
Christian Century, December 14, 1966.
Christian Science Monitor, May 4, 1967, October 17, 1970.
Globe and Mail (Toronto), July 26, 1986.
Journal of Asian Studies, November, 1983.
Library Journal, September 1, 1966, April 1, 1967.
Listener, September 24, 1970, August 18, 1977.
Los Angeles Times, April 16, 1984.

Manchester Guardian Weekly, June 14, 1981.
Nation, February 6, 1967, July 2, 1977.
National Review, July 30, 1963.
New Leader, April 10, 1978.
New Republic, May 13, 1967, July 9, 1977.
New Statesman, February 24, 1967, September 25, 1970.
Newsweek, December 31, 1962, July 1, 1963, January 17, 1977, January 30, 1978.
New York Herald Tribune Book Review, August 18, 1957.
New York Herald Tribune Books, June 16, 1963.
New York Post, January 10, 1962.
New York Review of Books, June 29, 1967, October 7, 1982.
New York Times, April 6, 1967, April 25, 1970, May 8, 1972, September 3, 1973, March 30, 1977, June 11, 1978, October 21, 1979, December 20, 1979, May 1, 1984, February 27, 1986.
New York Times Book Review, August 21, 1960, August 18, 1963, November 13, 1966, April 5, 1970, January 29, 1978, October 21, 1979, October 17, 1982, May 6, 1984, March 9, 1986.
New York Times Magazine, June 10, 1984.
Observer, March 18, 1962.
Publishers Weekly, January 3, 1985.
Reporter, May 4, 1967.
Saturday Review, August 17, 1957, November 12, 1966, April 29, 1967, April 25, 1970, May 20, 1972, January 22, 1977.
Spectator, May 12, 1961, October 4, 1963, July 28, 1984, May 31, 1986.
Times (London), October 19, 1972, June 15, 1977, July 5, 1984, June 8, 1985, May 15, 1986.
Times Literary Supplement, December 8, 1966, December 4, 1970, November 19, 1971, August 5, 1977, July 4, 1980, May 29, 1981, July 6, 1984, May 30, 1986.
Washington Post, December 28, 1982.
Washington Post Book World, January 20, 1980, July 25, 1982, March 9, 1986.
World Literature Today, autumn, 1983.

—*Sketch by Cheryl Gottler*

* * *

MELENDY, H(oward) Brett 1924-

PERSONAL: Born May 3, 1924, in Eureka, Calif.; son of Howard Burton (an assessor) and Pearl (Brett) Melendy; married Marian Robinson, March 29, 1952; children: Brenda Dale, Darcie Brett, Lisa Marie. *Education:* Attended Humboldt State College (now University), 1942-45; Stanford University, A.B., 1946, M.A., 1948, Ph.D., 1952. *Politics:* Democrat. *Religion:* Presbyterian.

ADDRESSES: Home—2010 University Ave., San Jose, Calif. 95128. *Office*—San Jose State University, San Jose, Calif. 95192.

CAREER: Theodore Roosevelt High School, Fresno, Calif., teacher, 1950-54; Fresno Junior College, Fresno, instructor, 1954-55; San Jose State University, San Jose, Calif., faculty member, 1955-70, professor of history, 1961-70, head of history department, 1958-65, chairman of department, 1965-69, assistant vice-president, 1968-69, acting vice-president, 1969; University of Hawaii, Honolulu, professor of history, 1970-79, interim dean for academic development, 1970, vice-president for community colleges, 1970-73; San Jose State University, professor of history emeritus, 1979—, dean of undergraduate studies, 1979-81, associate academic vice-president

for undergraduate studies, 1981-83, university archivist, 1983—. Reader in American history advanced placement exam, Educational Testing Service, 1961-74; visiting representative of Council on College-Level Examinations, College Entrance Examination Board, 1965-66. Chairman of Hawaii committee for the humanities, 1977-79.

MEMBER: American Historical Association, National Education Association, Masons.

AWARDS, HONORS: American Philosophical Society grant, 1962 and 1974; American Council on Education fellowship, 1967-68; National Endowment for the Humanities grant, 1975-76, 1976-78, 1979-81.

WRITINGS:

(With Benjamin F. Gilbert) *The Governors of California*, Talisman, 1965.
The Oriental Americans, Twayne, 1972.
Asians in America, Twayne, 1977.
Chinese and Japanese Americans, Hippocrene, 1984.
(Editor) *With Liberty and Justice for All! The Story of San Jose's Japanese Community*, City of San Jose, 1985.

CONTRIBUTOR

Roger Daniels and Spencer C. Olin, Jr., *Racism in California*, Macmillan, 1972.
Norris Hundley, Jr., editor, *The Asian American*, CLIO Book, 1976.
Emma Gee, editor, *Counterpoint: Perspectives on Asian America*, Asia American Studies Center, University of California, Los Angeles, 1976.
Dennis L. Cuddy, editor, *Contemporary American Immigration*, Twayne, 1982.
Lynwood Carranco, editor, *Redwood Country*, Star Publishing, 1984.
Paolo Coletta, editor, *U.S. Navy and Marine Corps Bases, Domestic*, Greenwood Press, 1985.
Hyung-Chan Kim, editor, *Dictionary of Asian American History*, Greenwood Press, 1986.

OTHER

Also contributor to *Encyclopaedia Britannica, Encyclopedia Americana, Harvard Encyclopedia of American Ethnic Groups, Encyclopedia of American Forest and Conservation History*, and to historical journals.

WORK IN PROGRESS: A biography, tentatively entitled *Walter F. Dillingham: Hawaii's Creative Genius*.

* * *

MERCER, David 1928-1980

PERSONAL: Born June 27, 1928, in Wakefield, Yorkshire, England; died of a heart attack, August 8, 1980, in Haifa, Israel; son of Edward (an engine driver) and Helen (Steadman) Mercer; married; wife's name Dafna; children: Rebecca. *Education:* University of Durham, B.A. (honors), 1953.

ADDRESSES: Home—37 Hamilton Gardens, London N.W. 8, England. *Agent*—Margaret Ramsay Ltd., 14 Goodwin Court, London W.C.2, England.

CAREER: Technician in pathological laboratory in England, 1943-48; teacher of general subjects, 1956-61; writer of television plays, stage plays, and screenplays.

MEMBER: Screenwriters Guild.

AWARDS, HONORS: Screenwriters Guild Award for best teleplay, 1962, for "A Suitable Case for Treatment"; *Evening Standard* award for most promising playwright, 1965; British Film Academy award for best screenplay, 1966, for "Morgan!"; best British original teleplay award, Writers Guild, 1967, for "In Two Minds"; best British original teleplay award, Writers Guild, 1969, for "Let's Murder Vivaldi"; French Film Academy award, 1977, for "Providence"; International Emmy for best drama of the season, for "A Rod of Iron."

WRITINGS:

PLAYS

"Where the Difference Begins" (first play in trilogy; also see below), broadcast by British Broadcasting Corp. (BBC-TV), 1961; stage adaptation first produced at Hull Arts Centre, May 19, 1970.

"A Climate of Fear" (second play in trilogy; also see below), broadcast by BBC-TV, 1962.

"A Suitable Case for Treatment" (also see below), broadcast by BBC-TV, 1962.

"The Buried Man," first produced at Manchester Library Theatre, 1962; broadcast by Associated Television, 1963.

"A Way of Living," broadcast by ABC-TV (England), 1963.

"The Birth of a Private Man" (third play in trilogy; also see below), broadcast by BBC-TV, 1963.

"For Tea on Sunday" (also see below), broadcast by BBC-TV, 1963.

"And Did Those Feet" (also see below), broadcast by BBC-TV, 1965.

Ride a Cock Horse (first produced on West End at Picadilly Theatre, 1965), Hill & Wang, 1966.

The Governor's Lady (first produced on West End at Aldwych Theatre, 1965), Methuen, 1968.

Belcher's Luck (first produced at Aldwych Theatre, 1966), Hill & Wang, 1967.

"In Two Minds" (also see below), broadcast by BBC-TV, 1967; stage adaptation first produced in London, 1973.

"The Parachute" (also see below), broadcast by BBC-TV, 1968.

"Let's Murder Vivaldi" (also see below), broadcast by BBC-TV, 1968; stage adaptation first produced in London at King's Head Theatre Club, 1972.

"On the Eve of Publication" (also see below), broadcast by BBC-TV, 1968.

(Contributor) Kenneth Tynan, *Oh! Calcutta!* (revue; first produced Off-Broadway at Eden Theatre, June 17, 1969; produced in London at Roundhouse Theatre, July 29, 1970), Grove, 1969.

After Haggerty (two-act; first produced at Aldwych Theatre, February 26, 1970), Methuen, 1970.

"The Cellar and the Almond Tree" (also see below), broadcast by BBC-TV, 1970.

"Emma's Time" (also see below), broadcast by BBC-TV, May 13, 1970.

Flint (two-act comedy; first produced on West End at Criterion Theatre, May 5, 1970; produced in Buffalo, N.Y., 1974), Methuen, 1970.

"White Poem," first produced in London at Institute of Contemporary Arts, 1970.

"Blood on the Table," first produced in London, 1971.

"The Bankrupt" (also see below), broadcast by BBC-TV, November 27, 1972.

"The Arcata Promise" (also see below), broadcast by Yorkshire Television, 1974.

Duck Song (first produced at Aldwych Theatre, February 5, 1974), Methuen, 1974.

"Huggy Bear" (also see below), broadcast by Yorkshire Television, 1976.

Cousin Vladimir [and] *Shooting the Chandelier* ("Cousin Vladimir" first produced at Aldwych Theatre, September 22, 1978), Methuen, 1978.

The Monster of Karlovy Vary [and] *Then and Now* ("Then and Now" first produced at Hampstead Theatre, London, May 21, 1979), Methuen, 1979.

"A Rod of Iron," broadcast by Yorkshire Television, 1980.

No Limits to Love (first produced in London at Warehouse Theatre, October 2, 1980), Methuen, 1981.

Also author of stage play "The Long Crawl through Time," 1965, and of television plays "You and Me and Him," "An Afternoon at the Festival," and "Barbara of the House of Grebe," all broadcast in 1973, and "Find Me," broadcast in 1974.

COLLECTED PLAYS

The Generations: A Trilogy of Plays (contains "Where the Difference Begins," "A Climate of Fear," and "The Birth of a Private Man"), J. Calder, 1964.

Three TV Comedies (contains "A Suitable Case for Treatment," "For Tea on Sunday," and "And Did Those Feet"), Calder & Boyars, 1966.

The Parachute and Two More TV Plays (contains "The Parachute," "Let's Murder Vivaldi," and "In Two Minds"), Calder & Boyars, 1967.

On the Eve of Publication and Other Plays, (contains "On the Eve of Publication," "Emma's Time," and "The Cellar and the Almond Tree"), Methuen, 1970.

The Bankrupt and Other Plays (contains "The Bankrupt," "You and Me and Him," "An Afternoon at the Festival," and "Find Me"), Methuen, 1974.

Huggy Bear and Other Plays (contains "Huggy Bear," "The Arcata Promise," and "A Superstition"), Methuen, 1977.

Collected TV Plays, Volume I (contains "Where the Difference Begins," "A Climate of Fear," "The Birth of a Private Man"), Volume II (contains "A Suitable Case for Treatment," "For Tea on Sunday," "And Did Those Feet," "Let's Murder Vivaldi," "In Two Minds," "The Parachute"), Riverrun Press, 1981.

SCREENPLAYS

"Morgan!" (based on his television play "A Suitable Case for Treatment"), Cinema V, 1966.

"Family Life" (based on his television play "In Two Minds"), Kestrel Films, 1971, released in America as "Wednesday's Child".

"A Doll's House" (based on the play by Ibsen), Reindeer Productions, 1972.

"Providence," Action Films, 1977, published as *Providence: Un film pour Alain Resnais,* translated by Claude Roy, Gallimard, 1977.

Also author of "Ninety Degrees in the Shade," 1965.

OTHER

(Contributor) *New Writers 3,* Calder, 1965.

(Author of introduction) *Leon Kossoff: Recent Paintings,* Whitechapel Art Gallery (London), 1972.

(Author of text) *Portrait of Adelaide,* drawings by Cedric Emanuel, Rigby, 1975.

Also author of a radio play, "Folie a Deux," 1974.

SIDELIGHTS: David Mercer was a prolific dramatist who wrote for theatre, film, and television. He was best known for his daring and original teleplays, which garnered him a reputation as a pioneering force in British television. Paul Madden observed in *Sight and Sound:* "[Mercer's] stage work may have enhanced his cultural respectability, but undoubtedly a larger part of his reputation must rest on his television plays, in their time startling and innovatory. . . . Through them it is possible to trace not only Mercer's growing stature as a (television) dramatist but also in microcosm a history of a particularly fertile period of British television drama, when taking risks was a *modus operandi,* elevated into an artistic principle."

Mercer's plays frequently are concerned with the effects of psychological and political disorientation. Mercer himself suffered a nervous breakdown in 1957, and began writing plays while receiving treatment at the British Institute for Psychoanalysis. Mercer's teleplay "A Suitable Case for Treatment" clearly reflects this period of his life, according to *Dictionary of Literary Biography* contributor Marianna Deeken. "Deeply rooted in Mercer's own past, the play expresses the conflict he felt between his political ideologies and his perceptions about the course of world affairs at the time of his own nervous breakdown, when the head of the British Institute for Psychoanalysis had pronounced him 'a suitable case for treatment.'" The teleplay is also viewed as evidence of Mercer's creative foresight. "In 'A Suitable Case for Treatment . . . ,'" wrote Madden, "Mercer was already looking forward to a TV drama that enjoyed the fluidity and freedom of film." "A Suitable Case for Treatment" won the Screenwriters Guild Award for best teleplay of 1962, and was adapted by Mercer into a film entitled "Morgan!," which won the British Film Academy award for best screenplay.

Mercer explores similar themes in his teleplay "In Two Minds," the story of a young girl's battle with schizophrenia. The teleplay represents the philosophy of psychiatrist R. D. Laing, who acted as consultant to the work. Mercer was impressed with the Laingian approach to therapy, and believed that Laing's assistance would help give the play the credibility and realism that Mercer demanded of his work. Like "A Suitable Case for Treatment," "In Two Minds" was named the best British teleplay of the year, and was also made into the film, "Family Life," for which Mercer wrote the screenplay.

In later years, Mercer's plays were "less stylistically adventurous," according to Deeken, "but he continued to explore the mind of man and his efforts to deal with the world and the people around him." Assessing Mercer's literary career, a London *Times* writer concluded: "Though [Mercer] could come through more surely in the relative freedom of television, his principal stage plays had often a pounding eloquence, as if wave upon wave were endeavoring—may be with less momentum in later life—to penetrate a barrier reef. . . . How they may appear to later generations is problematical; but Mercer during the 1960s and 1970s was certainly one of the powerful minds of his day."

BIOGRAPHICAL/CRITICAL SOURCES:

BOOKS

Contemporary Literary Criticism, Volume V, Gale, 1976.
Dictionary of Literary Biography, Volume XIII: *British Dramatists since World War II,* Gale, 1982.

PERIODICALS

Christian Science Monitor, May 20, 1970, February 26, 1971.

Dun's Review, summer, 1970, autumn, 1977, January, 1980, winter, 1981.
Listener, December 19, 1968.
London Magazine, September, 1970.
Nation, July 6, 1970.
New Statesman, March 6, 1970.
New York Times, May 4, 1970, November 16, 1977, March 19, 1979, June 4, 1982.
Plays and Players, June, 1970.
Sight and Sound, autumn, 1981.
Spectator, May 16, 1970.
Times Literary Supplement, January 15, 1970, June 25, 1970, September 25, 1970.
Transatlantic Review, summer, 1968.
Variety, March 11, 1970, February 24, 1971.

OBITUARIES:

PERIODICALS

New York Times, August 22, 1980.
Times (London), August 9, 1980.†

*   *   *

MICHAELS, Joanne 1950-

PERSONAL: Born December 30, 1950, in New York, N.Y.; daughter of Lawrence William (an accountant) and Renee (Pomer) Michaels; married Paul Fillingham, December 24, 1975 (divorced November 27, 1979); married Stuart Alan Ober (a financial consultant), September 20, 1981. *Education:* University of Connecticut, B.A., 1972.

ADDRESSES: Home—P.O. Box 888, Woodstock, N.Y. 12498. *Office*—JMB Publications, P.O. Box 425, Woodstock, N.Y. 12498.

CAREER: Viking Press, New York City, editorial assistant, 1972-74; Wyden Books, New York City, managing editor, 1974-75; David McKay, New York City, editor, 1975-77; St. Martin's Press, Inc., New York City, acquisitions editor, 1977-78; Beekman Publishers, Inc., Woodstock, N.Y., vice-president and marketing director, beginning 1978; *Hudson Valley,* Woodstock, editor-in-chief, 1982-86; JMB Publications, Woodstock, publisher, 1986—. Adjunct professor, Marist College, 1985.

MEMBER: Authors Guild, Authors League of America, Women in Communications, National Organization for Women, Ulster County Coalition for Free Choice.

AWARDS, HONORS: Nominated for investigative reporting award from American Society of Magazine Editors for *Redbook* article "The Teacher Hurt Me, Mommy."

WRITINGS:

Living Contradictions: The Women of the Baby Boom Come of Age, Simon & Schuster, 1982.
A Guide to the Best of the Hudson Valley and Catskills, Crown, 1988.
Woodstock Cooks, JMB Publications, 1988.

Contributor to *Redbook.*

SIDELIGHTS: Joanne Michaels told *CA:* "My article in *Redbook,* 'The Teacher Hurt Me, Mommy,' about a sex-abuse case at West Point's Day Care Center in January, 1986, was nominated for an award for investigative reporting by the American Society of Magazine Editors. Hopefully, a book will emerge from the story.

''I have traveled throughout Europe, Canada, Mexico, and the Caribbean and speak Spanish fluently. I wrote *Living Contradictions* because I felt no one had been a spokesperson for the women of my generation. The book is about women who came of age on the edge of change (the feminist movement, the sexual revolution, and the increasing questioning of values) without role models, and with only themselves as a source of direction.'' According to a *Los Angeles Times* contributor, Michaels discovers that ''liberation hasn't always brought content and satisfaction, let alone peace and freedom.'' *Living Contradictions* has been translated into Norwegian and Japanese.

BIOGRAPHICAL/CRITICAL SOURCES:

PERIODICALS

Los Angeles Times, May 6, 1982.

*   *   *

MICHELL, John (F.) 1933-

PERSONAL: Born February 9, 1933, in London, England; son of Alfred Henry and Enid (Carden) Michell. *Education:* Attended Eton College, 1946-51, and Trinity College, Cambridge, 1953-56.

ADDRESSES: Home—11 Powis Gardens, London W.11, England.

CAREER: Writer. *Military service:* Royal Navy, 1951-56.

WRITINGS:

The Flying Saucer Vision: The Holy Grail Restored, Sidgwick & Jackson, 1967.
The View over Atlantis, Garnstone Press, 1970, 3rd edition, Abacus, 1979.
City of Revelation: On the Proportions and Symbolic Numbers of the Cosmic Temple, McKay, 1972.
The Canon: An Exposition of the Pagan Mystery, Garnstone Press, 1974.
The Old Stones of Land's End, Garnstone Press, 1974.
The Earth Spirit: Its Ways, Shrines, and Mysteries, Avon, 1975.
A Little History of Astro-Archaeology: Stages in the Transformation of a Heresy, Thames & Hudson, 1977.
Secrets of the Stones: The Story of Astro-Archaeology, Penguin, 1977.
(With Robert J. M. Rickard) *Phenomena: A Book of Wonders,* Pantheon, 1977.
A Short Life at Land's End: J. T. Blight, F.S.A., Artist—Penzance, privately printed, 1979.
Simulacra: Faces and Figures in Nature, Thames & Hudson, 1979.
Megalithomania, Cornell University Press, 1982.
The New View over Atlantis, Harper, 1983.
Eccentric Lives and Peculiar Notions, Harcourt, 1984.
The Dimensions of Paradise, Thames & Hudson, 1987.

Also author of *Ancient Metrology* and, with Rickard, of *Living Wonders.* Contributor to *Listener, Spectator,* and other periodicals.

BIOGRAPHICAL/CRITICAL SOURCES:

PERIODICALS

Listener, June 27, 1968.
New York Times Book Review, January 20, 1985.

MIKOLAYCAK, Charles 1937-

PERSONAL: Surname is pronounced *Mike*-o-lay-chak; born January 26, 1937, in Scranton, Pa.; son of John Anthony and Helen (Gruscelak) Mikolaycak; married Carole Kismaric (an editor and writer), October 1, 1970. *Education:* Pratt Institute, B.F.A., 1958; attended New York University, 1958-59.

ADDRESSES: Home—64 East 91st St., New York, N.Y. 10128.

CAREER: Free-lance illustrator and designer, Du Crot Studios, Hamburg, Germany, illustrator and designer, 1959; Time-Life Books, New York, N.Y., designer, 1963-76; Syracuse University, Syracuse, N.Y., guest instructor, 1976—. *Military service:* U.S. Army, 1960-62; became sergeant.

AWARDS, HONORS: Books Mikolaycak designed or illustrated were included among the fifty best books of the year in American Institute of Graphic Arts Shows, 1967, 1968, 1970, 1973, 1974, 1977, 1980, and in Chicago Book Clinic Best of the Year Show, 1967, 1971, 1972; Printing Industries of America Graphic Design Awards, 1967, for *Great Wolf and the Good Woodsman,* 1970, for *Mourka, the Mighty Cat,* 1971, 1972, and 1973; Society of Illustrators Gold Medal for book art direction, 1970; *How the Hare Told the Truth about His Horse* was among the twenty-one books from which American Institute of Graphic Arts selected illustrations to enter in Biennial of Illustrations, Bratislava, 1973; *Shipwreck* and *The Feast Day* were included in American Institute of Graphic Arts Children's Book Show for 1973-74; *Shipwreck* was among twenty-seven books selected for Children's Book Showcase of Children's Book Council, 1975; Brooklyn Museum Art Books for Children citations, 1976, 1978, and 1979, for *Great Wolf and the Good Woodsman;* New York Graphics award, 1980, for *The Surprising Things Maui Did; Peter and the Wolf* was shown at Biennial of Illustrations, Bratislavia, 1984; *Babushka* was selected by the *New York Times* as one of the best illustrated books of 1984; Kerlan Award, University of Minnesota, 1987, in recognition of singular attainments in the creation of children's literature; Golden Kite Honor Book Award, 1987, for illustration of *Juma and the Magic Jinn.*

WRITINGS:

(Adapter with wife, Carole Kismaric, from Norwegian folktale, and illustrator) *The Boy Who Tried to Cheat Death* (juvenile), Doubleday, 1971.
(Adapter and illustrator) *Babushka,* Holiday House, 1984.

ILLUSTRATOR OF ADULT BOOKS; PUBLISHED IN JAPANESE

Feodor Dostoevski, *Crime and Punishment,* Kawade Shobo (Tokyo), 1966.
Feodor Dostoevski, *The Brothers Karamazov,* Kawade Shobo, 1967.

ILLUSTRATOR AND DESIGNER OF CHILDREN'S BOOKS

Helen Hoover, *Great Wolf and the Good Woodsman,* Parents' Magazine Press, 1967.
Jacob Grimm and Wilhelm Grimm, *Little Red Riding Hood,* C. R. Gibson, 1968.
J. Grimm and W. Grimm, *Grimm's Golden Goose,* Random House, 1969.
Jane Lee Hyndman (under pseudonym Lee Wyndham), *Mourka, the Mighty Cat,* Parents' Magazine Press, 1969.
Hyndman (under pseudonym Lee Wyndham), *Russian Tales of Fabulous Beasts and Marvels,* Parents' Magazine Press, 1969.

Cynthia King, *In the Morning of Time,* Four Winds, 1970.
Barbara Rinkoff, *The Pretzel Hero,* Parents' Magazine Press, 1970.
Eric Sundell, *The Feral Child,* Abelard-Schuman, 1971.
Margaret Hodges, reteller, *The Gorgon's Head,* Little, Brown, 1972.
Barbara K. Walker, *How the Hare Told the Truth about His Horse,* Parents' Magazine Press, 1972.
Edwin Fadiman, Jr., *The Feast Day,* Little, Brown, 1973.
Vera Cumberlege, *Shipwreck,* Follett, 1974.
Mirra Ginsburg, translator, *How Wilka Went to Sea and Other Tales from West of the Urals,* Crown, 1975.
Marion L. Starkey, *The Tall Man from Boston,* Crown, 1975.
Jerzy Ficowsky, *Sister of the Birds,* Abingdon, 1976.
Doris Gates, *A Fair Wind for Troy,* Viking, 1976.
Norma Farber, *Six Impossible Things before Breakfast,* Addison-Wesley, 1977.
Farber, *Three Wanderers from Wapping,* Addison-Wesley, 1978.
Barbara Cohen, *Binding of Isaac,* Lothrop, 1978.
Ewa Reid and Barbara Reid, *The Cobbler's Reward,* Macmillan, 1978.
Richard Kennedy, *Delta Baby and Two Sea Songs,* Addison-Wesley, 1979.
Jay Williams, *The Surprising Things Maui Did,* Four Winds, 1979.
Elizabeth Winthrop, *Journey to the Bright Kingdom,* Holiday House, 1979.
William Armstrong, *Tale of Tawny and Dingo,* Harper, 1979.
Ginsburg, *Twelve Clever Brothers and Other Fools,* Lippincott, 1979.
Ernesting Long, *Johnny's Egg,* Addison-Wesley, 1980.
Barbara Cohen, *I Am Joseph,* Lothrop, 1980.
Anne Pellowski, *Nine Crying Dolls,* Philomel, 1980.
Loretta Holz, *Christmas Spider,* Philomel, 1980.
Anne Laurin, *Perfect Crane,* Harper, 1981.
Bernard Evslin, *Signs and Wonder,* Four Winds, 1981.
Sergei Prokofiev, *Peter and the Wolf,* Viking, 1982.
Jan Wahl, *Tiger Hunt,* Harcourt, 1982.
Winthrop, *A Child Is Born,* Holiday House, 1983.
Alfred Noyes, *The Highwayman,* Lothrop, 1983.
Eve Bunting, *The Man Who Could Call Down Owls,* Macmillan, 1984.
Zilpha Snyder, *The Changing Maze,* Macmillan, 1985.
Winthrop, *He Is Risen,* Holiday House, 1985.
Joy Anderson, *Juma and the Magic Jinn,* Lothrop, 1986.
Jane Yolen, editor, *The Lullaby Songbook,* Harcourt, 1986.
Miriam Chaikin, *Exodus,* Holiday House, 1987.
Carole Kismaric, adapter, *The Rumor of Pavel and Paali,* Harper, 1988.
Kismaric, adapter, *A Gift from Saint Nicholas,* Holiday House, 1988.

PICTURE EDITOR AND/OR DESIGNER

Ken Dallison, *When Zeppelins Flew,* Time-Life, 1969.
Fred Freeman, *Duel of the Ironclads,* Time-Life, 1969.
Paul Williams, *The Warrior Knights,* Time-Life, 1969.
Kismaric, *On Leadership,* I.B.M., 1974.
Robert Elson, *Prelude to War,* Time-Life, 1976.
Robert Wernick, *Blitzkreig,* Time-Life, 1976.
Leonard Mosley, *The Battle of Britain,* Time-Life, 1976.
Robert Adams, *Beauty in Photography: Essays in Defense of Traditional Values,* Aperture, 1981.
Adams, *Summer Nights,* Aperture, 1985.

SIDELIGHTS: Charles Mikolaycak writes: "I am an illustrator because I must illustrate, and I am a book designer because I love books. Obviously the field in which the two meet is the one which makes me most happy—children's books. I can usually find something in most stories which makes me excited; be it a locale or period of time requiring great research, or a sense of fantasy which permits me to exercise my own fantasies pictorially, or great writing which forces me to try to match it in visual images.

"I am particularly fond of epics and folktales. I care not how many times they have been illustrated before; the challenge is to find the truth for myself and depict it. When I illustrate I am aware of many things; storytelling, graphic design, sequence of images and my own interest in which I can indulge. I never 'draw-down' to a projected audience. I feel children are most surprisingly capable of meeting a challenge and instinctively understand a drawing. Perhaps it will lead them to ask a question or wonder in silence—either will help them to learn or to extend themselves. I have experienced that if I am satisfied with one of my books, both children and adults will often get from it more than I ever realized I was putting into it."

Mikolaycak's children's book illustrations are in Kerlan Collection at University of Minnesota; several of his illustrations are in permanent collection of International Youth Library, Munich, Germany.

AVOCATIONAL INTERESTS: Reading, theatre, films, travel.

BIOGRAPHICAL/CRITICAL SOURCES:

BOOKS

Roginski, Jim, *Behind the Covers,* Libraries Unlimited, 1985.
Sebesta, Sam L. and William Iverson, *Literature for Thursday's Child,* Science Research Associates, 1975.
Something about the Author Autobiography Series, Volume IV, Gale, 1987.
Sutherland, Zena, *Children and Books,* Scott, Foresman, 1981.

PERIODICALS

Language Arts, October, 1981.

*   *   *

MILES, John
   See BICKHAM, Jack M(iles)

*   *   *

MILLER, Barbara D(iane)   1948-

PERSONAL: Born September 18, 1948, in Geneva, N.Y.; daughter of Donald E. (in business) and Genevieve A. (a bookkeeper) Miller; married Christopher A. Heaton, August 4, 1973 (separated April, 1987); children: Jack Ernest. *Education:* Syracuse University, B.A., 1971, M.A., 1976, Ph.D. (with distinction), 1978.

ADDRESSES: Home—240 Willamette Ave., Kensington, Calif. 94708. *Office*—Graduate Group in Demography, 2234 Piedmont Ave., University of California, Berkeley, Calif. 94720.

CAREER: Syracuse University, Syracuse, N.Y., senior research associate in local revenue administration at Maxwell

School of Citizenship and Public Affairs, 1979-86; University of California, Berkeley, Graduate Group in Demography, research anthropologist, 1987—.

AWARDS, HONORS: Woodrow Wilson fellowship in women's studies, 1976; Rockefeller-Ford Foundation grant in population and development policy, 1977-78; research grant, Wenner-Gren Foundation for Anthropological Research, 1983, 1984, research grant, National Science Foundation, 1987-88.

WRITINGS:

The Endangered Sex: Neglect of Female Children in Rural North India, Cornell University Press, 1981.
(Co-editor) *Local Government Finance in the Philippines,* Praeger, 1983.
(Co-author) *Internal Migration and Its Consequences in Sri Lanka,* Westview, 1987.

Contributor to academic journals.

WORK IN PROGRESS: Editing *The Anthropology of Gender Hierarchies,* a collection of papers presented at a conference funded by the Wenner-Gren Foundation for Anthropological research; a monograph on household structure and budgeting in Jamaica.

SIDELIGHTS: Barbara Miller told *CA:* "I was trained as an anthropologist, which can mean a lot of things. To me, anthropology must be useful; therefore I have tried consistently in the past few years to bring the expertise of anthropology to fields as diverse as demography and public finance. I have tried to think, speak, and write in a way that is interdisciplinary, that can be understood by people who work in different fields and in different areas of the world."

*   *   *

MILOSZ, Czeslaw 1911-
(J. Syruc)

PERSONAL: Surname is pronounced *Mee*-wosh; born June 30, 1911, in Szetejnie, Lithuania; defected to the West, 1951; came to the United States, 1960; naturalized citizen, 1970; son of Aleksander (a civil engineer) and Weronika (Kunat) Milosz. *Education:* University of Stephan Batory, M. Juris, 1934.

ADDRESSES: Office—Department of Slavic Languages and Literatures, University of California, 5416 Dwinelle Hall, Berkeley, Calif. 94720.

CAREER: Poet, critic, essayist, novelist, and translator. Programmer with Polish National Radio, 1935-39; worked for the Polish Resistance during World War II; cultural attache with the Polish Embassy in Paris, France, 1946-50; free-lance writer in Paris, 1951-60; University of California, Berkeley, visiting lecturer, 1960-61, professor of Slavic languages and literature, 1961-78, professor emeritus, 1978—.

MEMBER: American Association for the Advancement of Slavic Studies, American Academy and Institute of Arts and Letters, PEN.

AWARDS, HONORS: Prix Litteraire Europeen, 1953, for novel *La Prise du pouvoir;* Marian Kister Literary Award, 1967; Jurzykowski Foundation award for creative work, 1968; Institute for Creative Arts fellow, 1968; Polish PEN award for poetry translation, 1974; Guggenheim fellow, 1976; Litt.D., University of Michigan, 1977; Neustadt International Literary Prize for Literature, 1978; University Citation, University of California, 1978; Nobel Prize for literature, 1980; honorary

doctorate, Catholic University, Lublin, 1981; honorary doctorate, Brandeis University, 1983; Bay Area Book Reviewers Association Poetry Prize, 1986, for *The Separate Notebooks.*

WRITINGS:

Zniewolony umysl (essays), Instytut Literacki (Paris), 1953, translation by Jane Zielonko published as *The Captive Mind,* Knopf, 1953, reprinted, Octagon, 1981.
Rodzinna Europa (essays), Instytut Literacki, 1959, translation by Catherine S. Leach published as *Native Realm: A Search for Self-Definition,* Doubleday, 1968.
Czlowiek wsrod skorpionow: Studium o Stanislawie Brzozowskim (title means "A Man among Scorpions: A Study of St. Brzozowski"), Instytut Literacki, 1962.
The History of Polish Literature, Macmillan, 1969, revised edition, University of California Press, 1983.
Widzenia nad Zatoka San Francisco, Instytut Literacki, 1969, translation by Richard Lourie published as *Visions from San Francisco Bay,* Farrar, Straus, 1982.
Prywatne obowiazki (essays; title means "Private Obligations"), Instytut Literacki, 1972.
Moj wiek: Pamietnik nowiony (interview with Alexander Wat; title means "My Century: An Oral Diary"), edited by Lidia Ciolkoszowa, two volumes, Polonia Book Fund (London), 1977.
Emperor of the Earth: Modes of Eccentric Vision, University of California Press, 1977.
Ziemia Ulro, Instytut Literacki, 1977, translation by Louis Iribarne published as *The Land of Ulro,* Farrar, Straus, 1984.
Ogrod nauk (title means "The Garden of Knowledge"), Instytut Literacki, 1980.
Dziela zbiorowe (title means "Collected Works"), Instytut Literacki, 1980—.
Nobel Lecture, Farrar, Straus, 1981.
The Witness of Poetry (lectures), Harvard University Press, 1983.
The Rising of the Sun, Arion Press, 1985.
Unattainable Earth, translation from the Polish manuscript by Milosz and Robert Hass, Ecco Press, 1986.

POEMS

Poemat o czasie zastyglym (title means "Poem of the Frozen Time"), [Vilnius, Lithuania], 1933.
Trzy zimy (title means "Three Winters"), Union of Polish Writers, 1936.
(Under pseudonym J. Syruc) *Wiersze* (title means "Poems"), published by the Resistance in Warsaw, Poland, 1940.
Ocalenie (title means "Salvage"), Czytelnik, 1945.
Swiatlo dzienne (title means "Daylight"), Instytut Literacki, 1953.
Trak tat poetycki (title means "Treatise on Poetry"), Instytut Literacki, 1957.
Kontynenty (title means "Continents"), Instytut Literacki, 1958.
Krol Popiel i inne wiersze (title means "King Popiel and Other Poems"), Instytut Literacki, 1962.
Gucio zaczarowany (title means "Bobo's Metamorphosis"), Instytut Literacki, 1965.
Lied vom Weltende (title means "A Song for the End of the World"), Kiepenheuer & Witsch, 1967.
Wiersze (title means "Poems"), Oficyna Poetow i Malarzy (London), 1969.
Miasto bez imienia (title means "City without a Name"), Instytut Literacki, 1969.

Selected Poems, Seabury, 1973, revised edition published as *Selected Poems: Revised,* Ecco Press, 1981.

Gdzie wschodzi slonce i kedy zapada (title means "From Where the Sun Rises to Where It Sets"), Instytut Literacki, 1974.

Utwory poetyckie (title means "Selected Poems"), Michigan Slavic Publications, 1976.

The Bells in Winter, translation by Milosz and Lillian Vallee, Ecco Press, 1978.

Hymn O Perle (title means "Hymn to the Pearl"), Michigan Slavic Publications, 1982.

The Separate Notebooks, translation by Robert Hass and Robert Pinsky, Ecco Press, 1984.

NOVELS

La Prise du pouvoir, translation from the Polish manuscript by Jeanne Hersch, Gallimard (Paris), 1953, original Polish edition published as *Zdobycie wladzy,* Instytut Literacki, 1955, translation by Celina Wieniewska published as *The Seizure of Power,* Criterion, 1955 (published in England as *The Usurpers,* Faber, 1955).

Dolina Issy, Instytut Literacki, 1955, translation by Louis Iribarne published as *The Issa Valley,* Farrar, Straus, 1981.

EDITOR

(With Zbigniew Folejewski) *Antologia poezji spolecznej* (title means "Anthology of Social Poetry"), [Vilnius], 1933.

Piesn niepodlegla (Resistance poetry; title means "Invincible Song"), Oficyna, 1942, reprinted, Michigan Slavic Publications, 1981.

(And translator) Jacques Maritain, *Drogami Kleski,* [Warsaw], 1942.

(And translator) Daniel Bell, *Praca i jej gorycze* (title means "Work and Its Discontents"), Instytut Literacki, 1957.

(And translator) Simone Weil, *Wybor pism* (title means "Selected Works"), Instytut Literacki, 1958.

(And translator) *Kultura masowa* (title means "Mass Culture"), Instytut Literacki, 1959.

(And translator) *Wegry* (title means "Hungary"), Instytut Literacki, 1960.

(And translator) *Postwar Polish Poetry: An Anthology,* Doubleday, 1965, revised edition, University of California Press, 1983.

Lettres inedites de O. V. de L. Milosz a Christian Gauss (correspondence of Milosz's uncle, the French poet Oscar Milosz), Silvaire, 1976.

Founder and editor, *Zagary* (literary periodical), 1931.

TRANSLATOR

(With Peter Dale Scott) Zbigniew Herbert, *Selected Poems,* Penguin, 1968.

Alexander Wat, *Mediterranean Poems,* Ardi, 1977.

Ewangelia wedlug sw. Marka (title means "The Gospel According to St. Mark"), Znak, 1978.

Ksiega Hioba (title means "The Book of Job"), Dialogue (Paris), 1980.

Also translator of Anna Swir's *Happy as a Dog's Tail,* Harcourt.

SIDELIGHTS: One of the most respected figures in twentieth-century Polish literature, Czeslaw Milosz was awarded the Nobel Prize for literature in 1980. Born in Lithuania and raised in Poland, Milosz has lived in the United States since 1960. His poems, novels, essays, and other works are written in his native Polish and translated by the author and others into English. Having lived under the two great totalitarian systems of

modern history, National Socialism and Communism, Milosz writes of the past in a tragic, ironic style that nonetheless affirms the value of human life. Terrence Des Pres, writing in the *Nation,* states that "political catastrophe has defined the nature of our century, and the result—the collision of personal and public realms—has produced a new kind of writer. Czeslaw Milosz is the perfect example. In exile from a world which no longer exists, a witness to the Nazi devastation of Poland and the Soviet takeover of Eastern Europe, Milosz deals in his poetry with the central issues of our time: the impact of history upon moral being, the search for ways to survive spiritual ruin in a ruined world." Although Milosz writes in several genres, it is his poetry that has attracted the most critical acclaim. Several observers, Harold B. Segel writes in the *Washington Post Book World,* consider Milosz to be "the foremost Polish poet of this century." Similarly, Paul Zweig of the *New York Times Book Review* claims that Milosz "is considered by many to be the greatest living Polish poet." But Joseph Brodsky goes further in his praise for Milosz. Writing in *World Literature Today,* Brodsky asserts: "I have no hesitation whatsoever in stating that Czeslaw Milosz is one of the greatest poets of our time, perhaps the greatest."

Born in Lithuania in 1911, Milosz spent much of his childhood in Czarist Russia, where his father worked as a civil engineer. After World War I the family returned to their hometown, which had become a part of the new Polish state, and Milosz attended local Catholic schools. He published his first collection of poems, *Poemat o czasie zastyglym* ("Poem of the Frozen Time"), at the age of twenty-one. Milosz was associated with the catastrophist school of poets during the 1930s. Catastrophism concerns "the inevitable annihilation of the highest values, especially the values essential to a given cultural system. . . . But it proclaims . . . only the annihilation of certain values, not values in general, and the destruction of a certain historical formation, but not of all mankind," Aleksander Fiut explains in *World Literature Today.* The writings of this group of poets ominously foreshadowed the Second World War.

When the war began in 1939, and Poland was invaded by Nazi Germany and Soviet Russia, Milosz worked with the underground Resistance movement in Warsaw, writing and editing several books published clandestinely during the occupation. One of these books, a collection entitled *Wiersze* ("Poems") was published under the pseudonym of J. Syruc. Following the war, Milosz became a member of the new communist government's diplomatic service and was stationed in Paris, France, as a cultural attache. In 1951, he left this post and defected to the West.

The Captive Mind explains Milosz's reasons for defecting and examines the life of the artist under a communist regime. It is, Steve Wasserman maintains in the *Los Angeles Times Book Review,* a "brilliant and original study of the totalitarian mentality." Karl Jaspers, in an article for the *Saturday Review,* describes *The Captive Mind* as "a significant historical document and analysis of the highest order. . . . In astonishing gradations Milosz shows what happens to men subjected simultaneously to constant threat of annihilation and to the promptings of faith in a historical necessity which exerts apparently irresistible force and achieves enormous success. We are presented with a vivid picture of the forms of concealment, of inner transformation, of the sudden bolt to conversion, of the cleavage of man into two."

Milosz's defection came about when he was recalled to Poland from his position at the Polish embassy. He refused to leave. Joseph McLellan of the *Washington Post* quotes Milosz explaining: "I knew perfectly well that my country was becoming the province of an empire." In a speech before the Congress for Cultural Freedom, quoted by James Atlas of the *New York Times*, Milosz declares: "I have rejected the new faith because the practice of the lie is one of its principal commandments and socialist realism is nothing more than a different name for a lie." After his defection Milosz lived in Paris, where he worked as a translator and free-lance writer. In 1960 he was offered a teaching position at the University of California at Berkeley, which he accepted. He became an American citizen in 1970.

In *The Seizure of Power*, first published as *La Prise du pouvoir* in 1953, Milosz renders as fiction much of the same material found in *The Captive Mind*. The book is an autobiographical novel that begins with the Russian occupation of Warsaw at the close of the Second World War. That occupation is still a matter of controversy in Poland. As the Russian army approached the Nazi-held city, the Polish Resistance movement rose against the German occupation troops. They had been assured that the Russian army would join the fight the day after their uprising began. But instead the Russians stood by a few miles outside of the city, allowing the Nazis to crush the revolt unhindered. When the uprising was over, the Russian army occupied Warsaw and installed a communist regime. The novel ends with the disillusioned protagonist, a political education officer for the communists, emigrating to the West.

The Seizure of Power "is a novel on how to live when power changes hands," Andrew Sinclair explains in the London *Times*. Granville Hicks, in an article for the *New York Times Book Review*, sees a similarity between *The Captive Mind* and *The Seizure of Power*. In both books, "Milosz appeals to the West to try to understand the people of Eastern Europe . . . ," Hicks maintains. Told in a series of disjointed scenes meant to suggest the chaos and violence of postwar Poland, *The Seizure of Power* is "a novel of ineffable sadness, and a muffled sob for Poland's fate," Wasserman writes. Michael Harrington, in a review for *Commonweal*, calls *The Seizure of Power* "a sensitive, probing work, far better than most political novels, of somewhat imperfect realization but of significant intention and worth."

After living in the United States for a time, Milosz began to write of his new home. In *Native Realm: A Search for Self-Definition* and *Visions from San Francisco Bay*, Milosz compares and contrasts the West with his native Poland. *Native Realm*, Richard Holmes writes in the London *Times*, is "a political and social autobiography, shorn of polemic intent, deeply self-questioning, and dominated by the sense that neither historically nor metaphysically are most Westerners in a position to grasp the true nature of the East European experience since the First War." A series of personal essays examining events in Milosz's life, *Native Realm* provides "a set of commentaries upon his improbable career," as Michael Irwin maintains in the *Times Literary Supplement*. Milosz "has written a self-effacing remembrance composed of shards from a shattered life," Wasserman believes. "He tells his story with the humility of a man who has experienced tragedy and who believes in fate and in destiny. It is a work that reflects the stubborn optimism of his heart, even as it dwells on the pessimism of his intellect." Irving Howe, writing in the *New York Times Book Review*, finds *Native Realm* "beautifully writ-

ten." Milosz, Howe continues, "tries to find in the chaos of his life some glimmers of meaning."

In *Visions from San Francisco Bay*, Milosz examines his life in contemporary California, a place far removed in distance and temperament from the scenes of his earlier life. His observations are often sardonic, and yet he is also content with his new home. Milosz "sounds like a man who has climbed up, hand over hand, right out of history, and who is both amazed and grateful to find that he can breathe the ahistorical atmosphere of California," Anatole Broyard states in the *New York Times*. The opening words of the book are "I am here," and from that starting point Milosz describes the society around him. "The intention," Julian Symons notes in the *Times Literary Supplement*, "is to understand himself, to understand the United States, to communicate something singular to Czeslaw Milosz." Broyard takes this idea even further, arguing that Milosz "expresses surprise at 'being here,' taking this phrase in its ordinary sense of being in America and in its other, Heideggerian sense of being-in-the-world."

Although Milosz's comments about life in California are "curiously oblique, deeply shadowed by European experience, allusive, sometimes arch and frequently disillusioned," as Holmes points out, he ultimately embraces his adopted home. "Underlying all his meditations," Leon Edel comments in the *New York Times Book Review*, "is his constant 'amazement' that America should exist in this world—and his gratitude that it does exist." "He is fascinated," Symons explains, "by the contradictions of a society with enormous economic power, derived in part from literally non-human technical achievement, which also contains a large group that continually and passionately indicts the society by which it is maintained." Milosz, P. J. Kavanagh remarks in the *Spectator*, looks at his adopted country with "a kind of detached glee—at awfulness; an ungloomy recognition that we cannot go on as we are—in any direction. He holds up a mirror and shows us ourselves, without blame and with no suggestions either, and in the mirror he himself is also reflected." Edel believes that Milosz's visions "have authority: the authority of an individual who reminds us that only someone like himself who has known tyranny. . . can truly prize democracy."

The story of Milosz's odyssey from tyranny to democracy—from East to West—is also recounted in his poetry. Milosz's "entire effort," Jonathan Galassi explains in the *New York Times Book Review*, "is directed toward a confrontation with experience—and not with personal experience alone, but with history in all its paradoxical horror and wonder." Speaking of his poetry in the essay collection *The Witness of Poetry*, Milosz stresses the importance of his nation's cultural heritage and history in shaping his work. "My corner of Europe," he states, "owing to the extraordinary and lethal events that have been occurring there, comparable only to violent earthquakes, affords a peculiar perspective. As a result, all of us who come from those parts appraise poetry slightly differently than do the majority of my audience, for we tend to view it as a witness and participant in one of mankind's major transformations." "For Milosz," Helen Vendler explains in the *New Yorker*, "the person is irrevocably a person in history, and the interchange between external event and the individual life is the matrix of poetry." Writing in *TriQuarterly*, Reginald Gibbons states that Milosz "seems to wonder how good work can be written, no matter how private its subject matter, without the poet having been aware of the pain and threat of the human predicament."

Milosz sees a fundamental difference in the role of poetry in the democratic West and the communist East. Western poetry, as Alfred Kazin of the *New York Times Book Review* writes, is "'alienated' poetry, full of introspective anxiety." But because of the dictatorial nature of communist government, poets in the East cannot afford to be preoccupied with themselves. They are drawn to write of the larger problems of their society. "A peculiar fusion of the individual and the historical took place," Milosz writes in *The Witness of Poetry*, "which means that events burdening a whole community are perceived by a poet as touching him in a most personal manner. Then poetry is no longer alienated."

For many years Milosz's poetry was little noticed in the United States, though he was highly regarded in Poland. Recognition in Poland came in defiance of official government resistance to Milosz's work. The communist regime refused to publish the books of a defector, and so for many years only underground editions of his poems were secretly printed and circulated in Poland. But in 1980, when Milosz was awarded the Nobel Prize for Literature, the communist government was forced to relent. A government-authorized edition of Milosz's poems was issued. It sold a phenomenal 200,000 copies. One sign of Milosz's widespread popularity in Poland occurred when Polish workers in Gdansk unveiled a monument to their comrades who were shot down by the communist police. Two quotations were inscribed on the monument: one was taken from the Bible; the other was taken from a poem by Milosz.

The Nobel Prize also brought Milosz to the attention of a wider audience in the United States. Since 1980 a number of his earlier works have been translated into English and released in this country, while his new books have received widespread critical attention. Some of this critical attention has focused less on Milosz's work as poetry than "as the work of a thinker and political figure; the poems tend to be considered en masse, in relation either to the condition of Poland, or to the suppression of dissident literature under Communist rule, or to the larger topic of European intellectual history," as Vendler maintains. But most reviewers comment on Milosz's ability to speak in a personal voice that carries with it the echoes of his people's history. Zweig explains that Milosz "offers a modest voice, speaking an old language. But this language contains the resources of centuries. Speaking it, one speaks with a voice more than personal.... Milosz's power lies in his ability to speak with this larger voice without diminishing the urgency that drives his words."

This interweaving of the historical and personal is found in all of Milosz's poems. His early works focus on the Lithuania of his childhood and speak of the scenes and people from his own life; Milosz's later poems combine his memories of Europe with the images of his present life in the United States. "Milosz," Harlow Robinson writes in the *Nation*, "has rejected nothing of his long odyssey from the pagan green valleys of Lithuania to the emptying cafes of wartime Europe to the desolate concrete freeways of California." Clarence Brown of the *Village Voice* notes that when reading Milosz, "one has the impression that all his life experience is constantly available to him.... [His poetry] fuses the last waking thought with shards of distant or buried experience, foreshortens and warps the space-time of the poem, resulting in a sort of meta-tense, the everlasting now that came into being with Milosz (and thanks to these poems will outlast him)." This synthesis of personal and public, of past and present, is reflected in Milosz's combination of traditional poetic forms with a modern, individual sensibility. Louis Iribarne writes in the *Times Lit-*

erary Supplement that "the blending of private and public voices, the imaging of lyrical response to historical events, set off by a distinctly modern irony and a classical strictness of form, established the Milosz style."

Because he has lived through many of the great upheavals of recent history, and because his poetry fuses his own experiences with the larger events in his society, many of Milosz's poems concern loss, destruction, and despair. "There is a very dark vision of the world in my work," he tells Lynn Darling of the *Washington Post*. And yet Milosz goes on to say that he is "a great partisan of human hope." This essential optimism comes from his religious convictions. Milosz believes that one of the major problems of contemporary society—in both the East and the West—is its lack of a moral foundation. Writing in *The Land of Ulro*, Milosz finds that twentieth-century man has only "the starry sky above, and no moral law within." Speaking to Judy Stone of the *New York Times Book Review*, Milosz states: "I am searching for an answer as to what will result from an internal erosion of religious beliefs." Michiko Kakutani, reviewing *The Land of Ulro* for the *New York Times*, finds that "Milosz is eloquent in his call for a literature grounded in moral, as well as esthetic, values. Indeed, when compared with his own poetry, the work of many Westerners—from the neurotic rantings of the Romantics to the cerebral mind games of the avant-gardists—seems unserious and self-indulgent."

Because of his moral vision Milosz's writings make strong statements, some of which are inherently political in their implications. "The act of writing a poem is an act of fatih," Milosz claims in *The History of Polish Literature*, "yet if the screams of the tortured are audible in the poet's room, is not his activity an offense to human suffering?" His awareness of suffering, Joseph C. Thackery of the *Hollins Critic* writes, makes Milosz a "spokesman of the millions of dead of the Holocaust, the Gulags, the Polish and Czech uprisings, and the added millions of those who will go on dying in an imperfect world."

But Milosz also warns of the dangers of political writing. In a PEN Congress talk reprinted in the *Partisan Review*, he states: "In this century a basic stance of writers ... seems to be an acute awareness of suffering inflicted upon human beings by unjust structures of society.... This awareness of suffering makes a writer open to the idea of radical change, whichever of many recipes he chooses.... Innumerable millions of human beings were killed in this century in the name of utopia—either progressive or reactionary, and always there were writers who provided convincing justifications for massacre."

In *The Witness of Poetry* Milosz argues that true poetry is "the passionate pursuit of the Real." He condemns those writers who favor art for art's sake or who think of themselves as alienated. Milosz suggests, as Adam Gussow writes in the *Saturday Review*, that poets may have "grown afraid of reality, afraid to see it clearly and speak about it in words we can all comprehend." What is needed in "today's unsettled world," Gussow explains, are poets who, "like Homer, Dante, and Shakespeare, will speak for rather than against the enduring values of their communities."

This concern for a poetry that confronts reality is noted by Thackery, who sees Milosz searching "for a poetry that will be at once harsh and mollifying, that will enable men to understand, if not to rationalize, the debasement of the human spirit by warfare and psychic dismemberment, while simultaneously establishing a personal *modus vivendi* and a psychology of aesthetic necessity.'' Des Pres also sees this unifying quality in Milosz's poetry, a trait he believes Milosz shares with T. S. Eliot. ''The aim of both Milosz and Eliot,'' Des Pres states, ''is identical: to go back and work through the detritus of one's own time on earth, to gather up the worst along with the best, integrate past and present into a culminating moment which transcends both, which embraces pain and joy together, the whole of a life and a world redeemed through memory and art, a final restoration in spirit of that which in historical fact has been forever lost.'' Vendler believes that ''the work of Milosz reminds us of the great power that poetry gains from bearing within itself an unforced, natural, and long-ranging memory of past customs; a sense of the strata of ancient and modern history; wide visual experience; and a knowledge of many languages and literatures. . . . The living and tormented revoicing of the past makes Milosz a historical poet of bleak illumination.''

Upon receiving the Nobel Prize in 1980, Milosz hoped to ''continue with my very private and strange occupation,'' as McLellan quotes him. He has continued to publish books— some new titles and some older books appearing in English for the first time—and has spoken out at meetings of PEN, the international writers' organization, on such topics as censorship and totalitarianism. Darling explains that Milosz lives in Berkeley and writes, ''under the benevolent light of the California sun, in a country of easy consummation and temporary passion, poems about the past, about horror, about life in the abyss of the 20th century.''

Milosz's place in Polish literature is secure, while his influence and reputation in other nations continues to grow. As Galassi writes, ''few other living poets have argued as convincingly for the nobility and value of the poet's calling. Whatever its importance to Polish letters, Mr. Milosz's work, as poetry in English, presents a challenge to American poetry to exit from the labyrinth of the self and begin to grapple again with the larger problems of being in the world.'' ''Milosz has lived through, and participated in, some of the crucial political happenings of our century,'' Michael Irwin comments in the *Times Literary Supplement.* ''If he had never written a line he would be an intriguing figure merely by virtue of his survival. Since he in fact brought to bear upon his experiences a refined and resilient analytical intelligence, unusually combined with a poet's sensibility, his testimony is of unique importance. Attention must be paid to such a man.''

Because Milosz writes of recent Polish history, and decries the nation's political tragedies of the past thirty-five years, his work embodies a spirit of freedom that speaks powerfully to his countrymen as well as to others. ''Polish independence exists in this poet's voice,'' Brodsky maintains in the *New York Times.* ''This, at least, is one way to account for the intensity that has made him perhaps the greatest poet of our time.'' Milosz is one of three Poles who have come to international prominence during the 1980s, Norman Davies notes in the *New York Times Book Review.* Milosz, Pope John Paul II, and Lech Walesa, the leader of the Solidarity trade union challenging the Polish communist government, have ''each served in different ways to illuminate the depth and richness of their native Polish culture,'' Davies writes. In 1981, during his first visit to Poland in thirty years, Milosz met with Lech Walesa and the two men acknowledged their mutual indebtedness. ''I told him that I considered him my leader,'' Milosz recounts to Darling. ''He said that he had gone to jail because of my poetry.''

BIOGRAPHICAL/CRITICAL SOURCES:

BOOKS

Contemporary Literary Criticism, Gale, Volume V, 1976, Volume XI, 1979, Volume XXII, 1982, Volume XXXI, 1985.

Czarnecha, Ewe, *Prdrozny swiata: Rosmowy z Czeslawem Miloszem, Komentane,* Bicentennial, 1983.

Fiut, Aleksander, *Rozmowy z Czeslawem Miloszem,* Wydawnictwo Literackie (Cracow), 1981.

Gillon, A. and L. Krzyzanowski, editors, *Introduction to Modern Polish Literature,* Twayne, 1964.

Goemoeri, G., *Polish and Hungarian Poetry, 1945 to 1956,* Oxford University Press, 1966.

Hass, Robert, *Twentieth Century Pleasures: Prose on Poetry,* Ecco Press, 1984.

Milosz, Czeslaw, *The Captive Mind,* Knopf, 1953.

Milosz, Czeslaw, *The History of Polish Literature,* Macmillan, 1969, revised edition, University of California Press, 1983.

Milosz, Czeslaw, *The Witness of Poetry,* Harvard University Press, 1983.

Milosz, Czeslaw, *The Land of Ulro,* Farrar, Straus, 1984.

PERIODICALS

America, December 18, 1982.

American Poetry Review, January, 1977.

Books Abroad, winter, 1969, spring, 1970, winter, 1973, winter, 1975.

Book Week, May 9, 1965.

Book World, September 29, 1968.

Chicago Tribune, October 10, 1980.

Chicago Tribune Book World, May 31, 1981.

Commonweal, July 8, 1955.

Denver Quarterly, summer, 1976.

Eastern European Poetry, April, 1967.

Globe and Mail (Toronto), March 16, 1985.

Hollins Critic, April, 1982.

Ironwood, Number 18, 1981.

Los Angeles Times, January 14, 1987.

Los Angeles Times Book Review, May 10, 1981, August 22, 1982, June 5, 1983, August 24, 1984.

Nation, December 30, 1978, June 13, 1981.

New Republic, May 16, 1955, August 1, 1983.

New Statesman, October 24, 1980, December 17-24, 1982.

Newsweek, June 15, 1981, October 4, 1982.

New Yorker, November 7, 1953, March 19, 1984.

New York Review of Books, April 4, 1974, June 25, 1981.

New York Times, June 25, 1968, October 10, 1980, September 4, 1982, August 24, 1984, July 26, 1987.

New York Times Book Review, April 17, 1955, July 7, 1974, March 11, 1979, February 1, 1981, June 28, 1981, October 17, 1982, May 1, 1983, September 2, 1984, July 6, 1986.

Partisan Review, November, 1953, spring, 1977, Volume LIII, number 2, 1986.

Poetry, April, 1980.

Publishers Weekly, October 24, 1980.

Saturday Review, June 6, 1953, May-June, 1983.

Spectator, December 4, 1982.

Theology Today, January, 1984.

Times (London), July 16, 1981, January 6, 1983, May 19, 1983, February 9, 1985, May 27, 1987.

Times Literary Supplement, December 2, 1977, August 25, 1978, July 24, 1981, December 24, 1982, September 9, 1983.

TriQuarterly, fall, 1983.
Village Voice, May 2, 1974.
Virginia Quarterly Review, spring, 1975.
Washington Post, October 10, 1980, April 29, 1982.
Washington Post Book World, June 14, 1981.
World Literature Today, winter, 1978, spring, 1978.

—*Sketch by Thomas Wiloch*

* * *

MOHLER, James A(ylward)   1923-

PERSONAL: Born July 22, 1923, in Toledo, Ohio; son of Edward Francis (a teacher and writer) and Gertrude (Aylward) Mohler. *Education:* Xavier University, Cincinnati, Ohio, Litt.B., 1946; Bellarmine School of Theology, Ph.L., 1949, S.T.L., 1956; Loyola University, Chicago, Ill., M.S.I.R., 1960; University of Ottawa, Ph.D., 1964; University of St. Paul, S.T.D., 1965.

ADDRESSES: Home and office—John Carroll University, University Heights, Cleveland, Ohio 44118.

CAREER: Entered Society of Jesus, 1942, ordained Roman Catholic priest, 1955. St. Ignatius High School, Chicago, Ill., teacher of religion, mathematics, economics, and Latin, 1949-52; Jesuit Indian Mission, Sault Ste. Marie, Mich., teacher, 1954-56; John Carroll University, Cleveland, Ohio, instructor, 1960-65, assistant professor, 1965-69, associate professor, 1969-74, professor of religious studies, 1974—, director of Bernet Hall, 1960-62. Visiting scholar, Union Theological Seminary (N.Y.), 1966; research fellow at institutes, colleges, and universities in the United States and abroad, including Institute Saint Serge, Paris, 1968, Tien Educational Institute, People's Republic of China, 1972, St. Xavier's College, Bombay, 1974, and Yale University, 1978.

MEMBER: Catholic Theological Society of America, American Academy of Religion, College Theology Society, American Association of University Professors, Association for Asian Studies.

WRITINGS:

Man Needs God: An Interpretation of Biblical Faith, John Carroll University Press, 1966.
(With others) *Speaking of God,* edited by D. Dirscherl, Bruce Publishing, 1967.
The Beginning of Eternal Life: The Dynamic Faith of Thomas Aquinas, Origins and Interpretation, Philosophical Library, 1968.
Dimensions of Faith, Yesterday and Today, Loyola University Press, 1969.
The Origin and Evolution of the Priesthood, Alba, 1970.
The Heresy of Monasticism: The Christian Monks, Types and Anti-Types, Alba, 1971.
The School of Jesus: An Overview of Christian Education, Yesterday and Today, Alba, 1973.
Cosmos, Man, God, Messiah: An Introduction to Religion, John Carroll University Press, 1973.
Dimensions of Love: East and West, Doubleday, 1975.
Sexual Sublimation and the Sacred, John Carroll University Press, 1978.
The Sacrament of Suffering, Fides/Claretian, 1979.
Dimensions of Prayer, John Carroll University Press, 1981.
Love, Marriage, and the Family, Yesterday and Today, Alba, 1982.
Paradise: Gardens of the Gods, Satya Press, 1984.

Health, Healing and Holiness: Medicine and Religion, Satya Press, 1986.

Contributor to religious journals.

WORK IN PROGRESS: Books on suffering and the theology of work.

SIDELIGHTS: James A. Mohler is competent in Latin, Greek, French, Italian, and German.

AVOCATIONAL INTERESTS: Photography, horticulture, viticulture, fishing, the outdoors.

* * *

MONAGHAN, (Mary) Patricia   1946-

PERSONAL: Born February 15, 1946, in Brooklyn, N.Y.; daughter of Edward J. (a pilot) and Mary Margaret (a bookkeeper; maiden name, Gordon) Monaghan. *Education:* University of Minnesota, Duluth, B.A. (cum laude), 1967; University of Minnesota, Minneapolis, M.A., 1971; University of Alaska, M.F.A., 1981. *Politics:* Democrat. *Religion:* Society of Friends (Quakers).

ADDRESSES: Home—486 Ookpik Way, Fairbanks, Alaska 99709-6720. *Office*—Department of English, Tanana Valley Community College, Fairbanks, Alaska 99701. *Agent*—Michael Larsen-Elizabeth Pomada, 1029 Jones St., San Francisco, Calif. 92103.

CAREER: University of Alaska, Fairbanks, news editor, 1970-72; free-lance writer and editor, 1972-73; Model Cities, Minneapolis, Minn., reporter for *Southside Paper,* 1973; Walker Art Center, Minneapolis, public relations director, 1974; Minnesota Public Radio, St. Paul, editor of *Minnesota Monthly,* 1974-75; free-lance writer, 1975—; Alaska House of Representatives, Juneau, aide to majority caucus, 1976; *Daily News Miner,* Fairbanks, women's editor, 1976-77; Tanana Valley Community College, Fairbanks, instructor in English, 1977—. Consultant in public relations. Member of board of directors of *Tundra Times,* 1970-71; founder and director of Fireweed Press, 1975—. Member of board of directors of Women in Crisis, 1976-78; founding mother of Fairbanks Women's Writers Salon, 1981.

MEMBER: Authors Guild, Authors League of America, American Committee for Irish Studies, Phi Kappa Phi.

AWARDS, HONORS: Travel grant from Alaska State Arts Council, for Ireland, 1979; McCracken Award for poetry from University of Alaska, 1979, for ''Sedna's Daughters'' series; Alaska Fiction Competition award, 1979, for ''Slattery's Sheep''; Alaska State Poetry Competition purchase award, 1979, for ''In County Mayo,'' and individual artist award for poetry, 1981, all from Alaska State Council on the Arts.

WRITINGS:

The Book of Goddesses and Heroines, Dutton, 1981.
(Editor) *Hunger and Dreams* (anthology), Fireweed Press, 1982.
Lessons from the Witch (poems), Amazon Images Press, 1987.
(Editor) *Ten Irish-American Women Poets,* Fireweed Press, 1987.

Work represented in anthologies, including *Yearbook of American Magazine Verse.* Contributor of poems and articles to magazines, including *North American Review, Alaska,* and *Womanspirit,* and newspapers. Founding editor of *Friendly Woman,* 1974; editor of *Envoy.*

WORK IN PROGRESS: Oh Mother Sun!: A New View of the Cosmic Feminine, a survey of female solar myths, publication expected in 1988; *The Worship of Sex,* a feminist look at sex rituals in many cultures, completion expected in 1989.

SIDELIGHTS: Patricia Monaghan once told *CA:* "Although I was born in Brooklyn, N.Y., and spent my early years in Queens, I've lived most of my life in Alaska, which I consider home. Like many Alaskans, however, I've spent years Outside, in my case in Minnesota, where I retain strong professional and personal ties. In 1975 I returned to Fairbanks, living for nearly a year on a homestead seventy miles outside town. That 'bush' experience remains crucial to my writing.

"Both my parents are of Irish descent; much of my mother's family still resides in Bohola, County Mayo. I've traveled in Ireland a number of times and find the English spoken by rural Irish people a continuing source of pleasure and inspiration. I've studied at the Yeats School at Thoor Ballylee, County Galway, and am always thrilled when someone in a Claregalway pub stands up to recite William Butler Yeats—often with little provocation."

Monaghan more recently added: "The feminist spirituality movement continues to inspire not only my nonfiction but my poetry. Currently, I am researching sex rituals from many cultures with an eye to a feminist interpretation of such religions. I am especially interested in the transformational experiences continued in such traditions as Tantric Buddhism."

BIOGRAPHICAL/CRITICAL SOURCES:

PERIODICALS

Irish-America, May-June, 1987.
Times Literary Supplement, June 4, 1982.

*   *   *

MONTAGUE, Jeanne
See YARDE, Jeanne Betty Frances

*   *   *

MONTGOMERY, Max
See DAVENPORT, Guy (Mattison, Jr.)

*   *   *

MORGAN, Kenneth Owen   1934-

PERSONAL: Born May 16, 1934, in London, England; son of David James (a schoolmaster) and Margaret Morgan; married Jane Keeler, January 4, 1973; children: one son, one daughter. *Education:* Attended University College School, London, England, 1944-52; Oriel College, Oxford, M.A., 1958, D.Phil., 1958; Oxford University, D.Litt., 1985. *Politics:* Labour.

ADDRESSES: Home—63 Millwood End, Long Hanborough, Oxfordshire, England.

CAREER: University College of Swansea, Swansea, Wales, senior lecturer in history, 1958-66; Oxford University, Queen's College, Oxford, England, fellow in modern history and political science, 1966—. Columbia University, New York, N.Y., visiting fellow, 1962-63, visiting summer professor, 1965; television and radio broadcaster on political topics.

MEMBER: Royal Historical Society (fellow), British Academy (fellow), Honourable Society of Cymmrodorion, Welsh

Academy, British Association for American Studies, Historical Association, Oxford Union (life member).

AWARDS, HONORS: American Council of Learned Societies fellow, 1962-63; honorary fellow, University College of Swansea, 1985.

WRITINGS:

David Lloyd George: Welsh Radical as World Statesman, University of Wales Press, 1963, reprinted, Greenwood Press, 1982.
Wales in British Politics, 1868-1922, University of Wales Press, 1963, 3rd revised edition, 1980.
(Contributor) David E. Butler and Anthony King, editors, *The British General Election of 1964,* St. Martin's, 1965.
(Contributor) Butler and King, editors, *The British General Election of 1966,* St. Martin's, 1966.
Freedom or Sacrilege?: A History of the Campaign for Welsh Disestablishment, Church in Wales Publications, 1966.
Keir Hardie, Oxford University Press, 1967.
The Age of Lloyd George: The Liberal Party and British Politics, 1890-1929, Barnes & Noble, 1971.
(Editor) *Lloyd George: Family Letters, 1885-1936,* Oxford University Press, 1973.
Lloyd George, Weidenfeld & Nicolson, 1974.
Keir Hardie: Radical and Socialist, Weidenfeld & Nicolson, 1975.
Consensus and Disunity: The Lloyd George Coalition Government, 1918-1922, Oxford University Press, 1979.
(With wife, Jane Morgan) *Portrait of a Progressive: The Political Career of Christopher, Viscount Addison,* Oxford University Press, 1980.
Rebirth of a Nation: Wales, 1880-1980, Oxford University Press, 1981.
David Lloyd George, 1863-1945 (in English and Welsh), University of Wales Press, 1981.
Labour in Power, 1945-1951, Oxford University Press, 1984.
(Editor) *The Oxford Illustrated History of Britain,* Oxford University Press, 1984.
Labour People, Leaders and Lieutenants: Hardie to Kinnock, Oxford University Press, 1987.

Contributor of numerous articles and reviews to history journals, including *American Historical Review, Journal of Contemporary History,* and *History Today.* Editor, *Welsh History Review,* 1965—.

WORK IN PROGRESS: A history of Britain since 1945.

SIDELIGHTS: Kenneth Owen Morgan has been described as "the most productive and formidable historian currently writing on twentieth-century British politics" by Peter Clarke in the *Times Literary Supplement.* Although his writings cover a broad variety of subjects, ranging from a study of the Welsh church to a comprehensive history of Britain, Morgan sees himself primarily as a social and political historian; as he says in *History Today,* "Political history, indeed, is far more than the mere record of institutional development. [It] transcends sheer biography. It is concerned with groups, patterns, collective harmonies and conflicts, continuities and disjunctures. . . . Political history means the reinterpreting of any given unit or society—a town, a region, a people, a state or an international community—in terms of how power is sought, exercised, challenged, abused or denied."

Although Morgan is best known as an interpreter of Prime Minister Lloyd George and British Liberalism in the early years of the twentieth century and is gaining recognition as a general commentator on twentieth-century Britain, an overview of his work highlights two major areas of British history. In such books as *Keir Hardie: Radical and Socialist, Labour in Power 1945-1951* and *Labour People, Leaders and Lieutenants: Hardie to Kinnock*, he traces the history of the Labour movement from its beginnings in the early years of the century to its later efforts under Clement Attlee, and he chronicles the modern history of Wales in *Wales in British Politics, 1868-1922* and *Rebirth of a Nation: Wales, 1880-1980.*

Morgan's work is recognized for its definition of new ways in which to understand twentieth-century British history. For example, Max Beloff writes in *Books and Bookmen* of *Consensus and Disunity: The Lloyd George Coalition Government, 1918-1922,* "Morgan breaks largely new ground in his assessment of the political tactics adopted by Lloyd George [after the First World War]. . . . It is a most impressive performance and one that must inevitably be the starting point for future studies." Similar opinions are expressed by *Times Literary Supplement* critic John Griff, who says Morgan's "credentials are second to none . . . he writes with as near an approach to objectivity as anyone can, and with an apparatus of scholarship that very few can rival." Likewise, *Spectator* reviewer Stephen Koss states, "By his tour de force the author has made sure not only to stimulate debate, but also to raise it to a higher level of sophistication."

Many of Morgan's works have attracted critical attention because they cover areas previously unexamined by historians. *Rebirth of a Nation: Wales, 1880-1980* is such a book; the sixth volume, although the first to appear, of a standard history of Wales from earliest times, it concerns the reemergence of Welsh national identity as a factor in British politics. "For historians with no special interest in Wales," *New Society* contributor John Vincent says, "[*Rebirth of a Nation*] is still important as an exercise in total history, the history of a whole society, its culture, politics, art, scholarship, economy and religion, seen in continuous movement over a long period." Graham Hughes states in the *New York Review of Books,* "The book will be indispensible because, while there have been many articles and monographs on aspects of modern Welsh history, this is the first scholarly attempt to offer a full account of the struggle for Welsh identity over the last hundred years." Writing for the *Spectator,* Richard Cobb describes the same book as "a model of fairness, restraint and understatement offering occasional discreet hints of malice"; and John Keegan in the *New Republic* holds that "it sets standards of comprehensiveness, balance, and judgment that Dr. Morgan's fellow authors will have the greatest difficulty in meeting."

Peter Clarke, again writing for the *Times Literary Supplement,* suggests that because the events about which Morgan writes occurred in the recent past, his work tends to stir opposing emotions in different reviewers. Morgan's work on the Labour movement in Britain in particular has inspired controversy among critics. The Labour Party in Britain was formed in the early years of the twentieth century as a means for working-class people, especially those represented by unions, to have representation in Parliament. Important figures in Labour government included Keir Hardie, an avowed Socialist and first Labour Member of Parliament, Ramsay MacDonald, Prime Minister from 1929 to 1935, and Clement Attlee, deputy prime minister in the Churchill government during the war years and Prime Minister from 1945 to 1951.

Observer contributor A. J. P. Taylor commended Morgan's study, *Keir Hardie: Radical and Socialist,* when it first appeared in 1975. More recently the author's work has focused on Attlee's government. Anthony Howard, writing in the *Listener,* says of *Labour in Power, 1945-1951,* "What [Morgan] offers us is not so much a dispassionate record of Labour's first genuine bout of power, as an uninhibited tribute to what he plainly takes to be the most considerable government of the 20th century." A reviewer for the *Economist* feels differently: "'Labour in Power' represents the first attempt by a professional historian to tell the story of Attlee's administration as a whole. By any standards, it is a considerable achievement. Dr. Morgan's control over his diverse materials is total, and his judgments are dispassionate." Similarly, Merle Rubin states in the *Christian Science Monitor:* "Kenneth Morgan's unusually well-written history of this crucial era provides a compellingly readable inside view of Britain's postwar Labour governments. . . . [He] combines accuracy, vividness, and balance." *Times Literary Supplement* critic Peter Clarke says, "What Kenneth Morgan has done . . . is to pull all the available material together for the first time in a comprehensive and well-documented history of the Attlee government."

Labour People, Leaders and Lieutenants: Hardie to Kinnock, a compilation of biographical sketches about important figures in the Labour movement, has inspired less controversy. Peter Hennessy, a reviewer for the *Listener,* praises Morgan's "excellent collection of mini-biographies," and Peter Clarke observes in the *Times Literary Supplement* that "Morgan has produced some two dozen well-rounded biographical essays, unencumbered by footnotes but buttressed at every turn by an authoritative if tacit scholarship." In the *London Review of Books,* Brian Harrison lauds *Labour People*'s clear style, its very readable prose, its emphasis on secondary figures, and its range. He says, "There are very few historians who could now operate with such historical knowledge with a lively interest in current politics; he shows no coy academic inhibition about linking up the two, for he knows how amply each can enrich the other."

Reception of *Labour People* suffered somewhat because of the timing of its publication. As Hennessy and Clarke note, the book was written at a time when the Labour Party's future looked bright, before its disappointing showing in the 1987 national election. Clarke in particular says, "It is to be hoped that [*Labour People*] . . . is not temporarily cheated of its due by the vicissitudes of current politics." He considers *Labour People* a fine work of political history.

Kenneth Morgan himself recognizes the controversial nature of the subjects about which he chooses to write. He says in *History Today:* "Finally, political history should never be unduly rationalist. To assess the work of the 1945-51 Labour government, or any other group of politicians, in terms of academic logic or a timeless scale of values is a distortion of events. The historian, after all, is a comfortable, middle-class individual cocooned in his or her study or library, meditating in leisured tranquility on the crisis that engulfed former men and women in public life. He should never forget the pressures of time and circumstances which inexorably shaped the reactions of harassed politicians. They were not concerned with proclaiming universally valid truths, but with reconciling, managing, muddling through, relating their principles to the real, ravaged, terrifying world as they faced it in 1945."

The Oxford Illustrated History of Britain has been translated into French and Italian.

AVOCATIONAL INTERESTS: Sports, music, the theater, films, motoring in rural France, Inca archaeology.

BIOGRAPHICAL/CRITICAL SOURCES:

PERIODICALS

Books and Bookmen, April, 1980.
Christian Science Monitor, January 3, 1986.
Economist, March 10, 1984.
Guardian, March 26, 1981.
History Today, November, 1981, August, 1983, November, 1983, January, 1985.
Listener, March 15, 1984, April 16, 1987.
London Review of Books, June 4, 1987.
New Republic, April 25, 1981, September 17, 1984.
New Society, April 23, 1981, April 9, 1987.
New York Review of Books, November 18, 1982.
Observer, March 23, 1975, March 4, 1984, December 2, 1984, April 19, 1987.
Spectator, November 3, 1979, May 31, 1980, May 30, 1981, November 28, 1981, March 24, 1984.
Times (London), March 8, 1984.
Times Higher Education Supplement, May 15, 1981.
Times Literary Supplement, December 14, 1979, August 1, 1980, May 8, 1981, March 16, 1984, September 21, 1984, April 24, 1987.

—Sketch by Kenneth R. Shepherd

*   *   *

MORRIS, Michael (Spence Lowdell) 1940-

PERSONAL: Born January 31, 1940, in Cape Town, South Africa; son of Eric Spence (a military officer) and Freda (Lowell) Morris. *Education:* University of South Africa, graduated, 1968; Union College, Diploma in General Psychology, 1971; South African Police College, B.A., 1979; University of Cape Town, M.A., 1980.

ADDRESSES: Office—Terrorism Research, P.O. Box 1464, Cape Town 8000, South Africa.

CAREER: Associated with South African Police, 1960-72; Terrorism Research (originally Terrorism Research Centre), Cape Town, South Africa, founder and principal researcher, 1973—. Chairman of executive board of Portuguese Fighting Soldiers Comforts Fund (now Good Hope Comforts Fund), 1971-74.

MEMBER: International Association of Bomb Technicians and Investigators (associate member), Security Association of South Africa, Fire Protection Association of South Africa.

AWARDS, HONORS: Named Best Student of the Year at South African Police College; South African Police Medal for Combating Terrorism, 1969; Kwa Zulu Establishment Medal, 1986.

WRITINGS:

The Sweetness and the Sadness (poems), Universal, 1964.
A Passion for Home (poems), Argo, 1965.
Dreams of War (poems), Argo, 1967.
Now That I'm Dead (poems), Universal, 1968.
Redfive (poems), Poetry South, 1969.
Phoenix (poems), Poetry South, 1970.
Requiem (poems), Poetry South, 1971.
Terrorism in Southern Africa, Howard Timmins, 1971.
Fuzzversus: Police and Students in South Africa—Another View, J. Spence, 1973.
Armed Conflict in Southern Africa, J. Spence, 1974.
The Spirit of Michael Webfoot (prose), J. Spence, 1977.
Ant in a Stream (poems), J. Spence, 1980.

South African Security: Some Considerations for the 1980's, Terrorism Research Centre, 1980.
The Morality of Brutality: Reflections on Dedication in Political Violence, Terrorism Research Centre, 1980.
(With Helmoed Heitman) *Limpet-Mine Sabotage in South Africa: Weapon Data, Saboteur Tactics, Incident List,* Terrorism Research Centre, 1981.
(With Willem Steenkamp) *The South African National Congress Rocket Attack on Voortrekkerhoogte: Background Data, Characteristics, Tactics, and Illustrations,* Terrorism Research Centre, 1981.
(With Frederick Stoffberg) *Security Fencing: A Frank Appraisal,* Terrorism Research Centre, 1981.
South Africa: A Current Overview, Potchefstroom University, 1982.
Bombs and Bombers, Terrorism Research Centre, 1982.
South African Political Violence and Sabotage, three volumes, Terrorism Research Centre, 1982.
Soapy Water and Cabinda, Terrorism Research, 1985.
Joe Dunce in Blast Alley, Terrorism Research, 1986.
Dead Friend Dancing, Zurich Presse, 1986.
Sa Bomb Summary, Terrorism Research, 1986.
Goofs' Crusade, Terrorism Research, 1987.

Editor of general collections of *Poetry South.*

WORK IN PROGRESS: Dunlop Kentucky, the story of necklace executions in South Africa; *Blasted Employers, Landlords and Bus-Barons,* the use of bombs as recruiting tools; *Good Old Oliver,* case studies of bombings in South Africa; *Ringside in Bombsville,* researching political violence internationally.

SIDELIGHTS: Michael Morris told *CA:* "My high productivity is due to personal fascination with the topic, in which very few persons have specialized, and the fact that there is a burgeoning market for it. My independence means that I am able to write things as I perceive them, rather than present the hackneyed message of the propagandists. Terrorism, by whatever name it is called, is very much the topic of high interest in the seventies and eighties. Yet very, very few researcher-writers *really* analyze it, really have the solid academic *and* solid practical background combination and are able to communicate effectively. In this I am unusually fortunate and have been blessed to have those precious three attributes. It would be less than proper for me *not* to produce my specialist writings as rapidly as I am able, commensurate, of course, with thorough research, and careful checking and rechecking of detail. My major problem right now (and who are so lucky as to be able to say this?) is deciding what *not* to write—there is so much!"

*   *   *

MORSE, Roger A(lfred) 1927-

PERSONAL: Born July 5, 1927, in Saugerties, N.Y.; son of Grant D. (a superintendent of schools) and Margery A. (a teacher; maiden name, Saxe) Morse; married Mary Lou Smith, October 6, 1951; children: Joseph G., Susan A., Mary Ann. *Education:* Cornell University, B.S., 1950, M.S., 1953, Ph.D., 1955. *Politics:* Republican.

ADDRESSES: Home—425 Hanshaw Rd., Ithaca, N.Y. 14850. *Office*—Department of Entomology, Cornell University, Ithaca, N.Y. 14853.

CAREER: State Plant Board of Florida, Gainesville, apiculturist, 1955-57; University of Massachusetts, Field Station,

Amherst, assistant professor of horticulture, 1957; Cornell University, Ithaca, N.Y., assistant professor, 1957-64, associate professor, 1964-70, professor of apiculture, 1970—, chairman, department of entomology, 1986—. Visiting professor of apiculture, University of the Philippines, 1968, and University of Sao Paulo, 1978; guest lecturer at colleges and universities. Consultant to Food and Agriculture Organization of the United Nations, 1982. Member of Tompkins County Fair Board; member of Tompkins County Board of Representatives; former volunteer fire chief. *Military service:* U.S. Army, 1944-47; became staff sergeant.

MEMBER: International Union for the Study of Social Insects, International Bee Research Association (vice-chairman of council; chairman, American committee), Rotary International (former president, Ithaca section), Entomological Society of America, American Association for the Advancement of Science (fellow), Philippine Association of Entomologists, Eastern Apicultural Society, Florida Entomological Society, New York Academy of Science, Sigma Xi, Delta Sigma Rho.

AWARDS, HONORS: Fifteen travel and research grants from National Science Foundation, 1961—; research grant from U.S. Army, 1966; three research grants from National Institute of Health; three research grants from U.S. Department of Agriculture; two research grants from Environmental Protection Agency; Apimondia Gold Medal, 1979, for *Honey Bee Pests, Predators, and Diseases;* Apimondia Silver Medal, 1981, for *Making Mead.*

WRITINGS:

The Complete Guide to Beekeeping, Dutton, 1972, 3rd edition, 1986.
Bees and Beekeeping, Comstock, 1975.
(Contributor) Eva Crane, editor, *Honey,* Bee Research Association, 1975.
(Editor) *Honey Bee Pests, Predators, and Diseases,* Cornell University Press, 1978.
Comb Honey Production, Wicwas Press, 1979.
Rearing Queen Honey Bees, Wicwas Press, 1980.
Making Mead, Wicwas Press, 1981.
(Editor with Ted Hooper) *The Illustrated Encyclopedia of Beekeeping,* Dutton, 1984.
(With William L. Coggshall) *Beeswax,* Wicwas Press, 1985.

Also English editor of *Honey Bee Brood Diseases,* 1980. Contributor of hundreds of articles to conservation, natural history, and beekeeping journals. Research editor of *Gleanings in Bee Culture,* 1959—.

WORK IN PROGRESS: Pheromone Language of the Honey Bee; Honey: Harvesting, Extracting, Processing and Packaging.

SIDELIGHTS: Regarding *The Illustrated Encyclopedia of Beekeeping,* edited by Roger A. Morse and Ted Hooper, Dorothy Galton writes in the *Times Literary Supplement* that "every possible subject connected with honey-bees and bee-keeping (excluding bumble and other solitary bees) is covered in language as simple as the subject allows. . . . The *Encyclopedia* will answer practically every question the amateur and specialist may ask, and it can be recommended as replacement for all existing books on the subject written for readers using modern methods of beekeeping."

Roger A. Morse has spent a total of a year studying bees in Asia and has made numerous study trips to Europe, Africa, and South America. He also holds a U.S. patent on a method of making wine from honey. Some of Morse's books have been published in Russian and Italian editions.

AVOCATIONAL INTERESTS: Farming.

BIOGRAPHICAL/CRITICAL SOURCES:

PERIODICALS

Times Literary Supplement, August 23, 1985.

*   *   *

MOSTELLER, (Charles) Frederick   1916-

PERSONAL: Surname is pronounced *Moss*-teller; born December 24, 1916, in Clarksburg, W.Va.; son of William Roy (a road builder) and Helen (Kelley) Mosteller; married Virginia Gilroy, May 17, 1941; children: William Samuel, Gale Robin. *Education:* Carnegie Institute of Technology (now Carnegie-Mellon University), B.S., 1938, M.S., 1939; Princeton University, A.M., 1941, Ph.D., 1946.

ADDRESSES: Home—28 Pierce Rd., Belmont, Mass. 02178. *Office*—Department of Health Policy and Management, Harvard University, Cambridge, Mass. 02138.

CAREER: Office of Public Opinion Research, Princeton, N.J., research associate, 1942-44; Princeton University, Princeton, instructor in department of mathematics, 1942-44, research mathematician with Statistical Research Group, 1944-45; Harvard University, Cambridge, Mass., lecturer in department of social relations, 1946-48, associate professor, 1948-51, professor of mathematical statistics, 1951—, Roger I. Lee Professor, 1976-81, chairman of department of statistics, 1957-71, chairman of department of biostatistics, 1976-81, chairman of department of health policy and management, 1981—. Miller Research Professor, University of California, Berkeley, 1974-75. Teacher of National Broadcasting Company's television course in probability and statistics, 1960-61. Special consultant, research branch, U.S. War Department, 1942-43.

MEMBER: International Statistical Institute, American Epidemiological Society, American Academy of Arts and Sciences, American Philosophical Society, Institute of Mathematical Statistics (fellow; president, 1974-75), American Statistical Association (fellow; vice-president, 1963-65; president, 1967), American Association for the Advancement of Science (fellow; president, 1980), Mathematical Association of America, Psychometric Society (president, 1957-58), Biometric Society, Royal Statistical Society (honorary fellow), Sociological Research Association, National Academy of Sciences, Institute of Medicine.

AWARDS, HONORS: Fund for Advancement of Education fellow, University of Chicago, 1954-55; Center for Advanced Study in the Behavioral Sciences fellow, Stanford, Calif., 1962-63; Guggenheim fellow, 1969; D.Sc. from University of Chicago, 1973, and Carnegie-Mellon University, 1974; D.Soc. from Yale University, 1981; D.Sc. from Wesleyan University; Samuel S. Wilks Memorial Award, 1986.

WRITINGS:

(Co-author) *Gauging Public Opinion,* edited by Hadley Cantril, Princeton University Press, 1944.
Sampling Inspection, McGraw, 1948.
(With others) *The Pre-election Polls of 1948,* Social Science Research Council Bulletins, 1949.
(With R. R. Bush) *Stochastic Models for Learning,* Wiley, 1955.

(With R. E. K. Rourke and G. B. Thomas, Jr.) *Probability with Statistical Applications*, Addison-Wesley, 1961, revised edition, 1970.
(With Rourke and Thomas) *Probability: A First Course*, Addison-Wesley, 1962, revised edition, 1970.
(With D. L. Wallace) *Inference and Disputed Authorship: The Federalist*, Addison-Wesley, 1964.
Fifty Challenging Problems in Probability, Addison-Wesley, 1965.
(Co-author) *The National Halothene Study*, National Academy of Sciences, 1969.
(Co-author) *Statistics by Example*, Addison-Wesley, 1973.
(With Rourke) *Sturdy Statistics*, Addison-Wesley, 1973.
(With W. Fairley) *Statistics and Public Policy*, Addison-Wesley, 1977.
(With J. W. Tuker) *Data Analysis, Including Regression*, Addison-Wesley, 1977.
(With D. Hoaglin and others) *Data for Decisions*, Abt Associates, 1982.
(With J. A. Ingelfinger and others) *Biostatistics in Clinical Medicine*, Macmillan, 1983, 2nd edition, 1987.
Exploring Data Tables, Trends and Shapes, Wiley, 1985.

EDITOR

(Co-editor) *Statistics: A Guide to the Unknown*, Holden-Day, 1972.
(With J. P. Bunker and B. A. Barnes) *Costs, Risks, and Benefits of Surgery*, Oxford University Press, 1977.
(With D. Hoaglin and J. W. Tukey) *Understanding Robust and Exploratory Data Analysis*, Wiley, 1982.
(With J. C. Bailar III) *Medical Uses of Statistics*, NEJM Books, 1986.

OTHER

Contributor to journals.

*   *   *

MUIR, Richard   1943-

PERSONAL: Born June 18, 1943, in Harrogate, England; son of Kenneth (a hotelier) and Edna (Hugall) Muir; married Nina Rajpal (an academic editor), October 13, 1978. *Education:* University of Aberdeen, M.A. (with first class honors), 1967, Ph.D., 1970. *Politics:* "Liberal/Social Democrat."

ADDRESSES: Home and office—Waterfall Close, Station Road, Birstwith, Harrogate, North Yorkshire, HG3 3AG, England.

CAREER: University of Dublin, Trinity College, Dublin, Ireland, lecturer in geography, 1970-71; Cambridgeshire College of Arts and Technology, Cambridge, England, senior lecturer in geography, 1971-80; free-lance writer and landscape photographer, 1980—. Member of Council for the Protection of Rural England and of Medieval Village Research Group.

MEMBER: Green Alliance, Friends of the Earth, Society for Landscape Studies.

AWARDS, HONORS: Yorkshire Arts Literary Award, 1982-83.

WRITINGS:

Modern Political Geography, Macmillan, 1975.
(With R. Paddison) *Politics, Geography, and Behaviour*, Methuen, 1981.
History from the Air, M. Joseph, 1983.

(With J. R. Ravensdale) *East Anglian Landscapes: Past and Present*, M. Joseph, 1984.
Stones of Britain, M. Joseph, 1986.

AND PHOTOGRAPHER

The English Village, Thames & Hudson, 1980.
Riddles in the British Landscape, Thames & Hudson, 1981.
The Shell Guide to Reading the Landscape, M. Joseph, 1981.
Lost Villages of Britain, M. Joseph, 1982, revised edition, 1985.
(With Christopher C. Taylor) *Visions of the Past*, Dent, 1983.
(With Humphrey Welfare) *The National Trust Guide to Prehistoric and Roman Britain*, George Philip, 1983.
A Traveller's History of Britain and Ireland, M. Joseph, 1984.
(With Eric Duffey) *The Shell Countryside Book*, Dent, 1984.
The Shell Guide to Reading the Celtic Landscapes, M. Joseph, 1985.
The National Trust Guide to Dark Age and Medieval Britain, George Philip, 1985.
(With Nina Muir) *The National Trust Guide to Rivers of Britain*, H. Holt & Co., 1986.
Landscape and Nature Photography, George Philip, 1986.
(With N. Muir) *Hedgerows*, M. Joseph, 1987.
Old Yorkshire, M. Joseph, 1987.
The Countryside Dictionary, Macmillan, 1988.
Fields, Macmillan, in press.

OTHER

Also editor, National Trust Histories; editor, "Countryside Commission National Parks" series. Contributor to *Shell Book of Villages* and *The English World*. Contributor of photographs to BBC *History on Your Doorstep, National Trust Regional Histories of the Lake District, Wessex, Mid Anglia, and Cornwall*, and *The Domesday Inheritance*. Contributor to magazines and newspapers, including *Sunday Times, Observer, Geographical Magazine, Modern Political Geography*, and *New York Times*.

SIDELIGHTS: Richard Muir wrote: "In 1980 I resigned my senior lectureship in geography in order to write for the general reader on different aspects of the history of the British landscape. I had established a position as a leading authority on political geography, but thought I could do more service to the cause of conservation and return to my geographical grass-roots by this change of career. *The English Village* was a bestseller in the United Kingdom. *The Shell Guide to Reading the Landscape* is equally successful. I also specialize in landscape, historical, and archaeological photography.

"As a free-lance landscape historian and photographer, I spend much of my time visiting monuments and archaeological sites, all within the setting of the wonderful British and Irish landscapes I love. If I have a mission, it is to alert public opinion to the forces which threaten this incomparable heritage and to explain the evolution of the scenery. I have recently done radio broadcasts on the lost villages of England."

Commenting on Muir's landscape studies, Ronald Blythe of the *Sunday Times* noted that the author "has managed" to write his books "only by touring in every direction, reading every (it seems) relevant authority, taking all his own pictures and spurning the usual picture-banks, and generally letting his own philosophical, trenchant and always lively pen pour out facts with such verve, that no one without his zeal for the subject could possibly keep up." Blythe continued: Muir "is a missionary, not just a well-informed escort, and his aim is to produce followers in his steps, readers who will have absorbed enough of the deeper understanding of the landscape to be aware of the many dangers which now threaten it.''

BIOGRAPHICAL/CRITICAL SOURCES:

PERIODICALS

Los Angeles Times Book Review, August 10, 1980.
Sunday Times (London), May 24, 1981.
Times Literary Supplement, August 22, 1980.
Washington Post Book World, September 21, 1980.

* * *

MURDIN, Paul 1942-

PERSONAL: Born January 5, 1942, in Croydon, England; son of Robert (a draftsman) and Ethel (a clerk; maiden name, Chubb) Murdin; married Lesley Milburn (a lecturer), August 8, 1964; children: Benedict, Alexander, Louisa. *Education:* Oxford University, B.A., 1963; University of Rochester, Ph.D., 1970.

ADDRESSES: Home—"Woodside," 101 Hoads Wood Rd., Hastings, Sussex TN34 1BB, England. *Office*—Royal Greenwich Observatory, Hailsham, Sussex BN27 1RP, England.

CAREER: Royal Greenwich Observatory, Hailsham, England, principal, 1971-75; Anglo Australian Observatory, Epping, Australia, research scientist, 1975-78; Royal Greenwich Observatory, senior principal, 1978—.

MEMBER: International Astronomical Union, Royal Astronomical Society (fellow).

WRITINGS:

(With Patrick Moore) *The Astronomer's Telescope,* Brockhampton Press, 1964.
Radio Waves from Space, Brockhampton Press, 1965.
(With wife, Lesley Murdin) *New Astronomy,* Crowell, 1975.
(With David Allen and David Malin) *Catalog of the Universe,* Crown, 1979.
(With Malin) *Colours of the Stars,* Cambridge University Press, 1984.
(With L. Murdin) *Supernovae,* Cambridge University Press, 1986.

Contributor of more than one hundred articles to scientific journals.

WORK IN PROGRESS: Continuing astronomical research.

SIDELIGHTS: Paul Murdin wrote: "My books are attempts to communicate my excitement about astronomy."

* * *

MYERS, R(obert) E(ugene) 1924-

PERSONAL: Born January 15, 1924, in Los Angeles, Calif.; son of Harold Eugene and Margaret (Anawalt) Myers; married Patricia A. Tazer, August 17, 1956; children: Edward E., Margaret A., Hal R., Karen. *Education:* University of California, Berkeley, A.B., 1955; Reed College, M.A., 1960; further graduate study at University of Minnesota, 1960-63; University of Georgia, Ed.D., 1968. *Politics:* Democrat. *Religion:* Protestant.

ADDRESSES: Home—2846 Northwest Angelica Dr., Corvallis, Ore. 97330. *Office*—905 Fourth Ave. S.E., Albany, Ore. 97321.

CAREER: Elementary school teacher in Oregon, California, and Minnesota, 1954-61; Augsburg College, Minneapolis,

Minn., assistant professor of education, 1962-63; University of Oregon, Eugene, assistant professor of education, 1963-66; elementary school teacher in Eugene, 1966-67; University of Victoria, Victoria, British Columbia, associate professor of education and associate director of teacher education, 1968-70; Oregon State System of Higher Education, Teaching Research Division, associate research professor of education, 1970-73; Northwestern, Inc., Portland, Ore., filmmaker, 1973-74; University of Portland, Portland, Ore., associate professor of education, 1974-75; free-lance film producer, 1975-77; Oregon State Department of Education, Salem, learning resources specialist, 1977-81; Linn-Benton Education Service District, Albany, Ore., curriculum coordinator, 1981—. Visiting professor at San Diego State University, Northeastern Louisiana University, Winona State University, Oregon College of Education, University of Victoria, Paine College, and Texas Tech University. Has appeared on television programs. *Military service:* U.S. Merchant Marine, 1943-45.

MEMBER: International Reading Association, National Association for Gifted Children (member of board of directors, 1974-77), Mid-Valley Reading Council (member of board of directors).

AWARDS, HONORS: Outstanding book award from Pi Lambda Theta, 1972, for *Creative Learning and Teaching;* Golden Eagle from Council on International Nontheatrical Events, 1973, for "Feather."

WRITINGS:

(Contributor) E. Paul Torrance, editor, *Rewarding Creative Behavior,* Prentice-Hall, 1965.
(With Torrance) *Creative Learning and Teaching,* Dodd, 1970.

JUVENILE

(With Torrance) *Invitations to Thinking and Doing* (with teacher's guide), Ginn, 1965.
(With Torrance) *Invitations to Speaking and Writing Creatively* (with teacher's guide), Ginn, 1965.
(With Torrance) *Can You Imagine?* (with teacher's guide), Ginn, 1965, reprinted, Perceptive, 1986.
(With Torrance) *Plots, Puzzles, and Ploys* (with teacher's guide), Ginn, 1966.
(With Torrance) *For Those Who Wonder* (with teacher's guide), Ginn, 1966, reprinted, Perceptive, 1986.
(With Torrance) *Stretch* (with teacher's guide), Perceptive, 1968.
"Animal Friends" (film strip), A.I.M.S. Instructional Media, 1974.
"Exploring the Unexplained" (film strip), United Learning, 1974.
"Investigating the Unknown" (film strip), United Learning, 1974.
"Sing Along with Animals" (film strip), United Learning, 1975.
"Hand Tools: An Introduction to Working with Wood and Plastic" (film strip), A.I.M.S. Instructional Media, 1975.
It's a Butterfly! (with audio cassette), United Learning, 1977.
It's a Dolphin! (with audio cassette), United Learning, 1977.
It's a Squirrel! (with audio cassette), United Learning, 1977.
It's a Toad! (with audio cassette), United Learning, 1977.
It's an Alligator! (with audio cassette), United Learning, 1977.
Wondering, Creative Learning Press, 1984.
Imagining, Creative Learning Press, 1985.

FILMS

"Feather" (juvenile), ACI Media, 1973.

"Flexibility," Teaching Research, 1973.
"Learning Sets," Teaching Research, 1973.
"Perseveration," Teaching Research, 1973.
"Inducing a Creative Set: The Magic Net," Teaching Research, 1973.
"Elephants" (juvenile), ACI Media, 1974.

WORK IN PROGRESS: Revising *Creative Learning and Teaching;* writing booklets involving creative thinking about the future.

SIDELIGHTS: R. E. Myers writes: "My motivation for writing has always had two sides: self-expression and professional reasons. The latter generally deal with helping young people become more creative. I am interested in intelligence, learning, instructional materials and techniques, motivation, and personality. I've done research in all of these areas.

"In the past few years I've been involved in organizing, and giving workshops in, young authors festivals. Perhaps this stems from the fact that probably all four of my children surpass me in writing skills!"

N

NANDA, B(al) R(am) 1917-

PERSONAL: Born October 11, 1917, in Rawalpindi, India (now in Pakistan); son of P. D. and Shrimati Maya (Devi) Nanda; married Janak Khosla, May 24, 1946; children: Naren and Biren (sons). *Education:* Attended Government College, Lahore, 1935-39. *Religion:* Hundu.

ADDRESSES: Home—S-174 Panchshila Park, New Delhi 110017, India.

CAREER: Indian Railways, New Delhi, India, joint director, Ministry of Railways, 1962-64; Indian Institute of Public Administration, New Delhi, project director, 1964; Nehru Memorial Museum and Library, New Delhi, director, 1965-79.

AWARDS, HONORS: Rockefeller fellowship, 1964; Indian Council of Social Science Research national fellow, 1979-80; Dadabhai Naoroji Memorial Award, 1979, for *Gokhale: The Indian Moderates and the British Raj.*

WRITINGS:

Mahatma Gandhi: A Biography, Allen & Unwin, 1958, Beacon Press, 1959, abridged edition, Allen & Unwin, 1965, reprint of original edition, Oxford University Press, 1981.
The Nehrus: Motilal and Jawaharlal, Allen & Unwin, 1962, Day, 1963, Oxford University Press, 1985.
Motilal Nehru, Publications Division, Government of India (New Delhi), 1964.
(Editor) *Socialism in India,* Vikas Publications (Delhi), 1972.
Gandhi: A Pictorial Biography, Publications Division, Government of India, 1972.
Gokhale, Gandhi and the Nehrus: Studies in Indian Nationalism, St. Martin's, 1974.
(Editor) *Indian Foreign Policy: The Nehru Years,* International Book Distributors, 1976.
(Editor) *Science and Technology in India,* Vikas Publications, 1977, Advent Books, 1986.
Gokhale: The Indian Moderates and the British Raj, Oxford University Press, 1977.
(With P. C. Joshi and Raj Krishna) *Gandhi and Nehru,* Oxford University Press, 1979.
(Editor) *Essays in Modern Indian History,* Oxford University Press, 1980.
Jawaharlal Nehru: A Pictorial Biography, Publications Division, Government of India, 1980.

The Moderate Era in Indian Politics, Oxford University Press, 1981.
Gandhi and His Critics, Oxford University Press, 1985.
Gandhi, Pan-Islamism and Imperialism, Oxford University Press, in press.

WORK IN PROGRESS: In Gandhi's Footsteps: The Life of Jamnalal Bajaj.

SIDELIGHTS: B. R. Nanda told *CA:* "I have been trying to reconstruct the story of the Indian nationalist movement and the lives of some of its outstanding leaders who combined intense nationalism with a wide world view. I am fascinated by the subtle interplay of personalities and politics, and the insights such studies can yield for the understanding of political history. Though I have drawn largely on primary sources and written in a scholarly framework, my object has been to interest not only fellow historians but the general reader in India and abroad. Several of my books have been simultaneously published in India, Britain and U.S.A., and have been translated into Indian and European languages."

AVOCATIONAL INTERESTS: Visiting universities and institutions in India and abroad.

BIOGRAPHICAL/CRITICAL SOURCES:

PERIODICALS

Times Literary Supplement, November 23, 1962, February 3, 1978, February 6, 1987.

*   *   *

NAPIER, Mark
See LAFFIN, John (Alfred Charles)

*   *   *

NASH, Ronald H. 1936-

PERSONAL: Born May 27, 1936, in Cleveland, Ohio; son of Herman and Violet (Pankratz) Nash; married Betty Jane Perry, June 8, 1957; children: Jeffrey Alan, Jennifer Anne. *Education:* Barrington College, A.B., 1958; Brown University, M.A., 1960; Syracuse University, Ph.D., 1964. *Politics:* Republican. *Religion:* Baptist.

ADDRESSES: *Office*—Department of Philosophy/Religion, Western Kentucky University, Bowling Green, Ky. 42101.

CAREER: Barrington College, Barrington, R.I., instructor in philosophy, 1958-60; Houghton College, Houghton, N.Y., instructor in philosophy, 1960-62; Syracuse University, Syracuse, N.Y., instructor in philosophy, 1963-64; Western Kentucky University, Bowling Green, 1964—, began as associate professor, currently professor of philosophy. Baptist minister in churches in Penn Yan, N.Y., and Fall River, Mass., five years; has lectured in England, Wales, Ireland, and Scotland.

WRITINGS:

Dooyeweerd and the Amsterdam Philosophy, Zondervan, 1962.
The New Evangelicalism, Zondervan, 1963.
(Editor) The Philosophy of Gordon H. Clark: A Festschrift, Presbyterian & Reformed, 1968.
The Light of the Mind: St. Augustine's Theory of Knowledge, University of Kentucky Press, 1969.
(Editor) Ideas of History, Dutton, 1969.
(Contributor) Christianity and the Counter-Culture, Inter-Varsity Press, 1973.
Freedom, Justice, and the State, University Press of America, 1980.
The Word of God and the Mind of Man, Zondervan, 1982.
The Concept of God, Zondervan, 1983.
Social Justice and the Christian Church, Mott, 1983.
Christian Faith and Historical Understanding, Zondervan, 1984.
(Editor) Liberation Theology, Mott, 1984.
Christianity and the Hellenistic World, Zondervan, 1984.
Poverty and Wealth, Crossway, 1986.
Evangelicals in America, Abingdon, 1987.
(Editor) Process Theology, Baker, 1987.
(Editor) Evangelical Renewal in the Mainline Churches, Crossway, 1987.

*   *   *

NEW, Anthony (Sherwood Brooks) 1924-

PERSONAL: Born August 14, 1924, in London, England; son of Valentine Gill (an engineer) and Grace New; married Elizabeth Pegge, April 11, 1970; children: Susannah, Nicholas. *Education:* Attended Northern Polytechnic School of Architecture, 1941-51, and Enfield Technical College, 1943-45. *Religion:* Church of England.

ADDRESSES: *Home*—26 Somerset Rd., New Barnet, Hertfordshire EN5 1RN, England. *Office*—Priory Church of St. Bartholomew the Great, West Smithfield, London EC1A 7JQ, England.

CAREER: Architect in London, England, 1951—. Robert Cromie (architect), London, assistant, 1951-56; David Stokes (architect), London, assistant, 1956-58; Seely & Paget Partnership (architects), London, partner, 1958-86. *Military service:* Royal Navy, radio mechanic, 1945-47.

MEMBER: Royal Institute of British Architects (fellow), Institution of Structural Engineers, Society of Antiquaries (fellow), Art Workers Guild, Ecclesiastical Architects and Surveyors Association, Cathedral Architects' Association, Association for Studies in Conservation of Historic Buildings, Glaziers Company.

WRITINGS:

The Observer's Book of Postage Stamps, Warne, 1967.
The Observer's Book of Cathedrals, Warne, 1972.

A Guide to the Cathedrals of Britain, Constable, 1980.
Buildings at Work, London: A Guide to State-Owned Historic Buildings, Department of Environment, 1982.
(With others) British Standard Codes of Practice on External Cleaning of Buildings, British Standards Institution, 1983.
A Guide to the Abbeys of Britain, Constable, 1985.
A Guide to the Abbeys, Priories and Collegiate Churches of Scotland, Constable, 1988.

SIDELIGHTS: Anthony New told *CA:* "My professional work is chiefly concerned with historic buildings and their preservation and conservation, and it links naturally with sideline interests in touring and recording historic buildings in photographs, sketches, and words. I am less interested in modern architecture, except where it impinges on the old, for example in the problems of adding in a style of today to a building of the last century or older.

"A lifelong interest in stamps is allied to my interest in touring and travel but even more to my interest in design generally, and I am continually bothered by the fact that people who collect stamps per se are nearly blind to their aesthetic qualities. Architecture has been called 'frozen music,' but I liken stamps to music in the sense that these two arts alone have the power to travel, to cross frontiers, and to tell us about other nation's cultures and artistic concepts. That was really the theme of my first book."

BIOGRAPHICAL/CRITICAL SOURCES:

PERIODICALS

Times Literary Supplement, July 18, 1980.

*   *   *

NORDHAM, George Washington 1929-

PERSONAL: Born February 22, 1929, in Waldwick, N.J.; son of George (an architect) and Florence (Rockett) Nordham; married Jean Andrews, April 7, 1956 (died October 13, 1969); children: John Andrews. *Education:* George Washington University, B.A., 1949; University of Pennsylvania Law School, LL.B., 1952.

ADDRESSES: *Home*—67 East Prospect St., Waldwick, N.J. 07463. *Office*—Prentice-Hall, Inc., Englewood Cliffs, N.J. 07632.

CAREER: Admitted to the Bar of New York State, 1959; Morgan Guaranty Trust Co., New York City, trust administrator, 1955-60; Richardson-Vicks, Inc., New York City, assistant treasurer, 1960-66; Binney & Smith, Inc., New York City, corporate secretary, 1966-71; Prentice-Hall, Inc., Englewood Cliffs, N.J., legal editor, 1971-73; legal administrator for private law firms in New Jersey, 1973-77; Prentice-Hall, Inc., legal editor, 1977—. *Military service:* U.S. Army, Finance Corps, 1952-55; became second lieutenant.

MEMBER: American Bar Association, New York State Bar Association.

WRITINGS:

George Washington: Vignettes and Memorabilia, Dorrance, 1977.
George Washington's Women: Mary, Martha, Sally, and 146 Others, Dorrance, 1977.
George Washington and Money, University Press of America, 1982.
George Washington and the Law, Adams Press, 1982.

George Washington: A Treasury (short stories), Adams Press, 1983.
George Washington's Religious Faith, Adams Press, 1986.
George Washington, President of the Constitutional Convention, Adams Press, 1987.

Contributor of articles to periodicals, including *Daughters of the American Revolution*.

WORK IN PROGRESS: George Washington's Presidency.

SIDELIGHTS: Sharing both birthday and moniker with the first president of the United States, George Washington Nordham has built a lifelong avocation around his namesake. A collector of Washington memorabilia, he was encouraged in his hobby by his father, who, in 1932, purchased the first item for his son's collection—a replica of Jean-Antoine Houdon's life-sized bust of George Washington, finished in gold and weighing forty pounds. Since that time Nordham's collection has grown to include more than twenty-five busts, one hundred paintings, prints, and wall plates, hundreds of commemorative coins and stamps, paper currency, and a library of more than five hundred books on the founding father. Some of the items Nordham has acquired date back to the early 1800s.

Since the publication of his books on Washington, Nordham's expertise has been sought out by historical societies, and he has exhibited his Washington paraphernalia in several New Jersey cities.

BIOGRAPHICAL/CRITICAL SOURCES:

PERIODICALS

Americana, February, 1983.
GW Times, February, 1982.
New Jersey Monthly, February, 1986.
New York, February 25, 1980.

*　　　　*　　　　*

NORMAN, Cecilia   1927-

PERSONAL: Born November 7, 1927, in London, England; daughter of Hyman (a clergyman) and Esther (a suffragette; maiden name, Lev) Miller; married Laurie Norman (a chartered surveyor); children: Dilys Tauz, Kerry Lambert. *Education:* Attended Regent Polytechnic, 1948-50; Southgate College, teaching diploma, 1968.

ADDRESSES: Home—Apple Tree Cottage, 2B, South Hill Park, Hampstead, London NW3 2SB, England.

CAREER: Teacher of home economics; lecturer in communications; authority on microwave cooking; principal of microwave cooking school.

WRITINGS:

Microwave Cookery for the Housewife, Pitman, 1974.
The Heart-Watchers Cookbook, Hippocrene Books, 1975.
Freezer to Microwave, Pitman, 1978.
Colour Book of Microwave Cookery, Octopus Books, 1978.
Crepe and Pancake Cookbook, Barnes & Jenkins, 1979.
Microwave Cooking, Octopus Books, 1979.
Faster Cooking with Magimix and Microwave, I.C.T.C., 1981.
Sociable Slimmer's Cookbook, Hutchinson, 1981.
Cecilia Norman's Microwave Cookery Course, Granada Publishing, 1982.
The Pie and Pastry Book, Granada Publishing, 1983.
Barbecue Cooking, Granada Publishing, 1984.

Food Processor Cookbook, Granada Publishing, 1984.
Good Housekeeping Step by Step Cookbook, Ebury, 1985.
Sauces, Marinades and Dressings, Macdonald, 1985.
Microwave Menus, Marks & Spencer, 1985.
Microwave Cookery for One, Grafton, 1986.
Microwave Cookery: An Experimental Approach, Oxford University Press, 1986.
Thorson Vegetarian Microwave Cookbook, March, 1987.

Cookery correspondent, *Hornsey Journal*. Contributor to *Home Economics Journal*.

WORK IN PROGRESS: A new angle on microwaving; a vegetarian gourmet book.

SIDELIGHTS: Cecilia Norman wrote *CA:* "My writing career started when my husband gave me a cookery book for a present which had typographical errors. I did not think this right and complained to the editor, who promptly invited me to write a cookery book on microwaves. 'I cannot write and I know nothing about microwaves,' I pleaded. The reply was 'Well, my dear, its up to you.'

"I rose to the challenge and have repeated this story interminably to my college students in the hope that they too will pursue, persevere and prevail, as I have done.

"A lucky break is essential and one must recognise this if it happens and take full advantage of the chance."

*　　　　*　　　　*

NORRIE, Ian   1927-

PERSONAL: Born August 3, 1927, in Southborough, England; son of James Shepherd (a chemist) and Elsie (Tapley) Norrie; married Mavis Kathleen Matthews (a teacher), April 2, 1955; children: two daughters. *Politics:* "Pragmatist." *Religion:* None.

ADDRESSES: Home—75 Crescent West, Hadley Wood, Barnet, Herts, EN4 0EQ England. *Office*—High Hill Bookshops Ltd., 6-7 High St., Hampstead, London N.W. 3, England.

CAREER: High Hill Bookshops, London, England, manager, 1956-64, managing director, 1964—. Director of High Hill Press, 1968—.

MEMBER: Society of Bookmen (chairman, 1971-73), Garrick Club.

WRITINGS:

NOVELS

Hackles Rise and Fall, Dobson, 1962.
Quentin and the Bogomils, Dobson, 1966.
Plum's Grand Tour, Macdonald & Co., 1978.

NONFICTION

(With Frank Arthur Mumby) *Publishing and Bookselling*, J. Cape, 1974.
Hampstead, Highgate Village, and Kenwood: A Short Guide, with Suggested Walks, photos by Philip Greenall, drawings by Ronald Saxby, High Hill Press, 1977, revised edition, 1983.
Hampstead: London Hill Town, High Hill Press, 1981.
Publishing and Bookselling in the Twentieth Century, Bell & Hyman, 1982, corrected edition with new preface, 1984.
Sabbatical: Doing Europe for Pleasure, High Hill Press, 1983.
A Celebration of London, photos by Dorothy Bohm, Deutsch, 1984, reprinted as *Walks around London*, 1986.

Sixty Precarious Years, National Book League, 1985.

EDITOR

The Book of Hampstead, drawings by Moy Keightley, 1960, second revised edition, photos by Christopher Oxford, Colin Penn, L. H. Reader, and Edwin Smith, High Hill Press, 1968.
The Book of the City, photos by Smith and Ronald Saxby, High Hill Press, 1961.
The Heathside Book of Hampstead and Highgate, photos by Smith and Saxby, High Hill Press, 1962.
The Book of Westminster, photos by Smith and Saxby, High Hill Press, 1964.
Writers and Hampstead, High Hill Press, 1987.

Also a guest editor of *A Celebration of Books*, National Book League, 1975.

OTHER

Contributor to *Publishing News* and *Hampstead and Highgate Express*.

BIOGRAPHICAL/CRITICAL SOURCES:

PERIODICALS

Times (London), December 5, 1985.

*   *   *

NUNN, Walter (Harris)   1942-

PERSONAL: Born February 17, 1942, in Monticello, Ark.; son of Wallace Harris (a dry cleaner) and Margaret Eileen (Wicker) Nunn; married Rosemary Jean Smee (a social worker), July 5, 1969 (divorced, 1975); married Gale Booth, August 2, 1976; children: (first marriage) Amy, Robert. *Education:* Hendrix College, B.A. (with honors), 1964; University of Kansas, M.A., 1966. *Politics:* Democrat.

ADDRESSES: Home—5 Foxhunt Trail, Little Rock, Ark. 72207. *Office*—301 Louisiana, Little Rock, Ark. 72201.

CAREER: Citizens Conference on State Legislatures, Kansas City, Mo., research assistant, 1966-67; Arkansas Constitutional Revision Study Commission, Little Rock, senior research assistant, 1967; Constitutional Convention Advisory Commission, Little Rock, director, 1968; University of Arkansas, Little Rock, instructor in political science, 1968—. Owner of governmental affairs consultant firm, 1972—; director of Academic Press of Arkansas and president of Rose Publishing Co. (both Little Rock), 1973—. Fellow of Institute of Politics in Arkansas; research director of Arkansas Constitutional Convention, 1969-70; assistant director of Arkansans for the Constitution of 1970; management information officer of Little Rock Model Cities, 1970-72. Justice of the peace in Pulaski County, 1969-73; member of Pulaski County Democratic Committee.

MEMBER: National Municipal League, Common Cause, Pulaski County Mental Health Association, Little Rock Friends of the Library, Oak Forest Property Owners Association.

WRITINGS:

State Constitutional Provisions Affecting Legislatures, Citizens Conference on State Legislatures, 1967.
(With Calvin W. Clark) *Recent and Proposed Changes in Compensation for Legislators in the Fifty States*, Citizens Conference on State Legislatures (Kansas City), 1967.
(With Kay G. Collett) *Political Paradox: Constitutional Revision in Arkansas*, National Municipal League, 1972.
(With others) *Politics in Arkansas: The Constitutional Experience*, Academic Press of Arkansas, 1972.
(Editor) *Readings in Arkansas Government*, Rose Publishing, 1973.
Arkansas' Judge Pat Mehaffy, Parkin Printing and Stationary, 1977.

WORK IN PROGRESS: Arkansas Government and Politics.

O

O'DONNELL, Kevin, Jr.   1950-

PERSONAL: Born November 29, 1950, in Cleveland, Ohio; son of Kevin (a company president) and Ellen (Blydenburgh) O'Donnell; married Lillian Tchang (a marketing manager), September 7, 1974. *Education:* Yale University, B.A., 1972.

ADDRESSES: Home and office—3828 Abbey Court, Campbell, Calif. 95008. *Agent*—Howard Morhaim, 175 Fifth Ave., Rm. 709, New York, N.Y. 10010.

CAREER: Hong Kong Baptist College, Hong Kong, lecturer in English, 1972-73; American English Language Institute, Taipei, Taiwan, instructor in English, 1973-74; free-lance writer, 1976—; *Empire* (quarterly magazine for science fiction writers), New Haven, Conn., managing editor, 1979-81, publisher, 1981-83. Member of board of directors of Sherman Court Condominium Association, 1979-84, chairman, 1979-82.

AWARDS, HONORS: Second prize from *Galileo*, 1977, for short-short story, "Do Not Go Gentle"; Prix Litteraire Mannesmann Tally, 1987, for the French edition of *ORA:CLE*.

WRITINGS:

SCIENCE FICTION

Bander Snatch, Bantam, 1979.
Mayflies, Berkley Books, 1979.
Caverns, Berkley Books, 1981.
Reefs, Berkley Books, 1981.
War of Omission, Bantam, 1982.
Lava, Berkley Books, 1982.
ORA:CLE, Berkley Books, 1984.
Cliffs, Berkley Books, 1986.
(With Mary Kittredge) *The Shelter*, Tor Books, 1987.

OTHER

Contributor of more than fifty stories and articles to science fiction and mystery magazines.

WORK IN PROGRESS: Fire on the Border, a novel, "about clones, honor, and cultural conflict."

SIDELIGHTS: Kevin O'Donnell, Jr., commented: "I have traveled widely through eastern Asia, where I lived for four years (in Seoul, South Korea, 1966-68, in Hong Kong, 1972-73, and in Taipei, Taiwan, 1973-74). My linguistic competency—now sadly atrophied—once included French, Korean, Mandarin Chinese, and survival Japanese. The major motivating forces behind my choice of career are love of language, laziness, and the desire to be my own boss. The short commute-time helped, too."

AVOCATIONAL INTERESTS: Horticulture, microcomputers.

*   *   *

O'FLAHERTY, Wendy Doniger   1940-

PERSONAL: Born November 20, 1940, in New York, N.Y.; daughter of Lester L. (a publisher) and Rita (Roth) Doniger; married Dennis M. O'Flaherty (a lawyer), March 31, 1964; children: Michael Lester. *Education:* Radcliffe College, B.A. (summa cum laude), 1962; Harvard University, M.A., 1963, Ph.D., 1968; Oxford University, D.Phil., 1973.

ADDRESSES: Office—University of Chicago Divinity School, 1025 East 58th St., Chicago, Ill. 60637.

CAREER: University of London, London, England, lecturer in School of Oriental and African Studies, 1968-75; University of California, Berkeley, visiting lecturer in South and Southeast Asian studies, 1975-77; University of Chicago, Chicago, Ill., Mircea Eliade Professor of the History of Religions, 1978—. Lecturer at Graduate Theological Union, 1976—.

MEMBER: American Oriental Society, Association of Asian Studies (director), American Academy of Religion, American Association for the Study of Religion, California Dressage Society, Phi Beta Kappa.

AWARDS, HONORS: Lucy Allen Paton prize, 1961; National Endowment for the Humanities summer stipend, 1980; Guggenheim fellow, 1980-81.

WRITINGS:

(With R. Gordon Wasson) *Soma: Divine Mushroom of Immortality,* Harcourt, 1968.
Asceticism and Eroticism in the Mythology of Siva, Oxford University Press, 1973, published as *Siva: The Erotic Ascetic,* 1981.
(Translator from Sanskrit) *Hindu Myths: A Sourcebook,* Penguin (Harmondsworth), 1975.
The Origins of Evil in Hindu Mythology, University of California Press, 1976.

(Editor) J. Duncan M. Derrett, *The Concept of Duty in South Asia*, Vikas Publishing House (New Delhi), 1978.
(Editor) *The Critical Study of Sacred Texts*, Graduate Theological Union, 1979.
Women, Androgynes, and Other Mythical Beasts, University of Chicago Press, 1980.
(Editor) *Karma and Rebirth in Classical Indian Traditions*, University of California Press, 1980.
(Translator and compiler) *The Rig Veda: An Anthology—One Hundred and Eight Hymns*, Penguin (Harmondsworth), 1981.
(With Carmel Berkson and George Michell) *Elephanta: The Cave of Shiva*, photographs by Berkson, Princeton University Press, 1983.
Dreams, Illusion, and Other Realities, University of Chicago Press, 1984.
Tales of Sex and Violence: Folklore, Sacrifice, and Danger in the Jaiminiya Brahmana, University of Chicago Press, 1985.

Contributor to Asian and Oriental studies, theology, and literary journals. Editor, *Journal of the American Academy of Religion*, 1977—, *History of Religions*, 1979—.

WORK IN PROGRESS: Ancient Indian Horsemanship.

SIDELIGHTS: For Christopher Shackle in the *Times Literary Supplement*, Wendy Doniger O'Flaherty has a "reputation as the wittiest contemporary Western interpreter of classical Indian mythology." From her early work on the sex lives of Hindu gods, *Asceticism and Eroticism in the Mythology of Siva*, to her later analysis of what ancient dream tales reveal about Indian culture, *Dreams, Illusion and Other Realities*, reviewers commend O'Flaherty for making a major contribution to Indology: "Her unrivalled knowledge of classical Hindu mythology . . . provides succinct information about the gods and goddesses and other creatures. . . . One does not have to agree with some of her views, which are influenced by modern psychological research, to find them extremely stimulating," writes *Times Literary Supplement* critic J. C. Harle. O'Flaherty's work is said by reviewers to be mostly for the advanced student of Indology and mythology.

BIOGRAPHICAL/CRITICAL SOURCES:

PERIODICALS

New York Times Book Review, November 18, 1984.
Times Literary Supplement, January 18, 1974, February 6, 1976, January 13, 1978, October 31, 1980, September 4, 1981, April 13, 1984, October 25, 1985, August 29, 1986.
Village Voice, July 17, 1984.

*   *   *

O'LEVENSON, Jordan
     See LEVENSON, Jordan

*   *   *

O'REILLY, Timothy   1954-

PERSONAL: Born June 6, 1954, in Cork, Ireland; brought to the United States in 1954, naturalized citizen, 1971; son of Sean (a neurologist) and Anne (Hillam) O'Reilly; married Christina Feldmann (a writer and dancer), June 28, 1975; children: Arwen Kathryn, Meara Christina. *Education:* Harvard University, A.B. (cum laude), 1975.

ADDRESSES: Home—171 Jackson St., Newton, Mass. 02159.

CAREER: Brajer, O'Reilly & Associates (management and systems consultants), partner, 1978-81; O'Reilly & Associates, Inc. (technical writing consultants), Newton, Mass., president, 1981—.

MEMBER: Science Fiction Writers of America (affiliate member), Community for Conscious Evolution (member of board of directors, 1981), L-5 Society.

WRITINGS:

(Editor of abridgement and author of commentary) *George Simon: Notebooks, 1965-1973*, Community for Conscious Evolution, 1976.
Frank Herbert, Ungar, 1981.
(Editor with Martin Cohen) *Fragments of an Evolving Language*, Community for Conscious Evolution, 1981.
(Editor) Frank Herbert, *The Maker of Dune*, Berkley Publishing, 1987.
(With Dale Dougherty) *UNIX Text Processing*, Howard Sams, 1987.

Also author of technical manuals. Contributor to *Survey of Science Fiction Literature*.

WORK IN PROGRESS: The Mad Philosophers, translations of humorous anecdotes about the ancient Greek philosophers; *The Gift of Fire*, a biography and "philosophical apology" for the work of George Simon, pioneer researcher on consciousness.

SIDELIGHTS: Timothy O'Reilly commented: "In my writing, I want to communicate a sense of the experiential dimensions of ideas—to show truly original thought as a kind of perception, not a rehearsal of what is already known, but a participation in the unknown. I do not wish only to *talk* about such a dimension of thought, but to awaken it as I write.

"This approach is very much a product of my studies with George Simon. Watching Simon in his attempts to develop a 'language for consciousness' by distinguishing inner experiences and then finding the relationships between them, I became convinced that original thought does not come from the manipulation of other thoughts, but from grasping afresh at the nature of reality. (This is obviously true in the physical sciences, but less understood in literature and philosophy.) Simon himself has said 'perception and philosophy are one.' In my undergraduate work in classics, I studied Plato from this point of view and believe I uncovered many of the same dynamics in his work as I had seen in Simon's.

"As a literary critic, I have also been influenced by Colin Wilson, Stewart Brand, and John Cowper Powys. Each of these men in his own way appreciates books for the ideas they contain, and for the use those ideas have in enriching the life and awareness of the reader.

"As a writer of computer books, I try to help the user understand the basic principles of system operation, rather than just the mechanics. In this way the user can take more control, and hopefully get the computer to do more of the repetitive work it is especially good at."

*   *   *

ORMSBY, Frank   1947-

PERSONAL: Born October 30, 1947, in Enniskillen, Northern Ireland; son of Patrick and Anne Jane (McMahon) Ormsby; married Mary Elizabeth McCaffrey, 1968; children: Paula, Sean.

Education: Queen's University, Belfast, B.A., 1970, M.A., 1971.

ADDRESSES: Home—70 Eglantine Ave., Belfast BT9 6DY, Northern Ireland.

CAREER: Royal Belfast Academical Institution, Belfast, Northern Ireland, teacher of English, 1971—.

WRITINGS:

Ripe for Company (poems), Ulsterman Publications, 1971.
Business as Usual (poems), Ulsterman Publications, 1973.
A Store of Candles (poems), Oxford University Press, 1977.
Being Walked by a Dog (poems), Ulsterman Publications, 1978.
(Editor) *Poets from the North of Ireland*, Blackstaff Press, 1979.
A Northern Spring (poems), Secker & Warburg/Gallery Press, 1986.
(Editor) *Northern Windows: An Anthology of Ulster Autobiography*, Blackstaff Press, 1987.
(Editor) *The Long Embrace: Twentieth Century Irish Love Poems*, Blackstaff Press, 1987.

Editor of *Honest Ulsterman*, 1969—.

BIOGRAPHICAL/CRITICAL SOURCES:

PERIODICALS

Times Literary Supplement, February 15, 1980, November 21, 1986.

*   *   *

OSBORNE, Juanita Tyree   1916-

PERSONAL: Born August 31, 1916, in Irvine, Ky.; daughter of Charles G. (in railroad business) and Sally (Turpin) Tyree; married Harry C. Osborne (in insurance business), February 6, 1938; children: Jerry, Robert, Charles, Linda. *Education:* Attended Modesto Junior College. *Religion:* Presbyterian.

ADDRESSES: Home and office—1310 Stage Ave., Memphis, Tenn. 38127.

CAREER: Writer.

WRITINGS:

GOTHIC NOVELS; PUBLISHED BY BOUREGY

The Shrinking Pond, 1974.
The Wind-Bells of Lovingwood, 1974.
Rendezvous at the Hallows, 1975.
The Cottage at Barron Ridge, 1975.
Ashes of Windrow, 1976.
Shadow over Wyndham Hall, 1976.
The House on Hibiscus Hill, 1977.
Dark Season at Aerie, 1977.
Dwellers of Riven Oak, 1978.
Peril at Dorrough, 1979.
Fury of Fenlon, 1979.
The Curse of Wayfield, 1980.
The Dark Bayou, 1980.
A Nest of Hawks, 1980.
Terror at Tolliver Hall, 1981.
Cry of the Whippoorwill, 1981.
Menace at the Gate, 1982.
Walk with a Shadow, 1982.
The Hidden Fury, 1983.
Darkness at Middlebrook, 1983.

Mists of Revilla, 1983.
Menace at Brackstone, 1983.
Storm over Minitrea, 1984.
Hand of Evil, 1984.
Terror at Thor Mountain, 1984.
Heiress of Fear, 1985.
The Deadly Circle, 1985.
Voice of Vengeance, 1985.
Snare at Sycamore Grove, 1986.
Seed of Suspicion, 1986.

OTHER

Toronado (gothic novel), Ace Books, 1954.

Editor of *Scribblings* (literary magazine), Modesto Junior College, 1934-36.

WORK IN PROGRESS: The Remembering Heart; Where Danger Lies.

SIDELIGHTS: A number of Juanita Osborne's gothic romances have been published in foreign markets, including Germany and Denmark.

*   *   *

OWEN, Edmund
See TELLER, Neville

*   *   *

OZICK, Cynthia   1928-

PERSONAL: Born April 17, 1928, in New York, N.Y.; daughter of William (a pharmacist) and Celia (Regelson) Ozick; married Bernard Hallote (a lawyer), September 7, 1952; children: Rachel Sarah. *Education:* New York University, B.A. (cum laude), 1949; Ohio State University, M.A., 1950.

ADDRESSES: Home—34 Soundview St., New Rochelle, N.Y. 10805.

CAREER: Novelist, essayist, critic, translator, and author of short fiction. Filene's Department Store, Boston, Mass., advertising copywriter, 1952-53; New York University, New York City, instructor in English, 1964-65; City College of the City University of New York, New York City, distinguished artist-in-residence, 1981-82. Taught fiction workshop at Chautauqua Writers' Conference, July, 1966.

MEMBER: PEN, Authors League of America, American Academy of Arts and Sciences, Phi Beta Kappa.

AWARDS, HONORS: National Endowment for the Arts fellow, 1968; B'nai B'rith Jewish Heritage Award, Edward Lewis Wallant Memorial Award, and National Book Award nomination, all 1972, all for *The Pagan Rabbi, and Other Stories;* Jewish Book Council Award, 1972, for *The Pagan Rabbi, and Other Stories*, and 1976, for *Bloodshed and Three Novellas;* American Academy of Arts Award for Literature, 1973; O. Henry First Prize Award in fiction, 1975, 1981, and 1984; Pushcart Press Lamport Prize, 1980; Guggenheim fellow, 1982; National Book Critics Circle Award nomination, 1982 and 1983; Mildred and Harold Strauss Livings grant, American Academy and Institute of Arts and Letters, 1983; honorary degrees from Yeshiva University, 1984, Hebrew Union College, 1984, Williams College, 1986, and Hunter College of the City University of New York, 1987; Distinguished Service in Jewish Letters Award, Jewish Theological Seminary, 1984;

Distinguished Alumnus Award, New York University, 1984; PEN/Faulkner Award nomination, 1984; Phi Beta Kappa oration, Harvard University, 1985; Rea Award for the Short Story, Dungannon Foundation, 1986.

WRITINGS:

FICTION

Trust (novel), New American Library, 1966, reprinted, Dutton, 1983.
The Pagan Rabbi, and Other Stories, Knopf, 1971.
Bloodshed and Three Novellas, Knopf, 1976.
Levitation: Five Fictions, Knopf, 1982.
The Cannibal Galaxy (novel), Knopf, 1983.
The Messiah of Stockholm (novel), Knopf, 1987.

NONFICTION

Art and Ardor: Essays, Knopf, 1983.

Also author of *Metaphor and Memory* (essays), 1988.

CONTRIBUTOR

Erwin Glikes and Paul Schwaber, editors, *Of Poetry and Power: Poems Occasioned by the Presidency and by the Death of John F. Kennedy,* Basic Books, 1964.
Murray Mindlin and Chaim Bermont, editors, *Explorations: An Annual on Jewish Themes,* Quadrangle, 1968.
Harold U. Ribalow, editor, *My Name Aloud: Jewish Stories by Jewish Writers,* Yoseloff, 1969.
W. Moynihan, D. Lee, and H. Weil, editors, *Reading, Writing, and Rewriting,* revised and condensed edition, Lippincott, 1969.
Martha Foley and David Burnett, editors, *The Best American Short Stories, 1970,* Houghton, 1970.
Women in a Sexist Society, Basic Books, 1971.
·Foley, editor, *The Best American Short Stories, 1972,* Houghton, 1972.
Harry Harrison and Brian W. Aldiss, editors, *Best SF: 1971,* Putnam, 1972.
The First Ms. Reader, Warner Books, 1973.
C. Shrodes, H. Finestone, and M. Shugrue, editors, *The Conscious Reader: Readings Past and Present,* Macmillan, 1974.
Pat Rotter, editor, *Bitches and Sad Ladies: An Anthology of Fiction by and about Women,* Harper's Magazine Press, 1975.
Prize Stories 1975: The O. Henry Awards, Doubleday, 1975.
Joyce Field and Leslie Field, editors, *Bernard Malamud: A Collection of Critical Essays,* Prentice-Hall, 1975.
Foley, editor, *The Best American Short Stories, 1976,* Houghton, 1976.
Simon Wiesenthal, *The Sunflower: With a Symposium,* Schocken, 1976.
All Our Secrets Are the Same: New Fiction from Esquire Magazine, Norton, 1976.
Irving Howe, editor, *Jewish-American Stories,* Mentor, 1977.
Jeannette Webber and Joan Grumman, editors, *Woman as Writer,* Houghton, 1979.
The Penguin Book of Jewish Short Stories, Penguin, 1979.
Familiar Faces: Best Contemporary American Short Stories, Fawcett-Crest, 1979.
Robert Detweiler and Glenn Meeter, editors, *Faith and Fiction: The Modern Short Story,* Books on Demand, 1979.
Pushcart Prize V: Best of the Small Presses, 1980-1981 Edition, Pushcart Press, 1980.

Howard Schwartz and Anthony Rudolf, editors, *Voices within the Ark: The Modern Jewish Poets,* Avon, 1980.
Hortense Calisher and Shannon Ravenel, editors, *The Best American Short Stories, 1981,* Houghton, 1981.
William Abrahams, editor, *Prize Stories, 1981: The O. Henry Awards,* Prentice-Hall, 1981.
Abrahams, editor, *Prize Stories of the Seventies: From the O. Henry Awards,* Doubleday, 1981.
Jack Dunn, editor, *More Wandering Stars: An Anthology of Jewish Fantasy and Science Fiction,* Doubleday, 1981.
Susan Cahill, editor, *Motherhood: A Reader for Men and Women,* Avon, 1982.
Pushcart Prize VII: Best of the Small Presses, 1982-1983 Edition, Pushcart Press, 1982.
John Updike and Ravenel, editors, *The Best American Short Stories, 1984,* Houghton, 1984.
Abrahams, editor, *Prize Stories 1984: The O. Henry Awards,* Doubleday, 1984.
The Jewish Bible: Thirty-seven American Authors, Harcourt, 1987.

Also contributor to *Gates of the New City,* Avon.

CONTRIBUTOR OF TRANSLATIONS

Howe and Eliezer Greenberg, editors, *A Treasury of Yiddish Poetry,* Holt, 1969.
Howe and Greenberg, editors, *Voices from the Yiddish: Essays, Memoirs, Diaries,* University of Michigan Press, 1972.
Howe and Ruth Wisse, *The Penguin Book of Yiddish Verse,* Viking, 1987.

OTHER

(Author of foreword) Gertrud Kolmar, *Dark Soliloquy: The Selected Poems of Gertrud Kolmar,* Seabury, 1975.
(Author of foreword) Milton Hindus, editor, *The Worlds of Maurice Samuel: Selected Writings,* Jewish Publication Society of America, 1977.
(Author of introduction) Bill Henderson, editor, *Pushcart Prize XI: Best of the Small Presses, 1986-1987 Edition,* Pushcart Press, 1986.

Contributor to "About Books" column in *New York Times Book Review,* 1987. Contributor, under pseudonym Trudie Vocse, of article "Twenty-four Years in the Life of Lyuba Bershadskaya" to *New York Times Magazine.* Contributor of other articles, reviews, stories, poems, and translations to periodicals, including *Commentary, New Republic, Partisan Review, New Leader, New York Times Book Review, Ms., Esquire, New Yorker, American Poetry Review, Harper's,* and *New York Times Magazine.*

WORK IN PROGRESS: A novel.

SIDELIGHTS: Cynthia Ozick is "an important voice in American fiction, a woman whose intellect . . . is so impressive that it pervades the words she chooses, the stories she elects to tell, and every careful phrase and clause in which they are conveyed," writes Doris Grumbach in the *Washington Post Book World.* An acclaimed novelist, short story writer, essayist, and critic, Ozick is best known for her fiction, and in this regard "few contemporary authors have demonstrated her range, knowledge, or passion," says Diane Cole in the *Dictionary of Literary Biography.* Described by Elaine M. Kauvar in *Contemporary Literature* as a "master of the meticulous sentence and champion of the moral sense of art," Ozick writes on a variety of subjects, often mixing such elements as fantasy, mysticism, comedy, satire, and Judaic law and history, in a style that suggests a poet's perfectionism and a philosopher's dialectic. Although many of her works are steeped in Judaic culture and explore the conflict between the sacred and the profane, the epithet "Jewish writer"—as she has been called—is a misnomer according to many critics, including Ozick herself, who claims in *Art and Ardor* that the term is an oxymoron. Rather, to use the words of Robert R. Harris in *Saturday Review,* she is fundamentally a writer "obsessed with the words she puts on paper, with what it means to imagine a story and to tell it, with what fiction is. The result is a body of work at once as rich as Grace Paley's stories, as deeply rooted in Jewish folklore as Isaac Bashevis Singer's tales, [and] as comically ironic as Franz Kafka's nightmares."

While she has yet to attain the wide popularity of many best-selling authors, Ozick has attracted the attention of readers and reviewers of serious fiction ever since her first book, *Trust,* was published in 1966. Narrated by an anonymous young woman searching for real and psychological identity, *Trust* is a long, intricately plotted, literary novel about personal and political betrayal that, according to *New York Times Book Review* contributor David L. Stevenson and others, hearkens back to the tradition of Henry James, Joseph Conrad, and D. H. Lawrence. Martin Tucker points out in the *New Republic* that Ozick's "style, though shaped by the ancient moderns . . . is not self-consciously imitative. The outstanding achievement of her first novel is its play with words, its love of paradox." Other critics also praise Ozick's linguistic virtuosity in *Trust,* although several share Tucker's opinion that "sometimes the cleverness of her style is obtrusive." R. Z. Sheppard, for instance, writes in *Book Week* that *Trust* "introduces a novelist of remarkable intelligence, learning, and inventiveness—qualities that make the book an uncommonly rich reading experience, yet qualities so lavishly displayed they frequently hobble . . . Ozick's muse." Nevertheless, Sheppard believes Ozick "still manages a considerable achievement of passion and skill," and Tucker calls the novel "brilliant." Stevenson, moreover, hails the book as "that extraordinary literary entity, a first novel that is a genuine novel, wholly self-contained and produced by a rich, creative imagination."

Following *Trust,* Ozick published three award-winning collections of shorter fiction, *The Pagan Rabbi, and Other Stories, Bloodshed and Three Novellas,* and *Levitation: Five Fictions,* that firmly established her reputation as a writer of exceptional talent. In a *New York Times Book Review* article on the first of these collections, Johanna Kaplan says Ozick proves herself to be "a kind of narrative hypnotist. Her range is extraordinary; there is seemingly nothing she cannot do. Her stories contain passages of intense lyricism and brilliant, hilarious, uncontainable inventiveness—jokes, lists, letters, poems, parodies, satires." Reflecting on *Levitation* and the other two collections in the *New York Review of Books,* A. Alvarez concludes that Ozick is "a stylist in the best and most complete sense: in language, in wit, in her apprehension of reality and her curious, crooked flights of imagination. . . . Although there is nothing stiff or overcompacted about her writing . . . , she . . . has the poet's perfectionist habit of mind and obsession with language, as though one word out of place would undo the whole fabric." Such quality of invention prompts John Leonard to call the title story of *Levitation* "a masterpiece" in the *New York Times,* and leads *New York Times Book Review* contributor Leslie Epstein to regard *The Pagan Rabbi, and Other Stories* and *Bloodshed and Three Novellas* as "perhaps the finest work in short fiction by a contemporary writer."

Ozick's talent furthermore encourages *Newsweek*'s Peter S. Prescott to "fearlessly predict that when the chroniclers of our literary age catch up to what has been going on (may Ozick live to see it!), some of her stories will be reckoned among the best written in our time."

Because, as Kaplan notes, Ozick's range in these stories is so extraordinary, a brief summary cannot do them justice. Cole provides an indication of Ozick's stylistic virtuosity: "From page to page, Ozick will shift from an elevated Biblical inflection to the stilted Yiddish of the Russian immigrant to a slangy American vernacular; from sharply focused realism to fantastical flights into the supernatural. Magical transformations abound—of women into sea nymphs, trees into dryads, virile young poets into elderly androgynes." Similarly, Ozick's tales defy easy explication, in part because of their "thought-provoking dialectical quality," according to Harris and others. Carole Horn says in the *Washington Post Book World:* "You could think about the themes that run through 'Bloodshed,' 'Usurpation' and 'The Mercenary' at great length. . . . The more of the Jewish Idea, as Ozick calls it, you have at your command, the broader the levels of meaning you could explore. But you don't need that to find them interesting reading." Harris points out that because Ozick "deals with ideas—many of them steeped in Jewish Law and history—her stories are 'difficult.' But by difficult I mean only that they are not in the least bit fluffy. No word, emotion, or idea is wasted. They are weighty, consequential tales, lightened and at the same time heightened by their visionary aspects. . . . Her stories are elusive, mysterious, and disturbing. They shimmer with intelligence, they glory in language, and they puzzle."

The most frequently discussed theme in these stories is that of idol worship. "Again and again," writes Cole, ". . . characters are torn between the opposing claims of two religions. One is always pagan, whether it be the worship of nature or the idolatrous pursuit of art, whereas the other—Judaism—is sacred." Kaplan, among others, sees this theme in its broadest theological sense, as a "variant of the question: what is holy? Is it the extraordinary, that which is beyond possible human experience—dryads ('The Pagan Rabbi') or sea-nymphs ('The Dock-Witch')? Or is the holiness in life to be discovered, to be seen in what is ordinarily, blindly, unthinkingly discounted?" But Eve Ottenberg, author of a *New York Times Magazine* profile of Ozick, maintains that this theme has its greatest impact in a specifically Jewish context. "Over and over again," states Ottenberg, "[Ozick's] characters struggle, suffer, perform bizarre feats, even go mad as a result of remaining or finding out what it means to remain—culturally, and above all, religiously—Jewish in a world that for the most part is hostile. Her characters are often tempted into worshiping something other than God—namely, idols. And this struggle marks her characters with a singular aloneness—the aloneness of people who are thinking a great deal about who they are, and for whom thinking, not doing, is the most emotional and engaging aspect of their lives."

Idol worship is also the principal theme of Ozick's two subsequent novels, *The Cannibal Galaxy* and *The Messiah of Stockholm.* In fact, "idolatry is Cynthia Ozick's great theme," announces Edmund White in a *New York Times Book Review* appraisal of *The Cannibal Galaxy.* "In stories, essays and . . . in her second novel she meditates on this deep concern—the hubris of anyone who dares to rival the Creator by fashioning an idol." Harold Bloom declares in the *New York Times Book Review* that the central point of Ozick's work culminating in *The Messiah of Stockholm* has been to somehow reconcile her need to create fiction with her desire to remain a follower of the Jewish tradition. "Ozick's vision of literature," writes Bloom, "is conditioned by her anxiety about idolatry, her fear of making stories into so many idols. And her most profound insight concerns her ambivalence about the act of writing and the condemnation of the religion of art, or the worship of Moloch. This insight comes to the fore when she asks herself the combative question that governs every strong writer: 'Why do we become what we most desire to contend with?'"

As Bloom reports, Ozick's reply to this question in her early essays "was immensely bitter," and the same could be said for her early stories. The novella "Usurpation," collected in *Bloodshed and Three Novellas,* is ostensibly "a tale against tale telling," according to *Time*'s Paul Gray and others. "The thoroughly Jewish concern in this work," states Ruth R. Wisse in *Commentary,* "is the writing of fiction itself, in . . . Ozick's view an inheritance from the Gentiles and by nature an idolatrous activity. Art—in the Western tradition of truth to fiction as its own end—is against the Second Commandment, she says, and anti-Jewish in its very impulse. As a Jewish artist, . . . Ozick undertakes to subvert the aesthetic ideal by demonstrating its corrupting and arrogant presumption to truth."

Ozick has modified her position over time, though. "I've revised my thinking," she told Mervyn Rothstein of the *New York Times.* "The earlier way was an error. Now I have a better idea, I think, a larger, more penetrating thought—which I didn't come to myself. . . . Though the imagination does lead to the making of images, twist it up higher, require more of the imagination, put more pressure on it—and then and only then can you have monotheism. Because monotheism requires the highest possible imagination—in order to imagine that which no image can be made of, that which you cannot see, smell, touch. To imagine the unimaginable requires the hugest possible imagination."

Bloom considers Ozick's "triumph" in *The Messiah of Stockholm* to be "a developed awareness that her earlier view of art as idolatry was too severe. . . . The novel is a complex and fascinating meditation on the nature of writing and the responsibilities of those who choose to create—or judge—tales. Yet on a purely realistic level, it manages to capture the atmosphere of Stockholm and to be, at times, very funny indeed about the daily operations of one of the city's newspapers and Lar's [the protagonist's] peculiar detachment from everyday work and life."

In addition to these concerns, *The Messiah of Stockholm* has garnered praise for its stylistic vitality, a common characteristic of Ozick's work. Calling the book "a poetic yet often raucously comic epic" in the Chicago *Tribune Books,* Mona Simpson maintains that "of course, no work of Ozick's can be talked about without first acknowledging the simple brilliance of her prose." John Calvin Batchelor insists in the *Washington Post Book World* that *The Messiah of Stockholm* "is a superb read, with prose so deft that were it fisticuffs the author would be forbidden by law to combat mortals." But perhaps the finest compliment comes from Michiko Kakutani of the *New York Times:* "What distinguishes 'The Messiah of Stockholm' and lofts it above your run-of-the-mill philosophical novel is the author's distinctive and utterly original voice. . . . Ozick possesses an ability to mix up the surreal and the realistic, juxtapose Kafkaesque abstractions with Waugh-like comedy. Bizarre images . . . float, like figures in a Chagall painting, above precisely observed, naturalistic tableaux; and seemingly ordinary people suddenly become visionaries

capable of madness or magic. The result is fiction that has the power to delight us—and to make us think."

CA INTERVIEW

Cynthia Ozick answered *CA*'s questions by mail in April, 1986.

CA: Very early you loved stories and knew you were going to be a writer. Was there a lot of storytelling in your family?

OZICK: My mother and father led harried, anxious lives burdened by the long hours that were common for pharmacies during the Depression years. So the real storytelling came from my grandmother. I hesitate to say that she "lived with us." We simply lived together, in the extended family that seemed so natural in those times. She told stories all hours of the day: mainly of her childhood in the Russian village she had emigrated from. I remember them all. I remember, for instance, the story of how she and some other children were sent into the woods to gather mushrooms in their pinafores, and how, after a whole day of hard work heaping their harvest up in their aprons, they came home to learn that they had been picking poisonous toadstools instead. Many of her tales had lessons attached, not moralizing sermons, but simply the consequences of good and bad deeds. And she read Bible stories to me, before I could read myself. She gave me the lore and legend that belonged to these Biblical accounts—for instance, that the wickedness of Sodom included beastly behavior to guests! Tall visitors were given short beds.

My parents were unintentional storytellers. I would hear them discussing the small but stirring adventures of the people in our neighborhood, who confided their lives to our corner drugstore. When I think back to those late-night conversations, I realize that I was growing up in the middle of a Jane Austen or Trollope novel!

CA: In that lovely essay "A Drugstore in Winter" (collected in Art and Ardor) *you write about the magic of reading books and magazines in your father's pharmacy, finding in them pieces of yourself, escape from the awful reality of Public School 71, and reinforcement of the impetus to create your own fiction. Did the drugstore hours also shape the writing schedule you keep today?*

OZICK: The drugstore was shut at 1 A.M. This was certainly not unusual for those years. So it was at that hour that my parents came home, sat down at the kitchen table, and had their supper and tea. Consequently, I have never been a stranger to the night.

CA: In 1983, you won one of the first two Mildred and Harold Strauss Livings grants. Has that changed your approach to your work in any way?

OZICK: I have been relieved of teaching and lecturing, and have been given the great blessing of freedom to concentrate on reading and writing.

CA: Early on you wrote poetry, but then gave it up. Do you think the poetry writing somehow sharpened some of the skills that go into your fiction and essays?

OZICK: I think I would not have given up poetry had I been able to have a volume of it published. I tried and tried, and failed. But the poetry-impulse *is* still with me, and certainly I treat each sentence with the respect I would give to a line of a poem. I will not let it go until it is as "perfect" as I can make it.

CA: Dream and dreaming are words you often use yourself in talking about your writing. Do real dreams ever play a part in it?

OZICK: Only once did I ever put a real dream in a piece of writing. It was a nightmare. A long and horrifying set of teeth appeared up and down a human thigh. This is the only instance I know of.

CA: You told Eve Ottenberg for her New York Times Magazine article (April 10, 1983) about you that you are "hostile to the whole mystical enterprise," but still, "it's where the stories come from." Do you have any insight into how that works? Has it become clearer with time?

OZICK: In life I am simply a rationalist. I don't pursue the illogical, and I regard anything smacking of occultism as plain illusory folly. Superstitions of every kind make me lose patience. But in storytelling I am attracted to magic and mysticism and irrationalism and the strange vagaries of obsessiveness. Perhaps I've never gotten over my early rapture in the reading of fairy tales. Or perhaps stories are the true repository of the dream-mind, where illogical and irrational connections reign and sprites and spirits carry on: the underside of the controlled mind. The habitation of chaos and mystery.

CA: Do you find it hard to achieve a good balance between the solitude writers need to do the actual writing and the contact with the outside world they need to have fresh material and keep their work in perspective?

OZICK: I find I can't do without a lot of solitude. But after an extended period of such isolation, it becomes very hard to go out into the world for any occasion at all. It's like coming out of a cave into the light and blinking into the glare. Shyness gets exacerbated and I'm terrified of entering a room with people in it.

CA: Do you still see a lot of other writers?

OZICK: I see a few writers who are close both geographically and spiritually, and correspond with more.

CA: Are you continuing to study the Hebrew language and Judaic literature?

OZICK: I haven't actively studied Hebrew since college. My period of intensive reading in Jewish literature and philosophy and history was at its high point years ago, but I am still habitually drawn to such studies, especially history. It forms about a quarter of my general reading.

CA: When you talked with me for Dictionary of Literary Biography Yearbook: 1983, you said you felt you had a very small readership. Do you think it has grown since then?

OZICK: What a difficult question! Only the other day I was sent a transcript of a literary conference at which my name came up, and one of the speakers remarked, "She is a writer who is not much read in this country." I suppose this makes it sound as if I'm read in other countries! (Since we talked in 1983, there *has* been a flurry of translation and foreign pub-

lication all over Europe. Japan has been heard from, and China only last week. I feel this difference of being "noticed," of course.) But I discover that I am in the odd position of having achieved "recognition" without being in the least bit recognizable as a contemporary writer. I suppose that the only writers who become recognizable in this sense are those who are best-sellers and those who are taught in the classroom. I belong to neither of these categories. My readership, if it is large enough to be called that, remains minuscule. It's an idea I've grown used to, and I'm at an age where I can't any longer aspire toward the impossible.

CA: Can you tell me anything about the creation of your fine character Puttermesser, from Levitation? Is there a story about how she came into being?

OZICK: Puttermesser came into my head from bits and pieces, some of it autobiographical. The reading-lust is mine, I guess, and also the fudge-lust. The periodontic troubles too! The Crotona Park Library in the Bronx was the one used by my poet-uncle and his children in the 1940s; the Grand Concourse I knew from journeys to visit cousins who lived not on that broad avenue with its elegant apartment houses but off it, in a more modest Bronx setting. Some of Puttermesser's law clerk experience I took from a friend who underwent such trials, and all of her horrific miseries with the rottenness of New York City bureaucracy and patronage (all these chickens coming home to roost in the headlines nowadays) I picked up from someone very close to me who observed all this under several administrations, culminating in the current one, with its multiple scandals. And the idea of the golem came from reading the work of the great historian-philosopher of Jewish mysticism, the late Gershom Scholem. In short, Puttermesser is a ragbag of resentments, angers, memories, feelings, readings, jokes.

CA: "Shots," from the same collection, is a good story, told by your photographer-narrator. Have you done photography yourself?

OZICK: I've never "done" photography beyond the pushing of the button on the simplest and cheapest sort of camera. But I'm mysteriously lured by photographs, whether old family snapshots or the pages of photographic illustrations that often accompany literary biographies. I probably moon over the pictures in biographies as much as, or more than, the text itself.

CA: Bloodshed and Three Novellas was dedicated in part to Gordon Lish. I gather he gave you special encouragement on the book. Was he your editor?

OZICK: Gordon Lish was fiction editor of *Esquire* some time ago and began to publish my stories there. I dedicated *Bloodshed* to him partly because he had first published some of the stories in that volume, but also because he had made possible the publication of a controversial political-historical article I had written, which also appeared in *Esquire*—thanks to his strong advocacy and defense of it. We have remained good friends, and, though we rarely meet, letters fly back and forth between us, sometimes as often as once a week. We know our handwritings better than our faces, I believe.

CA: You've had a long and apparently happy relationship with the publishing house of Alfred A. Knopf. Would you like to comment on the reasons it has worked so well?

OZICK: I have been extraordinarily fortunate in my relationship with the house of Knopf. It began with the editor who published my first novel (though not with Knopf)—David Segal, a name that has become a legend. David Segal was William Gass's first publisher, for instance; he was devoted to deeply literary writers, and served them with all the idiosyncrasies of his heart and character. When David Segal died at age forty-two, Robert Gottlieb, Knopf's president, became my editor—and, I often think, my psychoanalyst! I can live for several years on a single afternoon's meeting with him. He nourishes, he supports, he understands, he causes understanding, he seizes and supplies insights. He is in possession of the double power of brilliance and kindness. I have been the recipient of unusual generosity in an industry where editors are not generally loyal to writers, i.e., to the whole work or developing body of work of a single writer. The practice is to think about the chances of one book at a time, not of the evolving vision of a writer's mind. Of course there are relentless economic reasons behind this. Bob Gottlieb for a long time spared me the logic of economics, and published books whether or not they were successful; and it goes without saying that they mostly weren't. Bob Gottlieb has been willing to go on publishing me whether or not I earned my keep, a huge act of faith that has shored me up and given me the breath to fight self-doubt and broken self-confidence. I am completely aware of how uncommon this is; I know how lucky I am, and I suffer on behalf of writer-friends who are in need of such loyalty from an editor and have not, in years of hard work, encountered it. One can't try to make art without editorial validation and encouragement. Bill Whitehead, formerly of Dutton and the founder of Dutton's paperback Obelisk line, is another editor whose backing (or paperbacking!) has brought light into my life. A writer works alone, but publishers are the bridge over the dark waters.

CA: What book review periodicals do you read and consider well done?

OZICK: I read the *New York Times Book Review, New York Review of Books, American Poetry Review,* and *American Book Review.* The reviews in the *New Republic* and the *New Leader* seem generally excellent. I also keep up with the reviews in *Harper's,* the *Atlantic,* the *New Yorker,* and *Commentary.* The book review as an essay of ideas seems to me to be in good health nowadays.

CA: Do you think we're getting away from what you've called the Ovarian Theory of Literature?

OZICK: No, I think we're drowning in it more and more. Oh, the paradox of it! It used to be the mode of anti-feminist writers to make a point of "women writers" and their psychological and experiential peculiarities. The aim of classical feminism was to put an end to such discriminatory thinking. Instead, the women's movement as currently conceived has come along to instigate and inflame the old prejudices *in the name of* feminism. I've written an essay on this: it appears in *Art and Ardor* and is called "Literature and the Politics of Sex: A Dissent." There I lament how "the pure, unqualified, unpolemical, unpoliticized word 'writer' begins all over again to refer to only half the writers there are." In fact, the Ovarian Theory of Literature and its segregationist politics has by now made a clean sweep of American universities. It was anti-feminist when practiced by bigoted males, and it remains anti-feminist even though implemented by so-called feminists. I used to think that in the end it would be detrimental to literature and writing.

But now I think the end is already with us; the damage has already been done, and will have its effects for a long time to come. When the community of writers is divided into two camps, "writers" and "women writers," and the "writers" are all men, how is *that* feminist progress? How can this be good for literature, which has always been a means of hope to unite humankind?

CA: At the PEN Congress in New York in January, 1986, there was a protest by some of the writers because so few women had been included on the panels. Could you talk about what happened, and what the outcome has been?

OZICK: Clearly there were very few women visible on the panels. But it seemed to me that the observation of the naked eye was not in this instance sufficient research, and the protest was launched without any reasonable investigation. A list of names of distinguished intellectuals was read out (by, as I recall, PEN President Norman Mailer), all of them women who had been invited to participate and who, for one reason or another not disclosed, had declined. Certainly the egregious absence of women on the panels ought to have been noted; but the protest, with its declamatory "We demand" tones of outrage, appeared premature. How can a reasoned judgment be made without information? It's equally true that no information was being provided by the Congress's organizers during the period of the protest itself, or, for all I've been able to discover, in the months since. I was myself invited to moderate a panel of East European writers, and declined because I did not know the work of all of them and felt improperly qualified. But I did participate in this same panel as a reader (and yes, as the only woman), and I remember the organizer telling me on the telephone, "We're desperately trying to get more women"—which suggests a genuine effort. The hugely critical questions remain unanswered until this moment: how many women were invited, what are their names, what countries did they represent, and, had they all accepted, would they have made an important difference on the panels?

After all, a similar argument can be made that many of the panels were improperly balanced (if such a balance is a just intent) on other not insignificant grounds: a representative range of the political spectrum was surely not to be found at the PEN Congress, at least not on the panels. V. S. Naipaul, for example (was he asked? did he refuse?), was not present to set his views against those of his fellow Indian, Salman Rushdie; the underrepresentation of women was not the only conspicuous omission. And certainly unpopular views were not only underrepresented but discounted, as I sadly found out when I tried to offer a statement of the record of former Austrian Chancellor Bruno Kreisky, a panel member, relative to his support for PLO and Libyan terrorist leadership. (I am sorry to say that a statement against the sources of terrorist action, the only one presented, constituted an "unpopular view" at the PEN Congress.)

Because there was no information attached to the "We protest" and "We demand" formulation of the women's position paper, and because it seemed to seek out agitation before discourse, I could not sign it. Instead, I submitted a separate statement (it immediately got lost in the waves of activity), in which I remarked on two forms of injustice. The first occurs when women are excluded solely on the basis of sex. The second occurs when women are included solely on the basis of sex. Both versions seem to me to be equally pernicious. As Susan Sontag commented, "Talent is not an equal opportunity employer."

You ask about the "outcome." One result that I know of was the convening of a meeting designed to air the whole problem of why women were underrepresented on the panels. The rule adopted for this meeting was that no men might attend. It struck me as odd, to say the least, that a protest involving exclusion on the basis of sex should itself commit an identical abuse.

The PEN Congress was one-sided in many respects. As an organization purporting to represent the diverse world community of writers, PEN is in need of major self-examination. If the women's protest, flawed as it was, helps bring about PEN's improved understanding of its mandate, I suppose something good will have come out of a precipitate action undertaken without facts. That the panels lacked women *was* a fact, but whether it was the controlling fact has never been established, and months after the Congress has turned into history (political, not literary, history), no one seems to know what really happened, and why.

CA: The Cannibal Galaxy was your first novel since Trust, and a gem of a book. How did you feel going back to the novel form?

OZICK: Joyful. I have since completed another novel about the same length as *The Cannibal Galaxy*. It is set in Sweden and is called *The Messiah of Stockholm*. I haven't yet typed it up for submission (no advent of the Computer Age here!), and plan to begin after the last word of this interview. It is one of my life's regrets that I haven't written enough fiction; certainly not enough novels.

CA: Can you tell at the beginning of a piece of work what length it's likely going to end up?

OZICK: Well, I began *The Messiah of Stockholm* thinking it was going to be a *very* short story that would take about two or three weeks to write. A year-and-a-quarter later, it appears to be a novel. And I had no idea it was heading toward that. Somewhere in the middle I realized this had occurred, but since I had already started another novel, I felt guilty and unhappy all the way through. Retrospectively, however, I am glad to have turned out another novel, even if accidentally. And now I have the interrupted novel to go on with.

BIOGRAPHICAL/CRITICAL SOURCES:

BOOKS

Alexander, Edward, *The Resonance of Dust: Essays on Holocaust Literature and Jewish Fate*, Ohio State University Press, 1979.

Berger, Alan L., *Crisis and Covenant: The Holocaust in American Jewish Fiction*, New York State University Press, 1985.

Bloom, Harold, editor, *Cynthia Ozick*, Chelsea House, 1986.

Cohen, Sarah Blacher, *Comic Relief: Humor in Contemporary American Literature*, University of Illinois Press, 1978.

Contemporary Literary Criticism, Gale, Volume III, 1975, Volume VII, 1977, Volume XXVIII, 1984.

Dictionary of Literary Biography, Volume XXVIII: *Twentieth-Century American-Jewish Fiction Writers*, Gale, 1984.

Dictionary of Literary Biography Yearbook, Gale, *1982*, 1983, *1983*, 1984.

Ozick, Cynthia, *Art and Ardor*, Knopf, 1983.

Pinksker, Sanford, *The Uncompromising Fictions of Cynthia Ozick*, University of Missouri Press, 1987.

Rainwater, Catherine and William J. Scheick, editors, *Three Contemporary Women Novelists: Hazzard, Ozick, and Redmon*, University of Texas Press, 1983.

Rainwater, Catherine and William J. Scheick, editors, *Contemporary Women Writers*, University of Kentucky, 1985.

PERIODICALS

Book World, June 19, 1966.

Chicago Tribune Book World, February 14, 1982, October 30, 1983.

Commentary, June, 1976, March, 1984, May, 1984.

Commonweal, December 2, 1966, September 3, 1971.

Contemporary Literature, spring, 1985, winter, 1985.

Critique, Volume IX, number 2, 1967.

Hudson Review, spring, 1984.

Los Angeles Times, March 11, 1987.

Los Angeles Times Book Review, May 29, 1983, September 18, 1983.

Nation, February 20, 1982, July 23-30, 1983.

New Republic, August 13, 1966, June 5, 1976.

Newsweek, May 10, 1971, April 12, 1976, February 15, 1982, May 30, 1983, September 12, 1983.

New York Review of Books, April 1, 1976, May 13, 1982, November 30, 1983, May 28, 1987.

New York Times, July 9, 1966, July 5, 1971, January 28, 1982, April 27, 1983, August 29, 1983, March 25, 1987, March 28, 1987.

New York Times Book Review, July 17, 1966, June 13, 1971, April 11, 1976, January 31, 1982, February 14, 1982, May 22, 1983, September 11, 1983, March 22, 1987.

New York Times Magazine, April 10, 1983.

Publishers Weekly, March 27, 1987.

Saturday Review, July 9, 1966, February, 1982.

Time, August 12, 1966, April 12, 1976, February 15, 1982, September 5, 1983.

Times (London), April 8, 1982.

Times Literary Supplement, January 26, 1967, April 23, 1982, January 20, 1984.

Tribune Books (Chicago), March 1, 1987.

Village Voice, February 10, 1982.

Washington Post Book World, June 6, 1971, March 13, 1977, February 28, 1982, July 3, 1983, September 25, 1983, March 8, 1987.

—*Sketch by James G. Lesniak*

—*Interview by Jean W. Ross*

P

PACKARD, Jerrold M(ichael) 1943-

PERSONAL: Born May 14, 1943, in Orange, Calif.; son of Lee R. (a printer) and Elizabeth (Miller) Packard. *Education:* Portland State University, B.A., 1967.

ADDRESSES: Home—Portland, Ore. *Agent*—Frederick Hill Associates, 2237 Union St., San Francisco, Calif. 94123.

CAREER: Blue Cross of Oregon, Portland, health administrator and manager of Medicare claims dept., 1969-73; Blue Cross of Northern California, Oakland, health administrator and utilization review manager, 1973-76; independent rare-book dealer in San Francisco, Calif., 1976-80; writer, 1980—. *Military service:* U.S. Air Force, 1961-65; became sergeant.

MEMBER: Authors League of America, Authors Guild.

WRITINGS:

The Queen and Her Court: A Guide to the British Monarchy Today (alternate selection of Book-of-the-Month Club), Scribner, 1981.
American Monarchy: A Social Guide to the Presidency, Delacorte, 1983.
Peter's Kingdom: Inside the Papal City (main selection of Catholic Digest Book Club), Scribner, 1985.
Sons of Heaven: A Portrait of the Japanese Monarchy, Scribner, 1987.

*   *   *

PAGELS, Heinz R(udolf) 1939-

PERSONAL: Born February 19, 1939, in New York, N.Y.; son of Heinz (an engineer) and Marie (Rosing) Pagels; married Elaine Hiesey (a professor of religion), June 7, 1969; children: Sarah. *Education:* Princeton University, A.B., 1960; Stanford University, Ph.D., 1965.

ADDRESSES: Office—New York Academy of Sciences, 2 East 63rd St., New York, N.Y. 10021. *Agent*—John Brockman Associates Inc., 2307 Broadway, New York, N.Y. 10024.

CAREER: University of North Carolina, Chapel Hill, research associate in theoretical physics, 1965-66; Rockefeller University, New York City, research associate, 1966-67, assistant professor, 1967-68, associate professor, 1968-80, adjunct professor of theoretical physics, 1980—; New York Academy of Sciences, New York City, executive director, 1980—. Member of board of trustees of Aspen Center for Physics, 1973-81; consultant to Brookhaven National Laboratory and Los Alamos National Laboratories.

MEMBER: International League for Human Rights (member of board of trustees, 1978—), Marconi International Council (trustee, 1981—), National Association of Science Writers (trustee, 1985—), Helsinki Watch (trustee, 1984—), American Physical Society, New York Academy of Sciences (member of board of governors, 1976—; vice-president, 1976-81; president, 1981; chairman of Physical Science Division, 1972-75, and human rights committee, 1976—), New York Hall of Science (trustee, 1981—).

AWARDS, HONORS: Sloan Foundation fellow, 1967-69; American Book Award nomination, 1983, for *The Cosmic Code: Quantum Physics as the Language of Nature.*

WRITINGS:

The Cosmic Code: Quantum Physics as the Language of Nature, Simon & Schuster, 1982.
(Editor) *Computer Culture: The Scientific, Intellectual, and Social Impact of the Computer,* New York Academy of Sciences, 1984.
Perfect Symmetry: The Search for the Beginning of Time, Simon & Schuster, 1985.

WORK IN PROGRESS: The Dreams of Reason: The Rise of the Sciences of Complexity.

SIDELIGHTS: Quantum physics, based on a concept of the physical universe as a structure of particles, is for Heinz R. Pagels the key to understanding the universe. In *The Cosmic Code: Quantum Physics as the Language of Nature,* Pagels declares, "The universe is a message, a message I call the cosmic code, and the job of scientists is to read the message. . . . The universe has a definite structure, from its largest to its smallest elements, and . . . this structure can be known by the human mind." In *The Cosmic Code* Pagels presents to the general reader his explanation of quantum physics and demonstrates the impact of quantum theory on technology and society. Then, according to Bart Everett in the *Los Angeles Times,* Pagels "announces in plain language that we are on the threshold of a new synthesis, a new physics."

306

"In one sense," Everett continued, "Pagels has written a lay history of the development of quantum theory . . . with excursions into philosophy and religion." Physics professor David Park, writing in the *Washington Post Book World*, criticized this aspect of *The Cosmic Code:* "To lead us into his subject Pagels gives us several chapters of historical introduction. They are pretty awful. History is not a discipline for Mr. Pagels." Park found other aspects of Pagels's book satisfying, however. He conceded: "Still, the book improves as it proceeds, and it is a good place to learn the modern ideas if one can stand the noise." Everett praised the book's inclusion of anecdotes and personal profiles, deeming them "at once understandable and lyrical." And Park concluded that *The Cosmic Code* reaches out "toward a reader who is interested in knowing where and what we are in the created universe, and what it means to know."

Pagels followed *The Cosmic Code* with *Perfect Symmetry: The Search for the Beginning of Time*, which, according to David N. Schramm in the *New York Times Book Review*, "is an attempt by a well-known elementary particle physicist to look at the first moments after creation [of the universe] and even to look at the creation event itself." Pagels claims that with the synthesis of the two scientific disciplines known as quantum physics and astrophysics, the origin of the universe can be explained mathematically and rationally. Even though astrophysicists have known for a long time that the universe is not perfectly symmetric, Pagels believes quantum physics introduces the possibility that the universe at the time of creation was perfect until the events of the Big Bang unfolded. *Washington Post Book World* reviewer Michael Guillen feels "Pagels' thesis in *Perfect Symmetry* is that we are at the threshold of being able to settle this possibility one way or the other." Whereas Guillen feels Pagels has backed his thesis with authority, it is also his feeling that Pagels may be overly optimistic concerning the cosmological resolutions of the near future: "Quantum physics . . . has created nearly as many compelling mysteries as it has resolved." *Times Literary Supplement* critic John Polkinghorne applauds Pagels for the inclusion of some "mildly philosophical comments at the end [of *Perfect Symmetry*]. Pagels is something of a scientific triumphalist, proclaiming 'nothing stands in the way of a rational description of the very origin of the universe, and someday this will be achieved."

Pagels told *CA:* "I want to communicate scientific ideas to non-scientists. Especially I want to describe the way in which science alters our intellectual culture and the perception of reality."

AVOCATIONAL INTERESTS: Mountains, hiking, climbing.

BIOGRAPHICAL/CRITICAL SOURCES:

BOOKS

Pagels, Heinz R., *Perfect Symmetry: The Search for the Beginning of Time*, Simon & Schuster, 1985.

PERIODICALS

Los Angeles Times, April 23, 1982.
Los Angeles Times Book Review, September 1, 1985.
New York Times Book Review, June 6, 1982, September 22, 1985.
Times Literary Supplement, July 29, 1983, November 22, 1985.
Washington Post Book World, March 28, 1982, August 25, 1985.

PALMER, Roy (Ernest) 1932-

PERSONAL: Born February 10, 1932, in Leicestershire, England; son of George Herbert (a truck driver) and Gwendoline (Cooper) Palmer; married Patricia Madin (a teacher), August 1, 1953; children: Simon James, Adam George, Thomas Eric. *Education:* University of Manchester, B.A., 1953, M.A., 1955. *Politics:* Labour Party. *Religion:* None.

ADDRESSES: Home—4 Victoria Rd., Birmingham B17 0AH, England.

CAREER: High school teacher, 1958-61, and grammar school teacher, 1961-63, both in Yorkshire, England; Shenley Court Comprehensive School, Birmingham, England, head of modern languages department, 1963-69, deputy headmaster, 1969-72; Dame Elizabeth Cadbury School, Birmingham, headmaster, 1972-83; freelance writer and lecturer, 1983—. Producer and performer on recordings and in the theater. *Military service:* British Army, 1955-57.

MEMBER: English Folk Dance and Song Society, Society for Oral History, Folklore Society.

WRITINGS:

(Contributor) *Folklore: Myths and Legends of Britain*, Reader's Digest Association, 1973.
Warwickshire Folklore, Batsford, 1976.
The Folklore of Leicestershire and Rutland, Sycamore Press, 1985.
Street Ballads in Birmingham: The Medium, the Message, the Music and the Words, Birmingham Museums and Art Galleries, 1987.
The Sound of History: Songs of Social Comment, Oxford University Press, 1988.

EDITOR

French Travellers in England, Hutchinson, 1960.
Room for Company, Cambridge University Press, 1971.
The Painful Plough, Cambridge University Press, 1972.
Songs of the Midlands, Norwood, 1972.
The Valiant Sailor, Cambridge University Press, 1973.
Love Is Pleasing, Cambridge University Press, 1974.
Poverty Knock, Cambridge University Press, 1974.
A Touch on the Times, Penguin, 1974.
(With Jon Raven) *The Rigs of the Fair*, Cambridge University Press, 1976.
The Rambling Soldier, Penguin, 1977.
(With A. Adams and R. Leach) *Feasts and Seasons*, four volumes, Blackie & Son, 1977-78.
(With R. Leach) *Folk Music in School*, Cambridge University Press, 1978.
A Ballad History of England, Batsford, 1979.
Birmingham Ballads, Birmingham Education Department, 1979.
Everyman's Book of English Country Songs, Dent, 1979, reissued as *The English Country Songbook*, Music Sales, 1985.
Everyman's Book of British Ballads, Dent, 1981.
Manchester Ballads, Manchester Education Department, 1982.
Folksongs Collected by Ralph Vaughan Williams, Dent, 1983.
The Oxford Book of Sea Songs, Oxford University Press, 1986.
British Soldiers' Songs of the Twentieth Century, Routledge & Kegan Paul, 1988.

OTHER

Also author of nine radio programs on the subjects of street ballads, Wellington's Army, the Battle of Waterloo, and songs of the Spanish Civil War, for British Broadcasting Corp., 1982,

1983, and 1986. Contributor of articles and reviews to magazines. Member of editorial board of *Folk Music Journal*.

WORK IN PROGRESS: A book on the folklore of Worcestershire; editing, with John Goodacre, "a manuscript ballad opera of the eighteenth century"; and the script "for an audio-cassette introducing English folk song to young people," for Sussex Publications.

SIDELIGHTS: Roy Palmer has produced, and performed for, Topic Records albums, "The Wide Midlands," 1971, "The Painful Plough," 1972, and "Room for Company," 1972; he produced "George Dunn," 1974, and "Cecilia Costello," 1975, both for Leader Records. Palmer was musical director and performer for "The Wellesbourne Tree" (a documentary drama), first produced in Birmingham, England at Cannon Hill Arts Centre, March, 1972; he has also acted as advisor to theatres, including the Traverse in Edinburgh, and the Duke of York's Theatre in Lancaster, and as song consultant to the television series, *Victorian Values* (Granada TV, 1987).

*   *   *

PAPPAS, Lou Seibert 1930-

PERSONAL: Born August 1, 1930, in Corvallis, Ore.; daughter of Emil E. (a wholesale grocer) and Norma (Helgesson) Seibert; married Nicholas Pappas (a consultant), November 21, 1956 (divorced July, 1983); children: Derek, Alexis, Christian, Niko. *Education:* Oregon State University, B.S., 1952.

ADDRESSES: Home—1201 Bryant St., Palo Alto, Calif. 94301.

CAREER: Sunset magazine, Menlo Park, Calif., staff home economist, 1952-58, 1964-71; De Anza College, Cupertin, Calif., instructor in home economics, 1972-78; food editor of *Peninsula Time Tribune*, 1978—. Consultant to western food firms, and to Ortho Books.

MEMBER: Home Economists in Business.

AWARDS, HONORS: Hope Chamberlain Award, Oregon State University, 1975; R. T. French C. Tastemaker Award, 1983, for *Vegetable Cookery*.

WRITINGS:

Crossroads of Cooking, Ritchie, 1973.
Greek Cooking, Harper, 1973.
Party Menus, Harper, 1974.
Bread Baking, Nitty Gritty Productions, 1975.
Crockery Pot Cookbook, Nitty Gritty Productions, 1975.
Egg Cookery, 101 Productions, 1976.
Casseroles/Salads, Nitty Gritty Productions, 1977.
Gourmet Cooking the Slim Way, Addison-Wesley, 1977.
International Fish Cookery, 101 Productions, 1979.
Entertaining the Slim Way, Addison-Wesley, 1979.
Cookies, Nitty Gritty Productions, 1981.
Entertaining in the Light Style, 101 Productions, 1982.
Vegetable Cookery, H.P. Books, 1982.
Creative Soups and Salads, Nitty Gritty Productions, 1983.
New American Chefs, 101 Productions, 1986.
(With Jane Horn) *Winemakers Cookbook*, Chronicle Books, 1986.

SIDELIGHTS: Lou Seibert Pappas once told *CA:* "Writing cookbooks, for me, is a great joy, an outpouring and sharing of great culinary discoveries. It is an intensive, well-disciplined time, brimming with working with great zeal. It is a way to consummate so many pleasures of travel and dining in one small compact volume. I write because I hope to bring pleasure to others with simple, sophisticated, delectable dishes."

AVOCATIONAL INTERESTS: Travel (has been to Europe, the Orient, and Mexico), daily swimming, gardening.

*   *   *

PARKER, (William George) Derek 1932-

PERSONAL: Born May 27, 1932, in Looe, Cornwall, England; son of George Nevin (an agriculturist) and Ivy Vashti (Blatchford) Parker; married Julia Louise Lethbridge (a consultant astrologer and author), July 27, 1957. *Education:* Attended schools in England until seventeen. *Politics:* Social Democrat. *Religion:* Agnostic.

ADDRESSES: Home—41 Elsham Rd., London W14 8HB, England; and Severalls, Foxton, Cambridgeshire SG8 6RP, England. *Agent*—David Higham Associates Ltd., 5 Lower John St., Golden Square, London W1R 4HA, England.

CAREER: Cornishman, Penzance, Cornwall, England, reporter, 1949-54; *Western Morning News*, Plymouth, Devonshire, England, drama critic, 1955-57; TWW-TV, Cardiff, Wales, interviewer and newscaster, 1957-58; free-lance writer and broadcaster, London, England, 1958—. Has made innumerable broadcasts on British radio and television; introduced "The Paperback Programme" weekly for the BBC World Service; lecturer on the history of astrology and on contemporary and classical English poetry.

MEMBER: Radiowriters' Association, Society of Authors (member of council), Royal Academy of Dancing (member of grand council), Royal Literary Fund (registrar).

WRITINGS:

The Fall of Phaethon (poems), Zebra Press, 1954.
(With Paul Casimir) *Company of Two* (poems), Zebra Press, 1955.
Byron and His World, Vanguard, 1968.
(Editor with John Lehmann) *Selected Letters of Edith Sitwell*, Macmillan, 1970.
Astrology in the Modern World, Taplinger, 1970.
The Question of Astrology: A Personal Inquiry, Eyre & Spottiswoode, 1970.
(With wife, Julia Parker) *The Compleat Astrologer*, McGraw, 1971, reprinted as *The New Compleat Astrologer*, Crown, 1984.
(With J. Parker) *The Compleat Lover*, McGraw, 1972.
The West Country, Hastings, 1973.
(Editor) *Sacheverell Sitwell: A Symposium*, Bertram Rota, 1975.
John Donne and His World, Thames & Hudson, 1975.
Familiar to All: William Lilly and Astrology in the Seventeenth Century, J. Cape, 1975.
(With J. Parker) *The Natural History of the Chorus Girl*, Bobbs-Merrill, 1975.
(With J. Parker) *The Immortals*, McGraw, 1976.
Radio: The Great Years, David & Charles, 1977.
The Complete Zodiac Name Book, Transatlantic, 1977.
(With J. Parker) *The Story and the Song*, Elm Tree, 1979.
The West Country and the Sea, Longman, 1980.
(With J. Parker) *How Do You Know Who You Are?*, Thames & Hudson, 1980.
(Editor) *An Anthology of Erotic Verse*, Constable, 1981.
(With J. Parker) *Do It Yourself Health*, Thames & Hudson, 1982.

(Editor with William Blatchford) *Grande Horizontal*, Stein & Day, 1983, published in England as *The Memoirs of Cora Pearl*, Granada, 1983.

(Editor) *Love Confessed*, Constable, 1983.

(With J. Parker) *A History of Astrology*, Deutsch, 1983.

(With J. Parker) *Dreaming, Remembering, Interpreting, Benefitting*, Crown, 1985.

(With J. Parker) *The Traveller's Guide to the Nile Valley*, J. Cape, 1986.

God of the Dance: Vaslav Nijinsky, Thorsons, 1988.

(With J. Parker) *The Traveller's Guide to Cyprus*, J. Cape, 1988.

Prophets and Predictions, Thorsons, in press.

CONTRIBUTOR

Charles Causley, editor, *Peninsula*, MacDonald & Co., 1957.

A. Borestone, editor, *Best Poems of 1965*, Pacific Books, 1966.

Arthur Russell, editor, *Ruth Pitter: Homage to a Poet*, Rapp & Whiting, 1969.

Cecil Woolf and Jean Moorcroft Wilson, editors, *Authors Take Sides on the Falklands*, Cecil Woolf Publishers, 1982.

Alan Bold, editor, *The Sexual Dimension in Literature*, Vision Press, 1982.

OTHER

Editor of *Poetry Review*, 1965-70, and *The Author*, 1986—.

BIOGRAPHICAL/CRITICAL SOURCES:

PERIODICALS

Times Literary Supplement, January 23, 1969, December 12, 1975, October 24, 1980.

*   *   *

PARKER, Julia (Louise) 1932-

PERSONAL: Born July 27, 1932, in Plymouth, England; daughter of Lester Francis and Edna Charity (Tapson) Lethbridge; married Derek William George Parker (an author), July 27, 1957. *Education:* Attended Plymouth College of Art, 1946-52; Faculty of Astrological Studies, D.F.Astrol.S., 1967. *Politics:* Liberal. *Religion:* Agnostic.

ADDRESSES: Home—41 Elsham Rd., London W14 8HB, England. *Agent*—David Higham Associates Ltd., 5-8 Lower John St., Golden Square, London W1R 4HA, England.

CAREER: Arts and crafts teacher at Plymouth College Preparatory School, 1953-57; Hammersmith Girls' Comprehensive School, London, England, art and dance teacher, 1959-64; Faculty of Astrological Studies, London, secretary, 1967-72, president, 1973-79. Professional dancer, 1953-57; set designer for TWW-TV, Cardiff, Wales, 1957.

MEMBER: Society of Authors, Astrological Association.

WRITINGS:

(With husband, Derek Parker) *The Compleat Astrologer*, McGraw, 1971, reprinted as *The New Compleat Astrologer*, Crown, 1984.

(With D. Parker) *The Compleat Lover*, McGraw, 1972.

(With D. Parker) *The Natural History of the Chorus Girl*, Bobbs-Merrill, 1975.

(With D. Parker) *The Immortals*, McGraw, 1976.

(With D. Parker) *The Story and the Song*, Elm Tree, 1979.

(With D. Parker) *How Do Know Who You Are?*, Thames & Hudson, 1980.

The Pocket Guides to Astrology, Simon & Schuster, 1981.

(With D. Parker) *Do It Yourself Health*, Thames & Hudson, 1982.

(With D. Parker) *A History of Astrology*, Deutsch, 1983.

(With D. Parker) *Dreaming: Remembering, Interpreting, Benefitting*, Crown, 1985.

(With D. Parker) *The Traveller's Guide to the Nile Valley*, J. Cape, 1986.

(With D. Parker) *The Traveller's Guide to Cyprus*, J. Cape, 1988.

WORK IN PROGRESS: The Zodiac Family.

SIDELIGHTS: Julia Parker wrote: "I am concerned to further a much wider knowledge of astrology, educating the public away from the simplistic Sun-sign columns common in newspapers and magazines. I see astrology as a helpful discipline, furthering man's awareness of himself and his potential, making life generally easier, pointing out how we can best develop our talents, develop positive characteristics, and negate negative traits.

"Astrology apart, my interests center around the arts: I paint and sculpt, and have been involved in classical ballet, teaching, choreographing, and performing for almost all my life. For the past six years I have been studying classical guitar.

"I feel strongly there should be a change in educational methods: with increasing leisure time becoming available, the only possible way to fulfillment is going to be in increased education for leisure, and an early encouragement of skills. Often the approach in art training, in particular, is far too narrow; greater versatility should be encouraged and aimed for, and the more attention that can be given to the development of new techniques in varying media the better for all concerned."

*   *   *

PATTERSON, Ward L(amont) 1933-

PERSONAL: Born December 26, 1933, in Killbuck, Ohio; son of Raymond Floyd and Florence May (Crosby) Patterson. *Education:* Cincinnati Bible Seminary, A.B., 1956, M.A., 1958; Fort Hays Kansas State College (now Fort Hays State University), M.S., 1960; graduate study at University of Melbourne, 1961; Indiana University at Bloomington, Ph.D., 1984. *Religion:* Undenominational Christian.

ADDRESSES: Home—3649 Morningside Dr., Bloomington, Ind. 47401. *Office*—707 East Eighth, Bloomington, Ind. 47401.

CAREER: Ordained minister of Christian Church, 1958; pastor of churches in Ohio and Indiana, 1955-58, and Hays, Kan., 1958-59; Fort Hays Kansas State College (now Fort Hays State University), Hays, instructor, 1959-60; professional artist specializing in archaeological designs from the Middle East, 1965—; Indiana University at Bloomington, associate instructor in speech, 1972-75, associate minister with Campus Christian Ministry, 1974-76, campus minister, 1976—, professor of speech communication, 1986—. Exhibitor at art shows.

MEMBER: Lambda Iota Tau, Phi Kappa Phi.

AWARDS, HONORS: Rotary International student exchange fellowship, 1960, for study in Australia.

WRITINGS:

Yesterday/Today, Standard Publishing, 1974.

Struggle, Crisis, and Victory, Standard Publishing, 1975.
At the Testing Tree, Standard Publishing, 1978.
Wonders in the Midst, Standard Publishing, 1979.
The Morality Maze, Standard Publishing, 1982.
(Contributor) *Your Family*, Inter-Varsity Press, 1982.
Triumph over Temptation, Standard Publishing, 1984.
Crisis in Genesis, Standard Publishing, 1985.
Under His Wings, Accent Books, 1986.
(Contributor) Andres Tapia, editor, *Guide to Campus Evangelism*, Inter-Varsity Press, 1987.
Out of His Heart, Accent Books, 1987.
Into His Love, Accent Books, 1988.

Also author of studies on ethics and leadership for Standard Publishing's "New Life Teen Studies" series. Creator of "The Adventures of Alan West," an illustrated comic strip for young people. Curriculum writer for Standard Publishing. Contributor to *Christian Standard, His, Lookout, Devotions,* and *Seek.*

WORK IN PROGRESS: Research on early Egyptian, Persian, Mesopotamian, and Greek art; dissertation on Grady Nutt and religious humor.

SIDELIGHTS: Ward L. Patterson writes: "My interests concern religion, history, archaeology, art, and travel. I spent nine years abroad, traveling for seven years on a 1946 motorcycle on which I visited over thirty countries of the Middle and Far East." He has trekked 500 miles into the high Himalayas of Nepal in order to reach Mount Everest, stayed in northern Afghan villages, climbed Mount Ararat, crewed on a yacht in the Mediterranean, worked as an extra in a movie being shot by Twentieth Century-Fox in Tunisia, and made a living as a "grave-rubber" in Egypt. He has acquired an extensive collection of rubbings of ancient Middle Eastern bas-reliefs.

More recently, Patterson combines his writing career with his duties as a minister and professor at Indiana University. He continues: "I find that the students and the college atmosphere stimulate me and help keep me in tune with contemporary trends in our society.

"My writing centers on religious subjects, though I am very interested in communication and leadership research. My graduate research has taken me into the area of religious humor and I hope to write more extensively on this subject. I find much personal fulfillment in writing, though I also find it laborious."

BIOGRAPHICAL/CRITICAL SOURCES:

PERIODICALS

Rotarian, October, 1972.

*   *   *

PEARL, Jack
    See PEARL, Jacques Bain

*   *   *

PEARL, Jacques Bain   1923-
    (Jack Pearl; pseudonyms: Stephanie Blake, Tricia Stevens, Trisha Stevens; Jake Logan, a house pseudonym)

PERSONAL: Born September 12, 1923, in Richmond Hill, N.Y.; son of Harold H. (an inventor) and Ada (Swales) Bain; married June Hewes, September 14, 1947; children: Jill, Janet.

Education: Columbia University, A.B., 1949, M.A., 1950. *Politics:* Democrat. *Religion:* Episcopal.

ADDRESSES: Home—915 Iris Dr., North Bellmore, N.Y. 11710. *Agent*—Scott Meredith Literary Agency, 580 Fifth Ave., New York, N.Y. 10036.

CAREER: Part-time advertising copywriter, 1947-50; "Gangbusters" television show, New York City, editor, 1952-53; MacFadden Publications, New York City, editor of *Saga,* 1953-60; free-lance writer, 1961—. *Military service:* U.S. Army, World War II; served in Africa, Sicily, and Italy.

MEMBER: Writers Guild of America, East.

WRITINGS:

UNDER NAME JACK PEARL

Blood-and-Guts Patton: The Swashbuckling Life Story of America's Most Daring and Controversial General, Monarch, 1961.
General Douglas MacArthur, Monarch, 1961.
Bruce Larkin, Air Force Cadet, Hammond, 1962.
Aerial Dogfights of World War II, Monarch, 1962.
The Young Falcons, Hammond, 1962.
Admiral "Bull" Halsey, Monarch, 1962.
Great Air Battles of World War II, Monarch, 1963.
Battleground, World War I: The Exciting Saga of the A.E.F. in France, Monarch, 1964.
The Dangerous Assassins, Monarch, 1964.
Stockade, Trident Press, 1964.
The Crucifixion of Pete McCabe, Trident Press, 1966.
The Space Eagle: Operation Doomsday, illustrated by Arnie Kohn, Whitman Publishing, 1967.
Garrison's Gorillas and the Fear Formula (based on television series), illustrated by Harvey Kidder, Whitman Publishing, 1968.
(With Edward Linn) *Masque of Honor,* Norton, 1969.
A Time to Kill . . . a Time to Die: A Novel, Norton, 1971.
The Plot to Kill the President, Pinnacle Books, 1972.
Victims: A Novel, Trident Press, 1972.
The Cops, Pinnacle Books, 1972.
Pollution Solution Revolution, Pyramid, 1972.
The Firefighters, Pinnacle Books, 1973.
Callie Knight (also see below), Saturday Review Press, 1974.
A Jury of His Peers: A Novel, Prentice-Hall, 1975.
Lepke, Pocket Books, 1975.
(With Nick Vasile) *Sado Cop,* Playboy Press, 1976.
(With David Toma) *The Affair of the Unhappy Hooker,* Dell, 1976.

Also author of *Divorce Court, No. 1* and *Divorce Court, No. 2,* Pocket Books, *Nancy,* Pyramid, *Exodus of the Damned* (novel), New American Library, and *Touch Us Not in Pity* (novel), Saturday Review Press; author of "Blood and Guts Patton," a film adaptation of *Blood and Guts Patton: The Swashbuckling Life Story of America's Most Daring and Controversial General,* Twentieth Century-Fox. Contributor of more than two hundred short stories and articles to magazines.

UNDER NAME JACK PEARL; NOVELIZATIONS OF MOTION PICTURE SCRIPTS

Robin and the Seven Hoods, Pocket Books, 1964.
The Yellow Rolls Royce, Pocket Books, 1965, reprinted, Amereon, c. 1987.
Our Man Flint, Pocket Books, 1965.
Ambush Bay, New American Library, 1966.
Garrison's Gorillas, Dell, 1967.

Funny Girl, Pocket Books, 1968.

UNDER PSEUDONYM STEPHANIE BLAKE

Flowers of Fire, Playboy Press, 1977.
Daughter of Destiny, Playboy Press, 1977.
Blaze of Passion, Playboy Press, 1978.
So Wicked My Desire, Playboy Press, 1979.
Secret Sins, Playboy Press, 1980.
Wicked Is My Flesh, Playboy Press, 1980.
Scarlet Kisses, Playboy Press, 1981.
Unholy Desires, Playboy Press, 1981.
Fires of the Heart, Playboy Press, 1982.
Callie Knight, Playboy Press, 1982.
A Glorious Passion, Jove, 1983.
Bride of the Wind, Jove, 1984.
Texas Lily, Jove, c. 1987.

OTHER

(Under pseudonym Tricia Stevens) *Hooker for a Day*, Pocket Books, 1975.
(Under pseudonym Trisha Stevens) *Bar Belles*, Pocket Books, 1976.

Also author of books under house pseudonym Jake Logan.

BIOGRAPHICAL/CRITICAL SOURCES:

PERIODICALS

First Novelist, spring, 1965.
New York Times, November 7, 1969.
Variety, October 28, 1960.

*   *   *

PERCY, Walker   1916-

PERSONAL: Born May 28, 1916, in Birmingham, Ala.; son of Leroy Pratt and Martha (Phinizy) Percy; married Mary Bernice Townsend, November 7, 1946; children: Ann Boyd, Mary Pratt. *Education:* University of North Carolina, B.A., 1937; Columbia University, M.D., 1941.

ADDRESSES: Home—Old Landing Rd., Covington, La. 70433. *Agent*—McIntosh & Otis, Inc., 475 Fifth Ave., New York, N.Y. 10017.

CAREER: Author.

MEMBER: American Academy and Institute of Arts and Letters (fellow).

AWARDS, HONORS: National Book Award for fiction, 1962, for *The Moviegoer*; National Book Award nomination, 1966, for *The Lost Gentleman*; National Institute of Arts and Letters grant, 1967; National Catholic Book Award, 1971, for *Love in the Ruins*; *Los Angeles Times* Book Prize, 1980, National Book Critics Circle citation, 1980, American Book Award nomination, 1981, Notable Book citation from American Library Association, 1981, and P.E.N./Faulkner Award nomination, 1981, all for *The Second Coming*; *Los Angeles Times* Book Prize for current interest, 1983, for *Lost in the Cosmos: The Last Self-Help Book*; St. Louis Literary Award, 1986.

WRITINGS:

FICTION

The Moviegoer, Knopf, 1961, reprinted, Avon, 1980.
The Last Gentleman, Farrar, Straus, 1966, reprinted, Avon, 1978.

Love in the Ruins: The Adventures of a Bad Catholic at a Time near the End of the World, Farrar, Straus, 1971, reprinted, Avon, 1978.
Lancelot, Farrar, Straus, 1977.
The Second Coming, Farrar, Straus, 1980.
The Thanatos Syndrome (Book-of-the-Month Club selection), Farrar, Straus, 1987.

NONFICTION

The Message in the Bottle: How Queer Man Is, How Queer Language Is, and What One Has to Do with the Other, Farrar, Straus, 1975.
Lost in the Cosmos: The Last Self-Help Book, Farrar, Straus, 1983.
Novel-Writing in an Apocalyptic Time (limited edition), Faust Publishing Company, 1986.

OTHER

(Author of introduction) William Alexander Percy, *Lanterns on the Levee: Recollections of a Planter's Son*, Louisiana State University Press, 1974.

Contributor of essays to scholarly journals and popular periodicals, including *Esquire, Commonweal, America, Harper's, Georgia Review, Saturday Review, Michigan Quarterly Review*, and *Personalist*.

SIDELIGHTS: Walker Percy is a highly respected American author who, through more than thirty years of writing, has balanced interesting, accessible fiction with serious ideas. With an "intellectual range and vigor few American novelists can match," to quote *New York Times Book Review* contributor Thomas LeClair, Percy seeks to understand the peculiar *angst* of the modern individual, adrift in the twentieth century. He uses novels to unite empirical practice with existentialist perception in the manner of some modern European writers, but his fictional milieus are invariably American—the fairways, subdivisions, and country clubs of the homogenized "New South" in which he lives. *Atlantic* essayist Richard Todd describes the author's theme as "the search for whatever it is that can banish despair" in this era when science and technology alleviate physical suffering but offer no solutions to spiritual crises. "Percy has spent his entire career debriding the same wound," Todd notes. "His work is narrow but it cuts deep." Since the publication of his National Book Award-winning novel *The Moviegoer* in 1961, the Alabama native has "claimed a position, never relinquished, as not only a major Southern novelist, but as one of the unique voices in American fiction," according to Malcolm Jones in the *New York Times Magazine*. As Charles Poore notes in the *New York Times*, Percy "shows us the modern world through the distorting mirrors that the modern world foolishly calls reality." Gail Godwin offers a concurrent description in the *New York Times Book Review*. "Walker Percy," Godwin writes, "has the rare gift of being able to dramatize metaphysics."

Epithets abound in critiques of Percy's work. The writer has been called "the moralist of the deep South," "the doctor of the soul," and even "the Dixie Kierkegaard." Simplistic as such appellations might seem, they nevertheless indicate Percy's central preoccupations: the nature of the cosmos and man's place in it, morality as opposed to mere civility, and sensitivity to the afflictions occasioned by the incomprehensibility of the self by itself. Jones claims that Percy "is one of our severest moralists, and one of our most philosophical novelists. . . . His [fictional] lawyers and doctors are not deaf to the imperatives of the past, but they are very much citizens of modern . . .

America, all searching for an answer to the question Percy himself once posed in an essay: 'Why does man feel so sad in the twentieth century?'" Lewis Jerome Taylor, Jr., elaborates in *Commonweal:* "Percy has keen and perceptive eyes for the despair underlying the increasing disarray of society, its root cause and its possible cure. It is not, however, knowledge about reality as such that primarily concerns him but the way by which a person can come to himself and begin to live his own life. Percy is an existentialist. A delightful thing about him, and one that continually carries over into his fictional characters, is that he is a man . . . who seems somehow to have moved into the realm of freedom."

The "realm of freedom" from which Percy works is that of the Christian—specifically Roman Catholic—faith. "Walker Percy is a Christian novelist," explains Peter Prescott in *Newsweek,* "which is not to say that he's a Christian who writes novels—there's no shortage of those—but that he's a novelist who writes about Christian concerns." Having immersed himself in the works of Christian philosophers such as Soeren Kierkegaard and Gabriel Marcel, Percy strives to convey "the Christian truth to an age for which the traditional words have worn so smooth that they no longer take effect," in Taylor's words. In a *Georgia Review* interview, Percy explains how his faith gives perspective to his writing: "To me, the Catholic view of man as pilgrim, in transit, in journey, is very compatible with the vocation of a novelist because a novelist is writing about man in transit, man as pilgrim." *New York Times Book Review* contributor John Romano takes the view that this particular perspective of Percy's "does not mean that plot and character are merely pretexts for philosophical investigations. Rather it refers to what is at stake in the outcomes of events that are tracked and lives that are examined. And although his best characters are fully realized and knowable persons, although he has brought great and careful energy to bear upon the study of a particular region of the country at a historically discreet moment, what is at stake in Percy's fiction is not finally personal or local. Instead he is testing certain concepts, traditional ones, such as the concept that one person might come to know and love another, and that language might actually assist rather than deter that process; or a concept that a life might be lived in some authentic relation to its own chief events . . . without the need to distort or repress or deny; or the concept that there are impulses, casual and shaping, that lie outside whatever scientific account we can take of ourselves."

Critics stress that Percy's Catholicism does not lead him to pen mere sermons exhorting the reader to seek Christian salvation. Instead, as Alfred Kazin notes in *Harper's,* Percy is "atypical" both as a Southerner and a Roman Catholic. "There is a singularity to his life," Kazin observes, "to his manifest search for a new religious humanism, there is a closeness to pain and extreme situations, that makes him extraordinarily 'sensitive'—to the existential theme of life as shipwreck—without suggesting weakness." In his fiction and nonfiction alike, Percy primarily diagnoses the American anomie, aware, as Kierkegaard was, that recognition of the presence of psychic woe is the first step to its cure. Prescott contends that Percy "writes about neurosis and existential terror, about malaise and the general breakdown of function in machines, in institutions and in people." Percy "started out, like any American writer, trying to capture ways of feeling," Richard Eder declares in the *Los Angeles Times Book Review.* "But Percy's hunt for contemporary pain led him to the mind. Our dramas may play out in our affections, our sex lives, our politics and

in the exercise and adornment of our egos, but their roots are in our metaphysics." Addressing himself to Percy's methods in *Walker Percy,* Jac Tharpe explains that whatever may be his character, the author "has a finely wrought ironic mind, a healthy approach to human antics through satire, and a good sense of humor" on which to build philosophical ideas central to human awareness.

Percy's youth in the deep South was far from ordinary; events from his formative years and young manhood often serve as the experiences upon which his fiction is based. He was born in 1916 in Birmingham, Alabama, and he spent his childhood there. When Percy was thirteen, his father committed suicide. His mother died two years later in an automobile accident. Percy and his two brothers were then adopted by their father's cousin, William Alexander Percy, a wealthy and learned gentleman who lived in Greenville, Mississippi. Uncle Will, as they called him, was himself a writer whose poetic memoir, *Lanterns on the Levee: Recollections of a Planter's Son* was a popular exploration of postwar gentility in the South. As a teenager, Percy encountered intellectuals of all sorts in his adoptive parent's home—historians, novelists, psychologists, and poets all enjoyed the elder Percy's hospitality. From such stimulating surroundings Percy left for college in 1934, planning to pursue a career in medicine. He studied chemistry at the University of North Carolina and in due course was admitted to medical school at the Columbia College of Physicians and Surgeons. He received his medical degree from that institution in 1941, and that same year he began his residency at Bellevue Hospital in New York City.

As a working pathologist in New York, Percy was called upon to perform autopsies on indigent alcoholics, many of whom had died of tuberculosis. Within a year Percy contracted the dreaded lung disease himself; he spent most of the following three years in a sanatorium. While convalescing he explored the humanistic interests that he had been unable to pursue during his medical training—French and Russian literature, philosophy and psychology. In 1944 Percy had recovered sufficiently to return to Columbia to teach pathology, but he suffered a relapse and decided to quit medicine. The illness was somewhat fortuitous, because Percy had become deeply interested in a whole new realm of intellectual endeavor. He told *Bookweek:* "If the first great intellectual discovery of my life was the beauty of the scientific method, surely the second was the discovery of the singular predicament of man in the very world which has been transformed by this science. An extraordinary paradox became clear: that the more science progressed and even as it benefited man, the less it said about what it is like to be a man living in the world." Percy searched for a solution to this paradox and began to consider a career, however humble, through which he could expose the unique modern conundrum. Writing provided him the means to that end. His first published works were philosophical essays that appeared in scholarly journals; these essays dealt with self-estrangement in the twentieth century, its causes and ramifications. Having married in 1946 and converted to Roman Catholicism in 1947, Percy and his wife moved to New Orleans, and then to Covington, Louisiana, living on an inheritance from a relative. When one of his children was born deaf, Percy became fascinated by a branch of philosophy that has consumed him ever since—semiotics, the study of symbols and how they are used in human communication.

Percy wrote two unpublished novels before beginning *The Moviegoer.* He finally found his fictive niche, however, when he decided to follow Albert Camus's example and write about a character who serves as "an embodiment of a certain pathology of the twentieth century," to use his own words from the *Southern Review*. He told the *New York Times* that in order to write meaningful fiction he had to overcome the American tendency "to distinguish between our reflections on our universal predicament and what can be told in fiction. . . . The French see nothing wrong with writing novels that address what they consider the deepest philosophical issues." *The Moviegoer* was published in 1961 when Percy was forty-five, and although the publisher, Alfred A. Knopf, did little to promote the book, it was discovered and accorded the National Book Award. Most critics feel that *The Moviegoer* presents most of the themes with which Percy has concerned himself in subsequent fiction and nonfiction. "What we don't see in Percy's novels is the changing vision of the world that we often get from a writer who publishes while he is young, and then continues to write," notes Andre Dubus in *Harper's*. "With *The Moviegoer* we were in the hands of a mature writer whose theme had already chosen him. He has been possessed by it ever since, and that is why he is not truly repetitious. . . . It's not repetition we're hearing, but the resonant sound of a writer grappling with his theme."

In *The Moviegoer* and subsequent novels, Percy introduces the concept of *Malaise*, a disease of "depression and despair, intensified by the awareness of a moral and metaphysical wasteland in which intellectuals claim to have outgrown the rituals and beliefs of organized religion," according to Tharpe. *Everydayness,* a term coined by Binx Bolling in *The Moviegoer*, serves as a precurser to—or substitute for—the malaise itself. Tharpe describes this condition as "the drag of uneventful, unchallenging life for those living in an environment so successful in satisfying physical needs that it encourages a man to be a content animal." Percy's protagonists move from the realm of everydayness into a search for self that brings them first to a recognition of the defects in the cult of technology, then to the awareness of shallowness in their own lives. His characters "are well-bred Southern gentlemen who, although endowed with all the trappings of contemporary comfort, are haunted by the fear that they lead meaningless and inauthentic lives," writes Francine du Plessix Gray in the *New York Times Book Review*. "They are all the more doomed because their gentility curbs them from that searing self-questioning which might jolt them into admitting their despair and exploring its roots." *Southern Review* essayist Richard Lehan suggests that Percy's fiction "takes place in a prolapsed world, often cut off from the ordinary workaday world, where characters are haunted by the past and bound by the absurdity of their situation. To this, Percy adds two states of narrative consciousness—one of perception and another of reflection—and also a sense of the grotesque. . . . Percy's alienated man is lonely and unloved, an isolated consciousness."

Coincident with their sense of alienation and inauthenticity, Percy's characters come to perceive a wider failure of human communication, the displacement of meaningful language by an array of cliches and elitist or technical jargon. In *Walker Percy: Art and Ethics*, Michael Pearson writes: "Percy's books are studies of man's inability to speak to his fellow-man, and affirmations of man's potential to communicate, to be fully human. . . . Percy asks the reader to view the mystery of language, to see that it can screen the world from sight or it can be a lens to clarify reality." Needless to say, Percy's wayfarers also neglect the divine, and consequently are apt to objectify other human beings, using or abusing them without full awareness of their humanity. At a crucial point in his search, Tharpe

notes, the Percy protagonist finds that "the world itself, made for his pleasure, has lost its value, though he cannot really escape it; and when he tries to live in it, he no longer has any familiarity with it or its ways. He cannot really operate at the transcendental realm, and his achievements and aspirations mean he is homeless in the immanent realm. Thus, he is more homeless and alienated than he ever was." According to *Dictionary of Literary Biography Yearbook 1980* contributor Joan Bischoff, this "cerebral main character shares many of the author's insights and obsessions: he is keenly aware of the paradoxes of being alive, the critical significance of language, and the corruption of contemporary American life."

How the individual has come to such an impasse in the twentieth century can be inferred from Percy's novels. The author also explores this conundrum in his nonfiction. Basically, Pearson explains, for Percy, "a careful look at language will point toward a clearer image of the human condition. All of his theories—linguistic, philosophical, and aesthetic—hinge on the central concept of symbolization. The germ of Percy's aesthetic theory begins with his disagreement with the behavioristic thesis that language can be explained as a stimulus-response mechanism. The flaw in the behavioristic thesis is that it makes no distinction between a sign and a symbol. . . . Naming sets human language apart from other forms of animal communication." In Percy's view, an investigation of the nature of language may yield a more spiritually satisfying theory about humankind than that currently propounded by the natural sciences. Scientific humanism, in fact, cannot adequately explain the sovereignty and individuality of human life, but it can serve to alienate man from his metaphysical strivings. Charles P. Bigger claims in *Walker Percy: Art and Ethics* that the author has, "with truly remarkable success, set himself to the task of restoring strangeness to the name and to ourselves, the users of names. Just as in his novels he has celebrated, often with comic irony, the violence and strangeness of man, so too through the resonance of the name he sets himself to uncover from the banalities of the behavioral sciences the peculiar mystery of being human."

A fresh perception of the uniqueness of language—of naming—is one method by which to overcome the malaise. Percy told the *Michigan Quarterly Review:* "It is the artist who at his best reverses the alienating process by the very act of seeing it clearly for what it is and naming it, and who in this act establishes a kind of community. It is a paradoxical community whose members are both alone yet not alone, who strive to become themselves and discover that there are others who, however tentatively, have undertaken the same quest." No technology, however advanced, can substitute for the quest, he told the *Washington Post*, for such searching is "integral to the human condition." Pearson writes: "It is Percy's hope that literature can be 'news,' the message that will deliver man from despair. For Percy, the 'news' is the Christian, specifically Catholic, message, but Percy is also attempting to renew faith in man as a sovereign knower in a universe of experience. . . . Percy does not view literature as a means to an end, but as an articulation of the previously unnamed."

The malaise and the alienation of self can also be overcome by love—the acceptance of another individual as a co-celebrant of being. According to Lehan, life thus becomes "a search for shared consciousness, for a communion of mind, for the affirmation of self which can only be found in the reflection of the other." Several of Percy's novels end with marriages; most end with intimations of epiphany, a divine love that will aid in the recovery of being. *New Republic* contributor Jonathan Yardley finds that as Percy's tales unwind, "there is an ultimate accommodation, an acceptance of pain in its various forms balanced, or made possible, by a discovery of love." In *Walker Percy: An American Search*, Robert Coles writes: "Every Percy novel ends on Marcel's theory of concreteness. . . . Grand designs, brilliant projects or propositions are put aside in favor of a step toward a person and a specific kind of life (a beginning of it) with that person." Without evangelizing, Percy stresses the positive ramifications of faith, good works, and family. "Tradition, accumulated wisdom," Yardley concludes, "is the bedrock. The 'deep abscesses in the soul of Western man' can be removed not by technology or theory but by the most fundamental respect for human dignity and diversity."

In the *New York Review of Books,* Thomas Nagel asserts that *The Moviegoer* "remains Percy's purest and most exact description of that malady of extreme detachment from perception and action which allows the victim to make contact with reality only when he is first dislodged, with greater or less violence, from his accustomed perch." The first-person narrative reveals the life of Binx Bolling, a Southerner of genteel background who becomes sensitive to the malaise as he goes through his middle-class routines in New Orleans. Kazin calls the work "a lean, tartly written, subtle, not very dramatic attack on the wholly bourgeois way of life and thinking in a 'gracious' and 'historic' part of the South. But instead of becoming another satire on the South's retreat from its traditions, it [is], for all the narrator's bantering light tone, an altogether tragic and curiously noble study in the loneliness of necessary human perceptions." Coles notes that at certain points in the novel, "Percy's didactic intentions appear, but never disruptively. The reader is free to glide through and beyond, simply enjoying a witty and charming Binx as he recalls his past or makes his clever appraisals." *New York Review of Books* contributor Robert Towers expresses the opinion that *The Moviegoer* is "Percy's best work, a perfect small novel whose themes, though important, are never allowed to overload the fictional craft. It is a book redolent of its time and place, a book with a thickly sensuous texture that can accommodate both the banalities of contemporary New Orleans and the glamorous aspects of Binx's now meaningless heritage. It is full of expertly realized characters." In the *Mississippi Quarterly Review,* John F. Zeugner concludes: "*The Moviegoer* seems to have been composed in joy—a muted celebration of Bolling's departure from despair. Written in the first person, shaped with a tranquil irony, *The Moviegoer* hums with the exhilaration of a man who has argued his way out of darkness."

Will Barrett, the protagonist of both *The Last Gentleman* and *The Second Coming,* must also argue his way out of darkness, but he is impeded in the first book by anmesia and in the second by attacks of heightened memory that return him to his traumatic past. Although both novels re-present Percy's philosophical and moral views, they also reveal "a man of fiction who clearly [enjoys] the old-fashioned virtues of the trade— storytelling, the amusement and edification of readers through the novelist's ability to use his imagination, conjure up all sorts of people, events, predicaments," to quote Coles. Tharpe feels that Percy uses Barrett's peculiar mental state and his social milieu as springboards from which to attack "christendom, with its two moral failures, sexual indulgence and enslavement of blacks." Those two issues are certainly explored, particularly in *The Last Gentleman,* but *New York Times Book Review* correspondent Peter Buitenhuis finds another level of

meaning in the fiction. *The Last Gentleman,* Buitenhuis writes, "succeeds brilliantly in dramatizing the contradictory nature of reality through characters who are at once typical of our condition yet saltily individual. Walker Percy's perception luminously lights up obscure depths of experience without at the same time explaining that experience easily away." In *The Second Coming* Barrett finally finds answers to his metaphysical quandary through his relationship with a young woman whose innovative use of language strengthens their bond. *Commonweal* reviewer Gerard Reedy writes: "The major change *The Second Coming* rings on the previous novels lies in its greater exploration of the peaceful, romantic images that have always been present in Percy's work and are here amplified to challenge, if not drown out, the discord of twentieth-century America." *Time* correspondent Paul Gray concludes that in all of its many convolutions, "*The Second Coming* is a meticulously crafted narrative, unobtrusively folding the distant past into a busy present."

Love in the Ruins and *The Thanatos Syndrome* also share the same protagonist—Dr. Tom More, a fictional descendant of the famous Tudor-era martyr, Sir Thomas More. Both works are set in the very near future; they reveal a morally bankrupt and politically polarized America where scientists use mechanical and technical means to distort human souls. Yardley contends that Percy's purpose "is not gloomy prognostication, though there is plenty of that. He is concerned wtih fantasizing the world as it now exists, with placing today's complaints in tomorrow's setting." *Saturday Review* contributor Joseph Catinella finds *Love in the Ruins* "a stunning satire conceived with mock-heroic intensity, peopled by absurd but recognizable human beings, and written with a gusto that makes most doomsday books look like effete comic strips." *The Thanatos Syndrome* finds More battling a group of scientists and social planners who contaminate public water supplies with a chemical that alters human nature. Malcolm Jones feels that the novel "slices deep with its uncompromising critique of the ethical, even religious pitfalls inherent in social engineering generally and euthanasia in particular." In a *Washington Post Book World* review, Yardley concludes that *The Thanatos Syndrome* is "a novel about ideas and issues that matter, a novel that looks beyond its own confines to the larger world outside, a novel that challenges the reader to think and imagine. . . . Its expansiveness and humanity are welcome reminders of what fiction can accomplish when it is written for more than the celebration of self or the adulation of a coterie."

Percy has also written two nonfiction books that present his semiotic explanation of the singular predicament of the self— *The Message in the Bottle: How Queer Man Is, How Queer Language Is, and What One Has to Do with the Other,* and *Lost in the Cosmos: The Last Self-Help Book. The Message in the Bottle* is a series of essays, some highly technical, that Percy wrote for journals over a period of twenty years; in the *Southern Review* Bigger calls it "an important work by a major novelist who is also even more impressive as a philosopher, one who lovingly seeks and strives for wisdom in and out of the conditions here and now with us in America." *Lost in the Cosmos* is clearly intended for a general audience. In a question-and-answer format, it presents a darkly humorous appraisal of the deficiencies in the comprehension of the self in an era when the sciences can explain everything else. Percy quietly mocks sex therapy, the "Phil Donahue Show," and efforts to contact extraterrestrial beings; he also explains his views on semiotics, using terms and diagrams the general reader can understand. *New Republic* reviewer Jack Beatty summarizes the work: "Our alienation from each other, our estrangement from religious faith, and our semiological pathos as the creature that can name everything in the cosmos except itself, have us in a permanently awful fix. Despite its subtitle, this book won't help, though it does contain one form of comfort: intellectual delight. It crackles with thought, ideas, exotic information." In *Time,* R. Z. Sheppard compares *Lost in the Cosmos* to Carl Sagan's *Cosmos,* a book that expresses hopes for an encounter with intelligent beings from outer space. "Percy's specialty is the gentle chiding of a generation that came of age blowing its mind and ended up blow-drying its hair," Sheppard writes. ". . . Percy's *Cosmos* is more challenging than Sagan's because the remote possibility of contacting extraterrestrials palls before a mankind that is alien to itself. Running off to the stars may be far simpler than exploring the black holes of human nature." Bigger offers this assessment of Percy's nonfiction in *Walker Percy: Art and Ethics:* "Percy once said that he wrote novels when he got philosophical cramps. One can say that his philosophy cures many philosophical cramps. By centering on one point, the mystery of naming as disclosing world, Percy has performed a remarkable service towards our recovery of strangeness. . . . The possibility of language discloses us as beings within and without the world."

Because he was born in the South and lives there still, Percy is inevitably considered a "Southern novelist," laboring within the tradition of William Faulkner, Eudora Welty, and Flannery O'Connor. Percy maintains, however, that a distinctive literature of the American South is not tenable as a concept in these days when regional impulses no longer mold the national character. "Faulkner and all the rest of them were always going on about this tragic sense of history, and we're supposed to sit on our porches and talk about it all the time," Percy told the *New York Times Book Review.* "I never did that. My South was always the New South. My first memories are of the country club, of people playing golf." Elsewhere in the *New York Times Book Review* the author added: "I lived a hundred miles from William Faulkner but he meant less to me than Albert Camus." Indeed, as Yardley sees it, "one does not immediately sense the South in Percy's work, . . . because he is telling us that the South is *not* the South any more, that it has been absorbed into the crassness and possibly the hopelessness of America. Percy's South has been violated not by Sherman's marauders but by . . . the masters of commerce and technology." *Saturday Review* contributor Bruce Cook likewise notes that Percy's fiction "lacks the local color—the magnolias and honeysuckle—and the Faulknerian, Old Testament sensibility for which [Southern] writers are noted. He is essentially a philosophical novelist; but a rare one, for there is such a crisp clarity to his writing, and such a lot of humor, that it is quite without pretension."

This is not to say that Percy's fiction lacks all sense of region. Godwin writes: "By choice as well as inclination, Mr. Percy is primarily a novelist of ideas, but he is a fine novelist of manners, too. He is uncommonly good at evoking the atmosphere and language of his region; he is dead on target when depicting the subtle, often devious locutions of Southern American talk." Nor does the author ignore the pertinent issues of modern Southern history, especially race relations, in his novels. "It's the great strength of Percy's fiction that he looks about him and sees a landscape of moral and emotional confusion, and refuses to offer handy sociological or economic wisdom by way of comforting explanation for it," Todd claims. "He speaks directly and challengingly to the private heart."

In a *New York Review of Books* essay, V. S. Pritchett praises Percy for "moving about, catching the smell of locality, and for a laughing enjoyment between his bouts with desperation and loss. . . . The sense of America as an effluence of bizarre locality is strong."

For all its serious portent, Percy's fiction is nevertheless imbued with comedy, satire, and intimations that mankind's case is not completely hopeless. He is also considered an engaging stylist whose accessible prose facilitates understanding of deep issues. As Joyce Carol Oates observes in the *New Republic,* Percy "has been wonderfully alive to the sounds and textures and odors of life, and his ability to render the baffling solidity of the world [makes] his prose sing with vitality. . . . It [is] hardly abstract notions of freedom, determinism, existential *angst,* alienation, etc. that [makes] these novels so irresistible. They [are] artistically and humanly rich, and beautifully crafted." In the *New Republic,* Yardley also describes what he views as the best aspect of Percy's work: "For all its seeming despair, for all its sad irony and wicked satire, it resolves into affirmation. In a cynical age it may seem sentimental. Human community, neighborliness, rootedness in the land, simple decency and honesty—those qualities are often acknowledged today, if at all, with embarrassed smirks. But the point of Percy's work, of the laughter he directs at our posturings, is that they are the best we have to fall back on. That he finds we have not yet lost them despite it all, that he is still not without hope, is a good word in a bad time."

Percy's works are popular among discerning readers both in America and abroad; he told the *Los Angeles Times* he thinks this is the case because "people realize that I'm just as screwed up as they are, and the only difference between us is that I have a way of writing about it." The author said in the *New York Times* that the rewards for a long writing career come when a novelist is "able to say something that everybody knows and yet doesn't know that he knows. The reader reads it and says, 'Why, that's me. I hadn't thought about it. I didn't know anybody else felt that way.'"

BIOGRAPHICAL/CRITICAL SOURCES:

BOOKS

Broughton, Panthea Reid, editor, *The Art of Walker Percy: Stratagems for Being,* Louisiana State University Press, 1979.

Bryant, Jerry H., *The Open Decision: The Contemporary American Novel and Its Intellectual Background,* Free Press, 1970.

Coles, Robert, *Walker Percy: An American Search,* Little, Brown, 1978.

Contemporary Literary Criticism, Gale, Volume II, 1974, Volume III, 1975, Volume VI, 1976, Volume VIII, 1978, Volume XIV, 1980, Volume XVIII, 1981.

Dabbs, James McBride, *Civil Rights in Recent Southern Fiction,* Southern Regional Council, 1969.

Dictionary of Literary Biography, Volume II: *American Novelists since World War II,* Gale, 1978.

Dictionary of Literary Biography Yearbook: 1980, Gale, 1981.

Douglas, Ellen, *Walker Percy's "The Last Gentleman": Introduction and Commentary,* Seabury, 1969.

Hoffman, Frederick J., *The Art of Southern Fiction: A Study of Some Modern Novelists,* Southern Illinois University Press, 1967.

Hyman, Stanley Edgar, *Standards: A Chronicle of Books for Our Time,* Horizon, 1966.

Lawson, Lewis A. and Victor A. Kramer, editors, *Conversations with Walker Percy*, University Press of Mississippi, 1985.

Lehan, Richard, *A Dangerous Crossing: French Literary Existentialism and the Modern American Novel*, Southern Illinois University Press, 1973.

Luschei, Martin, *The Sovereign Wayfarer: Walker Percy's Diagnosis of the Malaise*, Louisiana State University Press, 1972.

Murray, Albert, *South to a Very Old Place*, McGraw, 1971.

Poteat, Patricia Lewis, *Walker Percy and the Old Modern Age: Reflections on Language, Argument, and the Telling of Stories*, Louisiana State University Press, 1986.

Sheed, Wilfrid, *The Morning After*, Farrar, Straus, 1971.

Tanner, Tony, *The Reign of Wonder: Naivety and Reality in American Literature*, Cambridge University Press, 1965.

Tanner, Tony, *City of Words: American Fiction 1950-1970*, Harper, 1971.

Tharpe, Jac, editor, *Walker Percy: Art and Ethics*, University Press of Mississippi, 1980.

Tharpe, Jac, *Walker Percy*, Twayne, 1983.

PERIODICALS

America, January 5, 1957, January 12, 1957, July 20, 1957.
American Scholar, summer, 1968.
Atlantic, August, 1971, March, 1977, July, 1980.
Bookweek, December 25, 1966.
Book World, May 16, 1971.
Carleton Miscellany, Volume XVI, 1976-77.
Centennial Review, winter, 1968.
Chicago Tribune Book World, May 29, 1983, March 29, 1987.
Colorado Quarterly, spring, 1972.
Commonweal, July 6, 1956, December 13, 1957, June 5, 1959, December 22, 1961, October 29, 1971, May 10, 1974, October 25, 1974, August 29, 1980.
Detroit News, May 3, 1987.
Esquire, December, 1977, April, 1980.
Georgia Review, fall, 1971, winter, 1977, fall, 1978.
Globe & Mail (Toronto), May 9, 1987.
Harper's, April, 1965, June, 1971, April, 1977.
Hollins Critic, October, 1973.
Horizon, August, 1980.
Journal of Religion, July, 1974.
Los Angeles Times, August 10, 1983.
Los Angeles Times Book Review, June 5, 1983, April 12, 1987.
Michigan Quarterly Review, fall, 1977.
Mississippi Quarterly, winter, 1974-75.
Modern Age, fall, 1980.
Nation, August 8, 1966, April 30, 1977, August 16, 1980.
New Leader, October 13, 1975.
New Orleans Review, May, 1976.
New Republic, June 18, 1966, May 22, 1971, July 19, 1975, February 5, 1977, July 5-12, 1980, July 11, 1983.
Newsweek, May 17, 1971, February 28, 1977, July 7, 1980, June 13, 1983.
New York, July 28, 1980.
New Yorker, July 22, 1961, September 11, 1971, May 2, 1977, October 2, 1978, September 1, 1980.
New York Review of Books, July 28, 1966, July 1, 1971, September 18, 1975, March 31, 1977, August 14, 1980.
New York Times, June 16, 1966, May 15, 1971, February 17, 1977, July 3, 1980, June 11, 1983, April 1, 1987.
New York Times Book Review, May 28, 1961, June 26, 1966, May 23, 1971, July 4, 1971, June 8, 1975, February 20,
1977, June 29, 1980, June 5, 1983, August 4, 1985, April 5, 1987.
New York Times Magazine, March 22, 1987.
Notes on Mississippi Writers, fall, 1971, spring, 1978, summer, 1979.
Novel, fall, 1972.
Partisan Review, summer, 1966, spring, 1973.
Prairie Schooner, summer, 1968.
Publishers Weekly, March 21, 1977.
Saturday Review, June 18, 1966, May 15, 1971, November 6, 1973, June 28, 1975, March 19, 1977, April 1, 1978.
Sewanee Review, autumn, 1973.
Shenandoah, spring, 1967, winter, 1972, winter, 1976.
South Atlantic Bulletin, May, 1972.
South Atlantic Quarterly, summer, 1969.
Southern Literary Journal, fall, 1973, fall, 1977.
Southern Quarterly, January, 1978, Volume XVIII, number 3, 1980.
Southern Review, spring, 1968, October, 1970, spring, 1973, autumn, 1977, winter, 1977, spring, 1978, winter, 1978, winter, 1984.
Southern Studies, summer, 1979.
Southern Voices, May-June, 1974.
Southwest Review, spring, 1974.
Spectator, February 14, 1981.
Time, May 19, 1961, February 1, 1963, May 17, 1971, March 7, 1977, July 14, 1980, June 20, 1983, March 30, 1987.
Times Literary Supplement, December 21, 1967, October 1, 1971, January 23, 1981.
Village Voice, July 9-15, 1980, June 14, 1983.
Virginia Quarterly Review, summer, 1977.
Washington Post, May 14, 1987.
Washington Post Book World, February 27, 1977, July 20, 1980, June 19, 1983, March 22, 1987.
World Literature Today, spring, 1981, spring, 1984.
Yale Review, winter, 1976.

—*Sketch by Anne Janette Johnson*

*   *   *

PHIPSON, Joan
    See FITZHARDINGE, Joan Margaret

*   *   *

PIFER, Ellen 1942-

PERSONAL: Born June 26, 1942, in New York, N.Y.; daughter of Carl (in business) and Mae (Stein) Rosenberg; married Drury L. Pifer (a writer), December 30, 1962; children: Rebecca Anne. *Education:* University of California, Berkeley, B.A., 1964, M.A., 1969, Ph.D., 1976.

ADDRESSES: Office—Department of English, University of Delaware, 204 Memorial Hall, Newark, Del. 19716.

CAREER: University of California, Berkeley, acting instructor in comparative literature, 1974-76; University of Delaware, Newark, assistant professor, 1977-81, associate professor of English and comparative literature, 1981—. Member of planning board of Delaware Theatre Company, 1980-81. Director and faculty member of London Semester Abroad, University of Delaware. Consultant to various professional journals and university presses.

MEMBER: Modern Language Association of America, Vladimir Nabokov Society (program director, 1979), Saul Bellow Society.

WRITINGS:

Nabokov and the Novel, Harvard University Press, 1980.
(Contributor) *Dictionary of Literary Biography*, Volume XIV: *British Novelists since 1960*, Gale, 1983.
(Contributor) Phyllis A. Roth, editor, *Critical Essays on Vladimir Nabokov*, G. K. Hall, 1984.
(Contributor) Catherine Rainwater and William J. Scheick, editors, *Contemporary American Women Writers*, University Press of Kentucky, 1985.
(Editor and contributor) *Critical Essays on John Fowles*, G. K. Hall, 1986.

Co-author of "New West Magazine Competition," a column in *New West*, 1976-77. Contributor of articles and reviews to literature and Slavic studies journals and newspapers.

WORK IN PROGRESS: A book tentatively entitled *Saul Bellow Against the Grain*.

SIDELIGHTS: Writing about Ellen Pifer's *Nabokov and the Novel* in the *New York Times Book Review*, James Traub calls the book a "whirlwind tour [that] offers rich insights into almost all of Nabokov's works." Pifer's thesis that Nabokov's novels reflect a moral consciousness, however, "needs no proving," suggests Alex de Jonge in the *Times Literary Supplement*. And while de Jonge feels that Pifer defends Nabokov "against irrelevant charges," he recognizes that "she can also be very perceptive, when underlining the importance of individual perception, or emphasizing the importance of the theme of consciousness."

Pifer once told *CA:* "I am committed to studying literature in a comparative context. Even when I am writing on American literature exclusively, as I am right now, I find cross-cultural issues and influences most compelling. Current indifference in this country to the study of foreign languages and literatures, as well as to the humanities in general, is something that every literary critic, scholar, and teacher must oppose. The health, intelligence, and vitality of our own cultural life is at stake."

AVOCATIONAL INTERESTS: "Theatre and the other arts."

BIOGRAPHICAL/CRITICAL SOURCES:

PERIODICALS

New York Times Book Review, March 8, 1981.
Times Literary Supplement, August 7, 1981.

*   *   *

PLATE, Thomas 1944-

PERSONAL: Born May 17, 1944, in New York, N.Y.; married Andrea Darvi (a writer). *Education:* Amherst College, A.B., 1966; Princeton University, M.P.A., 1968.

ADDRESSES: Agent—Theron Raines, Raines & Raines, 71 Park Ave., Suite 4A, New York, N.Y. 10016.

CAREER: Newsweek, New York City, writer, 1968-70; *Newsday*, Garden City, N.Y., "Viewpoints" editor, 1970-72; *New York*, New York City, senior editor, 1972-74; free-lance writer, 1974—. Member of Amherst College Alumni Committee on Publications.

MEMBER: Princeton Club (New York City), Phi Beta Kappa.

WRITINGS:

Understanding Doomsday (nonfiction), Simon & Schuster, 1971.

(With others) *The Mafia at War*, New York Magazine Press, 1972.
Crime Pays!: An Inside Look at Burglars, Car Thieves, Loan Sharks, Hit Men, Fences, and Other Professionals in Crime (nonfiction), Simon & Schuster, 1975.
(With Patrick V. Murphy) *Commissioner: A View from the Top of American Law Enforcement* (nonfiction), Simon & Schuster, 1977.
(With wife, Andrea Darvi) *Secret Police: The Inside Story of a Network of Terror*, Doubleday, 1981.

Penthouse magazine, author of column "Crime," and contributing editor, 1977—.

WORK IN PROGRESS: Drifting Man, a novel, for Dell.

SIDELIGHTS: In his writings Thomas Plate has examined a number of serious questions related to current law enforcement, such as the reasons why a criminal breaks the law, the role and influence of police commissioner in a major American city, and the serious abuse of power wielded by secret police organizations.

Crime Pays!: An Inside Look at Burglars, Car Thieves, Loan Sharks, Hit Men, Fences, and Other Professionals in Crime explores Plate's theory that to many successful criminals, crime is a lucrative profession. As Charles Dollen writes in *Best Sellers:* "Can crime be considered a profession? [Plate] believes so, since most of the criminals caught by the police are 'amateurs,' men and women who make rather obvious mistakes." Agreeing, Frances Seamster remarks in *Library Journal* that in *Crime Pays!* "Plate attacks the belief that people become criminals because they are deprived victims of society: they go into crime because it pays, and Plate has figures to prove it." "[In *Crime Pays!*] we have the criminal elevated to the level of capitalist businessman," comments Lucinda Franks in the *New York Times Book Review*. "We have it complete with listings and charts showing the estimated annual salary of every specialist . . . , the working hours . . . , the overhead costs, such as police payoffs, fear and paranoia, and the small percentages of those professional criminals who are ever convicted."

In *Commissioner: A View from the Top of American Law Enforcement* Plate and co-author Patrick V. Murphy, former New York City Police Commissioner, write about the various qualities that make up good police management and the role of police commissioner. Otho Crawford writes in *Library Journal* that *Commissioner* is a "tour of sound police management ideas as well as a discussion of Murphy's role as police commissioner of New York during the Lindsay-Knapp Commission days." Peter Gardner states in *Saturday Review* that he found Plate's book "engrossing." Gardner goes on to write that *Commissioner* as an "analysis of what's wrong with the American police system is complemented by some eminently sensible suggestions about how the system can be improved."

In *Secret Police: The Inside Story of a Network of Terror*, Plate and co-author Andrea Darvi analyze the inner workings of police organizations operating in such countries as Chile, the Philippines, Iran, Haiti, and the Soviet Union. M. S. Stohl points out in *Library Journal* that *Secret Police* is "a carefully researched indictment of modern political life in all too many nations. . . . Plate and Darvi review the five major functions of the secret police—surveillance, search, arrest, interrogation, and indefinite detention." And a writer for *Choice* remarks that Plate and Darvi "conclude that these organizations of the political left and right have much in common and that there are important warnings and lessons to be learned by Americans about the dangers of secret police and intelligence operations."

BIOGRAPHICAL/CRITICAL SOURCES:

PERIODICALS

Best Sellers, August, 1975.
Choice, May, 1982.
Library Journal, June 15, 1975, December 15, 1977, October 1, 1981.
New York Times Book Review, July 6, 1975.
Saturday Review, February 4, 1978.†

*   *   *

PLAYFAIR, Guy Lyon   1935-

PERSONAL: Born April 5, 1935, in Quetta, India; son of I.S.O. (a military officer) and Jocelyn (Malan) Playfair. Education: Pembroke College, Cambridge, B.A. (with honors), 1959.

ADDRESSES: Office—7 Earls Court Sq., London SW5, England. Agent—David Bolt Associates, 12 Heath Dr., Send, Surrey GU23 7EP, England.

CAREER: Free-lance writer and photographer in Brazil, 1961-75; U.S. Agency for International Development, Information Office, Rio de Janeiro, Brazil, writer, 1967-71.

MEMBER: Society for Psychical Research, Society of Authors, College of Psychic Studies.

WRITINGS:

NONFICTION

The Unknown Power, Pocket Books, 1975.
The Indefinite Boundary, St. Martin's 1977.
(With Scott Hill) The Cycles of Heaven, St. Martin's, 1978.
This House Is Haunted: The True Story of a Poltergeist, Stein & Day, 1980.
If This Be Magic, J. Cape, 1985.
The Haunted Pub Guide, Harrap, 1985.
(With Uri Geller) The Geller Effect, Henry Holt, 1987.

OTHER

Contributor to The Unexplained, Orbis, 1980-82.

SIDELIGHTS: Guy Lyon Playfair told CA: "I am interested in border areas of human experience and in anomalous phenomena of all kinds. I find the influence of sunspots as interesting as the behavior of poltergeists or psychic surgeons, and I strongly object to finding my books classified as 'occult.' I am not concerned with the 'supernatural' but with unexplored areas of nature that are by definition natural."

Playfair is an amateur musician who has played trombone in several orchestras and jazz groups. He admits to having almost become a professional jazz musician, "but the life was too hectic." Now he owns a concert harpsichord, "which I keep meaning to learn to play properly. But however badly I play, it's better than watching television, which I gave up several years ago after reading Jerry Mander's Four Arguments for the Elimination of Television."

BIOGRAPHICAL/CRITICAL SOURCES:

PERIODICALS

Times (London), December 11, 1986.
Times Literary Supplement, February 7, 1986.

*   *   *

PLECK, Joseph H(ealy)   1946-

PERSONAL: Born July 14, 1946, in Evanston, Ill. Education: Harvard University, B.A., 1968, M.A., 1971, Ph.D., 1973.

ADDRESSES: Office—Wheaton College, Norton, Mass. 02766.

CAREER: University of Michigan, Ann Arbor, lecturer in psychology, 1973-77; University of Massachusetts—Amherst, associate professor of family studies, 1977-78; Wellesley College, Center for Research on Women, Wellesley, Mass., program director, 1978-86; Wheaton College, Norton, Mass., Luce Professor of Families, Change, and Society, 1986—.

MEMBER: American Psychological Association, American Sociological Association, National Council on Family Relations.

WRITINGS:

(Editor with Jack Sawyer) Men and Masculinity, Prentice-Hall, 1974.
(Editor with Elizabeth H. Pleck) The American Man, Prentice-Hall, 1980.
The Myth of Masculinity, MIT Press, 1981.
The Impact of Work Schedules on the Family, Institute for Social Research, 1983.
Working Wives, Working Husbands, Sage Publications, 1985.

BIOGRAPHICAL/CRITICAL SOURCES:

PERIODICALS

Chicago Tribune Book World, March 27, 1983.

*   *   *

POCOCK, Thomas Allcot Guy   1925-
(Tom Pocock)

PERSONAL: Born August 18, 1925, in London, England; son of Guy Noel (a writer) and Dorothy (Bowers) Pocock; married Penelope Casson, April 26, 1969; children: Laura Jane, Hannah Lucy. Education: Attended Westminster School and Cheltenham College, England. Religion: Church of England.

ADDRESSES: Home—22 Lawrence St., London S.W.3, England. Office—London Standard, 118 Fleet St., London E. C. 4, England.

CAREER: Leader, London, England, war correspondent, 1945, feature writer, 1945-48; Daily Mail, London, naval and military correspondent and special writer, 1949-52; Times, London, naval correspondent, 1952-55; Daily Express, London, Middle East correspondent and feature writer, 1955-57; Elizabethan, London, co-editor, 1957-59; Evening Standard Co. Ltd., London, Evening Standard, defense and war correspondent, 1960-74, travel editor, 1974-82, London Standard, special writer, 1982—. Member of board of governors of Foudroyant Trust, 1980—. Military service: Royal Navy, 1943-44.

MEMBER: Royal United Service Institution, Chelsea Society (member of council, 1965—), Garrick Club.

WRITINGS—Under name Tom Pocock:

Nelson and His World, Thames & Hudson, 1968.
Chelsea Reach: The Brutal Friendship of Whistler and Walter Greaves, Hodder & Stoughton, 1970.
London Walks, Thames & Hudson, 1973.
Fighting General, Collins, 1973.
Remember Nelson, Collins, 1977.
The Young Nelson in the Americas, Collins, 1980.
1945: The Dawn Came Up Like Thunder, Collins, 1983.
East and West of Suez: The Retreat from Empire, Bodley Head, 1986.

Author of documentary film scripts for public service groups. Contributor to magazines.

WORK IN PROGRESS: Biography of Lord Nelson.

SIDELIGHTS: Tom Pocock commented: "I am a journalistic rather than an academic historian, and have used my long experience as a newspaper correspondent (including covering wars in Algeria, Malaya, Arabia, Borneo, Cyprus, Aden, India, and Vietnam, as well as the end of World War II) to recreate the physical and emotional background to historical events. I have visited all the scenes of Lord Nelson's activities around the world, using the knowledge gained to give depth to material gathered through documentary research."

Critics have praised Pocock for his ability to recreate the pervading atmosphere of a particular historical period. For instance, in the London *Observer,* Vernon Bogdanor speaks of how Pocock "brilliantly evokes the sights and sounds of Britain and Europe" in his *1945: The Dawn Came Up Like Thunder.* And of his depiction of the United States, Bogdanor thinks that "Pocock conveys beautifully the sense of wonder which that land of riches, luxury and power across the Atlantic inspired in those days." Similarly, in Pocock's *East and West of Suez: The Retreat from Empire,* which reworks earlier stories to chronicle Britain's diminishing colonialism, "There are, in Pocock's colourful and unpretentious account, traces of make-believe which aptly convey the flavour of these events," writes John Luxmoore in the *Times Literary Supplement.* Although A. J. Stockwell suggests in *British Book News* that the "immediacy of his original despatches" is not completely recaptured, he feels that what is "successfully conveyed by [Pocock's] chilling accounts . . . is the dread risk run by journalists committed to bringing us world news."

BIOGRAPHICAL/CRITICAL SOURCES:

PERIODICALS

British Book News, October, 1980, October, 1986.
Observer (London), October 9, 1983.
Times Literary Supplement, October 23, 1970, December 19, 1980, December 19, 1986.

*   *   *

POCOCK, Tom
    See POCOCK, Thomas Allcot Guy

*   *   *

POLK, James   1939-

PERSONAL: Born September 1, 1939, in Miles City, Mont.; son of Raymond W. (a physician) and Lucille (a teacher and library consultant; maiden name, Carroll) Polk. *Education:*

University of Montana, B.A., 1961; Harvard University, M.A., 1962, Ph.D., 1968. *Religion:* "Lapsed Catholic."

ADDRESSES: Office—House of Anansi Press Ltd., 35 Britain St., Toronto, Ontario, Canada M5A 1R7. *Agent*—Elaine Markson Literary Agency, Inc., 44 Greenwich Ave., New York, N.Y. 10011.

CAREER: Idaho State University, Pocatello, instructor in English, 1964-65; University of Alberta, Edmonton, assistant professor of English, 1968-70; House of Anansi Press, Toronto, Ontario, editor, 1971-73, editorial director, 1973—.

AWARDS, HONORS: Woodrow Wilson fellowship, 1961-62; first prize for best first story in *Atlantic,* 1973, for "The Phrenology of Love."

WRITINGS:

Wilderness Writers (biographies of Canadian writers), Clarke, Irwin, 1972.
(Editor and author of introduction) A. S. Holmes, *Belinda; or, the Rivals,* Anansi, 1975.
(Contributor) McMullen, editor, *Twentieth Century Essays on Confederation Literature,* Tecumseh (Ottawa), 1976.
The Passion of Loreen Bright Weasel (novel), Houghton, 1981.
(Editor) Northrop Frye, *Divisions on a Ground: Essays on Canadian Culture,* Anansi, 1982.
"Vanity Press: A Comedy in Two Acts" (play), first produced in Toronto at Tarragon Theatre, March 13, 1987.

Contributor of stories and articles to periodicals, including *Atlantic, Oui, Mademoiselle, University of Toronto Quarterly, Canadian Literature,* and *Alphabet.*

WORK IN PROGRESS: Comic saga about a family's experiences in Hebb, Montana.

SIDELIGHTS: "*The Passion of Loreen Bright Weasel* is so rich in comic situations, quirky characters, and down-home talk that it is a good bet . . . for funniest novel of the year," said Canadian novelist David Williamson in the *Winnipeg Free Press.* At the heart of James Polk's comic satire is a young Indian woman, Loreen Bright Weasel, who zealously converts to Catholicism and sets out to redeem the town of Hebb, Montana. Among those Loreen targets with 'Corporate Works of Mercy' are Sheep Triumph, who wants to run for mayor and rid the town of his ex-wife's bordello, and Winn Triumph, Sheep's long-suffering wife and the only one in town "who knows anything about Caesar salads and smoked oysters."

Reviews include this response from Cathleen Hoskins, published in the *Toronto Star:* "Polk . . . obviously had great fun writing this book. The good-natured humor flows like a virtuoso performance of one-liners. Though his subjects are all easy marks—religion, small town death-in-life, the appalling botch-up of Indian-white relations, politics, marriage, midlife crisis—there's no denying he's bitten off quite a chunk to satirize and, for the most part, done a clever job of chewing." B. Derek Johnson, writing in the Toronto *Globe and Mail,* comments that "myopic religious zeal and small-town Western kitsch are an unlikely pair of targets for a single satire, yet James Polk . . . has successfully braided them into one hilarious short novel."

Reviewers also discuss the particular strengths of Polk's writing and the nature of his comedy. Johnson observes: "Polk writes like a lean, low-cholesterol version of Tom Robbins. He has a ball with hyperbole and will often chase a good joke at the risk of losing credibility. . . . His crisp, neatly-folded sentences reveal the sensibility of an editor rather than a writer. He lines up his words with a pool cue.'' Williamson states that ''Mr. Polk's comedy has all the richness and humanity of Roch Carrier's novels. His ability to pump new life into old cliches smacks of Peter De Vries, and his raunchy treatment of the contemporary American West brings to mind such fine writers as Larry McMurtry and John Nichols. But his style is distinctly his own; his comedy is never black, always compassionate, and all his characters are lovable.''

Polk once told *CA:* "*The Passion of Loreen Bright Weasel* took five years to write, coming together after my first published short stories in *Atlantic, Oui,* and *Mademoiselle* in the mid-1970s. I have been busy editing other writers for Anansi Press in Canada, but also I write very slowly, typing the paragraphs and sentences over and over, continually struggling with the octopus of plot. Since comedy depends so much on style and plot complications, it seems absolutely necessary to dawdle over words the way I do, but I hope my next novel won't take as long. I don't see how it can. I've been writing it concurrently with *Loreen* since I've found it healthier to be writing several things at once: When that black despair hits you over one project, there's always another palpitating in the wings.

"The critical response to *Loreen Bright Weasel* has been heartwarming. All have said (so far) that the book is funny—even 'great fun' (*Publishers Weekly*), 'hilarious' (Toronto *Globe and Mail*), and 'a ferociously funny first novel' (*New Yorker*). I hope some Catholic readers will also see that the book is cast in the traditional form of a saint's life, with the protagonist having visions, undergoing trials, and changing society through love. Of course, Loreen's energetic march to canonization brings total chaos in its wake, but she really does 'save' the other characters in that they are happier emotionally after she gets through with her Corporate Works of Mercy. Loreen herself suffers a 'passion' in the religious sense, too, since she experiences great anguish for the love of mankind, who doesn't ask for salvation to begin with and scarcely knows what to do with it.

"One review from the Virginia Kirkus Service accused Loreen's ministrations as being 'a dumb Indian act' and discerned a tinge of racism overall. This charge is so upsetting and so far from my purpose that it's worth emphasizing the obvious: Loreen is morally and spiritually good. She is not dumb: far from it. She's a bright student with her own eccentric ideas of the universe, and if anybody is dumb in the book it is the white society which expects her to mix martinis and understand the garbage disposal unit and which fills her mind with Catholic mythology. My book pokes fun at racist attitudes, yes, but my heroine is lovable and a kind of genius in her way; the whites really aren't so bad either. It's a plot where the Indian triumphs and prevails, and everybody is happy at the end. Oh, Virginia Kirkus, why can't you understand this?!

"I've been a lucky writer so far. I have done another nonfiction book, on Canadian animal-story writers, which was a lot of fun to research and put together. The reviews for my first novel have been good, and my publisher, Houghton Mifflin, is exemplary, with some of the editors referring to Loreen as if she were a real live person—the ultimate compliment. Also, my family and friends back in Miles City see *Loreen*'s satire on small-town life for what it is: not a put-down but a tongue-in-cheek celebration. Short of seeing *The Passion of Loreen Bright Weasel* opening in selected drive-ins across America as a major motion picture with Robert Redford and Barbara Streisand, what more could I ask?''

BIOGRAPHICAL/CRITICAL SOURCES:

PERIODICALS

Globe and Mail (Toronto), May 16, 1981.
Macleans, May 11, 1981.
Toronto Star, April 18, 1981.
Winnipeg Free Press, May 23, 1981.

*   *   *

POLLOCK, Bruce   1945-

PERSONAL: Born July 24, 1945, in Brooklyn, N.Y.; son of Joseph and Rose (Prager) Pollock; married Barbara Hoffman (an art teacher, poet, and painter), December 19, 1970. *Education:* City College of the City University of New York, B.A., 1972.

ADDRESSES: Home—130 Ferncliffe Rd., Fairfield, Conn. 06430.

CAREER: Managing editor, *Rock,* 1972-74; editor, *Contemporary Music,* 1974; managing editor, *Funny Papers,* 1975; senior editor, *Penthouse,* 1976; free-lance writer and editor, 1977—; editor in chief, *Guitar: For the Practicing Musician,* 1982—.

MEMBER: American Society of Composers, Authors and Publishers, American Society of Journalists and Authors.

AWARDS, HONORS: Dejur Award for fiction, 1971; Deems Taylor Award, 1973, for articles in *Rock;* Connecticut Commission on the Arts grant for fiction, 1978.

WRITINGS:

In Their Own Words: Songs and Songwriters, 1955-1974, Macmillan, 1975.
Playing for Change (novel), Houghton, 1977.
Me, Minsky and Max (novel), Houghton, 1978.
The Face of Rock and Roll: Images of a Generation, Holt, 1978.
The Disco Handbook, Scholastic Book Services, 1979.
It's Only Rock and Roll (novel), Houghton, 1980.
The Rock and Roll Fun Book, Scholastic Book Services, 1980.
When Rock Was Young: A Nostalgic Review of the Top Forty Era, Holt, 1981.
(Editor) *Popular Music: An Annotated Index of American Popular Songs* (annual series) Gale, 1979—.
Housework for Men, Planet Books, 1981.
When the Music Mattered: Rock in the 1960s, Holt, 1983.

Columnist for *Viva,* 1977, Gannett Westchester Newspapers, 1978—, and *Wilson Library Bulletin,* 1983—; writer of celebrity profiles, *Family Weekly,* 1979; video columnist, 1983-84, and celebrity journalist, both for *USA Today.* Contributor to *Playboy, Saturday Review, Cosmopolitan, New York Times, TV Guide, Oui, Redbook, Panorama,* and *Us.* Contributing editor, *Modern Hi-Fi and Music,* 1975; editor, *Tomorrow's Music,* 1978-79.

BIOGRAPHICAL/CRITICAL SOURCES:

PERIODICALS

Modern Hi-Fi and Music, July, 1975.

POLNER, Murray 1928-

PERSONAL: Surname is pronounced *Pole*-ner; born May 15, 1928, in Brooklyn, N.Y.; son of Alex (a salesman) and Rebecka (Meyerson) Polner; married Louise Greenwald (a teacher) June 16, 1950; children: Beth, Alex, Robert. *Education:* City College (now City College of the City University of New York), B.S.S., 1950; University of Pennsylvania, M.A., 1951; Columbia University, graduate study, 1951-53, 1955-57, certificate of Russian Institute, 1967; Union Graduate School, Ph.D., 1972. *Politics:* Liberal. *Religion:* Jewish.

ADDRESSES: Home—50-10 Concord Ave., Great Neck, N.Y. 11020. *Office—Present Tense,* 165 East 56 St., New York, N.Y. 10022. *Agent*—Julian Bach Literary Agency Inc., 747 Third Ave., New York, N.Y. 10017.

CAREER: Thomas Jefferson High School, Brooklyn, N.Y., teacher of social studies, 1956-66; Suffolk County Community College, Selden, N.Y. associate professor of history, 1966-69; executive assistant to the New York City Public Schools chancellor, Brooklyn, 1969-72; *Present Tense,* New York, N.Y., editor in chief, 1972—. Visiting lecturer in or professor of history and political science, 1965-76, at various institutions, including, Brooklyn College (now Brooklyn College of the City University of New York), Queens College (now Queens College of the City University of New York), Long Island University, Adelphi University, University of Maine at Orono, University of Prince Edward Island (Charlottetown), and St. Dunstan University (Canada). President, Lakeville Press, Inc. *Military service:* U.S. Naval Reserve, 1947-52. U.S. Army, 1953-55.

MEMBER: National Interreligious Service Board for Conscientious Objectors (member of board of directors), Jewish Peace Fellowship (vice-president, 1975—), Fellowship of Reconciliation.

WRITINGS:

Enriching Social Studies, Prentice-Hall, 1961.
(With Arthur Barron) *Where Shall We Take the Kids?,* Doubleday, 1961.
(With Barron) *The Questions Children Ask,* Macmillan, 1964.
(With Robert Schain) *The Use of Effective Discipline,* Prentice-Hall, 1964.
(Editor) *Reflections of a Russian Statesman,* University of Michigan Press, 1965.
(Editor) *"The Conquest of the United States by Spain" and Other Essays by William Graham Sumner,* Regnery, 1965.
(Editor with Alan Solomonow) *Roots of Jewish Nonviolence,* Jewish Peace Fellowship, 1970.
No Victory Parades: The Return of the Vietnam Veteran, Holt, 1971.
(Editor) *When Can I Come Home: A Debate on Amnesty for Antiwar Prisoners, Exiles and Others,* Doubleday, 1972.
Rabbi: The American Experience, Holt, 1977.
(With David Bresnick and Seymour P. Lachman) *Black, White, Red and Green,* Longman, 1978.
Branch Rickey: A Biography, Atheneum, 1982.
(Editor) *The Disarmament Catalog,* Pilgrim Press (New York, N.Y.), 1982.
(General editor) *American Jewish Biographies,* Facts on File, 1982.

CONTRIBUTOR TO ANTHOLOGIES

Robert Jay Lifton, editor, *America and the Asian Revolutions,* Aldine, 1970.

Gerald A. Bryant, Jr., and J. Burl Hogins, editors, *Reading for Insight,* Glencoe, 1970.
Alfred Balk and James Boylan, editors, *Our Troubled Press: Ten Years of the Columbia Journalism Review,* introduction by Elie Abel, Little, Brown, 1971.
Irving G. Hedrick and Reginald L. Jones, editors, *Crisis: Student Dissent in the Public Schools,* Houghton, 1971.
William Broen and James C. Coleman, editors, *Abnormal Psychology and Modern Life,* 4th edition, Scott, Foresman, 1972.

OTHER

Also author of *Discipline in the Classroom.* Contributor to *New Republic, New York Times Book Review, Commonweal, Christian Century, South Atlantic Quarterly, Nation, Washington Post,* and other journals and newspapers. Editor, *Shalom: Jewish Peace Fellowship.*

WORK IN PROGRESS: Books on Lt. Calley and My Lai, the 1960s, and the New York Giants baseball team.

BIOGRAPHICAL/CRITICAL SOURCES:

PERIODICALS

New York Times Book Review, January 1, 1978.
Saturday Review, July 31, 1971.
Washington Post Book World, July 18, 1982.

*   *   *

POLSBY, Nelson W(oolf) 1934-
   (Arthur Clun)

PERSONAL: Born October 25, 1934, in Norwich, Conn.; son of Daniel II (a businessman) and Edythe (Woolf) Polsby; married Linda Dale Offenbach, August 3, 1958; children: Lisa Susan, Emily Ann, Daniel Ralph. *Education:* Attended Brown University, 1955-56; Johns Hopkins University, A.B., 1956; Yale University, M.A., 1958, Ph.D., 1961.

ADDRESSES: Home—Berkeley, Calif. *Office*—Department of Political Science, University of California, Berkeley, Calif. 94720.

CAREER: University of Wisconsin—Madison, instructor in political science, 1960-61; Wesleyan University, Middletown, Conn., assistant professor, 1961-64, associate professor, 1964-67, professor of government, 1967-68; University of California, Berkeley, professor of political science, 1967—. Visiting member of faculty at Columbia University, 1963, Yale University, 1963, 1967, Hebrew University of Jerusalem, 1970, Stanford University, 1975, 1977, and Harvard University, 1986-87; fellow of Center for Advanced Studies in the Behavioral Sciences, Stanford, Calif., 1965-66, 1985-86; senior fellow, Roosevelt Center, Washington, D.C., 1982-83. Member of committee on public engineering policy of National Academy of Engineering, 1973-76. Member of commission on vice-presidential selection of Democratic National Committee, 1973-74; member of Council on Foreign Relations.

MEMBER: American Political Science Association (member of council, 1971-77), American Sociological Association, American Academy of Arts and Sciences, American Association for the Advancement of Science (fellow), Phi Beta Kappa.

AWARDS, HONORS: Social Science Research Council fellowship, 1959; Brookings Institution fellowship, 1959-60; Ford Foundation fellowship, 1970-71; Guggenheim fellowship, 1977-78, 1985-86; Wilbur Cross Medal, Yale University, 1985.

WRITINGS:

Community Power and Political Theory, Yale University Press, 1963, expanded edition, 1980.

Congress and the Presidency, Prentice-Hall, 1964, 4th edition, 1986.

(With Aaron Wildavsky) *Presidential Elections,* Scribner, 1964, 6th edition, 1984.

Congress: An Introduction, Rand McNally, 1968.

The Citizen's Choice: Humphrey or Nixon, Public Affairs Press, 1968.

Political Promises, Oxford University Press, 1974.

(With Geoffrey Smith) *British Government and Its Discontents,* Basic Books, 1981.

Consequences of Party Reform, Oxford University Press, 1983.

Political Innovation in America: The Politics of Policy Initiation, Yale University Press, 1984.

EDITOR

(With Robert A. Dentler and Paul A. Smith) *Politics and Social Life: An Introduction to Political Behavior,* Houghton, 1963.

(With R. L. Peabody) *New Perspectives on the House of Representatives,* Rand McNally, 1963, 3rd edition, 1977.

(With Wildavsky) *American Governmental Institutions,* Rand McNally, 1968.

Congressional Behavior, Random House, 1971.

Reapportionment in the 1970s, University of California Press, 1971.

The Modern Presidency, Random House, 1973.

(With Fred I. Greenstein, and contributor) *The Handbook of Political Science,* eight volumes, Addison-Wesley, 1975.

OTHER

Contributor, occasionally under pseudonym Arthur Clun, to political science periodicals, magazines, and newspapers, including *Harper's, Washington Post,* and *Wall Street Journal.* Managing editor of *American Political Science Review,* 1971-77; book review editor of *Transaction,* 1968-71; member of editorial advisory board of *Political Science Quarterly* and six other journals.

WORK IN PROGRESS: Further research on Congress, the Presidency, national politics, and comparative study of legislatures.

SIDELIGHTS: Nelson W. Polsby is referred to as the "Newton of the post-1968 political dynamics" by Edwin W. Yoder, Jr., in his *Washington Post Book World* review of *Consequences of Party Reform,* Polsby's explanation of how party reforms have altered the political landscape. Yoder believes the book to be "political science as it ought to be practiced but seldom is—the most searching work of analysis of its sort that I have read in years." Continues the critic: "Our ailing party system, which seems to be dying of the post-1968 'reforms' that were supposed to give it new life, has needed a master diagnostician for some time. In Nelson Polsby it has at last found one."

In his more recent *Political Innovation in America: The Politics of Policy Initiation,* Polsby analyzes the actual processes by which new programs and policies originate and flourish. Selecting examples since 1945 from "science policy (the creation of the Atomic Energy Commission), from foreign policy (the origins of the Truman Doctrine in 1947), and domestic policy (Medicare, the creation of the Peace Corps, the later community action program of Lyndon Johnson's 'war on pov-

erty')," notes Yoder in the *Washington Post Book World,* Polsby then "describes the dynamics by which lurking seeds of policy germinate and become actual programs, working some lasting and fundamental change in the political landscape." In the *New York Times Book Review,* William Schneider summarizes Polsby's argument, explaining that "innovation is now becoming routine in American politics because we have two groups of mutually dependent professionals—'policy entrepreneurs who specialize in identifying problems and finding solutions'... and politicians who are constantly in the market for new ideas." *Political Innovation in America,* remarks Yoder, is "as we have learned to expect of Nelson Polsby, a witty and instructive read."

BIOGRAPHICAL/CRITICAL SOURCES:

PERIODICALS

Los Angeles Times Book Review, May 8, 1983.
New York Times Book Review, May 13, 1984.
Times Literary Supplement, April 17, 1981, May 25, 1984.
Washington Post Book World, May 8, 1983, March 18, 1984.

*   *   *

PORTER, Andrew   1928-

PERSONAL: Born August 26, 1928, in Cape Town, South Africa. *Education:* University College, Oxford, M.A., 1950.

ADDRESSES: Office—New Yorker, 25 West 43rd St., New York, N.Y. 10036.

CAREER: Financial Times, London, England, music critic, 1950-74; *New Yorker,* New York, N.Y., music critic, 1972—. Visiting fellow at All Souls College, Oxford University, 1973-74; Regents Professor, University of California, Irvine, 1980; Bloch Professor, University of California, Berkeley, 1981. Member of music panel of Arts Council of Great Britain, 1962-72; member of music advisory committee of British Council, 1966-74; director of American Institute for Verdi Studies.

MEMBER: Royal Musical Association (member of council, 1964-72), American Musicological Society, American Academy of Arts and Sciences (fellow, 1985), Music Critics Association, Critics Circle of Great Britain (president, 1971, 1972), Donizetti Society (vice-president).

AWARDS, HONORS: Deems Taylor Award for criticism, from the American Society of Composers, Authors, and Publishers, 1975, 1976, and 1982.

WRITINGS:

(With Desmond Shawe-Taylor, Edward Sackville-West, and William Mann) *The Record Guide,* Collins, 1955.

A Musical Season: A Critic from Abroad in America, Viking, 1974.

Music of Three Seasons: 1974-1977, Farrar, Straus, 1978.

Music of Three More Seasons: 1977-1980, Knopf, 1980.

(Editor with David Rosen) *Verdi's "Macbeth": A Sourcebook,* Norton, 1984.

The Tempest (libretto, after Shakespeare's comedy, for John Eaton's opera), G. Schirmer, 1985.

TRANSLATIONS

Wagner's "Ring of the Nibelung," Norton, 1978.
Mozart's "Magic Flute," Faber & Faber, 1980.

Has also translated Alfano's "Resurrection," Gluck's "Orpheus and Eurydice," Handel's "Otho" ("Ottone"), Haydn's

"L'Incontro Improviso" (title means "The Unexpected Meeting") and "L'Infedelta Delusa" (title means "Deceit Outwitted"), Mozart's "Lucio Silla," "Idomeneo," "The Abduction from the Seraglio," "Figaro's Wedding," "Don Giovanni," and "Cosi fan tutte," Rossini's "The Turk in Italy" and "The Voyage to Rheims," Saint-Saens's "Henry VIII," Schoenberg's "Pierrot Lunaire," R. Strauss's "Intermezzo," Thomas's "Hamlet," Verdi's "Un Giorno di Regno" (title means "King for a Day"), "Nabucco," "Macbeth," "Rigoletto," G. Ricordi, "La Forza del Destino" (title means "The Force of Destiny"), G. Ricordi, "Don Carlos," "Otello," Riverrun Press, and "Falstaff," Riverrun Press, Wagner's "Tristan and Isolde," Riverrun Press, and "Parsifal," Riverrun Press, and many other operas.

OTHER

Editor of *Musical Times,* 1960-67, and newsletter of the American Institute of Verdi Studies; member of editorial board of *Opera,* 1953—; *Grove's Dictionary of Music and Musicians,* member of editorial executive committee, 6th edition, editorial advisor, new Berlioz edition.

WORK IN PROGRESS: Writing on Verdi.

SIDELIGHTS: Music of Three Seasons: 1974-1977, Music of Three Seasons: 1977-1980, and *A Musical Season: A Critic from Abroad in America* are collections of reviews Andrew Porter has written as music critic for the *New Yorker.* Reviewing the latter collection in the *New York Times Book Review,* John Yohalem notes that Porter has a "deep and wide-ranging erudition, the ability to discuss the history of apparently any aspect of music and related forms, traditions, sources, masters and disciples, editions, problems." Porter often applies his knowledge to the concerns of opera. According to *New Republic* contributor William Youngren, "Porter is firm and eloquent in his conviction that opera should be afforded productions that conform, as closely as possible, to the original intent of their composers.... Porter's wholly admirable and much needed campaign for authentic operatic production is part of a general plea for authenticity in all musical performance. He also convincingly advocated the appropriate use of Baroque pitch, eighteenth-century instruments (or good copies), and even the standard nineteenth-century orchestral seating arrangement." Porter makes one exception to his demand for authenticity; he believes that operas should be sung in translation. Porter explains his reasons in a *Publishers Weekly* interview with Genevieve Stuttaford: "Audiences should be able to understand what's being sung.... When you see 'Boris Godunov' performed in the original, you gain the sound of the Russian but lose the meaning of the words." According to Nicholas Kenyon, writing in the *New Yorker,* Porter hurdles such language barriers in his translation of Verdi's "La Forza del Destino." At one point during a California performance of the work, writes Kenyon, "Mr. Porter's translation, always a model of clarity and sensitivity, bec[ame]... a display of virtuosity, somehow managing to retain the puns and rhymes of the Italian while making sense in English."

Porter's musical taste isn't for everyone. In the opinion of *New Republic* reviewer B. H. Haggin, Porter writes "comparatively little about the music that interests most of his *New Yorker* readers, and a great deal about the music of today—by Boulez, Henze, Ginastera, Elliot Carter, George Crumb, and dozens of others." Youngren reports that he finds an "extraordinary imbalance in favor of vocal music in general and opera in particular" in *Music of Three Seasons: 1974-1977.* According to Youngren, Porter responded to the complaints

of his *New Yorker* readers with a review in which he contended that "'most music is vocal music'" and that "'most writing about music reflects the fact.'" Porter openly states his preference for vocal music. He told Stuttaford: "Opera is one of my strongest, or less weak, suits—however you like. It particularly interests me, so I write about it frequently."

George Bernard Shaw, known less well today as a music critic than as a playwright but considered one of the enduring writers in the form, is often mentioned as Porter's predecessor. Haggin contends that the connection is spurious: "Shaw is an example of a perceptive critic who is not a scholar; Porter is one of the exceedingly rare examples of a scholar who is also a perceptive critic.... As for style of writing, the striking difference between Shaw's and Porter's is precisely the appearance of high-spirited spontaneity in Shaw's as against the obvious studied crafting of Porter's that becomes tiresome." Other reviewers differ with Haggin's appraisal of Porter's style. Yohalem writes that "Porter's language is itself a thing musical. In a field that tends to strain verbal resources—there are just so many ways to describe a beautiful sound—Porter uses a vocabulary so wide it would do credit to a pornographer." Joseph McLellan notes in the *Washington Post Book World:* "Porter writes consistently well. At worst his prose is dryly informative, marked by clarity and precision. At best, it has a wit, an energy, a mastery of subtle variations in sentence-structure and vocabulary that any stylist might envy."

BIOGRAPHICAL/CRITICAL SOURCES:

BOOKS

Hitchcock, H. Wiley and Stanley Sadie, editors, *The New Grove Dictionary of American Music,* Groves Dictionaries of Music, 1986.
Nineteenth Century Music, Volume II, number 3, Taplinger, 1979.
Sadie, editor, *The New Grove Dictionary of Music and Musicians,* Volume XV, Macmillan, 1980.

PERIODICALS

New Republic, November 29, 1975, December 2, 1978.
New Yorker, May 12, 1980.
New York Times Book Review, July 7, 1974.
Opera News, January 5, 1980.
Publishers Weekly, October 23, 1978.
Southwest Review, spring, 1979.
Spectator, December 7, 1974.
Washington Post Book World, November 21, 1978, November 1, 1981.

*   *   *

PORTER, Laurence M(inot) 1936-

PERSONAL: Born January 17, 1936, in Ossining, N.Y.; son of Fairfield and Anne Elizabeth (Channing) Porter; married Elizabeth Hart (an architect), June 9, 1960 (divorced, 1979); married Laurel Melinda Cline (a social worker and writer), January 17, 1980; children: Leon Fairfield, Sarah Elizabeth, John Carl Fairfield. *Education:* Harvard University, A.B., 1957, A.M., 1959, Ph.D., 1965. *Politics:* "Anti-war and pro-human services." *Religion:* Agnostic.

ADDRESSES: Home—926 Sunset Lane, East Lansing, Mich. 48823. *Office*—Department of Romance and Classical Languages and Literatures, Michigan State University, Wells Hall, East Lansing, Mich. 48824.

CAREER: Michigan State University, East Lansing, instructor, 1963-65, assistant professor, 1965-69, associate professor, 1969-73, professor of French and comparative literature, 1973—. Co-director of National Colloquium on Nineteenth-Century French Studies, 1978; visiting Andrew W. Mellon Professor of Comparative Literature, University of Pittsburgh, 1980. *Military service:* U.S. Army Reserve, 1957-63.

MEMBER: International Comparative Literature Association, Modern Language Association of America, American Association of University Professors, American Comparative Literature Association, Sierra Club, Appalachian Mountain Club.

AWARDS, HONORS: Ford Foundation grant, 1966.

WRITINGS:

(Editor and translator, with Elisha Greifer) Joseph de Maistre, *On God and Society*, Regnery, 1959.
The Renaissance of the Lyric in French Romanticism, French Forum Monographs, 1978.
The Literary Dream in French Romanticism, Wayne State University Press, 1979.
(Editor with wife, Laurel Porter) *Aging in Literature*, International Book Publishers, 1984.
(Editor) *Critical Essays on Gustave Flaubert*, G. K. Hall, 1986.
The Interpretation of Dreams: Freud's Theories Revisited, Twayne, 1987.

Contributor to language and literature journals. Member of editorial board of *Degre Second*, 1976—, and *Nineteenth-Century French Studies*, 1982—.

WORK IN PROGRESS: *The Myth of the Devil from Milton to Mann; The Crisis of French Symbolism.*

SIDELIGHTS: Laurence M. Porter wrote: "As a critic and professor, I try to help people learn to read and write better. To me, this means helping people to recognize the nuance, hidden coherence, and significant detail which disclose the richness of artistic creation, and to articulate their own perceptions in a way which allows them to discover the wealth of their own individualities. 'How do I know what I mean till I see what I say?' I encourage people to profit from unlimited second chances which reading and writing, unlike life, can offer."

AVOCATIONAL INTERESTS: Singing in madrigal groups, running (including the Boston Marathon).

* * *

PRESCOTT, J(ohn) R(obert) V(ictor) 1931-

PERSONAL: Born in 1931 in Newcastle upon Tyne, England; son of George (a boilermaker) and Ada (a tailoress; maiden name, Howell) Prescott; married Dorothy F. Allen (a map curator), September 15, 1953; children: Margaret Prescott Frazer, Philip. *Education:* University of Durham, B.Sc., 1952, Diploma in Education, 1955, M.A., 1957; Birbeck College, London, Ph.D., 1961.

ADDRESSES: *Office*—Department of Geography, University of Melbourne, Parkville, Victoria 3052, Australia.

CAREER: University College (now University of Ibadan), Ibadan, Nigeria, lecturer in geography, 1956-61; University of Melbourne, Parkville, Australia, lecturer and reader in geography, 1961-85, professor of geography, 1985—. Visiting pro-

fessor at University of British Columbia, 1969-70. *Military service:* British Army, 1952-54; became lieutenant.

WRITINGS:

The Geography of Frontiers and Boundaries, Aldine, 1965, revised edition published as *Frontiers and Boundaries*, Croom Helm, 1978.
The Geography of State Policies, Aldine, 1968.
The Evolution of Nigeria's International and Regional Boundaries, 1861-1971, Tantalus, 1971.
Political Geography, Methuen, 1972.
The Political Geography of the Oceans, David & Charles, 1975.
The Map of Mainland Asia by Treaty, Melbourne University Press, 1975.
(With W. G. East) *Our Fragmented World: An Introduction to Political Geography*, Macmillan, 1975.
(With H. J. Collier and wife, Dorothy F. Prescott) *The Frontiers of Asia and Southeast Asia*, Melbourne University Press, 1976.
(With John Lovering) *The Last of Lands: Antarctica*, Melbourne University Press, 1979.
(Editor and contributor) *Australia's Continental Shelf*, Thomas Nelson, 1979.
Maritime Jurisdiction in Southeast Asia: A Commentary and Map, East-West Center (Honolulu, Hawaii), 1981.
The Maritime Political Boundaries of the World, Methuen, 1985.
Australia's Maritime Boundaries, Australian Institute for International Affairs, 1985.
Political Frontiers and Boundaries, Allen & Unwin, 1987.

WORK IN PROGRESS: Regional studies of maritime boundaries.

SIDELIGHTS: J. R. V. Prescott told *CA*: "In common with tenured academics throughout the English-speaking world, I have been very lucky to have a secure income and a post which requires me to spend some of my time writing books and papers.

"In my experience the benefit of writing books comes not from the royalties which might be earned, but from the contacts with readers. I value the invitations to address conferences, to work at the East-West Center in Honolulu, and to undertake work for governments more highly than the modest sums I have earned in royalties."

* * *

PRESTON, Harry 1923-
(Vanessa Cartwright)

PERSONAL: Born September 4, 1923, in Howick, Natal, South Africa; naturalized U.S. citizen, 1956; son of Richard Henry (a chemist) and Lillian Catherine (Walter) Pimm. *Education:* University of Natal, B.A., 1942. *Religion:* "Truth and honesty."

ADDRESSES: *Home*—4413 Clemson Dr., Garland, Tex. 75042.

CAREER: Singer, dancer, actor, and musician in South Africa, 1939-48; Cactus State Radio Network, Big Spring, Tex., program director, 1950-51; Big D Film Studio, Dallas, Tex., writer and director, 1952-55; WFAA-TV, Dallas, news editor, 1956-58; Metro-Goldwyn-Mayer Studios, Culver City, Calif., editorial analyst, 1959; Jam Handy Organization, Detroit, Mich., writer and director, 1960-62; independent film producer and director in Detroit, 1962-67; Bill Bailey Productions, Hollywood, Calif., writer and director, 1968; Harris-Tuchman Productions, Hollywood, writer and director, 1969; United States Air Force, Norton Air Force Base, California, writer, 1970-76; The Image House, Dallas, writer, 1977; *Spotlight Magazine*, Dallas, drama reviewer, 1978; *Dallas Times-Herald*, Dallas, book reviewer and feature writer, 1978-83; Omega Cinema Productions, Dallas, writer and director, 1980; Intowne Publications, Dallas, editor, 1985-86.

AWARDS, HONORS: Best Play, Texas Playwrights Contest, 1958, for comedy, "Time for Madness"; Best Supporting Actor in Southwest, 1959, for portrayal of Lord Brockhurst in Breck Wall's production of "The Boy Friend."

WRITINGS:

(With Vila Briley) *Housewives Guide to Extra Income: How to Make Your Spare Time Work for You,* Books for Better Living, 1972.
(With Jeanette Margolin) *Everything a Teenager Wants to Know about Sex and Should,* Books for Better Living, 1973.
Kicking Your Sex Hangups, Academy, 1973.
Erotic Africa, Academy, 1973.
(With Emil Halley) *The Natural Food Reducing Diet,* Books for Better Living, 1974.
Crucifixion of a Closet Queen, Academy, 1974.
How to Teach Your Children about Sex, Books for Better Living, 1974.
Queen of Darkness, Manor Books, 1976.
(With Ned Fritz) *The Sterile Forest,* Eakin Publishers, 1983.
(With John Marion Ellis) *Free of Pain,* Southwest Publishing, 1983.
(Editor) Stan DeFreitas, *Stan DeFreitas' Complete Guide to Florida Gardening,* Taylor, 1984.

SATIRICAL REVUES

"Bubblegum," first produced in Cape Town, South Africa, at Hofmeyr Theatre, 1944.
"You Gotta Be Kidding," first produced in Detroit, Mich., 1965, produced in Hollywood, 1967, produced in Dallas, 1980.

ROMANCE NOVELS; UNDER PSEUDONYM VANESSA CARTWRIGHT

Indigo Encounter, McFadden, 1978.
Wine of Love, McFadden, 1978.
Legacy of Love, McFadden, 1978.
Appointment in Antibes, McFadden, 1978.
Winter Wish, McFadden, 1978.
Summer in Stockholm, McFadden, 1978.
Escape to Happiness, McFadden, 1978.

OTHER

"Time for Madness" (play), first produced in Dallas at Dallas Institute of Performing Arts, 1958, produced in Dallas at Haymarket Theatre, 1980.

Also author, with Max Morales, of *The Other Side of the Alamo,* 1984; also author of "The Nostalgia Channel," a pilot, 1984. Author of seven book-length children's stories serialized in South African newspapers, 1936-39; author of more than four hundred industrial and documentary filmscripts. Contributor of more than two hundred short stories to newspapers and magazines.

WORK IN PROGRESS: I Remember Mau Mau, a humorous account of Preston's teen years touring with the circus and variety shows in South Africa; *Shot in Dallas,* a novel set in Dallas dealing with the would-be feature film industry in Texas; *Hustler,* a novel dealing with the relationship between a middle-aged homosexual and a young male hustler; "Time for Madness," a musical version of Preston's award-winning play.

SIDELIGHTS: Harry Preston once told *CA:* "As an eternal optimist, I find my hopes for harmony between the many races in Africa more idealistic than realistic. This is sad, because the country is one of the most beautiful in the world, and could be a paradise if people could only live together in peace, respecting each other's customs and cultures." Preston began writing at the age of ten, and was first published when he was fourteen. He reports he now writes an average of six hours a day, weekends included.

AVOCATIONAL INTERESTS: Cooking and gardening.

* * *

PRITCHARD, William H(arrison)   1932-

PERSONAL: Born November 12, 1932, in Binghamton, N.Y.; son of William (a lawyer) and Marion (a teacher; maiden name, La Grange) Pritchard; married Marietta Perl (a journalist), August 24, 1957; children: David, Michael, William. *Education:* Amherst College, B.A., 1953; Harvard University, M.A., 1956, Ph.D., 1960.

ADDRESSES: Home—86 Northampton Rd., Amherst, Mass. 01002. *Office*—Department of English, Amherst College, Amherst, Mass. 01002.

CAREER: Amherst College, Amherst, Mass., instructor, 1958-61, assistant professor, 1961-65, associate professor, 1965-70, professor, beginning 1970, currently Henry Clay Folger Professor of English.

AWARDS, HONORS: Guggenheim fellow, 1973-74; National Endowment for the Humanities fellow, 1977-78; American Council of Learned Societies fellow, 1981-82.

WRITINGS:

Wyndham Lewis, Twayne, 1968.
Wyndham Lewis: Profile in Literature, Humanities Press, 1972.
(Editor) *Penguin Critical Anthology: Yeats,* Penguin, 1972.
Seeing through Everything: English Writers, 1918-1940, Oxford University Press, 1977.
(Editor) *The Norton Anthology of American Literature,* Norton, 1979.
Lives of the Modern Poets, Oxford University Press, 1980.
Frost: A Literary Life Reconsidered, Oxford University Press, 1984.

Contributor to *Hudson Review, New York Times Book Review, New Republic, American Scholar,* and other publications. Advisory editor, *Hudson Review.*

SIDELIGHTS: William H. Pritchard's books of literary biography and criticism concentrate on the major British and American authors of the twentieth century. He has written full-length works on British novelist Wyndham Lewis and American poet Robert Frost, as well as survey volumes on periods in literary history. His *Frost: A Literary Life Reconsidered* has been instrumental in reestablishing Frost's literary reputation.

In his first two books, *Wyndham Lewis* and *Wyndham Lewis: Profile in Literature,* Pritchard examines the long and varied career of the British writer and artist. Lewis was a founder of the vorticist art movement, a co-editor with Ezra Pound of the avant-garde journal *Blast,* and the author of novels, plays, essays, and criticism during a career lasting nearly five decades. Because of the wide-ranging nature of Lewis's work, it has been difficult for many critics to adequately evaluate his accomplishments. And Lewis's outspoken political and literary views alienated other critics. But Pritchard's *Wyndham Lewis*, according to the *Times Literary Supplement* reviewer, "is the most reasoned and sensible view of Lewis's literary achievement that has yet appeared. . . . As an introduction to the scope of Lewis's achievement as an imaginative prose writer this study is admirably clear, concise and intelligent."

In *Seeing through Everything: English Writers, 1918-1940*, Pritchard writes of Lewis and sixteen others in an attempt, as he states in the book, to "come to terms with [the period's] most significant and enduring literary monuments." W. M. Hagen of *World Literature Today* sees the book as a study of "the process . . . by which writers, critics and ordinary readers salvage and organize experience. . . . [Pritchard's] criteria are sensible and clear throughout: technique should subserve the task of rendering and creating a human experience; the richest human experience is available through a voice or persona which encompasses and 'sees through' its subject and its own posture." Anatole Broyard of the *New York Times* admits that Pritchard's analysis "is persuasive enough to have disturbed two judgments I had grown complacent about" and he describes Pritchard as "a man who moves naturally and resourcefully through literary history, borrowing an apt phrase here and coining one there." When reading *Seeing through Everything*, Hagan believes that "instead of passively viewing yet another critic's parade of explicated masterpieces, the reader is engaged by the unfolding tradition of humane discourse."

In *Lives of the Modern Poets*, Pritchard studies how nine major poets from the first half of the twentieth century present themselves in their work, what Reed Whittemore of the *Washington Post Book World* describes as "the character that each poet provides himself in his poem—that is, his distinctive voice, tone, expressive manner." Pritchard's aim in this book, Jay Parini of the *New Republic* states, is "to provide the nonspecialist reader with an overview of the period and to offer revaluations of each 'life' for those of us already mired in vast private libraries of criticism on each poet mentioned. . . . Pritchard blows a fresh draft of air through the smoky corridors of contemporary criticism."

Pritchard's approach is conversational. As Deborah Pope explains in the *South Atlantic Quarterly*, "His voice is affable, low-key, quick to acknowledge his own shortcomings, telling over his favorite poems by each poet as confidingly as showing pictures in a wallet." This quality is also acknowledged by Richard Ellmann of the *New York Times Book Review*. Pritchard, Ellmann maintains, "writes pleasantly and confidingly, obsequiously follows or mildly diverges from other critics, rather haphazardly brings in biographical details and provides good talk about his subjects. His book is deliberately low-pitched, as if to sway by quiet rather than by noise." For John Leonard in the *New York Times*, Pritchard's accomplishment is "astonishing." *Lives of the Modern Poets*, Leonard writes, "makes this season of criticism a season of distinction. Mr. Pritchard, in making us listen as if we were children or about to die, to listen for the first and the last time, makes magic."

With his *Frost: A Literary Life Reconsidered*, published in 1984, Pritchard sought to counter the critical evaluations of American poet Robert Frost. As Donald Hall explains in the *Washington Post Book World*, "in his lifetime people tried simplifying [Frost] into a lovable rustic. . . . After his death,

Frost's biographer simplified him into an ogre of vanity and vengefulness." Pritchard's book is meant to provide a more balanced view of Frost, based on a reading of his own work. "In Mr. Pritchard's account," Helen Vendler writes in the *New York Times Book Review*, "the reader will see the best case that can be made for Frost as man and poet, a case made by a critic who has known the poems and lived with them for 30 years."

Pritchard primarily argues against the devastating biography of Frost written by Lawrance Thompson. A massive three-volume work of some 2,000 pages, Thompson's biography reveals Frost's "vindictive mind, petty, jealous, stunningly callous and ambitious," Joseph Parisi writes in the *Chicago Tribune Book World*. Its publication caused Frost's image to be radically transformed from a sage-like poet of rural New England into "what many regarded as a species of monster in human form," as Christopher Lehmann-Haupt maintains in the *New York Times*. But Thompson's examination of Frost's life contains a fundamental error in outlook, Pritchard believes. Thompson is too often literal-minded about many of Frost's poems and personal statements, ignoring what Pritchard sees as Frost's essentially playful approach. Thompson, Pritchard writes in the book, is "uncomfortable with the playful, complicated, devious Frost" and therefore misinterprets the poet.

But several critics find Pritchard's view of Frost too favorable. "It seems to me," Vendler remarks, "that Mr. Pritchard treats Frost's eccentricities rather too lightly." "Sometimes," Alfred Corn writes in the *New Republic*, "[Pritchard] whitewashes Frost's misdeeds or lets them pass without comment; sometimes he gives unconvincing justifications where better ones might be advanced; and sometimes he outdoes Thompson in indemnifying Frost." Still, Corn concludes that "perhaps it is time to allow that Frost had his failings petty and grand, but to consider that the best consolation for them now is his poetry."

Most critics note the success and importance of Pritchard's book. Vendler, for example, concludes that Pritchard's "deft, concise, readable literary life moves between its two genres—biography and criticism—with confidence and poise." "Pritchard has dispelled," Lehmann-Haupt believes, "the various caricatures of Frost, the folksy model as well as the monster glimpsed in the pages of Lawrance Thompson's biography. As the caricatures disperse, Frost's genius emerges. To judge from this intelligent study, that genius can be ranked among the masters of 20th century poetry."

BIOGRAPHICAL/CRITICAL SOURCES:

BOOKS

Contemporary Literary Criticism, Volume XXXIV, Gale, 1985.
Pritchard, William H., *Seeing through Everything: English Writers, 1918-1940*, Oxford University Press, 1977.
Pritchard, William H., *Frost: A Literary Life Reconsidered*, Oxford University Press, 1984.

PERIODICALS

Atlantic, May, 1980.
Chicago Tribune, November 18, 1984.
Detroit News, December 16, 1984.
Los Angeles Times Book Review, November 4, 1984.
New Republic, May 31, 1980, February 4, 1985.
Newsweek, October 29, 1984.
New York Review of Books, April 25, 1985.

New York Times, September 1, 1977, April 24, 1980, October 9, 1984.
New York Times Book Review, October 9, 1977, April 27, 1980, October 14, 1984.
South Atlantic Quarterly, autumn, 1981, summer, 1986.
Spectator, March 28, 1969.
Time, November 12, 1984.
Times (London), October 28, 1980.
Times Literary Supplement, February 27, 1969, April 7, 1972, February 3, 1978, September 26, 1980, August 2, 1985.
Washington Post Book World, May 11, 1980, October 7, 1984.
World Literature Today, winter, 1979, summer, 1981.
Yale Review, December, 1968.

—Sketch by Thomas Wiloch

Q-R

QUINN, Martin
See SMITH, Martin Cruz

*   *   *

QUINN, Simon
See SMITH, Martin Cruz

*   *   *

RAAT, W(illiam) Dirk 1939-

PERSONAL: Born July 1, 1939, in Ogden, Utah; son of Elmer W. (a plumber) and Iris (Calkins) Raat; married Geraldine (Koba) Corter, 1984; children: Kelly, David. *Education:* University of Utah, B.S., 1961, Ph.D., 1967; also attended National University of Mexico and Center for Intercultural Documentation, Cuernavaca, Mexico.

ADDRESSES: Home—132 Center St., Fredonia, N.Y. 14063. *Office*—Department of History, State University of New York College at Fredonia, Fredonia, N.Y. 14063.

CAREER: Moorhead State College, Moorhead, Minn., assistant professor, 1966-68, associate professor of history, 1968-70; State University of New York College at Fredonia, associate professor, 1970-77, professor of history, 1977—, chairman of department, 1973-74. Visiting professor of history, University of Utah, 1984-85. Member, Conference on Latin American History, Rocky Mountain Conference on Latin American Studies. Consultant to National Endowment for the Humanities. *Military service:* Utah National Guard, 1954-64.

MEMBER: Latin American Studies Association.

AWARDS, HONORS: James A. Robertson Award from Conference on Latin American History, 1968, for article "Leopoldo Zea and Mexican Positivism"; grant-in-aid, State University of New York, 1973, 1975, 1979; American Council of Learned Societies fellowship, 1976-77.

WRITINGS:

El positivismo durante el Porfiriato (title means "Positivism during the Porifiriato"), SepSetentas, 1975.
Revoltosos: Mexico's Rebels in the United States, 1903-23, Texas A & M University Press, 1981.

Mexico: From Independence to Revolution, 1810-1910, University of Nebraska Press, 1982.
The Mexican Revolution: Historiography and Bibliography, G. K. Hall, 1982.
(With William Beezley) *Twentieth-Century Mexico,* University of Nebraska Press, 1986.
Mexico and the U.S.: A Tale of Two Peoples, University of Georgia Press, c. 1988.

Contributor of over twenty articles and essays to history journals and books.

WORK IN PROGRESS: The FBI in Mexico.

SIDELIGHTS: W. Dirk Raat told *CA:* "Anyone desiring to be a historian should like to travel, have an excellent command of foreign languages, and be independently wealthy. As for myself, I do like to travel.

"More seriously, I believe that the historian has a special task to perform. Like the philosopher, he is analytical; unlike the great philosophers, he is seldom speculative. Like the social scientist, he is a researcher; unlike the sociologist, the historian has a story to tell. The telling of history is both a craft and an art. To create and publish a historical work is to engage in craftsmanship. To write well and effectively is the task of the artist."

*   *   *

RABY, William L(ouis) 1927-

PERSONAL: Born July 16, 1927, in Chicago, Ill.; son of Gustave E. (a painter) and Helen (Burgess) Raby; married Norma Claire Schreiner, September 8, 1956; children: Burgess, Marianne, Marlene. *Education:* Northwestern University, B.S., 1949; University of Illinois, C.P.A., 1950; University of Arizona, M.B.A., 1961, Ph.D., 1970.

ADDRESSES: Office—30 East Bishop, Tempe, Ariz. 85282.

CAREER: Swenson & Raby (certified public accountants), Rockford, Ill., partner, 1950-60; William L. Raby & Co. (certified public accountants), Tucson, Ariz., partner, 1961-69; Laventhol & Horwath (certified public accountants), Philadelphia, Pa., partner in Phoenix, Ariz., office, 1969-77; Touche Ross & Co., New York, N.Y., partner in Phoenix office, 1977-87. Lecturer in accounting, Rockford College, Rockford, Ill., 1954-55, and University of Arizona, 1958-70; associate professor of accounting, Ohio University, 1962-65; adjunct professor of taxation, New York University, 1978-81, and Arizona State University, 1983—. Member of Tax Court bar. *Military service:* U.S. Navy, 1942-45.

MEMBER: American Institute of Certified Public Accountants (chairman of Federal Tax Division, 1980-83, vice president, 1983-84), American Accounting Association (past president of American Taxation Association section), Arizona Chamber of Commerce (chairman elect), Beta Gamma Sigma (past president of Arizona alumni chapter), Delta Mu Delta, Beta Alpha Psi, Alpha Kappa Psi.

WRITINGS:

The Income Tax and Business Decisions, Prentice-Hall, 1964, 4th edition, 1978.
Building and Maintaining a Successful Tax Practice, Prentice-Hall, 1964.
(With Carl Riblet, Jr.) *The Reluctant Taxpayer,* Cowles, 1970.
Tax Practice Management, American Institute of Certified Public Accountants, 1974.
(With Victor Tidwell) *Introduction to Federal Taxation* (annual), Prentice-Hall, 1980—.
(With son, Burgess Raby) *Tax Practice Management: Client Servicing* (supplemental quarterly), Prentice-Hall, 1986.

Author of semi-weekly column for *PHANET* (Prentice-Hall information network). Senior author of "The Raby Report on Tax Practice Management." Contributor to professional journals. Member of editorial board, *Taxation for Accountants* and *Tax Advisor.*

* * *

RANDALL, Dudley (Felker) 1914-

PERSONAL: Born January 14, 1914, in Washington, D.C.; son of Arthur George Clyde (a Congregational minister) and Ada Viola (a teacher; maiden name, Bradley) Randall; married Ruby Hands, May 27, 1935 (marriage dissolved); married Mildred Pinckney, December 20, 1942 (marriage dissolved); married Vivian Spencer (a psychiatric social worker), May 4, 1957; children: (first marriage) Phyllis Ada (Mrs. William Sherron III). *Education:* Wayne University (now Wayne State University), B.A., 1949; University of Michigan, M.A.L.S., 1951; graduate study, University of Ghana, 1970. *Politics:* Independent. *Religion:* Congregational.

ADDRESSES: Home and office—12651 Old Mill Pl., Detroit, Mich. 48238.

CAREER: Ford Motor Co., River Rouge, Mich., foundry worker, 1932-37; U.S. Post Office, Detroit, Mich., carrier and clerk, 1938-51; Lincoln University, Jefferson City, Mo., librarian, 1951-54; Morgan State College, Baltimore, Md., associate librarian, 1954-56; Wayne County Federated Library System, Wayne, Mich., 1956-69, began as assistant branch librarian, became branch librarian, 1956-63, head, reference-interloan department, 1963-69; University of Detroit, Detroit, reference librarian and poet-in-residence, 1969-75. Visiting lecturer, University of Michigan, 1969. Founder and general editor, Broadside Press, Detroit, 1965-1977, consultant, 1977—. Founder, Broadside Poets Theater and Broadside Poetry Workshop, 1980. Member, Advisory Panel on Literature, Michigan Council for the Arts, and New Detroit, Inc., both since 1970. Has participated in several poetry seminars and festivals, including the East-West Culture Learning Institute's

Seminar on socio-literature at the University of Hawaii. *Military service:* U.S. Army, signal corps, 1942-46.

MEMBER: International Afro-American Museum, National Association for the Advancement of Colored People, American Library Association, Michigan Library Association, Michigan Poetry Society, Detroit Society for the Advancement of Culture and Education.

AWARDS, HONORS: Tompkins Award, Wayne State University, 1962, 1966; Kuumba Liberation Award, 1973; Arts Award in Literature, Michigan Foundation for the Arts, 1975; D.Litt., University of Detroit, 1978; Creative Artist Award in Literature, Michigan Council for the Arts, 1981; National Endowment for the Arts fellowship, 1981, senior fellowship, 1986; appointed First Poet Laureate of the City of Detroit by Mayor Coleman A. Young, 1981.

WRITINGS:

(Contributor) Rosey E. Pool, editor and author of introduction, *Beyond the Blues,* Hand and Flower Press, 1962.
(With Margaret Danner) *Poem Counterpoem,* Broadside Press, 1966.
(Editor and contributor with Margaret G. Burroughs) *For Malcolm: Poems on the Life and Death of Malcolm X,* Broadside Press, 1967, 2nd edition, 1969.
Cities Burning, Broadside Press, 1968.
(Editor) *Black Poetry: A Supplement to Anthologies Which Exclude Black Poets,* Broadside Press, 1969.
(Author of introduction) Sonia Sanchez, *We a BaddDDD People,* Broadside Press, 1970.
Love You, Paul Breman, 1970.
More to Remember: Poems of Four Decades, Third World Press, 1971.
(Editor and author of introduction) *The Black Poets,* Bantam, 1971.
(Contributor) Addison Gayle, Jr., editor, *The Black Aesthetic,* Doubleday, 1971.
After the Killing, Third World Press, 1973.
(With Gwendolyn Brooks, Keorapetse Kgositsile, and Haki R. Madhubuti) *A Capsule Course in Black Poetry Writing,* Broadside Press, 1975.
Broadside Memories: Poets I Have Known, Broadside Press, 1975.
A Litany of Friends: New and Selected Poems, Lotus Press, 1981, 2nd edition, 1983.
Homage to Hoyt Fuller, Broadside Press, 1984.
(Editor with Louis J. Cantoni) *Golden Song: The Fiftieth Anniversary Anthology of the Poetry Society of Michigan, 1935-1985,* Harlo, 1985.

Contributor of poems to anthologies, including *American Negro Poetry, New Negro Poets: USA, Ik Ben de Nieuwe Neger, La Poesie Negro-Americaine,* and *Kaleidoscope.* Contributor of poems, short stories, articles, and reviews to *Midwest Journal, Free Lance, Black World, Black Academy Review, Umbra, Negro Digest, Journal of Black Poetry, Beloit Review, Wayne Review,* and *New World Review.*

SIDELIGHTS: The influence of Dudley Randall, founder of Broadside Press and Detroit's first poet laureate, "has been one of the strongest—some say the strongest—in the black poetry movement of the last 15 years," writes Suzanne Dolezal. The 1982 article in *Detroit* magazine, a *Detroit Free Press* supplement, continues, "As publisher of Detroit's Broadside Press between 1965 and 1977, Randall provided a forum for just about every major black poet to come along during those years. And dozens of anthologies include his own rapid, emotional lyrics about Detroit's bag ladies, lonely old drunks, strapping foundry workers and young women with glistening, corn-rowed hair.'' R. Baxter Miller explains Randall's importance in the *Dictionary of Literary Biography: Afro-American Poets since 1955:* ''Beyond Randall's contributions as a poet, his roles as editor and publisher have proven invaluable to the Afro-American community.''

Randall's interest in poetry has been lifelong. Born in Washington, D.C., the son of a minister and a teacher, he wrote his first poem when he was four years old, moved to Detroit when he was nine, and saw his poems first published in the *Detroit Free Press* when he was thirteen. A bright student, Randall graduated early. After working in Ford's River Rouge foundry for five years and serving in the army, he extended his reputation for scholarship by earning a master's degree in library science from the University of Michigan and by studying the humanities. Randall, who became the reference librarian for Wayne County, also became fluent in Russian, visited Europe, Africa, and Russia, and later translated many Russian poems into English.

Randall's first books, however, did not display his range, Miller indicates. *Poem Counterpoem,* a unique volume in which ''ten poems each by [Margaret] Danner and Randall. . . . are alternated to form a kind of double commentary on the subjects they address in common,'' contains ''only the verses appropriately matched with Danner's,'' the essayist relates; and while *Cities Burning,* Randall's second opus, presents the spirit of the poet's urban environment and the politics of his times, it gathers only those poems that treat ''the theme of a disintegrating era.'' But the third and more inclusive collection *More to Remember: Poems of Four Decades* ''displays [Randall's] artistic breadth'' in poems that address universal themes and explore ''contradictions in human psychology and the black arts movement,'' observes Miller. Miller also sees ''Randall's aesthetic theory'' in poems that depict ''the artist as a modifier of both literary tradition and classical form.'' Randall defines this aesthetic himself in *Negro Digest:* ''Precision and accuracy are necessary for both white and black writers. . . . 'A black aesthetic' should not be an excuse for sloppy writing.'' He believes that for writers who adhere to the ''black aesthetic'' there is a future, ''as long as their rejection of 'white standards' rejects only what is false. . . . How else can a black writer write than out of his black experience? Yet what we tend to overlook is that our common humanity makes it possible to write a love poem, for instance, without a word of race, or to write a nationalistic poem that will be valid for all humanity.''

Later collections of Randall's poems also show his careful craftsmanship. Reviewing *After the Killing* (1973), Frank Marshall Davis declares, ''Dudley Randall again offers visual proof of why he should be ranked in the front echelon of Black poets.'' When the poet evades ''cliches and hackneyed rhymes, he excels at his craft,'' says Miller, who also believes that verses in *A Litany of Friends: New and Selected Poems* (1981) ''demonstrate Randall's technical skill.'' Brief notices about Randall's books in library trade journals are generally complimentary, in keeping with Davis's comment in *Black World* magazine and Miller's assessment.

Reviewers recognize Randall's work as a bridge between earlier black writers and the generation that raised its voice of affirmation in the 1960s. ''Exploring racial and historical themes, introspective and self-critical, his work combines ideas

and forms from Western traditional poetry as well as from the Harlem Renaissance movement,'' Miller notes. Writing in the *Negro Digest* in 1969, Ron Welburn concurs: ''[Randall's] is a keen functional awareness of what black poetry has been and remains, and there is no hint of an alienation from the ethos being developed by the new stylists.'' Welburn's review foresaw that younger poets would be somewhat influenced by Randall's voice and perhaps more potently by his example: ''he is contributing something to black literature that has a lasting value.''

Broadside Press—Randall's other contribution to black poetry in America—began in 1963. Randall had composed the poem ''Ballad of Birmingham'' after a bomb exploded in an Alabama church, killing four children. ''Folk singer Jerry Moore of New York had it set to music, and I wanted to protect the rights to the poem by getting it copyrighted,'' the publisher recalls in *Broadside Memories: Poets I Have Known.* Leaflets, he learned, could be copyrighted, so he published the poem as a broadside, a single sheet of paper that could be printed and sold for a minimal price. Randall's ''Dressed All in Pink,'' composed after John F. Kennedy's assassination, also recorded by Moore, became number two of the Broadside series, which was to include close to one hundred titles by 1982.

Randall became a book publisher when poets at a Fisk University conference nominated him to collect and publish ''the many poems being written about the slain black leader'' Malcolm X, reports Dolezal. The printing was delayed so that *For Malcolm: Poems on the Life and Death of Malcolm X* was not the first Broadside book published, but when it came out in 1967, it was a success. By that time aware that major publishers were seldom accepting works by young black poets, Randall ''became dedicated to giving the emerging black poetry the forum it needed,'' Dolezal notes. Indeed, Randall's encouragement was essential to the writing careers of several black poets. Etheridge Knight, for example, was in prison when he contributed three poems to the Broadside anthology *For Malcolm,* and Randall's visits ''convinced a hesitant Knight of his talent,'' Dolezal reports. Randall published first books for Knight and for Haki R. Madhubuti (formerly Don L. Lee), two poets who now enjoy international acclaim.

Altogether, the press produced nearly sixty volumes of poetry and criticism under Randall's tenure, all showcasing black writers, who rewarded his dedication by remaining loyal to Broadside even when larger publishing houses with generous promotion budgets beckoned. Gwendolyn Brooks insisted that Randall, not Harper & Row, would publish her autobiography; Sonia Sanchez preferred Broadside to the Third World Press, the small press founded by Madhubuti. Poet Nikki Giovanni explained to Dolezal, ''Broadside was neither mother nor father of the poetry movement, but it was certainly midwife. Dudley understood the thrust of the movement, which was essentially vernacular. He . . . allowed his poets to find their own voices. That was the charm of Broadside.''

By 1977, Randall's determination to supply low-priced books even to stores already in debt to him brought the small press, also deeply in debt, to the crisis point. The Alexander Crummell Memorial Center, a church in Highland Park, Michigan, bought the press, retaining Randall as its consultant. Though the poets he once published have found other publishers since the sale, Randall continues to be concerned for new poets, and anticipates the publication of more new works when the press revives. But Dolezal concludes that whether or not that hope materializes, ''Randall's achievement remains intact.'' Furthermore, as the poet laureate of a sprawling mid-western metropolis told *New York Times* contributor Harold Blum, there is always plenty to do: "[A poet] can change the way people look and feel about things. And that's what I want to do in Detroit."

BIOGRAPHICAL/CRITICAL SOURCES:

BOOKS

Barksdale, Richard K. and Keneth Kinnamon, editors, *Black Writers in America: A Comprehensive Anthology,* Macmillan, 1972.
Black Poets: The New Heroic Genre, Broadside Press, 1983.
Contemporary Literary Criticism, Volume I, Gale, 1973.
Dictionary of Literary Biography, Volume XLI: *Afro-American Poets since 1955,* Gale, 1985.
Gayle, Addison, editor, *The Black Aesthetic,* Doubleday, 1971.
King, Woodie, Jr., editor, *The Forerunners: Black Poets in America,* Howard University Press, 1981.
Randall, Dudley, *Broadside Memories: Poets I Have Known,* Broadside Press, 1975.
Randall, Dudley, *A Litany of Friends: New and Selected Poems,* Lotus Press, 1981, new edition, 1983.

PERIODICALS

Black American Literature Forum, Volume 17, number 3, 1983, February, 1984.
Black World, September, 1974.
Callaloo, Volume 6, number 1, 1983.
Detroit Free Press, April 11, 1982.
Library Journal, February 15, 1971, March 15, 1972.
Negro Digest, February, 1965, September, 1965, January, 1968, December, 1969.
New York Times, January 30, 1984.
New York Times Book Review, part 2, February 13, 1972.
Obsidian, Volume 2, number 1, 1976.

—*Sketch by Marilyn K. Basel*

*   *   *

RASBERRY, Salli   1940-

PERSONAL: Born September 21, 1940, in Cincinnati, Ohio; daughter of James R. (an investor) and Alicia (Marsh) Harrison; children: Sasha. *Education:* Attended Miami University, Oxford, Ohio.

ADDRESSES: P.O. Box 146, Bodega, Calif. 94922.

CAREER: Teacher and administrator at alternative school, 1967-71; Word Wheel Books, Inc., Palo Alto, Calif., partner, 1973-75; Multi-Media Resource, San Francisco, Calif., production associate and production editor, 1972-78; Glide Publications, San Francisco, partner, 1978-80; Specific Press, San Francisco, editorial consultant, 1978-79; commercial sheep rancher, 1979-85. International lecturer on small business; consultant to small business. Co-founder of San Francisco Friends of Books and Comics, 1971; sponsor of book fairs for small presses; partner, Clear Glass Publishing.

MEMBER: Norien Institute (founding member and partner), Briarpatch Network.

WRITINGS:

(With Robert Greenway) *Rasberry Exercises,* Freestone Publishing, 1970.
(With Michael Phillips) *Seven Laws of Money,* Random House, 1974.

(Editor) *Briarpatch Review Book,* Glide Publications, 1978.
(With Phillips) *Honest Business,* Random House, 1981.
(With Phillips) *Marketing without Advertising,* Nolo Press, 1986.
(With Phillips and Claude Whitmyer) *Running a One-Person Business,* Ten Speed Press, 1988.

Contributor to *Whole Earth Catalog.* Contributor to *Co-Evolution Quarterly.* Editor of *Ridge Review,* September, 1982.

SIDELIGHTS: Salli Rasberry once wrote: "I have participated in all aspects of book production and have helped other writers publish books. It's a magical, frustrating, vital industry, and I love it."

*   *   *

RAVEN, Ronald William   1904-

PERSONAL: Born July 28, 1904, in Coniston, England; son of Fredric William (a company director) and Annie Williams (Mason) Raven. *Education:* St. Bartholomew's Hospital and Medical College, M.R.C.S. and L.R.C.P., 1928, F.R.C.S., 1931. *Religion:* Plymouth Brethren.

ADDRESSES: Home and office—29 Harley St., London W1N 1DA, England.

CAREER: Resident in surgery, 1928-29; St. Bartholomew's Hospital, London, England, demonstrator in pathology, 1929-31; held various junior surgical appointments, 1931-35; Gordon Hospital (now Westminster Hospital), London, assistant surgeon, 1935-47; French Hospital, London, surgeon, 1936-69; Royal Cancer Hospital (now Royal Marsden Hospital), London, surgical registrar, 1935-39, assistant surgeon, 1939-46, surgeon, 1946-62, senior surgeon, 1962-69, consulting surgeon, 1969——. Registrar in statistics at National Radium Commission, 1931-34. Consulting surgeon at Eversfield Chest Hospital, 1937-48, and at Royal Star and Garter Home for Disabled Sailors, Soldiers, and Airmen, 1948-75; Westminster Hospital, surgeon, 1947-69, and consultant surgeon, 1969——. Conductor of surgical missions to Colombia, 1949, to Saudi Arabia, 1961, 1962, 1975, and 1976, and to United Arab Emirates, 1975 and 1985.

Honorary professor at National University of Colombia, 1949; visiting professor at Ein-Shams University, 1961, and at Maadi Hospital, Cairo, Egypt, 1974. Royal College of Surgeons of England, Arris and Gale Lecturer, 1933, Erasmus Wilson Lecturer, 1935, 1946, and 1947, Hunterian Professor, 1948, and Bradshaw Lecturer, 1975; joint lecturer in surgery at Westminster Medical School, University of London, London, 1951-69; Malcolm Morris Memorial Lecturer, London, 1954; Blair Bell Memorial Lecturer, London, 1960; Elizabeth Malthai Endowment Lecturer at Madras University, 1965; Edith A. Ward Memorial Lecturer, Barrow-in-Furness, England, 1966; first W. Emory Burnett Honor Lecturer at Temple University, 1966; Gerald Townsley Memorial Lecturer, Rochester, England, 1974; Ernest Miles Memorial Lecturer, London, 1980; first Kitty Cookson Memorial Lecturer, Royal Free Hospital, London, 1985. Marie Curie Memorial Foundation chairman of executive committee, 1948-61, and chairman of foundation, 1961——; vice-president and chairman of Royal Medical Foundation of Epsom College, 1954——. *Military service:* British Army, Royal Army Medical Corps, 1941-46; served in North Africa, Italy, and Malta; became colonel; named officer of Order of the British Empire, 1946; mentioned in dispatches; awarded Territorial Army decoration.

MEMBER: World Federation for Cancer Care (president, 1982—), Royal College of Surgeons of England (fellow; member of council, 1968-76; member of court of patrons, 1976—), Association of Head and Neck Oncologists of Great Britain (founding president, 1967-70), Royal Society of Medicine (president of proctology section and oncology section, 1973-74), British Association of Surgical Oncology (founding president, 1973-77), Department of Health and Social Security (member of subcommittee on cancer and advisory committee on cancer registration), Malta Memorial District Nursing Association (vice-president, 1982—), Freeman, City of London, 1956, Worshipful Company of Barbers (member of court, 1973—; master, 1980-81), American Society of Head and Neck Surgeons (corresponding foreign member), New York Academy of Sciences, Academy of Medicine of Colombia, Italian Society of Thoracic Surgeons, Czechoslovak Society of J. E. Purkyne, Roman Surgical Society, Society of Surgery of Bogota, Societe de Chirurgie de Lyon, Indian Association of Oncology, European Association of Oncology.

AWARDS, HONORS: Officer of the Order of St. John of Jerusalem in the British Realm, 1946; M.D. from University of Cartagena, 1949; received medal from International Stamp Exhibition, 1950; chevalier of French Legion of Honor, 1952; honored by American Society of Surgical Oncology, 1981, and by First Congress of European Society of Surgical Oncology, 1982; Academy of Athens membership, 1983; Diploma de Socio Honorario, Society de Cancerologia de El Salvador, 1983; Diploma de Honor al Merito, Liga Nacional de El Salvador, 1983; Royal Society of Medicine honorary fellow, 1987.

WRITINGS:

(Editor with Ernest Fletcher, and contributor) *War Wounds and Injuries,* Edward Arnold, 1940.
Treatment of Shock, Oxford University Press, 1942.
Surgical Care, Edward Arnold, 1942, 2nd edition, Butterworth, 1952.
(With P. E. T. Hancock) *Cancer in General Practice,* Butterworth, 1952.
(With Harold Burrows) *Surgical Instruments and Appliances,* Faber, 1952.
Handbook on Cancer for Nurses and Health Visitors, Butterworth, 1953.
Cancer and Allied Diseases, Duckworth, 1955.
(Contributor) Charles Rob and Rodney Smith, editors, *Operative Surgery,* Butterworth, 1956-57.
(Editor and contributor) *Cancer,* seven volumes, Butterworth, 1957-60.
Cancer of the Pharynx, Larynx, and Esophagus, and Its Surgical Treatment, Butterworth, 1958.
(Editor) *Cancer Progress,* Butterworth, Volume I, 1960, Volume II, 1963.
(Editor with Francis J. C. Roe) *The Prevention of Cancer,* Butterworth, 1967.
(Editor and contributor) *Symposium on the Prevention of Cancer,* Heinemann, 1970.
(Editor and contributor) *Symposium on the Rehabilitation of the Cancer Disabled,* Heinemann, 1971.
(Editor and contributor) *Symposium on Cancer Care: Assessment of the Present Position,* John Sherratt & Son, 1973.
(Editor and contributor) *Modern Trends in Oncology,* two volumes, Butterworth, 1973.
(Editor and contributor) *Cancer: The Patient and the Family,* John Sherratt & Son, 1974.

(Editor and contributor) *The Dying Patient,* Pitman Medical, 1975.
(Editor and contributor) *Principles of Surgical Oncology,* Plenum, 1977.
(Editor and contributor) *Outlook on Cancer,* Plenum, 1977.
(Editor and contributor) *Foundations of Medicine,* Heinemann, 1978.
(With I. W. F. Hannam and R. F. Mould) *Cancer Care: An International Survey,* Hilger, 1986.
Rehabilitation and Continuing Care in Cancer, Parthenon, 1986.
The Gospel according to St. John, Parthenon, 1987.

Senior editor of *Journal of Clinical Oncology,* 1979-82.

WORK IN PROGRESS: The History of Oncology, for Parthenon.

SIDELIGHTS: Ronald William Raven told *CA:* "On the completion of my work as registrar of statistics at the National Radium Commission, where I analyzed and published the results of the radium treatment of cancer achieved in the patients at all the radium centers in the United Kingdom (which was a pioneer work of great magnitude), I was appointed to the surgical staff of the Royal Cancer Hospital (now the Royal Marsden Hospital) where I worked with eminent cancer clinicians and researchers. I have devoted all my professional life to cancer—both clinical and research problems. I have witnessed and conributed to the great advances made in our understanding of the nature of the cancerous diseases, their prevention, diagnosis, and treatment.

"Our great hope for the future is in prevention; at least seventy-five percent of cancer can now be prevented by taking the appropriate action. For example, the dangerous tobacco cancers, especially in the lung, are preventable. The treatment triad—surgery, radiation, and chemotherapy—is saving many lives today. An important advance is the emergence of oncology—research, clinical, and social—where arts and sciences are combined for prevention and treatment. I am specially working in developing surgical oncology, both the theory and practice, and welcome the establishment of associations of surgical oncology throughout the world. There is a great need to develop national services for patients with persistent cancer, and in the United Kingdom I am much involved with the Marie Curie Memorial Foundation. The foundation, in addition to its research institute, has eleven nursing homes with four hundred and twenty beds, a nation-wide domiciliary day- and night-nursing service for cancer patients with near 4,000 part-time nurses. The foundation has established its Institute of Oncology to incorporate its rapidly expanding cancer education and training teaching cancer programmes, and to incorporate its Research Institute for Cancer. The foundation has sponsored the World Federation for Cancer Care, of which I am the first president. Our objective is to bring together all the countries of the world to share our knowledge and skills for the good of cancer patients everywhere and to fight our common enemy—cancer—which still causes a high international mortality.

"I derived great pleasure when the Russians translated *Treatment of Shock* into their language. *The Dying Patient* was translated into Japanese and Dutch."

AVOCATIONAL INTERESTS: "I have a deep interest in the arts, which developed as a child when I was introduced early to the life and works of John Ruskin, who was a lifelong friend of my paternal grandmother and stayed frequently with my grandparents. I have played the piano consistently throughout my life. This not only provides tremendous pleasure and re-laxation from work, but I feel sure pianoforte technique has contributed greatly to my manual dexterity in surgery. I also have an interest in ceramics, which was kindled by my mother, a direct descendant of Miles Mason, who developed the fa-mous Mason's Ironstone Porcelain so much sought after by collectors today. Other interests include collecting period fur-niture, pictures, and philately.''

*   *   *

REED, Barry
   See REED, Barry C(lement)

*   *   *

REED, Barry C(lement)   1927-
   (Barry Reed)

PERSONAL: Born January 28, 1927, in San Francisco, Calif.; son of Clement Barry and Julia A. (Donahue) Reed; married Marie T. Ash, June 2, 1951; children: Debra, Marie, Barry, Susan. *Education:* Holy Cross College, B.S., 1949; Boston College, L.L.B., 1954. *Politics:* Democrat. *Religion:* Roman Catholic.

ADDRESSES: Home—41 Cushing Rd., Westwood, Mass. 02090. *Office*—101 Tremont St., Boston, Mass. 02108.

CAREER: Admitted to the Bar of the State of Massachusetts; trial lawyer in Boston, Mass., 1955—. *Military service:* U.S. Army, 1945-47; became staff sergeant.

WRITINGS:

(With Elliot L. Sagall) *The Heart and the Law: A Practical Guide to Medicolegal Cardiology,* Macmillan, 1968.
(With Sagall) *The Law and Clinical Medicine,* Lippincott, 1970.
(Under name Barry Reed) *The Verdict* (novel), Simon & Schuster, 1980.

Contributor to journals, periodicals, and newspapers, includ-ing *American Bar Association Journal.*

SIDELIGHTS: Attorney Barry C. Reed's *The Verdict,* which was adapted into the critically acclaimed movie of the same title, tells the story of a down-and-out lawyer who represents a young paralyzed woman in a five million dollar malpractice suit against a prominent Roman Catholic hospital in Boston. As he becomes involved in the case, the lawyer finds himself pitted against the entire establishment of Boston—at one point he is even offered $300,000 from the Roman Catholic bishop to drop the suit—yet he becomes determined to fight for the entire amount of compensation he feels is due the woman. Culminating in a tense courtroom confrontation, *The Verdict* has been called by Clarence Petersen in the *Chicago Tribune Book World* ''one of the best courtroom dramas since 'Anat-omy of a Murder' . . . [and] a tale that rings with authentic-ity.'' Stanley Ellin in the *New York Times Book Review* adds that ''the book, digging deep into the mysteries of medical, legal and clerical practice, has everything going for it, and makes dramatically potent use of each element.''

The Verdict has been translated into eight foreign languages.

MEDIA ADAPTATIONS: The Verdict was made into a motion picture starring Paul Newman and released by Twentieth Cen-tury-Fox Film Corp. in 1982. The film received five Academy Award nominations.

BIOGRAPHICAL/CRITICAL SOURCES:

PERIODICALS

Chicago Tribune Book World, July 26, 1981.
New York Times Book Review, July 13, 1980.
Publishers Weekly, March 14, 1980.

*   *   *

RENDELL, Joan

PERSONAL: Born in Launceston, Cornwall, England; daugh-ter of Gervase (a senior civil servant) and Maud (Culley) Ren-dell. *Education:* Attended private schools in England and Scot-land and Ealing School of Art. *Religion:* Church of England.

ADDRESSES: Home—Tremarsh, Launceston, Cornwall, En-gland. *Agent*—Dieter Klein Associates, 1 Newburgh St., Lon-don W1V 1LH, England.

CAREER: Writer, broadcaster, lecturer and craftswoman. Free-lance contributor to programs produced by British Broadcast-ing Corp. and Independent Television Authority. Free-lance correspondent, *Western Morning News* and *Cornish and Devon Post.* Television and radio monitor, Tellex Monitors Ltd., London, England, 1965-75. Chairman of regional community groups committee, National Savings Movement; Launceston Floral Art Group, life member and chairman, 1965-69 and 1975—; member of regional Gas Consumer's Council, 1972-75.

MEMBER: British Matchbox Label and Booklet Society (life member; honorary editor), Federation of Old Cornwall Soci-eties (secretary), Launceston Old Cornwall Society (secre-tary), Dunheved Flower and Garden Group (secretary).

AWARDS, HONORS: Member of Order of the British Empire; Queen's Silver Jubilee Medal; named Bard of the Cornish Gor-seth.

WRITINGS:

(Contributor) Harold K. Starke, editor, *Young Collector's Book,* Burke, 1953.
Collecting Matchbox Labels, Arco, 1963.
Flower Arrangements with a Marine Theme, David & Charles, 1967.
Matchbox Labels, David & Charles, 1968.
Collecting Natural Objects, David & Charles, 1972, Castle Books, 1973.
Collecting Out of Doors, Routledge & Kegan Paul, 1976.
Your Book of Corn Dollies, Merrimack Book Service, 1976.
Country Crafts, Routledge & Kegan Paul, 1977.
Your Book of Pressed and Dried Flowers, Faber, 1978, Mer-rimack Book Service, 1979.
Along the Bude Canal, Bossiney Books, 1979.
Lundy Island, Bossiney Books, 1979.
Hawker Country, Bossiney Books, 1980.
Gateway to Cornwall, Bossiney Books, 1981.
(Contributor) *The Cornish Year Book,* Bossiney Books, 1982.
Cornish Churches, Bossiney Books, 1982.
The Match, the Box and the Label, David & Charles, 1983.
North Cornwall in the Old Days, Bossiney Books, 1983.
Around Bude and Stratton, Bossiney Books, 1985.
The Story of the Bude Canal, Stannary Press, 1987.

Contributor to magazines and regional newspapers in Great Britain.

SIDELIGHTS: Joan Rendell told *CA:* "I trained as an artist but took up writing in 1955 when I submitted an article to the regional newspaper 'The Western Morning News,' because I thought I could do as well as some of the articles they were publishing at that time! It was accepted and I was away! From then on I switched from painting to writing and found no shortage of work. I write non-fiction only and am particularly fond of doing topographical books. I fit in writing between a lot of voluntary work for various organizations and also do book reviewing, art reviews and general reporting for several newspapers and magazines, all of which makes for an interesting and varied life."

Joan Rendell has also been collecting matchbox labels since childhood. Her collection of well over 200,000 different lables and boxes is one of the largest in the world.

AVOCATIONAL INTERESTS: Collecting sand pictures and commemorative mugs, photography, and travel (Europe, United States, Africa, Middle East, and Mexico).

*   *   *

RICHARDS, Martin P(aul) M(eredith)   1940-

PERSONAL: Born January 26, 1940, in Cambridge, England; son of Paul Westmacott (a botanist) and Anne (a botanist; maiden name, Hotham) Richards. *Education:* Trinity College, Cambridge, B.A., 1962, M.A. and Ph.D., both 1965.

ADDRESSES: Home—57 Selwyn Rd., Cambridge, England. *Office*—Child Care and Development Group, Cambridge University, Cambridge, England.

CAREER: Princeton University, Princeton, N.J., visiting fellow in biology, 1966-67; Harvard University, Cambridge, Mass., visiting fellow at Center for Cognitive Studies, 1967; Cambridge University, Cambridge, England, research worker in medical psychology unit (now Child Care and Development Group), 1967—, lecturer in social psychology, 1970—.

MEMBER: International Society for the Study of Behavioral Develpment, Zoological Society, British Society for Social Responsibility in Science, Society for the Study of Animal Behaviour, Society for Research in Child Development.

AWARDS, HONORS: Postdoctoral fellowships from Science Research Council, 1965-67, Trinity College, Cambridge University, 1965-69, and Mental Health Research Fund, 1969-70.

WRITINGS:

(Editor with Kenneth Richardson and David Spears) *Race, Culture and Intelligence,* Penguin, 1972.
(Editor) *The Integration of a Child into a Social World,* Cambridge University Press, 1974.
(Editor with Tim Chard) *Benefits and Hazards of the New Obstetrics,* Heinemann Medical, 1977.
(Editor with F. S. W. Brimblecombe and N. R. C. Roberton) *Separation and Special Care Nurseries,* Heinemann Medical, 1978.
Infancy: The World of the Newborn, Harper, 1980.
(Editor with J. A. Davis and Roberton) *Parent-Infant Attachment in Premature Infants,* Croom Helm, 1983.
(Editor with P. Light) *Children of Social Worlds,* Polity Press/Harvard University Press, 1986.
(With J. Burgoyne and R. Ormrod) *Divorce Matters,* Penguin, 1987.

Contributor to scientific and popular journals. Member of editorial board of *Journal of Biosocial Science, Early Human Development, Birth, Journal of Infant and Reproductive Psychology,* and *Infant Mental Health Journal.* Adviser to Penguin Books, Inc.

WORK IN PROGRESS: A book on children and divorce; a book on obstetric services, with J. Garcia and R. Kilpatrick, for Oxford University Press.

SIDELIGHTS: Martin P. M. Richards writes *CA:* "I have longstanding doubts about the effectiveness of scientific research for producing beneficial change. Through writing, teaching, and other activities I have attempted to both expose the weaknesses and dangers in current scientific work and to strive to find better methods and strategies through my own scientific research."

*   *   *

RICHTER, Conrad (Michael)   1890-1968

PERSONAL: Born October 13, 1890, in Pine Grove, Pa.; died of a heart attack, October 30, 1968, in Pottsville, Pa.; son of John Absalom (a minister) and Charlotte Esther (Henry) Richter; married Harvena M. Achenbach, 1915; children: Harvena. *Education:* Attended public schools in Pennsylvania.

ADDRESSES: Home—11 Maple St., Pine Grove, Pa. *Agent*—Paul R. Reynolds & Son, 599 Fifth Ave., New York, N.Y.

CAREER: Editor and journalist for newspapers in Patton, Pa., Johnstown, Pa., and Pittsburgh, Pa., and private secretary in Cleveland, Ohio, 1910-1924; writer, 1924-68.

MEMBER: National Institute of Arts and Letters, Authors League, P.E.N.

AWARDS, HONORS: National Book Award nomination, 1937, for *The Sea of Grass;* Gold Medal for Literature from Society of Libraries of New York University, 1942, for *The Sea of Grass* and *The Trees;* Ohioana Library Medal, 1947; Pulitzer Prize for Fiction, 1951, for *The Town;* National Institute of Arts and Letters grant in literature, 1959; Maggie Award, 1959, for *The Lady;* National Book Award, 1961, for *The Waters of Kronos;* Litt.D., Susquehanna University, 1944, University of New Mexico, 1958, Lafayette College, 1966; LL.D., Temple University, 1966; L.H.D., Lebanon Valley College, 1966.

WRITINGS:

Brothers of No Kin and Other Stories, Hinds, Hayden & Eldredge, 1924, reprinted, Books for Libraries Press, 1973.
Human Vibration, Handy Book, 1925.
Principles in Bio-Physics, Good Books, 1927.
Early Americana and Other Stories, Knopf, 1936, reprinted, Gregg, 1978.
The Sea of Grass, Knopf, 1937, reprinted with new introduction by the author, Time, Inc., 1965.
The Trees (first volume in trilogy; also see below), Knopf, 1940, reprinted, Bantam, 1975.
Tacey Cromwell, Knopf, 1942, reprinted, University of New Mexico Press, 1974.
The Free Man, Knopf, 1943, reprinted, 1966.
The Fields (second volume in trilogy; also see below), Knopf, 1946, reprinted, 1964.
Smoke over the Prairie and Other Stories, Boardman, 1947.
Always Young and Fair, Knopf, 1947.
The Town (third volume in trilogy; also see below), Knopf, 1950, reprinted, Harmony Raine, 1981.
The Light in the Forest, Knopf, 1953, reprinted, 1966.

The Mountain on the Desert: A Philosophical Journey, Knopf, 1955.

The Lady, Knopf, 1957, reprinted, University of Nebraska Press, 1985.

Dona Ellen, Rauch, 1959.

The Waters of Kronos, Knopf, 1960.

A Simple, Honorable Man, Knopf, 1962.

Over the Blue Mountain (juvenile), Knopf, 1962.

Individualists under the Shade Trees in a Vanishing America, Holt, 1964.

The Grandfathers, Knopf, 1964.

A Country of Strangers, Knopf, 1966, Schocken, 1982.

The Awakening Land: I. The Trees, II. The Fields, III. The Town, Knopf, 1966.

The Wanderer, Knopf, 1966.

The Aristocrat, Knopf, 1968.

The Rawhide Knot and Other Stories, Knopf, 1978, reprinted, University of Nebraska Press, 1985.

Also author of monograph, *Life Energy*. Contributor to anthologies and magazines.

SIDELIGHTS: The late Conrad Richter brought the American past to life with his historical novels celebrating the hardy pioneer spirit. While many of his literary contemporaries bemoaned the malaise engendered by an industrial-technological society, Richter explored the world of his forebears, an era when seas of forest and grassland challenged a whole generation. A dedicated researcher, Richter took care to infuse his work with realistic dialogue, settings, and events, while creating a story the general reader could relish. The resulting novels and short stories were popular with the public but were also treated as serious fiction by the critics. Over the forty years of his writing career, Richter received several of the most prestigious awards the literary community bestows. He earned a Pulitzer Prize in 1951 for *The Town*, the final volume of his highly successful trilogy collected as *The Awakening Land*, and in 1961 he was given the National Book Award for *The Waters of Kronos*. *New York Herald Tribune Weekly Book Review* contributor Louis Bromfield observes that Richter's fiction reflects not only scholarly attention and sympathetic interpretation, but also creates for the reader "a world as real as the one in which he lives, a world which the reader enters on reading the first page and in which he remains until the last."

According to Marvin J. LaHood in *University Review*, Richter belonged "to that group of writers who are impressed with the strength and perseverance of the pioneer, and feel that this strength was a direct result of having dealt with the rigors of the frontier." In *The Trees, The Fields*, and *The Town*, brought together in *The Awakening Land*, Richter's frontier is the Ohio Valley, once an uncharted wilderness of pines. In *Early Americana and Other Stories* and *The Sea of Grass*, among others, the author wrote about the American West from the perspective of its first white settlers. "Painstaking research underlies these books," Dayton Kohler declares in *College English*, "but they illustrate the fact that the more a novelist knows about a region or a period the less his atmosphere depends on local color for its effect. . . . There is no surface decoration here—merely the facts of pioneer existence springing from a background of simple necessity. The remarkable fact is that [Richter] has accomplished so much with so little reference to actual history. . . . There are no novels quite like Richter's in the whole range of historical fiction. Together they probably give us our truest picture of the everyday realities of frontier life." LaHood draws a similar conclusion: "Conrad Richter's great-

est contribution to American letters [was] his tireless effort to put into fiction the setting and the people of an important moment in our nation's history. In the best of his novels and stories that moment lives again."

The son of a minister, Richter was deeply interested in philosophical issues. As Edwin W. Gaston, Jr., notes in the *Dictionary of Literary Biography*, Richter began his fiction-writing career with a "reasonably complete" philosophical system, a world view he explained in two works, *Human Vibration* and *Principles in Bio-Physics*. These books, and the 1955 title *The Mountain on the Desert*, "hold that man functions in response to bodily cellular vibrations which are regulated by the availability of physical and psychical energy," according to Gaston, who adds: "If the energy is plentiful, man is in harmony with life. . . . On the other hand, if energy is low, man is out of sorts with life. . . . To satisfy his energy hunger, man must engage in intense activity. Activity causes the strong cells in one's body to overflow, revitalizing the weak cells." Richter found this unscientific view quite satisfying; he felt the early American pioneers served as clear examples of people who achieved harmony with the environment through strenuous work and cooperation. As civilization advanced, however, the pioneers' children and grandchildren endured fewer hardships and therefore often suffered a resulting loss of character. In *The Old Northwest*, Dawn Wilson writes: "The major message of Richter's philosophy is that hard times have their own rewards; they provide the energy people need to grow. . . . Richter was so intrigued by the land and its settlers that he set out to portray in his fiction the courage and strength of the people, and the causes of the early settlers' enormous strength—causes which his own philosophy, by coincidence, so aptly explained. At last Richter had found the ideal topic for his fiction. He began writing tales of the frontier, authentic stories of danger and adventure on the early plains, which were in themselves both instances and examples of Richter's energy theories."

Richter was born in 1890 in Pine Grove, Pennsylvania, and grew up in a series of tiny coal mining towns through which his father moved as a Lutheran minister. The family always struggled to make ends meet; Richter's own formal schooling ended when he graduated from high school at the age of fifteen. For four years thereafter, Richter tried his hand at numerous jobs. He drove teams, worked on farms, cut timber, sold subscription magazines door-to-door, served as a bank teller, and clerked. Then, at nineteen, he became editor of a weekly newspaper called the Patton (Pennsylvania) *Courier*, and discovered that he enjoyed journalism. He left Patton for reporting jobs first in Johnstown and then in Pittsburgh, learning how to write "plain sentences against the discipline of a deadline," in the words of *Saturday Review* contributor John K. Hutchens. "Of his early jobs," claims Gaston, "reporting and editing most affected [Richter's] belletristic writing. As it had for Hemingway, journalism taught Richter concision of expression." Eventually Richter succumbed to wanderlust and took a job as private secretary to a wealthy Cleveland family who provided the means for wider travel. It was during this period that one of his first short stories was accepted. The work, entitled "Brothers of No Kin," was first published in *Forum* magazine and then was reprinted several times. Despite the piece's success, Richter had a very difficult time getting payment for it—and when the twenty-five-dollar check arrived, he was still disappointed. He told the *Saturday Review*: "I thought to myself, if that's all I get for the kind of story I want to write, why go on?"

Though convinced he would never be able to support his wife and daughter on a writer's salary, Richter persevered. In 1924 he published a collection of short fiction, *Brothers of No Kin and Other Stories*. *New Mexico Quarterly* essayist Bruce Sutherland characterizes these tales as "well-made" and "tailored for the trade." Some of them, the critic continues, "have elements of nativism and local color, some have a glimmer of characterization, but for the most part they give the impression of assembly-line mass production which at best gave the author practice in the art of writing." A major turning point in Richter's career occurred in 1928, when his wife's ill health forced him to move his family from Pennsylvania to Albuquerque, New Mexico. There, in the rugged terrain of the American Southwest, Richter "came upon a new world that he was to make his own," according to Hutchens. Poring through old newspapers and scrapbooks, and interviewing the oldest residents of the area, Richter became immersed in the folklore and history of his adopted state. "There was nothing new or startling about the Richter stories which began to appear in the magazines early in 1934," Sutherland writes. "On the surface they were Western stories of a high order, authentic, carefully conceived, and skillfully narrated. Closer scrutiny reveals how vastly different they are from the type of Western to which Americans have become accustomed. These are stories of pioneer fortitude aimed at a depression-ridden world; and the contemporary soul, battered and bewildered by life, through them is brought into closer contact with people of another age who also lived, loved, struggled, and died but whose lives form a pattern out of which emerges completeness and serenity." Richter's 1936 publication *Early Americana and Other Stories* is a collection of these Southwestern tales. It was followed in 1937 by *The Sea of Grass*, a novel that brought the author national recognition.

The Sea of Grass chronicles the nineteenth-century conflict between the free-ranging Western ranchers and the "nesters" who settled, fenced, and farmed. Sutherland describes the novel as the story "of change which destroys and builds at the same time, of the past which succumbs to the present and of the personal tragedy which attends the tide of progress." Kohler suggests that the Western theme caused critics to overlook the work at first, even though it transcends genre fiction. *The Sea of Grass,* writes Kohler, "is first a book about people. . . . We are not reading a local colorist. The surface decoration of most Western fiction—night herding, the roundup, cowboy sprees—is lacking here." Sutherland also finds *The Sea of Grass* "a completely successful short novel which meets even the most exacting literary standards." In all, Richter wrote three novels about the Southwest—*The Sea of Grass, Tacey Cromwell,* and *The Lady*. His main goal, Wilson contends, "was to recapture the essence of life in the past. All three Southwestern novels thus emphasize the idea that men and women of the past were of greater stature than the people of the present. . . . Thematically, he depicts the conflict between the old and the new in these novels, the lyrical quality of which is a result of the captivating power of the Southwestern landscape over his imagination."

Even as he labored on his books about the West, Richter continued to feel drawn toward the Pennsylvania Dutch country of his youth. His best-known and most highly regarded work, the trilogy *The Awakening Land*, gives a microcosmic overview of the settlement of the Ohio Valley. According to Orville Prescott in his book *In My Opinion: An Inquiry into the Contemporary Novel*, the three segments of the trilogy "are certain to rank among the fine novels of our time. Taken to-

gether as a vast epic of the American frontier seen in terms of one family they are a majestic achievement. . . . There is a rare quality in these glowing pages—the most finished yet unobtrusive artistry, and a profound understanding of the pioneer character as it was manifested in and affected by a way of life now vanished from the earth." Through the character of Sayward Luckett Wheeler—widely considered one of the most sensitively-drawn pioneer women in fiction—Richter portrayed the gradual replacement of the gloomy and dangerous forest wilderness by farming communities and then a thriving town. Most of the work is indebted to folklore; Richter took care to detail daily activities, superstitions, social mores, and special ceremonies, and his characters speak a dialect that has all but disappeared in modern America. In a *Midwest Folklore* essay, John T. Flanagan concludes that Richter's fiction "is the richer and the more convincing because he has seen fit to incorporate such material in his dialogue, action, and characterization." Individually and collectively, the three novels united in *The Awakening Land* have drawn critical acclaim. *Chicago Sunday Tribune* contributor Edward Wagenknecht finds the trilogy "unified in its design, sustained in its inspiration. It pulses from beginning to end with the passion of the land, this flesh, and the spirit. It has the American heartbeat in it. Cut it and it bleeds American."

In addition to the major works of his middle years and later life, Richter wrote a numer of minor novels. These include *The Free Man*, a story of a German indentured servant who fights in the Revolutionary War, *Always Young and Fair*, the psychological portrait of a woman robbed of her fiance by war, *The Light in the Forest*, an account of a white child raised by Indians, and *The Grandfathers*, a comic tale of Western Maryland hill folk. In his book *Conrad Richter*, Gaston observes that although such works created the impression of being interludes, they performed useful fictional functions for the author. They enabled Richter "to explore topics anterior to the subjects of his Ohio trilogy and thus to fill gaps helpful to greater appreciation of the larger novels." *Saturday Review* contributor Granville Hicks finds even these lesser works successful because Richter "has been a careful student of the relevant documents and because he has a deep sympathy with the life of earlier times." Hicks notes that Richter's prose is "direct and unpretentious," and his stories are capable of amusing and instructing without sentimentality. "Although his books have often been popular," the critic observes, "[Richter] has never written down to the masses. He has gone his own way, and he has no reason to regret it."

Two very personal, autobiographical novels—*The Waters of Kronos* and *A Simple, Honorable Man*, brought Richter further critical plaudits late in his career. Both books are set in Pennsylvania; in *The Waters of Kronos*, an aging writer named John Donner mystically visits his birthplace—a town submerged beneath the waters of the dammed-up Kronos River, and in *A Simple, Honorable Man*, Donner's father becomes a Lutheran minister and dedicates himself to serving his poorest and most needy parishioners. "Richter's nostalgia for the American past, so obvious in his carefully researched novels, brought him at seventy to an exact rendering of his relatives as he remembered them," LaHood explains in *University Review*. "It is an undertaking with few equals in American literature. But it is more than just a nostalgic family history, for in the two novels Richter wrestled with his own metaphysical problems." Most critics have praised the National Book Award-winning *The Waters of Kronos* and its prequel *A Simple, Honorable Man* for their dignified exploration of a nostalgic theme. "Seldom has a man written more candidly of himself and his relatives than has Richter,'' LaHood contends in *Conrad Richter's America*. ''. . . Richter honestly attempted to portray his struggles with life's most teasing intellectual and spiritual problems: man's existence before and after this life, the tenets of organized religion, the differences in character from person to person, the father-son relationship, and the old problem of fate versus free will. He also exhibited in these two novels a great pride in various ancestors from whom he received what he considered a priceless legacy.''

Richter spent most of the last twenty years of his life in Pennsylvania, his ancestral home. He died on October 30, 1968, within a few miles of his birthplace. According to Bruce Sutherland, the author's chief contribution to Americana ''is a restrained realism which depends greatly on brevity and understatement for its effect. This, combined with an understanding of people, a feeling for historical things which transcends mere knowledge, and the ability to think and write in terms of his characters and their environment places him among the chosen few who have made the past of America come alive.'' In his *Saturday Review* piece, Granville Hicks observes that Richter's name is not likely to come to mind as an important novelist of his period, but ''no careful history of American fiction in the twentieth century could ignore his work.'' Hicks concludes that Richter's career illustrates the notion ''that a man of talent and integrity may, with a little luck, thumb his nose at fashion and write the kind of books he wants to write.''

BIOGRAPHICAL/CRITICAL SOURCES:

BOOKS

Barnes, Robert J., *Conrad Richter*, Steck-Vaughn, 1968.
Contemporary Literary Criticism, Volume XXX, Gale, 1984.
Dictionary of Literary Biography, Volume IX: *American Novelists, 1910-1945*, Gale, 1981.
Edwards, Clifford Duane, *Conrad Richter's Ohio Trilogy: Its Ideas, Themes, and Relationships to Literary Tradition*, Mouton, 1971.
Gaston, Edwin W., Jr., *Conrad Richter*, Twayne, 1965.
LaHood, Marvin J., *Conrad Richter's America*, Mouton, 1975.
Lee, L. L., and Merrill Lewis, *Women, Women Writers, and the West*, Whitston, 1979.
Prescott, Orville, *In My Opinion: An Inquiry into the Contemporary Novel*, Bobbs-Merrill, 1952.
Stuckey, W. L., *The Pulitzer Prize Novels*, University of Oklahoma Press, 1966.

PERIODICALS

American Review, April, 1937.
Atlantic, November, 1943, June, 1946, April, 1947, August, 1950, June, 1964.
Books, February 7, 1937, March 3, 1940, November 1, 1942.
Book Week, August 22, 1943, March 31, 1946, June 7, 1964, May 22,1966.
Boston Transcript, March 2, 1940.
Chicago Sunday Tribune, April 23, 1950, May 26, 1957.
Christian Science Monitor, March 10, 1937, June 1, 1940, May 4, 1946, November 5, 1968, October 23, 1978.
College English, February, 1947, November, 1950.
Commonweal, November 10, 1967.
Critic, June-July, 1964.
English Journal, September, 1946.
Midwest Folklore, spring, 1952.
New Mexico Quarterly, winter, 1945.
New Republic, March 18, 1940, December 9, 1978.

New York Herald Tribune Book Review, March 30, 1947, April 23, 1950, May 17, 1953, July 3, 1955, May 19, 1957, April 17, 1960.
New York Herald Tribune Books, August 2, 1936, February 7, 1937, April 22, 1962.
New York Herald Tribune Weekly Book Review, August 22, 1943, March 31, 1946.
New York Times, March 3, 1940, August 8, 1943, March 31, 1946, March 30, 1947, April 23, 1950, June 5, 1955, May 1, 1960, October 10, 1968.
New York Times Book Review, August 2, 1936, October 25, 1942, May 1, 1960, May 6, 1962, May 24, 1964, July 10, 1966, September 18, 1966, October 6, 1968, December 24, 1978.
Northwest Ohio Quarterly, autumn, 1957.
Old Northwest, December, 1975.
San Francisco Chronicle, May 1, 1950, May 15, 1953, June 22, 1955, April 18, 1960.
Saturday Evening Post, October 12, 1946.
Saturday Review, May 16, 1953, May 25, 1957, April 16, 1960, April 28, 1962, May 14, 1966, December 21, 1968.
Saturday Review of Literature, February 27, 1937, April 22, 1950.
Southwest Review, summer, 1958.
Spectator, May 17, 1940.
Springfield Republican, March 14, 1937, November 8, 1942, June 23, 1957.
Time, May 1, 1950, April 18, 1960, September 27, 1968.
University Review, summer, 1964.
Yale Review, June, 1946.

OBITUARIES:

PERIODICALS

New York Times, October 31, 1968.†

—*Sketch by Anne Janette Johnson*

*   *   *

RICKS, Christopher (Bruce)   1933-

PERSONAL: Born September 18, 1933, in London, England; son of James Bruce and Gabrielle (Roszak) Ricks; married Kirsten Jensen, 1956 (divorced, 1975); married Judith Aronson, 1977; children: (first marriage) David, Julia, Laura, William; (second marriage) Alice, James, Sophie. *Education:* Balliol College, Oxford, B.A., 1956, B.Litt., 1958, M.A., 1960. *Religion:* Atheist.

ADDRESSES: Home—39 Martin St., Cambridge, Mass. 02138. *Office*—English Department, Boston University, Boston, Mass. 02215.

CAREER: Oxford University, Oxford, England, fellow and tutor at Worcester College and university lecturer, 1958-68; University of Bristol, Bristol, England, professor of English, 1968-75; Cambridge University, Cambridge, England, professor of English, 1975-86; Boston University, Boston, Mass., professor of English, 1986—. Visiting professor, Stanford University and University of California, Berkeley, 1965, Smith College, 1967, Harvard University, 1971, Wesleyan University, 1974, and Brandeis University, 1977, 1981, and 1984. *Military service:* British Army, 1951-53; became lieutenant in the Green Howards.

MEMBER: British Academy (fellow), Tennyson Society (vice-president).

WRITINGS:

Milton's Grand Style, Clarendon Press, 1963.
Tennyson's Methods of Composition, Oxford University Press, 1966.
Tennyson: A Biographical and Critical Study, Macmillan, 1972.
(Contributor) Roma Gill, editor, *William Empson: The Man and His Work*, Routledge & Kegan Paul, 1974.
Keats and Embarrassment, Oxford University Press, 1974.
The Force of Poetry, Oxford University Press, 1984.

EDITOR

(And author of introduction with Harry Carter) Edward Rowe Mores, *Dissertation upon English Typographical Founders and Foundries, 1788*, Oxford University Press, 1962.
(And author of introduction) *Poems and Critics: An Anthology of Poetry and Criticism from Shakespeare to Hardy*, Collins, 1966, Harper, 1972.
A. E. Housman: A Collection of Critical Essays, Prentice-Hall, 1968.
Alfred Lord Tennyson, *Poems of 1842*, Collins, 1968.
John Milton, *Paradise Lost and Paradise Regained*, New American Library, 1968.
The Poems of Tennyson, Longmans, Green, 1969, revised edition, 1987.
(And author of introduction) Elizabeth Barrett Browning and Robert Browning, *The Brownings: Letters and Poetry*, Doubleday, 1970.
English Poetry and Prose, 1540-1674, Barrie & Jenkins, 1970, reprinted, Peter Bedrick, 1987.
English Drama to 1710, Barrie & Jenkins, 1971.
(And author of introduction) *Selected Criticism of Matthew Arnold*, New American Library, 1972.
(With Leonard Michaels) *The State of the Language*, University of California Press, 1980.
The New Oxford Book of Victorian Verse, Oxford University Press, 1987.

OTHER

General editor, "English Poets" series, Penguin. Contributor of articles to professional journals. Former contributor of regular reviews to London *Sunday Times*. Co-editor, *Essays in Criticism*.

SIDELIGHTS: In *The Force of Poetry*, the highly respected English critic Christopher Ricks sheds new light on twelve poets by examining their techniques. Ricks, "a critical miniaturist," according to *Los Angeles Times Book Review* contributor Douglas Sun, "enlarges our understanding by presenting some aspect or facet of the poet's language we may have missed," as Helen Bevington explains. Her article in the *New York Times Book Review* lists the poets under scrutiny as A. E. Housman, William Empson, Stevie Smith, Robert Lowell, Philip Larkin, and Geoffrey Hill from the twentieth century, and John Gower (Geoffrey Chaucer's friend), Andrew Marvell, John Milton, Ben Johnson, William Wordsworth, and Thomas Lovell Beddoes from prior times, the earliest being Gower from the 14th century. "In each poet the marvelous resources of language appeal to [Ricks], and as critic and scholar he calls tremendously on his knowledge of literature past and present to provide new insights, aspects, and illuminations," Bevington observes. Ricks augments these essays, written over a period of twenty years, with essays on cliches, falsehoods, misquotations (particularly those of Walter Pater and Matthew Arnold), and the correspondence between slang and rapid change in America. Bevington deems Ricks "a lively critic, who as-

sures us through clarifying analysis of [poetry's] power and force in our lives."

BIOGRAPHICAL/CRITICAL SOURCES:

PERIODICALS

Chicago Tribune Book World, May 24, 1981.
Los Angeles Times Book Review, February 10, 1980, March 17, 1985.
New York Times Book Review, January 6, 1980, March 17, 1985.
Times (London), July 9, 1987.
Times Literary Supplement, February 22, 1980.
Washington Post Book World, February 17, 1980, May 10, 1981.

*   *   *

RILEY, Glenda   1938-

PERSONAL: Born September 6, 1938, in Cleveland, Ohio; daughter of George F. (a railroad employee) and Lillian (Knafels) Gates; children: Sean. *Education:* Western Reserve University (now Case Western Reserve University), B.A., 1960; Miami University, Oxford, Ohio, M.A., 1963; Ohio State University, Ph.D., 1967.

ADDRESSES: Office—Department of History, University of Northern Iowa, Cedar Falls, Iowa 50613.

CAREER: Teacher at public schools in Westlake, Ohio, 1960-62; Denison University, Granville, Ohio, instructor in history, 1967-68; Ohio State University, Columbus, visiting assistant professor of history, 1968-69; University of Northern Iowa, Cedar Falls, 1969-77, began as assistant professor, became associate professor, professor of history, 1977—; director of women's studies program, 1981-85. Mary Ball Washington Professor of American History (Fulbright lectureship), University College, Dublin, 1986-87.

MEMBER: American Historical Association, Organization of American Historians, Society for Historians of the Early American Republic, American Association for State and Local History, Coodinating Commission on Women in the Historical Profession, Conference Group in Women's History, National Organization for Women, National Women's Studies Association, National Council on Public History, Western History Association, Women Historians of the Midwest.

WRITINGS:

Frontierswomen: The Iowa Experience, Iowa State University Press, 1981.
Women and Indians on the Frontier, 1830-1915, University of New Mexico Press, 1984.
Inventing the American Woman: A Perspective on Women's History, 1607 to the Present, Harlan Davison, 1986.
The Female Frontier: A Comparative View of Women on the Prairie and Plains, University Press of Kansas, 1988.

Contributor to scholarly journals.

SIDELIGHTS: Glenda Riley told *CA:* "The central theme of my writing is to reconstruct women's historical experiences, particularly in the American West, while at the same time giving women the historical heritage and identity they have so long been denied. As a committed feminist and historical scholar, I find a great sense of satisfaction in doing such work. It's also exciting and pure fun to discover and retrieve the history of such a fascinating group of people."

AVOCATIONAL INTERESTS: Travel, aerobics, reading in human relations, nutrition, and folk medicine.

*　　*　　*

ROBERTSON, Don   1929-

PERSONAL: Born March 21, 1929, in Cleveland, Ohio; son of Carl Trowbridge (associate editor of the *Cleveland Plain Dealer*) and Josephine (Wuebben) Robertson; married second wife, Sherri Ann Heideloff, January 17, 1987. *Education:* Attended Harvard University, 1948-49, and Western Reserve University (now Case Western Reserve University), 1953-57. *Politics:* Democrat.

ADDRESSES: Agent—Clyde C. Taylor, 10 Astor Place, New York, N.Y., 10003.

CAREER: Cleveland Plain Dealer, Cleveland, Ohio, reporter, 1949-55, copy editor, 1955-57; *Cleveland News,* Cleveland, reporter, 1957-59; executive assistant to the Attorney General of Ohio, 1959-60; *Cleveland Plain Dealer,* reporter, 1963-66; *Cleveland Press,* Cleveland, columnist, 1968-82. Host of talk show on WVIZ-TV and WKBF-TV, 1967-70; movie and play reviewer on WKYC-TV, 1969 and 1971—. *Military service:* U.S. Army, 1946-48.

MEMBER: American Newspaper Guild.

AWARDS, HONORS: Putnam Award from G. P. Putnam's Sons, Inc., 1964, for *A Flag Full of Stars;* Cleveland Arts Prize, 1966.

WRITINGS:

NOVELS

The Three Days, Prentice-Hall, 1959.
By Antietam Creek, Prentice-Hall, 1960.
The River and the Wilderness, Doubleday, 1962 (published in England as *Games without Rules,* Barrie & Rockliff, 1962).
A Flag Full of Stars, Putnam, 1964.
The Greatest Thing since Sliced Bread (first novel in trilogy), Putnam, 1965.
The Sum and Total of Now (second novel in trilogy), Putnam, 1966.
Paradise Falls, Putnam, 1968.
The Greatest Thing That Almost Happened (third novel in trilogy), Putnam, 1970.
Praise the Human Season, A. Fields Books, 1974.
Miss Margaret Ridpath and the Dismantling of the Universe, Putnam, 1977.
Make a Wish, Putnam, 1978.
Mystical Union, Putnam, 1978.
Victoria at Nine, Ballantine, 1979.
Harv, John Zubal, 1985.
The Forest of Arden, John Zubal, 1986.
The Ideal, Genuine Man, Philtrum, 1987.

SIDELIGHTS: In a trilogy of tragicomic novels that begins with *The Greatest Thing since Sliced Bread,* author Don Robertson highlights events in the brief life of a boy named Morris Bird III. Morris is nine years old when readers first meet him in 1944 on Cleveland's east side. Accompanied by his younger sister and fortified with a jar of peanut butter, Morris picks up the handle of his little red wagon and sets out in search of his best friend, Stanley Chaloupka, who has recently moved to the other side of town. But a sudden explosion at the East Ohio Gas Company interrupts Morris's journey and turns him into an unexpected hero.

According to T. C. Vince of *Best Sellers,* Morris and his sister "are probably the two most appealing youngsters in fiction since Jem and Scout Finch crossed the pages of Harper Lee's *To Kill a Mockingbird.* . . . [Robertson] writes lovingly and well about his home town. . . . [*The Greatest Thing since Sliced Bread*] is a fine novel that can be unreservedly recommended to any one who still believes that the old verities of love, courage, and self-respect still count." Meyer Levin of the *New York Times Book Review* calls the story "delightful," noting that the author's "sentimental journey through boyhood [is] universal enough to send a twinge of nostalgia through any ex-boy." The *New Yorker* critic, too, is full of praise for *The Greatest Thing since Sliced Bread,* describing it as a "funny" book and declaring that "Robertson is a tremendously good writer." Concludes the *Saturday Review*'s Haskel Frankel: "Morris Bird III and every step he takes is completely, wonderfully alive. . . . [*The Greatest Thing since Sliced Bread*] is not a novel that will shatter you to the core, but it should warm you to the heart."

The second novel in the trilogy, *The Sum and Total of Now,* focuses on Morris as a thirteen-year-old coping with growing pains and the realization that his beloved grandmother is dying. Though the *New Yorker* critic finds that Morris "is just as likable and every bit as admirable as he was the first time we met him," he notes that Robertson's "highly individual style is being spoiled by a tendency to wordiness." Levin, commenting once again in the *New York Times Book Review,* also feels that *The Sum and Total of Now* lacks "the tautness that made [*The Greatest Thing since Sliced Bread*] appealing." On the other hand, *Book Week*'s Kenneth Lamott states that "Robertson writes so unpretentiously and effectively that I found myself thoroughly enjoying [his novel]. . . . [He] has a very good notion of what he is about and, consequently, his hero does become a person."

The Greatest Thing That Almost Happened marks the last chapter in the story of Morris Bird III. Morris, now seventeen years old, in love, and not-quite-a-star player on his high school basketball team, discovers he has leukemia. His struggle to come to grips with the inevitability of death forms the basis of the novel. Levin again notes Robertson's "flair for sentimentalizing the immediate past" but points out that "the juxtaposition of Morris's earthly ambitions with his impending doom is accompanied by heavy-handed pathos." Robert Cayton, writing in *Library Journal,* also believes that despite the author's success at sharpening "the pseudocynical style of the first two novels," *The Greatest Thing That Almost Happened* "is flawed in the last pages because Robertson moralizes about love. . . . Better to have Morris leave us while he remains still tragically unfulfilled, still galloping up the down escalator in the local department store." John Phillipson of *Best Sellers* finds this last novel in the trilogy "a less original work than *Sliced Bread,*" explaining that for him, at least, "it has clear echoes of J. D. Salinger [and] Holden Caulfield. Ellison's Owen Harrison Harding, Farrell's Danny O'Neil . . . and perhaps even John Gunther's son could enter into the composition of this fictional character." Nevertheless, concludes Phillipson, "Morris Bird III is believable and his story is touching."

MEDIA ADAPTATIONS: The Greatest Thing That Almost Happened was a made-for-television movie starring Jimmy Walker.

BIOGRAPHICAL/CRITICAL SOURCES:

PERIODICALS

Best Sellers, July 1, 1965, December 1, 1970, May, 1978.

Book Week, June 5, 1966.
Library Journal, June 15, 1965, April 15, 1966, January 1, 1971.
New Republic, December 9, 1978.
New Yorker, June 19, 1965, April 17, 1966.
New York Times Book Review, July 11, 1965, April 17, 1966, November 22, 1970, October 16, 1977, January 2, 1978.
Saturday Review, August 7, 1965, April 30, 1966.

*   *   *

RODEFER, Stephen 1940-
(Jean Calais)

PERSONAL: Born November 20, 1940, in Bellaire, Ohio; son of Howard Haydn (in glass industry) and Dorothy (a teacher; maiden name, Shackleford) Rodefer; children: Benjamin, Jesse, Felix. *Education:* Amherst College, B.A., 1963; State University of New York at Buffalo, M.A., 1967; San Francisco State University, M.F.A., 1981.

ADDRESSES: Home—6434 Raymond St., Oakland, Calif. 94609.

CAREER: State University of New York at Buffalo, instructor in English, 1966-67; University of New Mexico, Albuquerque, assistant professor of English and co-director of creative writing program, 1967-71; *Fervent Valley: A Magazine of the Arts,* Placitas, N.M., editor, 1972-75; language arts specialist at public schools in Berkeley, Calif., 1976-80; San Francisco State University, San Francisco, Calif., lecturer in English, 1981-83, lecturer and director of graduate program in Center for Experimental and Interdisciplinary Arts, 1983-85; University of California, San Diego, curator, Archive for New Poetry, 1985—. Artist in residence, Briarcombe Foundation, 1983; visiting lecturer, University of California, San Diego, 1985—.

MEMBER: American Literary Translators Association.

AWARDS, HONORS: Small Press Award, National Endowment for the Arts, 1975; Fulbright Senior Scholar Award, 1983-84; Annual Book Award, American Poetry Center (San Francisco), 1983, for *Four Lectures.*

WRITINGS:

POETRY

The Knife, Island Press, 1965.
(Translator) Carus Lucretius, *After Lucretius,* University of Connecticut Press, 1973.
(Translator under pseudonym Jean Calais) Francois Villon, *Villon,* Pick Pocket Series, 1976.
One or Two Love Poems From the White World, Duende, 1976.
Safety, Miam, 1977.
The Bell Clerk's Tears Keep Flowing, The Figures, 1978.
Plane Debris, Tuumba, 1981.
Four Lectures, The Figures, 1982.
(Translator) Ranier Maria Rilke, *Orpheus,* Tuscany Alley, 1983.
(With Benjamin Friedlander) *Oriflamme Day,* House of K, 1984.
Safety, Margery Cantor, 1985.
Emergency Measures, The Figures, 1987.

Contributor to *P-78: An Anthology of the One World Poetry Conference* (Amsterdam), and *Collection* (London).

OTHER

Author of plays "A & C: An Idyl in One Act" and "Ten-

nyson," 1983. Contributor to several periodicals, including the *New Mexico Quarterly, Ironwood, Choice, Downbeat,* and *Work.*

WORK IN PROGRESS: A long poem; a narrative fiction; translating the work of Rilke, Jean de Meun, and Villon.

SIDELIGHTS: Stephen Rodefer told *CA:* "My motivation is only to write. My circumstance often stands to circumvent this. Nothing is vital except what lives past its vitality. Only love and work are real. My writing is an improvement of my life and an addition to English literature."

BIOGRAPHICAL/CRITICAL SOURCES:

BOOKS

Bartlett, Lee, editor, *Talking Poetry: Conversations in the Workshop,* University of New Mexico, 1987.

*   *   *

RODOWSKY, Colby (F.) 1932-

PERSONAL: Born February 26, 1932, in Baltimore, Md.; daughter of Frank M. Fossett and Mary C. Fitz-Townsend; married Lawrence Rodowsky (an appeals court judge), August 7, 1954; children: Laurie, Alice, Emily, Sarah, Gregory, Katherine. *Education:* College of Notre Dame of Maryland, B.A., 1953. *Religion:* Roman Catholic.

ADDRESSES: Home—4306 Norwood Rd., Baltimore, Md. 21218. *Agent*—Gail Hochman, Brandt & Brandt, 1501 Broadway, N.Y. 10036.

CAREER: Teacher in public schools in Baltimore, Md., 1953-55, and in a school for special education, 1955-56; children's book reviewer, *Baltimore Sunday Sun,* 1977-84; librarian's assistant, Notre Dame Preparatory School, Baltimore, 1974-79.

AWARDS, HONORS: American Library Association Notable Book citation for *The Gathering Room,* and Best Books for Young Adults citation for *Julie's Daughter.*

WRITINGS:

JUVENILES

What about Me?, F. Watts, 1976.
P.S. Write Soon, F. Watts, 1978.
Evy-Ivy-Over, F. Watts, 1978.
A Summer's Worth of Shame: A Novel, F. Watts, 1980.
The Gathering Room, Farrar, Straus, 1981.
H, My Name Is Henley, Farrar, Straus, 1982.
Keeping Time, Farrar, Straus, 1983.
Julie's Daughter, Farrar, Straus, 1985.
Fitchett's Folly, Farrar, Straus, 1987.

OTHER

Contributor of fiction, essays, and reviews to periodicals, including *McCall's, Good Housekeeping, Christian Science Monitor, New York Times Book Review,* and *Washington Post.*

WORK IN PROGRESS: A novel; short stories.

SIDELIGHTS: The characters who populate the books by children's author Colby Rodowsky represent all age groups, and the challenges they face are difficult family relationships. Parents in the award-winning books struggle to adjust to the needs of family members with handicaps, or must learn to cope when a close friend is murdered or a spouse goes to prison. Their stories, however, are usually related by adolescents who try to understand their parents and to fathom their own sometimes ambivalent feelings about the stresses they face.

In Rodowsky's first book, *What about Me?*, a fifteen-year-old girl expresses her confused feelings toward a younger brother who has Down's syndrome. Dorrie's affection for "Fredlet," as she calls him, is as strong as her frustration when his special needs limit family activities. She feels the least affection for her retarded and heart-diseased brother when the family relocates to give him better care, and later when he dies. Far from being the solution to Dorrie's problems, her brother's death, as she feels it, seems only to take her mother farther away from Dorrie into grief. Unlike other books that portray the parents of the special child, *What about Me?* allows both Dorrie and her mother to have "reactions . . . complex enough to be believable," an *English Journal* reviewer states.

Rodowsky explores the impact of grief on parents and children again in *The Gathering Room,* in which nine-year-old Mudge befriends the characters who rest in peace in the cemetery where his father, Ned, is the caretaker. Ned has retreated from the world of business and society since the killing of his best friend, a politician, and he draws Mudge into protective isolation by schooling him in the gatehouse gathering room. At first, Mudge's only friends are the graveyard's residents, "so vividly sketched," says *Horn Book* contributor E. R. Twitchell, that it is "impossible to call them ghosts." Jane Langton says of them in the *New York Times Book Review*, "The supernatural inhabitants of Mudge's cemetery provide this simple, well-wrought story with a pleasant, if melancholy, sense of time and mortality. Puttering around their family plots, they help Mudge plumb his timid heart." But eventually, Ned's sister Ernestus arrives to ease Mudge and his parents back into the outside world. *Washington Post Book World* columnist Michele Slung explains the book's "19th century" flavor: "Mudge wanders back and forth between the worlds of the living and the dead, always himself, always confident. In this way he can be seen as a descendant of Lewis Carroll's Alice, Charles Kingsley's water baby, Tom, and all the children of L. Frank Baum's Oz. . . . Though this is a new book, it has a timelessness about it; where it's really set is in that land known as Classic Children's Literature."

In *H, My Name Is Henley*, a pre-teen girl chooses to stay with an aunt who leads a settled life rather than follow along when her restless, impulsive mother Patti decides to move on. Henley, who is twelve "going on forty-five," in her mother's view, narrates the story. The first-person point of view of this "tremendously moving book" lends "an immediacy and poignancy to Henley's dilemma," a *Bulletin of the Center for Children's Books* reviewer feels. Nancy C. Hammond thinks the narration "periodically lapses into melodrama," but on the other hand, Hammond's review in *Horn Book* claims, "the tension and conflict between mother and daughter, the strain on a child forced into adult responsibilities, and the characterization of Patti are intensely real." Furthermore, Barbara Lenchitz Gottesman, writing in the *Voice of Youth Advocates* magazine, believes that "Henley's feelings and insights" are accessible and potentially comforting to the children of "unresponsive" parents, and that "Rodowsky has created a masterpiece."

Keeping Time, referred to as "another winner" by Betsy Byars in a *Washington Post Book World* review, combines elements developed in earlier books. Drew Wakeman, the son of Baltimore street musicians, escapes like Mudge to a more inter-

esting world when family relationships are strained. And like Henley, Drew learns to communicate his frustrations to an unresponsive parent. Drew's two worlds are present-day Baltimore and 16th-century London, to which he slips back when singing the Old English ballad "Greensleeves." "The characters in both centuries are lively and entertaining (Colby Rodowsky's forte)," Byars writes. A *Horn Book* reviewer echoes, "What makes the novel impelling is the author's ability to develop distinctive characters through subtle imagery and plausible conversation."

A *Publishers Weekly* contributor deems *Julie's Daughter* "the most memorable of all [Rodowsky's] award winners." The book has three narrators: Julie, who once abandoned a baby daughter whose father she could not name; her daughter Slug, now seventeen and reunited with Julie; and their neighbor, the terminally ill Harper Tegges. Care and affection for Harper becomes the common ground for Julie and Slug's reconciliation. "All three are prickly characters, proud, selfish at times. Rodowsky surrounds them with equally strong peripheral figures," Elizabeth Castor notes in the *Washington Post Book World,* and the whole cast, "too strong to be called characters," leave "indelible impressions on the reader," the *Publishers Weekly* contributor concludes.

Readers and interviewers often ask Rodowsky where her characters come from, she relates in an article for *Writer* magazine. But perhaps more important than a character's origin is his ability to take over, leaving the author "trotting along behind," as she claims is often the case: "Once they're here . . . they frequently set off with an independence that astounds me, so that from time to time I have to catch up with them before I can determine where some of these people who stepped unbidden into my mind and my books come from." Once conceived, her characters "have a way of intruding" even when she is not writing, she adds. For instance, when Rodowsky attended her great aunt's funeral in the cemetery the author had portrayed in *The Gathering Room,* characters from the book seemed to be present. "I started to look around, casting quick surreptitious glances behind this angel, that vault or marble lamb. I knew, somehow, that they were all there. Mudge and his friends. . . . And, of course, Aunt Ernestus. That's how real they are to me. How real I try to make them to my readers."

CA INTERVIEW

CA interviewed Colby Rodowsky by telephone on October 10, 1986, at her home in Baltimore, Maryland.

CA: You've taught school and worked as a school librarian. Did those jobs help you in getting ideas for your novels?

RODOWSKY: I taught school a long time ago; I taught third grade and retarded children. But I was not a librarian, just a helper. I think ideas come from every place. Although my first book, *What about Me?,* was about a retarded child and I did teach retarded children, I kind of backed into it because I wanted to write about a child who had a younger brother or sister with a handicap. I just took that theme because I had taught the children and really loved them; I didn't set out to write about a retarded child.

CA: How did you come to be a writer?

RODOWSKY: I think I always wanted to be a writer. I wrote when I was a child. I was an English major in college and edited the literary magazine and all of those things. Then, after I got married and had six children, I somehow didn't quite get around to writing. But I don't think that time was wasted because everything that happens to you, you kind of store away. About fourteen years ago I went to visit a friend who had taught me in college. We weren't talking about writing; we were just talking about books. She finally stopped what she was saying and looked at me and said, "Just think: you have all your writing still ahead of you." It really kind of gives me cold chills even now when I think about it. I did not go home and write a book, but I went home thinking maybe I hadn't missed the boat on what I'd really wanted to do. Then I did eventually go back to the same teacher and take a writing tutorial, and I think that's what really got me back to writing. Perhaps the biggest thing I learned from that was discipline.

CA: So you didn't begin really early.

RODOWSKY: No. I was about forty, and at that time I thought if you hadn't done anything by forty, you never would. Now I know a lot better.

CA: Had you discussed the possibility of being a writer with your parents when you were very young?

RODOWSKY: Oh sure. When I was a kid, I was always going to be a writer. My mother was extremely supportive. I don't know whether it was because she was a doting mother or she really thought I could write, but she was very supportive. One of my regrets is that she didn't live to see the publication of my first book.

CA: Do your own children read your books and offer suggestions?

RODOWSKY: Good heavens, no. They read them when they're published. I almost never have them offer suggestions along the way, though once or twice I've gone to them for help if I've needed specific information about something. When I was working on a book called *Keeping Time*, I had a scene where some boys were trying to get Drew, the main character, to go to a ballgame. I went up and woke my son and said, "Come on. These kids are trying to get this other kid to not do what he's supposed to do and go to a ballgame. What would they say?" Very minor things like that. One daughter did read something in galleys because she was very anxious to read it. I also remember giving my youngest daughter a copy of one of the books when she was maybe twelve and not particularly interested in her mother's work. That book sat on her bedside table for ages. I would go up now and then and check to see where the book mark was. But now that she's twenty, she's very interested in my work.

I do discuss the books in progress with my husband. He's kind of my guinea pig. I give him sections to read and do awful things like sit and stare at him while he's reading and say, "Why are you frowning? You hate it." Or, "Why are you smiling? Is something funny?" Oddly enough, he doesn't read a great deal of fiction, but he's a wonderful critic. If he tells me there's something wrong, boy, I'd better believe him. I also send things piecemeal to my editor because I trust his judgment. But he's very careful about what he says at that point because he knows how fragile a work in progress is.

CA: You told Something about the Author *a few years ago about living in a very noisy house with six children, a dog,* and two cats. It must have been hard to find a quiet place and time for the writing.

RODOWSKY: It's not as noisy now because we only have one child at home (though there's still the dog—and three cats), but the others keep coming back for visits. It was hard. I started out the way everybody starts out, with a desk in a corner of my bedroom, and then as soon as my oldest daughter got married I got a room of my own to work in.

CA: What's your usual writing schedule?

RODOWSKY: I usually write all day. I try to start about 9:30 and work all morning, and then I do something active in the middle of the day, maybe go swimming or take a walk, and get back to the writing about 2:00. Now I can work until 5:00 or 5:30. I couldn't do that when my children were younger and they all arrived home at 3:00 or I had to go get them.

CA: Are you still writing for the Baltimore Sun?

RODOWSKY: No, I gave it up about two years ago. I was a children's book reviewer and I enjoyed it, but I spent the most incredible amount of time reading because the *Sun* would not send me just five or six books; all the children's books came here and I had to go through them. I did that for seven and a half years, and I thought that was long enough.

CA: Do you feel there's a glut of children's books on the market?

RODOWSKY: I don't know. I tend to not think about that. Now that I'm not reviewing children's books, I don't read as many of them as I used to, obviously, or as many of them as I would like to. I tend just to concentrate on what I'm working on and hope that if it's good enough, it will do well. I can't sit back and worry about how many books are being published. I feel that I have the absolutely best publisher there is, and I'm very happy to have them publish my books. I don't write books that I think are going to appeal to every child. Some, I think, are somewhat difficult and probably geared to good readers, but I don't see anything wrong with that. Every book isn't going to appeal to every child.

CA: Has there been any reaction to the language in your latest book, Julie's Daughter?

RODOWSKY: No. And if you're referring to Harper, that's just the way she would have spoken. I haven't gotten any bad feedback to it at all, and the book was on the ALA [American Library Association] Best Book for Young Adults list.

CA: So you haven't run into any kind of censorship problems?

RODOWSKY: I've never run into any problems of that kind. Not only that, but I've never had my editor tell me to take a word out because it would be difficult for children. We've done a lot of revisions, but always to try to make things better. I just felt that was the way Harper spoke. It's very true that characters take over, and I think they should. There's just no way she would have phrased things any differently. I have to be true to my characters—only in that way can I be true to my readers.

CA: With so many teenage pregnancies, there probably have been many young women who've identified with your char-

acter Julie Wilgus in Julie's Daughter. *Have you found that true?*

RODOWSKY: I don't know. Most of the feedback I've gotten from people has been about how much they like Harper or Slug. Slug appeared in an earlier book of mine called *Evy-Ivy-Over* as well as in the more recent book *H, My Name Is Henley.* Slug is kind of a favorite of mine. People ask me what's going to happen to Slug next, but I have no plans for her.

CA: When you begin a story, do you usually know where it's going?

RODOWSKY: I generally do. I usually have the ending in my mind, and very often I have written the last page first. However, when I wrote my first book, *What About Me?*, about a little boy with Down's syndrome, I had no idea when I started the book that he was going to die. So I don't always know what is going to happen.

CA: What about the book you're working on now?

RODOWSKY: I've just finished a book that's coming out in April. It's called *Fitchett's Folly,* and it's set in 1880 on what really was a barrier island off the Atlantic coast. The one I'm working on now I would prefer not to comment on.

CA: Your books usually take place close to home.

RODOWSKY: Some of them take place in Baltimore. Some of them take place in Baltimore but the place isn't identified as Baltimore. *The Gathering Room,* which was maybe one of my favorites (it was also an ALA Notable Book), takes place in an old cemetery in Baltimore, but I never mention this. A lot of them take place on the eastern shore of Virginia because that's where I spent the summers when I was a child, visiting my grandmother.

CA: You must have been very close to your grandmother.

RODOWSKY: I was very close to both of my grandmothers. In *Evy-Ivy-Over,* a book about Slug and her grandmother Gussie, I tried to describe the grandmother-grandchild relationship, though I must say neither of my grandmothers was at all like Gussie.

CA: Do you get many letters from your readers?

RODOWSKY: Some. They come in spurts. Sometimes you get letters from whole classes, sometimes just from individual students. It's difficult if you get a letter and it says you have to answer by a certain day and the date has already passed. This happens occasionally because the letter is sent to the publisher and it can take quite a while for me to get it.

CA: I imagine it could take a lot of time answering all the letters.

RODOWSKY: It does, but I really don't mind answering them.

CA: In your book Keeping Time, *you have Drew go back to Elizabethan England during part of the story. Did you do quite a bit of historical research?*

RODOWSKY: Yes, I did. I didn't quite know when I started that book where it was going. I knew I wanted to go back in

time, and I knew it had to have a musical connection because Drew is a musician. Oddly enough, I felt kind of spooky about the book. When I started working on it, my husband and I were downtown one night and there was a kind of festival at the harbor. There were street performers and musicians there, and one of the streets that was blocked off was called Cheapside Street. Eventually, when this whole thing was tied together, there was much of the Cheapside in London that played a part in the novel. I guess it started when I asked my son one night at dinner about a song that people would know today that was also known a long time ago. He suggested "Greensleeves."

CA: You made London of the time seem very vivid when you pointed out that the buildings were so close together, people could shake hands with one another from second-floor windows over the foul-smelling street below. I thought you must have done some research on things of this kind.

RODOWSKY: Yes, a lot. After the book was finished, we went to London and walked some of the same streets pictured in my novel.

CA: One thing that comes up frequently in your books is the difficulty of communication between young and old. Is this a major concern of yours?

RODOWSKY: I don't know that it's a major concern. I don't sit down and say to myself, Now I'm going to write a book about communication between kids and adults. I was an only child, which may have something to do with all this. Then suddenly I had a house full of children.

CA: You had your grandmothers to talk with, though, and could talk with them easily. But it was practically impossible for Henley to talk with her mother, and Drew had trouble talking with his father.

RODOWSKY: Patti was pretty impossible, but there are a lot of Pattis around. I've known some of them myself. I think Drew's father was just so laid back that his whole philosophy was to let people do what they wanted to do.

CA: Slug couldn't talk with her mother.

RODOWSKY: No, for the first seventeen years of her life Julie wasn't there, but she could talk with her grandmother. The whole thing of *Evy-Ivy-Over* was the very close relationship that Slug and Gussie had until Slug reached that age that I guess all kids get to, when she began to be embarrassed because Gussie was the town eccentric. She would go through town pulling a red wagon and taking things out of garbage cans and saving them.

CA: You've done short stories for adults as well as young adult fiction. Do you particularly enjoy the variety?

RODOWSKY: I really don't see any problem in writing for different ages. I think what you're writing about determines the age it's for. I don't think when you write for children that you ever consciously decide you're going to make something simpler, that you ever write down in any way. I get furious at people who think you write for children because that's where you start, and then you work up to writing for grownups. That's ridiculous. I don't think it's any easier to write for children than for adults.

CA: It seems to me that an aspiring teacher would do well to read children's novels instead of taking, say, education courses.

RODOWSKY: I'd love to have teachers read more children's novels. I'd love to have *parents* read more children's novels—if they'd read them in the spirit of wanting to share. My grandmother read a lot, and she used to read the books I read and give me things she'd liked. There's nothing better for any age than to talk about a book you love. When I was writing my column, that was one thing I did try to suggest off and on.

CA: What are some of your own favorite children's books?

RODOWSKY: One of my real favorites is *Unleaving* by Jill Paton Walsh. Another I really like is Madeleine L'Engle's *The Young Unicorns.*

CA: What kind of future plans do you have for the writing?

RODOWSKY: To get better. That's what we all want. What you always want somebody to say about your most recent book is that it's the best thing you've done. When I'm working on a book I tend not to be able to do anything else. I know there are people who can work on one book in the morning and then work on something else—another book, or a short story—in the afternoon. Whatever I do, I get totally involved in it. I am able to read other books when I'm writing a novel, though, and that's something I've heard some other writers can't do.

BIOGRAPHICAL/CRITICAL SOURCES:

BOOKS

Rodowsky, Colby, *H, My Name Is Henley,* Farrar, Straus, 1982.

PERIODICALS

Bulletin of the Center for Children's Books, July, 1980, January, 1983, September, 1985.
English Journal, October, 1979.
Horn Book, October, 1981, April, 1983, April, 1984.
Language Arts, May, 1982.
New York Times Book Review, October 25, 1981.
Publishers Weekly, June 14, 1985.
Times Educational Supplement, October 13, 1978.
Top of the News, winter, 1980.
Voice of Youth Advocates, April, 1983.
Washington Post Book World, October 11, 1983, November 6, 1983, August 11, 1985.
Writer, July, 1985.

—Sketch by Marilyn K. Basel

—Interview by Jean W. Ross

*   *   *

RODRIGUEZ, Judith Green 1936-
(Judith Green)

PERSONAL: Born February 13, 1936, in Perth, Australia; daughter of Gerald (in sales and management) and Dora (a teacher; maiden name, Spigl) Green; married Fabio Rodriguez, July, 1964 (divorced November, 1981); children: Sibila, Ensor, Rebeca, Zoe. *Education:* University of Queensland, B.A. (with first class honors), 1957; Girton College, Cambridge, M.A. (with first class honors), 1962; University of London, Certificate of Education, 1968. *Politics:* "Definitely, and how about education?" *Religion:* "Raised Anglican."

ADDRESSES: Home—Sydney, Australia. *Office*—Macarthur Institute of Higher Education, P.O. Box 108, Milperra 2122, Australia.

CAREER: University of Queensland, Brisbane, Australia, lecturer in external studies, 1959-60; Philippa Fawcett College of Education, London, England, lecturer in English, 1962-63; University of the West Indies, Kingston, Jamaica, lecturer in English, 1963-65; St. Giles School of English, London, teacher of English as a foreign language, 1965-66; St. Mary's College of Education, Twickenham, England, lecturer in English, 1966-68; La Trobe University, Bundoora, Australia, lecturer, 1969-75, senior lecturer in English, 1977-85; Macarthur Institute of Higher Education, Milperra, Sydney, Australia, lecturer in English, 1987—. Writer in residence, Rollins College, 1986; visiting fellow, West Australian Institute of Technology, 1986.

MEMBER: International PEN, Australian Society of Authors, Association for the Study of Australian Literature, South Pacific Association for Commonwealth Language and Literature Studies, Staff Association, Poets Union.

AWARDS, HONORS: Fellow of Arts Council of Australia, 1974, 1978, and 1983; biennial prize for literature from Government of South Australia, 1978, for *Water Life;* Victorian Regional Shell/*Artlook* Prize, 1979, for *Mudcrab at Gambaro's;* Peter Stuyvesant Prize for Poetry from International PEN, 1981, for *Mudcrab at Gambaro's.*

WRITINGS:

POETRY

(Under name Judith Green; with David Malouf, Rodney Hall, and Donald Maynard) *Four Poets,* F. W. Cheshire, 1962.
Nu-Plastik Fanfare Red, University of Queensland Press, 1973.
Water Life (self-illustrated), University of Queensland Press, 1976.
Shadow on Glass (self-illustrated), Open Door Press, 1978.
Mudcrab at Gambaro's (self-illustrated), University of Queensland Press, 1980.
Witch Heart, Sisters Publications, 1982.
(Editor) *Mrs. Noah and the Minoan Queen* (on Australian women poets), Sisters Publications, 1982.
Floridian Poems, Rollins College, 1986.
The House by Water: Selected and New Poems, University of Queensland Press, 1988.

OTHER

Author of poetry column, Sydney *Morning Herald,* 1984—. Contributor of articles, poems, and reviews (sometimes under name Judith Green) to scholarly journals and popular magazines, including *Age, Australian, Granta, Australian Literary Studies, Overland, Poetry Australia,* and *Westerly.* Poetry editor of *Meanjin Quarterly,* 1979-82.

WORK IN PROGRESS: Research on Australian poetry for children and on Canadian literature.

SIDELIGHTS: Judith Green Rodriguez told *CA:* "I have written poetry since I was small. Spurred on by late adolescent miseries (so helpful), I met my first stiffening criticism from John Manifold when I gave him half a dozen poems to look at in 1956. David Malouf, with whom I traveled extensively in Europe, has been a continual encouragement in thin times.

"My writing was very slow when I was first living abroad, 1960-68, a period which also saw my marriage and the birth of my first two children.

"I write to live more fully. At first I did not see the coherence in my own work, but gradually the poems themselves have forced me to see the continuing water symbolism in my thinking. Living is littoral for so many Australians; water—the need for it and enrichment by it—is a theme of our national life. Rather than changing, this theme goes on acquiring new aspects in my work, new branches, courses, beds, outlets.

"The seventies awakened me, with all my generation of women, to powerful sources of life and insight in *being* women and being women *now*. Children, the arts of printmaking and chamber music, poetry and love are behind and, I hope, in my writing. I have made linocuts since 1974, and I find them the natural visual accompaniment to my poems."

* * *

ROE, Derek A(rthur) 1937-

PERSONAL: Born August 31, 1937, in Hastings, Sussex, England; son of Arthur William and Marjorie (Barrow) Roe; married Fiona Greig (an archaeologist), July 11, 1964; children: Bridget Julia, Nicholas Derek. *Education:* Peterhouse, Cambridge, B.A., 1961, M.A., 1964, Ph.D., 1968.

ADDRESSES: Home—Oxford, England. *Office*—Donald Baden-Powell Quaternary Research Centre, Oxford University, 60 Banbury Rd., Oxford OX2 6PN, England.

CAREER: London Times, London, England, archaeological correspondent, 1961-65; Oxford University, Oxford, England, lecturer in prehistoric archaeology,1965—, director of Donald Baden-Powell Quaternary Research Centre, 1975—. St. Cross College, Oxford, fellow, 1970—, vice-master, 1985—. Governor of St. Edward's School, Oxford, England, 1970—.

MEMBER: The Prehistoric Society, Society of Antiquaries of London (fellow).

AWARDS, HONORS: D.Litt., Oxford University, 1984; Henry Stopes Memorial Medal, Geologists Association of London, 1985.

WRITINGS:

A *Gazetteer of British Lower and Middle Palaeolithic Sites,* Council for British Archaeology, 1968.
Prehistory: An Introduction, University of California Press, 1970.
The Lower and Middle Palaeolithic Periods in Britain, Routledge & Kegan Paul, 1981.
(Editor) *Adlun in the Stone Age: The Excavations of D. A. E. Garrod in Lebanon, 1958-1963,* two volumes, British Archaeological Reports, 1983.
(Ghost writer) Mary D. Leakey, *Disclosing the Post,* Doubleday, 1984.
(Editor) *Studies in the Upper Palaeolithic of Britain and Northwest Europe,* British Archaeological Reports, 1986.

Member of editorial board of *World Archaeology,* 1968-86, advisory board, 1986—; contributing editor of *Quarterly Review of Archaeology,* 1981—.

WORK IN PROGRESS: Researching and preparing articles and longer reports on earlier Stone Age archaeology in Britain, Europe, the Middle East, and Africa.

SIDELIGHTS: Derek A. Roe once told *CA:* "Though I have always enjoyed writing for its own sake, inevitably I am now mainly concerned with the presentation of archaeological material at various levels, from popular to highly technical. I see no reason why this cannot be achieved at a reasonably high literary level, or why even technical reports cannot be kept free from the needless use of jargon. Scholarly writing can still be made genuinely attractive to readers who have never studied in the discipline concerned. It seems to me that lucidity and warmth of style are the keys to this, and I shall continue to aim in that general direction."

Roe described his 1979 work, *Prehistory: An Introduction* as "a first introduction to the subject of prehistory, to the sequence of events in prehistoric times, and to some of the ways in which they are studied." A *Times Literary Supplement* reviewer judged the book "a most useful addition to the archaeological literature written for the general reader. The style is clear and attractive, the illustrations are well chosen and will include much that general readers will not have seen before, and the footnotes are genuinely informative and helpful."

In *The Lower and Middle Palaeolithic Periods in Britain,* Roe offers a technical discussion of how the archaeological evidence he first compiled and tabulated in his 1968 *Gazetteer* fits into a half-million-year time period. J. J. Wymer, in the *Times Literary Supplement,* strongly approved the book for even the general reader: "Roe is to be congratulated on the clarity with which he expounds his theme. This book reads so easily that I am sure he must have re-written it many times. He is never dogmatic nor does he shelter behind unnecessary jargon. For such a complex subject he has managed to retain a surprising amount of narrative. This is an ideal volume, indeed, from which to learn how Palaeolithic studies have progressed and where they now stand."

BIOGRAPHICAL/CRITICAL SOURCES:

PERIODICALS

Times Literary Supplement, May 21, 1971, January 29, 1982.

* * *

ROGERS, Rosemary 1932-

PERSONAL: Born December 7, 1932, in Panadura, Ceylon (now Sri Lanka); came to United States in 1962, naturalized citizen; daughter of Cyril Allan (an owner and manager of a private school) and Barbara Jansze; married Summa Navaratnam (divorced); married Leroy Rogers (divorced); married Christopher Kadison (a poet); children: (first marriage) Rosanne, Sharon; (second marriage) Michael, Adam. *Education:* University of Ceylon, B.A. *Politics:* Democrat. *Religion:* Episcopalian.

ADDRESSES: Home—Carmel, Calif. and New York, N.Y.

CAREER: Associated Newspapers of Ceylon, Colombo, writer of features and public affairs information, 1959-62; Travis Air Force Base, Fairfield, Calif., secretary in billeting office, 1964-69; Solano County Parks Department, Fairfield, secretary, 1969-74; writer. Part-time reporter for *Fairfield Daily Republic.*

MEMBER: Authors Guild, Authors League of America, Writers Guild.

WRITINGS:

Sweet Savage Love, Avon, 1974.
The Wildest Heart, Avon, 1974.
Dark Fires, Avon, 1975.
Wicked Loving Lies, Avon, 1976.
The Crowd Pleasers, Avon, 1978.

The Insiders, Avon, 1979.

Lost Love, Last Love, Avon, 1980, large print hardcover edition, G. K. Hall, 1984.

Love Play, Avon, 1981, large print hardcover edition, G. K. Hall, 1984.

Surrender to Love, Avon, 1982.

The Wanton, Avon, 1985, large print hardcover edition, G. K. Hall, 1986.

Bound by Desire, Avon, 1988.

WORK IN PROGRESS: A cookbook entitled *Sweet Savage Cooking;* a contemporary novel.

SIDELIGHTS: Rosemary Rogers, who writes lengthy historical and contemporary romances, has helped change the course of the genre by adding a new element: explicit sex in the previously G-rated love scenes. Relates Kathryn Falk in *Love's Leading Ladies:* "When Rosemary used to read historical novels as a young girl she often wondered why they didn't say a little more in the love scenes. 'Not that you want to be clinical like a sex manual,' [Rogers] explains. 'But I always felt you can go into a bit of detail and at the same time you can leave a little to the imagination.' This is what she attempts to do."

Formerly, romance novels required a virginal heroine who remained chaste until she married the hero, which usually occurred at the novel's conclusion. The beginnings of Rogers' books generally follow the traditional format. But before long, the hero forcefully awakens the heroine to her dormant passions. "The difference between R. R. and most of her rivals is intensity," writes Brad Darrach in *Time*. "Almost all the others write in pink ink about horse-and-carriage love and marriage; Rogers pumps out purple prose about red-blooded males and females living at white heat in electric-blue relationships." He adds that Rogers "perfected the soft-edge sex scene in which, just as the worst is about to happen, all the heavy breathing seems to steam the reader's glasses and the details fade discreetly into daydreams." Rogers' new formula has sold over fifty million copies of her books worldwide, disproving the theory that romances were "women's novels." Rogers includes men among her readers, some in unlikely places. "I have fan clubs in half the federal penitentiaries around the country!" she told *CA* interviewer Jean W. Ross.

"She's one author who looks and lives like one of her heroines," suggests Tom Huff, a romance writer quoted in *Love's Leading Ladies*. Rogers grew up in an environment similar to those depicted in her books. Her father owned and managed a group of private schools in Ceylon, and his eldest daughter was raised in a world of servants, chaperones, and European excursions. She wrote her first short story at the age of eight, read voraciously, and as a teenager wrote novels for pleasure. "At seventeen, initiating the pattern her heroines now follow, Rosemary rebelled against a feudal upbringing," writes a *Time* reporter. Rogers' rebellion took the form of being the first woman in her family to get a job. She became a feature writer for a Ceylon newspaper and worked there for three years. She also married a track star, who "often sprinted after other women," reports *Time*. A divorce followed, then another marriage, to Air Force Sergeant Leroy Rogers. The pair eventually moved to California, where she raised four children and continued to write. "Right through bringing up my own kids, through diaper time, instead of watching TV, I'd write stories," she told Falk.

But when her second marriage also ended, Rogers was left trying to support her family on a secretary's salary of $4,200 a year. About this time, her parents came to live with her after

fleeing the Marxist rebellion in Ceylon. In order to survive economically, Rogers decided to market one of her old stories, eventually rewriting it twenty-four times before sending the 636-page manuscript to Avon Books, whose name her daughter had found on the first page of *Writer's Market*. It arrived on editor Nancy Coffey's desk in the wake of Avon's successful publishing of *The Flame and the Flower* by Kathleen Woodiwiss. Recognizing another potential bestseller, Avon immediately offered Rogers a contract.

The novel was called *Sweet Savage Love* and Rogers promptly followed it up with another bestseller, *Dark Fires*. The first two books, plus a third, *Lost Love, Last Love* relate the lengthy, passionate, and sometimes violent romance between Steven Morgan, a womanizing adventurer, and Virginia Brandon, the spirited, initially virginal, heroine. While the public reacted enthusiastically to the books, critics were often less pleased. Weeks says "*Dark Fires*, though promoted as an epic historical love story, is in fact crammed with violence, sexual perversion and sado-masochism. . . . The theory behind *Dark Fires* assumes that females groove on violence and that rape is a shortcut to the joy of sex." Charles Madigan comments on *Lost Love, Last Love* in the *Chicago Tribune*: "Basically, it's about sex. Almost everyone in this 378-page book is interested in sex. Steve and Ginny, for example, mate with regularity. . . . Steve also couples with many other women, too. They are his mistresses. . . ." The word romance does not always denote moonlight and chivalry, either. "[Steve] never kisses Ginny; he lays such a lip lock on her that he almost breaks her neck. And Ginny, hey. She loves it," Madigan continues. Some critics have even labelled her books as pornographic. Rogers disagrees. In a note to *CA* she explained that she does not write pornography. She says her novels "are more like morality plays—exposing life the way it is."

Rape is a common and recurring theme in Rogers' novels. To the criticism that her heroines are masochistic women with rape fantasies, Rogers told Carol Lawson, *New York Times Book Review* contributor: "Most women *do* have a rape fantasy. But there is a difference between actual rape, which is horrifying, and fantasy. In the rape fantasy, you pick the man and the circumstances. It's not at all scary." In an interview with Patricia Goldstone for the *Los Angeles Times* she says of her heroines, "They end up getting raped a lot because, historically speaking, that's what happened to any woman who went out on her own."

"My heroines are partly me, partly women I have known or read about," Rogers told Goldstone. "They are Woman." A *West Coast Review of Books* reviewer describes the heroine of *The Wanton* a little differently, as "a beautiful and highly intelligent young woman, who is nevertheless the prisoner of her base passions and desires."

Still, many critics agree that the books provide an escape from life's everyday monotony. Writes Madigan, describing a woman reading her Rogers novel at the laundromat, "You are carried from the drudgery of the Buck-a-wash, from the rhythmic pounding of that washing machine and the whirring of those dryers and that offensive smell of bleach to a world of magnolias and women who smell like flowers and men who are so dashing you would never expect to meet one in the laundromat." Darrach quotes an Avon executive who relates why Rogers' books are so popular with American women. "They identify with Rosemary's heroines because the heroines do everything the average housewife longs to do—they travel to exotic places, meet famous people, have passionate affairs with fascinating men, and in the end fall madly in love and live happily ever after.'' Darrach continues that those who read the books "are force-fed events as the action mounts to a terrific climax in which lust sprouts little pink wings and Beauty fetters Beast with a golden wedding band.''

Rogers herself has undergone a Cinderella-type transformation with her books' successes. Elisabeth Busmiller of the *Washington Post* describes the now full-time author, who is also a grandmother: "She looks exactly as you would expect: Mink-wrapped (black, by Chloe) and jewelry-draped (one bracelet, two earrings, three necklaces and eight rings . . .). She is . . . tall, thin, olive-skinned, with cascading dark hair and full lips.'' Rogers now has two homes in California (one on Big Sur) and another home in Manhattan. She prefers to work at night, with music playing in the background.

Several elements, Rogers says, are necessary for a successful romance. "For me it has to have an element of adventure,'' she said in an interview with a *Chicago Tribune* reporter. Other requirements are "a strong male protagonist, a strong female who's a little bit feisty and rebellious, mystery, suspense, romance, and, above all, a happy ending. At the end, she's got to melt, but so does he.'' And while her readers want a happy ending, she continued, "They don't want sickening saccharine romance.'' She told Falk, "The basic thing is the chemistry. . . . If you have the attraction, then wherever you are becomes romantic. Society overdoes the candlelight, atmosphere bit. Love is a much abused word, nowadays. I believe in attraction at first sight, but love is precious and doesn't come too easily. It has a lot to do with liking. For love to last, it has to involve liking, friendship, and communication.'' What kind of book does she prefer to read? "I like something I can sink my teeth into,'' she added. "Something with action, mystery, and suspense.''

Unfavorable critical reviews don't bother Rogers too much; she is content with her enthusiastic audience. "I could never do things to please critics or an intellectual coterie,'' she told a *Time* reporter. "I write to please ordinary people—I write the kinds of books *I* want to read.'' Madigan says of *Lost Love, Last Love,* "This book and its predecessors . . . never will be candidates for the Nobel Prize for Literature. Rogers knows that, too. . . . She says they are pure entertainment, nothing less, nothing more.''

AVOCATIONAL INTERESTS: Reading, music, watching some sports (especially football), printing, cooking, opera, and disco dancing.

CA INTERVIEW

CA interviewed Rosemary Rogers by telephone on January 27, 1987, at her home in New York, New York.

CA: While you've obviously pleased millions of readers around the world, one has the feeling that you're also writing to please yourself. Are you still, on some level, the little girl in Ceylon happily telling stories to her brothers and sister?

ROGERS: I suppose in some way I am, except now everybody's grown up and I'm telling stories to myself. Sometimes when friends or members of my family are here, I bounce ideas off them and relate my story or the outline of whatever I'm doing.

CA: And you still enjoy the writing?

ROGERS: Yes, I do. This time I'm having a bit of a problem—not a real problem, except that I broke my wrist and had to have somebody come in and do dictation for my current book on the word processor, and he lost most of it.

CA: How awful! Was this for a book you were just starting?

ROGERS: No, it was a book I've been working on, the fourth novel in the Steve and Ginny saga. This one only starts with Steve and Ginny; it's mostly concerned with their twins, Laura and Franco. I had to start from scratch, so that's what I've done.

CA: When you started rewriting, did a lot of it come back to you easily, or from memory?

ROGERS: Some of it did, and the rest of it I had to improvise. What I have to work from, actually, is the first draft copy. It was the polished, finished copy that disappeared. I was devastated. It took me a couple of weeks to recover. And then I thought, Well, what's to be done? There's nothing to do but go ahead and start all over.

CA: You'd been writing for a long time before you sent the manuscript for Sweet Savage Love *to Avon in the early 1970s and thus launched your career. What finally gave you the courage to send some of the work off?*

ROGERS: It was more desperation than courage. I'd been writing for myself, for the family. Writing has always been my escape valve from harsh reality. There came a point when I had my parents and four children to support on a secretary's salary that was at that time $450 a month take-home pay. I had this huge, unwieldy pile of yellow notebooks in the closet which eventually became *Sweet Savage Love.* So I'd go to my office after hours and type with the janitors sometimes looking over my shoulder and making comments—"Hey, that's sexy!'' and that kind of thing. But I did it. And I did a lot of research in the library.

CA: Do you feel your early work as a journalist helped the fiction writing in any way?

ROGERS: No, not really. I had to adapt myself to the journalistic style. It's short, clipped, whereas my style is more—elongated, should I say! Sometimes I keep a sentence on and on and on with dashes and semi-colons, but I think it flows. It flows with my thoughts.

CA: You seem to believe very much in feelings, intuition, inspiration. You said in Love's Leading Ladies *that ideas for the writing come in "dreams and half-dreams.'' How does that work?*

ROGERS: What I mean by half-dreams is that state when I'm half asleep and half awake, just drifting off to sleep. Then all of a sudden these things come into my head. It could be an idea for a new story, or it could be a whole scene. At other times, I have what I call a story when I'm actually dreaming. There it is. I get up and I write it down—in rough form, of course. Then it becomes a book.

CA: You're very careful about eating properly and doing yoga. Do you think those practices contribute something to the state of mind that allows the inspiration to happen?

ROGERS: I think maybe so. Yoga is a form of self-discipline and meditation, and eating right keeps you healthy. If you're sick, it's hard to think or to function. In that way, yes, I think it has something to do with it.

CA: Does the writing go more easily when you're involved in a good romantic relationship yourself?

ROGERS: Actually, no. It has to do with what Freud called sublimation. I have to put everything in my libido, so to speak, into the writing itself. If I'm heavily involved in a romantic relationship, it's difficult to concentrate on the writing. My energy is being dissipated.

CA: Do you try to provide yourself a challenge in the writing by setting out with each new book to do something harder or something a little bit different?

ROGERS: Not really. It depends on what I feel like doing. For instance, this book I'm working on is historical, set in a very interesting period. As soon as it's over, I'm going to do a contemporary novel. It's just whatever I feel in the mood to do. That's the way I function.

CA: You told Patricia Goldstone for the Los Angeles Times, *"I prefer not to visit the places I write about, but to live there in my mind." Do you ever visit your setting after you've finished a book and get a chance to see how well you captured the place?*

ROGERS: Occasionally, very occasionally. And I find that it's worked out well. But I really still do prefer to read my research books, read diaries of the people who lived at the time, look at pictures. Then I can almost see it. Maybe this is my yoga coming in. I can imagine it and see it and almost feel how a place would have felt. I think it's better for me that way.

CA: Diaries must be especially useful, because you get a real sense of living with people if their diaries are good.

ROGERS: Even if they are not, even if they're the kind of diary that someone wrote just a few words a day in. Somebody gave me a copy of a diary that his great-grandmother had kept when the family went in a wagon train from Oregon to California. I found it fascinating. And, of course, being me, I'd make up things between the lines and between the entries. I remember one entry when she was very annoyed. Indians came up and were trading for sugar. She said that her brother teased her by offering her to the Indians, and one of the Indian men took it seriously. She wrote in her dairy, "Very upset"—just that, "Very upset." I like the real diaries, not the edited ones.

CA: Have you acquired a large personal library in the course of doing all the research for your books?

ROGERS: Yes, I certainly have! I have books everywhere—on shelves, piled up on the floor, on coffee tables and under coffee tables. And this applies not only to my New York apartment but to my two houses in Carmel [and] Big Sur as well.

CA: What do you want to give your readers? Is there something you set out to do for them each time you start a book?

ROGERS: I just want them to enjoy escaping into this fantasy world as much as I enjoy doing it while I'm writing. I have learned that they enjoy the historical books. The background is accurate, and it has interested a lot of people in history. Also, I guess in a way I'm expressing a sense of an individual's searching, whoever the individual is I'm writing about. Right now I'm immersed in my current book. Laura, who is Ginny and Steve's daughter, is really searching for herself. She knows everything on the surface—books, talk. She's sophisticated on the surface. But underneath, she worries about herself. I think all my characters, especially my heroines, are wandering and searching for something. To me, it doesn't matter what period I'm writing about. When I get immersed in it, I can feel the man's frustrations and feelings and emotions as well as I can feel the woman's. I feel that all of us, in some way, are looking for something, and that's what I'm trying to express.

CA: You've said that your readers include all ages, and a lot of men. What do men say in their letters about the books? What appeals especially to them?

ROGERS: Oh, dear. I have fan clubs in half the federal penitentiaries around the country! They all say, "Your books are fantastic; we love them. If you're like your heroines, boy would we ever like to meet you sometime!"

CA: It must be hard to respond to letters like that—if you even can.

ROGERS: I have responded to them, but in a kind of vague way, and without giving my address, of course. But I can see that. I write for men as well as for women. My male characters are just as strong. There's always a conflict between men and women; let's admit it. What I try to do is bring that conflict out. The way that men are brought up to think, and the way that women are, or were, brought up to think and told how to react—when it all breaks loose, the difference is there. I feel that what happens at the end of my books is that the women are discovering their equality as well as their love.

CA: I can't help wondering how your lead male characters can change so quickly from absolute bastards, sometimes, to such nice people. Is there a message in that?

ROGERS: Yes, I guess so. There *are* a lot of men who are absolute bastards. But, if they're made to realize that a woman can stand up to them and be strong for herself, they will respect her for it all the more.

CA: In "Prime Time for Sex" in Harper's Bazaar, *you wrote about the joys of sex past the first blush of youth, shall we say. Do you think Americans are beginning now to see older women in a more attractive light than in the past?*

ROGERS: I think so, because I think older women don't look and act the role of the little white-haired old grandmother wearing an apron. Older women *think* young. It's a matter of thinking young, keeping yourself fit and healthy, and being with young people, which I think is very important. I spend quite a bit of time with my children and their friends. Just seeing what they think, how they react to things, is essential. To stay young, you have to keep on growing. I don't think there's any problem with romances between the older woman and the younger man. But I don't think any woman has to be an "older woman." She's *a woman*, with that basic quality of being feminine.

CA: How do you divide your time now between your homes in New York City and Carmel, California?

ROGERS: Recently I've spent more time in New York City trying to finish this book, because my word processor is here.

CA: Can you write equally well in either place?

ROGERS: I prefer to write in my house in Big Sur, on the ocean. There's something very peaceful and soothing about it. I don't have to worry about neighbors if I want to turn my music on—I always have classical music in the background when I write. It's less distracting in California. Here there are distractions. I've been thinking more and more that I have to go back and be in peace and be surrounded by my family.

CA: Do you usually take time off between books to rest and catch up on other interests?

ROGERS: Most of the time, yes. I have two grandchildren now, whom I enjoy: a little girl, five, who's a joy and a delight; and a little boy, going on two.

CA: Some time ago you said there was a cookbook in the works. How's it coming along?

ROGERS: It's in embryo form. My agent is threatening; he says he's not going to do anything with it until I finish the novel I'm on.

CA: In the cookbook, will you make a connection between food and romance?

ROGERS: The way I have it planned out, it's going to have the titles of all my books. It's like the beginning and the middle and the ending of a romance, then the picking up again and the hope that something else is starting up. There's a little introduction to each. It's going to be called *Sweet Savage Cooking.*

CA: Is there any television work in the offing?

ROGERS: Not right now. I've been pretty much hibernating and trying to get the novel out. It's late because of having to start from scratch again after all those months of work. So I'm trying to have tunnel vision until I turn it in. Then, whoopee!

CA: You're interested in other things besides writing your books. For example, you've been a patron of the opera. Are you happy with your public image?

ROGERS: I don't really know what my public image is. I don't know how much of it is me and how much of it is publicity and how much of it is imagined by people who might read my books and then make up what they think about me. I remember certain occasions in the early times when people were amazed when they met me. They'd say, I read something about your age, and I thought I'd see a little old lady in tennis shoes. Well, thanks a lot. So often people make up their own fantasies.

CA: You told Savvy, *"I break all the rules." What rules are you proudest of having broken?*

ROGERS: I'm not conventional. I'm impulsive; I tend to leap before I look. And I say things outright. For instance, in any interview or in anything else I've ever done, I've never tried to cover up. If I don't want to answer a question, I'll say so. I believe in honesty. And I believe that if there were more honesty between people, half our problems wouldn't exist. I went through a time, when I was younger, of feeling I had to do certain things, had to pretend. But I don't now. I don't want to hurt anybody's feeling either—I never want to do that—but I have to be myself.

CA: Yes. One of the payoffs about getting older is feeling comfortable about whatever you are.

ROGERS: Exactly. For the first time I'm discovering I like being myself, being *able* to be myself and not being afraid of what people will think.

CA: What's the best part of the success?

ROGERS: Being able to feel free. Being able to travel. And being able to help my kids out, look after my father. There's so much more of a big world around, you know? Being able to go into a bookstore and buy armfuls of books—which is how I broke my wrist!

BIOGRAPHICAL/CRITICAL SOURCES:

BOOKS

Authors in the News, Volume I, Gale, 1976.
Falk, Kathryn, *Love's Leading Ladies,* Pinnacle Books, 1982.

PERIODICALS

Booklist, July 15, 1981, May 15, 1982, February 15, 1985.
Book World, January 21, 1979.
Chicago Tribune, June 14, 1981.
Chicago Tribune Magazine, June 5, 1983.
Detroit News, May 31, 1979.
Fort Worth Star-Telegram, December 31, 1974.
Harper's Bazaar, August, 1985.
Los Angeles Times, February 12, 1981.
New York Times, March 25, 1979.
New York Times Book Review, March 18, 1979.
Savvy, July, 1985.
Time, January 17, 1977.
Washington Post, May 22, 1980.
Washington Post Book World, September 14, 1975, September 3, 1978, January 21, 1979.
West Coast Review of Books, July, 1985.

—*Sketch by Jani Prescott*

—*Interview by Jean W. Ross*

*   *   *

ROOKE, Leon   1934-

PERSONAL: Born September 11, 1934, in Roanoke Rapids, N.C. *Education:* University of North Carolina, student, 1955-58, 1961-62. *Politics:* New Democrat.

ADDRESSES: Home—1019 Terrace Ave., Victoria, British Columbia, Canada V8S 3V2. *Agent*—Liz Darhansoff, 1220 Park Ave., New York, N.Y. 10128.

CAREER: Short story writer, novelist, and dramatist. University of North Carolina at Chapel Hill, writer-in-residence, 1965-66; University of Victoria, Victoria, British Columbia, lecturer in creative writing, 1971-72, visiting professor, 1980-81; Southwest Minnesota State College, Marshall, writer-in-residence, 1975-76; University of Toronto, Toronto, Ontario, writer-in-residence, 1984-85. *Military service:* U.S. Army, Infantry, 1958-60; served in Alaska.

MEMBER: PEN, Writers' Union of Canada.

AWARDS, HONORS: MacDowell fellowship, 1974; Canada Council theatre and fiction grants, 1974, 1975, 1976, 1979, 1983, and 1985; Yaddo fellowship, 1976; National Endowment for the Arts fellowship, 1978; Best Paperback Novel of the Year, 1981, for *Fat Woman;* Canada/Australia Prize, 1981, for overall body of work; Governor General's Literary Award for fiction, Canada Council, 1984, for *Shakespeare's Dog;* Author's Award for short fiction, Foundation for the Advancement of Canadian Letters, 1986.

WRITINGS:

STORY COLLECTIONS

Last One Home Sleeps in the Yellow Bed, Louisiana State University Press, 1968.
The Love Parlour: Stories, Oberon, 1977.
The Broad Back of the Angel, Fiction Collective, 1977.
Cry Evil, Oberon, 1980.
Death Suite, ECW Press (Toronto), 1981.
The Birth Control King of the Upper Volta, ECW Press, 1982.
Sing Me No Love Songs, I'll Say You No Prayers: Selected Stories, Ecco Press, 1984.
A Bolt of White Cloth, Ecco Press, 1985.

NOVELS

The Magician in Love, Aya Press (Toronto), 1981.
Fat Woman, Knopf, 1981.
Shakespeare's Dog (also see below), Knopf, 1983.

PLAYS

"Lady Physhie's Cafe," produced in Louisville, Kentucky, at Louisville Art Center, 1960.
Krokodile, Playwrights Co-op (Toronto), 1973.
"Ms. America" (three-act play), first produced in Toronto, Ontario, 1974.
Sword Play (one-act; first produced in Vancouver, Canada, at New Play Centre, March, 1973; produced Off-Off Broadway, 1975), Playwright's Co-op, 1974.
"Of Ice and Men" (two-act), produced in Toronto at Theatre Passe Muraille, 1985.
"Shakespeare's Dog" (one-man show), produced in Toronto at Theatre Passe Muraille, 1985.
"The Good Baby" (two-act), produced by Caravan Stage Company for British Columbia tour, 1987.

Also author of the play "Evening Meeting of the Club of Suicide," New Play Centre. Author of radio plays for Canadian Broadcasting Corporation, 1986-87.

CONTRIBUTOR TO ANTHOLOGIES

William Abrahams and Richard Poirier, editors, *Prize Stories of 1965: The O. Henry Awards,* Doubleday, 1965.
Jessie Rehder, editor, *Chapel Hill Carousel,* University of North Carolina Press, 1967.
John Metcalf, editor, *76: New Canadian Stories,* Oberon, 1977.
Statements, Fiction Collective, 1977.
Guy Owen, editor, *The North Carolina Short Story,* University of North Carolina Press, 1977.
Metcalf and Clark Blaise, editors, *Here and Now,* Oberon, 1977.
Edward Peck, editor, *Transitions II,* Comancept, 1978.
Metcalf, editor, *Stories Plus,* McGraw, 1979.
Stanley Elkin and Shannon Ravenel, editors, *Best American Short Stories, 1980,* Houghton, 1980.
Geoff Hancock, editor, *Magic Realism,* Aya Press, 1980.

Metcalf, editor, *80: Best Canadian Stories,* Oberon, 1980.
Hancock, editor, *Illusions,* Aya Press, 1981.
Paul Belserene, editor, *Canadian Short Fiction Anthology,* Intermedia Press, 1982.
Ron Smith and Stephen Guppy, editors, *Rainshadow: Stories from Vancouver Island,* Oolichon Books/Sono Nis Press, 1982.
Leah Flater, Aritha Van Herk, and Ruby Wiebe, editors, *West of Fiction,* NeWest Press, 1982.
Scholes and Sullivan, editors, *Elements of Fiction,* Oxford University Press, 1982.
Jack David and John Redfern, editors, *Introduction to Fiction,* Holt, 1982.
Donna Bennett and Russell Brown, editors, *An Anthology of Canadian Literature in English,* Volume II, Oxford University Press, 1983.
Metcalf, editor, *Making It New,* Methuen, 1983.
Hancock, editor, *The Shoe Anthology,* Aya Press, 1984.
New: West Coast Fiction, WCR/Pulp Press, 1984.
Canadian Short Stories, Oxford University Press, 1985.
Barbara E. Turner, editor, *Skeleton at Sixty,* Porcupines Quill, 1986.
Daniel Halpern, editor, *The Art of the Tale: An International Anthology of Short Stories, 1945-1985,* Viking, 1986.
Margaret Atwood and Robert Weaver, editors, *The Oxford Book of Canadian Short Stories,* Oxford University Press, 1986.
W. H. New, editor, *Canadian Short Stories: From Myth to Modern,* Prentice-Hall, 1986.
Ben Sonnenberg, editor, *A Grand Street Reader,* Summit Books, 1986.
Ian W. Mills and Judith H. Mills, editors, *The Arch of Experience,* Holt, 1986.
Peter Hinchcliffe and Ed Jewinski, editors, *Magic Realism and Canadian Literature: Essays and Stories,* University of Waterloo Press, 1986.
David Helwig and Sandra Martin, editors, *86: Best Canadian Stories,* Oberon, 1987.
Tesseracts 2: Canadian Science Fiction, Press Porcepic, 1987.
D. Helwig and Maggie Helwig, editors, *87: Best Canadian Short Stories,* Oberon, 1988.

OTHER

Vault, a Story in Three Parts: Conjugal Precepts, Dinner with the Swardians, and Break and Enter, Lillabulero Press, 1973.
(Editor with Metcalf) *81: Best Canadian Stories,* Oberon, 1981.
(Editor with Metcalf) *82: Best Canadian Stories,* Oberon, 1982.
(Editor with Metcalf) *The New Press Anthology: Best Canadian Short Fiction,* General Publishing (Toronto), 1984.
(Editor with Metcalf) *The Macmillan Anthology One,* Macmillan of Canada, 1988.

Contributor of short novels to *Carolina Quarterly, Noble Savage,* and *Descant.* Contributor of about 250 short stories to Canadian and U.S. literary magazines, including *Southern Review, Canadian Fiction Magazine, Antaeus, Yale Review, Mississippi Review,* and *Malahat Review.*

SIDELIGHTS: According to Toronto *Globe and Mail* reviewer William French, "Leon Rooke is unquestionably the most imaginative fiction writer currently practising in Canada. His closest competitor is probably Jacques Ferron, the Montreal fantasist, but Rooke is far more prolific than Ferron." Rooke has authored several volumes of short stories and a growing list of plays, and among his novels are *Fat Woman* and *Shake-*

speare's Dog. In the *New York Times Book Review*, Alberto Manguel finds Rooke hard to classify: "[Rooke's] style varies greatly not only from book to book but sometimes from page to page. It is impossible to speak of a typical Leon Rooke paragraph; each one sets out to explore different voices and textures."

Rooke's earliest short story collections, including *Last One Home Sleeps in the Yellow Bed, The Broad Back of the Angel,* and *The Love Parlour,* are noted for their experimental qualities and their intertwining of realism and surrealism. *Sewanee Review* critic George Garrett finds the collection *The Broad Back of the Angel* "mildly surrealist in matter and in manner . . . [like] a French surrealist movie of the late thirties, afflicted with poor subtitles. But Rooke is good at it and knows what he is doing well enough." Lesley Hogan comments in the *Canadian Fiction Magazine* that *The Broad Back of the Angel* and *The Love Parlour* "show masterful control of a variety of techniques. Rooke's concern is with love and the importance of personal relationships in an ever-increasingly impersonal society. . . . He maintains a delicate balance between the realms of reality and fantasy which gives his stories their double impact of strangeness and familiarity." In this same vein, Stephen Scobie claims in *Books in Canada* that "[one] feature of Rooke's fiction has been the way the ordinary lives of ordinary people coexist with the most extravagant and bizarre events and are presented in exuberantly experimental forms. . . . One key to such an approach is Rooke's insistence on *voice.* . . . Whooping and hollering, cajoling or complaining, Rooke's characters meet the world at an interface of language; their perception *is* their rhetoric."

Although reviewers generally find Rooke's earlier story collections impressive, they are not slow to address the unevenness of these volumes nor the fact that Rooke's avant-garde style, at times, fails. Regarding *The Broad Back of the Angel,* *Fiddlehead* contributor John Mills notes that although Rooke "writes excellent and sometimes poetic prose," *The Broad Back of the Angel* contains three stories about a magician that "are experimental, and in my opinion they fail—there is a coy air of self-congratulation about them." In turn, Sally Beauman expresses in her *New York Times Book Review* assessment of *Last One Home Sleeps in the Yellow Bed* that "there is a feeling of frustration" about these stories, "as if [Rooke] wanted to write, not short stories at all, but a novel. Not that it's such a bad fault to have themes which are too big for your medium."

With the advent of Rooke's collection entitled *Cry Evil* in 1980, critics detect a change in Rooke's posture. "From the very first words of [*Cry Evil*]," writes Russell M. Brown in the *Canadian Forum,* ". . . it becomes clear that we are dealing with a writer who is now trying out the self-conscious and self-reflexive mode of post-modernism. As we move through this book, we encounter something of the exhaustion, the labyrinths and the narrative games of writers like Barth." In *Canadian Literature,* Jerry Wasserman concurs: "The stories in *Cry Evil* are . . . [baroque and make great] demands on the reader, echoing Barth and Borges, Dostoevsky, Kafka, and Poe. They are not recommended for chronic depressives." Whereas the narrators in Rooke's earlier story collections were conventional, Brown finds that Rooke has informed *Cry Evil* with "a series of ingenious narrative variations that are evidence of the search for renewed creative energy." The story called "The Deacon's Tale," for instance, presents a deacon who has trouble telling his tale, partly due to his wife's incessant harping from the sidelines. Though Brown expresses

a degree of distaste for Rooke's drive toward inventive storytelling, he simultaneously maintains that "there is still emotion embedded in these stories, still human compulsions and neuroses," and he believes Rooke's stories contain a valuable depth beyond their wit.

Rooke's succeeding story collections, *Death Suite, The Birth Control King of Upper Volta, Sing Me No Love Songs, I'll Say You No Prayers: Selected Stories,* and *A Bolt of White Cloth,* have also sparked varied critical responses. "Rooke's hyperactive imagination occasionally betrays him, but the general quality of his output remains at an impressively high level," observes French. Of Rooke's 1985 endeavor *A Bolt of White Cloth,* *Canadian Forum* reviewer Barry Dempster feels Rooke "invents occurrences that are disappointingly unbelievable, endings that stumble and freeze in the unwelcome air," but Paul Steuwe declares in *Books in Canada* that "if for any reason you've been holding back from experiencing the world of Leon Rooke, this is as good a place as any to begin getting acquainted with a master craftsman of Canadian literature."

In the midst of Rooke's additions to his short story collections, he published his first novel, *Fat Woman,* in 1981. *Fat Woman* "is a slim novel with a big heart and a sizable funny bone," according to David Quammen in the *New York Times Book Review.* "Rooke puts us inside the copious body of Ella Mae Hopkins—an obese wife . . .—and we waddle with her through one traumatic day, sharing her secret worries and consolations, . . . her battles of gastronomic will. . . . The small miracle about 'Fat Woman' is that it remains entertaining despite its extreme simplicity of event. One large reason for this is the richness and rhythms and humor of Southern country language, which Rooke has captured wonderfully." Conversely, Timothy Down Adams notes in his *American Book Review* article that Rooke's "tampering with the slapstick humor characteristic of the worst of Southern fiction" almost kept *Fat Woman* from getting off the ground. Adams maintains that the book is redeemed by the development of the tender and humorous love relationship between the leading fat woman and her thin husband. "However," stresses Adams, "like its heroine, *Fat Woman* would have been easier to love if it were reduced by a third and tightened overall." For Tom Marshall in *Canadian Literature,* *Fat Woman* "is an enjoyable and absorbing read, and . . . has as a central aim an exploration of the dignity and even complexity of the lives of quite ordinary or socially marginal people."

Rooke's award-winning second novel, *Shakespeare's Dog,* is a "real sleeper, a veritable find, a novel to thoroughly delight and amuse the most jaded of readers," praises a *Publishers Weekly* reviewer. As a winner of the Governor General's Literary Award for fiction from the Canada Council in 1984, this highly imaginative tale aims at exposing Shakespeare during his married life with Anne Hathaway before he had ventured to London. The splendor of it all is that Shakespeare's philosophical cur, Mr. Hooker, is narrator. In what *New York Times Book Review* critic Jerome Charyn perceives as Rooke's "sad and funny novel about the ultimate talking dog[,] Hooker has caught Shakespeare's disease. His head is puffed with language, and the other dogs of Stratford poke fun at him. . . . [*Shakespeare's Dog*] would be a silly novel, imprisoned by its own narrow concerns, were it not for the vitality that . . . Rooke brings to the squabbling household of Hooke, Will Shakespeare and Anne Hathaway. . . . It parodies all the mysteries surrounding Master Will and seems to suggest that the real author of 'Hamlet' and 'Lear' was Hooker himself." Other reviewers proclaim that much of the novel's success stems from Rooke's gambol with language. John Bemrose writes in *Maclean's Magazine* that "*Shakespeare's Dog* is a triumph of Rooke's delight in the language, in how it can be twisted and even reinvented. It is written in pseudo-Elizabethan tongue that effortlessly carries its rich cargo of bawdy epithets and street poetry.'' And a reviewer in *Vogue* praises Rooke's language as "a breathless, randy mix of Joycean teasers, Elizabethan bawdies, newly-minted Rookisms—even a sprinkling of Shakespeare—that makes for a dark, ferocious lyricism and a whopping good story.''

Although there are reviewers who consider *Shakespeare's Dog* short on plot, overall the work is praised as yet another surprise from a writer whose range of talent seemingly knows no confines. S. Schoenbaum declares in the *Washington Post Book World* that "if there is a better novel than Rooke's dealing with Shakespeare's early days I'm not aware of it, although in fairness I'd have to add that his competition isn't that formidable. He has a highly original conception, and his spokespooch is a feisty (as well as intellectual) hound. . . . Through Hooker's eyes, sixteenth-century Stratford lives.''

BIOGRAPHICAL/CRITICAL SOURCES:

BOOKS

Contemporary Literary Criticism, Gale, Volume XXV, 1983, Volume XXXIV, 1985.

PERIODICALS

American Book Review, March-April, 1982.
Books in Canada, November, 1981, May, 1983, May, 1985.
Canadian Fiction Magazine, Numbers 30-31, 1979.
Canadian Forum, August, 1980, April, 1985.
Canadian Literature, summer, 1981, winter, 1981.
Fiddlehead, spring, 1978.
Globe and Mail (Toronto), January 5, 1985.
Harper's, May, 1983.
Kirkus Reviews, March 1, 1983.
Los Angeles Times, May 4, 1981.
Maclean's Magazine, January 11, 1982, May 16, 1983.
New York Times Book Review, March 2, 1969, January 1, 1978, May 17, 1981, May 29, 1983, April 1, 1984.
Publishers Weekly, March 11, 1983.
Quill and Quire, June, 1983.
Sewanee Review, summer, 1978.
Vogue, June, 1983.
Washington Post Book World, June 7, 1981, May 22, 1983, August 5, 1984.
WAVES, winter, 1982.

—*Sketch by Cheryl Gottler*

*   *   *

ROOT, Deane L(eslie) 1947-

PERSONAL: Born August 9, 1947, in Wausau, Wis.; son of Forrest Kent (a manufacturer's representative) and Marguerite (a financial secretary; maiden name, Fleenor) Root; married Doris Jane Dyen (an ethnomusicologist), August 27, 1972; children: Jessica Edith, Melanie Elizabeth. *Education:* New College, Sarasota, Fla., B.A., 1968; University of Illinois, M.Mus., 1971, Ph.D., 1977.

ADDRESSES: Home—Pittsburgh, Pa. *Office*—Stephen Foster Memorial, University of Pittsburgh, Pittsburgh, Pa. 15260.

CAREER: University of Wisconsin—Madison, lecturer in music history, 1973; Macmillan Publishers Ltd., London, En-

gland, editor of popular music and text editor of *The New Grove Dictionary of Music and Musicians,* 1974-76; University of Illinois at Urbana-Champaign, general editor of "Resources of American Music History'' project, 1976-80; University of Pittsburgh, Pittsburgh, Pa., curator of Stephen Foster Memorial and Foster Hall and adjunct assistant professor of music, 1982—, administrator of Heinz Memorial Chapel, 1983—. Manager of Suwannee River Bicycle Tours, 1980-81; lecturer and instructor at Lake City Community College, 1981-82; visiting research associate at Florida State University, 1981-82. Adjudicator for South Carolina Arts Commission, 1981; member, Lake City Playshop and chairman of public relations, 1981-82, Fine Arts Council of Lake City/ Columbia County and chairman, 1982, Blue-Gray Army, Inc. and historian and museum curator, 1982, Historic Preservation Board of Lake City and Columbia County and founding chairman, 1982, Columbia County Council on Aging and conductor of musical activities, 1982.

MEMBER: International Council of Traditional Music, American Musicological Society, American Association for the Advancement of the Humanities, Florida Folklore Society (founding member of board of directors, 1982), Society for Ethnomusicology, Sonneck Society (member of board of directors, 1979-80), Music Library Association, Greater Pittsburgh Museum Council (president, 1987), Columbia County Historical Society, Community Concert Association, Community Chorus, Pi Kappa Lambda.

AWARDS, HONORS: Woodrow Wilson fellow, 1968.

WRITINGS:

(General editor and contributor) *Resources of American Music History: A Directory of Source Materials From Colonial Times to World War II,* University of Illinois Press, 1981.
American Popular Stage Music, 1860-1880, UMI Publications, 1981.
Music of Florida Sites (monograph), Florida State University, 1983.

Contributor to *The New Grove Dictionary of Music and Musicians, The New Grove Dictionary of American Music, Yearbook for Inter-American Music Research,* and *Popular Music Yearbook.* Contributor to music journals. Editor of *Music of the American Theater,* a special issue of *American Music,* winter, 1984, and consulting editor of *The Complete Works of Stephen C. Foster (1826-1864),* Smithsonian Institution Press.

WORK IN PROGRESS: Series editor of *Nineteenth-Century American Musical Theatre,* facsimile reprints, for Garland Publishing.

SIDELIGHTS: Deane L. Root commented: "My work is motivated by the need to strengthen performing arts organizations at the local level, to provide access to information about our cultural history, and to promote awareness and participation in historic preservation. Throughout my career I have sought to direct scholarly attention toward the enduring qualities and customs of everyday life in America, especially as they are represented in so-called 'popular' and 'ephemeral' media. I have enjoyed musical performance as a trumpet player, and later as a tenor and conductor. As a historian, I have been most concerned with seeing beyond other historians' delineations and labelings of 'firsts' and 'great men' to discover the full richness of context in which historical figures operated. I have sought to provide accurate reference information for students and scholars of American music, to help demonstrate the abundant variety of musical activity in American life.''

ROTENSTREICH, Nathan 1914-

PERSONAL: Born March 31, 1914, in Sambor, Poland (now in U.S.S.R.); immigrated to Palestine (now Israel), 1932; son of Ephraim and Miriam (Eifermann) Rotenstreich; married Binah Metzger, March 3, 1936; children: Ephrat (Mrs. I. Balberg), Noa (Mrs. D. Schindler). *Education:* Hebrew University of Jerusalem, M.A., 1936. Ph.D., 1938; University of Chicago, postdoctoral study, 1949.

ADDRESSES: Home—7 Marcus St., Jerusalem, Israel. *Office*—Department of Philosophy, Hebrew University of Jerusalem, Jerusalem, Israel.

CAREER: Youth Aliyah Teachers Training College, Jerusalem, Israel, principal, 1944-51; Hebrew University of Jerusalem, Jerusalem, research fellow, 1949, senior lecturer in philosophy, Ahad Ha'am Professor of Philosophy, 1955—, dean of humanities, 1957-61, rector of university, 1963-69, head of Institute of Philosophy, 1971-74. Center for the Study of Democratic Institutions, visiting fellow, 1970, associate, 1972; visiting professor, City College of the City University of New York, 1969-70, and Harvard University, 1980.

MEMBER: International Institute of Philosophy, Israel National Academy of Sciences and Humanities (chairman, humanities section, 1974-80, 1983-86; vice-president, 1986—).

AWARDS, HONORS: Tscernichowski prize, 1955, for translation of *Critique of Pure Reason;* recipient of awards from municipalities of Tel Aviv, 1960, and Haifa, 1961; Israel Prize for Humanities, 1963; honorary Ph.D., Jewish Theological Seminary, 1975, Hebrew Union College-Jewish Institute of Religion, 1982, and Haifa University, 1986; Bublick Prize, Hebrew University of Jerusalem, 1987.

WRITINGS:

Between Past and Present: An Essay on History, foreword by Martin Buber, Yale University Press, 1958, 2nd edition, Kennikat, 1973.
The Recurring Pattern: Studies in Anti-Judaism in Modern Thought, Weidenfeld & Nicolson, 1963, Horizon Press, 1964.
Humanism in the Contemporary Era, Mouton & Co., 1963.
Spirit and Man: An Essay on Being and Value, Nijhoff, 1963.
Experience and Its Systemization: Studies in Kant, Nijhoff, 1965, 2nd edition, 1972.
Basic Problems of Marx's Philosophy, Bobbs-Merrill, 1965.
On the Human Subject: Studies in the Phenomenology of Ethics and Politics, C. C Thomas, 1966.
Jewish Philosophy in Modern Times: From Mendelssohn to Rosenzweig, Holt, 1968.
Tradition and Reality: The Impact of History on Modern Jewish Thought, Random House, 1972.
Philosophy: The Concept and Its Manifestations, Reidel, 1973.
From Substance and Subject: Studies in Hegel, Nijhoff, 1974.
Philosophy, History and Politics: Studies in Contemporary English Philosophy of History, Nijhoff, 1976.
Theory and Practice: An Essay in Human Intentionalities, Nijhoff, 1977.
Practice and Realization: Studies in Kant, Nijhoff, 1979.
(Editor with Yehuda Bauer) *The Holocaust as Historical Experience: Essays and a Discussion,* Holmes & Meier, 1981.
(Editor) *Essays on Zionism and the Contemporary Jewish Condition,* Herzl Press, 1981.
Man and His Dignity, Magnes Press, 1983.

Wege zur Erkennbarkeit der Welt, Alber (Freiburg), 1983.
(Editor with Norma Schneider) *Spinoza, His Thought and Work,* Israel Academy of Sciences and Humanities, 1983.
Reflection and Action, Nijhoff, 1985.

Also author of numerous works in Hebrew on philosophy, politics, history, philosophy of Judaism, and problems in Israeli society, including *'Al ha-shitah,* 1942, *ha-Mahashavah ha-yehudit,* 1945-49, 1950, *Yesodot ha-pilosoflyah shel Marks,* 1951-52, *'Al ha-temurah,* 1952-53, *Ben 'avar le-hoveh,* 1955, *Amat-midah,* 1958, *ha-Yahadut u-zekhuyot ha-Yehudim,* 1959, *ha-Ruah veha-adam,* 1959, *Sugyot be-filosofyah,* 1959, *Torat ha-midot veha-medinah,* 1963, *'Otsmah u-demutah,* 1963, *Sugyot be-hinukh,* 1964, *Ben 'am li-medinato,* 1965, *Galut Yisrael ba-mahashavah ha-yehudit shel Artsot ha-berit,* 1966, *'Iyun u-ma'aseh,* 1969, *'Al tehumah shel ha-filosofyah,* 1969, *ha-Ra'yon ha-tsiyoni be-sha'ah so* (with Ben Halpern), 1971, *'Al ha-kiyum ha-yehudi ba-zeman ha-zeh,* 1972, *Bikoret ha-tevunah ha-ma'asit,* 1973, *Zeman u-mashma'ut,* 1974, *'Iyunim ba-Tsiyonut ba-zeman ha-zeh,* 1977, *'Iyunim ba-mahashavah ha-yehudit ba-zeman ha-zeh,* 1978, and *Aharayutah shel medinat Yisrael la-tefutsot,* 1978. Also editor of *Hazut,* 1953.

Also translator into Hebrew, with S. H. Bergman, of the following works by Immanuel Kant: *Critique of Pure Reason, Critique of Practical Reason, Critique of Judgement,* and *Religion within the Limits of Reason Alone.*

WORK IN PROGRESS: Time and Meaning in History for Reidel; *Order and Might* for State University of New York Press.

SIDELIGHTS: Of *Jewish Philosophy in Modern Times: From Mendelssohn to Rosenzweig,* Arthur A. Cohen writes in the *New Republic:* "It is to the complex rethinking of classic Judaism in the light of the Kantian revolution that Nathan Rotenstreich's brilliant book, *Jewish Philosophy in Modern Times,* is directed. Rotenstreich, a careful and scrupulous scholar, shows how Jewish thinkers, disarmed by Kant's critique of *religious* metaphysics, sought to salvage Judaism by making ethics its quasi-autonomous essence."

BIOGRAPHICAL/CRITICAL SOURCES:

PERIODICALS

New Republic, March 15, 1969.

*   *   *

ROTHBLATT, Donald N(oah) 1935-

PERSONAL: Born April 28, 1935, in New York, N.Y.; son of Harry and Sophie (Chernofsky) Rothblatt; married Ann Vogel (a teacher), June 16, 1957; children: Joel M., Steven S. *Education:* City University of New York, B.Civil Engineering, 1957; Columbia University, M.S., 1963; Institute of Social Studies, The Hague, Netherlands, diploma in comprehensive planning, 1964; Harvard University, Ph.D., 1969.

ADDRESSES: Home—4051 Scripps Ave., Palo Alto, Calif. 94306. *Office*—Department of Urban and Regional Planning, San Jose State University, San Jose, Calif. 95192.

CAREER: New York City Planning Commission, New York City, planner, 1960-62; New York Housing and Redevelopment Board, New York City, planner, 1963-66; Harvard University, Cambridge, Mass., Center for Environmental Design Studies and John F. Kennedy School of Government, research fellow, 1965-70, instructor then assistant professor of city and regional planning, 1967-71, William F. Milton Research Fellow, 1970-71; San Jose State University, San Jose, Calif., professor of urban and regional planning and chairman of department, 1971—. Lady Davis Visiting Professor of Urban and Regional Planning at Hebrew University of Jerusalem and at Tel-Aviv University, 1978; visiting scholar, Indian Association of Architects, Bombay and New Delhi, 1979; visiting faculty member at Graduate School of Design, Harvard University, 1980; visiting scholar, Institute of Governmental Studies, University of California, Berkeley, 1980-87. Member of local citizens' community improvement committee. *Military service:* U.S. Army, Corps of Engineers, 1957-58; became first lieutenant.

MEMBER: American Institute of Certified Planners (member of task force on national urban policy, 1972-76), Association of Collegiate Schools of Planning (president, 1974-76), California Committee on Environmental Design Education (chairman, 1973-75).

AWARDS, HONORS: Traveling fellowship, Dutch Government, 1964; faculty research grant, National Science Foundation, 1972-79; Innovative Teaching Grant, California State University and Colleges, 1975-79; Best of West Award for informational public television, Western Educational Society for Telecommunication, 1976; research grant, California State University, 1977-88; award for architecture and planning, International Festival of Films, 1983; meritorious performance award, San Jose State University, 1986.

WRITINGS:

Human Needs and Public Housing, New York City Housing Library, 1964.
Thailand's Northeast, Center for Environmental Design Studies, Harvard University, 1967.
Regional Planning: The Appalachian Experience, Heath, 1971.
Allocation of Resources for Regional Planning, Appalachian Regional Commission, 1972.
(Editor) *National Policy for Urban and Regional Development,* Heath, 1974.
(Editor) *Regional Advocacy Planning: Expanding Air Transport Facilities for the San Jose Metropolitan Area,* San Jose State University, 1975.
(Editor) *Metropolitan-Wide Advocacy Planning: Dispersion of Low and Moderate Cost Housing in the San Jose Metropolitan Area,* San Jose State University, 1975.
(Editor) *Multiple Advocacy Planning: Public Surface Transportation in the San Jose Metropolitan Area,* San Jose State University, 1977.
(Editor) *A Multiple Advocacy Approach to Regional Planning: Open Space and Recreational Facilities for the San Jose Metropolitan Area,* San Jose State University, 1979.
(Co-author) *The Suburban Environment and Women,* Praeger, 1979.
Regional-Local Development Policy Making: The Santa Clara Valley Corridor, University of California, 1981.
Planning the Metropolis: The Multiple Advocacy Approach, Praeger, 1982.
(Co-author) *Comparative Suburban Data,* San Jose State University, 1983.
(Co-author) *Suburbia: An International Assessment,* St. Martin's, 1986.

Contributor to planning, urban studies, and regional studies journals.

WORK IN PROGRESS: Sunset in the Sunbelt: Retirement Communities in the Southwest.

ROTHSCHILD, Kurt Wilhelm   1914-

PERSONAL: Name indexed as Kurt William Rothschild in some sources; born October 21, 1914, in Vienna, Austria; son of Ernst (a salesman) and Phillipine (Hollub) Rothschild (a housewife); married Valerie Kunke (a secretary), August 10, 1938; children: Thomas, Elisabeth Rothschild Menzel. *Education:* University of Vienna, Dr. Juris, 1938; University of Glasgow, M.A. (with honors), 1940. *Politics:* Socialist. *Religion:* None.

ADDRESSES: Home—Doblinger Hauptstrasse 77A, A1190 Vienna, Austria.

CAREER: University of Glasgow, Glasgow, Scotland, lecturer in economics, 1940-47; Austrian Institute for Economic Research, Vienna, Austria, senior member of research staff, 1947-66; University of Linz, Linz, Austria, professor of economics, 1966-85, professor emeritus, 1985—. Member of Austrian Supreme Cartel Court, 1975-80; consultant to Austrian Institute for Economic Research.

MEMBER: American Economic Association, Royal Economic Society, Gesellschaft fuer Sozial- und Wirtschaftswissenschaften, Gesellschaft fuer National-oekonomie, Club of Rome.

AWARDS, HONORS: Award from city of Vienna, 1980, for distinguished work in the social sciences; science award from city of Linz, 1982.

WRITINGS:

Austria's Economic Development between the Two World Wars, Muller, 1947.
The Austrian Economy since 1945, Royal Institute of International Affairs, 1950.
The Theory of Wages, Basil Blackwell, 1954.
Lohntheorie (title means "Wage Theory"), F. Vahlen, 1963.
Marktform, Loehne und Aussenhandel (title means "Market Forms, Wages, and Foreign Trade"), Europa-Verlag, 1966.
Wirtschaftsprognose (title means "Economic Forecasting"), Springer-Verlag, 1969.
Development of Income Distribution in Western Europe, Organization for Economic Cooperation and Development, 1971.
(Editor) *Power in Economics,* Penguin, 1971.
(With Ewald Nowotny) *Bestimmungsgruende der Lohnbewegung* (title means "Determinants of Money Wage Movements"), Springer-Verlag, 1972.
(With H. J. Schmahl) *Beschleunigter Gerdwertschwund* (title means "The Decline in the Value of Money"), Weltwirtschaftliches Institut, 1973.
(With others) *The Utilization of Social Sciences in Policy Making,* Organization for Economic Cooperation and Development, 1977.
Arbeitslosigkeit in Oesterreich, 1955-1975 (title means "Unemployment in Austria, 1955-1975"), Institute for Labour Market Studies, 1977.
Einfuehrung in die Ungleichgewichts theorie (title means "Introduction to Disequilibrium Theory"), Springer-Verlag, 1981.
(Editor with H. Krupp) *Wege zur Vollbeschaeftigung* (title means "Roads to Full Employment"), Rombach-Verlag, 1986.

Also contributor to economic journals.

WORK IN PROGRESS: Research on income distribution and problems of working-time adjustments.

SIDELIGHTS: Kurt Wilhelm Rothschild told *CA:* "I always felt and still feel that economic theory, in spite of its weaknesses, can help to alleviate some of the pressing problems in this world. Unfortunately, too much of the present work is purely formal, career-oriented and often dealing with minor problems. I think that a greater drive for relevancy is the main task in economic science."

Rothschild also wrote: "I have a strong interest in economic, social, and political development. I want to improve the economic situation of less privileged groups. I am critical of entrenched interest groups. On all these matters economic theory could make a greater contribution if it did not get lost—too often—in unrealistic problems and sophisticated detail. In my writings I hope to find ways of turning research toward relevant questions and extracting usable answers from theoretical results."

AVOCATIONAL INTERESTS: Walking, climbing, theatre, film, and reading novels.

BIOGRAPHICAL/CRITICAL SOURCES:

BOOKS

Laski, K., and others, editors, *Beitraege zur Diskussion und Kritik der Neoklassischen Oekonomie: Festschrift fuer K. W. Rothschild und V. Steindl,* Springer-Verlag, 1979.

*   *   *

RUFFELL, Ann 1941-

PERSONAL: Born February 2, 1941, in Spalding, Lincolnshire, England; daughter of John William (a civil servant) and Agnes (a teacher; maiden name, Brown) Ruffell; married Bob Hounslow, April, 1965 (divorced, 1976); married William James Hood, July, 1981 (separated, 1986); children: (first marriage) Peter Timothy, Katharine Julia; (second marriage) Selina Judith. *Education:* Exeter University, B.A. (with honors), 1963. *Religion:* Church of England.

ADDRESSES: Home—46 St. Jude's Rd. W., Wolverhampton, West Midlands WV6 0DB, England.

CAREER: Daily Mirror Group, London, England, editorial researcher, 1963-66; Larchfield Preparatory School, Helensburgh, Scotland, teacher of English and music, 1969-71; Loretto School, Musselburgh, Scotland, teacher of piano, 1972-75. Free-lance writer, 1969—; private piano teacher, 1970—; musician, 1974—. Member of English Philharmonic Orchestra, 1979-81. Teacher of creative writing classes.

AWARDS, HONORS: Recipient of creative writing fellowship from Scottish Arts Council, 1980-82.

WRITINGS:

JUVENILES

A Piece of Earth, illustrations by Beryl Sanders, Dobson, 1977.
The Cuckoo Genius, Dobson, 1978.
Dragon Fire, illustrations by Nicole Goodwin, Hamish Hamilton, 1979, published with illustrations by Andrew Brown, Corgi Books, 1987.
Firebird, Dobson, 1979.
Blood Brother, F. Watts, 1980.
Dragon Water, illustrations by Goodwin, Hamish Hamilton, 1980.

The Horse Tree, illustrations by Sally Holmes, Hamish Hamilton, 1980.
Pyramid Power, F. Watts, 1981.
Dragon Earth, illustrations by Goodwin, Hamish Hamilton, 1981.
Dragon Air, illustrations by Goodwin, Hamish Hamilton, 1981.
(Contributor) Aidan Chambers, *Out of Time,* Harper, 1984.
Black Sand Miners, illustrations by Trevor Stubley, Hamish Hamilton, 1985.
The Bowley Boy, illustrations by Laszlo Acs, Hamish Hamilton, 1985.
Too Small, illustrations by Jennifer Bailey, Hamish Hamilton, 1985.
Friends for Keeps, Pan Books, 1985.
Secret Passion, Pan Books, 1985.
Baby Face, Pan Books, 1986.
Sun and Rain, illustrations by Caroline Ewen, Viking, 1986.
The Computer Cheat, illustrations by Maureen Bradley, Hamish Hamilton, 1987.

OTHER

Also author of *Dragon Wanted,* with illustrations by Dan Woods, 1986.

WORK IN PROGRESS: More novels for the teenage romance series "Heartlines" published by Pan Books.

SIDELIGHTS: Ann Ruffell told *CA:* "All my life I have been torn between two art forms: writing and music. I played piano and cello at school and at one time wanted to be a concert pianist. I was studying for this when I realized that I would never be good enough and that I couldn't bear to teach it. My other love was writing, so I turned to English literature and studied it at Exeter University. Music, however, was not forgotten. As I moved from one bedsitter to another, I invariably left an old piano in the last room. In those days you could pick up an ancient instrument very cheaply, even on a student's grant.

"I became a journalist. I don't think I was very good at this: I was afraid of telephones, afraid of meeting and talking to unknown people. I just wanted to write, but to write my own things, not to report other people's affairs. I had a few articles published in other magazines, but this was still not what I wanted.

"When I had my first baby, I decided this was the time to write a novel, so while the baby had his afternoon nap and during the early part of the evening when he was in bed, I sat in front of my typewriter and finished my first children's novel. It was dreadful! Fortunately no publisher wanted it, but, as any writer knows, writing is a kind of disease that stays in your bloodstream, like malaria, and I could not stop. I must have written four novels by the time my daughter was born three years later, and by now the publishers, though still rejecting them, were beginning to write kind letters explaining why.

"But now the music in me was claiming attention. I took lessons on the piano again and studied for a diploma in piano teaching—and began to teach the piano! At this time, I was living in Scotland and met members of a band who worked for Scottish television. By one of those strokes of luck that can happen, the pianist on a projected three-month tour of the United States and Canada was unable to go, and they asked me! It was hard leaving my two little children, but the experience was worth it. I returned home to the news that at last a novel, *A Piece of Earth,* had been accepted.

"I was now divorced and hard up. However, we were now in a period when people were beginning to tire of canned music and wanted to learn an instrument again. There was no lack of piano pupils. As I had to teach at home after school hours, this gave plenty of time during the day to write my books. I have found I work very well under pressure. A new daughter, however, created too much pressure even for me, and the next two years were unproductive in both music and writing. Then suddenly I found new strength and enthusiasm when Pan Books launched a new series of well-written romances for teenagers and asked me to join their team of writers. I am now teaching English to teenagers at a local school, gaining stimulus and new ideas from them."

S

SABRE, Dirk
See LAFFIN, John (Alfred Charles)

*   *   *

St. AUBYN, Fiona 1952-

PERSONAL: Born July 11, 1952, in Hassocks, England; daughter of Oliver Piers (a stockbroker) and Mary Baily (Southwell) St. Aubyn; married Robert Boyle, 1987. *Education:* Attended Le Fleuron College, Florence, Italy, 1969-70.

ADDRESSES: c/o The Royal Bank of Scotland PLC, Child & Co., 1 Fleet St., London EC4Y 1BD, England.

CAREER: Royal Opera House, Covent Garden, London, England, secretary, 1971-72; Winston Churchill Memorial Trust, London, press officer, 1974-76; New Zealand Consulate General, New York, N.Y., secretary, 1977-84; editor, 1984—; writer.

MEMBER: Army and Navy Club (London).

WRITINGS:

(With Stanley Ager) *Ager's Way to Easy Elegance,* Bobbs-Merrill, 1980, published as *The Butler's Guide,* Fireside Books, 1981.
(Contributor) James Wagenvoord, editor, *The Doubleday Wine Annual,* Doubleday, 1982.
(With Wagenvoord) *Clothescare,* Simon & Schuster, 1985.
A Portrait of Georgian London, David Leader, 1986.

SIDELIGHTS: A granddaughter of the third Lord St. Levan, Fiona St. Aubyn wrote *Ager's Way to Easy Elegance* with Stanley Ager, the man who served as her grandfather's butler for twenty-eight years.

AVOCATIONAL INTERESTS: Travel, ballet, antique porcelain.

BIOGRAPHICAL/CRITICAL SOURCES:

PERIODICALS

People, August 31, 1981.

SALMON, Wesley C(harles) 1925-

PERSONAL: Born August 9, 1925, in Detroit, Mich.; son of Wallis Samuel (an engineer) and Ruth (Springer) Salmon; married Nancy Pilson, November 26, 1949 (divorced, 1970); married Merrilee Hollenkamp Ashby, July 24, 1971; children: (first marriage) Victoria Anne. *Education:* Attended Wayne State University, 1943-44; University of Chicago, M.A., 1947; University of California, Los Angeles, Ph.D., 1950.

ADDRESSES: Office—Department of Philosophy, University of Pittsburgh, Pittsburgh, Pa. 15260.

CAREER: University of California, Los Angeles, instructor in philosophy, 1950-51; Washington State University, Pullman, instructor, 1951-53, assistant professor of philosophy, 1953-54; Northwestern University, Evanston, Ill., lecturer, 1954-55; Brown University, Providence, R.I., assistant professor, 1955-59, associate professor of philosophy, 1959-63; Indiana University at Bloomington, professor of the philosophy of science, 1963-67, Norwood Russell Hanson Professor of Philosophy of Science, 1967-73; University of Arizona, Tucson, professor of philosophy, 1973-81; University of Pittsburgh, Pittsburgh, Pa., professor of philosophy, 1981-83, university professor, 1983—. Visiting lecturer, University of Bristol, 1959; visiting professor, University of Minnesota Center for Philosophy of Science, 1963, 1985, University of Pittsburgh, 1968-69, University of Melbourne, 1978.

MEMBER: International Union for the History and Philosophy of Science (chairman of U.S. national committee, 1967-68; first vice-president of Division of Logic, Methodology, and Philosophy of Science, 1979-83), American Academy of Arts and Sciences (fellow), American Association for the Advancement of Sciences (fellow), American Philosophical Association (member of executive committee of Western Division, 1969-71; Pacific Division, vice-president, 1976-77, president, 1977-78), Philosophy of Science Association (vice-president, 1968-70; president, 1971-72), Sigma Xi.

AWARDS, HONORS: Fund for the Advancement of Science faculty fellow, 1953-54; M.A., Brown University, 1959; creative teaching award, University of Arizona, 1978.

WRITINGS:

Logic, Prentice-Hall, 1963, 3rd edition, 1984.

The Foundations of Scientific Inference, University of Pittsburgh Press, 1967.

(Editor) *Zeno's Paradoxes*, Bobbs-Merrill, 1970.

(With others) *Statistical Explanation and Statistical Relevance*, University of Pittsburgh Press, 1971.

Space, Time, and Motion: A Philosophical Introduction, Dickenson, 1975, 2nd edition, University of Minnesota Press, 1980.

(Editor) *Hans Reichenbach: Logical Empiricist*, D. Reidel, 1979.

Scientific Explanation and the Causal Structure of the World, Princeton University Press, 1984.

(Editor with Adolf Gruenbaum and contributor) *The Limits of Deductivism*, University of California Press, 1988.

(Editor with Philip Kitcher and contributor) *Scientific Explanation*, University of Minnesota Press, 1988.

CONTRIBUTOR

Sidney Hook, editor, *Psychoanalysis, Scientific Method, and Philosophy*, New York University Press, 1959.

Herbert Feigl and Grover Maxwell, editors, *Current Issues in the Philosophy of Science*, Holt, 1961.

Bernard H. Baumrin, editor, *Philosophy of Science: The Delaware Seminar II*, Wiley, 1963.

Henry E. Kyburg, Jr. and Ernest Nagel, editors, *Induction: Some Current Issues*, Wesleyan University Press, 1963.

Paul Feyerabend and Maxwell, editors, *Mind, Matter, and Method*, University of Minnesota Press, 1966.

Robert G. Colodny, editor, *Mind and Cosmos*, University of Pittsburgh Press, 1966.

Imre Lakatos, editor, *The Problem of Inductive Logic*, North-Holland Publishing, 1968.

David L. Arm, editor, *Vistas in Science*, University of New Mexico Press, 1968.

Nicholas Rescher, *Essays in Honor of Carl G. Hempel*, D. Reidel, 1969.

Colodny, editor, *The Nature and Function of Scientific Theories*, University of Pittsburgh Press, 1970.

Roger H. Stuewer, editor, *Historical and Philosophical Perspectives of Science*, University of Minnesota Press, 1970.

Joel Feinberg, editor, *Reason and Responsibility*, 2nd edition (Salmon was not associated with 1st edition), Dickenson, 1971, 3rd edition, 1975.

George Nakhnikian, editor, *Bertrand Russell's Philosophy*, Duckworth, 1974.

Maxwell and Robert M. Anderson, Jr., editors, *Induction, Probability, and Confirmation*, University of Minnesota Press, 1975.

S. Koerner, editor, *Explanation*, Yale University Press, 1975.

Peter Machamer and Robert G. Turnbull, editors, *Motion and Time, Space and Matter*, Ohio State University Press, 1976.

John S. Earman, Clark N. Glymour, and John Stachel, editors, *Foundations of Space-Time Theories*, University of Minnesota Press, 1977.

R. E. Butts and Jaakko Hintikka, editors, *Basic Problems in Methodology and Linguistics*, D. Reidel, 1977.

Hintikka, David Gruender, and Evando Agazzi, editors, *Probabilistic Thinking, Thermodynamics and the Interaction of the History and Philosophy of Science*, D. Reidel, 1981.

Robert McLaughlin, editor, *What? Where? When? Why?*, D. Reidel, 1982.

Colin Renfrew and others, editors, *Theory and Explanation in Archaeology*, D. Reidel, 1982.

Nicholas Rescher, editor, *The Heritage of Logical Positivism*, D. Reidel, 1985.

James H. Fetzer, editor, *Probability and Causality*, D. Reidel, 1988.

William Harper and Brian Skyrms, editors, *Probability and Causation*, D. Reidel, 1988.

OTHER

Editor with Joel Feinberg of Prentice-Hall's "Contemporary Prospectives in Philosophy" series. Contributor to *Encyclopedia Americana*. Also contributor to philosophy journals. Member of editorial board, *Journal of Philosophical Logic, Erkenntnis, American Philosophical Quarterly, Synthese, Synthese Library*, and *Pacific Philosophical Quarterly*.

*   *   *

SARRAUTE, Nathalie 1900-

PERSONAL: Born July 18, 1900, in Ivanovo, Russia (now in U.S.S.R.); daughter of Ilya (a chemist) and Pauline (a writer; maiden name, Chatounovsky) Tcherniak; married Raymond Sarraute (a barrister), July 28, 1925; children: Claude, Anne, Dominique. *Education:* Sorbonne, University of Paris, licence d'anglais, 1920, licence en droit, 1925; attended Oxford University, 1921; additional study in Berlin, 1921-22.

ADDRESSES: Home—12 avenue Pierre I de Serbie, 75116 Paris, France.

CAREER: Barrister from 1926 to 1932, when she began writing her first book, *Tropismes*.

AWARDS, HONORS: Formentor Prize ($10,000), 1964, for *The Golden Fruits;* doctor honoris causa, University of Dublin Trinity College, 1976; doctor honoris causa, University of Kent at Canterbury, 1980.

WRITINGS:

FICTION; IN ENGLISH TRANSLATION

Tropismes (sketches), Denoel (Paris), 1939, revised edition, Editions de Minuit (Paris), 1957, translation by Maria Jolas published as *Tropisms* (also see below), Braziller, 1967, reprinted, Riverrun Press, 1986.

Portrait d'un inconnu (novel), with preface by Jean-Paul Sartre, Robert Marin (Paris), 1948, reprinted, Gallimard (Paris), 1977, translation by Jolas published as *Portrait of a Man Unknown*, Braziller, 1958.

Martereau (novel), Gallimard, 1953, translation by Jolas published as *Martereau*, Braziller, 1959.

Le Planetarium (novel), Gallimard, 1959, 2nd edition, 1967, translation by Jolas published as *The Planetarium*, Braziller, 1960.

Les Fruits d'or (novel), Gallimard, 1963, translation by Jolas published as *The Golden Fruits*, Braziller, 1964.

Entre la vie et la mort (novel), Gallimard, 1968, translation by Jolas published as *Between Life and Death*, Braziller, 1969.

Vous les entendez? (novel), Gallimard, 1972, translation by Jolas published as *Do You Hear Them?*, Braziller, 1973.

"disent les imbeciles" (novel), Gallimard, 1976, translation by Jolas published as *"fools say"*, Braziller, 1977.

L'Usage de la parole (sketches), Gallimard, 1980, translation by Barbara Wright published as *The Use of Speech*, Braziller, 1983.

CRITICISM

L'Ere du soupcon: Essais sur le roman, Gallimard, 1956, translation by Jolas published as *The Age of Suspicion: Essays on the Novel* (also see below), Braziller, 1963.
Paul Valery et l'enfant d'elephant (first published in *Les Temps modernes*, January, 1947) [and] *Flaubert le precurseur* (first published in *Preuves*, February, 1965), Gallimard, c. 1986.

PLAYS

Le Silence [and] *Le Mensonge* (also see below; both plays first broadcast on German radio, both produced in Petit Odeon at Theatre de France, January 14, 1967), Gallimard, 1967, translation by Jolas published in England as *Silence* [and] *The Lie* (also see below), Calder & Boyars, 1969.
Isma; ou, Ce qui s'appelle rien (also see below; produced at Espace Pierre-Cardin, February 5, 1973) [and] *Le Silence* [and] *Le Mensonge*, Gallimard, 1970.
Theatre (contains "C'est Beau," first performed at Theatre d'Orsay, October 24, 1975, "Elle est la," first performed at Theatre d'Orsay, January 15, 1980, "Isma," "Le Mensonge," and "Le Silence"), Gallimard, 1978, translation by Jolas and Wright published as *Collected Plays of Nathalie Sarraute* (contains "It Is There," "It's Beautiful," "Izzum," "The Lie," and "Silence"), J. Calder, 1980, Braziller, 1981.

Also author of "For No Good Reason," first produced in New York City in 1985.

CONTRIBUTOR

Visages d'aujourd'hui, Plon (Paris), 1960.
The Writer's Dilemma, with an introduction by Stephen Spender, Oxford University Press, 1961.
Andrew Hook, editor, *The Novel Today: Edinburgh International Festival 1962—International Writers' Conference; Programme and Notes*, R. R. Clark (Edinburgh), 1962.
Jacqueline Levi-Valensi, editor, *Les Critiques de notre temps et Camus*, Garnier (Paris), 1970.
Violoncelle qui resiste, Eric Losfeld (Paris), 1971.
Gespraeche mit . . ., Europaverlag, 1972.
Jean Ricardou and Francoise von Rossum-Guyon, editors, *Nouveau roman: Hier, aujourd'hui* (text not reviewed by Sarraute), Union Generale d'Editions (Paris), 1972.
Words and Their Masters, Doubleday, 1974.
Comment travaillent les ecrivains, Flammarion (Paris), 1978.
Frida S. Weissman, editor, *Du monologue interieur a la sous-conversation*, Nizet (Paris), 1978.

OTHER

Tropisms [and] *The Age of Suspicion*, Calder & Boyars, 1964.
Enfance (autobiography), Gallimard, 1983, translation by Wright published as *Childhood*, Braziller, 1984.

Sarraute's works have been translated into twenty-five foreign languages, including German, Hebrew, Italian, Russian, and Spanish. Contributor to numerous journals and periodicals, including the *New York Times Book Review, Washington Post Book World, Times Literary Supplement, Cahiers Renaud Barrault, Le Monde, Les Temps modernes, Nouvelle revue francaise*, and *Preuves*.

SIDELIGHTS: As one of the outstanding writers and theoreticians of the "New Novel" in France, Nathalie Sarraute has consistently sought to create innovative forms of narrative that apprehend the psychological reality beneath the surface of daily events and conversations. Although she began writing in the 1930s, her work did not receive much critical attention until the 1950s and 1960s with the publication of her theoretical work, *L'Ere du Soupcon: Essais sur le roman (The Age of Suspicion: Essays on the Novel)*, and her novel *Les Fruits d'or (The Golden Fruits)*. Her novels are complex studies of human interaction that question traditional elements of character and plot. While sometimes considered difficult for the uninitiated, her books challenge the reader to reassess common assumptions about literature and its relationship to life. The rewards are well worth the effort, for Sarraute's works offer a poetic, humorous, and sometimes painful vision of life.

Although not inclined to discuss her personal life—feeling that biographical portraits erect their own "literary figures" according to codified conventions—Sarraute did provide some data to critics Mimica Cranaki and Yvon Belaval for their 1965 book, *Nathalie Sarraute*. In 1983, Sarraute also published *Enfance (Childhood)*, a literary investigation of her early childhood memories, which reveals glimpses of her past.

The only child of Russian Jewish intellectuals who divorced when she was two years old, Sarraute afterwards spent much of her early childhood moving back and forth between her parents in Russia and France, soon becoming fluent in the languages of both countries. Her mother, also a novelist, remarried a Russian historian and the three first settled in Paris when the child was two, and then in St. Petersburg (today called Leningrad) when the child was six. Here the young Nathalie tried writing a novel, but was discouraged when a friend of her mother's told her she should learn to spell first. At age eight, she returned to her father, who had remarried and started a dye factory in Paris. She remained there for the rest of her life, seeing her mother only twice.

Sarraute's rapport with her stepmother was at times difficult, but she struck up a warm relationship with her adoptive grandmother. A cultivated Russian who spoke several languages impeccably and who was an excellent musician, she gave Nathalie piano and German lessons. During the same period the young girl learned English as well. In 1909 Sarraute attended public elementary school where she thoroughly enjoyed the challenges of formal education, and then Lycee Fenelon, deriving special pleasure from writing assignments and the study of physics.

After completing her baccalaureat degree, Sarraute easily obtained a *licence* in English at the Sorbonne and studied at Oxford for a year, working on a B.A. in history. In the winter of 1921-1922, Sarraute studied sociology in Berlin and discovered German novelist Thomas Mann's *Tonio Krueger*, which reinforced her desire to write.

Upon her return to Paris, Sarraute enrolled in law school, where she met Raymond Sarraute, whom she married in 1925 and who proved to be a lifelong source of support and encouragement. Both received law degrees, and for about six years Mme. Sarraute practiced law. Between 1927 and 1933 their three daughters, Claude, Anne, and Dominique, were born. In 1932, Sarraute began the first texts of her *Tropismes (Tropisms)*, published in 1939 by Robert Denoel after being refused by Grasset and Gallimard. Although the book received little attention at first, Sarraute's literary career had officially begun, only to be delayed by the outbreak of World War II, when Sarraute was forced to pose as the governess of her own children in order to hide from the Germans. Since 1935, Sarraute has traveled extensively in Europe, Scandinavia, the Soviet Union, Cuba, and Israel, in addition to Egypt, the United

States, South America, Japan, and India, delivering lectures on college campuses.

One of the hallmarks of Sarraute's literary work is the "tropism." Borrowing the term from the biological sciences where it characterizes an involuntary reaction to external stimuli, as when a plant turns toward light or heat, Sarraute uses it to describe the subtle psychological responses of people to objects, words, and other human beings. In remarks published in the *Listener* in 1961, Sarraute explains tropisms as movements that "glide quickly round the border of our consciousness" and "compose the small, rapid, and sometimes very complex dramas concealed beneath our actions, our gestures, the words we speak, our avowed and clear feelings." Sarraute notes in the preface to her collection of critical essays, *The Age of Suspicion,* that she had intuited the tropistic movements during her childhood. *Tropisms* is composed of short texts that investigate what Valerie Minogue, in *Nathalie Sarraute and the War of the Words,* calls "the teeming sub-surface of life, anonymously yet intimately observed." The reader is thrust into the midst of a world of unidentified characters (nameless women gossiping in a tea salon, passersby in front of a shop window) who experience sensations that are dramatically and poetically rendered through imagery, rhythm, and repetition. Sarraute explains in the preface that "it was not possible to communicate [the tropisms] to the reader otherwise than by means of equivalent images that would make him experience analogous sensations." Character development and plot are minimal, she explains, because such novelistic traits tend to particularize experience and to "distract [the attention] of the reader," while Sarraute is interested in portraying an underlying psychological reality common to everyone.

In *The Age of Suspicion,* the author develops many of her critical and theoretical stances regarding the novel and clarifies her own creative goals. On the paperback cover the essays are described as the "first theoretical manifestation of the 'New Novel' school," whose representatives also include French writers Alain Robbe-Grillet, Michel Butor, Marguerite Duras, Claude Simon, and Claude Ollier. Sarraute argues that both novelists and readers have become suspicious of character types, the "unforgettable figures" of tightly knit, coherent plots in nineteenth-century novels by such earlier French writers as Honore de Balzac and Gustave Flaubert. According to Sarraute, these characters and their stories if written nowadays would appear as stereotypes that no longer ring true. Aligning herself with such novelists as Fedor Dostoevski, Marcel Proust, James Joyce, and Virginia Woolf, who investigate the human psyche, Sarraute advocates a new realism. In her interview for the 1984 special issue of *Digraphe* devoted to her work, Sarraute defines the "real" as "what hasn't yet taken on the conventional forms" and holds that the writer's task is not to copy or imitate accepted reality, but to invent new forms that will help the reader perceive new realities. In her investigation of the human psyche, Sarraute makes a case for formal innovations that shape the experience of the reader. Instead of calling for controlled analyses of carefully defined feelings, she develops in *The Age of Suspicion* the notion of the "subconversation" which renders verbally "what is dissimulated behind the interior monologue: a countless profusion of sensations, of images, of feelings, of memories . . . which no interior language expresses." She thus portrays instinctive, instantaneous reactions before they become fully understood and named, insisting that the passage from subconversation to dialogue must be continuous: no standard formulas like "she said" or "George murmured" are to interrupt the flow of

"these interior dramas made up of attacks, triumphs, defeats, caresses."

Imagery plays a major role in Sarraute's successful presentation of the unnameable sensations that make up the tropism. As Gretchen Rous Besser points out in *Nathalie Sarraute,* the novelist often utilizes the imagery of animals and insects "whose instinctive reactions are consonant with the prerational nature of tropistic reactions." The interpersonal struggles Sarraute portrays are sometimes enacted through the use of military terminology that dramatizes seemingly minor dissensions. Olga Bernal's 1973 *Modern Language Notes* article examines the symbolic oppositions developed in Sarraute's work between images of fluids and solids. This dichotomy contrasts the external world of appearances, solid, secure, and well-defined, with the invisible movements of the tropism, fluid, hesitant, vacillating, and oozing.

In his preface to Sarraute's first novel, *Portrait d'un inconnu (Portrait of a Man Unknown),* Jean-Paul Sartre characterizes the work as an anti-novel because it contests traditional novelistic conventions. Rene Micha, in *Nathalie Sarraute,* calls her novel "a long interrogation": a first person narrator, who remains a nameless voice, "is speaking or writing or dreaming or reflecting" about a couple, father and daughter, whose relationship fascinates and perhaps obsesses him. Sarraute herself has admitted in an interview with Serge Fauchereau and Jean Ristat in *Digraphe* that the father-daughter duo is inspired by Balzac's *Eugenie Grandet,* but the narrator explores the hidden side of Balzac's solid character types. The boundaries between the narrator's imagination and his actual knowledge about the couple tend to blur because there are no linguistic markers to distinguish between fact and fiction, between objective reality and creative interpretation. *Portrait of a Man Unknown* is reminiscent of a detective story, and as Jean V. Alter remarks in an article appearing in J. H. Matthews's collection *Un Nouveau Roman?:* "The reader finds himself involved in an inquiry regarding the reality of things." But unlike a third-person omniscient narrator, whose authority would guarantee the difference between an unquestionable evaluation of the couple and a personal interpretation, the narrator of Sarraute's novel can only reveal his hesitant, anguished questions and doubts about the accuracy of his perceptions. Other New Novelists, such as Robbe-Grillet in *The Erasers,* also use the detective story format while subverting it. But while Sarraute explores the depths of psychological reality, Robbe-Grillet prefers to remain at the surface, providing a minute description of external appearances that betray the depths.

Minogue argues that *Portrait of a Man Unknown* "contains a far-reaching critique of conventional characterization," putting on trial the notion of stable, definable characters (whether one is speaking of the narrator or the couple he watches) and ultimately questioning the way the reader constructs reality and personal identity. As in Sarraute's other novels and plays, there are no heroes and little action in the sense of an adventure outside the tropisms. Descriptions of places, historical events, and characters and their surroundings are either sketchy or completely lacking. Such omissions are strategies to keep the readers from resorting to old reading habits that would distance them from the text, for Sarraute wants her readers to take an active part in her works, to share in the invisible dramas.

Sarraute's second novel, *Martereau (Martereau),* increases the number of characters, including an aunt, uncle, cousin, and nephew (the first person narrator), and an outsider, Martereau, with his wife. With the social milieu expanded, the interaction becomes more complex. Although the purchase of a house is the basis for the external plot, Sarraute is again more concerned with drawing the reader into an anonymous world of relationships filtered through the vacillating perspectives of the narrating nephew. The family seems to provide Sarraute with a particularly favorable environment for depicting tropisms. Except for *Martereau,* characters are identified only by personal pronouns or family relationships. As in *Portrait of a Man Unknown,* the readers must make their way through this labyrinth of shifting connections by remaining attentive to certain repeated words and rhythms, which Minogue calls Sarraute's "signposts." But this radical indecision with respect to character identity is essential to Sarraute's work, because it stresses the common ground of the characters, instead of individualizing them according to an established set of reassuring categories. In all Sarraute's work, labels, proper names, and abstractions are shown to be ways of concealing the multifaceted aspects of life. Martereau, who does bear a name, is, at first, one of these stock individuals, a "traditional novel character," says Sarraute in her interview for *Digraphe,* "in the way that we see the people around us," that is, from the outside. But as the novel progresses, the external appearance disintegrates. As Minogue notes: "Martereau plays successively, in the mind of the narrator [and thus in ours], the roles of saint, adulterer, clown, and calculating crook," becoming a shadowy figure bereft of any "solidity." In her 1977 article in *PTL: A Journal for Descriptive Poetics and Theory of Literature,* Ann Jefferson explains the function of the named character: "To use a name is an index of the inauthentic in that it always goes with a deceitful venture of characterization and individuation which the novel's narrative refutes."

Regarding her novel *Le Planetarium (The Planetarium),* Sarraute remarked in the *Listener:* "Here I met with greater difficulties than in my previous books." In contrast to the first two, Sarraute's third novel is populated by a large cast of characters with proper names. However, as in most of Sarraute's works, the novel lacks elaborate descriptions of place and time. Sarraute may have chosen to name the characters in order to supply the reader with more recognizable markers because of the complex interaction between characters. Whatever the case, the names do not serve as a claim to uniqueness, for the novel concludes with the comment: "I think that we are all a little like that," and the characters' similarities ultimately loom larger than their differences. Although *The Planetarium* is written in the third person, there is no omniscient narrator to oversee and validate any one perspective. Instead, Sarraute uses the subconversation, which is reminiscent of Flaubert's free indirect discourse. The narrator (and reader) pass into the thoughts of a character, although the latter is referred to as a "she" or a "he," and the "thoughts" are more renderings of pre-verbal impressions than a discourse actually articulated by the character.

As Minogue points out, two social milieus dominate in *The Planetarium:* "the Parisian literary intellectuals on the one hand, and the conventional bourgeois family on the other." Objects, whether artistic or domestic, acquire importance in the social context because they trigger the antagonistic desires of the characters, who seek a form of esthetic triumph through the objects. The tropistic movements of repulsion and attraction toward objects (a door-handle, a pair of armchairs, a statue) coincide with a battle of wills raging amongst the characters. The intensity of the struggles contrasts, often comically, with their trivial pretexts: a woman tries to control her son-in-law by preparing a dish of grated carrots for him. But the son-in-

law strikes back by refusing it: "Alain told me he liked grated carrots. She is lying in wait. Always ready to pounce. She jumped on it, she holds it in her clenched teeth. . . . The hors-d'oeuvre dish in hand, she looks fixedly at him with gleaming eyes. But with a gesture, he gets away—a brief supple gesture of his raised hand, a movement of his head. . . . 'No, thank you . . .'." From the son-in-law's point of view, his mother-in-law resembles a wildcat about to devour its prey. From her perspective, she is only seeking to please and is rebuffed. Between the quotation's innocuous first and last sentences, a major struggle for power takes place. The minute movements from within are viewed at close range, as under a magnifying glass, and although novelistic time radically slows the action, in real time the drama happens in a fleeting instant. In her 1965 *Tel Quel* article, Lucette Finas comments on the quick psychological maneuvers and reversals: "All the dialogues have their victim and their tormenter who exchange roles from one page to the next, sometimes from one retort to the next."

With the publication of her next three novels, *Les Fruits d'or (The Golden Fruits), Entre la vie et la mort (Between Life and Death),* and *Vous les entendez? (Do You Hear Them?),* Sarraute adroitly focuses her attention on artistic creation and critical reception. Even more than her previous works, these novels exemplify the self-examining character of the "New Novel", implicitly and explicitly questioning Sarraute's own literary activity through discussions about the nature of artistic value and the process of creation. Humorous, moving, self-mocking, and intricate, they reveal Nathalie Sarraute's talent at its best.

According to Leah D. Hewitt's 1983 *Modern Language Studies* article, *The Golden Fruits* "traces the rise and fall of an imaginary novel, *also* called 'Les Fruits d'or,' as it is acclaimed, criticized and almost forgotten by its readers." The imaginary novel fulfills the same role as the various objects in *The Planetarium,* serving as a pretext around which a group of anonymous voices attempt to prove the superiority of their literary judgment. As in the novels that follow, *The Golden Fruits* juxtaposes everyday colloquial language and poetic metaphors that capture the underlying emotions of the moment. Also characteristic of Sarraute's style is the continual use of elliptical sentences that trail off without finishing. These fragmentary remarks underscore the commonplace quality of the discussions and, as Sarraute explains in a letter to *CA,* imply that the reader is "supposed to know how they would finish." But they also suggest that thoughts and impressions are formed and "cross our minds very quickly. There is no time to waste for building correct, well-rounded sentences."

The Golden Fruits centers around the way one reads, experiences, and evaluates literature, calling upon Sarraute's reader to participate actively in the interrogation. The tropism is not just a phenomenon to be perceived and understood by the readers: they re-enact it as they move toward and away from the speakers' comments about the imaginary novel. Although critical positions abound in the novel—ranging from the arrogant to the timid, from the "classical" which affirms that esthetic values are established and definable, to intimate, personal experiences of reading which can only offer subjective opinions—no single stance can triumph over the others. Through the extensive use of parody and cliches, Sarraute skillfully undermines positions of authority. Consider, for example, the jargon-ridden language of a pompous critic silencing dissenting opinion: "This book, I believe, installs in literature a privileged language that succeeds in encircling a correspondence that is its very structure. It is a very new and perfect appropriation of rhythmic signs that transcend by their tension what is inessential in all semantics.'' The parody is comically effective and ought to make any critic wary of obscurity.

Karlis Racevskis's study of Sarraute's irony in his 1977 *French Review* article shows that the reader of *The Golden Fruits* can neither wholly espouse nor wholly reject the positions of Sarraute's fictive readers, for just as he begins to accept or to dismiss a viewpoint, another voice intervenes to indicate its weaknesses or strengths. As Hewitt notes: ''Rather than providing a response to the question of value (an act which would deny the very problematic that she has dramatically set in motion), Sarraute creates a dialectical movement in which affirmations are always being undone.'' One voice comments near the end of the book: ''Art as you say, a work of art is never a sure value.... One is often wrong, that's natural. How can one know? Who can say that he knows?'' The open-ended questions of Sarraute's novel suggest that any work of art undergoes a continual re-evaluation according to the needs of a particular society at a given moment in history.

In *Between Life and Death,* Sarraute turns her attention to the writer's activity, pondering the act of creation from the inside, as well as the writer's interactions with his public. Minogue stresses the self-analyzing quality of the novel: ''[*Between Life and Death*] recreates in its pages the writer writing about writing—writing, indeed, about the specific writing we are reading.'' Nevertheless, on the paperback cover of her novel, Sarraute takes care to point out that it is not autobiographical and that the reader trying to construct a hero-writer will only find ''disparate parts'' which cannot hold together as a character. It would indeed prove difficult to identify the writer (sometimes a ''he,'' sometimes an ''I'') as one coherent being, because the ''factual'' elements from the past contradict each other. Racevskis aptly shows, for example, the humorous altering of details from one passage to the next. At one moment the writer maintains that he can compose only on the typewriter; at another, he uses a Bic ballpoint pen; at still another, he writes only with a pencil. Clearly, Sarraute is more concerned with problems in the perception of writers than with the portrait of a specific individual, even though there are references to particular situations and memories.

It is noteworthy that Sarraute refers to the writer as a ''he'' rather than a ''she,'' a technique that distances the author Sarraute from her work, avoiding an identification between them. As in most of her works, masculine voices tend to predominate for a strategic reason. In an interview with Bettina Knapp appearing in the *Kentucky Romance Quarterly* in 1969, Sarraute maintains that the masculine is as close as one can get to a neutral voice applicable to everyone. Sarraute feels that the feminine voice tends to be automatically considered as gender-specific and particularized, a characterization she wishes to avoid.

Micha observes that Sarraute had originally thought of naming her novel ''Le Cercle'' (''The Circle''), and Besser explains the circular structure of *Between Life and Death:* in the beginning, the writer is already established and well known to the public; then he returns to his childhood memories, early writing attempts, and the reactions of his family and friends; at the end, he is once again a successful writer, but still grappling with the creative process. No preconceived formula can guarantee successful creation and even the writer cannot explain how he writes. The reader shares in his solitary moments of joy and anguish as he labors over his manuscript, wondering whether his writing is original, facile, or interesting, whether

it is alive or dead. There is a certain magic in the way the words take shape, rising as if from a void, but the dangers of facility always lurk in the background, and the writer risks making his text too ''pretty,'' a stylistic accomplishment devoid of any vitality or emotional charge. Once he has written something, the writer splits himself in two to evaluate his effort. In a 1973 *Contemporary Literature* interview with Germaine Bree, Sarraute comments on this doubling: ''I think each writer, each artist . . . has a kind of double, who, from time to time as he works, stands back and looks at his painting or rereads his text. He is both himself and someone else. He often becomes a completely merciless judge.'' Besser points out that in *Between Life and Death* ''the process of autocriticism is rendered fictionally in the form of a dialogue between the artist's twin halves: his critical and creative faculties.''

In the childhood scenes, the writer-as-child shows an early sensitivity to words, which are fascinating playthings as well as sources of displeasure when used in certain ways or pronounced with certain intonations. The adults around him are quick to interpret his attention to language as a sign indicating his future career and pointing to an inability to deal adequately with his physical surroundings. While contesting the predestination of the writer, Sarraute does explore the relationship between an extreme preoccupation with language and the act of writing. Do the writer's words portray an extant reality or does he create one which refers only to itself? Other New Novelists such as Robbe-Grillet have maintained that there is no reality beyond the words, that writing is a purely self-reflexive activity, but Sarraute does not share this view. In *Between Life and Death,* the writer's struggle with words is an attempt to create something that exceeds the words but cannot be communicated to others without them. In *Nouveau Roman: Hier, aujourd'hui,* Sarraute speaks of this indeterminate ''something'' as a vibration, a vacillation, a vague sensation at the heart of the tropistic reactions which she brings to life through metaphor and analogy.

Most of *Between Life and Death,* like *The Golden Fruits* and *Do You Hear Them?,* entails an intricate web of dialogues and subconversations. Alternately humble and proud, the writer at times seeks positive recognition from his readers while remaining fearful that they will not approve of his work. At other times, when riding the wave of success, he becomes self-satisfied, considering himself a creative genius. When interacting with his readers, he finds that roles are imposed on him despite his wishes, as they transform his most innocuous gestures (preparing tea, for example) into romanticized ceremonial rituals that confirm his unique personality. Masks presenting a stereotyped view of ''The Writer'' are assigned to him, but at the same time, he uses such masks to defend himself against intrusions or to bolster his own importance. Ultimately, he is the only one who can judge his work: the novel concludes with the moving image of the anxious writer holding a mirror to his work to see if a breath will cloud it, thereby attesting to the work's vitality.

Sarraute completes the trilogy of *The Golden Fruits* and *Between Life and Death* with *Do You Hear Them?,* focusing, as she says in her interview with Bree, on ''the relationship between the work of art, the environment into which it falls, and its fate in general.'' In his home, a man and his friend contemplate a small stone figurine of primitive art while the man's children are heard laughing upstairs. The domestic drama lies in the tension between the father's love of the statue and his love for his children who rebel against what they see as his quasi-religious devotion to art, favoring free artistic creation untrammeled by rules and a weighty sense of tradition. The father interprets the children's effervescent laughter as, in turns, carefree and innocent or mocking and deceitful. Besser notes how the metaphorical descriptions of the children's gleeful voices pass from poetic cliche ("Tiny bells. Tiny drops. Fountains. Gentle water-falls. Twittering of birds.") to ominous images of persecution: "Soon the 'titters' grow 'sharp as needles,' and the water drips on its victim like a Chinese torture."

According to Besser, when asked which of the two opposing conceptions of art Sarraute would herself choose, the novelist responded that she could identify with both. Her answer is not surprising when one remembers that in *The Age of Suspicion* she had admired novelists of the past while nevertheless rebelling against certain novelistic conventions. In addition, Besser points out that, as in *Portrait of a Man Unknown*, "there is no delineation between 'real' and 'imagined' events," so that the boundaries separating the opposing positions of the father and children tend to blur. One cannot always distinguish between the father's viewpoint and the children's because the father often tries to identify with what he imagines his children are thinking. In the Bree interview, Sarraute corroborates this impression: "I wanted to show a kind of interaction between consciousnesses which are extremely close to one another to the extent that they almost fuse and communicate by a kind of osmosis. . . . What each one feels and attributes to another becomes any one of the others at any given moment."

In her next two works, *"disent les imbeciles"* (*"fools say"*) and *L'Usage de la parole* (*The Use of Speech*), Sarraute pushes the novelistic genre to the limit. In fact, *The Use of Speech* is often not considered a novel at all. In both works, there is no one story line or character to unite the fragmented episodes. Instead, the author creates a series of interpersonal exchanges in which anonymous voices react to the effects of linguistic labeling, to the power of cliches to imprison the individual in stock phrases and concrete descriptions. The unifying element lies in the relentless study of the way language intervenes in the development of ideas and of human identity. As in her other novels, the hypersensitive individuals of *"fools say"* writhe in discomfort as they find themselves condemned to play certain roles by virtue of the labels and categorizations that others ascribe to them. As Ellen W. Munley says in her 1983 *Contemporary Literature* article, "Sarraute scrutinizes the tropistic proximity and distance, the fusion and separation created by language. Words speak actions. . . . Words create a cast of characters erected at a distance: a grandmother 'sweet enough to eat,' a dual personality 'gifted but not intelligent,' 'fools'." Minogue describes the setting of *"fools say"* as "a terrorist world, against which Nathalie Sarraute raises a voice that insists that any idea, however comforting, or however disconcerting it may be, must be treated as an idea, not as an appurtenance of a personality, group, class, nation, or race."

The Use of Speech is a collection of ten essays or sketches more reminiscent of *Tropisms* than of a conventional novel. Again, Sarraute focuses her attention on the resonances of certain verbal expressions, investigating, for example, what is contained in the word "love" or in the phrase "Don't talk to me about that." But according to Munley, *The Use of Speech* differs from Sarraute's previous works in that "it contains a self-styled narrator-doctor of words who joins all of its loosely connected vignettes by virtue of her presence." Unlike the narrators of *Portrait of a Man Unknown* or *Martereau*, this speaker does not directly participate as one of the characters in the vignettes. The new use of a first person narrator in her

work perhaps anticipates Sarraute's subsequent interest in writing an account of her early years in *Childhood*.

Although Sarraute is best known for her novels, she also launched a playwriting career after the publication of *The Golden Fruits* in 1963. In "Le Gant retourne" ("The Inverted Glove"), published in the *Cahiers Renaud Barrault*, Sarraute explains that she had not considered writing for the theater until a young German, Werner Spies, asked her to write radio plays for Radio Stuttgart. After refusing several times, she finally decided to accept the challenge. Thus she composed two short plays, "Le Silence" ("Silence") and "Le Mensonge" ("The Lie"), which were first broadcast on German radio and then performed in Paris in 1967 at the Theatre de France under the direction of Jean-Louis Barrault. Sarraute was surprised at the richness of Barrault's staging, finding that the actors' work complemented her text.

Given Sarraute's enduring interest in the invisible, unspoken movements that underlie dialogue, the theater, as an oral, visual medium, presents special problems for the portrayal of tropisms. In the play format, the subconversations or pre-dialogues must be incorporated into the dialogue in order for the audience to witness and participate in them. Sarraute's dramatic dialogues are full of the hesitations, incomplete sentences, and trite expressions of everyday speech, and as in her novels, the characters are primarily anonymous, "even in the rare instances," as Besser notes, "when they are equipped with a name."

In "Silence" and "The Lie," Sarraute breaks down the social masks of commonplace dialogue with disruptive, although equally banal "events." In "Silence," one character in a group of friends remains silent for most of the play. His lack of participation in the exchange begins to bother another character, who eventually communicates his discomfort to everyone else. The silence produces a series of tropistic reactions and is interpreted in every way possible: it becomes in turns a positive, negative, or indifferent sign on the part of the silent man. As was the case with the title, *The Golden Fruits*, silence is transformed into a creative generator of meaning, the whole process eventually questioning the nature of meaning and interpretations of reality. In "The Lie," a seemingly trivial white lie disturbs one character and provokes not only a discussion of the differences between truth and untruth, between play-acting and authentic action, but a dramatic enactment of the issues as well.

Unlike many of her novels, Sarraute's plays do not use physical objects as catalysts for the tropisms; instead, elements of speech trigger reactions. But the cause for irritation is so slight that the characters are constantly repeating that it's nothing even as they respond to that "nothing." For example, in "Isma" ("Izzum"), first performed in 1970, the mannered pronunciation of words ending in "ism" causes an anonymous man and woman to vent their hostility toward a family named Dubuit. In the suffocating familial atmosphere of "C'est Beau" ("It's Beautiful"), first performed in 1975, a mother and father avoid saying the simple words "it's beautiful" in their son's presence because the phrase, as Besser says, "encompasses . . . all the ideas and principles that govern the parents' lives." Like the father of *Do You Hear Them?*, they cringe at the thought that their son might scorn their esthetic values.

Sarraute's next two plays, "Elle est la" ("It Is There"), which premiered in 1980, and "For No Good Reason," which premiered in New York in 1985, perhaps illustrate best that, in the struggles between individuals over truth or values, her characters are always seeking, as Sarraute said in her 1969 interview with Knapp, "fusion and contact with someone else." But such a desire is difficult to realize and in "For No Good Reason" an attempt at reconciliation between two old friends ends in a confirmation of their fundamental differences with respect to life-styles and values. It is paradoxically the desire to be close to another, to find the basis for agreement, that prompts the most intense antagonisms.

It might seem surprising that Sarraute, who has steadfastly questioned the status of personal identity and unequivocal factual truth, should have written *Childhood,* a series of autobiographical texts about her early relationships with her families and her first experiences in language. But for Sarraute, autobiography is still literature, another terrain for prospecting the subterranean tropisms of her own experiences. Instead of the singular "I" usually found in autobiography, this work contains *two* narrators in dialogue: while one voice narrates episodes from the past, the other admonishes, encourages, censures, and interprets what the first has presented. Sarraute makes no attempt to connect the various episodes she relates, for identity is conceived as split or fragmented, and interpretation is acknowledged in the text as a necessary component of memory. The author's personae and her past are recognized as fictive re-creations like those in her other literary works.

John Sturrock notes in his 1983 *Times Literary Supplement* review of *Childhood* that the theme of disobedience sets the stage for many of Sarraute's memories. The pleasure of self-affirmation in rebelling against parental rule seems to foreshadow the writer's subsequent revolt against established literary conventions. But at the same time, the reader is made aware of the child's intense need to be recognized and loved by her parents: her often frustrated efforts to feel an intimacy with her mother are poignant although never self-pitying. This aspect, too, reappears in her novels and plays, as characters move toward and away from each other in the difficult act of communication. One is particularly reminded of the writer in *Between Life and Death,* although Sarraute would be the first to deny that the novel is *her* story.

With *Childhood,* Sarraute captures the humor, joys, and pain of growing up in a divided family and in different languages in an original, enthralling autobiographical account. In 1985, after its 1984 Parisian premiere, *Childhood* was performed in New York under the direction of Simone Benmussa, with Glenn Close in the starring role.

As a New Novelist, Sarraute has successfully combined an investigation of language's ability to unsettle its own stale, rigid definitions, with an intimate, relentless study of the hazardous paths human beings explore in interacting. Her exploration of the tropism has given new life to the psychological novel, and her works continue to fascinate readers who, dissatisfied with conventional narrative forms that take "reality" for granted, turn to literature in search of new ways of understanding the changing relationships between language and the world.

STAGE ADAPTATIONS: Childhood was adapted as a play by Simone Benmussa and premiered in Paris in 1984. The American premiere, both adapted and directed by Benmussa, was produced in 1985 at the Samuel Beckett, New York City, featuring Glenn Close in the starring role.

BIOGRAPHICAL/CRITICAL SOURCES:

BOOKS

Alberes, R.-M., *Metamorphoses du roman,* Albin Michel (Paris), 1966.

Allemand, Andre, *L'Oeuvre romanesque de Nathalie Sarraute,* Editions de la Baconniere (Neuchatel), 1980.

Alter, Robert, *Partial Magic: The Novel as a Self-conscious Genre,* University of California Press, 1975.

Barrere, J.-B., *La Cure d'amaigrissement du roman,* Albin Michel, 1964.

Beja, Morris, *Epiphany in the Modern Novel,* University of Washington Press, 1971.

Bell, Sheila Margaret, compiler, *Nathalie Sarraute: A Bibliography,* Grant & Cutler, 1982.

Besser, Gretchen Rous, *Nathalie Sarraute,* Twayne, 1979.

Bloch-Michel, J., *Le Present de l'indicatif: Essai sur le nouveau roman,* Gallimard, 1963.

Boisdeffre, Pierre de, *Le Roman depuis 1900,* Presses Universitaires de France (Paris), 1979.

Butor, Michel, *Repertoire II,* Editions de Minuit, 1964.

Calin, Francoise, *La Vie retrouvee: Etude de l'oeuvre romanesque de Nathalie Sarraute,* Minard (Paris), 1976.

Chapsal, Madeleine, *Les Ecrivains en personne,* Julliard (Paris), 1960.

Contemporary Literary Criticism, Gale, Volume 1, 1973, Volume 2, 1974, Volume 4, 1975, Volume 8, 1978, Volume 10, 1979, Volume 31, 1985.

Cranaki, Mimica and Yvon Belaval, editors, *Nathalie Sarraute,* Gallimard, 1965.

Daellenbach, Lucien, *Le Recit speculaire,* Le Seuil (Paris), 1977.

Edel, Leon, *The Modern Psychological Novel,* revised edition, Grosset & Dunlap-Universal Library, 1964.

Eliez-Ruegg, Elizabeth, *La Conscience d'autrui et la conscience des objets dans l'oeuvre de Nathalie Sarraute,* Lang (Berne), 1972.

Frohock, W. M., editor, *Image and Theme: Studies in Modern French Fiction:* Harvard University Press, 1969.

Goldmann, Lucien, *Pour une sociologie du roman,* Gallimard, 1964.

Hassan, Ihab, *The Dismemberment of Orpheus,* Oxford University Press, 1971.

Heath, Stephen, *The Nouveau Roman: A Study in the Practice of Writing,* Temple University Press, 1972.

Jaccard, Jean-Luc, *Nathalie Sarraute,* Juris (Zurich), 1967.

Jansen, Steen, *Analyse de la forme dramatique du Mensonge de Nathalie Sarraute precedee de Nathalie Sarraute, Le Mensonge,* Akademisk Forlag, 1976.

Janvier, Ludovic, *Une Parole exigeante: Le Nouveau Roman,* Editions de Minuit, 1964.

Knapp, Bettina, *Off-Stage Voices: Interviews with Modern French Dramatists,* Whitston, 1975.

Kostelanetz, Richard, *On Contemporary Literature,* Avon, 1964.

Le Sage, Laurent, *The French New Novel,* Pennsylvania State University Press, 1962.

Matthews, J. H., editor, *Un Nouveau Roman?,* La Revue des Lettres Modernes, 1964.

Mauriac, Claude, *L'Alitterature contemporaine,* revised edition, Albin Michel, 1969.

McCarthy, Mary, *The Writing on the Wall and Other Literary Essays,* Harcourt, 1970.

Mercier, Vivian, *The New Novel: From Queneau to Pinget,* revised edition, Farrar, Straus, 1966.

Micha, Rene, *Nathalie Sarraute,* Editions Universitaires (Paris), 1966.

Minogue, Valerie, *Nathalie Sarraute and the War of the Words: A Study of Five Novels,* Edinburgh University Press, 1981.

Moore, Harry T., *Twentieth-Century French Literature since World War II*, Southern Illinois University Press, 1966.

Nadeau, Maurice, *The French Novel since the War*, translated by A. M. Sheridan-Smith, Methuen, 1967.

Newman, A. S., *Une Poesie des discours: Essai sur les romans de Nathalie Sarraute*, Droz (Geneva), 1976.

Peyre, Henri, *The Contemporary French Novel*, Oxford University Press, 1955.

Peyre, Henri, *French Novelists of Today*, Oxford University Press, 1967.

Podhoretz, Norman, *Doings and Undoings*, Farrar, Straus, 1953, revised edition, 1964.

Rahv, Betty T., *From Sartre to the New Novel*, Kennikat Press, 1974.

Raimond, Michel, *Le Roman depuis la revolution*, Armand Colin (Paris), 1967.

Ricardou, Jean, *Problemes du nouveau roman*, Le Seuil, 1967.

Ricardou, Jean, *Pour une theorie du nouveau roman*, Le Seuil, 1971.

Ricardou, Jean and Francoise von Rossum-Guyon, editors, *Nouveau Roman: Hier, aujourd'hui*, Union Generale d'Editions (Paris), 1972.

Ricardou, Jean, *Le Nouveau Roman*, Le Seuil, 1973.

Robbe-Grillet, Alain, *Pour un nouveau roman*, Gallimard, 1964.

Sarraute, Nathalie, *Portrait d'un inconnu*, with preface by Jean-Paul Sartre, Robert Marin, 1948, translation by Jolas published as *Portrait of a Man Unknown*, Braziller, 1958.

Sarraute, Nathalie, *L'Ere du soupcon: Essais sur le roman*, Gallimard, 1956, translation by Jolas published as *The Age of Suspicion: Essays on the Novel*, Braziller, 1963.

Sontag, Susan, *Against Interpretation and Other Essays*, revised edition, Farrar, Straus, 1966.

Temple, Ruth Z., *Nathalie Sarraute*, Columbia University Press, 1968.

Tison-Braun, Micheline, *Nathalie Sarraute ou la recherche de l'authenticite*, Gallimard, 1971.

Weightman, John, *The Concept of the Avant-Garde: Explorations in Modernism*, Alcove, 1973.

Wunderli-Mueller, Christine, *Le Theme du masque et les banalites dans l'oeuvre de Nathalie Sarraute*, Juris Druck Verlag (Zurich), 1970.

PERIODICALS

American Scholar, summer, 1963.
Arts, June 3-9, 1959.
Atlantic, June, 1960, March, 1973, May, 1977, April, 1984.
Books Abroad, autumn, 1972.
Book Week, February 9, 1964.
Bucknell Review, April, 1976.
Bulletin des jeunes romanistes, Volume 20, 1974.
Cahiers Renaud Barrault, Volume 89, 1975.
Christian Science Monitor, February 13, 1964, July 15, 1969, August 22, 1977, August 2, 1984.
Commonweal, December 18, 1959, August 22, 1969.
Contemporary Literature, spring, 1973, summer, 1983.
Critique (Paris), Volumes 86-87, 1954, Volumes 100-101, 1955, Volumes 111-112, 1956.
Critique: Studies in Modern Fiction, winter, 1963-64, Volume 14, number 1, 1972.
Digraphe, March, 1984.
Drama, autumn, 1981.
Esprit, Volume 376, 1968.
Essays in French Literature, Volume 3, 1966.
Etudes litteraires, Volume 17, number 2, 1984.
Express (Paris), April 29-May 5, 1968.

French Forum, Volume 5, 1980.
French Review, December, 1959, spring special issue, 1972, October, 1977, February, 1980, March, 1981, April, 1983.
French Studies, April, 1973, Volume 30, number 1, 1976.
Hudson Review, autumn, 1967, autumn, 1973.
International Fiction Review, January, 1974, January, 1977.
Kentucky Romance Quarterly, Volume 14, number 3, 1969.
Kenyon Review, summer, 1963.
Lettres francaises, February 4, 1960.
Lettres nouvelles, April 29, 1959.
Listener, March 9, 1961.
Los Angeles Times, April 17, 1984.
Mercure de France, Volume 336, 1959, Volume 345, 1962, Volume 348, 1963.
Modern Fiction Studies, winter, 1960-61.
Modern Language Notes, Volume 88, number 4, 1973.
Modern Language Review, July, 1978, July, 1982, January, 1986, January, 1987.
Modern Language Studies, Volume 13, number 3, 1983.
Ms., July, 1984.
Nation, March 23, 1962, March 2, 1964.
New Republic, March 21, 1964.
New Statesman, April 15, 1983.
Newsweek, February 10, 1964.
New Yorker, March 26, 1960, May 21, 1960, May 2, 1964, November 22, 1969, May 9, 1977, April 11, 1983.
New York Herald Tribune Book Review, August 3, 1958.
New York Review of Books, March 5, 1964, July 31, 1969, April 19, 1973, October 25, 1984.
New York Times, August 10, 1958, May 30, 1969, July 24, 1970, March 30, 1984.
New York Times Book Review, November 1, 1959, May 15, 1960, February 9, 1964, May 21, 1967, May 18, 1969, February 4, 1973, April 3, 1977, April 1, 1984.
Nouvelle Revue francaise, Volume 54, 1957, Volume 62, 1958, Volume 127, 1963.
Nouvelles litteraires, June 9, 1966.
Performing Arts Journal, winter, 1977.
Preuves, Volume 154, 1963.
PTL: A Journal for Descriptive Poetics and Theory of Literature, April, 1977.
Renascence, summer, 1964.
Revue de Paris, June, 1958.
Salmagundi, spring, 1970.
San Francisco Chronicle, July 10, 1960.
Saturday Review, August 2, 1958, January 2, 1960, June 11, 1960, March 16, 1963, February 15, 1964, May 6, 1967, May 24, 1969, April 2, 1977.
Symposium, winter, 1974.
Tel Quel, Volume 20, 1965.
Time, August 4, 1958, May 23, 1960, February 7, 1964.
Times Literary Supplement, January 1, 1960, January 30, 1964, July 29, 1965, July 11, 1968, January 1, 1970, February 25, 1972, July 11, 1975, April 4, 1980, July 30, 1982, June 10, 1983, April 11, 1986.
Village Voice, July 31, 1984.
Washington Post Book World, February 18, 1973, May 20, 1984.
World, July 4, 1972.
World Literature Today, summer, 1977, summer, 1979, spring, 1981, autumn, 1983, winter, 1983.
Yale French Studies, winter, 1955-56, summer, 1959, spring-summer, 1961, June, 1971.
Yale Review, winter, 1959, summer, 1960, autumn, 1973.

—*Sidelights by Leah D. Hewitt*

SCANLAN, Michael 1931-

PERSONAL: Born December 1, 1931, in Far Rockaway, N.Y.; son of Vincent Michael and Marjorie (O'Keefe) Scanlan. *Education:* Williams College, B.A., 1953; Harvard University, J.D., 1956; graduate study at Catholic University, 1963-64, and Boston University, 1965; Saint Francis Seminary, M.Div., 1975.

ADDRESSES: Home—Holy Spirit Monastery, Steubenville, Ohio 43952. *Office*—University of Steubenville, Steubenville, Ohio 43952.

CAREER: Admitted to the Bar of New York State, 1956; ordained Roman Catholic priest of Order of St. Francis (T.O.R.), 1964; College of Steubenville (now University of Steubenville), Steubenville, Ohio, lecturer in theology, 1964-66, acting dean, 1964-66, dean of college, 1966-69, director of general honors program, 1966-69; Saint Francis Major Seminary, Loretto, Pa., rector president, 1969-74; University of Steubenville, Steubenville, president, 1974—. Vice-chairman of board of trustees of Saint Francis College, Loretto, Pa., 1969-74; member of Pennsylvania Fulbright Committee, 1970. *Military service:* U.S. Air Force, member of Judge Advocate's staff, 1956-57.

MEMBER: New York Bar Association.

AWARDS, HONORS: Litt.D., College of Steubenville, 1972; LL.D., Williams College, 1978.

WRITINGS:

The Power in Penance, Ave Maria Press, 1972.
Inner Healing, Paulist-Newman, 1974.
(With Ann Therese Shields) *And Their Eyes Were Opened,* Servant Books, 1976.
Prayers and Blessings (booklet), College of Steubenville, 1978.
A Portion of My Spirit, Carillon Books, 1979.
(With Randall J. Cirner) *Deliverance from Evil Spirits,* Servant Books, 1980.
Turn to the Lord: A Call to Repentance, Servant Books, 1984.
Titles of Jesus, Franciscan University Press, 1985.
Let the Fire Fall, Servant Books, 1986.
Appointment with God, Franciscan University Press, 1987.

Contributor to religion periodicals.

SIDELIGHTS: Michael Scanlan wrote *CA:* "All I write comes from prayer. I go into solitude and after prayer reflect on the struggle in the [Catholic] Church today. Writing then is a release of fire from within."

* * *

SCHERTLE, Alice 1941-

PERSONAL: Surname rhymes with "turtle"; born April 7, 1941, in Los Angeles, Calif.; daughter of Floyd C. (a real estate investor) and Marguerite (a teacher; maiden name, Soucie) Sanger; married Richard Schertle (a general contractor), December 21, 1963; children: Jennifer, Katherine, John. *Education:* University of Southern California, B.S. (cum laude), 1963.

ADDRESSES: Home—La Habra Heights, Calif.

CAREER: Highland School, Inglewood, Calif., elementary school teacher, 1963-65; writer, 1965—.

WRITINGS:

JUVENILES

The Gorilla in the Hall, illustrations by Paul Galdone, Lothrop, 1977.
The April Fool, Lothrop, 1981.
Hob Goblin and the Skeleton, illustrations by Katherine Coville, Lothrop, 1982.
In My Treehouse, Lothrop, 1983.
Bim Dooley Makes His Move, Lothrop, 1984.
Goodnight Hattie, My Dearie, My Dove, Lothrop, 1985.
My Two Feet, Lothrop, 1985.
That Olive!, Lothrop, 1986.
Jeremy Bean's St. Patrick's Day, Lothrop, 1987.
Bill and the Google-Eyed Goblins, Lothrop, 1987.
Gus Wanders Off, Lothrop, 1988.
William and Grandpa, Lothrop, 1988.
That's What I Thought, Harper, 1988.
Witch Hazel, Harper, 1988.

"CATHY AND COMPANY" SERIES; ALL ILLUSTRATED BY CATHY PAVIA

Cathy and Company and Mean Mr. Meeker, Childrens Press, 1980.
. . . and Bumper the Bully, Childrens Press, 1980.
. . . and the Green Ghost, Childrens Press, 1980.
. . . and the Nosy Neighbor, Childrens Press, 1980.
. . . and the Double Dare, Childrens Press, 1980.
. . . and Hank the Horse, Childrens Press, 1980.

SIDELIGHTS: Alice Schertle wrote: "I live with my husband and three children on almost two acres of land in La Habra, California. Adding to the general confusion are two dogs, four cats, eight chickens, two hives of bees, and assorted birds and butterflies. When I'm not feeding anybody or writing anything, I like to spend my time in my vegetable garden. I find the garden quiet and peaceful, a good place to germinate seeds and ideas for stories.

"*In My Treehouse* was inspired by my son's adventures in his own treehouse. As a child, I spent a good deal of time in trees, so I took John up on his invitation to join him in his house in a big fruitless mulberry. In fact, I did a lot of writing up there, though I find they're not making treehouses as big as they used to. Treehouses have a lot more ants nowadays, too.

"I write children's books because I love them—always have. The various seasons of my childhood are identified in my memory with the books that were important to me then. There was the year Mary Poppins floated into the lives of Jane and Michael Banks and me. And my sixth grade year I think I spent with the Black Stallion and King of the Wind. There were countless times Nancy Drew and I fought crime in River Heights; and there was the wonderful summer I read *Little Women* and *The Yearling*—and the summers when I reread them.

"As for my own writing, I want it to tell a good story, one with a definite beginning, and ending, and something in between that ties the two together in a logical way. Sounds simple.

"One of the nicest things about being an author is that it gives me the opportunity to talk to classes of children about books and writing. I always tell them that the best way to learn to write is to read and read and read. It's advice I take myself. There's a tall stack of books precariously balanced on my bedside table, and a good many of them are children's books."

BIOGRAPHICAL/CRITICAL SOURCES:

PERIODICALS

Los Angeles Times Book Review, April 3, 1983.

*   *   *

SCOTT, John Anthony 1916-

PERSONAL: Born January 20, 1916, in London, England; became U.S. citizen, 1943; son of Philip (a dentist) and Nora (Mort de Bois) Scott; married Maria Malleville Haller (a teacher), August 27, 1940; children: Elizabeth, John Wardlaw, Robert Alan. *Education:* Trinity College, Oxford, B.A. (with first class honors), 1937, M.A. 1945; Columbia University, M.A., 1947, Ph.D., 1950. *Politics:* Independent.

ADDRESSES: Home—3902 Manhattan College Pkwy., New York, N.Y. 10471. *Office*—School of Law, Rutgers University, Newark, N.J. 07102.

CAREER: Columbia University, New York City, instructor in European history, 1946-48; Amherst College, Amherst, Mass., instructor in European history, 1948-51; Fieldston School, New York City, instructor in United States history and chairperson of department, 1951-67; Rutgers University, School of Law, Newark, N.J., visiting professor of legal history, 1967—. Instructor at Seminar on American Culture, Cooperstown, N.Y., 1963. Instructor in folksong at seminars of teachers. Sometime ballad singer at Old Sturbridge Village. Civil rights movement organizer, 1956-63, aiding in organization of Prayer Pilgrimage to Washington, 1957, and two youth marches for integrated schools, 1958 and 1959; New York metropolitan coordinator for March on Washington for Equal Rights and Jobs, August, 1963. Director, Bronx Draft Information and Counselling Service, 1967-73. Consultant, National Humanities Faculty and National Faculty, 1970—. *Military service:* U.S. Army, Armored Forces and Intelligence, 1942-45; served in Europe; became staff sergeant; received Field Citation.

MEMBER: American Historical Association, Association for the Study of Negro Life and History, Organization of American Historians, Society for Historians of the Early American Republic, Southern Historical Association.

AWARDS, HONORS: M.A. from Oxford University, 1945; Social Science Research Council fellow.

WRITINGS:

Republican Ideas and the Liberal Tradition in France, Columbia University Press, 1951.
The Ballad of America: The History of the United States in Song and Story, Bantam, 1966, 2nd edition, Southern Illinois University Press, 1983.
Settlers on the Eastern Shore, 1607-1750, Knopf, 1967.
The Trumpet of a Prophecy: Revolutionary America, 1763-1783, Knopf, 1969.
Teaching for a Change, Bantam, 1972.
Fanny Kemble's America, Crowell, 1973.
Hard Trials on My Way: Slavery and the Struggle against It, 1800-1860, Knopf, 1974.
Woman against Slavery: The Life of Harriet Beecher Stowe, Crowell, 1978.
The Story of America, National Geographic Society, 1984.
Make Way for Liberty: The Life of John Brown of Harper's Ferry, Facts on File, 1987.

(Contributor) Randall M. Miller and John D. Smith, editors, *Dictionary of Afro-American Slavery*, Greenwood Press, 1987.

EDITOR

Introduction to Contemporary Civilization in the West, Columbia University Press, 1946.
Frances Anne Kemble, *Journal of a Residence on a Georgian Plantation in 1838-1839*, Knopf, 1961, 2nd edition, University of Georgia Press, 1984.
Living Documents in American History, Washington Square Press, Volume I: *From Earliest Colonial Times to the Civil War*, 1963, Volume II: *From Reconstruction to the Outbreak of World War I*, 1968.
(And translator and contributor) *The Defense of Gracchus Babeuf before the High Court of Vendome*, Gehenna Press, 1964, University of Massachusetts Press, 1967.
Thomas More, *Utopia*, Washington Square Press, 1965.
(And author of introduction) Frank Moore, compiler, *The Diary of the American Revolution, 1775-1781*, Washington Square Press, 1967.
James M. McPherson, *Marching toward Freedom: The Negro in the Civil War, 1861-1865*, Knopf, 1968.

General editor of "The Living History Library" series, Knopf, 1965-76 and of "Makers of America" series, Facts on File, 1985—.

OTHER

Also author of scripts and producer of recordings for Heirloom Records, including "The New Deal through Its Songs and Ballads," "Irish Immigration through Its Songs and Ballads," "The Negro People through Their Songs and Ballads," "New England Whaling through Its Songs and Ballads," "New York City through Its Songs and Ballads," "The Story of the Cowboy through His Songs and Ballads," "The American Revolution through Its Songs and Ballads," and, with Bill Bonyun, "The Civil War through Its Songs and Ballads." Contributor of articles to *Teaching and Learning, New York Folklore Quarterly, Activist, Journal of Negro History, Sing Out, Rutgers University Law Review, Journal of the Early Republic*, and to other folklore and education journals.

WORK IN PROGRESS: The Origins of Anglo-American Law.

SIDELIGHTS: John Anthony Scott wrote *CA:* "I write for young people of all ages, from elementary school to the graduate level. Much of my writing has been inspired by students' questions, by the dozens of ideas thrown up by discussions with these students. Then I start collecting materials—books, letters, documents, songs, all the things that are the lifeblood of the historian's craft; and sooner or later a new book emerges.

"Writing I find both difficult and necessary. Necessary because an historian tries to contribute to historical truth, to add to what is known about people and life, or to make easily available the literary materials that are the historical heritage of the American public. Difficult, because writing is a way of investigating reality, a reality that is not always easy to understand. And then, again, writing is a craft that takes effort and patience to try and say what you mean, and to say it as briefly and as simply as possible."

AVOCATIONAL INTERESTS: Tennis, swimming, running, bicycle riding, cross-country skiing, hiking, canoeing, and travelling.

BIOGRAPHICAL/CRITICAL SOURCES:

PERIODICALS

Book Review, February 25, 1968.
Horn Book, April, 1968, August, 1978.
New York Times Book Review, February 25, 1968.
Time, June 1, 1962.

*   *   *

SEGAL, Marilyn 1927-

PERSONAL: Born August 9, 1927, in Utica, N.Y.; daughter of Abraham L. (a financier) and Alice (Lyons) Mailman; children: Betty, Wendy, Richard, Patricia, Debra. *Education:* Wellesley College, B.A., 1948; McGill University, B.S., 1949; Nova University, Ph.D., 1969. *Politics:* Democrat. *Religion:* Jewish.

ADDRESSES: Home—919 S.S. Lake Dr., Hollywood, Fla. 33019. *Office*—Family Center, Nova University, 3301 College Ave., Fort Lauderdale, Fla. 33314.

CAREER: The Pre-School, Hollywood, Fla., administrator, 1965-68; social worker in Boston, Mass., 1969; Nova University, Fort Lauderdale, Fla., director of University School, 1970-71, assistant professor of early childhood, 1971-79, professor of developmental psychology, 1979-87, director of Institute of Early Childhood and Open Education, 1971-72, chief investigator, School for Parents program, 1971-72, director of Family Center, 1979—. Member of board of governors, University School, 1969-82; member of board of trustees, University of Miami, 1969—. Chairman of board of directors, A. L. Mailman Family Foundation, 1982—.

WRITINGS:

Run Away Little Girl, Random House, 1965.
(Contributor) *You Are Your Baby's First Teachers,* Nova University Press, 1973.
"Play and Learn" for Parents and Infants, Nova University Press, 1974.
From Birth to One Year: Play and Learn, Nova University Press, 1974, published as *From Birth to One Year,* B. L. Winch, 1978.
(With Don Adcock) *From One to Two Years: Play and Learn,* Nova University Press, 1976, published as *From One to Two Years,* B. L. Winch, 1978.
(With Adcock) *From Two to Three Years: Social Competence* (also see below), B. L. Winch, 1979.
(With Adcock) *From Two to Three Years: Play and Learning* (also see below), B. L. Winch, 1979.
(With Adcock) *Feelings: Social and Emotional Development in the Preschool Years,* Humanics, 1980.
(With Adcock) *Play and Learn Volume I and II and III* (includes revised editions of *From Two to Three Years: Social Competence* and *From Two to Three Years: Play and Learning*), Oak Tree Publications, 1981.
(With Adcock) *Just Pretending,* Prentice-Hall, 1981.
(With Len Tomasello) *Nuts and Bolts: Organization and Management Techniques for an Interest Centered Pre-School Classroom,* Humanics, 1981.
(With Adcock) *Play Together, Grow Together: A Cooperative Curriculum for Teachers of Young Children,* Mailman Family, 1983.
(With Adcock) *Making Friends: Ways of Encouraging Social Development in Young Children,* Prentice-Hall, 1983.

(Contributor) Irving E. Sigel, editor, *Parental Belief Systems: The Psychological Consequences for Children,* L. Earlbaum Associates, 1985.
Your Child at Play: Birth to One Year, Newmarket, 1985.
(With Adcock) *Your Child at Play: One to Two Years,* Newmarket, 1985.
(With Adcock) *Your Child at Play: Two to Three Years,* Newmarket, 1985.
(With Adcock) *Your Child at Play: Three to Five Years,* Newmarket, 1986.
(Contributor) Jaipul L. Roopnarine and James E. Johnson, editors, *Approaches to Early Childhood Education,* C. E. Merrill, 1987.

Also author, with Abbey Manburg, of *All About Child Care;* also author of scripts for "To Reach a Child" television series for the Office of Child Development, 1973. Contributor to periodicals, including *Child Care Center, Inquiry, Journal of Applied Developmental Psychology, Journal of Reading Behavior, Parents Magazine, Reader's Digest, Research in Education, Scholastic Preschool Today,* and *Woman's Day.*

*   *   *

SHANNON, Doris 1924-
(E. X. Giroux)

PERSONAL: Born August 7, 1924, in Elmira, N.Y.; daughter of Edwin (an engineer) and Elizabeth (a telephone operator; maiden name, Graham) Giroux; married Frank Shannon (a customs officer), August 1, 1947; children: Patricia Anne, Deborah Elizabeth. *Education:* Attended Napanee Collegiate Institute, 1939-42.

ADDRESSES: Home—16268 Southglen Place, Surrey, British Columbia, Canada.

CAREER: Writer, 1969—. Royal Bank of Canada, teller in Napanee, Ontario, 1942-47, in Vancouver, British Columbia, 1948-49.

AWARDS, HONORS: Writer's Digest creative writing award, 1969, for short story "And Then There Was the Youngest."

WRITINGS:

NOVELS

The Whispering Runes, Lenox Hill, 1972.
Twenty-two Hallowfield, Fawcett, 1974.
The Seekers, Fawcett, 1975.
Hawthorn Hill, St. Martin's, 1976.
The Lodestar Legacy, Popular Library, 1976.
Cain's Daughters, St. Martin's, 1978.
Beyond the Shining Mountains, St. Martin's, 1979.
The Punishment, St. Martin's, 1981.
Little Girls Lost, St. Martin's, 1981.
Family Money, St. Martin's, 1984.

"ROBERT FORSYTHE MYSTERY" SERIES; UNDER PSEUDONYM E. X. GIROUX

A Death for Adonis, St. Martin's, 1984.
A Death for a Darling, St. Martin's, 1985.
A Death for a Dancer, St. Martin's, 1985.
A Death for a Doctor, St. Martin's, 1986.
A Death for a Dilettante, St. Martin's, 1987.

WORK IN PROGRESS: A Death for a Dietitian, the sixth book in the Robert Forsythe mystery series.

SIDELIGHTS: Doris Shannon told *CA* that at the age of forty, "without quite realizing my own motivation I turned to writing. Much to my surprise . . . editors expressed . . . confidence in a talent I had never realized I possessed. . . . Writing appears to be a profession where gray hair and age are not signals that one's working life is over. I share with many writers the desire to write that special book, the fine one, and also eventually I should like to teach creative writing."

* * *

SHANNON, George (William Bones) 1952-

PERSONAL: Born February 14, 1952, in Caldwell, Kan.; son of David W. (a professor) and Doris (Bones) Shannon. *Education:* Western Kentucky University, B.S., 1974; University of Kentucky, M.S.L.S., 1976.

ADDRESSES: Home—648 Galloway St., No. 3, Eau Claire, Wis. 54703.

CAREER: Librarian at public schools of Muhlenberg County, Ky., 1974-75; Lexington Public Library, Lexington, Ky., librarian, 1976-78; professional storyteller/lecturer, 1978—. Guest lecturer at University of Kentucky, autumn, 1977. Member of external advisory board, Cooperative Children's Book Center, Madison, Wis.

WRITINGS:

Humpty Dumpty: A Pictorial History, Green Tiger Press, 1981.
Folk Literature and Children: An Annotated Bibliography of Secondary Materials, Greenwood Press, 1981.
(With Ellin Greene) *Storytelling: A Selected Annotated Bibliography,* Garland Publishing, 1986.
Unlived Affections, Charlotte Zolotow/Harper, 1988.

JUVENILE

The Gang and Mrs. Higgins, illustrations by Andrew Vines, Greenwillow, 1981.
The Piney Woods Peddler, illustrations by Nancy Tafuri, Greenwillow, 1981.
Lizard's Song, illustrations by Jose Aruego and Ariane Dewey, Greenwillow, 1981.
Dance Away!, illustrations by Aruego and Dewey, Greenwillow, 1982.
The Surprise, illustrations by Aruego and Dewey, Greenwillow, 1983.
Bean Boy, illustrations by Peter Sis, Greenwillow, 1984.
Stories to Solve: Folktales from around the World, Greenwillow, 1985.
O I Love, Bradbury, 1988.

OTHER

Contributor of articles to magazines, including *Horn Book, Catholic Library World,* and *Wilson Library Bulletin,* and of reviews to *School Library Journal.*

WORK IN PROGRESS: A critical study of Arnold Loebel's fiction for Twayne; "various fiction projects and studying."

SIDELIGHTS: George Shannon wrote *CA:* "In recent years my focus in fiction has evolved from plot to characterization—especially how people live and feel between times of major events. While my focus has changed, my concern for distilled form has not. Less will always be more, for it creates the connective bridge between writer and reader as the reader invests himself in the story to create its full life."

SHAW, George
See BICKHAM, Jack M(iles)

* * *

SHAW, Linda 1938-

PERSONAL: Born November 28, 1938, in El Dorado, Ark.; married Bennett Shaw (a planning engineer), June 20, 1957; children: Randy, Shelley, Tim. *Education:* North Texas State University, B.Mus., 1977.

ADDRESSES: Home and office—500 Pecan St., Keene, Tex. 76059.

CAREER: Professional organist, 1972—. Piano teacher in Gainesville, Tex., 1972-77.

WRITINGS:

NOVELS; PUBLISHED BY SILHOUETTE BOOKS

December's Wine, 1982.
All She Ever Wanted, 1982.
After the Rain, 1983.
The Way of the Willow, 1983.
A Thistle in the Spring, 1983.
A Love Song and You, 1984.
One Pale, Fawn Glove, 1985.
The Sweet Rush of April, 1985.
Kisses Don't Count, 1985.
Something about Summer, 1986.
Fire at Dawn, 1987.
Santiago Heat, 1987.

OTHER PUBLISHERS

Ballad in Blue, Ballantine, 1979.
The Satin Vixen, Gallen, 1981.
An Innocent Deception, Gallen, 1981.
Prior Claim, Pocket Books, 1987.

WORK IN PROGRESS: Disarray and an untitled work, both for Silhouette Books.

SIDELIGHTS: Linda Shaw told *CA:* "I would like to see the romance genre develop a fine quality of writing and an experienced authorship that will command respect within the publishing industry. I would also like to see romance novels deal with the contemporary woman in a credible fashion."

She has twenty-seven titles in foreign translation, including Italian, Greek, Japanese, French, German, and Portuguese editions.

* * *

SHEBL, James M(ichael) 1942-

PERSONAL: Born July 1, 1942, in Tacoma, Wash.; son of Joseph J. (a physician) and Mary Ellen (Hurley) Shebl; married Patricia A. Pedroni, August 22, 1964; children: Bonnie Marie, Catherine Theresa. *Education:* Creighton University, B.A., 1965; University of Nebraska, M.A., 1969; University of the Pacific, Ph.D., 1974. *Politics:* "Left Conservative." *Religion:* Roman Catholic.

ADDRESSES: Home—3517 Stone River Cir., Stockton, Calif. 95209. *Office*—St. Joseph's Health Care Corp., 1800 North California St., Stockton, Calif. 95204.

CAREER: Worked as U.S. Air Force civilian instructor in swimming and diving, 1964-65, and as inspector of agricultural crops in California, 1969-70; University of the Pacific, Stockton, Calif., assistant to academic vice-president, 1972-78, assistant professor of humanities, 1975-83, associate director of Pacific Center for Western Historical Studies, 1975-80, assistant dean of Raymond-Callison College, 1978-79, director of foundation support, 1980-83; St. Joseph's Health Care Corp., Stockton, Calif., director of community relations, 1983—. Consultant to Knotts Berry Farm and Cahuilla Indian Reservation.

MEMBER: Westerners International, Modern Language Association of America, American Association of University Professors, Western Literature Association, Western History Association, Southwestern American Literature Association, Southwest Mission Research Center, Phi Kappa Psi (past president), Phi Kappa Phi (past president).

AWARDS, HONORS: Nominated for gold medallion for western writing by Commonwealth Club of California, 1974, for *King, of the Mountains;* U.S. Department of Interior fellowship in historic preservation.

WRITINGS:

(Author of introduction) Clarence King, *Mountaineering in the Sierra Nevada,* University of Nebraska Press, 1969.
King, of the Mountains, University of the Pacific Press, 1974.
(Co-editor and contributor) *Daddy Boy: Jack London's Inscriptions to His Wife Bessie,* Pacific Center for Western Studies, University of the Pacific, 1976.
(Contributor) *Pioneer or Perish: A History of the University of the Pacific, 1947-1972,* University of the Pacific, 1976.
In This Wild Water: The Suppressed Poems of Robinson Jeffers, Ritchie, 1976.
(Editor) *The Tulebreakers: The Story of the California Dredge,* Westerners (Stockton), 1982.
This Great Work: The Story of St. Joseph's Hospital, St. Joseph's Hospital (Stockton, Calif.), 1983.
Weber!: The Story of Charles M. Weber, Founder of Stockton, San Joaquin County Historical Society, 1987.

Contributor to *Valley Trails* (Westerners annual), 1980, and to *Arizona and the West, Pacific Historian, California Historian,* and *Far Westerner.* Former editor, *Far Westerner.*

WORK IN PROGRESS: Green Gold, a historical novel of the Salinas Valley; *Dear Una,* a drama of the early years of Robinson Jeffers; *Bear Faced Lies and Other True Stories . . . of California Bears.*

SIDELIGHTS: James M. Shebl told *CA:* "I have a keen interest in the past—especially as it influences the present, the future. I hope my work reflects, in part, the continuum of the American consciousness. Our history is wonderfully ambiguous; we have so much to learn and remember—but even the work of learning and remembering is enriching, I hope enough to improve our performance."

AVOCATIONAL INTERESTS: International travel, reading, athletics, Spanish California missions, the Sierra Nevada, backand horse-packing.

*   *   *

SHEPARD, Ernest Howard   1879-1976

PERSONAL: Born December 10, 1879, in St. John's Wood, London, England; died March 24, 1976, in Lodsworth, England; son of Henry Dunkin (an architect) and Harriet Jessie (Lee) Shepard (daughter of William Lee, watercolor painter); married Florence Eleanor Chaplin, September 28, 1904 (died, 1927); married Norah Radcliffe Mary Carroll, 1944; children: (first marriage) Mary Eleanor (illustrator of the *Mary Poppins* books; Mrs. E.G.V. Knox), Graham Howard (killed in World War II while serving with the Royal Navy). *Education:* Attended St. Paul's School, London, 1892-94, Heatherleys Art School, 1896, Royal Academy Schools, 1897-1902.

CAREER: Exhibited his work in many galleries, beginning 1901. Began drawing for *Punch* magazine, 1907, joined the round table, 1921, senior staff editor, 1929-45, political cartoonist, 1940-45 and afterwards until his retirement in 1953. *Military service:* Royal Artillery, 1915-19; became major; awarded military cross.

MEMBER: Art Worker's Guild, National Art Collections Fund, Artists General Benevolent Institution, Savage Club.

AWARDS, HONORS: Landseer Scholarship from the Royal Academy of Schools, 1898; British Institution Prize, 1900; Ohioana Award, 1952, for illustrations in *Enter David Garrick;* Spring Book Festival award, 1955, for illustrations in *Crystal Mountain;* Lewis Carroll Shelf Award, 1958, for *The Wind in the Willows* and *The World of Pooh,* 1962, for *The World of Christopher Robin,* and 1963, for *The Reluctant Dragon;* University of Southern Mississippi Medallion, 1970; Order of the British Empire, 1972.

WRITINGS:

SELF-ILLUSTRATED

Fun and Fantasy (drawings), Methuen (London), 1927.
(Compiler) Edward V. Lucas, *As the Bee Sucks* (verses), Methuen, 1937.
Drawn from Memory (autobiography; also see below), Lippincott, 1957, new edition, Penguin, 1975.
Drawn from Life (autobiography; also see below), Methuen (London), 1961, Dutton (New York), 1962.
Pooh, His Art Gallery: Prints from the World of Pooh and the World of Christopher Robin (drawings), Dutton, 1962.
Ben and Brock (juvenile), Methuen, 1965, Doubleday, 1966.
Betsy and Joe (juvenile), Methuen, 1966, Dutton, 1967.
Drawn from Memory; Drawn from Life: The Autobiography of Ernest H. Shepard, Methuen, 1986.

ILLUSTRATOR; BOOKS BY A. A. MILNE

When We Were Very Young (poems; also see below), Dutton, 1924, new edition, Methuen, 1934, Dutton, 1935, edition with foreword by Sir James Pitman, Dutton, 1966.
The King's Breakfast (also see below), Dutton, 1925.
Fourteen Songs from "When We Were Very Young" (also see below), Dutton, 1925.
Teddy Bear, and Other Songs from "When We Were Very Young," music by H. Fraser Simson, Dutton, 1926.
Winnie-the-Pooh (also see below), Dutton, 1926, new edition, Methuen, 1934, Dutton, 1935, edition with foreword by Sir James Pitman, Dutton, 1966, full color edition, Methuen, 1973, Dutton, 1974.
Now We Are Six (poems; also see below), Dutton, 1927, new edition, 1934, revised edition, 1961.
The House at Pooh Corner (also see below), Dutton, 1928, new edition, Methuen, 1934, Dutton, 1935, revised edition, Dutton, 1961, full color edition, Methuen, 1974.
The Christopher Robin Story Book (from *When We Were Very Young, Now We Are Six, Winnie-the-Pooh,* and *The House at Pooh Corner;* also see below), Dutton, 1929.

The Very Young Calendar, 1930 (verses), Dutton, 1929.
The Christopher Robin Calendar, Methuen, 1929.
When I Was Very Young, Fountain Press (New York), 1930.
Tales of Pooh (selections from *Winnie-the-Pooh* and *The House at Pooh Corner*), Methuen, 1930.
The Christopher Robin Birthday Book, Methuen, 1930, Dutton, 1931.
The Christopher Robin Verses (*When We Were Very Young* and *Now We Are Six* with new color illustrations), Dutton, 1932, published as *The Christopher Robin Book of Verse,* Dutton, 1967.
Songs from "Now We Are Six," Dutton, c. 1935.
More "Very Young" Songs, Dutton, 1937.
The Hums of Pooh (also see below), Dutton, 1937.
Sneezles, and Other Selections, Dutton, 1947.
Old Sailor, and Other Selections, Dutton, 1947.
Introducing Winnie-the-Pooh, and Other Selections, Dutton, 1947, Garden City Publishing, 1950.
Year In, Year Out, Dutton, 1952.
The World of Pooh (includes *Winnie-the-Pooh* and *The House at Pooh Corner;* with new illustrations in full color), Dutton, 1957.
The World of Christopher Robin (includes *When We Were Very Young* and *Now We Are Six;* with new illustrations in full color), Dutton, 1958.
Pooh's Library (contains *Now We Are Six, Winnie-the-Pooh, When We Were Very Young,* and *The House at Pooh Corner*), four volumes, Dutton, 1961.
The Pooh Song Book (contains *The Hums of Pooh, The King's Breakfast,* and *Fourteen Songs from "When We Were Very Young"*), Dutton, 1961, reprinted, Godine, 1985.
Pooh's Birthday Book, Dutton, 1963.
The Pooh Story Book (with decorations and illustrations in full color), Dutton, 1965, Methuen, 1982.
The Christopher Robin Story Book, Dutton, 1966.
The Christopher Robin Book of Verse (selections from *When We Were Very Young* and *Now We Are Six,* with decorations and illustrations in full color), Dutton, 1967 (published in England as *The Christopher Robin Verse Book,* Methuen, 1969, cased edition, 1983).
Pooh's Pot O' Honey (stories originally published in *Winnie-the-Pooh*), four volumes, Dutton, 1968.
The Hums of Pooh: Lyrics by Pooh, Methuen, 1972.
Pooh's Alphabet Book, Elsevier-Dutton, 1975.
Eeyore Has a Birthday, Methuen, 1975.
An Expotition to the North Pole, Methuen, 1975.
Kanga and Baby Roo Come to the Forest, Methuen, 1975.
Piglet Meets a Heffalump, Methuen, 1975.
Pooh Goes Visiting and Pooh and Piglet Nearly Catch a Woozle, Methuen, 1975.
Winnie-the-Pooh and Some Bees, Methuen, 1975.
Christopher Robin Gives a Pooh Party (story taken from *Winnie-the-Pooh*), Methuen, 1975.
A House Is Built at Pooh Corner for Eeyore (story taken from *The House at Pooh Corner*), Methuen Children's, 1976.
Piglet Is Entirely Surrounded by Water (story taken from *Winnie-the-Pooh*), Methuen, 1976.
Pooh Invents a New Game (story taken from *The House at Pooh Corner*), Methuen Children's, 1976.
Tigger Comes to the Forest and Has Breakfast (story taken from *The House at Pooh Corner*), Methuen, 1976.
Tigger Is Unbounced (story taken from *The House at Pooh Corner*), Methuen Children's, 1976.
Pooh's Quiz Book, Elsevier-Dutton, 1977.

Eeyore Finds the Wolery (story taken from *The House at Pooh Corner*), Methuen Children's, 1977.
Piglet Does a Very Grand Thing (story taken from *The House at Pooh Corner*), Methuen, 1977.
Tiggers Don't Climb Trees (story taken from *The House at Pooh Corner*), Methuen Children's, 1977.
Pooh's Bedtime Book (collection of stories and poems), Elsevier-Dutton, 1980.
Pooh's Counting Book, Dutton, 1982.
Where Is Eeyore's Tail?, Methuen, 1983.
Who Are Pooh's Friends?, Methuen, 1983.
Pooh's Rainy Day, Methuen, 1983.
Pooh and Piglet Build a House, Methuen, 1983.
What Does Tigger Like?, Methuen, 1984.
The King's Breakfast: A Selection of Verse from "When We Were Very Young," Methuen Children's, 1984.
Winnie-Ille-Pu: A Latin Version of A. A. Milne's "Winnie-the-Pooh," translated by Alexander Lenard, Dutton, 1984.
Winnie-the-Pooh's Calendar Book, 1986, Dutton, 1985.
Brian Sibley, compiler, *The Pooh Book of Quotations: In Which Will Be Found Some Useful Information and Sustaining Thoughts by Winnie-the-Pooh and His Friends,* Methuen, 1986.
The Winnie-the-Pooh Journal, Dutton, 1986.

Shepard's illustrations also appear in *Winnie-the-Pooh's Calendar Book, 1977* and annual revisions, published by Dutton.

ILLUSTRATOR; BOOKS BY LAURENCE HOUSMAN

Victoria Regina: A Dramatic Biography, J. Cape, 1934, Scribner, 1935.
Golden Sovereign (play), Scribner, 1937, J. Cape, 1940.
We Are Not Amused [and] *Happy and Glorious* (play), J. Cape, 1939.
Bedchamber Plot (play), J. Cape, 1939.
Suitable Suitors (play), J. Cape, 1939.
Stable Government (play), J. Cape, 1939.
Promotion Cometh (play), J. Cape, 1939.
Primrose Way (play), J. Cape, 1939.
Great Relief (play), J. Cape, 1939.
Go-Between (play), J. Cape, 1939.
Firelighters (play), J. Cape, 1939.
Enter Prince (play), J. Cape, 1939.
Comforter (play), J. Cape, 1939.
Gracious Majesty (scenes from the life of Queen Victoria), J. Cape, 1941, Scribner, 1942.

ILLUSTRATOR; BOOKS BY KENNETH GRAHAME

The Golden Age (limited autographed edition), John Lane, 1928, Dodd, 1929, edition with new illustrations, 1954, 5th edition, Bodley Head, 1973.
Dream Days (also see below), new edition, John Lane, 1930, Dodd, 1931, edition with new illustrations, Dodd, 1954, reprinted, Bodley Head, 1973.
The Wind in the Willows (first edition published in 1908 without Shepard illustrations), Methuen, 1931, Scribner, 1933, new edition, 1953, edition with new color plates, Methuen, 1959, new edition with introduction and study guide by Marsden V. Dillenbeck and Ellen W. Brooks, Scribner, 1964, simplified edition by Sue Ullstein, Longman, 1982, with preface by Margaret Hodges, Macmillan, 1983.
The Reluctant Dragon (previously published as a chapter in *Dream Days*), Holiday House, 1938, Deutsch, 1986.
Bertie's Escapade (first published in *First Whisper of the Wind in the Willows*), Lippincott, 1949, Harper, 1977.
Toad's Tale, Methuen, c. 1982.

ILLUSTRATOR; BOOKS BY MALCOLM SAVILLE

Susan, Bill and the Wolf-Dog, Ted Nelson, 1954.
Susan, Bill and the Ivy-clad Oak, Ted Nelson, 1954.
Susan, Bill and the Vanishing Boy, Ted Nelson, 1955.
Susan, Bill and the Golden Clock, Ted Nelson, 1955.
Susan, Bill and the "Saucy Kate," Ted Nelson, 1956, reprinted, White Lion Publishers, 1976.
Susan, Bill and the Dark Stranger, Ted Nelson, 1956, reprinted, White Lion Publishers, 1973.

ILLUSTRATOR; BOOKS BY OTHER AUTHORS

Thomas Hughes, *Tom Brown's Schooldays,* c. 1904, new edition, Ginn, 1956.
Hugh Walpole, *Jeremy,* Cassell, 1919.
A. C. Benson and Sir Lawrence Weaver, editors, *Everybody's Book of the Queen's Doll's House,* Methuen, 1924.
Edward Verrall Lucas, *Playtime and Company,* Doubleday, Doran, 1925, published as *A Book of Children's Verse,* 1925.
Samuel Pepys, *Everybody's Pepys,* abridged and edited by O. F. Morshead, G. Bell, 1926, Harcourt, 1931.
Charles Dickens, *The Holly-tree, and Other Christmas Stories,* Scribner, 1926.
Eva Violet Isaacs (Marchioness of Reading), *The Little One's Log,* Partridge (London), 1927.
Georgette Agnew, *Let's Pretend* (poems), Putnam, 1927.
Lucas, *Mr. Punch's County Songs,* Methuen, 1928.
Anthony Armstrong (pseudonym of Anthony Armstrong Willis), *Livestock in Barracks,* Methuen, 1929.
James Boswell, *Everybody's Boswell,* abridged and edited by F. V. Morley, Harcourt, 1930, Bell & Hyman, 1980, new edition published as *The Life of Samuel Johnson and The Journal of a Tour to the Hebrides with Samuel Johnson,* Harper, 1966.
John Drinkwater, *Christmas Poems,* Sidgwick & Jackson, 1931.
Jan Struther (pseudonym of Joyce Maxtone Graham), *Sycamore Square* (verse), Methuen, 1932.
Richard Jeffries, *Bevis: The Story of a Boy,* new edition, P. Smith, 1932, abridged edition, Puffin Books, 1974.
Boswell, *The Great Cham (Dr. Johnson),* G. Bell, 1933.
Everybody's Lamb, abridged and edited by A. C. Ward, G. Bell, 1933, with new title page by E. H. Shepard, 1950.
Patrick R. Chalmers, *The Cricket in the Cage* (verse), Macmillan, 1933.
Lady Winifred Fortescue, *Perfume from Provence,* Blackwood, 1935.
Euphan (pseudonym of Barbara Euphan Todd), *The Seventh Daughter,* Burn Oats, 1935.
Struther, *The Modern Struwelpeter,* Methuen, 1936.
John Collings Squire, editor, *Cheddar Gorge,* Collins, 1937, Macmillan (New York), 1938.
(Frontispiece) Fortescue, *Sunset House,* Blackwood, 1937, published as *Sunset House: More Perfume from Provence,* Chivers, 1974.
Roland Pertwee, *The Islanders,* Oxford University Press, 1950.
Anna B. Stewart, *Enter David Garrick,* Lippincott, 1951.
Eleanor Farjeon, *The Silver Curlew,* Oxford University Press, 1953, Viking, 1954.
Juliana Ewing, *The Brownies, and Other Stories,* Dutton, 1954.
Mary Louisa Molesworth, *The Cuckoo Clock,* Dutton, 1954.
E. and Herbert Farjeon, *Glass Slipper,* Oxford University Press, 1955, Viking, 1956, reprinted, Goodchild, 1983.
Pertwee, *Operation Wild Goose,* Oxford University Press, 1955.
Susan Colling, *Frogmorton,* Collins, 1955, Knopf, 1956.
Roger L. Green, editor, *Modern Fairy Stories,* Dutton, 1955.

George MacDonald, *At the Back of the North Wind,* Dutton, 1956.
B. D. Rugh, *The Crystal Mountain,* Riverside Press, 1956.
Francis Hodgson Burnett, *The Secret Garden,* Heinemann, 1956.
Shirley Goulden, *Royal Reflections,* Methuen, 1956.
J. Fassett, editor, *The Pancake,* Ginn, 1957.
Green, editor, *Old Greek Fairy Tales,* Bell & Hyman, 1958, reprinted, 1978.
Fassett, editor, *Briar Rose,* Ginn, 1958.
Hans Christian Andersen, *Fairy Tales,* translated by L. W. Kingsland, Oxford University Press, 1961, Walck, 1962.
J. Compton, editor, *A Noble Company,* Ginn, 1961.
Emile Victor Rieu, *The Flattered Flying Fish, and Other Poems,* Dutton, 1962.
Virginia H. Ellison, *The Pooh Cook Book,* Dutton, 1969.
Ellison, *The Pooh Party Book,* Dutton, 1971.
Katie Stewart, *The Pooh Cook Book: Inspired by "Winnie-the-Pooh" and "The House at Pooh Corner" by A. A. Milne,* Methuen Children's, 1971.
Patsy Kumm, *The Pooh Party Book: Inspired by "Winnie-the-Pooh" and "The House at Pooh Corner" by A. A. Milne,* Methuen, 1975.
Ellison, *The Pooh Get-Well Book: Recipes and Activities to Help You Recover from Wheezles and Sneezles,* Dell, 1975.
Rawle Knox, editor, *The Work of E. H. Shepard,* Methuen, 1979, Schocken, 1980.
Benjamin Hoff, *The Tao of Pooh,* Methuen, 1982.
Brian Sibley, editor, *The Pooh Sketch Book,* Methuen, 1982, Dutton, 1984.
Lady Arabella Boxer, *The Wind in the Willows Country Cook Book: Inspired by "The Wind in the Willows" by Kenneth Grahame,* Scribner, 1983.
Ethan Mordden, *Pooh's Workout Book,* Dutton, c. 1984.
Stewart, *Pooh's Fireside Recipes: Inspired by "Winnie-the-Pooh" and "The House at Pooh Corner" by A. A. Milne,* Methuen Children's, 1985.
Stewart, *Pooh's Picnic Recipes,* Methuen Children's, 1985.

Also illustrator of *Tom Brown's Schooldays* by Thomas Hughes; *Toby* by Grace Allingham; *David Copperfield* by Charles Dickens; *Aesop's Fables,* adapted by Rev. G. Henslow; *Henry Esmond* by W. M. Thackeray; *Play the Game!* by Harold Avery; *Money or Wife* by Effie Adelaide Rowlands; and *Smouldering Fires* by Evelyn Everett Green; all published between 1900 and 1914.

OTHER

Contributor of drawings to *Punch* and other illustrated magazines.

SIDELIGHTS: British artist, illustrator, cartoonist, and author Ernest Howard Shepard was a master of line, "the last of the great Victorian [pen-and-ink draughtsmen]," Bevis Hillier writes in *The Work of E. H. Shepard.* The book's author, Rawle Knox, observes that Shepard gave a "lightness and movement . . . to everything he drew or painted," but figures drawn for Kenneth Grahame's *The Wind in the Willows* and A. A. Milne's *Winnie-the-Pooh* are the artist's most famous works. As Knox explains, "The visual characters that Shepard made of . . . Milne's inspired collection of Christopher Robin's friends are universally known." Roy Strong comments in the foreword to *A Pooh Sketch Book* that "Shepard's illustrations to . . . [the] Pooh stories form without a doubt one of the great classics of children's book illustration."

Shepard began to draw as a boy, to illustrate his sister's stories. He disclosed in *Drawn from Memory* that his father "had quite decided that I should be an artist when I grew up, though I myself considered an artist's life to be a dull one and looked for something more adventurous.'' But his mother, the daughter of William Lee, the watercolorist, also encouraged his drawing, and when she died, the young Shepard ''missed her companionship terribly and determined to justify her faith'' in his abilities, he related in *Drawn from Life*. He attended art schools, won competitions and scholarships, and exhibited his work for the first time in 1901.

Shepard illustrated books and contributed cartoons to *Punch* magazine for twenty years before the *Pooh* books brought him fame. R. G. G. Price recalls in *A History of Punch* that Shepard's drawings made the rest of the magazine ''look static.'' Figures drawn by others sat ''heavily'' on their chairs, but ''even when the scene in Shepard was a conversation,'' says Price, it captured the feeling ''that there was a wind in the room and that someone had just moved and that someone else was about to move.'' Brian Sibley suggests in his introduction to *The Pooh Sketch Book* that ''Shepard's talent lay in his gentleness as an observer of life, and in the accuracy and precision of his draughtsmanship.''

Shepard's drawings first accompanied Milne's verses ''When We Were Very Young'' in a 1924 issue of *Punch*. The combination sold out on the first day it was published in book form. Its success moved E. V. Lucas to invite Shepard to illustrate *Playtime and Company*, and ''for the rest of the decade, commissions came in thick and fast,'' reports Knox. Shepard made sixty drawings for *Everybody's Pepys*, another instant success that prompted G. Bell and Sons to publish *Everybody's Boswell* and *Everybody's Lamb* with new illustrations by Shepard. During these years the artist produced what is generally considered to be his best work. His illustrations for *Bevis: The Story of a Boy* by Richard Jeffries made the book popular for the first time since its appearance in 1882. Shepard also illustrated Laurence Housman's published plays during this period, and a number of children's books, notably *The Golden Age*, *The Wind in the Willows*, and *The Reluctant Dragon* by Grahame, and Lady Winifred Fortescue's *Perfume from Provence*.

Work on Milne's *Winnie the Pooh* began with a visit to the author's home to sketch scenes from Ashdown Forest in which Christopher Robin, Tigger, Piglet, Eeyore, Kanga, and Roo would share the title figure's adventures. Studies and photos of Milne's son Christopher and the boy's stuffed toys were also made. Figures in the book were drawn from these originals, except for Pooh, who was modeled after Growler, a stuffed bear that had belonged to Shepard's own son, Graham. A similar visit to Kenneth Grahame's country home resulted in sketches that convinced the wary author that Shepard could interpret *The Wind in the Willows* more to his satisfaction than previous illustrators. ''As with Milne's Pooh books, . . . Shepard's pictured animal characters took over the printed page,'' Knox says of Toad, Rat, Mole and Badger as they appeared in the last edition of the book approved before Grahame's death. Shepard's renditions preserved Grahame's affection for the creatures of *The Wind in the Willows* and sustained more popular appeal than those of other illustrators, writes Knox.

With two autobiographies, *Drawn from Memory* and *Drawn from Life*, the famous illustrator began a second career as a writer when he was eighty; when nearing ninety, he wrote the children's books *Ben and Brock*, in which a boy discovers smugglers in a badger's cave, and *Betsy and Joe*, which blends

a kidnap-and-rescue story with an old tramp's memories of World War I. All the while, Knox points out, the demand for Pooh illustrations steadily increased, as ''the public devotion to Pooh developed . . . almost into a fetish.'' To meet this demand, Shepard added color to early line drawings and produced so many new ones during the 1960s that he said he was getting rather tired of that ''silly bear,'' Knox relates. The bear's popularity—and Shepard's fame—spread as Milne's classics were translated and published around the world. A Russian translation of *Winnie the Pooh* and *The House at Pooh Corner*, for instance, ''has become one of the most popular children's books in that country,'' reports an *Ann Arbor News* article. Shepard was ninety when he did his last work, adding color to original drawings of *Winnie the Pooh* and *The House at Pooh Corner* for their new editions. By then, 1972, admiration for his work had grown such that he was given the Order of the British Empire for his life's work. Blindness brought that work to an end several years before Shepard's death in 1976.

The Kerlan collection at the University of Minnesota includes some of Shepard's works; originals of his *Punch* cartoons are at the University of Kent; original sketches for *Winnie-the-Pooh* and *The House at Pooh Corner* are kept at the Victoria and Albert Museum; and paintings made by Shepard during his years as a soldier in World War I are housed at the Imperial War Museum.

MEDIA ADAPTATIONS: ''Winnie the Pooh and the Honey Tree,'' based on Shepard's illustrations, was filmed by Walt Disney Productions in 1965.

AVOCATIONAL INTERESTS: Gardening, reading.

BIOGRAPHICAL/CRITICAL SOURCES:

BOOKS

Crouch, Marcus, *Treasure Seekers and Borrowers*, Library Association, 1962.
Field, Eleanor Whitney, editor, *Horn Book Reflections on Children's Books and Reading*, Horn Book, 1969.
Knox, Rawle, editor, *The Work of E. H. Shepard*, Schocken, 1980.
Oxbury, H. F., *Great Britons: Twentieth-Century Lives*, Oxford University Press, 1985.
Price, R. G. G., *A History of Punch*, Collins, 1957.
Shepard, Ernest Howard, *Drawn from Memory* (autobiography), Lippincott, 1957.
Shepard, Ernest Howard, *Drawn from Life* (autobiography), Methuen, 1961.
Sibley, Brian, editor, *The Pooh Sketch Book*, Methuen, 1982, Dutton, 1984.

PERIODICALS

Ann Arbor News, January 1, 1987.
Christian Science Monitor, March 21, 1963, May 5, 1966.
McCalls, August, 1970.
New York Review of Books, December 18, 1980.
Times Educational Supplement, November 12, 1982.
Times Literary Supplement, January 12, 1962.

OBITUARIES:

PERIODICALS

Bookseller, April 3, 1976.
New York Times, March 27, 1976.

Publishers Weekly, April 12, 1976.
School Library Journal, May, 1976.†

—*Sketch by Marilyn K. Basel*

*   *   *

SHEPPARD, Joseph 1930-

PERSONAL: Born December 20, 1930, in Owings Mills, Md.; son of Joseph E. and Edna (Marquiss) Sheppard; divorced; children: Jonathan, William, Joseph. *Education:* Maryland Institute of Art, fine art certificate, 1952; studied privately with Jacques Maroger.

ADDRESSES: Home—Regnalla 6, Valdicastello, Pietrasanta, Lucca 55045, Italy; and P.O. Box 276, Camden, Del. 19934.

CAREER: Artist. Artist-in-residence and instructor in oil painting, Dickinson College, 1955-57; instructor in oil painting, Maryland Institute of Art, 1963-75. One-man shows at Butler Institute of American Art, 1964 and 1972, Westmoreland County Museum, 1966 and 1972, and Davenport Municipal Art Gallery, 1967; work included in many public and private collections including Baltimore Museum of Art, Columbus Museum of Fine Arts, University of Arizona Museum, Brooks Memorial Art Gallery, Fine Arts Museum of the South, and the Malcolm Forbes Collection. Also painter of commissioned works for organizations.

MEMBER: Allied Artists of America, National Sculpture Society, Society of Animal Artists, Knickerbocker Artists (New York).

AWARDS, HONORS: Emily Lowe Prize, Allied Artists exhibition, 1956; Guggenheim fellowship, 1957-58; John F. and Anna Lee Stacy Award, 1958; Bronze Medal of Honor, Allied Artists of America Exhibition, 1959; Prize for Figure Painting, Allied Artists of America, 1963; first purchase award, Butler Institute of American Art, 1963; John J. McDonough Prize, Butler Institute of American Art, 1967; Governor's Prize, Maryland Artists' Exhibition, 1971; Tallix Foundry Prize, National Sculpture Society Exhibition, 1983; Award of Merit, Society of Animal Artists, 1983; Paul Puzinas Award, Allied Artists of America, 1984; William Meyerowitz Memorial Award, Allied Artists of America, 1985; Agop Agopoff Memorial Prize, National Sculpture Society Exhibition, 1986.

WRITINGS:

Anatomy: A Complete Guide for Artists, Watson-Guptill, 1975.
Drawing the Female Figure, Watson-Guptill, 1975.
Illustrations for Socrates, Stemmer House, 1975.
Drawing the Male Figure, Watson-Guptill, 1976.
Learning from the Masters, Watson-Guptill, 1979.
Illustrations for Keeping Christmas, Stemmer House, 1981.
The Work of Joseph Sheppard, Georgi & Gambi, 1982.
Drawing the Living Figure, Watson-Guptill, 1984.
Bringing Textures to Life, Watson-Guptill, 1987.

SIDELIGHTS: Anatomy: A Complete Guide for Artists, Drawing the Female Figure, and *Drawing the Male Figure* have been translated into Japanese; *Drawing the Living Figure* has been translated into Italian and German.

BIOGRAPHICAL/CRITICAL SOURCES:

BOOKS

Sheppard, Joseph, *The Work of Joseph Sheppard,* Georgi & Gambi, 1982.

SHERIDAN, Eugene Robert 1945-

PERSONAL: Born January 23, 1945, in New York, N.Y.; son of Eugene Bernard (a steelworker) and Muriel Ann (Roche) Sheridan; married Sylvia Ann Deprez, June 8, 1968; children: Maureen Mary. *Education:* Fordham University, B.A., 1966; University of Wisconsin—Madison, M.A., 1968, Ph.D., 1972. *Politics:* Independent. *Religion:* Roman Catholic.

ADDRESSES: Home—46 Pine Knoll Dr., Lawrenceville, N.J. 08648. *Office*—Department of History, Princeton University, 129 Dickinson Hall, Princeton, N.J. 08540.

CAREER: Massachusetts Historical Society, Boston, history editor of "John Adams Papers," 1972-73; Library of Congress, Washington, D.C., history editor of "Letters of the Continental Congress," 1973-81; Princeton University, Princeton, N.J., history editor of "The Thomas Jefferson Papers," 1981—.

MEMBER: Organization of American Historians, Institute of Early American History and Culture (associate), Association of Documentary Editors.

AWARDS, HONORS: Fellow of American Philosophical Society, 1973-74; fellow of New Jersey Historical Commission, 1973-74, 1978-79, and 1985-87; Alfred E. Driscoll Prize, New Jersey Historical Commission, 1980, for *Lewis Morris, 1671-1746: A Study in Early American Politics;* Book Prize, Society of Colonial Wars, 1983; History Prize, Society of the Cincinnati, 1986.

WRITINGS:

(Editor with Paul H. Smith and others) *Letters of Delegates to Congress, 1774-1789,* eleven volumes, U.S. Government Printing Office, 1976-81.
(Contributor) Robert J. Taylor and others, editors, *Papers of John Adams,* Volumes I-II, Harvard University Press, 1977.
Lewis Morris, 1671-1746: A Study in Early American Politics, Syracuse University Press, 1981.
(Editor with Charles T. Cullen and others) *Papers of Thomas Jefferson,* Princeton University Press, Volume XXI: *1760-1791* (includes index to Volumes I-XX), 1982, Volume XXII: *August 6-December 31, 1791,* 1986, Volume XXIII: *January 1-May 31, 1792,* 1987.
(Author of introduction) D. W. Adams, editor, *Jefferson's Extracts From the Gospels,* Princeton University Press, 1983.
Congress at Princeton, Princeton University Press, 1985.
(Editor) *Papers of Lewis Morris, 1691-1746,* two volumes, New Jersey Historical Society, in press.

Contributor to history journals.

*   *   *

SHOOK, Robert L. 1938-

PERSONAL: Born April 7, 1938, in Pittsburgh, Pa.; son of Herbert M. (an insurance executive) and Belle (Slutsky) Shook; married Roberta Gay Wolk, April 18, 1962; children: Faith Caroline, Robert James, Michael David. *Education:* Ohio State University, B.S., 1959. *Religion:* Jewish.

ADDRESSES: Home—261 South Columbia Ave., Columbus, Ohio 43209.

CAREER: Shook Associates Corp., Columbus, Ohio, chairman of board, 1961—, partner in Atlantic Division, 1964-78; American Executive Corp., Columbus, chairman of board, 1973-

78; American Executive Life Insurance Co., Phoenix, Ariz., chairman of board, 1973-78; full-time writer, 1978—. Has appeared on more than six hundred radio and television talk shows, including "David Susskind," "Sally Jessy Raphael," and "Today." Director, J. Ashburn Youth Center, 1974—. Member of board, Columbus Film Association, 1980-82, American Cancer Society, 1984-87, and Players Theatre and Opera, Columbus, both 1986-87. *Military service:* U.S. Army, 1960; U.S. Army Reserves, 1960-61.

WRITINGS:

(With father, Herbert M. Shook) *How to Be the Complete Professional Salesman,* Fell, 1974.
(With Ronald L. Bingaman) *Total Commitment,* Fell, 1975.
Winning Images: Nothing Succeeds Like the Appearance of Success, Macmillan, 1977.
Ten Greatest Salespersons (Fortune Book-of-the-Month selection), Harper, 1978.
The Entrepreneurs, Harper, 1980.
The Real Estate People, Harper, 1980.
The Chief Executive Officers, Harper, 1981.
(Ghostwriter) *Mary Kay* (autobiography), Harper, 1981.
(With Martin Shafiroff) *Successful Telephone Selling in the 80's,* Harper, 1982.
Why Didn't I Think of That?, New American Library, 1982.
The Shaklee Story, Harper, 1982.
The Book of Why, Hammond, Inc., 1983.
(With daughter, Carrie Shook) *What to Name Your Dog,* Tribeca Communications, 1983.
Survivors: Living with Cancer, Harper, 1983.
(With Stephanie Simonton) *The Healing Family,* Bantam, 1984.
(With Joe Gandolfo) *Joe Gandolfo's How to Make Big Money Selling,* Harper, 1984.
(Ghostwriter) *Mary Kay on People Management,* Warner Books, 1984.
(With Buck Rodgers) *The IBM Way: Insights into the World's Most Successful Marketing Organization,* Harper, 1986.
(With David Sams) *Wheel of Fortune,* St. Martin's, 1987.

WORK IN PROGRESS: Honda: An American Success Story.

SIDELIGHTS: Robert L. Shook writes: "I have a business background and have always been sales-oriented. In considering an idea for a book I always address myself to the questions: What is my market? Who will want to buy a book on this subject? After all, like any other businessperson, an author has a product that must be sold. In negotiating with publishers, I always offer to help market the book in many non-traditional ways (outside retail book stores). I believe that an author must make every effort to help sell his book. My motto is, 'Nothing happens until something is sold.'"

BIOGRAPHICAL/CRITICAL SOURCES:

PERIODICALS

Los Angeles Times Book Review, July 18, 1982.
New York Times Book Review, April 13, 1980.
Wall Street Journal, February 5, 1986.
Washington Post, October 23, 1981.

*   *   *

SICHEL, Werner   1934-

PERSONAL: Born September 23, 1934, in Munich, Germany (now West Germany); son of Joseph and Lilly (Greenwood) Sichel; married Beatrice Bonne, February 22, 1959; children:

Lawrence, Linda. *Education:* New York University, B.S., 1956; Northwestern University, M.A., 1960, Ph.D., 1964.

ADDRESSES: Home—5046 Merryweather Lane, Kalamazoo, Mich. 49007. *Office*—Department of Economics, Western Michigan University, Kalamazoo, Mich. 49008.

CAREER: Roosevelt University, Chicago, Ill., assistant professor, 1959-60; Western Michigan University, Kalamazoo, instructor, 1960-64, assistant professor, 1964-66, associate professor, 1966-72, professor of economics, 1972—; chairman of department, 1985—. Instructor, Lake Forest College, 1959-62; Fulbright senior lecturer, University of Belgrade, 1968-69; visiting scholar, Hoover Institution, Stanford University, 1984-85.

MEMBER: American Economic Association.

WRITINGS:

(With Peter Eckstein) *Basic Economic Concepts: An Aid to the Study of Economic Problems,* Rand McNally, 1974, 2nd edition, 1977, Volume I: *Microeconomics,* Volume II: *Macroeconomics.*
(With Martin Bronfenbrenner and Wayland Gardner) *Economics,* with study guide, instructor's manual, and test bank, Houghton, 1984, 2nd edition, 1987, Volume I: *Macroeconomics,* Volume II: *Microeconomics.*
(With wife, Beatrice Sichel) *Economic Journals and Serials: An Analytical Guide,* Greenwood Press, 1986.

EDITOR

Industrial Organization and Public Policy: Selected Readings, Houghton, 1967.
Antitrust Policy and Economic Welfare, Bureau of Business Research, University of Michigan, 1970.
(With Thomas G. Gies) *Public Utility Regulation: Change and Scope,* Heath, 1975.
The Economic Effects of Multinational Corporations, Bureau of Business Research, University of Michigan, 1975.
Salvaging Public Utility Regulation, Lexington Books, 1976.
Economic Advice and Executive Policy: Recommendations from Past Members of the Council of Economics Advisers, Praeger, 1978.
Public Utility Rate Making in an Energy Conscious Environment, Westview, 1979.
(With Gies) *Applications of Economic Principles in Public Utility Industries,* Division of Research, Graduate School of Business Administration, University of Michigan, 1981.
(With Gies) *Deregulation: Appraisal before the Fact,* Division of Research, Graduate School of Business Administration, University of Michigan, 1982.

OTHER

Contributor of articles to professional journals, including *Journal of Risk and Insurance, St. John's Law Review, Antitrust Bulletin, Antitrust Law and Economic Review,* and *Journal of Economic Issues.*

*   *   *

SIMOONS, Frederick J.   1922-

PERSONAL: Born November 2, 1922, in Philadelphia, Pa.; son of Frederick J. and Stephanie M. (Ryckboer) Simoons; married in 1949. *Education:* Rutgers University, B.A., 1949; Harvard University, graduate study, 1949-50; University of California, Berkeley, M.A., 1952, Ph.D., 1956.

ADDRESSES: Home—2927 Salem Ave., Davis, Calif. 95616. *Office*—Department of Geography, University of California, Davis, Calif. 95616.

CAREER: Ohio State University, Columbus, instructor, 1956-57; University of Wisconsin—Madison, assistant professor, 1957-60, associate professor, 1960-64, professor of geography, 1964-66; Louisiana State University, Baton Rouge, professor of geography, 1966-67; University of Texas at Austin, professor of geography, 1967-69; University of California, Davis, professor of geography, 1969—, chairman of department, 1973-77. Consultant, National Institute of Child Health and Human Development. *Military service:* U.S. Army, 1944-46; became sergeant.

MEMBER: International Organization for the Study of Human Development.

AWARDS, HONORS: John Simon Guggenheim Memorial Foundation fellow, 1963-64.

WRITINGS:

Northwest Ethiopia: Peoples and Economy, University of Wisconsin Press, 1960, reprinted, Greenwood Press, 1983.
Eat Not This Flesh: Food Avoidances in the Old World, University of Wisconsin Press, 1961, reprinted, Greenwood Press, 1980.
(With Elizabeth S. Simoons) *A Ceremonial Ox of India: The Mithan in Nature, Culture, and History,* University of Wisconsin Press, 1968.

*   *   *

SIMPER, Robert   1937-

PERSONAL: Born December 12, 1937, in Blaxhall, Suffolk, England; son of Norman Edward (a farmer) and Lillian (Turner) Simper; married Pearl Bater, July 18, 1959; children: Caroline Sara, Joanna Eleanor, Jonathan Robert. *Education:* Attended Royal Agricultural College, 1957-58. *Politics:* "Middle of the road."

ADDRESSES: Home—Sluice Cottage, Ramsholt, Woodbridge, Suffolk 1P12 3AD, England.

CAREER: Worker on Simper Farms (family farm), 1953—, partner, 1962—; director, N. E. Simper & Son (farming company), Suffolk, England; sailor and writer on agriculture, sailing, traditional vessels, and travel, 1962—.

MEMBER: Society for Nautical Research, American National Maritime Historical Society, Old Gaffers Association (vice-president, 1977-82; president, 1983—).

WRITINGS:

Over Snape Bridge, East Anglian Magazine, 1967.
Woodbridge and Beyond, East Anglian Magazine, 1972.
East Coast Sail, David & Charles, 1972.
Scottish Sail, David & Charles, 1974.
North East Sail, David & Charles, 1976.
British Sail, David & Charles, 1977.
(Contributor) Spencer Smith, editor, *Yachtsman's Winterbook,* McKay, 1978.
Victorian and Edwardian Yachting from Old Photographs, Batsford, 1978.
Gaff Sail, Argus Books, 1979.
Traditions of East Anglia, Boydell Press, 1980.
Suffolk Show, East Anglian Daily Times, 1981.
Britain's Maritime Heritage, David & Charles, 1982.

Sail in the Orwell, Maritime Ipswich, 1982.
Beach Boats of Britain, Boydell Press, 1984.
Sail: The Surviving Tradition, Conway Maritime Press, 1984.
East Anglian Coast and Waterways, East Anglian Magazine, 1985.
(Contributor) *Under Sail,* BBC Publications, 1986.
The Suffolk Sandlings: Alde, Deben and Orwell Country, East Anglian Magazine, 1986.

Author of column "Sail Review" in *Sea Breezes,* 1966—. Contributor to agriculture and sailing magazines and newspapers.

SIDELIGHTS: Robert Simper told *CA:* "I began writing accidently because of a prolonged back injury. The result has been that my living has remained in farming, an occupation I get a great deal of pleasure from, but writing satisfies the creative side of my nature. Much of my writing is intended to encourage people to preserve traditional working craft. I have researched, so far, throughout the British Isles, Western Europe, the West Indies, the eastern United States, Canada, and Kenya.

"I am a believer in democracy and working towards some form of stable world peace. Every area should retain its own individual identity and culture, but co-exist with its neighbour. This belief means that Britain should stay firmly united and part of the Western European community."

AVOCATIONAL INTERESTS: Photography (has used several of own photographs to illustrate books), meeting people, travel.

*   *   *

SINCLAIR, Donna   1943-

PERSONAL: Born December 24, 1943, in Englehart, Ontario, Canada; daughter of Frank A. (a railroad employee) and Margaret (MacQueen) Knapp; married James Sinclair (a minister), July 1, 1966; children: David, Andrew, Tracy. *Education:* University of Toronto, B.A., 1964. *Religion:* United Church of Canada.

ADDRESSES: Home and office—1400 Pinegrove Cres., North Bay, Ontario, Canada P1B 4B8.

CAREER: Teacher of English, history, and art at collegiate institute in Toronto, Ontario, 1964-67; Knob Lake Protestant School, Schefferville, Quebec, teacher of history and geography, 1967-69; free-lance writer, 1969—. Leader of workshops and seminars, 1975—; creative writing teacher at Canadore College, 1979-81, and 1982-87.

WRITINGS:

The Pastor's Wife Today, Abingdon, 1981.
"A Time to Mourn, a Time to Dance" (screenplay), United Church of Canada, 1981.
Worth Remembering, Woodlake Books, 1984.
Living Together in Marriage, United Church of Canada, 1985.

Contributor to magazines, including *Financial Post* and *Christian Ministry.* Editor of "Kidspace," in *United Church Observer,* 1975-77, contributing editor, 1979—.

WORK IN PROGRESS: Research on children and "in the area of dreams and their interpretation by/for 'ordinary' people."

SIDELIGHTS: Donna Sinclair wrote: "My writing, generally, is informed by my ongoing task of balancing the creative life in writing with the creative life in nurturing children, in working out how to balance the sense of solitude required to write and the sense of otherness required to live in the world and maintain relationships. I am deeply interested in Jungian psychology; and I have a particular interest in both the very young, and the very old, especially in the things they share (a different attitude to productivity than the other generations, perhaps).

"Another 'item to balance' in the struggle to make enough time for real productivity in writing is the part of my life devoted to conducting workshops and seminars on various subjects—usually concerning children and family, or sometimes creative writing, and sometimes dreams as ways to spiritual growth."

BIOGRAPHICAL/CRITICAL SOURCES:

PERIODICALS

Globe and Mail (Toronto), March 29, 1986.

* * *

SINGER, Milton Borah   1912-

PERSONAL: Born July 15, 1912, in Poland; brought to the United States in 1920, natualized citizen, 1921; son of Julius M. and Esther (Greenberg) Singer; married Helen Goldbaum, October 1, 1935. *Education:* University of Texas, Main (now University of Texas at Austin), B.A., 1934, M.A., 1936; University of Chicago, Ph.D., 1940.

ADDRESSES: Office—Department of Anthropology, University of Chicago, Chicago, Ill. 60637.

CAREER: University of Chicago, Chicago, Ill., member of faculty, beginning in 1941, professor of social sciences, 1950-52, Paul Klapper Professor of Social Sciences, 1952-79, Paul Klapper Professor of Social Sciences Emeritus, 1979—, professor of anthropology, 1954-79, professor emeritus, 1979—, chairman of social sciences staff, 1947-53, executive secretary of committee on Asian studies, 1955-67, chairman of committee, 1967-70, chairman of civilization studies and member of governing board of New Collegiate Division, 1966-71, associate director of Redfield project on comparative civilizations, 1951-61, co-director of South Asia Language and Area Center, 1959-63. Center for Psychosocial Studies, Chicago, Ill., research advisor, 1979—. Senior anthropologist at Institute of International Studies, University of California, Berkeley, 1956; fellow of Center for Advanced Studies in the Behavioral Sciences, Palo Alto, Calif., 1957-58; fellow of American Institute of Indian Studies, 1964; visiting professor at University of Hawaii, 1966-67, and University of California, San Diego, 1971.

MEMBER: International Society for the Comparative Study of Civilization (honorary member), American Academy of Arts and Sciences (fellow), American Anthropological Association (fellow), American Institute of Indian Studies (vice-president, 1961-64), Association for Asian Studies, Phi Beta Kappa.

AWARDS, HONORS: Quantrell Award for excellence in undergraduate teaching, University of Chicago, 1948; Distinguished Scholarship Award, Association for Asian Studies, 1984; Silver Pen Award for learned publication from the Journal Fund.

WRITINGS:

(Translator with wife, Helen Singer) A. Gratry, *Logic,* Open Court, 1944.
(With Gerhart Piers) *Shame and Guilt: A Psychoanalytic and a Cultural Study,* Norton, 1953, 2nd edition, 1973.
(Editor) *Introducing India in Liberal Education: Proceedings of a Conference Held at University of Chicago, May 17, 18, 1957,* University of Chicago, 1957.
(Editor and contributor) *Traditional India: Structure and Change,* American Folklore Society, 1959.
(Editor and contributor) *Kishna: Myths, Rites, and Attitudes,* East-West Center Press, 1966.
(Editor with Bernard S. Cohn, and contibutor) *Structure and Change in Indian Society,* Wenner-Gren Foundation for Anthropological Research, 1968.
When a Great Tradition Modernizes: An Anthropological Approach to Indian Civilization, Praeger, 1972.
(Editor and contributor) *Entrepreneurship and Modernization of Occupational Cultures in South Asia,* Duke University, 1973.
Man's Glassy Essence: Explorations in Semiotic Anthropology, Indiana University Press, 1984.
(Contributor) H. Varenne, editor, *Symbolizing America,* University of Nebraska Press, 1986.
(Contributor) M. Case and G. Barrier, editors, *Essays in Honor of Edward C. Dimock, Jr.,* Manohar (Delhi), 1986.
(Contributor) P. Hockings, editor, *Essays in Honor of David Mandelbaum,* Mouton (Berlin), 1987.
(Contributor) D. Jordan and M. Swartz, editors, *Essays in Honor of Melford Spiro,* University of Georgia Press, 1987.

Co-editor of "Comparative Studies of Cultures and Civilizations," a series, 1953-58, AAA Memoirs and University of Chicago Press. Contributor to scholarly journals.

* * *

SMITH, Duane A(llan)   1937-

PERSONAL: Born April 20, 1937, in San Diego, Calif.; son of Stanley W. (a dentist) and Ila (Bark) Smith; married Gay Woodruff, August 20, 1960; children: Laralee Ellen. *Education:* University of Colorado, B.A., 1959, M.A., 1961, Ph.D., 1964.

ADDRESSES: Home—2911 Cedar Ave., Durango, Colo. 81301. *Office*—Department of History, Fort Lewis College, Durango, Colo. 81301.

CAREER: Fort Lewis College, Durango, Colo., assistant professor, 1964-67, associate professor, 1967-72, professor of history, 1972—.

MEMBER: Society for American Baseball Research, Organization of American Historians, Western History Association, Colorado Historical Society, Montana Historical Society, Phi Alpha Theta.

AWARDS, HONORS: Huntington Library research grants, 1968, 1973, and 1978; Hafen Award, 1971, for outstanding magazine article; Certificate of Commendation, 1974, for *Horace Tabor,* and Award of Merit, 1981, both from American Association for State and Local History; Westerners' Little Joe Award, 1977, for *Colorado Mining;* Society for Technical Communication Award of Distinction, 1980, for *Secure the Shadow,* and 1983, for *Song of the Hammer and Drill: The Colorado San Juans, 1860-1914.*

WRITINGS:

Rocky Mountain Mining Camps: The Urban Frontier, Indiana University Press, 1967.

(With M. Benson and C. Ubbelohde) *A Colorado History,* Pruett, 1972, revised edition, 1987.

Horace Tabor: His Life and the Legend, Colorado Associated University Press, 1973.

Silver Saga: The Story of Caribou, Colorado, Pruett, 1974.

Colorado Mining: A Photographic History, University of New Mexico Press, 1977.

(With D. Weber) *Fortunes Are for the Few: Letters of a Forty-Niner,* San Diego Historical Society, 1977.

Rocky Mountain Boom Town: A History of Durango, University of New Mexico Press, 1980.

Secure the Shadow: Lachlan McLean, Colorado Mining Photographer, Colorado School of Mines Press, 1980.

(With D. Vandenbusche) *A Land Alone: Colorado's Western Slope,* Pruett, 1981.

Song of the Hammer and Drill: The Colorado San Juans, 1860-1914, Colorado School of Mines Press, 1982.

(Editor) *Natural Resources in Colorado and Wyoming,* Sunflower University Press, 1982.

(Editor) *A Taste of the West: Essays in Honor of Robert G. Athearn,* Pruett, 1983.

When Coal Was King: A History of Crested Butte, Colorado, 1880-1952, Colorado School of Mines, 1984.

(With Fay Metcalf and Thomas Noel) *Colorado: Heritage of the Highest State,* with teacher's guide and activity tablet, Pruett, 1984.

(With Richard D. Lamm) *Pioneers and Politicians: Ten Colorado Governors in Profile,* Pruett, 1984.

Mining America: The Industry and the Environment, 1800-1980, University Press of Kansas, 1987.

Shadows of the Centuries: A History of Mesa Verde National Park (tentative title), University Press of Kansas, 1987.

Also author of *Our Once Happy Land: Civil War Colorado, 1861-65* (tentative title).

WORK IN PROGRESS: The 8th Illinois Cavalry and *High Country Frontier.*

SIDELIGHTS: Duane A. Smith told *CA:* "Probably the most important motivation for research on mining camps was the desire to uncover a more realistic and honest history as opposed to much of the literature which passes for the true history of the mining frontier.

"I believe that history is not dull, but writers and teachers of it often make it so. Therefore, my goal as a writer is to make history come alive for the reader, to 'hook' people on history."

AVOCATIONAL INTERESTS: Jogging and other sports, conservation, gardening, and politics.

*   *   *

SMITH, Louis
    See BARZINI, Luigi (Giorgio, Jr.)

*   *   *

SMITH, Martin
    See SMITH, Martin Cruz

SMITH, Martin Cruz   1942-
    (Martin Smith; pseudonyms: Martin Quinn, Simon Quinn; Nick Carter, Jake Logan, house pseudonyms)

PERSONAL: Original name, Martin William Smith; born November 3, 1942, in Reading, Pa.; son of John Calhoun (a musician) and Louise (a jazz singer and Indian rights leader; maiden name, Lopez) Smith; married Emily Arnold (a chef), June 15, 1968; children: Ellen Irish, Luisa Cruz, Samuel Kip. *Education:* University of Pennsylvania, B.A., 1964.

ADDRESSES: Home—240 Cascade Dr., Mill Valley, Calif. 94941. *Agent*—Knox Burger Associates Ltd., 39½ Washington Sq. S., New York, N.Y. 10012.

CAREER: Writer. Worked for local television stations, newspapers, and as a correspondent for Associated Press; *Philadelphia Daily News,* Philadelphia, Pa., reporter, 1965; Magazine Management, New York, N.Y., 1966-69, began as writer, became editor of *For Men Only.*

MEMBER: Authors League of America, Authors Guild.

AWARDS, HONORS: Edgar Award nomination, Mystery Writers of America, 1972, for *Gypsy in Amber,* 1976, for *The Midas Coffin,* 1978, for *Nightwing,* and 1982, for *Gorky Park;* Gold Dagger, Crime Writers Association, 1982.

WRITINGS:

Nightwing (suspense novel; also see below), Norton, 1977.
The Analog Bullet (novel), Belmont-Tower, 1978.
(With Steve Shagan and Bud Shrake) "Nightwing" (screenplay; based on his novel of the same title), Columbia, 1979.
Gorky Park (novel; Book-of-the-Month Club selection), Random House, 1981.
Stallion Gate (novel), Random House, 1986.

UNDER NAME MARTIN SMITH

The Indians Won (novel), Belmont-Tower, 1970, reprinted under name Martin Cruz Smith, Leisure Books, 1981.
Gypsy in Amber (mystery novel), Putnam, 1971.
Canto for a Gypsy (mystery novel), Putnam, 1972, reprinted under name Martin Cruz Smith, Ballantine, 1983.

UNDER PSEUDONYM MARTIN QUINN

The Adventures of the Wilderness Family (movie novelization), Ballantine, 1976.

UNDER PSEUDONYM SIMON QUINN; NOVELS

His Eminence, Death, Dell, 1974.
Nuplex Red, Dell, 1974.
The Devil in Kansas, Dell, 1974.
The Last Time I Saw Hell, Dell, 1974.
The Midas Coffin, Dell, 1975.
Last Rites for the Vulture, Dell, 1975.
The Human Factor (movie novelization), Dell, 1975.

UNDER HOUSE PSEUDONYM JAKE LOGAN

North to Dakota, Playboy Press, 1976.
Ride for Revenge, Playboy Press, 1977.

OTHER

Gorky Park has been translated into Russian. Also author of several other genre novels under various pseudonyms, including Nick Carter. Contributor of stories to *Male, Stag,* and *For Men Only* and of book reviews to *Esquire.*

WORK IN PROGRESS: A novel.

SIDELIGHTS: In 1972, a struggling young writer named Martin William Smith approached his publisher, G. P. Putnam's Sons, with an idea for a different sort of mystery. Inspired by a *Newsweek* review of *The Face Finder,* a nonfiction book recounting the efforts of Soviet scientists to reconstruct faces from otherwise unidentifiable human remains, Smith outlined a plot involving a partnership between a Soviet detective and his American counterpart as they attempt to solve an unusual murder. (As the author later revealed in the *Washington Post,* his original inclination was to portray a sort of "Butch Cassidy and the Sundance Kid, but one [partner would be] Russian.") Putnam's liked Smith's proposal and agreed to pay him a $15,000 advance.

For the next five years, Smith eked out a living writing several dozen paperback novels, often under one of his various pseudonyms. ("I didn't want to be associated with those books," he told *Newsweek*'s Peter S. Prescott.) Whenever he had accumulated enough to live on for awhile, he did research for his murder mystery; in 1973, he even managed to make a trip to Moscow where he spent almost a week wandering through the city jotting down notes on how it looked and sketching scenes he hesitated to photograph. Later denied permission for a return visit, Smith instead spent hours pumping various Russian emigres and defectors for details about life in the Soviet Union "on everything from the quality of shoes . . . to whether a ranking policeman would have to be a member of the Communist Party," as Arthur Spiegelman of the *Chicago Tribune* notes. "I would write a scene and show it to one of my Russian friends," Smith recalled. "If he would say that some Russian must have told me that, then I knew it was OK."

By this time, Smith knew he no longer wanted to write a conventional thriller. "I suddenly realized that I had something," he commented in the *Washington Post.* "This [was] the book that [could] set me free." He abandoned the idea of a partnership between detectives, deciding instead to focus on the challenge of making the Soviet detective his hero. Putnam's, however, was less than enthusiastic about the change in plans, for they doubted that such a book would have much commercial appeal. Smith was urged to stick to more marketable plots—namely, those featuring an American hero.

The year 1977 proved to be a turning point of sorts for Smith; he not only bought back the rights to his novel from Putnam's (after a long and bitter battle) and changed his middle name from William to Cruz (his maternal grandmother's name), he also received approximately a half million dollars when *Nightwing,* his vampire bat horror-thriller, became a surprise success. The following period of financial security enabled Smith to put the finishing touches on his "simple detective story," which by now had grown into a 365-page novel. In 1980, he and his agent began negotiating with Random House and Ballantine for the publishing rights. Despite the lack of interest Putnam's had shown in his work, Smith was confident that his book would indeed be published—and at a price *he* would name. As he remarked to Prescott: "Every time I looked at the novel I decided to double the price. When I wrote the last line, I *knew;* I have never been so excited in my life, except for the birth of children, as when I wrote the last line of [that book]. Because I knew it was just right. I had this marvelous book and I was *damned* if I was going to sell it for anything less than a marvelous price. The words 'one million' seemed to come to mind." Before the end of the year, Smith *was* $1 million richer and Random House was preparing to

gamble on an unusual 100,000-copy first printing of what soon would become one of the most talked-about books of 1981—*Gorky Park.*

The product of eight years of research and writing, *Gorky Park* chronicles the activities of homicide detective Arkady Renko as he investigates a bizarre murder. Three bullet-riddled bodies—two men and a woman—have been discovered frozen in the snow in Moscow's Gorky Park, their faces skinned and their fingertips cut off to hinder identification. Renko immediately realizes that this is no ordinary murder; his suspicions are confirmed when agents of the KGB arrive on the scene. But instead of taking over the investigation, the KGB suddenly insists that Renko handle the affair. From this point on, the main plot is complicated by an assortment of sub-plots and a large cast of characters, including a greedy American fur-dealer, a visiting New York City police detective who suspects one of the murder victims might be his radical brother, and a dissident Siberian girl with whom Renko falls in love. Before the end of the story, the detective has tracked the killer across two continents and has himself been stalked and harassed by the KGB, the CIA, the FBI, and the New York City police department.

As Spiegelman observes in his article, "First comment on *Gorky Park* has bordered on the ecstatic." Many reviewers, even those who find fault with a few aspects of the book, describe it as a novel that "transcends the genre" in the tradition of such acknowledged masters as John Le Carre, Eric Ambler, Len Deighton, and Graham Greene. They praise its exceptionally vivid and authentic images of Moscow and the way of life in the Soviet Union, as well as its skillful depiction of characters who are not mere *types,* but *people.*

Peter Andrews's comments in the *New York Times Book Review* are typical. "Just when I was beginning to worry that the large-scale adventure novel might be suffering from a terminal case of the Folletts," he writes, "along comes *Gorky Park* . . . , a book that reminds you just how satisfying a smoothly turned thriller can be. Mr. Smith fulfills all of the requirements of the adventure novel and then transcends the genre. . . . *Gorky Park* is a police procedural of uncommon excellence." Margaret Cannon of *Maclean's* agrees that "on its surface, *Gorky Park* is a police procedural." But "at its heart," she says, "it's a novel of greed and betrayal in the best form of Le Carre or Graham Greene." The *Washington Post Book World*'s Peter Osnos also compares Smith to Le Carre. He writes: "*Gorky Park* is not at all a conventional thriller about Russians. It is to ordinary suspense stories what John Le Carre is to spy novels. The action is gritty, the plot complicated, the overriding quality is intelligence. You have to pay attention or you'll get hopelessly muddled. But staying with this book is easy enough since once one gets going, one doesn't want to stop."

One reason readers of *Gorky Park* find it difficult to stop, says Prescott of *Newsweek,* stems from Smith's ability to bring to life "the inside of a world that he, as an American, cannot have experienced." The *New Yorker* critic, too, finds Smith's portrait "astonishingly" real, with all "the texture and substance of reality," while Osnos declares that "more perhaps than any other recent work of American fiction, [*Gorky Park*] conveys a feeling for the Soviet Union, its capital, its moods and its people."

Smith's characterization is another feature of *Gorky Park* that critics single out for praise. Robert Lekachman of the *Nation,* for example, attributes the book's success to the fact that "Smith has invented some genuinely complicated individuals and placed them in challenging ethical predicaments. . . . [*Gorky Park*'s] characters will linger in memory for quite a while.'' Perhaps because he is the protagonist, Arkady Renko in particular seems to have impressed reviewers the most, though Osnos, among others, points out that Smith avoids making *any* of his characters into the "sinister stick figures" common in other novels about the Soviets. Stefan Kanfer of *Time,* for example, states that "despite his country of origin, Arkady is not the customary exotic beloved by lending-library readers.'' A slightly seedy but totally decent and competent man, Arkady is, according to Osnos, "a Russian-style Sam Spade, skilled yet vulnerable, solitary yet capable of love.'' The *New Republic*'s Tamar Jacoby regards the detective as an "unusual and winning . . . moral hero without a trace of righteousness, an enigmatic figure as alluring as the mystery he is trying to solve. . . . This is what makes *Gorky Park* so extraordinary among thrillers where the heroes are up against simple villains or enemy organizations. Smith sees to it that there is nothing easy or superior about the moral insight that Arkady earns.''

While on the whole *Gorky Park* has met with a positive response from critics, it has also generated a few negative comments. Some reviewers, for example, do not think it is worthy of comparison to the work of authors who regularly "transcend the genre." Julian Symons, commenting in the *New York Review of Books,* insists its principal novelty lies in the fact that its hero is Russian and its setting is Moscow. "*Gorky Park* is much above the average thriller,'' he admits, "but almost equally far below the best of Ambler, Deighton, and Le Carre. Its outstanding virtue is the conviction with which the Moscow settings are rendered, and the assurance with which they are given to us in detail; its particular weaknesses are feeble characterization and an overindulgence in violence.'' Symons goes on to state that Arkady Renko emerges in the story as a "near-immortal hero'' in the conventional role of "a good guy in a bad organization, with many people ready to deceive him, most hands against him,'' while some of the plot twists and "all-too-plentiful action'' strike Symons as "outrageously improbable.''

The "conventional'' ending of *Gorky Park,* a bloody shootout on New York's Staten Island, also disappoints some critics. Richard J. Walton of the *Chicago Tribune Book World,* who otherwise feels the book is a "brilliant'' work of "stunning originality,'' remarks in his review that "it is only when . . . the story comes to New York that [*Gorky Park*] begins to limp a little.'' Kanfer notes that "when the characters act for themselves, *Gorky Park* maintains its credibility and force. Only at the end, when the lines of Soviet intrigue are played out, does Smith allow action to rule character. In New York the story degenerates to shootout, and authenticity gives way to violence and the requisite antiromantic finale.'' Nevertheless, he adds, "it hardly matters. Beneath its contrivances, *Gorky Park* provides a rich social context and a knowledgeable portrait of Eastern Europe.''

The *New York Times*'s Christopher Lehmann-Haupt, who criticizes what he calls the novel's "cliched international shoot'em-up'' ending, agrees that the ending "hardly matters,'' because we are still "under the spell of its beginning and middle. . . . For its first two-thirds . . . *Gorky Park* is superb. It is superb in its sense of mystery. . . . It is superb in its detective work. . . . It is superb in its pacing. . . . Most of all, it is superb in its evocation of the Moscow atmosphere.''

Concludes Kanfer: "*Gorky Park* [is] the first thriller of the '80s with polish, wit and moral resonance. . . . This is no small achievement for any novel. For what is essentially an espionage tale, it is a signal for rejoicing. In Arkady Renko, the U.S.S.R. finally has an exportable sleuth. In Martin Cruz Smith, . . . the U.S. at last has a domestic Le Carre.'' Despite such words of praise, Smith remains somewhat wary of success. "I always assume that there are angry gods,'' he told the *Washington Post,* "and that if you presume too much, they will take it all away.'' He added that the success of *Gorky Park* had not made that much of a difference in his life. "Before, I was treated as an idiot,'' Smith said. "Now, I'm treated as an idiot-savant.''

In his most recent novel, *Stallion Gate,* Smith sets his fiction among the scientists and military personnel of the Manhattan Project, those men and women who gathered near Los Alamos, New Mexico, to develop and test the first atom bomb. "Where *Gorky Park*'s subject was Russian,'' writes Stephen Pickles in the *Spectator,* "in this novel Martin Cruz Smith turns to something very American, taking on one of the 20th century's most crucial historical moments.'' Yet, even with this more familiar setting, Smith recognized the need to investigate his subject in order to reanimate the now famous scientists and to reconstruct the historical setting. Explains Pickles, "He researched the subject for 18 months, interviewing survivors and anyone who knew or worked with those involved with the Manhattan Project.''

Though closer to home, the backdrop for Smith's novel of intrigue gives it an alien quality much as Moscow colored *Gorky Park;* notes Pickles, "Los Alamos . . . gives the author a conveniently exotic and bizarre setting for this varied and self-consciously cinematic narrative.'' From this desert landscape, as R. Z. Sheppard observes in *Time,* Smith "shapes images that contain haunting affinities: wild horses and Army jeeps; rattlesnakes and coils of electrical cable; the lustrous surfaces of ceremonial pottery and the polished plutonium core of the atom bomb.'' Together with this setting and its images, Smith uses, in the words of *Washington Post Book World* contributor Ross Thomas, "a dry, controlled, almost laconic style to tell his tale of treachery, obsession and betrayal.'' The result, according to Thomas, is "an extraordinarily good novel.''

At the test site are J. Robert Oppenheimer, Edward Teller, Enrico Fermi, Brigadier General Leslie Groves, Harry Gold, and Klaus Fuchs—the real heroes and villains of the effort to build the first atomic bomb. Also present are the Indians of the area, some displaced by the scientists, some members of the project's support staff. All are part of the genesis of what the camp psychiatrist calls "the primary anxiety of the rest of history.'' "Through the Indians, the author develops a magical dimension within the story,'' writes Pickles. Through the chief of security, an army captain who suspects Oppenheimer of passing project secrets to the Soviets, Smith involves his main character and his readers in his story of suspense. Yet, in the view of *New York Review of Books* contributor Thomas R. Edwards, "This is only reluctantly a thriller. Smith, himself part Indian, is interested in the cultural collision between modern science and native beliefs and folkways of New Mexico.'' For this reason, as Thomas observes, "*Stallion Gate* is crammed with facts about the customs of the various Indian tribes that dwell in New Mexico, and of another tribe, this one composed of scientists.''

At the center of the story is Sergeant Joe Pena, a man with ties to each of the groups gathered in the New Mexico desert.

"Pena is as memorable as Arkady Renko, the Moscow policeman of 'Gorky Park,'" Tony Hillerman comments in the *Los Angeles Times Book Review*. "He is a Pueblo Indian, a sometime prize fighter, a jazz pianist and an Army misfit who appeals to the wrong women." He is also a boyhood friend of the physicist Oppenheimer, a relationship that prompts the suspicious security chief to spring Pena from a military jail to spy on the scientist.

As with *Gorky Park,* many reviewers of *Stallion Gate* focus on the characterization in the book. "I'm afraid that Pena is merely a device of plot and theme and not a person," comments Edwards. This reviewer maintains that "the sheer mass of his duties to the narrative constricts his human interest, especially since Smith insists that he be right at the center of everything." In Edwards's final judgement, "[Smith's] wish to make a star of Joe Pena ensures that *Stallion Gate* can be neither a good suspense story nor a serious historical novel." Sheppard offers a different view: "The sergeant is a winning creation, even though he stretches belief by conducting a lot of personal business as a noncom assigned to a super-secret project." In Thomas's estimation, Smith handles well the demands placed upon him by the unique main character he has conceived: "Sergeant Pena . . . is a major accomplishment since it's no mean feat to turn a soldier, boxer and be-bop pioneer into a sympathetic and even sensitive progtagonist." And G. E. Murray, in an article in the *Chicago Tribune Book World*, points to the value of Pena's role even as a plot device, noting that "through Pena's extraordinary 180 degree vision we experience an underbelly view of the dawning of the Atomic Age, like it or not."

Although some reviewers such as John Ziman in the *London Review of Books* find that "the historical figures [in *Stallion Gate*] are little more than cardboard cutouts," Thomas believes that "Smith skillfully mixes his real characters in with his fictional ones." Commenting on the background characterization as well as the historical backdrop, Hillerman contends, "Smith's skill at showing us just a little and letting our imagination work often moves us past craftsmanship into poetry." And as Murray suggests, the novel is more than a historical portrait of the pioneers of the atomic age; it is more than a study of Joe Pena. "Certainly Smith's main purpose here is the making of a popular psychological drama . . . ," writes the reviewer. "But in doing so, he also addresses such questions as the loss of innocence both individual and national, and shifting rationales for destruction, real or promised."

Because of the praise *Gorky Park* earned its author—the comparisons to works by the masters of genre writing—*Stallion Gate*'s reception has been influenced by expectations of a book from the same mold. And although similarities exist between the two books, the intent of each book, Smith has explained, is different. "I wanted to do an American story after *Gorky Park*," he writes in *Publishers Weekly*, "and I thought the most American story would be a New Mexican story." He elaborates in his *CA* interview: "The primary idea of the book is to get across 1945 New Mexico . . . in almost an elegiac fashion with some of the rhythms of jazz." *New York Times Book Review* contributor Howard Frank Mosher recognizes Smith's effort; he comments that "no one should fault a novelist for striking out in new directions. 'Gorky Park' was highly entertaining," he adds, "but in some ways 'Stallion Gate' is a more ambitious book." In his review of *Stallion Gate*, Tony Hillerman concludes, "Martin Cruz Smith, master-craftsman of the good read, has given us another dandy."

MEDIA ADAPTATIONS: "Gorky Park," a film starring William Hurt and Lee Marvin based on Smith's novel of the same title, was released by Orion Pictures in 1983.

CA INTERVIEW

CA interviewed Martin Cruz Smith by telephone on September 30, 1986, at his home in Mill Valley, California.

CA: Though Nightwing *did very well financially and got you some exposure,* Gorky Park *was the book that caught everybody's attention. When you began to realize during the writing that it was going to be a big book, a very important book, did it get scary?*

SMITH: No, it just got enjoyable.

CA: One of the most amazing things about Gorky Park *is that you were able to create such an authentic Moscow although you'd spent only about five days there and didn't know the language. How had you prepared before your visit to get the most research out of it?*

SMITH: I had done a great deal of reading, and I had my plot written out. So when I went there, I went to those places that I knew I would have in the book; I went to Gorky Park and I went to the prosecutor's office—outside, not inside—and to militia headquarters. Some things, however, I decided to use while I was there, like Mosfilm, for example. I had not intended to use it, but once I was there I decided to try to crash into Mosfilm. I spent half a day there, trying to get inside, *not* getting inside, but being there long enough to see who went to Mosfilm, who worked there. Later on, when I got back to this country, I was able to talk to a couple of people who worked at Mosfilm.

CA: You talked with a lot of Russians in this country after you got back, didn't you?

SMITH: Yes. I spent I cannot tabulate how many hours doing that, because the writing went on for years, and a number of the Russians who helped me would in fact come and live with me and my family.

CA: The plot of Gorky Park *is quite intricate. How did you manage to keep up with it yourself in the writing? Was it tricky?*

SMITH: I was totally confused. I couldn't keep up with it. At the last second I was still going back and trying to make things mesh.

CA: There are so many different things going on in the story. But that's part of what made it good, I think.

SMITH: Yes, I think the intricacy is something that people like in that kind of book. It was intricate in part because I wanted to have so many things in it. You want to have so much life in a book; you want people to be alert, and the one way to get them alert is to give them the sense that there might be some clues in it.

CA: Were you pleased with the way the movie came out?

SMITH: No. I think it's rare that anybody ever is. I thought it was a movie that took a fairly two-dimensional approach. It was basically decided to make it an anti-Soviet film. You can be critical and *should* be critical of a number of Soviet attitudes, but I think you also have to recognize that an awful lot of the people who work within that system are both human and humane. That was somewhat the point of Arkady Renko, and to make him such a cold fish in the movie, I think, missed the point of the book.

CA: Your fascination with the Russians and the years of working on Gorky Park *must give you a different kind of view of the current spy happenings from that most Americans have.*

SMITH: Well, one thing you learn is the Russians' attitude towards us, which is partly that our journalists are spies. Because their own journalists are so closely tied to the KGB, they actually do make an assumption that our journalists are tied to the CIA. So it's always good to keep their perception in mind when we are dealing with these people. There's almost an innocence to their paranoia.

CA: You lived with your Gorky Park *characters a long time and most of them were very genuine, real people. Was there a kind of grief when you had to let them go?*

SMITH: No, I was happy to let them go. I mean happy for *their* sake, because I felt they would be appreciated. I was especially pleased with Pribluda, because I thought he was in many ways closest to the Russian character, and I wanted people to appreciate him.

CA: How did the habits you learned from the early work—the newspaper reporting, magazine writing, the paperbacks written under several pseudonyms—help or hinder you in the later writing?

SMITH: All that writing does is tell you get it down on paper, to do it, not to sit around making diagrams for six months. If you're writing for a newspaper, it has to be done that afternoon, it has to be done in ten minutes. So it forces you not to contemplate too long. On the other hand, you have to learn at some point to do some thinking and to pace yourself a little bit. So it goes back and forth: sometimes the lessons learned from that are useful and sometimes they are not. You have to be aware whether you are using good training or suffering from a bad habit.

CA: Were mysteries and crime fiction something you loved early on and thought you'd someday like to write?

SMITH: I don't think I had any particular ambition. When I read something like *Look Homeward, Angel,* I was aware that this was something that intrigued me; the great bulk of it was intriguing, and the characters were intriguing. At the same time, I've always appreciated and quite naturally in my own writing tended to lean towards the tautness of a different kind of writing. And in that sort of taut writing mysteries naturally find themselves. It's an easy way to create character because the reader is so alert for it.

CA: Mysteries and crime stories seem to be enjoying tremendous popularity now.

SMITH: Some of the best American writers have been writing in that style, with that particular tautness of, let's say, Dashiell Hammett. James Cain is a very underrated writer. Also Hemingway certainly had that tautness in mind.

CA: For Gypsy in Amber *and* Canto for a Gypsy, *you created the Gypsy detective Roman Grey. How did you decide to make him an antique dealer?*

SMITH: Well I wanted to have somewhat of a contradiction within the character himself and to have him a Gypsy. I wanted to give him a particular trade that would be different from other trades, but also be very different from the Gypsy stereotype.

CA: Were all the details of Gypsy life and language in the books from specific research, or did you know something about them before the books were conceived?

SMITH: They were simply book research.

CA: Was that information hard to get?

SMITH: It wasn't at all. I didn't know when I started that my wife's grandfather, the Reverend Frederick Arnold, had been a Gypsyologist. He spoke Romany and had built up quite a sizeable private library on Gypsies. After my two books came out, some of his own work on the Gypsy language, a dictionary of Romany, and studies of the Gypsies then were published by the Gypsy Lore Society.

CA: There was a lot of wonderful food in Gypsy in Amber. *Your wife is or has been a professional chef, I believe. Can any connection be made here, or do you just happen to love good food?*

SMITH: I have had the opportunity to love food myself because she is so good and has been a professional cook, so some of the things in there, like Gypsy caviar, are simply things that she has been making for a long time herself. Even in *Gorky Park* we ate Russian for quite a long time, though I think it was more pre-Revolutionary Russian.

CA: In Nightwing *you dealt with Indian ways and had some Indian characters, including main character Youngman Duran. Again in the 1986 book* Stallion Gate *you had an Indian main character, Joe Pena, and some Indian lore. Did all the Indian knowledge come from your Pueblo heritage on your mother's side, or was it something you'd consciously researched?*

SMITH: I didn't grow up on reservations as these characters do. Part of the knowledge is simply from going to the reservations. The problem with *Nightwing* was that I *didn't* go; I relied on my own background and research because I did not have the money to go and do it on the reservations. Writing the book without that made it not as good as it otherwise would have been; if I had actually gone to Hopi land, I think the book would have been significantly better.

CA: Do you think readers would have been aware of that?

SMITH: No, but you know yourself.

CA: You've talked elsewhere about growing up in the East, where it wasn't in any way a disadvantage to be part Indian. When did you begin to be interested in your Indian background?

SMITH: I've never been particularly interested in it. I've frankly avoided, if possible, being a professional Indian, and I always find myself surprised to be writing about Indians, though I've done it three times now. Maybe that's enough; maybe I'm now free. I have not made it a mission of mine to educate the white man in the ways of the Indian or to expand on Indian mysticism. But the attitudes of the Indians are an integral part of these stories I've written.

CA: Did you feel you were taking any sort of risk in Stallion Gate *by having the real characters—Robert Oppenheimer, Klaus Fuchs, Leslie R. Groves?*

SMITH: Yes. But I think it worked well. The book has not had the kind of reception I wanted it to have, in part, I think, because the research is folded so deeply within the style of the book itself. The primary idea of the book is to get across 1945 New Mexico. To tell all of this in almost an elegiac fashion with some of the rhythms of jazz was a conscious decision on my part. I'm glad I did it because I like that book, but it meant that all the research that was done on the book, on the physics and the time and on Indian mores, is deep within the book and pared down to essentials. I haven't made it easy for people to appreciate how much information is in fact in the book. The more you know about Los Alamos in 1945 and the more you know about the Pueblos in 1945, the more, perhaps, you can appreciate what is said as well as how it is said.

CA: Do you particularly enjoy doing the research for the books?

SMITH: Well, it constantly lets me know how little I know about the world, but I always enjoy it. For one thing, writing itself is so intensely boring, in the social context: you're all by yourself, nobody else is there. That's one reason why I pick characters that I'm going to like, because I'm going to be stuck with them for a couple of years. But in research you're always going out and meeting people that you've always wanted to meet, or people you *didn't* know you wanted to meet but happen to find, people out there with these stories that you can remake, that you can bring to life in a different way.

CA: The character Anne in Nightwing *mentioned John Cheever's short story "The Swimmer." Was Cheever a particular literary hero of yours?*

SMITH: No. He would have been for her, though. When I was a kid, I was very strong on Aldous Huxley. I loved things like *Brave New World, After Many a Summer Dies the Swan,* and *Eyeless in Gaza.* Then I was hooked on Evelyn Waugh, and then I was hooked on T. E. Lawrence, and then started reading lots and lots of Americans, basically what everybody else reads, which is Malamud and Bellow. I think what matters is that you do a enormous amount of reading from an enormous number of directions. Anne, in *Nightwing,* mentions Cheever because she grew up in Scottsdale, which is one of the very few suburbs of Arizona. The one thing that she was responding to was a description of suburban life in Connecticut. It's suburban life; that's why she mentions it.

CA: You seem to have an invaluable help in your agent, Knox Berger. Would you like to comment here on the relationship and why it works so well?

SMITH: Part of the reason we work so well together is that Knox is a very good editor. I've been fortunate in having a good editor at Random House, and having a wife who is the best editor of all, in fact. It's important to have an editor who knows when you're writing well and when you're faking it, who knows when you really *seem* to be writing well but you're

actually not saying anything that's worth saying, and is capable of telling you so. Of course you have to have the ability to listen.

CA: When did you make the move from New York to California?

SMITH: Just before Christmas of 1981.

CA: Does being there instead of in New York affect your writing in any way?

SMITH: Yes, it does. New York is totally work-oriented. It's much harder to write in a place that is so delightful to be in, where there's so much more to see when you look out the window. When you look out the window in Manhattan, you're looking out at people rushing to work. When you look out the window here you see people strolling around in clogs. It doesn't give you the same Calvinistic impulse to go sit yourself down and do some labor.

CA: From remarks you've made in earlier interviews, one has the impression that success wasn't something you coveted mainly for the money it would bring. What's the best part of it for you?

SMITH: I think the best part of it is to be able to write what you want to write, not having to write what anybody else wants you to write. And of course it gives you the opportunity to *write, period,* not to be doing something else. I think that many American writers who have achieved the ability to simply write are aware that there is a phantom life, their alter ego, the one who is trapped, that somewhere there is a ghost of themselves writing advertising copy, and that somehow they have escaped that.

CA: So many writers are teaching, too, which seems to be both good and bad for most of them.

SMITH: That is both good and bad. I enjoy teaching myself and have been doing it for years here. But I do it once a week, not five days a week.

CA: Are you teaching in a college?

SMITH: No, I prefer elementary school or middle school or high school. Really, of them all, I prefer the elementary school.

CA: And you're actually having the kids do some writing?

SMITH: Yes.

CA: Since the Roman Grey books, you haven't done any two at all alike. Is there something completely different in the works now?

SMITH: What I want to do right now is something else that I've had an idea about for years, but I can't tell you anything about it; I hate to talk about it. I hope it's going to be different.

BIOGRAPHICAL/CRITICAL SOURCES:

BOOKS

Contemporary Literary Criticism, Volume XXV, Gale, 1983.

PERIODICALS

Best Sellers, June, 1981, August, 1986.

Business Week, April 6, 1981.
Chicago Tribune, March 25, 1981.
Chicago Tribune Book World, April 19, 1981, May 11, 1986.
Christian Science Monitor, April 13, 1981.
Detroit News, April 12, 1981, August 16, 1981.
London Review of Books, September 4, 1986.
Los Angeles Times Book Review, April 19, 1981, May 11, 1986.
Maclean's, May 4, 1981.
Nation, April 4, 1981.
New Republic, May 9, 1981.
Newsweek, April 6, 1981, May 25, 1981, April 14, 1986.
New Yorker, April 6, 1981.
New York Review of Books, June 11, 1981, May 8, 1986.
New York Times, March 19, 1981.
New York Times Book Review, April 5, 1981, May 3, 1981, May 4, 1986.
People, May 25, 1981.
Publishers Weekly, March 20, 1981, January 4, 1985.
Spectator, September 12, 1981, July 5, 1986.
Time, March 30, 1981, May 12, 1986.
Times (London), June 19, 1982.
Times Literary Supplement, June 5, 1981.
Washington Post, April 10, 1981.
Washington Post Book World, March 29, 1981, April 20, 1986.

—Sketch by Bryan Ryan

—Interview by Jean W. Ross

* * *

SMITH, Vivian (Brian) 1933-

PERSONAL: Born June 3, 1933, in Hobart, Tasmania, Australia; son of Vivian and Sibyl (Daniels) Smith; married Sybille Gottwald, February 15, 1960; children: Vanessa, Gabrielle, Nicholas. *Education:* University of Tasmania, M.A., 1956; University of Sydney, Ph.D., 1971.

ADDRESSES: Home—19 McLeod St., Mosman, New South Wales 2088, Australia. *Office*—Department of English, University of Sydney, Sydney, New South Wales 2006, Australia.

CAREER: University of Tasmania, Hobart, lecturer in French, 1955-67; University of Sydney, Sydney, Australia, lecturer, 1967-74, senior lecturer, 1974-82, reader in English, 1982—; poet.

MEMBER: Poetry Society of Australia, Australian Society of Authors.

AWARDS, HONORS: New South Wales' Premier's Prize for Poetry, and the Grace Leven Prize for Poetry, both 1983.

WRITINGS:

The Other Meaning (poems), Edwards & Shaw, 1956.
James McAuley, Lansdowne Press, 1965.
An Island South, Angus & Robertson, 1967.
Les Vige en Australie (juvenile; title means "The Vige Family in Australia"), Longmans, Green (Melbourne), 1967.
(Editor) *Australian Poetry,* Angus & Robertson, 1969.
The Poetry of Robert Lowell, University of Sydney Press, 1974.
Vance and Nettie Palmer, Twayne, 1975.
Letters of Vance and Nettie Palmer, National Library (Canberra), 1977.
Familiar Places (poems), Angus & Robertson, 1978.
Tide Country (poems), Angus & Robertson, 1982.
(Co-editor) *Quadrant: Twenty-five Years,* University of Queensland Press, 1982.

Tasmania and Australian Poetry (essay), University of Tasmania, Hobart, 1984.
Selected Poems, Angus & Robertson, 1985.
(Co-editor) *Effects of Light: The Poetry of Tasmania,* Twelvetrees Press, 1985.
(Editor) *Poetry Australia 1986,* Angus & Robertson, 1986.
(Editor) *Portable Australian Authors: Nettie Palmer,* University of Queensland Press, 1988.

CONTRIBUTOR OF POEMS TO ANTHOLOGIES

Howard Sergeant, editor, *Young Commonwealth Poets '65,* Heinemann, 1965.
G. P. Dutton, editor, *Modern Australian Writing,* Fontana, 1966.
Sergeant, editor, *Commonwealth Poems of Today,* John Murray, 1967.
David Campbell, editor, *Modern Australian Poetry,* Sun Books, 1974.
James McAuley, editor, *A Map of Australian Verse,* Oxford University Press, 1975.
H. P. Heselline, editor, *Modern Australian Poetry,* Penguin, 1980.
R. Hall, editor, *Collins Book of Australian Verse,* Collins, 1981.
Oxford History of Australian Literature, Oxford University Press, 1981.

OTHER

Contributor to Australian newspapers and literary journals. Literary editor of *Quadrant,* 1975—.

SIDELIGHTS: Vivian Smith told *CA:* "Most of my life—apart from trips overseas—has been spent in the two oldest cities in Australia: Hobart, where I was born and lived until I was thirty-three, and Sydney, where I have lived and worked for the last twenty years. The sense of place is of major importance in my poetry and I should like to leave a series of poems that are as evocative of these places as are the paintings of Edith Holmes or Haughton Forrest.

"The principal themes in my work are the search for continuity, the sense of decay and transcience, a preoccupation with what endures: persistence and renewal—'How things change, and how they hold,' as I put it in my poem 'Back in Hobart.'"

AVOCATIONAL INTERESTS: Translating from French and German.

* * *

SMUCKER, Barbara (Claassen) 1915-

PERSONAL: Born September 1, 1915, in Newton, Kan.; daughter of Cornelius W. (a banker) and Addie (Lander) Claassen; married Donovan E. Smucker (a minister and professor of sociology and religion), January 21, 1939; children: Timothy, Thomas, Rebecca. *Education:* Kansas State University, B.S., 1936; further study at Rosary College, River Forest, Ill., 1963-65, and University of Waterloo, 1975-77. *Politics:* Democrat. *Religion:* Mennonite.

ADDRESSES: Home and office—57 McDougall Rd., Waterloo, Ontario, Canada N2L 2W4.

CAREER: Public high school teacher of English and journalism in Harper, Kan., 1937-38; *Evening Kansas Republican,* Newton, Kan., reporter, 1939-41; Ferry Hall School, Lake Forest, Ill., teacher, 1960-63; Lake Forest Bookstore, Lake

Forest, bookseller, 1963-67; Kitchener Public Library, Kitchener, Ontario, children's librarian, 1969-77; Renison College, Waterloo, Ontario, head librarian, 1977—. Has also worked as an interviewer for Gallup Poll.

MEMBER: American Association of University Women, Canadian Association of University Women, Canadian Society of Children's Authors, Canadian Writers Union, Illustrators and Performers, Children's Reading Roundtable.

AWARDS, HONORS: Children's Book Center named *Underground to Canada* one of the fifty best books of all time in Canada, 1978; Brotherhood Award from National Conference of Christians and Jews, 1980, top honors from All-Japan Library Committee and from Catholic Teachers Association of West Germany, for *Underground to Canada;* children's literary award from Canada Council and Ruth Schwartz Foundation Award, both 1980, both for *Days of Terror;* distinguished service award from Kansas State University, 1980, for children's literature; senior honorary fellow, Renison College, 1982. Dr.Litt., honoris causa, University of Waterloo, 1986.

WRITINGS:

JUVENILES

Henry's Red Sea, Herald Press, 1955.
Cherokee Run, Herald Press, 1957.
Wigwam in the City, Dutton, 1966, reprint published as *Susan,* Scholastic Book Services, 1978.
Underground to Canada, Clark, Irwin, 1977, published as *Runaway to Freedom: A Story of the Underground Railway,* Harper, 1978.
Days of Terror, Clarke, Irwin, 1979.
Amish Adventure, Clarke, Irwin, 1983.
White Mist, Clarke, Irwin, 1985.
Jacob's Little Giant, Viking, 1987.

OTHER

Also contributor to *American Educator Encyclopedia.*

WORK IN PROGRESS: A children's book based on Barnum's famous elephant.

SIDELIGHTS: Barbara Smucker's juvenile novels bring history to life while educating their readers. To produce historical novels relevant to contemporary social issues, Smucker mixes some of her personal insights with actual past events. For example, *Underground to Canada,* a novel about slavery and the underground railroad, was born out of the author's concern for the civil rights movement, an interest that was previously challenged by a black student who questioned Smucker's ability to empathize with circumstances and feelings she had never experienced. A resident of Mississippi until the 1960s, the author settled in Canada and extended her interest to include Canada's role in the underground railroad and its famous "conductor," Alexander Ross.

Underground to Canada recounts the unhappy lives of fourteen-year-old Julilly and the crippled Liza, two slaves who work over eighteen hours every day and live in small, crowded huts in the Deep South. In the novel, Ross leads the girls and two other slaves to St. Catharine's, Ontario, where they must contend with freedom as it really is, however different than they anticipated it would be. "*All* children should read [*Underground to Canada*]," wrote Virgina Hamilton of the *New York Times Book Review.* "We need scrupulously honest books like this one to inform subsequent generations that a great

crime was committed against a people, and that we must always be on guard against victimization and genocide."

Similar to *Underground to Canada,* Smucker's other novels deal with the struggles and triumphs of ethnic or religious groups. *Wigwam in the City* illustrates the plight of Native Americans once they move from reservations to jobs in cities, and several books look at the history of the Mennonites. *Henry's Red Sea,* which is used as an educational tool in Mennonite schools, describes the perilous movement of wartime refugees from Russia to Germany to Paraguay. Another book, *Days of Terror,* recalls when Mennonites fled to Canada to maintain their religious freedom during the Russian Revolution of 1917. And *Cherokee Run* tells of the institution of Mennonite settlements in Oklahoma.

Smucker's books have been published in sixteen countries and translated into French, German, Japanese, Swedish, Spanish, Dutch, and Danish.

BIOGRAPHICAL/CRITICAL SOURCES:

BOOKS

Children's Literature Review, Gale, Volume X, 1986.
Michele Landsberg's Guide to Children's Books, Penguin Books, 1986.

PERIODICALS

Globe and Mail, November 30, 1985.
In Review, fall, 1977.
Mennonite Quarterly Review, January, 1981.
New York Times Book Review, April 30, 1978.
Saturday Night, November, 1979.

*   *   *

SNELLGROVE, L(aurence) E(rnest)   1928-

PERSONAL: Born February 2, 1928, in London, England; son of Ernest George and Emily (Wren) Snellgrove; married Jean Hall, April 5, 1951; children: Peter Laurence. *Education:* Culham College, 1948-52, Associate of College of Preceptors, B.A., 1953. *Religion:* Church of England.

ADDRESSES: Home—Kitty Hawk, 23 Harvest Hill, East Grinstead, Sussex RH19 4BU, England.

CAREER: Assistant master of Rose Hill School, Oxford, England, 1950-53, Cheshunt County Secondary School, Hertfordshire, England, 1953-55, and Yaxley School, Huntingdonshire, England, 1955-57; Caterham Valley County Secondary School, Surrey, England, head of history department, 1957-66; de Stafford Comprehensive School, Caterham, Surrey, head of history department, 1966-73; writer and lecturer, 1973—. *Military service:* Royal Air Force, 1945-48; became leading aircraftsman.

WRITINGS:

From Kitty Hawk to Outer Space: The Story of the Aeroplane, illustrated by Andrew Dodds and Bartley Powell, Longmans, Green, 1960.
From Steam Carts to Minicars: A History of Motor Cars, illustrated by T. Jacques and G. Lane, Longmans, Green, 1961.
From Coracles to Cunarders, illustrated by Rosemary Grimble and Winston Megoran, Longmans, Green, 1962.
From Rocket to Railcar: An Outline of Rail Development since 1804, illustrated by Harry Toothill, Longmans, Green, 1963.

Suffragettes and Votes for Women, illustrated by Toothill, Longmans, Green, 1964, 2nd edition, Longman, 1984.

Franco and the Spanish Civil War, Longmans, Green, 1965, McGraw, 1968, reprinted, Longman, 1980.

The Modern World since 1870, Longmans, Green, 1968, 2nd edition, Longman, 1980, expanded edition (with K. Greenberg) published in Rhodesia (now Zimbabwe) as *The Modern World since 1900,* Longman Rhodesia, 1973.

(With Richard J. Cootes) *The Ancient World,* Longman, 1970.

The Early Modern Age, Longman, 1972.

Hitler, Longman, 1974.

World War II, Longman, 1974.

(With John Roy Charles Yglesias) *Mainstream English,* six volumes, Longman, 1974-75.

(With Ron Sandford) *Picture the Past,* Longman, Volume I: *Gods, Greeks and Romans,* 1978, Volume II: *Knights, Priests and Peasants,* 1978, Volume III: *Kings, Queens and Jacks,* 1978, Volume IV: *Men, Machines and Masters,* 1980, Volume V: *War, Welfare and Science,* 1982.

Wide Range History, four volumes with activity books, Oliver & Boyd, 1978-79.

History around You, Oliver & Boyd, Volume II, illustrated by Terry Gabbey and Hamish Gordon, 1982, Volume IV, illustrated by Tim Marwood, Jeremy Gower, and Donald Harley, 1983.

Britain since 1700, Longman, 1985.

Storyline History, Oliver & Boyd, Volume I, illustrated by Donald Harley, 1985, Volume II, illustrated by Jennifer Campbell, 1985, Volume III, illustrated by Stephen Gibson, 1985, Volume IV, illustrated by Colin Andrew and others, 1985.

The Modern World since 1870, The Ancient World, and *The Early Modern Age* have been translated into Japanese. Also contributor to *New Schoolmaster, Storyteller,* and *Times Educational Supplement.*

SIDELIGHTS: L. E. Snellgrove told *CA:* "I started to write when I was very young; the love of words has always been there. At 14 I broadcast one of my own short stories on a B.B.C. programme called 'Youth Magazine.' My historical writing arose directly out of my teaching. I have always loved history but I think it only fair and honest to say that, although I would and have written for nothing, I do like the idea of earning a living from writing. I hope that my books will give readers a fair, accurate and reasonably up-to-date version of history—a much abused subject. My stories for younger readers have given me an opportunity to play with words and develop the purely artistic and technical side of telling a story.

"Of the literary scene today I know little and care even less. Writing, at its best, should be about people in relation to the world. 'Literary scenes' are about as real as cardboard cutouts of people. . . . I never read reviews of my work and I should think 'incisive' reviews are quite rare. Most reviewers seem to write about themselves although they pretend to be reviewing somebody's book. The only honest reviewer I can think of off-hand was Bernard Shaw. In his musical reviews he did not bother too much about the music if he could explain the uniqueness of himself. Incidentally, Shaw as a stylist was an influence on me.

"My advice to aspiring writers is to work hard, preferably by writing some sort of diary each day. Go back over the work and cut out any word or phrase which could have been expressed more simply. Remember words are about communication. The real failure is not to be understood."

AVOCATIONAL INTERESTS: Music, theatre, swimming, and sitting in a deckchair during the short English summer.

*   *   *

SPEAR, Hilda D(oris) 1926-

PERSONAL: Born August 27, 1926, in Pinner, England; daughter of Joseph Charles (in Royal Navy) and Blanche Elizabeth (a nurse; maiden name, Collins) King; married Walter E. Spear (a university professor), 1952; children: Gillian Spear Dolan, Kathryn. *Education:* Birkbeck College, London, B.A. (with honors), 1951, M.A., 1953; University of Leicester, Ph.D., 1972.

ADDRESSES: Office—Department of English, University of Dundee, Dundee DD1 4HN, Scotland.

CAREER: Teacher of English at secondary schools in London, England, 1946-48, and Leicester, England, 1952-56; Purdue University, West Lafayette, Ind., lecturer in English, 1957-58; lecturer in English and education at colleges of education in Leicester, 1958-60; University of Leicester, Leicester, lecturer in English and education, 1965-68; University of Dundee, Dundee, Scotland, lecturer in English, 1969-87, senior lecturer, 1987—, senior adviser of studies, 1978-87. Guest lecturer at schools and universities in Great Britain, the United States, Japan, China, and India. Member of Bursaries Panel, Scottish Arts Council, 1981-86.

MEMBER: International Biographical Association (fellow), English Association, Dundee Literary Society.

AWARDS, HONORS: Prizes from Scottish Arts Council, 1978, for *The Poems and Selected Letters of C. H. Sorley,* and 1980, for *Remembering, We Forget;* awards from British Academy and Carnegie Trust, 1979, for *Remembering, We Forget.*

WRITINGS:

(Editor) *The English Poems of Charles Stuart Calverley,* Leicester University Press, 1974.

(Editor) *The Poems and Selected Letters of C. H. Sorley,* Blackness Press, 1978.

Remembering, We Forget, Davis-Poynter, 1979.

Hardy, "The Mayor of Casterbridge": Notes, Longman, 1980.

Lawrence, "The Rainbow": Notes, Longman, 1980.

Conrad, "Youth" and "Typhoon": Notes, Longman, 1981.

Golding, "The Inheritors": Notes, Longman, 1981.

Emily Bronte: Wuthering Heights (study outline), Macmillan, 1985.

Golding, "The Spire": Notes, Longman, 1986.

Forster: A Passage to India (study outline), Macmillan, 1986.

(With Abdel Moneim Aly) *Forster in Egypt,* Woolf, 1987.

CONTRIBUTOR

Boris Ford, editor, *Pelican Guide to English Literature,* Volume V, Penguin, 1957, 2nd edition, 1982.

James Vinson and D. L. Kirkpatrick, editors, *Great Writers of the English Language,* Macmillan, 1980.

Ford, editor, *A Guide for Readers,* Penguin, 1984.

Alvin Sullivan, editor, *British Literary Magazines,* Greenwood Press, 1986.

OTHER

Also author of *Your Bright Promise: An Evocation of the Life of Charles Sorley,* a dramatic narration first performed in 1986. Contributor to language and literature journals, including *The Use of English, English, Four Decades of Poetry, English*

Literature in Transition, Durham University Journal, Scottish Review, and *Lines Review.*

WORK IN PROGRESS: Research on the literature of World War I, on Forster, and on other modern novelists.

SIDELIGHTS: Hilda D. Spear told *CA:* "I find writing and research both absorbing and enjoyable. I also enjoy teaching, particularly passing on to students my own enthusiasms in reading and research. Literature should always give the reader pleasure of some kind.

"I suppose that, like many writers and academics, I am a dissident liberal, I don't know the answers and wish I did; but I am aware of the problems! It is this which makes a study of war literature so especially fascinating.

"However, I believe that concentrated work on any area of literature brings its rewards; I very rarely find that I am unable to receive intellectual pleasure from poems, novels or plays that I happen to be working on. My dramatic narration *Your Bright Promise* was the result of a public performance to accompany an exhibition on the life and work of Sorley. It was one of the results of a sabbatical year; the other results were mainly academic but the year off has made me realise how important it is to be able, occasionally, to stand back and have leisure to think and to brood. I shouldn't like it all the time; I suspect that I am a bit of a workaholic; at least I enjoy working!"

*   *   *

SPENCE, Jonathan D(ermot) 1936-

PERSONAL: Born August 11, 1936, in England; son of Dermot Gordon Chesson and Muriel (Crailsham) Spence; married Helen Alexander, September 15, 1962; children: Colin Chesson, Ian Alexander. *Education:* Cambridge University, B.A., 1959; Yale University, Ph.D., 1965.

ADDRESSES: Office—Department of History, Yale University, New Haven, Conn. 06520.

CAREER: Yale University, New Haven, Conn., assistant professor,1965-71, professor of Chinese history, beginning 1971, currently George Burton Adams Professor of History and chairman of department. *Military service:* British Army, 1954-56; became first lieutenant.

AWARDS, HONORS: Christopher Book Award, 1975, for *Emperor of China: Self-Portrait of K'ang-Hsi;* Los Angeles Times Book Award, 1982, and Harold D. Vursell Memorial Award, American Academy-Institute of Arts and Letters, 1983, both for *The Gate of Heavenly Peace: The Chinese and Their Revolution, 1895-1980.*

WRITINGS:

Ts'ao Yin and the K'ang-Hsi Emperor, Bondservant and Master, Yale University Press, 1966.
To Change China: Western Advisers to China, 1620-1960, Little, Brown, 1969 (published in England as *The China Helpers: Western Advisers to China, 1620-1960,* Bodley Head, 1969).
Emperor of China: Self-Portrait of K'ang-Hsi, Knopf, 1974.
The Death of Woman Wang (novel), Viking, 1978.
(With John E. Wills, Jr.) *From Ming to Ch'ing: Conquest, Region and Continuity in Seventeenth-Century China,* Yale University Press, 1979.
The Gate of Heavenly Peace: The Chinese and Their Revolution, 1895-1980, Viking, 1981.

The Memory Palace of Matteo Ricci, Viking, 1984.

WORK IN PROGRESS: Studies in Chinese local and political history, 1550 to the present.

SIDELIGHTS: Jonathan D. Spence writes books of Chinese history which employ novel modes of organization and approach. "No one writes history—Chinese or any other kind—exactly as Spence does," Harrison E. Salisbury claims in the *Chicago Tribune Book World.* In his *Emperor of China: Self-Portrait of K'ang-Hsi,* Spence splices together contemporary accounts of a seventeenth-century Chinese ruler to fashion a kind of autobiography. In *The Death of Woman Wang,* he fuses the official history of a seventeenth-century Chinese province, the memoirs of a local magistrate, and a collection of contemporary short stories into a historical novel. *The Gate of Heavenly Peace: The Chinese and Their Revolution, 1895-1980* presents recent Chinese history as seen and lived by China's writers and artists. And *The Memory Palace of Matteo Ricci* is a biography of a sixteenth-century Jesuit missionary to China organized around the mental images used in a Medieval memory system. Because he "brings imagination and literary flair to his material," these books have won Spence "a high reputation," as John Gross reports in the *New York Times.*

Perhaps Spence's most successful book has been *The Gate of Heavenly Peace,* winner of two major awards in the field of historical writing. Tracing the turbulent history of modern China, *The Gate of Heavenly Peace* does not tell of the political leaders of the time nor of the common people. It focuses instead on China's intelligensia and records how they both inspired and served the forces of political change and were often the first victims of those changes. As Kenneth J. Atchity explains in the *Los Angeles Times Book Review,* "Spence shows us history through the perceptions of individuals who—in a more or less minor key, relative to Sun Yat-sen and Mao—were affected by these movements and whose souls helped shape these dreams." In particular, the book follows the careers of three people: the Confucian scholar Kang Youwei, the writer Lu Xun, and the novelist Ding Ling.

"No one has quite done Chinese history like this before," Jay Mathews writes in the *Washington Post Book World.* Mathews believes that Spence "brings alive the men and women who made the revolution, uncovering their bedtime fantasies, personality conflicts, sexual weaknesses and irrational rages." Similarly, Richard Harris of the London *Times* calls *The Gate of Heavenly Peace* "a book that brings China to life better than almost any other written about China since [the revolution]."

Spence's book also provides a valuable insight into the nature of the Chinese revolution. As Stuart Schram writes in the *Times Literary Supplement,* "Spence illuminates in a way no one else has done before, important aspects of the revolution, and in the process brings us closer to a full understanding of its meaning." "Spence has woven a magical symphony," Salisbury writes, "that tells us as no conventional history could of the agony of a nation in awesome labor, giving birth, as it were, to its own future."

In *The Memory Palace of Matteo Ricci,* Spence recreates the China of the sixteenth century and the work of the Jesuit missionaries of the time. In doing so, he also sketches a panoramic overview of the relationship between Europe and the East. The book's title comes from Ricci's memory system, which he used to remember vast amounts of information. His memory feats astounded his Chinese friends. At one gathering, Ricci was given a list of 500 Chinese characters to memorize. He read them back correctly and then, to the astonishment of the Chinese, recited them correctly in backward order as well. The system he used was based on a mental "memory palace"—a series of vividly-imagined rooms. In each room was stored visual representations of the items to be remembered. As the user of the system imagines a walk through these rooms, the visual images trigger the proper memories in the proper order.

The Memory Palace of Matteo Ricci is organized around eight pictures—four used in Ricci's memory system and four religious wood-cuts he chose to illustrate one of his books. Spence uses these pictures as starting-points to discuss such topics as sixteenth-century warfare, commerce, and religious thought. "Spence cuts across the fabric of history from many different angles and directions," H. J. Kirchhoff writes in the Toronto *Globe and Mail*, "allowing Ricci's choices of illustration and explication to direct our gaze toward the Chinese of the sixteenth century, and toward the Jesuits who so determinedly and imaginatively proselytized them." As Marvin R. O'Connell observes in the *Washington Post Book World*, "Spence has employed Ricci's preoccupation with mnemonics to fashion an ingenious structure in which to bring together a history of China and Europe during Ricci's lifetime. . . . [It is] a genuine tour de force."

Spence's unique presentations of history, Michael Feingold maintains in the *Voice Literary Supplement*, "may be on the thin edge of ethical procedure. For the lay reader, however, they're infinitely more entertaining than the ponderous sobriety, overlaid with econometric tables and French theorizing, that history as a field has become. . . . If Spence's tactics are maddening, they're also revelatory, making us think about the life behind history as a drier recitation of facts never could." David Lattimore of the *New York Times Book Review* cites *Emperor of China, The Death of Woman Wang,* and *The Gate of Heavenly Peace* as works in which Spence "employs a similar method of delicate interweaving and transition. These are works of carefully thought out, accurately annotated history, which, with their well-observed detail and extensive quotations, propel us among the very sights and sounds and emotions of the time. They exemplify a high historical art, worthy tributes to Clio, muse of history." Salisbury describes Spence as "a poet-historian of China, whose images bring to us the true fragrance of the East, the limitless breadth of China, the deep wells of its culture, the harshness of its cruelties, the continuity of the Chinese ethos."

BIOGRAPHICAL/CRITICAL SOURCES:

PERIODICALS

Chicago Tribune Book World, October 11, 1981.
Globe and Mail (Toronto), June 29, 1985.
Los Angeles Times Book Review, December 27, 1981, November 25, 1984.
Nation, September 2, 1978.
Newsweek, May 22, 1978, November 9, 1981.
New York Review of Books, May 18, 1978.
New York Times, October 12, 1981, November 21, 1984.
New York Times Book Review, July 16, 1969, June 11, 1978, October 18, 1981, December 2, 1984.
Times (London), February 18, 1982.
Times Literary Supplement, August 19, 1983, September 27, 1985.
Voice Literary Supplement, December, 1984.

Washington Post Book World, November 22, 1981, December 23, 1984.
Yale Review, autumn, 1969.

—*Sketch by Thomas Wiloch*

* * *

SPENCER, Harold (Edwin) 1920-

PERSONAL: Born October 1, 1920, in Corning, N.Y.; son of Clayton Judson (an industrial worker) and Hazel (McCaslin) Spencer; married Editha Mary Hayes, September 13, 1947; children: David Hayes, Robert Alan, Eric James, Mark Edward. *Education:* Studied at Art Students' League, New York, 1941-42, and U.S. Merchant Marine Academy, 1942-43; University of California, Berkeley, A.B., 1948, M.A., 1949; Harvard University, Ph.D., 1969.

ADDRESSES: Home—R.R. 1, Box 56, Ashford, Conn. 06278. *Office*—School of Fine Arts, University of Connecticut, Storrs, Conn. 06268.

CAREER: Blackburn College, Carlinville, Ill., member of faculty and chairman of art department, 1949-62; Occidental College, Los Angeles, Calif., associate professor of art history, 1962-68, chairman of department of art, 1963-68; University of Connecticut, Storrs, associate professor, 1968-69, professor of art history, 1969—, administrative associate to department head, 1972-73, associate department head, 1977-79. *Military service:* U.S. Merchant Marine, 1942-46; became lieutenant junior grade.

MEMBER: American Association of University Professors, Connecticut Academy of Arts and Sciences, College Art Association, Phi Kappa Phi.

AWARDS, HONORS: Awards for painting and drawing.

WRITINGS:

(Editor) *Readings in Art History,* Scribner, Volume I: *Ancient Egypt through the Middle Ages,* 1969, 3rd edition, 1982, Volume II: *The Renaissance to Present,* 1969, 3rd edition, 1982.
(Editor and author of introduction) *The American Earls* (exhibition catalogue), William Benton Museum of Art, University of Connecticut, 1972.
The Image Maker: Man and his Art, Scribner, 1975.
Criehaven: A Bellows Pastoral (bulletin), William Benton Museum of Art, University of Connecticut, 1977.
(Editor) *American Art: Readings from the Colonial Era to the Present,* Scribner, 1980.
Reflections on American Impressionism, Smithsonian Institute, 1982.

Also author of *Reflections on Impressionism, Its Genesis and American Phase,* 1980 and *On Some Works by Maurice Prendergast,* 1985.

WORK IN PROGRESS: A biography of English travel-artist, Augustus Earle, a biography of American painter, Charles W. Hawthorne, and a history of the American landscape.

* * *

SPENCER, William 1922-

PERSONAL: Born June 1, 1922, in Erie, Pa.; son of Herbert Reynolds (a manufacturer) and Rachel (Davis) Spencer; married Martha Jane Brown, February 6, 1948 (divorced); married

Elizabeth Bouvier (an artist and teacher), May 18, 1969; children: (first marriage) Christopher, Meredith, Anne. *Education:* Princeton University, A.B., 1948; Duke University, A.M., 1950; American University, Ph.D., 1965. *Politics:* Democrat. *Religion:* Episcopalian.

ADDRESSES: Home—P.O. Box 1702-52, Gainesville, Fla. 32602.

CAREER: St. Lawrence University, Canton, N.Y., instructor in English, 1950-51; U.S. Information Agency, Turkish-American Association, Ankara, Turkey, teacher of English, 1954-56; *Middle East Journal,* Washington, D.C., assistant editor, 1956-57; George Washington University, Washington, D.C., associate professor of political science, 1957-60; U.S. Office of Education, Washington, D.C., international programs specialist, 1960-62; UNESCO, Paris, France, chief of publications, 1962-64; American University, Washington, D.C., director of Institute of Non-Western Studies, 1965-68; Florida State University, Tallahassee, professor of Middle East history, 1968-80; freelance writer and newspaper columnist, 1980—. Visiting professor of politics, Rollins College, 1982-85. Member of Islam Centennial Fourteen National Academic Advisory Board, Walden University Board of Academic Advisors, and of several community service boards, including Florida Heritage Foundation, Central Florida Community Action Agency, and Partners Enchancing Porter's, an inner-city social service foundation. Former advisor to the government of Morocco for the establishment of African Research Center in Public Administration in Tangier. Consultant to Board of Advisors, University of North Africa. *Military service:* U.S. Army, 1943-46; cadet, Army Specialized Training Program (Turkish); Signal Intelligence Service, India; received Presidential Citation.

MEMBER: Phi Kappa Phi, Pi Sigma Alpha, Phi Alpha Theta.

AWARDS, HONORS: Distinguished Service Award, U.S. Junior Chamber of Commerce, 1958; Carnegie fellowship; U.S. Office of Education Title V grant; Fulbright-Hays Award; Florida State University research grant.

WRITINGS:

The Land and People of Turkey, Lippincott, 1958, revised edition, 1972.
Political Evolution in the Middle East, Lippincott, 1962.
The Land and People of Morocco, Lippincott, 1965, revised edition, 1973.
The Land and People of Tunisia, Lippincott, 1967, revised edition, 1972.
The Land and People of Algeria, Lippincott, 1969.
The Story of North Africa, McCormick-Mathers, 1975.
Algiers in the Age of the Corsairs, University of Oklahoma Press, 1976.
Historical Dictionary of Morocco, Scarecrow Press, 1980.

Also author of *Global Cultures: The Middle East,* 1986, 2nd edition, 1988, and of several government reports.

Author of weekly column, "Micanopy," in *Gainesville Sun,* 1980—. Contributor to *World Book Encyclopedia, World Book Year Book,* and *Grolier Encyclopedia Year Book.* Contributor of over 500 articles and book reviews to national journals and newspapers.

WORK IN PROGRESS: A complete revised edition, tantamount to a new book, updating *The Land and People of Turkey* for Lippincott; contributing travel pieces regularly to the *Gainesville Sun* and other periodicals; a series on Mexico; a

comic novel, *The CIA and the Twelfth Imam* is on the back burner.

SIDELIGHTS: William Spencer told *CA:* "Writing for me tends to alternate between periods of intense activity and equally intense burnout. Thus, the writing of *Global Cultures: The Middle East* was an exhausting effort—three months of steady writing, then a break, then several more months of editing and revision. As a change of pace, I became involved in volunteer work in the community and, in time, organized a small non-profit, church-related foundation which has again absorbed all my time and energy. But it has been an invaluable experience in terms of material, human interest stories, giving me another dimension as a writer. I'm excited about the upcoming revisions of two of my books, not merely for sales but also for reputation, since I moved out of Middle Eastern scholarship with retirement. But I look forward with equal eagerness to working on other types of writing, even fiction, drawn from my community work. These are wonderful times in which to live and to record life as a writer."

*   *   *

SPINGARN, Lawrence P(erreira)   1917-

PERSONAL: Born July 11, 1917, in Jersey City, N.J.; son of Joseph and Ann (Birnbaum) Spingarn; married Sylvia Georgina Wainhouse (an English instructor), June 19, 1949; children: one son, one daughter. *Education:* Bowdoin College, B.S., 1940; University of Michigan, M.A., 1948; University of California, Los Angeles, additional study, 1949.

ADDRESSES: Home—13830 Erwin St., Van Nuys, Calif. 91401. *Office*—Perivale Press, 13830 Erwin St., Van Nuys, Calif. 91401.

CAREER: Library of Congress, Washington, D.C., Hispanic desk, special librarian, 1941-43; United Service Organizations, New York, N.Y., publicity, 1944-45; free-lance writing and work in own business, New York City and Los Angeles, Calif., 1945-49; Ponoma College, Ponoma, Calif., instructor, 1948-49; affiliated with Los Angeles Valley College, Van Nuys, Calif., 1948-59, professor of English, 1959-85, professor emeritus, 1985—. Publisher and senior editor, Perivale Press, 1968—.

MEMBER: International Institute of Arts and Letters, Poetry Society of America, Poetry Society of London, PEN.

AWARDS, HONORS: Bread Loaf fellowships, 1941, 1942; McDowell resident fellowships, 1946, 1981; Huntington Hartford Foundation award, 1950, fellowships, 1955, 1956; Yaddo resident fellowship, 1958; Hawthornden fellowship, Scotland, 1986; "Best Poem," Poetry Society of America, 1975; "Best Poem of the Year," *Yankee Magazine,* 1981.

WRITINGS:

Rococo Summer and Other Poems (Book-of-the-Month Club recommendation), Dutton, 1947.
The Lost River: Poems, Heinemann, 1951.
Letters from Exile: Poems, Longmans, 1961.
Madame Bidet and Other Fixtures: Poems, Perivale Press, 1968.
Freeway Problems and Others: Poems, Perivale Press, 1970.
(Editor) *Poets West: Contemporary Poems from the Eleven Western States,* Perivale Press, 1975.
The Blue Door and Other Stories, Perivale Press, 1977.
The Black Cap: A Story, Mudborn Press, 1978.

The Dark Playground: Poems, Perivale Press, 1979.
The Belvedere: A Story, Typographeum, 1982.
Moral Tales: Fictions and Parables, Perivale Press, 1983.

CONTRIBUTOR TO ANTHOLOGIES

The Poetry Society of America, Fine Editions Press, 1946.
Poetry Awards, University of Pennsylvania Press, 1949.
Best American Short Stories, Houghton, annual volumes, 1950-53, 1955-56, 1961, and 1968.
Poetry Los Angeles, Villiers Publications, 1958.
The Golden Year: The Poetry Society of America, Fine Editions Press, 1960.
The Complete Imbiber, Vista Press, 1961.
The New York Book of Poems, Viking, 1969.
Great American World Poets: A Golden Treasure of American Verse, Poet Press (Madras, India), 1976.
Poems of Death and Suicide, Shell Press Chapbook, 1978.
A Long Line of Joy, W. J. Robson, 1978.
Contents Under Pressure, Moonlight Publications, 1981.
Fiction 83, Exile Press, 1983.

Also anthologized in *American Writing,* 1942 and 1943.

OTHER

Contributor of poetry, fiction, essays, and general articles to numerous magazines and newspapers, including *Harper's, Kenyon Review, Modern Age, New Yorker, New York Times, Paris Review, Poetry, Saturday Review, Southern Review,* and *Yale Review;* contributor to numerous professional journals in Canada, France, Great Britain, and West Indies, as well as the United States. Founding editor, *California Quarterly,* 1950-53; contributing editor, *Trace,* 1961-64.

WORK IN PROGRESS: The Overture, a novel.

SIDELIGHTS: Lawrence P. Spingarn told *CA:* "I have traveled extensively, but not exclusively, in countries of the mind."

BIOGRAPHICAL/CRITICAL SOURCES:

PERIODICALS

Los Angeles Times, August 8, 1985.

* * *

SPYERS-DURAN, Peter 1932-

PERSONAL: Born January 26, 1932, in Budapest, Hungary; son of Alfred (a colonel) and Maria Balogh (Almassy) Spyers-Duran; married Jane F. Cumber, March 21, 1964; children: Kimberly, Hilary, Peter II. *Education:* University of Budapest, certificate, 1955; University of Chicago, M.A.L.S., 1960; Nova University, E.D., 1975.

ADDRESSES: Home—517 Kimberly, Birmingham, Mich. 48009. *Office*—Department of Libraries and Library Science, Wayne State University, Detroit, Mich. 48002.

CAREER: Chicago Public Library, Chicago, Ill., reference librarian, 1959-60; University of Wichita, Wichita, Kan., head of circulation department, 1960-62; American Library Association, Chicago, assistant executive secretary, 1962-63; University of Wisconsin—Milwaukee, assistant director of libraries and assistant professor, 1963-67, associate director of libraries and associate professor, 1967; Western Michigan University, Kalamazoo, associate professor, 1967-69, professor, 1969-70, director of libraries, 1967-70; Florida Atlantic University, Boca Raton, professor and director of libraries and chairman of library science program, 1970-76; California State

University, Long Beach, executive director of library and learning resources, 1976-83; Wayne State University, Detroit, Mich., dean of Libraries and Library Science, 1983—. Institutional repesentative to Center for Research Libraries and International Federation of Library Associations.

MEMBER: American Library Association, American Society for Information Science, Association for Library and Information Science Education, Southeastern Library Association, Florida Library Association, Florida Association of Public Junior Colleges, California Library Association, California Academic and Research Libraries, Michigan Library Association.

WRITINGS:

Moving Library Materials, University of Wisconsin—Milwaukee Library Associates, 1964, revised edition, American Library Association, 1965.
A Survey of Fringe Benefits Offered by Public Libraries in the United States, American Library Association, 1966.
Basic Fringe Benefits for Public Libraries in the United States, Libraries Unlimited, 1967.
(Contributor) Theodore Samore, editor, *Problems in Library Classification, Dewey 17 and Conversion,* University of Wisconsin, 1968.
(Editor) *Approval and Gathering Plans in Academic Libraries,* Western Michigan University, 1970.
(Editor) *Advances in Understanding Approval Plans in Academic Libraries,* Western Michigan University, 1970.
Economics of Approval Plans, Greenwood Press, 1972.
(Co-editor) *Management Problems in Serials Work,* Greenwood Press, 1973.
Prediction of Resource Needs: A Model Formula Budgeting System for Upper Division University Libraries, Nova University Press, 1975.
Issues in Automated Cataloging, Greenwood Press, 1979.
Shaping Library Collections for the 1980's, Oryx, 1981.
Austerity Management in Academic Libraries, Scarecrow, 1983.
Financing Information Services, Greenwood Press, 1985.
Issues in Academic Librarianship, Greenwood Press, 1985.

Contributor of reviews and articles to professional journals, including *Wilson Library Bulletin, Incipit, Library Quarterly,* and *College Research Libraries.*

AVOCATIONAL INTERESTS: Riding, tennis, swimming, the theater, music, deep-sea fishing, and boating.

* * *

SQUIRE, Jason E(dward) 1948-

PERSONAL: Born November 3, 1948, in Brooklyn, N.Y.; son of Sidney (a judge) and Helen (Friedman) Squire. *Education:* Syracuse University, B.S., 1969; University of California, Los Angeles, M.A., 1972.

CAREER: WAER-FM (radio station), Syracuse, N.Y., program director, 1968-69; Talent Associates Ltd., Studio City, Calif., television production associate, 1969-70; Avco Embassy Pictures Corp., Los Angeles, Calif., production associate, 1970; United Artists Corp., New York City, assistant to senior production vice-president, 1971-73; E.P.A. Films, Inc., New York City and Los Angeles, executive in charge of development, 1974-78; currently associate director of television movies, Twentieth Century-Fox Film Corp., Los Angeles.

MEMBER: Writers Guild of America West, Tau Theta Upsilon, Alpha Epsilon Rho, Sigma Delta Chi, Sigma Tau Rho.

WRITINGS:

(Editor with A. William Bluem) *The Movie Business: American Film Industry Practice* (textbook), Hastings House, 1972.

(Editor) *The Movie Business Book,* Prentice-Hall, 1983.

Also author of screenplay "Red Harvest," based on Dashiell Hammett's novel of the same title, for E.P.A. Films.

WORK IN PROGRESS: A second textbook on the film industry.

*   *   *

STARBUCK, George (Edwin) 1931-

PERSONAL: Born June 15, 1931, in Columbus, Ohio; son of George W. (a professor) and Margaret Beiswanger; name legally changed to Starbuck; married Janice King, April 25, 1955; married second wife, Judith Luraschi (an artist), July 28, 1962; married third wife, Kathryn Dermand, May 18, 1968; children: (first marriage) Margaret Mary, Stephen George, John Edward; (second marriage) Anthony Luigi, Joshua Beiswanger. *Education:* Attended California Institute of Technology, 1947-49, University of California, 1950-51, University of Chicago, 1954-57, and Harvard University, 1957-58. *Politics:* "Pinko; that is, domestically a libertarian meliorist; in foreign policy, close to AFSC." *Religion:* "One of my major interests."

ADDRESSES: Office—Office of Graduate Programs, Boston University, Boston, Mass. 02215.

CAREER: Houghton Mifflin Co., Boston, Mass., editor in trade department, 1958-61; American Academy in Rome, Italy, fellow, 1961-63; State University of New York at Buffalo, librarian and lecturer, 1963-64; University of Iowa, Writers Workshop, Iowa City, associate professor, 1964-67, director, 1967-70; Boston University, Boston, Mass., professor of creative writing and director of graduate programs, 1971—. *Military service:* U.S. Army, 1952-54; served as corporal in Military Police Corps.

MEMBER: PEN, Modern Language Association of America, New University Conference, New England College English Association.

AWARDS, HONORS: Yale Series of Younger Poets Award, 1960; John Simon Guggenheim Memorial fellowship, 1961; American Academy and Institute of Arts and Letters award in literature, 1983; Prix de Rome of American Academy of Arts and Letters.

WRITINGS:

POETRY

Bone Thoughts, Yale University Press, 1960.
White Paper, Little, Brown, 1966.
Elegy in a Country Church Yard, Pym-Randall, 1975.
Desperate Measures, David Godine, 1978.
Talkin' B.A. Blues: The Life and a Couple of Deaths of Ed Teashack, or, How I Discovered B.U., Met God, and Became an International Figure, Pym-Randall, 1980.
The Argot Merchant Disaster: Poems, New and Selected, Little, Brown, 1982.

Contributor of poetry to periodicals, including *New Yorker, Atlantic, Poetry, New Republic, Saturday Review,* and *Yale Review.*

SIDELIGHTS: George Starbuck's songs of protest are usually concerned with love, war, and the spiritual temper of the times. John Holmes believes that "there hasn't been as much word-excitement . . . for years," as one finds in *Bone Thoughts.* Harvey Shapiro points out that Starbuck's work is attractive because of its "witty, improvisational surface, slangy and familiar address, brilliant aural quality . . . ," and adds that Starbuck may become a "spokesman for the bright, unhappy young men. . . ."

Thomas Gunn, on the other hand, believes that Starbuck "is not even very elegant," but, Louise Bogan writes, his daring satire "sets him off from the poets of generalized rebellion."

After reading *Bone Thoughts,* Holmes hoped for other books in the same vein; R. F. Clayton finds that, in *White Paper,* the verse again stings with parody. Although Robert D. Spector wasn't sure of Starbuck's sincerity in *Bone Thoughts,* he rates the poems in *White Paper,* which range "from parody to elegy to sonnets, and even acrostic exercises," as "generally superior examples of their kind." In particular, Spector writes, when Starbuck juxtaposes McNamara's political language and a Quaker's self-immolation by burning, or wryly offers an academician's praise for this nation's demonstration of humanity by halting its bombing for "five whole days," we sense this poet's genuine commitment.

Starbuck reads French, speaks Italian, and "covets" Chinese.

BIOGRAPHICAL/CRITICAL SOURCES:

PERIODICALS

New Yorker, March 26, 1960.
New York Herald Tribune Book Review, June 12, 1960.
New York Times Book Review, October 23, 1960.
Saturday Review, February 11, 1967.
Yale Review, June, 1960.†

*   *   *

STEVENS, Tricia
See PEARL, Jacques Bain

*   *   *

STEVENS, Trisha
See PEARL, Jacques Bain

*   *   *

STEWART, Will
See WILLIAMSON, John Stewart

*   *   *

STINCHCOMBE, Arthur L. 1933-

PERSONAL: Born May 16, 1933, in Clare County, Mich.; son of Frank Homer (a high school counselor) and Christina (Stratton) Stinchcombe; married Barbara E. Bifoss, July 1, 1953 (divorced); married Carol A. Heimer, December 30, 1980; children: (first marriage) Maxwell Benjamin, Amy Lenore, Adam Michael, Kirk Thomas; (second marriage) Kai Heimer, Der Heimer. *Education:* Central Michigan University, A.B., 1953; University of California, Berkeley, Ph.D., 1960. *Politics:* Socialist.

ADDRESSES: Office—Department of Sociology, Northwestern University, Evanston, Ill. 60201.

CAREER: Johns Hopkins University, Baltimore, Md., assistant professor, 1959-65, associate professor of social relations and chairman of department, 1965-67; University of California, Berkeley, 1967-75, began as associate professor, became professor of sociology, chairman of department, 1971-73; University of Chicago, Chicago, Ill., professor of sociology and senior study director of National Opinion Research Center, 1975-80; University of Arizona, Tucson, professor of sociology, 1980-83; Northwestern University, Evanston, Ill., professor of sociology, 1983—. Visiting professor, University of Essex, 1968-69, and University of Bergen, 1979-80. Staff member and researcher in Venezuela and elsewhere, Harvard University-Massachusetts Institute of Technology Joint Center for Urban Studies, 1964-65; fellow, Netherlands Institute for Advanced Study, 1973-74; senior research sociologist, Institute of Industrial Economics, Bergen, 1979-87. *Military service:* U.S. Army, Medical Corps, 1953-55.

MEMBER: American Sociological Association, American Academy of Arts and Sciences (fellow).

WRITINGS:

Rebellion in a High School, Quadrangle, 1965.
Constructing Social Theories, Harcourt, 1968.
(With Rene Marder and Zahava Blum) *Creating Efficient Industrial Administration,* Academic Press, 1974.
Theoretical Methods in Social History, Academic Press, 1978.
(With Calvin Jones and Paul Sheatsley) *Dakota Farmers Evaluate Crop and Livestock Surveys,* National Opinion Research Center, 1979.
(With others) *Crime and Punishment: Changing Attitudes in America,* Jossey-Bass, 1980.
Economic Sociology, Academic Press, 1983.
(With wife, Carol A. Heimer) *Organization Theory and Project Management,* Norwegian University Press, 1985.
Stratification and Organization, Cambridge University Press, 1986.

CONTRIBUTOR

James G. March, editor, *Handbook of Organizations,* Rand McNally, 1965.
Neil J. Smelser, editor, *Sociology: An Introduction,* Wiley, 1967, revised edition, 1973.
Instructor's Guide to Sociology Today, CRM Books, 1971.
K. Land and S. Spilerman, editors, *Social Indicator Models,* Russell Sage, 1975.
Nelson Polsby and Frederick Greenstein, editors, *Handbook of Political Science,* Volume III, Addison-Wesley, 1975.
Louis A. Coser, editor, *The Idea of Social Structure,* Harcourt, 1975.
Coser and Otto N. Larsen, editors, *The Uses of Controversy in Sociology,* Free Press, 1976.
Dwight Perkins, editor, *Small Scale Industry in China,* University of California Press, 1978.
Walter G. Stepahn and Joe R. Feagin, *School Desegregation: Past, Present and Future,* Plenum, 1980.
Social Science Information, Sage Publications, 1980.

Also contributor to *Encyclopedia of the Social Sciences.*

OTHER

Contributor of articles and reviews to professional journals.

*   *   *

STONE, Irving   1903-

PERSONAL: Name legally changed; born July 14, 1903, in San Francisco, Calif.; son of Charles Tannenbaum and Pauline (Rosenberg) Tannenbaum Stone; married Jean Factor (his editor since 1933), February 11, 1934; children: Paula Hubbell, Kenneth. *Education:* University of California, Berkeley, B.A., 1923, graduate study, 1924-26; University of Southern California, M.A., 1924. *Politics:* Independent. *Religion:* Jewish.

ADDRESSES: Home—Beverly Hills, Calif. *Office*—c/o Doubleday & Co., 501 Franklin Ave., New York, N.Y. 11530.

CAREER: University of Southern California, Los Angeles, instructor in economics, 1923-24; University of California, Berkeley, instructor in economics, 1924-26; writer, 1926—. Visiting professor of creative writing, University of Indiana, 1948, University of Washington, 1961, and Gustavus Adolphus College, 1982; lecturer, University of Southern California and California State Colleges, 1966, New York University and Johns Hopkins University, 1985. Specialist on cultural exchange for U.S. State Department to Soviet Union, Poland, and Yugoslavia, 1962; contributing member, American School of Classical Studies, Athens, Greece, 1965—. Member of advisory board, University of California Institute for Creative Arts, 1963—; founder, California State Colleges Committee for the Arts, 1967; member, Center for the Study of Evolution and the Origin of Life, University of California, Los Angeles, 1985. Member, U.S. delegation to Writers Conference, Kiev, Soviet Union, 1982; panelist, Nobel Conference on "Darwin's Legacy"; member, Soviet-American Writers Conference, Pepperdine University, 1984; Regents' professor, University of California, Los Angeles, 1984—.

Member of California Civil War Centennial Commission, 1961-65, California Citizens' Committee for Higher Education, 1964, and California State Committee on Public Education, 1966-67. Member of Eleanor Roosevelt Memorial Foundation, 1963; vice-president, Eugene V. Debs Foundation, 1963—; trustee, Douglass House Foundation, 1967-74; chairman, Allan Nevins Memorial Fund, Huntington Library, 1972—. Member of American Assembly, Columbia University, 1963-67; president, Beverly Hills Improvement Association, 1964-65. Founder with wife, Jean Stone, of two annual $1000 awards for the best biographical and historical novels published; founder, Jean and Irving Stone Honors Commons, University of California, Los Angeles, 1985.

MEMBER: Authors League of America, PEN, Society of American Historians, National Society of Arts and Letters (member of advisory council, 1976—), Academy of American Motion Picture Arts and Sciences, Academy of Political Science, Academy of American Poets (founder), Western Writers of America, Renaissance Society of America, California Writers Guild (president, 1960-61), California Writers Club (honorary life member), Historical Society of Southern California, Fellows for Schweitzer (founder and president, 1955—), Berkeley Fellows (charter member), Los Angeles Dante Alighieri Society (president, 1968-69).

AWARDS, HONORS: Christopher Award and Silver Spur Award from Western Writers of America, both 1957, for *Men to Match My Mountains;* Golden Lily of Florence, Rupert Hughes Award from Author's Club, Gold Medal from Council of American Artist Societies, and Gold Medal from Commonwealth Club of California, all for *The Agony and the Ecstasy;* named commendatore of Republic of Italy; American Revolution Round Table Award and Literary Father of the Year Award, both 1966, for *Those Who Love;* Gold Trophy from American Women in Radio and Television, 1968; Herbert Adams Memorial Medal from National Sculpture Society, 1970; Golden Plate Award from American Academy of Achievement, 1971; Alumnus of the Year from University of California, Berkeley, 1971; honorary citizen of Athens, Greece, 1972; Corpus Litterarum Award from Friends of the Libraries, University of California, Irvine, 1975; Distinguished Alumni Award from Los Angeles Unified School District, 1976; Author of the Year Award from Book Bank USA, 1976.

Distinguished body of work annual award, Los Angeles PEN Center, 1980; Rupert Hughes Award for excellence in writing from Author's Club, 1980; Call Achievement Award from University of Southern California, 1980; named Grand Ufficiale of the Italian Republic, 1982; Neil H. Jacoby Award from International Student Center, University of California at Los Angeles, 1983; honorary citation from Union of Soviet Writers, 1983; Commandeur dans l'Ordre des Arts et des Lettres from French Ministry of Culture, 1984. D.L. from University of Southern California, 1965; D.Litt. from Coe College, 1967, and California State Colleges, 1971; LL.D. from University of California, Berkeley, 1968; H.H.D. from Hebrew Union College, 1978.

WRITINGS:

Pageant of Youth, A. H. King, 1933.

Lust for Life (biographical novel about Vincent van Gogh; also see below), Longmans, Green, 1934, published with foreword by the author, Modern Library, 1939, reprinted, 1962, published with reader's supplement, Washington Square Press, 1967, published as limited edition with portfolio of drawings by van Gogh, Franklin Library, 1980.

(Editor with wife, Jean Stone) *Dear Theo: The Autobiography of Vincent van Gogh,* Doubleday, 1937, reprinted, New American Library, 1969.

Sailor on Horseback (biographical novel about Jack London), Houghton, 1938, published as *Jack London, Sailor on Horseback,* Doubleday, 1947, reprinted, New American Library of Canada, 1969, published with twenty-eight stories by London as *Irving Stone's Jack London, His Life, Sailor on Horseback,* Doubleday, 1977.

False Witness (novel), Doubleday, 1940.

Clarence Darrow for the Defense (biography), Doubleday, 1941, abridged edition, Bantam, 1958, reprinted, New American Library, 1971.

Immortal Wife (biographical novel about Jessie Benton Fremont; also see below), Doubleday, 1944, condensed edition, 1954, reprinted New American Library, 1972.

They Also Ran: The Story of the Men Who Were Defeated for the Presidency, Doubleday, 1945, reprinted, New American Library, 1966.

Adversary in the House (biographical novel about Eugene V. Debs), Doubleday, 1947, reprinted, New American Library, 1969.

Earl Warren: A Great American Story (biography), Prentice-Hall, 1948.

The Passionate Journey (biographical novel about John Noble), Doubleday, 1949.

We Speak for Ourselves: A Self-Portrait of America, Doubleday, 1950.

The President's Lady (biographical novel about Rachel and Andrew Jackson; also see below), Doubleday, 1951, reprinted, New American Library, 1968.

Love Is Eternal (biographical novel about Mary Todd and Abraham Lincoln), Doubleday, 1954, reprinted, New American Library, 1969, condensed large type edition, Ulverscroft, 1976.

Men to Match My Mountains: The Opening of the Far West, 1840-1900, Doubleday, 1956, reprinted, Berkley Publishing, 1982.

The Agony and the Ecstasy (biographical novel about Michelangelo Buonarroti; also see below), Doubleday, 1961, illustrated edition, 1963, published with illustrations by Bruce Waldman, Franklin Library, 1977, abridged juvenile edition with illustrations by Joseph Cellini published as *The Great Adventures of Michelangelo,* Doubleday, 1965.

(Editor with J. Stone) *I, Michelangelo, Sculptor: An Autobiography through Letters,* translated by Charles Speroni, Doubleday, 1962.

(Editor with Allan Nevins) *Lincoln: A Contemporary Portrait,* Doubleday, 1962.

Two Faces of Love: Lust for Life [and] Immortal Wife, Doubleday, 1962.

The Irving Stone Reader, Doubleday, 1963.

The Story of Michelangelo's Pieta, Doubleday, 1964.

Those Who Love (biographical novel about Abigail and John Adams), Doubleday, 1965.

(Editor and author of introduction) *There Was Light: Autobiography of a University; Berkeley,* Doubleday, 1970.

The Passions of the Mind (biographical novel about Sigmund Freud; Collectors Edition Club choice), Doubleday, 1971.

The Greek Treasure (biographical novel about Henry and Sophia Schliemann), Doubleday, 1975.

The Origin (biographical novel about Charles Darwin), Doubleday, 1980.

Irving Stone: Three Complete Novels (includes *Lust for Life, The Agony and the Ecstasy,* and *The President's Lady*), Avenel Books, 1981.

Depths of Glory (biographical novel about Camille Pissarro and the French impressionists), Doubleday, 1985.

The Science, and the Art, of Biography (Naumburg Memorial lecture; monograph), Division of Honors, University of California, Los Angeles, 1986.

CONTRIBUTOR

The People's Reader, Consolidated, 1949.

Isabel Leighton, editor, *The Aspirin Age,* Simon & Schuster, 1949.

Rudolf Flesch, editor, *Best Articles, 1953,* Hermitage House, 1953.

Three Views of the Novel: Lectures by Irving Stone, John O'Hara, and MacKinlay Kantor, Library of Congress, 1957.

American Panorama: West of the Mississippi, Doubleday, 1960.

The Good Housekeeping Treasury, Simon & Schuster, 1960.

Bucklin Moon, editor, *A Doubleday Anthology,* Doubleday, 1962.

Donald C. Rehkoff, editor, *Portraits in Words,* Odyssey, 1962.

Roy Newquist, editor, *Counterpoint,* Rand McNally, 1964.

My Most Inspiring Moment, Doubleday, 1965.

Bromberg and Greene, editors, *Biography for Youth,* Globe, 1965.

Tanner and Vittetoe, editors, *A Guide for Objective Writing,* Ginn, 1968.

Charles L. Hamrum, editor, *Nobel Conference XVII: Darwin's Legacy,* Harper, 1983.

OTHER

"Magnificent Doll" (screenplay), Universal, 1946.

(Author of introduction) *The Drawings of Michelangelo,* Borden Publishing, 1961.

Also author of *The Biographical Novel: A Lecture Presented at the Library of Congress*, 1957, *Evolution of an Idea*, 1965, and *Mary Todd Lincoln: A Final Judgment?*, 1973. Author of plays "The Dark Mirror," 1928, "The White Life" (about Baruch Spinoza), 1929, and "Truly Valiant," 1936, all produced in New York. Also contributor to *Fourteen Radio Plays*, edited by Arch Oboler, Random House. Art critic for the *Los Angeles Times Mirror*, 1959-60. Contributor to popular magazines, including *American Weekly, California Monthly, Catholic Digest, Coronet, Family Weekly, Good Housekeeping, Holiday, Horizon, Life, Saturday Evening Post, Saturday Review* and *Suburbia Today*.

SIDELIGHTS: "Irving Stone is far and away the most magisterial of all the popular novelists working today," writes Peter Andrews in the *New York Times Book Review*. Although he has written both fiction and biography, Stone is considered the "undisputed king of the literary genre he terms 'biographical novel'" by critics such as Edwin McDowell of the *New York Times Book Review*. Ever since the publication more than fifty years ago of *Lust for Life*, his popular and enduring fictionalized biography of Vincent van Gogh, Stone has written best-selling biographical novels about such influential figures as Michelangelo in *The Agony and the Ecstasy*, Sigmund Freud in *The Passions of the Mind*, Charles Darwin in *The Origin*, and more recently, Camille Pissarro and the French impressionists in *The Depths of Glory*. While critics have been somewhat reluctant to appreciate the genre itself—considering it a mongrelized form that ultimately fails as biography as well as fiction—and have faulted Stone for what they perceive to be tedious, fact-laden tomes, they nonetheless commend his perseverance and meticulous research. "Searching relentlessly for evidence—letters, documents, records, scraps of paper—Stone has written a series of widely acclaimed books," says Marshall Berges in the *Los Angeles Times*, ". . . each time focusing on a long-departed giant and vividly restoring not only the era and the scene but most of all the person."

"I have always loved human stories, both the reading and the writing of them," relates Stone in a *Contemporary Authors Autobiography Series* essay. "I decided early on that I would read all the great tales that had been written, and those which had not yet been set down I would create myself." Although Stone studied economics and political science in college, the desire to become a writer ultimately proved to be more powerful than the inclination to complete his doctorate and eventually led him to Paris in the 1920s. "During my fifteen months in Paris, Antibes and Florence, I wrote seventeen full-length plays, thirty-one one-act plays, several essays and random chapters of novels that never got any further," continues Stone. "The work literally poured out of my fountain pen; yet in some dim way I knew that this was an act of regurgitation rather than creativity." The plays were unsuccessful, but Berges notes that Stone, having been "dazzled" by detective stories as a child, "supported himself by writing penny-a-word detective stories. Later, he adopted detective-like methods to become one of the world's best-selling authors."

In the introduction to *The Irving Stone Reader*, Joseph Henry Jackson observes that working on these early detective stories taught Stone "the necessity of careful plotting, the trick of keeping a narrative on the move, the techniques of construction." Jackson suggests, however, that "the kind of spark that would fire his imagination . . . was character-ready-made, the story of someone who had lived, whose acts could be found in the record and whose motives might be traced by patient, careful, sympathetic investigation." What motivates Stone to

bring a given character to life is "any suspicion that such a character had been misunderstood, perhaps even misrepresented through historical accident or through an early biographer's prejudice." While critical response to Stone's work has not paralleled his popularity, Peter Gorner maintains in the *Chicago Tribune* that most people are probably indebted to Stone for what they know about van Gogh, Freud, and Michelangelo, and that "Stone also has written about lesser-known folks he felt people should learn about. . . . And he has been quick to portray great lives he believes were unfairly wounded by cheap shots."

In *The Science, and the Art, of Biography* (his Naumburg Memorial Lecture at the University of California, Los Angeles), Stone presents his thoughts on the genre he has fostered and on the author's responsibility toward it: "The biographical novel is a true and documented story of one human being's journey across the face of the years, transmuted from the raw material of life into the delight and purity of an authentic art form. It is based on the conviction that the best of all plots lie in human character; and that human character is endlessly colorful and revealing. The biographical novel sets out to document this truth, for character is plot; character development is action; and character fulfillment is resolution." Stone also explains that while biography involves three persons—the subject, the reader, and the author as a mediator between them—the biographical novel involves but two, since the author merges with his subject: "The author becomes the main character by years of intense study of his diaries, journals, correspondence, recorded dialogues, writings about him, his finished work, his character, personality, his manner of speaking, acting; geographic place in the world. The author slips slowly and authentically into his bloodstream, the millions of cells in his brain, the feelings in his gut and nervous system. A total portrait of this one human being's values, his beatings and failures, accomplishments and fulfillments."

Stone indicates to Grace Glueck in the *New York Times* that his preference for the biographical novel over nonfictionalized biography is partially due to the opportunity it affords him to use the "novelistic skills" he acquired during his early attempts at writing plays. But he also says: "I know from experience that biographies have a limited audience. We have thousands of readers who love [the biographical novel] and are thrilled by it, who'd never get near a conventional biography." In *The Science, and the Art, of Biography*, Stone asserts that "the research, dedication and techniques of the biographical novelist are identical to those of the biographer. The major difference is one of dramatization." Perhaps because of his efforts to champion the underdog or to set the historical record straight, Stone is aware of his responsibility for accurate representation in his work and has produced monumentally impressive research for each book. Moreover, Stone's patient and careful research has brought much previously unpublished and important information into print. In addition to the letters of Michelangelo, Stone has had access to van Gogh's letters and Freud's papers, as well as access to the friends and relatives of his more contemporary subjects.

The persistent effort to uncover remnants of an individual's existence calls for ingenuity and tenacity as well as stamina; but to revivify such an existence also requires creative imagination. Stone suggests in Roy Newquist's *Counterpoints* that "even if there is endless documentation it would be impossible to know what a man thought inside his own mind." A vital question is thereby raised, says Stone: "Do you push your character around, and distort history, or do you study [him] so carefully, identify him so totally and with such honesty, that when you come to the point where documentation leaves off, and you must put yourself inside the heart and mind of this man or woman, can you think and feel as he (or she) would have, in the given circumstances? This is the creative part of the book, and if you are honest, if you are sincere, if you have worked hard, if you are determined to be true and to achieve exact identity and to plumb the depths of a man's feelings, I think you have a good chance of doing the job proudly.''

Stone's research for *Lust for Life* included a stay not only in van Gogh's asylum cell but also, on the fortieth anniversary of his death, in the very room in which van Gogh died. As Stone recalls in *The Science, and the Art, of Biography:* "On the very night that Vincent died I went to bed about midnight, surrounded by colored reproductions of his canvases. I pored over them until one o'clock when I began to feel faint. I could not understand why until I realized that Vincent had died in that very bed at 1:20 in the morning. I grew fainter, until finally at 1:19 I threw off the covers, dashed to the back window, stuck my head out and took in deep lungsful of the night air.''

Stone's intense identification with his subjects has prompted several critics to question the extent of his objectivity. In a review of *Lust for Life* in the *Nation,* for instance, Robert Morse suggests that "from a novelist one might have hoped for a dispassionate and honest attempt to clarify and explain the behavior of an extremely interesting human being. . . . I began to suspect that . . . Stone had fallen into the old attitude of unquestioning sentimental identification with his hero.'' However, a reviewer for the *Boston Transcript* notes in his defense of the novel: "Stone did not need to call this fiction. Many biographers have taken more liberties with less results. There is reality here, pathos, humor, a knowledge of art and artists, and a delightful, nonchalant style which keeps us fascinated . . . to the end.''

Decrying Stone's method of interpreting the life and motivation of his subject by "becoming" that character, some critics suggest that Stone tends toward idealization. R. J. Clements, for example, finds *The Agony and the Ecstasy* "an important and thoroughly enjoyable novel," but says in the *Saturday Review* that "Stone's Michelangelo is an idealized version, purged not only of ambisexuality, but of the egotism, faultfinding, harsh irony, and ill temper that we know were characteristic of Michelangelo.'' And although a *Kirkus Reviews* contributor calls *The Agony and the Ecstasy* "an enormous book, in scope, in historical background, in depth perception and characterization," others feel it is simply not a very good novel. Moreover, despite the enormous sales of his novels, many critics seem to agree that Stone is better suited to historical and biographical nonfiction. In the *New York Herald Tribune Lively Arts,* for example, Richard Winston distinguishes between Stone's weaknesses and his obvious talent: "How elegant and convincing some of . . . Stone's shrewd guesses and fictional insights might have been in a straight biography—whereas here they are so often embarrassing and give rise to uneasiness and dissatisfaction.''

The critics' obvious admiration for Stone's impressive research does not prevent them from questioning his manipulation of the collected data. In the *Atlantic,* Steven Marcus praises Stone's fictionalized biography of Freud, *The Passions of the Mind,* for its bibliography, calling it "daunting in its compendiousness, impressive evidence of the earnestness with which

[Stone] has taken this work to himself.'' However, he also believes that "the novel constitutes itself by an incessant, indiscriminate, and incontinent regurgitation of second-hand information.'' Similarly, Richard Locke refers to the book in the *New York Times* as "a 'massively researched' erector set of a novel crammed with biographical, architectural, gastronomical, geographical, medical, historical details.'' And while Edwin Fadiman, Jr. observes in *Saturday Review* that "the author's integrity is revealed in every line," he adds that "it is precisely this glacial earnestness, this obsession with detail that make *The Passions of the Mind* praiseworthy yet dull.'' In *Time,* Brad Darrach calls Stone "the taxidermist of biography" and suggests that he "seems more interested in the facts than he is in Freud.'' Several critics think that the accumulation of detail inhibits the reader's awareness of any inner evolution on the part of the subject. Marcus, for instance, writes: "There is suggested none of the pathological involvement without which a genius of Freud's magnitude is almost unthinkable. It is Freud without the warts.'' Yet Rosalind Wade calls the book "a magnificent memorial to Freud's achievement" in the *Contemporary Review.* "Apart from being an excellent narrative in its own right the book affords an illuminating blue-print of the means by which psychotherapy was belatedly accepted during the 'twenties and 'thirties in the London teaching hospitals.''

Stone's techniques may have an undesired effect, suggests Redmond O'Hanlon in the *Times Literary Supplement:* "The making of lists, the fussy accumulation of historical detail, far from bringing a period to life, may actually museum it away, stiff and distant.'' And some reviewers even wonder whether a profusion of facts, no matter how comprehensive, can disclose accurately a sense of the individual. Calling Stone's *The Origin* "743 pages of catalogues," Anthony Astrachan writes in the *Washington Post Book World* that the novel "conveys nothing of Darwin's emotions, and little of his intellect beyond what can be gleaned from documents.'' Further, Astrachan finds that "nowhere . . . is there any of the one thing that would justify a novel about Darwin: a re-creation of the feelings and the mental processes of one of the great figures of the nineteenth century.'' Webster Schott acknowledges in the *New York Times Book Review* that the book is "a work of vast research, much pleasure and modest insights," yet he also senses that it "seldom seems to reach the essence of the man who went through physical anguish . . . as he wrestled with conflicts created by his extraordinary ideas and their public reception.'' Perhaps Stone has "encountered a character he can observe in almost limitless detail, but not fully reveal," suggests Schott.

Noting, however, that Darwin poses a "severe challenge for a biographical novelist," S. J. Gould adds in *Science* that "Stone's success with such a recalcitrant subject is a testimony to the power of an art that he has promoted assiduously for many years.'' While Christopher Lehmann-Haupt of the *New York Times* admits that *The Origin* "does sound a few major chords amid its endless stream of notes," he thinks that "such chords could have just as well been sounded by a conventional biography.'' And despite the shared belief that "there is little sense of the man . . . and no large attempt to follow the intricacies of his work," O'Hanlon maintains that "this is far and away . . . Stone's best researched and best written book to date.''

Some critics feel that because Stone's research is so thorough he may be overwhelmed by its sheer mass. Susan Isaacs, for example, finds that Stone's book about Camille Pissarro and the French impressionists, *The Depths of Glory*, "lacks the verve, narrative device and structure that made his earlier work so enjoyable." She adds in the *New York Times Book Review* that "this book is little more than mere data." Believing the purpose of detail should be "to flesh out character or add texture to the setting," Isaacs thinks "Stone seems overwhelmed by the piles of information he's gathered, and manages only the weakest narrative thread." However, Daniel Fuchs notes in the *Los Angeles Times Book Review* that Stone "willingly forgoes the useful devices of fiction—the suspense that comes from organized plot and drama, the winning, fictional characters, the manufactured pleasures and excitement and surprise of the actual event." Stone expressed to Glueck that he would like to see Camille Pissarro become as well-known as Vincent van Gogh, and Glueck remarks that "though as a subject, Pissarro lacks the glamour of Van Gogh and Michelangelo . . . Stone has spared no detail that might pique the reader's interest. He gives a full picture of Pissarro's travails as a painter and a family man . . . and conjures up a Paris art world where the schmaltz runs deep."

Stone admits that as a writer he may be verbose. His wife edits all his work and routinely cuts about ten percent of it before a finished product is achieved—a finished product which some reviewers may claim is still too long. Stone and his work, though, have prevailed over the critics, whom he refers to in *The Science, and the Art, of Biography* as "my sometimes critics—and how barren an author's life would be without critics!" The popularity of his work is certainly confirmed by the many languages into which it has been translated: French, German, Spanish, Italian, Greek, Swedish, Turkish, Arabic, Japanese, Russian, Finnish, Norwegian, Danish, Dutch, Portuguese, Polish, Hungarian, Rumanian, Czech, Slovene, Hebrew, Assamese, Hindu, Tamil, Gujarati, Kannada, Marathi, Kanarese, Bengali, Malayan, Latvian, Serbo-Croatian, Persian, Bratislavian, and Icelandic. Surmising that "the secret of the popularity of . . . Stone's novels may very well lie in their unreadability," Peter Andrews remarks in the *New York Times Book Review* that getting through one of his books "gives one a sense of accomplishment." Perhaps, however, the secret rests in the formula Stone uses for his books. "The recurring theme," notes Gorner, "is one man (or woman) against the world, succeeding no matter what." Stone elaborated on this theme to Berges: "My goal always is to tell a universal story, meaning it's about a person who has an idea, a vision, a dream, an ambition to make the world somewhat less chaotic. He or she suffers hardships, defeats, miseries, illnesses, poverty, crushing blows. But ultimately that person accomplishes a big, beautiful, gorgeous job of work, leaving behind a testimonial that the human mind can grow and accomplish fantastic ends."

MEDIA ADAPTATIONS: Stone's novel *False Witness* was filmed by Republic in 1941 as "Arkansas Judge" and was released in Great Britain under its original title; *Immortal Wife* became a film by Twentieth Century-Fox in 1953 under the title "The President's Lady," starring Charlton Heston and Susan Hayward; *Lust for Life* was filmed by Metro-Goldwyn-Mayer in 1956 and starred Kirk Douglas and Anthony Quinn in an Academy Award-winning performance; *The Agony and the Ecstasy* was filmed by Twentieth Century-Fox in 1963 and starred Charlton Heston and Rex Harrison.

AVOCATIONAL INTERESTS: Collecting art.

CA INTERVIEW

CA interviewed Irving Stone by telephone on February 7, 1987, at his home in Beverly Hills, California.

CA: In your 1986 Naumburg Memorial Lecture at UCLA, The Science, and the Art, of Biography, *you described the extraordinary experience of staying in the hotel room where Vincent van Gogh died, and feeling on the anniversary of his death, to the hour, an increasingly deathly faintness. Was this a stronger-than-usual demonstration of the empathy you feel with your subjects?*

STONE: I would say that not only was it a stronger feeling, but it was self-hypnosis. I don't have any spiritualist leanings whatever. I don't believe in ESP or any of the rest of it—at least I say that I don't; it seems to happen once in a while. But I think I worked myself up to that. Knowing all the surrounding details of Vincent's death, I think I just relived it in his capacity as I tried to relive every part of the book *Lust for Life*.

CA: In the biographical novel, as you pointed out in the Naumburg Memorial Lecture, as opposed to biography, "the author becomes the hero *and the reader becomes* the hero, *with total emotional identification." Have you ever studied a subject that you later found you couldn't become, couldn't get into the skin and mind of?*

STONE: Yes, I have, but the particular case was on a slightly different tangent. It was the story of Henry Ford's relationship to his son Edsel and the intervening character of Colonel Bennett. Bennett was the hard-fisted man whom Henry Ford used against the workers. I had a friend from Laguna Beach who had owned the local newspaper there and had done a column for it every week; and also owned the Ford agency. When World War II broke out, he was called back by Henry Ford to start a daily plant newspaper in Dearborn. He stayed there the entire four years of the war and then came back to Laguna Beach and told me these tremendous stories of the conflict and defeat of Edsel Ford and his battles with Colonel Bennett. It looked to me like a good drama that had never been told, and my friend wanted me to write it.

When I was next in New York on some other business, perhaps a month or two later, I called together the three editors who listened to my story ideas back then. I told my story about Henry Ford and Edsel Ford and Colonel Bennett in one hour, as I always did when I had a story I wanted to try on them, outlining the dramatic conflicts and what I thought was the importance of the story in American history; and also the characterizations. When I had finished my hour-long stories previously, I had always had enormously enthusiastic reactions from all my editors. This time there was a very strange silence. You know, there are many different kinds of silences. This was one I had never heard before, and I was puzzled.

Several minutes went by, and then Ken McCormick, who was my editor for forty-five years or more, until he retired, said to me in a very gentle voice, "Irving, you know, you have no hero." With that, I realized that this was not a book I could write. There wasn't anybody there that I liked. I felt compassion for Edsel and hatred for Colonel Bennett. I was puzzled by Henry Ford, but there was no hero. And I said immediately, "Of course you're right. This is not a story for me." That is the only time that, having gone into a story, I talked myself out of it.

CA: How do you pick your subjects? What do they absolutely have to have in order to appeal to you?

STONE: There are a number of criteria. First of all, they have to have what I conceive to be great human stories, with conflict and opposition and defeat and failure, arising again and again and again to accomplish some modest part of what they have set out to accomplish in a realization or a vision of what was needed. So the human story comes first.

Secondly, I have to have a very genuine affection, or you might even use the word *love,* for my main character because I don't have the capacity to get inside the mind or heart or spirit or body of someone I dislike or disapprove of. That's a very special attribute. There are some people who love to write out of hate, which is a contradiction in terms. I can't do that. I have to feel that this is a life I would like to have lived, and might even have been worthy of living.

The third criterion would be that this individual man or woman— I have four books about women—has been on the side of the angels, on the side of human justice and human rights, and has sought to accomplish something that in some modest way would improve the lot of mankind and make life a little more intelligible, a little more beautiful, a little more peaceable. The person has to have had a worthwhile life with some striving over the years to accomplish something not merely for himself or herself—which may have been a by-product and perhaps not even thought of—but something that would in some way better the lot of humanity in this crazy world that is controlled by so much greed and lust and all of the other vices that we cherish and promulgate.

CA: Did the women pose any special challenges to your imagination by being of the opposite sex?

STONE: Yes. At the beginning, that posed an almost insuperable problem. My first book about a woman was *Immortal Wife,* about Jessie Benton Fremont. I had encountered her story while I was working for my Ph.D. at the University of California at Berkeley. I read an article in the *American Mercury* at that time about her life, and I fell in love with the lady. I decided at that point that I would marry in that image— which I did long years later, by the way. When I wrote *They Also Ran,* the story of the defeated presidential candidates, of course I had to write a chapter about John Charles Fremont. He was the first nominee of the new Republican party, in 1856. In researching his life, again I came to Jessie Benton Fremont and the magnificent part she had played in his life, not only in terms of loyalty and devotion, but also in helping him move forward to carve out new empires and write his then very popular books and keep his life in a straight direction, which was not always easy.

So I decided I would like to write a book about Jessie Benton Fremont, but I didn't think I could become a woman. I didn't think I could put myself into the mind and heart and nervous system of a woman. I took my problem to my wife, Jean. I told her of my uncertainties and doubts and yet my very strong desire to write this story, because I thought it was one of the truly great American stories. She said, "Why don't you go ahead and try? After all, we belong to the same species." I said, "Thank you. With that encouragement, I will."

I then completed my research and wrote a fairly long first chapter. I wrote it very tremulously, with great doubt and hesitations. I hoped I had become Jessie Benton Fremont, but I couldn't convince myself. When I finished the chapter, I took it from my studio to Mrs. Stone's office, which is always at the other end of the house or the property. I laid it on her desk and said, "I don't know. I just don't think I've been able to identify with Jessie Benton Fremont. I'm not sure that this is right. But you read it and tell me what you think, honestly." She said she would. A couple of days later she came back into my studio with the manuscript marked a little bit, and she said, "You're all right. Under these circumstances, this is the way a woman would think and feel and act."

Enormously buoyed up and with total confidence now, I dashed into the second section, Chapter 2, which I wrote very fast and full-bloodedly. I took it in to my wife when I was finished and said, "Here. I think you're going to love this." She came back a few hours later holding the chapter at the end of her arm like a dead fish and said, "No woman in the world ever thought or felt or acted like this. Throw it away. Go back to your first chapter and get into that frame of mind, where you *did* identify, and write the second chapter in that same mood or with that same understanding."

That's how we went through the entire book, with my wife telling me I had not quite made the identification and how I could correct it and actually become Jessie Benton Fremont. I must have succeeded in some measure, because the press on that book was ecstatic. We were on top of the *New York Times* bestseller lists for about thirteen months. It was read by millions of women and I didn't get any letters of protest, so I guess I made the transition. After that, doing the stories about Abigail and John Adams, Mary Todd Lincoln, and Rachel Jackson, I had no further difficulty. I simply *became* the women. I had confidence that I could, and apparently I did.

CA: A tremendous amount of all kinds of research goes into your books, down to working in the marble quarries in Carrara, as Michelangelo had done, for The Agony and the Ecstasy. *Does the love of research go all the way back to the early detective stories you wrote?*

STONE: There was no research for the detective stories. They were plain made-up fiction. I sat down at six or seven in the morning, and by six or seven at night I had concocted a murder story. The research goes back to my years at the University of California at Berkeley and also my one year at the University of Southern California, where I took a master's. I entered Berkeley on August 9, 1920. We had no courses in research, and although I took some history courses along with all the others I had to take and wanted to take, the professors were lecturing to large audiences—I remember that Herbert Bolton, a great professor of Spanish history who wrote many wonderful books, was lecturing to a class of seven or eight hundred. They had no time or inclination to teach us how to research.

By trial and error, fumbling and stumbling, I learned how to go about it. I learned to find out how things happened, and where and when. But what I learned that was most important, that has been my mainstay ever since, was that beyond that first answer to the *why,* there are another hundred. And you must never stop. You relentlessly pursue it until you've gotten to the bottom of the barrel of *why*s.

This takes, first of all, a certain love for the work. Research for me is sheer pleasure, because—to go back to your question—I treat it as though it were a detective story, a mystery. I look for clues. When I don't find the answers in the first twenty-five or fifty places I look, I know that it's my fault, that I haven't thought of the right place to look. So I go on, and I find it in the sixtieth or seventieth place. If you have a doggedness so that nothing can put you off the trail, eventually you will find everything that it's possible for a human being to find.

CA: Do you feel you have to have every answer before you begin writing?

STONE: No. That's not possible. I usually work for about two-and-a-half years on the research before I decide that I not only have enough to start, but I have all that I'm able to get at that particular time. Then when I return, let's say, from Italy, where I did *The Agony and the Ecstasy,* or from Greece and Turkey, where I did *The Greek Treasure,* or from England, where I did *The Origin,* about Charles Darwin, I come home to my own desk, where I am sitting in the warm sunshine right now. I keep stringers in all the places where my material is—Athens, Turkey, wherever—it may be all over the world. Then I write letters to them with any number of questions I need answers to, and some of the places where they might find them. Two or three times a week I have material pouring in answering my questions. I tell these people what I must have and that they must provide it. And nine times out of ten, they get it.

CA: You've done the ordinary kind of biography, of course, as well as the biographical novel. Did you find the former too constraining?

STONE: I think I found certain stories, such as *Sailor on Horseback,* about Jack London, and *Clarence Darrow for the Defense,* so unusual and dramatic that I was afraid to put them into novel form for fear they would be thought of by readers as fiction. In those two cases, I didn't want them to be thought of as fiction. Recently I received a book from the University of Chicago Press; they wanted me to give them a quote. The author had said, "You must not think of this book as a novel, though it will appear to be." I thought that was strange. Doubleday had published *Sailor on Horseback* for many years as a novel, and I kept telling them, "It's *not* a novel. Don't do that." They thought they'd sell more books if they called it a novel.

I looked at it again, and I looked at *Clarence Darrow for the Defense* again, vis-a-vis a lot of straight academic biographies I've been reading of late, and I saw that you really could call both of those books novels if you wanted to. Instead of using the indirect, I staged a drama under a proscenium so that the reader is there. It's not a case of the reader going through a biographer to a distant character whom he may or may not understand. In both of those books, the reader acutally identifies with the main characters and lives their lives. In that sense I suppose they are novels even though I didn't intend them to be.

CA: Do you have favorite biographies?

STONE: I have whole shelves of them: as a few examples Leon Edel's biography of Henry James, the first two volumes of the new Joseph Frank biography of Dostoevski. I've read the Lytton Strachey biographies; I've read the English and those that are translated from French and German and Russian. The Henri Troyat biography of Pushkin, I think, is one of the best that's ever been written. I have a library full of stories of political figures, scientists, philosophers et al. I enjoy them very much—except when they start back a hundred years before the hero was born and we get a hundred pages of great-grandparents and grandparents and it takes so long to get up

to the character you're interested in that sometimes the biographer loses you. That's why I've always insisted on starting my books at the Moment of Truth, as the Spaniards call it, that episode which decides the entire future of the individual.

CA: You commented in your 1986 lecture on "how barren an author's life would be without critics!" Do you feel you've learned anything from them?

STONE: I don't know. I'm like all other writers, I suppose: I'm pleased when there are good reviews, and I'm unhappy when there are bad ones. But in the latter years I've followed something Ernest Hemingway told me way back in 1936 down at his home in Key West. He said, "If you don't read the good reviews, you're not obliged to read the bad ones." I try very hard not to see reviews. They're sent to me, and I look at the space, and occasionally I happen to see a headline which is either very good or bad.

What happens, though, is that your friends and relatives and associates always manage to let you know when there's been a bad review. They either phone or visit or write to sympathize with you and call the critic dirty names, but they make sure you get the bad review. That's how I see my bad reviews. I can tell from the publishers if there's been a crippling review, which happens occasionally. But by and large I have fared extremely well with the press. I have no complaints.

CA: Art has been at the heart of several of your books, including the most recent, Depths of Glory, *the story of Camille Pissarro and the French impressionists. Were you collecting art before you began to write about artists?*

STONE: No. I wrote *Lust for Life* back in 1930 and '31, when I was penniless. I managed to get back to Europe on the trail of van Gogh by writing six straight murder stories in six days and selling five of them. On that money I walked across the face of Belgium, Holland, and France with a rucksack on my back, wearing a beret. I was very young. I wore a mustache so that people wouldn't think I was *too* young. I had no money; I couldn't buy anything then. We started collecting after *Sailor on Horseback,* when we had a few spare dollars. We collected pre-Columbian art at first, and then we started buying American and European paintings. We have a good collection now, but it took place gradually over a lot of years.

CA: What do you consider most important in teaching the writing of biography?

STONE: Mrs. Stone and I gave a class in biography last year at UCLA, where we are Regents' professors. The research I can teach the students. The idea of structure I can teach them. I can try to teach them a sense of place, how to describe character, the virtues of dialogue to ease up the narrative. I can teach them twenty or thirty different aspects of the technique of writing. Technique can be conveyed. The art of writing cannot. I cannot teach them how to write with grace and beauty and liquidity. That's something that flows in your blood. It's in your brain cells and the marrow of your bones.

I refused to believe it until just recently because I rejected the idea, but I am now afraid that that particular talent is something you're born with. I don't think the writing of *literature* can be taught. That depends not only on your style and your grace; it depends on your values and the depth of your IQ. How much do you perceive about people? How much do you understand? How much do you know about how the world has functioned in earlier times and how it's functioning now? How much compassion do you have for the whole of the human race? These things you can't teach. Character and personality are buried deep in your genes and nurtured as you are raised by your parents and your teachers and your peers. Everyone has a different means of expression, and I think this is the key: everyone has a different depth. I know lots of writers who are shallow. They can spin a good plot; they're good action people who can write a strong narrative. But they have no particular values. They don't understand what I'm talking about when I speak of human and world values.

CA: There's a great deal of oral history being done now. How do you think it rightfully fits into the practice of biography?

STONE: It's an enormous help. It was started by one of my very dear friends and great teachers, Allan Nevins, at Columbia University. He used his own money to bring in people like Frances Perkins, who was Franklin Delano Roosevelt's secretary of labor and the first woman cabinet member. It spread from there, and people are now going into organized and disciplined oral history groups and getting down material that would never get down otherwise.

It cannot, though, be trusted on its face. You can quote from it, but you have to question it. I use the method of what I call the triple check. If I have only a double check on a piece of historicity, I'm not all that happy about it; I like to get a triple check so that I know I'm not just using something a man or a woman may have remembered fragmentarily or may have used imagination to polish off to make it appear a little better for the teller. But oral history is certainly getting us documents that we couldn't get any other way.

CA: I won't ask you to break your rule and talk about work in progress, but is there a dream book, one you've always wanted to write but haven't been able to?

STONE: I have half a dozen I've always wanted to do. I've wanted to write a biographical novel about Beethoven, but I cannot understand anything that's written about music. It sounds to me like speaking in tongues. I love music; I've been a symphony-goer since I went to Berkeley at sixteen, and I go to opera and all the rest of it. But I cannot write about it. So I refused a brilliant contract on that book.

I wanted to write a biographical novel about Albert Schweitzer, but his daughter wanted approval of anything that would appear to be critical of him—not in my mind, but in her mind. I wanted to write a biographical novel about Karl Marx as one of the four men who created the modern world. I've done two of them, Freud and Darwin, and the other two I've wanted to write about over the years are Marx and Einstein. But I got to Marx very late, and I didn't get there until I read some of his poetry. I hadn't known that he was a poet, and when I read some of his poetry, I realized that there was another story here that might make this worthwhile, in particular because I would guess that about a quarter of humanity today is controlled by the political ideology that emerged from Marx and Engels.

Einstein I was stopped on for two reasons. First of all, his papers were locked up for many years at Princeton by his executor, who would allow nobody to see them. Now they're at the University of Jerusalem, where they're being catalogued and codified. But the major reason I couldn't write about Ein-

stein is that I don't understand mathematics or physics. I can manage a row of figures, but that's about all. I only got through algebra because a very charming, youngish woman teacher helped me. So I realized I could never get inside Einstein's mind, and I would not be able to write the book. There are others like that, but those are four examples of books I would write if I had another twenty or thirty years.

BIOGRAPHICAL/CRITICAL SOURCES:

BOOKS

Authors in the News, Volume I, Gale, 1976.
Contemporary Authors Autobiography Series, Volume III, Gale, 1986.
Contemporary Literary Criticism, Volume VII, Gale, 1977.
Newquist, Roy, *Counterpoint,* Rand McNally, 1964.
Stone, Irving, *The Irving Stone Reader,* introduction by Joseph Henry Jackson, Doubleday, 1963.
Stone, Irving, *The Science, and the Art, of Biography* (Naumberg Memorial Lecture), Division of Honors, University of California, Los Angeles, 1986.

PERIODICALS

Atlantic, May, 1961, April, 1971.
Books, September 30, 1934, October 19, 1941.
Boston Transcript, September 26, 1934.
Catholic World, August, 1961.
Chicago Sunday Tribune, March 26, 1961.
Chicago Tribune, August 26, 1980.
Christian Science Monitor, October 17, 1934, September 27, 1951, October 14, 1954, August 30, 1962.
Contemporary Review, July, 1971.
Fort Lauderdale News, January 10, 1975.
Forum, October, 1938.
Kirkus Reviews, July 15, 1956, January 15, 1961.
Los Angeles Times Book Review, November 18, 1984, October 20, 1985.
Nation, November 7, 1934.
New Republic, September 21, 1938, June 5, 1971.
Newsweek, November 1, 1965.
New York Herald Tribune, September 26, 1934.
New York Herald Tribune Book Review, September 28, 1947, August 22, 1954, September 30, 1956.
New York Herald Tribune Lively Arts, March 19, 1961.
New York Times, September 30, 1934, September 18, 1938, April 14, 1940, November 9, 1941, October 1, 1944, March 27, 1971, August 7, 1980, October 16, 1985.
New York Times Book Review, March 19, 1961, August 26, 1962, March 14, 1965, November 7, 1965, March 14, 1971, October 12, 1975, September 14, 1980, August 9, 1981, September 16, 1984, October 20, 1985.
San Francisco Chronicle, October 7, 1951, September 23, 1956, March 17, 1961.
Saturday Review, August 21, 1954, March 18, 1961, May 15, 1965, November 20, 1965, April 10, 1971, May 27, 1972, August, 1980.
Saturday Review of Literature, September 30, 1944, September 29, 1951.
Science, January 16, 1981.
Springfield Republican, September 30, 1956, August 19, 1962.
Time, September 19, 1938, November 5, 1965, April 5, 1971, September 15, 1975, October 10, 1977, November 11, 1985.
Times Literary Supplement, July 13, 1967, April 6, 1971, January 2, 1976, June 19, 1981.
Washington Post, April 2, 1971.

Washington Post Book World, August 22, 1980.
World Literature Today, winter, 1980.

—Sketch by Sharon Malinowski
—Interview by Jean W. Ross

*   *   *

STONE, Robert (Anthony) 1937-

PERSONAL: Born August 21, 1937, in New York, N.Y.; son of C. Homer and Gladys Catherine (a teacher; maiden name, Grant) Stone; married Janice G. Burr, December 11, 1959; children: Deidre M., Ian A. *Education:* Attended New York University, 1958-60, and Stanford University, 1962-64.

ADDRESSES: Agent—Candida Donadio & Associates, 231 West 22nd St., New York, N.Y. 10011.

CAREER: Novelist and screenwriter. *New York Daily News*, New York City, copyboy and caption writer, 1958-60; worked at various jobs, 1960-62, in a coffee factory and as an actor in New Orleans, La., and as an advertising copywriter in New York City; *National Mirror*, New York City, writer, 1965-67; free-lance writer in London, England, Hollywood, Calif., and Saigon, South Vietnam (now Ho Chi Minh City, Vietnam), 1967-71; Princeton University, Princeton, N.J., writer in residence, 1971-72, faculty member, 1985 and 1986; Amherst College, Amherst, Mass., associate professor of English, 1972-75, writer in residence, 1977-78; writer in residence at Stanford University, 1979, University of Hawaii at Manoa, 1979-80, and Harvard University, 1981; faculty member at University of California, Irvine, 1982, New York University, 1983-84, and University of California, San Diego, 1985. *Military service:* U.S. Navy, 1955-58; served in amphibious force of the Atlantic Fleet and as senior enlisted journalist on Operation Deep Freeze Three in Antarctica; became petty officer third class.

MEMBER: PEN (member of executive board), Authors League of America, Authors Guild, Writers Guild of America, West.

AWARDS, HONORS: Wallace Stegner fellowship, Stanford University, 1962-64; Houghton-Mifflin literary fellowship, 1967, and William Faulkner Foundation Award for notable first novel, 1968, both for *A Hall of Mirrors;* Guggenheim fellowship, 1971; National Book Award, 1975, for *Dog Soldiers;* nomination for best script adapted from another medium, Writers Guild of America, 1979, for "Who'll Stop the Rain"; *Los Angeles Times* Book Prize, 1982, for *A Flag for Sunrise;* nominations for American Book Award, National Book Critics Circle Award, and PEN/Faulkner Award, all 1982, all for *A Flag for Sunrise;* runner-up for Pulitzer Prize in fiction, 1982, for *A Flag for Sunrise;* American Academy and Institute of Arts and Letters Award, 1982; John Dos Passos Prize for literature, 1982; National Endowment for the Arts fellowship, 1983; grant from National Institute of Arts and Letters.

WRITINGS:

NOVELS

A Hall of Mirrors, Houghton, 1967.
Dog Soldiers, Houghton, 1974.
A Flag for Sunrise, Knopf, 1981.
Children of Light, Knopf, 1986.

SCREENPLAYS

"WUSA" (based on his novel *A Hall of Mirrors*), Paramount, 1970.

(With Judith Roscoe) "Who'll Stop the Rain" (based on his novel *Dog Soldiers*), United Artists, 1978.

CONTRIBUTOR

Richard Scowcroft and Wallace Stegner, editors, *Twenty Years of Stanford Short Stories*, Stanford University Press, 1966.
New American Review 6, New American Library, 1969.
David Burnett and Martha Foley, editors, *Best American Short Stories, 1970*, Houghton, 1970.
James B. Hall and Elizabeth Hall, editors, *The Realm of Fiction: Seventy-four Short Stories*, McGraw, 1977.
Theodore Solotaroff, editor, *American Review 26*, Bantam, 1977.
William O'Rourke, editor, *On the Job: Fiction about Work by Contemporary American Writers*, Vintage, 1977.
Rust Hills and Tom Jenks, editors, *Esquire Fiction Reader*, Volume I, Wampeter, 1985.
Images of War (nonfiction), Boston Publishing, 1986.

Also contributor to *Who We Are*, a collection of articles on aspects of the war in Vietnam.

OTHER

Contributor of articles and reviews to periodicals, including *Atlantic, Harper's, Life, New York Times Book Review, Manchester Guardian*, and *TriQuarterly*.

WORK IN PROGRESS: A novel set in New England.

SIDELIGHTS: In just four novels, Robert Stone has established himself as one of America's most stringent political voices and an artist of considerable caliber. His books, many critics acknowledge, are not for everyone. A typical Stone protagonist is a down-and-out, cynical drifter engrossed in the drug culture or otherwise at odds with the law. Stone's stories have taken readers to the bowels of society, from the underbelly of New Orleans to the jungles of Vietnam, from the brutality of war-torn Central America to the artificial glamour of Hollywood. In this way the author is often compared to Graham Greene, Joseph Conrad, John Dos Passos, and Nathanael West, but Stone's individuality ultimately distinguishes him as "the apostle of strung out," as *New York Times Book Review* critic Jean Strouse sees him.

Stone has earned that epithet. A native of Brooklyn, New York, a product of Catholic school upbringing, the young man started his career in the 1950s as a newspaper copyboy, but soon Stone and his wife dropped their conventional life to see America. "They got as far as New Orleans, where they both worked at a variety of menial jobs that never lifted them above the poverty level," reports Sybil Steinberg in *Publishers Weekly*. Finally, the Stones, joined by a daughter born in a charity hospital, returned to New York City. There the author joined the emerging bohemian scene, counting Jack Kerouac among his confederates, and the group's dedication to discovery took them to northern California and to Ken Kesey.

His days in New Orleans undoubtedly provided Stone with the background material for his first novel, *A Hall of Mirrors*. While the story of a young man's encounter with class politics is set in this city, the book is really about all of America, as several reviewers suggest. "The unspoken theme of *A Hall of Mirrors* is the relation between the prosperous official society and its necessary underworld of drop-outs and cast-offs," notes *Commonweal* critic Emile Capouya. "These parallel systems meet in the persons of two characters. One is the millionaire demagogue, who wants to get more power than he already has by exploiting the fears of the poor white trash. The other is

Rheinhardt, the pattern of the available 'intellectual,' the dis-abused journeyman liar of the communications industries.'' The communications industry in question is WUSA, a right-wing propagandist radio station that Rheinhardt infiltrates. The author's ''breadth of mind and . . . seriousness [set] him apart from any number of merely talented writers, for he instinctively makes the connection between the accidents of his fable and the world of his readers' experience,'' says Capouya, adding that Rheinhardt is ''[Albert] Camus' Stranger in a less abstract, less absolute form.''

''Stone's language is a joy,'' declares Ivan Gold in his *New York Times Book Review* piece on *A Hall of Mirrors*. ''Rich yet unobtrusive, self-effacing but in complete control—there is a growing sense of awe, once one has finished the book, at what the effort must have cost him. When so accomplished a style is joined to an ear which encompasses the dictions of hippies, and senators, and a good portion of the worlds in between; which seems incapable of producing or reproducing a line of dialogue which does not ring true, it takes an act of willfulness on the part of the reader not to be drawn in, and moved, and altered.''

The serious scholarly attention accorded Stone's first novel is summed up in the words of L. Hugh Moore, who says in *Critique: Studies in Modern Fiction:* ''Stone's vision of the modern world and society is a profoundly pessimistic one. The implications of his main, related metaphors—the undersea world and evolution—are, indeed, disturbing. To see the world as an environment, an ecological system, that is as cold, hostile, and brutal as the sea floor is hardly new. Nor is his view of his characters as denizens of the deep profoundly original. What disturbs and what makes the novel contemporarily relevant is the fact that Stone offers no melioristic possibility. To survive in the new ice age is immoral; neither work, bitter humor, nor withdrawal is humanly possible. 'Despair and die' is the final message of the novel.''

Suspenseful, convincing, cruel, funny and frightening are just some of the words critics use to describe Stone's next novel, *Dog Soldiers*. Like *A Hall of Mirrors*, this book exposes corruption and greed, this time in settings ranging from Saigon to California. During the waning days of the Vietnam war, journalist John Converse, stationed in Saigon, gets an offer he cannot refuse: If he smuggles three kilograms of pure heroin back to the States, he will earn $40,000. Engaging an accomplice, Ray Hicks, into the scheme, Converse manages to get the package to California and to leave it in possession of his wife, Marge. ''The stark evil in this plan quickly flows into nightmare,'' *Time*'s Paul Gray writes, as Converse and his cohorts are pursued by agents for a corrupt federal officer.

Dog Soldiers ''is more than a white-knuckled plot; it is a harrowing allegory,'' continues Gray. ''The novice smugglers evade a sense of their own villainy through sophistry or indifference. Converse rationalizes that in a world capable of producing the horrors of war, 'people are just naturally going to want to get high.' '' *New York Review of Books* critic Roger Sale takes a different view. ''The more seriously Stone takes his characters, the more carefully he brings their aimlessness to a decision, the more he eventually either jettisons the aimlessness or falsifies the decisiveness and its importance. I'm not sure how he could better have pondered his materials and his wonderful first half, but the remainder is good writing that seems divorced from a wider purpose than its own existence, and so seems just like writing.''

Despite his reservations, however, Sale concludes that *Dog Soldiers* ultimately shows the author's ''clear eye for detail and clear-eyed determination to see these lives through to some end without sentimentalizing them. Throughout, thus, his integrity gives us a sense of learning at first hand what most of us have known only as hearsay or freakout. He brings the news, as novelists are supposed to do; he makes one think we have only begun to understand our immediate past.'' And a *Washington Post Book World* reviewer, labeling *Dog Soldiers* the most important novel of the year, adds that ''Stone writes like a Graham Greene whose God is utterly dead, and he favors the same sort of setting, the same juxtaposition of the exotic and the banal.''

Stone's third novel, *A Flag for Sunrise*, ''is about Catholics—a nun, a priest, an anthropologist, a drifter—caught up among spies, gun runners, murderers, maniacs, and revolutionaries in a poor Central American country ruled by American business interests and the CIA through a local military regime,'' summarizes Leonard Michaels in the *Saturday Review*. ''The plot is complicated and built upon short scenes, some of them so intensely dramatic they could be published independently. What holds them together is suspenseful action, an atmosphere of neurasthenic menace, and Stone's prose style. Lean, tough, quick, and smart, it is perfect for violent action, yet lyrical enough for Stone's nun as she contemplates her own mind, her 'inward place.' ''

To *Los Angeles Times Book Review* writer Carolyn See, Stone ''does American imperialism so well it is possible to read his third novel as a purely aesthetic experience. The decay is so attractive, so muted, so 'literary,' that reading it is . . . like curling up with Graham Greene in Africa or Joseph Conrad in the deep Pacific.'' William Logan finds distinct ties between the author's first and third books. *A Flag for Sunrise*, he notes in the *Chicago Tribune Book World*, ''so carefully duplicates the structure of 'A Hall of Mirrors,' even to the rhythm of its title. In each, the narration emanated from three characters whose careless intertwinings led to a cataclysm only one escaped alive.''

Jonathan Yardley has criticism for the author's style. While Stone ''writes very well, [creating] plausible characters [with] a deft hand for dramatic incident,'' the critic says in the *Washington Post Book World*, the author ''is a preacher masquerading in novelist's clothing, indulging himself in rhetoric right out of SDS or the IWW. It is the politics of his novels rather than the craft of them that seems ultimately to interest him the most; the problem is that there is nothing interesting about his politics.'' Elaborating, Yardley points out that the nun character, Sister Justin, ''is clearly intended to be the novel's moral center, but she is simply too good to be true.'' Also, Stone ''trivializes what he hopes to glorify. The stock roles that his characters play and the stock rhetoric that they utter are nothing more than safe, comfortable responses to a situation that is considerably more complex and ambiguous than Stone appears to realize.'' However, Yardley remarks, when the author ''gets off his soapbox and pays attention to the craft of fiction, he is very good.''

On the other hand, *Commonweal* critic Frank McConnell calls *A Flag for Sunrise* ''an important political novel precisely because it is such a perceptive religious novel.'' Further, Stone offers ''an indication of a new trend in the American sensibility. For Conrad, Greene, and [John] LeCarre can be considered the elegists of Britain's dreams of empire and the explorers of that vaster, richer territory of the spirit that lies beyond the hope of triumph over history. Robert Stone is the first American writer I know of who shares that melancholy, that maturity, and that bitter sanity. And if his novel is fierce in its despair, it is even fiercer in its unvoiced suggestion of a sensibility that renders despair itself mute before the absurd, unending possibility of love.'' ''*Flag* is a disturbing book in many ways, some of them not intended,'' in Richard Poirier's opinion. Poirier, in the *New York Review of Books,* adds that he is ''not referring to Stone's politics as such but to the degree to which they may reveal more about his opportunism as a novelist than about his anxieties as a citizen.''

Stone's first two novels were made into feature films. While he contributed to both screenplays, ''WUSA,'' based on *A Hall of Mirrors,* and ''Who'll Stop the Rain,'' based on *Dog Soldiers,* are remarkable for the unfavorable response both received from film critics and audiences. Many factors go into the fate of a film, however—the work of the director, cast, crew and production company included—and Stone has stated in interviews that the finished products were never even close to the screen treatments he had originally conceived. Still, his experiences in film provided the author with the impetus for his fourth novel, *Children of Light.* Set on the location of a film, it chronicles the wasted days of a washed-up screenwriter and a schizophrenic actress; the novel offers ''a fine, complex, often funny tale, full of lights and shadows, with great dialogue and a sharp sense of character and place,'' according to Jean Strouse in the *New York Times Book Review.*

The book ''is jampacked with people pretending to be other than they are, people with masks, people who have become their lies. Even the film location, Mexico pretending to be Lousiana, is schizoid. The only sane person is the mad one, [the actress] Lee Verger,'' notes *Washington Post Book World* critic Stephen Dobyns. The author ''has taken some spectacular risks, particularly with his climax,'' says Christopher Lehmann-Haupt. ''His drama plays, and one's sense of dread builds up like a bank of storm clouds.''

Lehmann-Haupt, commenting in a *New York Times* article, continues that while *Children of Light* is Stone's ''most dramatically coherent performance to date,'' nevertheless ''there is a mechanical quality about the way [he] manipulates his characters that keeps the reader's mind divided. Part of one's reaction is to be amazed at the effects he is pulling off, but another part is to wonder why his characters are so remorselessly condemned to their respective fates. Why is [main character] Gordon Walker a drunk and a coke addict? Why is Lee Verger schizophrenic? Why are all the film types so wiseacre, heartless and nasty? What do all the drugs and alcohol mean? Are they no more than God's way of telling Hollywood that it has too much money? Not that this reader was able to figure out.''

Again, Stone's dialogue wins wide praise. Not only does the author's language ''snap like a bullwhip,'' feels *Globe and Mail* reviewer Norman Snider, but the author, ''having paid hard dues in Hollywood, has an acute sense of how the patois of the film biz equally encompasses relationships as well as professional arrangements. [A character's] husband, for instance, 'takes a walk' out of the marriage in exactly the same way performers or directors would walk off a film they suspect will damage their career.''

Children of Light ''seems far more slanted than anything Stone has written before,'' in A. Alvarez's opinion. ''He has always kept apart from the current fashion that confuses fiction with the art of the self and is suspicious of anyone with a strong gift for narrative. Stone, who has a strong imaginative grip on the contemporary American scene and writes like an angel—

a fallen, hard-driving angel—is also a marvelous storyteller. He does not take sides and is as much at one with Pablo, the murderous speed freak, as he is with Holliwell, the liberal intellectual,'' writes Alvarez in the *New York Review of Books.* The critic sums up that in order for the author to reach his own level of truth, ''he has sacrificed the intricate, gallows-humor detachment that has made him, in his previous books, one of the most impressive novelists of his generation.''

In a 1981 *Washington Post* interview, Stone explained his reasons for telling the stories he does: He believes that by exposing readers to the darker side of society, he is abetting ''the awareness of ironies and continuities, showing people that being decent is really hard and that we carry within ourselves our own worst enemy.''

AVOCATIONAL INTERESTS: Scuba diving, acting.

CA INTERVIEW

CA interviewed Robert Stone by telephone on March 25, 1987, at his home in Connecticut.

CA: Children of Light, *your latest book, bears the title of the Robert Lowell poem you used as an epigraph for your first novel,* A Hall of Mirrors. *Beyond the title, is there a creative connection that spans the years between the two books?*

STONE: At first I was going to use *Children of Light* for the title of the book that became *A Hall of Mirrors.* Later, when I was writing about people who were involved with movies, I thought that this was a way to use it, that it was just as apt for this book, even perhaps more apt. But there's a connection between the books, I think, insofar as the people in *Hall of Mirrors* are people who are being undermined by illusions—in a somewhat different way from *Children of Light,* but that is going on in both books. I think there's a connection in the level of artifice and illusion that gets between the characters and each other and gets between them and themselves.

CA: Children of Light *seems a less complex story than your earlier ones in that it isn't played against the backdrop of the '60s, Vietnam, or the U.S. involvement in Central America. Did you set out deliberately this time to narrow your focus in that sense?*

STONE: Yes. I saw this as a simpler story in every sense. It didn't have the complexity of the others; it was a single-line story. It came to me all at once, and I wanted to get it down. It's different from the other three in certain ways. I don't know what it means in terms of what direction my work is going to take. I think the book I'm doing now is more complicated; it has a larger canvas.

CA: At the end of Children of Light, *Gordon Walker is drinking Perrier and writing again. His wife has returned. He says, ''I thought that at my present age I might stop going with the flow.'' Does he seem to you less doomed than your earlier survivors?*

STONE: I think I leave that in question. There's a certain irony in his survival: in a way he took his own misfortune and disaster and inflicted it on Lu Anne. I tried to convey that he survived altogether at her expense. That is what Shelley is reproaching him for at the end. I think we can see him in a way as saving himself, as perhaps being less doomed, because somehow he's done the emotional equivalent of that James

Bond scene where Bond falls out of an airplane and falls on top of somebody's parachute and takes the parachute off the person. Gordon Walker does that at Lu Anne's expense.

CA: There have been the predictable suggestions from reviewers that the book may to some extent reflect your own dealings with moviemaking. Is that worth a comment?

STONE: I know a lot of people see it as an attack on the film industry, but it's really not that. It's much more than that. Of course it reflects my experiences in movies, but I don't do portraits from life, and I'm not an autobiographical writer. I'm trying to use the situation of the artist in films as analogous for a number of other things. On the other hand, it's certainly not untrue to say that it reflects my experience in movies.

CA: Joseph Epstein said in Commentary *that you can "speak out of the mouths and minds of a vast range of characters." When you start to write a book, have you already lived with your characters long enough to know them pretty well?*

STONE: Yes. I think I start from character more than anything else. As soon as I know who the people are, I know a great deal about the book I'm going to write, because in novels, in fiction generally, character is literally fate. If you know who the people are, you know what they sound like, you know what they think like, and to some extent you know what's going to happen.

CA: Lu Anne in Children of Light *and Sister Justin in* A Flag for Sunrise *are among my favorites. Do you feel they are related somehow?*

STONE: They are related, I think, although Justin is really whole; she's not a broken person the way Lu Anne is. Lu Anne is in a very bad place. Psychologically, spiritually, Justin is a person whose integrity remains unbroken. There's a kind of upward progression. Justin's despair is redeemed, even though what happens to her is fatal, whereas Lu Anne's never is quite. I try and evoke a kind of mercy for her, which is entirely hope, maybe a forlorn hope. Those characters are related, but what happens to them is very different. They both die, but what I see them going through is quite different. Lu Anne's plight is much worse.

CA: You seem to love even the most unlovable of your characters, and you've spoken previously about being quite bereft when Hicks died, in Dog Soldiers, *and Geraldine, in* A Hall of Mirrors. *Do the survivors go on in your imagination beyond their books?*

STONE: Not very far beyond the books. For some reason I feel that I have to close off speculation about them. I might be able to picture a certain day in their lives. Sometimes I might think, what would Reinhardt or Converse or Holliwell be thinking at this particular moment? But I never really speculate on what's going to happen to them after the book is over. I feel I don't really know. I have to know everything about them except that. I only have to know where they are at the end of the book, then everything becomes arbitrary and open to question again. Everything has to be thus and so in the area for which I'm responsible, but I close off speculation about the future.

CA: Are there characters you've had a hard time getting straight in your head so that you could start writing about them?

STONE: Some were harder than others. Hicks and Justin were two that I had to spend a lot of time thinking about before I could write them.

CA: In an interview with Eric James Schroeder published in Modern Fiction Studies, *you said that "the best writing about Vietnam, the best fiction, goes beyond the realistic mode." Do you think any of the movies about Vietnam have been able to capture the surreal quality of the experience that I think you were referring to in that statement?*

STONE: I think "The Deer Hunter" was almost a very good movie, showing the people from this Pennsylvania town caught up in the war. I think it could have been wonderful if it had just dealt with the effect of the Vietnam War on the people of this town. In terms of rendering the effect of the war on America, it was off to a great start. But it got lost in metaphor. And there's a lot of confusion between metaphor and verisimilitude in the Vietnamese parts of the movie, which are the weakest parts. "Platoon," I think, is very good in terms of rendering the experience, particularly among the soldiers of the 25th Division. I know the area that is being described—although I know it was filmed in the Philippines. The plot is a little bit melodramatic, but "Platoon" does the best job of any of the movies, I think, in evoking the experience of the war.

CA: Do you keep up with the growing body of work on Vietnam?

STONE: Only incidentally and somewhat fortuitously I come across a book, but I don't make it a point to read everything that comes out. I've read a lot of the historical interpretations of the war, but I have by no means read all the novels. There are so many.

CA: Do you feel your own perspective on Vietnam was influenced by having seen it after living in England for a couple of years rather than in the States?

STONE: Very much so. I was out of touch in a lot of ways. I really got back to America by going to Vietnam. And of course I'd been seeing the war in a very strange perspective, from the perspective of Western Europe, which made my attitude toward it very complicated indeed.

CA: Was that period after you finished A Hall of Mirrors *but before you went to Vietnam, when you were doing free-lance journalism, a time when you had no clear vision of your future direction as a writer?*

STONE: Yes. It was a time when I was a bit at sea. I'd had to work for a long, long time on my first book, and when I finished it I didn't know exactly what to do with myself. I made a couple of false starts on another book, and I took a long time to get myself together and know what I wanted to do.

CA: What do you think about the influence of the Beats on current writing? You were to some extent a part of that scene.

STONE: We are created by our history. Many writers my age were influenced by them, I think. The Beats were kind of a payoff; that was the work of people who read Hemingway and Steinbeck and Thomas Wolfe, a certain kind of romantic attitude toward America, toward the land and toward The Road.

I think this has gone into the making of the contemporary American fictional sensibility; it's all part of our history, so it's definitely part of our sensibility.

CA: You've expressed your disapproval of drugs, and certainly they've gotten your characters into a mess of trouble. Yet you have said that you got some important and lasting insights on drugs. Is there a moral contradiction here?

STONE: In the early '60s, like a number of artists in northern California, I experimented with psychedelic drugs. We saw ourselves as pursuing an experimental tradition we associated with painters like Joan Miro. The drugs with which we experimented were not habit-forming drugs. I have never anywhere had anything good to say about habit-forming drugs.

CA: You've said that you write on a word processor, but you do some parts in longhand when you're having to work especially hard at getting them right. What do you think it is about the latter method that makes it seem more precise?

STONE: One thing is that you have to slow down, and you have to give every word its weight. It slows you down enough that you're compelled to lucidity. You have to live with the resonances. You're supposed to do that even on a word processor, of course.

CA: The machine sometimes seems to be waiting rather impatiently for action.

STONE: Yes. A friend of mine has a very complicated method for making the cursor stop blinking. He somehow had it programmed off. I got him to do the same thing for mine so it doesn't flash on and off. Sometimes it can look like Times Square flashing on and off.

CA: Your dialogue has a very special quality. Does it get revised and polished many times over?

STONE: I think dialogue is very important, so I want to get it right. I usually know the sound I want, and I work it over until I get it. I don't take any liberties there.

CA: In an interview with Maureen Karagueuzian in Tri-Quarterly *you talked about Hemingway's "technical discoveries about how to utilize the difference between the way people actually speak and dialog that reads like people speaking." What did you learn from him in that regard?*

STONE: It's very difficult to put into words; it's not ineffable, but it's very close. I think the answer is all in the story "Hills Like White Elephtants," a story largely told in dialogue without a single adverb. Everything that one could learn about dialogue from Hemingway could be learned by reading "Hills Like White Elephants." Using the white space, as they say; using words to create attention, to invoke secondary and tertiary meanings—to invoke the *connotive* meaning.

CA: Do you ever write down bits of overheard real-life dialogue to use in some fictional form later?

STONE: I don't write them down, usually, but they do tend to stay with me. I don't often write things down.

CA: You've done a lot of teaching. How well do you think the combination of teaching and writing works for you?

STONE: I think it works rather well. It tends to give the week a certain kind of shape, and it doesn't hurt to talk about writing, because it helps me find out what I believe about writing. The great thing about writing courses is that even if you can't teach anybody to write—which you certainly can't—you get to talk about everything. Writing courses are really more the philosophy of composition than they are anything else. You can't teach people how to write, but you can talk about life, about how it is, how people are. That's not a bad way to pass a couple of hours.

CA: As Joyce Carol Oates said in Esquire, *you are "one of a fairly small number of contemporary American writers of prose fiction who concern themselves not with minimalist subjects but with politics and current history." How do you feel about the so-called minimalist writing that's being done now?*

STONE: Let each writer serve his or her own muse. I don't believe in opposing one school of fiction to another.

CA: You've recently gone from Knopf to the New York offices of Weidenfeld & Nicolson. What do you hope to find in the new writer-publisher relationship?

STONE: I always want the sense that the people who are publishing my books really believe in me, believe in what I'm doing, value my work. I have that sense at Weidenfeld.

CA: Is it too early to talk about the next book?

STONE: It's a contemporary book, set in New England.

CA: You said not long ago that you were interested in writing something comic, and certainly the party scene in Children of Light *was very funny, in spite of its seriousness. Are you still interested in doing a comic novel?*

STONE: Yes. I would like to write one altogether comic novel. I hope to do that someday.

BIOGRAPHICAL/CRITICAL SOURCES:

BOOKS

Contemporary Literary Criticism, Gale, Volume V, 1976, Volume XXIII, 1983, Volume XLII, 1987.

PERIODICALS

Atlantic, November, 1981.
Chicago Tribune Book World, October 25, 1981, March 9, 1986.
Commentary, March, 1982.
Commonweal, April 5, 1968, March 12, 1982, May 23, 1986.
Critique: Studies in Modern Fiction, Volume XL, number 3, 1969.
Encounter, September, 1975.
Esquire, August, 1985.
Globe and Mail (Toronto), April 26, 1986.
Harper's, April 28, 1975.
Los Angeles Times Book Review, November 8, 1981, March 23, 1986.
Modern Fiction Studies, spring, 1984.
New Boston Review, February, 1982.
New Republic, January 4, 1975, November 18, 1981, April 28, 1986.
Newsweek, November 11, 1974, October 26, 1981, March 17, 1986.

New York Review of Books, April 3, 1975, December 3, 1981, April 10, 1986.
New York Times, October 31, 1974, October 16, 1981, March 13, 1986.
New York Times Book Review, September 24, 1967, November 3, 1974, October 18, 1981, April 15, 1984, March 16, 1986.
Publishers Weekly, March 21, 1986.
Saturday Review, November, 1981.
Time, November 11, 1974, October 26, 1981, March 10, 1986.
Times Literary Supplement, May 30, 1975, December 4, 1981, March 21, 1986.
TriQuarterly, winter, 1982.
Washington Post, November 15, 1981.
Washington Post Book World, December 8, 1974, November 1, 1981, March 23, 1986.

—Sketch by Susan Salter

—Interview by Jean W. Ross

*   *   *

STORER, J(ames) D(onald)   1928-

PERSONAL: Born January 11, 1928, in Hemsworth, England; son of James Arthur (a teacher) and Elizabeth M.G. (a teacher; maiden name, Pirie) Storer; married Shirley Anne Kent (a secretary), May 28, 1955; children: J. Martin, Carol Anne. *Education:* City and Guilds of London Institute, associate, 1947; Imperial College of Science and Technology, London, B.Sc.Eng. (with honors), 1948.

ADDRESSES: Home—52 Thomson Rd., Currie, Edinburgh EH14 5HW, Scotland. *Office*—Royal Museum of Scotland, Chambers St., Edinburgh EH1 1JF, Scotland. *Agent*—Rupert Crew Ltd., King's Mews, Gray's Inn Rd., London WC1N 2JA, England.

CAREER: British Aircraft Corp., Weybridge, England, worked in design office, 1948-66; Royal Scottish Museum, Edinburgh, assistant keeper, 1966-78, keeper of department of technology, 1978-85; National Museums of Scotland, Edinburgh, keeper of Department of Science, Technology, and Working Life, 1985—. Past chairman of British Aviation Preservation Council; public speaker.

MEMBER: Royal Aeronautical Society, University of Edinburgh Staff Club.

AWARDS, HONORS: Chartered Engineer, 1966.

WRITINGS:

FOR CHILDREN

Steel and Engineering, Longmans, Green, 1959.
Behind the Scenes in an Aircraft Factory, Dent, 1965.
It's Made Like This: Cars, John Baker, 1967.
The World We Are Making: Aviation, Methuen, 1968.
A Simple History of the Steam Engine, John Baker, 1969.
How to Run an Airport, John Baker, 1970.
How We Find Out About Flight, John Baker, 1973.
Flying Feats, Hamlyn, 1977.
Book of the Air, Hamlyn, 1979.
Great Inventions, Hamlyn, 1980.
(Co-author) *The World's Transport*, Hamlyn, 1983.
(Contributor) *Encyclopedia of Transport*, Hamlyn, 1983.
(Co-author) *East Fortune: Museum of Flight and History of the Airfield*, RSM Publication, 1983.

(Contributor) *The Silver Burdett Encyclopedia of Transport: Air*, Silver Burdett, 1984.
Ship Models in the Royal Scottish Museum, RSM Publication, 1986.

Contributor to *Transport Museums Yearbook, Marshall Cavendish Encyclopedia, World Pictorial Map Series*. Contributor to periodicals, including *Child Education* and *Museums Journal*.

SIDELIGHTS: J. D. Storer told *CA:* "My first book was for a series edited by my uncle, Mr. T. Herdman, who introduced me to writing for children. My interest is to present technical subjects in a simple manner."

*   *   *

STORR, Catherine (Cole)   1913-
(Irene Adler, Helen Lourie)

PERSONAL: Born July 21, 1913, in London, England; daughter of Arthur Frederick (a lawyer) and Margaret (Gaselee) Cole; married Anthony Storr (a psychiatrist and writer), February 6, 1942; married Lord Balogh (an economist), 1970; children: (first marriage) Sophia, Cecilia, Emma. *Education:* Studied at Newnham College, Cambridge, 1932-36 and 1939-41, and West London Hospital, 1941-44. *Religion:* Agnostic.

ADDRESSES: Home—No. 5, 12 Froghal Gardens, London N.W.3, England. *Agent*—A. D. Peters, 10 Buckingham St., London W.C.2, England.

CAREER: West London Hospital, London, England, assistant psychiatrist, 1948-50; Middlesex Hospital, London, England, assistant psychiatrist, 1950-62; now full-time writer.

WRITINGS:

Ingeborg and Ruthy, Harrap, 1940.
Clever Polly, Faber, 1951.
Stories for Jane, Faber, 1952.
Clever Polly and the Stupid Wolf, Faber, 1955, reprinted, 1979.
Polly, the Giant's Bride, Faber, 1956.
The Adventures of Polly and the Wolf, Faber, 1957.
Marianne Dreams, Faber, 1958.
Marianne and Mark, Faber, 1960.
Magic Drawing Pencil, A. S. Barnes, 1960.
Lucy, Bodley Head, 1961.
Lucy Runs Away, Bodley Head, 1962.
(Under pseudonym Helen Lourie) *A Question of Abortion*, Bodley Head, 1962.
Robin, Faber, 1962.
(Under pseudonym Irene Adler) *Freud for the Jung*, Cresset, 1963.
The Catchpole Story, Faber, 1965.
The Merciful Jew (adult), Barrie & Rockcliff, 1968.
Polly and the Wolf, Penguin, 1968.
Rufus, Faber, 1969, Gambit, 1970.
Puss and Cat, Faber, 1969.
Thursday, Faber, 1971, Harper, 1972.
Black God, White God, Barrie & Rockcliff, 1972.
Kate and the Island, Faber, 1972.
The Painter and the Fish, Faber, 1975.
Adolescence, Hutchinson, 1975.
The Chinese Egg, Faber, 1975.
Unnatural Fathers (adult), Quartet, 1975.
Story of the Terrible Scar, Faber, 1976.
Tales from the Psychiatrist's Couch, Quartet, 1977.
Hugo and His Grandma, Dinosaur, 1977.

Hugo and His Grandma's Washing Day, Dinosaur, 1978.
Winter's End, Macmillan, 1978.
Pebble, Macmillan, 1979.
Pen Friends, Macmillan, 1979.
Clever Polly and the Hungry Wolf, Faber, 1980.
Vicky, Faber, 1981.
February Yowler, Faber, 1982.
It Can't Happen to Me, Dinosaur, 1982.
Cold Marble and Other Ghost Stories, Faber, 1985.
The Sword in the Stone, Raintree Publishers, 1985.
Competitions and Ponies, Macmillan, 1986.
The Boy and the Swan, Deutsch, 1987.
The Underground Conspiracy, Faber, 1987.

"RAINTREE STORIES CLIPPERS" SERIES; PUBLISHED BY RAINTREE PUBLISHING

The Pied Pier of Hamelin, 1984.
Rip Van Winkle, 1984.
Robin Hood, 1984.

"RAINTREE STORIES" SERIES; PUBLISHED BY RAINTREE PUBLISHERS

Joan of Arc, 1985.
King Midas, 1985.
The Trojan Horse, 1985.
Dick Whittington, 1985.
The Flying Dutchman, 1985.
Odysseus and the Enchanters, 1985.
Theseus and the Minotaur, 1985.
The Three Musketeers, 1985.

"PEOPLE OF THE BIBLE" SERIES; PUBLISHED BY RAINTREE PUBLISHERS

Jesus Begins His Work, 1982.
Noah and His Ark, 1982.
The Birth of Jesus, 1982.
Joseph and His Brothers, 1982.
Adam and Eve, 1983.
Jonah and the Whale, 1983.
Miracles by the Sea, 1983.
The Prodigal Son, 1983.
Abraham and Issac, 1985.
David and Goliath, 1985.
Moses and the Plague, 1985.
St. Peter and St. Paul, 1985.
Jesus and John the Baptist, 1985.
Jesus the Healer, 1985.
Joseph and the Famine, 1985.
King David, 1985.
Moses in the Wilderness, 1985.
Ruth's Story, 1985.
Samson and Delilah, 1985.
The Trials of Daniel, 1985.

OTHER

Contributor of articles to *Nova* and *Cosmopolitan*.

WORK IN PROGRESS: *The Castle Boy*.

BIOGRAPHICAL/CRITICAL SOURCES:

BOOKS

Children's Literature in Education/1, APS Publications, Inc., 1970.

PERIODICALS

Horn Book, April, 1973.

New York Times Book Review, October 1, 1972.
Times Literary Supplement, November 20, 1981, March 26, 1982, July 13, 1984.

*   *   *

STRATI, Saverio 1924-

PERSONAL: Born August 16, 1924, in Italy; son of Paolo (a mason) and Agatha (Romeo) Strati; married Hildegard Fleig, 1958; children: Giampaolo.

ADDRESSES: Home—Via Giotto, Scandicci, Firenze, Italy.

CAREER: Full-time writer.

MEMBER: Sindacato degli Serittori.

AWARDS, HONORS: Charles Veilon International Prize (Lausanne) for *Tibi e Tascia;* Sila Prize for *Gente in viaggio;* Napoli Prize for *Noi lazzaroni;* Campiello Prize for *Il Selvaggio di Santa Venere;* Pomarico Prize for *Il Diavolaro;* Prize Saverese cittao di Enna for *I Cari Parenti;* Prie Citta di Ciro Marina for *La Conca degli aranci.*

WRITINGS:

La Marchesina, Mondadori (Milan), 1956.
La Teda, Mondadori, 1957, translation published as *Terrarossa*, Abelard, 1957.
Tibi e Tascia, Mondadori, 1959.
Mani vuote, Mondadori, 1960, translation by Peter Moule published as *Empty Hands*, Abelard, 1964.
Avventura in citta, Mondadori, 1962, translation by Angus Davidson published as *The Lights of Reggio*, J. Murray, 1962.
Il nodo, Mondadori, 1965.
Gente in viaggio, Mondadori, 1966.
Il codardo, Bietti (Milan), 1970.
Noi lazzaroni, Mondadori, 1972.
E' il nostro turno, Mondadori, 1975.
Il Selvaggio di Santa Venere, Mondadori, 1977.
I centro bambini, Lerici (Cosenza), 1977.
Il visionario e il ciabattino, Mondadori, 1978.
Terra di emigranti, Salani (Florence), 1979.
Il Diavolaro, Mondadori, 1980.
Piccolo grande Sud, Salani, 1981.
I Cari Parenti, Mondadori, 1982.
Ascolta, Stefano, Mursia, 1983.
La Conca degli aranci, Mondadori, 1987.

*   *   *

STRAUS, Dennis
   (Ascher/Straus, a joint pseudonym)

PERSONAL: Born in New York, N.Y.; son of Frank and Roslyn (Bassin) Straus. *Education:* Brooklyn College, B.A.; Columbia University, M.A.

ADDRESSES: Home—118-07 Newport Ave., Rockaway Park, N.Y. 11694.

CAREER: Writer, 1973—.

AWARDS, HONORS: Experimental fiction prize from *Panache* magazine, 1973, for story "City/Edge"; Pushcart Prize from Pushcart Press, 1978-79, for excerpt from novel titled "Even after a Machine Is Dismantled, It Continues to Operate, with or without Purpose"; New York State Creative Artists Public Service fellowship in fiction, 1981-82; Treacle Press First Novel Prize, 1982, for *The Menaced Assassin.*

WRITINGS:

WITH SHEILA ASCHER, UNDER JOINT PSEUDONYM ASCHER/STRAUS

Letter to an Unknown Woman (story), Treacle Press, 1980.
The Menaced Assassin (novel), Treacle Press, 1982.
Red Moon/Red Lake (novella), Top Stories, 1984.

SPACE NOVELS; WITH ASCHER, UNDER JOINT PSEUDONYM ASCHER/STRAUS

"As It Returns," first presented in New York at Contemporary Arts Gallery of New York University, May, 1975, published in *Seventh Assembling,* 1977.
"The Blue Hangar," first presented in New York at Gateway National Recreation Area, August 2-3, 1975, published in *Coda,* April/May, 1976, in *Queen Stree T Magazine,* Spring, 1977, and in *Interstate,* 1979.
"Twelve Simultaneous Sundays," first presented in New York at Gegenschein Vaudeville Placenter, September 19-December 5, 1976.

CONTRIBUTOR TO ANTHOLOGIES

Pushcart Prize Anthology III, Pushcart Press, 1978-79.
Likely Stories, Treacle Press, 1981.
Chelsea: A Retrospective, Chelsea Associates, 1984.
Chouteau Review: Ten Year Retrospective, Chouteau Review, 1985.

OTHER

Also co-publisher with Ascher of "Green Inventory," partially published by Ghost Dance Press, winter, 1975-76, and spring, 1977. Creator of language art gallery installations, including "Language and Structure in North America," Toronto, "Beyond the Page," Philadelphia, "Last Correspondence Show," Sacramento, "First New York Post Card Show," New York, "International Mail Art Exhibition," Northampton, Mass., "TELIC Exhibition," Kansas City, Mo., and "Assembling Exhibition," New York. Contributor to journals, including *Chicago Review, Interstate, Exile, Chouteau Review, Sun and Moon, Chelsea, Paris Review, Beyond Baroque, Gallimafry, Panache, Aspen Anthology, Aphra, Tamarisk, Zone, Annex, Benzene, Fifth Assembling, Ghost Dance, Neoneo Do-Do, Telephone, Sixth Assembling, Gegenschein Quarterly, Source, Eighth Assembling, Margins,* and *Precisely.*

WORK IN PROGRESS: A novel; a volume of related stories; a multi-volume novel with Ascher called *Monica's Chronicle;* "a volume of 'chamber' texts, minimal narratives that test the essential properties of fiction as well as the deployment of language on the page."

SIDELIGHTS: Dennis Straus told *CA:* "Hannah Arendt wrote that the greatest threat to the continued development of the novel as a high art form is not the popular novel, but the serious, middlebrow novel, novels of big ideas or rhetorical playfulness that don't continue the major adventure of the novel as the ultimate art form. Artificial, philosophical, musical, painterly, achitectural, poetic, cinematic—within a ground of storytelling, the novel can be anything, discontinuous and inclusive, not without governing principles, but generating new ones.

"The culture's strictures against adventuous fiction are severe, oddly more severe in regard to the homegrown product than the imported. And nothing less than total commitment, writing as *first* profession no matter what the risks and sacrifices, is sufficient to accomplish anything under such cultural conditions.

"More than anything, I suppose, the literary alliance with Sheila Ascher has been a way (pooling materials, resources, survival techniques as well as more narrowly technical services, editing and the like, though rarely collaborating in the ordinary sense of the word) of maintaining an uncompromising commitment. The only area where Sheila and I are co-authors in anything approaching the traditional sense is in a series of 'environmental' narratives: 'As It Returns,' 'The Blue Hangar,' and 'Twelve Simultaneous Sundays.'

"Along the same lines, a writer should lose his youthful anger. A certain revulsion for what exists is what makes things new. And this anger or revulsion, beyond any particular theory (all theories advance sets of conventions), the anger and revulsion of the author for what exists and for what is merely assumed in language, structure, and general approach to the reader is what gives moral and aesthetic energy to writing."

For additional information see *CA* entry for Sheila Ascher in this volume.

BIOGRAPHICAL/CRITICAL SOURCES:

PERIODICALS

Chelsea, Number 36, 1977.
Cumberland Journal, spring, 1981.
Interstate 12, 1979.
Library Journal, October 1, 1981.
Village Voice, October 19, 1982.
Zone, spring/summer, 1981.

*   *   *

SULZBERGER, C(yrus) L(eo II)   1912-

PERSONAL: Born October 27, 1912, in New York, N.Y.; son of Leo Sulzberger and Beatrice (Josephi) Sulzberger Kahn; married Marina Tatiana Lada, January 21, 1942 (died, 1976); children: Marina Beatrice (Mrs. Adrian Berry), David Alexis. *Education:* Harvard University, B.S. (magna cum laude), 1934.

ADDRESSES: Home—25 boulevard du Montparnasse, 75006 Paris, France; and Spetsai, Greece. *Agent*—Julian Bach, 747 Third Ave., New York, N.Y. 10017.

CAREER: Pittsburgh Press, Pittsburgh, Pa., reporter and re-write man, 1934-35; United Press, Washington, D.C., reporter, 1935-38; *London Evening Standard,* London, England, foreign correspondent, 1938-39; employed abroad by United Press, North American Newspaper Alliance, and Columbia Broadcasting Corp., 1939-40; *New York Times,* New York, N.Y., correspondent, covering the Balkans, Russia, and the Middle East, 1940-44, chief of global foreign service, based in Paris, 1944-54, foreign affairs columnist, 1954-77.

MEMBER: Phi Beta Kappa, Metropolitan Club (Washington, D.C.).

AWARDS, HONORS: Overseas Press Club of America award, 1941, for best reporting on the German-Russian front, 1951, for best consistent reporting from abroad, and 1973, for best book on foreign affairs, *An Age of Mediocrity: Memoirs and Diaries, 1963-1972;* Pulitzer Prize special citation in journalism, 1951; Overseas Press Club of America citation for excellence, 1957 and 1970.

WRITINGS:

Sit-Down with John L. Lewis, Random House, 1938.

The Big Thaw: A Personal Exploration of the "New" Russia and the Orbit Countries, Harper, 1956.

What's Wrong with U.S. Foreign Policy, Harcourt, 1959.

My Brother Death, Harper, 1961.

The Resistentialists, Harper, 1962, published as *Unconquered Souls: The Resistentialists,* Overlook Press, 1973.

The Test: De Gaulle and Algeria, Harcourt, 1962.

Unfinished Revolution: America and the Third World, Atheneum, 1965.

(With the editors of American Heritage) *The American Heritage Picture History of World War II,* American Heritage Publishing, 1966, abridged edition published as *World War II,* 1970.

A Long Row of Candles: Memoirs and Diaries, 1934-1954, Macmillan, 1969.

The Last of the Giants (sequel to *A Long Row of Candles*), Macmillan, 1970.

The Tooth Merchant (novel), Quadrangle, 1973.

An Age of Mediocrity: Memoirs and Diaries, 1963-1972, Macmillan, 1973.

The Coldest War: Russia's Game in China, Harcourt, 1974.

Postscript with a Chinese Accent: Memoirs and Diaries, 1972-1973, Macmillan, 1974.

Go Gentle into the Night, Prentice-Hall, 1976.

The Fall of Eagles (Literary Guild alternate selection), Crown, 1977.

Seven Continents and Forty Years: A Concentration of Memoirs, foreword by Andre Malraux, Quadrangle, 1977.

The Tallest Liar, Crown, 1977.

(Editor) Marina Sulzberger, *Marina: Letters and Diaries,* Crown, 1978.

How I Committed Suicide: A Reverie, Ticknor & Fields, 1982.

Such a Peace: Yalta Revisited, Continuum, 1982.

The World and Richard Nixon, Prentice-Hall, 1987.

SIDELIGHTS: In spite of his family ties in the newspaper business (his late uncle, Arthur Hays Sulzberger, published the *New York Times*), C. L. Sulzberger chose to establish his career on an earned reputation as a journalist, rather than on his family name. When the *Times* eventually sought out his services in 1940, it was on the basis of his aggressive, objective reporting on the turmoil in Europe in 1938-1940.

During World War II, Sulzberger covered almost every major front in Europe, the Middle East, and in Russia. Millions of Americans followed the progress of the war through his front-page news stories and his feature articles in the *Times*. In his long and distinguished career as a foreign correspondent, Sulzberger worked on all seven continents, witnessed many of the major events of contemporary history, and became close to most of the great and near-great figures of our time—Churchill, de Gaulle, and Eisenhower among many others.

Critics have been dismayed at times by the massive detail of people, places, and events in Sulzerger's memoirs, *A Long Row of Candles, The Last of the Giants, An Age of Mediocrity,* and *Postscript with a Chinese Accent,* all of which are drawn from a vast file of working notes accumulated over the years. But Christopher Lehmann-Haupt of the *New York Times* believes that if Sulzberger had reworded "the raw material of journalism [material not originally written for publication] into a more elegant literary form," he would have stripped "a historical goldmine." Lehmann-Haupt points out that *A Long Row of Candles* "is not really about C. L. Sulzberger at all. It is more an autobiography of the world from 1938 to 1954, . . . not so much a book you read as it is a total historical environment through which you wander, pausing only to examine

what catches your eye." Similarly, in the *New York Times Book Review,* Walter Laquer praises the historical value of *An Age of Mediocrity,* calling it "essential reading for an understanding of American foreign policy before and during detente."

Reviewing *Seven Continents and Forty Years,* a combined condensation of Sulzberger's four earlier memoirs, Paul Grimes of the *New York Times* also considers the accounts helpful "as footnotes to history." But as to Sulzberger's ability to gain access to important policy-makers, Grimes questions "whether it was Mr. Sulzberger's skill that prompted world leaders to talk profusely to him, or whether it was that, [because of his membership in the family controlling the *New York Times,*] they knew he was a far better conduit than other competent journalists to get maximum attention for their views." Nevertheless, Grimes believes that much of *Seven Continents and Forty Years* is "just plain fun, especially the sharp, succinct portraits" of famous world leaders.

BIOGRAPHICAL/CRITICAL SOURCES:

BOOKS

Sulzberger, C. L., *A Long Row of Candles: Memoirs and Diaries, 1934-1954,* Macmillan, 1969.

Sulzberger, C. L., *The Last of the Giants,* Macmillan, 1970.

Sulzberger, C. L., *An Age of Mediocrity: Memoirs and Diaries, 1963-1972,* Macmillan, 1973.

Sulzberger, C. L., *Postscript with a Chinese Accent: Memoirs and Diaries, 1972-1973,* Macmillan, 1974.

Sulzberger, C. L., *Seven Continents and Forty Years: A Concentration of Memoirs,* Quadrangle, 1977.

PERIODICALS

Chicago Tribune Book World, February 20, 1983.

Los Angeles Times Book Review, June 21, 1987.

New York Times, May 26, 1969, March 30, 1977, April 21, 1977, March 10, 1982.

New York Times Book Review, May 25, 1969, November 25, 1973, August 2, 1987.

Publishers Weekly, June 16, 1969.

Saturday Evening Post, July 12, 1958.

Time, March 11, 1966, October 21, 1966.

*   *   *

SUMMERS, Anthony (Bruce) 1942-

PERSONAL: Born December 21, 1942, in Bournemouth, England; son of Frederick Ernest (a hotelier) and Enid Elizabeth (a hotelier; maiden name, Shaw) Summers; married; children: two sons. *Education:* New College, Oxford, B.A. (with honors), 1964.

ADDRESSES: Home—Republic of Ireland. *Agent*—Sterling Lord Agency, 660 Madison Ave., New York, N.Y. 10021.

CAREER: Swiss Broadcasting Corp., Berne, Switzerland, newsreader and writer, 1964; British Broadcasting Corp., London, England, newswriter, 1965, researcher and senior producer of "Panorama," and "24-Hours," 1965-73; writer, 1974—.

MEMBER: National Union of Journalists, Association of Broadcasting Staff, Association of Cinema Technicians.

WRITINGS:

(With Tom Mangold) *The File on the Tsar: The Fate of the Romanovs . . . Dramatic New Evidence,* Harper, 1976.

Conspiracy, McGraw, 1980.
Goddess: The Secret Lives of Marilyn Monroe, Macmillan, 1985, revised edition, New American Library, 1986.
(With Stephen Dorrill) *Honeytrap: The Secret Worlds of Stephen Ward,* Weidenfeld & Nicolson, 1987.

Producer of documentary presentations on foreign affairs and politics for British Broadcasting Corp.

SIDELIGHTS: "Anthony Summers . . . has a habit of taking worn-out subjects and making them seem fresh and alive again," writes Christopher Lehmann-Haupt in the *New York Times.* Using the investigative skills he learned as a reporter for the British Broadcasting Corporation, Summers has offered readers a new look at such controversial historical incidents as the fate of the last Russian tsar, the assassination of President John F. Kennedy, and the life of film star Marilyn Monroe. Although some critics have questioned the conclusions Summers draws in his journalistic inquiries, it is generally admitted that his books give interested readers comprehensive analyses of their topics.

In *The File on the Tsar,* Summers and co-author Tom Mangold question the official version of the death of Nicholas II and his family. The tsar, his wife, and his five children supposedly were slain by the Bolsheviks in a Siberian cellar on July 16, 1918. Summers's re-examination of the evidence led him to suggest that, while Nicholas and his son may have been captured and executed somewhere in Siberia that night, Tsarina Alexandra and her four daughters were spared for some six months before being put to death—and one of the daughters, Anastasia, may have survived and resided in the United States as "Anna Anderson" until her death in 1984.

New York Times Book Review contributor Richard Pipes dismisses *The File on the Tsar* as "gossip, innuendo, unanswered questions. None of this proves anything except that the violent death of a head of state stimulates fantasies." But *Spectator* reviewer Ronald Hingley takes the book far more seriously, believing that Summers and Mangold "have demolished the old story and replaced it with a version far more tentative but far more credible." With their "brilliant detective work," the authors "have made their mark on history," claims Hingley. "No one, surely, will be able to write of the Romanov deaths again without taking their findings into account." A *New Yorker* writer also praises the book, but stresses its value as entertainment: "The book sets forth the facts with great ingenuity: on each page the reader weighs some new bit of evidence, sizes up some new witness, makes some imaginative connection—it's better than a jigsaw puzzle."

Political assassination again concerned Summers in *Conspiracy,* an examination of the shooting of President John F. Kennedy. "There have been so many books written about the assassination of President Kennedy—and among them so many of dubious merit and provenance—that the mind tends to freeze over at the prospect of yet another," remarks Lehmann-Haupt in his *New York Times* review of Summers's offering. Yet *Conspiracy* is highly rated by Lehmann-Haupt and others; it is a "huge, exhaustive, deeply unsettling book," finds Eliot Fremont-Smith of the *Village Voice.* Summers organizes the confusing jumble of theories and evidence surrounding the crime in a "readable, understandable style," writes Bill Boyarsky in the *Los Angeles Times,* and in so doing, he demonstrates the superficiality of the Warren Commission's report, which attributed Kennedy's death solely to Lee Harvey Oswald.

Conspiracy shows Oswald's connections with the CIA and anti-Castro groups that may have worked with organized crime to arrange the assassination. It suggests that Oswald was not the only gunman to fire at the President, and that Oswald's own shooting death by Jack Ruby was a part of the total conspiracy. Summers does not claim to explain exactly what happened in Dallas in November, 1963, but as Nicholas Walter states in *Spectator,* his "aim is not so much to answer questions as to show what questions must be asked, and his achievement is not so much to establish certainty as to illuminate uncertainty." Andrew Hacker in the *New York Review of Books* adds "[*Conspiracy*] is exceptionally well-written, with all the tone and tension of an Eric Ambler thriller."

John F. Kennedy also figured prominently in Summers's third book because of his alleged liaison with film star Marilyn Monroe. Monroe's life and death, like Kennedy's assassination, have been the subject of many volumes. In *Goddess: The Secret Lives of Marilyn Monroe,* Summers again succeeded in turning up new material on a well-worn topic, according to many reviewers. His research included reading the thirty-eight books published about the actress before his own appeared, as well as over six hundred interviews with people associated with her. He focuses on Monroe's last years, including her relations with President Kennedy and his brother, Robert F. Kennedy, and the suspicious circumstances surrounding her suicide. Summers suggests that Robert Kennedy may have been with Marilyn Monroe on the night she died.

The result of Summers's work, writes Michael Musto in *Saturday Review,* is "a voraciously readable smarmfest done with a journalistic integrity. *Goddess* puts a brick wall of substance behind the kind of salaciousness *roman a clef* authors can only dream of. . . . But the true litmus test of a biography is whether all of its diggings amount to any new revelations and not just rewordings of old ones, and *The Goddess* passes the test with honors." And in his *New York Times* review, Lehmann-Haupt again salutes Summers's style, writing, "Whether [or not] the case that Mr. Summers makes proves ultimately valid, it makes for extraordinary reading. Instead of bludgeoning the reader with his theories, he lures one on, and the drama of his presentation is nearly as great as what it finally reveals."

BIOGRAPHICAL/CRITICAL SOURCES:

PERIODICALS

Los Angeles Times, July 17, 1980.
Los Angeles Times Book Review, October 27, 1985.
New Yorker, January 31, 1977.
New York Review of Books, March 31, 1977, July 17, 1980.
New York Times, November 9, 1976, July 22, 1980, September 19, 1985.
New York Times Book Review, December 12, 1976, June 29, 1980.
Saturday Review, November, 1985.
Spectator, September 11, 1976, May 17, 1980.
Time, January 10, 1977, September 30, 1985.
Times (London), May 22, 1980, October 8, 1986.
Times Literary Supplement, November 22, 1985.
Village Voice, June 25, 1980.
Washington Post, September 4, 1985.

—*Sketch by Joan Goldsworthy*

*   *   *

SUTHREN, Victor (James Henry) 1942-

PERSONAL: Born March 2, 1942, in Montreal, Quebec, Canada; son of Joseph William (an engineer) and Emily Anne (a nurse; maiden name, Roberts) Suthren; married Lindsay Scott (an artist), July 12, 1969; children: Scott, Caedi, Amy. *Education:* Bishop's University, B.A., 1965; graduate study at McGill University, 1966; Concordia University, Montreal, Quebec, M.A., 1970.

ADDRESSES: Home—36 Bellwood Ave., Ottawa, Ontario, Canada K1S 1S7.

CAREER: La Maison del Vecchio, Montreal, Quebec, restorer, 1967-68; Parks Canada, National Historic Sites Service, Montreal, research historian, 1970-71; Fortress of Louisbourg National Historic Park, Cape Breton, Nova Scotia, staff historian, 1971-73; Parks Canada, Atlantic Region, Halifax, Nova Scotia, regional historic interpretive specialist, 1973-74; Parks Canada, National Historic Sites Service, Ottawa, Ontario, research historian, 1974-75; Canadian War Museum, Ottawa, curator of war art, 1975-76, curator of exhibitions, planning, and design, 1976-80, deputy chief curator of museum, 1980-86, director, 1986—. Member of infantry drill unit of Fort Henry Guard, Kingston, Ontario, summers, 1964-65, 1967; seaman aboard the schooner *Bluenose II*, out of Halifax, summer, 1967. Member of Canadian sub-commission of International Commission for Maritime History. Guest on television and radio programs. *Military service:* Royal Canadian Navy Reserve, 1964-71; became sub-lieutenant.

MEMBER: North American Society for Oceanic History, Canadian Museums Association, Royal Society of Arts (fellow).

WRITINGS:

"PAUL GALLANT" TRILOGY; HISTORICAL NOVELS

The Black Cockade, Collins, 1977.
A King's Ransom, Collins, 1980, St. Martin's, 1981.
In Perilous Seas, St. Martin's, 1984.

"EDWARD MAINWARING" SERIES; HISTORICAL NOVELS

Royal Yankee, St. Martin's, 1987.
The Golden Galleon, St. Martin's, 1988.

OTHER

Oxford University Press Book of Canadian Military Anecdotes, Oxford University Press, in press.

Contributor to history and social studies journals and newspapers.

SIDELIGHTS: Victor Suthren told *CA:* "I continue to find the writing of historical fiction the most immediate way to develop a sense of the past, and as I feel a sense of roots to be fundamental to a society's health, I am glad to contribute to the development of that sense. Writing has drawn me into efforts to relive for brief periods key moments in the past, whether by crewing on a replica schooner or trekking with snowshoes and a blanket coat into the depths of a winter pine forest. There was such a qualitative richness to the doing even of mundane things in the so-called pioneer era, that to experience it is to take a holiday away from our fast-food society as refreshing as any travel getaway. Perhaps, as Tofler wrote, we will survive by creating our own immediate minicultures as a defense against a mass world culture; to do that by drawing on the physical as well as philosophical lessons of the past may well prove the most satisfying form of that defense. It will be so only if it is used as a contrast to an eagerly embraced future, and not as a replacement."

SWARD, Robert (Stuart)   1933-

PERSONAL: Born June 23, 1933, in Chicago, Ill.; son of Irving Michael (a doctor) and Gertrude (Huebsch) Sward; married second wife, Diane Kaldes, February, 1960 (divorced, 1969); married Judith Essenson, March 21, 1969 (divorced, 1972); children: (second marriage) Cheryl Ann, Barbara Anne, Michael Paul; (third marriage) Hannah, Nicholas. *Education:* University of Illinois at Urbana-Champaign, B.A. (with honors), 1956; Middlebury College, Bread Loaf School of English, graduate study, summers, 1956-58; University of Iowa, M.A., 1958; University of Bristol, graduate study, 1960-61. *Religion:* Jewish.

ADDRESSES: Home—P.O. Box 7062, Santa Cruz, Calif. 95061-7062.

CAREER: Connecticut College, New London, instructor in English, 1958-59; Cornell University, Ithaca, N.Y., instructor in English, 1962-64; University of Iowa, Writers' Workshop, Iowa City, writer-in-residence, 1967; University of Victoria, Victoria, British Columbia, assistant professor of English and writer-in-residence, 1969-73; Hancock House Publishers, Victoria, editor, 1976-79; free-lance writer, editor, and technical writer, 1979—. Visiting writer, University of California, Santa Cruz, 1986—, and Monterey Peninsula College, Monterey, Calif., 1986—. Associate fellow, Strong College, York University, Canada, 1984—. Editor and publisher, Soft Press, 1970-77. Free-lance broadcaster for Canadian Broadcasting Corporation (CBC-Radio). Participant, Writers in the Schools program, 1979—, Ontario Arts Council, 1979-85; visiting Writer in the Schools, Cultural Council of Santa Cruz County, 1986—. Sward has exhibited his poetry, stories, photographs, and lithographs on occasion. Has worked as a gardener. *Military service:* U.S. Navy, 1951-53.

MEMBER: Modern Poetry Association, Writers' Union of Canada, League of Canadian Poets, Committee of Small Magazine Editors and Publishers, Periodical Writers Association, Phi Beta Kappa.

AWARDS, HONORS: Dylan Thomas Poetry Award; poetry fellow, Bread Loaf Writers' Conference, 1958; Fulbright scholar, 1960-61; Guggenheim fellowship, 1964-65; D. H. Lawrence fellowship, University of New Mexico, 1966; Canada Council grants, 1973-74 and 1981; Explorations grant, 1982; MacDowell Colony and Yaddo fellowships.

WRITINGS:

The Jurassic Shales (novel), Coach House Press, 1975.
The Toronto Islands: An Illustrated History (also see below), Dreadnaught Press (Toronto), 1983.

POETRY

Advertisements, introduction by Fred Eckman, Odyssey Chapbook Publications, 1958.
Uncle Dog and Other Poems, Putnam (London), 1962, published as *Kissing the Dancer and Other Poems,* introduction by William Meredith, Cornell University Press, 1964.
The Thousand-Year-Old Fiancee and Other Poems, Cornell University Press, 1965.
Horgbortom Stringbottom, I Am Yours, You Are History, Swallow Press, 1970.
Hannah's Cartoon, Soft Press, 1970.
(With Mike Doyle) *Quorum/Noah,* Soft Press, 1970.
Gift, Soft Press, 1971.
Songs from the Jurassic Shales, Soft Press, 1972.
Five Iowa Poems and One Iowa Print, Stone Wall Press, 1975.

Honey Bear on Lasqueti Island, B.C. (contains photographs and prints), Soft Press, 1978.

Six Poems, League of Canadian Poets (Toronto), 1980.

Twelve Poems, Island House Books (Toronto), 1982.

Movies: Left to Right, South Western Ontario Poetry (London, Ontario), 1983.

Half a Life's History, Poems: New and Selected, 1957-1983, introduction by Earle Birney, AYA Press (Toronto), 1983.

(With Robert Priest and Robert Zend) *The Three Roberts: Premiere Performance*, HMS Press (Scarborough, Ontario), 1984.

(With Priest and Zend) *The Three Roberts on Love*, Dreadnaught Press, 1984.

(With Priest and Zend) *The Three Roberts on Childhood*, Moonstone Press (St. Catharines, Ontario), 1985.

EDITOR

Vancouver Island Poems (poetry anthology), Soft Press, 1973.

Cheers for Muktananda (poetry anthology), Soft Press, 1976.

Edythe Hembroff-Schleicher, *Emily Carr: The Untold Story*, Hancock House, 1978.

Allen T. Denison and Wallace K. Huntington, *Victorian Architecture of Port Townsend, Washington*, Hancock House, 1978.

Phil J. Thomas, *Songs of the Pacific Northwest*, Hancock House, 1979.

Leslie Drew and Douglas Wilson, *Agillite: The Art of the Haida*, Hancock House, 1980.

(With Penny Kemp) *Contemporary Verse Two: Spiritual Poetry in Canada*, Volume VI, numbers 1-2, University of Manitoba, 1981-82.

CONTRIBUTOR TO ANTHOLOGIES

Edwin Glikes and Paul Schwaber, editors, *John F. Kennedy Memorial Anthology: Of Poetry and Power*, Basic Books, 1964.

Robert Kelly and Paris Leary, editors, *A Controversy of Poets: The Anchor Book of Contemporary American Poetry*, Doubleday Anchor, 1965.

Lucien Stryk, editor, *Heartland: Poets of the Midwest*, Northern Illinois University Press, 1967.

George MacBeth, editor, *Penguin Book of Animal Poetry*, Penguin (London), 1967.

Walter Lowenfels, editor, *Where Is Vietnam?*, Doubleday, 1967.

Earle Stibitz, editor, *Illinois Poetry*, Southern Illinois University Press, 1968.

Mark Strand, editor, *The Contemporary American Poets: American Poetry since 1940*, World Publishing, 1970.

Hayden Carruth, editor, *The Voice That Is Great within Us*, Bantam, 1970.

Robert Vas Dias, editor, *Inside Outer Space: New Poems of the Space Age*, Doubleday Anchor, 1970.

Silver Screen ("Neue Amerikanische Lyrik"): An Anthology of Modern American Poetry Translated into German, Verlag Kiepenheuer & Witsch (West Germany), 1970.

Rolf Dieter Brinkmann, editor, *Acid Anthology: Modern American Poetry in German Translation*, Verlag Kiepenheuer & Witsch, 1970.

The New Yorker Book of Poems, Viking, 1970.

Dunning, Lueders, and Smith, editors, *Some Haystacks Don't Even Have Any Needle and Other Modern Verse*, Scott, Foresman, 1970.

Roxanne Knudson, editor, *Sports Poems*, Dell, 1971.

Dana Atchley, editor, *Space Atlas* (poetry and graphics), [Victoria, British Columbia], 1971.

Carli and Kilman, editors, *The Now Voices*, Scribner, 1972.

The Rhetoric of Yes, Holt, 1972.

William Cole, editor, *Poems One Line and Longer*, David Grossman, 1973.

George Chambers, editor, *Out of Sight*, Number 26, Out of Sight Library, 1973.

David Swanger, editor, *The Poem as Process*, Harcourt, 1974.

Alice Fleming, editor, *America Is Not All Traffic Lights*, Little, Brown, 1976.

Susan Mernit and Rochelle Ratner, editors, *Handbook* (poetry), Spring Street, 1976.

John Robert Colombo, editor, *Poets of Canada*, Hurtig Publishers (Alberta), 1978.

Fred Candelaria, editor, *New: West Coast Anthology*, Intermedia, 1978.

Dennis Maloney, editor, *On Turtle's Back: A Biogeographic Anthology of New York State Poetry*, White Pine Press, 1978.

William Harmon, editor, *The Oxford Book of American Light Verse*, Oxford University Press, 1979.

P. K. Page, editor, *To Say the Least: Canadian Poets from A to Z*, Press Porcepic (Victoria), 1979.

LaVerne Harrell Clark, editor, *The Face of Poetry: 101 Poets*, foreword by Richard Eberhart, Heidelberg Graphics, 1979.

Sheridan Baker, Northrop Frye, and George Perkins, editors, *The Practical Imagination: Stories, Poems, Plays*, Harper, 1980.

Sarah Provost, editor, *Carpet of Sparrows: Poems for Young Readers*, Nocturnal Canary Press, 1980.

Ursula Heller, compiler, *Village Portraits* (collection of photographs and interviews; contains edited versions of interviews from Sward's *The Toronto Islands: An Illustated History*), Methuen (Toronto), 1981.

Florence McNeill, editor, *Here Is a Poem*, League of Canadian Poets, 1983.

Benjamin Spencer, editor, *A Canine Testament*, Harper, 1985.

Also contributor to *New: American and Canadian Poetry*, edited by John Gill, 1973, and *Signal Hill Broadsides*, 1977.

RADIO BROADCASTING

"Spiritual Poetry in Canada" (contains interviews with Margaret Atwood, Earle Birney, John Robert Colombo, Joy Kogawa, David McFadden, and others), CBC-Radio, April, 1983.

"Poetry as Performance," CBC-Radio, June, 1984.

Also author of a radio anthology with singer-songwriter Leonard Cohen for CBC-Radio, December, 1984.

OTHER

(Contributor) *The New Canadian Encyclopedia*, Hurtig Publishers, 1985.

Also author of the holograph *Letter to a Straw Hat*, with byline omitted, Soft Press, 1976. Sward's poetry is featured in the premiere issue of the journal *Santa Cruz*, 1985. Contributor of poems, reviews, stories, and features to over two hundred periodicals in the United States, Canada, South America, England, Germany, Switzerland, New Zealand, and Australia, including *Poetry, Paris Review, Transatlantic Review, New Yorker, Poetry Canada*, and *Neue zuercher*.

WORK IN PROGRESS: Golden Oldies and New Releases (poetry); *Toronto Island Suite*, a collection of poems, interviews, stories, and photographs focusing on the Toronto Island community; *How to Cure a Broken Heart*, short stories; *Adven-*

tures with Authors and Eagles, a comic novel; *Journey to Ganeshpuri,* a nonfiction work discussing the experience of living in a spiritual community in India; editor with Pat Keeney Smith of a work tentatively entitled *From Impulse to Art: Interviews with Twenty Poets and Novelists* which will contain interviews with Margaret Atwood, Saul Bellow, Leonard Cohen, Ted Hughes, Mark Strand, and D. M. Thomas.

SIDELIGHTS: Robert Sward began his writing career at sea during a four-year stint with the U.S. Navy. A United States citizen by birth, Sward lived in Canada for a number of years and considers himself "a North American poet." "I don't feel bound to any one particular place," he told *Excalibur*'s Stuart Ross. "If it's possible to belong to both places, I do."

In a review of Sward's *Kissing the Dancer and Other Poems,* John Malcolm Brinnin of the *New York Times Book Review* notes that "many of [the author's] poems are honed to a spareness that recalls the vernacular simplicity of William Carlos Williams. To his credit, the endeavor reveals a voice and not a repetition. . . . [Sward] is fierce, new-minted and convincing." Though he writes primarily in idiomatic American English, Sward does give his poetry a "sinewy linguistic texture," according to the *Carleton Miscellany*'s Lawrence Lieberman. Describing this as "the most singular quality of his poetry," Lieberman goes on to say that "the word-thickness . . . revives a tradition in English that many critics feel reached a dead end in the work of Hopkins and Hart Crane, two poets who . . . cultivated special vocabularies while retaining a large measure of literary or 'poetical' vocabulary."

William Meredith speculates in the preface to *Kissing the Dancer and Other Poems* that Sward's poems have been turned down by many publishers "because they are so original as to be unrecognizable as poetry by a conventional eye. They have gone off to respectable publishers with praise from Stanley Kunitz, Louise Bogan, even Robert Lowell, and come back with the embarrassed confession that they simply escaped the respectable editors. . . . Like other good works of art, these poems have the air of having been made for people rather than for other artists. They contain high-toned gossip rather than aesthetics, or the aesthetics are hidden and acted out like charades. A lot of the poems are unpleasant in places, like life itself, but none of them contains any fashionable despair. . . . There is that humility about them that comes from paying a blasphemous attention, God's own attention, to oneself."

There is also in these poems an attention to things which results in a kind of mysticism. "The mysticism of objects, of thingness," observes Lieberman, "is an inversion and, in a way, a bizarre parody of conventional mysticism. With Wordsworth, we 'see into the life of things.' In Sward's world, things work their way inside *our* life, become parts of our psyche, dominate our minds and take us over, *make* us over, entirely." Adds Meredith: "I have come to the conclusion that when [Sward] works on [his poems] he is paying perfect, slightly mystical attention to . . . (1) himself as an example of a man; (2) his vocabulary as a butterfly net to catch the experiences the man has; and (3) a passion for simplicity. His simplicity is not that of Zen . . . or of Thoreau, but something more like that of Blake or Emily Dickinson."

Much of the mysticism in Sward's poetry can be traced to his involvement with yoga. In fact, the poet regards the connection between poetry, yoga, and meditation as "the whole process of communication between two people, an intermingling of one consciousness with another. I guess I'm constantly trying to simplify my language and my approach. I write primarily

for myself, but the next inclination is to see whether other people can connect with it. I don't think there's anybody who poetry cannot reach."

"The Islanders," a traveling exhibition of Robert Sward's poems on the Toronto Island community, accompanied by the photographs of Ursula Heller, opened in the Toronto City Hall in November, 1980, and was subsequently seen by more than sixty thousand people in various libraries and community centers. Collections of Sward's manuscripts are housed in the Washington University Libraries, St. Louis, Mo., in the City Hall Archive, Toronto, Ontario, and in the National Library of Canada, Ottawa, Ontario. Additional material of Sward's is housed in the Special Manuscript Collection in the Rare Books Library at the University of Victoria, Victoria, British Columbia.

MEDIA ADAPTATIONS: The Thousand-Year-Old Fiancee and Other Poems, read by Sward, was recorded by Western Michigan University Aural Press in 1965 and by New Letters on the Air, University of Missouri—Kansas City, March, 1985.

AVOCATIONAL INTERESTS: Swimming, meditating, yoga, photography.

BIOGRAPHICAL/CRITICAL SOURCES:

BOOKS

The Face of Poetry, Heidelberg Graphics, 1979.
Sward, Robert, *Kissing the Dancer and Other Poems,* introduction by William Meredith, Cornell University Press, 1964.
Sward, Robert, *Half a Life's History, Poems: New and Selected, 1957-1983,* introduction by Earle Birney, Volume IV, AYA Press, 1983.

PERIODICALS

Canadian Literature, spring, 1985.
Carleton Miscellany, spring, 1967.
Excalibur, April 2, 1981.
Monday Magazine (Victoria), October 13, 1975.
New York Review of Books, March 31, 1966.
New York Times Book Review, October 25, 1964, April 17, 1966.
Pacific Northwest Review of Books, April, 1978.
Poetry, April, 1963.
Times Literary Supplement, August 18, 1966.

*　　*　　*

SYRUC, J.
See MILOSZ, Czeslaw

*　　*　　*

SZULC, Tad   1926-

PERSONAL: Surname is pronounced Schulz; born July 25, 1926, in Warsaw, Poland; came to United States, 1947; naturalized, 1954; son of Seweryn and Janina (Baruch) Szulc; married Marianne Carr, July 8, 1948; children: Nicole, Anthony. *Education:* Attended University of Brazil, 1943-45.

ADDRESSES: Home and office—4515 29th St. N.W., Washington, D.C. 20008. *Agent*—Morton L. Janklow Associates, 598 Madison Ave., New York, N.Y. 10022.

CAREER: Associated Press (AP), reporter in Rio de Janeiro, Brazil, 1945-46; United Press International (UPI), correspondent at United Nations, 1949-53; *New York Times,* New York, N.Y., 1953-72, served as correspondent in Southeast Asia, Latin America, Portugal, Spain, Eastern Europe, the Middle East, and with the Washington Bureau; author and foreign policy commentator, 1973—. Visiting professor, Fletcher School of Law and Diplomacy, Tufts University, Medford, Mass., 1979. Lecturer on foreign affairs at universities, government seminars, for Peace Corps, and on radio and television.

MEMBER: Cosmos Club and Federal City Club (both Washington, D.C.), Overseas Press Club (New York).

AWARDS, HONORS: Maria Moors Cabot Gold medal of Columbia University for advancement of international friendship in the Americas, 1959; Overseas Press Club, citations, 1966, 1974, 1975, 1977, 1978, award for best magazine interpretation of foreign affairs, 1976, award for best book on foreign affairs, 1979 and 1986; Sigma Delta Distinguished Service Award, 1968; Knight of the Order of the Legion of Honor (France), 1983; D.H.L., American College of Switzerland, 1987; distinguished medal, World Business Council, 1987.

WRITINGS:

Twilight of the Tyrants, Holt, 1959.
New Trends in Latin America, Foreign Policy Association, 1960.
(With Karl E. Meyer) *The Cuban Invasion: The Chronicle of a Disaster,* Praeger, 1962.
Latin America, Encyclopaedia Britannica, 1965.
Dominican Diary, Delacorte, 1965.
The Bombs of Palomares, Viking, 1967.
Czechoslovakia since World War II, Viking, 1971.
(Editor and author of preface) *The United States and the Caribbean* (American Assembly series), Prentice-Hall, 1971.
Portrait of Spain, American Heritage Press, 1972.
Compulsive Spy: The Strange Case of E. Howard Hunt, Viking, 1973.
The Illusion of Peace: Foreign Policy in the Nixon Years, Viking, 1978.
Diplomatic Immunity (novel), Simon & Schuster, 1981.
Fidel: A Critical Portrait (Book-of-the-Month Club selection), Morrow, 1986.

FOR YOUNG PEOPLE

The Winds of Revolution: Latin America Today and Tomorrow, Praeger, 1963, revised edition, 1965.
Innocents at Home: America in the 1970s, Viking, 1974.
The Energy Crisis, F. Watts, 1974, revised edition, 1978.
The Invasion of Czechoslovakia, August, 1968: The End of a Socialist Experiment in Freedom, F. Watts, 1974.

OTHER

Contributor to *New Yorker, New York Times Magazine, Parade, Foriegn Policy Quarterly, New Republic, Saturday Review, New York, Forbes,* and other magazines and newspapers. Member of editorial board of *Foreign Policy,* 1976—.

WORK IN PROGRESS: A study of the consequences of World War II, for Morrow.

SIDELIGHTS: During his twenty-year tenure as foreign and diplomatic correspondent for the *New York Times,* Tad Szulc's investigative prowess sometimes got him into trouble: he was expelled from both Portugal and Czechoslovakia, for example. Even in the United States his skills were not entirely appreciated: his phone was tapped during the Nixon administration because of his candid reporting on delicate political issues.

Despite these intrusions on his work, Szulc has been able to turn his experiences on four continents into a series of widely reviewed books on foreign affairs and foreign policy. In *Portrait of Spain,* for instance, Szulc draws on his background as a *New York Times* correspondent in Madrid from 1965 to 1968, while in *Czechoslovakia since World War II* Szulc gives his eye-witness account of the Soviet invasion of that country.

Szulc's familiarity with Washington politics and foreign affairs is never more evident than in *The Illusion of Peace: Foreign Policy in the Nixon Years,* a study of foreign policy decisions made between 1969 and 1974 by President Nixon and Henry Kissinger, who served as Nixon's special adviser on national security until being named secretary of state in 1973. The work is praised by Alex Beam in *Nation* and William Bundy in *Saturday Review.* Beam calls it "the most complete and well-informed account of the Nixon diplomacy to date." Bundy notes: "There is to be sure a wealth of information in the book. Szulc was a superb investigative reporter before that term was invented."

At the same time, however, Bundy questions Szulc's approach to crediting sources. "He obviously had good sources, with the National Security Council staff and the CIA, in particular. But his overwhelming reliance on such 'reporter's sources' at one extreme and on the public record at the other leaves out a whole layer of background knowledge and research in between. . . . Szulc's failure to cite his sources is not merely frustrating, it is also confusing." Bundy feels that more complete citations would aid the reader: "It is one thing to protect confidential personal sources but another to omit sources that would enable the reader to check the provenance and context of the public material cited."

Richard H. Ullman echoes Bundy's criticism, writing in the *New York Times Book Review* that "analysts will have a needlessly difficult time retracing . . . Szulc's steps" because his "book is totally devoid of . . . footnotes, lists of sources and other means to let a reader know the nature of evidence an author used to form his opinions." Although Ullman finds "'The Illusion of Power' . . . absorbing, even compelling reading," and notes that "much of its information is new, sometimes startlingly so," he also observes that the "information [is] often impossible to evaluate." These objections aside, Ullman contends that Szulc's book is "by far the best extant account of the Nixon Administration's foreign policy."

After writing more than a dozen nonfiction books, Szulc turned his foreign policy experiences into a novel, *Diplomatic Immunity.* While not a bestseller, the book has elicited some positive comments from reviewers. Robert Sherrill writes in the *New York Times Book Review,* "Aside from its other merits, 'Diplomatic Immunity' is, because of . . . Szulc's expertise, a liberal education in State Department metaphysics." In the *Chicago Tribune Book World* Michael Hutchinson notes, "The author's firsthand knowledge of how U.S. foreign policy . . . works is illuminating, turning this into a first-rate thriller." Both Sherrill and Hutchinson emphasize the role of Szulc's own foreign experiences in making the characters and foreign intrigue of the plot believable.

Szulc apparently had little difficulty turning to fiction after writing nonfiction for so many years. He told *Library Journal:* "I think I was greatly aided by the notion, which occurred to me when I started [writing the novel], that fiction is essentially story-telling in the same sense as reporting on a war, a revolution, a diplomatic negotiation—or a fire. With this in mind, the story just flowed from the typewriter."

While Szulc deals in *Diplomatic Immunity* with ambassadors, dictators, and CIA officials who are fictional, in real life the author counts such powerful people as friends. In *Publishers Weekly*, Dave Masello notes Szulc's "close personal ties to such figures as Francois Mitterand, John and Robert Kennedy and Pope John Paul II." Another of Szulc's acquaintances, Cuban leader Fidel Castro, is the subject of the journalist's *Fidel: A Critical Portrait.*

Szulc's fluency in Spanish (he also speaks Polish, Portuguese, and French) gave him easy access to existing Cuban and other Spanish-language biographical material and allowed direct communication with Castro regarding information for *Fidel.* Szulc met the Cuban leader nearly thirty years ago when the two were introduced by *New York Times* editorial board member Herbert Matthews. Szulc reminisces in *Publishers Weekly:* "Herbert . . . introduced me to Fidel, and that was the first all-night session I had with Castro. We sat all night in the kitchen—Fidel's favorite place to meet with people—of the Havana Hilton. . . . Then the three of us went to the First People's Beach and sat until 4 a.m. drinking Cokes in the sand."

After being announced in advance by Szulc's publisher, the first full-length Castro biography was eagerly awaited because of Szulc's solid reputation as a journalist and also because Castro would cooperate fully with the author. Judging by post-publication public interest and critical acclaim, *Fidel: A Critical Portrait* has lived up to its expectations. "Szulc has sketched a meticulously honest, painstakingly detailed and essentially complete portrait of the revolutionary," writes Jorge G. Casteneda in the *Los Angeles Times Book Review.* In the Toronto *Globe and Mail* John D. Harbon observes, "Szulc . . . has written a highly readable study about Castro and his era," and Leonard Bushhoff claims in the *Christian Science Monitor* that Szulc's *Fidel* "makes fascinating reading."

Because of Szulc's familiarity with his subject, *Fidel* includes previously unknown details of Castro's rise to power. Szulc maintains, for example, that Castro became a Communist as early as 1948—long before he officially claimed to be one. The author also reveals that in the 1950s the CIA secretly gave funds to Castro's 26th of July Movement to help overthrow then-Cuban dictator Fulgencio Batista. Finally, as Frank del Olmo notes in the *Los Angeles Times,* the book "offers new insights from Castro on his tumultuous, and often dangerous relationships with the United States, including the 1961 Bay of Pigs invasion and the Cuban missile crisis of the following year."

Though highly praised, *Fidel* has elicited its share of criticism, some of which is directed at the book's focus on the period leading up to the 1959 coup d'etat at the expense of Castro's years in power. Casteneda notes, for example, that the longest portion of Szulc's book details Castro's activities before 1959, and the reviewer wishes more information had been provided on Castro's later years. George de Lama similarly observes in the Chicago *Tribune Books* that "by focusing almost entirely on Fidel's early years—a worthy goal in itself—the book gives sparse treatment to the last twenty years of Castro's rule." De Lama adds, "Unfortunately, the lack of attention given to the last two decades' developments in Cuba make this book half a loaf."

Robert Sherill seems to sum up Szulc's career as a journalist when he writes in the *New York Times Book Review,* "As a foreign correspondent, Tad Szulc has been filing exciting dispatches for a generation." Now in his post-correspondent pe-riod, Szulc continues to excite readers' interest and critics' praise. Without a doubt his journalistic background is the key to his books' popularity because, as Masello notes, Szulc's years as a correspondent allowed him to be a "witness to this generation's most resonant, historical episodes."

MEDIA ADAPTATIONS: Motion picture and television rights to *Fidel: A Critical Portrait* have been sold to Jazbo Productions, Los Angeles, California.

CA INTERVIEW

CA interviewed Tad Szulc by telephone on December 15, 1986, at his home in Washington, D.C.

CA: Let's begin by talking about your latest book, Fidel. *What made you decide to write a biography of Fidel Castro?*

SZULC: No one else had done it. As far as I know, mine is the first real biography, as compared to bits and fragments from here, there, and elsewhere. Castro is one of the few truly interesting people in the world today, and since I've known him for twenty-eight years, I thought it was a good time to do a biography, and so I did it.

CA: Was there a moment of inspiration in which you realized it would be a good book to write?

SZULC: I was in Cuba in January 1984, almost three years ago, on assignment for a magazine, and Castro and I spent a great deal of time together—three days and three nights. I suddenly realized that his memory was beginning to falter a bit, that people were dying, and there was no real record of the Cuban Revolution and no real biography of Castro. I asked him if he planned on writing his autobiography, and he said he'd been thinking about it for twenty years, but he didn't see how he could get around to it. At some point it occurred to me that a biography was something one should do. I wouldn't call it inspiration, but it was a thought that came to me, and we began to toss it back and forth. We kept in touch through most of 1984, sending messages back and forth, and by the end of the year we had pretty much agreed on the terms—essentially that this was an unofficial, not authorized, biography, but I would have full access to him and his people and the materials, such as they are. I hadn't realized, even at that point, how little there is available that's of any value.

CA: It must have been curious to you that there was no biography of him.

SZULC: It is curious. What you find in Cuba, in Spanish, are very superficial, fragmentary, brief, and partially one-sided basic propaganda accounts of his life. There is a biography called *The Young Fidel,* which covers only his youth. At the same time my book came out, there was another one published here, written by Peter Bourne, a man who worked for Jimmy Carter in the White House. The basic flaw of that book is that the author never met Castro on a one-to-one basis.

CA: And you'd known him since the beginning of the Revolution?

SZULC: Yes. My work with him began back in 1959 and continued to 1961 at the Bay of Pigs. Then there was a very long gap during which I was on assignment in Europe, one thing and another happened, and it was some time before we got together again. I returned again to Cuba in 1984 and 1985, when I spent most of the time researching the book.

CA: Was Castro a cooperative subject?

SZULC: He was reasonably available, certainly enough for my purposes. With Castro, the problem is that he tends, as I discovered, to be extremely repetitious. I went to the obvious trouble of reading endless interviews which he had granted in the past, and essentially there are no terribly new ideas; mainly he was repeating the same themes in the same words. In all I had maybe a dozen conversations with him. Everything was taped and transcribed and donated to the University of Miami in Coral Gables, Florida, and in part to the Kennedy Library at Harvard. It's available to scholars; there are certain restrictions placed on the material. It was five thousand pages of transcripts of different interviews with Castro and his associates.

CA: In the book, you called Castro a moody introvert. In public he seems to project the opposite image.

SZULC: The public's view of him is based on television and news photos in which he obviously appears at his dramatic best. The private Castro is different. He seldom broods publicly. He's very conscious of his public persona. But this is not unusual. There are scads of people who appear jolly to the outside world, but when alone are introspective. Castro is a very reserved and sometimes moody person as well.

CA: What is your assessment of what Castro has done for the Cuban people since he has been in power?

SZULC: I think he did a lot during the initial period, but now I think it's all going down the drain. The current economic situation is the worst crisis they've had since he came into power, simply because nothing works. Even the material gains of the Revolution are in question twenty-five years later. So you begin to wonder. My book was never meant to be a history or an assessment of the Revolution, because that would be a seven-thousand-page book instead of what it is. It's an attempt to stick to the subject, Castro himself. But I think it describes the rise, the peaking, and the beginning of the descent which I believe we're observing now. I want to be very careful to stay away from prophecy, however.

CA: Aside from the frontispiece, there are no photographs in the book. Were you prohibited from taking pictures in Cuba?

SZULC: What happened was a classical publishing situation. My publisher originally planned—and said so in one of his early catalogues—to include twenty or thirty pages of pictures. The book was never planned to be so long, but there was such a marvelous amount of rich material that it became very, very long. We were on a fast schedule with the book, so, for example, we skipped galleys altogether to save time. A decision had to be made by the publisher to sacrifice the pictures to make room for more words. My British publisher feels strongly that photos should be included, and the British edition will have a section of photographs, which we are providing. The explanation is that simple. And there are really no new pictures of Castro. There are pictures of Castro as a baby that have already been published in the *New York Times*. There's a batch of pictures with me, and we used one of them on the jacket. But both my editor and I felt strongly that the enormously long

chapter notes had to be kept, and that meant the pictures had to go.

CA: Has Castro commented on the book?

SZULC: No, and I don't think he ever will. It's just one of those situations where he will not say whether he likes part of it or hates other parts or whatever. I may get word through third parties, either Cuban or others, which I expect will be critical of certain passages of the book.

CA: You've written other books and many articles on Latin America. In your book Winds of Revolution, *which came out in 1963 and was later revised, you speak of the winds of revolution blowing more strongly every day. How do you see it more than twenty years later?*

SZULC: Hindsight is such a beautiful thing. In Latin America there is a turning away from Marxist Cuba because in the Third World there is a realization that this system of government does not work. I think the return of democratic systems in Brazil and Argentina has defused those pressures for the time being, but at the same time they are occurring elsewhere. Look at Africa, which is running a generation behind Latin America. I haven't the faintest idea what will happen next in Angola or Namibia or South Africa. But evidently something bloody awful is coming there. We see the same thing in parts of Asia. So I think that revolutions, but not of the 1959 Castro type, will occur elsewhere. As long as there is mass unemployment, overpopulation, and starvation, revolution is possible. Mexico is a case in point. I'm much more concerned with what is going on in that country than with Nicaragua's going communist. At the present time Mexico has a population of seventy million, but by the year 2000 it will have increased to a hundred million. Mexico is bound to blow up because of its infrastructure. So the winds of revolution still have the same causes they had twenty-five years ago.

CA: You were born in Poland, and by some accounts fled Poland before the beginning of World War II. Is that accurate?

SZULC: No. I was exported before the beginning of the war, sent to a boys' prep school, Le Rosey in Switzerland, through foresight on the part of my parents. I was there for two years, then World War II came and I lived in France for a year until the German occupation. Then I went to Brazil because my father had lived there. And while I was in Brazil, I attended school there.

CA: You eventually left Brazil for New York. According to an article in Time *magazine, you met your future wife at a party five days before your visa expired, married her five days later, and have lived in the United States ever since.*

SZULC: That's correct. And we're still married thirty-eight years later; we were married in 1948. I went to work for the United Press in early 1949, and then moved over to the *New York Times* in May of 1953. I stayed with the *Times* for almost twenty years.

CA: Much of your work has been as an investigative news correspondent.

SZULC: Well, I shy at the word *investigative* because it's a redundant expression. If a reporter doesn't investigate, he isn't a reporter. Most of my career was on the *Times*. I spent a year and a half in New York as a correspondent. I had spent one year in the Far East and six years in Latin America. I had about twelve years as a foreign correspondent. I was twice in the Washington bureau.

CA: When tragedy has struck around the globe, you seem to have been in the right place at the right time. Do you think you were just lucky?

SZULC: Obviously I was lucky. I was assigned by the *Times* to Europe. I had no idea that Prague would explode. That was in 1968, when I was in charge of the Prague bureau.

CA: You had no inkling that something was afoot there?

SZULC: I think everyone who covered Prague at that time knew that sooner or later there would be a confrontation. Bearing in mind what had happened in Budapest in 1956, it was obvious that the Soviets would tolerate what was going on in Czechoslovakia only so long and no longer. My wife and our two children and I came home in July for home leave, and my family went to Cape Cod. I got very nervous and didn't want to be away, so I went back to Prague on a Thursday and the invasion came on the following Tuesday. I would have hated myself forever had I been on Cape Cod at that time.

CA: You are often credited with breaking the story of the Bay of Pigs invasion. How true is that?

SZULC: I would say it's true only up to a point. I don't want to take credit for more than I did. It had been published some months earlier that Cuban exiles were being trained in Guatemala for something of this kind. My contribution was to say that this something was being set in motion and when and how it would occur. In that sense it's fair to say that I did break the story.

CA: One account says that you were visiting friends in Miami, and it was there that you uncovered details about the impending attack.

SZULC: I was being reassigned by the *New York Times* from Latin America, where I was a correspondent for six years, to the Washington bureau. What I was doing in March and April of 1961 was traveling very slowly north, stopping at all the cities which were in my territory to say good-bye to people I had known during those six years. On this trip I hit Miami—as it happened, on Easter weekend—and spent the long weekend there with friends. It was there that I first became aware of the coming invasion, and the more I heard, the more I became alarmed. So I asked permission to go to New York and talk to the managing editor and the publisher. I was told to return to Miami and start a war bureau, and the rest of the story you know.

CA: In 1981 your first and, to date, only novel, Diplomatic Immunity, *was published. Is it pretty much based on fact?*

SZULC: It's the usual composite of people. The situation itself is invented, obviously. There never was a U.S. woman ambassador in Central America. There was an American woman ambassador whom I know elsewhere in the Caribbean, but it was just a dramatic device to use a woman as an ambassador. The mythical country in the book is a composite of Nicaragua and El Salvador, and the leader is modeled to some extent on

Somoza. It was kind of fun to do because I'd never done it before, and I enjoyed it very much.

CA: Had you planned to write a novel for some time?

SZULC: I had played with the idea of doing a novel for quite a while, but I was always caught up with other things. My agent, Morton Janklow, kind of talked me into it. It was great fun inventing facts instead of gathering them. It doesn't purport to be serious literature, but for what it is, I think it's reasonably plausible. Basically I wanted to establish in my own mind that I was capable of writing it and having it published. It was not a runaway bestseller, but it did get some nice reviews.

CA: You're not connected at all now with the New York Times?

SZULC: No. I left exactly fourteen years ago. I retain a marvelous relationship with them. I write for the op-ed page and for the magazine. In fact, the magazine did me a service by running a whole chapter of the Fidel book prior to the publication date. And since the magazine has a million and a half readers, that was a great help to me.

CA: So you're more or less a free-lance writer now?

SZULC: Yes, though I prefer the word *independent*. But I'm very close to everybody at the *Times*.

CA: You've written for younger audiences too, haven't you?

SZULC: Yes, I have, by some accident of history. I was once asked to do a young people's version of the book which I did on Czechoslovakia in 1968. That was a young people's book published by Franklin Watts. I don't even list it separately among the fifteen books I've written. It's such a small thing.

CA: Do you ever lecture to young audiences?

SZULC: There was a time when I was doing a lot of lecturing in colleges. I've been doing much less lately. During the promotion for *Fidel* I've done quite a bit of that. I spoke here in Washington; I spoke at USC at Los Angeles, at the professional journalism center. I spoke at the University of Miami. Colleges are not as interested in foreign policy as they were once upon a time. The bookings are far more on domestic problems. When I was younger and I was doing much less writing I had a very nice flourishing business speaking at colleges. But that was during the Kennedy period when the Peace Corps was started as well as the Alliance for Progress. When the Vietnam War came, interests changed a good deal. Today only foreign policy experts like Henry Kissinger and half a dozen others draw large audiences. I spent a semester in 1979 as a visiting professor at Fletcher in Cambridge, Massachusetts, and that was unusual in that the course was devoted to foreign policy.

CA: Will you write another novel?

SZULC: Maybe, at some point. I just finished a month-long promotion tour on *Fidel*, and I'm trying to get myself organized. I just haven't come to a decision about what I want to do next. My publisher is very nice about it. He wants me to write another book, whatever I'm comfortable with. But I don't want to rush. When you rush, it never comes out right. Things have to happen in their own good time.

CA: Do you have any idea what your next book will be about?

SZULC: No. I'm playing with ideas and chatting with my agent. Castro was such an obvious idea it didn't take a great deal of thought once it became clear in my mind that it was feasible in terms of sources and access. But I don't see anything quite so obvious now. You know, the world is lacking in terribly interesting leaders right now.

BIOGRAPHICAL/CRITICAL SOURCES:

PERIODICALS

Business Week, March 9, 1987.
Chicago Tribune Book World, August 15, 1982.
Christian Science Monitor, June 12, 1967, June 26, 1978, January 6, 1987.
Globe and Mail (Toronto), January 24, 1987.
Library Journal, October 1, 1981.
Listener, May 18, 1967.
Los Angeles Times, December 17, 1986.
Los Angeles Times Book Review, October 1, 1981, November 16, 1986.

Nation, May 20, 1978, January 24, 1987.
National Review, October 11, 1974, February 13, 1987.
New Leader, July 3, 1967, May 3, 1971.
New Republic, May 20, 1967, December 30, 1981, January 19, 1987.
Newsweek, November 24, 1986.
New Yorker, May 22, 1978.
New York Times, July 8, 1967, November 4, 1986.
New York Times Book Review, April 23, 1967, January 17, 1971, October 1, 1972, June 18, 1978, September 27, 1981, November 30, 1986.
Publishers Weekly, June 14, 1985, December 5, 1986.
Saturday Review, January 30, 1971, June 10, 1978.
Times Literary Supplement, July 6, 1967, April 30, 1982.
Tribune Books (Chicago), January 18, 1987.
Washington Post Book World, October 12, 1981, November 2, 1986.

—*Sketch by Marian Gonsior*

—*Interview by Walter W. Ross*

T

TANGERMAN, Elmer John 1907-

PERSONAL: Surname is pronounced *Tan*-jer-man; born August 8, 1907, in Hammond, Ind.; son of William John (an inventor and factory superintendent) and Josephine (Karsten) Tangerman; married Mary M. Christopher, September 7, 1929; children: John Tilden (deceased), Mary Tangerman Salerno, Judith Tangerman Hickson. *Education:* Purdue University, B.S.M.E., 1929, M.E., 1937. *Politics:* Republican.

ADDRESSES: Home—111 Ivy Way, Port Washington, N.Y. 11050.

CAREER: American Machinist, New York City, assistant editor, 1929-32; *Power,* New York City, assistant editor, 1932-34, associate editor, 1934-36, managing editor, 1937; *American Machinist,* assistant manager, 1938-42; *Power,* business manager, 1942-45; *American Machinist,* managing editor, 1945-50, executive editor, 1950-56; *Product Engineering,* New York City, chief editor, 1957-65, associate publisher, 1965-66; McGraw-Hill Publications, New York City, designer of office of planning and development, 1966-69; writer, 1969—. General manager of *Nucleonics,* 1947-49. Woodcarver, with exhibitions of work; judge of woodcarving competitions; public speaker. Past president of local play troupe.

MEMBER: Junior Engineering Technical Society (member of board of directors, 1960-66; president, 1963-64), National Society of Professional Engineers (past chairman of New York Chapter), American Society of Mechanical Engineers, National Wood Carvers Association (vice-chairman, 1975-81), Society of American Value Engineers (honorary member), Tau Beta Pi, Pi Tau Sigma, Sigma Delta Chi, Kappa Phi Sigma, Lambda Chi Alpha, Scabbard and Blade.

AWARDS, HONORS: Medal from Freedoms Foundation, 1955, for *Man and His Tools;* Jesse Neal Award of Merit from Associated Business Publications, 1958, for a report on the Soviet Union, 1960, for a report on engineering futures, and 1961, for a report on quality control and redundancy.

WRITINGS:

(Editor) *Power Operator's Guide: One Thousand One Practical Helps,* McGraw, 1935.
Whittling and Woodcarving, McGraw, 1936, reprinted, Dover, 1962.
(Editor) *Power's Question and Answer Book,* Power, 1938.

Design and Figure Carving, McGraw, 1940, reprinted, Dover, 1964.
(Editor) *Power's New Question and Answer Book,* Power, 1944.
Horizons Regained: Seventy Selected Editorial Essays, Product Engineering, 1964.
(Editor with Reynold Bennett) *Living Tomorrow, Today: The Magic of New Science and Technology,* J. G. Ferguson, 1969, reprinted as *Living Tomorrow, Today!: Science of the Seventies,* 1972.
The Modern Book of Whittling and Wood-Carving (Better Homes and Gardens Book Club selection), McGraw, 1973.
One Thousand One Designs for Whittling and Woodcarving (Popular Science Book Club selection), McGraw, 1976.
Build Your Own Inexpensive Dollhouse with One Sheet of 4' x 8' Plywood and Home Tools (booklet), Dover, 1977.
Carving Wooden Animals (also see below), Sterling, 1979.
Carving Religious Motifs in Wood, Sterling, 1980.
Carving Faces and Figures in Wood (also see below), Sterling, 1980.
Carving Flora and Fables in Wood, Sterling, 1981.
Capturing Personality in Wood, Sterling, 1981.
Relief Woodcarving (also see below), Sterling, 1982.
Carving the Unusual, Sterling, 1982.
Basic Whittling and Woodcarving, Sterling, 1983.
Carving Birds in Wood, Sterling, 1984.
Complete Guide to Woodcarving, Sterling, 1985.
Woodcarver's Pattern and Design Book, Sterling, 1986.
The Woodcarver's Library (collection; contains *Carving Wooden Animals, Carving Faces and Figures in Wood,* and *Relief Woodcarving*), Greenwich House, 1986.

PLAYS; JUVENILES

''Jack and the Beanstalk,'' first produced in Port Washington, N.Y., 1957.
''Pinocchio,'' first produced in Port Washington, 1961.
''The Pied Piper of Hamelin,'' first produced in Port Washington, 1966.

OTHER

Also author of *Man and His Tools.* Author of ''Tangents,'' a column in *Chip Chats.* Contributor to technical journals. Technical editor of *Wing* and *McGraw-Hill Digest,* 1942-45.

WORK IN PROGRESS: A book to supplement two earlier books written for Sterling; articles for periodicals in the United States and England.

418

SIDELIGHTS: Elmer John Tangerman commented: "I began writing for publication as a member of the staff of the *Purdue Exponent,* the daily newspaper of Purdue University (where there is no journalism school) and became chief editor in my senior year. This led me to McGraw-Hill and engineering journalism and away from a strictly engineering career. Early in the Depression, I began to write articles for *Popular Mechanics, Popular Science,* and *Scouting.* About 1935, I suggested changes in the requirements for the Boy Scout merit badge in woodcarving and rewrote the instruction manual. At the same time I prepared a booklet for the Remington Arms Company, then a big manufacturer of pocket knives. 'Things to Do with a Pocket Knife' was distributed free to perhaps seven hundred fifty thousand people. This all led to my first book, *Whittling and Woodcarving,* followed by *Design and Figure Carving.* Both went out of print in 1958, but were reprinted as paperbacks in the early sixties.

"The great bulge in craft interest in the United States began in the early sixties, and shortly thereafter I began writing again on whittling and woodcarving, but this time for *Chip Chats,* the magazine of the National Wood Carvers Association, and for the bulletin of the International Wood Collectors Society.

"All of my recent books include not only my own work, but also typical examples of folk carving from all over the world, material collected from my own travels over the past forty years. As an engineering editor I traveled widely, then supplemented my business trips with personal travel as well.

"Since I retired in 1969 I have devoted my time to woodcarving and whittling, doing a great many commissioned pieces. I have had a number of shows and exhibits, have won some awards, lectured to woodcarving groups all over the country, judged shows (including the two big ones in Davenport, Iowa, and Toronto, Ontario), and taught locally as well as in Nebraska, Ohio, Georgia, and North Carolina."

*   *   *

TEC, Nechama 1931-

PERSONAL: Born May 15, 1931, in Lublin, Poland; came to United States in 1952, naturalized in 1960; daughter of Roman (a businessman) and Esther (Hachamoff) Bawnik; married Leon Tec (a child psychiatrist), February 14, 1950; children: Leora, Roland. *Education:* Columbia University, B.S. (cum laude), 1954, M.A., 1955, Ph.D., 1963.

ADDRESSES: Home—11 Rockyfield Rd., Westport, Conn. 06880. *Office*—Department of Sociology, University of Connecticut, Scofieldtown Rd., Stamford, Conn. 06903.

CAREER: New York State Department of Mental Hygiene, New York, N.Y., research sociologist in biometrics, 1956-57; Columbia University, New York, N.Y., lecturer in School of General Studies, 1957-60; Rutgers University, Douglass College, New Brunswick, N.J., instructor in sociology, 1959-60; Columbia University, lecturer in sociology, 1968-71; Trinity College, Hartford, Conn., visiting professor of sociology, 1971-72; University of Connecticut, Stamford, associate professor, 1974-87, professor of sociology, 1987—. Research director, Mid-Fairfield Child Guidance Center, Norwalk, Conn., 1968—.

MEMBER: American Sociological Association, Authors Guild, Authors League of America, Phi Beta Kappa.

WRITINGS:

Gambling in Sweden, Bedminster, 1964.

Grass is Green in Suburbia: A Sociological Study of Adolescent Usage of Illicit Drugs, Libra Publishers, 1974.
Dry Tears: The Story of a Lost Childhood, Wildcat Publishing, 1982, edition with new epilogue, Oxford University Press, 1984.
When Light Pierced the Darkness: Christian Rescue of Jews in Nazi-Occupied Poland, Oxford University Press, 1986.

Contributor to numerous journals and periodicals, including *Adolescence, Contemporary Sociology, Journal of Marriage and Family, Journal of Social Problems, Journal of Social Science and Medicine,* and *Social Forces.*

WORK IN PROGRESS: Anatomy of a Rescuer (tentative title) for Oxford University Press.

SIDELIGHTS: Based on interviews with both rescuers and survivors, Nechama Tec's *When Light Pierced the Darkness: Christian Rescue of Jews in Nazi-Occupied Poland* "celebrates one segment of Polish society—men and women from many backgrounds and social circumstances who risked their lives to help Jews escape," writes Michael R. Marrus in the *Washington Post Book World.* Yet, as Gene Lyons notes in *Newsweek,* "to read *When Light Pierced the Darkness* is to encounter the Holocaust anew from a unique and bewildering angle." Jan Tomasz Gross in the *New York Times Book Review* elaborates, stating, "what is unusual about [the] book is that it both emphasizes Polish rescue efforts and reveals a ubiquitous hostility towards Jews." A reviewer in *Publishers Weekly* writes that "balancing a scientist's dispassion and her own clearly passionate attitudes toward both the Holocaust and Poland, Tec presents systematic sociological evidence about the characteristics of people apt to risk their lives to save others, characteristics rare if universal but especially pertinent in the climate of Poland." While Timothy Garton Ash in the *New York Review of Books* comments that "Tec concludes . . . the only sociological generalization that can safely be made about people who helped Jews is that *peasants* were the class least likely to do so," Gross observes that "most of the rescuers . . . had a strong sense of independence and individuality . . . ready to defy their own society."

In her 1982 book *Dry Tears: The Story of a Lost Childhood,* Tec tells how she survived the Holocaust in Poland disguised as a Catholic schoolgirl. "It was the book, plus Tec's promise of anonymity," writes Lyon, "that persuaded both survivors and protectors to grant her the extensive interviews that form the basis for [*When Light Pierced the Darkness*]."

BIOGRAPHICAL/CRITICAL SOURCES:

PERIODICALS

Kirkus Reviews, November 15, 1985.
Newsweek, January 27, 1986.
New York Review of Books, December 19, 1985.
New York Times Book Review, January 12, 1986.
Publishers Weekly, November 15, 1985.
Washington Post Book World, March 30, 1986.

*   *   *

TELLER, Neville 1931-
(Edmund Owen)

PERSONAL: Born June 10, 1931, in London, England; son of Hyman (a company director) and Sarah (Ephron) Teller; married Sheila Brown, October 20, 1958; children: Richard Henry Marshall, Adam James Grenville, Matthew David

Alexander. *Education:* St. Edmund Hall, Oxford, B.A. (with honors), 1955, M.A., 1963.

ADDRESSES: Home—15 Ewhurst Close Cheam, Surrey, England. *Office*—Department of Health and Social Security, Alexander Fleming House, Elephant & Castle, London S.E.1, England. *Agent*—Lorna Vestey, 33 Dryburgh Rd., London S.W. 15, England.

CAREER: Butterworth & Co. Ltd. (publisher), Sevenoaks, England, marketing manager, 1966-68; Granada Publishing Ltd., St. Albans, England, marketing director, 1968-69; *Times,* London, England, marketing coordinator, 1969-70; Department of Health and Social Security, London, civil servant, 1970—. Free-lance radio writer.

MEMBER: Society of Authors.

WRITINGS:

Bluff Your Way in Marketing, Wolfe, 1966, 2nd revised edition, 1969.

EDITOR

Whodunit: Ten Tales of Crime and Detection, Edward Arnold, 1970.
(With Jane Cicely Saunders and D. H. Summers) *Hospice: The Living Idea,* Edward Arnold, 1981.
British Construction Profile, McMillan Martin, 1985.

EDITOR; "BRITISH ARCHITECTURAL DESIGN AWARD" SERIES

British Architectural Design Awards, 1983, Templegate, 1984.
. . . , *1984,* McMillan Martin, 1985.
. . . , *1985-86,* McMillan Martin, 1986.

OTHER

Also adaptor, sometimes under pseudonym Edmund Owen, of works for radio dramatization, including *Party Going* by Henry Green, *The Serpent's Smile,* by Olga Hesky, *The Sword in the Stone* by T. H. White, *The Daughter of Time,* by Josephine Tey, and *Shadows of Doubt* by Palma Harcourt.

WORK IN PROGRESS: A radio dramatization of *Regency Buck* by Georgette Heyer.

SIDELIGHTS: Neville Teller wrote: "I have been a radio writer since 1956, mainly though not exclusively for the British Broadcasting Corp. I specialize in abridgement, adaptation, dramatization, and serialization for reading on the air. The number of programs I have scripted runs into the thousands. I have researched and scripted such literary and historical features as 'The Horror at Bly,' an investigation of Henry James's *The Turn of the Screw;* 'The Queen and the Kaiser,' a study of the relationship between Queen Victoria and her grandson; a fifteen-part abridgement of *The Franchise Affair* by Josephine Tey; and 'Dizzy and the Faery Queen,' a feature on Queen Victoria and Disraeli.

"I have been fascinated by radio since boyhood—television and film have never held the same appeal. At university, as a committee member of the Oxford University Dramatic Society and secretary of the Experimental Theatre Club, I specialized in radio productions, and later moved very quickly into writing free-lance for radio, while pursuing a career in marketing and general management.

"In 1970 I moved out of the business world into the civil service, but continued and gradually extended the scope of my radio work. The range of artistic and technical possibilities

inherent in the sound medium for interesting, moving and communicating with people, as individuals and en masse at one and the same time, is a never-ending source of wonder and delight. The radio writer's intense satisfaction stems from blending the words, sounds, music, and technical devices on his palette to produce in the mind's eye of his listening audience and on their emotions a precisely calculated effect.

"I pity those benighted parts of the civilized world where radio has degenerated into a form of aural wallpaper, and where artisty and craftsmanship by writer, producers, and actors for radio has atrophied. *Floreat* the BBC!"

*   *   *

TENNISON, Patrick Joseph   1928-

PERSONAL: Born July 16, 1928, in Brisbane, Australia; son of James and Clarice (Ransom) Tennison; married Olga Massey, March 17, 1955; children: Max, Katrina.

ADDRESSES: Home and office—375 High St., Ashburton, Melbourne, Victoria, Australia.

CAREER: Modern Times, Brisbane, Australia, reporter, 1948-50; *Geelong Advertiser,* Geelong, Australia, reporter, 1950-51; *Melbourne Sun,* Melbourne, Australia, reporter, 1951-63; Radio Australia, Melbourne, commentator, 1961-78; commentator for 3AW (radio), 1977-83; Channel 10 (television), commentator, 1982—; 3DB (radio), commentator, 1985—. Commentator for Voice of America, 1973-78. Television writer.

MEMBER: Australian Society of Authors, Fellowship of Writers, Sydney Journalists Club, Melbourne Press Club (president, 1971-73).

WRITINGS:

NONFICTION

Meet the Gallery, Sun Books, 1968.
The Marriage Wilderness, Angus & Robertson, 1972.
Defence Counsel, Hill of Content, 1973.
Lucky Country Reborn, Hill of Content, 1976.
(Editor) *Heyday or Doomsday?,* Hill of Content, 1977.
Family Court: The Legal Jungle, Tennison Enterprises, 1983.
Mastering the Interview, Information Australia, 1986.

SIDELIGHTS: Patrick Tennison commented: "From a father who was a great raconteur, reciter of poetry, and enthusiast for knowing what was happening in the world, I inherited an appreciation and affection for words and ideas, and for the way they are transmitted. I remain fascinated by the magic of the communication process—how an idea is passed from one mind to another. We live in a bountiful world of people and events. I see the journalist, for newspapers, radio, and television, as the chronicler and interpreter of current history. It is ideal life participation to be involved in that process.

"I write mainly about legal, sociological, political, and psychological topics—since these are what most affect our lives. Although most people are aware of this, they often find them difficult to understand. It is therefore the journalist's job to 'inform and interpret' what they mean, how they operate, how they may best be used."

*   *   *

THOMPSON, Francis George   1931-

PERSONAL: Born March 29, 1931, in Stornoway, Scotland;

son of Frank (an engineer) and Georgina (Jappy) Thompson; married Margaret Elaine Pullar (a secretary), April 23, 1960; children: Rona, Ewan, Fay, Eilidh. *Education:* Attended Nicolson Institute, Stornoway, Scotland, 1936-46. *Religion:* Church of Scotland.

ADDRESSES: Home—5 Rathadna Muilne, Stornoway, Isle of Lewis PA87 2TZ, Scotland. *Agent*—Maclean-Dubois Ltd., 3 Rutland Sq., Edinburgh, Scotland.

CAREER: North of Scotland Hydro-Electric Board, Stornoway, Scotland, supply electrician, 1947-57; Associated Electrical Industries, Manchester, England, technical author, 1957-59; Bruce Peebles Ltd., Edinburgh, Scotland, assistant publicity manager, 1959-63; Inverness Technical College, Inverness, Scotland, lecturer in electrical engineering, 1963-77; Lews Castle College, Stornoway, lecturer, 1977—. Managing editor of Club Leabhar Ltd. *Military service:* British Army, Royal Electrical and Mechanical Engineers, 1949-51.

MEMBER: Institution of Electrical and Electronic Engineers (fellow), Association of Supervisory and Executive Engineers, Society of Antiquaries of Scotland (fellow).

AWARDS, HONORS: Grants from Scottish Arts Council, 1979, 1981.

WRITINGS:

Harris Tweed: The Story of a Hebridean Industry, David & Charles, 1968.
Problems in Electrical Installation: Craft, Theory, and Practice, Longmans, Green, 1968.
Electrical Installation and Workshop Technology, Longmans, Green, Volume I, 1968, revised edition, 1978, Volume II, 1969, revised edition, 1975, Volume III, 1972.
Harris and Lewis: Outer Hebrides, David & Charles, 1968, revised edition, 1973.
Our Community at Work, Longmans, Green, 1969.
St. Kilda and Other Hebridean Outliers, Praeger, 1970.
Highland Smugglers, Graphis Publications, 1972.
Highland Waterway: The Caledonian Canal, Graphis Publications, 1972.
The Ghosts, Spirits, and Spectres of Scotland, Bell, 1973.
(Editor) *Highland Ways, and Byways*, Club Leabhar, 1973.
The Highlands and Islands, R. Hale, 1974.
The Uists and Barra, David & Charles, 1974.
Void—Air Aite Falamh: A Poem Sequence from "The Memory-Books of Donald MacLeod" on the Highland Clearances, Graphis Publications, 1975.
Victorian and Edwardian Highlands from Old Photographs, Batsford, 1976.
Supernatural Highlands, R. Hale, 1976.
Scottish Bestiary: The Lore and Literature of Scottish Beasts, Molendinar Press, 1978.
Murder and Mystery in the Highlands, Transatlantic, 1978.
The Highlands and Islands Advisory Panel: A Review of Its Activities and Influence, 1946-1964, An Comunn Gaidhealach, 1979.
Portrait of the Spey, R. Hale, 1979.
The National Mod, Acair Ltd., 1979.
Crofting Years, Luath Press Ltd., 1984.
Shell Guide to Northern Scotland and the Islands, Michael Joseph, 1987.
The Scottish Yules, Scotpress U.S.A., 1987.

Member of editorial board and contributor to *Books in Scotland.* Co-editor of *Sruth Newspaper,* 1966-70.

WORK IN PROGRESS: A research project on Edward Dwelly, maker of the illustrated *Gaelic Dictionary;* research on the collectors of Gaelic oral traditions in the last century; a book in progress on the Highland soldier as mercenary.

SIDELIGHTS: Francis George Thompson told *CA:* "My main area has been socio-economic and cultural aspects of the highlands and islands of Scotland. I have long been involved in Scottish national politics (formerly as a member of the Scottish National party) and the struggle to gain legal status for the Gaelic language in Scotland. I am also involved in aspects of living in the Outer Hebrides and the impact of state impositions on island communities. Writing concentrates the mind wonderfully, in particular the great discipline of poetry."

*   *   *

THOMPSON, Hunter S(tockton)   1939-

PERSONAL: Born July 18, 1939, in Louisville, Ky.; son of Jack R. (an insurance agent) and Virginia (Ray) Thompson; married Sandra Dawn, May 19, 1963; children: Juan. *Education:* Attended public schools in Louisville, Ky. *Politics:* Anarchist. *Religion:* None.

ADDRESSES: Home—Owl Farm, Woody Creek, Colo. 81656.

CAREER: New York Herald Tribune, New York, N.Y., Caribbean correspondent, 1959-60; *National Observer*, New York, N.Y., South American correspondent, 1961-63; writer, 1963—. National affairs editor, *Rolling Stone* (magazine), 1969-74. *Military service:* U.S. Air Force, 1956-58.

MEMBER: Overseas Press Club, American Civil Liberties Union, National Rifle Association.

WRITINGS:

Hell's Angels: A Strange and Terrible Saga, Random House, 1966.
Fear and Loathing in Las Vegas: A Savage Journey to the Heart of the American Dream, illustrated by Ralph Steadman, Random House, 1972.
Fear and Loathing on the Campaign Trail '72, illustrated by Steadman, Straight Arrow Books, 1973.
The Great Shark Hunt: Strange Tales from a Strange Time, Summit Books, 1979.
The Curse of Lono, illustrated by Steadman, Bantam, 1983.

Contributor to *Esquire, New York Times Magazine, Nation, Reporter, Harper's,* and other publications.

WORK IN PROGRESS: The Silk Road, a novel set in the Florida Keys during "The Great Cuban Freedom Flotilla."

SIDELIGHTS: Hunter S. Thompson ranks among the first and foremost practitioners of New Journalism, a genre that evolved in the 1960s to reflect the particular mood of those times. Thompson, who has called his contributions "Gonzo Journalism," was among the most visible—and vituperative—of New Journalism correspondents; as national affairs editor for *Rolling Stone* and author of such widely read books as *Hell's Angels: A Strange and Terrible Saga, Fear and Loathing in Las Vegas: A Savage Journey to the Heart of the American Dream,* and *Fear and Loathing on the Campaign Trail '72,* he caught both the disillusionment and the delirium of a volatile era. According to Morris Dickstein in *Gates of Eden: American Culture in the Sixties,* Thompson "paraded one of the few original prose styles of recent years," a style that indulged in insult and stream-of-invective to an unparalleled degree. He pioneered a new approach to reporting, allowing the story of covering an event to become the central story itself, while never disguising the fact that he was "a half-cranked geek journalist caught in the center of the action," to quote Jerome Klinkowitz in *The Life of Fiction.*

Critics have responded enthusiastically to Thompson's mad, drug-ridden forays into the heart of a corpulent and complacent America. *Saturday Review* contributor Joseph Kanon notes that Thompson has brought a great originality to his work. "There is no one quite like him," Kanon writes, "and we turn to [him] not for 'objective' reporting . . . but to watch an interesting sensibility engaged in high drama. . . . His eccentricity works for him—he seems a rare individual voice in a world of homogenized telecasts. His raving excess is what we read him *for,* and, as with all good writers, his style—a wild mishmash of put-on, fantasy, and cultivated lunacy—seems an extension of personality. He is the kind of writer who talks to you right on the page." Klinkowitz, among others, praises Thompson for employing the technique "of simultaneously leading the parade and heckling oneself from the curb, to capture the spirit of the age in himself." By this means, Klinkowitz contends, Thompson "turns himself into a laboratory for the study of what's going on in contemporary America." *New York Times Book Review* correspndent Leo E. Litwak observes that Thompson's "language is brilliant, his eye is remarkable, and his point of view is reminiscent of Huck Finn's. He'll look at anything; he won't compromise his integrity. Somehow his exuberance and innocence are unaffected by what he sees." In his book *Wampeters Foma & Granfalloons,* Kurt Vonnegut, Jr., concludes that Thompson "is that rare sort of American author who must be read. He makes exciting, moving collages out of carefully selected junk."

Thompson was considered a seasoned journalist while still in his twenties. Between 1959 and 1965 he served as a Caribbean correspondent for the *New York Herald Tribune* and South American correspondent for the *National Observer* and also contributed to magazines such as the *Nation, Harper's, Reporter* and *Scanlan's.* His early works were conventional, but as his own experiments with drugs increased, and the tenor of the nation began to change, he embraced the nascent New Journalism style. *New York Times Book Review* contributor Crawford Woods explains that New Journalism's roots lay in "the particular sense of the nineteen-sixties that a new voice was demanded—by the way people's public and private lives were coming together in a sensual panic stew, with murder its meat and potatoes, grass and acid its spice. How to tell the story of a time when all fiction was science fiction, all facts lies? The New Journalism was born." Dickstein notes that the genre "developed parallel to the chief organs of information, influencing them only subtly and gradually, in tandem with the influence of the age. . . . This work included a broad spectrum of underground writing—political, countercultural, feminist, pornographic, and so on—that dealt with cultural developments ignored, distorted, or merely exploited by the media." Riding and drinking with the Hell's Angels motorcycle gang, taking massive quantities of hallucinogenic drugs, and careening to assignments on little food and less sleep, Thompson became the "professional wildman" of the New Journalists, to quote *Village Voice* contributor Vivian Gornick. He also became a nationally-known figure whose work "in particular caused currents of envy in the world of the straight journalists, who coveted his freedom from restraint," according to an *Atlantic* essayist.

In *Critique: Studies in Modern Fiction,* John Hellmann writes: "By conceiving his journalism as a form of fiction, Thompson has been able to shape actual events into meaningful works of literary art." Thompson's "Gonzo Journalism" narratives are first-person accounts in which the author appears as a persona, sometimes Raoul Duke, but more commonly Dr. Hunter S. Thompson, a specialist variously in divinity, pharmaceuticals, or reporting. Hellmann describes this self-caricature in his book *Fables of Fact: The New Journalism as New Fiction.* It is "a paradox of compulsive violence and outraged innocence, an emblem of the author's schizophrenic view of America. . . . But the persona also has a determined belief in the power of good intentions and right methods which runs counter to his violent impulses. Despite the psychotic threatening, his artistic aims include the corrective impulse of satire." Hellmann elaborates: "The created persona is essentially defined by the title phrase 'fear and loathing,' for it embodies both the paranoia with which the persona perceives the ominous forces pervading actuality, and the aggression with which he seeks to survive it. This latter trait is particularly crucial, for despite the comic buffoonery and paranoia delusions, Thompson's persona is hardly a passive anti-hero. A descendant of the trickster character of folklore, the Vice of medieval drama, the picaro of early prose narratives, he is a self-portrait of the journalist as rogue. . . . But as a journalist and a human being attempting to report contemporary events, the dangers he meets are psychological and spiritual. Defining himself through opposition, he counters them with violence and laughter."

With talent and a significant measure of recklessness, Thompson has created "fantasies which record the spirit—if not the misleading 'actual' facts—of the life they've experienced," according to Klinkowitz. The critic suggests that Thompson "multiplies himself" in his works through several methods: by "making as much of the conditions under which he's writing as he does of the subject matter itself," by "including references to his own mythology as a writer," by "dividing his own personality into mutually exclusive personae," and by "constantly downgrading his own paranoid fantasies in proportion to the raving madness of the so-called straight world." Gornick sees Thompson's work in a simpler light. "He poses variously as a maverick journalist, a nonstop drug user, an enemy of Main Street America and the Corporate State," she writes, "but being wild is really what his profession is. . . . Savaging everything in sight is his real target." Whatever his aims and methods might be, however, Hellmann notes in *Fables of Fact* that Thompson "has developed a journalism which communicates, both formally and thematically, his black humorist vision. The pervasive theme of Thompson's work is one of 'doomed alienation on your own turf.' In his 'fear and loathing' works he has expressed this malaise through an innovative application of the same parodic devices found in black-humor fictions. The result is journalism which reads as savage cartoon."

Hell's Angels, Thompson's 1966 account of the infamous California motorcycle gang, is the most conventional of his book-length works. The young author rode with the Angels for almost a year, recording their road rallies, their home lives, and their sexual adventures. The book strives to present the gang objectively while exposing the fact that its brutal reputation was primarily the creation of the scandal-mongering media. *New Republic* contributor Richard M. Elman observes that in *Hell's Angels* Thompson has "managed to correct many popular misconceptions about [the Angels], and in the process, provided his readers with a tendentious but informative participant-observer study of those who are doomed to lose.'' In the *Nation,* Elmer Bendiner likewise notes that throughout the book "Thompson's point of view remains eminently sane and honest. He does not weep for the Angels or romanticize them or glorify them. Neither does he despise them. Instead, he views them as creatures of an irresponsible society, given their image by an irresponsible press, embodying the nation's puerile fantasy life. He sees the menace not so much in the Hell's Angels themselves, as in the poverty of spirit and perennial adolescence that spawned them.'' *Hell's Angels* has garnered a mixture of critical reactions. *Atlantic* correspondent Oscar Handlin contends that Thompson's ''lurid narrative, despite its sympathy for his subjects, reveals the threat they pose.'' Conversely, William Hogan in *Saturday Review* calls the work ''a jarring piece of contemporary Californiana, as well as an examination of a weird branch of present-day show business.'' According to Elman, Thompson's ''fascinating invocation to, evocation *of,* and reportage *about* the Hell's Angels . . . is certainly the most informative, thorough, and vividly written account of this phenomenon yet to appear.''

In 1972 Thompson published *Fear and Loathing in Las Vegas,* perhaps his best known work. Hellmann describes the book in *Fables of Fact:* "*Fear and Loathing in Las Vegas* is, in barest outline, the author's purported autobiographical confession of his failure to fulfill the magazine's assignment to 'cover' two events in Las Vegas, the Fourth Annual 'Mint 400' motorcycle desert race and the National Conference of District Attorneys Seminar on Narcotics and Dangerous Drugs. It is more exactly the author's (or 'Raoul Duke's') tale of his hallucinations and adventures while with a 300-pound Samoan attorney called Dr. Gonzo, actually a Chicano lawyer named Oscar Zeta Acosta, . . . who serves as a parody of noble savage 'sidekicks' from Chingachgook to Tonto. The book is, then, even in its most general subject and presentation, either a report of an actual experience which was largely fantasy or an actual fantasy which is disguised as report.'' The author poses as Raoul Duke in the first-person narrative, and he relates a series of episodic adventures revolving around drug use and *carte blanche* access to Las Vegas's finest hotels. *National Observer* contributor Michael Putney calls the book ''a trip, literally and figuratively, all the way to bad craziness and back again. It is also the most brilliant piece of writing about the dope subculture since Tom Wolfe's *Electric Kool-Aid Acid Test* and, at the same time, an acid, wrenchingly funny portrait of straight America's most celebrated and mean-spirited pleasure-dome, Las Vegas.''

Critics have argued about how much of *Fear and Loathing in Las Vegas* is fact or ''journalism,'' and how much of it is fiction, but most have praised the work for its originality and humor. *New York Times* columnist Christopher Lehmann-Haupt finds favor with the book's ''mad, corrosive prose poetry,'' and in *Fables of Fact* Hellmann calls it ''an important report on the American unreality of the late 1960's.'' Woods writes that *Fear and Loathing in Las Vegas* is ''a custom-crafted study of paranoia, a spew from the 1960's and—in all its hysteria, insolence, insult, and rot—a desperate and important book, a wired nightmare. . . . The book's highest art is to be the drug it is about, whether chemical or political. To read it is to swim through the highs and lows of the smokes and fluids that shatter the mind, to survive again the terror of the politics of unreason.''

Thompson continues to explore ''the politics of unreason'' in his 1973 book *Fear and Loathing on the Campaign Trail '72,* a collection of articles that first appeared in *Rolling Stone*

magazine. *Nation* correspondent Steven d'Arazien calls the work ''a New Journalism account of the [1972 presidential] campaign from before New Hampshire to Miami and beyond. . . . It will be regarded as a classic in the genre.'' As national affairs editor for *Rolling Stone,* Thompson travelled with the press corps who followed George McGovern; Dickstein notes that the author ''recorded the nuts and bolts of a presidential campaign with all the contempt and incredulity that other reporters must feel but censor out.'' According to Jules Witcover in *Progressive* magazine, the book's ''heavily personalized writing-on-the-run, riddled here and there by the clear eye of hindsight, does convey an honest picture of a political writer picking his way through all the hoopla, propaganda, tedium, and exhaustion of a campaign.'' Critics' opinions on the book depend on their assessment of Thompson's reporting style. *Columbia Journalism Review* essayist Wayne C. Booth characterizes the work as ''an inflated footnote on how [Thompson] used the campaign to achieve a 'very special kind of High.''' The critic concludes: ''Cleverness, energy and brashness cannot, finally, make up for ignorance and lack of critical training.'' On the other hand, Kanon finds *Fear and Loathing on the Campaign Trail '72* ''the best political reporting in some time—it manages to give politics, after years of televised lobotomy, some flesh.'' In the *New York Times,* Lehmann-Haupt concludes that while Thompson ''doesn't exactly see America as Grandma Moses depicted it, or the way they painted it for us in civics class, he does in his own mad way betray a profound democratic concern for the polity. And in its own mad way, it's damned refreshing.''

Thompson's two subsequent books, *The Great Shark Hunt: Strange Tales from a Strange Time* and *The Curse of Lono,* continue to mine his vein of personal, high-energy reporting. *Los Angeles Times Book Review* correspondent Peter S. Greenburg notes that *The Great Shark Hunt* ''is not so much an attack on America as it is a frightfully perceptive autopsy of our culture. . . . In each story—or rather adventure—he leads us on a scattered but very personal journey of experience. The bottom line is that he's really a Charles Kuralt for crazy people, but Thompson's version of 'On the Road' is filled with so many detours that ultimately there isn't just one fork in the road but a complete service for eight. Nevertheless, there seems to be method in his madness. He is the master of the cosmic metaphor and combines this talent with all the subtlety of a run at someone's jugular with a red-hot rail spike.'' In *The Curse of Lono* Thompson recounts his antics during a visit to Hawaii with his longtime illustrator, Ralph Steadman. Once again the author demonstrates his ''very nearly unrelieved distemper,'' an attribute William F. Buckley describes as ''the Sign of Thompson'' in the *New York Times Book Review.* *Washington Post Book World* reviewer Michael Dirda claims of the work: ''No one writes like Hunter Thompson, though many have tried, and *The Curse of Lono* dispenses pages rabid with his hilarious, frenzied rantings, gusts of '60s madness for the stuffy '80s.''

Needless to say, Thompson's paeans to hallucinogenic drugs and his bouts of colorful invective have not found universal favor. In the *Washington Monthly,* Joseph Nocera calls the author ''a manifestation of an old and ignoble strain in American journalism. We have always had our share of writers more interested in being fashionable, or snide, or above the fray than in understanding or enlightening.'' Nocera concludes his essay with the remark that Thompson ''has given New Journalism a bad name, and the damage he did may take a long time to undo.'' Likewise, *London Magazine* contributor Jonathan Raban finds Thompson "a professionally unreliable witness; you feel you are listening to an impossible skein of truth mixed up with falsehood, and he implores you to quit bothering about which is which." According to a *New Republic* reviewer, Thompson is either unwilling or unable to get beneath what he sees, and therefore is "yet another carrier of journalism's current typhus: he transmits surface description as analysis."

More critics praise Thompson than disparage him, however. Klinkowitz writes: "For all of the charges against him, Hunter S. Thompson is an amazingly insightful writer. His 'journalism' is not in the least irresponsible. On the contrary, in each of his books he's pointed out the lies and gross distortions of conventional journalism.... Moreover, his books are richly intelligent." According to Gornick, Thompson's talent "lies in his ability to describe his own manic plunge into drink, drugs, and madness through a use of controlled exaggeration that is truly marvellous. There are many moments in his stories—all having to do with paranoia finally induced after hours and days of swallowing, snorting, slugging down amounts of pills, powders, and alcohol that would long ago have killed an army of Berbers—that are so wonderfully funny you are left shaking with laughter and the happiness of literary creation." John Leonard expresses a similar opinion in the *New York Times*. Thompson, Leonard writes, "became, in the late 1960's, our point guard, our official crazy, patrolling the edge. He reported back that the paranoids were right, and they were. The cool inwardness, ... the hugging of the self to keep from cracking up, is not for him. He inhabits his nerve endings; they are on the outside, like the skin of a baby; he seeks thumbprints.... He is also, as if this needs to be said, hilarious."

The dust jacket of *Fear and Loathing in Las Vegas* describes Thompson as an author who "continues to work his own strange tangents, seemingly oblivious [to] public outrage, acclaim, or criticism of any sort. He is known, to his handful of friends, as a compulsive hermit with an atavistic fondness for the .44 Magnum and extremely amplified music." Thompson's own self-parody has served to inspire another parodist of modern culture. Garry Trudeau, author of the "Doonesbury" cartoon strip, has modeled his "Uncle Duke" character on Thompson and his manic exploits. A denizen of Woody Creek, Colorado—where he once ran for sheriff on the "Freak Power" ticket—Thompson works, he says, only when he needs money to "crank up" his lifestyle. He told the *New York Times Book Review:* "I never liked to write very much. For me, journalism was just a way to have someone pay you to get out there and see what was happening."

BIOGRAPHICAL/CRITICAL SOURCES:

BOOKS

Contemporary Literary Criticism, Gale, Volume IX, 1978, Volume XVII, 1981, Volume XL, 1986.
Dickstein, Morris, *Gates of Eden: American Culture in the Sixties*, Basic Books, 1977.
Hellmann, John, *Fables of Fact: The New Journalism as New Fiction*, University of Illinois Press, 1981.
Klinkowitz, Jerome, *The Life of Fiction*, University of Illinois Press, 1977.
Thompson, Hunter S., *Fear and Loathing in Las Vegas: A Savage Journey to the Heart of the American Dream*, illustrated by Ralph Steadman, Random House, 1972.
Thompson, Hunter S., *The Great Shark Hunt: Strange Tales from a Strange Time*, Summit Books, 1979.

Vonnegut, Kurt, Jr., *Wampeters Foma & Granfalloons*, Delacorte, 1974.

PERIODICALS

Atlantic, February, 1967, July, 1973.
Columbia Journalism Review, November-December, 1973, September-October, 1979.
Commonweal, April 7, 1967.
Critique: Studies in Modern Fiction, Volume XXI, number 1, 1979.
Detroit News, August 26, 1979, November 27, 1983.
Harper's, July, 1973.
London Magazine, June-July, 1973.
Los Angeles Times Book Review, August 12, 1979.
Nation, April 3, 1967, August 13, 1973, October 13, 1979.
National Observer, August 5, 1972.
New Republic, February 25, 1967, October 14, 1972, October 13, 1973, August 25, 1979.
Newsweek, March 6, 1967.
New Yorker, March 4, 1967.
New York Review of Books, October 4, 1973.
New York Times, February 23, 1967, June 22, 1972, May 18, 1973, August 10, 1979.
New York Times Book Review, January 29, 1967, March 5, 1967, July 23, 1972, July 15, 1973, December 2, 1973, August 5, 1979, October 14, 1979, January 15, 1984.
Progressive, July, 1973.
Saturday Review, February 18, 1967, April 21, 1973.
Times (London), May 12, 1982.
Times Literary Supplement, January 11, 1968, November 3, 1972.
Village Voice, November 19, 1979.
Washington Monthly, April, 1981.
Washington Post Book World, August 19, 1979, December 18, 1983.

—*Sketch by Anne Janette Johnson*

*   *   *

TIERNEY, Tom   1928-

PERSONAL: Born October 8, 1928, in Beaumont, Tex.; son of John Taylor (an accountant) and Mary Lou (Gripon) Tierney. *Education:* University of Texas, B.F.A., 1949; attended Pratt Institute, 1953, Art Students League, 1955, Cartoonists and Illustrators School (now School of Visual Arts, N.Y.), 1955. *Politics:* "Not committed." *Religion:* "Not committed."

ADDRESSES: Home—151 West 74th St., New York, N.Y. 10023. *Office*—Tom Tierney Studio, Inc., Drawer D, Hopewell Jct., N.Y. 12533.

CAREER: Tom Tierney Studio, Inc., New York, N.Y., freelance illustrator. *Military service:* U.S. Army, 1951-52; served as a recruiting illustrator; became sergeant.

MEMBER: "None (I am a rabid non-joiner!)"

AWARDS, HONORS: Purchase Award, Texas General Exhibition, 1952, for watercolor; First Prize, Beaumont Art Museum, 1953, for oil painting.

WRITINGS:

SELF-ILLUSTRATED

Thirty from the Thirties (paper dolls), Prentice-Hall, 1974.

Glamorous Movie Stars of the Thirties (paper dolls), Dover, 1978.
Attitude: An Adult Paper Doll Book, St. Martin's, 1979.
Rudolph Valentino Paper Dolls, Dover, 1979.
Marilyn Monroe Paper Dolls, Dover, 1979.
John Wayne Paper Dolls, Dover, 1981.
Vivien Leigh Paper Dolls in Full Color, Dover, 1981.
Pavlova and Nijinsky Paper Dolls in Full Color, Dover, 1981.
Cut and Assemble a Toy Theater/The Nutcracker Ballet: A Complete Production in Full Color, Dover, 1981.
Judy Garland Paper Dolls in Full Color, Dover, 1982.
Carmen Miranda Paper Dolls, Dover, 1982.
Great Empresses and Queens Paper Dolls, Dover, 1982.
American Family of the Colonial Era: Paper Dolls in Full Color, Dover, 1983.
Cat Snips (paper dolls), Tribeca, 1983.
Joan Crawford Paper Dolls in Full Color, Dover, 1983.
Santa Claus Paper Dolls in Full Color, Dover, 1983.
Great Fashion Designs of the Belle Epoque: Paper Dolls in Full Color, Dover, 1983.
Fashion Designers of the Twenties Paper Dolls, Dover, 1983.
Famous Modern Dancers (paper dolls), Dover, 1983.
Nancy Reagan Fashion Paper Dolls in Full Color, Dover, 1984.
Pope John Paul II Paper Dolls, Dover, 1984.
Ronald Reagan Paper Dolls in Full Color, Dover, 1984.
Great Black Entertainers Paper Dolls, Dover, 1984.
(More) Erte Fashions (paper dolls), Dover, 1984.
Cut and Assemble a Toy Theater: Peter Pan, Dover, 1984.
Fashion Designers of the Thirties (paper dolls), Dover, 1984.
Cupie (paper dolls), Dover, 1984.
Opera Stars of the Golden Age (paper dolls), Dover, 1984.
Greta Garbo (paper dolls), Dover, 1985.
Princess Diana and Prince Charles (paper dolls), Dover, 1985.
Legendary Baseball Stars (paper dolls), Dover, 1985.
Gibson Girl Fashions (paper dolls), Dover, 1985.
Paul Poiret's Fashions (paper dolls), Dover, 1985.
Fashion Designers of the Fifties (paper dolls), Dover, 1985.
American Family of the Civil War Era (paper dolls), Dover, 1985.
Ziegfield Follies Paper Dolls, Dover, 1985.
Clarke Gable (paper dolls), Dover, 1986.
Grace Kelly (paper dolls), Dover, 1986.
Supergirl (paper dolls), Putnam, 1986.
Chanel's Fashion Review (paper dolls), Dover, 1986.
American Family of the Victorian Era (paper dolls), Dover, 1986.
Little Cupie Paper Dolls, Dover, 1986.
Three Little Kittens (paper dolls), Dover, 1986.
Diaghilev's Ballets Russe (paper dolls), Dover, 1986.
American Family of the Puritan Era (paper dolls), Dover, 1987.
Teddy Bear Paper Dolls, Dover, 1987.

ILLUSTRATOR

Clip Art: Children's Illustrations, Dover, 1982.
Clip Art: Women's Head Illustrations, Dover, 1982.
Clip Art: Men's Head Illustrations, Dover, 1982.
Clip Art: Hand Illustrations, Dover, 1983.
Day-to-Night Barbie Paper Doll Book, Western, 1985.
Clip Art: Wedding Illustrations, Dover, 1986.
A Sleep Over Visit, Golden, 1986.
Kovacs, Deborah, *Battle of the Bands*, Golden, 1986.
Hallock, Rusty, *Night of a Thousand Earrings*, Golden, 1986.
Weinberg, Larry, *Spoils of Success*, Golden, 1986.

Abbott, Jennie, *Dance Club Magic*, Golden, 1986.
Turner, T. P., *Secret Star*, Golden, 1986.
Hughes, Sara, *Surprise at Starlight Mansion*, Golden, 1986.
Packard, Mary, *Video Mischief*, Golden, 1986.
Barbie and the Rockers: The Fan, Golden, 1986.
Barbie and the Rockers: The Hottest Group in Town, Golden, 1986.
Barbie and the Rockers Stamp Book, Paninni, 1986.

OTHER

Contributor of illustrations to *Harper's Bazaar, Sports Illustrated,* and *Show Magazine,* among others.

WORK IN PROGRESS: More paper doll books for Dover.

SIDELIGHTS: Tom Tierney told *CA:* "My training has been as a visual artist, painting, sculpture, etc., so most of my interests have been in these areas. I have always been a film enthusiast—this, coupled with my fashion art career, led to *Thirty from the Thirties.*" Tierney created the book of paper dolls as a gift for his mother, who still owned paper dolls collected during her childhood. His mother enthusiastically showed the dolls to several friends, including a literary agent. Soon after, *Thirty from the Thirties* was published, and in 1978 Dover persuaded the successful fashion illustrator to make more books of paper dolls. Tierney, whose clients in the retail fashion industry include Lane Bryant and Macy's, explained, "These paper doll books are unique in that they are designed for the serious collector of nostalgia buff. They include biographical data and notes, while the costumes are researched and rendered for maximum accuracy. The series seems assured of success."

AVOCATIONAL INTERESTS: Ballet, singing.

*   *   *

TOCH, Hans (Herbert)   1930-

PERSONAL: Born April 17, 1930, in Vienna, Austria; U.S. citizen. *Education:* Attended high school in Havana, Cuba; Brooklyn College (now Brooklyn College of the City University of New York), B.A. (summa cum laude), 1952; Princeton University, Ph.D., 1955.

ADDRESSES: Office—School of Criminal Justice, State University of New York, Albany, N.Y. 12222.

CAREER: Michigan State University, East Lansing, instructor, 1957-58, assistant professor, 1958-61, associate professor, 1961-66, professor of psychology, 1966-67; State University of New York at Albany, School of Criminal Justice, professor of psychology, 1968-86, distinguished professor, 1986—. Visiting lecturer, department of social relations, Harvard University, 1965-66. Consultant to National Commission on the Causes and Prevention of Violence, 1968-69; member of Governor's Advisory Panel on Violent Juvenile Delinquents, 1975. *Military service:* U.S. Naval Reserve, active duty as enlisted man (morale researcher), 1955-57; reserve officer, 1957-66.

MEMBER: American Psychological Association (fellow), Phi Beta Kappa, Sigma Xi.

AWARDS, HONORS: Fulbright senior research fellowship to Oslo, Norway, 1963-64; Hadley Cantril Memorial Award, 1976, for *Men in Crisis: Human Breakdowns in Prison.*

WRITINGS:

(Editor and contributor) *Legal and Criminal Psychology*, Holt, 1961.

The Social Psychology of Social Movements, Bobbs-Merrill, 1965.

(Editor with H. C. Smith and contributor with others) *Social Perception: The Development of Interpersonal Impressions*, Van Nostrand, 1968.

Violent Men: An Inquiry into the Psychology of Violence, Aldine, 1969, revised edition, Schenkman, 1980.

(With J. D. Grant and R. Galvin) *Agents of Change: A Study in Police Reform*, Schenkman, 1975.

Men in Crisis: Human Breakdowns in Prison, Aldine, 1975.

Peacekeeping: Police, Prisons and Violence, Lexington Books, 1976, published as *Police, Prisons, and the Problem of Violence*, U.S. Government Printing Office, 1977.

Living in Prison: The Ecology of Survival, Free Press, 1977.

(Editor and contributor) *The Psychology of Crime and Criminal Justice*, Holt, 1979.

(Editor and contributor) *Therapeutic Communities in Corrections*, Praeger, 1980.

(With Grant) *Reforming Human Services*, Sage Publications, 1982.

(Editor with R. Johnson and contributor) *Pains of Imprisonment*, Sage Publications, 1982.

AUTHOR OF FOREWORD

R. Johnson, *Culture and Crisis in Confinement*, Lexington Books, 1976.

B. McCarthy, *Easy Time: The Experiences of Female Inmates on Temporary Release*, Lexington Books, 1979.

D. E. Georges and K. Harries, *Crime: A Spatial Perspective*, Columbia University Press, 1980.

D. Lockwood, *Prison Sexual Aggression*, Elsevier-North Holland, 1980.

L. X. Lombardo, *Guards Imprisoned: Correctional Officers at Work*, Elsevier-North Holland, 1981.

CONTRIBUTOR

(With M. Rokeach and T. Rottman) Rokeach, *The Open and Closed Mind*, Basic Books, 1960.

(With A. Hastor and W. Ittelson) F. P. Kilpatrick, editor, *Explorations in Transactional Psychology*, New York University Press, 1961.

E. Hartley and R. Hartley, editors, *Readings in Psychology*, Crowell, 1965.

S. I. Hayakawa, editor, *Our Language and Our World*, Harper, 1969.

(With M. MacLean) K. K. Serano and C. D. Mortensen, *Readings in Communication Theory*, Harper, 1969.

M. Levitt and B. Rubenstein, *Rebels and the Campus Revolt*, Prentice-Hall, 1969.

(With S. Milgran) G. Lindzey and E. Aronson, *Handbook of Social Psychology*, Volume IV, Addison-Wesley, 1969.

(With R. M. Schulte) W. Nord, editor, *Concepts and Controversy in Organizational Behavior*, Goodyear Publishing, 1970.

E. I. Magaree and J. E. Hokanson, editors, *The Dynamics of Aggression*, Harper, 1970.

(With MacLean) H. W. Hepler and I. Campbell, *Dimensions in Communication*, 2nd edition (Toch was not associated with earlier edition), Wadsworth, 1970.

N. K. Denzin, *The Values of Social Science*, Aldine, 1970.

Sociological Realities: A Guide to the Study of Society, Harper, 1971.

B. Danto, editor, *Jailhouse Blues: Suicide in Jail and Prison*, Epic Publications, 1972.

G. Leinward, editor, *The Police*, Pocket Books, 1972.

Y. R. Snibbe and H. M. Snibbe, *The Urban Policeman in Transition*, C. C Thomas, 1973.

D. Chappell and J. Monahan, editors, *Violence and Criminal Justice*, Heath, 1975.

M. O'Neill and K. R. Martensen, *Criminal Justice Group Training*, University Associates, 1975.

(With MacLean) R. L. Applebaum and others, *Speech Communication: A Basic Anthology*, Macmillan, 1975.

A. Cohen and others, editors, *Prison Violence*, Heath, 1976.

B. D. Sales, editor, *Perspectives in Law and Psychology: The Criminal Justice System*, Plenum, 1977.

(With MacLean) T. M. Steinfatt, *Readings in Interpersonal Communication*, Bobbs-Merrill, 1977.

S. I. Safa and G. Levitas, *Social Problems in Contemporary America*, Transaction Books, 1979.

(With D. Svendsen and R. Rommetveit) Rommetveit and R. M. Blakar, *Studies of Language Thought and Verbal Communication*, Academic Press, 1979.

N. Farberrow, editor, *The Many Faces of Suicide: Indirect Self-destructive Behavior*, McGraw, 1980.

(With MacLean) Ben W. Morse and Lynn A. Phelps, *Interpersonal Communication: A Relational Perspective*, Burgess, 1980.

J. R. Hays, K. S. Solway, and T. K. Roberts, editors, *Violence and the Violent Individual*, Spectrum, 1981.

D. A. Ward and K. F. Schoen, *Confinement in Maximum Custody*, Heath, 1981.

R. Ross, editor, *Correctional Officer*, Butterworth (Ontario), 1981.

(With Joan Grant and J. D. Grant) V. J. Konecni and E. B. Ebbesch, editors, *Social-Psychological Analysis of the Legal Process*, W. H. Freeman, 1982.

G. M. Stephenson and J. H. Davis, editors, *Progress in Applied Social Psychology*, Volume II, Wiley, 1984.

A. Campbell and J. Gibbs, editors, *Violent Transactions*, Basil Blackwell, 1986.

A. Blumberg and A. Niederhoffer, editors, *The Ambivalent Force: Perspectives on the Police*, Blaisdell, in press.

E. Eldefonso, *Introduction to Police Science*, Glencoe, in press.

A. Rosenblatt and W. Ilchman, editors, *Coping and Caring*, Rockefeller Institute, in press.

M. Gottfredson and T. Hirschi, editors, *Positive Criminology: Essays in Honor of Michael J. Hindelang*, Sage Publications, in press.

P. Anderson and L. T. Winfree, editors, *The Expert Witness*, State University of New York Press, in press.

OTHER

Also author of research reports for U.S. Naval Personnel Research Field Activity, San Diego, Calif.; editor of conference proceedings for School of Criminal Justice, New York University. Contributor to *Correctional Institutions*, 3rd edition, *Criminology Review Yearbook*, Volume II, Sage Publications, 1980, and proceedings of several professional conferences. Also author of column, "Ripples on Lake Success," *United Nations World*, 1949-50; book reviewer for government agencies. Contributor of book reviews and articles on communication, public opinion, criminology, psychology of religion, and experimental psychology to journals, including *American Journal of Psychology, American Behavioral Scientist, Criminology, Police, Humanist, Corrections Magazine*, and *Journal of Criminal Justice*. Editor of *Journal of Research in Crime and Delinquency*, 1974; member of editorial boards of several journals.

WORK IN PROGRESS: Coping: Maladaptation in Confinement.

SIDELIGHTS: Hans Toch told *CA:* "[I feel that] academic writing has become needlessly stilted and full of private language and obscuratisms. . . . [I] also feel that social science must deal with real life situations without loss of respect for scientific rigor."

* * *

TOLAND, John (Willard) 1912-

PERSONAL: Born June 29, 1912, in La Crosse, Wis.; son of Ralph (a concert singer) and Helen (Snow) Toland; married present wife, Toshiko Matsumura, March 12, 1960; children: (previous marriage) Diana, Marcia; (present marriage) Tamiko (daughter). *Education:* Williams College, B.A., 1936; attended Yale University, 1937.

ADDRESSES: Home—1 Long Ridge Rd., Danbury, Conn. 06810. *Agent*—Carl D. Brandt, Brandt & Brandt Literary Agents Inc., 1501 Broadway, New York, N.Y. 10036.

CAREER: Writer. Advisor to the National Archives. *Military service:* U.S. Air Force, six years; became captain.

MEMBER: Overseas Press Club, Writers Guild, PEN.

AWARDS, HONORS: Overseas Press Club award, 1961, for *But Not in Shame,* 1967, for *The Last 100 Days,* 1970, for *The Rising Sun: The Decline and Fall of the Japanese Empire, 1936-1945,* and 1976, for *Adolf Hitler;* L.H.D., Williams College, 1968; Van Wyck Brooks Award for nonfiction, 1970, and Pulitzer Prize for nonfiction, 1970, both for *The Rising Sun;* L.H.D., University of Alaska, 1977; National Society of Arts and Letters gold medal, 1977, for *Adolf Hitler;* Accademia del Mediterrano, 1978; L.H.D., University of Connecticut, 1986.

WRITINGS:

Ships in the Sky, Holt, 1957.
Battle: The Story of the Bulge, Random House, 1959.
But Not in Shame, Random House, 1961.
The Dillinger Days, Random House, 1963.
The Flying Tigers (juvenile), Random House, 1963.
The Last 100 Days, Random House, 1966.
The Battle of the Bulge (juvenile), Random House, 1966.
The Rising Sun: The Decline and Fall of the Japanese Empire, 1936-1945, Random House, 1970.
Adolf Hitler, Doubleday, 1976.
Hitler: The Pictorial Documentary of His Life, Doubleday, 1978.
No Man's Land: 1918, The Last Year of the Great War, Doubleday, 1980.
Infamy: Pearl Harbor and Its Aftermath, Doubleday, 1982.
Gods of War (novel), Doubleday, 1985.
Occupation (novel), Doubleday, 1987.

Contributor of articles to *Look, Life, Reader's Digest, Saturday Evening Post,* and other magazines.

SIDELIGHTS: John Toland's "approach to history," Diana Loercher writes in the *Christian Science Monitor,* "is that of an investigative reporter." For each of his books Toland interviews the participants in a historic event, sometimes several hundred of them, in order to get all sides of a story from those people who know it best. He then presents these interviews as objectively as is possible. "I believe it's my duty," Toland

explains, "to tell you everything and let you draw your own conclusions. I keep my opinions to a minimum."

Among Toland's more popular books are the Pulitzer Prize-winning *The Rising Sun: The Decline and Fall of the Japanese Empire, 1936-1945;* his *Adolf Hitler,* a biography; *No Man's Land: 1918, The Last Year of the Great War; Infamy: Pearl Harbor and Its Aftermath;* and the novel *Gods of War.* Many of these titles have been best-sellers and have helped to establish Toland as "a superb popular historian of World War II," as Jack Lessenberry states in the *Detroit News.*

Toland's most successful book is *The Rising Sun,* which traces the collapse of the Japanese Empire after its fatal decision to wage war during the 1930s. It is a "big, absorbing and finally very moving history of the Pacific war, told primarily from the Japanese viewpoint," as Walter Clemons explains in the *New York Times.* William Craig of the *Washington Post Book World* believes that "nowhere in American literature has the Japanese side of the war in the jungles been so well told."

To uncover the Japanese version of the Second World War, Toland interviewed hundreds of participants, "ranging from former generals and admirals to former first-class privates of the Imperial Army and housewives who somehow lived through Hiroshima," the *Times Literary Supplement* critic states. He interweaves this material with relevant written documents to produce a narrative history of Imperial Japan. "Although in the main a narrative account," the *Times Literary Supplement* critic writes, "[*The Rising Sun*] is not devoid of passages of shrewd analytical insight." Craig believes that "*The Rising Sun* makes a significant contribution to our knowledge of the recent past. . . . Toland has fashioned a compelling portrait of Japan at the brink of national suicide."

The extensive research for *The Rising Sun* resulted in the clearing up of historical inaccuracies and the unearthing of new information. Toland found, for example, that a simple misunderstanding during Japanese-American negotiations prior to World War II was one of the reasons Japan went to war. During these negotiations, the United States had demanded that the Japanese remove their troops from China. Although agreeable to a withdrawal from China, the Japanese assumed that this demand included Manchuria, an area of China they wished to keep, and so refused to withdraw. In fact, the United States had not meant to include Manchuria in its demand. If this point had been clarified, Japanese-American relations may have been normalized and the subsequent war averted. "In showing how just about all of the Japanese leaders in 1941 sincerely hoped to avoid war," notes F. X. J. Homer in *Best Sellers,* "Toland makes it possible for us to recognize that Pearl Harbor was the result of failings on the part of American diplomacy as well as of Japanese aggression. . . . Toland adds a new dimension to orthodox military history in going beyond grand strategy to portray the human side of the conflict."

In *Adolf Hitler,* a study of the National Socialist leader of World War II Germany, Toland's research again uncovered new facts and dispelled some widely believed misinformation. As with Toland's previous books, *Adolf Hitler* relies on extensive interviews. Toland spoke to almost two hundred people who knew or worked with Hitler. Piecing together their accounts, he constructs a multi-faceted portrait of one of the pivotal figures of the war. Because this portrait presents observations from "generals and diplomats [and] some of Hitler's closest friends and attendants," as W. Warren Wagar notes in the *Saturday Review, Adolf Hitler* contains "hundreds of chatty anecdotes and odd glimpses into Hitler's life that help to give him a human, if often unpleasing, face.''

Toland's book reveals that until the Second World War began, Hitler was overwhelmingly popular in Germany. He had brought his country out of a depression, instituted a series of massive building programs that provided much-needed jobs, established sweeping social reforms, and given the German people a sense of common purpose. Internationally, Hitler enjoyed an equally favorable reputation. Gertrude Stein believed he deserved a Nobel Peace Prize. George Bernard Shaw praised him in newspaper articles. The Vatican cooperated with him. Toland states that ''if Hitler had died in 1937 . . . he would undoubtedly have gone down as one of the greatest figures in German history.''

Critical reaction to *Adolf Hitler* particularly praised the sheer mass of information that Toland gathers into one book. ''Put simply,'' Peter S. Prescott comments in *Newsweek*, ''Toland tells us more about Hitler than anyone knew before.'' And because of the vast amount of information provided in the book, *Adolf Hitler* is one of the most comprehensive studies of its subject available. ''Not only is 'Adolf Hitler' marvelously absorbing popular history,'' Christopher Lehmann-Haupt writes in the *New York Times*, ''it also must be ranked as one of the most complete pictures of Hitler we have yet had.'' ''Toland's book,'' Eliot Freemont-Smith claims in the *Village Voice*, ''is very good, in most ways the best Hitler biography so far. . . . What makes it 'best' is Toland's superb command of an enormous amount of detail, of where to place emphasis in order to increase our understanding and of tone.''

In *No Man's Land: 1918, The Last Year of the Great War*, Toland turned from his studies of the Second World War to look at how the First World War had ended. The last year of that conflict saw stunning military reversals and massive casualties. It began with a stalemate on the Western Front, where soldiers on both sides endured a stagnant and bloody trench warfare. But in the spring of 1918 the Kaiser completed a peace treaty with Russia and was able to move troops from the Russian front to the Western Front. With some 600,000 men, far more than the French and British armies could muster, the Germans launched ''the greatest military assault in history,'' as Timothy Foote writes in *Time*. It appeared as if the Germans would soon capture Paris.

But in July the Allies counterattacked, driving the German army back some twenty miles. The French and British armies then captured some 50,000 German soldiers in one battle near Amiens and put an end to the Kaiser's hopes of victory. When American troops began to arrive shortly thereafter, at the rate of some 250,000 a month, the German high command realized that the war was lost. Toland's account of the dramatic finish of the First World War is ''scrupulously accurate while at the same time absorbing and dramatic,'' according to Richard M. Watt of the *New York Times Book Review*.

Some reviewers were critical of Toland's approach. Brian Bond of the *Times Literary Supplement* calls *No Man's Land* ''essentially a story without any real attempt to analyse issues, reappraise evidence or reach conclusions.'' In the *Detroit News*, Bernard A. Weisberger complains that Toland ''seems to have relied on first-hand accounts by soldiers who still had some notion of the war as an adventure.'' But the London *Times'* Laurence Cotterell praises Toland's objectivity. ''While describing in exhaustive detail the direction and course of battle,'' writes Cotterell, ''Toland displays remarkably little partisanship [and] yet evokes all the intrinsic colour and passion

of the situation, enabling the reader to form his or her own conclusions.''

With *Infamy: Pearl Harbor and Its Aftermath*, Toland examined the tragic attack which brought the United States into the Second World War. Some 2,400 American servicemen died when the Japanese fleet staged a surprise attack on the naval base at Pearl Harbor, Hawaii, on December 7, 1941. Toland had written about this event in his *The Rising Sun* in 1970. But, he tells Andrew R. McGill of the *Detroit News*, ''I made a mistake in *The Rising Sun* by saying the attack was a total surprise. . . . Subsequently, enough people came to me with contrary information that I learned I had fallen into a trap.''

Toland argues in *Infamy* that President Franklin D. Roosevelt and a handful of top government officials wanted to provoke a war with Japan but were held back by the isolationism of the American people. Their provocations finally drove the Japanese to plan an attack on Pearl Harbor, America's largest naval base in the Pacific. When Roosevelt learned of the upcoming attack, he and his aides deliberately kept the information from the Naval commanders at Pearl Harbor. Roosevelt's purpose was to make the Japanese fire the first shot and ''make Americans so mad they'd abandon their isolationism and plunge into the confrontation with fascism,'' as Jeff Lyon explains in the *Chicago Tribune Book World*.

Reaction to Toland's assertion that Roosevelt knew of the coming Pearl Harbor attack and did nothing to stop it drew some harsh criticism. ''I'm getting the greatest hatred on this,'' Toland told Lyon. And yet, his conclusions are based on what D. J. R. Bruckner of the *New York Times Book Review* calls ''tons of documents unsealed by the Freedom of Information Act.'' Among the evidence are reports that radio messages from the Japanese naval force were intercepted days before the attack; that a Dutch diplomat who visited the navy's Washington command center in early December of 1941 watched as intelligence officers tracked the Japanese fleet on its way to Hawaii; and that a British double agent alerted the United States that a Pearl Harbor attack was planned. ''The evidence [Toland] has gathered . . . ,'' Lyon writes, ''is fresh and compelling.'' Bill Stout of the *Los Angeles Times Book Review* finds that *Infamy*'s evidence amounts to ''a strong indictment of Franklin D. Roosevelt and most of his wartime inner circle.''

After writing for more than twenty years about recent history, particularly about the Second World War, Toland decided in 1985 to transform historical fact into fiction. *Gods of War*, his first novel, traces the experiences of two families during World War II: the McGlynns are an American family; the Todas, a Japanese family. Together, their stories provide a panoramic look at the entire war in the Pacific. ''Toland makes a majestic sweep of conditions, events and personalities,'' Webster Schott explains in the *New York Times Book Review*.

Although Lessenberry believes that *Gods of War* ''is a ponderous, 598-page pedestrian work in which the substance of characters range from cardboard to knotty pine,'' other critics find much to praise. While admitting that ''Toland is an analyst of history, not personality,'' and that ''his characters act rather than struggle,'' Schott concludes that *Gods of War* ''is compelling as information and impressive as performance. It's history dressed as fiction. Very well dressed.'' Noel Barber of the *Washington Post Book World* maintains that, ''small faults aside, this is a massive novel, broad in its scope and fascinating in its detail. Like all good sagas based on recent war history, it cannot fail.''

BIOGRAPHICAL/CRITICAL SOURCES:

PERIODICALS

American Historical Review, February, 1972.
Ann Arbor News, June 6, 1982.
Best Sellers, February 1, 1971.
Books and Bookmen, July, 1977.
Book World, January 3, 1971.
Chicago Tribune Book World, September 28, 1980, May 15, 1982, April 14, 1985.
Christian Science Monitor, March 3, 1966, October 27, 1976.
Detroit News, October 19, 1980, June 13, 1982, March 10, 1985.
Los Angeles Times, December 28, 1980.
Los Angeles Times Book Review, May 9, 1982, March 3, 1985.
Modern Age, fall, 1966.
Nation, January 22, 1977.
National Review, April 29, 1977.
New Republic, November 20, 1976, June 16, 1979.
Newsweek, March 7, 1966, December 28, 1970, September 20, 1976.
New York Herald Tribune Book Review, February 18, 1966.
New York Review of Books, May 26, 1977, December 18, 1980, May 27, 1982.
New York Times, December 7, 1970, October 12, 1976.
New York Times Book Review, November 29, 1970, September 26, 1976, November 12, 1980, August 22, 1982, April 21, 1985.
North American Review, summer, 1977.
Progressive, February, 1977.
Saturday Review, March 12, 1966, January 2, 1971, September 18, 1976, September, 1980.
Time, December 7, 1970, December 6, 1976, September 22, 1980.
Times (London), December 11, 1980.
Times Literary Supplement, September 1, 1972, February 6, 1981.
Village Voice, November 15, 1976.
Virginia Quarterly Review, summer, 1977.
Wall Street Journal, February 28, 1966.
Washington Post, October 27, 1980, May 3, 1982, October 29, 1987.
Washington Post Book World, January 3, 1971, September 5, 1976, April 23, 1985.
Yale Review, June, 1971.

—*Sketch by Thomas Wiloch*

*   *   *

TOWNS, James E(dward)   1942-
(Jim Towns)

PERSONAL: Born February 27, 1942, in Clovis, N.M.; son of Verney Edward (a businessman) and Mona (Hancock) Towns. *Education:* Hardin-Simmons University, B.A., 1965; Southern Illinois University, M.A., 1966, Ph.D., 1970. *Politics:* Democrat. *Religion:* Baptist.

ADDRESSES: Home—Box 6174, S.F.A. Station, Nacogdoches, Tex. 75962. *Office*—Department of Communication, Stephen F. Austin State University, Nacogdoches, Tex. 75962.

CAREER: Stephen F. Austin State University, Nacogdoches, Tex., instructor, 1966-68, assistant professor, 1970-77, associate professor, 1977-81, professor of communication, 1981—. Speaker at religious conferences and retreats; conducts workshops for families and single adults. Communication consultant for businesses and local churches.

MEMBER: Speech Communication Association of America, Southern Speech Communication Association, Texas Speech Communication Association, Phi Kappa Phi.

WRITINGS:

Faith Stronger than Death: How to Communicate with a Person in Sorrow, Warner Press, 1975.
The Social Conscience of W. A. Criswell, Crescendo, 1976.
One Is Not a Lonely Number, Crescendo, 1977.
(Editor under name Jim Towns) *Solo Flight,* Tyndale, 1980.
Life: Joy in Being, Broadman, 1981.
Growing through Grief, Warner Press, 1984.
(Under name Jim Towns) *Singles Alive,* Pelican Publishing, 1984.
(Under name Jim Towns) *A Family Guide to Death and Dying,* Tyndale, 1987.

WORK IN PROGRESS: Research and writing on the subjects of death education, single adult life, and interpersonal communication.

*   *   *

TOWNS, Jim
See TOWNS, James E(dward)

*   *   *

TRIPP, Wallace (Whitney)   1940-

PERSONAL: Born June 26, 1940, in Boston, Mass.; son of Kenneth and Frances Whitney Tripp; married Marcia Bixby (president of Pawprints, Inc.) in 1965; children: two sons, one daughter. *Education:* Received diploma from Boston Museum School; and B.Ed. from Keene State College; graduate study at University of New Hampshire.

ADDRESSES: Home—Jaffrey, N.H., 03452. *Office*—Sparhawk Books, Inc., Box 446, Jaffrey, N.H., 03452.

CAREER: Has worked as an English teacher. Free-lance illustrator and author, 1965—; Pawprints Greeting Cards, illustrator, 1972—; Sparhawk Books, Jaffrey, N. H., president and creative director, 1981—.

MEMBER: Authors League of America, Authors Guild.

AWARDS, HONORS: Recipient of Boston Globe-Horn Book award for illustrations, 1977, for *Granfa' Grig Had a Pig; A Great Big Ugly Man Came Up and Tied His Horse to Me* appeared on the American Library Association's notable book list.

WRITINGS:

SELF-ILLUSTRATED; JUVENILES

The Tale of a Pig: A Caucasian Folktale, McGraw, 1968.
(Compiler) *A Great Big Ugly Man Came Up and Tied His Horse to Me: A Book of Nonsense Verse,* Little, Brown, 1973.
My Uncle Podger: A Picture Book (based on a passage from *Three Men in a Boat* by Jerome K. Jerome), Little, Brown, 1975.
(Compiler) *Granfa' Grig Had a Pig and Other Rhymes without Reason from Mother Goose* (verse), Little, Brown, 1976.
Sir Toby Jingle's Beastly Journey (Junior Literary Guild selection), Coward, 1976.

(Compiler) *Rhymes without Reason from Mother Goose*, World's Work, 1980.

(Compiler) *Marguerite, Go Wash Your Feet!* (verse), Houghton, 1985.

ILLUSTRATOR; CHILREN'S FICTION

Reginald B. Hegarty, *Rope's End*, Houghton, 1965.

Lisa Tsarelka, *Stay Away From My Lawnmower*, Houghton, 1965.

Ruth Christoffer Carlsen, *Henrietta Goes West*, Houghton, 1966.

Carlsen, *Hildy and the Cuckoo Clock*, Houghton, 1966.

Ilse Kleberger, *Grandmother Oma*, Atheneum, 1967.

Andrew Lang, editor, *Read Me Another Fairy Tale*, Grosset, 1967.

Katherine E. Miller, *Saint George: A Christmas Mummers' Play*, Houghton, 1967.

Gerald Dumas, *Rabbits Rafferty*, Houghton, 1968.

Carlsen, *Sam Bottleby*, Houghton, 1968.

Felice Holman, *The Holiday Rat, and the Utmost Mouse* (short stories), Norton, 1969.

John Erwin, *Mrs. Fox*, Simon & Schuster, 1969.

Scott Corbett, *The Baseball Bargain*, Little, Brown, 1970.

Tom Paxton, *Jennifer's Rabbit*, Putnam, 1970.

Rene Guillot, *Little Dog Lost*, translated by Joan Selby-Lowndes, Lothrup, 1970.

Betty Brock, *No Flying in the House*, Harper, 1970.

Ferdinand N. Monjo, *Pirates in Panama*, Simon & Schuster, 1970.

Robert Sidney Bigelow, *Stubborn Bear*, Little, Brown, 1970.

Julian Bagley, *Candle-Lighting Time in Bodidalee* (folktales), foreword by Alfred V. Frankenstein, American Heritage Publishing Co., 1971.

Peggy Parish, *Come Back, Amelia Bedelia*, Harper, 1971.

Victor Sharoff, *The Heart of the Wood*, Coward, 1971.

Marguerita Rudolph, adapter, *The Magic Egg, and Other Folk Stories of Rumania*, Little, Brown, 1971.

Peter Hallard, *Puppy Lost in Lapland*, F. Watts, 1971.

Patricia Thomas, *''Stand Back,'' Said the Elephant, ''I'm Going to Sneeze!,''* Lothrup, 1971.

Miriam Anne Bourne, *Tigers in the Woods*, Coward, 1971.

Tony Johnston, *The Adventures of Mole and Troll*, Putnam, 1972.

Cynthia Jameson, adapter, *Catofy the Clever* (folktale), Coward, 1972.

Liesel Moak Skorpen, *Old Arthur*, Harper, 1972.

Parish, *Play Ball, Amelia Bedelia*, Harper, 1972.

Carolyn Lane, *The Voices of Greenwillow Pond*, Houghton, 1972.

Boris Vladimirovich Zakhoder, *The Crocodile's Toothbrush*, translated by Marguerita Rudolph, McGraw, 1973.

Malcolm Hall, *Headlines*, (Junior Literary Guild selection), Coward, 1973.

Johnston, *Mole and Troll Trim the Tree*, (Junior Literary Guild selection), Putnam, 1974, revised edition, 1980.

Jan Wahl, *Pleasant Fieldmouse's Halloween Party*, Putnam, 1974.

Robert Fremlin, *Three Friends*, Little, Brown, 1975.

Ernest Lawrence Thayer, *Casey at the Bat: A Ballad of the Republic, Sung in the Year 1888* (verse), Coward, 1978.

Hilaire Belloc, *The Bad Child's Book of Beasts*, revised edition, Sparhawk, 1982.

OTHER

Wallace Tripp's Wurst Seller, (humor for adults), Sparhawk, 1981.

AVOCATIONAL INTERESTS: Classical music, traveling, aviation.

BIOGRAPHICAL/CRITICAL SOURCES:

BOOKS

Lee Kingman and others, *Illustrators of Children's Books: 1967-76*, Horn Book, 1978.

PERIODICALS

New York Times Book Review, March 5, 1968, May 27, 1973, September 12, 1976.

Times Literary Supplement, December 5, 1968, December 6, 1974.

*   *   *

TSIEN, Tsuen-hsuin   1909-

PERSONAL: Born December 1, 1909, in Kiangsu, China; naturalized U.S. citizen; son of Wei-chen (a scholar) and Chuan-shih (Hsu) Tsien; married Wen-ching Hsu (a lecturer at University of Chicago), August 31, 1936; children: Ginger, Gloria, Mary Dunkel. *Education:* University of Nanking, B.A., 1932; University of Chicago, M.A., 1952, Ph.D., 1957.

ADDRESSES: Home—1408 East Rochdale Pl., Chicago, Ill. 60615. *Office*—Joseph Regenstein Library, University of Chicago, Chicago, Ill., 60637.

CAREER: National Library of Peiping (Peking), Shanghai, China, editor and chief of Shanghai office, 1937-47; University of Chicago, Chicago, Ill., professorial lecturer, 1949-58, associate professor, 1958-64, professor of Chinese literature and library science, 1964-79, professor emeritus, 1979—, curator of Far Eastern Library, 1949-78, curator emeritus, 1978—. Visiting professor of Asian studies, University of Hawaii, summer, 1959; affiliated with Science and Civilization Project, Cambridge University, 1968—; director, Institute of Far Eastern Librarianship, summer, 1969; research fellow, Needham Research Institute, 1982. Chinese Student and Alumni Services, Inc., member of board of directors, 1958—, president, 1960-62; member of Task Force on Libraries and Research Materials, American Council of Learned Societies and Social Science Research Council, 1974-76. Advisor, Government/Academic Interface Committee on International Education of the Task Force on Library and Information Resources, American Council of Education, 1974. Member of delegation of American librarians to China, 1979.

MEMBER: International Association of Oriental Librarians (advisor, 1968-72), Association for Asian Studies (chairman, committee on East Asian Libraries, 1966-68, executive member of China and Inner-Asia Council, 1970-72), Association of College and Research Libraries (executive member, Asian and African section, 1972-73), American Library Association.

AWARDS, HONORS: Distinguished Service Awards, Chinese Ministry of Education, 1943, Committee on East Asian Libraries, 1978, Chinese-American Librarians Association, 1985; American Council of Learned Societies grant, 1968-69; National Science Foundation and National Endowment for the Humanities grants, 1977-82, for the study of paper and printing in Chinese civilization.

WRITINGS:

Western Impact on China through Translation, Department of

Photographic Reproduction, University of Chicago Library, 1952.

The Pre-Printing Records of China, Department of Photographic Reproduction, University of Chicago Library, 1957.

Asian Studies in America, University of Hawaii, 1959.

(With G. Raymond Nunn) *Far Eastern Resources in American Libraries,* 1959.

(Contributor) *Asian Studies and State Universities,* Indiana University, 1959.

(Contributor) *A Guide to Historical Literature,* Macmillan, 1961.

Written on Bamboo and Silk: The Beginnings of Chinese Books and Inscriptions, University of Chicago Press, 1962.

(Editor with Howard W. Winger) *Area Studies and the Library,* University of Chicago Press, 1966.

(Editor) *Library Resources on East Asia,* Inter-Documentation Co. (Zug, Switzerland), 1968.

A Guide to Reference and Source Materials for Chinese Studies, Graduate Library School, University of Chicago, 1969, supplement, 1977.

(Contributor) *Collected Essays Dedicated to Dr. Chiang Fu-tsung in Honor of His Seventieth Birthday,* National Central Library (Taipei), 1969.

Terminology of the Chinese Book: Bibliography and Librarianship, Graduate Library School, University of Chicago, 1972.

(Contributor) *Resources on the History of Chinese Books and Printing,* Lung Men Press (Hong Kong), 1974.

A History of Writing and Writing Materials in Ancient China, Chinese University of Hong Kong Press, 1975.

Current Status of East Asian Collections in American Libraries, 1974-1975, Association of Research Libraries, 1976.

History of Chinese Printing and Publishing: Outline and Bibliography, Graduate Library School, University of Chicago, 1977.

Introduction to Chinese Bibliography: Outline and Bibliography, Graduate Library School, University of Chicago, 1977.

Chinese Bibliography and Historiography: Outline and Bibliography, Graduate Library School, University of Chicago, 1977.

(With James K. M. Cheng) *China: An Annotated Bibliography of Bibliographies,* G. K. Hall, 1978.

(Contributor) Yves Hervouet, editor, *Sung Bibliography,* Chinese University of Hong Kong, 1978.

(Editor with David T. Roy) *Ancient China: Studies in Early Civilization,* Chinese University of Hong Kong Press, 1978.

(Contributor) *Cooperation among East Asian Libraries,* Cornell University Libraries, 1979.

(Contributor) Joseph Needham, *Science and Civilization in China,* Volume V, Cambridge University Press, 1980.

Paper and Printing in Chinese Civilization (monograph), Cambridge University Press, 1982.

(Contributor) *Essays in Commemoration of the Golden Jubilee of the Fung Ping Shan Library,* Hong Kong University Press, 1982.

(Contributor) *Explorations in the History of Science and Technology in China,* [Shanghai], 1982.

(Contributor) Soeren Edgren, editor, *Chinese Rare Books in American Collections,* China Institute in America, 1984.

(Contributor) *Proceedings of the Workshop on the Authentication and Preservation of Chinese Rare Books,* Library Association of China (Taipei), 1985.

Collected Papers on Chinese-American Cultural Relations, Lien Ching Ch'u-Pan-Kung-Ssu, 1987.

Also author, with J. K. M. Cheng, of *China: A Reference and Research Guide,* G. K. Hall, and of papers presented to professional conferences. Contributor to William Boltz and Michael Lowe, editor, *Proceedings of the Third International Conference on the History of Chinese Science,* and Zheng Rusi, editor, *Chinese Books and Written Records before the Invention of Printing,* Printing Industry Publishing House (Peking), revised edition, *International Cooperation in Oriental Librarianship, Biographical Dictionary of the Republic of China, Dictionary of Ming Biography, Sung Biography, Encyclopedia of Library and Information Science, Bibliophilia Sinica,* and *Handbook on Early Chinese Texts.* Contributor of articles on China and library science and of book reviews to periodicals in the United States, China, and Japan, including *Journal of Asian Studies, College and Research Libraries, Harvard Journal of Asiatic Studies,* and *Ming Pao Monthly.* Advisory editor of *Tsing Hua Journal of Chinese Studies,* 1959—, and member of editorial board of *Library Quarterly,* 1980—.

WORK IN PROGRESS: Pre-printing Books and Documents of China; History of the Book, Paper and Printing in Chinese Culture; Chinese-American Literary Relations.

SIDELIGHTS: Tsuen-hsuin Tsien collects letter openers and early printing and manuscripts from China where, he points out, not only was block printing invented in the seventh century, but movable type was used four hundred years before Gutenberg.

BIOGRAPHICAL/CRITICAL SOURCES:

PERIODICALS

Bulletin of East Asian Libraries, number 81, 1987.
Chicago Sun-Times Midwest Magazine, January 20, 1960.
Hong Kong Times, April 7, 1965.
Library Quarterly, Volume XX, 1952, Volume XXIX, 1959, Volume XXXV, 1965.

U

ULANOFF, Stanley M(elvin) 1922-

PERSONAL: Surname is pronounced *You*-la-noff; born May 30, 1922, in Brooklyn, N.Y.; son of Samuel H. (a stockbroker) and Minnie (Druss) Ulanoff; married Bernice "Tooty" Mayer (an interior decorator), June 15, 1947; children: Roger, Amy, Lisa, Dory Kennedy. *Education:* University of Iowa, B.A., 1943; Hofstra College (now University), M.B.A., 1955; New York University, Ph.D., 1968; attended U.S. Army Command and General Staff College, Intelligence School, and Infantry School.

ADDRESSES: Home—17 The Serpentine, Roslyn, N.Y. 11576. *Office*—Department of Marketing, Bernard M. Baruch College of the City University of New York, New York, N.Y. 10010.

CAREER: New York Times, New York City, promotion copywriter, 1946-49; Cecil & Presbrey Advertising Agency, New York City, newswriter and advertising copywriter, 1946-49; free-lance writer and advertising and public relations consultant, 1951—; Executive Broadcasting Corp. (operator of radio station WTYM), Springfield, Mass., president, 1959-62; State University of New York at Stony Brook, assistant to the president, 1962-65; Bernard M. Baruch College of the City University of New York, New York City, associate professor of marketing, 1964-86, head of Co-op Work Training Program, former head of Advertising and Public Relations Division.

Member of faculty, Intensive Business Training Program, City College (now City College of the City University of New York), 1946-49; member of faculty, Evening Division, State University of New York at Farmingdale, 1961-62; adjunct assistant professor of business administration, C. W. Post College of Long Island University, 1962-64; associate professor of business, Kingsborough Community College of the City University of New York, 1964-65; adjunct professor of communication arts and supervisor of Externship Program, Graduate School, New York Institute of Technology, 1974—. Assistant to the president, Compton Advertising; president, Advisions, a video production company, 1974—. Introduced and closed series of video documentaries on World War II for Goodtimes Home Video, Corp., 1986. Consultant to businesses and to U.S. Department of Defense. *Military service:* U.S. Army, Counter Intelligence Corps, 1942-46; served in European Theater as special agent, as officer in charge of public information, and as head of *The History of CIC Operations in Europe* writing project; became second lieutenant. U.S. Army Reserve, 1946—; served as economics officer in Civil Affairs, commanding officer of a Military Intelligence detachment, information officer at Fort Drum, and U.S. Government researcher attached to U.S. Merchant Marine Academy; retired as brigadier general; received U.S. Army Commendation Medal, 1977, and U.S. Army Achievement Medal, 1982.

MEMBER: American Academy of Advertising, Public Relations Society of America, American College Public Relations Association, American Association of University Professors, Society of Professional Journalists, Direct Mail Advertising Association, Military Intelligence Reserve Society (president), Reserve Officers Association (chapter president), Alpha Delta Sigma, Pi Sigma Epsilon.

AWARDS, HONORS: Lewis Kleid Advertising Scholarship grant, 1966; Russell Sage Foundation Scholarship grant, 1968; Chevalier dans L'ordre des Palmes Academiques (France), 1968; American Association of Advertising Agencies fellowship, 1969; named "Very Important Professor," Specialty Advertising Association, 1970; Certified Advertising Specialist degree, University of Missouri and Specialty Advertising Association, 1970; U.S. Government Certificate of Achievement, 1971, for research; Eastman-Kodak fellowship, 1971, for television film; Conspicuous Service Cross, State of New York, 1975; Meritorious Service Medal, U.S. Government, 1975; Legion of Merit, U.S. Government, 1976; Alumni Distinguished Service Award (gold), Hofstra University.

WRITINGS:

Illustrated Guide to U.S. Missiles and Rockets, Doubleday, 1959, revised edition, 1962.
(Editor) *Fighter Pilot,* Doubleday, 1962, revised edition, Prentice-Hall, 1986.
MATS: The Story of the Military Air Transport Service, F. Watts, 1964.
Ace of Aces, Doubleday, 1967.
(Editor) William Avery Bishop, *Winged Warfare,* Doubleday, 1967, revised edition, Arco, 1981.
(Editor) Duncan William Grinnell-Milne, *Wind in the Wires,* Doubleday, 1968.
Flying Fury, Doubleday, 1968.

Fighting Airmen: The Way of the Eagle, Doubleday, 1968.
Man in the Green Beret, Scholastic Book Services, 1969.
The Red Baron, Doubleday, 1969.
Ace of the Iron Cross, Doubleday, 1970.
Flying in Flanders, Ace Books, 1971.
(Editor) Harold Evans Hartney, *Up and at 'Em*, Doubleday, 1971.
Illustrated History of World War I in the Air, Arco, 1971.
(Editor) *Bombs Away: True Stories of Strategic Airpower form World War I to the Present*, Doubleday, 1971.
World War II Aircraft in Combat, Arco, 1976.
Advertising in America: Principles of Persuasive Business Communication, Hastings House, 1976.
American Wars and Heroes (Doubleday Military Book Club selection), Arco, 1984.
Handbook of Sales Promotion, McGraw, 1984.
Israeli Air Force, Arco, 1985.
Fighting Israeli Air Force, Arco, 1985.

Also author of *Comparison Advertising: An Historical Retrospective*, 1975. Contributor of articles and reviews to periodicals, including *New York Times*. Consulting editor, *Journal of Advertising*, 1975.

SIDELIGHTS: Stanley M. Ulanoff told *CA:* "While I have been a professor of marketing (advertising, public relations, and sales promotion) and do consulting and writing in those areas, the bulk of my writing is in military history and aviation or aerospace. I write because I enjoy recounting the tales of high adventure, human endurance, and achievement that have gotten lost through time and are overshadowed by more recent events." Ulanoff speaks or reads Spanish, French, German, and Hebrew.

AVOCATIONAL INTERESTS: Travel, skiing, model-aircraft building, collecting military memorabilia, coins, and stamps.

*   *   *

UNSTEAD, R(obert) J(ohn)   1915-

PERSONAL: Born November 21, 1915, in Deal, Kent, England; son of Charles Edmond and Elizabeth (Nightingale) Unstead; married Florence Margaret Thomas (her husband's secretary), March 15, 1939; children: Judith, Mary, Susan. *Education:* Attended Goldsmith's College, University of London, 1934-36. *Religion:* Church of England.

ADDRESSES: Home—"Reedlands," Lakeside, Thorpeness, Suffolk, England.

CAREER: Schoolmaster in St. Albans, England, 1936-40; headmaster in Letchworth, England, 1947-57; free-lance author, 1957-87. Director, R. J. Unstead Publications Ltd. *Military service:* Royal Air Force, 1940-46; became flight lieutenant.

MEMBER: Society of Authors, National Book League (both London).

WRITINGS:

Cavemen to Vikings (also see below), A. & C. Black, 1953.
The Middle Ages (also see below), A. & C. Black, 1953.
Tudors and Stuarts (also see below), A. & C. Black, 1954.
Queen Anne to Elizabeth II (also see below), A. & C. Black, 1955.
Looking at History: Britain from Cavemen to the Present Day (contains *Cavemen to Vikings, The Middle Ages, Tudors and Stuarts,* and *Queen Anne to Elizabeth II*), A. &

Black, 1955, Macmillan (New York), 1956, 3rd edition, A. & C. Black, 1966, new edition, 1975.
People in History, A. & C. Black, Book I: *From Caractacus to Alfred*, 1955, Book II: *From William the Conqueror to William Caxton*, 1955, Book III: *Great Tudors and Stuarts*, 1956, Book IV: *Great People of Modern Times*, 1956, published in America in one volume as *People in History: From Caractacus to Alexander Fleming*, Macmillan, 1957.
A History of Houses, A. & C. Black, 1958.
Travel by Road Through the Ages, A. & C. Black, 1958, 2nd edition, 1969.
Looking at Ancient History, A. & C. Black, 1959, Macmillan, 1960.
(Editor with William Worthy, and contributor) *Black's Children's Encyclopaedia*, A. & C. Black, 1961.
Monasteries, Dufour, 1961, 2nd edition, A. & C. Black, 1970.
Some Kings and Queens (also see below), Odhams, 1962, Follett, 1967.
A History of Britain, A. & C. Black, Book I: *The Medieval Scene, 787-1485*, 1962, Book II: *Crown and Parliament, 1485-1688*, 1962, Book III: *The Rise of Great Britain: 1688-1837*, 1963, Book IV: *The Century of Change, 1837-Today*, 1963.
Royal Adventurers (also see below), Odhams, 1963, Follett, 1967.
Men and Woman in History, A. & C. Black, Book I: *Heroes and Saints*, 1964, Book II: *Princes and Rebels*, 1964, Book III: *Discoverers and Adventurers*, 1965, Book IV: *Great Leaders*, 1966.
Britain in the Twentieth Century, A. & C. Black, 1966.
Kings and Queens in World History (contains *Some Kings and Queens* and *Royal Adventurers*), Odhams, 1966.
The Story of Britain, A.& C. Black, 1969, Thomas Nelson, 1970.
(With W. F. Henderson) *Homes in Australia*, A. & C. Black, 1969.
British Castles, Crowell, 1970 (published in England as *Castles*, A. & C. Black, 1970).
My World, Herder, 1970.
(With Henderson) *Transport in Australia*, A. & C. Black, 1970.
(With Henderson) *Pioneer Home Life in Australia*, A. & C. Black, 1971.
Living in a Medieval City, A. & C. Black, 1971.
Living in a Castle, illustrated by Victor Ambrus, A. & C. Black, 1971.
Living in a Medieval Village, Addison-Wesley, 1971.
Living in a Crusader Land, A. & C. Black, 1971.
A History of the English-speaking World (eight volumes), Silver Burdett, 1971-74.
The Twenties, Silver Burdett, 1973.
(Editor) *World War One, World War Two*, R. J. Hoare, 1973.
Invaded Island, Addison-Wesley, 1974.
Kings, Barons and Serfs, Addison-Wesley, 1974.
Years of the Sword, Addison-Wesley, 1974.
Struggle for Power, Addison-Wesley, 1974.
Emerging Empire, Addison-Wesley, 1974.
Freedom and Revolution, Addison-Wesley, 1974.
Age of Machines, Addison-Wesley, 1974.
Incredible Century, Addison-Wesley, 1974.
Living in the Elizabethan Court, Addison-Wesley, 1974.
Living in Samuel Pepys' London, Addison-Wesley, 1974.
Living in the Time of the Pilgrim Fathers, Addison-Wesley, 1974.

The Thirties, Silver Burdett, 1974.
Living in Aztec Times, Addison-Wesley, 1974.
Living in Ancient Egypt, Addison-Wesley, 1976.
A Dictionary of History, Ward, Lock, 1976.
Living in Pompeii, Addison-Wesley, 1977.
See Inside a Castle, Hutchinson, 1977.
Greece and Rome, A. & C. Black, 1978.
Egypt and Mesopotamia, A. & C. Black, 1978.
A Book of Kings and Queens, Ward, Lock, 1978.
The Egyptians, Ward, Lock, 1980.
The Assyrians, Ward, Lock, 1980.
Cities of Long Ago, Hutchinson, 1980.
A History of the World, A. & C. Black, 1983.

General editor, "Looking at Geography" series, five books, A. & C. Black, 1957-60, "Black's Junior Reference Books," thirty-five books, A. & C. Black, 1958-80, and "See Inside" series, twelve books, Hutchinson, 1977-80.

Also author, with Henderson, of *Police in Australia* and *Sport and Entertainment in Australia,* both published by A. & C. Black. Contributor to *Encyclopeadia Americana.*

BIOGRAPHICAL/CRITICAL SOURCES:

PERIODICALS

Best Sellers, February 15, 1971.
New Statesman, November 12, 1971, November 4, 1977, May 19, 1978.
Times Literary Supplement, July 2, 1971, July 5, 1974.

*   *   *

URBANSKI, Edmund Stefan
   See URBANSKI, Edmund Stephen

*   *   *

URBANSKI, Edmund Stephen   1909-
  (Edmund Stefan Urbanski)

PERSONAL: Born July 6, 1909, in Poland; naturalized U.S. citizen; son of Andrew and Leokadia (Winkler) Urbanski; children: Jane Mercedes, Wanda Marie. *Education:* Classic College (Poland), B.A., 1930; University of Lund, certificate, 1939; National University of Mexico, M.A., 1943, Ph.D., 1946; University of Barcelona, diploma, 1955; University of San Marcos, certificate, 1959; postdoctoral study at University of California and Middlebury College.

CAREER: National University of Mexico, Mexico City, associate professor of Slavic philology, 1942-45; Marquette University, Milwaukee, Wis., instructor in Spanish language and Spanish American literature and civilization, 1946-48; University of San Francisco, San Francisco, Calif., assistant professor of Spanish language and Spanish American literature and civilization, 1949-50; Idaho State University, Pocatello, assistant professor of Spanish language and Spanish American literature and civilization, 1950-55; University of Notre Dame, South Bend, Ind., assistant professor of Spanish language and Spanish American literature, 1955-56; John Carroll University, Cleveland, Ohio, assistant professor of Spanish American literature and civilization, 1956-60; University of Buffalo, Buffalo, N.Y., visiting associate professor of Spanish American literature and civilization, 1960-62; Western Illinois University, Macomb, associate professor of Spanish American literature and civilization, 1962-65; Western Michigan University, Kalamazoo, associate professor of Spanish American literature

and civilization, 1965-67; Howard University, Washington, D.C., professor of Spanish American literature and civilization, 1967-75; University of Warsaw, Warsaw, Poland, visiting professor, 1976-78; Federal University of Parana, Brazil, visiting professor, 1979; researcher and writer, 1980—. Guest lecturer at universities in Colombia, Ecuador, Guatemala, Peru, Mexico, Paraguay, Poland, Holland, and Spain; has conducted archaeological and historic-literary field research in Spain and Latin America; consultant to Peace Corps, Inter-American Defense College, and Canada Council.

MEMBER: International Congress of Americanists, International Association of Hispanists, Instituto Internacional de Literatura Iberoamericana, Instituto Interamericano (fellow), International Social Science Honor Society (life member), Modern Language Association of America, American Association of Teachers of Spanish and Portuguese, Association of Latin American Studies, Anthropological Association of Canada (fellow), Instituto de Estudios Humanos (honorary member), Sociedad Nacional Hispanica (honorary member), Academia de Historia de Santander (Colombia), Anthropological Association of Washington.

AWARDS, HONORS: Gold medal from Instituto de Estudios Humanos, Lima, Peru, 1966; five research grants and honorary diploma from Centro Cultural, Literario e Artistico, Portugal.

WRITINGS:

Problem szkolnictwa zawodowega na Wybrzezu (title means "Problems of Professional Education on the Polish Coast"), Dokada, 1938.
Los eslavos ayer, hoy y manana (title means "Slavs Yesterday, Today and Tomorrow"), Ediciones Ibero-Americanas, 1943.
Polonia los eslavos y Europa (title means "Poland, Slavs and Europe"), Ediciones Ibero-Americanas, 1944.
Breve historia de la literatura polaca (title means "Brief History of Polish Literature"), Editorial Pax, 1946.
Studies in Spanish American Literature and Civilization, Western Illinois University Press, 1964.
Angloamerica e Hispanoamerica (title means "Anglo-America and Hispanic America"), Ediciones Studium, 1965.
(With Gonzalo Humberto Mata) *Sobre Montalvo o demistificacion de un mixtificador* (title means "About Montalvo or Unmystifier of a Mystifier") Editorial Cenit, 1969.
Hispanoamerica: Sus razas y civilizaciones (title means "Hispanic America, Its Races and Civilizations"), foreword by Manuel M. Valle, Eliseo Torres, 1972, translation by Frances Kellam Hendricks and Beatrice Berler published as *Hispanic America and Its Civilizations: Spanish Americans and Anglo-Americans,* foreword by Carl Compton, University of Oklahoma Press, 1978, 2nd edition, 1980.
Hispanoameryka i jej cywilizacje, P.W.N. (Warsaw), 1980.
Poles in Latin America, Charaszkiewicz Foundation, 1982.

Contributor to proceedings. Contributor of more than one hundred articles to scholarly journals in the United States, Canada, Latin America, and Europe, including *Estudios, Critica, Humanitas, Journal of World History, Current History, Americas, Journal of Inter-American Studies, Hispania, Modern Mexico, Inter-American Review of Bibliography, Cultures* (Paris), and *Anthropological Journal of Canada.*

WORK IN PROGRESS: Research on ethno-cultural values in Spanish American literature and civilization; *Strange Notions of the New World in Early European Cartography.*

V

Van CAENEGEM, R(aoul) C(harles)   1927-

PERSONAL: Surname is pronounced Van *Kane*-ham; born July 14, 1927, in Ghent, Belgium; married Patricia Carson, August, 1954. *Education:* University of Ghent, D.Laws, 1951, D.History, 1953; also studied at University of Paris, 1951-52, and London School of Economics and Political Science, London, 1952-54.

ADDRESSES: Home—Veuestraat 47, 9821 Gent-Afsnee, Belgium. *Office*—Faculteit de Letteren, Blandijnberg 2, University of Ghent, Ghent, Belgium.

CAREER: University of Ghent, Ghent, Belgium, assistant to Prof. F. L. Ganshof, 1954-60, lecturer, 1960-64, professor of medieval and legal history in Faculty of Letters and Faculty of Law, 1964—.

MEMBER: Royal Commission for History (Belgium), Royal Commission for Old Laws and Ordinances (Belgium), Royal Academy of Sciences of the Netherlands (foreign member), Royal Academy of Sciences of Belgium, Royal Historical Society (England; fellow), British Academy (corresponding fellow), Societe d'Histoire du Droit (France), Max Planck Institute for European Legal History (member of scientific advisory council), Mediaeval Academy of America (fellow).

WRITINGS:

Geschiedenis van het strafrecht in Vlaanderen van de XIe tot de XIVe eeuw, Royal Flemish Academy, 1954.
Geschiedenis van het strafprocesrecht in Vlaanderen van de XIe tot XIVe eeuw, Royal Flemish Academy, 1956.
Royal Writs in England from the Conquest to Glanvill: Studies in the Early History of the Common Law, Selden Society (London), 1959.
(With F. L. Ganshof) *Kurze Quellenkunde des westeuropaeishen Mittelalters*, [Goettingen], 1964.
The Birth of the English Common Law, Cambridge University Press, 1973.
Guide to the Sources of Medieval History, North-Holland Publishing, 1978.
Geschiedenis van Engeland van Stonehenge tot het tijdperk der vakbonden, Nijhoff, 1982.
Judges, Legislators and Professors: Chapters in European Legal History, Cambridge University Press, 1987.

Contributor to *International Encyclopaedia of Comparative Law*, 1973.

*   *   *

VANDENBERG, Philipp   1941-
(Klaus Dieter Hartel)

PERSONAL: Original name Klaus Dieter Hartel; name legally changed in 1972; born September 20, 1941, in Breslau, Germany (now Wroclaw, Poland). *Education:* Attended University of Munich, 1963-64. *Politics:* None. *Religion:* None.

ADDRESSES: Home—D 8157 Baiernrain, Villa Vandenberg, Germany.

CAREER: Passauer Neue Presse (newspaper), Passau, Bavaria, local editor, 1964-67; *Abendzeitung*, Munich, Germany, news editor, 1967-69; *Quick* (magazine), Munich, editor and writer, 1969-74; *Playboy*—Germany, Munich, nonfiction editor, 1974-76; full-time writer, 1976—.

WRITINGS:

IN ENGLISH TRANSLATION

Der Fluch der Pharaonen, Scherz, 1973, translation by Thomas Weyr published as *The Curse of the Pharaohs*, Lippincott, 1975.
Nofretete: eine archaeologische Biographie, Scherz, 1975, translation by Ruth Hein published as *Nefertiti: An Archaeological Biography*, Lippincott, 1978.
Der vergessene Pharao: Unternehmen Tut-ench-Amun, das groesste Abenteuer der Archaeologie, Bertelsmann, 1978, translation published as *The Forgotten Pharaoh*, Macmillan, 1980.

IN GERMAN

(Under name Klaus Dieter Hartel) *Martin Luther King: Vorkaempfer fur Frieden und Menschenwuerde*, Brunnen, 1968.
Nofretete, Echnaton und ihre Zeit: Die glanzvollste Epoche Aegyptens in Bildern, Berichten und Dokumenten, Scherz, 1976.
Auf den Spuren unserer Vergangenheit, Goldmann, 1977.
Ramses der Grosse: eine archaeologische Biographie, Scherz, 1977.

Das Geheimnis der Orakel: Archaeologen entschluesseln das bestgehuetete Mysterium der Antike (first part of title means "The Secret of the Oracles), Bertelsmann, 1979.
Nero: Kaiser und Gott, Kuenstler und Narr, Bertelsmann, 1981.
Der Gladiator (fiction), Heyne, 1982.
Das Tal: Auf den Spuren der Pharaonen, Bertelsmann, 1983.
Die Hetaere (fiction), Heyne, 1984.
Die Pharaonin (fiction), Heyne, 1984.
Das versunkene Hellas: Die Wiederentdeckung des antiken Griechenland, Bertelsmann, 1984.
Caesar und Kleopatra, Bertelsmann, 1986.
Der Pompejaner (fiction), Luebbe, 1986.
Das Tal der Pharaonen, Heyne, 1986.

SIDELIGHTS: Philip Vandenberg's books have been published in twenty-five languages, including Japanese, Turkish, Spanish, Finnish, Swedish, Polish, Rumanian, Italian, and French.

* * *

VanderZWAAG, Harold J.   1929-

PERSONAL: Surname is pronounced VanderSwog; born June 26, 1929, in Spring Lake, Mich.; son of John H. (a factory foreman) and Clara (Knoll) VanderZwaag; married Jane E. Barker (a speech therapist), February 11, 1956; children: John, Carol, George, Charles. *Education:* Calvin College, A.B., 1951; University of Michigan, M.A., 1952, Ph.D., 1962. *Politics:* Non-partisan. *Religion:* Lutheran.

ADDRESSES: Home—16 Aubinwood Rd., Amherst, Mass. 01002. *Office*—Department of Sport Studies, School of Physical Education, University of Massachusetts, Amherst, Mass. 01002.

CAREER: U.S. Coast Guard Reserve, active duty, 1952-59, instructor in physical education at Coast Guard Academy, New London, Conn., 1957-59, inactive duty, 1959—, with present rank of commander; DePaul University, Chicago, Ill., assistant professor of physical education, 1962-64; University of Illinois at Urbana-Champaign, associate professor of physical education, 1964-67; University of Massachusetts—Amherst, professor of physical education, 1967—, head of department of physical education for men, 1967—.

MEMBER: North American Society for Sport History and Sport Management, American Association for Health, Physical Education, and Recreation, American Academy of Physical Education (fellow), National College Physical Education Association for Men, Philosophic Society for the Study of Sport.

WRITINGS:

(With Earle F. Zeigler) *Physical Education: Progressivism or Essentialism,* Stipes, 1968.
(With Karl W. Bookwalter) *Foundations and Principles of Physical Education,* Saunders, 1969.
Toward a Philosophy of Sport, Addison-Wesley, 1972.
(With Thomas Sheehan) *An Introduction to Sport Studies: From the Classroom to the Ball Park,* W. C. Brown, 1978.
Sport Management in Schools and Colleges, Wiley, 1984.
Policy Development in Sport Management, Benchmark Press, 1987.

* * *

Van DYKE, Vernon Brumbaugh   1912-

PERSONAL: Born November 5, 1912, in Pocatello, Idaho;

son of Irvin Cloyd and Sara (Hope) Van Dyke; married Evadean Dickey, April 1, 1934; children: Joan Van Dyke Fouts, Marcia Van Dyke Shaffer. *Education:* Manchester College, B.A., 1933; University of Chicago, M.A., 1934, Ph.D., 1937.

ADDRESSES: Home—201 First Ave. #209, Iowa City, Iowa 52240. *Office*—Department of Political Science, University of Iowa, Iowa City, Iowa 52242.

CAREER: DePauw University, Greencastle, Ind., associate professor, 1937-44; Yale University, New Haven, Conn., assistant professor, 1946-49; University of Iowa, Iowa City, professor of political science, 1949—. *Military service:* U.S. Navy, 1944-46, became lieutenant in Naval Reserve.

MEMBER: American Political Science Association (member of executive council, 1961-63), Midwest Conference of Political Scientists (president, 1966-67), International Studies Association (president, 1966-67).

AWARDS, HONORS: Social Science Research Council, senior research award in governmental affairs, 1962-63; National Endowment for the Humanities senior fellowship, 1972-73; Woodrow Wilson International Center for Scholars senior fellowship, 1972-73.

WRITINGS:

International Politics, Appleton, 1957, 3rd edition, 1972.
Political Science: A Philosophical Analysis, Stanford University Press, 1960.
Pride and Power: The Rationale of the Space Program, University of Illinois Press, 1964.
Human Rights, the United States, and World Community, Oxford University Press, 1970.
(Editor) *Teaching Political Science: The Professor and the Polity,* Humanities, 1977.
The Human Rights, Ethnicity, and Discrimination, Greenwood Press, 1985.
Introduction to Politics, Nelson-Hall, 1988.

Contributor to professional journals. Editor, *Midwest Journal of Political Science,* 1960-62.

* * *

VERHOEVEN, Cornelis   1928-

PERSONAL: Born February 2, 1928, in Udenhout, Netherlands; son of Johannes (a farmer) and Johanna Verhoeven; married Janine Van de Kamp (a teacher), July 10, 1965 (divorced). *Education:* University Nymegen, Ph.D., 1956.

ADDRESSES: Home—Uilenburg 30, 5211 EV 's Hertogenbosch, Netherlands.

CAREER: Jeroen Bosch College, 's Hertogenbosch, Netherlands, teacher of Greek and Latin, 1955-82; University of Amsterdam, Amsterdam, Netherlands, professor of Greek philosophy, 1982-87, professor of metaphysics, 1987—. Weekly columnist, 1966—.

MEMBER: Maatschappy der Nederlandse Letterkunde.

AWARDS, HONORS: Anne Frank Prize, Dutch Government, 1964; Pieter Cornelisz Hooft Prize, Dutch Government, 1979.

WRITINGS:

Symboliek van de Voet (title means "The Symbolism of the Foot"), Van Gorcum, 1957.
Symboliek van de Sluier (title means "The Symbolism of the Veil"), Standaard, 1961.

(With Frederik Jacobus Johannes Buytendijk) *Taal en gezond-heid* (title means "Language and Health"), Spectrum, 1969.

Een verleden als bezit (title means "A Past as a Property"), Deventer, 1977.

PUBLISHED BY AMBO

Rondom de Leegte (title means "Around Emptiness"), 1965.
Het grote gebeuren (title means "The Great Event"), 1966.
Tegen het geweld (title means "Against Violence"), 1967.
Inleiding tot de verwondering, 1967, translation by Mary Foran published as *The Philosophy of Wonder,* Macmillan, 1972.
Omzien naar het heden: De mythe van de vooruitgang (title means "Look Back at the Present"), 1968.
Afscheid van Brabant? (title means "A Farewell to Brabant?"), 1968.
Voor eigen gebruik (title means "For the Use of Myself"), 1969.
Bijna niets (title means "Hardly Anything"), 1970.
(With Cas Eijsbouts) *Zakelijkheid en ethiek* (title means "Facts and Ethics"), 1971.
Het Leedwezen: Beschouwingen over troost en verdriet, leven en dood (title means "Mourning: Essays about Consolation and Sorrow"), 1971.
Het gewicht van de Buitenstaander (title means "The Importance of the Outsider"), 1972.
Het axioma van Geulincz (title means "The Axiom of Geulincz"), 1973.
Parafilosofen (title means "Paraphilosophers"), 1974.
De Resten van het vaderschap (title means "The Rests of Fatherhood"), 1975.
Een Vogeltje in myn buik (title means "A Little Bird in My Belly"), 1976.
Folteren om bestwil (title means "Torture for the Good"), 1977.
Herinneringen aan mijn moedertaal (title means "Memories of My Vernacular Language"), 1978.
De schaduw van een haar (title means "The Shadow of One Hair"), 1979.
Tractaat over het spieken (title means "An Essay about Cribbing"), 1980.
Merg en Been (title means "Marrow and Bone"), 1981.
Mensen in een grot (title means "People in a Cave"), 1983.
De duivelsvraag (title means "The Devil's Question"), 1983.
Voorbij het begin: De griekse filosofie in haar spiegel (title means "Beyond the Beginning: The Greek Philosophy in Her Mirror"), two volumes, 1984-85.
De letter als beeld (title means "The Letter as a Figure"), 1987.

Het medium van de waarheid (title means "The Medium of Truth"), 1988.

Also author of *Weerloos Denken* (title means "Defenseless Thinking").

OTHER

Editor of *Raam,* 1961-75.

*   *   *

VIOLA, Herman J(oseph)   1938-

PERSONAL: Born February 24, 1938, in Chicago, Ill.; son of Joseph (a carpenter) and Mary (Incollingo) Viola; married Susan Bennett (a librarian), June 13, 1964; children: Joseph, Paul, Peter. *Education:* Marquette University, B.A., 1960, M.A., 1964; Indiana University, Ph.D., 1970.

ADDRESSES: Office—Museum of Natural History, Smithsonian Institution, Washington, D.C. 20560.

CAREER: National Archives, Washington, D.C., archivist, 1966-68; *Prologue: Journal of the National Archives,* Washington, D.C., founding editor, 1968-72; Smithsonian Institution, National Anthropological Archives, Washington, D.C., director, 1972-86, Museum of Natural History, director of Quincentenary Programs, 1986—. *Military service:* U.S. Navy, 1962-64.

MEMBER: Society of American Archivists, Organization of American Historians, Western History Association.

WRITINGS:

Thomas L. McKenney: Architect of America's Early Indian Policy, 1816-1830, Swallow Press, 1974.
The Indian Legacy of Charles Bird King, Smithsonian Institution Press, 1976.
(Editor with Robert Kvasnicka) *The Commissioners of Indian Affairs,* University of Nebraska Press, 1979.
Diplomats in Buckskins: A History of Indian Delegations in Washington City, Smithsonian Institution Press, 1981.
The National Archives of the United States, Abrams, 1984.
(Editor with Carolyn Margolis) *Magnificent Voyagers,* Smithsonian Institution Press, 1985.
Exploring the West: A Smithsonian Book, Smithsonian Institution Press, 1987.

BIOGRAPHICAL/CRITICAL SOURCES:

PERIODICALS

Los Angeles Times Book Review, September 30, 1984.
Washington Post Book World, August 23, 1981.

W

WADDELL, D(avid) A(lan) G(ilmour) 1927-

PERSONAL: Born October 22, 1927, in Edinburgh, Scotland; son of David and Helen (Gilmour) Waddell; married Barbara Box, 1951; children: Louise, Clive, Adrian. *Education:* University of St. Andrews, M.A., 1949; St. John's College, Oxford, D.Phil., 1954.

ADDRESSES: Home—2 Airthrey Castle Yard, Stirling FK9 4LH, Scotland. *Office*—Department of History, University of Stirling, Stirling FK9 4LA, Scotland.

CAREER: University College of the West Indies, Kingston, Jamaica, lecturer, 1954-59; University of Edinburgh, Edinburgh, Scotland, lecturer, 1959-63, senior lecturer, 1963-68; University of Stirling, Stirling, Scotland, professor of modern history, 1968—. Visiting lecturer, University of West Indies, Trinidad, 1964-65, Universidad del Valle, Colombia, 1967, University of California, Irvine, 1971, and University of California, Santa Barbara, 1986. *Military service:* Royal Air Force, 1949-51, became Flying Officer.

MEMBER: Royal Historical Society (fellow).

WRITINGS:

British Honduras: A Historical and Contemporary Survey, Oxford University Press for Royal Institute of International Affairs, 1961, reprinted, Greenwood Press, 1981.
(Contributor) Robin Winks, editor, *The Historiography of the British Empire-Commonwealth,* Duke University Press, 1966.
The West Indies and the Guianas, Prentice-Hall, 1967.
(Contributor) Burton Benedict, editor, *Problems of Smaller Territories,* Athlore Press, 1967.
(Contributor) Peter Walne, editor, *Guide to Manuscript Sources for the History of Latin America and the Caribbean in the British Isles,* Oxford University Press, 1971.
(Contributor) John Lynch, editor, *Andres Bello: The London Years,* Richmond Publishing Co., 1982.
Gran Bretana y la Independencia de Venezuela y Colombia, Ministry of Education, Caracas, 1983.
(Contributor) Leslie Bethell, editor, *Cambridge History of Latin America,* Cambridge University Press, Volume III, 1985.
(Contributor) Alberto Filippi, editor, *Bolivar y Europa,* Presidency of the Republic, Caracas, Volume I, 1986.

Contributor to historical journals.

WORK IN PROGRESS: Venezuela, in "World Bibliographical Series," for Clio Press; British neutrality and Spanish American independence, a research project.

*   *   *

WAIN, John (Barrington) 1925-

PERSONAL: Born March 14, 1925, in Stoke-on-Trent, Staffordshire, England; son of Arnold A. (a dentist) and Anne Wain; married Marianne Urmston, 1947 (divorced, 1956); married Eirian James, 1960; children: William, Ianto, Tobias. *Education:* St. John's College, Oxford, B.A., 1946, M.A., 1950.

ADDRESSES: Home—17 Wolvercote Green, Oxford OX2 8BD, England.

CAREER: St. John's College, Oxford University, Oxford, England, Fereday Fellow, 1946-47; University of Reading, Reading, England, lecturer in English literature, 1947-55; writer and critic, 1955—. Churchill Visiting Professor at University of Bristol, 1967; visiting professor at Centre Experimental de Vincennes, University of Paris, 1969; George Elliston Lecturer on Poetry at University of Cincinnati; Professor of Poetry at Oxford University, 1973-78. Director of Poetry Book Society's festival, London, 1961.

MEMBER: Oxford Union Society.

AWARDS, HONORS: Somerset Maugham Award, 1958, for *Preliminary Essays;* Royal Society of Literature fellow, 1960; Brasenose College creative arts fellowship from Oxford University, 1971-72; James Tait Black Memorial Prize and Heinemann Award from Royal Society of Literature, both 1975, both for *Samuel Johnson;* Whitbread Literary Award, 1985, for *The Free Zone Starts Here.*

WRITINGS:

FICTION

Hurry on Down (novel), Secker & Warburg, 1953, published as *Born in Captivity,* Knopf, 1954, published as *Hurry on Down,* Viking, 1965, reprinted with a new introduction by the author, Secker & Warburg, 1978.
Living in the Present (novel), Secker & Warburg, 1955, Putnam, 1960.

The Contenders (novel), St. Martin's, 1958.
A Travelling Woman (novel), St. Martin's, 1959.
Nuncle and Other Stories (short stories), Macmillan (London), 1960, St. Martin's, 1961.
Strike the Father Dead (novel), St. Martin's, 1962.
The Young Visitors (novel), Viking, 1965.
Death of the Hind Legs and Other Stories (short stories), Viking, 1966.
The Smaller Sky (novel), Macmillan, 1967.
A Winter in the Hills (novel; also see below), Viking, 1970.
The Life Guard (short stories), Macmillan, 1971, Viking, 1972.
King Caliban and Other Stories, (short stories), Macmillan, 1978.
The Pardoner's Tale (novel), Macmillan, 1978, Viking, 1979.
Lizzie's Floating Shop (juvenile), Bodley Head, 1981.
Young Shoulders (juvenile), Macmillan, 1982, published as *The Free Zone Starts Here,* Delacorte, 1982.

POETRY

Mixed Feelings, University of Reading, 1951.
(Contributor) D. J. Enright, editor, *Poets of the Fifties,* [London], 1955.
A Word Carved on a Sill, St. Martin's, 1956.
(Contributor) Robert Conquest, editor, *New Lines,* [London], 1956.
Weep before God, St. Martin's, 1961.
A Song about Major Eatherly, Qara Press (Iowa City), 1961.
(Contributor) Chad Walsh, editor, *Today's Poets,* Scribner, 1964.
Wildtrack, Macmillan, 1965, Viking, 1966.
Letters to Five Artists, Macmillan, 1969, Viking, 1970.
The Shape of Feng, Covent Garden Press, 1972.
Feng, Viking, 1975.
Poems for the Zodiac (limited edition), Pisces Press, 1980.
Thinking about Mr. Person, Chimaera Press (Kent), 1980.
Poems, 1949-1979, Macmillan, 1981.
The Twofold, Hunting Raven Press (Somerset), 1981.
Mid-week Period Return: Home Thoughts of a Native, Celandine Press (Stratford-upon-Avon), 1982.

PLAYS

"Harry in the Night," first produced in Stoke-on-Trent, England, 1975.
"You Wouldn't Remember" (radio play), first produced by British Broadcasting Corporation (BBC), 1978.
"A Winter in the Hills" (radio play; adapted from the author's novel), 1981.
Frank (radio play; first produced by BBC), Amber Lane Press, 1984.
"Good Morning Blues" (radio play), first produced by BBC, 1986.

NONFICTION

Preliminary Essays, St. Martin's, 1957.
Gerard Manley Hopkins: An Idiom of Desperation, Oxford University Press, 1959, reprinted, Folcroft Editions, 1974.
(Contributor) Tom Maschler, editor, *Declaration,* MacGibbon & Kee, 1959.
Sprightly Running: Part of an Autobiography, Macmillan, 1962, St. Martin's, 1963.
Essays on Literature and Ideas, St. Martin's, 1963.
The Living World of Shakespeare: A Playgoer's Guide, St. Martin's, 1964.
Arnold Bennett, Columbia University Press, 1967.

A House for the Truth: Critical Essays, Macmillan, 1972, Viking, 1973.
Samuel Johnson (biography; Book-of-the-Month Club selection), Macmillan, 1974, Viking, 1975.
Professing Poetry, Macmillan, 1977, Viking, 1978.
Dear Shadows: Portraits from Memory, J. Murray, 1986.

EDITOR

Contemporary Reviews of Romantic Poetry, Barnes & Noble, 1953.
Interpretations: Essays on Twelve English Poems, Routledge & Kegan Paul, 1955, Hillary, 1957, 2nd edition, Routledge & Kegan Paul, 1972.
International Literary Annual, two volumes, J. Calder, 1958, 1959, Criterion, 1959, 1960.
Frances Burney d'Arblay, *Fanny Burney's Diary,* Folio Society, 1961.
Anthology of Modern Poetry, Hutchinson, 1963.
(Author of introduction and notes) *Pope,* Dell, 1963.
(Author of introduction) Thomas Hardy, *The Dynasts,* St. Martin's, 1966.
Selected Shorter Poems of Thomas Hardy, Macmillan, 1966.
Selected Stories of Thomas Hardy, St. Martin's, 1966.
Shakespeare: Macbeth; a Casebook, Macmillan, 1968, Aurora Publications, 1970.
Shakespeare: Othello; a Casebook, Macmillan, 1971.
Johnson as Critic, Routledge & Kegan Paul, 1973.
Samuel Johnson, *Lives of the English Poets,* Dent, 1975, Dutton, 1976.
Johnson on Johnson: A Selection of the Personal and Autobiographical Writings of Samuel Johnson, Dutton, 1976.
Edmund Wilson: The Man and His Work, New York University Press, 1978 (published in England as *An Edmund Wilson Celebration,* Phaidon Press, 1978).
Personal Choice: A Poetry Anthology, David & Charles, 1978.
(With wife, Eirian Wain) *The New Wessex Selection of Thomas Hardy's Poetry,* Macmillan, 1978.
Anthology of Contemporary Poetry: Post-War to the Present, Hutchinson, 1979.
Everyman's Book of English Verse, Dent, 1981.
Arnold Bennett, *The Old Wives' Tale,* Penguin, 1983.
James Hogg, *The Private Memoirs and Confessions of a Justified Sinner,* Penguin, 1983.

OTHER

(With Ted Walker) *Modern Poetry* (sound recording), BFA Educational Media, 1972.
The Poetry of John Wain (sound recording), Jeffrey Norton, 1976.
Geoffrey Halson, editor, *A John Wain Selection,* Longman, 1977.
(Translator from Anglo-Saxon) *The Seafarer,* Grenville Press, 1982.

Contributor to numerous periodicals, including *New Republic, Observer, New Yorker, Times Literary Supplement, Saturday Evening Post, Harper's Bazaar,* and *Ladies' Home Journal.* Founding editor of *Mandrake,* 1944.

SIDELIGHTS: For more than thirty years, John Wain, a British man of letters, has devoted his energies primarily to writing. The diversity of his output demonstrates his commitment to his craft—since 1951 he has penned novels, short stories, poetry, critical essays, and a highly acclaimed biography, *Samuel Johnson.* According to *Dictionary of Literary Biography* contributor A. T. Tolley, Wain's novels and stories "make up one of the more substantial bodies of contemporary fiction in English,'' while his poetry ''stands as an important contribution to his total achievement and displays that concern with the life of literature in our day that has permeated his work.'' Wain is likewise commended for his critical judgments that prove him ''adamantly committed to the mystery of literary truths that can advance the universal human experience,'' in the words of *Dictionary of Literary Biography* essayist Augustus M. Kolich. Kolich calls Wain ''an iconoclast who is uncompromising in his dedication to the belief that in a world where 'destruction and disintegration' are the norm, only the artist's creative language can clear the ruins and establish a foundation for heroic individualism.'' Wain's writings pursue this high ideal in an unpretentious and readable style; Susan Wood notes in the *Washington Post Book World* that the author, while an Oxford graduate, ''is no dour Oxford don. . . . Instead, he typifies the very best of what one might call 'Englishness'—good sense, moderation, a feeling for language, erudition without pretension, and wit.''

Addressing Wain's fiction specifically, *Esquire* critic Geoffrey Wolff comments: ''From his first novel, *Hurry on Down* (1953), Wain has concerned himself with contemporary English manners, with the small choices that comprise a program of values. . . . Wain writes about boredom, the killing regularity of diminished, stunted lives; because he is so skilled a writer, he creates an accurate evocation of the awful coziness and regularity of English conventions.'' Wain is also preoccupied, in much of his work, with the survival of individual dignity and purpose in a world where bullying and domination often prevail. Kolich states: ''In Wain's criticism of contemporary English society, his target is clearly the totalitarian consciousness which has as its object the manipulation and domination of the small child in all of us—that part of our self-concept that naturally sees through folly and pretense and always expects to be left uncontrolled and free. Hence, Wain's fiction is above all morally pledged to a set of values that aim at offending the status quo, when it seems either silly, absurd, or oppressive, and championing commonsense individualism, whenever it can be championed in a world of antiheroes.''

This theme of individual rebellion is particularly prevalent in *Hurry on Down*, the novel that established Wain among the clan of writers known as ''angry young men'' in postwar Great Britain. Set in a provincial town similar to the one in which Wain himself was raised, *Hurry on Down* describes the picaresque adventures of Charles Lumley, a cynical youth who contrives to avoid the respectable middle class lifestyle expected of him by his education and upbringing. *Times Literary Supplement* reviewer Blake Morrison suggests that Lumley could be seen ''as representative of a 'less deceived' post-war generation hostile to old values and intent upon radical political change. He and other new heroes in fiction were the subject of much journalistic discussion—discussion which ensured *Hurry on Down*'s success.'' According to Kolich, Wain came to be identified with his alienated protagonist, even though the author was never comfortable with the way most critics associated him with the ''angry decade'' movement. Morrison even suggests that the true political significance of the Lumley character ''lies in his concern to avoid commitments and his willingness to adapt himself—both features of an era when not anger and rebellion but 'Butskellism' and 'the End of Ideology' were dominant ideals.'' In any case, *Hurry on Down* was a commercial and critical success for Wain. *South Atlantic Quarterly* contributor Elgin W. Mellown claims that the work ''holds the reader by its verisimilitude and artfully contrived

though seemingly unposed candid-camera shots of English life in the late forties and early fifties.'' In his book *Tradition and Dream: The English and American Novel from the Twenties to Our Time,* Walter Allen concludes that *Hurry on Down* made Wain ''the satirist of this period of social change.''

Disillusioned Englishmen figure in many of Wain's subsequent novels, including *Strike the Father Dead, The Contenders,* and *The Smaller Sky.* Kolich writes: ''In the process of breaking away from the confines of economic and social success and the seductive powers of competitive capitalism, Wain's heroes still must face the unsettling business of reordering their lives outside the conventional set plans that either religion or business might offer. . . . Very often, . . .they seem lost and unable to cope with the shifting emotional currents generated by those toward whom they feel drawn.'' In general, critics have found Wain's novels of the late 1950s and 1960s less successful than his debut fiction work. As Mellown describes it, Wain ''commands an almost flawless technique and can write in a truthful, accurate, and revealing way about human beings interacting on the personal level; but when he looks beyond these individuals and attempts to put them into a larger focus or to give them a wider significance, their thoughts and beliefs condemn them as second-rate.'' In his book entitled *Postwar British Fiction: New Accents and Attitudes,* James Gindin contends: ''For the kind of point Wain is making about the contemporary world that he depicts with such specificity, force, and intelligence, he does require some tangible expression of the value of the personal and the humane. But the form of expression often lacks a comic richness that would avoid both the brittle gimmick and the heavy sediment of emotion.'' Undaunted by the sometimes harsh criticism, Wain has continued to produce fiction. His more recent works have found favor with reviewers, and, in retrospect, his seriousness of purpose and sheer productivity have led Mellown to suggest that ''these [early] novels are the most impressive output of any of the postwar British writers.''

Kolich describes *A Winter in the Hills,* Wain's 1970 novel, as ''perhaps the most typical . . . in terms of themes and characters.'' The story concerns a philologist who moves to North Wales and becomes involved in a local bus driver's efforts to thwart a business takeover. *Newsweek* contributor Raymond A. Sokolov finds the work ''an unashamedly romantic, heroic, plot-heavy, character-ridden, warm piece of narration with a beginning, a middle and an end. . . . Wain proves there is still much life in the old tricks.'' A *Times Literary Supplement* reviewer asserts that *A Winter in the Hills* ''goes farther, perhaps, in defining and developing Mr. Wain's basic concerns as a writer than most of his earlier works; and does it with a growing maturity and conviction.'' The reviewer notes Wain's continuing interest in the quality of individual living, and adds, ''Observing social situations, catching hints of character and motive in conversational habits, contriving elaborate and efficient plots—these continue to be [Wain's] strengths.''

The Pardoner's Tale, published in 1978, has proven even more popular than *A Winter in the Hills.* In *Time,* R. Z. Sheppard calls the work a ''thoughtful treatment of two middle-aged men joyfully making fools of themselves over younger women.'' The book is a novel-within-a-novel; an author, Giles Hermitage, seeks to resolve his own romantic misadventures by writing about a fictitious businessman and *his* encounter with a woman. The resulting pastiche of stories evokes ''a steady sensuous glow that warms the brain,'' according to Sheppard. *Saturday Review* correspondent Carole Cook contends that it is Wain himself who ''shines as the hero'' in *The Pardoner's*

Tale. "He has beaten the clock," Cook writes, "enticed us into the game, and held us so captivated by his voice of a man desperate for a second chance at life that it becomes, word by word, our own." Amy Wilentz argues a different viewpoint in the *Nation.* She finds *The Pardoner's Tale* a "well-intentioned book," but subsequently declares that there is "so little true atmosphere in Wain's book that his characters, who are sporadically well drawn, also seem shadowy and displaced." Conversely, D. A. N. Jones praises the novel in the *Times Literary Supplement.* "The lineaments of gratified desire are persuasively drawn," Jones asserts. "Precise details of plot and character dissolve into an amorous haze, spreading delight. . . . John Wain's novel is written in a warmly forgiving spirit; and this, together with its engaging riggishness, contributes to the reader's delight."

In an essay for the *Contemporary Authors Autobiography Series,* Wain claims that his book about Samuel Johnson was "the most successful work of my middle life." *Samuel Johnson* provides a comprehensive biography of one of England's leading literary figures, written expressly for the general reader. Most critics praise the account not only for its accessibility to the non-academic public, but also for its subtle reflections on the literary life in any age. *Harper's* reviewer Jack Richardson writes: "To John Wain, Johnson is not only a great figure in literature, he is also a magnificent companion, someone who brings with him a feeling of good company when met for the first time or recalled for the hundredth; and it is this feeling which Wain wishes to celebrate, and which makes *Samuel Johnson* more than anything else a narrative of friendship." In the *Nation,* Robert L. Chapman states: "John Wain's own stature as a literary-academic person assures us a voice both authoritative and eloquent" in *Samuel Johnson,* but the author is still "less interested in the precise delineation of a dead man than in the appraisal of an immortal colleague. . . . I cherish the lively, novelistic quality of [Wain's] book, where I can see an idea being born, growing, and at last enforcing itself as the prime focus of meaning."

Anatole Broyard offers further commendations for *Samuel Johnson* in the *New York Times:* "A good biography of a great man is one of the best ways to define the society he concentrated in himself. Mr. Wain's 'Samuel Johnson' is a brilliant picture of 18th-century England, too." *New York Times Book Review* contributor Christopher Ricks calls the work "vividly humane" and suggests that it "does justice to the range and depth of this just and merciful man. . . . It is a noble story nobly told." Ricks adds: "Johnson's was essentially a commemorative spirit, and Mr. Wain's biography is a dignified achievement because it too is undertaken in a commemorative spirit. Not 'let me tell you about this man,' but 'let us remember together this man.'" As George Gale concludes in the *Spectator,* Wain's biography "is at the end seen to be a very substantial work of synthesis, intuitive understanding and intellectual grasp. . . . We are left with . . . a work which, by persuading us of the stature of its subject, establishes at the same time a very considerable stature of its own."

Wain's poetry is also seen as a significant contribution to the body of English letters since 1945. Tolley explains that, in his early poems, Wain is "affronting the whole modernist poetic, where the emphasis had been on the image, on the maximization of sensory impact, and where generalizations had been seen as the enemies of the poetic. Wain . . . is comfortable with a poetry of statement. However, these [early] poems are far from being doctrinaire literary stunts. Many stand out as simple and passionate statements on what have proved to be

some of Wain's abiding themes: love, isolation, honesty, and sympathy for the deprived. . . . Poems . . . seemingly artificial . . . survive as expressions of tenderness." Wain is perhaps better known for his long poems such as *Wildtrack, Feng,* and *Letters to Five Artists.* "Wain's devotion to the long poem," writes Tolley, ". . . is at once courageous and surprising in view of his steady adherence to the realistic tradition in his novels. Whatever may be said about his attainment in his longer poems, he has not been content with the diminished ambitions that have often led to diminished poetry in Britain the last quarter of a century." According to Philip Gardner in the *Times Literary Supplement,* Wain, "concerned with the communication both of humane values and of an imaginative response to experience, . . . sometimes errs on the side of too much clarity: over-insistent, he button-holes the reader or goes on too long." Derek Stanford expresses a different opinion in *Books:* "Wain's unitary theme is the relationship between art and life—particularly that between the individual work and the individual producer. . . . All in all, *Letters to Five Artists* is full of vigorous poetry, written in sinewy masculine language but without any of that paraded toughness sometimes indulged in by the New Movement." A *Times Literary Supplement* reviewer concludes that there is "no deliberate order or consistency in Mr. Wain's reflections, except for the unity given by an underlying compassion."

In 1973 Wain was elected to the prestigious Professor of Poetry chair at Oxford. He held the chair for five years, giving lectures on subjects that reflected his critical concerns. These lectures are collected in *Professing Poetry,* his most recent volume of criticism. Kolich contends that, as a literary critic, Wain projects an iconoclasm "derived from a privately felt moral sense of self-determination, a concept that he hopes can be shared by a community of equals, scholars and artists, working toward 'the establishment of a hierarchy of quality.'" According to Herbert Leibowitz in the *New York Times Book Review,* Wain "detests the art chatter and sensationalism of the modern age, with its denial of complexity and the rich diapason of language. For Wain, the imagination is under siege by an 'insistence on explicitness,' 'intellectual slapstick' replaces thought, and our art 'abandons the search for standards' by stupidly rejecting the past." As might be expected of one educated at and honored by Oxford, Wain's critical judgments reside "in his devotion to the idea that the study of the best literature that has been written can provide the criteria for the best judgments," Kolich concludes.

"As a writer I have regarded my basic material as the word rather than as this or that literary form," Wain states in the *Contemporary Authors Autobiography Series.* Wain refuses to be classified as "primarily" one specific sort of writer—novelist, poet, or essayist. "I am always primarily what I am doing at the moment," he explains. The author also claims that he knew from an early age that he intended to write, the career being "not a profession but a condition." He offers these thoughts on literature: "The books I most admire are those that take human life as I know it and live it from day to day and describe it honestly and lovingly, and illuminate it fearlessly. As a novelist I have always seen myself as contributing to the central tradition of the novel, the tradition that grew up in the eighteenth century, which means recognisable human beings in familiar settings, doing the kind of things that you and I do, with all the usual consequences. . . . Everything important, everything lyrical and tragic and horrifying and uplifting and miraculous, is there in our ordinary lives if we can open our eyes and see it."

Mellown observes that Wain, who labors "within a tradition sustained by the living presence of earlier literature," is a writer who has consciously developed his skills over three decades. Of all the so-called former "angry young men," according to Mellown, Wain "represents perhaps better than any other the traditional British novelist. His output (in both quantity and versatility) and its quality cause him to be reckoned an outstanding figure of his generation." In *Atlantic*, Benajmin DeMott concludes that in his sober manner, Wain has avoided gags, touched on hard subjects, celebrated classic authors, and produced, on occasion, "an elevated, unironic, unself-protective case for Art-in-the-large." The author, who now divides his time between homes in Oxford and Wales, continues to work—as he puts it in his memoir *Dear Shadows: Portraits from Memory*—"entirely at my own pace and my own sweet will."

AVOCATIONAL INTERESTS: Walking, canoeing.

BIOGRAPHICAL/CRITICAL SOURCES:

BOOKS

Allen, Walter, *Tradition and Dream: The English and American Novel from the Twenties to Our Time*, Phoenix House, 1964.

Allen, Walter, *The Modern Novel*, Dutton, 1965.

Allsop, Kenneth, *The Angry Decade*, P. Owen, 1958.

Burgess, Anthony, *The Novel Now: A Guide to Contemporary Fiction*, Norton, 1967.

Contemporary Authors Autobiography Series, Volume IV, Gale, 1986.

Contemporary Fiction in America and England, 1950-1970, Gale, 1976.

Contemporary Literary Criticism, Gale, Volume II, 1974, Volume XI, 1979, Volume XV, 1980.

Dictionary of Literary Biography, Gale, Volume XV: *British Novelists, 1930-1959*, 1983, Volume XXVII: *Poets of Great Britain and Ireland, 1945-1960*, 1984.

Enright, D. J., *Conspirators and Poets*, Dufour, 1966.

Fraser, G. S., *The Modern Writer and His World*, Penguin, 1964.

Gerard, David, *My Work as a Novelist: John Wain*, Drake Educational Associates (Cardiff, Wales), 1978.

Gindin, James J., *Postwar British Fiction: New Accents and Attitudes*, University of California Press, 1962.

Karl, Frederick R., *The Contemporary English Novel*, Farrar, Straus, 1962.

Maschler, Tom, editor, *Declaration*, MacGibbon & Kee, 1959.

O'Connor, William Van, *The New University Wits and the End of Modernism*, Southern Illinois University Press, 1963.

Ries, Lawrence R., *Wolf Masks: Violence in Contemporary Poetry*, Kennikat, 1977.

Salwak, Dale, *John Braine and John Wain: A Reference Guide*, G. K. Hall, 1980.

Salwak, Dale, *John Wain*, G. K. Hall, 1981.

Wain, John, *Sprightly Running: Part of an Autobiography*, Macmillan, 1962, St. Martin's, 1963.

Wain, John, *Dear Shadows: Portraits from Memory*, John Murray, 1986.

PERIODICALS

Atlantic, May, 1979.
Best Sellers, October 15, 1971.
Books, February, 1970, June, 1970.
Books Abroad, summer, 1967.

Books and Bookmen, October, 1967.
Commonweal, February 10, 1967.
Contemporary Review, October, 1978, January, 1979.
Esquire, April 10, 1979.
Globe and Mail (Toronto), June 16, 1984.
Harper's, July, 1975, July, 1979.
Listener, October 12, 1967, October 26, 1978.
London Magazine, November, 1956, October, 1967.
Los Angeles Times, May 17, 1970.
Los Angeles Times Book Review, August 6, 1978.
Nation, October 5, 1970, April 19, 1975, April 7, 1979.
New Leader, July 3, 1978.
New Republic, March 15, 1975.
New Statesman, October 6, 1967, May 19, 1978.
Newsweek, September 14, 1970, February 17, 1975.
New Yorker, April 28, 1975, May 7, 1979.
New York Review of Books, April 14, 1966, March 23, 1967, February 20, 1975.
New York Times, February 13, 1975, December 26, 1978, April 6, 1979.
New York Times Book Review, January 25, 1959, October 24, 1965, December 18, 1966, September 13, 1970, March 19, 1972, July 29, 1973, March 16, 1975, March 25, 1979.
Observer, October 8, 1967, May 3, 1970, December 20, 1970.
Poetry, February, 1978.
Punch, October 11, 1967.
Saturday Review, May 7, 1955, July 27, 1957, October 16, 1965, December 3, 1966, February 8, 1975, April 28, 1979.
South Atlantic Quarterly, summer, 1969, autumn, 1979.
Spectator, May 16, 1970, November 30, 1974, May 3, 1986.
Stand, Volume XVII, number 1, 1975-76.
Time, April 2, 1979.
Times (London), January 7, 1984, April 24, 1986.
Times Educational Supplement, July 20, 1956.
Times Literary Supplement, July 26, 1963, July 29, 1965, September 30, 1965, October 3, 1966, October 5, 1967, July 3, 1969, February 12, 1970, April 30, 1971, November 19, 1971, March 8, 1974, November 22, 1974, September 26, 1975, February 24, 1978, May 19, 1978, October 13, 1978, November 17, 1978, February 27, 1981, July 10, 1981, October 15, 1982, April 25, 1986.
Washington Post Book World, February 23, 1975, October 8, 1978, April 22, 1979, May 13, 1984.
Wilson Library Bulletin, May, 1963.
World Literature Today, spring, 1979.
Yale Review, winter, 1967.

—Sketch by Anne Janette Johnson

*   *   *

WALKER, Robert H(arris)   1924-

PERSONAL: Born March 15, 1924, in Cincinnati, Ohio; married Grace V. Burtt, 1953; children: three. *Education:* Northwestern University, B.S., 1945; Columbia University, M.A., 1950; University of Pennsylvania, Ph.D., 1955.

ADDRESSES: Home—3915 Huntington St. N.W., Washington, D.C. 20015. *Office*—George Washington University, Washington, D.C. 20052.

CAREER: U.S. Military Government, Shizuoka, Japan, education specialist, 1946-47; Carnegie Institute of Technology (now Carnegie-Mellon University), Pittsburgh, Pa., instructor, 1950-51; University of Pennsylvania, Philadelphia, instructor,

1953-54; Haverford College, Haverford, Pa., instructor, 1954-55; University of Wyoming, Laramie, assistant professor of American studies, 1955-59, acting director of School of American Studies, 1956-59; George Washington University, Washington, D.C., associate professor of American literature, 1959-63, professor of American civilization, 1963—, director of American Studies Program, 1959-66, and 1968-70. Visiting instructor at Jamestown College, 1961, Kyoto-Doshisha, 1964, Stetson University, 1965, and University of Hawaii, 1967. Director of Peace Corps training in American studies and other disciplines at several universities, 1962-65; director, division of education public programs, National Endowment for the Humanities, 1966-68. Commissioner, Japan-U.S. Friendship Commission, 1977-81; consultant to U.S. Information Agency, 1959—, and to other government and private agencies. Director, Rose Bibliographical Project, 1974-75; Washington editor, Algonquin Books, 1983—. *Military service:* U.S. Naval Reserve, 1942-61; on active duty, 1943-46; became lieutenant junior grade.

MEMBER: American Studies Association (national president, 1970-71), Phi Beta Kappa, Cosmos Club.

AWARDS, HONORS: U.S. Department of State specialist grants to Japan, 1964 and 1975, Germany, 1965 and 1986, Sweden, 1965 and 1983, Thailand, Iran, and Greece, all in 1975, Israel, 1980, Brazil, 1981, and Italy, 1986; research grants from Washington S.T.A.R., 1966-67, and National Endowment for the Humanities, 1966-69; Fulbright grants to Australia, New Zealand, and Philippines, all in 1971, and Sweden, 1987; fellow, George Lieb Harrison, 1952-53 and 1954-55, Woodrow Wilson International Center, 1972-73, Rockefeller Research Center, 1979, Huntington Library, 1980, and Hoover Institution, 1980.

WRITINGS:

American Studies in the United States, Louisiana State University Press, 1958.

The Poet and the Gilded Age: Social Themes in Late Nineteenth-Century American Verse, University of Pennsylvania Press, 1963.

Everyday Life in the Age of Enterprise, Putnam, 1967, published as *Life in the Age of Enterprise,* Capricorn Books, 1971.

(Contributor) *New Directions in Graduate Education,* Council of Graduate Schools in the U.S., 1968.

(Contributor) A. B. Callow, editor, *American Urban History,* Oxford University Press, 1968.

(Contributor) *Histoire du Development Culturel et Scientifique de l'Humanite,* United Nations Educational, Scientific and Cultural Organization, 1969.

(Contributor) *Notable American Women,* Belknap, 1971.

(Author of introduction) Kenneth Schuyler Lynn, editor, *Visions of America: Eleven Historical Essays,* Greenwood Press, 1973.

(Author of introduction) Ralph H. Gabriel, editor, *American Values: Continuity and Change,* Greenwood Press, 1974.

(Editor and author of introduction) *American Studies Abroad,* Greenwood Press, 1976.

(Editor and author of introduction) *The Reform Spirit in America: A Documentation of the Patterns of Reform in the American Republic,* Putnam, 1976.

(Editor and author of introduction) *American Studies: Topics and Sources,* Greenwood Press, 1976.

(Contributor) C. L. Cooper, editor, *Growth in America,* Greenwood Press, 1976.

(Author of introduction) Robert Ernest Spiller, editor, *Milestones in American Literary History,* Greenwood Press, 1977.

(Author of introduction) Leonard Doob, editor, *Ezra Pound Speaking: Radio Speeches of Ezra Pound,* Greenwood Press, 1978.

(Contributor) J. C. Mickelson, editor, *Images of the American in the Arts,* Kendall/Hunt, 1978.

(Author of introduction) Joseph S. Tulchin, editor, *Hemispheric Perspectives on the United States,* Greenwood Press, 1978.

(Author of introduction) W. A. Linn, *Horace Greeley,* Chelsea, 1980.

(Contributor) *The Chinese Ideal and the American Dream,* Academia Sinica, 1980.

American Society, Nan'Un Do, 1980.

(Contributor) Richard Dorson, editor, *Handbook of American Folklore,* Indiana University Press, 1983.

(Editor and author of introduction, both with Jefferson Kellogg) *Sources for American Studies,* Greenwood Press, 1983.

(Contributor) Stephen B. Oates, editor, *Portrait of America,* Volume II, Houghton, 1983.

(Author of introduction) Clifford Brown and Robert J. Walker, compilers, *A Campaign of Ideas: The 1980 Anderson/Lucey Platform,* Greenwood Press, 1984.

Reform in America: The Continuing Frontier, University Press of Kentucky, 1985.

(With Gabriel) *The Course of American Democratic Thought,* 3rd edition, Greenwood Press, 1986.

Editor of "Contributions in American Studies" monograph series, Greenwood Press, 1970—. Contributor of articles and book reviews to literary and historical journals, including *American Historical Review, American Literature, American Quarterly, American Studies International, Christian Science Monitor, Commonweal, Pennsylvania Literary Review,* and *Shenandoah.* Editor, *American Quarterly,* 1953-54; senior editor, *American Studies International,* 1970-81.

WORK IN PROGRESS: The history of ideas as an organizing principle in cultural history; a study of social attitudes in Middle America, and further work on reform.

*   *   *

WALKER, Robert W(ayne) 1948-

PERSONAL: Born November 17, 1948, in Corinth, Miss.; son of Richard Herman and Janie (McEachern) Walker; married Cheryl Ann Ernst, September 8, 1967; children: Stephen Robert. *Education:* Northwestern University, B.S., 1971, M.S., 1972, additional study, 1975. *Politics:* "Nonpartisan."

ADDRESSES: Home—Route 2, Old Market Rd., Potsdam, N.Y. 13676. *Agent*—Adele Leone, 26 Nantucket Place, Scarsdale, N.Y. 10583.

CAREER: Forest Road Junior High School, LaGrange, Ill., English teacher, 1971-72; Northwestern University, Evanston, Ill., associate registrar, 1972-76; American Dietetic Association, Chicago, Ill., assistant coordinator of records in education department, 1976-81; currently a full-time free-lance writer and substitute teacher.

MEMBER: Authors Guild, Authors League of America.

WRITINGS:

Sub-Zero! (suspense novel), Leisure Books, 1979.

Daniel Webster Jackson and the Wrongway Railway (young adult novel), Oak Tree, 1982.
(With Donald W. Kruse and others) *There's a Skunk in My Trunk,* May Davenport, 1984.
Brain Watch, Leisure Books, 1985.
Search for the Nile (young adult novel), Bantam, 1986.
Spotty (juvenile picture book), May Davenport, 1986.
Salem's Child, Leisure Books, 1987.
Aftershock, St. Martin's, 1987.
Disembodied, St. Martin's, 1988.

Also author of *Bloodroot,* an adult historical novel, and *Indian Brigades in the Civil War,* nonfiction. Creator of "Battlestormer" (computer software), Home Computer Software, 1985. Contributor of articles, stories, and reviews to magazines.

WORK IN PROGRESS: "Body Parts," a series of adult horror novels, book number one entitled *Floaters.*

SIDELIGHTS: Robert W. Walker writes: "I begin a murder mystery with a chapter which raises untold questions, for which no one knows the answers, not even me. All my books require an evolutionary period in which plot and character percolate, grow, ripen, and answer the questions created in the first chapter. I combine the murder mystery and horror with science fiction/science fact in a 'what if' plot. All of my science fiction is careful to build on science fact. A 'what if' plot is the basic tool of the science fiction and mystery writer. What if the sun doesn't come up tomorrow? What if it starts to rain and never stops? What if all the plants begin to die? What happens to people?

"My purpose in writing at all is to fulfill a need in myself and to speak to people through my writing. I feel empty when I'm not writing, and I get *irritable.* All my books, horror or history, popularize a body of knowledge, science or field: meteorology, brain research, medicine, or history, for instance, as a backdrop to murder. *Brain Watch,* I hope, makes brain research fascinating and understandable for the general public. *Salem's Child* goes into historic horror and genealogy when a detective goes looking for a serial killer and finds a demon.

"I began writing in the horror genre late, but looking back at my early attempts at writing, the *fantastic* was always there. Horror writing is the most exciting field right now, and like the mystery, it teaches you to plot tightly. Most importantly, it teaches you to write in a compelling manner, so that any 'dull' science or 'history' can be made exciting if someone's become a 'victim' of the science or the history, as in *Salem's Child.*

"I still write historical novels but am turning them into 'mystery histories.' In effect, the principles used in writing a winning murder mystery can and should be applied to writing historical fiction to culminate in a fast-paced historical novel that enhances and retains the integrity of historic fact.

"Every novel I've written, no matter the category, has taught me the truth of doing: writing is an activity. Learning to write is not theoretical classroom stuff. It's a professional activity. No class can teach the craft. You become a craftsman at writing by doing it—picking up pen, pencil, typewriter, and going after the words. 'Write' is active, so if you're going to write, do it actively. Write your novel and don't look back. If the draft you complete is a terrible novel, you rewrite it or you go on to another, but in the original writing (and rewriting) you learn more than anyone can teach. It's little different from an architect who learns with each new project.

"Publishers are turning to the manuscripts that come to them in polished, final form, so make yours the best it can be. Visualize every scene. This is 90 percent of what is called the imagination."

BIOGRAPHICAL/CRITICAL SOURCES:

PERIODICALS

Elgin Herald, July 2, 1979.
Esprit, July, 1979.
Publishers Weekly, May 28, 1979, June 4, 1982.
Syracuse Herald-American, February 3, 1985.
Watertown Daily Times, January 28, 1985, February 25, 1985, April 3, 1985.

*   *   *

WALKER, Willard (Brewer)   1926-

PERSONAL: Born July 29, 1926, in Boston, Mass.; son of William H. C. and Helen (Brewer) Walker; married C. Pearline Large, October 18, 1952; children: Christopher William, Andrew Francis. *Education:* Harvard University, A.B., 1950; University of Arizona, M.A., 1953; Cornell University, Ph.D., 1964.

ADDRESSES: Home—Culver Lane, Portland, Conn. 06480. *Office*—Department of Anthropology, Wesleyan University, Middletown, Conn. 06457.

CAREER: University of Chicago, Chicago, Ill., research associate of Carnegie Corporation Cross-Cultural Education Project, 1964-66; Wesleyan University, Middletown, Conn., began as assistant professor, became associate professor, 1966-77, professor of anthropology, 1977—. *Wartime service:* American Field Service ambulance driver, 1945; received Italy Star from British Army.

MEMBER: American Anthropological Association, Society for Applied Anthropology, Linguistic Society of America, American Ethnological Society, American Society for Ethnohistory.

WRITINGS:

Cherokee Primer, [Tahlequah, Okla.], 1965.
(With Watt Spade) *Cherokee Stories,* Laboratory of Anthropology, Wesleyan University, 1966.
(Contributor) Walter Goldschmidt, editor, *Exploring the Ways of Mankind,* Holt, 2nd edition, 1971.
(With father, William H. C. Walker) *A History of World's End,* Trustees of Reservations, Inc. (Milton, Mass.), 1973.
(Contributor) James P. Spradley and Michael A. Rynkiewich, editors, *The Nacirema: Readings on American Culture,* Little, Brown, 1975.
(Contributor) M. Dale Kinkade, K. L. Hale, and O. Werner, editors, *Linguistics and Anthropology: In Honor of C. F. Voegelin,* Peter de Ridder Press, 1975.
(Contributor) James J. Crawford, editor, *Studies in Southeastern Indian Languages,* University of Georgia Press, 1975.
(Contributor) W. C. Sturtevant, editor, *Handbook of North American Indians,* Volume IX, Smithsonian Institution Press, 1979.
(Contributor with Gregory Buesing and Robert H. Conkling) Ernest Schusky, editor, *Political Organization of Native North Americans,* University Press of America, 1980.
(Contributor) Charles Ferguson and Shirley Brice Heath, editors, *Language in the USA,* Oxford University Press, 1981.

(Contributor) George P. Castile and Gilbert Kushner, editors, *Persistent Peoples,* University of Arizona Press, 1981.
(Editor with Lydia L. Wyckoff) *Hopis, Tewas, and the American Road,* Wesleyan University Press, 1983.

*   *   *

WALL, Robert Emmet, Jr. 1937-

PERSONAL: Born April 29, 1937, in New York, N.Y.; became naturalized Canadian citizen, 1976; son of Robert Emmet (a salesman) and Sabina (Daly) Wall; married Regina Palasek (a college professor), August 1, 1959; children: Elizabeth Ann, Regina Ellen, Amy Victoria, Christopher, Craig. *Education:* Holy Cross College, A.B., 1960; Yale University, M.A., 1961, Ph.D., 1965.

ADDRESSES: Home—523 West 9th St., Erie, Pa. 16502. *Office*—Gannon University, Erie, Pa. 16541.

CAREER: Duke University, Durham, N.C., instructor in history, 1963-65; Michigan State University, East Lansing, assistant professor, 1965-70, associate professor of history, 1970; Concordia University, Montreal, Quebec, associate professor, 1970-72, professor of history, 1972-80, chairman of department, 1972-77, provost, 1977-80; Fairleigh Dickinson University, Rutherford, N.J., provost, 1980-84, acting vice president, 1984-85; Gannon University, Erie, Pa., vice president, 1986—.

MEMBER: American Historical Association, Organization of American Historians.

WRITINGS:

Massachusetts Bay: The Crucial Decade, 1640-1650, Yale University Press, 1972.
The Canadians, Seal Books, Volume I: *Blackrobe,* 1981, Volume II: *Bloodbrothers,* 1981, Volume III: *Birthright,* 1982, Volume IV: *The Patriots,* 1982, Volume V: *Inheritors,* 1983, Volume VI: *Dominion,* 1984, Volume VII: *Brotherhood,* 1985.
The Acadians, Seal Books, 1984.
Sierra Gold, Seal Books, 1987.

Contributor to *William and Mary Quarterly* and *Journal of American History.*

WORK IN PROGRESS: Eden, a novel of sixteenth-century North America; *The Cat and the Rat,* a novel spy-thriller.

*   *   *

WARNER, Matt
See FICHTER, George S.

*   *   *

WARNER, Val 1946-

PERSONAL: Born January 15, 1946, in Harrow, England; daughter of Alister Alfred (a schoolmaster) and Ivy Miriam (a teacher; maiden name, Robins) Warner. *Education;* Somerville College, Oxford, B.A. (with honors), 1968. *Politics:* Socialist. *Religion:* Atheist.

ADDRESSES: Office—c/o Carcanet, 208-12 Corn Exchange Buildings, Manchester M4 3BQ, England.

CAREER: Teacher for Inner London Education Authority and librarian in London, England, 1969-72; free-lance writer in London, England, 1972, and in Scotland, 1981—. Writer in residence, University College of Swansea, 1977-78, and University of Dundee, 1979-81.

AWARDS, HONORS: Translators' grant from Arts Council of Great Britain, 1972, for Corbiere translations; Gregory Award for Poetry, 1975.

WRITINGS:

These Yellow Photos (poems), Carcanet, 1971.
Under the Penthouse (poems), Carcanet, 1973.
(Translator and author of introduction) Corbiere, *The Centenary Corbiere: Poems and Prose of Tristan Corbiere,* Carcanet, 1974.
(Editor) Charlotte Mew, *Collected Poems and Prose,* Virago Press, 1982.
Before Lunch, Carcanet, 1986.
(Contributor) *PEN New Fiction 2,* Quartet, 1987.

Contributor of poems, translations, short stories, and reviews to more than fifty periodicals, including *Encounter, Poetry Wales, Scotsman, Pequod, Scrievins, Green River Review, Tribune, Poetry Nation, Antaeus, Poetry Review, Dublin Magazine, Outposts, Ambit,* and *Critical Quarterly.*

WORK IN PROGRESS: A novel.

BIOGRAPHICAL/CRITICAL SOURCES:

PERIODICALS

Times Literary Supplement, December 4, 1981.

*   *   *

WARREN, Dave
See WIERSBE, Warren W(endell)

*   *   *

WATERS, John F(rederick) 1930-

PERSONAL: Born October 27, 1930, in Somerville, Mass.; son of Herbert M. (a tradeshow director) and Magdelena (Robinson) Waters; married Barbara Seaver (an educator) May 16, 1959; children: Herbert, Sandra, Lane, Duane. *Education:* University of Massachusetts, B.S., 1959.

ADDRESSES: Home—Box 735, Chatham, Mass. 02633.

CAREER: Cape Cod Standard Times, Hyannis, Mass., reporter, 1959-60; elementary teacher in Falmouth, Mass., 1960-66; full-time writer, 1966—. *Military service:* U.S. Army; became sergeant.

MEMBER: Twelve O'Clock Scholars.

AWARDS, HONORS: Outstanding Science Book Award, National Science Teachers Association, 1972, for *Some Mammals Live in the Sea* and *Green Turtle Mysteries,* 1973, for *The Mysterious Eel,* 1974, for *Carnivorous Plants,* and 1975, for *The Continental Shelves* and *Creatures of Darkness.*

WRITINGS:

JUVENILE

Marine Animal Collectors, Hastings House, 1969.
The Sea Farmers, Hastings House, 1970.
What Does an Oceanographer Do, Dodd, 1970.
Saltmarshes and Shifting Dunes, Harvey House, 1970.
The Crab from Yesterday (Junior Literary Guild selection), Warne, 1970.

Turtles, Follett, 1971.
Neighborhood Puddle (Junior Literary Guild selection), Warne, 1971.
Some Mammals Live in the Sea, Dodd, 1972.
Green Turtle Mysteries, Crowell, 1972.
The Royal Potwasher, Methuen, 1972.
Seal Harbor, Warne, 1973.
The Mysterious Eel, Hastings House, 1973.
Giant Sea Creatures, Follett, 1973.
Hungry Sharks, Crowell, 1973.
Camels: Ships of the Desert, Crowell, 1974.
Carnivorous Plants, F. Watts, 1974.
Victory Chimes, Warne, 1975.
The Continental Shelves, Abelard, 1975.
Creatures of Darkness, Walker & Co., 1975.
Maritime Careers, F. Watts, 1977.
Summer of the Seal, Warne, 1978.
Fishing, F. Watts, 1978.
The Hatchlings, Walker & Co., 1979.
Crime Labs, F. Watts, 1979.
A Jellyfish Is Not a Fish, Crowell, 1979.

OTHER

Exploring New England Shores, Stone Wall Press, 1974.

WORK IN PROGRESS: An adult novel and a cookbook.

SIDELIGHTS: John F. Waters told *CA:* "I'm now only writing fiction. It is more enjoyable because I can use my imagination and create people. Writing in any form is fun, but I write because I have to—otherwise I'd suffocate under the pile of unused words! I still write every day of the week except Sunday and enjoy it so much. Since turning to novels my writing has improved tremendously, but as yet I have not sold an adult piece of fiction. I may never; however, I will keep on trying because I believe I was meant to do it and can't imagine doing anything else. Big blind love for one's writings grows like wild zucchini."

*   *   *

WEAVER, Richard L. II 1941-

PERSONAL: Born December 5, 1941, in Hanover, N.H.; son of Richard L. (a professor) and Florence B. (a teacher; maiden name, Grow) Weaver; married Andrea A. Willis, 1965; children: R. Scott, Jacquelynn M., Anthony K., Joanna C. *Education:* University of Michigan, A.B., 1964, M.A., 1965; Indiana University, Ph.D., 1969.

ADDRESSES: Home—9583 Woodleigh Court, Perrysburg, Ohio 43551. *Office*—Department of Interpersonal and Public Communication, Bowling Green State University, Bowling Green, Ohio 43403.

CAREER: University of Massachusetts—Amherst, instructor, 1968-69, assistant professor, 1969-74; Bowling Green State University, Bowling Green, Ohio, associate professor, 1974-79, professor of speech, 1979—, director of basic speech communication course, 1974—. Visiting professor at University of Hawaii at Manoa, 1981-82.

MEMBER: International Communication Association, International Society for General Semantics, Speech Communication Association, Central States Speech Association, Midwest Basic Course Director's Conference, Ohio Speech Association.

WRITINGS:

(With Saundra Hybels) *Speech/Communication,* D. Van Nostrand, 1974, 2nd edition, 1979.
Speech/Communication: A Reader, Collegiate Publishing, 1975, 2nd edition, 1979.
Speech Communication: A Student Manual, Collegiate Publishing, 1976, 2nd edition, 1979.
Understanding Interpersonal Communication, Scott, Foresman, 1978, 4th edition, 1987.
(With Raymond K. Tucker and Cynthia Berryman-Fink) *Research in Speech Communication,* Prentice-Hall, 1981.
Speech/Communication: Skills, Collegiate Publishing, 1982.
(Editor) *Foundations of Speech Communication: Perspectives of a Discipline,* University of Hawaii, 1982.
Understanding Public Communication, Prentice-Hall, 1983.
Understanding Business Communication, Prentice-Hall, 1985.
(With Hybels) *Communicating Effectively,* Random House, 1986, 2nd edition, in press.

Contributor of more than sixty articles to speech-communication, education, and history journals. Associate editor of *Communication Education,* 1979-81.

WORK IN PROGRESS: Books on innovative instructional strategies, relationships, motivation, as well as articles on imaging, mentoring, and other instructional techniques.

SIDELIGHTS: Richard L. Weaver II told *CA:* "Writing, for me, is an extension of my teaching; I put teaching as my highest priority and commitment. Like teaching, writing is an opportunity to reach out and directly touch college students in a deep and meaningful manner. I write from my teaching experience; I want my writing to be easy to understand, comfortable, and enjoyable. The more students can relate to my writing, identify with my examples, and feel they are being addressed specifically and directly, the more they are likely to comprehend and learn from what they read.

"When I am writing, I put myself in the place of my readers. How are they likely to think? How will they respond? How will they feel? Writing is a personal experience for me, but it is also a fulfilling interpersonal one as well because I feel as if I am having a conversation with my readers. In a sense, when I am writing I am 'in relationship' with them; it is a transactional experience in which I am actually creating an image of them and communicating with that image as I write.

"Writing is also an enjoyable experience for me. I seldom approach it with dread, as a chore, or as something I must get out of the way. Often, I cannot wait to finish other activities so that I can return to writing. It is both cathartic and a way to channel my energies. It is also an escape, because part of writing is an intense, internal experience; you enter the world of the imagination where you can have dialogues with yourself. You can explore and challenge, question and probe. I like to write more than almost anything else.

"When people who read my books say they can really feel me talking to them through my words and ideas, for me that is a valuable, cherished compliment. Although directness, informal style, and specific examples help achieve this, the discipline of speech communication also contributes. I write about a topic that permeates the very core of people's lives. Thus, it is easy to find stimulus for writing from daily encounters, including the acute questions of my students. Much of the substance of my writing comes from the exciting drama and experience of everyday living—something everyone can relate to.

"No matter what career people enter, no matter what profession they pursue, no matter what activity they engage in, speech communication is often a major force in their effectiveness and success. If the concepts and principles I write about help in even the slightest way to make readers' lives more significant, effective, or satisfying, I feel richly rewarded.

"What writing has done for me is to force me out of myself and into the lives of others. It is like the effect that teaching has on my life. It makes me a lover of people, and when you become a lover of people it has an influence on the whole business of living. Once we learn to love people, we learn the true art of living."

AVOCATIONAL INTERESTS: Travel, camping, outdoor activities, hiking, swimming, music, reading.

*   *   *

WEBB, Phyllis 1927-

PERSONAL: Born April 8, 1927, in Victoria, British Columbia, Canada. *Education:* University of British Columbia, B.A., 1949; attended McGill University, 1953.

ADDRESSES: Home—R.R. 2, Mt. Baker Cr., C-9, Ganges, British Columbia, Canada V0S 1EO.

CAREER: Secretary in Montreal, Quebec, 1956; University of British Columbia, Vancouver, member of staff, 1961-64; Canadian Broadcasting Corporation (CBC), Toronto, Ontario, program organizer, 1964-67, executive producer, 1967-69; freelance writer and broadcaster. Guest lecturer, University of British Columbia, 1976-77. University of Victoria, sessional lecturer, 1977-78 and 1982-84, visiting assistant professor, 1978-79. Writer-in-residence, University of Alberta, 1980-81. Conductor of writing workshops at the Upper Canada Writers Workshop in Kingston, Ontario, and at the Banff Center.

AWARDS, HONORS: Overseas Award from Government of Canada, 1957; Canada Council grant, 1963, senior fellowship, 1969, Senior Arts Award, 1981; Governor General's Award for poetry, 1982, for *The Vision Tree*.

WRITINGS:

POEMS

(With Gael Turnbull and Eli Mandel) *Trio*, Contact Press, 1954.
Even Your Right Eye, McClelland & Stewart, 1956.
The Sea Is Also a Garden: Poems, Ryerson Press, 1962.
Naked Poems, Periwinkle Press, 1965.
Selected Poems, 1954-1965, edited and introduced by John Hulcoop, Talonbooks, 1971.
Wilson's Bowl, Coach House Press, 1980.
Sunday Water: Thirteen Anti Ghazals, Island Writing Series, 1982.
The Vision Tree: Selected Poems, edited and introduced by Sharon Thesen, Talonbooks, 1982.
Water and Light: Ghazals and Anti Ghazals, Coach House Press, 1984.

ESSAYS

Talking, Quadrant Editions, 1982.

SIDELIGHTS: "I'm a pressure-cooker writer. I have to let the psychic pressure build up until it is almost unbearable," says Canadian poet Phyllis Webb in a *Books in Canada* interview. The interviewer, Eleanor Wachtel, explains, "[Webb] writes

quickly, in bursts, after long silences." Webb's first creative surge carried into print *Trio, Even Your Right Eye, The Sea Is Also a Garden: Poems*, and *Naked Poems*. These poems for the most part were collected in *Selected Poems: 1954-1965* and published by Talonbooks as part of its Canadian poetry series. The next surge began with Webb's decision in 1969 to leave her position as executive producer of the Canadian Broadcasting Corporation's "Ideas" program to devote herself to poetry. Returning to Canada's west coast, Webb settled on Salt Spring Island and discovered the Indian petroglyphs that account for "some of the Indian themes that appear" in the poems, Webb told *CA*. Though she began to write *The Kropotkin Poems*, she "abandoned" that "study of power and anarchism," she related, "as my political commitment shifted away from anarchism to feminism."

The poems that resulted from this second period appeared in 1980 as *Wilson's Bowl*. In 1982, Talonbooks issued a second collection, *The Vision Tree: Selected Poems*, which received the Governor General's Award for poetry. This period also marked a change in critical opinion regarding Webb's importance. As critic John F. Hulcoop comments in the *Dictionary of Literary Biography*, "Before publication of *Wilson's Bowl*, Webb was seen as a major minor poet whose relatively small creative output was perfect in its way, but whose increasing need of self-isolation seemed to be silencing her poetic voice. Since 1980, however, a radical revision of opinion has occurred. She is acknowledged as what it has taken her thirty years to become: a major twentieth-century Canadian poet whose influence is both widespread and seminal."

Poems from *Even Your Right Eye* and *The Sea Is Also a Garden* drew applause for their precision and refinement, but reviewers found the sharpest economy of phrase in *Naked Poems*, which Webb referred to at a 1963 poetry reading as "bone-essential" statements. "This valuable collector's item," Hulcoop notes, is a "slim volume, containing forty-one poems, many of which consist of less than ten words (the last for example, is one word '*Oh?*'—a characteristic Webb question), designed and printed by west coast painter Takao Tanabe." Keith Garebian points out in *Books in Canada* that by writing lean poems, Webb "tries to elude 'The Great Iambic Pentameter'"—the traditional rhythm of poetry in English—that she calls "the Hound of Heaven in our stress" in *The Sea Is Also a Garden*.

Garebian's survey of the early books also mentions "a growing pessimism" in the poems—the component that elicited negative responses from John Bentley Mays in *Open Letter* and Frank Davey in *From Here to There*. Robert Weaver explains in a *Saturday Night* article, "Webb is an intensely, painfully personal writer," one who "causes very personal responses in her readers." Pain is frequently the subject of Webb's poems, which often raise "painful questions," writes Hulcoop. One such inquiry from "Lament" in *Trio* asks "what can love mean in such a world, / and what can we or any lovers hold in this immensity / of hate and broken things?" Gail Fox writes of the despair in such poems and others that treat resignation and suicide, but argues in *Canadian Forum* that detractors who find the poems "neurotic, or self-pitying" have missed the causes for despair catalogued in Webb's canon.

Webb told *CA* that more recent "feminist reinterpretations" of her poems "have led to a more balanced view of the work to date." For example, Sharon Thesen maintains in the introduction to *The Vision Tree* that Webb's "canonization as a sort of priestess of pain hasn't, I think, been warranted. Webb's candour—both in her poetry and in her prose—about the difficulties of her vulnerability, has invited some curious looks into her psyche, some decidedly more competent and respectful than others, but all seeking to explain the sense of loss, futility, and despair that her poems document. The error of such psychologizing, of course, is that it seeks to identify the origins of this sense of loss in terms of a personal grief, whereas more often than not it is anguish's human universality that is expressed.'' Hulcoop suggests that history and poetics are Webb's other concerns: "What begins to emerge in these poems is an arresting, because unique, combination of politics and lyric form: a tightly controlled but feeling expression of moods/states of mind/emotions that have to do with rebellion against the political status quo, with socialist ideals, and, eventually, with anarchy.''

In 1970, Webb set out to explore Piotr Alekseyevich Kropotkin's vision of anarchist utopia in long-lined pieces to be called *The Kropotkin Poems,* but she later set the project aside for a different frame of reference. Webb told *Books in Canada* interviewer Wachtel: "The Kropotkin utopia enchanted me for a while until I saw that [it] was yet another male-imaginative structure for a new society. It would probably *not* have changed male-female relations.''

Webb's increasingly feminist perspective is reflected in *Wilson's Bowl* and subsequent works of the 1980s. The introduction to *Wilson's Bowl* and the prose pieces in *Talking* articulate Webb's perception of the political implications inherent in various poetic forms, particularly the long line, which she sees as a male-imaginative structure. The long line, she says in *Talking,* "comes from assurance (or hysteria), high tide, full moon, open mouth, big-mouthed Whitman, yawp, yawp & Ginsberg—howling. Male.''

In *Sunday Water: Thirteen Anti Ghazals* and *Water and Light: Ghazals and Anti Ghazals* Webb employs a poetic form that she finds more conducive to feminine language. The ghazal is an ancient Persian love song usually written in five couplets that are loosely linked by associative leaps rather than by linear logic. Webb discovered the form in John Thompson's *Stilt Jack.* Seeing him adapt the form to his own purposes led her to also play a game of breaking some of the form's traditional rules. According to Hulcoop in *Canadian Literature,* Webb's anti ghazal maintains the intricate rhyme and syllabic schemes of the classical ghazal while it rejects the latter's romantic ideals. Hulcoop sees her adaptations as "an act of liberation: a liberation of self-as-woman from male socio-sexual, political, and poetic conventions.... Her autonomy as a woman poet, her growing need to disconnect from a male-dominated tradition, and her profound desire to be disobedient [in an otherwise conventional life] . . . all find expression in the ghazal.''

Water and Light, published in 1984, is the last of five books that make up Webb's second "burst" of creativity. Though these works mark some important new directions for Webb, Hulcoop maintains that the books since 1980 further her progress along a path she began to explore in the books of her first efflorescence. The later books show the poet emerging from a protective isolation, symbolized by poems about imprisonment, "*outwards* . . . into the public world where 'the great dreams pass on / to the common good,'" he writes in *Essays on Canadian Writing,* ending with lines from *Wilson's Bowl.* An awareness of the mythic significance of things in the physical world expressed in spiritual symbols also persists. Wachtel relates that "Christian mysticism and Buddhism provided met-

aphors for poetic expression'' in the early books because "Webb sees parallels between the poetic search and a religious search.'' Garebian demonstrates how this "iconography" appears in the later books. "Webb envisions a tree akin to the Tree of Life or the shaman's magic sky-ladder" rooted near "Wilson's Bowl, the ancient petroglyph bowl carved into the shoreline rock" of Salt Spring Island, he says. Both represent a link between heaven and earth, and are "eternal centres from which the poet [speaks].''

Webb feels there may be more to discover, and perhaps another "silence," beyond the writing of anti ghazals. She senses the approach of "hard times" that may compel her "to go deeper.'' Speaking to Wachtel, Webb said, "I think [the ghazals are] a transitional thing for me. A little bit superficial, perhaps. Before I go into the cave again for the big spiritual stuff.'' But in any case, as Hulcoop maintains in *Essays in Canadian Literature,* "Webb's work stands out like an object in a landscape, a guide to all adventuring critics whose job it is to fathom the depths . . . and explore the farthest reaches of Canadian poetry—a guide also to younger poets whose vocation it is to acknowledge and overcome their great precursors.''

BIOGRAPHICAL/CRITICAL SOURCES:

BOOKS

Contemporary Literary Criticism, Volume XVIII, Gale, 1981.
Davey, Frank, and others, *From There to Here: A Guide to English-Canadian Literature since 1960,* Press Porcepic, 1974.
Dictionary of Literary Biography, Volume LIII: *Canadian Writers since 1960, First Series,* Gale, 1986.
Lecker, Robert and Jack David, editors, *The Annotated Bibliography of Canada's Major Authors,* Volume VI, ECW, 1985.
Neuman, Shirley and Smaro Kamboureli, editors, *A Mazing Space: Writing Canadian Women Writing,* Longspoon/Newest, 1986.
Webb, Phyllis, Gael Turnbull, and Eli Mandel, *Trio,* Contact Press, 1954.
Webb, Phyllis, *The Sea Is Also a Garden: Poems,* Ryerson Press, 1962.
Webb, Phyllis, *Selected Poems, 1954-1965,* edited and introduced by John Hulcoop, Talonbooks, 1971.
Webb, Phyllis, *Wilson's Bowl,* Coach House Press, 1980.
Webb, Phyllis, *The Vision Tree: Selected Poems,* edited and introduced by Sharon Thesen, Talonbooks, 1982
Webb, Phyllis, *Talking,* Quadrant Editions, 1982.
Webb, Phyllis, *Sunday Water: Thirteen Anti Ghazals,* Coach House Press, 1984.

PERIODICALS

Books in Canada, May, 1981, June, 1981, November, 1982, November, 1983.
British Columbia Library Quarterly, October-January, 1972-1973.
Canadian Forum, May, 1972, August, 1981.
Canadian Literature, summer, 1961, spring, 1967, spring, 1972, summer, 1986.
Essays on Canadian Writing, summer, 1983, Number 30, 1984-1985.
Line, spring, 1984.
Maclean's, March 30, 1981.
Open Letter, 1973.

Saturday Night, November, 1971.
Victoria's Monday Magazine, April 15, 1983.

—*Sketch by Marilyn K. Basel*

* * *

WEINSTEIN, Howard 1954-

PERSONAL: Born September 16, 1954, in Queens, N.Y.; son of Abraham (an optometrist) and Lillian Weinstein. *Education:* University of Connecticut, B.A., 1975.

ADDRESSES: Home—485 Lakeville Lane, East Meadows, N.Y. 11554. *Agent*—Sharon Jarvis, 260 Willard Ave., Staten Island, N.Y. 10314.

CAREER: Writer, 1974—; New York Diabetes Association, New York, N.Y., public information director and editor, 1978—. Guest speaker at "Star Trek" and science fiction conventions; story development consultant for "Star Trek IV: The Voyage Home," Paramount, 1986.

AWARDS, HONORS: CAPRA Award from Community Agencies Public Relations Association and Good Sam Award from American Advertising Federation, both 1980, for writing and producing radio public service announcements for the New York Diabetes Association.

WRITINGS:

"The Pirates of Orion" (episode of the animated version of "Star Trek"), National Broadcasting Co., 1974.
The Covenant of the Crown (Star Trek novel), Pocket Books, 1981.
(With A. C. Crispin) *V: East Coast Crisis,* Pinnacle Books, 1981.
V: Prisoners and Pawns, Pinnacle Books, 1985.
Deep Domain (Star Trek novel), Pocket Books, 1987.
V: Path to Conquest, Pinnacle Books, 1987.

Contributor of columns to *Newsday* and *New York Times.*

WORK IN PROGRESS: Science fiction books; television and film scripts on contemporary issues and relationships.

SIDELIGHTS: Howard Weinstein told *CA:* "Although science fiction isn't the only thing I write, it's an area I hope to stay involved with. Science fiction has been called 'the literature of ideas,' and it also happens to be fun and challenging. The only limits are the limits of your own imagination.

"As far as 'Star Trek' is concerned, I've been a fan since I was twelve, and a 'Star Trek' TV script was my first writing sale when I was nineteen. Now into its third decade, 'Star Trek' has proved durable beyond anyone's expectations. And with more than twenty years' perspective, it's not hard to see why the series has lasted. It directly and intelligently addresses some terribly important questions: What will the future be like? Will we even *have* a future? And what can we do to shape it?

"At their best, science fiction in general and 'Star Trek' in particular prod us to take probing looks at our own world. And while there's plenty that's ugly—war, greed, corruption, injustice, cruelty and just plain indifference—we can also find a few flowers growing among the weeds. In my stories, whether science fiction or contemporary, I try to highlight that streak of stubborn optimism that enables people to get up each day and face a world that's a lot more rotten than we'd like it to be.

"'Star Trek' faces that squarely, in a cautionary way. In these late twentieth century years, humanity is at a crossroads. More than ever before in our history, decisions we make and courses we embark upon today will decide the fate of the earth and every living thing on it. This fact is our special burden—and, at the same time, a wondrous opportunity. Maybe we *can't* change the world . . . maybe we can't make it better. But, on the other hand, maybe we can. We won't know if we never try. That's what I care about, and that's what I try to write about."

* * *

WELLS, Joel F(reeman) 1930-

PERSONAL: Born March 17, 1930, in Evansville, Ind.; son of William Jackson (an engineer) and Edith (Strassell) Wells; married Elizabeth Hein, June 5, 1952; children: William, Eugenia, Susan, Steven, Daniel. *Education:* University of Notre Dame, B.A. (journalism), 1952; Northwestern University, graduate study, 1963. *Religion:* Roman Catholic.

ADDRESSES: Home—827 Colfax St., Evanston, Ill. *Office*—Thomas More Association, 225 West Huron St., Chicago, Ill. 60610.

CAREER: Thomas More Association, Chicago, Ill., promotion director, 1955-64, editor of *Critic* (magazine), 1964—, editor of Thomas More Press, 1971—, vice-president and director. Rosary College, River Forest, Ill., lecturer, 1963—. *Military service:* U.S. Navy, 1952-55; became lieutenant junior grade.

AWARDS, HONORS: Doctor of Letters, Rosary College, 1982.

WRITINGS:

(Editor with Dan Herr) *Bodies and Souls,* Doubleday, 1961.
(Editor with Herr) *Blithe Spirits,* Doubleday, 1962.
(Editor with Herr) *Bodies and Spirits,* Doubleday, 1964.
(Editor with Herr) *Through Other Eyes,* Newman, 1965.
Grim Fairy Tales for Adults, Macmillan, 1968.
A Funny Thing Happened to the Church, Macmillan, 1969.
Second Collection, Thomas More Press, 1973.
Bad Children's Book, Argus, 1976.
(Editor) *Pilgrim's Regress,* Thomas More Press, 1979.
How to Survive with Your Teenager, Thomas More Press, 1983.
Coping in the 80s, Thomas More Press, 1986.

Contributor of fiction, articles, and parodies to newspapers and periodicals including *New York Times, National Catholic Reporter, Woman's Day, Chicago Tribune, New Republic,* and *Christian Century.*

* * *

WELSH, David
See HILLS, C(harles) A(lbert) R(eis)

* * *

WESCOTT, Glenway 1901-1987

PERSONAL: Born April 11, 1901, in Kewaskum, Wis.; died February 22, 1987, in Rosemont, N.J.; son of Bruce Peters (a farmer) and Josephine (Gordon) Wescott. *Education:* Attended University of Chicago, 1917-19.

CAREER: Writer.

MEMBER: Authors Guild of the Authors League of America (member of council), National Institute of Arts and Letters (president, 1959-62), American Academy of Arts and Letters.

AWARDS, HONORS: Harper Prize, 1927, for *The Grandmothers: A Family Portrait;* D.Litt., Rutgers University, 1963.

WRITINGS:

The Bitterns: A Book of Twelve Poems, Monroe Wheeler, 1920.
The Apple of the Eye (novel), Dial, 1924.
Natives of Rock: XX Poems, 1921-1922, Francisco Bianco (New York), 1925.
. . . Like a Lover (stories), Monroe Wheeler, 1926.
The Grandmothers: A Family Portrait (novel), Harper, 1927.
Good-bye, Wisconsin (stories), Harper, 1928, reprinted, Books for Libraries Press, 1970.
The Babe's Bed (novella), Harrison (Paris), 1930.
Fear and Trembling (essays), Harper, 1932.
A Calendar of Saints for Unbelievers, Harrison, 1932, reprinted, Leete's Island Books, 1976.
The Pilgrim Hawk: A Love Story, Harper, 1940.
(Contributor) Margaret Mayorga, editor, *The Best One-Act Plays of 1940,* Dodd, 1941.
Apartment in Athens (novel), Harper, 1945, reprinted, Greenwood Press, 1972.
(Editor and author of introduction) *The Maugham Reader,* Doubleday, 1950.
(Editor and author of introduction) *Short Novels of Colette,* Dial, 1951.
(Adaptor) *Twelve Fables of Aesop,* Museum of Modern Art, 1954.
Images of Truth: Remembrances and Criticism, Harper, 1962.
The Best of All Possible Worlds: Journals, Letters, and Remembrances, 1914-1937, Farrar, Straus, 1975.

Also author of *Elizabeth Madox Roberts: A Personal Note,* 1930, and of "The Dream of Audubon," a ballet libretto.

WORK IN PROGRESS: Wescott's extensive journals are being readied for publication.

SIDELIGHTS: Glenway Wescott made his reputation in the 1920s with the novel *The Grandmothers: A Family Portrait* and the story collection *Good-Bye, Wisconsin.* Both are autobiographical works set in Wescott's native Wisconsin. The critically acclaimed novel *The Pilgrim Hawk: A Love Story* appeared in 1940, and the best-selling *Apartment in Athens* in 1945. But for the last forty years of his life Wescott was to publish no new fiction. The reason for his long silence is still a matter of speculation among critics.

Wescott was first known as an Imagist poet, publishing his first collection of poems at the age of nineteen. But it was as a writer of fiction that he earned critical recognition. In *The Apple of the Eye, The Grandmothers,* and *Good-Bye, Wisconsin,* Wescott fashioned his memories of his rural Wisconsin childhood into fiction. "Wescott," Bruce Bawer explained in the *New Criterion,* "was elaborately, almost compulsively, exploring his roots." In each of these works, Sy M. Kahn wrote in the *Dictionary of Literary Biography,* "Wescott employs a central young narrator. . . . Nostalgically and elegaically, each of these narrators imaginatively recreates the American past, as symbolized in rural characters from Wisconsin, and in so doing he reveals the involvement, and, ultimately, the rebellion of his own mind and sensibility."

The Apple of the Eye, Wescott's first novel, was published when the author was twenty-three years old. "Though it has

many of the shortcomings of youthful first works," William Rueckert of the *Dictionary of Literary Biography* commented, "it is an impressive, quite original first novel." It tells the story of Dan Strane, a Wisconsin teenager who comes to a bitter awareness of the puritanical restrictions of his rural upbringing and takes steps to free himself from them. Bawer described the novel as "a peculiar hodge-podge" and believed that Wescott's "metaphors and similes . . . feel particularly forced and overdone." Writing in his *Glenway Wescott: The Paradox of Voice,* Ira Johnson admitted that *The Apple of the Eye* possessed "a limited though powerful and rhetorical narrative voice. [But] two serious flaws are evident: the novel's didacticism, due to Wescott's conception of *image* and *truth,* and the disparity between the omniscient narrator and the rest of the work."

Wescott's second novel, *The Grandmothers,* "established him as one of the major American novelists of his generation," Bawer wrote. A series of short narratives based on the pictures in a family album, *The Grandmothers* recounts many actual events in Wescott's family history. As Kahn explained, "Wescott first conceived *The Grandmothers* as a history of his own family rather than a work of fiction, but as the work grew, it compelled his imagination to transcend memory, and the work was transmuted from a personal memoir to a skillful and successful novel."

Critics of the time praised *The Grandmothers* as a major work of uniquely American fiction. Burton Rascoe of *Bookman,* for example, called it "a novel not only with its roots in the American soil, but it is a novel of those roots and of that soil. It is a novel that gives a new significance to American life." In similar terms, C. P. Fadiman of the *Nation* believed that "Wescott's very beautiful and moving chronicle is possibly the first artistically satisfying rendition of the soul of an American pioneer community and its descendants."

The care with which Wescott prepared the novel, and the depth of his concern for the people he portrays, are qualities highlighted by several commentators. The *Atlantic*'s M. E. Chase believed that the novel "stands out as a book which has been conceived in deep and quiet perceptions and born in pride, care, and patience." Reviewing the book for the *New York Times,* J. Carter called it "a fine piece of work, conceived and matured in all seriousness and thoroughness of workmanship." Allan Nevins of the *Saturday Review of Literature* emphasized the emotional quality of Wescott's narrative. "It is," Nevins wrote, "the ebullient freshness and force, the tenderness as well as the keenness of the insight into human motives and ideals and frailties, and the sincerity of the author's reverence for what he calls 'ghosts of the little local history' . . . , which give the uneven, inchoate narrative the inspiration it unquestionably has." Bawer maintained that "there is something wonderfully mature about [*The Grandmothers*], about its quiet recognition that we are all the products of our families, and that the better we understand them the better we can understand—and create—ourselves."

A year after the appearance of *The Grandmothers,* Wescott published a collection of stories entitled *Good-Bye, Wisconsin,* which again explores the scenes and events of his own childhood. The opening piece, an essay explaining the book's subject matter, "is not a piece of objective social analysis," Johnson wrote, "but an attack, which presents in terms of his personal vision the reasons why Wescott finds the Middle West and America a place that in countless ways prevents the development of the self." As Rueckert explained: "The stories of *Good-Bye, Wisconsin* tell over and over again the sad lives of those who have been victims of the Midwest and found it impossible to flourish there.''

By the time *Good-Bye, Wisconsin* was published, Wescott had already left the United States to live in France. He was to spend eight years there. But despite his distance from his native region, Wescott continued to write of Wisconsin. ''Wescott was an expatriate, living in France,'' as Walter Allen explained in his *The Modern Novel in Britain and the United States,* ''but, on the evidence of his fiction, still unable to escape from Wisconsin, his native state, which seems at times almost as much a state of mind as a place.'' His *The Babe's Bed,* a short novella-length work published in a limited edition, is set in Wisconsin although, as Rueckert argued, ''the story is not really an examination of the region at all; instead, it expresses for the first time Wescott's self-doubts about himself as a fiction writer.''

Because of his growing self-doubts, Wescott did not publish any fiction for ten years. His reputation suffered during this time, partly because his two nonfiction books of this period—*Fear and Trembling* and *A Calendar of Saints for Unbelievers*—were failures. But with the 1940 novel *The Pilgrim Hawk,* Wescott regained critical acceptance while finally moving beyond his Wisconsin background.

The Pilgrim Hawk is an autobiographical work set in 1920s France. It revolves around a group of people who spend a day together in the countryside: the narrator Alwyn Tower, who is an American novelist, his cousin Alexandra Henry, and two of Alexandra's friends, Larry and Madeleine Cullen. The Cullens have brought a pet falcon with them and it becomes the central metaphor of the novel. Subtitled *A Love Story,* the book ultimately concerns the Cullens' marriage and the reaction of Alwyn, an old bachelor, to it. The falcon's captivity is seen by Alwyn as a symbol for the marriage. But when at novel's end the falcon is released, soars high into the air exuberantly, only to return again, Alwyn discerns a new depth to the marriage relationship.

A ''haunting, poetic, compressed story of love and art, freedom and captivity,'' as a London *Times* writer described the novel, *The Pilgrim Hawk* was widely acclaimed. Wescott, A. L. Graham of *Library Journal* wrote, ''has created a strange, tense atmosphere, while telling the story with delicacy and charm.'' Writing in *Books,* Rose Feld called *The Pilgrim Hawk* ''a tightly bound little tale that has depths and flights far beyond the surface of the human entanglements it covers.'' Rueckert called the novel Wescott's ''one authentic masterpiece,'' while Johnson found it ''the culmination of his career as a fiction writer.'' Bawer believed *The Pilgrim Hawk* to be perhaps Wescott's ''most nearly perfect work—taut, subtle, and exquisitely ordered.''

In 1945 Wescott published *Apartment in Athens,* a novel quite different from his earlier efforts. It concerns a family in occupied Greece during the Second World War who must allow a German soldier to stay at their apartment. The tensions between the family and their unwanted guest are described ''with the minimal amount of fictional distortion. It is the attempt of an essentially romantic, lyric, naturally symbolic novelist to write realistic fiction,'' as Rueckert explained.

''It was,'' Kahn wrote of *Apartment in Athens,* ''a popular success but is considerably below the artistic achievement of his two most distinguished works, *The Grandmothers* and *The Pilgrim Hawk.*'' But Edmund Wilson disagreed. Writing in

his *Classics and Commercials,* Wilson believed that ''the cramped physical and moral conditions, the readjustments in the relationships of the family, the whole distortion of the social organism by the unassimilated presence of the foreigner—all this is most successfully created.''

After the success of *Apartment in Athens* in 1945, Wescott was to publish no more fiction. *Images of Truth: Remembrances and Criticism,* a collection of his nonfiction, appeared in 1962; *The Best of All Possible Worlds: Journals, Letters, and Remembrances, 1914-1937* was published in 1975. But Wescott's fiction remained unpublished. He claimed to have finished manuscripts with which he was unsatisfied stored in trunks. ''Any explanation,'' Rueckert wrote, ''of Wescott's diminishing career is probably psychological and personal.'' Bawer speculated after Wescott's death in 1987 that one reason for the long silence may have been Wescott's homosexuality; he had lived since his teens with Monroe Wheeler. An autobiographical writer, Wescott had already successfully written about his childhood and coming of age. ''But few readers, at that time anyway, would have regarded [a] sensitive and candid novel based upon Wescott's adult domestic life,'' Bawer commented, ''with anything other than horror.''

Whatever the reasons for Wescott's forty years of silence, he holds, Rueckert claimed, ''a significant, if minor place in the literary history of our time.'' And *The Pilgrim Hawk,* Rueckert believed, ''will remain one of [our] finest short novels.'' ''To read the body of work that [Wescott] has left behind,'' Bawer commented, ''is not only to marvel at its charm and polish but to admire its probity and seriousness of purpose. . . . That Glenway Wescott has fallen into near-obscurity is a measure less of his own failings than of the misbegotten values of the literary culture that has allowed him to fall.'' The London *Times* commentator believed that despite his years of silence, Wescott ''did enough to be remembered so long as fiction is read.''

BIOGRAPHICAL/CRITICAL SOURCES:

BOOKS

Allan, Walter, *The Modern Novel in Britain and the United States,* Dutton, 1965.
Contemporary Literary Criticism, Volume XIII, Gale, 1980.
Dictionary of Literary Biography, Gale, Volume IV: *American Writers in Paris, 1920-1939,* 1980, Volume IX: *American Novelists, 1910-1945,* 1981.
French, Warren, editor, *The Twenties: Fiction, Poetry, Drama,* Everett/Edwards, 1975.
Hicks, Granville, *The Great Tradition: An Interpretation of American Literature since the Civil War,* Macmillan, 1933.
Johnson, Ira, *Glenway Wescott: The Paradox of Voice,* Kennikat, 1971.
Rueckert, William H., *Glenway Wescott,* Twayne, 1965.
Wilson, Edmund, *Classics and Commercials,* Farrar, Straus, 1950.
Zabel, Morton Dauwen, *Craft and Character: Texts, Method and Vocation in Modern Fiction,* Viking, 1957.

PERIODICALS

Atlantic, October, 1927.
Bookman, September, 1927, October, 1928.
Books, September 23, 1928, December 8, 1940.
Bulletin of Bibliography, Number 22, 1956.
College English, March, 1957.
Commonweal, October 12, 1962.
Dial, December, 1924, November, 1927.

Library Journal, November 1, 1940.
Nation, October 12, 1927, December 21, 1940.
New Republic, December 9, 1940.
New Yorker, September 29, 1962.
New York Times, August 28, 1927, December 1, 1940.
New York Times Book Review, October 21, 1962.
Papers on English Language and Literature, summer, 1965.
Saturday Review, October 6, 1962.
Saturday Review of Literature, September 24, 1927, November 30, 1940.
Time, September 28, 1962.
Washington Post Book World, May 25, 1986.

OBITUARIES:

PERIODICALS

International Herald Tribune, March 2, 1987.
New Criterion, May, 1987.
New York Times, February 24, 1987.
Times (London), February 27, 1987.
Trentonian, February 24, 1987.
Trenton Times, February 24, 1987.†

—*Sketch by Thomas Wiloch*

*   *   *

WHITE, Jude Gilliam 1947-
(Jude Deveraux)

PERSONAL: Born September 20, 1947, in Louisville, Ky.; daughter of Harold J. (an electrician) and Virginia (Berry) Gilliam; married Richard G. Sides, February 4, 1967 (divorced February, 1969); married Claude B. White (a contractor), June 3, 1970. *Education:* Murray State University, B.S., 1970, College of Santa Fe, teaching certificate, 1973; University of New Mexico, remedial reading certificate, 1976.

ADDRESSES: Home—1937 Tijeras Rd., Santa Fe, N.M. 87501.

CAREER: Worked as elementary school teacher in Santa Fe, N.M., 1973-77; writer.

MEMBER: Romance Writers of America, Costume Society of America.

WRITINGS—Under pseudonym Jude Deveraux:

The Enchanted Land, Avon, 1978.
The Black Lyon, Avon, 1980.
The Velvet Promise, Pocket Books, 1981.
Casa Grande, Avon, 1982.
Highland Velvet, Pocket Books, 1982.
Velvet Song, Pocket Books, 1983.
Velvet Angel, Pocket Books, 1983.
Sweetbriar, Pocket Books, 1983.
Counterfeit Lady (first book of "James River" trilogy), Pocket Books, 1984.
Lost Lady (second book of "James River" trilogy), Pocket Books, 1985.
River Lady (third book of "James River" trilogy), Pocket Books, 1985.
Twin of Ice, Pocket Books, 1985.
Twin of Fire, Pocket Books, 1985.
The Temptress, Pocket Books, 1986.
The Raider, Pocket Books, 1987.
The Princess, Pocket Books, 1987.
The Maiden, Pocket Books, 1988.
The Awakening, Pocket Books, 1988.

SIDELIGHTS: Jude Deveraux, who has had several books on the *New York Times* best seller lists, told *CA:* "I started writing romances because I was tired of reading rape sagas. I was tired of women who hid behind some granite cheeked taciturn man who fought off villains and later threw her on a bed. I'd had enough of women who did little more than stamp their feet and say, 'How dare you?' The heroes also bothered me because they seemed to be cut out of the same mold, afraid to sit down and talk to anyone.

"I wanted to write about women who had some power, who could create things, could make things happen. I consider myself a feminist, a believer in equality between men and women. I don't like being told I must like housekeeping because women are supposed to like that sort of thing. Nor do I believe all men should be expected to be go-getters, hustlers, merely because they are men.

"Although some people say it's a contradiction in terms to be a feminist and a romantic, I am both. I believe in the family, in love between men and women but not in a love where the man gives all the orders and the woman meekly stands by and obeys. It must be a relationship of give and take.

"In starting a book, I take two characters, such as in *The Velvet Promise,* where I had a hero who'd spent most of his life with men, and gave him a heroine who'd been trained to be a nun. In medieval times a nun could become an abbess before she was thirty and as such she learned to rule estates and manage people. The conflict came when the hero, who believed women should be sweet and nice, was married to a woman who ran his business better than he did.

"In another book, titled *Highland Velvet,* the heroine is the laird of a Scottish clan and she's married to an Englishman who believes he's going to teach the Scots how things should be done. Instead, he learns to compromise, as she does.

"All my books concern people learning to work together, growing and developing. Which brings me to one of my most heartfelt causes. Depending upon the section of the country, romance novels comprise forty-five to fifty-five percent of all sales. In spite of romances being the backbone and most of the muscle of the publishing industry, romance writers are not respected, either by the media or the public. Personally, I've had many people say, 'I thought you were a "real" writer.' The media seems to think romances are easier than other novels, do not require the discipline other novelists must have, or the work. They constantly denigrate romance writers, saying that they are merely frustrated housewives. If a person writes a work of science fiction, or a contemporary novel about insane people, he/she is immediately said to be a writer. A romance writer, even if she has fifty novels in print selling millions of copies, is still called a housewife, and referred to with a smirk.

"I would be the first to admit that romances are fantasies, that they aren't related to our real world, but if they are fantasies, why aren't they treated with respect? Why is a created story about goblins and fairies praised and a story about pirates and beautiful women laughed at?

"All the romance writers I have met are hard-working women, with a firm grasp of what goes into making a good story, and above all, a strong sense of self discipline. In other words, they have all the qualities that go into making a good writer. But even women who call themselves feminists look down on romance writers, seeming to say that all the writers' work means little because they write stories of love.

"The new romances are about strong women, women who fight and travel, women who are restless and want more from life than a sinkful of dishes. Because the heroines also want an interesting, talented man to love does not lessen the story. In the contemporaries, the heroines always have careers. In *Highland Velvet*, my heroine is an architect who wins a design contest but because the house is to be built away from a town, the overseeing architect, the hero, says a woman cannot work on the crew. My heroine proves to him that she can hold her own by doing well in her studies as well as in the construction."

AVOCATIONAL INTERESTS: Body building, costume history.

*   *   *

WHITE, Paul Hamilton Hume   1910-
(Jungle Doctor)

PERSONAL: Born February 26, 1910, in Bowral, New South Wales, Australia; son of Richard Sibford (a farmer) and Rose (Morgan) White; married Beatrice Mary Bellingham, August 11, 1936; children: David Hamilton, Rosemary Helen. *Education:* Sydney University, M.B., B.S., 1934. *Religion:* Anglican Church in Australia.

ADDRESSES: Home—6 Newark Cres., Lindfield, Sydney, New South Wales, Australia 2070.

CAREER: Royal North Shore Hospital, Sydney, Australia, resident medical officer, 1935; Ryde District Soldiers' Memorial Hospital, Sydney, resident medical officer, 1936; Church Missionary Society Hospitals, Tanganyika (now United Republic of Tanzania), East Africa, medical superintendent, 1937-40; New South Wales Community Hospital, Sydney, rheumatologist, 1947; professional practice as specialist in rheumatic diseases, 1947-73. Chairman of directors, Ambassador Press Pty. Ltd., and Piligrim Productions Ltd. Made weekly "Jungle Doctor" radio broadcasts in Australia, 1942-78, some programs were aired in the United States, South America, Philippines, and elsewhere; has made television appearances in Australia as "Jungle Doctor." General secretary, Inter-Varsity Fellowship, 1942-52. Australian chairman, African Enterprise, 1978—.

WRITINGS:

Doctor of Tanganyika, Dash, 1941.
Yakobo in Slippery Place, African Christian Press, 1973.

PUBLISHED BY PATERNOSTER

Jungle Doctor, 1942, revised edition, 1950, reprinted, Eerdmans, 1964.
Jungle Doctor on Safari, 1943, revised edition, 1950, reprinted, 1975.
Jungle Doctor Operates, 1944, revised edition, 1950.
Jungle Doctor Attacks Witchcraft, 1947, revised edition, 1950, reprinted, 1975.
Jungle Doctor's Enemies, 1948, revised edition, 1950.
Jungle Doctor Meets a Lion, 1950.
Jungle Doctor to the Rescue, 1951.
Jungle Doctor's Casebook, 1952, reprinted, 1975.
Jungle Doctor and the Whirlwind, 1952.
Eyes on Jungle Doctor, 1953.
Jungle Doctor Looks for Trouble, 1953, reprinted, 1975.

Jungle Doctor Goes West, 1954.
Jungle Doctor Stings a Scorpion, 1955.
Jungle Doctor's Fables, 1955, reprinted, Moody, 1971.
Jungle Doctor Hunts Big Game, 1956, reprinted, 1975.
Jungle Doctor's Monkey Tales, 1957, reprinted, 1972.
Jungle Doctor on the Hop, 1957.
Jungle Doctor's Tug-of-War, 1958, reprinted, 1972.
Jungle Doctor's Crooked Dealings, 1959, reprinted, 1975.
Jungle Doctor Panorama, 1960.
(With David Britten) *Ranford Mystery Miler*, 1960.
(With Britten) *Ructions at Ranford*, 1961.
(With Britten) *Ranford Goes Fishing*, 1962.
Jungle Doctor's Progress, 1962.
Jungle Doctor Spots a Leopard, Eerdmans, 1964.
Jungle Doctor Pulls a Leg, 1964.
(With Britten) *Ranford in Flames*, 1965.
Jungle Doctor's Hippo Happenings, 1966.
Jungle Doctor Sees Red, 1967.
Donkey Wisdom, 1973.
Monkey in a Lion's Skin, 1973.
Reflections of Hippo, 1973.
Famous Monkey Last Words, 1973.
The Monkeys and the Eggs, 1975.
Monkey Crosses the Equator, 1975.
Jungle Doctor's Rhino Rumblings, 1975.
Sweet and Sour Hippo, 1975.
The Cool Pool Story, 1975.
Get Moving: Motivation for Living, 1976.
Alias Jungle Doctor: An Autobiography, 1977.
Monkey in the Bog, 1978.
The Monkeys Who Didn't Believe in the Crocodile, 1978.
The Wisdom of Donkeys, 1978.
The Goat Who Wanted to Become a Lion, 1978.
The Great Wall, 1978.
The Helpfulness of Hippo, 1978.
Knots Untied, 1978.
Little Leopards Become Big Leopards, 1978.
Out on a Limb, 1978.
Safe as Poison, 1978.
The Sticky End, 1978.
Jungle Doctor Meets Mongoose, 1979.
(With Brian Booth) *Booth to Bat*, 1983.
(With Booth) *Cricket and Christianity*, 1985.
(With Glen Threlfo) *Children's Nature Books*, 1986.
(With Threlfo) *The Bird that Walks on Water*, 1986.
(With Threlfo) *Glen Threlfo and the Theatre in the Rain Forest*, 1986.
(With Threlfo) *Glen Threlfo Explores a River*, 1986.

OTHER

Author of weekly column, "Through My Stethoscope," *Challenge* (New Zealand). Editor, *Inter-Varsity*, 1942-50; editor, *Cap and Cuffs*, Australian Nurses Christian Movement, beginning 1945.

SIDELIGHTS: Many of Paul Hamilton Hume White's "Jungle Doctor" books have been translated for publication in other countries, with some available in as many as 110 languages. White is competent in Swahili and Cigogo, one of the central Tanzanian languages.

*   *   *

WHITTINGTON, Peter
See MACKAY, James (Alexander)

WIERSBE, Warren W(endell)   1929-
(Dave Warren)

PERSONAL: Born May 16, 1929, in East Chicago, Ind.; son of Fred and Gladys (Forsberg) Wiersbe; married Betty Warren, June 20, 1953; children: David, Carolyn, Robert, Judy. *Education:* Attended Indiana University, Calumet Extension, 1947-48; Northern Baptist Seminary, Th.B., 1953; additional study at Roosevelt University, 1954-55. *Religion:* Baptist.

ADDRESSES: Home—441 Lakewood Dr., Lincoln, Neb. 68510. *Office*—P.O. Box 82808, Lincoln, Neb. 68501.

CAREER: Central Baptist Church, East Chicago, Ind., pastor, 1950-57; Youth for Christ International, Wheaton, Ill., publications director, 1957-59, editor, *Youth for Christ Magazine* (now *Campus Life*), 1959-61; Calvary Baptist Church, Covington, Ky., associate pastor, 1961-62, pastor, 1962-71; Moody Church, Chicago, Ill., senior minister, 1971-78; radio and conference speaker, 1978—. "Back to the Bible" broadcast, associate teacher, 1980-85, general director, 1985—. Speaks at ministerial seminars and denominational conferences.

AWARDS, HONORS: D.D., Temple Seminary (Chattanooga, Tenn.), 1965 and Trinity Evangelical Divinity School, 1986; Litt.D. from Cedarville College, 1987.

WRITINGS:

A Guidebook to Ephesians, Zondervan, 1957.
A Guidebook to Galatians, Zondervan, 1958.
(Editor) *Teen-Age Rock!*, Zondervan, 1959.
Quaran-teen, Zondervan, 1960.
(With Ted W. Engstrom) *Fifty-two Workable Junior High Programs*, Zondervan, 1960.
Byways of Blessing: A Daily Devotional Guide, Moody, 1961.
Teen-Agers Anonymous, Zondervan, 1961.
How to Study Successfully, Zondervan, 1962.
Teens Triumphant!, Moody, 1962.
(Editor) *Successful Christian Living for Twentieth-Century Teens*, Zondervan, 1962.
Be a Real Teenager!, Revell, 1965.
Creative Christian Living, Revell, 1967.
The Wonderful World of Teens, Moody, 1969.
Thoughts for Men on the Move: Strength for the Journey, Moody, 1970.
Be a Real Teen, Moody, 1971.
Be Real, Victor Books, 1972.
(With Howard Sugden) *When Pastors Wonder How*, Moody, 1973, published as *Confident Pastoral Leadership, William Culbertson: A Man of God*, Moody, 1974.
Be Joyful: A Practical Study of Philippians, Victor Books, 1974.
Be Free: An Expository Study of Galatians, Victor Books, 1975.
Live Like a King: Make Beatitudes Work in Daily Life, Moody, 1976.
Be Rich: Are You Losing the Things That Money Can't Buy?; An Expository Study of the Epistle to the Ephesians, Victor Books, 1976.
His Name is Wonderful, Tyndale, 1976.
Walking with the Giants: A Minister's Guide to Good Reading and Great Preaching, Baker Book, 1976.
Be Right: An Expository Study of Romans, Victor Books, 1977.
(Editor) A. W. Tozer, *Treasury of the World's Great Sermons*, Kregel, 1977.
Five Secrets of Living, Tyndale, 1978.

Be Mature: An Expository Study of the Epistle of James, Victor Books, 1978.
Be Ready, Victor Books, 1979.
Meet Yourself in the Parables, Victor Books, 1979.
The Strategy of Satan: How to Detect and Defeat Him, Tyndale, 1979.
The Bumps Are What You Climb On: Encouragement for Difficult Days, Baker Book, 1980.
Listening to the Giants: A Guide to Good Reading and Great Preaching, Baker Book, 1980.
(Editor) John Bunyan, *The Annotated Pilgrim's Progress*, Moody, 1980.
Meet Your King, Victor Books, 1980.
Be Complete, Victor Books, 1981.
Be Faithful, Victor Books, 1981.
(Editor) *Giant Steps*, Baker Book, 1981.
A Basic Library for Bible Students, Baker Book, 1981.
(Editor) James Marchant, compiler, *Anthology of Jesus*, Kregel, 1981 (originally published in 1926).
Listen! Jesus Is Praying!, Tyndale, 1982.
Be Confident, Victor Books, 1982.
Be Dynamic: Acts 1-12, Victor Books, 1987.
Be Daring: Acts 13-28, Victor Books, 1988.
So That's What a Christian Is, Tyndale, 1988.

Also author of *Expository Outlines on the Old Testament* and *Expository Outlines on the New Testament*, both Calvary Book Room. Also editor of W. A. Quayle, *The Pastor-Preacher*, and A. W. Tozer, *The Best of A. W. Tozer*.

*   *   *

WILLEMS, J. Rutherford   1944-
(James Lassen-Willems)

PERSONAL: Born October 11, 1944, in Coronado, Calif.; son of Everleigh Durward (a naval officer) and Miriam May (Shepul) Willems; married Morgan Kathleen MacGowan, July 4, 1965 (died February 20, 1968); married Patricia Diyan Crawford (a teacher in an experimental school), May 20, 1969; married Coryl J. Lassen (an Episcopal priest), January 22, 1981; children: (second marriage) Aaron Nikolai. *Education:* San Diego State College (now University), B.A., 1966, graduate study, 1966-68; Episcopal Divinity School, Cambridge, Mass., M.Div., 1984; Boston College, graduate study in theology, 1984—. *Politics:* Socialist. *Religion:* Anglican.

ADDRESSES: Home—56 Broad St., Pascoag, R.I. 02859. *Agent*—Peter Marin, 750 Mission Oaks Lane, Santa Barbara, Calif. 93108.

CAREER: Poet. San Francisco State University, San Francisco, Calif., director of Experimental College, 1968-69, program developer for teacher corps, 1971-74; theologian and Episcopal priest, 1981—. President, Isthmus Poetry Foundation, 1970-77. Consultant to Carnegie Foundation, 1968, and to Artists in San Francisco, 1972-77.

MEMBER: PEN American Center.

WRITINGS:

And She Finishes, Isthmus Press, 1973.
Opening the Cube, Tree, 1975.
Amidamerica, Tooth of Time, 1976.
The Harlequin Poems, Isthmus Press, 1976.

Contributor to literary magazines, including *Vort, Tree, Invisible City, Boulder, Hyperion, San Francisco Fault, Painted*

Bride Quarterly, and *Strange Faeces.* Also contributor of theological reviews and articles to journals, including the *Anglican Theological Review.* Editor of *Isthmus Review.*

WORK IN PROGRESS: The Fugues: Eye/Aur; Spiritual Direction with Women; The Horizon of Hope; Thinking Reconciliation: Personal and Social Transformation; Politics and Religion: Towards a New Paradigm; The Abrahamic Accord: Beyond Jewish Christian Dialogue.

*   *   *

WILLIAMS, William P(roctor)   1939-

PERSONAL: Born September 1, 1939, in Glade, Kan.; son of Joseph Earl (a farmer) and Berneice (Richardson) Williams; married Karen McKinley, August 19, 1962; children: Elizabeth, William II. *Education:* Kansas State University of Agriculture and Applied Science (now Kansas State University), B.A., 1961, M.A., 1964, Ph.D.,1968; Oxford University, Certificate, 1962. *Religion:* Episcopalian.

ADDRESSES: Home—1020 Garden Rd., DeKalb, Ill. 60115. *Office*—Department of English, Northern Illinois University, DeKalb, Ill. 60115.

CAREER: Kansas State University of Agriculture and Applied Science (now Kansas State University), Manhattan, instructor in English, 1966-67; Northern Illinois University, DeKalb, assistant professor, 1967-70, associate professor, 1970-76, professor of English, 1976—; director of summer session at University College, Oxford University, 1970, 1971, 1976, and 1977.

MEMBER: Modern Language Association of America, Renaissance Society of America, Bibliographical Society, Midwest Modern Language Association, Central Renaissance Conference, Bibliographical Society of Northern Illinois (cofounder).

AWARDS, HONORS: Fellow of Folger Shakespeare Library, 1972; American Philosophical Society fellow, 1972-73; Newberry Library fellowship, 1974; National Endowment for the Humanities fellow, 1978; American Council of Learned Societies fellow, 1973, 1979.

WRITINGS:

(Compiler) *A Descriptive Catalogue of Seventeenth-Century English Religious Literature in the Kansas State University Library,* Kansas State University Libraries, 1966.
(Compiler with Charles Pennel) *Elizabethan Bibliographies,* Volume IV: *George Chapman and John Marston,* Volume VIII: *Francis Beaumont, John Fletcher, Philip Massinger, John Ford, and James Shirley,* Nether Press, 1968.
(Compiler with Robert Gathorne-Hardy) *A Bibliography of the Writings of Jeremy Taylor to 1700,* Northern Illinois University Press, 1971.
(Editor and compiler) *Jeremy Taylor, 1700-1976: An Annotated Checklist,* Garland Publishing, 1979.
(Compiler) *An Index to the Stationers' Register, 1640-1708,* Nether Press, 1980.
(With Craig S. Abbott) *An Introduction to Bibliographical and Textual Studies,* Modern Language Association of America, 1985.

Contributor to *Dictionary of Anonymous and Pseudonymous English Literature* (revised edition), and to literature journals. Associate editor of *English Literature in Transition,* 1969-71; editor of *Analytical and Enumerative Bibliography,* 1977—.

WORK IN PROGRESS: A critical edition of the dramatic work of Cosmo Manuche.†

*   *   *

WILLIAMSON, Jack
See WILLIAMSON, John Stewart

*   *   *

WILLIAMSON, John Stewart   1908-
(Jack Williamson; pseudonym, Will Stewart)

PERSONAL: Born April 29, 1908, in Bisbee, Arizona Territory (now the state of Arizona); son of Asa Lee (a rancher and teacher) and Lucy Betty (a onetime teacher; maiden name, Hunt) Williamson; married Blanche Slaten Harp (a merchant), August 15, 1947; children: (stepchildren) Keigm Harp, Adele Harp Lovorn. *Education:* Taught at home by parents until he was twelve, then attended high school in Richland, N.M.; studied at West Texas State Teachers College (now West Texas State University), 1928-30, at University of New Mexico, 1932-33; Eastern New Mexico University, B.A. (summa cum laude) and M.A., 1957; University of Colorado at Boulder, Ph.D., 1964. *Politics:* Democrat. *Religion:* Methodist.

ADDRESSES: Home—Box 761, Portales, N.M. 88130. *Agent*—Eleanor Wood, Spectrum Literary Agency, 432 Park Ave. S., Rm. 1205, New York, N.Y. 10016.

CAREER: Fantasy and science fiction writer, 1928—; *News Tribune,* Portales, N.M., wire editor, 1947; creator of comic strip "Beyond Mars" for New York *Sunday News,* 1953-56; New Mexico Military Institute, Roswell, instructor in English, 1957-59; University of Colorado at Boulder, instructor in English, 1960; Eastern New Mexico University, Portales, associate professor, 1960-69, professor, 1969-77, currently Distinguished Research Professor in English. Guest of honor, Thirty-fifth World Science Fiction Convention, Miami, Florida, 1977, and at numerous regional conventions.

MEMBER: Science Fiction Writers of America (president, 1978-80), National Council of Teachers of English, Masons, Rotary Club.

AWARDS, HONORS: First Fandom Science Fiction Hall of Fame Award, 1968; Pilgrim Award, from Science Fiction Research Association, 1973; Grand Master Award for lifetime achievement, from Science Fiction Writers of America, 1976; Hugo Award, 1985, for *Wonder's Child: My Life in Science Fiction.*

WRITINGS:

SCIENCE FICTION NOVELS; UNDER NAME JACK WILLIAMSON

(With Miles J. Breuer) *The Girl from Mars,* Stellar, 1929.
The Legion of Space (also see below), illustrated by A. J. Donnell, Fantasy Press, 1947.
The Humanoids (originally published in *Astounding* as *And Searching Mind*), Simon & Schuster, 1949, reprinted, Ultramarine, 1980.
One against the Legion (also see below), Fantasy Press, 1950, published with novella *Nowhere Near,* Pyramid Books, 1967.
The Green Girl, Avon, 1950.
The Cometeers (also see below), illustrated by Ed Cartier, Fantasy Press, 1950.
Dragon's Island, Simon & Schuster, 1951, published as *The Not-Men,* Belmont, 1968.

The Legend of Time, Fantasy Press, 1952, published as *The Legion of Time* and *After Worlds End*, two volumes, Digit, 1961.

Dome around America, Ace Books, 1955.

(With James E. Gunn) *Star Bridge*, Gnome Press, 1955.

The Trial of Terra, Ace Books, 1962.

Bright New Universe, Ace Books, 1967.

Trapped in Space (juvenile), illustrated by Robert Amundsen, Doubleday, 1968.

The Moon Children, Putnam, 1972.

The Power of Blackness, Berkley Publishing, 1976.

Brother to Demons, Brother to God, Bobbs-Merrill, 1979.

The Humanoid Touch (sequel to *The Humanoids*), Holt, 1980.

Three from the Legion (contains *The Legion of Space*, *The Cometeers*, and *One against the Legion*), Doubleday, 1981.

(With Breuer) *The Birth of a New Republic: Jack Williamson—The Collector's Edition*, Volume II, P.D.A. Enterprises, 1981.

Manseed, Ballantine, 1982.

The Queen of the Legion, Pocket Books, 1983.

Lifeburst, Ballantine, 1984.

Firebird, Bluejay, 1986.

"JIM EDEN" SCIENCE FICTION SERIES; UNDER NAME JACK WILLIAMSON; WITH FREDERIK POHL

Undersea Quest, Gnome Press, 1954.

Undersea Fleet, Gnome Press, 1956.

Undersea City, Gnome Press, 1958.

"THE STARCHILD TRILOGY"; UNDER NAME JACK WILLIAMSON; WITH POHL

The Reefs of Space (also see below), Ballantine, 1964.

Starchild (also see below), Ballantine, 1965.

Rogue Star (also see below), Ballantine, 1969.

The Starchild Trilogy (contains *The Reefs of Space*, *Starchild*, and *Rogue Star*), Doubleday, 1977.

"CUCKOO'S SAGA"; UNDER NAME JACK WILLIAMSON; WITH POHL

Farthest Star (also see below), Ballantine, 1975.

Wall around a Star (also see below), Ballantine, 1983.

The Saga of Cuckoo (contains *Farthest Star* and *Wall around a Star*), Doubleday, 1983.

SCIENCE FICTION SHORT STORY COLLECTIONS; UNDER NAME JACK WILLIAMSON

Lady in Danger, Utopian, 1945.

(With Murray Leinster and John Wyndham) *Three Stories*, Doubleday, 1967 (published in England as *A Sense of Wonder: Three Science Fiction Stories*, edited by Sam Moskowitz, Sidgwick & Jackson, 1967).

The Pandora Effect, Ace Books, 1969.

People Machines, Ace Books, 1971.

The Early Williamson, Doubleday, 1975.

Dreadful Sleep, Weinberg (Chicago), 1977.

The Best of Jack Williamson, introduction by Pohl, Ballantine, 1978.

The Alien Intelligence: Jack Williamson—The Collector's Edition, Volume I, P.D.A. Enterprises, 1980.

(With others) *Medea: Harlan's World*, edited by Harlan Ellison, illustrated by Kelly Freas, cartography by Diane Duane, Bantam, 1985.

CONTRIBUTOR; UNDER NAME JACK WILLIAMSON

Lloyd Arthur Eshbach, editor, *Of Worlds Beyond*, Fantasy Press, 1947.

O. J. Friend and Leo Margulies, editors, *My Best Science Fiction Story*, Merlin Press, 1949.

Robert Silverberg, editor, *The Mirror of Infinity*, Harper, 1970.

Robin Scott Wilson, editor, *Those Who Can: A Science Fiction Reader*, New American Library, 1973.

Ben Bova, editor, *The Science Fiction Hall of Fame*, Doubleday, 1973.

Willis E. McNelly, editor, *The Academic Awakening*, CEA, 1974.

Isaac Asimov, *Before the Golden Age*, Doubleday, 1974.

Reginald Bretnor, editor, *Science Fiction: Today and Tomorrow*, Harper, 1974.

Bretnor, editor, *The Craft of Science Fiction*, Harper, 1976.

Thomas D. Clareson, editor, *Voices for the Future: Essays on Major Science Fiction Writers*, Volume I, Bowling Green University, 1976.

Terry Carr, editor, *The Best Science Fiction of the Year, Number Six*, Holt, 1977.

SCIENCE FICTION NOVELS; UNDER PSEUDONYM WILL STEWART

Seetee Shock (sequel to *Seetee Ship*; originally published serially), Simon & Schuster, 1950, reprinted under name Jack Williamson, Lancer Books, 1968.

Seetee Ship (originally published serially), Gnome Press, 1951, reprinted under name Jack Williamson, Lancer Books, 1968.

OTHER; UNDER NAME JACK WILLIAMSON

Darker than You Think (novel), Fantasy Press, 1948.

Golden Blood (novel), Lancer Books, 1964.

The Reign of Wizardry (novel), Lancer Books, 1964, reprinted, Phantasia Press, 1979.

Teaching Science Fiction (nonfiction), privately printed, 1973.

(Editor) *Teaching Science Fiction: Education for Tomorrow* (essays), Owlswick, 1980.

Wonder's Child: My Life in Science Fiction (autobiography), Bluejay, 1985.

Also author, with Pohl, of *Land's End*, Bluejay. Most science fiction magazines have carried his stories, with novels, novelettes, and short stories appearing in *Amazing Stories*, *Science Wonder Stories*, *Air Wonder Stories*, *Astounding Stories*, *Wonder Stories*, *Weird Tales*, *Astounding Science Fiction*, *Argosy*, and others.

SIDELIGHTS: Jack Williamson was born in Arizona Territory, moved to Mexico, then Texas, and then, by covered wagon, to a homestead in eastern New Mexico. "We lived on isolated farms and ranches, far from anybody, and when I was young I knew very few other kids; so I lived to a great extent in my imagination. . . . Life would have been absolutely empty without imagination," records Rosemary Herbert in *Publishers Weekly*. Because his family's ranch failed to prosper, Williamson was unable to pursue his ambition of becoming a scientist. However, by employing both his imagination and his interest for science, Williamson has become a pivotal author in the genre of science fiction.

While he was living in the desertland of New Mexico, Williamson discovered Hugo Gernsback's new magazine called *Amazing Stories*: "Here were space craft taking off from other worlds, travel in time and all sorts of wonderful inventions!" quotes Herbert. Williamson thereby took a chance at the genre and sold his first story, "The Metal Man," to *Amazing Stories* in 1928. Thirteen of his first twenty-one published stories were spectacular enough to gain covers in the early science fiction magazines, often appearing in installments. Williamson says he generally earned his living writing for these magazines for as little as half-a-cent per word.

"If science-fiction writing is an art that can be taught, there is probably no one in the world better qualified to teach it than Jack Williamson," remarks Sam Moskowitz in *Seekers of Tomorrow: Masters of Science Fiction*. "[Williamson is] an author who pioneered superior characterization in a field almost barren of it, realism in the presentation of human motivation previously unknown, scientific rationalization of supernatural concepts for story purposes, and exploitation of the untapped story potentials of antimatter." As an academic, Williamson also legitimized science fiction as a field deserving of literary attention. In recognition of his contributions, he received the Grand Master Award for lifetime achievement from the Science Fiction Writers of America in 1976.

Williamson initially attracted attention in the science fiction genre as a master of the space opera. *The Legion of Space* (1934), the first book of what was to become a series, put Williamson on equal ground with such science fiction writers as John W. Campbell and Edward E. "Doc" Smith. Set in the thirtieth century, *The Legion of Space*'s authenticity rests on the development of the memorable comic figure Giles Habibula. Alfred D. Stewart writes in the *Dictionary of Literary Biography: Twentieth-Century American Science Fiction Writers*: "Developed in Dickensian fashion through distinctive traits of speech and character, [Habibula] is modeled on Shakespeare's Falstaff; he is a born thief who whines about his ills and threats to his personal safety throughout the series." In his second book of the series, *The Cometeers*, Williamson introduces another interesting character, Orco. During the course of the story, Orco discovers, to his distress, that he is not a true human. While the characterization in these early stories was found to be rather striking by reviewers, Moskowitz claims that Williamson's true expertise at characterization came in the stories that followed. "Realism was present in the characterization as well as in the plotting of [his later] stories. Giles Habibula had been a milestone, but Garth Hammond, aptly labeled 'a hero whose heart is purest brass,' in [the short story "Crucible of Power"], was a giant step towards believability in science fiction. Hammond was the man who made the first trip to Mars and built a power station near the sun for sheer selfish, self-seeking gain. . . . There had never been anything as blunt as this in science fiction before. . . . After [Williamson] showed the way, not-completely-sympathetic and more three-dimensional people began to appear" in science fiction.

Reviewers label Williamson's early writing, such as the "Legion of Space" novels, fantasy literature. Stewart stresses that such novels were "vehicles for cosmic plotting and pseudo-scientific devices, not for the examination of man's possibilities. Williamson's [eventual] fascination with Darwin, H. G. Wells, and evolution led him, in his best thought-out and best written books, to deal with real possibilities for man, not exaggerated romantic vagaries." Williamson's writing, beginning in the forties, became more grounded in logical scientific explanations. He wrote his "Seetee" series in the early forties under the pseudonym Will Stewart, and to some they are considered the best expositions on the subject of antimatter ever written. (The concept of antimatter, or contra-terrene, is the condition in which positive and negative charges are reversed from that which is typical on earth.) In *Seetee Ship*, the earth has become morally and politically stagnant, and scientists, known as "asterites," strive to legalize the use of antimatter as a means of reestablishing freedom and progress for mankind. But the asterites and the Establishment are at odds. In the sequel, *Seetee Shock*, the conflict has expanded—the asterites are convinced the power of antimatter should be available to all inhabitants on all planets. When the novel's hero, Nick Jenkins, manages to turn on a special transmitter, the Fifth Freedom results, destroying governments and establishing freedom for all in the universe.

Williamson's most famous novel, *The Humanoids*, also strives for human freedom, but the outcome is disastrous. The humanoids are small robots who have as their goal the protection and happiness of man. However, Stewart says, "As Williamson remarked in a talk at the 1977 World Science-Fiction Convention, 'Their built-in benevolence goes too far. Alert to the potential harm in nearly every human activity, they don't let people drive cars, ride bicycles, smoke, drink or engage in unsupervised sex. Doing everything for everybody, they forbid all free action. Their world becomes a luxurious but nightmarish prison of total frustration.'" Eventually man must regain his freedom and does so by developing psychic powers. A contributor to the *New York Herald Tribune Book Review* believes *The Humanoids* "deals, essentially, with the conflict that began when the wheel and the lever were invented: the battle between men and machines." Does advanced technology cause man to progress or regress? Williamson questions. Thirty years later Williamson wrote the sequel to *The Humanoids* entitled *The Humanoid Touch*, which some reviewers found disappointing. "Williamson is able to offer only a partial answer to the humanoid challenge—a utopia the hero escapes to, where the psychic and biological sciences have achieved ultimate perfection," notes a critic in *Publishers Weekly*.

Several of Williamson's other works focus on genetic engineering, advanced human evolution, and a number of additional evolutionary possibilities. Four distinct species of man exist in *Brother to Demons, Brother to Gods:* premen, trumen, mumen, and stargods. Because of the varying abilities and moralities of these four species, a power struggle arises and the only hope for universal peace is the evolution of "ultiman," a being of perfect love and power. According to Stewart, "*Brother to Demons, Brother to Gods* focuses in the end on humanity's stupendous potential." Williamson is both the optimist and the pessimist. Indeed, Moskowitz credits Williamson as "one of the most adaptable science fiction writers alive." Stewart believes "the future of science fiction is now as unlimited as the future of science itself, and Jack Williamson is one of the pioneer writers who made it so."

Williamson wrote to *CA:* "Though retired from actual teaching, I'm still a full-time science fiction writer, happy that ideas still happen, that I enjoy making them into stories, that editors and readers still seem interested—sometimes, anyhow.

"With so many old and dear friends gone, I have probably been writing science fiction longer than anybody else who is still writing science fiction. Unlike those who dislike the label 'science fiction' on their work, I've always been proud of it. Though some apologists claim too much for the genre, I think some of our claims are justified. It's a way of thinking and feeling about change, about the impacts of science and technology on our minds and our lives—impacts that keep coming harder and faster. Some of the things that some science fiction writers do, at least some of the time, are akin to what some scientists do. For one small example, newspaper reporters who interview me these days give me credit for coining the phrase 'genetic engineering'—for a novel, *Dragon's Island*, first published in 1951, a couple of years before Watson and Crick broke the genetic code and touched off the current exciting transfomation of imagined possibility into hard science.

"Since I discovered science fiction—back in 1926, before it had been named science fiction—it has been half my life. For the first twenty years and more, writing it paid barely enough to let me keep writing it, but in recent decades the rewards in recognition as well as in royalties have been more generous than I had ever dared expect. Looking back on a life of being reasonably well rewarded for doing exactly what I wanted to do, I feel pretty lucky. Pretty optimistic, too, about the ability of homo sapiens to keep on surviving crises as it has always survived them, and about my own ability to survive a little longer as a science fiction writer."

Williamson's work has been translated into numerous European and Asian languages. A collection of his work can be found at Eastern New Mexico University in Portales, New Mexico.

BIOGRAPHICAL/CRITICAL SOURCES:

BOOKS

Clareson, Thomas D., editor, *Voices for the Future: Essays on Major Science Fiction Writers*, Volume I, Bowling Green University, 1976.
Contemporary Literary Criticism, Volume XXIX, Gale, 1984.
Dictionary of Literary Biography, Volume VIII: *Twentieth-Century American Science Fiction Writers*, Gale, 1981.
Moskowitz, Sam, *Seekers of Tomorrow: Masters of Science Fiction*, World Publishing, 1966.
Myers, Robert E., editor, *Jack Williamson: A Primary and Secondary Bibliography*, G. K. Hall, 1980.
Williamson, Jack, *Wonder's Child: My Life in Science Fiction* (autobiography), Bluejay, 1985.

PERIODICALS

Amazing Stories, October, 1964.
Los Angeles Times, October 21, 1980.
New York Herald Tribune Book Review, October 9, 1949.
Publishers Weekly, September 12, 1980, May 23, 1986.
Science Fiction Horizons, Number 1, 1964.
Washington Post Book World, September 30, 1984, September 28, 1986.

—*Sketch by Cheryl Gottler*

*   *   *

WILLIS, Ted 1918-
(George Dixon)

PERSONAL: Born January 13, 1918, in Tottenham, Middlesex, England; son of Alfred John (a bus driver) and Maria Harriett (Meek) Willis; married Audrey Mary Hale (a former actress), August 18, 1944; children: John Edward, Sally Ann Hale. *Education:* Educated in England.

ADDRESSES: Home—5 Shepherds Green, Chislehurst, Kent, England. *Agent*—ALS Management, 67 Brook St., London W.1, England.

CAREER: Free-lance journalist; writer of plays for stage, films, and television. Director of a film production company; member of board of governors, National Film School, London. *Military service:* British Army, World War II; served in Royal Fusiliers, then as writer of War Office films and Ministry of Information documentaries.

MEMBER: Royal Society of Arts (London; fellow), Writers Guild of Great Britain (president, 1959-69).

AWARDS, HONORS: Berlin Festival Award and London Picture-Goer Award, both for "Woman in a Dressing Gown"; Edinburgh Festival Award for "Story of Achievement"; created Lord Willis of Chislehurst, 1963; Pye Special Award and Variety Club Award, both for distinguished service to television; Bookseller Award for most popular library book; Royal Society of Arts Silver Medal.

WRITINGS:

PLAYS

"Buster," produced in London, England, at Arts Theatre Club, July, 1943.
God Bless the Guv'nor: A Moral Melodrama in Three Acts in Which the Twin Evils of Trades Unionism and Strong Drink Are Exposed, New Theatre Publications, 1945.
The Lady Purrs: A Farcical Comedy in Three Acts, Baker's Plays, 1950.
George Comes Home: A Play in One Act for Women, Samuel French, 1955.
(With Richard Gordon) *Doctor in the House* (three-act comedy; based on the novel by Gordon), Evans Brothers, 1957, Samuel French, 1966.
Woman in a Dressing Gown, and Other Television Plays, Barrie & Rockliff, 1959, title play published separately as *Woman in a Dressing Gown* (also see below), Evans Brothers, 1964.
Hot Summer Night (three-act), Samuel French, 1959.
(With Henry Cecil) *Brothers in Law: A Comedy in Three Acts* (based on the novel by Cecil), Samuel French, 1959.
The Eyes of Youth (two-act; adapted from the novel *A Dread of Burning* by Rosemary Timperley), Evans Brothers, 1960.
The Little Goldmine (one-act television play), Samuel French, 1962.
"Dead on Saturday," produced in Leatherhead, England at the Thorndike, January 26, 1971.

Also author of produced plays "No Trees in the Street," 1948, "The Magnificent Moodies," 1952, "Kid Kenyon Rides Again," 1954, "The Eyes of Youth," 1959, "Mother" (adapted from the novel by Maxim Gorky), 1961, "Doctor at Sea" (adapted from the novel by Richard Gordon), 1962, "A Slow Roll of Drums," 1964, "A Murder of Crows," 1965, "Queenie" (musical), 1968, "A Fine Day for Murder," 1970, "Yellow Star," "All Change Here," "When in Rome," "Duel at Wapping Creek." Author of television plays, including "What Happens to Love," "The Young and the Guilty," "Look in Any Window," "Strictly for the Sparrows," "Accent of Fear," "The Four Seasons of Rosie Carr," "Old Soldiers," "Doctor on the Boil," and "Stardust."

NOVELS

The Blue Lamp (based on film script of the same name; also see below), Convoy Publications, 1950.
The Devil's Churchyard, Parrish, 1957.
Seven Gates to Nowhere, Parrish, 1958.
(With Charles Hatton; under pseudonym George Dixon) *Dixon of Dock Green: My Life* (also see below), William Kimber, 1960.
Death May Surprise Us, Macmillan, 1974.
The Left-Handed Sleeper, Macmillan, 1975.
Man-Eater, Macmillan, 1976.
The Churchill Commando, Macmillan, 1977.
The Buckingham Palace Connection, Macmillan, 1978.

The Lions of Judah, Macmillan, 1979.
The Naked Sun, Macmillan, 1980.
The Most Beautiful Girl in the World, Macmillan, 1982.
Spring at the Winged Horse, Macmillan, 1983.
A Problem for Mother Christmas, Gollancz, 1986.

FILM SCRIPTS

"It's Great to be Young," Columbia, 1946.
"Holiday Camp," Gainsborough Pictures, 1947.
"Good Time Girl," Sydney Box, 1950.
"The Blue Lamp," Ealing Studios, 1950.
"Trouble in Store," Two Cities Films, 1953.
"Top of the Form," J. Arthur Rank, 1953.
"Up to His Neck," J. Arthur Rank, 1954.
"Woman in a Dressing Gown," Godwin-Willis, 1957.
"No Trees in the Street," Associated British-Pathe, 1958.
"Flame in the Streets," Atlantic Pictures Corp., 1962.

Also script writer for "Burnt Evidence," 1952, "The Young and the Guilty," 1957, "Bitter Harvest," 1960, "The Undefeated," (with Gerard Bryant) "The Huggetts Abroad," "The Wallet," "The Horsemaster," "Last Bus to Banjo Creek," "Mrs. Harris, M.P.," "Mrs. Harris Goes to New York," and "Mrs. Harris Goes to Moscow." Author of scripts for television series, including "Patterns of Marriage" and "Dixon of Dock Green," both for British Broadcasting Corp., "Big City" for International Television, "A Place for Animals," and "Racecourse," both for German television, and "Flower of Evil," "Outbreak of Murder," "Crime of Passion," "Virgin of the Secret Service," "Hunters Walk," and "Black Beauty."

OTHER

Whatever Happened to Tom Mix?: The Story of One of My Lives (autobiography), Cassell, 1970.

Author of pamphlet *Fighting Youth of Russia: The Story of the Young Men and Women of the Soviet Union*, Russia Today Society, 1942. Writer of about fifty scripts for War Office films and Ministry of Information documentaries.

SIDELIGHTS: Ted Willis's plays have been performed in many countries around the world. Several books based on film or television scripts by Willis have been published, notably Mabel and Denis Constanduros' *The Huggetts Abroad*, Sampson Low, Marston & Co., 1949, Douglas Enefer's *The Days of Vengeance*, World Distributors, 1961, and John Burke's *Flame in the Streets*, Four Square Books, 1961. In 1969 John Long published *Sergeant Cork's Second Casebook* by Arthur Swinson, a book of stories from the A.T.V. television series featuring Willis's character, Sergeant Cork. Willis appears in the *Guiness Book of Records* as the writer who has created the greatest number of television series.

AVOCATIONAL INTERESTS: Tennis, badminton, football, traveling (with special interest in Australia and South America).

BIOGRAPHICAL/CRITICAL SOURCES:

PERIODICALS

Observer Review, October 25, 1970.
Stage and Television Today, November 26, 1970.

*   *   *

WILSON, Erica

PERSONAL: Born in England; came to the United States, 1952; married Vladimir Kagan (a furniture designer). *Education:* Attended Royal School of Needlework.

ADDRESSES: Office—717 Madison Ave., New York, N.Y., 10021.

CAREER: Teacher of needlework at home and at Cooper Union Museum, New York City; owner of Erica Wilson Needle Works, retail stores in New York City and Nantucket, Mass.; author and lecturer on needlework. Organizer of needlework seminars, 1974—; has appeared on her own Public Broadcasting System television series, "Erica."

WRITINGS:

Crewel Embroidery, Scribner, 1962, abridged edition published as *Craft of Crewel Embroidery*, 1971.
Fun with Crewel Embroidery, Scribner, 1965.
Erica Wilson's Embroidery Book, Scribner, 1973.
Needleplay, Scribner, 1975.
Ask Erica, Scribner, 1977.
The Animal Kingdom, Scribner, 1978.
New World of Plastic Canvas, Scribner, 1978.
Say It with Stitches, Scribner, 1978.
More Needleplay, Scribner, 1979.
Quilts of America, Oxmoor, 1979.
Christmas World, Scribner, 1980.
Erica Wilson's Needlework to Wear, Oxmoor, 1982.
Erica Wilson's Children's World, Scribner, 1983.

Also author of four-part video series, "Needlepoint," "Quilting," "Knitting," and "Cross Stitch."

WORK IN PROGRESS: Knitting Book, for Scribner; *Book for the Bride*, for Little, Brown.

BIOGRAPHICAL/CRITICAL SOURCES:

PERIODICALS

Book and Author Magazine, March/April, 1984.

*   *   *

WILSON, Robert Renbert   1898-1975

PERSONAL: Born October 10, 1898, in Hillsboro, Tex.; died April 29, 1975, in Durham, N.C.; son of Edgar Thomas (a merchant) and Sophia (Richardson) Wilson; married Marea Cappon Van Noppen, December 22, 1928; children: Robert Renbert, Jr. *Education:* Austin College, A.B., 1918; Princeton University, M.A., 1922; Harvard University, Ph.D., 1927. *Politics:* Democrat. *Religion:* Presbyterian.

ADDRESSES: Home—717 Anderson St., Durham, N.C. 27706. *Office*—Department of Political Science, Duke University, Durham, N.C. 27706.

CAREER: Austin College, Sherman, Tex., college registrar, 1919-21; Duke University, Durham, N.C., assistant professor, 1925-27, associate professor, 1927-29, professor of political science and international law, 1929-61, James B. Duke Professor, 1961-66, Emeritus James B. Duke Professor, 1966-75, chairman of department of political science, 1934-48, director of graduate studies, 1937-47, 1949-66, lecturer in Law School, 1948-66, chairman of Commonwealth Studies, 1959-66. Visiting professor at University of Texas, 1926, 1928, 1935 (summers), Stanford University, 1939 (summer), University of North Carolina, 1940; Fulbright professor, University of Istanbul, 1951-52. Adviser on commercial treaties to U.S. State Department.

MEMBER: International Law Association, American Society of International Law (president, 1957-58), Southern Political Science Association (past president), Cosmos Club.

AWARDS, HONORS: Carnegie fellowship in international law for graduate study, 1922-23, 1924-27; LL.D. from Austin College, 1940.

WRITINGS:

International Law in Treaties, Turkish Institute of International Law, 1949.
The United Nations Organization and the Organization of American States, Turkish Institute of International Law, 1952.
The International Law Standard in Treaties of the United States, Harvard University Press, 1953.
A Decade of New Commercial Treaties, Lancaster, 1956.
(Contributor) *Some Questions of Legal Relations between Commonwealth Members,* Lancaster, 1957.
(Contributor) David R. Deener and R. Taylor Cole, editors, *Commonwealth Perspectives,* Duke University Press, 1958.
(With others) *United States Commercial Treaties and International Law,* Hauser Press, 1960.
(Contributor) Deener, editor, *Canada-United States Treaty Relations,* Duke University Press, 1963.
(Editor and contributor) *The International Law Standard and Commonwealth Developments,* Duke University Press, 1966.
(Editor and contributor) *International and Comparative Law of the Commonwealth,* Duke University Press, 1968.
(Contributor) *A Decade of Legal Consultation: Asia-African Collaboration,* Center for Commonwealth Studies, Duke University, 1968.
International Law and Contemporary Commonwealth Issues, Duke University Press, 1971.

Member of board of editors, *American Journal of International Law,* beginning 1937.

BIOGRAPHICAL/CRITICAL SOURCES:

BOOKS

Deener, David R., editor, *De Lege Pactorum,* Duke University Press, 1970.

OBITUARIES:

PERIODICALS

Durham Morning Herald, April 30, 1975.†

*   *   *

WINN, Charles S.   1932-

PERSONAL: Born April 15, 1932, in Utah; son of David G. (an educator) and Edith (Hughes) Winn; married Ann Crandall, August 7, 1953; children: Steven, Julie, Sally, Kathy. *Education:* University of Utah, B.S., M.S., Ed.D.

ADDRESSES: Home—720 South 850th E., Bountiful, Utah 84010. *Office*—Utah State Board of Education, 250 East 500th S., Salt Lake City, Utah 84111.

CAREER: Federal Reserve Bank, Salt Lake City, Utah, management trainee, 1957-59; Utah Technical College, Salt Lake City, member of staff, 1959-61; Hercules Powder Co., Salt Lake City, Utah, training coordinator, 1961-63; Utah State Board of Education, Salt Lake City, educational supervisor,

1963—. *Military service:* U.S. Air Force, 1954-57. Utah Air National Guard; became lieutenant colonel.

MEMBER: Sales and Marketing Executives International, American Vocational Association, National Business Education Association, National Association of State Supervisors of Distributive Education.

WRITINGS:

FOR YOUNG PEOPLE; "CAREERS IN FOCUS" SERIES; PUBLISHED BY McGRAW

Careers in Focus Program Guide, 1975.
(With M. C. Baker) *Exploring Occupations in Food Service and Home Economics,* 1975.
(With C. Healy) *Discovering You,* 1975.
(With L. Heath) *Exploring Occupations in Electricity and Electronics,* 1975.
(With B. J. Vorndran) *Exploring Occupations in Personal Services, Hospitality, and Recreation,* 1975.
(With others) *Exploring Occupations in Agribusiness and Natural Resources,* 1975.
(With others) *Exploring Occupations in Public and Social Services,* 1975.
(With others) *Exploring Marketing Occupations,* 1975.
(With L. A. Walsh) *Exploring Transportation Occupations,* 1976.
Exploring Careers in Construction, 1976.
(With L. M. Davis) *Exploring Careers in Science, Fine Arts, and Humanities,* McGraw, 1976.
(With M. Peterson) *Exploring Business and Office Occupations,* 1976.
(With others) *Exploring Health Occupations,* 1976.
(With others) *Exploring Occupations in Communication and Graphic Arts,* 1976.
(With others) *Exploring Occupations in Engineering and Manufacturing,* 1976.

WORK IN PROGRESS: Careers in Manufacturing and Repair; Careers in Construction, new edition.†

*   *   *

WINTERS, Jon
See CROSS, Gilbert B.

*   *   *

WOODIWISS, Kathleen E(rin)   1939-

PERSONAL: Born June 3, 1939, in Alexandria, La.; daughter of Charles Wingrove, Sr., and Gladys (Coker) Hogg; married Ross Woodiwiss (a retired U.S. Air Force major), July 20, 1956; children: Sean Alan, Dorren James, Heath Alexander. *Education:* Attended schools in Alexandria, La. *Politics:* Republican.

ADDRESSES: Home—Princeton, Minn. *Office*—Avon Books, Hearst Corporation, 959 Eighth Ave., New York, New York 10019.

CAREER: Writer.

WRITINGS:

NOVELS

The Flame and the Flower, Avon, 1972.
The Wolf and the Dove, Avon, 1974.
Shanna, Avon, 1977.

Ashes in the Wind, Avon, 1979.
A Rose in Winter, Avon, 1982.
Come Love A Stranger, Avon, 1984.

SIDELIGHTS: Kathleen E. Woodiwiss is a pioneering writer of romance fiction whose first novel is generally credited with creating the sub-genre known as "erotic historical" romance. When *The Flame and the Flower* was published in 1972 the field of romance writing was dominated by "contemporary gothics" produced by writers such as Mary Stewart, Victoria Holt, and Phyllis Whitney. *The Flame and the Flower* differed from its predecessors in that it was substantially longer, but also because it contained lengthy, often detailed passages describing the sexual encounters of the hero and heroine. The immediate success of *The Flame and the Flower* cleared the way for writers like Rosemary Rogers and Laura McBain, authors who, along with Woodiwiss, have helped to make the historical romance an enormously popular form.

The novels following *The Flame and the Flower* continued to be ground-breakers and assured Woodiwiss a large and loyal readership. *Shanna,* Woodiwiss's third book, made publishing history by becoming the first historical romance released in a trade paperback edition. *Shanna* went on to sell over three million copies and spent a full year on the *New York Times* bestseller list. In 1979 Avon published *Ashes in the Wind* with a first printing of 1.5 million copies and backed the book with a huge promotional campaign, including full-page advertisements in national women's magazines and commercials on network television. The publicity paid off almost immediately as *Ashes in the Wind* sold over two million copies and went into a third printing within a month of its release. All told, Woodiwiss's books have sold over ten million copies.

In spite of her remarkable success, Woodiwiss's initial motives for writing were rather simple. "I couldn't find anything good to read, a good romantic book to pass a few hours away, so I decided to write one myself," she told Judy Klemesrud in the *New York Times Book Review.* "I just started pecking away at this story set during the American Revolution. It wasn't anything I could get completely absorbed in. I had three boys at home, and there were always dishes to be put in the dishwasher." Woodiwiss finished the book and, following the advice of her husband and friends, submitted it to half-a-dozen publishers. After they had all rejected it, she sent the book to Avon where an editor, Nancy Coffey, picked it out of a group of submitted manuscripts known as the "slush pile." The book became *The Flame and the Flower* and went on to launch Woodiwiss into a successful writing career.

Historical romances vary in some respects but share fundamental similarities. Settings are typically exotic and frequently change from continent to continent. Heroes are characteristically handsome and commanding while heroines are beautiful and sensitive. Often innocent, the heroine is usually introduced to the hero with whom she falls in love, only to be parted from him for much of the story. The book inevitably ends with the heroine being united with her true love. *The Flame and the Flower* clearly embodies the traditions of its genre. The heroine, Heather, is a teenager throughout a story that begins around 1800 in England and moves to the American Carolinas. A beautiful and proper girl who becomes the ward of a cruel aunt, Heather is raped by a handsome Yankee who in turn is forced to marry her. After many adventures, the pair reunite and their initial hatred for each other turns to love. *The Flame and the Flower* also maintains the traditional structural relationship of males as dominant to and protective of females.

Where *The Flame and the Flower* and other Woodiwiss novels break with tradition is in their frank depiction of the sexual relationship between the hero and the heroine. Yet while her books contain occasional sexual passages, Woodiwiss objects to charges that her books are "erotic." "I'm insulted when my books are called erotic," she told an interviewer in *Cosmopolitan.* "I don't think people who say that have read my books. I believe I write love stories. With a little spice. Some of the other current romances are a bit savage, though. They make sex dirty. It's embarrassing to read them. But women are looking for the love story. I get a lot of fan mail, and they tell me that."

Woodiwiss's enormous success does not seem to have greatly affected her lifestyle. She still spends much of her time with her family at their home in rural Minnesota. As she told Klemesrud, "I enjoy cooking and cleaning, my family and my home." Writing is something of a family affair for Woodiwiss. In scheduling her books she does her writing primarily during the school year, because, as she explained to Klemesrud, "when the boys are home in the summer, I like to spend time with them." Woodiwiss's husband, a retired Air Force major, often gets involved in the writing process by giving Woodiwiss ideas for her books. In fact, he wrote the poems that begin and end both *Shanna* and *Ashes in the Wind.*

That her books are generally ignored by "serious" reviewers does not seem to bother Woodiwiss, nor does it make her wish to change her approach to writing. As she told Klemesrud: "I never started out to win any prizes for my writing. I wanted to appease a hunger for romantic novels, and that is what I shall continue to do."

CA INTERVIEW

CA interviewed Kathleen E. Woodiwiss by telephone on February 10, 1987, at her home in Princeton, Minnesota.

CA: According to John Bowers in Cosmopolitan, *the writer you most admire is Winston Churchill rather than any of the storytellers of fiction. Did Churchill's writing appeal to you primarily because of your interest in history?*

WOODIWISS: I enjoyed it very much when I was doing research for *The Flame and the Flower.* As far as pleasure reading goes, I think some of the romantic books appeal to me more. But I enjoyed Churchill's writing quite a bit; I enjoyed reading history from his standpoint.

CA: You're said to have become interested in writing because you weren't happy with anything you were reading. What was missing?

WOODIWISS: Actually, I had the desire to write many, many years before that. I just came to a point where I was looking for a good book and couldn't find a romantic one that appealed to me in every way. I thought, Why don't I write my own?

CA: You've said that when you sat down and started work on The Flame and the Flower, *the book that's credited with beginning the current paperback historical romance genre, you were doing it mainly to entertain yourself. At what point did you begin to think you had a salable book on your hands?*

WOODIWISS: About three-quarters of the way through I let some friends read it, and they encouraged me to finish it and start sending it around. That was the beginning.

CA: You seem to care a lot about getting the historical and social details correct. Was research a skill you had to acquire somewhere in the writing of the first book, or were you already adept at it?

WOODIWISS: I have been interested in history all my life. Digging through the books for *The Flame and the Flower,* I didn't think of myself as honing my skills. It was just a matter of trying to find some facts that I needed. I sought them until I found them.

CA: That seems to be a part of the work you enjoy especially.

WOODIWISS: Yes, I do.

CA: Do you look for something other than standard books—things like diaries and newspapers?

WOODIWISS: With *Ashes in the Wind,* which was set in the Civil War, I was able to gain some knowledge from newspaper accounts. Mostly my books are in time periods where newspapers weren't published that much.

CA: I've noticed you write a lot of good detail about the clothing your characters wear. Is this a particular interest of yours?

WOODIWISS: Oh yes. I'm a clothes hog. At one point in my life I was doing some art work, and I thought of becoming a dress designer. That was a passion of mine. I didn't realize that I was sort of throwing aside this desire to write, too. I thought writing a book was something someone else could do, but not me. That was when I first decided to do it for my own pleasure.

CA: Have you acquired quite a large personal library in the course of your work?

WOODIWISS: Yes. I belong to the History Book Club, and I buy books as I go along. I usually have a couple of plots in my head for the future, and I start ahead collecting books for that time period.

CA: So the plot comes before the setting.

WOODIWISS: Yes. The plot comes first, and I set it in a time period where it can work.

CA: Of the time periods you've used in your books, is there one you feel the most kinship with or interest in?

WOODIWISS: I enjoy the eighteenth century best of all. To me, it's the most romantic and exciting period to write about. I feel a sense of comfort when I'm writing about that era, as if it's become an old friend that I know.

CA: Do you live with the characters for a while mentally before you start writing?

WOODIWISS: Not really. When I start, it's very sketchy. I struggle quite a bit trying to know the characters and figure out what they would do. Once I reach a point where I know the characters, it's much easier to determine what they would do in certain instances.

CA: So they're firming up as you write, in the beginning?

WOODIWISS: Yes.

CA: Do you have a particular method for picking the characters' names?

WOODIWISS: I like unusual names, unique names. I just search until I find them. I have a couple of name books, but I think I'm wearing those out. Shanna I thought I had invented until I was autographing books and came across a few Shannas. Actually, it's a Jewish word that means *beauty,* but I didn't know that when I was writing.

CA: Do you have a favorite among your characters?

WOODIWISS: My characters are like children to me, something I've created. I really don't have any favorites, but I think I enjoyed doing Shanna and Ruark the most because I didn't have any deadlines to meet and I wasn't under pressure to get the book out at a certain time.

CA: What do you like to feel you're giving your readers?

WOODIWISS: Enjoyment. Escape. I would like to be able to give the reader a time period of relaxation and pleasure, a time of being able to put the worries and everything aside and just enjoy and relax.

CA: You're always described as shy. Has this been a problem in doing promotion appearances for your books?

WOODIWISS: I've gone on tour. I think getting up and speaking to a big crowd or anything like that would be difficult. I was not born to be a speechmaker. I was born to be a writer, and I think I'm best avoiding those kinds of promotion things. I'm not terribly shy; it's not as though I'd put my head in a hole in the ground. I think I'm reserved and live a quiet life, and I prefer it that way.

CA: Do you see much of other writers?

WOODIWISS: Not terribly much. I haven't gone to any of the conventions. But I do have friends. Laurie McBain is a friend of mine, and I think she's a very sweet girl. We talk on the telephone now and then.

CA: Is your work usually over when you submit a manuscript to the publisher, or do you often do revisions after that point?

WOODIWISS: With the last couple of books, I was handing in papers as I finished them. There weren't any revisions afterwards except minor things. Prior to that I've sent in whole manuscripts, and there were very few changes made. I like to present a book that is as completed as possible.

CA: Do you feel you've gotten much direction and help from editors?

WOODIWISS: I can't really say that I have. Walter Meade refreshed my memory about proper English. By the time I started writing, I was in my thirties and I had forgotten a few things. But as far as the plot goes, it's what I create, and nobody in the publishing world has lent to the storyline.

CA: Your sons were young when you began to get your books published. How did they respond to your success? Did they realize Mom was a writer?

WOODIWISS: I think they took it in stride and still do. I'm just Mom to them. As far as thinking of me as any great writer, I don't believe they think in that light.

CA: You were quoted in Love's Leading Ladies *as having said, "I don't agree with ERA and the women's movement." Have you changed your thinking on that since?*

WOODIWISS: I think they've taken that a little bit out of context. I am a woman. I believe I am just as capable as a man doing certain things. I don't think a man is smarter than a woman or a woman more intelligent than a man; but an individual can be more gifted or have a higher IQ than another individual. I'm rather independent. My father died when I was twelve, and we were mainly a house full of women. I might have been the first ERA representative! But as far as trying to compete on a masculine level goes, I'd much rather be a woman. I'm proud to be a woman, and I appreciate men opening doors for me and all of that.

CA: Have you had time to go back at all to the painting?

WOODIWISS: No, I haven't had time, and it will probably be one of the things I'll never go back to. I think you really have to keep yourself polished to do art work, and I have been a long time away from it.

CA: Have your writing habits changed over the years?

WOODIWISS: Because my time is demanded other places, I find it harder to get to my work, but I still like writing on a daily schedule and sticking with a book. There comes a point when I just have to tell everybody, Hey, I'm working on a book; I'll see you when it's finished.

CA: What part of the work do you find most challenging?

WOODIWISS: I think putting down the first draft of the book is the most challenging. After I begin to know the characters and the flow of the story, things become much easier.

CA: Would you like to do something completely different in the writing, maybe a setting you haven't done any previous reading on, or even a new genre?

WOODIWISS: I don't think so. I started out writing what I wanted to write, and I haven't changed in that aspect.

CA: You don't seem to have been swept off your feet by the money your books have brought. What do you feel is the best part of the success?

WOODIWISS: It gives me a few more comforts than I had before. I have always liked my home, and I like being able to furnish it and decorate it as I want. I have done that.

CA: Can you talk about what you're working on now?

WOODIWISS: I usually don't talk about my plot until the book comes out, but I can say that it will be set in the Elizabethan period. Another historical romance! I hope to be finished with it the latter part of this year. I was really rushed with the last one, and I swore after that I'd always hand in a book that I felt good about. When I feel good about the book, then I will hand it in.

BIOGRAPHICAL/CRITICAL SOURCES:

BOOKS

Falk, Kathryn, *Love's Leading Ladies*, Pinnacle Books, 1982.

PERIODICALS

Cosmopolitan, February, 1978.
New York Times Book Review, November 4, 1979.
Publishers Weekly, January 31, 1977, May 30, 1977.
Village Voice, May 9, 1977.
Washington Post Book World, October 7, 1979.†

—*Interview by Jean W. Ross*

*   *   *

WOODMAN, Anthony John   1945-

PERSONAL: Born April 11, 1945, in Newcastle upon Tyne, England. *Education:* University of Newcastle upon Tyne, B.A., 1965; King's College, Cambridge, Ph.D., 1970.

ADDRESSES: Office—Department of Classics, University of Durham, Durham DH1 3EU, England.

CAREER: University of Newcastle upon Tyne, Newcastle upon Tyne, England, lecturer in classics, 1968-79, reader in Latin literature, 1979-80; University of Leeds, Leeds, England, professor of Latin, 1980-84; University of Durham, Durham, England, professor of Latin, 1984—.

MEMBER: Classical Association of England and Wales, Society for the Promotion of Roman Studies, Cambridge Philological Society.

WRITINGS:

(Contributor) Jacqueline Bibauw, editor, *Hommages a Marcel Renard* (title means "Studies in Honor of Marcel Renard"), Latomus (Brussels), 1968.
(Editor with David West and contributor) *Quality and Pleasure in Latin Poetry*, Cambridge University Press, 1975.
(Contributor) T. A. Dorey, editor, *Empire and Aftermath: Silver Latin II*, Routledge & Kegan Paul, 1975.
Velleius Paterculus, Cambridge University Press, Volume I: *The Tiberian Narrative*, 1977, Volume II: *The Caesarian and Augustan Narrative*, 1983.
(Editor with West and contributor) *Creative Imitation and Latin Literature*, Cambridge University Press, 1979.
(Editor with West and contributor) *Poetry and Politics in the Augustan Age*, Cambridge University Press, 1983.
(Editor with I. S. Moxon and J. D. Smart) *Past Perspectives: Studies in Greek and Roman Historical Writing*, Cambridge University Press, 1986.
From Thucydides to Tacitus: Four Studies in Historical Narrative, Croom Helm, 1988.

Contributor to classical journals.

WORK IN PROGRESS: A commentary on *Tacitus;* (with R. H. Martin) *Annals* 4.

AVOCATIONAL INTERESTS: Football, mountains, poetry, table tennis, and "the Great War, World War II."

*   *   *

WOODS, John   1926-

PERSONAL: Born July 12, 1926, in Martinsville, Ind.; son of Jefferson Blount and Doris (Underwood) Woods; married Emily Newbury, December 1, 1951 (deceased); children: David Warren, Richard William. *Education:* Indiana University, B.S., 1949, M.A., 1954; University of Iowa, graduate study, 1957-58.

ADDRESSES: Home—6411 Hampton St., Portage, Mich. 49002. *Office*—English Department, Western Michigan University, Kalamazoo, Mich. 49008.

CAREER: Western Michigan University, Kalamazoo, assistant professor, 1955-61, associate professor, 1961-65, professor of English, 1965—. Visiting professor, University of California at Irvine, 1967-68; visiting professor and poet-in-residence, Purdue University, 1975. *Military service:* U.S. Army Air Force, 1944-46.

MEMBER: American Association of University Professors, Associate Writing Programs.

AWARDS, HONORS: Theodore Roethke Award from *Poetry Northwest*, 1969; Publication Award from National Endowment for the Arts, 1970; Distinguished Faculty Scholar Award from Western Michigan University, 1978; Distinguished Michigan Artist Award, 1978; Michigan Individual Artist Grant, 1981; National Endowment for the Arts Fellowship, 1982.

WRITINGS:

POETRY

The Deaths at Paragon, Indiana University Press, 1955.
On the Morning of Color, Indiana University Press, 1961.
The Cutting Edge, Indiana University Press, 1966.
Keeping Out of Trouble, Indiana University Press, 1968.
The Knees of Widows (broadsheet), Westigan Review, 1971.
Turning to Look Back: Poems, 1955-70, Indiana University Press, 1972.
(With James Hearst and Felix Pollack) *Voyages to the Inland Sea*, Wisconsin State University at LaCrosse, 1972.
Alcohol, Pilot Press, 1973.
Bone Flicker, Juniper Books, 1974.
Striking the Earth, Indiana University Press, 1976.
Thirty Years on the Force, Juniper Press, 1977.
The Night of the Game, Raintree Press, 1982.
The Valley of Minor Animals, Dragon Gate, 1982.
The Salt Stone: Selected Poems, Dragon Gate, 1984.

CONTRIBUTOR

American Literary Anthology, Viking, 1970.
Just What the Country Needs, Wadsworth, 1971.
Contemporary American Poetry, Penguin, 1971.
A Geography of Poets, Bantam, 1979.

OTHER

Contributor of poems, stories, plays, and reviews to *Poetry, Shenandoah, Folio, Kenyon Review, Chicago Review, Epoch, Western Review, Paris Review, Fresco, Calliope, Saturday Review, Prairie Schooner, Poetry Northwest, Massachusetts Review, Critic, Choice, CCC Journal, Western Humanities Review*, and numerous other magazines. Has recorded his poetry for the Library of Congress and for Aural Press (where he was poetry editor, 1964-65).

*   *   *

WRAGG, E(dward) C(onrad)   1938-

PERSONAL: Born June 26, 1938, in Sheffield, England; son of George William (a florist) and Maria (Brandstetter) Wragg; married Judith King, December 29, 1960; children: Josephine, Caroline, Christopher. *Education:* University of Durham, B.A. (with first class honors), 1959, diploma in education, 1960, University of Leicester, M.Ed., 1967; University of Exeter, Ph.D., 1972

ADDRESSES: Office—School of Education, University of Exeter, Exeter EX1 2LU, England.

CAREER: Teacher in grammar school in Wakefield, England, 1960-63; teacher of German and head of department in boys' school in Leicester, England, 1964-66; University of Exeter, Exeter, England, lecturer in education, 1966-73; University of Nottingham, Nottingham, England, professor of education, 1973-78; University of Exeter, professor of education, 1978—, director of School of Education, 1978—. Chairman, BBC School Broadcasting Council; specialist adviser, Parliamentary Select Committee on Education; director, Teacher Education Project, Department of Education and Science, 1976-81; member, Council for National Academic Awards.

MEMBER: British Educational Research Association (president), Universities Council for the Education of Teachers.

WRITINGS:

(Author of adaptation) Wolfgang Ecke, *Krimis*, Longmans, Green, 1967.
Life in Germany, Longmans, Green, 1968.
Teaching Teaching, David & Charles, 1974.
Classroom Interaction, Open University, 1976.
Teaching Mixed Ability Groups, David & Charles, 1976.
A Handbook for School Governors, Methuen, 1980.
Class Management and Control, Macmillan, 1981.
A Review of Research in Teacher Education, National Foundation for Educational Research, 1982.
Swineshead Revisited, Trentham, 1982.
Classroom Teaching Skills, Croom Helm, 1984.
More Pearls from Swineshire, Trentham, 1984.
The Domesday Project, BBC Publications, 1985.
Education: An Action Guide for Parents, BBC Publications, 1986.
Teacher Appraisal, Macmillan, 1987.

Editor of teaching series for David & Charles. Regular columnist for *Times Educational Supplement*. Contributor to language and education journals.

WORK IN PROGRESS: Research on teacher education, classroom interaction, and curriculum development.

SIDELIGHTS: E. C. Wragg told *CA:* "Writing a regular column for a national newspaper in which I try to bring out the humorous side of education has made me realise how hilarious human behavior is. I think of all those wasted years I took it seriously."

AVOCATIONAL INTERESTS: Sport, reading, travel, media.

*   *   *

WRIGHT, Charles (Penzel, Jr.)   1935-

PERSONAL: Born August 25, 1935, in Hardin County, Tenn.; son of Charles Penzel and Mary Castleman (Winter) Wright; married Holly McIntire, April 6, 1969; children: Luke Savin Herrick. *Education:* Davidson College, B.A., 1957; University of Iowa, M.F.A., 1963; postgraduate study, University of Rome, 1963-64.

ADDRESSES: Home—940 Locust Ave., Charlottesville, Va. 22901. *Office*—Department of English, University of Virginia, Charlottesville, Va. 22903.

CAREER: University of California, Irvine, 1966-83, began as assistant professor, became professor of English; affiliated with University of Virginia, Charlottesville, 1983—. Fulbright lecturer in Venice, Italy, 1968-69. *Military service:* U.S. Army, Intelligence Corps, 1957-61.

MEMBER: PEN American Center.

AWARDS, HONORS: Fulbright scholar at University of Rome, 1963-65; Eunice Tietjens Award, *Poetry* magazine, 1969; Guggenheim fellow, 1975; Melville Cane Award, Poetry Society of America, and Edgar Allan Poe Award, Academy of American Poets, both 1976, both for *Bloodlines;* Academy-Institute Award, American Academy and Institute of the Arts, 1977; PEN translation award, 1978; Ingram Merrill fellow, 1980; runner-up for Pulitzer Prize in poetry, 1982, for *The Southern Cross;* American Book Award in poetry (shared with Galway Kinnell), 1983, for *Country Music/Selected Early Poems;* National Book Critics Circle award in poetry nomination, 1984, for *The Other Side of the River.*

WRITINGS:

POETRY

The Dream Animal (chapbook), House of Anansi (Toronto), 1968.
The Grave of the Right Hand, Wesleyan University Press, 1970.
The Venice Notebook, Barn Dream Press, 1971.
Hard Freight, Wesleyan University Press, 1973.
Bloodlines, Wesleyan University Press, 1975.
China Trace, Wesleyan University Press, 1977.
The Southern Cross, Random House, 1981.
Country Music/Selected Early Poems, Wesleyan University Press, 1982.
The Other Side of the River, Random House, 1984.
Zone Journals, Farrar, Straus, 1988.

TRANSLATOR

Eugenio Montale, *The Storm,* Field Editions, 1978.
Montale, *Motets,* Windhover, 1981.
Dino Campana, *Orphic Songs,* Field Editions, 1984.

SIDELIGHTS: Charles Wright's reputation has increased steadily with each poetry collection he has published. Today, he is widely regarded as one of the most important poets living in the United States. From his first collection, *The Grave of the Right Hand,* to more recent works, such as *The Southern Cross* and *The Other Side of the River,* Wright has worked in a style which creates a feeling of immediacy and concreteness by emphasizing objects and personal perspective. Many critics believe that Wright's youth in rural Tennessee remains a vital force in his writing, for he shows a typically Southern concern for the past and its power. He began writing poetry while serving in Italy with the U.S. Army. While there he "began using Ezra Pound's Italian Cantos first as a guide book to out-of-the-way places, then as a reference book and finally as a 'copy' book," quotes *Dictionary of Literary Biography Yearbook: 1982* essayist George F. Butterick.

Ezra Pound's influence is obvious in *The Grave of the Right Hand,* Wright's first major collection. These poems "have the polished clarity one would expect from a master of the plain style," *Georgia Review* contributor Peter Stitt observes. "They are obviously meant to speak to the reader, to communicate something he can share." At the same time, *The Grave of the Right Hand* is the most symbolic of all Wright's works, with images of gloves, shoes, hands, and hats recurring throughout. Through these images, the poet introduces themes that recur in all his later work, described by Butterick as "mortality, the uses of memory, the irrepressible past, states of being, per-

sonal salvation, the correspondence between nature and the spiritual work, and, most broadly, the human condition."

Wright is credited with finding his own voice in *Hard Freight,* which Peter Meinke calls in a *New Republic* review "less Poundian, less hard-edged, than his first book, *The Grave of the Right Hand.*" John L. Carpenter praises Wright for reaching for his own style in a *Poetry* review of *Hard Freight:* "It is less incisive and less deliberate than the first book, but it is more experimental, less ironclad and defensive." It is in this volume that the poet first exhibits his technique of creating poetry by compiling catalogs of fragmented images. It is a device which requires "that the reader assist in the creative activity," finds *Washington Post Book World* contributor Edward Kessler. "[Wright's] almost spastic writing can at times be enlivening and fascinating, like watching the changing fragments of a kaleidoscope." But this technique is not praised by all critics. Some find it excessive, including Sally M. Gall, who protests in *Shenandoah:* "He frantically piles up details, images, similes, and metaphors as if sheer quantity can replace quality of perception. His catalogues can be perniciously boring rather than enlightening." Kessler disagrees: "His senses are awake, and even when he cannot quite bring his *things* of the world into a satisfying shape, his fragments are rife with suggestions. This man is feeling his way toward a personal definition."

Bloodlines continues in the same vein as *Hard Freight,* but many reviewers feel that Wright's voice is even stronger in this volume, including J. D. McClatchy, who writes in *Yale Review,* "Charles Wright has come completely home in *Bloodlines,* a book that confirms and emphasizes his reputation." Carol Muske also notes the power of this collection in *Parnassus: Poetry in Review:* "[Wright] is on the move. His poems fairly explode from the page in hurly-burly refrain, elliptical syntax, and giddy shifts that recall Hopkins." McClatchy adds, "He recreates not aspects but images of his past experiences—prayer meetings, sexual encounters, dreams—mingling memory and fantasy. The poems are suffused with remembered light."

Hard Freight, Bloodlines and *China Trace* comprise what Wright thinks of as a trilogy of poetry collections. Explains Kathleen Agena in *Partisan Review,* "Like Wallace Stevens, Wright has conceived of his work as a whole. Individual poems are arresting but none of them quite has its meaning alone. The poems elucidate and comment on each other, extending and developing certain key metaphors and images." In *China Trace,* Wright again considers universal connections to the past. According to Butterick, the poet describes this collection as "a book of Chinese poems that don't sound like Chinese poems and aren't Chinese poems but are *like* Chinese poems in the sense that they give you an idea of one man's relationship to the endlessness, the ongoingness, the everlastingness of what's around him, and his relationship to it as he stands in the natural world."

Agena contends that Wright's power comes from his faith in "the mad sense of language" and his willingness to abandon himself to it. She summarizes: "When Charles Wright's poems work, which is most of the time, the poetic energies seem to break the membrane of syntax, exploding the surface, reverberating in multiple directions simultaneously. It is not a linear progression one finds but rather a richocheting, as if, at the impact of a single cue, all the words bounced into their pockets, rearranged, and displaced themselves in different directions all over again. And it seems to happen by accident, as if Wright simply sets the words in motion and they, playing a game according to their own rules, write the poem.''

BIOGRAPHICAL/CRITICAL SOURCES:

BOOKS

Contemporary Literary Criticism, Gale, Volume VI, 1976, Volume XIII, 1980, Volume XXVIII, 1984.
Dictionary of Literary Biography Yearbook: 1982, Gale, 1983.
Friebert, Stuart and David Young, editors, *A Field Guide to Contemporary Poetry and Poetics*, Longman, 1980.

PERIODICALS

American Poetry Review, September/October, 1982.
Antioch Review, spring, 1982.
Choice, September, 1976.
Georgia Review, summer, 1978, spring, 1982.
Hudson Review, spring, 1974, autumn, 1975.
Los Angeles Times Book Review, February 7, 1982.
Michigan Quarterly Review, fall, 1978.
New Republic, November 24, 1973, November 26, 1977.
New Yorker, October 29, 1979.
New York Times Book Review, February 17, 1974, September 7, 1975, December 12, 1982, July 1, 1984.
Parnassus: Poetry in Review, spring-summer, 1976.
Partisan Review, volume XLIII, number 4, 1976.
Poetry, December, 1974, December, 1978.
Sewanee Review, spring, 1974.
Shenandoah, fall, 1974.
Times Literary Supplement, March 1, 1985.
Washington Post Book World, May 5, 1974.
Yale Review, autumn, 1975.

—*Sketch by Joan Goldsworthy*

*   *   *

WRIGHT, William   1930-

PERSONAL: Born October 22, 1930, in Philadelphia, Pa.; son of William Connor and Josephine (Hartshorne) Wright. *Education:* Yale University, B.A., 1952.

ADDRESSES: Home—New York, N.Y. 10028. *Agent*—The Helen Brann Agency Inc., 157 West 57th St., New York, N.Y. 10019.

CAREER: Holiday, New York City, associate editor, 1960-65; *Venture*, New York City, articles editor, 1968-70; *Chicagoan Magazine*, Chicago, Ill., editor, 1969-71; *Leisureguide*, Chicago, editor, 1971-74; *Chicago Magazine*, Chicago, interim editor, 1974; full-time writer,1974. General manager of Gian Carlo Menotti's Spoleto Festival, 1965. *Military service:* U.S. Army, Chinese translator, 1952-55.

WRITINGS:

NONFICTION

Ball: A Year in the Life of the April in Paris Extravaganza, Saturday Review Press, 1972.
The Washington Game, Dutton, 1974.
Heiress: The Rich Life of Marjorie Merriweather Post, New Republic Books, 1979.
(With Luciano Pavarotti) *Pavarotti: My Own Story*, Doubleday, 1981.
The Von Buelow Affair, Delacorte, 1983.
Lillian Hellman: The Image, the Woman, Simon & Schuster, 1986.

OTHER

Rich Relations (novel), Putnam, 1980.

Contributor to *Oui, Travel, Leisure, Town & Country*, and *Vanity Fair*.

WORK IN PROGRESS: A play.

SIDELIGHTS: As a biographer and writer of general nonfiction, William Wright has received the most critical attention for his books *The Von Buelow Affair* and *Lillian Hellman: The Image, the Woman*. In the former, Wright offers an account of what led to the sensational 1982 conviction of Claus Von Buelow for the attempted murder of his wife, Martha "Sonny" Von Buelow, the heiress to a $75 million natural gas fortune. In the opinion of *Washington Post Book World* reviewer Susan Jacoby, "Wright has written a fascinating social and legal history that not only clarifies many of the issues in the case but illustrates the deficiencies of daily journalism—in particular, television journalism—in dealing with a complicated running story. Wright also casts considerable light on the mystifying phenomenon of popular sympathy for Von Buelow, symbolized in 'Free Claus' buttons and T-shirts. He attributes this phenomenon partly to the sketchiness of news reports, partly to the popular suspicion that Sunny's two children by a former marriage had brought accusations against their stepfather . . . , and partly to the psychological process of identification with the accused rather than the victim.''

Reviewer Taki, a friend to Von Buelow, writes in *Spectator* that "three fourths of Wright's book deals with the trial. It is not a bad read as such books go. Wright seems to be fascinated with the rich, so much so that he performs one of the subtlest hatchet jobs I have yet to come across in print. Buelow is consistently portrayed as a greedy, gigolo type of fortune hunter whose only ambition is to better himself socially.'' Taki points out several "miscarriages of justice'' in the Von Buelow case and concludes: "Wright is obsessed with getting the reader to believe [Von Buelow] guilty.'' Whereas Dudley Clendinen in the *New York Times Book Review* considers Wright's account the best of several he had read by that time, "particularly as it dispels the aura in which the very rich are veiled . . . and gives back to Sunny . . . a measure of the dignity that was stolen from her,'' a *Time* critic believes "for all its malicious detail, *The Von Buelow Affair* never really answers the question that nags at every reader: Did Claus really do it? . . . . The case that had everything still needs a book that has everything—including a plausible solution to the crime.''

Playwright Lillian Hellman penned in her later years three memoirs, *An Unfinished Woman, Pentimento*, and *Scoundrel Time*, which obscured rather than clarified her life story. As a means of bringing the edges into better focus, Wright approached Hellman for authorization to do her official biography. Hellman refused and did much to obstruct Wright's path. Even so, notes Paul Roazen in the Toronto *Globe and Mail*, "Wright succeeded in interviewing more than 150 people who had known her. Out of the welter of contradictory material, Wright has fashioned a remarkably fair-minded book, [*Lillian Hellman: The Image, the Woman*].'' According to Patricia Goldstone in her *Los Angeles Times Book Review* article, "in this meticulously researched, evenhanded and intuitive biography of America's arguably greatest female playwright, author William Wright . . . has written three books in one. 'Lillian Hellman' is a book about theater, a book about women and success, and a book about the political forces shaping the American intellectual left since the 1930s. . . . The most pruriently fascinating aspect of the book is of course Hellman the Woman, who appears, at least in some aspects, as monstrous as her most memorable dramatic creation, Regina in 'The Little Foxes.'''

According to the *New York Time*'s Frank Rich, ''Wright seems an unlikely candidate to sort out the Hellman story. As it happens, he possesses an essential attribute that more passionate writers who either loved or reviled his subject do not: he really is an objective observer.... His main concern is facts, which he has diligently collected, documented and analyzed.... Wright's biography replaces the saintly, often fictive Lillian Hellman of her memoirs with a flawed, real-life Lillian Hellman.'' Though Rich commends Wright for his fact-based account, he nevertheless feels Hellman, ''no little fox, continues to outrun anyone who might attempt to cage her.'' Similarly, Laura Shapiro states in *Newsweek* that with Wright's book ''we're no closer to Hellman herself than we were when she wrote her last paragraph.... [Wright] puts an astonishing amount of faith in Hellman's FBI files, as if he'd never heard of the errors and misconceptions rampant in the bureau's communist watch. He even dabbles in two-penny psychology.... Wright's lack of faith permeates every page of this biography and reduces its subject to straw. Hellman deserves better.''

In contrast to Rich's assertion that Wright has fashioned a biography of facts, David Richard's complaint in the *Washington Post Book World* is that Wright's book is excessively conjectural. Though Wright claims to get at the ''truth behind the legend,'' for Richards, ''Wright ends up with lots of speculations of his own and his text is dotted with such prudent verbal caveats as 'may well have been,' 'it might be assumed' and 'it is possible that'.... If some of Wright's theories are provocative, you can't help feeling throughout this book that

you are being lured out onto the thin ice of hypothesis.'' Roazen, however, defends the biography which he believes ''does not purport to be definitive.... Doubtless there will be substantial literature on Hellman, but in this first biography Wright does a fine job of recreating a remarkable woman's life.'' As for *New Republic* critic Eric Breindel, Hellman had cause for concern when Wright approached her to chronicle her life: ''She was right to be concerned. Wright's excellent book punctures many myths.''

BIOGRAPHICAL/CRITICAL SOURCES:

BOOKS

Contemporary Literary Criticism, Volume XLIV, Gale, 1987.
Wright, William, *Lillian Hellman: The Image, the Woman,* Simon & Schuster, 1986.

PERIODICALS

Chicago Tribune Book World, November 9, 1986.
Globe and Mail (Toronto), January 17, 1987.
Los Angeles Times Book Review, January 4, 1987.
New Republic, March 30, 1987.
Newsweek, November 24, 1986.
New Yorker, January 26, 1987.
New York Times, November 17, 1986.
New York Times Book Review, July 2, 1978, July 3, 1983, November 23, 1986.
Spectator, August 6, 1983.
Time, July 4, 1983.
Times (London), May 21, 1987.
Washington Post Book World, June 6, 1983, November 23, 1986.

—Sketch by Cheryl Gottler

Y-Z

YARDE, Jeanne Betty Frances 1925-
(Joan Hunter, Jeanne Montague)

PERSONAL: Born October 17, 1925, in Bath, England; daughter of Louis (a musician) and Winifred (a musician; maiden name, Smaggasgale) Field; married Graham Herbert Treasure, August 14, 1943 (divorced July, 1976); married Michael Andrew "Hank" Yarde, December 23, 1981; children: (first marriage) Anthony, Vanessa Coultas, Louise, Bruce. *Education:* Attended Bath College of Art. *Politics:* Conservative. *Religion:* "Christened Church of England but follow the Old Religions."

ADDRESSES: Home and office—23 Vicarage St., Warminster, Wiltshire BA12 8JG, England. *Agent*—June Hall Literary Agency, 19 College Cross, London N1 1PT, England.

CAREER: Associated with Citizen House (theatrical costumers), Bath, England, 1941-42 and 1945-47; writer, 1970—.

WRITINGS:

UNDER PSEUDONYM JOAN HUNTER; HISTORICAL ROMANCES

Courtney's Wench, R. Hale, 1973, published as *Roxanna,* Pocket Books, 1975.
The Falcon and the Dove, R. Hale, 1974, published as *Under the Raging Moon,* Pocket Books, 1975.
Rupert the Devil, R. Hale, 1976, published as *Cavalier's Woman* (bound with *Cavalier*), Pocket Books, 1977.
Cavalier, R. Hale, 1977.
The Lord of Kestle Mount, Pocket Books, 1979.

UNDER PSEUDONYM JEANNE MONTAGUE

Touch Me with Fire, Macdonald Futura, 1981, published as *Passion Flame,* Ace Books, 1983.
Flower of My Heart, Macdonald Futura, 1981.
So Cruel My Love, Macdonald Futura, 1982.

UNDER PSEUDONYM JEANNE MONTAGUE; GOTHIC ROMANCES

The Clock Tower, Century Publishing, 1983, St. Martin's, 1984.
Midnight Moon, St. Martin's, 1985.
The Castle of the Winds, Century Hutchinson, 1986, St. Martin's, 1987.

UNDER PSEUDONYM JEANNE MONTAGUE; "DAWN OF LOVE" SERIES OF HISTORICAL ROMANCES FOR YOUNG READERS

Brave Wild Heart, Dragon Books, 1987.
The Power of Love, Dragon Books, 1987.
Vengeance Is Mine, Dragon Books, 1987.
Sword of Honour, Dragon Books, 1987.

WORK IN PROGRESS: Under pseudonym Jeanne Montague, a gothic romance for Century Hutchinson with the tentative title *Tigers of Wrath.*

SIDELIGHTS: Jeanne Betty Frances Yarde wrote to *CA:* "I was born of musical parents and, being the only child, had much care and attention lavished on me. I wanted to be an opera singer, but World War II prevented this.

"The atmosphere of the beautiful old city of Bath and the fact that both my parents loved historical novels and read them aloud to me, developed my taste for this form of literature. I started writing as early as ten years old, but was torn between my love of painting and my desire to sing and write.

"Being a highly romantic and somewhat solitary child, I fell in love early—too early, in fact, and was married by the time I was seventeen. My husband was an artist, but trouble soon started as he is a Virgo of a very conventional, Methodist background, whereas I am a Libra from a liberal, musical, theatrical family. The two just did not jell. One of the major bones of contention was that I adore babies and would have had a dozen if I could. I only managed four. He didn't really want children at all.

"I had never entirely given up writing and, in 1970, I sold my first romantic historical novel. I carried on against many difficulties. When I left my husband, I lived for a year with my widowed mother in Bath. I was joined by my eldest daughter, Vanessa, and her small daughter. She too had just ended a relationship. Together we bought our present home in Warminster. This is an eighteenth-century house, very old and interesting.

"I write all the time to make a living, sometimes as much as fifteen hours a day, seven days a week. It is hard but rewarding work, not so much in the way of finance, as it is a struggle to make much money at writing, but for the joy, satisfaction and sense of achievement it gives me. There have been numerous occasions when I've gone through a bad patch and we've been down to bread and jam, literally—wondering which bill to pay off first! However, things are brighter now and I work only on books that have been commissioned by publishers. Gone are the hit and miss days! I do a great deal of research, fussy about period atmosphere and accuracy, and will tackle almost any genre that my agent or editor suggests. My ambition would be to write a science fantasy novel, but I'm too busy with romance. I would also like to produce a really chilling modern occult book. I've tried this in *Hellspawn,* but haven't yet found a publisher for it. In the pipeline are suggestions for another historical, and a contemporary glitz and glamour book. My working life has been considerably helped by the fact that I now use a word processor. I recommend that every writer get one. Wonderful little robots!

"If I get time to read for relaxation, then I'll pick up the works of my favourite poets: Shelley, Byron, Coleridge and Charles Baudelaire, or I'll read horror novels—particularly Bram Stoker's *Dracula* or the books by Graham Masterson. I love the novels of Victorian writers, Wilkie Collins and Henry James, for example. But I get little time for reading for pleasure.

"I particularly enjoyed writing the four books for younger readers in the 'Dawn of Love' series. These concerned the adventures of the same heroine, a kind of female Scarlet Pimpernel, set in the time of the French Revolution. To do this, I had to think back to the novels which used to inspire me in my early teens: *The Three Musketeers* by Dumas, and the novels by Rafael Sabatini, *Captain Blood* and *The Black Swan.* So they are swashbuckling books, with a light dash of love-interest. These were a pleasant change from the steamy romances I've been writing recently, and I hope they will also inspire young readers with a sense of chivalry and high adventure. There's lots of swordplay and galloping about on horseback and rescuing aristocrats from a bloody death on the guillotine!

"As for my Gothics, well, they are dark; some critics say they're brooding and intense, rather downbeat and bitter. My editor of these, Rosemary Cheetham, thinks them worthwhile books which will still be on the shelves in ten years time. I hope so. The emphasis in these is on chills and thrills, and the love-scenes are earthy, rather than romantic. The really sexy ones were the two I did for Macdonald Futura, *Touch Me with Fire* and *Flower of My Heart.* These, incidentally, are the ones that are borrowed most often from the lending libraries. Library rights returns show that they go out twice as often as the others!"

The Clock Tower has been translated into French and was published as *Rendez-vous a Alexandrie* by Flamme in 1984.

AVOCATIONAL INTERESTS: Watching television, film videos, operas, ballet, and concerts; the occult; sunbathing; weight training; and family.

* * *

YOURCENAR, Marguerite 1903-1987

PERSONAL: Born June 8, 1903, in Brussels, Belgium; originally French citizen; naturalized U.S. citizen, 1947; name legally changed in 1947; died December 17, 1987, in Maine; daughter of Michel and Fernande (de Cartier de Marchienne) de Crayencour. *Education:* Educated privately.

ADDRESSES: Home—Mount Desert Island, Maine.

CAREER: Writer, 1921-87. Professor of comparative literature at Sarah Lawrence College, 1940-50.

MEMBER: Academie Francaise, Academie Royale de langue et de litterature francaises de Belgique, American Academy and Institute of Arts and Letters, American Civil Rights Association.

AWARDS, HONORS: Prix Femina-Vacaresco, 1951, for *Memoires d'Hadrien;* Page One Award from Newspaper Guild of New York, 1955; L.T.D. from Smith College, 1961; Prix Combat, 1963, for ensemble of work; Prix Femina, 1968, for *L'Oeuvre au noir;* L.T.D. from Bowdoin College, 1968; L.T.D. from Colby College, 1972; Prix Monaco, 1973, for ensemble of work; Grand Prix National des Lettres from French Ministry of Culture, 1975; Grand Prix de la Litterature from Academie Francaise, 1980; L.T.D. from Harvard University, 1981; National Arts Club Medal of Honor for Literature, 1985; commander of Legion of Honor (France).

WRITINGS:

IN ENGLISH TRANSLATION

Alexis; ou, Le Traite du vain combat (novel), [Paris], 1929, revised edition, Plon, 1965, translation by Walter Kaiser published as *Alexis,* Farrar, Straus, 1984.

Dernier du reve (novel), Grasset, 1934, revised edition, 1959, translation by Dori Katz published as *A Coin in Nine Hands,* Farrar, Straus, 1982.

Feux (poems), [Paris], 1936, revised edition, Gallimard, 1974, translation by Katz published as *Fires,* Farrar, Straus, 1981.

Nouvelles Orientales (short stories), Gallimard, 1938, translation by Alberto Manguel published as *Oriental Tales,* Farrar, Straus, 1985.

Le Coup de grace (novel), Gallimard, 1939, translation by Grace Frick published as *Coup de Grace,* Farrar, Straus, 1957, reprinted, 1981.

Memoires d'Hadrien (novel), Plon, 1951, translation by Frick published as *Memoirs of Hadrian,* Farrar, Straus, 1954, reprinted, Modern Library, 1984.

Les Charites d'Alcippe (poems), [Brussels], 1956, translation published as *The Alms of Alcippe,* Targ Editions, 1982.

Sous benefice d'inventaire (essays), Gallimard, 1962, revised edition, 1978, translation by Richard Howard published as *The Dark Brain of Piranesi and Other Essays,* Farrar, Straus, 1984.

L'Oeuvre au noir (novel), Gallimard, 1968, translation by Frick published as *The Abyss,* Farrar, Straus, 1976.

Theatre (plays), two volumes, Gallimard, 1971, translation by Katz published as *Plays,* Performing Arts Journal Publications, 1985.

Les Yeux ouverts: Entretiens avec Matthieu Galey, Centurion, 1980, translation by Arthur Goldhammer published as *With Open Eyes: Conversations with Matthieu Galey,* Beacon Press, 1986.

Mishima; ou, La Vision du vide (biography), Gallimard, 1981, translation by Manguel published as *Mishima: A Vision of the Void,* Farrar, Straus, 1986.

Comme l'eau qui coule (short stories), Gallimard, 1982, translation by Kaiser published as *Two Lives and a Dream,* Farrar, Straus, 1987.

IN FRENCH

La Nouvelle Eurydice (novel), Grasset, 1931.
Pindare, Grasset, 1932.
Les Songes et les sorts, Grasset, 1938.
Electra; ou, La Chute des masques, Plon, 1954.

(Author of critique and translator from the Greek with Constantin Dimaras) *Presentation critique de Constantin Cavafy, 1863-1933*, Gallimard, 1958, reprinted, 1978.

Le Mystere d'Alceste [and] *Qui n'a pas son minotaure?*, Plon, 1963.

(Translator from the English) *Fleuve profond, sombre riviere: Les Negro spirituals*, Gallimard, 1964.

(Author of critique and translator from the English) *Presentation critique d'Hortense Flexner*, Gallimard, 1969.

Le Labyrinthe du monde, Gallimard, Volume I: *Souvenirs pieux*, 1974, Volume II: *Archives du nord*, 1977.

Suite d'estampes pour Kou-Kou-Hai, High Loft, 1980.

Discours de reception de Mme Marguerite Yourcenar a l'Academie Francaise et reponse de M. Jean d'Ormesson, Gallimard, 1981.

Oeuvres romanesques, Gallimard, 1982.

Le Temps, ce grand sculpture: Essais, Gallimard, 1983.

Blues et gospels, Gallimard, 1984.

Also author of *Anna Sonor*, 1979, and *Un Homme obscur*, 1982.

OTHER

Translator of works by Henry James, Virginia Woolf, and ancient Greek poets. Contributor to French journals and periodicals, including *Le Monde*, *Le Figaro*, and *Nouvelle Revue Francaise*.

WORK IN PROGRESS: The third volume of the trilogy *Le Labyrinthe du monde; Quoi?: L'Eternite*, a volume of quotations.

SIDELIGHTS: When author Marguerite Yourcenar was elected to the Academie Francaise in 1981, she became the first woman to receive the French state's highest literary honor. Throughout its three hundred fifty years of existence, the Academie Francaise had elected only men until the octogenarian novelist was asked to join its ranks. The honor was formidable, and most critics agree that Yourcenar, long a resident of Mount Desert Island off the coast of Maine, deserves such unprecedented acclaim. She has written fiction, essays, poetry, and a biography, but she is best known for two thought-provoking historical novels, *Memoirs of Hadrian* and *The Abyss*, first published in France as *Memoires d'Hadrien* and *L'Oeuvre au noir*. According to Moses Hadas in the *Saturday Review*, Yourcenar's "highest usefulness and greatest success is in a field beyond the range of the orthodox historian, a field to which only the imaginative writer can be adequate." Her example, Hadas adds, "is to be commended to all writers of historical fiction." *Los Angeles Times Book Review* contributor Frances McConnel offers a similar appraisal of the Belgian-born writer: "Whatever magic she is about, Yourcenar crosses barriers of century, discipline, language, myth and history with no sense of impropriety or danger. The path her mind takes through these landscapes is always stepping-stone easy to follow, yet everywhere full of bold jumps and staggering views." In *World Literature Today*, Alexander Coleman concludes that an open-minded reader "will discover in all Yourcenar's writings a luminous and keenly magisterial intelligence."

Yourcenar has lived primarily in America since 1939, although she has travelled widely, and received United States citizenship in 1947. She has always written in French, however, having been taken to France by her family shortly after her birth, and her French citizenship was restored to her in 1980. *Saturday Review* essayist Stephen Koch suggests that Yourcenar has for many years found herself in "the anomalous—

indeed, unique—position of being a major French writer and an American citizen." If her summer domicile is in Maine, critics note, Yourcenar's style and substance are still clearly French. In the *Times Literary Supplement*, John Weightman contends that her novels "show an extraordinary range of knowledge in various fields, and a quite exceptional awareness of the whole French literary tradition. Although . . . she protests that she has never been a systematic scholar, she must be one of the most learned practitioners of the French novel in her time." Addressing his comments to Yourcenar's style, Hugh Lloyd-Jones claims in the *New York Times Book Review* that the author "writes an ornamental and mellifluous French prose, studded with the literary allusions which come so easily to such a cultivated writer." *New York Review of Books* contributor Mavis Gallant elaborates: "Writers who choose domicile in a foreign place, for whatever reason, usually treat their native language like a delicate timepiece, making certain it runs exactly and no dust gets inside. Mme. Yourcenar's distinctive and unplaceable voice carries the precise movement of her finest prose, the well-tended watch." Gallant also observes that Yourcenar's "mind, her manner, the quirks and prejudices that enliven her conclusive opinions, the sense of caste that lends her fiction its stern framework, her respect for usages and precedents, belong to a vanished France."

Commentary essayist Joseph Epstein discusses the theme that arises from much of Yourcenar's fiction. "Intricate moral questions are usually not at the center of Marguerite Yourcenar's work," Epstein writes. "Human destiny, its meaning and even more its mysteries, are. She has a clearer sense than anyone now writing of the tragedy yet also the hope inherent in human lives. . . . The effect of reading her novels is to be reminded of the difficulty of life and of its heroic possibilities—hardly a thing that contemporary literature does best, if at all. Most of us are undone by life. Ours is but to do, then die. Marguerite Yourcenar's novels make us question why. This is what major writers have always done. This is why she is among their number." In the *Times Literary Supplement*, George Steiner reflects on the notion that through strong central characters, Yourcenar "argues her vision of essential human solitude, of the radical incapacity of human beings, particularly and paradoxically when they are most self-conscious and articulate, to communicate to others, even to those they love best, the final quality or truth of their convictions. This, indeed, is the Yourcenar leitmotif." The vision is sometimes bleak; *New York Times Book Review* contributor Michael Wood feels that Yourcenar's characters "make tremendous demands of themselves and generally despair of others," but erudition and estimations of human potential for intellectual and spiritual sovereignty alleviate the solemnity. In a *New York Times Book Review* piece, Koch calls Yourcenar "one of the great scholar-artists," who provides ". . . riches for anyone interested in history, humanism or the psychology of power."

Yourcenar "had an ideally vagrant and unsettling youth for a writer of historical fiction," according to John Sturrock in the *New York Times Book Review*. She was born in Brussels in 1903; her father was French and her mother Belgian. Yourcenar lost her mother to a fever shortly after her birth, so her father undertook sole responsibility for her care. Together they travelled extensively in England, France, Italy and Switzerland, using the family name of de Crayencour that Yourcenar later scrambled to form her unusual nom de plume. As a youngster, Marguerite de Crayencour was educated privately, largely by her father. Weightman writes of him: "M. de Crayencour must have been a curious mixture of playboy and free-thinking, gentleman-scholar, because it was he who gave [Yourcenar] a grounding in Latin and Greek and read many of the French classics with her; nor does he seem to have imposed on her any of the conventional restraints of the time. Father and daughter were fairly constant companions until his death in 1929, after which she continued the nomadic life, in undefined circumstances but with apparently adequate financial resources, sharing her time between France, Italy, Greece and other countries." Yourcenar began writing while still in her teens, and she was twenty-six when her first novel, *Alexis; ou, Le Traite du vain combat,* was published. *New Republic* contributor Anne Tyler reflects on how Yourcenar's unsettled youth—interrupted by both World Wars—influences her writings: "Her physical distance from her Belgian homeland and her psychological distance from the country she has adopted [the United States,] combine to give a picture of someone watching the world at one remove—as Marguerite Yourcenar most certainly does. Her concern is man's relationship with history. Her characters are most often tiny, lonely figures in a vortex of political events."

In 1934 Yourcenar made the acquaintance of Grace Frick, an American visiting Paris. They became inseparable companions, and in 1939 Yourcenar moved to the United States because of the outbreak of war. She taught comparative literature at Sarah Lawrence College for ten years and continued to write short stories, novels, essays, and plays. If her life can be said to have had a turning point, it may have occurred shortly after the Second World War, when a friend sent Yourcenar some personal belongings and papers she had left in France. Yourcenar told the *Washington Post* of a discovery she made while burning some of this old correspondence: "As I unfolded and threw mechanically into the fire that exchange of dead thoughts between a Marie and a Francois or a Paul, long since disappeared, I came upon four or five typewritten sheets, the paper of which had turned yellow. The salutation told me nothing: 'My dear Mark. . . .' Mark . . . what friend or love, what distant relative was this? I could not recall the name at all. It was several minutes before I remembered that Mark stood here for Marcus Aurelius, and that I had in hand a fragment of [a] lost manuscript. From that moment there was no question but that this book must be taken up again, whatever the cost."

The book in question is *Memoirs of Hadrian,* hailed in France and America as a classic achievement in postwar fiction. In the *Spectator,* Miranda Seymour calls the work "arguably the finest historical novel of this century." Likewise, *New York Herald Tribune Book Review* contributor Geoffrey Bruun notes that *Memoirs of Hadrian* "is an extraordinarily expert performance. . . . It has a quality of authenticity, of verisimilitude, that delights and fascinates." Drawing on her vast knowledge of ancient Rome, Yourcenar has recreated the world of the Emperor Hadrian, who, in a series of first-person letters to his newphew Marcus Aurelius, reminisces about his life and times. James Boatwright describes the work in the *Washington Post Book World:* "In a prose of exquisite clarity and grace, the Emperor Hadrian . . . reveals himself as both a creator and worshiper of beauty, a man of keen intelligence and strong passion, powerful and magnanimous, a poet, a lover, a prince 'who was *almost* wise.'" According to Epstein, the novel's outlook "is worldly; its tone philosophical; its feeling completely Roman. The book is a triumph of historical ventriloquism; it is impossible to read it and not think that, had Hadrian left memoirs, this is how they would have read. . . . To bring off such a book requires not only artistry and scholarship but intelligence of a very high order."

Other critics are similarly impressed with *Memoirs of Hadrian.* In the *Nation,* Stanley Cooperman calls it "historical fiction at its best" and adds that Yourcenar "has avoided the usual hack plot and romantic baubles and produced a moving and scholarly recreation of a fascinating scene and epoch—Hadrian's Rome." Cooperman further comments that *Memoirs of Hadrian* reaches "deeply into the blend of humanism and cruelty, decadence and power, art and economics referred to inadequately as 'pagan Rome.'" Hadas writes: "Even a reader indifferent to history and historical personages must find the Hadrian here presented a full and sensitive man well worth knowing. . . . Miss Yourcenar breathes life into the enigmatic data concerning the man and communicates a vivid sense of the multifarious empire he ruled." *Washington Post* correspondent Michael Kernan expresses the opinion that it "is hard to find a reader who refuses to love 'Hadrian.' The man comes through so clearly, in the loneliness of his intelligence, in his practiced but wary handling of his own immense power, in his grief over the death of his young lover Antinous, that we feel this is what greatness must be like." *New Yorker* columnist George Steiner goes so far as to suggest that *Memoirs of Hadrian* earned Yourcenar her invitation to join the Academie Francaise. "It is in [Hadrian's] eminent glow," Steiner concludes, "that the new Academician took her historic seat."

The Abyss, published in France as *L'Oeuvre au noir,* first appeared in English translation in 1976. Another historical/philosophical novel, the work follows the life of a fictitious Renaissance physician, Zeno of Bruges. In a *New York Times Book Review* assessment of the French edition, Marc Slonim calls the book "at the same time a study of the Renaissance and a picture of that turbulent era as seen through the eyes of a poet. . . . What gives this fateful story a singular dimension is its high intellectual content. . . . 'L'Oeuvre au noir,' written in the compact, poetic language so typical of Mme. Yourcenar, is a stirring, unusual and often disturbing experience for the contemproary reader." Once again critics have praised *The Abyss* for its authenticity and intellectual content. As Muriel Haynes notes in *Ms.* magazine, Yourcenar's "immense erudition and meticulous scholarship recreate this period of dissolution. . . . Beneath this richly textured surface, the book is a compendium of ideas, a philosophical examination of the abyss in which humankind is plunged still. . . . Like *Memoirs of Hadrian* it is a meditation on history in which the past is seen as both present and eternal." Kernan likewise feels that the work "is a brilliant tapestry of western Europe in the Middle Ages, . . . so rich in smells and sounds and scenes that it seems like superb reporting." Haynes suggests that although Zeno is a fictitious character, "his cast of mind, his convictions and experiences, are a kind of collage of those of actual personages who shared his century," and a *Times Literary Supplement* reviewer offers the compliment that the novel "will delight historians of this period."

One consequence of Yourcenar's inclusion in the Academie Francaise is that more of her work has been translated and published in English. Novels such as *Alexis, Coup de Grace,* and *A Coin in Nine Hands* have all been issued or reprinted since 1981. These works precede *Memoirs of Hadrian* in a chronological listing of Yourcenar's oeuvre, but the author has revised them extensively since their first publications between 1929 and 1939. In these novels, Yourcenar explores the contemporary world through tales of unrequited love, homosexuality, and political assassination. They are generally considered secondary offerings, dwarfed in importance by *Memoirs of Hadrian* and *The Abyss,* but critics nonetheless cite them for interesting characterization and cogent style. Seymour, for instance, claims that *A Coin in Nine Hands* "is among [Yourcenar's] best work, a testament to her extraordinary ability to turn stereotypes into archetypes, to invoke the past to illuminate the present." *A Coin in Nine Hands* charts the progress of an Italian coin as it passes from person to person in Italy during the dictatorship of Mussolini. *Times Literary Supplement* reviewer Michael Tilby calls the work "at heart an ironic and even playful novel. The omniscient narrator, endowed with a roving cinematographic eye, creates a deliberate impression of stylization, as does the mingling of the straightforwardly mimetic and the world of myth, or the abrupt changes of style and tone." In the *Los Angeles Times Book Review*, Doris Grumbach lists the novel's distinctions: "vivid characters, passages that move close to poetry and a story that belongs to both literature and history."

In addition to her novels, Yourcenar has published poetry, essays, and stories, and many of these have also been made available in English translation. *Fires* is a collection of poetic monologues based on classical Greek and Judeo-Christian stories; Boatwright contends that the pieces "are variations on the theme of absolute love, its terrible price and transcendent rewards, whatever its form." *Times Literary Supplement* contributor Oswyn Murray feels that the poems in *Fires* demonstrate "those qualities which were to make [Yourcenar] a great novelist—empathy, a sense of individuality, and wisdom." *Oriental Tales* offers a series of folktales from various European and Far Eastern cultures. In the *New York Times Book Review*, Koch states that the stories "are wonderful. . . . [Each] of them seems a small window opened, magically, on some quite real but lost world. For Miss Yourcenar, scholarship is the entryway to the imagination, and, like all her work, these borrowed stories are simultaneously efforts at reconstruction and new creation. . . . At once immemorial and new, they show us the fabulist as mythographer and sage." Yourcenar's first essay collection, *Sous benefice d'inventaire*, published in the United States as *The Dark Brain of Piranesi and Other Essays*, has also garnered critical praise. Assessing the work in the *New York Times*, John Gross concludes that Yourcenar's essays "make it clear that she is . . . an outstanding critic. They are forceful, deeply pondered, the record of a full imaginative response."

Marguerite Yourcenar is an intensely private person who prefers to avoid the literary circles in both New York and Paris. For half the year she lives in the cottage on Mount Desert Island that she and the late Grace Frick purchased together; Yourcenar told the *New York Times* that she stays there both to avoid autograph-seekers and because she likes the "village rhythm" and the beautiful scenery. Although Gross, among others, notes that the author "is reticent about her private life, and . . . more preoccupied with long perspectives than with the fashion of the hour," Yourcenar has published some books about herself. One ongoing project is *Le Labyrinthe du monde;* its completed components, *Souvenirs pieux* and *Archives du nord* describe her parents' families in the century before she was born. She is working on a third volume to complete the trilogy. She has also released a series of interviews the English translation of which is entitled *With Open Eyes: Conversations with Matthieu Galey*. Gross claims that the views expressed in that book "are all of a piece—those of a liberal and a humanitarian who believes that 'the social problem is more important than the political problem,' and whose deepest public concerns tend to be cultural and ecological."

Mavis Gallant feels that Yourcenar "stands among a litter of flashier reputations as testimony to the substance and clarity of the French language and the purpose and meaning of a writer's life." Well into her eighties, the author continues to write, travel, and contemplate historical and philosophical issues central to the human condition. "Some novelists pull us more deeply into our own time;" Epstein observes, "she pulls us away from it—or rather above it. Marguerite Yourcenar's subject is human destiny. It was the only serious subject for the Greeks, whom she so much admires. It has always been the great subject of the novel, and always will be, even though few writers in our day have been able to find the means to take it on, let alone so directly as Marguerite Yourcenar has done." In his *Saturday Review* essay, Koch concludes: "As an artist and thinker—for Yourcenar's novels must be regarded as simultaneously art, scholarship, and profound philosophical meditation—Marguerite Yourcenar writes squarely in defense of the very highest standards and traditions of that enlightened humanism which Hadrian promulgated for an empire and to the agonized rebirth of which her Zeno dies a martyr. It is, to say the least, heartening to find a writer so deeply committed to that humanism who is producing major art at this moment in our own history. It is, in fact, inspiring."

BIOGRAPHICAL/CRITICAL SOURCES:

BOOKS

Contemporary Literary Criticism, Gale, Volume XIX, 1981, Volume XXXVIII, 1986.
Yourcenar, Marguerite, *Le Labyrinthe du monde,* Gallimard, Volume I: *Souvenirs pieux,* 1974, Volume II: *Archives du nord,* 1977.
Yourcenar, Marguerite, *Les Yeux ouverts: Entretiens avec Matthieu Galey,* Centurion, 1980, translation by Arthur Goldhammer published as *With Open Eyes: Conversations with Matthieu Galey,* Beacon Press, 1986.

PERIODICALS

Chicago Tribune, December 29, 1986.
Chicago Tribune Book World, June 28, 1981, October 27, 1985.
Commentary, August, 1982.
Commonweal, September 6, 1957, October 23, 1981.
Globe & Mail (Toronto), November 16, 1985, November 15, 1986, January 24, 1987.
Harper's, October, 1984.
Hudson Review, winter, 1976-77.
Los Angeles Times, November 28, 1986, June 26, 1987.
Los Angeles Times Book Review, October 3, 1982, February 3, 1985, November 3, 1985.
Ms., August, 1976.
Nation, December 25, 1954, October 30, 1976.
New Republic, January 10-17, 1983.
Newsweek, June 28, 1976.
New Yorker, June 14, 1976, August 17, 1981, February 11, 1985.
New York Herald Tribune Book Review, November 21, 1954.
New York Review of Books, October 14, 1976, October 10, 1985, December 5, 1985.
New York Times, December 3, 1979, March 7, 1980, December 27, 1984, April 10, 1987.
New York Times Book Review, August 25, 1968, July 11, 1976, October 4, 1981, January 30, 1983, September 16, 1984, February 24, 1985, September 22, 1985, December 14, 1986, April 19, 1987.

Saturday Review, November 27, 1954, July 20, 1957, June 12, 1976, June, 1981.

Spectator, June 19, 1982, February 19, 1983, November 12, 1983.

Times (London), July 8, 1982, November 17, 1983, May 10, 1984, July 16, 1987.

Times Literary Supplement, October 3, 1968, August 6, 1971, August 23, 1974, March 3, 1978, April 4, 1980, May 29, 1981, August 13, 1982, October 8, 1982, April 1, 1983, July 22, 1983, February 17, 1984, November 30, 1984, November 8, 1985.

Village Voice, November 4-10, 1981.

Washington Post, August 8, 1983.

Washington Post Book World, July 11, 1976, September 6, 1981, December 19, 1982, September 2, 1984, September 22, 1985, December 28, 1986, June 14, 1987.

World Literature Today, autumn, 1978, autumn, 1979, autumn, 1981, spring, 1982, autumn, 1984, summer, 1985, summer, 1986.

—Sketch by Anne Janette Johnson

*   *   *

ZILIOX, Marc
    See FICHTER, George S.